1994 ANNUAL EDITION

THE ANTIQUE TRADER

Antiques & Collectibles
PRICE GUIDE

Edited by
Kyle Husfloen

A comprehensive price guide to the entire field of
antiques and collectibles for the 1994 market.

Illustrated

The Antique Trader
P.O. Box 1050
Dubuque, Iowa 52004

II

STAFF

Assistant Editor		Subscription Manager	Bonnie Rojemann
Assistants	Marilyn Dragowick	Publisher	Ted Jones
	Carolyn Clark		
	Louise Paradis		
	Aaron Roeth		
	Ruth Willis		

ISBN: 0-930625-09-9
Library of Congress Catalog Card No. 85-648650

Additional copies of this book may be ordered from:

The Antique Trader
P.O. Box 1050
Dubuque, Iowa 52004

$12.95 plus $2.00 postage and handling.

A WORD TO THE READER

The Antique Trader has been publishing a Price Guide for twenty-three years. *The Antique Trader Price Guide to Antiques and Collectors' Items* has been available by subscription and on newsstands across the country, first as a semi-annual and then as a quarterly publication, and since 1984 it has been published on a bi-monthly basis.

In 1985, in response to numerous requests to combine the material of the bi-monthly issues and provide a large, complete price guide, the first edition of *The Antique Trader Antiques & Collectibles Price Guide* was issued. The book you now hold in your hands is the 1994 guide, our Tenth Annual Edition.

This book is the most current price listing available. We think it is also the most reliable book for dealers and collectors to turn to for realistic values of antiques and collectibles. Prices listed in this guide have not been unrealistically set at the whim of an editor who has no material at hand to substantiate the listed values. The Antique Trader Price Guide staff has always used a very methodical compilation system that is supported by experts from across the country as we select listings for the various categories. Prices are derived from antiques shops, advertisements, auctions, and antiques shows, and on-going records are maintained. Items are fully described and listings are carefully examined by experts who discard unreasonable exceptions to bring you the most reliable, well-illustrated and authoritative Price Guide available.

Our format enables us to maintain a wide range of both antique and collectible items in a running tabulation to which we are continually adding information and prices. Items are diligently researched and clearly described. As new areas of collecting interest develop, new categories are added and if a definite market is established, this material becomes a part of the Price Guide. A new category in the Glass Section this issue is Westmoreland Glass.

Six popular areas of collecting are highlighted in well-illustrated "Special Focus" features which provide background material and tips on collecting. Our 1994 edition includes focuses on Dugan-Diamond Glass, Collecting Ice Skates & Skating Memorabilia, Collecting Letter Openers, Collecting Playing Card Decks, Revival Style Furniture and U.S. Coin Glass.

This book should be used only as a *guide* to prices and is not intended to set prices. Prices do vary from one section of the country to another and auction prices, which are incorporated into this guide, often have an even wider variation. Though prices have been double-checked and every effort has been made to assure accuracy, neither the compilers, editor nor publisher can assume responsibility for any losses that might be incurred as a result of consulting this guide, or of errors, typographical or otherwise.

This guide follows an alphabetical format. All categories are listed in alphabetical order. Under the category of Ceramics, you will find all types of pottery, porcelain, earthenware, parian and stoneware listed in alphabetical order. All types of glass, including Carnival, Custard, Depression, Pattern and so on, will be found listed alphabetically under the category of Glass. A complete Index and cross-references in the text have also been provided.

We wish to express sincere appreciation to the following authorities who help in selecting material to be used in this guide: Sandra Andacht, Little Neck, New York; Lillian Baker, Gardena, California; Marilyn Dipboye, Warren, Michigan; Robert T. Matthews, West Friendship, Maryland; Cecil Munsey, Poway, California; Ruth Schinestuhl, Marmora, New Jersey; and Tim Timmerman, Beaverton, Oregon.

The authors of the "Special Focus" segments deserve special recognition: "Dugan-Diamond Glass" by Dr. James Measell, Berkley, Michigan; "Letter Openers," by Diane Levin, Chicago, Illinois; "Ice Skates & Skating Memorabilia," by Ann J. Bates, Land O' Lakes, Wisconsin; "Collecting Playing Card Decks," by Ray Hartz; "Revival Style Furniture," by Connie Morningstar, Salt Lake City, Utah; and "U.S. Coin Glass," by Tim Timmerman, Beaverton, Oregon.

Photographers who have contributed to this issue include: E.A. Babka, East Dubuque, Illinois; Al Bagdade, Northbrook, Illinois; Stanley L. Baker, Minneapolis, Minnesota; Dorothy Beckwith, Platteville, Wisconsin; Donna Bruun, Galena, Illinois; David Carter, Stillwater, Oklahoma; Herman C. Carter, Tulsa, Oklahoma; J.D. Dalessandro, Cincinnati, Ohio; Bill Freeman, Smyrna, Georgia; Jeff Grunewald, Chicago, Illinois; Kevin McConnell, Pilot Point, Texas; the late Don Moore, Alameda, California; Gale Morningstar, Salt Lake City, Utah; Louise Paradis, Galena, Illinois; Joyce Roerig, Waltersboro, South Carolina; and Ruth Schinestuhl, Marmora, New Jersey.

For other photographs, artwork, data or

permission to photograph in their shops, we sincerely express appreciation to the following auctioneers, galleries, museums, individuals and shops: Mark Aldrich, Malden, Massachusetts; Americana Shop, Chicago, Illinois; Antique Alley, Phoenix, Arizona; Antique Manor, Albuquerque, New Mexico; Antique Trove, Scottsdale, Arizona; Arizona Antique Gallery, Tempe, Arizona; Adele Armbruster, Dearborn, Michigan; Auctioneers International, Salt Lake City, Utah; Donna Bauerly, Dubuque, Iowa; Bell Tower Antique Mall, Covington, Kentucky; Bider's, Lawrence, Massachusetts; Block's Box, Trumbull, Connecticut; Bradbury's Antique Bazaar, Phoenix, Arizona; Norm & Diana Charles, Hagerstown, Indiana; Christie's, New York, New York; Classic Century Square, Albuquerque, New Mexico; David Cobb Doll Auctions, Columbus, Ohio; Collector's Auction Services, Seneca, Pennsylvania; Gail De Pasquale, Leavenworth, Kansas; William Doyle Galleries, New York, New York; Marilyn Dragowick, Dubuque, Iowa; DuMouchelle's, Detroit, Michigan; Dunning's Auction Service, Elgin, Illinois; T. Emert, Cincinnati, Ohio; Frasher's Auctions, Oak Grove, Missouri; Garth's Auctions, Inc., Delaware, Ohio; Glass-Works Auctions, East Greenville, Pennsylvania; Glentiques, Ltd., Coral Springs, Florida; Glick's Antiques, Galena, Illinois; Morton M. Goldberg Auction Galleries, New Orleans, Louisiana; Grand Antique Mall, Apache Junction, Arizona; and Grunewald Antiques, Hillsborough, North Carolina.

Also to Gary Guyette & Frank Schmidt, Inc., West Farmington, Maine; Vicki Harmon, San Marcos, California; the Gene Harris Antique Auction Center, Marshalltown, Iowa; the late William Heacock, Marietta, Ohio; House of the Seven Fables, Somonauk, Illinois; International Carnival Glass Assoc., Mentone, Indiana; Jewel Johnson, Tulsa, Oklahoma; James Julia, Fairfield, Maine; Peter Kroll, Sun Prairie, Wisconsin; Beverly Kubesheski, Dubuque, Iowa; L.F.K. Art & Antiques, Kansas City, Kansas; Joy Luke Gallery, Bloomington, Illinois; J. Martin, Mt. Orab, Ohio; McMasters Doll Auctions, Cambridge, Ohio; Dr. James Measell, Berkley, Michigan; Rosemary Meyer, Dubuque, Iowa; J. Nard Auctions, Milan, Pennsylvania; Neal Auction Company, New Orleans, Louisiana; New Orleans Auction Galleries, New Orleans, Louisiana; Nostalgia Galleries, Elmont, New York; Nostalgia Publications, Inc., Hackensack, New Jersey; O'Gallerie, Inc., Portland, Oregon; Pence Auction Company, Liberty, Missouri; Dave Rago Arts & Crafts, Trenton, New Jersey; R.A.M. Quality Auctions, Joliet, Illinois; Raven & Dove, Wilmette, Illinois; Jane Rosenow, Galva, Illinois; Tammy Roth, East Dubuque, Illinois; Simmons & Ross Auctioneers, Richmond, Missouri; Robert W. Skinner, Inc., Bolton, Massachusetts; Sotheby's, New York, New York; Doris Spahn, East Dubuque, Illinois; Stephens Consignment Gallery, Santa Fe, New Mexico; Michael Strawser, Wolcottville, Indiana; Sun Cities Auction Gallery, Sun City, Arizona; Rose Mary Taylor, Pecatonica, Illinois; Theriault's, Annapolis, Maryland; Time Was Museum, Mendota, Illinois; Tin Pan Alley Antiques, Galena, Illinois; Town Crier Auction Service, Burlington, Wisconsin; Don Treadway Auction Service, Cincinnati, Ohio; Tri-State Auction & Realty, Dubuque, Iowa; Lee Vines, Hewlett, New York; Doris Virtue, Galena, Illinois; Chris Walker Auctions, Potosi, Wisconsin; Wolf's Auctioneers and Appraisers, Cleveland, Ohio; Woody Auctions, Douglass, Kansas; and Yesterday's Treasures, Galena, Illinois.

The staff of *The Antique Trader Antiques & Collectibles Price Guide* welcomes all letters from readers, especially those of constructive critique, and we make every effort to respond personally.

Kyle Husfloen, Editor

ABC PLATES

These children's plates were popular in the late 19th and early 20th centuries. An alphabet border was incorporated with nursery rhymes, maxims, scenes or figures in an apparent attempt to "spoon feed" a bit of knowledge at mealtime. They were made of ceramics, glass and metal. A boon to collectors is the fine book, A Collector's Guide to ABC Plates, Mugs and Things *by Mildred L. and Joseph P. Chalala.*

CERAMIC

5" d., humorous scene, bust portrait of a young officer in uniform in green surrounded by a comic verse, embossed alphabet border w/narrow rope-band border trimmed in red (wear, stains, small chips) $110.00

5" d., Oriental boy w/a whip making a small dog jump through a hoop, "Jumping Through the Hoop," brown transfer 135.00

5 1/8" d., adult activities, black transfer-printed center scene of a couple working in the fields, polychrome enamel trim, embossed alphabet border (stains) 55.00

5¼" d., domestic animals, transfer-printed scene of Whippet dog in center, Germany 75.00

5 3/8" d., children's activities, black transfer-printed center scene of children & dog w/"These children are trying as you see, to teach their dog polite to be," polychrome trim, embossed alphabet border (stains, wear, hairline) 45.00

6" d., domestic animals, a black transfer-printed center scene of three cats, blue rim 90.00

6" d., Franklin Maxim, "Poor Richard's Way to Wealth - Little Strokes...," w/black transfer-printed center scene of a woodsman, embossed alphabet border (some wear & stains) 115.00

6" d., Y is a youth, Staffordshire 67.00

6 1/8" d., wild animal series, transfer-printed standing zebra w/polychrome trim, embossed alphabet border, Powell & Bishop, 1876-78 (stains, wear) 105.00

6 3/8" d., children's activities, red transfer-printed center scene of a children's tea party w/sign language around the inner edge, embossed alphabet border, blue rim band (dark stains) 165.00

6½" d., "The Donkey," brown transfer-printed scene 65.00

7" d., Franklin Maxim, "Constant Dropping Wears Away Stones and Little Strokes Fall Great Oaks" . . . 95.00

7¼" d., boy w/stringed instrument near bird on fence, brown transfer, embossed alphabet border, Adams 75.00

7¼" d., farm animals, polychrome transfer-printed scene of an elderly man & child carrying a reluctant donkey over a wooden bridge (slight browning in one area) 75.00

7½" d., nursery tales series, "Old Mother Hubbard," brown transfer-printed framed scene of Mother Hubbard & dog to lower right side, polychrome enamel trim, alphabet above & to left of scene, marked "Tunstall," ca. 1887 . . . . . . 200.00

8 1/8" d., Deaf & Dumb (so-called) sign language series, blue transfer decoration depicting two fashionably dressed rabbits & sign language alphabet center, embossed standard alphabet border, H. Aynsley & Co., Longton, England, 1904 . . . . 170.00

GLASS

Clock Face ABC Plate

6" d., clock face center w/Arabic & Roman numerals, alphabet border, frosted & clear (ILLUS.) 65.00

6" d., dog standing on grass beside tree center scene, alphabet border, clear 65.00

6" d., Little Bo Peep center scene, raised alphabet border 45.00

TIN

3½" d., Girl on Swing lithographed center scene, printed alphabet border 55.00

4¼" d., two kittens playing w/sewing basket lithographed center scene, printed alphabet border . . . 75.00

8" d., embossed center scene of six frogs playing leapfrog, embossed alphabet border 125.00

ADVERTISING ITEMS

Chesterfield Ashtray

Thousands of objects made in various materials, some intended as gifts with purchases, others used for display or given away for publicity, are now being collected. They range from ash and drink trays to toys. Also see AUTOMOTIVE COLLECTIBLES, BANKS, BASEBALL MEMORABILIA, BIG LITTLE BOOKS, BOTTLE OPENERS, BOTTLES & FLASKS, BUSTER BROWN COLLECTIBLES, CALENDAR PLATES, CANS & CONTAINERS, CARNIVAL GLASS, CHARACTER COLLECTIBLES, COCA-COLA ITEMS, COOKBOOKS, FANS, KITCHENWARES, JEWEL TEA AUTUMN LEAF WARES, OLD SLEEPY EYE POTTERY, SALESMAN'S SAMPLES, SCOUTING ITEMS, STICKPINS, TOYS, TRADE CARDS, TRADE CATALOGS, WATCH FOBS and WORLD'S FAIR COLLECTIBLES.

Ashtray, "Chesterfield Cigarettes," lithographed tin, oval w/indentations at each end, printed to look like a football stadium viewed from overhead, printed in green, red & silver w/white lettering reading "And another all-star eleven -" & "They Satisfy" in red, ca. 1940, minor scuffing, 5¼ x 6¼" (ILLUS.) $22.00

Ashtray, electric company, clear glass w/silk-screened "Reddy Kilowatt" figure center, 4" sq. 15.00

Ashtray, "Goodrich Silvertown Tires," rubber tire shape w/clear glass insert, 6" d. 25.00

Ashtray, "Michelin" tires, molded rubber & plastic, a molded rubber figure of the Michelin man seated atop one side of oblong black molded plastic tray base, ca. 1940's, 5½" w., 4¾" h. 275.00

Baby's spoon w/long handle, "Gerber's," silver plate 12.00

Backbar bottle, "C. Sandhegers Sour Mash Bourbon," clear w/handles.............. 75.00

Backbar bottle, "Paul Jones Whiskey," clear glass w/enameled picture of a man pouring whiskey into a glass..................... 375.00

Baking pan, "Hershey's - The Chocolate That Is Pure," metal, 10 x 18"........................ 198.00

Bank, "Dodge," tin, 55 gallon drum shape, one side lettered "Switch to Dodge & Save Money," other side states "Owners Report Dodge Saves Up to 6 Barrels of Gas in a Year," red w/white lettering, 3¼" h. (closure missing) 50.00

Bank, "Planters Peanuts," cast iron, figural Mr. Peanut, 8" h. 80.00

Barometer, "Mustro Bros. Radio & Hardware," wooden 45.00

Barrel end label, "The Sleepy Eye Mills," round colored lithographed paper on cardboard, the wide red border band printed in white w/"The Sleepy Eye Mills, Sleepy Eye, Minn. - Sleepy Eye Cream," at the center of each side an oval floral reserve, one printed w/"196 Lbs. Net When Packed," the other w/"Highest Patent Flour," the center printed w/a colorful bust portrait of "Old Sleepy Eye," ca. 1910, framed, 16" d. (two tiny tears & two tiny holes) 330.00

Bill hook, "LeRoy Plow," hook w/cardboard back, illustration of a plow, ca. 1905 .... 25.00

Blotter, "Pepsi-Cola," reads "Pepsi and Pete - The Pepsi-Cola Cops," illustrations include Pepsi bottles & pictures of Pepsi & Pete, ca. 1930, 4 x 9" 75.00

Blotter, "Royal Corona Range," pictures a range, ca. 1900 .... 10.00

Book, "Boy Blue Ammonia," entitled "Boy Blue Ammonia Fairy Story," illustrated 17.00

Book, "Chase & Sanborn Coffee," entitled "Eddie Cantor's N.B.C. Picture Book," w/large fold-out page 20.00

Booklet, "Alka-Seltzer - Miles Laboratory," entitled "Our Presidents," 1930 .... 7.00

Booklet, "American Cereal Co. - Quaker Oats," entitled "The Frolic Grasshopper Circus," w/grasshoppers & clowns, whimsical circus scenes, 1895 .... 62.00

Booklet, "Jell-O," entitled "The Jell-O Girl Entertains," eight color illustrations signed by Rose O'Neill 25.00

Booklet, "Quaker Oats," entitled "Dick Darling from Quaker Oats" 15.00

Booklet, "Shredded Wheat," entitled "A Visit to the Home of Shredded Wheat," 1933 .... 12.00

Booklet, "White Mountain Ice Cream Freezers," pictures woman making ice cream, early 1900's 25.00

Bootjack, "Musselman's Plug Tobacco," cast iron 149.00

Box, "Borden's None Such Mince Meat," pictures girl slicing pie, unopened, 1939 .... 25.00

Bride's basket, "Palace Clothing & Shoes, 421 Main Street, Joplin, MO," Hobnail patt. w/ruffled rim bowl, cranberry opalescent glass, in silver plate frame, inscription is on the handle, bowl 10" d. 295.00

Broom holder, "Gold Medal Flour," tin 375.00

Broom holder, "Wiley Bros. - G.E. Appliances, Pillsbury, PA.," metal 15.00

Calendar, 1892, "Prudential Insurance," pictures girl inside a seashell 60.00

Calendar, 1893, "Aetna Insurance Co.," picture depicting dwarfs at various pursuits in a firehouse, framed (minor damage to one corner) 412.50

Calendar, 1899, "Metropolitan Life Insurance Co.," pictures eight children, 12 x 20" 85.00

Calendar, 1902, "Bemis Bag Co.," w/pictures of game birds 225.00

Calendar, 1904, "Christian Herald," pictures four children's heads encased by butterflies, framed, 18 x 36" 350.00

Calendar, 1914, "McCormick Reapers," scene entitled "The Home Makers," 12 x 21" 85.00

Calendar, 1918, "DeLaval - Cawker City, Kansas," pictures girl & horse, 12 x 17" 125.00

Calendar, 1918, "Hood's Sarsaparilla," complete 45.00

Calendar, 1943, "Hercules Gunpowder," full pad 150.00

Calendar, 1946, "Tip-Top Bread," full-color illustration 3.00

Calendar, 1960, "Continental Trailways," pictures three older buses 20.00

Calendar holder, "Phoenix Assurance Co.," bronze, desk-type, 1932 .... 25.00

Calendar plate, 1898, "Prudential Insurance" 75.00

Candy bag, "Ox Heart Milk Chocolate," glassine, ca. 1915 .... 10.00

Candy box, "Baby Ruth," 2c Halloween candy bars, decorated w/children in costume 45.00

Candy wrapper, "Butterfinger," 1936 .... 32.00

Cereal box, "Post Toasties Corn Flakes," 1941, mint condition 50.00

Charm, "Kendall Shoe Co.," metal, shoe-shaped, 1½" 15.00

Charm bracelet, "Planters Peanuts," chain w/plastic Mr. Peanut & peanut charms 17.50

Cigarette carton, "Chesterfield," pictures service men & families waiting at train station on Christmas eve, W.W. II era 10.00

Early Aspinall's Enamel Clock

Clock, "Aspinall's Enamel," wall-mounted regulator, large round top w/advertising around dial w/Roman numerals, the round drop w/a half-round match holder decorated as a paint can & brush, ca. 1895 (ILLUS.) 1,210.00

Clock, "Cooper Cordless Tires," wall-mounted neon-type, orange, royal blue & white, 18" w. 475.00

Keen Kutter Electric Clock

Clock, "Keen Kutter," wall-mounted electric, round red metal case w/white metal dial printed w/red logo & "E.C. Simmons Keen Kutter - Cutlery - Tools - The Recollection of QUALITY remains long after the PRICE is forgotten" (ILLUS.) ... 900.00

Clothes brush, "Bolter's Men's Apparel 55th Anniversary - Boston," folding brush w/plastic case 15.00

Coal shovel, "Round Oak Stove," premium from "The Beckwith Co., Dowagiac, Michigan," 1890-1905 .. 125.00

Coffee bag w/coffee, "Valor Roasted Coffee," pictures steaming coffee cup, "Victory War Bonds" & the Minuteman, ca. 1940 .... 35.00

Coffee measure, "Wood Coffee," brass, w/figural swami handle ... 18.00

Coffee scoop, "Navarre," metal, spade-shaped, "Use Navarre Golden Sun Coffee," 3½" l. 38.50

Cookie cutter, "Davis Baking Powder," tin, rabbit-shaped 15.00

Counter display, "Bond & Lillard Whiskey," easel-back cardboard, 15 x 18" 185.00

Counter display, "Borden's," wood & tin, model of a milk wagon 335.00

Counter display, "DeLaval," paper, punch-out type, model of a cow & calf, 1950's 25.00

Counter display, "J.C. Penney," paper, entitled "Christmas Toyland Parade," includes 20 stand-up figures, ca. 1930, in original envelope 30.00

Counter display, "Wrigley's Doublemint Gum," the green Arrow Man emblem standing between fold-out boxes for the gum (some wear) 495.00

Counter display box, "PayDay Candy Bar," 1960's 24.00

Counter display carton, "Smokey City Antiseptic Laundry Flakes," cardboard, rectangular w/deep sides, contains 24 packages of the product, ca. 1930 (one tear in carton) 60.50

Columbian Fruit Display Case

Counter display case, "Columbian Fruit - Tuxedo - Pepsin Phosphate" (gum), glass & wood, curved glass front printed w/"Columbian Fruit - Tuxedo - Pepsin Phosphate," ca. 1900 (ILLUS.)......................... 750.00

Counter display case, "Mansfield Pepsin Gum," lithographed tin, a tall square container w/a panel at the top w/a small color picture of an elegant 1890's lady beside wording "Mansfield Pepsin Gum - It Has No Equal," lower case divided into sections labeled "Wintergreen," "Blood Orange" & "Peppermint," on a shaped, oak base, base 7" sq., 15½" h. 1,760.00

Counter display case, "Planters Peanuts," curved glass front & glass sides in narrow wood framing, Mr. Peanut decals on the glass top & forming a solid sheet across the inside bottom 180.00

Counter display figure, "Chiclet Gum," die-cut tin w/easel back, model of a monkey, dated 1916, 6 1/8" w., 9½" h. 2,500.00

Counter display figure, "Esso," plaster, model of a reclining German Shepherd dog, 36" l. 48.50

Counter display figure, "General Electric Radio," jointed wood, figure of a standing soldier in red & white uniform, tall top hat w/G.E. logo, jointed at the legs & arms, 18½" h. 550.00

Rare Planters Peanuts Figure

Counter display figure, "Planters Peanuts," papier-mache', electric, standing Mr. Peanut w/blinking eyes, on a flaring square base printed "Planters," restored (ILLUS.) 6,820.00

Counter display figure, "Poll Parrot Shoes," chalkware, model of the parrot, 12" h. 225.00

Counter display figure, "RCA Victor," stuffed cloth, model of dog Nipper, 1940's, 30" h............ 175.00

Counter display figure, "Red Goose Shoes," model of a goose, w/sign attached, pull head down & it lays a gold plastic egg, 12 x 22 x 25" 895.00

Counter display jar, cov., "LikEm Nuts," clear glass, "LikEm Nuts" embossed on two sides & ribbing decoration, metal cover, 8" h. 75.00

Counter display jar, cov., "Planters Peanuts," clear glass "football" shape & original glass lid w/peanut finial 275.00

Counter display jar, cov., "Planters Peanuts," clear glass slant-front "streamline" jar & metal lid 92.50

Counter display jar, cov., "Robertson Candy Co. - New York, U.S.A.," aqua blue glass w/tin cover, 3 qt. 95.00

Counter display jar, cov., "Tom's Peanuts," clear glass, embossed "Eat Tom's Toasted Peanuts," cover w/red knob finial 38.00

Crate, "American Brand Citrus," wooden, dovetailed, fruit trees & American flags etched in the wood 45.00

Jell-O China Dish

Dish, "Jell-O," china, oblong, printed in the center w/a color portrait of the Jell-O girl above "Jell-O - The Dainty Dessert," tiny glaze crack on side of face, ca. 1910, 4 1/8" l. (ILLUS.) 275.00

Doll, "Chiclets Gum," raccoon, uncut cloth, 1916 . . . . 125.00

Doll, "Cracker Jack," Sailor boy, by Vogue Dolls, in original unopened box 42.50

Doll, "Imperial Granum Co.," girl w/blonde "spit curls" around face, uncut cloth, 1915 . . . . 95.00

Doll, "Kellogg's," Dandy Duck, uncut cloth, 1935 . . . . 68.00

Doll, "Kellogg's," Freckles the Frog, uncut cloth 105.00

Doll, "Planters Peanuts," Mr. Peanut, wood-jointed, 8½" h. 195.00

Doll, "Planters Peanuts," Mr. Peanut, cloth, 19" h. 18.00

Doll, "Puritan Flour," Pilgrim man, printed stuffed cloth, printed w/facial features & traditional Pilgrim outfit, lettered "Puritan

Flour" on broad collar & buttons spell out "Puritan," 16" h. (some fading, fabric coming apart under left arm) 75.00

Dolls, "Silver Dust Twins," two girls holding the product, uncut cloth . . 100.00

Door push plate, "Salada Tea," porcelain 65.00

Egg separator, "T & S Flour," tin 13.50

Fan, "Emerson's Drugs," cardboard, colorful scene of pretty girl playing tennis 35.00

Fan, "Putnam Dyes," cardboard, colored lithograph w/"General Putnam escapes British Dragoons," & drugstore advertising, 6½ x 8½" 22.50

Figure, nodding-type, "Planters Peanuts," ceramic, Mr. Peanut w/cane over one arm & other hand raised to hat 99.00

Fire chief hat, "Texaco Gasoline," felt, child-size 35.00

Flour sack, "Crete Mills," pictures black & white dolls 37.50

Football, "Kentucky Fried Chicken," rubber, pictures Colonel Sanders, sports giveaway item, 12" l. 15.00

Goblet, "Medicine Glass - Dr. Carter's," w/picture of bottle, clear glass 19.00

Humidor, cov., "Tuxedo Tobacco," glass, square w/rounded sides . . . 44.00

Ice cream spoons, "Lowney's," brass w/shell-shaped bowl, 4" l., set of 5 . . . . 75.00

Indian headdress, "Honey Krust Bread," paper 7.00

Jigsaw puzzle, "Baby Ruth," reads "1c Baby Ruth," 1920's, w/original mailer 55.00

Jigsaw puzzle, "Cocomalt," entitled "The Flying Family," w/original map & envelope, 1932 . . . . 35.00

Jigsaw puzzle, "Eveready Flashlights," pictures a Christmas scene & reads "Is That You Santa Claus," 1930's, in original envelope 35.00

Jug, miniature, "Jones Bros. Blue Grass Belle Vinegar, Louisville, KY," pottery, jug marked "Red Wing" 295.00

Knife, butter-type, "Planters Peanuts," Carlton silver plate 35.00

Knife, pocket-type, "Armours Dry Sausage," celluloid handle 25.00

Knife, pocket-type, "Star Brand Shoes - Roberts, Johnson & Rand," shoe-shaped 65.00

Knife, fork & spoon, "Planters Peanuts," blue plastic, 3 pcs. 50.00

Letter opener, "Armour," celluloid, detailed rooster head on handle . . 55.00

Letter opener, "Needham Oil, Mass," green plastic 5.00

Marshmallow toaster, "Cracker Jack Co.," embossed "Angelus Marshmallow Toaster," mint in original box 52.50

Measuring cup, "Adco Dry Clng. Prod., Sedalia, Mo., Since 1908," white graniteware 40.00

Mirror, pocket-type, "ABS Cement," round, pictures a happy/sad man 35.00

Mirror, pocket-type, "Automobile Invincible Oil," oval, pictures an oil barrel 95.00

Mirror, pocket-type, "Berry Bros. Toy Wagons," pictures children playing 150.00

Mirror, pocket-type, "Compliments of the Oak Cafe," round, pictures young girl w/flowers 125.00

Mirror, pocket-type, "Delta Lines, Mississippi Shipping Co., Inc., New Orleans, LA," 3½" d. 85.00

Mirror, pocket-type, "Drink Golden Dome Whiskey," round, pictures a whiskey bottle 55.00

Company, Directory Department," 3½" d. 45.00

Mirror, pocket-type, "Murphy Mills Clothing Co.," oval, bust profile of a young woman 110.00

Mirror, pocket-type, "Oliver Chilled Plow Works," pictures James Oliver 145.00

Mirror, pocket-type, "Oxford Chocolates," oval, bust portrait of a young woman graduate 110.00

Mirror, pocket-type, "Queen Quality Shoes," oval, bust portrait of Queen Louise w/star tiara . . . . .50.00 to 75.00

Mirror, pocket-type, "Red Seal Lye," round, pictures a can of lye 75.00

Mirror, pocket-type, "Savoy Theatre," w/decorative metal border . . 34.00

Mirror, pocket-type, "Sterling Range Has No Equal," round, pictures a range 110.00

Mirror, pocket-type, "Union Furniture," oval, profile bust portrait of a young woman within a heartshaped reserve 95.00

Duffy's Pocket Mirror

Mirror, pocket-type, "Duffy's Malt Whiskey," oval, celluloid, inventor pictured (ILLUS.) 95.00

Mirror, pocket-type, "Dyer & Brady Clothiers, Long Beach, Ca.," picture of a beautiful woman (some edge wear) 99.00

Mirror, pocket-type, "First National Bank, Gallatin, Tenn. - We Appreciate your Patronage," red & white decoration 69.00

Mirror, pocket-type, "Horlick's Malted Milk," round, pictures a girl w/cow, white border 45.00

Mirror, pocket-type, "Kyanize Varnishes," pictures a happy/sad man 35.00

Mirror, pocket-type, "Mountain States Telephone & Telegraph

Penna Bottling & Supply Mug

Mug, "Penna Bottling & Supply Co.," pottery, name above a scene of doves on a branch over "Dove Brand - Ginger Ale," shaded brown ground, ca. 1900, 5 1/8" h. (ILLUS.) 71.50

Mug, "Round Oak Stove," pottery, pictures Indian brave Doe-Wah-Jack on shaded brown ground, 1905 . . . . 110.00

Napkin dispenser, restaurant-type, "Royal Crown Cola," metal, cubeshaped 225.00

Needle threader, "Prudential Insurance," tin 6.50

Oven mitt, electric company, w/illustration of "Reddy Kilowatt" 12.00

Package, "Big Kick Chewing Tobacco," w/original contents 10.00

Packing box, "Woonsocket Rub-

bers," wooden, pictures an elephant, 18 x 20" 98.00
Paint book, "Dutch Boy Paint," 1921,
unused 17.00
Paint book, "Planters Peanuts," entitled "Mr. Peanut Happy Time
Paint Book".................... 15.00
Paper dolls, "Es-Ki-Mo Rubber-
boots," eskimos & polar bears on
arctic backdrop, uncut 40.00
Paperweight, "Borden's," glass, illustrates Elsie, copyright "Bor-
dens," 1940 .... 125.00
Paperweight, "Players Navy Cut,"
glass dome, multicolor millefiori
decoration, sailor's head & a ship
on the base 59.00
Party kit, "Kellogg's," entitled "Singing Lady Party Kit," includes
masks & punch-outs, 1936, uncut........................... 60.00
Pen, ballpoint, "Arvin Glaesman -
Ready Mix Concrete - Leola,
SD" 65.00
Pen & pencil set, "Parbeaco - Best
Nibs," Japan, in original box 95.00

Baker's Pencil Sharpener

Pencil sharpener, "Baker's Choco-
late," metal, figural La Belle
Chocolatiere (ILLUS.)............ 65.00
Phonograph record, "Remington
Shaver," entitled "Music To Shave
By, The Adjustable Remington
Shaver," 1948 .... 15.00
Photographs, "Chesterfield Cig-
arettes," photograph signed "Best
Chesterfield Wishes, Helen For-
rest, Corky Corcourau & Johnny
McAlfie," includes pictures of Har-
ry James & His Chesterfield Music
Makers & the full band pictures,
5 x 7", set of 4 .... 45.00
Pin, "Aunt Jemima Breakfast Club,"
3" d., mint condition 60.00
Pinback button, "Baker Windmills,"
celluloid, w/colorful picture in-
cluding windmills, 7/8" d........ 50.00
Pinback button, "The Bulletin,"
Philadelphia newspaper, "Happy
New Years," ca. 1920-30 .... 30.00

Pinback button, "Shoot Peter's
Shells," celluloid, 7/8" d. 40.00
Plaque, "Atwater Kent Radio," cast
brass, pictures a galleon, 3 x 4" .. 15.00
Plate, "Baltimore Dairy," china,
6" d.......................... 20.00
Plates, ice cream parlor-type, "Borden's Ice Cream," cardboard
w/fluted rim, pictures a Borden's
ice cream carton & fruit......... 15.00
Plate, "Union Pacific Tea Co.,"
lithographed tin, center color bust
portrait of a pretty turn-of-the-
century girl w/long blonde curls &
a big ribbon in her hair, wide border design of children & bears
having snowball fights, printed on
the back "Presented and copyright
1907 by The Union Pacific Tea
Co.," 8 1/8" d. 110.00
Platter, "Chicken in the Rough,"
white china, 9½" oval 25.00
Platter, "Texaco," Mayer China,
14" oval 100.00
Playing cards, "Chair City Motor Express Co., Sheboygan, WI" 25.00
Playing cards, "Clark's Spool Cotton," boxed................... 15.00
Playing cards, "Hard A Port Cut
Plug," each card pictures a different beautiful woman in scanty attire, w/Joker (1 card missing,
some poor condition) 132.00
Playing cards, "Planters Peanuts,"
pictures Mr. Peanut in canoe
w/umbrella woman, w/original
box 150.00
Policy case, "Prudential Insurance
Co.," leather, snap lock, dated
"1932" 50.00
Postcard, oversized, "Carnation Ice
Cream," pictures a billboard,
2c postage.................... 20.00
Pot scraper, "King Midas Flour,"
w/illustration of a little girl 225.00
Print, "Pears Soap," "Where Are
You Going My Pretty Maid?,"
in color, w/original frame,
17 x 24½" 125.00
Puppet, hand-type, "Procter & Gam-
ble," cloth, witch Glinda of the
Wizard of Oz 25.00
Radio, "Coors Beer," can-shaped,
mint in box 50.00
Radio, "Pepsi-Cola," soda fountain
syrup dispenser-shaped, "Say
'Pepsi please'," ca. 1960, 12", mint
in box....................... 900.00
Ruler w/1919 calendar, "Glory Soap
Chips," celluloid, fold-up type 15.00
Salt shaker, "White Coffee Pot
Restaurants," glass, pictures wait-
ress holding tray 15.00

Salt & pepper shakers, "Double Cola," aqua glass w/red logos, bottle-shaped, 4¼" h., pr. 25.00

Salt & pepper shakers, "Ken-L-Ration," plastic, models of dogs, one embossed "Fido," the other "Fifi," 1950, pr. 12.00

Salt & pepper shakers, "Planters Peanuts," ceramic, figural Mr. Peanut, pr. 95.00

Screwdriver, "Ferris Bondman Auto Ins., Cincinnati, Ohio," cast iron . . 20.00

Serving tray & recipe booklet, "Betty Crocker," aluminum tray & booklet entitled "Company For Supper," pictures Betty Crocker, 1947, 2 pcs. 15.00

Sheet music, "Anheuser-Busch," entitled "Under the Anheuser-Busch," pictures a man & woman toasting 25.00

Shipping crate, "Cleveland's Superior Baking Powder," wood w/lithographed paper label 45.00

Advertising Shot Glasses

Shot glass, "Old Kentucky Liquors, Cripple Creek, Colo." (ILLUS. left) 28.00

Shot glass, "Old Yucca Rye - Wm. Theobald & Co., St. Paul, MN," clear glass w/etching 49.00

Shot glass, "Red Fox Rye" (ILLUS. right) 42.00

Spatula, "Beechnut Gum," cast iron, 12½" l. 45.00

Stickpin, "Burk Pork Packers, Philadelphia," model of a pig, ca. 1900 . . . . 30.00

Tape measure, "Edison Mazda," celluloid, color graphics 55.00

Tape measure, "Lydia Pinkham," celluloid, picture and "Yours for Health Lydia E. Pinkham," 1¾" d. (ILLUS. top next column) 38.00

Teaspoon, "Heinz," sterling silver, pickle-shaped handle 30.00

Teaspoon, "Towle's Log Cabin Syrup," silver plate, figural cabin at top of handle (ILLUS. top next column) 20.00

Thermometer, "Happy Jim Chewing Tobacco," tin, pictures a hobo 35.00

Lydia Pinkham Tape Measure

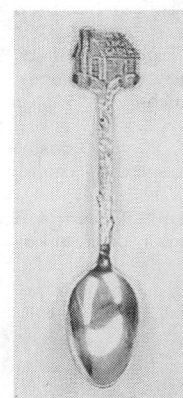

Towle's Log Cabin Syrup Teaspoon

Thermometer, "Nesbitt's Orange," tin, lithographed picture of a bottle 65.00

Tie tack, "Dictaphone Family," copper & blue enamel, model of an early Dictaphone 15.00

Toy, "General Electric," paper punch-out "Wild West Rodeo," in original envelope, 1950's 35.00

Toy wrist watch, "Cracker Jack," lithographed tin, ca. 1940 . . . . 75.00

Toy yo-yo, "Mobile Oil," "Little Ace" by Duncan Yo-yo Co., 1½" d. 135.00

Tumbler, baby, "Pet Milk," milk white glass w/two spouts & ounce measurements, embossed "My Pet Cup," pictures rabbit, duck & cat 25.00

Valentine, "Fleers 'Bang' Gum," pictures a boy pilot, unopened gum stick forms plane 40.00

Whiskey barrel, "Private Stock of Carl Hanekers," wooden w/wooden spigot, 2 gal. 40.00

Window display, "Hohner Harmonica," w/oversized harmonica 125.00

Wrist watch, "Planters Peanuts," w/Mr. Peanut on watch face, in original mailer 43.50

Wrist watch, "Starkist Tuna," pic-
tures Charlie the tuna, 1971 . . . . . .   85.00
Yardstick, "Moxie," wooden 200.00

ALMANACS

*Almanacs have been published for decades.
Commonplace ones are available at $4 to $12;
those representing early printings or scarce
ones are higher.*

Ayer's American Almanac, 1886 . . . . $18.00
Centaur Liniment Almanac, 1873 . . . .   12.50
Dr. Harter's Almanac, 1884 . . . .   8.00
Family Christian Almanac, 1879 . . . . .   8.00
Flying Red Horse Almanac, 1944 . . . .   6.00
Hazeltine's Almanac, 1893,
    1½ x 2" 4.00
Herbalist Almanac, 1943 . . . .   3.00
Herrick's Almanac, 1861 . . . .   8.00
Hostetter's Almanac, 1889 . . . .   10.00
Indianapolis News Almanac, 1894 . . .   12.00
Leavitt's Almanac, 1868 . . . .   7.00
Maine Farmer's Almanac, 1892 . . . . .   14.00
New England Farmer's Almanac,
    1850 . . . .   20.00
Phinney's Western Almanac, 1883,
    48 pp. 4.50
Swamproot Almanac, 1909, Indian
    on cover 35.00

ARCHITECTURAL ITEMS

Early Baroque Doors

*In recent years the growing interest in and
support for historic preservation has spawned
a greater appreciation of the fine architectural
elements which were an integral part of early buildings, both public and private. Where,
in decades past, fine structures might be
razed and doors, fireplace mantels, windows,*
*etc., hauled to the dump, today all interior and
exterior details from unrestorable buildings
are salvaged to be offered to home restorers,
museums and even builders who want to include a bit of history in a new construction
project.*

Attic door, decorated chestnut,
    board & batten construction, rec-
    tangular w/one top corner
    notched, w/original brown grain-
    ing on a salmon ground, original
    iron latch & added bolt, 19th c.,
    25½ x 60¾" $110.00
Door, poplar w/old blue & orange
    paint, four-panel, early 19th c.,
    35¾ x 80¼", 1 1/8" thick (some
    damage at hinges) 319.00
Door, redwood, Arts & Crafts style,
    recessed & paneled construction
    surrounding a stained glass win-
    dow showing the Libby family
    crest, designed by Greene &
    Greene for the Arthur Libby
    home, original finish & hardware,
    ca. 1905, 42½" w., 7' 4" h. (re-
    placed glass) 1,760.00
Doors, brass, inset at the top w/tall
    rectangular Prairie School design
    leaded glass window w/squared
    geometric designs in clear & cara-
    mel slag glass w/red textured
    glass accents, a lower recessed
    panel, early 20th c., 17½" w.,
    39" h., pr. 1,210.00
Doors, fruitwood marquetry, Ba-
    roque style, each w/three
    paneled reserves inlaid w/flower-
    filled urns surmounted by tas-
    selled baldaquin & raised on
    elaborate bracket supports & ta-
    ble tops, all within ebonized back-
    ground & door frames, Europe,
    first quarter 18th c., 19½" w.,
    6' 3" h., pr. (ILLUS.) 7,150.00

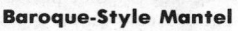

Baroque-Style Mantel

Fireplace mantel, carved oak,
    Baroque-Style, the long rectangu-
    lar shelf w/curved & notched
    corners above a wide central pan-

el carved w/ornate leafy blossom scrolls centered by a cartouche, the end w/full-figure classical ladies standing on outset bases, 19th c., one arm missing (ILLUS.) 4,675.00

Fireplace mantel, hand-hammered copper & bronze, Aesthetic Movement style, the rectangular overmantel panel in hammered copper depicting an arrangement of chestnut leaves, blossoms & berries in bas-relief within a cast-bronze surround above a narrow rectangular mantel above a latticework section raised on molded stiles, England, ca. 1880, 50¾" l., 4' 8" h. 1,760.00

Fireplace mantel, painted pine, Federal style, the projecting shelf above a stepped cornice over an urn-carved tympanum, the sides w/leaf-carved & fluted pilasters topped w/carved urns, painted light green, Massachusetts, early 19th c., overall 91¼" l., 4' 7½" h. 880.00

Fireplace surround, oil paint on panels, the top panel decorated w/a row of round openings, the center three w/owl heads poking through, further round openings down the sides all decorated w/interwoven ivy vines, American-made, unsigned, late 19th - early 20th c., 37 x 43" (minor scattered abrasions & retouch, craquelure) 3,575.00

Keystone, trapezoidal, sandstone carved w/the large head of a lion, dark greyish red stone w/worn white paint, 18" h. 214.50

Plaque, terra cotta, modeled in the half-round w/the figure of a running newsboy, mouth open, presumably crying "Read All About It!," his right arm raised holding a copy of the *Saturday Globe*, the figure posed before a hemispheric globe set within a 'tombstone' arch w/molded edge, now mounted on a black-painted rectangular wooden base, formerly on the Saturday Globe Building, Utica, New York, stamped "H.A. Lewis, South Boston," Massachusetts, 1883-87, 61" w., 5' 1" h. . .14,300.00

Shutters w/movable louvers, painted wood, top rectangular panel w/a cut-out crescent moon & star, old worn blue paint, found in New Hampshire, 17½ x 74½", pr. (age cracks in one top panel) 440.00

Snow eagles, cast iron, w/original

shaft straps, ca. 1865, set of 8 (one is missing lower part of wing & strap) 325.00

Staircase riser, cast iron, the rectangular panel cast w/a frieze of Celtic-inspired decorations including concentric circles & starburst elements, designed by Louis Sullivan for the Chicago Stock Exchange Building, 1893, 42¾" l. . . . 770.00

ART DECO

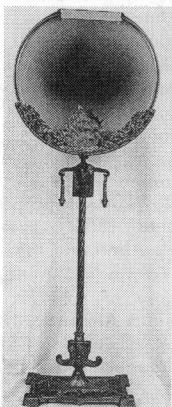

Art Deco Fish Bowl on Stand

Interest in Art Deco, a name given an art movement stemming from the Paris International Exhibition of 1925, is at an all-time high and continues to grow. This style flowered in the 1930's and actually continued into the 1940's. A mood of flippancy is found in its varied characteristics—zigzag lines resembling the lightning bolt, sometimes steps, often the use of sharply contrasting colors such as black and white and others. Look for Art Deco prices to continue to rise.

Belt, hip hugger-type, orange & black beading w/Bakelite dividers $110.00

Candleholders, cast metal, figural nudes, Krome-Kraft, 8½" h., pr. . . 75.00

Carpet, wool, the rectangular grey ground w/fringed ends centering an oval field in teal blue strewn w/stylized rose blossoms & leafage in shades of red, pink, orange, beige, tan & mint green, France, ca. 1930, 6' 3½" x 10' . . .4,675.00

Clock, table model, circular face in clear glass revealing the movement, w/chrome chapter ring & silver plated hands, raised on a stepped glass base, designed by

Maison Desny, France, ca. 1925,
13 3/8" h....................1,760.00

Clock, table model, aluminum, rectangular molded case w/stepped sides & a decorative floral pattern, the top mounted w/a floral bouquet in a vase, ca. 1930's, 14" h........................ 121.00

Fish bowl, flattened moon-shaped green glass bowl raised on a brass-plated metal stand w/a sailing ship scene at the top & raised on a slender twisted standard w/drops continuing down to a pierced rectangular base, ca. 1930's, 42" h. (ILLUS.)........... 550.00

Mirror, wall-type, wrought iron, the oval mirror plate within a conforming surround wrought w/stylized rose blossoms & leafage around lower half w/large scrolls at either side, ca. 1925, 40½" w., 19" h. 1,320.00

Tea set: cov. coffeepot, cov. teapot, cov. sugar bowl & creamer; sterling silver, all of octagonal form w/curved wooden handles & rectangular wooden finials w/a pierced stylized monogram, each impressed "JEAN E. PUIFORCAT," France, largest pot 6" h., the set 8,800.00

ART NOUVEAU

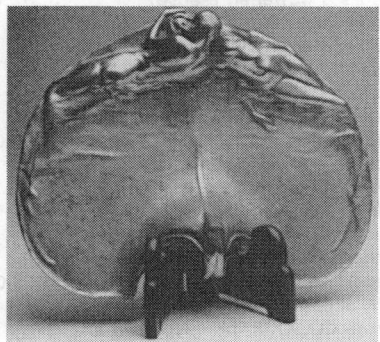

Art Nouveau Tray

Art Nouveau's primary thrust was between 1890 and 1905 but commercial Art Nouveau productions continued until about World War I. This style was a rebellion against historic tradition in art. Using natural forms as inspiration, it is primarily characterized by undulating or wave-like lines. Many objects were made in materials ranging from glass to metals. Interest in Art Nouveau still remains high, especially for jewelry in the Nouveau taste.

Belt, sterling silver, designed as six panels modeled as busts of women w/long flowing hair, joined together by a chain, all attached to a satin ribbon, marked "Kerr," 24" l. $715.00

Chalice, silver, goblet-form, the stem applied w/three ribbon-like supports terminating in repousse' poppies, the foot engraved "1880 16 SEPTEMBER 1905," impressed mark "800 POSEN," Europe, 13" h. 935.00

Dresser set: hand mirror & brush; sterling silver frame w/large repousse' poppy blossoms joined by whiplash swirls, marked "Sterling," mirror 9 5/8" l., 2 pcs. 115.00

Lamp, table model, the sinuous metal harp supporting a ribbed floriform fabric-covered shade raised on a gilt-bronze standard cast w/ribs & expanding at the base w/stylized lotus leaves, by Edward Colonna, inscribed "Colonna," designed for L'Art Nouveau shop, Paris, France, ca. 1900, 18¾" h. 5,500.00

Mirror, wall-type, hammered silver-colored metal & brass, the arch-topped rectangular beveled mirror plate within conforming wooden surround, decorated w/applied hammered silver-colored metal w/stylized blossoms & leafage about a textured brass ground, first quarter 20th c., 43" w., 6' ¾" h. 3,575.00

Tray, bronze, lily pad-shaped w/stem as handle & male & female figures embracing in relief at one side, impressed mark, France, ca. 1900, 11½ x 14½", 2½" h. (ILLUS.) 660.00

Vase, brass, waisted cylindrical body w/flaring rim, decorated w/an applied iris & foliage, 14¼" h. 286.00

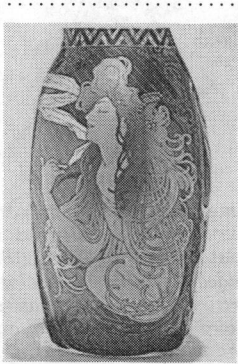

Art Nouveau Portrait Vase

Vase, glass, bulbous w/triangular
opening, clear olive green glass
enameled w/a Mucha-type portrait of a girl w/a cigarette
against a burgundy ground,
10 7/8" h. (ILLUS.) 1,320.00
Vase, porcelain, slightly tapering
cylindrical footed body w/a rounded shoulder below the wide, tall
& gently flaring neck, decorated
around the lower section w/two
maidens in stylized costumes
within a whiplash bordered reserve, the remaining sides w/in-
trelac devices in various colors
w/a stylized floral border at the
neck, all in overglaze colors
& enamels trimmed in gold, factory marked, Austria, ca. 1900,
12 1/8" h. 1,925.00
Wall sconces, bronze, five-light
candle-type, a swelled teardrop-
form wall mount w/pierced ribs
tapering out to issue an arm w/a
down-turned tip suspending a
bell-form cap suspending three
chains composed of small balls
which suspend a pierced disc
w/five short candlearms w/sock-
ets, unsigned, France, ca. 1900,
23" l., pr. 825.00

AUDUBON PRINTS

Broad-winged Hawk

John James Audubon, American ornithol-
ogist and artist, is considered the finest
nature artist in history. About 1820 he con-
ceived the idea of having a full color book pub-
lished portraying every known species of
American bird in its natural habitat. He spent
years in the wilderness capturing the beau-
ty in vivid color only to have great difficulty
finding a publisher. In 1826 he visited
England, received immediate acclaim, and
selected Robert Havell as his engraver.
"Birds of America," when completed, consist-
ed of four volumes of 435 individual plates,
double-elephant folio size, which are a com-
bination of aquatint, etching and line engrav-
ing. W.H. Lizars of Edinburgh engraved the
first ten plates of this four volume series.
These were later retouched by Havell who
produced the complete set between 1827 and
early 1839. In the early 1840's, another defini-
tive work, "Viviparous Quadrupeds of North
America," containing 150 plates, was pub-
lished in America. Prices for Audubon's origi-
nal double-elephant folio size prints are very
high and beyond the means of the average col-
lector. Subsequent editions of "Birds of
America," especially the chromolithographs
done by Julius Bien in New York (1859-60)
and the smaller octavo (7 x 10½") edition of
prints done by J.T. Bowen of Philadelphia in
the 1840's are those that are most frequent-
ly offered for sale.

American Widgeon - Plate CCCXLV,
hand-colored engraving by Robert
Havell, Jr., London, 1827-38,
25 3/8 x 38 1/8" (minor staining,
scattered foxing, transfer to
reverse, nicks & edge tears) $1,870.00
Baltimore Oriole - Plate XII, hand-
colored engraving by Robert
Havell, Jr., London, 1827-38,
framed, 20 5/8 x 25 7/8" (very
light foxing & discoloration, small
tears & flattened crease) 3,575.00
Barred Owl - Plate XLVI, hand-
colored engraving by Robert
Havell, Jr., London, 1827-38,
25¾ x 38¾" (few tiny tears &
creases, old binding holes, some
staining) 3,080.00
Black-billed Cuckoo - Plate XXXII,
hand-colored engraving by Robert
Havell, Jr., London, 1827-38, matted, 25½ x 38" (handling marks &
creases, very minor lower edge
tear) 4,125.00
Black Skimmer or Shearwater -
Plate CCCXXIII, hand-colored engraving by Robert Havell, Jr., London, 1827-38, 25½ x 38" (faint
transfer & ink penetration, fox
marks on margin, minor handling
marks & creases) 2,970.00
Black-Tailed Hare - Plate LXIII,
hand-colored lithograph by J.T.
Bowen, Philadelphia, ca. 1845,
framed, 15¾ x 23 5/8" (pale
traces of mat stain in margins) . .2,090.00
Black-Winged Hawk - Plate CCCLII,
hand-colored engraving by Robert
Havell, Jr., London, 1827-38,

framed, 21¼ x 30 1/8" (slight soiling & fox marks in margin) . . . 1,430.00

Boat-Tailed Grackle - Plate XXXVII, hand-colored engraving by Robert Havell, Jr., London, 1827-38, framed, 20½ x 25 5/8" (slight traces of soiling & fox marks, stitch holes & traces of glue on disbound edge, small margin tears & slight discoloration) 2,475.00

Bonapartian Gull - Plate CCCXXIV, hand-colored engraving by Robert Havell, Jr., London, 1827-38, 16¾ x 21" (tear, creases, some foxing & staining) 1,100.00

Broad-winged Hawk - Plate 91, hand-colored engraving by Robert Havell, Jr., London, 1827-38, matted, laid down, pale foxing & light staining, handling marks & creases at edges, 25¼ x 38 3/8" (ILLUS.) 1,320.00

Canada Otter - Plate LI, hand-colored lithograph by J.T. Bowen, Philadelphia, ca. 1845, 17¾ x 25" (light soiling, small repaired tears in margins, two creases, tiny skinned spot in margin corner) . . . 880.00

Columbia Jay - Plate XCVI, hand-colored engraving by Robert Havell, Jr., London, 1827-38, 27½ x 37¼" (small rubbed spots, scattered foxing, minor stains & tears, backed) 4,400.00

Dusky Duck - Plate CCCII, hand-colored engraving by Robert Havell, Jr., London, 1827-38, framed, 24¾ x 37 5/8" (pale foxing, conserved vertical crease through center, pale mat staining, minor edge nicks & tears) 3,850.00

Eider Duck - Plate CCXLVI, hand-colored engraving by Robert Havell, Jr., London, 1827-38, 23¼ x 35 7/8" (slight discoloration, small tears & losses in margins, few creases & larger losses along disbound edge, lower corner broken off) 17,600.00

Gadwall Duck - Plate CCCXLVIII, hand-colored engraving by Robert Havell, Jr., London, 1827-38, 25½ x 37 7/8" (minor rubs in image, nick & tears to edges, handling creases & marks) 1,870.00

Golden-Eye Duck - Plate CCCXLII, hand-colored engraving by Robert Havell, Jr., London, 1827-38, 38 3/8" w., 25¾" h. (slight soiling & mat stain in margins, small razor cut in extreme upper margin at left, few small tears along disbound edge) 3,300.00

Goshawk; Stanley Hawk - Plate

CXLI, hand-colored engraving by Robert Havell, Jr., London, 1827-38, 25½ x 38 1/8" (minor soiling, nicks & losses to edges, tape residue upper edge) 1,540.00

Great Cinerous Owl - Plate CCCLI, hand-colored engraving by Robert Havell, Jr., London, 1827-38, 25 x 37½" (pale water stain in lower margin, trimmed at corners, minor soiling) 4,400.00

Hooded Merganser

Hooded Merganser - Plate CCXXXII, hand-colored engraving by Robert Havell, Jr., London, 1827-38, framed, some discoloring & foxing, minor creases & nicks in margins, 20¾ x 25¾" (ILLUS.) 2,310.00

Labrador Falcon - Plate CXCVI, hand-colored engraving by Robert Havell, Jr., London, 1827-38, 25 x 38" (repaired tears, pale time staining) 2,090.00

Mallard Duck - Plate CCXXI, hand-colored engraving by Robert Havell, Jr., London, 1827-38, matted, 25 1/8 x 38 1/8" (mount staining, scattered foxing, nicks & tears to edges, unobtrusive abrasions to image) 11,000.00

Mottled Owl - Plate 97, hand-colored engraving by Robert Havell, Jr., London, 1827-38, framed, 20½ x 25 5/8" (small spots of soiling, pale discoloration & small losses & tears in margins) 2,200.00

Orchard Oriole - Plate 42, hand-colored engraving by Robert Havell, Jr., London, 1827-38, 20¾ x 25¾" (pale scattered foxing & time staining) 2,090.00

Raccoon (Male), Plate LXI, hand-colored lithograph by J.T. Bowen, Philadelphia, ca. 1845, 27 1/8" w., 21" h. (margins w/some soiling & mat stain, verso w/slight mottled discoloration) 6,600.00

Raven - Plate CI, hand-colored engraving by Robert Havell, Jr., London, 1827-38, 25 5/8 x 38 5/8" (repaired tear, pale soiling) 4,620.00

Red-headed Woodpecker - Plate 27, hand-colored lithograph by Robert Havell, Jr., London, 1827-38, 21¾ x 25 3/8" (repaired tear at top, pale staining) 2,200.00

Red-Shouldered Hawk, Plate LVI, hand-colored engraving by Robert Havell, Jr., London, 1827-38, 25 7/8 x 38 7/8" (very minor tape along binding edge, several unobtrusive foxing marks, two minute nicks along lower edge) 3,400.00

Ruff-necked Humming-bird - Plate CCCLXXIX, hand-colored engraving by Robert Havell, Jr., London, 1827-38, matted, 25½ x 38" (foxing in margins, minor handling creases & marks, minor nicks in edge) 2,090.00

White-headed Eagle - Plate 31, hand-colored engraving by Robert Havell, Jr., London, 1827-38, 26 x 38¾" (paper losses, tears & tack holes at edges) 2,860.00

Wild Turkey, Female - Plate VI, hand-colored engraving by Robert Havell, Jr., London, 1827-38, 25 3/8 x 38¼" (image slightly trimmed, several small tears & losses, some discoloration & foxing on verso) 7,150.00

Yellow-billed Magpie; Stellers Jay; Ultramarine Jay; Clark's Crow - Plate CCCLXII, hand-colored engraving by Robert Havell, Jr., London, 1827-38, 25 5/8 x 38" (rub to plate mark, pale foxing, minor nicks & edge tears) 2,310.00

AUTOGRAPHS

Letter from Abraham Lincoln

Values of autographs and autograph letters depend on such factors as content, scarcity and the fame of the writer. Values of good autograph material continue to rise. A.L.S. stands for *"autographed letter signed,"* L.S. for *"letter signed,"* D.S. for *"document signed"* and S.P. for *"signed photograph."*

Brahms, Johannes, (1833-97) German composer, S.P. $1,320.00

Bronson, Charles, (1922-) American actor, S.P., 8 x 10" 8.00

Burr, Aaron C., (1756-1836) 3rd Vice President of the United States, A.L.S., signed to Mr. Hedges, Esquire, dated New York, July 8th, 1829, one page (creases) 467.50

Correll, Charles, (1890-1972) radio personality, played "Andy" in the 'Amos & Andy' series, S.P., black & white movie still showing the two characters, inscribed "To Miss Thompson - This scene is taken from our picture. Best Wishes, Chas. Correll - Andy, Amos & Andy" 165.00

DiMaggio, Joe, (1914-) baseball player, S.P., vintage wire photo, Joe pictured w/Ken Kiltner, 7 x 10" 100.00

Edison, Thomas A., (1847-1931) American inventor, signed calling card dated "April 23, 1878," together w/an early engraved portrait, 2 pcs. (slight rust damage) . . 330.00

Garbo, Greta, (1906-90) actress, signed bank card, inscribed "Greta Garbo *In Trust For* Sven Gustafson - *Residence* 165 Maberry Road Santa Monica Cal. - *Married* no - *Date of Birth* Sept. 18 - *Occupation* actress - *Father's Name* Karl Gustafson - *Mother's Maiden Name* Anna Gustafson - *Kin* Brother - *Date of Birth* July 26," similar typewritten information on the back, 3 x 5" 1,430.00

Gibson, Hoot, (1892-1962) American actor, S.P., 8 x 10" 150.00

Grable, Betty, (1916-73) American actress, S.P., 8 x 10" 90.00

Harlow, Jean, (1911-37) American movie star, S.P., black & white photo of the actress standing wearing a white riding habit & holding the leash of a large dog, inscribed "To Miss Y.A.M. sincerely & Kindly Jean Harlow," 8 x 10" 715.00

Harrison, Benjamin, (1833-1901) 23rd President of the United States, D.S., appointment of George C. French as Notary Public for the District of Columbia, cosigned by the Attorney General, dated March 24, 1890, on paper, unframed 725.00

Holiday, Billie, (1915-59) American

singer, S.D., typed letter to Mr. Bill Robinson authorizing the deduction of monies from the Oasis club appearances, August 24 through September 5, signed in blue ballpoint pen, dated April 3, 1954, 8½ x 11" 440.00

Johnson, Andrew, (1808-75) 17th President of the United States, D.S., nomination of George H. French as Major by Brevet in the U.S. Volunteers, co-signed by Edwin Stanton, Secretary of War, dated at Washington, June 30, 1866, on vellum, unframed 1,550.00

Lincoln, Abraham, (1809-65) 16th President of the United States, A.L.S., to T.C. Durant regarding a telegram, dated October 16, 1883, on White House stationery, framed w/a photograph of Lincoln, overall 13½ x 19½" (ILLUS.) 28,600.00

Madison, James, (1751-1836) 4th President of the United States, D.S., signature on printed land grant, awarding one hundred acres for military service, dated 1815, framed, 16¾" w., 12¾" h........................330.00

Monroe, James, (1758-1831) 5th President of the United States, D.S., signed land grant dated August 6, 1823 .... 715.00

Presley, Elvis, (1935-77) American singer & actor, S.P., color photograph of Elvis in military uniform w/his acoustic guitar, inscribed "Best Wishes - Elvis," 8 x 10"..... 330.00

Rand, Sally, (1904-79) American exotic dancer, S.P., promotional photo from "The Click" theatre restaurant, Philadelphia, ca. 1930's 65.00

Rockwell, Norman, (1894-1978) American artist, L.S., on personal stationery 65.00

Roosevelt, Franklin D., (1882-1945) 32nd President of the United States, book entitled "The Democratic Book of 1936" signed on a page at the front picturing the White House 417.00

Roosevelt, Franklin D., (1882-1945) 32nd President of the United States, signature clipped from White House stationery 192.50

Roosevelt, Theodore, (1858-1919) 26th President of the United States, signed program of the Hamilton Club of Chicago, September 10, 1910, together w/guest list & envelope, the group 325.00

Stanton, Edwin M., (1814-69) Secretary of War under Abraham Lincoln, A.L., signed at the War Department, advising George H. French of his appointment as First Lieutenant of the Invalid Corps, dated October 27, 1863 .... 280.00

Turner, Lana, (1920-) American actress, S.P., 8 x 10" 25.00

Signed Photo of Rudolph Valentino

Valentino, Rudolph, (1895-1926) American movie star, S.P., sepia bust picture signed in lower right "Sincerely Rudolph Valentino," further inscribed at upper left "To Johnny Johnson In memory of my Brother Rudolph with deep appreciation Alberto Valentino," photo marked in lower right hand corner "Henry Waxman V.P. 181," 8 x 10" (ILLUS.) 550.00

Washington, George, (1732-99) 1st President of the United States, A.L.S., six & a half pages handwritten on two leaves, addressed to Tobias Lear & dated Philadelphia, December 21, 1794 (minor discoloration on verso along fold lines, minute losses at edge of fold lines)....................38,500.00

Welk, Lawrence, (1903-92) American musician, S.P., color, 8 x 10" 25.00

Wood, Natalie, (1938-81) American actress, S.P., 8 x 10" 125.00

AUTOMOBILE LITERATURE

Book, "Automobile Engineering Volume V," welding, shops, garages, motorcycles, steam cars, illustrated, ca. 1920 .... $15.00

Book, "Dyke's Auto Encyclopedia," 1912, second edition, St. Louis.... 75.00

Book, "Official Automobile Blue Book," 1915................... 32.00

Buick owner's manual & service poli-
cy, 1933 .... 20.00
Buick Six owner's manual, 1920 ..... 15.00
Chevrolet owner's manual, "Instruc-
tions for Your 1937 Chevrolet" 25.00
Chevrolet owner's manual, 1955 .... 10.00
Chrysler Town & Country dealer's
fold-out brochure, shows cars,
1946 .... 26.00
Corvair shop manual, 1960 .... 20.00
Dodge dealer's brochure, 1957 ..... 20.00
Edsel shop manual, 1958, large 33.00
Ford Falcon catalog, 1963, full color
photographs, Peanuts cartoon
characters, 28 pp. 35.00
Ford Model T owner's manual,
1915 .... 15.00
Ford owner's supply book, 1927,
128 pp. 25.00
Ford service manual, 1925, detailed
instructions for servicing Ford
cars 30.00
Ford Thunderbird owner's manual,
1955 .... 12.00
GMC military shop manual, 1941 ... 18.00
Graham-Paige owner's manual, ca.
1920's 15.00
Jaguar dealer's brochure, show-
room-type, 1953 Jaguar XK120
convertible model, illustrated 21.00
Magazine, Automobile Digest, 1930,
July 5.00
Magazine, Auto Trade Journal, 1917,
November, Commercial Motor Car
Number, 388 pp. 29.00
Magazine, Motor Age, 1943,
September 12.50
Oldsmobile dealer's brochure, 1924,
fold-out type, depicts Oldsmobile
8 Model 46, w/specifications de-
scription, 16 x 18" unfolded 15.00
Oldsmobile dealer's brochure,
1954 .... 10.00
Oldsmobile shop manual, 1940 ..... 20.00
Oldsmobile Six dealer's brochure,
1931 .... 25.00
Packard dealer's brochure, fold-out
type, 1951 .... 10.00
Rambler sales booklet, 1905, suede-
like cover, 16 pp., 9½ x 12¼" ... 30.00
Reo Eight dealer's brochure, 1931 ... 10.00
Reo Flying Cloud dealer's brochure,
1929 .... 25.00
Thomas Auto Top Company catalog,
August, 1920, Muncie, fabric, radi-
ators, hood covers, w/specs.,
prices, etc., most cars, illustrated,
20 pp. 25.00
Western Auto owner's supply book,
1929, 128 pp. 25.00
Willys military shop manual, 1941 ... 18.00

AUTOMOBILES

1940 Cadillac Convertible

Austin, 1967 Mini-Mook, good running condition, 10,000 original
miles $3,200.00
Cadillac, 1940 Convertible, black exterior w/white top, V-8 engine,
141" wheel base, limited production, restored (ILLUS.) 65,000.00
Chevrolet, 1956 Bel Air, butterscotch
& white paint, original motor, restored interior 3,500.00
Chevrolet, 1957 210 Series, four-
door, power brakes, new paint,
no rust, odometer reading
81,901 ....5,500.00
Chevrolet, 1961 Corvair pickup
truck, w/rampside, factory-made,
fully restored 5,500.00
Ford, 1921 pickup truck, all-wood
body, runs well, driveable 5,800.00
Ford, 1927 Model T, two-passenger,
good running condition 8,000.00
Ford, 1958 Edsel Ranger, four-door,
completely restored 4,700.00
Jaguar, 1963 MK II sedan, six-
cylinder, white exterior w/blue interior, standard transmission,
odometer reads 89,970 miles 6,050.00
LaSalle, 1939 hearse, mechanically
sound, original condition, from
California 9,500.00
Mercedes-Benz, 1969 300 SEL, four-
door sedan, automatic transmission, eight-cylinder engine, dark
green exterior w/matching leather interior, odometer reading
46,446 miles 13,200.00

AUTOMOTIVE COLLECTIBLES

Air compressor, portable, figure of
the Michelin man seated astride
the oblong bullet-shaped cast
metal compressor housing, flat
gauge on top below the rubber
bail handle, brass plate on front
end reads "R. Toussaint & Co. -
Wageor & Cou.Finhal," ca.
1920-30, 11" h. (some paint
drips)........................$1,650.00

Antenna decoration, furry Breeze Tail, "For Autos, Bicycles & Tricycles," mint in package depicting a car & a boy on bicycle, ca. 1950's 20.00

Ashtray, chrome, figural Mack Bulldog on headlight reflector, Central Die Casting, Chicago (small pit spot) 65.00

Book, "Official Automobile Blue Book - 1918," Volume 2, covers the region of New England, eastern Canada & the Maritime Provinces, features early advertising, hard covers 132.00

Book, "Why You Should Buy An Oakland," 1920, hardbound 25.00

Chauffeur's badge, 1911, Missouri, No. 1214 (missing pin) 55.00

Chauffeur's badge, 1917, Pennsylvania 47.50

Chauffeur's badge, 1923, California 75.00

Chauffeur's badge, 1925, New York 27.50

Gasoline pump globe, "Atlantic White Flash," milk white glass, white lettering on a red & blue background, ca. 1946-53, 16½" d. 330.00

Gasoline pump globe, "Gargoyle Mobiloil," oval milk white glass, raised black lettering "Gargoyle" above a raised gargoyle logo in maroon & black above "Mobiloil," before 1938, 16¼" w., 12¼" h. (some paint restoration) 1,650.00

Gasoline pump globe, "Metro," milk white glass, red bands above & below a wide white center band printed w/"Metro" in green w/red outlining, ca. 1930-40, 16½" d. ... 385.00

Mobilgas Gas Pump Globe

Gasoline pump globe, "Mobilgas," milk white glass w/red Pegasus logo above "Mobilgas" in blue, ca. 1936-47, 15" d., 15½" h. (ILLUS.)........................ 341.00

Gasoline pump globe, "Sinclair Diesel," milk white glass, green background w/white lettering, ca. 1959-70, 16½" d. 198.00

Gear shift knob, green & cream swirl glass 45.00

Hood ornament, "Pontiac," metal & glass, 1947 .... 45.00

Hood ornament, "Pontiac Super Chief," lighted, w/instructions, 1950, mint in box 225.00

Hubcap, "Bentley," 1949 .... 35.00

Hubcaps, "LaSalle," 1940, set of 4 (one w/small dent) 100.00

Hubcaps, "Packard," 1956, mint in original Studebaker Packard envelopes, set of 4 .... 35.00

Indian headband w/real feathers, "Pontiac," promotional item, 1952 .... 30.00

License plate, 1914, Massachusetts, porcelain ....150.00 to 200.00

License plate, 1915, Illinois, front, slotted, 90% original paint 49.50

License plate, 1925, South Dakota .. 10.00

License plate, 1937, Texas 12.50

License plate, motorcycle, 1930, Georgia 15.00

Lug wrench, Model T Ford 25.00

Medallion, "Ford," bronze, 'Henry Ford Centennial, 1863-1963,' made by Medallic Art Co., New York, given to owners of Ford dealerships, 2¼ x 3½" oval 350.00

Oil Pouring Can

Oil pouring can, "Monamobile Oil," metal, wide strap handle & broad pouring spout at rim, large printed label showing four planes, a boat & an early touring car & bicycle & "Monamobile Oil - for All Motor Vehicles...," printed in silver & blue, ca. 1910-20, some label wear, 8" h. (ILLUS.) 198.00

Oil-testing thermometer, brass, a tall slender cylinder cut out along one side to hold the thermometer tube & temperature scale, conical top & heavy brass bail handle at top, marked along tube "Red Reading Mercury - Property of Socony Vacuum Oil - Palmer, Cin.O.," ca. 1910-20, 1¾" d., 16" h. 55.00

Pen, mechanical, "Dodge," dealer item, tiny blue Dodge car floats in oil inside pen, ca. 1940's 45.00

Pinback button, "Plymouth Hotter Than a Firecracker," celluloid, w/ribbons attached, ca. 1940 ..... 38.00

Plate, dinner, china, "Ford" in script w/rotunda building scene, 9" d. ... 65.00

Promotional decoration, silvered bronze figure of a winged female standing above a crested tray bearing the Rolls-Royce double "R" trade-mark, cast Rolls-Royce logo front & back, inscribed "Gorham Founders 08AU," 5½" d., 5¼" h. 660.00

Radiator cap, Art Deco style, figure of a male golfer, Weidlich, 6" h... 150.00

Radiator cap, "Dodge," metal, figural ram, 1932 .... 50.00

Radio, "Ford," 1940 deluxe model... 200.00

Shoulder patch, cloth, round, "Oldsmobile Service," ca. 1940 .... 24.00

Taillight lens, "Chevrolet," 1934 .... 12.00

Tire pressure gauge, for Model A Ford, 1927-30 .... 100.00

Tire pump, portable, a large figure of the Michelin man riding on top of cast-iron pump fitted on carriage w/two rubber wheels at back below the long metal loop handle wrapped w/the air hose, ca. 1930's, 12½" w., 32½" h. (paint worn) 1,980.00

Turn signals, novelty, "Monsturn," model of Frankenstein w/turn signal light bulbs in each hand, hooks up to the car battery, ca. 1960's 200.00

AVIATION COLLECTIBLES

Recently much interest has been shown in collecting items associated with the early days of the "flying machine." In addition to relics, flying adjuncts and literature relating to the early days of flight, collectors also seek out items that picture the more renowned early pilots, some of whom became folk-heroes in their own lifetimes, as well as the early planes themselves.

Book, "The Aeroplane Speaks," by H. Barber, 1928, Robert McBride Co., New York, ninth edition, black & white illustrations, plane styles, engine specs, 6½ x 10", 200 pp. $65.00

Book, "National Air Race Directory," 1939, 19th anniversary, wraps, 10 x 13", 64 pp. 65.00

Book, "We," by Charles Lindbergh, 1927 .... 42.00

Book, "What's That Plane?," 1943, Penguin Paperback, identification of American & Japanese planes, illustrated, wraps, 223 pp. (small tear to cover) 15.00

Book, "Your Wings," by Assen Jordanoff, 1939, Funk & Wagnall, black & white illustrations, cartoons, instructions, 7½ x 9¾", w/dust jacket, 282 pp. (small repaired tear & light soil to dust jacket) 65.00

Book ends, bronzed metal, bust of Charles Lindbergh, signed "Verona," ca. 1930, 6 1/8" h., pr. 35.00

Bust of Charles Lindbergh, goldwashed metal, Lindbergh depicted wearing aviator's cap & goggles, detailed features, signed "N. Tregor - 3," 6" h. 50.00

Catalog, Nicholas Bealey Airplane Co., 1929 .... 75.00

Lunch box, child's, scene entitled "History of Aviation," oval, ca. 1930's 120.00

Medallion, brass, commemorating "First East to West Transatlantic Flight, April 12-13, 1928," w/busts of flyers reverse & airplane "Bremen" 35.00

Model, "FH-105 Thunderchief," heavily polished aluminum, w/stand .. 385.00

Photograph, "International Aviation Meet," panoramic, black & white, depicts plane over lakefront at Chicago, 1911, 7¾ x 20" 200.00

Pinback button, Charles Lindbergh pictured, New York to Paris, 1927 .... 60.00

Print, "Spirit of St. Louis," by Zula Kenyon, scene of plane flying over water, in original frame, 10 x 13" 55.00

Propeller, laminated hard-rock maple w/copper edge & tips, 6' l. ... 475.00

Puzzle, jigsaw-type, "Pan American Clipper," Jaymar 20.00

Schedule brochure, "Northwest Airlines," 1939 .... 15.00

Table cover, hand-crocheted, scene of plane in center & "The Spirit of St. Louis," 17½ x 25" 95.00

Tapestry, woven, commemorating Charles Lindbergh's flight from New York to Paris, New York City

& Paris skylines w/Spirit of St.
Louis in center, France, 19 x 52".. 175.00
Ticket, Mitchell Trophy Race air
show, Selfridge Field, Mt. Clemens, Michigan, 1938 .... 30.00

BABY MEMENTOES

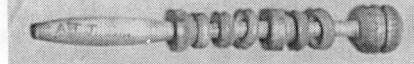

Early Wooden Rattle

*Everyone dotes on the new baby and
through many generations some exquisite
and unique gifts have been carefully selected with a special infant in mind. Collectors
now seek items from a varied assortment of
baby mementoes, once tokens of affection to
the newborn babe. Also see CHILDREN'S
BOOKS and CHILDREN'S MUGS.*

Blanket, hand-made, fine beige
twill, sateen back, hand-
embroidered blue ribbons, ca.
1920's, 36" sq. $50.00
Breakfast set: mug & plate; china,
decorated w/a scene of Dutch
children on tan ground, Syracuse
China, ca. 1960 .... 50.00
Carriage, Landau-style, decorated
wood & leather, a shallow curved
wood body painted black w/ele-
gant yellow pinstriping & w/a
tufted leather seat, a fold-down
leather top w/three oval windows, curved handles w/turned
wooden crossbar, on steel springs
raised on two large back wheels
& two smaller front wheels
w/delicate spokes, S.H. Kimball,
Boston, Massachusetts, ca. 1870,
40" l. 5,500.00
Feeding dish, china, depicts kids
teaching a dog to smoke a pipe,
Germany 125.00
Feeding spoon, gold-washed sterling
silver, loop handle, "Baby" on
handle w/enameled reserve, "Little Miss Muffet" scene in bowl ... 49.00
Rattle, celluloid, depicts Old King
Cole on drum, w/delicate swan
finial, 7" l. 135.00
Rattle, celluloid, model of an Art
Deco-style peacock, full-length
plumage, green & yellow,
5" l. 55.00
Rattle, celluloid, model of a stork
w/baby 65.00
Rattle, celluloid, model of a turtle .. 15.00
Rattle, sterling silver, dumbbell-
shaped, heavy, 3" l. 40.00

Rattle, sterling silver w/mother-of-
pearl, decorated w/an etching of
a bunny 55.00
Rattle, turned wood, cylindrical
shaft w/slight swelling for handgrip at one end, the other end in
the form of a compressed ball
w/incised band at middle, shaft
w/seven loose rings that slide up
& down, carved "A.T. Junior,"
14" l. (ILLUS.) 60.50
Teething ring, mother-of-pearl,
w/sterling silver bell 55.00

BAKELITE

*Bakelite is the trade-mark for a group of
thermoplastics invented by Leo Hendrik
Baekeland, an American chemist who invented this early form of plastic in 1909, only
twenty years after immigrating to New York
City from his native Belgium where he had
taught at the University of Ghent. Bakelite
opened the door to modern plastics and was
widely used as an electrical insulating material replacing the flammable celluloid. Jewelry
designers of the 1920's considered Bakelite
the perfect medium to create pieces in the Art
Deco style and today Bakelite bracelets, earrings and pins of this period are finding favor with another generation of modish
women.*

Belt, lady's, link-type, orange &
amber $15.00
Belt buckle, model of a horseshoe,
large........................ 37.50
Bracelet, bangle-type, carved, dark
green w/molded butterscotch
rope 40.00
Bracelet, bangle-type, painted cherry red & geometrically carved to
reveal white 30.00
Dresser box, cov., hexagonal,
brown & black marbleized, ribbed
cover, w/reverse "K," 9" w....... 100.00
Manicure scissors, red Bakelite
handles 12.00
Mechanical pencil, green, rifle-
shaped, engraved "Good Luck
Soldier" 35.00
Napkin ring, figural elephant
w/ball 85.00
Napkin ring, figural Scottie dog,
red 35.00
Pencil sharpener, model of an
airplane 30.00
Pencil sharpener, model of an Army
tank 25.00
Pin, bullet-shaped, w/carved wood
U.S. Army jeep hanging from it .. 125.00

Pin, carved heart-shape, red w/red
   balls hanging from center, large . . 125.00
Pin, model of a Scottie dog,
   brown 25.00

BANKS

Original early mechanical and cast-iron still banks are in great demand with collectors and their scarcity has caused numerous reproductions of both types and the novice collector is urged to exercise caution. The early mechanical banks are especially scarce and some versions are seldom offered for sale but, rather, are traded with fellow collectors attempting to upgrade an existing collection. Numbers before mechanical banks refer to those in John Meyer's Handbook of Old Mechanical Banks. *However, a recently published book,* Penny Lane - A History of Antique Mechanical Toy Banks, *by Al Davidson, provides updated information and the number from this new volume is indicated in parenthesis at the end of each mechanical bank listing.*

In past years, our standard reference for cast-iron still banks was Hubert B. Whiting's book Old Iron Still Banks, *but because this work is out of print and a beautiful new book,* The Penny Bank Book - Collecting Still Banks *by Andy and Susan Moore pictures and describes numerous additional banks, we will use the Moore numbers as a reference preceding each listing and indicate the Whiting reference in parenthesis at the end. The still banks listed are old and in good original condition with good paint and no repair unless otherwise noted. An asterisk (*) indicates this bank has been reproduced at some time.*

MECHANICAL

Boy Scout Camp Bank

1   Acrobat (PL 1) . . $4,500.00 to 5,500.00
7   Artillery - eight-sided Block
   House, no soldier 2,420.00
   Blacksmith w/sledge hammer
   in hand hammers penny

into anvil, embossed "Bank
on John Deere Quality," ca.
1950, figure stands 7" h.,
4¾" sq. base, overall
9½" h. 150.00
21   Boy Scout Camp, PL 52
   (ILLUS.) . . . . . 15,000.00 to 20,000.00
24   Bread Winner (PL 54) 38,500.00
   Called Out Bank, soldier
   standing on top of pyramid, J. & E. Stevens Co.,
   Connecticut, ca. 1900
   (PL 95) 8,800.00

Chief Big Moon Bank

42   Chief Big Moon, PL 108
   (ILLUS.) 6,325.00
49   Clown on Globe
   (PL 127) . . . . 2,000.00 to 2,400.00
51   Confectionery Store
   (PL 131) . . . . 8,000.00 to 8,500.00
54   Creedmore - New (Tyrolese
   Bank), PL 358 . . . . . 750.00 to 800.00
53   Creedmore - Soldier aims Rifle at Target in Tree trunk
   (PL 137) 935.00
57   Dentist (PL 152) 12,100.00
58   Dinah (PL 153) . . . . . 400.00 to 600.00
63   Dog - Bulldog Bank - Coin on
   Nose (PL 64) 1,210.00
65   Dog - Bulldog - Standing
   (PL 66) 715.00
67   Dog on Turntable (PL 159) . . . 1,650.00
80   Elephant, modern
   (PL 174) . . . . 550.00 to 650.00
   Elephant, w/Howdah,
   w/tusks, pull tail
   (PL 175) . . . . 450.00 to 500.00
106   Germania Exchange
   (PL 211) 23,100.00
116   Goat - Butting
   (PL 91) . . . . 650.00 to 1,000.00
   Grenadier Bank
   (PL 223) . . . . 700.00 to 775.00
124   Home Bank - Door w/three-
   paneled window on each
   side & three steps leading
   to door, man in doorway,
   4¼ x 4½ x 5½" (PL 243) . . 1,100.00
   Horse Race, w/straight base
   (PL 246) 3,080.00
129   Indian Shooting Bear
   (PL 257) 2,475.00

132   Jolly Nigger - Shepard Hard-
      ware Co., Buffalo, N.Y.,
      March 14, 1882 (PL 275) ...1,430.00
138   Jonah and the Whale
      (PL 282) ....4,500.00 to 5,000.00
139   Jonah and Whale on Pedestal
      (PL 283)................55,000.00

Kiltie Bank

Kiltie - Scotsman's Head,
      PL 290 (ILLUS.) ....700.00 to 800.00
145   Lighthouse (PL 298) 1,980.00
131   Little Jocko Musical Bank
      (PL 303).................7,700.00
154   Magician
      (PL 315) ....6,500.00 to 8,500.00
159   Mikado (PL 326) 55,000.00
164   Monkey and Organ Grinder
      (PL 334)........700.00 to 1,000.00
169   Mule Entering Barn
      (PL 342) ....1,800.00 to 2,000.00
173   National Bank (PL 356) 26,400.00
176   Novelty, House (PL 361) 1,100.00
179   Organ Bank - with Monkey on
      Top (PL 371) ...1,500.00 to 1,900.00
184   Owl with Book - Slot in Book
      (PL 373) ....450.00 to 550.00

Picture Gallery Bank

192   Picture Gallery, PL 385
      (ILLUS.) .....9,000.00 to 10,500.00
196   Pony - Trick, worn paint
      (PL 484) ....1,200.00 to 1,500.00
203   Punch & Judy (PL 404).......2,310.00
208   Red Riding Hood (PL 412) ...57,200.00
216   Scotchman - tin
      (PL 434) ....600.00 to 700.00

Stump Speaker Bank

222   Stump Speaker, PL 453
      (ILLUS.) 2,860.00
224   Tammany (PL 455)...450.00 to 550.00
226   Teddy and the Bear in Tree
      (PL 459)................2,420.00
231   Uncle Sam with Satchel
      & Umbrella
      (PL 493) ....3,500.00 to 5,000.00
237   William Tell
      (PL 565) ....750.00 to 900.00
244   World's Fair Bank - with
      Columbus and Indian
      (PL 573) ....1,350.00 to 1,650.00

STILL

Aunt Jemima Bank

219   "Andy Gump Savings Bank,"
      lead, General Thrift
      Products, 1920's,
      5¾ x 5¾"................ 500.00
1424   Armoured Car, World War I
      mobile army unit, cast iron,
      A.C. Williams Co., Ohio,
      1914-27, 6¾" l., 3¾" h.
      (W. 160) 2,500.00
1498   Armoured Truck Bank, metal,
      Callen Mfg. Corp., Ameri-
      can-made, 2¾ x 5¼"...... 150.00
1482   Automobile - Limousine, with
      driver, cast iron w/steel
      wheels, Arcade Mfg. Co.,
      Illinois (No. 05 model),
      ca. 1921, 8 1/16" l.,
      3½" h. 2,200.00

907 Barrel - White City Barrel
     No. 1 on Cart, cart w/two
     wheels, cast iron, Nicol,
     patd. 1894, 5" l. cart
     (W. 286)..........300.00 to 350.00

715 Bear - Begging Bear, cast
     iron, A.C. Williams, ca.
     1910 & Arcade, 1910-25,
     5 3/8" h. (W. 330) * 80.00

693 Bear - Bear Stealing Pig,
     original gold paint,
     American-made,
     5½" h...........850.00 to 950.00

713 Bear - Mean Standing Bear,
     w/paws clasped at waist &
     coin slot from side to side,
     cast iron, Hubley Mfg. Co.,
     Pennsylvania, ca. 1906,
     5½" h. (W. 329) * 135.00

683 Beehive Bank, cast iron,
     Kyser & Rex, Pennsylvania,
     1882, 2½" h. *....135.00 to 175.00

598 Bird (Owl) - "Be Wise Owl,"
     "Be Wise - Save Money" on
     stump, cast iron, A.C. Wil-
     liams, 1912-20's, 2½" w.,
     4 7/8" h. ......150.00 to 175.00

24   Black Boy - Save & Smile
     Money Box, caricature head
     w/gold hat w/lettering on
     brim, cast iron, Sydenham
     & McOustra or Chamberlain
     & Hill, England, 4" w.,
     4¼" h. (W. 46) * ..325.00 to 350.00

170 Black Boy - Young Negro,
     bust, embossed "The Young
     Nigger Bank" on back, cast
     iron, England, 4½" h.
     (W. 42) 220.00

168 Black Woman - Aunt Jemima
     (Mammy with Spoon), cast
     iron, A.C. Williams,
     1905-30's, 5 7/8" h.,
     W. 17 * (ILLUS.) 137.50

1623 Book - "Scrappy Bank," book-
     shaped, covered metal,
     key-locked trap, Zell
     Products Co., 3 1/8" w.,
     3¼" h. 45.00

984 Building - Blackpool Tower,
     cast iron, Chamberlain
     & Hill, ca. 1908,
     2 7/8 x 4 3/8",
     7 3/8" h. ....150.00 to 200.00

954 Building - Castle Bank, cast
     iron, Kyser & Rex, 1882,
     1 13/16 x 2 13/16", 3" h.
     (W. 354) 175.00

991 Building (Church) - Old South
     Church, cast iron, Ameri-
     can-made, 4½ x 7½",
     13" h., W. 448 (ILLUS. top
     next column) 4,675.00

958 Building (Church) - Westside

Old South Church Bank

Presbyterian Church, back
door opens w/key, cast
iron, American-made, ca.
1916, 3½" w., 3¾" h.
(W. 282).........400.00 to 500.00

1182 Building - Domed "Bank,"
     building w/cast iron mesh
     sides & solid cast iron
     domed roof, A.C. Williams,
     1899-1934, 2 x 3¼", 4½" h.
     (W. 422) 70.00

999 Building (House) - Bungalow
     Bank (Cottage with Porch),
     cast iron, Grey Iron,
     1918-28, 3 x 3¼",
     3¾" h. (W. 377)........... 275.00

993 Building (House) - Colonial
     House (House with Porch),
     cast iron, A.C. Williams,
     1910-31, 2 1/8 x 2 5/8",
     3" h. (W. 404)............ 605.00

1002 Building (House) - Two
     Story House, cast iron,
     A.C. Williams, 1931-34,
     1 13/16 x 2 1/8", 3 1/16" h.
     (W. 355)..................   70.00

1211 Building - Independence Hall,
     complete w/side wings,
     cast iron, American-made,
     ca. 1876, 3 x 11", 6 3/8" h.
     (W. 449) 800.00

1053 Building - U.S. Treasury Bank,
     replica of Sub-Treasury
     Building in New York, cast
     iron w/sheet metal base,
     Grey Iron, 1925-28,
     3¼ x 3¾", 3¼" h.
     (W. 379)...........75.00 to 100.00

1041 Building - Woolworth Build-
     ing, cast iron, Kenton
     Hardware Mfg. Co., Ohio,
     1915, 1¾ x 2¼",
     7 7/8" h. ....75.00 to 100.00

242 Buster Brown & Tige (paint
     variation), cast iron, A.C.
     Williams, 1920's, 5½" h.
     (W. 2) * 125.00

768 Camel - Camel, Small, cast
iron, Hubley & A.C. Wil-
liams, 1920-30's, 4¾" h. 90.00

770 Camel - Kneeling Camel,
wearing pack, cast iron,
Kyser & Rex, 1889,
4 7/8" l., 2½" h. (W. 256).. 600.00

1425 Cannon, on wheels, cast iron,
Hubley, ca. 1914, 6 7/8" l.,
3" h. (W. 165) 2,750.00

367 Cat - Cat seated with fine
lines, cast iron, ca. 1912,
American-made, 3 x 4" 175.00

358 Cat - Cat on Tub, cast iron,
A.C. Williams, 1920-34,
4 1/8" h. (W. 53) 125.00

352 Cat - Cat with Ball, cast iron,
A.C. Williams, 1905-19,
5 11/16" l., 2½" h.
(W. 247) 225.00

364 Cat - Cat with Bow, cast iron,
Grey Iron, 1922, 2 7/8" w.,
4 3/8" h. 175.00

1553 Clock - Mantel Clock, lead,
key locked trap, Ingram
Co., American-made,
6 7/8" l., 6 7/8" h. 75.00

1548 Clock - Street Clock, cast iron
& steel, A.C. Williams,
1920's-31, 6" h. (W. 219) ... 300.00

1546 Clock - "Time is Money" embossed on face, cast iron,
A.C. Williams, 1909-31,
3 5/8" h. (W. 225) * 60.00

1315 "Coronation Bank" (George
V), cast iron, Sydenham
& McOustra (?), England,
1911, 4 1/8" w.,
6 5/8" h. * ....100.00 to 125.00

31 Devil - Two-Faced Devil (Devil
Head Toy Bank), cast iron,
A.C. Williams, 1904-12,
4¼" h. (W. 41) * 500.00

421 Dog - Boston Bull Terrier,
standing animal, cast iron,
Vindex Toys, 1931, 5¾" l.,
5¼" h. (W. 112) ..100.00 to 125.00

411 Dog - Husky, cast iron, possibly by Grey Iron, ca. 1910,
5" h....................... 450.00

440 Dog - Newfoundland, standing animal, cast iron,
Arcade, 1910-mid-30's,
5 3/8" l., 3 5/8" h.
(W. 107) 75.00

442 Dog - Puppo on Pillow, bee
on side, cast iron, Hubley,
1920's, little paint,
6" w., 5 5/8" h.
(W. 336) * ....175.00 to 225.00

437 Dog - St. Bernard with Pack
(large), cast iron, A.C. Williams, 1901-30's, 7¾" l.,
5½" h. (W. 113) * ..75.00 to 100.00

Water Spaniel Bank

438 Dog - Water Spaniel with
Pack ("I Hear a Call"), cast
iron, American-made, ca.
1900, 7 7/8" l., 5 3/8" h.
(ILLUS.)..................   55.00

499 Donkey (small), with saddle,
cast iron, Arcade, 1913-32
& A.C. Williams, 1910-34,
4 5/8" l., 4½" h.
(W. 198) * ....65.00 to 85.00

1314 "Dreadnought Bank," embossed "United We Stand,"
w/clasped hands & Eng-
lish flags, cast iron, probably by Sydenham & Mc-
Oustra, ca. 1915, 7" h.
(W. 363).........450.00 to 525.00

615 Duck Bank, cast iron, A.C.
Williams, 1909-35, 4 7/8" h.
(W. 211).........125.00 to 150.00

16 Dutch Girl, cast iron, Grey
Iron (?), 6½" h. (W. 24) ... 600.00

450 Elephant - Art Deco Elephant,
w/"G.O.P." on side,
trunk uplifted, cast iron,
American-made, 5½" l.,
4 3/8" h. (W. 72) 165.00

462 Elephant - Circus Elephant,
seated animal wearing
child's straw sailor hat
w/ribbon, cast iron, Hub-
ley Mfg. Co., Pennsylvania,
1930-40, 3 7/8" h. 195.00

480 Elephant - Elephant No. 479
(no chariot holes), cast
iron, Hubley, 1906, 7¾" l.,
4¾" h. (W. 62) 200.00

484 Elephant - Elephant on Tub,
w/blanket, cast iron, A.C.
Williams Co., Ohio,
1920-34, 5 3/8" h.
(W. 60) * 175.00

1630 Elephant - Elephant with Howdah (short trunk), cast iron,
Hubley, 1910, 4¾" l.,
3¾" h. (W. 64) 125.00

474 Elephant - Elephant with Howdah (large), cast iron,
A.C. Williams, 1910-30's,
6 3/8" l., 4 7/8" h., W. 63 *
(ILLUS. top next page) 60.00

Elephant with Howdah Bank

477 Elephant - Elephant with How-
     dah (small), trunk curled
     out, cast iron, A.C. Wil-
     liams, 1905-20's, 5" l.,
     3½" h. * 72.00

445 Elephant - Seated Elephant
     with Turned Trunk, cast
     iron, American-made,
     4¼" h., (W. 66) 500.00

1658 Fox Head, cast iron, Uni-
     cast US, 1973, 2 3/8" w.,
     4½" h. 45.00

320 Foxy Grandpa (Grandpa
     Bank), w/screw, cast iron,
     Wing Mfg. Co., Illinois, ca.
     1900 & Hubley, 1920's,
     5½" h. (W. 23) * 350.00

546 Hen on Nest, cast iron,
     American-made, early
     1900's, 3" h. (W. 253) 800.00

532 Horse - "Beauty," cast iron,
     Arcade Mfg. Co., Illinois,
     1910-32, 4¾" l., 4 1/8" h.
     (W. 82) 60.00

509 Horse - Horse on Tub, Deco-
     rated, cast iron, A.C.
     Williams Co., 1920-34,
     5 5/16" h. (W. 56) * 165.00

Horse on Wheels Bank

512 Horse - Horse on Wheels,
     cast iron, A.C. Williams, ca.
     1920, 4¼" l., 5" h., W. 87
     (ILLUS.) 135.00

523 Horse - Saddle Horse (small),
     cast iron, A.C. Williams,
     1934, 3 3/16" l., 2¾" h.
     (W. 86) 175.00

Humpty Dumpty Bank

337 Humpty Dumpty, Seated,
     white metal, American-
     made, 5¼" h. (ILLUS.) 35.00

228 Indian with Tomahawk, cast
     iron, Hubley, ca. 1915-30,
     5 7/8" h. 225.00

782 Liberty Bell - Liberty Bell
     ("1926"), embossed "Sesqui-
     1926-Centennial," cast iron,
     Grey Iron Casting Co.,
     Pennsylvania, 1928, 3¾" h.
     (W. 281) * 95.00

756 Lion - Fine Haired Mane, cast
     iron, American-made,
     4¾" l., 3¾" h............. 50.00

747 Lion - Lion on Tub, small, cast
     iron, A.C. Williams Co.,
     4 1/8" h. (W. 61) 125.00

Lion Bank

754 Lion - Lion, Tail Right, cast
     iron, A.C. Williams,
     1905-31, 6¼" l., 5¼" h.,
     W. 89 (ILLUS.) 73.00

177 Mulligan (Policeman), cast
     iron, A.C. Williams,
     1905-32 & Hubley, 1914,
     5¾" h. (W. 8) * ...150.00 to 200.00

629 Pig - "I Made Chicago
     Famous" (small), cast
     iron, J.M. Harper, 1902,
     4 1/8" l., 2 1/8" h.
     (W. 177).........150.00 to 180.00

582 Pig - Seated Pig, cast iron,
     A.C. Williams Co., 1910-34,
     3" h. (W. 179) * 60.00

566 Rabbit - Begging Rabbit, cast iron, A.C. Williams Co., 1908-1920's, 5 1/8" h. (W. 98) * ....100.00 to 125.00

820 Radio - Crosley Radio, small, model No. 70, Kenton, 1931-36, cast iron, 4" w., 4 5/16" h. (W. 141) 300.00

40 Recruit, aluminum, England, 1918, 5 7/8" h. (W. 48) 150.00

1329 "Royal Bank" (George V), bust portraits of King George V & Queen Mary & cornucopias cast in relief, cast iron, Chamberlain & Hill, England, 1910, 5¼" h. 295.00

882 Safe - "Arabian Safe," wording on front & desert scenes on sides, cast iron, key locked trap, w/key, Kyser & Rex, Pennsylvania, ca. 1882, 4 1/8 x 4¼", 4 9/16" h. (W. 346) 220.00

Burglar Proof House Safe Bank

Safe - "Burglar Proof House Safe," nickel-plated cast iron, marked on base "Key Combination Safe No. 40 - J. & E. Stevens Co. - Cromwell Conn. - U.S.A. - Patd Aug. 17, 1897," small piece missing from right bottom side, 4¾" w., 5 7/8" h. (ILLUS.) 38.50

1585 Shoe - Red Goose Shoe, tin, American-made, 5¾" l., 2¾" h. 90.00

1474 Trolley Car, cast iron, Kenton, 1904-22, 5¼" l., 2 11/16" h. 275.00

587 Turkey - Small Turkey, cast iron, A.C. Williams, 1905-35................. 130.00

POTTERY

Advertising, model of an acorn, lettered "Acorn Stoves will save half

your fuel money," green glaze, 3" h. 55.00

Child's head, amber glaze, 3½" h... 55.00

Cylindrical w/applied hen & chicks, redware, 12" h. 540.00

Dog's head, a retriever-type animal w/molded fur & facial details, greenish glaze on dark brown clay, 3½" h. (small chips) 225.50

Jug-form, wide ovoid body tapering to a button finial, overall brown Albany slip glaze, 6 3/8" h. 181.50

Ovoid domed shape w/flat bottom, tanware w/brown slip glaze, the surface tooled overall w/a tree bark design, applied knobs & star at top near coin slot, 6¾" h. (chipped, wear to slip).......... 165.00

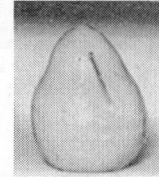

Pear Pottery Bank

Pear, realistic yellow-green glaze w/pink blush, 3 7/8" h. (ILLUS.) .. 95.00

Pig, seated, white clay w/brown glaze & yellow splotches, 3 5/8" h. 30.00

TIN

Tin Clown Bank

Advertising, "Red Circle Coffee," yellow w/black lettering, red circle, 3 7/8" h. 24.00

Barrel, "Happy Days," J. Chein & Co. 22.00

Bird in birdhouse, mechanical, put penny on bird perch & crank handle, bird comes out, takes penny & goes back in 400.00

Clown head, lever-operated semi-mechanical, multicolored, J. Chein & Co., 5" h., PL 118 (ILLUS.) 65.00

Mailbox, embossed w/"Save for Savings Bonds," red, white & blue, 9" h...................... 50.00

Monkey tips hat, semi-mechanical,
J. Chein Co., ca. 1940
(PL 336) .... 65.00 to 85.00

BARBERIANA

*A wide variety of antiques related to the
tonsorial arts have been highly collectible for
many years, especially 19th and early 20th
century shaving mugs and barber bottles and,
more recently, razors. We are now combining
these closely related categories under one
heading here for easier reference. A selection
of other varied pieces relating to barbering
will also be found below.*

BARBER BOTTLES

Mary Gregory-style Barber Bottle

Amethyst blown glass, bulbous base
tapering to a lady's leg neck, h.p.
white enamel Mary Gregory-style
decoration of a profile bust portrait of a young lady w/long flowing hair about the word "Vege-
derma," ca. 1900, 7 7/8" h. $385.00
Amethyst blown glass w/interior
ribbing, bulbous base tapering to
a thick bulbous lady's leg neck,
white enamel Mary Gregory-style
decoration of a young girl standing among feathery trees, ca.
1900, 7 3/8" h. (ILLUS.) 93.50
Bright green glass, bulbous base
tapering to a lady's leg neck,
white enamel Mary Gregory-style
decoration of a young girl among
flowers, ca. 1900, 7 7/8" h. 231.00
Clear "label-under glass," four-sided
w/rounded edges tapering to a
tall slender neck w/porcelain
stopper, label reads "Cooling
Head Rub Hair Fixative Rubex For
Dandruff" on red, gold & green
label & "Koken St. Louis U.S.A."
on smooth base, ca. 1890-1920,
7 5/8" h. 176.00

Cobalt blue blown glass, bulbous
base tapering to a tall lady's
leg neck, white enamel Mary
Gregory-style decoration of a
young boy playing tennis, ca.
1900, 8" h. 165.00
Cobalt blue blown glass, double bulbous base tapering to a 'stick'
neck, interior ribbing, white
enameled floral decoration, ca.
1880-1920, 8" h. 121.00
Cobalt blue blown glass, bulbous
base w/tall swelled neck w/rolled
lip, interior ribbing, enameled
w/white & orange flowerheads
& white dotting decoration, ca.
1880-1920, 8½" h. 61.50
Cranberry cut to clear blown glass,
bulbous base tapering to a tall
swelled cylindrical neck, h.p.
white enamel Mary Gregory-style
decoration of a young girl in a
garden, the neck cut to clear w/a
design of ovals beneath rim & at
base w/cut rings at the center,
8¼" h. 577.50
Cranberry opalescent glass, Coin
Spot patt., 7¼" h. 150.00
Cranberry opalescent glass, bulbous
body tapering to a tall slender
neck w/rolled rim, Stars & Stripes
patt., 7 1/8" h. 325.00
Cranberry opalescent glass, corset-
shaped, tall cylindrical neck
w/rolled rim, molded Herringbone
patt., 7 3/8" h. 154.00
Emerald green blown glass, tapering
bell-shaped body w/a cylindrical
ringed neck & ground rim, h.p.
small blossom heads & a rope-
twist band in orange, white & yellow enamels, ca. 1900, 8¼" h. ... 231.00
Frosted amber glass, bulbous base
tapering to a tall lady's leg neck,
molded internal ribbing, the body
h.p. in an Art Nouveau design
w/long slender leaves & blossoms
in green, white & gold, another
small h.p. band around the neck,
ca. 1900, 8" h. 368.50
Iridescent violet-blue glass, Loetz-
type, bulbous body tapering to a
tall lady's leg neck, overall iridized oilspot decoration, ground
rim, ca. 1900, 8 1/8" h. (shallow
chip on lip) 495.00
Lavender blue opaque glass, cylindrical body w/rounded shoulder
to the slender neck w/thick rolled
rim, h.p. up the side & neck w/a
heavy enamel floral bouquet in
green, yellow & white & the
words "Bay Rum" in gold, ca.
1900, 8 5/8" h. 412.50

Medium amber blown glass, bulbous base tapering to a slender lady's leg neck, h.p. dotted bands & dotted blossom heads in white, yellow & orange enamel, ca. 1900, 8 1/8" h. 82.50

Milk white glass, bulbous conical base tapering sharply toward the bottom & at the shoulder, a tall slender neck w/rolled rim, decorated w/two small blossom clusters at the shoulder above "Bay Rum," marked on the bottom "Koken Barber Supply Co., St. Louis, U.S.A.," ca. 1900, 7¾" h. ... 33.00

Milk white glass, footed ovoid form tapering to a wide cylindrical neck w/ringed rim, multicolored floral decoration & "Sea Foam" on one & "Hair Tonic" on the other, pontil scarred bases, ca. 1880-1910, 8¾" h., pr. 605.00

Pink amethyst blown glass, ovoid base w/tall swelled neck & original brass stopper, molded ribbing, white enameled "Bay Rum" & mill scene, ca. 1880-1920, 8" h. 385.00

Robin's egg blue opaque glass, cylindrical body w/a rounded shoulder to the tall cylindrical neck w/thick rolled rim & shaker top, h.p. w/a large colorful flying bird above reeds, ca. 1900, 8¾" h. 264.00

Teal blue glass, cylindrical tapering to a tall neck & rolled rim, h.p. in polychrome enamels w/large daisies & a banner inscribed "COLOGNE" or "BAY RUM," ca. 1900, 10½" h., pr. 412.50

Turquoise blue opalescent glass, bulbous base tapering to a slender neck w/rolled rim, Fern patt., ca. 1900, 6¾" h. 82.50

Turquoise blue opalescent glass, tall cylindrical base tapering to a short narrow cylindrical neck w/rolled lip, Coin Spot patt., ca. 1880-1920, 10 1/8" h. 230.00

Yellowish amber glass, ovoid body tapering to a cylindrical neck, Hobnail patt., ca. 1900, 6¾" h. (slight inside stain) 99.00

RAZORS

Safety razor, "Collins," windup, silver plate, dated 1915, w/case & blades 75.00

Safety razor, "Enders Speed," green Catalin handle 22.50

Safety razor, "Gem," gold-plated w/white handle, plastic case, ca. 1940 .... 10.00

Safety razor, "Pacific," w/long hollow handle to store the styptic pencil 12.00

Safety razor, "Schick," brass, dated 6-18-26 .... 10.00

Safety razor, "Star," take-apart type, brochure in top, razor blades in base compartment, complete in advertising tin, Kampfe Bros., New York, patented 1899 .. 45.00

Safety razor, "Valet," rear release, boxed 25.00

Safety razor & strop, "Pal," Model C outfit, includes a newspaper advertisement from "The Community Weekly of Character," 1920's, 3 pcs. 15.00

Straight razor, blade decorated w/three gold medallions & "The Admirals," one medallion depicts Admiral Dewey & is inscribed "Dewey - Manilla," another depicts Admiral Sampson & is inscribed "Sampson - Santiago," the third depicts Admiral Schley & is inscribed "Schley - Santiago" 150.00

Straight razor, #76 Country Club, black handle, w/box 17.50

Straight razor, "Sears Craftsman," celluloid handle, in box 35.00

Straight razor, "Yankee Cutlery," celluloid handle, depicts nude woman, in box 65.00

SHAVING MUGS

(Porcelain unless otherwise noted)

Fraternal

Benevolent & Protective Order of Elks, "T.J. McCutcheon" in gold Gothic lettering, depicts elk & bird encircled in ribbon & "Unity, Benevolence & Concord," advertising on bottom in red for "Eugene Bernhaus, Cinn, OH., Climax," barber chair in center, Germany.. 150.00

Fraternal Order of the Eagles, flying eagle decoration 175.00

Fraternal Order of the Eagles, "Freedom, Charity, Friendship," decoration & name in gold, T & V blank 85.00

Grand Army of the Republic, shows the medal of the G.A.R., w/"G.R. Durkee," base marked "9346," ca. 1880-1920 (usual loss of gilt around base & rim)............. 264.00

Improved Order of Red Men, h.p. bust portrait of an American Indian chief in feather bonnet w/a landscape in the background & above the letters "T.O.T.E.," name across the top, marked on the base "T. & V. France," ca. 1900... 935.00

Knights of Columbus & Knights of the Mystic Chain, w/symbols for both, name in gold worn, T & V blank 150.00

Patriotic Order of Sons of America, depicts shield w/bust of George Washington & crossed swords on front, name in gold (worn but readable)..................... 115.00

Occupational

Butcher's Shaving Mug

Artist, decorated w/an artist's palette, name in gold at bottom, "T & V France" stamped on base, ca. 1880-1920 .... 412.50

Bartender, scene of a bartender & four people in a bar.....450.00 to 500.00

Bicyclist, h.p. man standing beside an early safety bicycle, name at the top, marked "CFH/GDM," ca. 1900 (some gilt wear, professional repairs)....... 357.50

Blacksmith, h.p. scene of two men working at an anvil, workbench, forge & tools shown, name at the top, stamped on the base "T. & V. Limoges France," ca. 1900 .... 467.50

Blacksmith, decorated w/a blacksmith standing by an anvil holding a hammer at his side, name in gold at top, base is marked "Natl.," ca. 1880-1920............ 687.50

Butcher, depicts a steer & butchering tools, w/name (ILLUS.) ....200.00 to 250.00

Carpenter, a scene of a carpenter at his workbench 350.00

Clergy, decorated w/a church scene surrounded by flowers, name in gold at top, "A. Kern" debossed on base, ca. 1880-1920 (some loss to gilt around base & rim) 412.50

Fireman, h.p. scene of fireman on a horse-drawn fire engine, name at the top, "Germany" on the base, ca. 1900 (minor gilt wear)........ 742.50

Gambler, decorated w/horseshoe & clover...................... 250.00

Grocery wagon driver, scene of man driving a horse-drawn covered wagon lettered "Groceries & Provisions" against a maroon ground, name in gold, bottom marked "Barber Supply Co.," T & V blank (crack to back)................. 195.00

Horseman, finely drawn head of horse in black & white, name in gold, T & V blank 185.00

Hunter, man standing in wooded landscape firing his rifle at flying ducks, his dog running to retrieve, name at the top, ca. 1900 (slight gilt wear) 357.50

Jeweler, h.p. watch face at the top above the name over the wording "Jeweler - 531 Warren St. - Hudson, N.Y.," ca. 1900 (minor gilt loss) 253.00

Lathe operator, h.p. scene of a man standing at a large lathe, name at the top, marked "G.S." on base, ca. 1900 .... 375.00

Oil field worker, h.p. oil derrick w/building in background, name in gold at the top, stamped on bottom "By Koken Barbers Supply, Congress Chair, Best in the World, St. Louis, Mo.," ca. 1900 (some gilt wear) 495.00

Pharmacist, decorated w/a mortar & pestle, name in gold at bottom, base is marked "T & V France," ca. 1880-1920 .... 121.00

Salesman, decorated w/a salesman showing a bolt of cloth to a woman customer, decorated w/colorful sprigs of flowers on each side, name in gold at top, base is marked "Weyer, St. Joe," ca. 1880-1920 (thin spider crack in base glaze, some loss to gilt around base & rim)............. 385.00

Telegraph operator, decorated w/a telegraph key, name in gold at top, "Aug. Kern Barber Supply Co. (Trade Mark Always Upright) St. Louis, MO." stamped on base, ca. 1880-1920...................... 330.00

Watchmaker, decorated w/a detailed watch & chain above name in gold 495.00

Writer, scene of man seated at a desk writing w/a pen 325.00

General

Buff clay, slightly waisted cylinder, round soap dish attached to exterior rim, ribbed strap handle, mottled brownish glaze, 3½" h. (small flakes & repaired rim chips) 49.50

China, depicts two black men, one

in suit & tie, the other in pink
shirt & trousers w/suspenders,
reads "A Close Shave" 295.00
China, colorful decoration w/church,
mountains & lake scenery 285.00
China, h.p. eagle w/two flags &
gold band trim, "William J. Gray"
& roses in latticework scroll,
unmarked 125.00
China, ferns & calla lilies on black
ground, "R.H. Lindsay" in gold,
T. & V. Limoges blank 95.00
China, decorated w/flowers, lettered "E.P. Myers," O & EG Royal
Austria blank 35.00
China, h.p. rose & blossom clusters
at the top & bottom flanking the
name in the center, designed &
painted by Curt Grimm, Koken's
decorating department, base
stamped "Decorated by Koken
Barbers Supply Co., St. Louis,
Mo.," ca. 1900 .... 49.50
China, h.p. winter landscape w/a
small house in background & two
birds on a bare branch in foreground, worn gold name at the
bottom 22.00
Porcelain, figural, bust of a black
man, ca. 1920................. 335.00
R.S. Prussia china, decorated
w/shaded pink florals, turquoise
blue shadow flowers & gold
florals around top, beaded rim,
w/mirror on front (mirror w/slight
wear) 185.00
R.S. Prussia china, Morning Glory
mold, decorated w/pink roses,
unmarked 85.00

GENERAL ITEMS

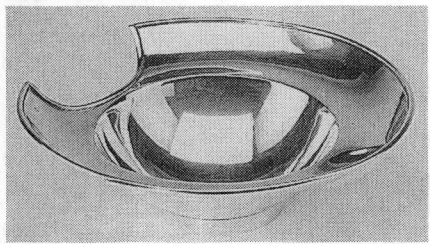

Silver Barber Bowl

Barber bowl, silver, circular w/a
notched rim applied w/a bead
molding, the curving brim w/a
well for soap, on a circular foot,
maker's mark of William Moul-
ton IV, Newburyport, ca. 1815,
10¼" d., 3 1/8" h. (ILLUS.) 5,500.00
Barber chair, oak & cast iron, ornate casting, round seat & back,
Koken 1,850.00

Barber pole, carved & painted pine,
tall tapering cylindrical form
w/ball finial, painted w/the traditional red, white & blue diagonal
stripes, mounted on a black-
painted rectangular base, America, late 19th - early 20th c.,
8' 10" h. (some abrasions &
wear) 2,750.00
Barber pole, leaded glass, "Koken,"
Victorian 975.00

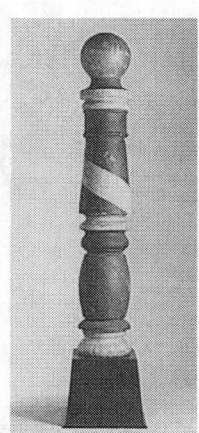

Late 19th Century Barber Pole

Barber pole, turned & painted wood,
the turned standard w/silvered
ball finial, painted the traditional red, white & blue diagonal
stripes, mounted on a black pedestal stand, America, late 19th c.,
overall 7' 4" h. (ILLUS.) 3,300.00
Cabinet & mirror, oak storage cabinet w/white marble top above
single drawer above cupboard
w/pull-down door, the whole surmounted by a tall narrow beveled
mirror in an oak frame w/ornate
crest & compressed ball finials,
Koken 2,200.00
Cotton jar, cov., clambroth glass,
ovoid footed body w/a domed
cover & pointed finial, printed in
green on the side "Antiseptic Cotton," fancy raised embossing on
the cover, marked "JHK" on the
base, ca. 1920, 7½" h. 66.00
Hair clippers, "Keen Kutter K543" ... 20.00
Hair wax case w/product, "Butch
Hair Wax," each bottle depicts
boy w/crew cut, twelve full bottles in case, w/display sign, ca.
1940's 69.00
Mustache curling iron, cast iron, on
cast iron stand 85.00
Razor blade bank, china, model of a
donkey, advertising Listerine 16.00

Razor blade sharpener, "Twinplex,"
  boxed 31.00
Razor hone, "Keen Kutter," in tin
  box 50.00
Razor strop, "Keen Kutter K-80" 30.00
Shaving brush, aluminum handle,
  Germany 6.00
Shaving brush, "Made Rite" 10.00

Federal Shaving Mirror

Shaving mirror, Federal, carved
  ebonized mahogany, the rectangular mirror plate pivoting between reeded & scrolled uprights
  above a rectangular base w/three
  short drawers, on ball feet, Boston, Massachusetts, ca. 1820,
  20¾" w., 24" h. (ILLUS.) 1,100.00
Shaving mirror, mahogany, the oval
  mirror plate crested by an open
  basket & foliage, swiveling above
  a serpentine base w/three short
  drawers, on ogee feet, w/overall
  stringing, George III period, England, last quarter 18th c., 17" w.,
  26" h. 5,280.00
Shaving paper vase, amethyst blown
  glass, cylindrical, white enamel
  Mary Gregory-type decoration of
  a boy & girl playing tennis, tooled
  lip, ca. 1890, 8" h. 962.50
Shaving soap, "Colgate," unopened
  roll w/eight cakes 45.00

BASEBALL MEMORABILIA

Baseball was named by Abner Doubleday as he laid out a diamond-shaped field with four bases at Cooperstown, New York. A popular game from its inception, by 1869 it was able to support its first all-professional team, the Cincinnati Red Stockings. The National League was organized in 1876 and though the American League was first formed in 1900, it was not officially recognized until 1903. Today, the "national pas-

time" has millions of fans and collecting baseball memorabilia has become a major hobby with enthusiastic collectors seeking out items associated with players such as Babe Ruth, Lou Gehrig, and others, who became legends in their own lifetimes. Though baseball cards, issued as advertising premiums for bubble gum and other products, seem to dominate the field there are numerous other items available.

Babe Ruth-Signed Baseball

Baseball, autographed by Joe
  DiMaggio $132.00
Baseball, autographed by Mike
  Greenwell, Rawlings American
  League ball 28.00
Baseball, autographed by Babe Ruth
  (ILLUS.) 2,530.00
Baseball, autographed by 1941
  Brooklyn Dodgers, includes Pee
  Wee Reese, Leo Durocher, Joe
  Medwick & 19 other signatures, in
  original Spalding box 500.00
Baseball card, 1934, Big League
  Chewing Gum, Frank Hogan,
  No. 20, w/"Lou Gehrig Says..." on
  back 95.00
Baseball card, 1951, Bowman Gum,
  Mickey Mantle rookie card,
  No. 253 . . . . .4,000.00
Baseball card, 1952, Look'n See,
  Babe Ruth, No. 15 . . . . 143.00
Baseball card, 1953, Topps Gum,
  Satchell Paige, No. 220 . . . . 400.00
Baseball card, 1954, Topps Gum,
  Hank Aaron rookie card,
  No. 128 . . . . 770.00
Baseball card, 1955, Topps Gum,
  Sandy Koufax rookie card,
  No. 123 . . . . 330.00
Baseball card, 1955, Topps Gum,
  Roberto Clemente, No. 164 . . . . 357.50
Baseball card, 1956, Topps Gum,
  Hank Aaron, No. 31 . . . . 99.00
Baseball card, 1958, Topps Gum,
  Ted Williams, No. 1 . . . . 121.00
Baseball card, 1960, Topps Gum,
  Carl Yastrzemski rookie card,
  No. 148 (ILLUS.) 176.00

Carl Yastrzemski Rookie Card

Baseball card, 1965, Topps Gum,
Steve Carlton rookie card,
No. 477 .... 425.00
Baseball card, 1966, Topps Gum,
Willie Mays, No. 1 .... 77.00
Baseball card, 1967, Topps Gum,
Pete Rose, No. 430 .... 50.00
Baseball card, 1969, Topps Gum,
Rollie Fingers, No. 597 .... 85.00
Baseball card, 1973, Topps Gum,
Reggie Jackson, No. 255 .... 20.00
Baseball card, 1975, Topps Gum,
George Brett rookie card,
No. 228 ....175.00 to 180.00
Baseball card, 1979, Topps Gum,
Robin Yount, No. 95 .... 10.00
Baseball card, 1980, Topps Gum,
Rickey Henderson rookie card,
No. 482 .... 176.00
Baseball card, "Pfeister," Old Mill
Tobacco insert card, white bor-
der, back intact, early 20th c.,
1 7/16 x 2 5/8" (slight crease) 770.00
Bat, miniature, wood, advertising-
type, the knob end pulls out to
open a red & white striped pleat-
ed paper fan, the sides of the bat
printed w/"Always deposit your
savings at Colonial Trust Co. -
Make a safe hit," ca. 1920's,
7¾" l. 49.50
Bat, wood, marked "Louisville Slugger - 40 T.C - Hillerich & Bradsby
Co. - Made in U.S.A. - Louisville,
Ky. - Trade mark Reg. U.S. Pat.
Off.," color decal label near end
w/figure of Ty Cobb batting above
wording "Georgia Peach - Ty
Cobb," ca. 1919, label nearly complete, 34" l. 1,430.00
Bat, autographed by Babe Ruth,
on a Burke-Hanna No. B bat,
overall good w/first "B" a little
faded.........................4,860.00
Book, "Ball Players are Humans,
Too," by Ralph Houk, New York
Yankees, 1962, 253 pp. 25.00
Book, "How to Pitch," by Bob Feller,
1948, New York, illustrated,
w/dust jacket 12.50

Book, "Play Ball, Son!," Ford Motor
Co. premium, endorsed by Boston
Red Sox 25.00
Books, "DeWitt's Baseball Guide,"
15 bound volumes, 1869 to 1883,
board covers, the group 3,850.00
Bottle opener, figural, advertising-
type, "Isaac Leisy Brewery,"
Cleveland, Ohio, figure of a base-
ball player, dated "1914" 75.00
Button, pinback, Cincinnati Reds Na-
tional League Champions, 1939 ... 25.00
Button, pinback, 1970 World Series,
Cardinals vs Royals, 3" d......... 5.00
First Day mail cover, Centennial of
baseball, photo of Honus Wagner
on one end, dated 1939,
3 5/8 x 6½" 148.50
Game, board-type, "Babe Ruth's
Official Baseball Game," w/origi-
nal box, 17 x 25"................ 302.50
Game, "Bagatelle Pinball," metal
frame, wood base, steel balls,
great baseball graphics, mint in
original box, ca. 1930's 150.00
Game, skill-type, "Peg Base Ball,"
Parker Bros., like new in box 49.50
Glove, leather, Robin Roberts model, produced by MacGregor,
1950's, w/original box (glove
worn w/some fraying, box
w/some creases & stains) 99.00
Inflatable figure, Yogi Berra,
w/catcher's mitt, used for pitching
practice, facsimile signature of
Yogi Berra on mitt, 1963, 36" h. .. 75.00
Jersey, 1975 Oakland A's white
home version, Reggie Jackson's
#9, size 44.................... 412.50
Pencil, mechanical, blue plastic
model of a baseball bat w/simu-
lated "Joe DiMaggio" signature &
"Louisville Slugger" marking 95.00

Early Baseball Tintype
Photograph, tintype, shows two
players in uniforms, one holding a
bat, the other a ball, "Taylors"
shown on the shirts, ca. 1870,
2 7/8" h. (ILLUS.) 385.00

Plate, china, a picture of a cartoon
elephant holding a pennant, the
body composed of the faces of
members of the 1911 Philadelphia
Athletics World Champions, the
figure of Connie Mack seated
on the elephant's neck, 10" d. 1,375.00
Poster, "Old German Beer," depicts
full color shot of Ebbets Field
w/game in progress & head pictures of American League & National League All Stars, also has
schedules, records & other stats,
ca. 1950, 16 x 34" 550.00
Print, "Champion Nine of the Atlan-
tic Baseball Club of Brooklyn,
L.I.," Harper's Weekly, 1865 . . . . . .   35.00
Program, 1945, Detroit Tigers vs
Chicago Cubs, at Briggs Stadium. . 154.00
Program book, 1926 World Series,
St. Louis vs Yankees . . . .550.00 to 600.00
Program book, 1956 World Series,
Yankee edition, Larsen's perfect
game scored inside 495.00
Program book, 1966 World Series,
Dodgers vs Orioles 65.00
Program book, 1968 World Series,
Tigers vs Cardinals, autographed
by Tony Kubek, 120 pp. 125.00
Scorecard, Chicago vs Philadelphia,
1882 . . . . .1,320.00
Scorecard, official 1893 Brooklyn BB
Club vs Philadelphia, at Eastern
Park, gilt detailing (creased) 880.00
Scorecard-folder, 1954, Washington
Nationals 15.00
Sheet music, "Take Me Out To the
Ball Game," title superimposed
on baseball, w/small inset photo-
graph of lady, framed 22.00
Sign, advertising "E. & J. Burke -
Finest Pale Ale," color litho-
graphed paper, shows the cap-
tains of the Chicago and New
York champion teams seated in
front of a striped tent toasting
each other, dated 1881, framed,
20 x 26" 33,000.00
Ticket, 1912 World Series "rain
check" ticket, game one, Polo
Grounds, New York vs Boston, on
an album sheet 137.50
Ticket book, 1903 season, for the
Detroit Base Ball & Amusement
Co., complete 412.50
Trade sign, carved & painted wood,
model of a large baseball bat
w/remnants of original paint, late
19th - early 20th c., 36" l. 330.00
Yearbook, 1952 Chicago White
Sox 50.00
Yearbook, 1958 Los Angeles
Dodgers 200.00

BASKETS

Miniature "Buttocks" Basket

*The American Indians were the first bas-
ket weavers on this continent and, of necessity, the early Colonial settlers and their
descendants pursued this artistic handicraft
to provide essential containers for berries,
eggs and endless other items to be carried or
stored. Rye straw, split willow and reeds are
but a few of the wide variety of materials
used. The Nantucket baskets, plainly and
sturdily constructed, along with the baskets
woven by American Indians and at the Shaker settlements, would seem to draw the
greatest attention in an area of collecting
where interest has stabilized because of the
wide availability of fine baskets by contemporary basket weavers for art and craft shows
across the country.*

*Also see INDIAN ARTIFACTS &
JEWELRY and SHAKER ITEMS.*

"Buttocks" basket, miniature, 10-rib
construction, woven splint, old
varnish finish, 6 x 6½", 3¾" h.
plus bentwood handle $95.00
"Buttocks" basket, miniature, 12-rib
construction, woven splint
w/splint ash handle, 19th c.,
5¼" l., 4" h. plus handle (some
minor breaks) 137.00
"Buttocks" basket, miniature, 16-rib
construction, woven splint, well-
made, old patina, 4 x 4½", 2" h.
plus bentwood handle (minor
damage) 250.00
"Buttocks" basket, miniature, 16-rib
construction, woven splint,
4 x 4½", 2½" h. plus bentwood
handle 130.00
"Buttocks" basket, miniature, 16-rib
construction, woven splint in natural & dark brown, 4¼ x 5¾",
4½" h. plus bentwood handle 250.00
"Buttocks" basket, 18-rib construction, woven splint, old patina,
8 x 9", 4¾" h. plus bentwood
handle (minor breaks) 125.00
"Buttocks" basket, miniature, 22-rib
construction, woven splint, good
color, 4 x 4½", 2 5/8" h. plus
bentwood handle (some dam-
age) 155.00
"Buttocks" basket, 24-rib construc-
tion, woven splint, good brown

patina, 10½ x 12", 6" h. plus
bentwood handle 175.00
"Buttocks" basket, 24-rib construc-
tion, woven splint, worn patina,
14 x 15", 7½" h. plus bentwood
handle (minor damage) 115.00
"Buttocks" basket, miniature, 28-rib
construction, woven splint, America, 19th c., 5" l., 4½" h. plus
bentwood handle (ILLUS.) 192.50
"Buttocks" basket, 30-rib construction, woven splint, very deep incurved oblong form w/twisted
sapling handle at the center,
15 x 27½", 10½" h. plus handle,
(wear, damage) 115.00
Cheese basket, honeycomb design
woven splint, round top & hexagonal base, good old patina,
12" d. (small breaks, minor dam-
age) 200.00
Cheese basket, woven splint in
honeycomb design, wrapped rim,
grey scrubbed finish, 21½" d.,
8" h. (some damage) 275.00
Cotton-picking basket, woven splint,
deep rounded sides w/a square
bottom tapering to a conical neck
w/a wrapped round rim, leather
shoulder strap across the top, old
worn blue paint, 18" h. (some
damage) 302.50
Field (or gathering) basket, woven
splint, old worn dark finish,
12½ x 14", 4½" h. plus bentwood
handle 175.00
Field (or gathering) basket, woven
splint, rectangular, bentwood rim
handles, dark patina, 12 x 16¼",
6½" h. (minor damage) 75.00
Field (or gathering) basket, rectangular, woven splint w/radiating
ribs, 12 x 16", 7¼" h. plus bent-
wood handle 85.00
Field (or gathering) basket, woven
splint, two swivel bentwood handles, 12½ x 16½", 8" h. (minor
damage) 55.00
Field (or gathering) basket, woven
splint, round w/shallow sides & a
high, arched bentwood handle,
old green paint, 9½" d. (some
damage) 145.00
Field (or gathering) basket, woven
splint, low sides, curving up
slightly at ends, high bentwood
handle, 12 x 18½" 55.00
Gathering basket, woven splint,
decorated w/red & green paint,
19th c., 14" d. (imperfections) 715.00
Laundry basket, woven splint, rectangular bottom w/deep swelling
sides to the oblong wrapped rim,
a decorative woven band around

the middle & near the rim,
19 x 27", 11" h. (minor damage) . . 71.50
Market basket, woven splint, square
bottom & deep sides w/rounded,
wrapped rim & bentwood handle,
dark natural patina w/green &
yellow, 7¾" w., 4¼" h. plus han-
dle (minor damage) 93.50
Market basket, woven splint, very
sturdy, 10½ x 12", 7" h. plus
bentwood handle 100.00
Melon basket, woven splint, 12-rib
construction, center bentwood
handle, light color, 6½ x 7", 4" h.
plus bentwood handle 140.00
Melon basket, woven splint, 16-rib
construction w/integral side handles, good age & color, 12½" d.,
6" h. (some damage) 99.00

Nantucket Work Basket

Nantucket work basket, cov., finely
woven splint, wrapped rim, minor
splint breaks, circular wooden
base, bentwood swing handle,
base w/partial paper label
"...ma.. by A.D. Williams... Orchard... Nantucket," A.D. Williams, Nantucket Island, Massachusetts, 20th c., 9" d., 8½" h.
plus handle (ILLUS.) 1,210.00
Nantucket basket, finely woven
splint & cane, round, a wrapped
rim above deep sides & a turned
& incised wooden base, wooden
swing handle across the top, late
19th c., 13½" d., 9" h. (some
splint breaks) 935.00
Picnic basket, split hickory, bent-
wood handles, hinged cover,
8 x 12 x 17" 25.00
Single-egg basket, woven splint,
natural color, carved ash swing
handle, America, 19th c., 6" l.,
overall 6" h. 330.00
Storage basket, cov., woven rye
straw, round slightly tapering
sides, flat fitted cover, good col-
or, 20" d., 14" h. (wear) 115.50

Storage basket, woven rye straw,
oval w/deep flaring sides & a
wide flat bottom, 15 x 20", 7" h.
(some damage) 148.50

Utility basket, woven rye straw,
round w/flaring sides, integral
rim hanging loop on the rim,
11½" d., 4" h. 137.50

Utility basket, woven splint, rectangular w/wrapped rim & bentwood
end handles, old mustard brown
paint, 11½ x 14", 5" h. plus
handles 203.50

Utility basket, woven splint,
wrapped oval rim & a rectangular
base, dark varnish stain finish,
14½ x 18", 8½" h. plus bentwood
handle 60.50

Utility basket, woven splint,
wrapped rim, 10 x 14", 8¾" h.
plus well-shaped bentwood
handle 192.50

BELLS

Bronze Temple Bell

Bell metal bell, w/cast iron yoke &
clapper, molded decorative details
& inscription "G.W. Coffin & Co.
Buckeye Bell Foundry, Cincinnati,"
overall 21" h. $225.00

Brass bell, model of two Spaniel
dogs handle, 2¾" d., 4" h. 65.00

Figural bell, bisque, full-skirted
woman, stockinged legs clapper,
5½" h. 200.00

Figural bell, china, boy dressed in
white coat w/blue & orange flowers & blue trim, holding paper in
his hands, overall gold trim,
2½" d., 6½" h. 145.00

Figural bell, china, lady in pink, yellow & white dress holding large
bouquet of lavender flowers,
2½" d., 4½" h. 65.00

Figural bell, sterling silver, cast in
the shape of a standing woman
w/a shawl over her face, marked
"A. Mano - Peru - 925," 4" h. 85.00

Glass bell, cranberry, clear handle,
5½" h. 55.00

School teacher's hand bell, brass,
turned wood handle w/brass fini-
al, 4½" d., 7½" h. 50.00

Sterling silver bell, the plain domed
bell applied around the base
w/vining ivy, the figural handle in
the form of a standing classical
maiden, Tiffany & Co., New York,
ca. 1875, 5½" h. 1,045.00

Temple bell, bronze, tapering form
w/serpentine rim, banded rib
decoration & panels of inscriptions, surmounted by animalistic
figure (possibly later addition),
Oriental, late 17th - early 18th c.,
25" h. (ILLUS.) 2,860.00

Trolley bell, metal, foot-operated,
"Bermuda Carriage Bell," New
York 50.00

Wedding bell, cranberry glass,
w/clear glass applied handle,
glass clapper, Victorian, 5½" d.,
12" h. 185.00

BICYCLES

Columbia "Deluxe," girl's, red,
working horn & light, 1953 . . . . . . $600.00

J.C. Higgins "Deluxe," girl's, ca.
early 1950's. 800.00

Monarch "Super Deluxe," boy's,
1947, original 550.00

Montgomery Ward & Co. "Haw-
thorne," lady's, ca. 1950 . . . . 750.00

Montgomery Ward & Co. "Haw-
thorne," man's, ca. 1950's 550.00

Schwinn "Jaguar Mark V," springer
front, all original & perfect. 550.00

Schwinn "Red Phantom" 1,250.00

Western Flyer, 1953 (needs some
parts) 500.00

BIG LITTLE BOOKS

*The original "Big Little Books" and "Bet-
ter Little Books" small format series were
originated in the mid-30's by Whitman Publishing Co., Racine, Wisconsin, and covered
a variety of subjects from adventure stories
to tales based on comic strip characters and
movie and radio stars. The publisher originally assigned each book a serial number. Most*

prices are now in the $15.00 - $40.00 range with scarce ones bringing more.

Arizona Kid on the Bandit Trail,
No. 1192, 1936 . . . . $15.00

Blondie, Who's Boss?, No. 1423,
1942 . . . . 26.50

Blondie & Dagwood, Everybody's
Happy, No. 1438, 1948 . . . . 25.00

Buccaneer (The), No. 1470, 1938 . . . . 20.00

Buck Jones and the Rock Creek Cat-
tle War, No. 1461, 1938 . . . . 35.00

Captain Midnight and the Moon
Woman, No. 1452, 1943 . . . . 30.00

Captain Midnight & the Secret
Squadron vs the Terror of the Ori-
ent, No. 1488, 1942 . . . . 40.00

Chester Gump in the City of Gold,
No. 1146, 1935 . . . . 40.00

Clyde Beatty, Daredevil Lion and Tiger Tamer, No. 1410, 1938 . . . . 30.00

Dan Dunn Secret Operative 48,
No. 1116, 1934 . . . . 37.50

Dan Dunn Secret Operative 48 and
the Crime Master, No. 1171,
1937 . . . . 40.00

Dan Dunn Secret Operative 48 on
the Trail of Wu Fang, No. 1454,
1938 . . . . 45.00

Dick Tracy and His G-Men, "movie
flip" page corners, No. 1439,
1935 . . . . 30.00

Dick Tracy and the Stolen Bonds,
No. 1105, 1934 . . . . 26.00

Dick Tracy, From Colorado to Nova
Scotia, No. 749, 1933 . . . . 18.00

Dick Tracy on the High Seas,
No. 1454, 1938 . . . . 30.00

Don Winslow, U.S.N., Lieutenant
Commander, No. 1107, 1935 . . . . . . 40.00

Flash Gordon in the Water World of
Mongo, No. 1407, 1937 . . . . 36.00

Freckles and the Lost Diamond
Mine, No. 1164, 1937 . . . . 18.00

Gang Busters Step In, No. 1433,
1939 . . . . 20.00

Gene Autry and Raiders of the
Range, No. 1409, 1946 . . . . 22.50

G-Man on the Crime Trail, No. 1118,
1936 . . . . 40.00

Inspector Wade Solves the Mystery
of the Red Aces, No. 1448, 1937 . . 30.00

In the Name of the Law, No. 1155,
1937 . . . . 35.00

Little Annie Rooney and the Orphan
House, No. 1117, 1936 . . . . 40.00

Little Orphan Annie, No. 708,
1933 . . . . 125.00

Little Orphan Annie and Chizzler,
No. 748, 1933 . . . . 25.00

Little Women, No. 757 (O), 1934 . . . . 24.00

Lone Ranger and His Horse Silver,
No. 1181, 1935 . . . . 30.00

Perry Winkle and the Rinkeydinks,
No. 1199, 1936 . . . . 23.50

Popeye and the Jeep, No. 1405,
1937 . . . . 22.00

Powder Smoke Range, No. 1176,
1935 . . . . 23.50

Radio Patrol, No. 1142, 1935 . . . . 18.50

Sequoia, No. 1161 (O), 1935 . . . . 15.00

Tailspin Tommy and the Lost Trans-
port, No. 1413, 1939 . . . . 35.00

Tailspin Tommy in the Famous Pay-
roll Mystery, No. 747, 1933 . . . . 40.00

Tailspin Tommy, The Dirigible Flight
to the North Pole, No. 1124,
1934 . . . . 50.00

Tarzan Escapes, No. 1182, 1936 . . . . . 42.50

Tarzan of the Screen, No. 778,
1934 . . . . 35.00

Tillie the Toiler and the Wild Man of
Desert Island, "movie flip" page
corners, No. 1442, 1941 . . . . 12.00

Tiny Tim (The Adventures of),
No. 767, 1935 . . . . 15.00

Tom Mix and Tony, Jr. in Terror
Trail, No. 762 (O), 1935 . . . . 60.00

Tom Mix in the Fighting Cowboy,
No. 1144, 1935 . . . . 31.50

Treasure Island, movie edition
w/Jackie Cooper, No. 1141 (O),
1934 . . . . 22.00

West Point of the Air, movie edition
w/Wallace Beery, No. 1164 (O),
1935 . . . . 14.50

World War in Photographs,
No. 779 (O), 1934 . . . . 12.00

RELATED BOOKS

Adventures of Jim Bowie, Big Little
Book TV Series, No. 1648, 1958 . . . 6.00

Buck Rogers on the Planetoid Eros
(The Adventures of), Big Big
Books, No. 4057, 1934 . . . . 97.50

Gentleman Joe Palooka, Jumbo
Books, No. 1176, 1940 . . . . 30.00

Little Orphan Annie (The Story of),
Big Big Books, No. 4054, 1934 . . . . 125.00

Tom Mix, The Trail of the Terrible
Six, Ralston Purina Company
premium, 3 x 3½", 1937 . . . . 30.00

Will Rogers (The Story of), Little Big
Book, No. 1096, 1935 . . . . 35.00

BLACK AMERICANA

*Over the past decade or so this field of col-
lecting has rapidly grown and today almost
anything that relates to Black culture or illustrates Black Americans is conside
desirable collectible. Although n
representations of Blacks, especially on
and early 20th century advertising pieces*

housewares, were cruel stereotypes, even these are collected as poignant reminders of how far American society has come since the dawning of the Civil Rights movement, and how far we still have to go. Other pieces relating to this category will be found from time to time in such categories as Advertising Items, Banks, Character Collectibles, Kitchenwares, Cookie Jars, Signs and Signboards, Toys and several others.

Reference books dealing with Black Americana include Black Collectibles *by Lynn Morrow (1983);* Collecting Black Americana *by Dawn E. Reno (Crown Publishers, 1986); and* Black Collectibles, Mammy and her friends *by Jackie Young (Schiffer Publishing Ltd., 1988).*

Ambrotype of Black Soldier

Ambrotype, quarter-plate, in a half-case, a member of the 54th Massachusetts Infantry Regiment, Company I, in Civil War uniform, ca. 1863-64 (ILLUS.) $3,450.00
Book, "The Black Phalanx," by J.T. Wilson, American Publishing Co., history of black soldiers in wars 1775-1812 & 1861-65, 56 illustrations, 528 pp., cloth cover, 1890 .. 150.00
Book, "Ole Mammy's Torment," black dialect, dated 1897 .... 110.00
Book, "When Malindy Sings," by Paul Laurence Dunbar, 1903, Dodd & Mead Co., w/several photographs of blacks at turn of the century........................ 125.00
Book, "White Side of a Black Subject," by N.B. Wood, 1894, Chicago, illustrated, first edition, vindication of African-American race in America................ 50.00
Booklet, "Celebration of the Colored Peoples Educational Monument Assn. in Memory of Abraham Lincoln, Presidential Grounds, July 1865," 5 x 9", 34 pp. 40.00
Bus schedule, Greyhound, Mississippi, 1935, cover depicts blacks w/watermelon 20.00

Calendar, 1896, advertising for a hardware store, colorful scene of a comical dancing black man wearing a frock coat, derby hat & juggling a variety of heads attached to strings, each w/a different expression, framed 135.00
Coloring book, "Little Brown Koko," 1941, unused 65.00
Doll, bisque baby, painted features, three pigtails, jointed, wearing a diaper, marked "Japan," 4" h..... 45.00
Doll, cloth, "Uncle Mose," Aunt Jemima premium, 1924 .... 120.00
Doorstop, cut-out wood, Mammy w/exaggerated features, ca. 1920's 175.00
Fan, large black face, "Pickaninny" menu on back, 14" l. 30.00
Figurine, china, black boy on potty & holding a watermelon, marked "Japan," 3¾" h. 35.00
Game, "Chucklers," box depicts two black men, ca. 1931, complete (little wear on box sides).......... 90.00
Kitchen towels, cross-stitched Mammy & days of the week, complete & unused, the set 150.00
Lamp base, chalkware, full-figure black child, ca. 1940's 225.00

"Sprinkling Sambo" Lawn Sprinkler

Lawn sprinkler, "Sprinkling Sambo," cut-out wood, silhouetted figure of a black boy dressed in green overalls w/a yellow & black-striped shirt, label reads "The Firestone Tire and Rubber Co.," w/a metal spike base, minor scratches, paint nicks & soiling, 39" h. (ILLUS.) 247.50
Marriage certificate, pictures black couple, minister & cherubs, 1910, 16 x 20"........................ 50.00
Matchbook w/matches, "Coon Chicken Inn".................... 25.00

Match holder, chalkware, figural sitting boy w/watermelon between legs.......................... 55.00

Photograph, family portrait, three children & parents, in walnut frame, ca. 1890, 14 x 16"....... 105.00

Playing cards, deck of 52 including comic black character cards, marked "Harlequin playing cards, Tiffany & Co., Copyright 1879 by Chas. E. Capryl" (minor soiling & title card marked in ink)......... 148.50

Print, "A Bright Future," by Harry Roseland, depicts a black fortune teller, in original walnut frame, 16 x 20".......................... 125.00

Puppet, "Little Black Sambo," w/large features, 1952, mint in box.......................... 150.00

Salt shaker, ceramic, figural black chef, marked "Brayton," 5" h..... 45.00

Salt & pepper shakers, ceramic, figural Mammy & chef, marked "Japan," 9" h., pr.............. 30.00

Salt & pepper shakers, ceramic, figural Mammy & chef, Pearl China, 3" h., pr................... 65.00

Smoking stand, wrought iron, tin & brass, the figure of a black man w/very long legs wearing a tuxedo & holding an ashtray flanked by a match holder & cup, mounted on a square base, painted decoration, ca. 1920, 35½" h........ 770.00

Toy, die-cut cardboard, "Dancing Sambo," w/articulated legs, in original envelope, 12" h......... 30.00

Toy, windup celluloid-type, black dancer in front of tin sign w/"Lenox Ave & 125 St.," Occupied Japan.......................... 475.00

Tumbler, china, decorated w/two black boys w/"Two Little Nigger Boys" between them, w/gold trim, Grafton China, England, ca. early 1900's, 3¾" h.................. 265.00

BOOK ENDS

Bronze, modeled as the head of a bulldog, marked "Solid Bronze," ca. 1930's, 4½" h., pr...........$100.00

Bronze, model of a Russian wolfhound, copyrighted 1929, 5¾" h., pr................................. 80.00

Bronze, modeled as a silhouette of a daffodil, by G. Thew, impressed marks, 1928, 6" h., pr........... 209.00

Bronze, molded arches centering a seated Buddha, gold dore' finish

impressed "Tiffany Studios - New York - 1025," 6" h., pr.......... 275.00

Bronze, figural, cast as an animated jester mounted on stepped plinth, chocolate brown patina, signed in the bronze "Zach," impressed "ARGENTOR WIEN," 6¾" h., pr.....1,100.00

Bronze, Art Deco style, figural, nude figures sculpted facing the books, marked by Armor Bronze & dated 1927, 7¼" h., pr.............. 150.00

Bronze, "Zodiac" patt., the wide flat uprights w/arched tops engraved w/swirling discs alternating w/discs framing various signs of the zodiac each colorfully enameled, impressed "TIFFANY STUDIOS - NEW YORK 1091," pr... 302.50

Bronze-plated metal, figural Art Deco-style dancing nudes, Pompeiian Bronze, 8" h., pr........ 350.00

Cast iron, figural knight on horse, pr................................. 40.00

Cast iron, model of a flower basket, pr................................. 40.00

Cast iron, model of a horse & foal, on a wooden base, pr.......... 65.00

Cast metal, deeply molded relief design of a seated cherub against the book-shaped backplate, dark bronze finish & gilded edge, 6¼" h., pr..................... 75.00

Ceramic, Art Deco style, figural stylized turkeys in crackled cream & silver glaze, impressed "C.H. FRANCE," 6¾" h., pr.......... 150.00

Chalkware, carnival-type, model of nude lady on sea shell, pr........ 48.00

Copper, hand-hammered, the rectangular uprights w/a square cutout center, the sides stamped w/arched & intertwined slender loops, original dark patina, marked "The Jarvie Shop," early 20th c., 5½" l., 4½" h., pr....... 440.00

Gilt-bronze, irregular flattened archform inscribed w/bands of Aztecinspired designs, stamped "TIFFANY STUDIOS NEW YORK 2010," 5" h., pr.....................1,430.00

Patinated white metal, Art Deco style, one w/the figure of a man playing pipes, the other a woman w/cymbals, green patina, medallion mark w/"Fabrication Francais, Paris," France, ca. 1930's, 3 7/8 x 7 1/8", 6½" h., pr. (slight chip on one marble base)........ 190.00

Sewer tile pottery, model of an owl, short rounded body w/well-defined feathering, on square, stepped base, incised initials "E.T.E.," 5 5/8" h., pr........... 425.00

Soapstone, carved overall w/reticu-

lated floral designs, China, early
20th c., 5¾" h., pr. 55.00
White metal, Art Nouveau style,
cast as the figure of a dancing
girl, patinated, American-made,
early 20th c., 6¾" h., pr. 90.00
Wood, Art Deco style, sculpted as
the head of a girl, ca. 1930's,
6¼" h., pr. 60.00

BOOKS

ANTIQUES RELATED

American Historical Catalog Collection (The), "Pennsylvania Glassware 1870-1904," paperback, first
edition, 156 pp. $20.00
Belknap, E. McCamly, "Milk Glass,"
1959, Crown Publishers 45.00
Bleier, Paul & Meta, "John Rogers'
Groups of Statuary," 1971, pictorial guide, paperback, 134 pp. 25.00
Bryant, Gilbert Ernest, "The Chelsea
Porcelain Toys. Scent bottles, bon-
bonnieres, etuis, seals and
statuettes made at the Chelsea
factory, 1745-1769 and Derby
Chelsea, 1770-1784," 1925, limited
edition published by the Medici
Society, numbered, signed by author, 10 x 12½" 125.00
Camehl, Ada W., "Blue China
Book," 1946, 200 photographs of
historical American transfers,
322 pp., w/dust jacket 29.00
Chippendale, Thomas, "The Gentleman and Cabinet-Makers Director," 1938, w/presentation
inscription by Joe Kindig, Jr.,
12½ x 18¼" (minor damage)..... 135.00
Edwards, Ralph, "The Dictionary of
English Furniture," 1954, revised
edition, volumes I-III, the set 1,650.00
Finley, Ruth E., "Old Patchwork
Quilts," 1929, 96 photographs,
100 drawings, 202 pp., w/dust
jacket 25.00
Greaser, Arlene & Paul, "Cookie
Cutters and Molds," 1969, autographed by authors, 6¼ x 9¼"... 65.00
Hawley, Walter A., "Oriental Rugs,
Antique and Modern," 1937, hard
cover, 324 pp., w/dust jacket 74.00
Huxford, Sharon & Bob, "The Collec-
tor's Encyclopedia of Fiesta," first
edition, autographed 130.00
Koch, Robert, "Louis C. Tiffany -
Rebel in Glass," 1964, Crown Publishers, New York, illustrated,
243 pp., hard cover 90.00

Lee, Ruth Webb & Rose, James,
"American Glass Cup Plates,"
1948, first edition, autographed by
Ruth Webb Lee, 6½ x 9½"....... 65.00
Lichten, Frances, "Folk Art of
Rural Pennsylvania," 1946,
9½ x 12¼" 55.00
McClinton, Katharine Morrison, "Col-
lecting American 19th Century Sil-
ver," 1968, hard cover 20.00
Metz, Alice H., "Early American Pattern Glass," 1975, spiral bound,
2 vols. 40.00
Palmer, Brooks, "The Book of
American Clocks," 1950, 312 illus-
trations, 180 clock makers, hard
cover 29.00
Pearson, J. Michael, "Encyclopedia
of American Cut and Engraved
Glass - Volume I: Geometric Con-
cepts," 1975, 272 pp., 9 x 11¼" .. 70.00
Pearson, J. Michael & Dorothy T.,
"American Cut Glass for the Dis-
criminating Collector," 1965, Van-
tage Press, New York, 204 pp.,
8¾ x 10¾" 170.00
Purviance, Louise, Evan Purviance &
Norris F. Schneider, "Zanesville
Art Pottery in Color," 1968 ...... 20.00
Rainwater, Dorothy, "American
Spoons," 1968.................. 30.00
Remise, Jac & Fondin, Jean, "The
Golden Age of Toys," 1967,
10¼ x 12".................... 75.00
Santore, Charles, "The Windsor Style
in America," 1981, autographed,
10½ x 10½" 125.00
Sonn, Albert, "Early Ameri-
can Wrought Iron," Bonanza,
8¾ x 11¼" 55.00
Stoudt, John Joseph, "Pennsylvania
German Folk Art," 1966, Pennsyl-
vania German Folklore Society,
Allentown, Pennsylvania,
6½ x 9¼" 155.00
Wiener, Herbert & Lipkowitz, Freda,
"Rarities in American Cut Glass,"
1975, Collectors House of Books
Publishing Co., Houston, 294 pp.,
8¾ x 11¼" 180.00

CIVIL WAR RELATED

*More books have been written about the
Civil War era (1861-65) than any other period in the history of our country. The following listing includes books by and about those
directly involved in the fighting, overall history of the conflict and the years following.*

"American Conflict," by Horace
Greeley, 1864-66, Volumes 1 & 2,
leather-bound.................. 75.00
"Bullet & Shell, War As The Soldier

Saw It," by Major Williams, 1882,
Forbes, New York, illustrated 45.00

"Capture & Execution of John
Brown," by Elijah Avey, 1906, Elgin, illustrated 15.00

"Face of Robert E. Lee in Life & Legend (The)," by R. Meredith, New
York, 1947, first edition, illustrated, w/dust jacket 35.00

"Following The Flag," by Coffin,
1865, Boston, illustrated 14.00

"Gray Ghosts of Confederacy," by
Brownlee, 1958, Baton Rouge, first
edition, w/dust jacket, signed by
author 25.00

"History of the Civil War," 1895, by
Frank Leslie 130.00

"History of the 15th Iowa Volunteer
Infantry," 1887, 664 pp. 175.00

"History of the 61st Pennsylvania
Volunteer Infantry," 1911,
234 pp........................ 145.00

"Jeb Stuart, Last Cavalier," by Burke
Davis, 1957, New York, first edition, signed by author 30.00

"Life of Jefferson Davis," by Al-
friend, 1868, first edition, 645 pp.
(little cover wear) 45.00

"Nurse & Spy In the Union Army,"
by Emma Edmonds, 1865, first edition, illustrated 25.00

"Robert E. Lee and the Southern
Confederacy," by Henry White,
1910, illustrated 25.00

"Secession of Southern States," by
G.W. Johnson, New York, 1933,
w/dust jacket 25.00

"Second Battle of Bull Run," by J.
Cox, Fitzjohn Porter Case, Cincinnati, 1882, first edition 28.50

"Secret Service (The)," by Richardson, 1865, a contemporary Civil
War account 35.00

PRESIDENTS & HISTORICAL FIGURES

*The following listing includes a wide cross-
section of books by and about former Presidents of the United States and other persons
of note.*

"Abe Lincoln," by W. Wisdon, 1949,
Pidgeon Creek, New York, first
edition 8.50

"The Achievements of Stanley &
Other American Explorers," by
Headley 20.00

"Administration of President Lincoln," by Raymond, 1864, New
York, first edition 15.00

"Belle Star, Bandit Queen," by Ras-
coe, 1941 .... 7.00

"Booker T. Washington," by Frederick E. Drinker, 1915, memorial

edition, 32 photographic pictures,
352 pp. (back loose) 45.00

"Brigham Young," by Werner, 1925,
first edition (cover rub, pencil
markings) 25.00

"Challenge to Liberty," by Herbert
Hoover, 1934 .... 20.00

"East of the Sun," by Theodore
Roosevelt & Kermit Roosevelt,
1926, 284 pp. 35.00

"James A. Garfield," by C.C. Coffin,
1880 .... 20.00

"Life & Deeds of General Sherman,
by Northrop, 1891, Philadelphia .. 10.00

"Life & Military Career of Thomas J.
(Stonewall) Jackson," by Markin-
field Addey, 1863, New York, first
edition, 240 pp. (cover faded) 48.50

"Life & Times of Washington," by
John Schroeder, 1857, New York,
two volumes 55.00

"Life of Benjamin Harrison," by L.
Wallace, 1888 .... 35.00

"Life of General Sherman," by Johnson, 1891, New York, illustrated,
first edition 10.00

"Life of Sitting Bull & History of the
Indian War of 1890-91," by Fletcher Johnson (complete but loose) .. 49.50

"Lincoln, His Life & Public Service,"
by Powers, 1884 .... 45.00

"The Memoirs of Herbert Hoover,"
1952, 3 vols. 17.00

"My Life and Works," by Henry
Ford, 1922 .... 8.00

"Portfolio of Official Portraits of
Presidents & First Ladies," 1929,
limited edition, from Washington
to Hoover, Coleman Engraving
Co., gold embossed cover &
pages, 14 x 20" 250.00

"The Real Lincoln," by J. Weik, 1922,
Boston, first edition, illustrated,
323 pp........................ 28.50

"Theodore Roosevelt, The Boy and
the Man," by George Seaver,
1920 .... 11.00

"Warren G. Harding, Memorial Volume," 1924, United States Government Printing Office 25.00

STATE & LOCAL

CALIFORNIA

"History of Sacramento County,
California," 1923 .... 45.00

"San Francisco & Oakland Visitor's
Guide," 1923, published by Rand
McNally, w/colorful fold-out map
of the region, Pacific states
& United States, hard cover,
85 pp......................... 25.00

"What I Saw in California," by

Bryant, 1846, a journal of going
West, w/map 65.00

ILLINOIS
"Chicago & Its Cesspools of Infamy,"
1910 .... 10.00
"George Rogers Clark's Conquest of
Illinois - Wabash Towns 1778 &
79," by Consul W. Butterfield,
1904, Columbus, 815 pp. 35.00
"Illinois & Winnebago Co. Atlas,"
1872, pictures farms & homes,
w/maps of all counties in Illinois 150.00
"U.S. Biographical Dictionary & Picture Gallery, 1883," Illinois edition, full tooled leather cover 55.00

IOWA
"Atlas of Allamakee County, Iowa,"
1917 .... 50.00
"Atlas of Plymouth County, Iowa,"
1914 .... 25.00
"50 Years in Iowa," J.M.D. Burrows,
1888, Davenport 75.00
"History of Chickasaw & Howard
Counties, Iowa," by Alexander,
1883 .... 85.00
"History of Fremont County, Iowa,"
Des Moines, Iowa Historical Co.,
1881, cities, towns, geneology, illustrated, 778 pp., cloth & leather
cover 100.00
"Who's Who In Iowa," 1940,
1,322 pp. 37.50

KANSAS
"Atlas of Saline County, Kansas,"
1903 (spine cover gone) 55.00
"History of Linn County," 1928 ...... 40.00
"History of the State of Kansas," by
A.T. Andreas, 1883 .... 80.00

MASSACHUSETTS
"Atlas of Berkshire, Massachusetts,"
1876, steel engravings 95.00
"Atlas of the State of Mas-
sachusetts," published by Walling
& Grey, 1871 .... 200.00
"Births, Marriages & Deaths, 1635-
1850, Concord, Massachusetts" ... 50.00
"History of Martha's Vineyard, Mas-
sachusetts," Volume 3, 1925, fami-
ly geneologies 17.50
"Professional & Industrial History of
Suffolk Co., Massachusetts," Vol-
ume 1, 1894 .... 45.00

MINNESOTA
"Atlas of Rock County, Minnesota,"
1935 .... 60.00
"History of Goodhue County, Minnesota," 1878 .... 60.00

MISSOURI
"Encyclopedia of the History of St.
Louis," 1899, published by South-
ern History Company, 3 vols...... 45.00
"History of Randolph County, Mis-
souri," 1910................... 110.00
"Missouri State History of the
Daughters of the American Revo-
lution," many photos, 832 pp. 30.00

NEBRASKA
"Atlas of Fillmore County, Nebras-
ka," 1918..................... 60.00
"Biographical Record of Butler, Polk,
Seward, York & Fillmore Counties,
Nebraska," 1899 .... 65.00
"Nebraska," American Guide Series,
1939, w/folding map 29.00
"Plat Atlas Book, Clay County,"
1908 .... 75.00

WISCONSIN
"History of Southwestern Wisconsin -
Old Crawford County," 1932, four
volumes 110.00
"Wisconsin, Story & Biography," by
Ellis Usher, 1914, Lewis, Chicago,
illustrated, 8 volumes (faded red
covers) 150.00

BOOTJACKS

Folding Revolver Bootjack

Cast iron, figural "Naughty Nellie,"
9½" l. $78.00
Cast iron, folding-type, cast as
a hinged revolver w/"American
Bull Dog Boot-Jack," 8¼" l.
(ILLUS.) ....125.00 to 150.00
Cast iron, model of a cricket,
marked "Webster Bros. & Co.,
Reading, Pa.," 10½" l........... 55.00
Cast iron, traveling-type, lacy design
w/"V" shaped hinged iron shoe
holder sliding back into groove,
brass pivot allows extensions to
flare out, two front feet fold
down 75.00
Wooden, painted pine, primitive
form, old blue paint, 13½" l...... 27.50

Wooden, fish-shaped w/a heart-
pierced handle, painted black,
19th c., 23½" l. 440.00

BOTTLE OPENERS

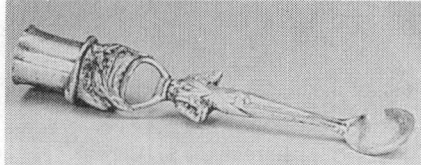

Figural Silver Plated Opener

*Corkscrews were actually the first bottle
openers and these may date back to the mid-
18th century, but bottle openers, as we know
them today, are strictly a 20th century item
and came into use only after Michael J.
Owens invented the automatic bottle machine
in 1903. Avid collectors have spurred this relatively new area of collector interest that requires only a modest investment. Our listing,
by type of metal, encompasses the four basic types sought by collectors: advertising
openers; full figure openers which stand alone
or hang on the wall; flat figural openers such
as the lady's leg shape; and openers with embossed, engraved or chased handles.*

*The numbers following figural openers are
taken from Mike Jordan's book* Figural Bottle Openers *(1981).*

Advertising, "Hudepohl," enameled
red & white. $32.00
Advertising, "Iroquois Beer," red
plastic figural caricature of an
Indian 17.50
Brass, full figure beaver (J-72). 75.00
Brass, full figure nude lady w/arms
above head, 4" 20.00
Brass, full figure stylized Dachshund
dog (J-96) 65.00
Cast iron, full figure Canada goose,
polychrome paint, Wilton Products
(J-108) 75.00
Cast iron, full figure cowboy at sign
post, leg out, polychrome paint,
John Wright Co., some wear,
4¼" h. (J-19) . . . . .150.00 to 250.00
Cast iron, full figure Dinky Dan,
polychrome paint, Gadzik (J-33) . . 450.00
Cast iron, full figure dog, Irish Setter, John Wright Co. (J-94) 40.00
Cast iron, full figure donkey, seat-
ed, ears together, traces of polychrome paint, Wilton Products,
3 5/8" h., J-74 (worn paint) 35.00
Cast iron, full figure drunk in top
hat & tails, legs apart, one arm

out, the other raised w/hand
curved to hold onto shelf, 5½" h.
(worn polychrome paint) 65.00
Cast iron, full figure elephant, seat-
ed w/trunk curled back touching
forehead, head tilted back, Wilton
Products, polychrome paint, some
wear, 3 5/8" h. (J-88). 32.50
Cast iron, full figure flamingo, hol-
low blow mold, polychrome paint,
Wilton Products (J-122) 125.00
Cast iron, full figure foundryman,
polychrome paint, John Wright
Co., 3½" h. (J-18) 105.00
Cast iron, full figure goat, seated
(Billy Goat), polychrome paint,
John Wright Co. (J-105) 200.00
Cast iron, full figure Jayhawk, styl-
ized Jayhawk bird strutting on
round base (J-113) 250.00
Cast iron, full figure lobster, John
Wright Co. (J-134) 33.00
Cast iron, full figure Mallard
duck, standing on base, poly-
chrome paint, Wilton Products
(J-106) . . . . .50.00 to 75.00
Cast iron, full figure monkey,
seated next to tree stump,
black paint, John Wright Co.
(J-109) . . . . .225.00 to 250.00
Cast iron, full figure parrot (large),
large notched crest & long tail on
perch, John Wright Co., 3" h.
(J-61) 45.00
Cast iron, full figure rooster, stand-
ing bird w/arched tail, polychrome paint, 3 1/8" h., J-97
(worn paint) 93.50
Cast iron, wall-mounted, bear's
head, polychrome paint, John
Wright Co. (J-165) 135.00
Cast iron, wall-mounted, four-eyed
bald-headed man w/mustache,
polychrome paint, minor wear,
3¾" h. (J-169) 45.00
Cast iron, wall-mounted head of a
clown, polychrome paint w/polka
dot bow tie, John Wright Co.,
4 3/8" h. (J-158) . . . . .100.00 to 150.00
Silver plate, figural caricature of
Congressman Volstead, man
wearing top hat, mouth forms
opener, spoon at the bottom end,
marked "Pat. 8.16.32 U.S.A.," ca.
1933, 9 5/8" l., light wear & tar-
nish (ILLUS.) 143.00
Sterling silver & stainless steel,
Acorn patt., Georg Jensen, Denmark, 20th c., w/original box,
6 3/8" l. 95.00
Warthog tusk handle w/sterling cap
& studs, ca. 1910 . . . . 80.00

BOTTLES & FLASKS

BITTERS

(Numbers with some listings below refer to those used in Carlyn Ring's For Bitters Only.*)*

Baker's Orange Grove Bitters

African Stomach Bitters, Spruance, Stanley & Co., round, reddish amber, 9 5/8" h....................$130.00

Allen's (William) Congress Bitters, rectangular, olive amber, 10" h. . . . 900.00

Amazon Bitters - Peter McQuade, New York, square, applied mouth, smooth base, amber, ca. 1890-1900, 9" h. 242.00

American Life Bitters - P.E. Iler, Manufacturer, Tiffin, Ohio - American Life Bitters, cabin-shaped, amber, 8 7/8" h........3,600.00

American Stomach Bitters, Rochester, N.Y., oval, tooled lip, smooth base, amber, ca. 1880-90, 7 7/8" h. 240.00

Ayer (Dr. M.C.) Restorative Bitters, Boston, Mass., rectangular, smoky grey, 8 7/8" h.................. 170.00

Baker's Orange Grove - Bitters, square w/roped corners, applied mouth, smooth base, medium to dark puce, shallow sliver in bottom corner, 9½" h. (ILLUS.) 187.00

Baker's Orange Grove - Bitters, square w/roped corners, applied mouth, smooth base, medium apricot puce, 9½" h. 440.00

Big Bill Best Bitters, square, orange amber, w/paper labels, 12 1/8" h. 132.00

Blakes (Dr.) - Aromatic Bitters - New York, rectangular, pontil, aqua, 7" h.............150.00 to 175.00

Blue Mountain Bitters, rectangular, aqua, 7 7/8" h. 95.00

Bohlin's (Doctor) - Norman Bitters, square, clear, 8 7/8" h........... 130.00

Boyer's Stomach Bitters, Cincinnati, round w/ribs around shoulder & base, clear, 11" h. 95.00

Brophy's Bitters within a crescent, above a five-pointed star over "Trade Mark," & "Nokomis, Illinois" at base, square, aqua, 7½" h....................... 70.00

Brown & Lyon's - Blood Bitters - Binghamton N.Y., square, yellow olive, 10 7/8" h.................1,350.00

Brown's Celebrated Indian Herb Bitters - Patented Feb. 11, 1868, figural Indian Queen, rolled lip, smooth base, deep chocolate, ca. 1870-80, 12½" h. 1,375.00

Buhrer's Gentian Bitters - S. Buhrer, Proprietor, square, amber, 8 9/16" h. 82.50

Caldwell's (Dr.) Herb Bitters (below) The Great Tonic, triangular, amber, 12¾" h. ....100.00 to 150.00

Campbell's (Dr.) Scotch Bitters, strap-sided flask, amber, ¼ pt., 6 1/8" h. 150.00

Canton (star) Bitters, round w/lady's leg neck, amber, 12¼" h................325.00 to 350.00

Carmeliter Bitters For All Kidney & Liver Complaints - Carmeliter Burhenne & Dorn Proprietors Brooklyn, New York, w/"Capacity 23 ozs." horizontally at base of panels, square, amber, 10½" h. . . 150.00

Caroni - Bitters (on shoulders), embossed "Caroni Bitters" on base, cylindrical, olive green, 5 1/16" h. 55.00

Clarke's Vegetable Sherry Wine Bitters, Sharon, Mass., aqua, gal., 14" h. 500.00

Coleman's (Dr. A.W.) - Anti Dyspeptic and Tonic Bitters, rectangular, applied mouth, iron pontil, deep emerald green, ca. 1840-50, 9¼" h. 2,475.00

Columbo Peptic Bitters - L.E. Jung & Co., New Orleans, La., square, partial labels, amber, 9" h. 55.00

Constitution Bitters - A.M.S.2 1864 (on two sides) - Seward & Bentley, Buffalo, N.Y., rectangular, amethyst, 9¼" h.................1,650.00

Copp's (Dr.) White Mountain (in shield) Bitters, J. Copp & Co., Manchester, N.H., w/"JHC" monogram, oval, tooled mouth w/collar, aqua, pt., 8¼" h. 125.00

Devil-Cert - Stomach Bitters - Fred Kalina, 409 Water St., Pittsburgh, PA, round, clear, 4" h. ....25.00 to 50.00

Digestine Bitters, P.J. Bowlin Liquor Co., Sole Proprietors, St. Paul, Minn., rectangular, amber, 8" h. 300.00

Drake's Plantation Bitters - Patented 1862, cabin-shaped, six-log, arabesque variant, light honey amber, 10" h. (D-102) . . . . 50.00 to 75.00

Drake's Plantation Bitters - Patented 1862, cabin-shaped, six-log, arabesque variant, true yellow, 10" h. (D-102) 595.00

Drake's (S T), 1860 Plantation Bitters - Patented 1862, no "X," cabin-shaped, four-log, amber, 10¼" h. (D-110) 55.00

Drake's (S T) 1860 Plantation Bitters - Patented 1862, no "X," cabin-shaped, four-log, golden amber, 10¼" h. (D-110) 60.50

Drake's (S T) 1860 Plantation Bitters - Patented 1862, no "X," cabin-shaped, six-log, golden amber, 10" h. (D-103) 120.00

Drake's (S T) 1860 Plantation X Bitters - Patented 1862, cabin-shaped, six-log, medium burgundy, 10" h. (D-105) 220.00

Drake's (S T) 1860 Plantation X Bitters - Patented 1862, cabin-shaped, six-log, medium yellowish amber, 10" h. (D-105) 405.00

Drake's (S T) 1860 Plantation X Bitters - Patented 1862, cabin-shaped, six-log, peach, 10" h. (D-105) 286.00

Drake's (S T) 1860 Plantation X Bitters - Patented 1862, cabin-shaped, six-log, yellow w/orange cast, 10" h. (D-105) 110.00

Drake's (S T) 1860 Plantation X Bitters - Patented 1862, cabin-shaped, six-log, apricot, 10" h. (D-108) 231.00

Drake's (S T) 1860 Plantation X Bitters - Patented 1862, cabin-shaped, six-log, deep cherry puce, 10" h. (D-108) 240.00

Drake's 1860 Plantation Bitters

Drake's (S T) 1860 Plantation X Bitters - Patented 1862, cabin-shaped, six-log, pinkish amber, 10" h., D-108 (ILLUS.) 467.50

"Electric" Brand Bitters - H.E. Bucklen & Co., Chicago, Ill., square, amber, 8 5/8" h. . . . . 25.00 to 35.00

English Female Bitters - Louisville, KY - Dromgoole - 12 Fl. Ozs., rectangular, clear w/light amethyst tint, 8½" h. 90.00

Fenner's (Dr. M.M.) - Capitol Bitters - Fredonia, N.Y., rectangular, aqua, 10½" h. 65.00

Ferro Quina Stomach Bitters, Blood Maker, Mfg. by D.P. Rossi, San Francisco, Cal, square w/lady's leg neck, amber, 9" h. 75.00

Fischs (Doctor) Bitters - W.H. Ware, Patented 1866, figural fish, amber, 11¾" h. . . . . 135.00 to 195.00

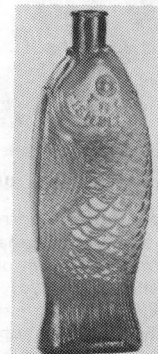

The Fish Bitters

Fish (The) Bitters - W.H. Ware, Patented 1866, figural fish, amber, 11½" h. (ILLUS.) 160.00

Fish (The) Bitters - W.H. Ware, Patented 1866, figural fish, yellow, 11 3/8" h. 575.00

German Balsam Bitters, W.M. Watson & Co. Sole Agents for U.S., square, milk white, 9" h. 400.00

German - Hop - Bitters - 1880 - Dr. C.D. Warner's - Reading, Mich., square, amber, 9½" h. 125.00

Gillmore's (Dr.) Laxative Kidney & Liver Bitters, oval, clear, 10 3/8" h. 200.00

Globe Bitters, Manufactured only by - Byrne Bros & Co., New York, (also on shoulder) Globe Bitters - Byrne Bros. & Co., New York, round, amber shading to yellow, 11" h. 425.00

Godrey's - Celebrated Cordial Bitters, square, applied mouth, aqua, 10" h. . . . . 850.00 to 1,100.00

Goff's (S.B.) - Herb Bitters - Camden, N.J., rectangular, aqua, 7¾" h. . . . . 30.00 to 40.00

Greeley's Bourbon Bitters, barrel-
shaped, ten rings above & below
center band, amber, w/paper la-
bel, 9 3/8" h. . . . . .225.00 to 250.00

Greeley's Bourbon Bitters, barrel-
shaped, ten rings above & below
center band, copper amber,
9 3/8" h. 302.50

Greeley's Bourbon Bitters, barrel-
shaped, ten rings above & below
center band, medium olive green,
9 3/8" h. .1,250.00

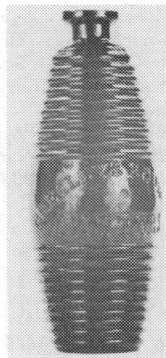

Greeley's Bourbon Bitters

Greeley's Bourbon Bitters, barrel-
shaped, ten rings above & below
center band, medium plum puce,
9 3/8" h. (ILLUS.) 247.50

Hall's Bitters - E.E. Hall, New Haven,
Established 1842, barrel-shaped,
medium amber, w/paper label,
. . . . 9 1/8" h. 330.00

Hall's Bitters - E.E Hall, New Haven,
Established 1842, barrel-shaped,
yellow w/amber tone, w/paper
label & paper wrapper, 9¼" h. 522.50

Hellman's - Congress Bitters - St.
Louis. Mo, square, amber,
2 5/8" sq., 8¾" h. 320.00

H.P. Herb Bitters Bottle

Herb (H.P.) Wild Cherry Bitters,
Reading, Pa., cabin-shaped,

square w/cherry tree motif &
roped corners, deep amber,
10" h. (ILLUS.) 275.00

Hibernia Bitters, square, applied
mouth, smooth base, yellowish
amber, 9¾" h. 198.00

Holtzermans Patent Stomach Bitters
(on shoulders), cabin-shaped
w/four roofs, amber, w/paper la-
bel, 9 5/8" h. . . . . .250.00 to 300.00

Hopkins (Dr. A.S.) Union Stomach
Bitters, Hartford, Conn., square,
light amber, 9¾" h. 115.00

Hops & Malt, T (sheaf of wheat motif) M, Bitters, square, amber,
3 5/8" h. . . . . .250.00 to 300.00

Hostetter's (Dr. J.) Stomach Bitters,
square, smooth base, applied
mouth, yellowish olive green,
9" h. 231.00

Hutchings - Dyspepsia Bitters - New
York, rectangular, applied mouth,
open pontil, aqua, ca. 1830-60,
9½" h. 302.50

John's (Dr. Herbert) - Indian Bitters -
Great Indian Discoveries, square
w/beveled corners, amber,
8 5/8" h. 302.50

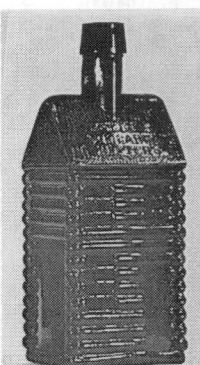

Kelly's Old Cabin Bitters Bottle

Kelly's Old Cabin Bitters - Patd
March 1870, cabin-shaped, amber,
9¼" h. (ILLUS.) 467.50

Keystone Tonic Bitters - McLain
Bros., Foreston, Ills, "A. & D.H.C."
embossed on smooth base, ap-
plied mouth, amber, 9" h. 330.00

Langley's (Dr.) Root & Herb Bitters -
99 (numbers backwards) Union
St., Boston, round, whittled, aqua,
8¼" h. 52.50

Langley's (Dr.) Root & Herb Bitters,
99 Union St., Boston, round, applied mouth, smooth base, medium bluish aqua, ca. 1865-80,
8½" h. 412.50

Litthauer Stomach Bitters (paper label), Hartwig Kantorowicz, Posen,

Ham - burg, Paris, square case
gin-shape, milk white, miniature,
3¾" h. 71.50

Litthauer Stomach Bitters, Hartwig
Kantorowicz, Posen, Berlin, Hamburg, Germany, flattened oval
w/heavy rib up each side, smooth
base, applied mouth, bright yel-
lowish green, 10 3/8" h. 1,100.00

Marshall's Bitters - The Best Laxative and Blood Purifier, square,
amber, 8 5/8" h. 45.00

Mishler's Herb Bitters - Table Spoon
Graduation (ruled marker) - Mish-
ler Herb Bitters Co. - 40 Med.
Doses, embossed "Stoeckels Grad
Pat. Feb 6 '66" on base, square,
yellowish amber, 9" h. 69.00

Mishler's Herb Bitters - (ruled marker) 1 oz., 5 oz., 10 oz., 15 oz., Table Spoon Graduation - Mishler's
Herb Bitters - 40 Med. Doses -
Stoeckels Grad Pat Feb. 11 '66,
square, medium orangish amber,
2¾" w., 9" h. 30.00

Moffat (Jno.) - Price $1 - Phoenix
Bitters - New York, rectangular
w/wide beveled corners, pontil
scarred base, applied mouth, ol-
ive amber, 5½" h. 440.00

National Bitters - Patent 1867,
figural ear of corn, yellowish am-
ber, 12 5/8" h. 365.00

Nectar Bitters w/HB monogram, lady's leg shape, applied mouth,
smooth base, medium orangish
amber, ca. 1870-80, 12½" h. (½"
stress crack in neck while being
made). 495.00

Old Homestead Wild Cherry Bitters -
Patent (on shoulders), cabin-
shaped, amber, 9 7/8" h. 250.00

Old Sachem Bitters and Wigwam
Tonic, barrel-shaped, ten-rib,
medium amber, ca. 1860-70,
9½" h. 385.00

Parker's Celebrated Stomach Bitters,
square, amber, 7 13/16" h. 245.00

Parker's Celebrated Stomach Bitters,
square, light honey amber,
7 13/16". 295.00

Philadelphia Hop Bitters & embossed
picture of a black man holding a
bottle, square, applied mouth,
smooth base, ca. 1860-70,
9½" h. 880.00

Pipifax Celebrated Bitters, square,
light amber, 2¼" w., 9 5/8" h. . . . 160.00

Prickly Ash Bitters Co., square, amber, ¾ qt., 9¾" h. (P-142) 42.00

Red Jacket Bitters, Bennet Pieters &
Co., square, amber, 9½" h. 198.00

Reed's Bitters, cylindrical, lady's leg

neck, amber, smooth base, ap-
plied mouth, amber, 12½" h. 242.00

Roback's (Dr. C.W.) Stomach Bitters,
Cincinnati, O, barrel-shaped, am-
ber, 9 3/8" h. 220.00

Rose's (E.J.) Magador Bitters For
Stomach, Kidney & Liver, square,
amber, 8 5/8" h. . . . . .135.00 to 175.00

Saint Jacob's Bitters, square, dark
blackish amber, 8¾" h. 130.00

Sawen's (Dr.) Life Invigorating Bitters - Utica, N.Y., square, light
amber, 9 1/8" h. 210.00

Sazarac Aromatic Bitters, lady's
leg neck, medium amber,
10 1/8" h. 330.00

Schroeder's Bitters, Louisville and
Cincinnati, Established 1845 - S B
& G Co., lady's leg neck, tooled
lip, smooth base, amber, 9" h. . . . 495.00

Soule (Dr.) - Hop - Bitters - 1872
(embossed on shoulders), hop
flowers & leaf motif one side
(same side has "1872" on shoulder), square, dark amber,
9¾" h. 88.00

Soule (Dr.) - Hop - Bitters - 1872
(embossed on shoulders), hop
flowers & leaf motif one side
(same side has "1872" on shoulder), square, yellow, 9¼" h.
(wear & scratches on corners) 88.00

Dr. Stoever's Bitters Bottle

Stoever's (Dr.) Bitters - Established
1837 - Kryder & Co., Philadelphia,
square, dark amber, 9½" h.
(ILLUS.). 165.00

Suffolk Bitters - Philbrook & Tucker,
Boston, model of a pig, medium
amber, 10 1/8" l. 852.50

Swiss - Stomach Bitters - WM. F.
Zoeller - Pittsburgh, PA., w/paper
label, rectangular, applied mouth,
smooth base, amber, ca. 1870-80,
9¼" h. 715.00

Toneco Stomach Bitters - Appetizer
& Tonic, square, clear, 9" h. 48.00

Wahoo & Calisaya Bitters -
Jacob Pinkerton - Jacob
Pinkerton, square, amber,
9 5/8" h. . . . . .250.00 to 275.00
Wahoo & Calisaya Bitters - Jacob
Pinkerton - Jacob Pinkerton,
square, light golden amber,
9 5/8" h. 410.00
Warner's Safe Bitters, embossed
safe & Trade Mark, Rochester
N.Y., oval, smooth base, applied
mouth, amber, 7½" h. 357.50
West India Stomach Bitters - St.
Louis, Mo. - Wim Co., square, am-
ber, 8½" h. 46.00
Wheat Bitters, rectangular, amber,
9½" h. 154.00
Youngs (Dr.) Wild Cherry Bitters,
Brooklyn, N.Y., rectangular, am-
ber, 8½" h. 357.50
Zingari Bitters - F. Rahter (embossed
on shoulders), cylindrical,
lady's leg neck, amber,
12" h. . . . . .200.00 to 250.00

CONTEMPORARY

Ezra Brooks

Elk

Bengal Tiger 30.00
Big Red No. 1 . . . . 33.00
Christmas Tree 19.50
Clown, Cowboy (No. 2) 23.50
Clown, Pagliacci (No. 3) 20.00
Clown, Tramp (No. 6) (1982) 24.50
Corvette, 1962 Mako Shark (1979) . . . 25.00
Elk (ILLUS.) 34.00
Kachina Doll No. 2 (1973) 70.00
Old Ez, Eagle Owl, No. 2 (1978) 62.00
Red Fox (1980-81) 42.50
Shrine King Tut (1979) 16.50
Snow Leopard (1980-81) 32.00
Thunderbird, Ford, blue 82.50
West Virginia Mountaineer 86.00

Jim Beam

Ambulance, 1931 Ford 25.00
Antique Trader, 1968 (ILLUS.) 19.50

Antique Trader

Baggage Car (1981) 52.00
Bobby Unser Racing Car, Olsonite
Eagle (1975) 55.00
Box Car, yellow 54.00
Buffalo Bill (1971) 12.00
Caboose, red (1980) 62.50
Cardinal, male (1968) 31.50
Conventions
   1972 No. 2 Anaheim 44.00
   1975 No. 5 Sacramento 19.00
   1979 No. 9 Houston 39.50
Dining Car (1982) 69.50
Dog, Setter (1958) 44.00
Ducks Unlimited
   1974 Mallard (No. 1) 40.00
   1978 Mallard (No. 4) 41.50
   1979 Canvasback Drake (No. 5) . . . 35.50
Executives
   1959 Tavern Scene 54.00
   1961 Golden Chalice 56.00
   1965 Marbled Fantasy 58.00
   1972 Regency 15.00
Figaro w/base & paperweight 215.00
Fire Engine, 1867 Mississippi Steam
Engine (1978) 114.00
Fire Truck, 1930 Model "A" Ford
(1983) 135.00
Football Hall of Fame (1972) 15.50
Fox
   1965 Green Fox 29.00
   1974 Rennie The Runner 14.00
Harolds Club
   1964 Nevada, Silver 150.00
   1967 VIP 64.50
   1977 VIP 32.50
International Petroleum (1971) 10.50
Jackelope (1971) 12.00
Light Bulb (1979) 12.50
Locomotive
   J.B. Turner (1982) 88.00
Model T Ford, green & black
(1974) 59.00
Monterey Bay Club (1977) 8.50
New Jersey Yellow (1963) 51.00
Paddy Wagon (1984) 105.00
Pearl Harbor (1972) 19.50

Screech owl, red or grey (1979)..... 18.50
Stutz Bearcat (1977), yellow & black
or grey & black, each............ 59.00
Telephone Pioneers
1975 1907 Wall Telephone
(No. 1)...................... 39.00
1980 1919 Dial Telephone
(No. 4)..................... 56.00
Twin Bridges Club (1971)........... 47.00
Volkswagen (1973), red or blue,
each.......................... 50.00
West Virginia (1963)............. 152.00

FIGURALS

Carry Nation Bottle

Barrel, brilliant lavender glass,
smooth base, tooled lip, ca. 1880-
1900, 9¼" h. 93.50
Bear, Kummel-type, black opaque
glass, 11" h..............70.00 to 85.00
Bunker Hill Monument w/ground
neck, clear glass, 12" h. 48.00
Bust of O'Connell ESQ' (Daniel), pot-
tery, tan & brown glaze, "Irish Re-
form Cordial Daniel O'Connell
Esq" embossed on front & back &
"Dourne Denby Made in England"
stamped on base, ca. 1830-50,
7¾" h......................... 176.00
Cannon, clear glass, embossed
"Phalon & Son" within a shield,
for cologne, smooth base, tooled
lip, ca. 1880-1900, 7 1/8" h. 253.00
Carry Nation, clear glass, 8¾" h.
(ILLUS.) ....110.00 to 135.00
Coachman, amber glass, "Van
Dunck's" 135.00
Coachman, pottery, Bennington-type
tan & brown mottled glaze, em-
bossed "1830, J. Smith The
Mormon Prophet," ca. 1840-50,
8 7/8" h. (½" chip off corner of
base) 385.00
Corn stalk, aqua glass, 6½" h. 50.00
Ear of corn w/tooled lip, clear glass,
6" h.......................... 32.00
Elephant (standing) w/trunk around
a tree, clear glass, 3¾" h. 50.00

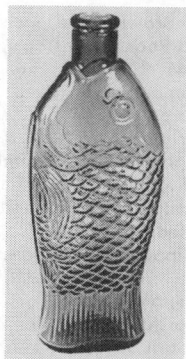

Fish Bottle

Fish, amber glass, mid-20th c.,
9¾" h. (ILLUS.) ....15.00 to 20.00
Guitar, clear glass, 21" l. 25.00
Gun, amber glass, "Patent applied
For" embossed above trigger,
smooth base, tooled lip, ca. 1880-
1900, 10" l. 72.50
Hand holding a pistol, clear glass,
13" l. 35.00
Lighthouse, clear glass, embossed
"Patent Applied For - Geo. Miller
& Son" on smooth base, ground
lip w/original metal screw cap,
ca. 1890-1910, 7" h. 198.00
Man in the moon, yellow glass on
black amethyst glass base, 95%
original face paint, metal pour
spigot, ground lip, overall
13" h. 632.50
Negro waiter, miniature, clear glass
w/original paint 1,800.00

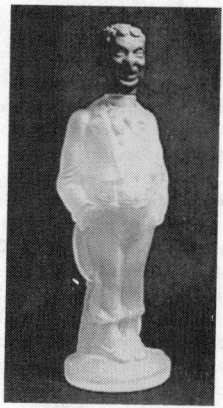

Negro Waiter Bottle

Negro waiter, frosted glass body
w/black glass head stopper, 1880-
1920, 12¼" h. (ILLUS.) 450.00
Our Lady of Lourdes, clear glass,
6¼" h......................... 28.00
Pig, pottery, tan & brown glaze, ca.
1870-90, 6 3/8" l................ 154.00

Pig, pottery, brown glaze, incised "Good Old Peach in a Hog's," ca. 1880-90, 8½" l. 412.50

Pineapple, amber glass, 9" h. 100.00

Potato, aqua glass, 5¼" l. 18.00

Potato, clear glass, 4¼" l. 15.00

Shoe, clear glass w/ornate embossing, pontil 30.00

Shoe, laced high top-type, clear glass, tooled top, 4". 35.00

Shoe, low slipper w/opening in upturned toe, embossed "L.M.," clear glass, 5½" l. 22.00

Spanish senorita, milk white glass, smooth base, ca. 1920-30, 11 7/8" h. 71.50

Turkey, amber glass 60.00

Zucchini, medium cobalt blue glass, pontiled, ca. 1880-1900, 8¾" l. . . . 93.50

FLASKS

(Numbers used below refer to those used in the McKearin's American Bottles & Flasks.*)*

Columbia Bust Flask

GI-2 - Washington bust below "General Washington" - American Eagle w/shield w/seven bars on breast, head turned to right, edges w/horizontal beading w/vertical medial rib, plain lip, pontil, light green, pt. 231.00

GI-10 - Washington bust below "G. Washington" - American Eagle below 11 stars & standing on oval frame w/inner band of 15 small pearls, plain lip, horizontal beading w/vertical medial rib, pontil, aqua, pt. 467.50

GI-11 - Washington bust below branches - American Eagle w/head turned right & body curving, wings partly raised, three arrows in right talons & olive branch in left, sunrays above eagle's head & 13 small stars, horizontal beading w/vertical medial rib, plain lip, pontil mark, aqua, pt. . . 715.00

GI-20 - Washington bust (facing right) below "Fells," "Point" below bust - Baltimore Monument w/"Balto" below, plain lip, vertical medial rib, pontil, aqua, pt. . . 132.00

GI-26 - Washington bust - American Eagle w/shield w/eight vertical & two horizontal bars on breast, head turned to right, plain lip, pontil, aqua, qt. 137.50

GI-32 - "Washington" above bust, uniform without bars on lapel - "Jackson" above bust, plain lip, pontil, olive amber, pt. 165.00

GI-33 - "Washington" above bust, uniform without bars on lapel - "Jackson" above bust, plain lip, pontil, olive amber, pt. 137.50

GI-51 - Washington bust - Taylor bust, smooth edges, flat sloping collar, pontil, medium sapphire blue, qt. 495.00

GI-54 - Washington bust without queue - Taylor bust in uniform, open pontil, light bluish aqua, qt., 8¾" h. 60.50

GI-71 - Taylor bust, facing left, w/"Rough and Ready" below - Ringgold bust, facing left, w/"Major" in semicircle above bust & "Ringgold" in semicircle beneath bust, heavy vertical ribbing, plain lip, pontil mark, clear w/smoky grey tint, pt. 302.50

GI-71 - Taylor bust, facing left, w/"Rough and Ready" below - Ringgold bust, facing left, w/"Major" in semicircle above bust & 'Ringgold" in semicircle beneath bust, heavy vertical ribbing, plain lip, pontil mark, light yellowish green, pt. 176.00

GI-80 - "Lafayette" above bust & "T.S." & bar below - "De Witt Clinton" above bust & "Coventry C-T" below, plain lip, horizontally corrugated edges, pontil, olive amber, pt. 700.00

GI-92 - Lafayette bust facing right below Masonic Arch & a fleur-de-lis, "Genl Lafayette" along sides - American Eagle w/shield on breast below seven stars all in an oval & "Wheeling" in semicircle above upper part of panel & "Knox & McKee" in semicircle around lower panel, smooth edges, plain lip, pontil mark, aqua, pt. 4,675.00

GI-93 - Lafayette bust facing right below Masonic Arch & above a fleur-de-lis, " Genl Lafayette" along side - American Eagle w/shield on breast below seven stars all in an oval, vertical ribbing on edges, plain lip, emerald green, pt. 2,915.00

GI-96 - Franklin bust below "Benjamin Franklin" - Dyott bust below "T.W. Dyott, M.D.," edges embossed "Eripuit Coelo Fulmen. Sceptrumque Tyrannis" and "Kensington Glass Works, Philadelphia," plain lip, pontil, pinkish amethystine, qt. 1,540.00

GI-99 - "Jenny Lind" above bust - View of Glasshouse w/"Glass Works" above & "Huffsey" below, calabash, smooth sides, broad sloping collar, pontil, aqua, qt. . . .   99.00

GI-104 - "Jeny (sic) Lind" above bust - View of Glasshouse, calabash, vertically ribbed edges, rounded collar, pontil, deep bluish aqua, qt., 9¾" h. 130.00

GI-107 - "Jenny Lind" above bust - View of Glasshouse w/"Fislerville Glass Works" above, calabash, vertically fluted edges, broad sloping collar, pontil, emerald green, qt. 25.00

GI-117 - Columbia bust w/"Kensington" below - American Eagle w/head turned to right & w/"Union. Co." below, aqua, pt. (ILLUS.). 650.00

GI-121 - Columbia bust - American Eagle w/"B & W" in script below, vertically ribbed edges, plain lip, pontil, aqua, pt. 425.00

GI-128 - Christopher Columbus bust w/"Columbian Exposition" above & "A.E.M. Bros. & Co." below - "Pennsylvania Pure Rye, Baker, Whiskey," smooth base, tooled lip, medium amber, pt. 1,000.00

GI-131 - Taylor bust, facing left, w/"Rough & Ready" in semiellipse below - Ringgold bust, facing left, w/"Major" in semicircle beneath bust, heavy vertical ribbing, plain lip, pontil mark, light amethystine, pt. 632.50

GII-24 - American Eagle above oval obverse & reverse, ribbon & two semicircular rows of stars above & elongated eight-point star in oval below, edges corrugated horizontally w/vertical medial rib, plain lip, pontil, amber, pt. 1,050.00

GII-24 - American Eagle above oval obverse & reverse, ribbon & two semicircular rows of stars above & elongated eight-point star in oval below, edges corrugated horizontally w/vertical medial rib, plain

lip, pontil, deep olive green, pt. 2,750.00

GII-38 - American Eagle facing right, poised on a rock formation which supports an American shield, "E Pluribus Unum" inscribed on ribbon held in eagle's mouth - "Dyottville Glass Work's" in semicircle & "Philada." below in slightly curved line, smooth edges, plain lip, aqua, pt. 110.00

GII-40 - American Eagle on oval, obverse & reverse, heavy vertical ribbing, short, sheared neck, pontil, emerald green, pt. 907.50

GII-48 - American Eagle on oval - American flag w/"Coffin & Hay." above & "Hammonton" below, vertically ribbed edges, plain lip, pontil, emerald green, qt. 2,090.00

GII-53 - American Eagle w/head erect & turned right, on shield w/olive branches below - "For Our Country" below U.S. flag w/20 stars, vertically ribbed edge, plain lip, open pontil, aqua, pt. . . 145.00

GII-54 - American Eagle on Shield w/olive branches below - "For Our Country" below U.S. flag w/20 stars, vertically ribbed edges, plain lip, open pontil, aqua, pt. 150.00

GII-61 - American Eagle below "Liberty" - inscribed in four lines, "Willington - Glass, Co - West Willington - Conn," smooth edges, reddish amber, qt. 253.00

GII-63 - American Eagle below "Liberty" - inscription in five lines, "Willington - Glass - Co - West Willington - Conn.," smooth edges, plain lip, amber, ½ pt. . . . 170.00

GII-69 - American Eagle w/head turned left w/thunderbolt in left talon & olive branch in right - Inverted cornucopia filled w/produce, horizontally beaded w/vertical medial rib, plain lip, pontil mark, aqua, ½ pt. 330.00

GII-69 - American Eagle w/head turned left w/thunderbolt in left talon & olive branch in right - Inverted cornucopia filled w/produce, horizontally beaded w/vertical medial rib, plain lip, pontil mark, clear, ½ pt. 770.00

GII-72 - American Eagle w/head turned right & standing on rocks - Cornucopia with Produce, vertically ribbed edges, plain neck, yellowish amber, pt. 77.00

GII-74 - American Eagle w/head turned to the right & standing on rocks - Cornucopia w/produce &

"X" on left, smooth edges, plain lip, pontil mark, brilliant green, pt. 440.00

GII-80 - American Eagle above oval inscribed "Granite. - Glass Co." obverse, reverse the same except inscribed "Stoddard - NH," vertical rib about 3/8" w., round collar, golden amber, qt. 93.50

GII-81 - American Eagle above oval inscribed "Granite. - Glass Co." obverse, reverse the same except inscription "Stoddard - NH," narrow vertical rib, plain lip, pontil mark, yellowish amber, pt. 264.00

GII-83 - American Eagle above oval obverse & reverse, frame 3/8" from base on obverse & 5/8" from base on reverse, plain lip, yellowish amber, pt. 110.00

American Eagle Flask

GII-87 - American Eagle above oval obverse & reverse, "X" in oval frame on obverse, plain lip, pontil, tiny open bubble on side, olive amber, ½ pt. (ILLUS.) 88.00

GII-88 - American Eagle above oval w/bead obverse, reverse same except bead 1/8" larger, vertically ribbed edges, plain lip, pontil, yellowish amber, ½ pt. 88.00

GII-106 - American Eagle above oval obverse & reverse, w/"Pittsburgh, PA" in oval on obverse, narrow vertical rib on edges, some mouth roughness, forest green, pt. 143.00

GII-107 - American Eagle above oval obverse & reverse, w/"Pittsburgh, PA" in oval obverse, narrow vertical rib, light blue, pt. 120.00

GII-143 - American Eagle w/plain shield in talons & pennant in beak, calabash, four vertical flutes on edges, bright yellow green, qt. 145.00

GIII-4 - Cornucopia with Produce - Urn with Produce, vertically ribbed edges, plain lip, pontil, green, pt. 77.00

GIII-7 - Cornucopia with Produce - Urn with Produce, vertically ribbed edges, sheared lip, pontil, medium green, ½ pt. 170.00

GIII-7 - Cornucopia with Produce - Urn with Produce, vertically ribbed edges, sheared lip, pontil, olive amber, ½ pt. 71.50

GIII-7 - Cornucopia with Produce - Urn with Produce, vertically ribbed edges, sheared lip, pontil, yellowish amber, ½ pt. 55.00

GIII-10 - Cornucopia with Produce - Urn with Produce, vertically ribbed edges, heavy medial rib, plain lip, pontil mark, olive amber, ½ pt. 55.00

GIII-11 - Cornucopia with Produce - Urn with Produce, vertically ribbed edges, plain lip, pontil, yellowish olive, ½ pt. 187.00

GIII-12 - Cornucopia with Produce & curled to right - Urn with Produce, plain lip, vertically ribbed edges, pontil, golden amber, ½ pt., 5½" h. 55.00

GIII-16 - Cornucopia with Produce & curled to right - Urn with Produce & w/"Lancaster.Glass.Works N.Y." above, sheared mouth, vertically ribbed edges, iron pontil, golden amber, pt. 2,900.00

GIV-1 - Masonic Emblems - American Eagle w/ribbon reading "E Pluribus Unum" above & "IP" (Old-fashioned J) below in oval frame, tooled mouth, five vertical ribs, bright bluish green, pt. 137.50

GIV-5 - Masonic Arch - American Eagle holding shield w/eight dots (representing stars), banner above, oval frame w/eight-pointed star below, vertically ribbed, tooled mouth, medium yellowish green, pt. 480.00

GIV-18 - Masonic Arch, pillars & pavement w/Masonic emblems - American Eagle without shield on breast, plain oval frame below w/"KCCNC" inside, smooth edges w/single vertical rib, plain lip, pontil, yellowish amber, pt. 214.50

GIV-24 - Masonic Arch, pillars & pavement w/Masonic emblems - American Eagle grasping large balls in talons & without shield on breast, plain oval frame below, smooth edges w/single medial rib, plain lip, pontil, bright amber, ½ pt. 99.00

GIV-32 - Masonic Arch w/"Farmer's

Arms," sheaf of rye & farm implements within arch - American Eagle, w/shield w/seven bars on breast, head turned to right, "Zanesville" above eagle on oval frame w/"Ohio" inside & "J. Shepard & Co." beneath, vertically ribbed edges, open pontil, brilliant orange amber, pt. 335.00

GIV-36 - Masonic Arch w/"Farmer's Arms," sheaf of rye & farm implements within arch - full rigged frigate sailing to right, "Franklin" below, edges horizontally beaded w/medial rib, plain lip, pontil, light green, pt. 1,320.00

GIV-38 - Clasped hands above square & compass all inside shield w/"Union" above shield - American Eagle carrying plain shield above plain oval frame, smooth edges, rounded collar, aqua, qt... 65.00

GV-3 - "Success to the Railroad" around embossed horse pulling cart - similar reverse, sheared lip, pontil, light yellow, pt. 500.00

GV-3 - "Success to the Railroad" around embossed horse pulling cart - similar reverse, sheared lip, pontil, yellowish amber, pt. 176.00

"Success to the Railroad" Flask

GV-6 - "Success to the Railroad" around embossed horse pulling cart obverse & reverse, w/"Success" above scene, open pontil, vertically ribbed edges, olive green, pt. (ILLUS.) 165.00

GV-8 - "Success to the Railroad" around embossed horse pulling cart - large American Eagle w/head turned left & holding a shield w/seven vertical & two horizontal bars on breast, seventeen large five-pointed stars surround eagle, vertically ribbed edges w/heavy medial rib, plain lip, pontil mark, light yellowish olive, pt. 195.00

GVI-3 - "Baltimore" above monument - "Liberty & Union," smooth edges, plain lip, pontil mark, aqua, pt. 247.50

GVI-4 - "Baltimore" below monument - "Corn For The World" in semicircle above ear of corn, smooth edges, plain lip, pontil mark, aqua, qt. 93.50

GVIII-3 - Sunburst w/twenty-four rounded rays obverse & reverse, horizontal corrugated edges, plain lip, pontil mark, light green, pt. ... 450.00

GVIII-8 - Sunburst w/twenty-eight triangular sectioned rays, obverse & reverse, center raised oval w/"KEEN" on obverse & w/"P & W" on reverse, pontil, olive amber, pt. 302.50

GVIII-10 - Sunburst w/twenty-nine triangular sectioned rays, center raised oval w/"Keen" reading from top to bottom on obverse & reverse, sheared lip, pontil, bright green, ½ pt. 390.00

GVIII-28 - Sunburst w/sixteen rays obverse & reverse, rays converging to a definite point at center & covering entire side of flask, horizontally corrugated edges, plain lip, open pontil, clear w/faint amethystine, ½ pt. 253.00

GIX-2 - Scroll w/two six-point stars obverse & reverse, vertical medial rib, long neck w/plain lip, deep olive green, qt. 550.00

Scroll Flask

GIX-11 - Scroll w/two eight-point stars obverse & reverse, many seed bubbles, 1/8" stress crack on shoulder, teal blue, pt. (ILLUS.)... 467.50

GIX-14 - Scroll w/six-point star above seven-point star obverse & reverse, vertical medial rib on edge, plain lip, pontil, light apple green, pt. 132.00

GIX-44 - Scrolls w/large pearl below each curved line at base of inner frame & two large pearls below scrolls at top of outer frame - fleur-de-lis w/two large pearls below top scroll left & right, vertical medial rib, plain lip, pontil mark, aqua, pt. 253.00

GX-6 - Cannon, "Genl Taylor Never Surrenders" inscribed in semicircle around cannon - vine & grape form a semicircular frame containing the inscription "A Little More Grape Capt Bragg," vertically ribbed w/heavy medial ribbing, open pontil, aqua, ½ pt. 187.00

GX-7 - Sailboat (sloop) w/pennant on waves - inscription running lengthwise parallel to panel "Bridgetown" on right from top to bottom & "New Jersey" on left from top to bottom, vertically ribbed w/heavy medial rib, plain lip, pontil mark, aqua, ½ pt. 99.00

GX-8 - Sailboat (sloop) w/pennant on waves - eight-point star w/three-pointed ornaments, vertically ribbed sides, pontil, medium green, ½ pt. 300.00

GX-19 - Summer Tree - Winter Tree, plain lip, smooth edges, pontil, aqua, qt. 115.00

GXI-9 - "For Pike's Peak" above prospector w/tools & cane standing on oblong frame "Old Rye" - American Eagle w/pennant above frame "Pittsburgh PA.," smooth edges, deep aqua, pt. 125.00

GXI-24 - "For Pike's Peak" above prospector w/tools standing on oblong frame - American Eagle w/pennant above oblong frame, smooth edges, bright yellowish green, qt. 605.00

GXI-41 - "For Pikes Peak" above prospector w/tools & cane - American Eagle w/pennant above oval frame, molded collar, plain edges, aqua, pt. 110.00

GXII-1 - Clasped hands above oval, all inside shield, w/"Union" above - American Eagle above oval frame, medium yellow olive, qt. . . 357.50

GXII-6 - Clasped hands above oval, all inside shield - American Eagle above oval frame, honey yellow, qt. 467.50

GXII-18 - Clasped hands above oval, all inside shield - American Eagle w/plain shield above oval frame, base w/"L & W" inside disc-shaped frame, amber, pt. 214.50

GXII-25 - Clasped hands above oval w/"Old Rye" all inside shield below "Union" - American Eagle

w/shield & pennant in beak inscribed "A & D H C," above cartouche panel w/"Pittsburgh, PA," medium yellowish green, pt. 605.00

GXII-40 - Clasped hands above oval w/"FA & Co.," all inside shield w/"Union" above - Small cannon & large American flag, smooth base, golden amber, pt. 264.00

GXII-43 - Clasped hands above square & compass above oval w/"Union" all inside shield - American Eagle, calabash, round collar, aqua, qt. 75.00

GXIII-4 - Hunter facing left wearing flat-top stovepipe hat, short coat & full trousers, game bag hanging at left side, firing gun at two birds flying upward at left, large puff of smoke from muzzle, two dogs running to left toward section of rail fence - Fisherman standing on shore near large rock, wearing round-top stovepipe hat, V-neck jacket, full trousers, fishing rod held in left hand w/end resting on ground, right hand holding large fish, creel below left arm, mill w/bushes & tree in left background, calabash, edges w/wide flutes, iron pontil, apricot, qt. 275.00

GXIII-4 - Hunter facing left wearing flat-top stovepipe hat, short coat & full trousers, game bag hanging at left side, firing gun at two birds flying upward at left, large puff of smoke from muzzle, two dogs running to left toward section of rail fence - Fisherman standing on shore near large rock, wearing round-top stovepipe hat, V-neck jacket, full trousers, fishing rod held in left hand w/end resting on ground, right hand holding large fish, creel below left arm, mill w/bushes & tree in left background, calabash, edges w/wide flutes, iron pontil, medium peach, qt. 440.00

GXIII-12 - Soldier standing on patch of ground holding rifle & pointing to drum above bevel-edged narrow rectangular bar inscribed "BALT. MD." - Ballet dancer on patch of ground holding tambourine above bevel-edged narrow rectangular bar inscribed "CHAPMAN," plain lip, smooth edges, light yellowish green, pt. 121.00

GXIII-31 - Sheaf of Grain above large oval frame - plain reverse, smooth edges, reddish puce, pt. . . 300.00

GXIII-35 - Sheaf of Grain w/rake &

pitchfork crossed behind sheaf - "Westford Glass Co., Westford Conn," smooth sides, medium olive amber, pt. 121.00

GXIII-39 - Sheaf of Grain above crossed rake & pitchfork - large five-pointed star, smooth edges, teal blue, pt. 412.50

GXIII-49 - Anchor w/fork-ended pennants inscribed "Baltimore" & "Glass Works" - Sheaf of Grain w/rake & pitchfork crossed behind sheaf, smooth edges, peach amber, ½ pt. 425.00

GXIII-60 - Anchor w/fork-ended pennants inscribed "Spring Garden" & "Glass Works," w/a rectangular panel below - three-quarter view of log cabin w/a rectangular panel below, smooth edges, plain collar, aqua, ½ pt. 187.00

GXIII-66 - Anchor across side, cable forming S-curve behind - plain reverse, wide flat band edges, round collar w/lower bevel, amber, ½ pt. 66.00

GXV-1 - "Clyde Glass Works" in semicircle, plain reverse, smooth edges, medium amber, qt. 110.00

GXV-15 - "Newburgh Glass Co." upper half of circle & "Patd Feb 27th 1866" in lower half of circle - plain reverse, smooth edges, applied mouth, black amber, pt. 330.00

Chestnut, 20 swirled ribs, amber, probably Pittsburgh, late, 16" h. . . 115.00

Chestnut, expanded diamond "popcorn" design, clear, 5¼" h. 95.00

Chestnut, light green, collared lip, ½ pt. 82.50

Nailsea-type, clear w/white loopings, pontil, 7¼" l. 125.00

Nailsea-type, white & red loopings, 7" l. 165.00

Pitkin, 36 broken ribs swirled to the right, half-post neck, pontil, olive yellow, pt., 6¼" h. 577.50

INKS

Umbrella-type Ink Bottle

Boat-shaped, cobalt blue mold-blown glass, applied lip, two pen ledges, 1 5/8 x 2 1/8", 2 1/8" h. 39.00

Cathedral, six Gothic arch panels, sapphire blue glass, embossed "Carter" around bottom edge, smooth base, qt., 9¾" h. 75.00

Cone-shaped, aqua glass, "W.E. Bonney, So Hanover, Mass.," 2 3/8" d., 2 3/8" h. 75.00

Cone-shaped, clear glass, w/original paper label "G.H. Gilbert Co. of West Brookfield, Massachusetts". . 154.00

Cylindrical, master size, amber glass, "Sanford's Inks - One Quart - and Library Paste" on paper label, smooth base, ca. 1915-20, 9 3/8" h. 66.00

Cylindrical, amber glass w/puce tinges, mold-blown w/applied lip, 1 15/16" d., 2 11/16" h. 100.00

Cylindrical, aqua glass, embossed "E. Waters, Troy, N.Y.," 2 1/8" d., 3 11/16" h. 357.50

Cylindrical, master size, olive amber glass, mold-blown, smooth base, applied mouth w/pouring lip, ca. 1855-65, 9 5/8" h. 49.50

Domed w/central neck, aqua glass, embossed "J. Raynald," smooth base, ground lip w/screw threads, ca. 1880-1900, 2¼" h. 187.00

Domed w/central neck, dark olive green mold-blown glass, embossed "Bertinguiot," 2½" d., 2" h. 225.00

Log cabin-shaped, clear glass, smooth base, tooled lip, ca. 1870-80, 1 11/16 x 2½", 2½" h. . . 660.00

Octagonal, aqua glass, embossed "Harrison's Columbian Ink," open pontil, rolled lip, 1 5/8" h. 143.00

Octagonal, aqua glass, embossed "Harrison's Columbian Ink," open pontil, 2½" h. 85.00

Square, aqua glass, mold-blown w/applied lip, embossed "J. Field" on the side & "J H" on the base, 1½" sq., 2 3/16" h. 10.00

Square, medium apple green glass, mold-blown w/tooled & flared lip, pontil scarred base, ca. 1820-40, 1 7/8" h. 495.00

Teakettle-type fountain inkwell w/neck extending up at angle from base, cobalt blue glass, 2 7/16" h. 550.00

Umbrella-type (8-panel cone shape), clear glass, open pontil, rolled lip, 2½" h. 357.50

Umbrella-type (8-panel cone shape), clear glass w/greyish tint, open

pontil, rolled lip, 2 3/8" h. (ILLUS.
previous page) 412.50
Umbrella-type (8-panel cone shape),
deep olive green glass, open pon-
til, rolled lip, 2¼" h. 132.00
Umbrella-type (8-panel cone shape),
light cornflower blue glass, open
pontil, rolled lip, 2½" h. 1,155.00
Umbrella-type (8-panel cone shape),
light emerald green glass, open
pontil, rolled lip, 2½" h. 143.00
Umbrella-type (8-panel cone shape),
medium green glass, open pontil,
rolled lip, 2¼" h. 440.00
Umbrella-type (8-panel cone shape),
reddish amber glass, pontil
scarred base, sheared lip creates
a pouring spout, 2½" h. 198.00
Umbrella-type (8-panel cone shape),
yellowish olive green glass, open
pontil, rolled lip, 2½" h. 220.00
Umbrella-type (16-panel shape),
master size, cobalt blue glass,
10" h. 60.00

MEDICINES

W. Henderson & Co. Bottle

Acker's English Remedy - For All
Throat & Lung - W.H. Hooker &
Co., Proprietors, New York,
U.S.A., cobalt blue, 5 3/8" h. 30.00
Allen's Lung Balsam - J.N. Harris &
Co. - Cincinatti (sic), rectangular,
aqua, 8" h. 12.00
American - Medicinal - Oil - Burkes-
ville KY, rectangular, applied
mouth, open pontil, aqua, ca.
1830-50, 6 1/8" h. 495.00
Atherton's (Dr.) Wild Cherry Syrup,
E.W. Hall, Whitehall, N.Y., rolled
lip, aqua, 5 1/8" h. 32.00
Baker's (Dr.) - Pain Panacea, rectan-
gular, pontil, aqua, 5" h. 50.00
Bell's (Dr.) Pine-Tar-Honey, The E.E.
Sutherland Medicine Co., aqua,
6½" h. 10.00

Blackman's (Dr.) - Genuine - Healing - Balsam, eight-sided, rolled
lip, open pontil, clear, 1½" w.,
5 5/8" h. 27.50
Brinkerhoff's Health Restorative,
New York, rectangular, pontil, ol-
ive green, 7" h. 412.50
Brown (J.T.) - 292 Washington St.,
Boston - Select - Preparation, rectangular w/indented panels, applied mouth, open pontil, aqua,
ca. 1830-50, 6¼" h. 55.00
Caldwell's Syrup Pepsin, Mf'd. by
Pepsin Syrup Company, Monticello, Illinois, rectangular, aqua,
3" h. 17.50
Chamberlain's Colic, Cholera and Di-
arrhoea Remedy, Des Moines, Ia.,
rectangular, aqua, 4½" h. 20.00
Clark (N.L.) & Co. - Peruvian Syrup,
rectangular, applied mouth, aqua,
8¾" h. 15.00
Couley's Fountain of Health -
No. (embossed fountain) 5, Balti-
more St, Baltimore, applied
mouth, open pontil, aqua, ca.
1840-50, 9½" h. 143.00
Craig's Kidney & Liver Cure, oval-
shaped, golden amber, 9½" h. 150.00
Crook's (Dr.) Wine of Tar, A. &
D.HC. on the base, deep aqua,
8¾" h. 45.00
DeWee's (Dr.) Worm Syrup - P.T.
Wright Co. - Philadelphia, open
pontil, aqua, 4" h. 40.00
Drake's (Dr.) German Croup Remedy
- Findlay, Ohio - The Glessner
Med. Co., rectangular, tooled lip,
light aqua, 6¼" h. 28.00
Fort's Western Liniment Good for
Man, Good for Beast, E.M. Fort
Lowell, Mich., applied lip, aqua,
6¼" h. 125.00
Fowler (Prof. F.C.), Moodus, Conn. -
Strength - Health, rectangular
w/beveled corners, smooth base,
tooled lip, cobalt blue, 3 3/8" h. . . 71.50
The Great South American Nervine
Tonic Trade (monogram) Mark and
Stomach & Liver Cure, oval, clear,
9½" h. 90.00
Guinn's Pioneer Blood Renewer -
Macon Medicine Co. - Macon,
GA., amber, 10 7/8" h. . . 100.00 to 125.00
Guysott's (Dr.) Compound Extract of
Yellow Dock & Sarsaparilla, rec-
tangular w/beveled edges, pontil,
aqua, 9" h. 209.00
Hart's Swedish Asthma Cure, rectan-
gular, amber, 5" h. 20.00
Haskin's Nervine - Haskin Medicine
Co. - Binghamton, N.Y., rectangu-
lar, citron, 8½" h. (light haze) . . . 50.00
Hawes' Healing Extract, A.F. Whitte-

more, Essex, Conn., round, pontil,
aqua, 3¼" h. 30.00

Henderson (W.) & Co. - Extract of
Sarsaparilla - Pittsburgh," rectangular w/sunken panels, deep
aqua, ca. 1850, 9" h. (ILLUS.) 990.00

Hunter's Pulmonary Balsam or
Cough Syrup, J. Curtis Prop., Ban-
gor, Me., rectangular, aqua,
6" h. 100.00

Hunt's Liniment - prepared by G.E.
Stanton - Sing Sing, N.Y., rectan-
gular, aqua, 4¾" h. 50.00

Hurd's Cough Balsam, rectangular
w/beveled corners, partial label,
open pontil, aqua, 4½" h. 160.00

Jayne's (Dr. D.) Carminative Balsam,
round, aqua, 5¼" h. . . . ., 25.00

Johnson's (W.M.) Pure Herb Tonic
Sure Cure For All Malarial Diseases, mold-blown, applied lip,
square w/beveled corners, am-
ber, 8¾" h. 190.00

Kendall's (Dr. B.J.) Spavin Cure (embossed around the shoulder),
Enosburg Falls, VT (embossed on
base), 12-sided, aqua, 5½" h. 28.00

Kendall's (Dr. B.J.) Spavin Cure (embossed around the shoulder),
Enosburg Falls, VT (embossed on
base), 12-sided, w/full paper la-
bel, amber, 5½" h. 44.00

Kennedy's (Dr.) Rheumatic Liniment,
Roxbury, Mass., rectangular w/in-
dented panels, aqua, 6 5/8" h. . . . 100.00

Kerr (Dr. M.G.) & Bertloet - Compound Asiatic Balsam - Norris-
town, Pa., rectangular, aqua,
4 5/8" h. 50.00

Kilmer's (Dr.) Autumn-Leaf Extract
for Uterine Injection, rectangular,
aqua, 4¼" h. 49.00

Kilmer's (Dr.) Ocean Weed Heart
Remedy, The Blood Specific, rectangular, embossed heart, aqua,
8½" h. 110.00

H. Lake's Indian Specific

Lake's (H.) Indian Specific, rectangu-

lar w/deeply beveled corners &
raised frame around embossing,
ring on neck, aqua, 8¼" h.
(ILLUS.) 275.00

Langenbach's Dysentery Cure,
cylindrical, blob top, amber,
5 5/8" h. 32.00

Lyon's Powder - B&P N.Y. (lettering
on shoulder), cylindrical, wine
red, 4" h. . . . . .100.00 to 125.00

Magic Cure Liniment, E.I. Barnett,
Easton, PA, aqua, w/contents &
full paper label, 6¼" h. 50.00

Magnetic Aether, Halstead & Co.,
w/paper label reading "Magnetic
Aether or Fluid of Restoration, H.
Halstead & Co., Physicians &
Chemists, Rochester, NY," nine-
sided, open pontil, flared lip,
aqua, 4¼" h. 110.00

Marine Hospital Service, embossed
Marine symbol, "2798," "U.S."
star, "1871 - 251 CC," cylindrical,
smooth base w/applied flared
mouth, amber, 9" h. 77.00

McLane's (Dr.) American Worm
Specific, round, open pontil, aqua,
3 7/8" h. 30.00

Merchant (G.W.), Lockport, N.Y.,
rectangular w/beveled corners,
dark green, 5" h. . . . . .75.00 to 100.00

Mexican Mustang Liniment, round,
pontil, aqua, 4" h. 25.00

Mixer's Cancer & Scrofula Syrup,
Hastings, Michigan, clear 30.00

Moore's (Dr. J.P.) Essence of Life,
round, pontil, aqua, 3¾" h. 25.00

Morse's Celebrated Syrup, Prov. R.I.,
large, oval-shaped, huge iron
pontil, deep aqua, 9½" h. 125.00

Morse's Celebrated Syrup, Prov. R.I.,
large, oval-shaped, huge iron
pontil, applied mouth, medium
green, 9½" h. 385.00

National Kidney & Liver Cure,
square w/beveled corners, am-
ber, 9" h. 55.00

One Minute Cough Cure - E.C.
Dewitt & Co. - Chicago, U.S.A.,
rectangular, aqua, w/label, con-
tents & box, 5½" h. 36.00

Osgood's - India Cholagogue - New
York, rectangular, pontil, aqua,
5 3/8" h. 50.00

Paine's - Celery Compound, square,
amber, 9¾" h. (ILLUS. top next
page) 15.00

Pettit's American Cough Cure,
Howard Bros. (all on front panel),
aqua, 6¾" h. 32.00

Pettit's (Dr. J.) Canker Balsam, oval,
open pontil, clear, 3¼" h. 35.00

Polar Star Diarrhea Cure, rectangu-
lar, aqua, 5" h. 23.00

Paine's Celery Compound

Preston's (William R.) Veg Purifying
Catholicon, Portsmouth, New
Hampshire, open pontil, aqua,
9¾" h..................200.00 to 250.00

Race's Indian Blood Renovator,
aqua, 9" h.......................   40.00

Radam's Microbe Killer, The Water
of Life, pictures man beating
skeleton, all the embossing on
base, amber, large..............   82.50

Radway's Ready Relief (R.R.R.), One
Dollar, New York, rectangular
w/beveled corners, applied sloping collared mouth, pontil, aqua,
ca. 1840-60, 8" h............... 176.00

Roberts's (M.B.) Vegetable Embroca-
tion, cylindrical, pontil, light lime
green, 5" h............100.00 to 125.00

Roger's (Dr. A.) Liverwort, Tar
and Canchalagua - A.L. Scovill -
Cincinnati, rectangular, aqua,
8" h....................75.00 to 100.00

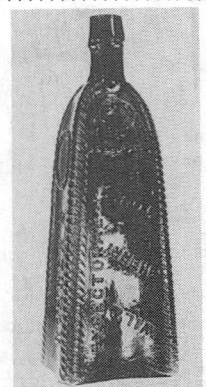

Rohrer's Wild Cherry Tonic Expectoral

Rohrer's Wild Cherry Tonic Expectoral, Lancaster, Pa., tapered square
w/roped corners, collared mouth,
iron pontil, amber, 10½" h.
(ILLUS.) ....150.00 to 200.00

Rose's (Dr.) - Philada - For All Lung
& Throat Diseases - Cough Syrup,

open pontil, applied mouth, aqua,
5½" h.........................   71.50

Sanford's Extract of Hamamelis or
Witch Hazel, rectangular w/bev-
eled corners, sapphire blue,
1 5/8 x 2 3/8", 7¼" h........... 210.00

Scovell Blood & Liver Syrup, Cincinnati, aqua, 9½" h..............   35.00

Seminole Indian Medicine Co.,
Boone, Iowa, rectangular, light
amethyst, 8½" h...............   40.00

Shaker Syrup No. 1, Canterbury,
N.H., rectangular, aqua, 7¼" h. .. 435.00

Southworth's (Dr.) Blood & Kidney
Remedy, rectangular, aqua,
8¾" h..........................   38.00

Sperry's Rheumatic & Nerve Liniment, open pontil, aqua 140.00

Stearn (Frederick) & Co., Detroit,
Mich., w/paper label reading
"Stearns Wine of Cod Liver Oil
with Peptonate of Iron, Detroit,
Mich.," triangular, smooth base,
tooled lip, amber, 10 1/8" h. 82.50

Swaim's - Panacea - Philada., cylindrical paneled, aqua, 8" h.......   45.00

Swaim's - Panacea - Philada., cylindrical paneled, applied mouth,
pontil scar, deep olive amber,
8" h.......................... 253.00

Taylor's Cough Syrup, Leraysville,
PA, rectangular w/indented pan-
el, tooled lip, aqua, 7¾" h......   25.00

Thompson's Vermifuge, Philada,
open pontil, aqua, 4" h. 40.00

Townsend's (V.P.D) Liniment - JNO.
T. Steel, Prop'r, New York, oval,
tooled lip, aqua, 6¾" h. 10.00

Tus Sano Cures Coughs and Colds -
C.I. Hood & Co. - Lowell, Mass,
aqua, 6¾" h...................   37.00

Warner's Safe Cure Co. - Rochester,
N.Y. - Free Sample, round, amber, 4¼" h. 42.00

Warner's Safe Cure (Concentrated),
w/safe, oval, amber, 5½" h......   42.00

Warner's Safe Cure, London,
w/safe, oval, smooth base, applied mouth, olive green, pt.,
9 3/8" h. 330.00

Warner's Safe Cure, London, Eng.,
Toronto Canada, Rochester N.Y.,
w/safe, oval, dark amber,
9½" h. 55.00

Warner's Safe Cure, Melbourne,
Aus. - London, Eng. - Toronto,
Can. - Rochester, NY. USA,
w/safe, oval, applied double collar mouth, smooth base, root beer
amber, ca. 1880-90, 9¾" h. 49.50

Warner's Safe Kidney & Liver Cure,
Rochester, N.Y., w/embossed picture of a safe, oval, amber,
9¾" h.........................   20.00

Weaver's (Dr. S.A.) Canker & Salt
Rheum Syrup, oval, whittled, iron
pontil, aqua, 9" h. . . . . .50.00 to 75.00
Wetherell's Cream of Benzoin and
Roses, w/paper label reading
"Wetherell's Cream of Benzoin
And Roses, A.S. Wetherell,
Apothecary, Exeter, N.H.," rectangular w/beveled edges, smooth
base, tooled lip, milk white,
5" h. 88.00
Wilson (B.O. & G.C.), Botanic Drug-
gist, Boston, open pontil, applied
mouth, aqua, 9½" h. 264.00
Winslow's (Mrs.) Soothing Syrup,
Curtis & Perkins Proprietors, cylindrical, aqua, 5 1/8" h. 25.00
Wyeth (John) & Bro., Philadelphia,
w/dose cap, "Pat. May 16, 1899"
on base, & "Take Next Dose At"
on neck, cobalt blue, 6½" h. 20.00

MILK

Thatcher's Dairy Bottle

Amber, embossed "Bramlage Dairy -
Established 1900" bust of Lincoln -
Trade Mark - Pomeroy, O. - To Be
Washed and Returned," smooth
base, tooled lip, ca. 1900-10, qt.
(two 1/8" chips off inner edge of
lip) 632.50
Amber, embossed "Fort Wayne -
Dairy Co's - Buttermilk," smooth
base, tooled lip, ca. 1900-10,
½ pt. 852.50
Amber, embossed "Peoria Sanitary
Milk Co. - Wash and Return,"
smooth base, tooled lip, ca.
1900-10, ½ pt. 176.00
Aqua, embossed "Warren Creamery
- 323 Warren St. - This Bottle To
Be Washed and Returned," tin
lid & wire bail, tooled lip, ca.
1900-10, qt. 88.00
Clear, "Borden's" & illustration of El-
sie, red pyroglaze paint, ½ pt. . . . 10.00
Clear, embossed "Wm. Brewer Farm
Prop. Dairy" & "J.B. Brooks, 86

Fulton St., New York Maker" on
base, qt. 125.00
Clear, enameled "Brookfield,"
w/embossed baby face, ½ pt. 75.00
Clear, embossed "Cop the Cream,"
face of cop & "Glenside Dairy,
Deep Water, N.J. - It Whips!,"
& patent number embossed
on smooth base, ABM lip, ca.
1930-40, pt. 198.00
Clear, embossed "Ideal Dairy -
N. Ray Bourbonnais, Ill. - This
Side Up - Cream Separator Bottle
Inc.," smooth base, ABM lip, ca.
1925-35, qt. 77.00
Clear, embossed "Litchfield Co. -
L.W. Melahn - Milk & Cream -
5%-12% - Whiteman's Patent Feb.
18, 1890 - Standard Cream Line -
Not To Be Bought or Sold" &
"York" embossed on smooth base,
tooled lip, original tin lid stamped
"Patd. Jan. 5th 1875, Reissued
June 5th. Patd. April 3," wire bail,
ca. 1890-1900, qt. 962.50
Clear, embossed "Lyon Brook Dairy
- Aerated Milk - E.L. Haynes,
Prop. - 1554 B'Way. B'klyn" & embossed lion head above the word
"Brook" & embossed "Registered"
on smooth base, tooled lip, original tin lid & wire bail, ca.
1890-1900, qt. 385.00
Clear, "Metzgers," w/embossed
baby face, qt. 75.00
Clear, embossed baby face & "Mur-
phys Dairy - Neenah - Sealed,"
smooth base, ABM lip, ca.
1920-40, ½ pt. 165.00
Clear, embossed "Standard Cream
Line - Whiteman's Patent Feb 18,
1890 - This Bottle to be Washed
and Returned" & on base "Whiteman - Maker - 144 Chambers St. -
New York," tooled lip, original
glass lid w/wire bail, ca. 1890-
1900, qt. 132.00
Clear, embossed "Thatcher's Dairy,"
& embossed man milking cow,
1884 patent (ILLUS.) 250.00
Clear, "Use Sealtest Dairy Products -
Buy War Bonds, Everybody Every
Payday 10% - No Better Home
Guard, Buy War Bonds & Stamps"
etc. in red & blue pyroglaze paint
& "Toledo, Ohio" embossed on
base, ABM lip, ca. 1941-45, qt. . . . 247.50
Clear w/amethystine tint, embossed
"R.F.S. - R.F. Stevens Co. - 90-92-
94 - Third Ave, Brooklyn - R.F.S. -
To Be Washed and Returned" &
embossed "S" on smooth base,
ABM lip, tin lid & wire bail, ca.
1910-20, qt. 77.00

Deep violet purple, embossed "Hotel Sherman - College Inn," smooth base, tooled lip, ca. 1900-10, ½ pt. 176.00

Pale green, embossed "Chicago Sterilized Milk Company" & on smooth base "S.B.& G.CO.," tooled blob lip, original 'lightning' closure & wire bail, ca. 1890-1900, pt. 165.00

Pale green, smooth base embossed "A.G.S. - Patent - App'd For - & Co." (A.G. Smalley), metal lid, wire bail & handle, ca. 1890-90, pt. 242.00

MINERAL WATERS

Adirondack Spring, Whitehall, N.Y., Saratoga-type, emerald green, pt. 190.00

Blount Springs Natural Sulphur Water - Trade (logo) Mark, blue 125.00

Boardman (J.), N.Y. Mineral Water, eight-sided, iron pontil, cobalt blue 250.00

Bochert Spring Mineral Waters, amber, qt. 40.00

Boyd - Balt, ten-pin shape, smooth base, applied mouth, medium yellowish green, ca. 1855-65, 8 7/8" h. 605.00

Champlain Spring Mineral Water, Highgate, VT., green 350.00

Clarke (John), New York, cylindrical w/sloping collared mouth w/ring, smooth base, yellowish olive, qt. 121.00

Congress & Empire Spring Co., Hotchkiss & Sons, CW Saratoga, yellowish olive, pt. 145.00

Congress & Empire Spring Co., Hotchkiss & Sons, CW Saratoga, green, pt. 65.00

Dearborn (J & A) - New York - Mineral Water, eight-sided, iron pontil, applied mouth, deep sapphire blue, 7" h. 209.00

Great Bear Spring - Trade Mark - Fulton, N.Y., "This Bottle Is Loaned And Never Sold" on bottom, glass stopper, blob top, aqua, 7" h. 50.00

Henniker HN - Magnetic Spring (embossed in half circle), Saratoga-type, golden amber, qt. 286.00

High Congress Spring - C. & W., light olive green, qt. 195.00

High Congress Spring - C. & W., olive green, pt. 140.00

High Congress Spring - C. & W., yellowish olive, pt. 132.00

Highrock Congress Spring, cylindrical w/sloping collared mouth w/ring, teal blue, pt. (some exterior roughness including two small pick marks & some inside stain) 209.00

Improved Mineral Water, short tapered top, graphite pontil, cobalt blue, 7½" h. (light stain inside) .. 150.00

Improved Mineral Water, short tapered top, graphite pontil, sapphire blue, 7½" h. (small flake in lip) 95.00

Knowlton (D.A.), Saratoga, N.Y., whittled, olive green, pt. 60.00

Koldrok, embossed w/pine trees & mountains, w/original ceramic lightning stopper, clear 60.00

Lancaster - X - Glassworks - XX, cylindrical, applied mouth, iron pontil, medium cobalt blue, 7" h. 176.00

Lynch & Clarke, New York, Saratoga-type, pontil, crude, olive amber, pt. ....300.00 to 350.00

Missisquoi "A" Springs, embossed squaw & papoose on reverse, cylindrical w/sloping collared mouth w/ring, smooth base, emerald green, qt. 88.00

Missisquoi "A" Springs, embossed squaw & papoose on reverse, honey amber, qt. 80.00

Newcomb & Brown - Boston, ten-pin shape, smooth base, applied mouth, aqua, ca. 1870-80, 9" h. .. 385.00

Oak Orchard, Acid Springs, C.W. Merchant, Lockport, N.Y., Saratoga-type, emerald green, qt. 70.00

Peerless Mineral Water, Martin & Cherry, New York 1873, Saratoga-type, aqua...................... 20.00

Poland (Moses) Water, cylinder, aqua, w/label 125.00

Premium - Mineral Water - S, eight-sided, iron pontil, applied mouth, green w/hint of yellow, ca. 1850-60, 7½" h. 154.00

Ryan (John), Excelsior Mineral Water 1859, Savannah, Ga., cobalt blue 150.00

Smith (Tarr.) & Clark - Boston - Mineral Water, cylindrical tapering to a heavy collared mouth, iron pontil mark, bright green, ca. 1845-60, ½ pt. 159.50

Star Spring Co., amber, pt......... 95.00

POISONS

Amber, coffin-shaped, embossed "Poison" surrounded by small raised diamonds, smooth base, tooled lip, 3½" h. 440.00

Amber, octagonal, embossed "Jacob Hull - Not to be taken - Strychnine" 39.00

Amber, rectangular, embossed "POISON" on each side, "P.D. & CO." on smooth base & "Corrosive Sublimate" on paper label, tooled lip, ca. 1890-1910, 2 7/8" h. 55.00

Amber, rectangular w/embossed criss-cross design on the edges, embossed "POISON" on side panels & paper label w/"Mercury Bichloride, Parke Davis & Co." on front panel, smooth base, tooled lip, ca. 1890-1910, 5¾" h. 110.00

Amber, triangular, huge embossed "POISON" reading vertically on one side, "J.T.M. & CO." on smooth base, tooled lip, ca. 1890-1910, 3" h. 77.00

Amber, triangular, huge embossed "POISON" reading vertically on one side, "J.T.M. & CO." on smooth base, & "Mercury Bichloride" on paper label, tooled lip, ca. 1890-1910, 5 1/8" h. 687.50

Cobalt blue, cylindrical, raised lattice & diamond design, smooth base, tooled lip, ca. 1890-1900, 4 3/8" h. 66.00

Cobalt blue, cylindrical, diamond quilted design, flared mouth, smooth base, 10" h. 385.00

Cobalt blue, flask-shaped, embossed "POISON," diamond quilted design, ½ pt. 139.00

Cobalt blue, paneled, embossed "POISON" vertically on two front side panels flanking a panel w/two embossed stars & skull & crossbones, smooth base embossed "S&D 173" & paper label w/"Mercury Bichloride Tablets" on the back, ABM lip, ca. 1910-15, 2¾" h. 522.50

Cobalt blue, rectangular w/embossed ribbed edges, embossed "POISON" on each side & "JNO. WYETH & BROS, Philadelphia" on the front panel, smooth base, tooled lip, ca. 1890-1910, 2 5/8" h. 99.00

Cobalt blue, rounded rectangular form, fine horizontal ribbing on side panels, embossed "Melvin & Badger Apothecaries, Boston, Mass." on center panel & "G.L.G. & Co., Patent Appl'd For" on smooth base, tooled lip, ca. 1880-1910, 6¼" h. 104.50

Cobalt blue, triangular, embossed "Poison" on one side, an owl sitting on mortar on one side & "The Owl Drug Co." on the third side, smooth base, tooled lip, ca. 1890-1910, 5¼" h. 220.00

Pale green, flask-shaped, mold-

blown overall hob design, pontil scarred base, sheared lip, ca. 1845-60, 5 5/8" h. 154.00

Turquoise blue, triangular, embossed "POISON," embossed lattice & diamond design, smooth base, tooled lip, ca. 1890-1910, 5¼" h. 412.50

Yellowish amber, hexagonal, embossed "POISON" on center panel, diamond quilted design on other panels & "Pat Appl'd For, N.B. & Co." on smooth base, tooled lip, ca. 1890-1910, 2½" h. 88.00

SNUFF

Amber glass, ground lip, glass lid & zinc band, w/original paper label "Maccoby Cherry Snuff," 7½" h. ... 45.00

Amber glass, rectangular w/beveled corners, tooled & flared lip, smooth base, embossed "J.M. Venable & Co. - Petersburg, Va.," ca. 1850-70, 4¼" h. (two shallow flakes & minor iridescent bruise on edge) 176.00

Amber glass, square w/beveled corner panels, tooled & flared lip, open pontil, ca. 1820-40, 4¼" h. ... 82.50

Medium olive amber glass, rectangular w/beveled corners, pontil, tooled & flared lip, embossed "E. Roome - Troy - New York," ca. 1830-40, 4 3/8" h. 132.00

Olive amber glass, rectangular w/beveled corners, sheared & flared lip, smooth base, ca. 1850-60, 9½" h. 143.00

Yellowish amber glass, rectangular w/beveled corners, tooled & flared lip, pontil, embossed "E. Roome - Troy - New York," ca. 1830-40, 4¼" h. 231.00

Yellowish amber glass, rectangular w/beveled corners, tooled & flared lip, open pontil, embossed "J.J. Mapes - No 61 Front St. - N-York," ca. 1830-40, 4 3/8" h. 412.50

SODAS & SARSAPARILLAS

Brennan & Graham, J.H., Stuebenville O, cylindrical, applied mouth, iron pontil, aqua, ca. 1850-60, 7¼" h. 93.50

Buffum's Sarsaparilla & Lemon Mineral Water, Pittsburgh, ten-sided, applied mouth, iron pontil, cobalt blue, ca. 1840-50, 7¾" h. ... 467.50

Bull (A.H.) Extract of Sarsaparilla, Hartford, Conn., rectangular, aqua, 7" h. 115.00

Byrne (W.P.) American Soda, cylindrical tapering to a blob top, aqua, 9" h. 250.00

Carpenter & Cobb Knickerbocker
Soda Water, Saratoga Springs,
ten-sided, applied lip, iron pontil,
deep aqua..................... 200.00

Carpenter & Cobb Knickerbocker
Soda Water, Saratoga Springs,
ten-sided, applied lip, iron pontil,
peacock blue 335.00

Clark (John) - F.P. - Balto - C, applied mouth, iron pontil, cobalt
blue, ca. 1840-50, 7 1/8" h. 687.50

Clark (John) - F.P. - Balto - C, applied mouth, iron pontil, deep
emerald green, ca. 1840-50,
7¼" h......................... 110.00

Coca-Cola, embossed "Mar-
shalltown, IA," soda, square,
clear 20.00

Coca-Cola, embossed "Coca-Cola
Bottling Works, Rochester, N.Y.,"
soda, cylindrical, 8" h........... 45.00

Coca-Cola, embossed "Rockwood,
TN," soda, square, clear 20.00

Coughlan, Balto., ten-pin shape
w/Baltimore round bottom, applied mouth, smooth base, bright
medium yellowish green, ca.
1850-65, 8¾" h................. 687.50

Coughlan (W.), Balto., applied
mouth, iron pontil, olive green,
ca. 1840-50, 7" h. 275.00

Coughlan (Wm.), Balt., ten-pin
shape w/Baltimore round bottom,
applied mouth, smooth base,
deep olive green, ca. 1850-65,
8½" h......................... 907.50

Cox (D.T.), Fort Jervis, N.Y., Hones-
dale Glassworks, cylindrical, applied mouth, iron pontil, cobalt
blue, ca. 1845-55, 7¼" h. (some
outside stain & scratching) 825.00

Dinets (J.), Superior Soda Water,
Chicago, six-sided, iron pontil, applied mouth, cobalt blue, ca.
1850-60, 8 1/8" h. 852.50

Dodge (W.), 114 N. Front St., This
Bottle Never Sold, applied mouth,
smooth base, yellowish amber, ca.
1870-80, 8½" h. (light haze) 467.50

Eagle (Wm), New York, Premium
Soda Water, eight-sided, applied
mouth, iron pontil, cobalt blue,
ca. 1840-50, 7¼" h............. 104.50

Guyette & Company, Registered,
Detroit, Mich., This Bottle Is
Never Sold & "G" embossed on
smooth base, soda, Hutchinson
stopper, rolled lip, medium cobalt
blue, ca. 1890-1910, 7" h. 198.00

Hagen (W.E.) & Co., Troy, N.Y.,
soda, eight-sided, cobalt blue 105.00

Harvey (J.) & Co., Canal St., Providence R.I., pontil, forest green ... 95.00

Hennessy & Nolan, Albany, N.Y.,

Empire State & embossed capitol
building (trade-mark), soda,
tooled lip, smooth base, clear, ca.
1880-1900, 7 1/8" h. 66.00

Italian Soda Water Manufactory, San
Francisco, iron pontil scar, medium green........................ 180.00

Kelley (J.L.) & Co., Chemist, Portland, ME., sarsaparilla, open pontil, aqua, 7¾" h. (light haze) 225.00

Kinsella (S.B.) & Hennessy, soda,
squat shape, green (dug) 45.00

Leon's Sarsaparilla, Belfast, Maine,
aqua, 7¾" h..................... 67.50

Log Cabin Sarsaparilla, Rochester,
N.Y. on paper label & "Pat Sept
6th 1886" embossed on smooth
base, rectangular, applied mouth,
dark amber, 8 7/8" h. 231.00

Marshall's (Dr.) Extract of Sarsaparilla & Dandelion, aqua,
8½" h.......................... 40.00

Maui Soda Works & "W" on smooth
base, soda, Hutchinson stopper,
tooled lip, aqua, ca. 1890-1900,
7¾" h.......................... 44.00

Pioneer Soda Works, a shield w/the
word "Trade" on one side &
"Mark" on the other, blob top,
aqua, 7½" h. 85.00

Plummer (J.P.) - Boston, cylindrical
tapering to a blob top, cobalt
blue, ½ pt. (exterior case
wear) 302.50

Premium - Soda Water - WM Eagle,
eight-sided, iron pontil, applied
mouth, 7¼" h................... 132.00

Smith (S.) - Auburn, N.Y. - 1856 -
KR. S - Water, twelve-sided, iron
pontil, applied mouth, cobalt blue,
ca. 1856-60, 7¼" h. 231.00

Smith (S.) - Auburn, N.Y. - 1857,
ten-sided, iron pontil, cobalt
blue 345.00

Southwick & Tuppes, New York, ten-
pin shape, red graphite pontil,
deep green 195.00

Standard Bottling Works - Minneapolis, Minn. & "H.R." embossed on
smooth base, soda, Hutchinson
stopper, tooled lip, deep root
beer amber, ca. 1890-1910,
6¼" h. 385.00

Townsend's (Dr.) - Sarsaparilla - Albany, N.Y., square w/beveled
corners, iron pontil, applied
mouth, dark bluish green,
9½" h.......................... 98.00

Twedle's Celebrated - Soda or
Mineral Waters - Courtland Street
- 38 - New York, applied mouth,
iron pontil, medium emerald
green, ca. 1840-55, 7" h......... 104.50

Wight (J.P.), Ginger Pop, cylindrical,

stoneware w/cobalt slip band
around neck & across wording,
American-made, ca. 1840-60,
6 7/8" h. 330.00

WHISKEY & OTHER SPIRITS

Thufeldt & Co. Case Gin

Beer, "O.O. Chituzte, J.N. Ham-
mond - Bottle Not Sold," stoneware, cylindrical, upper one-
third w/mottled brown glaze,
American-made, ca. 1840-60,
9 7/8" h. 198.00
Beer, "O.B. Cook & Co, Detroit,
Mich," stoneware, cylindrical, tan
w/speckled brown glaze overall,
American-made, ca. 1840-60,
6½" h. 143.00
Beer, "Paul Fick," stoneware, cy-
lindrical, upper half w/dark
brown glaze, American-made, ca.
1840-60, 10" h. 176.00
Beer, "S.C. Heald, Bottle Not Sold,
1852," stoneware, cylindrical,
some light mottled olive brown
glaze overall, American-made, ca.
1840-60, 9½" h. 187.00
Beer, "Hoppe & Strub B. Co. Toledo,
Ohio," w/original wire bail, am-
ber, qt. 20.00
Beer, "Morton & Richardson, 1853,"
stoneware, cylindrical, deep
brown slip around entire neck
& mouth, American-made, ca.
1840-60, 9¼" h. 231.00
Beer, "Pabst Branch E.O. Jones Co.,
Youngstown, O.," amber. 40.00
Beer, "Pentucket Ale, Bottle Not
Sold," stoneware, cylindrical,
dark cobalt blue slip around
blob mouth, American-made, ca.
1840-60, 9½" h. 357.00
Beer, "Potosi Brewing Co. Potosi,
Wis.," w/porcelain top & bail,
blob top, amber, ½ gal. 26.00
Beer, "Schlitz," royal ruby, 7 oz.,
w/original labels 50.00

Beer, "J. Simonds, 1854," stoneware, cylindrical, cobalt blue slip
around mouth & across lettering,
American-made, ca. 1840-60,
10" h. 187.00
Beer, "Tacoma Bottling Co., San
Francisco, Cal.," blob top, amber,
qt. 25.00
Beer, "Van Coutren Bros. Kewanee,
Ill.," w/original wire bail, amber,
qt. 20.00
Beer, "Claus Wreden Brewing Com-
pany, San Francisco," amber,
qt. 30.00
Bourbon, "Bininger (A.M.) & Co.,
Old Kentucky, Distilled in 1848,
1849 Reserve Bourbon, 19 Broad
St. N.Y.," barrel-shaped, smooth
base, applied mouth, medium am-
ber, 7 7/8" h. 187.00
Bourbon, "Good Old Bourbon - In a
Hog," pig-shaped, tooled lip,
medium amber, 6¾" l. 302.50
Case gin, "Hoytema & Co.," flared
lip, olive green 26.00
Case gin, "Messinger (R.E.) & Co. -
Cordial Gin," pontil-scarred base,
applied mouth, 85% paper label,
olive green, 7¾" h. 275.00
Case gin, "Henry H. Thufeldt & Co. -
Rye Malt (crown) - Gin," smooth
base, yellowish amber, ca. 1880,
9¾" h. (ILLUS.) 33.00
Case gin, dip-molded, wide flared
rim, large open pontil, medium
yellowish olive, ca. 1770-1800,
10 1/8" h. 1,210.00
Case gin, dip-molded, open pontil,
medium olive yellow, 11" h. 110.00
Case gin, dip-molded, open pontil,
flared lip, medium amber olive,
12 1/8" h. 150.00

Bininger Old London Dock Gin
Gin, "A.M. Bininger & Co. - No. 338
Broadway - Old London Dock -
Gin," rectangular w/cut corners,
smooth base, few tiny nicks, dark
yellowish green, 9¾" h. (ILLUS.) . . 55.00

Gin, "Bouvier's Buchu Gin," clear,
4½" h. 26.00
Gin, "Charles - London - Cordial
Gin," square w/beveled corners, smooth base, dark green,
9½" h. 11.00
Gin, "J.J. Peters - Hamburg," sunk-
en panel under bottom, light am-
ber, 8½" h. 65.00
Schnapps, "Ajentes Dominguez YC
Nueva York - Schnapps Aromati-
co," square w/beveled edges,
smooth base, applied mouth, olive
amber, 7¼" h. 121.00
Schnapps, "Dunbar Schiedam Cordial
Schnapps," olive green 125.00

Udolpho Wolfe's Schnapps

Schnapps, "Udolpho Wolfe's - Aromatic - Schnapps - Schiedam,"
rectangular w/cut corners, iron
pontil, olive green, 8¼" h.
(ILLUS.) 49.50
Schnapps, "Udolpho Wolfe's - Aro-
matic - Schnapps - Schiedam,"
Stoddard-type, open pontil, crude,
olive amber, qt. 85.00
Sloe gin, "Rudy Sloe Gin," short la-
dy's leg neck, amber 20.00
Spirits, "F.J.O." on applied bottle
seal, applied mouth, pontil scar,
Ricketts Glass Works, Bristol,
England, yellowish green, ca.
1820-40, 10½" h. 110.00
Spirits, onion-form, pontil scarred
base, applied string lip, England,
ca. 1720-30, deep olive amber,
4" d., 6 1/8" h. (slight roughness
to edge of lip) 253.00
Spirits, shaft- & globe-form, tall
neck w/applied ring, pontil mark,
probably England, ca. 1650, deep
green, light wear, slight iridescence at base, 5 5/8" d., 7½" h.
(ILLUS. top next column) 825.00
Whiskey, "A.M. Bininger & Co.,
19 Broad St., N.Y.," cannon-
shaped, sheared mouth, smooth

Early Spirits Bottle

base, golden amber, ca. 1860-80,
12½" h. (interior haze & some
mouth roughness) 412.50
Whiskey, "A.M. Bininger & Co,
19 Broad St. N.Y.," cannon-
shaped, smooth base, sheared lip,
medium amber, 12½" h. 330.00
Whiskey, "Bininger's Night Cap,
No. 19 Broad St. N.Y.," flask-
shaped, smooth base, applied
mouth, yellow w/amber over-
tones, 7¾" h. 357.50
Whiskey, "Bininger's Peep-O-Day,
No. 19 Broad St. N.Y.," flask-
shaped, smooth base, applied
mouth, amber, 7¾" h. 550.00
Whiskey, "Chestnut Grove, C. Whar-
ton," cylinder, embossed vertical
rib pattern, smooth base, applied
mouth, amber, 9¼" h. 412.50

Chestnut Grove Whiskey Bottle

Whiskey, "Chestnut Grove Whiskey
C.W.," globular-form, pontil,
applied mouth & handle, amber,
9" h. (ILLUS.) 242.00
Whiskey, "Dyottville Glass Works
Philada." on base, cylinder, ap-
plied mouth, aqua, 11 3/8" h. 71.50
Whiskey, "Dyottville Glass Works,
Phila." on base, "Patent" on

shoulder, & "Class of 1846" on applied seal, applied mouth, medium olive amber, 11¼" h. 715.00

Whiskey, "J.T. Gayen, Altona,"
cannon-shaped, large round collared mouth, smooth base, ca.
1860-80, deep reddish amber,
13¾" h. 880.00

Whiskey, "I.W. Harper," bottle encased in wicker, graduated collar,
light amber, qt., 9¾" h. 65.00

Whiskey, "Pure Old Rye - Hart &
Amberg," encased in wicker
w/handle, lovely lady on multicolored label-under-glass, cylindrical, amber, 12¼" h. 247.50

Whiskey, "E.P. Middleton & Bro.
Wheat Whiskey, 1825, Philada.,"
deep olive amber, ca. 1860-70,
9½" h. 145.00

Whiskey, "Potter & Bodine," base
embossed w/"Patent," cylindrical
w/lady's leg shaped neck, applied
mouth, yellowish olive amber,
11½" h. 198.00

Whiskey, "H. Ricketts & Co. Glass
Works Bristol" on pontil scarred
base, "Revd. J. E. Melhuish" on
black glass seal, cylinder, applied
mouth, olive amber, England, ca.
1830-40, 10 7/8" h. 302.50

Whiskey, "Something Good In A
Hogs - He Won't Squeal," pig-
shaped, smooth base, tooled lip,
clear, 4 3/8" l. 99.00

Whiskey, "Turner Brothers, New
York," barrel-shaped, smooth
base, applied mouth, medium reddish puce, 9 7/8" h. 231.00

Whiskey, "Rothschild Bros., 1868,
Phil" on applied seal, squatty
shape, orange amber (tiny nick on
neck) 68.00

Whiskey, "Whartons Whiskey 1850
Chestnut Grove," w/applied handle, tooled lip & pour spout, amber, 10" h. (handle cracked)...... 125.00

Wine, "Riesling German Wine Cellars," paper label of vineyard &
shipping docks, amber.......... 20.00

(End of Bottles Section)

BOXES

Band box, wallpaper-covered, deep
oval form covered w/floral pattern paper printed in pink, brown
& white on a yellow ground, printed paper label under lid for Hannah Davis, Jaffrey, New Hampshire, 1825-55, 13" l., 7½" h. (imperfections)....................$440.00

Band box, wallpaper-covered cardboard, covered w/a leaf design
paper in red, green & brown
on off-white, lined w/an 1839
Hagerstown, Maryland newspa-
per, 7¾" l. 275.00

Band box, printed paper-covered,
oval form w/removable cover
depicting soldiers on horseback
w/swords raised, the sides depicting a log cabin w/an American
flag, two gentlemen in the foreground w/a steamship behind,
Baltimore, Maryland, labeled, ca.
1840, 20" l., 14½" h. (some
wear) 4,675.00

Bible box, carved oak, rectangular
top lifting above well, the outside
base chip-carved w/arched band
of palmette-style leaves, wrought-
iron lock & hasp, old dark finish, England, early, 18¼ x 28",
10" h. 700.00

Bride's box, painted & decorated
bentwood pine, oval, the top
painted w/a scene of a couple
holding hands above the German
inscription "Thou Goest with me &
I with thee...." sides decorated
w/intricate polychrome floral designs on a black ground, 18¾" l.
(minor wear, lid lacing incomplete
& lid has minor edge damage) ...2,310.00

Candle box, carved & painted wood,
the shaped black-painted lid centering a red-painted carved posy
sliding into a black-painted box
further decorated w/a red-painted
carved posy on the front, molded
base, 7¼ x 9¼", 5" h. 7,150.00

Candle box, hanging-type, gumwood, Chippendale, the arched
pediment centering a pierced
heart flanked by pierced ovals
above a rectangular sliding lid
centering an applied molded reserve, Connecticut, late 18th c.,
18½" h. 1,045.00

Candle box, walnut, square peg
construction, rectangular w/slid-
ing lid, old dark finish, 10¾" l.... 150.00

Copper w/silver mountings, rectangular, four silver bead feet,
"Athenic" patt., the sides &
hinged domed cover applied
w/scrolling silver strapwork
panels over the hammered patinated surface, the lock escutcheon engraved w/initials, wood
interior, Gorham Mfg. Co., Providence, Rhode Island, ca. 1901,
8¼" l........................2,640.00

Cut glass, domed hinged lid above the rectangular tapered body, cut in a design of reeded panels alternating w/plain panels, surrounded by ormolu borders chiseled w/floral & foliate devices, raised on splayed ormolu feet cast w/masks, Charles X period, France, second quarter 19th c., 6¾" w., 4¼" h.........3,575.00

Document box, gilded & painted wood, rectangular, the top decorated w/a woman & man on horseback in front of a neo-Grec home set in a pastoral landscape surrounded by gilded banding, the case painted black w/gilt banding, inscribed "May E. Turner," ca. 1830, 7 3/8 x 11", 3 5/8" h. 220.00

Document box, inlaid bird's-eye maple, rectangular, the hinged lid w/a central compass inlay, opening to a removable compartmentalized shelf, 8 x 12" 440.00

Games box, tortoiseshell, the rectangular canted lid opening to a scarlet silk interior, the underside of the rectangular case inset w/printed directions for the game 'simple multiplication,' Victorian, England, second quarter 19th c., 10" l....................2,640.00

Glass box, round w/metal-hinged cover & rim mounts, amber decorated w/orange & lavender fuchsias & green leaves on the cover, flowers & leaves around the sides, late 19th c., 4" d., 3 5/8" h. 158.00

Glass box, egg-shaped w/metal-hinged cover & rim mounts, frosted light green decorated w/white enameled flowers w/yellow & orange centers, green leaves & gold trim, late 19th c., 2½" d., 4" h. ... 125.00

Early Pine Hat Box

Hat box, pine, tricorn-type, the triangular top compartment

w/hinged front cover above a rectangular case w/two thumb-molded short drawers over a long drawer, on a molded base, late 18th c., 24" w., 31" h. (ILLUS.) ...3,050.00

Jewelry box, carved rosewood, model of a house, w/removable gabled roof w/chimneys & windows, opening to compartments, the facade decorated w/windows, a door & projecting staircase, England, late 19th c., 8½ x 12", 12" h. 4,125.00

Jewelry box, silver plate, heavy embossed florals on the base, pincushion fitted into bead & scalloped cover, Derby Silver Co., late 19th c. 85.00

Knife box, flame grain mahogany, slanted lid w/inlaid star opening to a divided interior, silver fittings, England, 13½" h. (some veneer damage).................. 660.00

Painted & Stenciled Box

Painted & stenciled box, rectangular w/hinged lid opening to a compartmented interior w/slide, the top & sides stenciled w/fruit-filled compotes & flowers in silver, white & red on a black ground, probably New England, mid-19th c., 6½ x 9¾", 5" h. (ILLUS.) 2,200.00

Patch box, enameled, green & white ground inscribed "I present this to you as a trifling mark of my esteem," England, late 18th - early 19th c., 1 7/8" l., 7/8" h. 275.00

Pill box, micro-mosaic & brass, the hinged lid's circumferences decorated w/a filigree scrolling, centered by a bouquet of multi-colored daisies on a blue ground worked in micro-mosaic, the sides adorned in filigree w/stylized flowers, circles & applied enamel white stars on a black ground, 19th c., 2¼" d. 44.00

Pipe box, painted pine, the scroll-cut sides & backplate pierced for hanging, w/folded front corners & single drawer below, painted dark green, New England, 1770-90, 5½" x 5¾", 16¼" h. 2,475.00

Sterling silver box, plain rectangular form, monogrammed, w/wood liner, Tiffany & Co., New York, 1907-38, 9½" l. 880.00

Storage box, grain-painted poplar, rectangular w/a domed top, New England, early 19th c., 14¼ x 28", 11½" h. .1,100.00

Storage box, oval bentwood, laced lappet seams, pine w/green repaint, 15¼" l. 225.50

Tobacco box, brass, oval domed hinged top opening over a conforming molded base, the top & bottom engraved w/courting couples & mottoes in Dutch reading *"Mijn Lief Mijn Kaant"* & *"Mijn Arou Ontwangh,"* Holland, 18th c., 5" l. 1,430.00

BREWERIANA

Collectible Beer Glasses

Beer is still popular in this country but the number of breweries has greatly diminished. More than 1,900 breweries were in operation in the 1870's but we find fewer than 40 supplying the demands of the country a century later. The small local brewery has either been absorbed by a larger company or forced to close, unable to meet the competition. Advertising items used to promote the various breweries, especially those issued prior to Prohibition, now attract an ever growing number of collectors. The breweriana items listed are a sampling of the many items available. Also see BOTTLES.

Ashtray, milk white glass, "Tuborg Beer" $15.00

Beer glass, "Drink Allweiden Beer," printed (ILLUS. left) 65.00

Beer glass, "Berghoff," etched 20.00

Beer glass, "Wm. Bierbaw Brewing Co., Mankato, Minnesota," etched 195.00

Beer glass, "Burgie! please," a Hamm's brand, printed (ILLUS. second from left) 151.00

Beer glass, "Enterprise, San Francisco," etched 75.00

Beer glass, "Everett Brewing, Everett, Washington," etched 65.00

Fresno and Hack & Simon Glasses

Beer glass, "Fresno Brewing Co., Fresno, Calif.," w/picture of the brewery, printed (ILLUS. left) 85.00

Beer glass, "Hack & Simon - Elite Export - Vincennes, Ind.," w/ornate logo, printed (ILLUS. right) . . 72.00

Beer glass, "Hamm's Beer," printed (ILLUS. second from right, first photo) 43.00

Beer glass, "Hamm's, Excelsior, St. Paul, MN," etched w/eagle & banner, tapered 25.00

Beer glass, "A & J Hochstein, Hudson, Wisconsin," etched 150.00

Beer glass, "Indianapolis Brewing Co. - Indianapolis...," w/ornate logo, printed 71.00

Beer glass, "India Wharf Brewing Co. - Brooklyn, New York - U.S.A.," w/scene of brewery, printed 83.00

Beer glass, "Jax Beer Preferred Quality," straight-sided, 3½" h. . . . 20.00

Beer glass, "Kiewel's Beer," w/logo, printed (ILLUS. far right, first photo) 46.00

Beer glass, "Los Angeles Brewing, Mission Santa Barbara," etched . . . 65.00

Beer glass, "Premium Atlantic Beer" 79.00

Beer glass, "Regal Beer," red & white graphics, straight-sided, 5" h. 10.00

Beer glass, "The Virginia Brewing Co. - Southern Progress - Roanoke, VA," w/logo, printed . . . 66.00

Calendar, 1909, "Schlitz," long narrow format w/lithograph of beautiful Indian maiden 286.00

Calendar, 1910, "Schlitz," long narrow format depicting scene of Indians above bust portrait of

Pilgrim woman over scene of Pilgrims leading cow 220.00
Can, cone-top, "Bohemian Club" 27.50
Can, cone-top, "Golden Age" 27.50
Can, cone-top, "Milwaukee Club" ... 33.00
Can, cone-top, "Schmidt's Cream Ale" 27.50
Clock, wall-type, neon, "Bottle of Pearl Lager Beer, Please," yellow center 395.00
Corkscrew, steel, "Anheuser-Busch," model of a bottle, ca. 1897, 2" h. 40.00
Display bottle, "Frank Fehr Brewing Co.," complete neck & body labels, 20" h. (cap w/minor wear) 145.00

Collectible Beer Mugs

Mug, pottery, Budweiser Beer 1984 Los Angeles Olympic Games commemorative (ILLUS. left) 205.00
Mug, pottery, "Natural Light" w/Anheuser-Busch logo (ILLUS. right) 126.00
Mug, pottery, Budweiser post-convention souvenir, decorated w/Anheuser-Busch logo & portrait of founder 110.00
Mug, pottery, Budweiser "San Francisco" commemorative, embossed trolley design 158.00
Photograph, Anheuser-Busch Clydesdale team depicted in front of a hotel, hand-tinted, pine frame, embossed photographer's stamp, w/brass plate, all original, early, 23 x 29" 375.00
Plate, china, "Krug Brewery," pictures Fred Krug on front, brewery on back & dates "1859-1909," 1909 .... 120.00
Salt & pepper shakers, glass, "Fort Pitt Beer," miniature bottle-shaped, in original box, pr. 12.00
Sign, "Leisey's Light Beer," wall-type, electric, round, blue & white design w/logo in center, neon band around rim, 15" d. (ILLUS.) .. 220.00

Leisey's Beer Sign

Sign, "Old Topper Ale," reverse-painted on glass w/a light, for placing atop a cash register, ca. 1920-40, 12" w., 6¾" h. (minor paint loss at edges) 44.00

Budweiser Commemorative Steins

Stein, pottery w/metal lid, Budweiser 1980 commemorative, embossed wagon scene (ILLUS. left) 175.00
Stein, pottery w/domed metal lid, Budweiser commemorative CSL2, embossed wreath design w/Anheuser-Busch logo, band w/horses & wagon around the base (ILLUS. right) 275.00
Tap head, "Schmidt City Club Beer," ornate three-color enamel design 85.00
Tap spigot, "Schlitz," large cylindrical disc at top 16.50

BROWNIE COLLECTIBLES

The Brownies were creatures of fantasy created by Palmer Cox, artist-author, in 1887. Early in this century numerous articles with depictions of or in the shape of Brownies appeared.

Brownies "Nine-pins" Game

Candlestick, ceramic, figural "Bobby," marked "2889-44," 7½" h. . . . $300.00

Candlestick, ceramic, figural sailor,
"Defender," marked "2972-9,"
9" h. 325.00

Candlestick, ceramic, figural sailor,
"Volunteer," marked "2872-9,"
9" h. 300.00

Candlestick, ceramic, figural "Uncle
Sam," marked "2887-21," 9" h. . . 325.00

Candy dish, silver plate, ball footed
w/fancy handles & turned over
sides, decorated w/fifteen
Brownies, fancy etched decoration
reads "Forget Me Not," "Sweetest
Kisses for Little Misses," etc.,
marked "Tufts," 5½ x 7" 195.00

Cigar holder-ashtray, silver plate,
w/full figure Brownie, marked
"Pairpoint 1063" 330.00

Doll, "Indian," stuffed cloth, Arnold
Print Works, 1892 . . . . 110.00

Game, "Nine-pins," includes nine
wooden stand-up cut-out figures
of Brownies in various costumes,
together w/original illustrated
box, McLoughlin Bros., the set
(ILLUS.) 1,900.00

Humidor, cov., ceramic, figural
police officer, marked "3265,"
6" h. 350.00

Humidor, cov., ceramic, figural
sailor, "Defender," 6" h. 450.00

Knife, fork & spoon, silver plate,
depiction of a little Brownie at top
of each, ca. 1900's, the set 140.00

Magazine, "Busy Brownies," Jan-
uary 5, 1897, No. 1 . . . . 85.00

Paper doll, "Esquimau," Lion coffee
advertising insert 18.00

Pitcher, china, scene of Brownies
playing golf against a tan ground,
6" h. 300.00

Plate, china, five Brownies wrapped
in tattered American flag,
7½" d. 49.00

Rubber stamps, depicting Brownies
at various pursuits, set of 10 . . . . . 35.00

Salt shaker, pressed opaque blue
glass, square w/four panels separated by beaded corners, each
panel w/embossed Brownie, Mt.
Washington Glass Co. 135.00

Tea tiles, china, depict dancing
Brownies, 6¼" d., set of 6 (two
worn) 95.00

Toothpick holder, silver plate,
depicts Brownies w/umbrella 450.00

Tray, china, self-handled, w/two
fencing Brownies, 4½ x 6¼" 75.00

BUTTER MOLDS & STAMPS

Eagle & Cow Butter Stamps

*While they are sometimes found made of
other materials, it is primarily the two-piece
wooden butter mold and one-piece butter
stamp that attract collectors. The molds are
found in two basic styles, rounded cup form
and rectangular box form. Butter stamps are
usually round with a protruding knob handle
on the back. Many were factory made items
with the print design made by forcing a metal die into the wood under great pressure,
while others had the design chiseled out by
hand.*

Acorn w/two leaves stamp, deeply
carved maple, round w/knob han-
dle, ca. 1820, 3¼" d. $220.00

Acorns & leaves mold, carved wood,
2 lb. size, 5½ x 11" 110.00

Berries & leaves stamp, carved
wood, round, three large round
berries w/cross-hatched design
above cluster of long, pointed &
serrated leaves, serrated rim,
one-piece turned handle, old pati-
na, 4½" d. (age cracks) 65.00

Bird & flowers stamp, carved wood,
rectangular, well detailed backwards looking bird & flowers
within a chip-carved border, old
patina & dark stains, inserted
turned handle, 1¾ x 2½",
4¾" l. 225.00

Cherries cased mold, carved wood,
oblong w/almond-shaped indented mold carved w/a stylized cluster of cherries on a leafy twig, a
serrated border, two-part, dark
finish, 10½" l. (age cracks) 85.00

Clover stamp, carved wood, round,
a sprig w/three round leaves on

slender stem, narrow border bands, one-piece turned handle, old refinishing, 2 7/8" d. 95.00

Cornflower mold, hand-carved maple, round, New York state origin, ca. 1830, 4¾ x 9" 90.00

Cow cased mold, carved wood, rectangular, the incised center carved w/a large standing cow, a small tree at one end & a small fence at the other, varnished, 3½ x 7½" 150.00

Cow stamp, carved wood, carved rope border, turned threaded handle, scrubbed finish, 3 7/8" d. 125.00

Cow stamp, carved wood, round, a blocky-looking animal w/a punch-patterned coat stands between deeply incised bands, serrated rim, one-piece turned handle, old patina, age cracks, 4 1/8" d. (ILLUS. right) 155.00

Eagle stamp, carved wood, spread-winged eagle & foliage above a banner carved w/"J. Richardson," old patina, turned handle, 3¾" d. (age cracks in design) 325.00

Eagle stamp, carved wood, round, spread-winged eagle w/foliage & starflowers, old patina, turned handle, 4¼" d. 175.00

Eagle & star stamp, carved wood, round, spread-winged bird facing right w/star above left shoulder, serrated rim, one-piece turned handle, old patina, 3¾" d. (ILLUS. left) 225.00

Floral stamp, carved wood, boat-shaped, stylized long-stemmed flower w/veined leaves, old patina, 8¾" l. 159.50

Floral "lollipop" stamp, carved wood, stylized flowers within chip-carved edge, further carved w/initials, natural patina, 6 5/8" l. 375.00

Fox stamp, carved running animal, scrubbed finish, one-piece turned handle, 3½" d. 632.50

Geometric stamp, wheel-type, carved wood, a thick wheel disc w/incised dashes & leaf bands along the edge, mounted in a one-piece bracket w/turned handle, old refinishing, 5½" l. (minor age cracks) 65.00

Heart, anchor & cross insignia mold, carved wood, dished form w/fluted sides, old brown patina, 4 5/8" d., 2" h. (minor age cracks) 75.00

Leaf stamp, round, carved wood, a sprig of three large serrated leaves in the center framed by

thin chip-carved borders, w/a turned handle, 3¾" d. (wear, age crack) 60.50

Sheaf of wheat stamp, crudely carved sheaf flanked by clusters of 'dashes,' one-piece turned handle, old dark finish, 3 7/8" d. 82.50

Sheaf of wheat stamp, carved wood, rectangular, scrubbed finish, chunky handgrip on back, 3½ x 4½" 99.00

Starflower stamp, six-point star w/short petals between each of the longer ones, inserted turned handle, scrubbed finish, 3¾" d. . . . 121.00

Starflower stamp, concave circle reverse, carved wood, old patina, 3¾" d. 75.00

Starflower "lollipop" stamp, carved thin hardwood w/a delicate 12-point star inside a gently swagged border band, flat & flaring stick handle, grey scrubbed finish, 6½" l. 302.50

Starflower "lollipop" stamp, pine, deeply carved six-petal flower w/a carved "almond" device between each petal, incised narrow border band, flattened flaring angled side handle, worn dark finish, 8¾" l. 550.00

Starflower & star stamp, carved wood, central starflower within center of intricately carved six-pointed star, oval-shaped devices at edge between points, chip-carved edge, back further decorated w/a well-carved relief design w/a scratched-out area, carved handle, old patina, 6¼" d. (minor age cracks) 300.00

Strawberry sprig stamp, a large carved berry on a leafy stem w/a small blossom, one-piece whittled handle, scrubbed finish, 4¼" d. (some wear) 165.00

Swan mold, carved wood, cased, old finish, 5" d. (age crack in case) . . . 104.50

Swan stamp, carved wood, round, swan center within carved border, 4 1/8" d. 350.00

Tulip stamp, primitively carved blossom w/long slender petals flanked by tiny starflowers on thin stems, turned handle, scrubbed soft finish, 4½" d. 357.50

Vase of flowers stamp, carved wood, round, simple vase containing bouquet of flowers center, one-piece turned handle, old scrubbed finish, 2¾" d. 45.00

CALENDAR PLATES

1912 Calendar Plate

Calendar plates have been produced in this country since the turn of the century, primarily of porcelain and earthenwares but also of glass and tin. They were made earlier in England. The majority were issued after 1909, largely intended as advertising items.

1907, Santa Claus center, River
Falls, Wisconsin advertising,
9¼" d. $65.00
1908, four cat faces & "Merry Christ-
mas, B.L. Schermerhorn, Lowville,
New York," 9¼" d. 39.00
1908, portrait of a lady center,
Detroit, Michigan advertising 50.00
1910, cherubs decoration, Daven-
port, Iowa advertising 75.00
1910, girl & horse heads center 25.00
1910, colorful horseshoe encircling
hunter w/dog, "Compliments of
Rhoads & Bros.," 8¼" d. 39.00
1911, scene of hunter, dog & quail
center, "Compliments of F.A.
Middlekauf, Mt. Morris, Illinois" . . 39.00
1912, biplane center, Cincinnati,
Ohio grocery advertising 85.00
1912, flowers & cherubs center,
8½" d. 25.00
1912, scene of Indian maiden sitting
by fire husking corn, "Home Bank,
De Witt, Arkansas" advertising . . . 39.00
1912, owl on open book w/calendar
on pages, Augusta, Illinois adver-
tising, 7½" d. (ILLUS.) 35.00
1914, sandpiper center, signed "R.K.
Beck," 9½" d. 45.00
1919, flag center, "Lubbers Co.,
East Saugatuck, Michigan" adver-
tising 35.00

CANDLESTICKS & CANDLEHOLDERS

Candelabra, Britannia metal, four-
light, Art Nouveau-style, the standard formed as an elegantly
draped lady, her flowing skirt
forming a circular base, the figure
holding beside her head a vase issuing three sinuous arms w/a
taller central arm, each arm terminating in a leafy bud candle
socket, w/removable bobeches,
produced by the Wurtembergische
Metallwaren-Fabrik, Germany, ca.
1900, w/the "WMF" mark, 19" h.,
pr. $8,250.00
Candelabra, silver, four-light, com-
posed of two intersecting arched
arms ending in bobeches supported on a circular base, the surface
w/a hammered finish, impressed
"800 - POSEN" & w/impressed factory marks, Austria, dated "1920,"
6¾" h., pr. 1,100.00
Candelabra, wrought iron, three-
light, each cylindrical candlecup
w/flaring rim set on an arched
support riveted to a U-form standard enclosing a stylized flowerhead & coiling leafage above a
paneled circular base, impressed
"COBERG," ca. 1925, 13 3/8" h.,
pr. 2,750.00
Candleholder, wrought iron, a
square plate base raised on three
small strap feet & supporting a
slender twisted upright w/hook
end & fitted w/a loop spring can-
dle clip, 8½" h. 440.00
Candleholders, chromium-plated
metal, the J-shaped tubular support w/detachable circular
bobeche at each end, on a circular base, stamped "CHASE" w/the
firm's centaur logo, ca. 1930-36,
9¾" h., pr. 220.00
Candleholders, copper, the C-
shaped arm on a flat circular
base, w/a cylinder supporting a
circular bobeche, designed by A.
Reimann, stamped w/the Chase
firm's centaur logo & "CHASE DE-
SIGN BY REIMANN," ca. 1930's,
8 3/8" h., pr. 660.00
Candlestand, wrought iron, the
hook-ended rod above an octagonal plate supporting a candleholder on a tripod base
w/scrolled feet, 24" h. 770.00
Candlestick, brass, figural, the inverted bell-form candle holders
above highly stylized rearing
horses & a terrier, raised on a
trumpet-form base w/spherical
knop, impressed "HAGENAUER -
WIEN" w/monogram & "MADE IN
- AUSTRIA," numbered "1005 -

Unusual Brass Candlestick

2064," ca. 1930, 15¾" h. (ILLUS.) 2,310.00
Candlestick, bronze & glass, the twisted standard enclosing two amber iridescent glass spheres & supporting a larger sphere enclosing a candle socket w/bobeche, raised on a pierced radiating base resembling an exotic flowerhead, each petal set w/an amber iridescent glass cabochon, impressed "TIFFANY STUDIOS - NEW YORK - 1223," 1899-1918, 14¾" h. 15,400.00
Candlestick, oak & copper, a thick wooden cross-form base on angled block feet, centered by a short copper candle socket, original dark patina, incised mark of Charles Rohlfs, early 20th c., 6" w., 2½" h. 137.50
Candlestick, pressed flint glass, Petal & Loop patt., the sapphire blue petal socket applied w/a wafer to the milky clambroth loop base, attributed to the Boston & Sandwich Glass Co., ca. 1850, 6¾" h. (slight roughage under socket petals) . . . 935.00
Candlestick, pressed flint glass, a large hexagonal tulip-shaped socket above a shaped & ring-molded hexagonal shaft flaring to the round, slightly domed foot, cobalt blue, Pittsburgh area, ca. 1850, 9 5/8" h. 660.00
Candlestick, wrought iron "hog scraper" type w/push-up & lip hanger, 9" h. (brass ring dented) 275.00
Candlesticks, brass, flaring bobeche above a molded candlecup & knopped stem, on an incised lobed foot, stamped "Geo. Grove," Birmingham, England, mid-18th c., 7¼" h., pr. 1,540.00
Candlesticks, brass, Queen Anne

style, a domed flaring round foot w/scalloped rim supports a simple cylindrical shaft w/a swelled disc below the ringed cylindrical candlecup w/a flared scalloped rim, England, ca. 1750, 9 7/8" h., pr. . . 550.00
Candlesticks, brass, flattened circular foot, elongated hourglass-form standard, w/bobeches, cast "Jarvie," Robert Jarvie, ca. 1910, 13½" h., pr. 3,300.00
Candlesticks, bronze, standing nude maiden holding aloft a small urn to hold a candle, mounted on a large lotus leaf raised on four feet, inscribed "GRACE HELEN TALBOT - 1922" & "ROMAN BRONZE WORKS N.Y.," dated 1922, 17¼" h., pr. 5,225.00
Candlesticks, hand-hammered copper, Arts & Crafts style, tall slender tapering shaft w/a ring above the wide domed base on a hexagonal foot, a wide flat drip pan below the candle socket at the top, original patina, Stickley Brothers, Model 135, unmarked, 5½" d., 10" h., pr. 495.00
Candlesticks, pewter, molded cylindrical nozzle above a stepped flaring drip pan, double knopped stem, domed molded base, Continental, 18th c., 10" h., pr. 2,420.00
Candlesticks, porcelain, figural tree trunk shaft in brown w/two gold & black owl figures applied, also applied w/white & pink roses & green leaves, impressed hand & sword mark, Germany, 19th c., 2¼" d., 7½" h., pr. 245.00
Candlesticks, miniature, pressed flint glass, hexagonal foot & socket & baluster-form hexagonal shaft, canary yellow, New England, ca. 1840, 2" h., pr. 357.50
Candlesticks, Sheffield plate & cut glass, telescopic, on domed crested base w/lobed borders supporting barrel-shaped glass knop cut in diamond pattern, extending cylindrical stem, lobed vase-shaped sconce, detachable nozzle, reeded border, Matthew Boulton Plate Co, ca. 1800, extended 12¼" h., pr. 1,540.00
Candlesticks, silver, Grapevine patt., flat disc base, expanding cylindrical stem, cupped bobeche enclosing the socket, Georg Jensen Silversmithy, Copenhagen, Denmark, after 1945, numbered 263A, 5 7/8" h., pr. 5,500.00
Candlesticks, sterling silver, candle socket above a fluted Corinthian

column standard on round foot,
weighted base, Gorham Mfg. Co.,
Providence, Rhode Island, 12" h.,
pr. 1,100.00
Candlesticks, tole, columnar stand
w/removable nozzle on a square
tapering plinth, decorated w/por-
trait medallions on a striped
ground, George III period, Eng-
land, late 18th c., 6¼" h., pr. . . .1,045.00

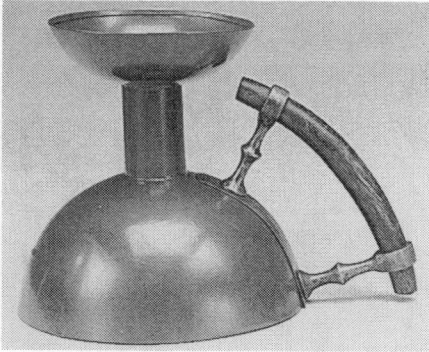

Unique 19th Century Chamberstick

Chamberstick, enameled brass &
wood, composed of two semi-
spheres joined by a cylinder,
enameled in red, the larger semi-
sphere mounted w/a curved
wooden handle held by a brass
fixture, stamped "C. DRESSER'S
DESIGN" & w/registration lozenge
for 1883, impressed w/"PERRY,
SON & CO." folded rope mark,
5½" h. (ILLUS.) 1,320.00
Chamberstick, mahogany & hand-
hammered copper, a triangular
wooden base on three tab feet
supports a conforming paneled
block w/curved side handle, the
top fitted w/a copper triangular
dish w/pinched corner tabs, incised mark of Charles Rohlfs, dat-
ed 1902, 10½" l., 5" h. 385.00
Taper jack, silver, circular pan
w/beaded rim & foliate handle
supporting a slender standard
w/flying scroll pincer-form device
to one side & saucer-form drip
pan at other, w/acorn finial,
George III period, John Wakelin &
William Taylor, London, England,
1778, 5 5/8" h. 1,540.00

CANDY CONTAINERS (Glass)

**Indicates the container might not have
held candy originally. +Indicates this container might also be found as a reproduction.*

‡*Indicates this container was also made as
a bank. All containers are clear glass unless
otherwise indicated. Any candy container
that retains the original paint is very desirable and readers should follow descriptions
carefully realizing that an identical candy container that lacks the original paint will be less
valuable.*

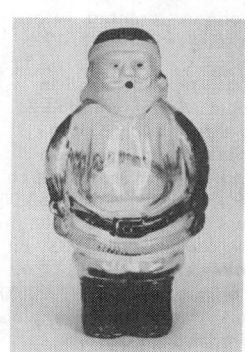

Santa Claus Candy Container

Airplane - "P-38" Lightning, all
glass, 5½" l., 7 1/8" wing
span . . . .$95.00 to 145.00
+Automobile - electric runabout,
w/tin closure at top, ca. 1914,
3½" l. 80.00
*Bell - "1776 Liberty Bell Bank,"
green, amber or blue, 4" base d.,
4 1/8" h., each 85.00
*Boat - "Remember the Maine,"
two-piece dish container, 7¼" l... 75.00
Bus - "Victory Lines Special," paint-
ed, w/closure, 4 7/8" l. 65.00
Charlie Chaplin beside barrel - fig-
ure beside barrel marked "Geo.
Borgfeldt & Co." on base & w/tin
closure on barrel slotted for use
as bank, ca. 1915, 3 7/8" h. figure
w/paint . . . . .130.00 to 170.00
"Chicken on the Nest" - marked on
cardboard closure, J.H. Millstein,
4 5/8" h. 40.00
Dirigible - "Los Angeles" marked on
side, Victory Glass Co., aluminum
screw-on cap closure, painted, ca.
1929, 5¾" l. 150.00
Duck - with large head & bill, paint-
ed, w/tin closure, 1900's,
3¼" h. 135.00
Elephant - marked "G.O.P." on side,
painted grey, marked "V.G. Co.,"
w/tin closure, ca. 1925, 2 7/8" l.,
2¾" h. 175.00
*Elk's tooth, w/screw-on lid, milk
white 125.00
*Elk's tooth, w/clock logo, milk
white, good paint, no closure 350.00
Gun - marked "Kolt" on grip &
"V.G." on barrel, w/round tin clo-

sure on handle grip, ca. 1925,
4¼" l. 50.00

House - one-story bungalow w/dor-
mer in roof, painted, w/tin closure, early 1900's, 2¾ x 2 1/8",
2 3/8" h. 160.00

Iron - electric-type w/string as cord,
4½" l. (no closure) ....25.00 to 35.00

+Jackie Coogan - painted, w/origi-
nal "marked" closure, ca. 1925,
5" h. 1,025.00

Lantern - barn-type enclosed in
glass frame w/wire bail handle
attached through top of glass
frame, clear, metal screw-on closure at base, West Bros. Co., ca.
1913, 4½" h. ....50.00 to 75.00

Locomotive - Stough's "E 3 S" engine
w/narrow cab, marked "E3S" on
boiler below stack & "1028" below
window on cab, 4" l. ......20.00 to 25.00

Locomotive - American-type engine
w/lithographed tin closure, ca.
1924, 4 3/16" l. 85.00

Nursing Bottle - "Lynne Doll Nurs-
er," w/rubber nipple, 2¾" h. 22.50

Pencil - marked "Baby Jumbo,"
w/closure, 5½" l. 50.00

+Piano - upright model, painted in
gilt, w/tin slide on back & also
slotted for use as bank, early
1920's, 2 13/16" h. ......135.00 to 160.00

Powder horn, nickel screw cap
marked "Pat Appl'd for," clear,
Cambridge Glass Co., ca. 1916,
5" l. 49.00

Pumpkin Head Witch - original
paint, w/closure, 4½" h. 425.00

Rabbit Family on Base - painted rabbits, clear base, marked "V.G.
Co., etc.," w/tin closure, 1920's,
4¾" h. ....500.00 to 600.00

*Rubber boot, embossed strap &
buckle on instep, embossed on
both sides "Wale's Goodyear,"
heavy glass, early, 3 7/8" l.,
2 1/8" h. 120.00

Safety First - baby with oversized
safety pin on diapers standing beside barrel, 3¾" h. .....350.00 to 475.00

Santa Claus with Plastic Head -
marked "J.H. Millstein Co." etc.
inside plastic head, parts of
Santa airbrush-painted, 1940's,
5 5/8" h. (ILLUS.)................ 85.00

"Spark Plug" - marked on side of
horse wrapped in blanket, painted, marked "King Feature Syndicate, Inc." on base, w/tin closure,
1923, 3". ....90.00 to 135.00

Telephone - candlestick-type, tall
musical toy, w/wooden receiver,
ca. 1950, 4¼" h. 30.00

Telephone - "Victory Glass Co.," Dial

Type," wire hanger & wooden receiver, ca. 1944, 4 7/8" h. 47.50

Telephone - candlestick-type,
"Tall," w/wooden receiver,
marked "V.G. Co." on base,
7½" h. 160.00

Windmill, "Five Windows," red tin
blades, w/closure, 3 7/8" h. 160.00

CANES & WALKING STICKS

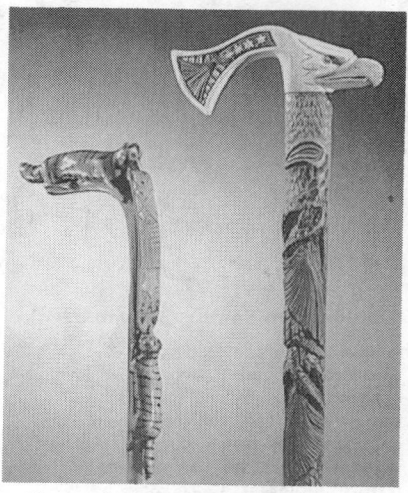

Unusual Carved & Painted Canes

*Canes have been used for thousands of
years and probably collected for hundreds of
years. Seventeenth and eighteenth century
court "dandies" often owned numerous canes,
coordinating their use to various costumes
and occasions. Today's collector looks for
canes made of unique materials in a unique
form. Gadget canes, such as those that con-
vert into a weapon or conceal a whiskey flask
in the handle, are probably the most elusive
type for the collector to acquire.*

Bamboo cane, angled cylindrical ivory handle set in a sterling silver
ferrule w/scrolled trim, 36" l. $185.00

Bamboo walking stick, sterling silver
knob handle set w/a small clock
w/enameled face marked "Bre-
vete," silver marked "Sterling,"
32¾" l. (clock lens cracked)...... 225.00

Black lacquer gold-headed cane, a
chased & engraved 14k yellow
gold handle mounted on a black
lacquered shaft, Victorian........ 275.00

Glass cane, clear cased over a
1" w. opal ribbon w/a red stripe
down one edge & a blue stripe
down the other, shepherd's crook
handle w/fancy knurl, 36" l. 245.00

Glass cane, pale green, ribbed, tapered twist last 18", twist in handle, 1½" d., 52" l. 250.00

Ivory-handled cane, the handle carved as the stylized body of a dog, silver ferrule, ebonized shaft, ca. 1900 . . . . 247.50

Pine cane, carved & painted, the handle carved in the form of a recumbent striped cat tugging at a plaque w/relief-carved American eagle, crossed cannon, flag & stars along w/the initials "GAR" w/two hearts, the tapering shaft carved in relief w/another figure of a striped cat pulling at the other end, late 19th c., 35" l. (ILLUS. left) 1,870.00

Pine cane, carved & painted, the handle carved in low-relief in the form of a bald eagle head w/a hatchet-like extension carved w/leaf & six-pointed stars & painted red, white & blue, the tapering shaft carved w/pine needles, cones, branches & berries, probably New England, early 20th c., 37" l. (ILLUS. right) 2,750.00

Rosewood walking stick, stippled red & black shaft & ornate sterling silver knob handle 125.00

Wooden cane, the handle carved w/a stylized head of a bearded man, a tassled cord carved on the shaft, attributed to the "Bally Carver," southeastern Pennsylvania, 19th c., 35" l. (split at top) . . . 605.00

CANS & CONTAINERS

Between the Acts Cigar Box

The collecting of tin containers has become quite popular within the past several years. Air-tight tins were at first produced by hand to keep foods fresh and, after the invention of the tin-printing machine in the 1870's, containers were manufactured in a wide variety of shapes and sizes with colorful designs.

Antifreeze, Cities Service Koldpruf 1 qt. can, cylindrical, purple background on top portion w/white lettering, white band w/dark lettering across bottom, ca. 1957-65 . . . . $44.00

Antifreeze, Frigidtest 1 qt. can, white, blue & red arctic scene on front w/polar bears, post-war, 5½" h. (top missing) 176.00

Automotive supplies, Whiz Auto Top Dressing 1 pt. tin, flat rectangle, early car pictured on cream background, blue borders w/yellow accents, ca. 1910, 4¾" h. 60.00

Baby powder, ZBT tin 10.00

Baking powder, Baker's Delight tin, depicts blacks, 14¼" h. 149.00

Baking powder, Rumford sample tin 20.00

Baking powder, Snow King sample tin, w/contents 25.00

Biscuit, Huntley & Palmers "Bookstand," books in case, 1905, 4¼" w., 6¼" h. (some wear) 143.00

Biscuit, Huntley & Palmers "Toby Jug," 1911, 6½" h. 400.00

Blasting caps, Hercules round tin . . . 45.00

Candy, Bonomo's Hard Candy tin . . . 25.00

Candy, Greenfield's Persian 1 lb. tin 18.00

Candy, Monarch "Teenie Weenie" Toffies tin w/150 packages, lion logo center w/elf on either side, mint condition 412.50

Candy, Ripley's Toffee tin, depicts "Canadian Mountie on Patrol" 10.00

Candy, Whitman's "Salamagundi" 1 lb. box, bust of Art Nouveau lady 20.00

Cigarettes, Chesterfield flat fifties tin 15.00

Cigarettes, Lucky Strike flat fifties, green, red & gold 17.50

Cigarettes, Marshall's Prepared Cubeb box. 150.00

Cigarettes, M. Melachrino & Co. long tin, "The Assorted Package of Melachrino Egyptian Cigarettes" 22.50

Cigarettes, Old Gold round fifties tin 20.00

Cigarettes, Peacock round fifties tin, depicts colorful peacock, unopened. 45.00

Cigarettes, Royal Jamaica flat tin . . . 30.00

Cigars, Between the Acts box, 3 x 3¼" (ILLUS.) 12.00

Cigars, Bugle round tin 100.00

Cigars, Camel tin, man riding camel, yellow ground, rectangular w/rounded corners, holds 50 cigars, Factory No. 1, Ohio 80.00

Cigars, Chancellor tin, 1 x 3 x 5" . . . 18.00

Cigars, El Roi-Tan horizontal box, 1 x 3 x 4" 18.00

Cigars, Galleon tin chest, colorful
   embossed sailing ships 20.00
Cigars, Goal Cigars tin, pictures
   football 195.00
Cigars, La Palina tin, 1 x 3 x 5" 35.00
Cigars, Little Tom horizontal box,
   1 x 2 x 3" 18.00
Cigars, Muriel canister, Spanish lady's portrait, 5¼" d., 5¼" h...... 22.00
Cigars, Webster horizontal box,
   bust portrait of Daniel Webster,
   1 x 3 x 4" 35.00
Cigars, White Ash round tin 45.00

White Owl Squires Box

Cigars, White Owl Squires rectangu-
   lar box, large (ILLUS.) 18.00
Cinnamon, A&P Great American Tea
   Co. tin, depicts cockatoo mascot,
   ca. 1860's...................... 90.00
Cocoa, Borden's 5 lb. can 90.00
Cocoa, Droste 1 lb. square tin,
   Dutch girl & boy decoration, ca.
   1904 .... 23.50
Cocoa, Hershey's 10 lb. can 75.00
Cocoa, Rawleigh's sample tin....... 125.00
Coconut, Schepp's 1 lb. pail, mon-
   keys playing, black & green 260.00

After Glow Coffee Can

Coffee, After Glow 4 lb. pail
   (ILLUS.)........................ 49.00
Coffee, Alice Foote MacDougall 1 lb.
   can 45.00
Coffee, Atwood's tall 1 lb. tin,
   blue 80.00

Coffee, Beech-Nut sample tin, key-
   wind lid 45.00
Coffee, Berma Coffee 1 lb. tin,
   screw-on lid 45.00
Coffee, Big Hit can, key-wind lid ... 60.00
Coffee, Bird Brand 3 lb. can 185.00
Coffee, Breakfast Delight tin 12.00
Coffee, Brown Betty 1 lb. can 45.00
Coffee, Burma 1 lb. tin, black &
   gold, screw-on lid 25.00
Coffee, Butter-Nut 1 lb. can, key-
   wind lid 19.00
Coffee, Chock Full O'Nuts 4 oz. tin,
   key-wind lid 20.00
Coffee, Comrade 1 lb. can,
   lithographed dog bust, 7½" h. ... 65.00
Coffee, Condor can, key-wind lid ... 30.00
Coffee, Fairview 3 lb. can, depicts
   black men picking coffee 600.00
Coffee, Folger's 1 lb. can, key-wind
   lid 40.00
Coffee, Forbes Culture can, key-
   wind lid 50.00
Coffee, Franklin 3 lb. tin 2,000.00
Coffee, French Market can, key-
   wind lid 60.00
Coffee, Giant 5 lb. tin 65.00
Coffee, Glendora sample size tin ... 24.00
Coffee, Hersh's Best 1 lb. can 80.00
Coffee, Holland 1 lb. can 82.50
Coffee, Holstad's 5 lb. pail 42.00
Coffee, Home Brand 5 lb. pail, bail-
   handled, Briggs & Cooper, St.
   Paul ....50.00 to 75.00
Coffee, Hostess 3 lb. can 125.00
Coffee, IGA 1 lb. can, key-wind
   lid 17.00
Coffee, Kleeko 1 lb. tin 65.00
Coffee, Luzianne sample
   tin ....175.00 to 200.00
Coffee, Luzianne 1 lb. container,
   mammy pictured 46.00
Coffee, Luzianne Coffee & Chicory
   3 lb. tin, dated 1928 .... 100.00
Coffee, Mammy's Favorite 4 lb.
   pail, black mammy on orange
   ground ....200.00 to 225.00
Coffee, Medaglia D'Oro 1 lb. can,
   key-wind lid 24.00
Coffee, MJB 4 lb. pail 65.00
Coffee, Mohican tall 1 lb.
   tin ....125.00 to 150.00
Coffee, Morning Glow 1 lb. can,
   depicts sailing ship 28.00
Coffee, Morning Joy 1 lb. tin 30.00
Coffee, Mother's Joy 1 lb. can,
   screw-on lid 45.00
Coffee, Old Master 1 lb. can, old
   gentleman portrait in oval, screw-
   on lid ....50.00 to 75.00
Coffee, Pickwick 1 lb. tin 38.00
Coffee, Richelieu 5 lb. can 40.00
Coffee, Roundy's 2 lb. can 36.00

Coffee, Sears Special Combination
10 lb. pail 70.00
Coffee, Silver Dollar 3 lb. can 125.00
Coffee, Thomas J. Webb 1 lb. can .. 50.00

Wak-Em Up Coffee Pail

Coffee, Wak-Em Up 5 lb. pail, Indian
profile in round medallion
(ILLUS.) 125.00
Coffee, WGY 1 lb. can, screw-on lid,
blue decoration, 4¼" d., 6" h. ... 75.00
Coffee, White Bear 1 lb. can 75.00
Cooking oil, Planters High Hat 1 pt.
can, full 85.00
Dental cream, Colgate Dental Cream
sample box 15.00
Denture powder, Hope Denture
Powder sample tin, depicts den-
tures & hand, orange, w/brass
cover 60.00
Face powder, Hudnut Face Powder
sample tin 15.00
Flea powder, Hartz Mountain tin,
depicts girl w/terrier 15.00
Food coloring, Peacock 25 lb. can,
very colorful 127.00
Grease, Co-Op 1 lb. can, w/handle,
1933 .... 50.00
Grease, Mica Axle Grease 5 lb.
tin 40.00
Grease, Texaco 1 qt. can, w/con-
tents, 1954 .... 35.00
Gun powder, Dupont Supreme tin,
elliptical-shaped, red paper label,
Wilmington, Delaware, brass
screw cap, patented 1859,
1½ x 4¼ x 6" 85.00
Ice cream, Fairmont Imperial Ice
Cream 1 qt. tin 20.00
Lighter fluid, Pep Boy's can 10.00
Livestock spray, Jim Dandy 1 qt. upright tin, w/handle, depicts cow &
chicken logo, ca. 1920's 35.00
Louse powder, Lee's Louse Powder
can 27.00
Malted milk, Horlick's 10 lb.
container 45.00
Marshmallows, Heidi's None Finer
can 55.00

Marshmallows, Starlight Marshmal-
low 5 lb. tin, Cracker Jack Co. ... 100.00
Marshmallows, UNICY 5 lb. tin 30.00
Motor oil, Enarco 1 qt. can 35.00
Motor oil, Golden Leaf 1 qt. can 60.00
Motor oil, Gulf Lube Motor Oil 1 qt.
can, checkerboard design 45.00
Motor oil, Pennzoil 1 qt. can, depicts
three owls 30.00
Motor oil, Zerolube 1 qt. can,
depicts polar bears 45.00
Needles, Verona tin 35.00
Nuts, Kemp's tin, depicts a marching
band, 1931, 6" l. 27.00
Nuts, Peterson's tin, copyright 1928,
1 7/8 x 4½ x 6¾" 15.00
Oysters, Wentworth 1 gal. pail 75.00
Patent medicine, Cloverine salve
tin 4.00
Patent medicine, Scott's Blood
Tablets tin, pretty lady on lid,
sealed w/original contents 65.00
Peanut butter, Armour's Veribest
12 oz. tin, w/lid 165.00
Peanut butter, Armour's Veribest
1 lb. pail, Mother Goose scenes .. 110.00
Peanut butter, Clark's Wilderness
pail 400.00
Peanut butter, Climax 1 lb. pail 68.00
Peanut butter, Derby Peter Pan
sample tin 85.00
Peanut butter, Fi-Na-St 1 lb. pail,
man in white jacket in center 77.00
Peanut butter, Frontenac 12 oz.
pail 75.00
Peanut butter, G.W.C. 1 lb. tin 1,500.00
Peanut butter, Hoody's 1 lb. pail,
w/picture of kids teetering on a
peanut ....400.00 to 450.00
Peanut butter, Jackie Coogan 12 oz.
pail 250.00
Peanut butter, Monarch "Teenie
Weenie" 1 lb. pail, pictures car-
toon kids, ca. 1920's 195.00
Peanut butter, Pickaninny 1 lb.
pail ....250.00 to 275.00
Peanut butter, Pond 2 lb. can 55.00
Peanut butter, Shedd's 5 lb. pail,
elves 20.00
Peanut butter, Sultana 1 lb. pail,
children, orange 65.00
Peanut butter, Yankee pail........ 220.00
Peanuts, Giant Salted 10 lb. tin,
pictures giant w/club & castle
in background, red, white &
blue ....175.00 to 200.00
Peanuts, Pickaninny Brand 10 lb. tin,
pictures black girl w/doll 450.00
Peanuts, Planters Sal-in-Shell 10 lb.
tin w/lid ....700.00 to 775.00
Peanuts, Planters Pennant Salted
Peanuts 10 lb. canister, blue & red
lettering on black background,
pennant w/Mr. Peanut across cen-

ter, w/original lid, 8½" d.,
10" h. . . . . .125.00 to 150.00
Pest control product, Kill A Pest can,
depicts a rat 25.00
Phonograph needles, Bagshaw's Bril-
liantone tin 20.00

Victor Phonograph Needles Tin

Phonograph needles, RCA Victor tin,
dog & phonograph pictured
(ILLUS.) 35.00
Popcorn, Doye O'Dell 1 gal. tin, pic-
tures cowboy 135.00
Popcorn, Jolly Time pail, depicts
children playing, ca. 1927 . . . . 90.00
Popcorn, Monarch "Teenie Weenie"
1 lb. pail . . . . .225.00 to 250.00
Shortening, Gunn's 5 lb. can, w/bail
handle 32.00
Skin powder, Merit Skin Powder
tin 25.00
Soft drink, Grape-Ola tin, embossed
design of grapes in a basket 250.00
Spice, Jack Sprat Allspice tin 12.50

G.F. Foster's Spice Tins

Spice, G.F. Foster's Parrot Brand
Cinnamon & Ginger tins, colorful
parrot picture, 5" h., 2 pcs.
(ILLUS.) 35.00
Spice, Regoes Sage round tin,
depicts a turkey, colorful 20.00
Spice, Windsor Brand Whole Cloves
tin 15.00
Stove polish, Mason's tin, black
pictured 45.00
Sugar butter, Purity Brand pail, EE
Post, Utica, New York, turquoise
& black lettering, depicts child &
maid 50.00
Syrup, Towle's Log Cabin tin, cabin-
shaped, "Stockade School" 100.00

Talcum powder, As The Petals tin,
depicts dancing girl 150.00
Talcum powder, Colgate Dactylis
sample tin, depicts a pretty girl . . 65.00
Talcum powder, D'Jer Kiss tin 15.00
Talcum powder, Johnson & Johnson
sample tin 55.00
Talcum powder, Mennen's Borated
Talcum sample tin, lithographed
picture, 1¾" d. 35.00
Talcum powder, Santox tin, depicts
nurse 100.00
Talcum powder, Tiny Tot tin, depicts
baby 68.00
Talcum powder, Vantine's tin,
depicts Oriental boy w/kite 40.00
Talcum powder, Winchester tin,
depicts a dog, hunter & gun 145.00
Tea, Montgomery Ward 3 lb. tin 95.00
Tea, Sahib C.B. 1 lb. tin 25.00
Tea, Vesper's ¼ lb. tin, colorful
depiction of a Colonial woman,
ca. 1920's 14.00

Ace Tobacco Store Tin

Tobacco, Ace (Popper's) store tin,
deep bluish green w/glass top,
lettered in gold, cream & black,
overall paint chipping, 6 x 7",
8¾" h. (ILLUS.) 660.00
Tobacco, Ace High flat pocket tin . .3,000.00
Tobacco, Baby's Bottom tin 14.00
Tobacco, Bagdad pocket tin 70.00
Tobacco, Bambino pocket tin,
baseball player swinging bat on
front . . . . .1,825.00 to 2,400.00
Tobacco, B & L's flat pocket tin, red
label 75.00
Tobacco, Belfast tin 40.00
Tobacco, Big John Plug Cut tin,
w/paper label 25.00
Tobacco, Blue Boar tin 35.00
Tobacco, Bowl of Roses pocket tin,
short 155.00
Tobacco, Buckingham pocket tin 100.00
Tobacco, Buffalo Bill tin, depicts
Buffalo Bill on horseback chasing
buffalo 2,950.00
Tobacco, Campbell's Shag pocket
tin 550.00

Tobacco, Capstan Navy Cut tin, ca.
1920's, unopened w/contents 20.00
Tobacco, Carolina Gem square
box 25.00
Tobacco, Carte Blanche pocket tin . .   50.00
Tobacco, Central Union canister
w/small top 215.00

Central Union Cut Plug Box

Tobacco, Central Union Cut Plug
box, 6" l., 3¼" h. (ILLUS.) 40.00
Tobacco, Coach & Four pocket tin . . .   280.00
Tobacco, Craven Mixture round tin,
depicts a cat, unopened 27.50
Tobacco, Derby concave pocket tin,
½ x 2½ x 4½" 20.00
Tobacco, Dill's Best pocket tin,
marked "Complimentary regular
size free".   72.00
Tobacco, Dill's Best Rubbed pocket
tin 45.00
Tobacco, Doctor's Mixture tin 68.00
Tobacco, Edgeworth Junior vertical
pocket tin 52.00
Tobacco, English Bird's Eye square
box 37.50
Tobacco, Epicure pocket tin 145.00
Tobacco, Erinmore Flake tin, full &
unopened, ca. 1920's 15.00
Tobacco, Eve Cube Cut pocket tin . . .   150.00
Tobacco, Fairmont pocket tin, 10c on
scroll 195.00
Tobacco, Fast Mail pocket tin 350.00
Tobacco, Fountain canister, early
fountain w/figures 425.00
Tobacco, Four Roses flip-top pocket
tin 75.00
Tobacco, Freyer's round tin, monk
on lid, w/1926 stamp, unopened . .   35.00

Game Fine Cut Store Tin

Tobacco, Game Fine Cut store tin,
male & female grouse depicted in
blue scene, orange & black lettering, dent on top & left side, paint
loss overall on lid, scratches,
8 x 11½", 6½" h. (ILLUS.) 313.50
Tobacco, Granulated Cut Plug pock-
et tin 1,100.00
Tobacco, Guide pocket tin 225.00
Tobacco, Half & Half pocket tin,
telescopic-type 24.00
Tobacco, Herbert Tareyton smoking
mixture tin, 3" 32.00
Tobacco, Hickey's Perique
tin, green, black & gold,
2 x 3½ x 5" 35.00
Tobacco, Hi-Ho pocket tin 1,475.00
Tobacco, Hindoo pocket tin 810.00
Tobacco, Hollandia tin, colorful
depiction of windmill & sailboat,
New York distributor, w/con-
tents 20.00
Tobacco, Honest Labor Cut Plug
tin 20.00
Tobacco, In-B-Tween tin,
1 x 2½ x 4" 30.00
Tobacco, Kentucky Club 14 oz. tin . .   12.00
Tobacco, Kentucky Club square tin,
depicts horse & jockey, 2" sq. 22.50
Tobacco, Laredo tin, 4 x 6" 40.00
Tobacco, London Sherbet pocket
tin . . . . .150.00 to 175.00
Tobacco, Louisiana Perique round
tin, Christian Pepper Co., small,
unopened 20.00
Tobacco, Lucky Strike 1 lb. can 45.00
Tobacco, Maryland Club horizontal
box, 1 x 2 x 3" 69.00
Tobacco, Maryland Club upright
tin 225.00
Tobacco, Medallion pail 100.00
Tobacco, North Pole, Peary pictured,
w/handle, 6 x 6" 425.00
Tobacco, Old Brier box, large 15.00
Tobacco, Old Colony (Bagley's) con-
cave pocket tin 250.00
Tobacco, Paris Mutuals tin 30.00
Tobacco, Pat Hand pocket tin 115.00
Tobacco, Patterson's Lucky Strike
Cut Plug tin. 32.00
Tobacco, Preferred Stock tin, Ameri-
can Tobacco Co. 85.00
Tobacco, Pride of Virginia flat pock-
et tin, blue 75.00
Tobacco, Prince Albert pocket tin,
w/knife offer 15.00
Tobacco, Revelation pocket tin,
telescopic-type 22.00
Tobacco, Squadron Leader pocket
tin 75.00
Tobacco, Stag pocket tin, short
(ILLUS. top next page) 47.50
Tobacco, State Express tin, w/1926
stamp, unopened. 25.00

Stag Pocket Tin

Tobacco, Sterling store bin, plaid ... 110.00
Tobacco, Sweet Tips (Bagley's) pock-
    et tin 52.00
Tobacco, Taxi upright pocket tin ...3,000.00
Tobacco, Three Feathers pocket
    tin.....................250.00 to 325.00
Tobacco, Tiger Brand horizontal box,
    blue, 1 x 3 x 5" 175.00
Tobacco, Tiger Brand horizontal box,
    red, 1 x 3 x 5" 95.00
Tobacco, Top pocket tin........... 18.00
Tobacco, Uncle Sam pocket tin 2,800.00
Tobacco, Virginia Dare box, square
    cornered 180.00
Tobacco, Whalen 1½ oz. tin, un-
    opened........................ 50.00
Tobacco, Wild Fruit (Bagley's)
    horizontal box, 3 x 4 x 6" 40.00
Tobacco, Windmill tin, depicts
    windmill...................... 45.00
Turtle food, Hartz Mountain Turtle
    Food tin 15.00
Typewriter ribbon, Cavalier tin 7.00
Typewriter ribbon, Codo Super Fiber
    tin 7.00
Typewriter ribbon, International
    tin 45.00
Typewriter ribbon, KeeLox tin,
    depicts Oriental girl 6.00
Typewriter ribbon, Old Town tin,
    depicts secretary & typewriter, un-
    opened, key-wind lid, ca. 1930's .. 15.00
Typewriter ribbon, U.S. Brand tin ... 12.00
Typewriter ribbon, Wonder tin, pic-
    tures Art Deco style girl looking
    into mirror 25.00
Veterinary medicine, Bickmore Gall
    Salve tin, "For Horses & Cattle,"
    depicts horse, ca. early 1900's,
    mint unopened condition......... 25.00
Veterinary medicine, Fleischmann's
    Yeast tin, depicts Terrier......... 10.00

CAROUSEL FIGURES

*The ever-popular amusement park merry-go-round or carousel has ancient antecedents but evolved into its most colorful and com-*plex form in the decades from 1880 to 1930. In America a number of pioneering firms, begun by men such as Gustav Dentzel, Charles Looff and Allan Herschell, produced these wonderful rides with beautifully hand-carved animals, the horse being the most popular. Some of the noted carvers included M.C. Illions, Charles Carmel, Solomon Stein and Harry Goldstein.*

Today many of the grand old carousels are gone and remaining ones are often broken up and the animals sold separately as collectors search for choice examples. A fine reference to this field is Painted Ponies, American Carousel Art, *by William Manns, Peggy Shank and Marianne Stevens (Zon International Publishing Company, Millwood, New York, 1986).*

Herschell-Spillman Frog

Cat, w/bird in mouth, Gustav Dent-
    zel & Co. $33,000.00
Frog, green-painted body, shown
    leaping, wearing a yellow waist-
    coat & orange shorts, Herschell-
    Spillman, North Tonawanda, New
    York, ca. 1914, 42" l. (ILLUS.) ...19,800.00
Horse, jumper, w/flame mane, M.C.
    Illions & Sons (restored) 33,000.00
Horse, outside row jumper, elegant-
    ly carved w/original paint, Gustav
    Dentzel & Co., ca. 1880 (some
    paint restored on trappings) 14,950.00
Horse, outside row stander, animat-
    ed animal w/finely carved bridle
    & saddle furnishings w/tassels,
    well-painted, Gustav Dentzel &
    Co., ca. 1895 (replaced wooden
    tail) 23,000.00
Horse, second row jumper, w/origi-
    nal dappled body paint, black
    mane & hooves, blue trappings
    w/deep rose floral decoration,
    Gustav Dentzel, ca. 1908, 52" l.,
    52" h. (restoration to trappings
    paint) 8,250.00

Horse, stander, w/cherub on side of
    saddle, Gustav Dentzel & Co. ... 42,900.00
Horse, stander, heavily jeweled,
    Charles Carmel, jewels added by
    Borelli 29,700.00

CASH REGISTERS

National Model 311

*James Ritty of Dayton, Ohio, is credited
with inventing the first cash register. In 1882,
he sold the business to a Cincinnati salesman,
Jacob H. Eckert, who subsequently invited
others into the business by selling stock. One
of the purchasers of an early cash register,
John J. Patterson, was so impressed with the
savings his model brought to his company,
he bought 25 shares of stock and became a
director of the company in 1884, eventually
buying a controlling interest in the National
Manufacturing Company. Patterson thor-
oughly organized the company, conducted
sales classes, prepared sales manuals and established salesman's territories. The success
of the National Cash Register Company is
due as much to these well organized origins
as to the efficiency of its machines. Early
"National" cash registers, as well as other
models, are deemed highly collectible today.*

Brass, "National," Model 5, candy
    store model $900.00
Brass, "National," Model 7, detail-
    adder, candy store model 325.00
Brass, "National," Model 12, candy
    store model .... 750.00 to 900.00
Brass, "National," Model 250, candy
    store model .... 650.00 to 750.00
Brass, "National," Model 311, candy
    store model (ILLUS.) ..... 650.00 to 750.00
Brass, "National," Model 312, candy
    store model 475.00
Brass, "National," Model 313, candy
    store model, restored .. 950.00 to 1,000.00
Brass, "National," Model 317, candy
    store model 475.00

Brass, "National," Model 327, candy
    store model ....650.00 to 750.00
Brass, "National," Model 552-5,
    standing oak base.............. 450.00
Brass, "National," Model 1040, pat-
    ent dated "8-30-1913" 300.00

CASTORS & CASTOR SETS

Early German Castor Set

*Castor bottles were made to hold condi-
ments for table use. Some were produced in
sets of several bottles housed in silver plated frames. The word also is sometimes spelled
"Caster."*

Castor set, 2-bottle, silver-mounted
    cut glass bottles engraved w/a
    crest on hinged covers & partly
    pierced & forked handles, the
    open frame applied w/a shell-
    work cartouche enclosing an
    engraved crest, on four scroll sup-
    ports w/rococo shell termi-
    nals, George II period, Samuel
    Wood, London, England, 1750,
    10¼" h. $2,475.00
Castor set, 3-bottle, green glass
    shaded to clear bottles cut
    w/panels, ornate silver plate
    frame, 3½ x 4", 5" h. 165.00
Castor set, 3-bottle, Rubina glass
    bottles cut w/panels, ornate silver
    plate frame, 3½ x 4¼", 5" h. 175.00
Castor set, 4-bottle, cobalt blue
    glass bottles w/silver plate tops
    fitted in an oval galleried silver
    plate frame w/four columns sup-
    porting a pierced cupola, together
    w/a similar salt dip w/blue glass
    liner, Germany, ca. 1795, 14½" h.
    (ILLUS.) 4,675.00
Castor set, 4-bottle, opalescent
    glass bottles w/horizontal ribbing
    & a vertical band in front

enameled w/colored flowers, original ornate silver plate footed & handled frame, marked Simpson, Hall, Miller & Co. 245.00

Castor set, 5-bottle, clear pressed glass Daisy & Button patt. bottles, ornate silver plate frame w/a bell at top (resilvered) 550.00

Rare Gothic-Form Castor Set

Castor set, 6-bottle, clear cut glass bottles fitted in a Gothic turret-form stand w/pointed top w/ball finial above the six-lobed revolving silver plate frame w/arched panels embossed w/trophies of game & opening at the turn of a button to reveal the bottles in flower-chased frames, on four pierced & scroll-molded feet, stamped "PATENTED DEC. 1, 1857," 17" h. (ILLUS.) 3,738.00

Pickle castor, amber glass w/enamel decorated bulbous insert, footed silver plate frame, 8½" h. 300.00

Pickle castor, apricot to pink mother-of-pearl satin glass Herringbone patt. insert, ornate silver plate frame 750.00

Pickle castor, Burmese blown glass insert w/applied flowers, silver plate frame w/square bottom on paw feet, swing bail handle 425.00

Pickle castor, clear pressed glass Block patt. insert, silver plate frame w/tongs, marked Pairpoint 130.00

Pickle castor, clear pressed glass Hexagonal Button & Bar patt. insert, ornate silver plate footed frame, marked Reed & Barton 145.00

Pickle castor, cranberry glass Inverted Thumbprint patt. finger bowl-shaped insert, heavily decorated silver plate frame w/hook for lid to hang on 295.00

Pickle castor, cranberry glass Optic patt. paneled bulging insert w/enameled gold flowers & leaves & clear applied shell rigaree all around, ornate silver plate frame w/cut-out lacy sides & top & on claw-and-ball feet, w/tongs 425.00

Pickle castor, opaque pink shading to rose glass insert w/molded shells halfway up body & enameled w/blue & pink forget-me-nots & gold scrolls, square ornate footed silver plate frame w/beading around rim & side handles, space for pickle fork, marked Knickerbocker Silver Company 350.00

Pickle castor, Peach Blow satin-finished cased glass insert w/enameled decoration, silver plate frame w/dark patina, embossed hand on tongs, marked James W. Tufts 695.00

Pickle castor, sapphire blue glass Inverted Thumbprint patt. insert w/bulged-out center & decorated w/yellow & white caterpillars & gold leaves, ornate scalloped silver plate frame decorated w/pickles & leaves, marked Derby Silver Company 495.00

Pickle castor, soft pink, green & white cased spatter glass insert w/eight rows of molded horizontal threading, ornate silver plate frame, marked Wilcox Silver Plate Company 395.00

Pickle castor, topaz facet-cut glass insert, silver plate frame w/loop decoration & fancy tongs, marked Meriden Britannia Company 200.00

Pickle castor, white opalescent glass Swirl patt. hourglass-shaped insert, footed double-handled ornate silver plate frame 295.00

Pickle castor, yellow cased glass Cone patt. insert, ornate silver plate frame 450.00

CAT COLLECTIBLES

General:

Animation cel, Figaro, from "Pinocchio" $2,000.00

Animation cel, full-figure scene of Felix, signed by Joe Oriolo 225.00

Bank, figural cat, by Kliban 18.00

Biscuit jar, cat face, painted black, mint condition, 6" h. 55.00

Candy pail, Felix the Cat pictured . .2,750.00

Carousel animal, cat w/bird in
mouth, Dentzel 33,000.00
Character jug, Cook & Cheshire Cat,
Royal Doulton, 7" h. (discon-
tinued) 140.00

"Miss Priss" Cookie Jar

Cookie jar, cov., Lefton's "Miss
Priss," blue & pink, floral design,
perky facial expression, #1502
(ILLUS.) 40.00
Cookie jar, cov., black & white
striped cat w/blue scarf w/fish
design, © Coco Dowley, 12" h. . . . 40.00
Cookie jar, Puss 'n Boots, w/gold
trim, Shawnee Pottery . . .350.00 to 400.00
Creamer, "calico" cat, Brayton Lagu-
na Pottery 45.00
Cup, yellow w/blue cat handle,
double crown mark, Goebel,
Germany 85.00
Doorstop, unusual black cat, mint . . 280.00
Doorstop, cat w/bell & ribbon,
10" h. 250.00
Felix the Cat candlestick, Felix in
the "Keeps on Walking" pose,
5½" h. 930.00
Felix the Cat salt & pepper shakers,
ceramic, pr. 1,030.00
Felix the Cat figural perfume bottle,
5" h. 135.00
Felix the Cat advertising figure for
Felix Chevrolet (CA), plaster of
Paris, 53" h. 2,750.00

Figural Firescreen

Firescreen, wrought iron & mesh,
the rectangular black-painted
wrought-iron frame w/two applied cats reserved against a
mesh ground, raised on double
scrolling supports, paint chipped,
minor rust, in the manner of Wilhelm Hunt Diederich, ca. 1930,
42" w., 32¼" h. (ILLUS.) 385.00
First Day Covers (FDC) all using the
22c cat stamps (block of 4):
Cats, artist Kribbs, single
stamp 40.00
Cats, Poorman, hand-
drawn, hand-painted,
LE125 . . . . .100.00 to 125.00
Cats, Olde Well Cachets/Dolly
La Manna (Multicolor), overall, hand-drawn, hand-
painted; complete set on two
covers - cream Persian and
kitten on one; British short
hair & kitten on the other,
LE40 sets . . . . .125.00 to 150.00
Game, "Cats and Mice," McLoughlin
Bros., in original box 350.00
Game, "Three Cats Lotto," McLough-
lin Bros., in original box 120.00
Lamp, table-model, cast-bronze,
model of a lion w/jeweled hammered copper shade, Art Nouveau
period 275.00
Lamp, table model, ceramic, cat &
the fiddle, possibly American
Bisque, w/pleated shade, overall
15" h. 75.00
Models of cats:
Bisque, white w/black spots,
standing cat on oval base,
4½" l., 5" h. 30.00
Bisque, grey "alley cat," tall &
lean, "Lefton" paper label,
#1087, 8" h. 25.00
Ceramic, Persian (model came in
black, white & grey), discontinued model, "Shafford," 9" l.,
5½" h. 32.50
Chalkware, brown-spotted, wear-
ing red collar, 19th c., 15" h. . .9,000.00
Chalkware, seated cat w/spotted
coat, 6½" h. 195.00
Fornasetti, porcelain, sleeping
cat, black splotches on white,
12" l., 4¾" h. 275.00
Pierce, Howard (California), pot-
tery cat family: 9½" h. mother
& two kittens, each 4" l. &
4" h.; cream & brown w/dark
brown eyes, the set 48.00
Porcelain, tan & white cats
w/blue balls of yarn; one model
cat is sitting, 5" l., one model
cat lying on its back, 5½" l.,
NAO (Spain), each 85.00

Porcelain, cat in lying down
stalking position, white w/grey
& black striped tail and top of
head, "Ardalt Japan" paper label, 6" l. 48.00

Porcelain, sleeping cat, black &
white, marked "Erphilia Germany," 8" h. 110.00

Pottery, unglazed, pair of kittens,
"Van Briggle," 3" l............ 65.00

Pottery, brown cat, sitting up,
green bow, yellow ball of yarn,
Royal Copley, 7" h............ 28.00

Royal Doulton figures w/cats (all
discontinued):
Dorothy, HN 3098 .....225.00 to 250.00
The Favourite, HN 2249 .... 150.00
Forty Winks,
HN 1974...........225.00 to 250.00
Pussy (or Black Cat), HN 18
& 507 ....6,000.00 to 7,000.00
Save Some For Me, Childhood
Days series, HN 2959 .... 125.00
Solitude, HN 2810 .... 125.00
Twilight, HN 2256 .... 250.00

Sebastian miniature, figure group
"Three Little Kittens" from
"Now's the Time for Jell-O"
series, 1956................. 400.00

Steiff, mohair, Siamese cat
w/jointed neck, original tag,
1950 .... 175.00

Steiff, "Gruffy" 70.00

Wade Pottery (England) cartoon
characters, Tom and Jerry,
pr........................... 160.00

Zoratti, Silvio P. (Ohio), wooden,
white pouncing cat w/blue
marble eyes & a mischievous
grin........................ 500.00

Perfume bottle, glass, figural Felix
the Cat, 5" h. 135.00

Perfume bottle, ceramic, black cat,
marked "Japan," 6" h.......... 50.00

Pitcher, Minton-type, cobalt blue &
floral decoration, cat handle,
8¾" h. 1,000.00

Plate, cat looking at a dragonfly,
signed "L. Coudert," Limoges,
9¾" d. 175.00

Playing cards, double deck (never
unwrapped) in plastic case, Siamese (pink cards), long-haired cat
(blue cards) signed "Robert Gay-
man Forbes".................. 12.50

Puzzle, jigsaw-type, "Wedding in
Catland," artwork by Louis Wain,
mint in box 300.00

Rooftop cat, clay body w/majolica-
type glaze, glass eyes, original
paper label, France, 24" h....... 500.00

Salt & pepper shakers, Siamese
cats, tall & short, Ceramic Arts
Studio, pr..................... 115.00

Sheet music:
"What Does the Pussy Cat Mean
When She Says 'ME-OW'," Leo
Feist, Inc., New York, picture
on cover of a cat w/the moon
in background, below is a city
skyline 12.00
"A China Clock and a Dresden
Cat (Tic Toc)," words by C.P.
McDonald, music by W.C.
Powell; picture on cover of two
cats looking up at a mantel
clock (cover shows wear) 7.00

Figural Table Base

Table base, steel & bronze, cat
stalking bird on crossbars, Llana
Goor, 1989 (ILLUS.) 1,980.00

Teapot, cov., gold striped cat
w/green bow, marked "Pussyfoot
HJ Wood England," 9¾" h........ 52.00

Toy, Felix Movie Cat, Nifty, w/origi-
nal box, 1920's 5,570.00

Artwork:

Chessie Print by Bracker

Chessie, print by Charles E. Bracker, "Peake" has returned home
from the war, in wooden frame,
13¼ x 13¼" (ILLUS.) 85.00

Oil Painting of Two Kittens

Oil on canvas, two kittens, one peeking out of box, one lying on a drape of fabric, signed "C. Brunell Neuville," 15 x 18¼" (ILLUS.) 1,900.00

Oil on canvas, "Busy Moments," mom cat observing her three kittens (two on a rug draped over a table and one atop an opened decorative box), signed by J. Leroy (Jules Leroy, French, 1833-1865), 17 x 19¼" 16,500.00

Oil on board, "Unexpected Visitor," four kittens near bowl of milk watch as a dog exits the doorway, signed by J. Dolph (American, 19th c.), 8 x 10¼"......... 1,500.00

Painting of Two Cats on Porcelain

Painting on porcelain, two cats in a grassy setting, delicate foliage in background, Chinese characters along left edge, China, ca. 1920, wooden frame w/black outer frame (four different pictures to represent the four seasons), 15½ x 21½", each (ILLUS. of one) 450.00

Two grey kittens looking at a grasshopper, water-color, deep tan

Water-color Painting of Kittens

mat, ca. 1920, in brown wooden frame, 9 x 11" (ILLUS.)........... 38.00

White cat, primitive, painted on barn wood, signed & dated 1983, 11 x 16½" 20.00

CERAMICS

ABINGDON

From about 1934 until 1950, Abingdon Pottery Company, Abingdon, Illinois, manufactured decorative pottery, mainly cookie jars, flowerpots and vases. Decorated with various glazes, these items are becoming popular with collectors who are especially attracted to Abingdon's novelty cookie jars.

Cookie jar, "Clock" (Cookie Time) .. $95.00
Cookie jar, "Hippo," white glaze.... 165.00
Cookie jar, "Humpty Dumpty" ....200.00 to 250.00
Cookie jar, "Jack-in-the-Box" ....175.00 to 200.00
Cookie jar, "Little Girl," w/'O's in "Cooky" forming her eyes........ 95.00
Cookie jar, "Little Old Lady," green glaze 135.00
Cookie jar, "Miss Muffet" ..250.00 to 300.00
Cookie jar, "Money Bag"........... 80.00
Cookie jar, "Pineapple" 65.00
Cookie jar, "Pumpkin" (Jack o' Lantern)..................275.00 to 325.00
Cookie jar, "Three Bears" 92.00
Cookie jar, "Wigwam" 950.00
Planter, modeled to resemble a large bowknot, light green glaze, No. 484, 4½ x 8" 25.00
Vase, 15" h., fern leaf design, matte white glaze, No. 433 ...... 185.00

Wall pocket, double-lily, matte turquoise glaze, No. 375 . . . .　45.00
Wall pocket, sunflower . . . .　55.00

ADAMS

Palestine Pattern Plate

*Members of the Adams family have been
potters in England since 1650. Three William
Adamses made pottery, all of it collectible.
Most Adams pottery easily accessible today
was made in the 19th century and is im-
pressed or marked variously ADAMS, W.
ADAMS, ADAMS TUNSTALL, W.
ADAMS & SONS, or W. ADAMS & CO.
with the word "England" or the phrase
"Made in England" added after 1891. Wm.
Adams & Son, Ltd. continues in operation to-
day. Also see STAFFORDSHIRE TRANS-
FER WARES under Ceramics.*

Bowl, 10½" d., 2½" h., "gaudy" floral decoration w/four large stylized blossoms on leafy stems
radiating from the center, in
shades of red, blue & green, English registry mark & "Adams Tunstall - England," late 19th - early
20th c. . . . .　$65.00
Cup & saucer, oversized, black
transfer-printed design of "The
Farmer's Arms" w/polychrome
trim, marked "Adams England,"
late 19th - early 20th c. (wear, minor damage, hairline at base of
handle) . . . .　195.00
Plates, 7½" d., Palestine patt., red
transfer-printed scene, set of 18
(ILLUS. of one) . . . .　495.00
Plate, 10" d., Cries of London
decoration. . . . .　55.00
Platter, 12½" l., oval, green
feather-edged border design, impressed mark "Adams" (stains,
pinpoint flakes) . . . .　130.00

Platter, 15" l., oval, Palestine patt.,
red transfer-printed scene (minor
wear) . . . .　181.50
Soup plates w/flanged rims, Pales-
tine patt., red transfer-printed
scene, 10½" d., set of 5 . . . .　247.50

AUSTRIAN

*Numerous potteries in Austria produced
good-quality ceramic wares over many years.
Some factories were established by American
entrepreneurs, particularly in the Carlsbad
area, and other factories made china under
special brand names for American importers.
Marks on various pieces are indicated in
many listings. Also see ROYAL VIENNA.*

Bowl, 9 7/8" d., ornate floral
transfer-printed decoration w/gold
trim, ca. 1900 . . . .　$70.00
Cake plate, open handles, oranges
w/violets & foliage, gold rim,
pearlized finish, 11" (M Z Aus-
tria) . . . .　29.00
Chocolate pot, cov., Bluebird patt.,
10" h. . . . .　125.00
Chocolate pot, cov., decorated w/a
scene of a courting couple, artist-
signed (Victoria Austria) . . . .　40.00
Chocolate set: cov. chocolate pot &
six cups & saucers; decorated
w/roses, matte finish & gold trac-
ery, 13 pcs. . . . .　400.00
Creamer, model of a moose head . .　28.00
Dresser tray, h.p. roses & gold trim,
6 x 9" (M Z Austria) . . . .　52.00
Dresser tray, white & pink roses
on green & white ground,
7½ x 10" . . . .　35.00
Ewer, squatty, chrysanthemum blos-
soms in various shades of tan
against a blue & cream ground,
gold handle & spout, artist initialed, 7" d., 5" h. (Crown Vienna
Austria) . . . .　95.00
Ewer, "Pompadour," h.p. portrait
depicting Madame Pompadour
against a green relief-molded
ground, reticulated handle,
7" h. . . . .　150.00
Hatpin holder, decorated w/laven-
der asters on white ground, gold
trim (M.Z. Austria) . . . .　80.00
Plate, 6" d., scalloped rim, decorat-
ed overall w/roses, gold trim
(M.Z. Austria). . . . .　15.00
Plate, 8½" d., portrait of Louis XIV
(Victoria Carlsbad) . . . .　65.00
Plate, 9¾" d., portrait of a pretty
blonde lady, "Constance," formal
gold tracery, turquoise & green
border, artist-signed . . . .　110.00

Tray, oval w/pierced handles, Alhambra patt., oval center reserve, bold triangular panels around the border, 11 x 16½" 245.00

Vases, 6" h., lozenge-shaped w/narrow neck & reticulated handles, h.p. violets decoration, pr. 90.00

Vase, 7 7/8" h., 3 3/8" d., ovoid body w/flared rim raised on three slender curved legs w/hoof feet & headed by small lions' heads on a triangular foot, decorated w/pink flowers & green leaves outlined in gold on a beige satin ground, gold legs & foot, marked "B.H." & crown above "Austria," late 19th c. 135.00

Vase, 14½" h., heavily enameled fuchsias in realistic coloring, cobalt blue on handles extending down sides & around base 360.00

Vase, 15" h., narrow neck w/flared rim, scalloped foot, ornate gold handles, a transfer-printed scene of Falstaff & Mrs. Ford against an emerald green & gold spatter ground, ca. 1900 .... 85.00

BAVARIAN

Ceramics have been produced by various potteries in Bavaria for many years. Those appearing for sale in greatest frequency today were produced in the 19th and early 20th centuries.

Bowl, 9½" w., 2¾" h., colorful plumed bird & foliage on white ground, iridescent gold rim band $25.00

Bowl, 9½" d., profusely decorated w/large orange poppies & green leaves 65.00

Bowl, 6¾ x 11½" oval, 2¼" h., scene of lady & boy picking wheat in center panel, blue sides, pierced white rim, marked "Schumann" 36.00

Cake plate, open handles, decorated w/pink roses, large 30.00

Chocolate pot, cov., decorated w/wide gold bands & pink flowers, gold handle, crown mark, 9½" h. 75.00

Chocolate pot, cov., dainty pink & blue floral vines on white, fancy handle w/gilt thumb rest, 10¾" h. 60.00

Coffee set: cov. coffeepot, creamer, cov. sugar bowl, 12" d. serving plate, four 8" d. plates & four

cups & saucers; poppy decoration, 16 pcs. 250.00

Cruet w/original stopper, body & stopper decorated w/violet blossoms & foliage, signed "R.A.K. 1915," marked "Bavaria," 6½" h. 300.00

Cup & saucer, h.p. forget-me-nots decoration & brushed gold trim ... 25.00

Game plate, center scene of elk, blue ground, gold tracery & trim, blue beehive mark, 12" d. 125.00

BELLEEK

Belleek china has been made in Ireland's County Fermanagh for many years. It is exceedingly thin porcelain. Several marks were used, including a hound and harp (1865-1880), and a hound, harp and castle (1863-1891). A printed hound, harp and castle with the words "Co. Fermanagh Ireland" constitutes the mark from 1891. Belleek-type china also was made in the United States last century by several firms, including Ceramic Art Company, Columbian Art Pottery, Lenox Inc., Ott & Brewer and Willets Manufacturing Co. Also see LENOX.

AMERICAN

Bowl, 5¼" d., three-footed, pearl lustre & green w/gold trim (Willets) $42.00

Bowl, 8" d., 3½" h., silver deposit swirl design around top 100.00

Bowl, 8¾" d., shallow ruffled sides w/roses decoration, artist-signed (Willets) 295.00

Bowl, 9½" d., shallow, ruffled rim, decorated w/lovely roses (Willets) 295.00

Chalice, h.p. monk smoking a cigar, 12" h. (Willets) ....650.00 to 690.00

Charger, h.p. gold & bronze enamel floral center w/scalloped rim, 10½" d. (Willets) 185.00

Creamer, pale pink w/gold paste florals, lavender palette mark, 4" h. (Ceramic Art Co.) 75.00

Creamer & cov. sugar bowl, Art Nouveau style floral band decoration, marbleized base, gold trim, artist-signed, green palette mark, pr. (Lenox) 250.00

Cup & saucer, Bouquet patt. (Coxon) 135.00

Cup & saucer, eggshell quality, gold paste flowers, wishbone handle (Ott & Brewer) 135.00

Demitasse set: cov. coffeepot, cov. sugar bowl, creamer & four footed cups; each h.p. w/the Harvard

University tiger & crest on a white ground, gold trim, one cup damaged, ca. 1899, 7 pcs. (Willets) 995.00

Egg stand, footed flat plate pierced w/six holes, centered by figural dolphin handle, applied gold floral decoration & sponged gold (Ott & Brewer) 950.00

Hatpin holder, decorated w/delicate gold scrolling & ovals composed of tiny soft green enameled dots on top & base, gold trim & top ... 225.00

Ott & Brewer Jar

Jar, cov., spherical ivory colored body, the front decorated in shaded gilding w/a spray of daisies & wheat against sponged gilt stripes continuing around the reverse, the rim & cover rim (very small chip) w/slightly worn gilt edges, the cover finial formed as a girl's head emerging from two concentric rows of molded petals, late 19th c., 4 13/16" h., Ott & Brewer (ILLUS.) 1,100.00

Mug, decorated w/cards, poker chips, dice, pipe & whiskey bottle entwined w/snake, "Zeke" inked on handle, artist-signed, 3¾" h. (Willets) 195.00

Mug, monk portrait, ornate handle (Ceramic Art Company) 125.00

Pitcher, lemonade, 7" h., 8" d., scalloped top w/gold trim, gold scroll handle, the body decorated w/yellow, orange, green & white water lilies outlined in gold (Willets) 250.00

Salt dip, h.p. flowers (Willets) 25.00

Salt dip, h.p. roses, 1¼" h. (Willets) 50.00

Stein, h.p. scene of monk drinking from bottle, other bottles tucked in his apron, green palette mark, 7¼" h. (Lenox) 135.00

Vase, 6" h., bulbous body tapering to narrow neck, shades of lemon, tan & light green w/Art Nouveau florals & swirling ribbons overall,

artist-signed, palette mark (Lenox) 345.00

Vase, 12½" h., slender neck w/flared rim, pedestal base, decorated w/pastel pink & yellow roses, gold handles at neck, ca. 1889 (Ceramic Art Company) 325.00

IRISH

Bust of Clytie

Bust of Clytie, satin finish, leaves & pedestal in glossy finish, 7½" d., 11 1/8" h., 1st black mark (ILLUS.) 1,995.00

Bust of Sorrow, 10" h., 2nd black mark 2,800.00

Compote, open, 9¾" d., 4¾" h., openwork edge, Greek patt., aqua trim, 2nd black mark 650.00

Cornucopia-vase, model of a cherub holding a cornucopia, 7" h., 1st black mark 1,600.00

Cracker jar, cov., Diamond patt., Victoria Tea Ware, 8" h., 1st black mark 1,000.00

Cracker jar, cov., Shell patt., Victoria Tea Ware, 8" h., 2nd black mark 1,000.00

Creamer, Irish patt., footed, yellow iridized interior & handle, 3" h., 3rd black mark 50.00

Creamer, double, Lifford patt., 1st black mark 195.00

Creamer, Lifford patt., w/armorial crests, 3rd black mark 175.00

Creamer, Lily patt., green handle & trim, 3½" h., 2nd black mark 50.00

Creamer, Lotus patt., pink handle & trim, 3" h., 2nd black mark 55.00

Creamer, Shamrock-Basketweave patt., footed, kettle-shaped, brown twig handle, 3" h., 2nd black mark 50.00

Creamer & open sugar bowl, Ivy patt., 3rd black mark, pr. 95.00

Creamer & open sugar bowl, Lily patt., 1st green mark, pr......... 60.00

Creamer & sugar bowl, Ribbon patt., 1st green mark, pr. 50.00

Cup & saucer, Grass patt., 1st black
mark 250.00
Cup & saucer, Harp Shamrock patt.,
3rd black mark 110.00
Cup & saucer, Shamrock-
Basketweave patt., 2nd black
mark 100.00
Egg cups w/matching holder, Sydney
patt., six egg cups w/basketweave
design fit into basketweave
holder w/hand holding ring handle at center, 1st black mark,
6" d., 5½" h. 1,100.00
Plates, 7" d., Shamrock-Basket-
weave patt., 3rd black mark,
pr. 85.00
Sugar bowl, cov., Shamrock-
Basketweave patt., small, 3rd
black mark 60.00
Sugar bowl, open, Shamrock-
Basketweave patt., 2nd black
mark 105.00
Tea kettle, cov., Shamrock-
Basketweave patt., 4" h., 2nd
black mark 425.00
Teapot, cov., Limpet patt., 3rd black
mark 275.00

Neptune Pattern Teapot

Teapot, cov., Neptune patt., green
trim, 2nd black mark (ILLUS.) 275.00
Teapot, cov., Tridacna patt., 1st
green mark 250.00
Vase, 6 1/8" h., model of three-
branch tree stump, Shamrock
patt., 3rd black mark 95.00
Vase, 13" h., 8¼" d., Amphora
Vase, ovoid body w/flaring trumpet neck, the base tapering to a
point & raised on three curved
legs w/hoof feet, overall embossed design on body, creamy
lustre glaze, 2nd black mark 650.00

BENNINGTON

*Bennington wares, which ranged from
stoneware to parian and porcelain, were made
in Bennington, Vermont, primarily in two
potteries, one in which Captain John Norton
and his descendants were principals, and the*
*other in which Christopher Webber Fenton
(also once associated with the Nortons) was
a principal. Various marks are found on the
wares made in the two major potteries, including J. & E. Norton, E. & L.P. Norton,
L. Norton & Co., Norton & Fenton, Edward
Norton, Lyman Fenton & Co., Fenton's
Works, United States Pottery Co., U.S.P. and
others.*

*The popular pottery with the mottled
brown on yellowware glaze was also produced
in Bennington, but such wares should be referred to as "Rockingham" or "Bennington-
type" unless they can be specifically attributed to a Bennington, Vermont factory.*

Bennington Candlestick

Book flask, binding impressed "Ladies Suffering G," mottled Flint
Enamel glaze, Lyman Fenton &
Company, ca. 1850, 5¼" h. (im-
perfections) $412.50
Bust of a young girl w/a bird on her
shoulder, Parian, 5" h. 55.00
Candlestick, bell-shaped socket
above a four-sided flaring shaft
w/indented panels above a round,
flaring foot, mottled Flint Enamel
glaze, 7¾" h. 385.00
Candlestick, the cylindrical candle
socket w/a flattened flaring rim
above a shaft w/two flaring,
stepped segments above the
wide, round foot, mottled brown
Rockingham glaze, 8 3/8" h.
(ILLUS.) 368.50
Figurine, Parian, boy standing w/a
basket of eggs on one shoulder,
round base, 9¾" h. 110.00
Jug, stoneware, semi-ovoid,
brushed cobalt blue leafy blossom
sprig, impressed mark "Norton &
Fenton, East Bennington, Vt. 2,"
2 gal., 13" h. 275.00
Name plate, rectangular w/mold-
ed rectangular center panel, mottled brown Rockingham glaze,
3 3/8 x 7¼" (corner chips) 308.00

Pipkin, cov., tall ovoid melon-lobed body w/long S-shaped side handle, domed & ribbed cover w/button finial, mottled dark brown Rockingham glaze, indistinctly marked, Lyman Fenton & Co., ca. 1850, 6¼" h. (chips) 990.00

Pitcher, 12½" h., footed tapering octagonal body w/a high arched spout & angled handle, mottled Flint Enamel glaze, base marked "E," Lyman Fenton & Co., ca. 1850 . . . . 825.00

Syrup pitcher w/original hinged metal lid, Parian, ovoid body molded w/long scroll ribs dividing the body into six panels, ribbon mark, ca. 1852-58, 5¼" h. 175.00

Vase, 6½" h., figural, model of an upright clenched fist, mottled Flint Enamel glaze, Lyman Fenton & Co., ca. 1850 . . . . 275.00

Vase, 9" h., tulip-shaped w/an octagonal flaring bowl raised on a flaring octagonal foot, mottled Flint Enamel glaze, Lyman Fenton & Co., ca. 1850 (chips) 385.00

BERLIN (KPM)

Berlin Dinner Service

The mark, KPM, was used at Meissen from 1723 to 1725, and was later adopted by the Royal Factory, Konigliche Porzellan Manufaktur, in Berlin. At various periods it has been incorporated with the Brandenburg sceptre, the Prussian eagle or the crowned globe. The same letters were also adopted by other factories in Germany in the late 19th and 20th centuries. With the end of the German monarchy in 1918, the name of the firm was changed to Staatliche Porzellan Manufaktur and though production was halted during World War II, the factory was rebuilt and is still in business. The exquisite paintings on porcelain were produced at the close of the 19th century and are eagerly sought by collectors today.

Centerpiece, figural, the main body composed of a molded cluster of tall, scrolling reeds trimmed w/gilt & partially entwined w/a ribbon band held by two putti figures at the base, all atop a flaring ornately scroll-molded base w/scroll feet & applied at the center base w/a putti head, the front of the base w/a large panel h.p. w/a river landscape scene in autumnal hues, marked w/the "KPM" & underglaze-blue sceptre marks, ca. 1890, 37¾" h. (minor chips) $15,312.00

Dinner service: 13 each service plates, dinner plates, salad plates, bread & butter plates & 11 each cups & saucers & cream soup bowls & liners; porcelain & bisque, Art Deco style relief medallion decoration, ca. 1945, the set (ILLUS. of part) 3,300.00

Figure of a classically robed goddess w/a fox seated at her feet, all-white, underglaze-blue Berlin mark, 7" h. 220.00

Plaque, oval, decorated w/a standing figure of a young queen in a white silk & lace gown, her crown on the table beside her, artist-signed, impressed "K.P.M." & sceptre mark, giltwood frame, 4 x 5¼" 770.00

Plaque, rectangular, depicting a half-length portrait of a young gypsy woman w/long flowing dark hair raising one arm above her head w/a languid expression on her face, impressed "K.P.M." & sceptre mark, in a carved giltwood frame, 10¼ x 12½" 8,525.00

Urn, two handles w/goat's head masks, sides decorated w/floral bouquets, stamped mark, late 19th c., 20" h. 990.00

Vase, 10¼" h., a large egg-shaped bowl h.p. w/a center oval reserve of a sailboat scene flanked by water lily reserves above a relief-molded applied band of flowers resting on the shoulders of a cherub seated on a turtle, incised "3523," orb mark & "KPM" in red, sceptre mark in blue, 19th c. 1,100.00

Vases, 24" h., wide ovoid body on a short pedestal w/an octagonal base, the wide shoulder tapering to a slender neck w/flaring rim, decorated w/putti riding dolphins, the neck flanked by foliate scrolled & mask-modeled handles, sceptre mark in blue, printed orb mark in red, third quarter 19th c., pr. 3,575.00

BISQUE

Figure of a Young Girl

Bisque is biscuit china, fired a single time but not glazed. Some bisque is decorated with colors. Most abundant from the Victorian era are figures and groups, but other pieces from busts to vases were made by numerous potteries in the U.S. and abroad.

Busts of young French children, girl w/brown hair & wearing a blue hat w/bow, boy in feathered hat & lace collar, floral bases, 11" h., pr. $325.00

Centerpieces, model of a footed conch shell, one w/a seated boy in pink pants & red hat, the other w/a seated girl in a pink & blue dress highlighted w/delicate flowers, 7 x 8", pr. 375.00

Figure of a reclining nude woman w/red flapper hat, marked No. S29, Germany, 2½" l. 200.00

Figure of a baby in a barrel, the small child in molded shift & bonnet seated inside a barrel turned on its side, the child w/painted blue eyes, molded & painted blonde hair & closed mouth, holding one hand to its mouth, barrel white w/brown bands, unmarked, 3½" h. (top of one toe chipped) .. 55.00

Figure of a little "googlie-eyed" boy dressed in a sailor suit w/"U.S.N." on his cap, toy boats at his feet, possibly Schafer & Vater, 1 7/8" d., 3¾" h. 45.00

Figure, free-swinging little blonde-haired Victorian girl seated in a swing suspended from cords, dressed in pastel blue w/blue shoes & hat & tan trim, 3¼" w., 5¼" h. 95.00

Figure of a boy sitting on a high back chair w/gold cup in hand, blue & white, Germany, 6½" h. .. 60.00

Figure of a little girl, the standing round-faced winking child

w/blonde hair wearing an orange skirt, striped top, on a rectangular platform base incised across the front "I Do Like Kissing," 2½" w., 7" h. 118.00

Figure of a girl gracefully holding the hem of her pleated skirt in each hand, one foot extended, blue intaglio eyes, molded & painted curly blonde hair, green & white pleated dress & shoes, clothing colored on front only, on a flower covered base, Heubach "sunburst" mark, 8" h. (ILLUS.) ... 175.00

Figure of a young girl, wearing a pink dress w/a blue bow, seated on a floral plinth w/pleated baskets on either side, 8 x 10¼" 75.00

Figure, smiling, dancing girl in aqua dress w/sanded surface, pink bow, white lace collar, multi-colored base, Heubach, 11½" h... 510.00

Figures, a peasant man & lady, he standing wearing tan knee-breeches, greenish brown jacket & green hat & carrying a dog bowl & leash, she standing holding a puppy in her pale blue apron, w/a red skirt & gold head scarf, 4" d., 13" h., pr. 345.00

Ornate Bisque Figures

Figures, elaborate couple in fancy 18th c. costume, ornate molded details & delicate painted details, on round base, George Jones, England, 1861-73, slight damage on one, 24" h., pr. (ILLUS.) 3,850.00

Figure group, a Bacchic maiden & cherub in a drunken dance, brightly decorated, Europe, 19th c., 17" h. 209.00

Figure group, a little Victorian boy & girl each seated on a chamber pot, dressed in white w/lavender & green trim, Germany, 3" w., 4½" h. 65.00

Figure group, standing young man &
woman in 18th century costume,
shades of green & rust, 13" h..... 225.00
Piano baby, baby boy holding a ball,
4¾" h......................... 115.00
Piano baby, baby girl holding a toy,
4¾" h......................... 115.00

Large Bisque Piano Baby

Piano baby, seated w/legs crossed,
curly blond hair, wearing a yellow
dress w/a pink bow & gold bead-
ing, unsigned, 8" h. (ILLUS.) 295.00
Vase, double, 10" h., 10½" w.,
joined in the center by a lady on
a swing hung from branches issuing from the vases, ornate applied roses & lavish gold beading 235.00

BLUE & WHITE POTTERY

*The category of blue and white or blue and
grey pottery includes a wide variety of pottery, earthenware and stoneware items widely
produced in this country in the late 19th century right through the 1930's. Originally marketed as inexpensive wares, most pieces featured a white or grey body molded with a
fruit, flower or geometric design and then
trimmed with bands or splashes of blue to
highlight the molded pattern. Pitchers, butter crocks and salt boxes are among the
numerous items produced but other kitchenwares and chamber sets are also found.
Values vary depending on the rarity of the
embossed pattern and the depth of color of
the blue trim; the darker the blue, the better.
The pattern names used with our listings are
taken from two references,* Blue & White
Stoneware, Pottery, Crockery *by Edith Har-
bin (Collector Books, 1977) and* Blue & White
Stoneware *by Kathryn McNerney (Collector
Books, 1981).*

Bowl, 5" d., embossed Wedding
Ring patt. $75.00

Bowl, 9" d., embossed Greek Key
patt., advertising "Thoren Bros.,
Rock Grove, IL" 160.00
Bowl, 9½" d., embossed Daisy &
Waffle patt. 110.00
Butter crock, cov., blue flowers on
side, embossed Star of David on
cover, bail handle 125.00
Butter crock w/wooden lid, em-
bossed Apricot patt............. 95.00
Butter crock w/wooden lid, em-
bossed Cows & Fence patt....... 225.00
Chamber pot, Open Rose & Spear
Point Panels patt. 95.00
Mug, embossed Bow Tie patt.
w/printed bluebird 110.00
Mug, embossed Monk patt., 3½" d.,
4½" h........................ 69.00
Pitcher, 7" h., embossed Dutch Boy
& Girl Kissing patt......125.00 to 150.00
Pitcher, 7" h., printed Dutch Farm
patt. 195.00
Pitcher, 7¾" h., embossed Peacock
patt. 410.00
Pitcher, 8" h., embossed Avenue of
Trees patt. 325.00
Pitcher, 8" h., embossed Grape with
Rickrack patt., cream & blue 140.00
Pitcher, 8" h., embossed Indian in
War Bonnet patt................ 300.00
Pitcher, 8" h., embossed Monastery
(or Castle) & Fishscale patt. 175.00
Pitcher, embossed Fishscale & Wild
Roses patt., large 95.00
Pitcher, stenciled Wildflower patt.,
double blue band ....175.00 to 200.00
Pitcher & bowl, embossed Rose on
Trellis patt., set.........250.00 to 275.00
Salt box, original lid, hanging-type,
embossed Apricot patt. 149.00
Salt box, cov., hanging-type,
embossed Good Luck (Swastika)
patt..................275.00 to 300.00
Water cooler, cov., embossed Cu-
pid patt., Monmouth Potteries,
15" h........................ 450.00

BLUE RIDGE DINNERWARES

*The small town of Erwin, Tennessee was
the home of the Southern Potteries, Inc.,
originally founded by E.J. Owen in 1917 and
first called the Clinchfield Pottery.*

*In the early 1920's Charles W. Foreman
purchased the plant and he revolutionized the
company's output, developing the popular
line of hand-painted wares sold as "Blue
Ridge" dinnerwares. Free-hand painted by
women from the surrounding hills, these
colorful dishes in many patterns, continued
in production until the plant's closing in 1957.*

Bonbon, flat shell shape, Chintz
  patt. $45.00
Bowl, soup, lug handled, Poinsettia
  patt. 7.00
Cake plate w/loop handle, maple
  leaf-shaped, French Peasant
  patt. 55.00
Candy box, cov., vitreous china,
  Katherine patt., 6" d. 110.00
Casserole in chrome holder, Rock
  Rose patt., 9 x 13" 36.00
Celery tray, French Peasant patt.,
  peasant woman decoration 95.00
Celery tray, leaf-shaped, Ridge
  Daisy patt. 30.00
Character jug, Pioneer Woman,
  6½" h. 400.00
Chocolate pot, cov., French Peasant
  patt., pedestal base 289.00
Cigarette box, cov., vitreous china,
  Rose Step patt., 4½ x 5½". 110.00
Creamer & sugar bowl, individual-
  sized, Yellow Nocturne patt.,
  pr. 49.00
Creamer & sugar bowl, Rose Marie
  patt., pedestal base, pr. 65.00
Cup & saucer, demitasse, Sungold
  No. 2 patt. 25.00
Cup & saucer, demitasse, Sweet Clo-
  ver patt. 35.00
Cup & saucer, Dresden Doll patt. . . . 16.00
Pitcher, 5¾" h., vitreous china, Big
  Blossom patt., Grace shape 59.00
Pitcher, 7" h., vitreous china, Sculp-
  tured Fruit patt., 40 oz. 65.00
Plate, 8" d., Ham 'n Eggs patt. 30.00
Plate, 9½" d., Hawaiian Fruit
  patt. 8.00
Plate, dinner, 10" d., Petunia patt. . . 10.00
Plate, 10½" d., Betty patt., Candle-
  wick shape 12.00
Relish dish, vitreous china, shell-
  shaped, Tussie Mussie patt. 27.50
Salt & pepper shakers, vitreous chi-
  na, Nove Rose patt., pr. 49.50
Salt & pepper shakers, Chickens
  patt., yellow w/brown, hen
  4" h., rooster 4¾" h., pr. 120.00
Teapot, cov., Beaded Apple patt.,
  Colonial shape 65.00
Teapot, cov., Cherry Coke patt. 98.00
Teapot, cov., Country Road patt.,
  Colonial shape 69.00
Teapot, cov., Forest Fruit patt., Sky-
  line shape 32.00
Teapot, cov., Wild Strawberry patt.,
  Colonial shape 85.00
Tray, handled, maple leaf-shaped,
  Easter Parade patt. 49.00
Tray, vitreous china, loop-handled,
  Serenade patt. 62.50
Vase, 9¼" h., ruffled top, Calico
  patt. 120.00

Vegetable bowl, cov., Green Briar
  patt. 40.00
Vegetable bowl, open, oval, French
  Peasant patt. 75.00

BOCH FRERES

Boch Freres Lamp

The Belgian firm, founded in 1841 and still
in production, first produced stoneware art
pottery of mediocre quality, attempting to upgrade their wares through the years. In 1907,
Charles Catteau became the art director of the
pottery and slowly the influence of his work
was absorbed by the artisans surrounding
him. All through the 1920's wares were decorated in distinctive Art Deco designs and are
now eagerly sought along with the hand-
thrown gourd-form vessels coated with earth-
tone glazes that were produced during the
same time. Almost all Boch Freres pottery
is marked, but the finest wares also carry the
signature of Charles Catteau in addition to
the pottery mark.

Compote, open, 8¼" h., the hexagonal base & bowl joined by a
  columnar standard, white w/a
  blue & aqua diamond design,
  marked $242.00
Jardiniere, wide ovoid body w/wide
  flat mouth, incised & glazed in
  blue, aqua & black w/grazing
  deer, on a cream crackled
  ground, designed by Charles Catteau, firm's mark & Catteau's
  facsimile signature & "D.943,"
  8" h. 1,100.00
Lamp, table model, ovoid body
  tapering to a short, cylindrical
  neck, decorated around the sides
  w/a band of full-length parading
  penguins incised & colored in
  black & pale green, drilled &
  fitted w/electric fittings & a

wooden base, ca. 1920's, 11" h. (ILLUS.) 770.00

Plate, comic scene of hunters, guns, dog & rabbit, titled "Les Sports - Le Chasse" 65.00

Vase, 9" h., cylindrical central section surrounded by curved panels of varying heights, continuing to a circular foot, incised & glazed in bright yellow & black w/geometric forms resembling buildings & balloons against a crackled white ground, printed in overglaze "KERAMIS - MADE IN BELGIUM," & "D1283" & impressed "1068," ca. 1925 . . . . 1,100.00

Vase, 9½" h., 8½" d., bulbous ovoid body w/a wide shoulder & short wide mouth w/flat rim, incised on each side w/a figure of a large stag & geometric & leaf bands around the shoulder & base, blue, green & black enamels against a white crackled ground, stamped "Made in Belgium - D.943" 660.00

Vase, 10¼" h., ovoid body tapering sharply to a narrow neck w/widely flaring rim, incised & glazed in orange, yellow, grey & black w/a geometric design of rows of diamonds, scattered dots & pointed bands, on a crackled cream ground, company mark & "D.1210" 528.00

Vase, 11¼" h., ovoid body w/everted rim, the shoulder incised & painted w/stylized cream & dark brown blossoms on a matte mottled putty-colored ground, inscribed "Gres. Keramis" w/firm's mark & painted "D.863A" 440.00

Vase, 11¾" h., tall ovoid body tapering to a short narrow neck w/rolled rim, decorated w/six vertical stripes of tan & black circles on a crackled cream ground, designed by Charles Catteau, signed "Ch.Catteau D.831," & inscribed "Gres. Keramis" & w/the company stamp 715.00

Vase, 12¼" h., tall ovoid body tapering slightly to short neck w/flat rim, decorated in chocolate brown w/a central band of stylized birds against an unglazed tan ground, designed by Charles Catteau, printed company marks, facsimile Catteau signature & "D.1086A" 990.00

Vases, 11½" h., swelled cylindrical body, painted w/spiraling borders & central band of spirals & star-shaped blossoms in yellow, orange & blue on a dark brown ground, stamped w/blue wolf mark & impressed "895," painted "MB D. 1091 L.D.," pr. 1,760.00

BOEHM PORCELAINS

Although not antique, Boehm porcelain sculptures have attracted much interest as Edward Marshall Boehm excelled in hard porcelain sculptures. His finest creations, inspired by the beauties of nature, are in the forms of birds and flowers. Since his death in 1969, his work has been carried on by his wife at the Boehm Studios in Trenton, New Jersey. In 1971, an additional studio was opened in Malvern, England, where bone porcelain sculptures are produced. We list both limited and non-limited editions of Boehm.

ANIMALS & BIRDS

Baby Blue Jay, No. 436, introduced in 1957, 4½" h. . . . . $150.00 to 175.00

Baby Cedar Waxwing, No. 432, 1957-73, 3" h. 165.00

Baby Chickadee, No. 461, 1962-72, 3" h. . . . . 150.00 to 175.00

Baby Robin, No. 437D, introduced in 1957, 3½" h. 150.00

Carolina Wren w/Mushrooms, Malvern Studio, England, No. 200-23, introduced in 1975, 7 x 7½" 600.00

Chick, yellow glaze, No. 412, introduced in 1954, 3½" h. 175.00

Cygnet (Baby Bird of Peace) on Lily Pad, No. 400-13, introduced in 1971, 3 x 6" . . . . 375.00 to 400.00

Fledgling Blue Jay, 3½" w., 4½" h. . . . . 175.00 to 200.00

Jenny Wren, bird on rocks w/white flowers, Malvern Studio, England, No. 2001, introduced in 1971, 4 x 6" 350.00

Little Owl, on stump, Malvern Studio, England, No. 1002, 1971-73, 6 x 9" 600.00

Mallards, in flight, No. 406, 1952-60's, 11½" from wing tip to wing tip, 11" h., pr. 2,055.00

Orchard Oriole on Blossoming Tulip, No. 400-11, 1970-75, 11" l., 14" h. 550.00

Panda, Giant Panda Cub, reclining on bamboo, No. 400-47, introduced in 1975, 6½ x 8" 400.00

Ruffed Grouse, male, No. 456, 1960-66, 12" h. 1,300.00

Slate-Colored Junco on Pyracantha, No. 400-12, introduced in 1970, 10½ x 11½" 850.00

Varied Thrush w/Parrot Tulips,
No. 400-29, 1974-76, 10" w.,
18" h. 715.00

BUFFALO POTTERY

Buffalo Pottery was established in 1902 in Buffalo, New York, to supply pottery for the Larkin Company. Most desirable today is Deldare Ware, introduced in 1908 in two patterns, "The Fallowfield Hunt" and "Ye Olden Times," which featured central English scenes and a continuous border, Emerald Deldare, introduced in 1911, was banded with stylized flowers and geometric designs and had varied central scenes, the most popular being from "The Tours of Dr. Syntax." Reorganized in 1940, the company now specializes in hotel china.

DELDARE

Deldare Humidor

Bowl, 12" d., 5" h., The Fallowfield
Hunt - Breakfast at the Three
Pigeons $595.00
Card tray, Ye Lion Inn, artist-signed,
7¾" d. 302.50
Cup & saucer, Ye Village Street 330.00
Humidor, cov., bulbous, There
was an Old Sailor, etc., 8" h.
(ILLUS.) . . . . .850.00 to 900.00
Matchbox holder w/ashtray, Scenes
of Village Life in Ye Olden Days,
artist-signed, 1924, 6½" w.,
3¼" h. 500.00
Mug, The Fallowfield Hunt, artist-
signed, 4" h. . . . . .350.00 to 400.00
Pitcher, 8" h., octagonal, The Fallowfield Hunt - The Return 650.00
Plaque, pierced to hang, The Fallowfield Hunt - Breakfast at the
Three Pigeons, 12" d. . . .475.00 to 525.00
Plaque, Thursday, scene of monks
fishing, artist-signed, 1917,
12" d. .1,320.00

Plaque, Friday, scene of monks
seated at a long table dining,
artist-signed, 1914, 12" d. 1,100.00
Plate, 9¼" d., The Daughters of the
Revolution, artist-signed, 1909 . . .1,980.00
Plate, 9½" d., 1910 calendar 1,550.00
Plate, chop, 14" d., An Evening at
Ye Lion Inn, artist-signed, ca.
1908 . . . . 395.00

Deldare Chop Plate

Plate, chop, 14" d., The Fallow-
field Hunt - The Start
(ILLUS.) . . . . .575.00 to 600.00
Teapot, cov., Scenes of Village Life
in Ye Olden Days, 3¾" h. 375.00
Tea set: cov. teapot, cov. sugar
bowl & creamer; Ye Olden Days,
creamer 3" h., sugar bowl
4½" h., teapot 5¾" h., 3 pcs. . . .1,000.00
Tea tile, The Fallowfield Hunt -
Breaking Cover, artist-signed,
6" d. 285.00
Tea tile, Traveling in Ye Olden
Days, 6" d. . . . . .350.00 to 400.00

EMERALD DELDARE

Candlesticks, hexagonal base, abstract bayberry motif, artist-
signed, 9" h., pr. 1,100.00
Fern dish, butterfly decoration 700.00
Humidor, cov., Doctor Syntax
returned Home, artist-signed,
1911, 6¼" d., 7" h. 1,430.00
Plate, 10" d., Dr. Syntax Making a
Discovery 550.00

MISCELLANEOUS

Bowl, 4" d., 2½" h., Blue Willow
patt. 5.00
Bowl, 8" l., 6½" h., oval, Blue Wil-
low patt. 25.00
Candlestick, Abino Ware 650.00
Casserole, cov., Blue Willow patt.,
round 200.00
Casserole, cov., Blue Willow patt.,
square 225.00
Charger, Rouge Ware, h.p. scene of
Morgan's Road Coach Tavern,
11½" d. 350.00

Chocolate pot, cov., cream w/decoration of roses 135.00

Cup, demitasse, Blue Willow patt. ... 8.00

Game plates, different design on each, signed, 9½" d., set of 6.... 100.00

Game set: 10½ x 15" platter & six 9" d. plates; each w/a different game animal in a wooded landscape, green & gold border, artist-signed, 7 pcs. 230.00

Pitcher, milk, 6" h., chrysanthemum decoration...................... 90.00

Pitcher, jug-type, 7" h., The Whirl of the Town one side & the Foxhunt reverse, butterscotch lustre ground 495.00

Pitcher, 8¼" h., bulbous paneled base below a wide flaring neck, Mason patt., transfer-printed Neapolitan fisherman & Roman ruins scenes around the neck, stylized fruits & flowers between columnar bands around the base, 1907 .... 850.00

Pitcher, jug-type, 9¼" h., Gloriana, teal green 495.00

Pitcher, jug-type, Pink Rose patt. ... 95.00

Plate, 7½" d., commemorative, Improved Order of Red Men, Indian head in polychrome (professional repair on back) 135.00

Plate, 9" d., Blue Willow patt. 6.00

Plate, 10" d., Gaudy Willow patt. 100.00

Plate, 10¼" d., Roosevelt Bears series, five single bear scenes & five action scenes around border, one large action scene in center of plate........................... 615.00

Platter, 11 x 14" rectangle, buffalo hunting scene.................. 375.00

CANTON

Canton Candlesticks

This ware has been decorated for nearly two centuries in factories near Canton, China. In-

tended for export sale, much of it was originally inexpensive blue-and-white hand decorated ware. Late 18th and early 19th century pieces are superior to later ones and fetch higher prices.

Bowl, 9¼" d., shallow tightly scalloped sides, ca. 1825 .... $550.00

Candlesticks, tall slender cylindrical shaft flaring at the base, flattened rim, 19th c., 7½" h., pr. (ILLUS.) 2,200.00

Candlesticks, tall slender cylindrical shaft flaring at the base, w/a flat rim at top, 9¾" h., pr........... 1,800.00

Creamer, footed wide ovoid body w/a high flat rim & pinched spout, C-scroll handle, 4 3/8" h. 295.00

Hot water plate, 9¼" d. 350.00

Mug, cylindrical, entwined handle, 4½" h. 400.00

Plates, 10" d., group of 10 (minor flakes) 750.00

Plate, chop, 14" d., 19th c. 220.00

Platter, 13" l., oval, orange peel glaze 450.00

Platter, 11 x 14¼", rectangular w/canted corners, ca. 1850 ...... 467.50

Platter, 15¼" l., octagonal, late 19th c. (glaze imperfections) 467.50

Platter, 15 7/8" l., oblong w/canted corners, early 19th c............ 935.00

Platter, 17 x 20", molded well & tree, 19th c. 880.00

Teapot, cov., cylindrical body w/shoulder tapering to a small mouth w/inset cover & berry finial, intertwined strap handle, ca. 1840, 8¾" l., 5½" h. 440.00

Tureen, cov., deep rounded flaring sides raised on flaring footring, boar's head handles at ends, low domed cover w/sprig finial, 12½" l. 500.00

Vegetable dish, cov., almond-shaped, marked "China," 9¼" l... 50.00

Vegetable dish, cov., rectangular w/deep, flaring sides, slightly domed cover w/fruit finial, 9¼" l. 275.00

Vegetable dish, cov., rectangular w/notched corners, domed cover w/molded pine cone finial, 19th c., 8 x 9½" (chips) ..330.00 to 360.00

CAPO DI MONTE

Production of porcelain and faience began in 1736 at the Capo-di-Monte factory in Naples. In 1743 King Charles of Naples established a factory there that made wares with relief decoration. In 1759 the factory was moved to Buen Retiro near Madrid, operating until 1808. Another Naples pottery was opened in 1771 and operated until 1806 when its molds were acquired by the Doccia factory of Florence, which has since made reproductions of original Capo-di-Monte pieces with the "N" mark beneath a crown. Some very early pieces are valued in the thousands of dollars but the subsequent productions are considerably lower.

Capo Di Monte Urns

Coffeepot, cov., decorated w/relief-molded nude figures & trees near a lake, cover w/pear finial, ca. 1890, 6" h. $195.00

Figure group, a young boy kneeling w/a camera taking a photo of a young girl seated on a low brick wall, Crown "N" mark, 8½ x 9½" 175.00

Tureen, cover & undertray, the ovoid body molded overall w/cavorting figures, the interior decorated w/floral sprigs, the cover surmounted by a drunken cherub finial, the undertray similarly decorated, 13" l., the set.... 715.00

Urn, campana-form, loop handles at base of bowl raised on a flaring pedestal & round foot, the body molded in relief w/semi-nude women & men amid grapevines, trimmed in colorful enamels, 13½" h. 350.00

Urns, cov., baluster-shaped w/domed covers, the sides molded in relief w/cupids & grapevines, molded in relief florals on cover & molded Bacchus heads at base of handles, 15" h., pr. 450.00

Urns, cov., waisted ovoid w/band of full-figure cherubs engaged in playing music & dancing above four applied masks of men & women, reticulated cover surmounted by dancing cherub, on a low square base, repairs & losses, 31" h., pr. (ILLUS.) 1,760.00

CATALINA ISLAND POTTERY

The Clay Products Division of the Santa Catalina Island Co. produced a variety of wares during their brief ten-year operation. The brainchild of chewing-gum magnate, William Wrigley, Jr., owner of Catalina Island at the time, and his business associate D.M. Retton, the plant was established at Pebbly Beach, near Avalon in 1927. Its two-fold goal was to provide year-round work for the island's residents and building material for Wrigley's ongoing development of a major tourist attraction at Avalon. Early production consisted of bricks and roof and patio tiles. Later, art pottery, including vases, flower bowls, lamps and home accessories, were made from a local brown-based clay and, about 1930, tablewares were introduced. These early wares carried vivid glazes but had a tendency to chip readily and a white-bodied, more chip-resistant clay, imported from the mainland, was used after 1932. The costs associated with importing clay eventually caused the Catalina pottery to be sold to a California mainland competitor in 1937. These wares were molded and are not hand-thrown but some pieces have hand-painted decoration.

Ashtray-pipe holder, figural, an irregular oblong shape modeled w/a sleeping Mexican in the center flanked by a depression for ashes on one side & an indentation for a pipe on the other, bright enamel decoration on the scarf & sombrero, ca. 1927-37 .... $250.00

Bowl, 14", green & yellow glaze 35.00

Candleholders, pedestal form, pink glaze, Shape No. 606, 4" h., pr. ... 120.00

Coffee server w/wooden handle, yellow glaze, 7 x 8" 38.00

Decanter w/stopper, bulbous body, glossy yellow glaze, 7½" h. 95.00

Platter, 14" d., scalloped, blue matte glaze 95.00

Vase, 5" h., 6" d., bulbous body w/three-tier stepped design on the shoulder, square open handles from the flat mouth to the base of the shoulder, early clay body, impressed mark 357.50

Vase, 13½" h., 9¾" d., wide fluted trumpet-form body on a round disc foot, overall orange glaze, marked 330.00

CELADON

Celadon is the name given a highly-fired Oriental porcelain featuring a glaze that ranges from olive through tones of green, *blue-green and grey. These wares have been made for centuries in China, Korea and Japan. Fine early celadon wares are costly, later pieces are far less expensive. Japanese celadon wares are called "Seiji."*

Early Celadon Vase

Bottles, globular body & tall slender
neck, decorated w/carved peonies
& palmettes on base & part of
neck, Kangxi period, China,
18¼" h., pr. $11,000.00
Bowl, 6" d., carved foliage decora-
tion, Yaozhou, Northern Song Dy-
nasty, China 1,430.00
Bowl, 8" d., lotus-form, molded on
the exterior w/long petals, set on
an elaborate wooden stand w/a
disc of long curved petals raised
on six long slender scrolled legs,
Southern Song Dynasty, China,
13th c. (rim frits) 1,100.00
Charger, carved in the center w/a
quatrefoil barbed panel of inter-
linked 'cash' diaper pattern, the
well w/a swiftly executed lotus
scroll similarly repeated around
the exterior, all under a rich
celadon glaze, Longquan, Ming
Dynasty, China, 18¼" d. 2,090.00
Saucer, octagonal, molded lightly on
the interior w/a single lotus blossom below the angled cavetto &
everted rim, all under a rich sea
green glaze falling short of the
flat base w/concave center,
Northern Song Dynasty, China,
4" w. 1,100.00
Vases, 6" h., baluster-form body,
the neck flanked by loop handles
suspending rings, fitted on wood-
en base, China, 13th - 14th c., pr.
(ILLUS. of one) 1,210.00
Vase, 11" h., baluster-form, decorat-
ed w/black floral sprays at shoulder, Koryo Dynasty, Korea, 13th -
14th c. 1,045.00
Vase, 23 3/8" h., wide baluster-form

body w/a tall cylindrical flaring
neck, the body molded w/a broad
peony scroll, the flowers & buds
enclosed by a slender undulating
stem w/small leaves, above a
two-tiered band of overlapping
petals encircling the base, the
neck rising from a deep groove
on the shoulders & decorated
w/three concentric grooves on the
flared mouth, covered overall w/a
sea green glaze, Longquan, Yuan
Dynasty, China (hairline crack,
restored chip, rim ground) 8,250.00

CERAMIC ARTS STUDIO
OF MADISON

Founded in Madison, Wisconsin in 1941 by two young men, Lawrence Rabbitt and Reuben Sand, this company began as a "studio" pottery. In early 1942 they met an amateur clay sculptor, Betty Harrington and, recognizing her talent for modeling in clay, they eventually hired her as their chief designer. Over the next few years Betty designed over 460 different pieces for their production. Charming figurines of children and animals were a main focus of their output in addition to models of adults in varied costumes and poses, wall plaques, vases and figural salt and pepper shakers.

Business boomed during the years of World War II when foreign imports were cut off and, at its peak, the company employed some 100 people to produce the carefully hand-decorated pieces.

After World War II many poor-quality copies of Ceramic Arts Studio figurines appeared and when, in the early 1950's, foreign imported figurines began flooding the market, the company found they could no longer compete. They finally closed their doors in 1955.

Since not all Ceramic Arts Studio pieces are marked, it takes careful study to determine which items are from their production.

Figurine, Accordion Boy, 5" h. $45.00
Figurine, Angel, praying on knees,
4½" h. 35.00
Figurine, Aphrodite, black & tan,
7¾" h. 120.00
Figurine, Bali-Gong, 5½" h. 35.00
Figurine, Balinese Dancer, 9½" h. . . 42.00
Figurine, Boy in Chair, blue, green &
brown, 2¼" h. 15.00
Figurine, Drummer Girl, 4¼" h. 78.00
Figurine, Girl in Chair, 2¼" h. 15.00
Figurine, Guitar Boy, 5" h. 45.00
Figurine, Isaac, 10½" h. 79.00

Figurine, Jill, 4¾" h.	18.00
Figurine, Little Jack Horner, 4½" h.	58.00
Figurine, Pioneer Susie, standing girl w/broom, 5½" h.	35.00
Figurine, Pixie Girl, kneeling, 2½" h.	28.00
Figurine, Promenade Lady, 7¾" h.	53.00
Figurine, Rebekah, 10 1/8" h.	79.00
Figurine, Saxophone Boy, blue, 5½" h.	35.00
Figurine, Shadow Dancer, 7" h.	65.00
Figurine, Shepherdess, 8½" h.	40.00
Figurine, Southern Belle, blue, 7" h.	24.00
Figurine, Sultan on pillow, 4¾" h.	29.00
Figurines, Beth & Bruce, dancers, 5" & 6½" h., pr.	60.00
Figurines, Black Sambo & Tiger, 5" l., 3½" h., pr.	150.00
Figurines, Colonial Dancing Boy & Girl, 5" & 5¼" h., pr.	42.00
Figurines, Comedy & Tragedy, 10" h., pr.	115.00
Figurines, Encore Man & Lady, 8¼" & 8¾" h., pr.	175.00
Figurines, Gypsy Tambourine Girl & Violin Boy, pr.	165.00
Figurines, Lu Tang & Wing Sang, 6¼" h., pr.	70.00
Figurines, Peter Pan & Wendy, on bases w/tall leafy plants, pr.	60.00
Figurines, Spanish Dance Man & Woman, 7" & 7½" h., pr.	140.00
Figurines, Square Dance Boy & Girl, 6" & 6½", pr.	55.00
Figurine, shelf-sitter, Farmer Girl, blue clothes	35.00
Figurines, shelf-sitters, Colonial Boy & Girl, on bench, pr.	85.00
Figurines, shelf-sitters, Dutch Boy & Girl, pr.	37.00
Lamps, Fire Man & Fire Woman, on bases, pr.	250.00
Model of a cat, kitten playing w/ball of yarn	25.00
Model of a cat, kitten scratching, white, 2" h.	15.00
Model of a cat, Tom	25.00
Model of lovebirds, joined, pr.	25.00
Model of a Skunk, Baby Boy	22.00
Models of Mother Skunk & Baby, pr.	45.00
Pitcher, jug-type, 5½" h., brown w/monk decoration, artist-signed	400.00
Planters, models of heads, Manchu & Lotus, pr.	160.00
Salt & pepper shakers, figural Chihuahua & dog house, pr.	70.00
Salt & pepper shakers, figural deer & fawn, pr.	50.00
Salt & pepper shakers, figural elephants, pr.	45.00

Salt & pepper shakers, figural Gingham Dog & Calico Cat, pr.	65.00
Salt & pepper shakers, figural Mr. & Mrs. Penguin, pr.	50.00
Salt & pepper shakers, figural Mother & Baby Cow, pr.	70.00
Salt & pepper shakers, figural Wee Chinese Boy & Girl, pr.	28.00
Salt & pepper shakers, figural Wee French Boy & Girl, pr.	48.00
Salt & pepper shakers, figural Wee Indians, pr.	50.00
Wall plaque, pierced to hang, model of a cockatoo	39.50
Wall plaques, pierced to hang, figural Dutch boy & girl dancing, pr.	72.00
Wall plaques, pierced to hang, figural Harlequin & Columbine, pr.	112.50

CHELSEA

Chelsea Reticulated Basket

This ware was made in London from 1754 to 1770 in England's second porcelain factory. From 1770 to 1783 it was operated as a branch of the Derby Factory. Its equipment was then moved to Derby. It has been reproduced and ceramics made elsewhere are often erroneously called Chelsea.

Basket, oval w/deep reticulated sides & upright end loop handles, the interior painted in shades of rose, blue, iron-red, yellow, green, grey & brown w/a floral bouquet amid scattered sprigs & two insects, the exterior molded w/open wickerwork beneath a brown-edged scalloped rim, puce-bound stem end handles ending in yellow & brown mottled branches bearing iron-red blossoms & green leaves, ca. 1755, slight glaze abrasion, handle ends chipped, 12 1/8" l. (ILLUS.) $550.00

Dish, leaf-shaped, modeled as two overlapping cos-lettuce leaves w/puce veins & edged in a bright

green, Red Anchor mark above
"8," ca. 1755, 9 7/8" l. (slight surface wear) 1,210.00

Dish, leaf-shaped, modeled as a
large cabbage leaf w/puce veins
& painted in color w/figs, a turnip, scattered flowers & insects
within a brown line rim, Brown
Anchor mark, ca. 1755, 11¾" l.
(rim chips, some wear) 3,300.00

Figure of a young sportsman,
modeled wearing a black hat, a
dotted pink neckerchief, a turquoise jacket w/rose cuffs, a
gold, black & iron-red fan-
patterned waistcoat, pale yellow
breeches & tan-topped black
boots, holding a bird in his right
hand & another brown bird between his feet, his brown rifle
(barrel tip chipped) to his left & a
recumbent brown-spotted white
hound to his right before a tree
stump bearing iron-red berry
clusters & green leaves (chips),
on a scroll-molded mound base
trimmed in turquoise & gold,
Gold Anchor mark, ca. 1765,
7 1/16" h. 1,100.00

Plates, 9 5/16" d., scalloped border,
each painted in shades of rose,
iron-red, yellow, blue, purple,
brown, green & grey w/small floral sprigs between a larger sprig
& a bouquet on either side of the
brown-edged rim, tiny Red Anchor
marks, ca. 1755, pr. (three small
chips on one) 440.00

Platter, 13 5/16" l., oval w/scal-
loped rim, the mottled rose
ground reserved w/four
cornucopia-shaped cartouches
painted in iron-red, blue, yellow,
puce & black w/birds in flight
within gilt C-scrolls & trellises issuing tooled gilt floral sprays &
supporting garlands suspended
from gilt bowknots at the gilt
dentil-edged rim, Gold Anchor
mark, ca. 1760-65 (some central
scratching & wear to the gilt
rim) 1,540.00

CHINESE EXPORT

*Large quantities of porcelain have been
made in China for export to America from the
1780's, much of it shipped from the ports of
Canton and Nanking. A major source of this
porcelain was Ching-te-Chen in the Kiangsi
province but the wares were also made elsewhere. The largest quantities were blue and*

*white. Prices fluctuate considerably depend-
ing on age, condition, decoration, etc.*

Chinese Export Hot Water Pot

Candlesticks, *famille verte* palette,
European silver form w/a cylindrical candle nozzle painted w/bor-
ders of yellow & green *ruyi* heads
& leaves, the triple-knopped stem
w/a central lightly fluted sphere
striped in blue, yellow, green &
pale aubergine between two iron-
red-ground spheres reserved
w/white stylized floral designs &
all divided by narrow rings, the
low conical base molded w/petal
designs above a yellow-ground
border of gilt-centered blue &
iron-red chrysanthemum blossoms
& scrolling green foliage, 1700-15,
8¾" h., pr. (one nozzle cracked,
one repaired, some fritting &
chips) $6,050.00

Cider pitcher, cov., jug-type, domed
cover w/a reclining fu-dog finial,
entwined strap handle, white
w/gilt band trim & shield-shaped
reserves framing monogram "DH"
beneath drapery swags & a pair
of birds, ca. 1800, 10½" h. 1,100.00

Coffeepot, cov., baluster-form body
w/molded spout, applied interlaced handle, centering on both
sides pseudo arms of New York,
the circular domed lid w/blue enamel rim, gilt stars & gilt strawberry finial, ca. 1790-1800,
5½" w., 8½" h. 2,750.00

Compote, open, 8¾" d., 8½" h.,
flaring pierced basketweave sides
on a rounded base raised on a
slender pedestal above a square
foot, trimmed w/gilt banding,
1827-38 (some gilt wear) 2,860.00

Creamer, helmet-shaped w/branch
handle, the flaring lip decorated
in apple green & gold w/diaper-
ing & bellflowers, under the spout

an oval reserve painted in polychrome w/the arms of the State
of Rhode Island, early 19th c.,
5" h. 605.00
Dish, rectangular w/rounded,
notched corners, *famille rose* palette, the center painted w/a butterfly hovering above two iron-red
grisaille & gold cocks in a con-
frontation amid fungi, peonies &
prunus growing by rockwork, the
rim w/a border of brown-spotted
white bamboo entwined w/a rose,
iron-red, blue, gold & green
flowering vine, ca. 1750, 14" l.
(gilt rubbed, hairline & repaired
chip on rim, some enamel
chips) 4,675.00
Hot water pot, cov., ovoid
w/shaped spout, entwined handle
terminating in relief-molded leafage, decorated w/the Arms of
Smale (or Smalley), very minor
imperfections, late 18th - early
19th c., 9¼" h. (ILLUS.) 550.00

Chinese Export Mantel Garniture Set

Mantel garniture set: a pair of tall
cylindrical vases w/flaring rims &
a baluster-form jar w/domed cover & figural finial; each decorated
w/blue bands around the rim &
base, the center of the side h.p.
w/a large footed, covered urn
w/bird finial, 19th c., vases
10" h., jar 11½" h., 3 pcs.
(ILLUS.) 1,210.00
Models of quail, each bird w/a
black-dashed aubergine head,
neck & yellow breast, & white &
black-delineated green back
plumage & aubergine & yellow
wing & tail feathers, the eyes
picked out in black, & w/a yellow beak, legs & feet, modeled
perched on deeply incised &
pierced aubergine rockwork, together w/fitted hardwood bases,
19th c., 7" h., pr. (beak tip restored, one toe missing & others
touched up) 2,530.00

Monteith bowl, blue "Fitzhugh"
patt., deeply scalloped rim, ribbed
sides & low flaring foot, interior
enamel decorated w/a variation
of the arms of Elphinstone, late
18th - early 19th c., 9 7/8" d.
(restoration) 825.00
Mug, cylindrical, blue & white, deco-
rated w/a molded-edge reserve
panel containing an urn trailing
w/*famille rose* floral garlands, the
underglaze-blue borders of fruiting & flowering vines, interlaced
strap handle, ca. 1870, 6" h. (gilt
rubbed, handle restored) 352.00
Pitcher, cov., milk, 4 13/16" h., jug-
shaped, *famille rose* palette, the
pear-shaped body painted w/a
continuous scene depicting Jupiter
dressed as a shepherd approaching Mnemosyne seated beneath a
tree by a clearing, the cover w/a
landscape vignette encircling the
worn gilt tear-shaped knop, ca.
1740 (handle restored) 990.00
Pitchers, 9¼" h., wide ovoid body
w/a wide flaring neck w/flaring
pinched lip, C-scroll handle, white
decorated in gilding & blue enamel w/bow-tied foliate wreaths
& paired lyres, ca. 1827-38, pr.
(wear to gilt) 5,500.00
Plate, 9" d., Tobacco Leaf patt.,
painted w/a green-centered rose,
purple & yellow tobacco blossom
superimposed against a gilt-
trimmed underglaze-blue leaf &
surrounded by smaller blossoms &
leaves in shades of rose, iron-red,
purple, yellow, turquoise, pink,
green & gold, the underside of
the scalloped rim w/three
underglaze-blue & iron-red flowering branches, 1770-85 (some frit-
ting & wear) 1,725.00
Platter, 21" l., oval, blue "Fitzhugh"
patt., 19th c. (minor rim chips) . . . 825.00
Punch bowl, *famille rose* palette,
deep rounded sides on a thick
footring, painted in shades of
rose, blue, iron-red, turquoise,
green, white, black & gold on the
front of the exterior w/peonies,
chrysanthemums & other flowers
growing by rockwork in a fenced
garden, & on the reverse & the interior w/a flowering peony
branch, the rim edge showing
traces of gilding, ca. 1740,
13 3/8" d. (some gilt rubbing,
repaired rim chip) 2,750.00
Sugar bowl, cov., the bowl of globu-
lar form w/symmetric applied interlaced handles, waving blue

banding w/gilt stars at neck, blue
enamel decoration to foot, centering sepia & gilt shield & swags,
the domed lid w/plain rim decorated w/band of blue enamel &
gilt stars, centering a strawberry
finial, ca. 1790-1810, 6" w.,
5¾" h........................ 330.00

Teapot, cov., *famille rose* palette,
spherical body & domed cover,
iron-red ground patterned w/gilt
scrolling lotus vines & reserved on
either side w/a black- and gold-
edged panel finely painted on the
pot w/a Chinese lady & youth in
an interior, on the cover w/a pink
& green flowering peony or chrysanthemum branch, ca. 1740,
5 3/8" h. (two chips on cover) 660.00

Tureen, cov., oval, blue "Fitzhugh"
patt., decorated w/the crest
of the Beale family, 19th c.,
10¾" l......................1,980.00

Vases, 11¼" h., square bottle-form,
blue & white, each side painted
w/a court scene, including
dancers performing before noble-
women & mounted huntresses
outside a fortress, borders of
crosshatch & diaper, flowering
branches on the square neck,
ribbon-tied artemesia leaf marks
in recessed squares on the base,
Kangxi period, pr. (one neck
w/restoration, some fritting).....3,300.00

Chinese Export Wine Cooler

Wine coolers, Rococo-style, each
molded around the lower body
w/gold- and iron-red feathered
rocaillerie extending up to form
scroll handles at the sides, painted in the rocaillerie & on the body
above in rose, purple, iron-red &
green w/floral bouquets & sprays,
the scalloped rim lightly fluted,
the scalloped foot w/an iron-red
& gilt chain border, 1775-80,
one handle on each slightly
chipped, rim w/small chips &
frits, 10½" w., 6" h., pr. (ILLUS.
of one) 9,900.00

CLARICE CLIFF DESIGNS

"Bizarre" Demitasse Set

*Clarice Cliff was a designer for A.J. Wilkin-
son, Ltd., Royal Staffordshire Pottery, Burslem, England when they acquired the
adjoining Newport Pottery Company whose
warehouses were filled with undecorated
bowls and vases. About 1925 her flair with
the Art Deco style was incorporated into designs appropriately named "Bizarre" and
"Fantasque" and the warehouse stockpile
was decorated in vivid colors. These hand-
painted earthenwares, all bearing the printed signature of designer Clarice Cliff, were
produced until World War II and are now
finding enormous favor with collectors.*

Bone dish, Tonquin patt., black $30.00
Bowl, 8" w., 4¼" h., "Bizarre"
ware, octagonal, h.p. w/Original
Bizarre patt., large crudely painted bands of maroon, dark orange
& dark blue diamonds above an
ochre base band, ink mark....... 880.00

Bowl, 9½" d., 4½" h., h.p. orange,
green & blue poppies decoration.......................... 495.00

Condiment set: two jars w/silver-
plated lids & a small open bowl
fitted in a silver-plated frame w/a
looped center handle; each piece
h.p. w/stylized red & blue flowers
on an ivory ground, marked, tray
4½ x 5", the set (small chip on
one piece) 522.50

Demitasse set: cov. coffeepot, six
demitasse cups & saucers, creamer & open sugar bowl; "Bizarre"
ware, Fantasque patt., decorated
w/a stylized tree on one side, the
other w/stylized hollyhocks, small
chip to one saucer, 15 pcs. (ILLUS.
of part) 2,750.00

Dinner set: service for six w/8" d.,
9" d. & 10" d. plates, three oval
platters, two cov. serving dishes
& one pitcher; "Bizarre" ware,
stepped geometric border design
in orange, blue & black against
an ivory ground, all marked, the
set.......................... 990.00

Gravy boat & underplate, Tonquin
patt., black 40.00

Pitcher, 7½" h., 7¼" d., "Bizarre"
ware, My Garden patt., bulbous
base below a wide cylindrical
body flaring slightly at the rim, an
arched bumpy branch handle in
mottled purple w/long sprigs of
molded green leaves at the base
on the all-black matte-glazed
body, ink mark (small repaired
chip on handle) 412.50

Pitcher, 9¾" h., 7¾" d., jug-type,
"Bizarre" ware, Isis shape, Sum-
merhouse patt., decorated
w/trees & gazebos in yellow,
green, purple, red & blue against
an ivory ground, marked 3,300.00

Plate, 9" d., "Bizarre" ware, Blue
Chintz patt., decorated w/styl-
ized flowers in green, blue &
pink against an ivory ground,
marked 522.50

Plate, 9" d., "Fantasque" line, h.p.
Melon patt., a wide band of stylized fruit in yellow, orange, red,
blue & green w/an orange center
circle & a narrow orange rim
band, ink mark (minor wear)..... 660.00

Plate, dinner, Tonquin patt.,
lavender 28.00

Sauceboat & undertray, Tonquin
patt., green 29.00

Sugar shaker, "Bizarre" ware, Bon-
jour shape, a flattened upright
oval w/tiny feet across the base,
h.p. Nasturtium patt., stylized orange, red & yellow blossoms &
pale green leaves, white at top &
burnt orange at the bottom, ink
mark, 1¾" w., 5" h............. 245.00

Sugar shaker, "Bizarre" ware, Cone
patt. 350.00

Vase, 9" h., 4½" d., "Bizarre" ware,
baluster-shaped w/a short, wide
slightly flaring neck, decorated on
the upper half w/a wide band of
triangles in purple & burnt orange
against a burnt orange body,
Shape No. 14D, marked 1,760.00

Vase, 9" h., 4¾" d., "Bizarre" ware,
baluster-shaped, h.p. in the Original Bizarre patt., a wide middle
band of multicolored triangles
flanked by a dark blue rim band
& yellow & orange base bands,
No. 264, ink mark (minor wear)..1,650.00

Vase, 9½" h., 6½" d., "Bizarre"
ware, Isis shape, ovoid body
tapering to a wide, flat rim, decorated in the Melon patt., bold
stylized abstract fruits in dark
red, blue, orange, green & yellow
around the middle flanked by
wide dark orange bands, ink
mark 2,860.00

COALPORT

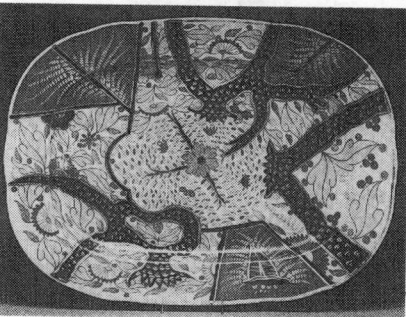

Japan Pattern Coalport Platter

*Coalport Porcelain Works operated at Coal-
port, Shropshire, England, from about 1795
to 1926 and has operated at Stoke-on-Trent
as Coalport China, Ltd., making bone china
since then.*

Bough pots, D-shaped, each painted
in shades of iron-red, rose, purple, green & yellow w/anemones,
ranunculus & roses or poppies,
convolvulus, ranunculus & roses
against a black ground in a rectangular panel flanked by lightly
fluted pilasters, the sides
w/slightly recessed panels painted in rose against the gold
ground w/neoclassical foliate
scrolls issuing from demi-eagles
above urns in ovals, & raised on
four gilt ball feet, now fitted
w/brass covers pierced w/three
large & four small circular apertures, ca. 1810, 8 11/16" l., pr.
(one w/footrim chip, small hairline in back, small rim chip, star
crack on base) $9,200.00

Dessert service: pair oval fruit
stands, pr. scalloped lozenge-
shaped dishes, pr. square dishes,
pr. shell-shaped dishes & 12
plates; 'Rock and Tree' patt., each
piece painted in an expanded Imari palette of underglaze-blue,
iron-red, green, salmon & gold
w/an acacia tree & peonies growing by a double rock in a fenced
garden, the rim w/a 'brocade'
border of floral, foliate & cell diaper panels within a gilt edge, ca.
1805-10, fruit stands 11 7/8" &
12 1/8" l., 20 pcs. 7,475.00

Platter, 21 3/8" l., oval, 'Japan'
patt., painted w/a central gilt
blossom on a field of green & yellow foliage surrounded by gilt-
dashed underglaze-blue trees,
iron-red, green & yellow blos-

soms, berries & leaves, & iron-red
ground panels of underglaze-blue
& gilt stylized plants bearing yellow leaves, the wavy rim edged
w/a gilt band, wear to gilt band,
ca. 1805 (ILLUS.) 1,495.00

Vase, 8 13/16" h., 'Church Gresley'
patt., decorated around the flaring cylindrical neck w/a colorful
floral garland between gilt
hatched & berried foliate band
borders repeated in variation
around the shield-shaped body &
flaring circular foot & enclosing an
elaborate pattern of yellow hexa-
gons reserved w/gilt ovals painted w/cornflowers & surrounded
by rose sprigs in diamond-shaped
panels alternating w/rectangular
panels of green & iron-red ovals,
the front reserved w/a gilt-edged
floral panel, the lower body w/a
gilt border of arches & sprigs
above the knopped ankle & the
integral square base fully gilded,
painted probably in the London
studio of James Giles, ca. 1805
(ankle repaired) 1,150.00

COPELAND & SPODE

Parian Bust of Veiled Maiden

*W.T. Copeland & Sons, Ltd., have operat-
ed the Spode Works at Stoke, England, from
1847 to the present. The name Spode was
used on some of its productions. Its predeces-
sor, Spode, was founded by Josiah Spode
about 1784 and became Copeland & Garrett
in 1843, continuing under that name until
1847. Listings dated prior to 1843 should be
attributed to Spode.*

Bowl, 10 5/8" d., 4½" h., overall
pure white sculptured floral decoration, marked "Spode, Impl. Eng-
land," 1930's $125.00

Bust of a veiled maiden, a floral
wreath around her head, on a socle base, signed on back "R. Monti 1861," inscribed on pedestal
foot "Crystal Palace Art Union,"
17½" h. (ILLUS.) 1,155.00

Pitcher, milk, 6" h., Spode's Tower
patt., blue 135.00

Plates, luncheon, 8½" d., Imari
patt., ca. 1900, set of 8 . . . . 330.00

Platter, 13 x 16", Spode's Tower
patt., blue 275.00

Relish tray, handled, Italian patt.,
blue 46.00

Teapot, cov., spherical body
w/cream ground w/a deep blue
wide band decorated w/white-
relief classical figures in a Dancing Hours design, 4¼" d.,
4¾" h. 125.00

Teapot, cov., Romney patt. 215.00

COWAN

Cowan Lamp

*R. Guy Cowan first opened a studio pottery
in 1913 in Cleveland, Ohio. The pottery continued to operate almost continuously, at various locations in the Cleveland area, until it
was forced to close in 1931 due to financial
problems. This fine art pottery, which was
gradually expanded into a full line of commercial productions, is now sought out by collectors.*

Bowl, 7" d., 3" h., deep rounded
sides, fine iridescent gold & crackled celadon glaze, marked "R.G.
Cowan" & "RC" $330.00

Console set, 8" h. fan-shaped
vase & matching 4½" h. candleholders w/figural sea horse
bases, 3 pcs. 135.00

Flower frog, figural mushroom, ivo-
ry glaze 135.00

Lamp, table-type, Art Deco style, ovoid body molded w/a stylized orchard design w/a glossy blue & green glaze, mounted w/a heavy & elaborate silvered-metal base & electric fittings, overall 25" h. (ILLUS.). 467.50

Rare 'Jazz' Punch Bowl

Punch bowl, 'Jazz' design, deep flaring sides on a low foot, carved on the exterior w/symbols of the Jazz Age, glazed in black & bright blue, designed by Viktor Schreckengost, ca. 1932, base impressed "Viktor Schreckengost" & "Cowan," 13¾" d., 8½" h. (ILLUS.) 13,200.00
Toothpick holder, molded sea horse decoration 35.00
Trivet, woman's face surrounded by a garland of flowers on blue ground, 6½" d. 275.00
Vase, 5" h., fan-shaped, apple green glaze w/gold specks. 90.00
Vase, 8" h., fan-shaped, sea horse at base, lavender glaze 75.00

CYBIS

Though not antique, fine Cybis porcelain figures are included here because of the great collector interest. They are produced in both limited edition and non-numbered series and thus there can be a wide range available to the collector.

Baby lamb "Mandy," No. 6002, 1979-82, 4" l., 4¼" h. $100.00
Burro, "Fitzgerald," No. 632, 1964-83, 7" l. . . . . .135.00 to 150.00
Christopher, The Sea Listener, No. 4009, 1979-84, 6" w., 6½" h. 295.00
Duckling, "Baby Brother," No. 361, 1962-79, 4½" h. . . . . .100.00 to 125.00
Elephant, "Alexander - He's the Greatest," No. 682, 1975, 6½" l., 7½" h. 350.00
Elizabeth Ann, No. 490, 1976, 5" h. . . . . .265.00 to 300.00

Eros (Cupid) Head on base, No. 477, 1974, 10" h. 275.00
First Flight, No. 410, 1966-73, 4½" h. 200.00
Heidi, No. 432, 1966-73, 7½" h. 250.00
Jane Eyre, No. 4047, 1981-84, 12" h. 1,250.00
Jeanie With The Light Brown Hair, No. 4012, 1979-81, 9½" h. 565.00
Little Bo Peep, No. 498, 1977-82, 10½" h. 335.00
Peter Pan, No. 430, 1958-70, 7½" h. 650.00
Rebecca, No. 443, 1964-72, 6½" h. . . . 325.00
Rumples, the Pensive Clown, No. 4014, 1979-81, 7" h. 300.00
Sleeping Beauty, No. 4060, 1982, 7½" h. 1,100.00
Wendy, No. 433, 1957-82, 6½" h. . . . . .200.00 to 250.00
Wood Wren & Dogwood, No. 336, 1963-64, 5½" h. 300.00

DAVENPORT

Davenport Porcelain Bulb Pot

The Davenport factory operated under various names at Longport, England, from about 1794 to 1887. They produced a wide range of good quality earthenware dinnerwares as well as some finer porcelain pieces. Various marks were used, including the well known anchor. Also see FLOW BLUE.

Bulb pot, cov., porcelain, D-shaped body painted in puce monochrome on the front w/a rustic bridge over a waterfall in a hilly landscape, decorated on the sides w/a distant ruin or cottage in a landscape, all within recessed panels divided by orange & gold pilasters above four gilt ball feet & bordered on the lower body w/similarly colored molded arches, the gilt-edged cover (repaired chips) pierced w/three small circular apertures between three orange-lined bulb holders (restored) decorated around their exteriors w/gilt sprigs, impressed "Davenport" & anchor mark, 1807-12, star crack in base, some restoration to base & one end, 7½" l. (ILLUS.) $2,475.00

Plate, 8½" d., Cyprus patt., black transfer, incised anchor mark, ca. 1850 .... 60.00

Sauce tureen on attached stand, cover & ladle, pearlware, each piece molded w/overlapping oak leaves shaded in green, yellow, turquoise & brown & edged on the rim in black (some wear), the ends of the tureen & the cover w/olive green (some wear) twig handles, impressed "Davenport" & anchor mark, 1810-15, incised "15" on tureen & cover, base 7 15/16" l. (small chip on stand rim) 1,760.00

Soup plate w/flange rim, pearlware, rim w/green feathered edging, center w/stylized house decoration in orange, brown & yellow, 8 1/8" d. (minor wear & tiny flakes) 425.00

DEDHAM

Dedham "Tapestry Lion" Plate

This pottery was organized in 1866 by Alexander W. Robertson in Chelsea, Massachusetts, and became A.W. & H. Robertson in 1868. In 1872, the name was changed to Chelsea Keramic Art Works and in 1891 to Chelsea Pottery, U.S.A. About 1895, the pottery was moved to Dedham, Massachusetts, and was renamed Dedham Pottery. Production ceased in 1943. High-fired colored wares and crackle ware were specialties. The rabbit is said to have been the most popular decoration on crackle ware in blue.

Since 1977, the Potting Shed, Concord, Massachusetts, has produced quality reproductions of early Dedham wares. These pieces are carefully marked to avoid confusion with original examples.

Bowl, 4½" d., 2" h., Turtle $357.50
Bowl, 5" d., decorated w/a central medallion w/Scottie dogs.......1,430.00
Bowl, 7" d., 3" h., Grape 192.50
Bowl, whipped cream, 7¼" d., 2½" h., w/flanged rim, Iris 220.00
Celery tray, oblong, Azalea, ink & impressed marks, 6¼ x 10" 110.00
Charger, Elephant, 12" d. 880.00
Charger, Turtle, 12" d. 2,475.00
Creamer, squatty bulbous body w/pinched spout, Azalea, ink mark, 5½" d., 2¼" h. 55.00
Cup & saucer, Magnolia, cup 4¾" d., 2¼" h. 137.50
Pitcher, 5¼" h., 5½" d., ovoid body w/pinched spout, Night & Morning design w/birds, ink mark 715.00
Pitcher, 6½" h., spherical body tapering to a short cylindrical neck w/pinched spout, Turtle 3,575.00
Plate, 6¼" d., Rabbit 80.00
Plate, 8¼" d., the center decorated w/a stylized landscape scene, a simple corn crib house border (glaze skips) 412.50
Plate, 8½" d., Flying Serpent 4,180.00
Plate, 8½" d., Grouse 2,750.00
Plate, 8½" d., Iris 185.00
Plate, breakfast, 8½" d., Mushroom, marked 825.00
Plate, breakfast, 8½" d., Tapestry Lion, marked (ILLUS.) 1,870.00
Plate, 8½" d., Water Lily 192.50
Plate, 8¾" d., scalloped rim, Dolphin 1,640.00
Plate, 9" d., Cat 4,840.00
Plate, 10" d., Clover.............. 825.00
Plate, 10" d., Dolphin & Mask, "CPUS" clover mark.............2,420.00
Platter, 10 x 18", oblong, Crab.....3,630.00
Salt & pepper shakers, model of a rabbit, 3½" h., pr. 450.00
Tray, round w/raised rim, two-ear Rabbit, ink mark, 13¼" d. 770.00
Vase, 5¼" h., 5¾" d., bulbous ovoid body tapering to a wide flat mouth, thick dripping green glaze on upper half above a grey lower body, incised mark & "HR" (inmaking firing lines at rim) 660.00
Vase, 5 5/8" h., wide baluster-form body, experimental glaze in mottled green w/traces of blue on white stoneware, designed by Hugh Robertson, impressed "Dedham Pottery HCR" 330.00
Vase, 8" h., 2¾" d., ovoid body

tapering to a tall cylindrical neck w/flat rim, iridescent greenish grey mottled glaze dripping over red, incised mark & "HR" 935.00

DELFT

Early Delft Bowl

In the early 17th century Italian potters settled in Holland and began producing tin-glazed earthenwares, often decorated with pseudo-Oriental designs based on Chinese porcelain wares. The city of Delft became the center of this pottery production and several firms produced the wares throughout the 17th and early 18th century. A majority of the pieces featured blue on white designs, but polychrome wares were also made. The Dutch Delftwares were also shipped to England and eventually the English copied them at potteries in such cities as Bristol, Lambeth and Liverpool. Although still produced today, Delft peaked in popularity by the mid-18th century.

Barber bowl, round w/notched flanged rim, decorated in blue, the center w/a large stylized leafy tree & blossom, the rim w/a swag band, England or Europe, 18th c., 13¼" d. (minor rim flakes) $825.00

Bowl, 9" d., inscribed in blue "One More and Then," England or Europe, 18th c.................... 550.00

Bowl, 10" d., deep flaring sides on footring, decorated in blue w/oblong reserves w/flowers framed by diamond trellis designs, England or Europe, second quarter 18th c., rim flakes (ILLUS.) 687.50

Bowl, 12" d., deep slightly tapering sides on footring, exterior decorated in blue, iron-red & green w/leafy foliage & overall scattered stylized flowers & iron-red "stars," the interior w/a floral spray & stylized foliage, probably Bristol, England, ca. 1740 (cracks, rim chips) 3,500.00

Bowl, 12" d., fluted rim, the interior painted in blue w/a large Oriental island landscape featuring a large house, bridge & centering a tall willow tree, England or Europe, 18th c. 1,100.00

Bulb bowl, shallow rounded dish w/a slightly concave top pierced w/numerous small holes & a larger central hole, the top & sides h.p. overall w/blue scrolling flower & leaf designs, England, ca. 1750, 8½" d. 1,045.00

Charger, decorated in blue, the dished center w/large stylized Oriental blossoms, the flanged rim decorated w/reserves of a large blossom & tiny leafy vines, England or Europe, 18th c., 12¼" d. (rim flakes)............ 522.50

Charger, polychrome, the center decorated w/a large stylized flower-filled urn within a peacock feather border, in shades of yellow, green, iron-red, blue & aubergine, Holland, 18th c., 16½" d. 522.50

Dish, blue & white, the center w/a half-length portrait of William of Orange in crown & ermine robes within concentric bands of fluting enriched w/blue stylized half flowerheads, Holland, ca. 1690, 9 5/8" d. (chips, some glaze losses)........................4,400.00

Figure group, a seated milkmaid beside a large standing cow, each decorated w/overall scrolling colorful flowers & vines, on a shaped platform base w/a scroll-decorated edge band, Holland, 19th c., 9" l. 605.00

Flower brick, rectangular block w/the narrow top pierced w/holes, the front h.p. in blue w/an Oriental landscape, England, mid-18th c., 6¼" l. (rim flakes) 605.00

Model of a cow, polychrome floral decoration, Holland, early 20th c., 5¾" h......................... 66.00

Model of a lady's high heel shoe, white ground decorated overall w/h.p. blue leafy vines & blossoms, a strip down the front decorated w/a band of scrolls, England, ca. 1700, 6¼" l...........1,540.00

Planter, flaring foot tapering to tall cylindrical sides w/a flaring molded rim, applied C-scroll handles, decorated in blue w/stylized leafy floral vines, England or Europe, 18th c., 5¾" h. (ILLUS. top next page) 715.00

Early Delft Planter

Plate, 8½" d., blue & white, the center w/half-length portraits of William & Mary in crowns & court robes within double blue lines, England, ca. 1690 (restoration to rim, crack, rim chip, some glaze loss to rim) 3,300.00

Plate, 10 3/8" d., the initials "RLM" & "1688" within a tasseled cartouche flanked by winged half-griffins centering a mask & surmounted by a crown, England or Holland, 1688 (rim chips) 1,210.00

DERBY & ROYAL CROWN DERBY

Early Derby Chestnut Basket

William Duesbury, in partnership with John and Christopher Heath, established the Derby Porcelain Works in Derby, England, about 1750. Duesbury soon bought out his partners and in 1770 purchased the Chelsea factory and six years later, the Bow works. Duesbury was succeeded by his son and grandson. Robert Bloor purchased the business about 1814 and managed successfully until illness in 1828 left him unable to exercise control. The "Bloor" Period, however, extends from 1814 until 1848, when the factory closed. Former Derby workmen then resumed

porcelain manufacture in another factory and this nucleus eventually united with a new and distinct venture in 1878 which, after 1890, was known as Royal Crown Derby.

Chestnut basket, cov., the footed base w/deep flaring sides decorated w/gilt-centered rose florettes within a molded honeycomb pattern, the cover (married & restored) w/similar rose florettes within pierced arches surrounding a central oval of turquoise pierced basketweave beneath the green & yellow flower-applied twig handle, the base w/similar applied flower & twig handles (repaired), the sides of the base & gilt-edged cover painted w/purple, iron-red, yellow & brown insects, the base interior & foot rim (minor chip) painted w/small sprigs of iron-red berries & green leaves, ca. 1765, 8¼" l. (ILLUS.) $1,430.00

Figure of 'Discretion,' modeled as Cupid w/pink-tinged wings (one w/a small chip), wearing a turquoise-lined gold drapery (upper end chipped) sprigged in rose & a yellow quiver suspended on a gilt-patterned strap, standing before a gilt-trimmed urn-on-pedestal entwined w/a leafy tree (losses), on a pierced rockwork base mottled in light brown & green, molded w/a small blue rivulet, & applied w/pastel-colored flowers, shells, green leaves & moss, possibly modeled by Pierre Stephan, ca. 1775, 8 5/16" h................ 880.00

Plate, 10¼" d., King's patt., underglaze blue w/gold trim, Royal Crown Derby 65.00

Tea set: cov. teapot, cov. sugar bowl & creamer; Kedleston patt., ca. 1920's, 3 pcs................ 275.00

Tureens & covers, each naturalistically modeled as a partridge on a nest of wheat, grasses & feathers, the plumage in brown & rust respectively, ca. 1770, 6¾" l. overall, pr. (both covers restored, chips to grasses & feathers & one base) 1,100.00

Vases, 6" h., bulbous form w/a tall cylindrical neck, mask handles, gold decoration on cranberry ground, ca. 1880, pr. 467.00

Vases, cov., 12" h., bulbous ovoid body raised on a flaring domical foot & w/a short flaring neck supporting a domed cover w/pointed finial, the neck flanked by a pair of low pierced gilt handles, the cream-glazed body decorated w/large pendent flowers in iron-red & blue w/heavy gilt trim against a shaded cobalt blue ground, Royal Crown Derby, 19th c., pr. 852.50

Derby "Japan" Pattern Vase

Vases, 13 3/8" h., tall urn-form body on a square foot, the sides flanked by long scroll handles, Japan patt., decorated on the front & back w/a cobalt blue ground panel patterned w/gilt dots & reserved w/gilt-edged salmon diamonds & green-dotted circular & tear-shaped floral designs all edged in gold & surrounded by gilt floriate motifs, the sides, waisted neck & foot decorated w/cobalt blue, iron-red, green & gold flowering branches interrupted at the sides by gilt foliate-molded handles (cracked or repaired), the foot (small chips) w/a gold & cobalt blue-bordered edge, ca. 1825-30, pr. (ILLUS. of one) 3,300.00

DOROTHY DOUGHTY BIRDS

These magnificent porcelain birds were created by the talented artist Dorothy Doughty for the Royal Worcester Porcelain Factory in Worcester, England, beginning in 1935. They are life-sized, beautifully colored and crafted with the greatest artistry.

Bewick's Wrens and Yellow Jasmine, ca. 1955, 9 1/3" h., pr. $385.00
Blue-Grey Gnatcatchers, ca. 1955, 10¾" h., pr. (leaf damage) 467.50
Blue-Tit Cock and Pussy Willow in Spring, ca. 1984, 7¾" h., pr. 275.00

Cactus Wrens and Prickly Pear, ca. 1958, 10¼" h., pr. (thorn missing) 550.00
Canyon Wrens with Wild Lupin, ca. 1959, 6¾" h., pr. 550.00
Cardinals, ca. 1950, 9½" h., pr. 495.00
Cerulean Warblers and Red Maple, ca. 1965, 8½" h., pr. 440.00
Chiff Chaff on Hogweed, ca. 1964, 17" h. 330.00
Downy Woodpeckers and Pecans, ca. 1959, 10" h., pr. 440.00
Hooded Warblers and Cherokee Rose, ca. 1961, 10½" h., pr. (minor chips) 550.00
Indigo Buntings and Blackberry Sprays, ca. 1955, 8" h., pr. 275.00
Kingfisher and Autumn Beech, ca. 1964, 11½" h. 330.00
Lark Sparrow with Red Gild and Twinpod Growing in Volcanic Ash, ca. 1966, 5¾" h. 220.00
Lesser White Throats and Wild Rose, ca. 1964, pr. 412.50
Magnolia Warblers and Magnolia, ca. 1957, 13" h., pr. 990.00
Mocking Birds and Peach Blossoms, ca. 1940, 10" h., pr. (minor chips) 330.00
Mountain Bluebirds and Spleenwort Niger, ca. 1959, 8¾" h., pr. 302.50
Oven Birds with Crested Iris and Lady's Slipper, ca. 1960, 9¾" h., pr. 605.00
Parula Warblers and Sweet Bay, ca. 1957, 8¼" h., pr. (one w/base crack) 330.00
Phoebes and Flame Vine, ca. 1958, 10" h., pr. (base hairline, branch off) 440.00
Red-Eyed Vireos and Swamp Azalea, ca. 1954, 7¾" h., pr. 440.00
Redstarts on Gorse, ca. 1968, 10¼" h., pr. 880.00
Robin, ca. 1964, 6½" h. 220.00

Ruby-Throated Hummingbirds

Ruby-Throated Hummingbirds and Fuchsia, ca. 1954, 9¼" h., pr. (ILLUS.) 935.00

Scarlet Tanagers and White Oak, ca.
1956, 11½" h., pr. 330.00
Scissor-Tailed Flycatcher, ca. 1962,
24" l. 330.00
Yellow Throats and Water Hyacinth,
ca. 1959, 11" h., pr. 550.00

DOULTON & ROYAL DOULTON

Doulton & Co., Ltd., was founded in Lambeth, London, about 1858. It was operated there till 1956 and often incorporated the words "Doulton" and "Lambeth" in its marks. Pinder Bourne & Co., Burslem was purchased by the Doultons in 1878 and in 1882 became Doulton & Co., Ltd. It added porcelain to its earthenware production in 1884. The "Royal Doulton" mark has been used since 1902 by this factory, which is still in production. Character jugs and figurines are commanding great attention from collectors at the present time.

ANIMALS & BIRDS
Cat, "Lucky," K 12 . . . .$115.00
Cat, kitten, lying on back, brown,
HN 2579 . . . . 54.00
Cat, kitten, sitting licking hind paw,
HN 2580 . . . . 40.00
Dog, Airedale, HN 996, 8" 750.00
Dog, Alsatian, K 13 . . . . 75.00
Dog, Bulldog, HN 1043 . . . . 325.00
Dog, Bulldog, HN 1045 . . . . 550.00
Dog, Bulldog, brown & white,
HN 1047, small . . . . 125.00 to 150.00
Dog, Bulldog, "Union Jack," British
flag over back, HN 6407, 2 x 4",
2½" h. . . . . 125.00 to 150.00
Dog, Bulldog, sitting, K 1,
2¼" h. . . . . 70.00 to 90.00
Dog, Cairn Terrier, "Charming
Eyes," HN 1035, 3¼" 89.00
Dog, Cairn Terrier, begging,
HN 2589, 4" 59.00
Dog, Character Dog, running w/ball,
HN 1097 . . . . 52.00
Dog, Character Dog, w/brown ball,
HN 1103, 2½" 59.00
Dog, Cocker Spaniel, black & white,
HN 1078, 3½" 99.00
Dog, Cocker Spaniel, golden,
HN 1187, 5" 80.00
Dog, Cocker Spaniel, K 9 . . . . 50.00
Dog, Collie, "Ashstead Applause,"
HN 1058, 5" 199.00
Dog, Collie, "Ashstead Applause,"
HN 1059, 3½" 80.00
Dog, Dachshund, "Shrewd Saint,"
HN 1129, 3" 275.00
Dog, Dachshund, K 17, 2½" h. 55.00

Dog, English Setter, "Maesydd Mus-
tard," HN 1050, 5¼" 75.00
Dog, Foxhound, sitting, K 7,
2½" . . . . .50.00 to 75.00
Dog, Fox Terrier, "Charley Hunter,"
HN 1013, medium 175.00
Dog, Irish setter, HN 1056,
small . . . . .100.00 to 130.00
Dog, St. Bernard, lying down, K 19,
miniature, 1¾" 49.00
Dog, Scottish Terrier, Ch. "Albourne
Arthur," HN 1016, small 125.00
Dog, Sealyham, "Scotia Stylist,"
HN 1032, small 265.00
Dog, Sealyham, K 3, 2¾" 110.00
Dog, Springer Spaniel, HN 2516 . . . . . 250.00
Dog, Springer Spaniel, HN 2517 . . . . . 225.00
Duck, Mallard drake, HN 806 . . . . . . 125.00
Horse, "Merely A Minor," grey,
HN 2531, large . . . . 850.00 to 950.00
Horse, "Merely A Minor," grey,
HN 2567, small 295.00
Horse, "Merely A Minor," brown,
HN 2571, small . . . . 365.00 to 385.00

CHARACTER JUGS

Captain Hook Character Jugs

Apothecary, small, 3½" h. 55.00
'Ard of 'Earing, large,
6" h. . . . . .800.00 to 900.00
'Arriet, tiny, 1¼" h. 175.00
'Arriet, miniature, 2¼" h. 96.00
Auld Mac, tiny, 1¼" h. . . . .150.00 to 200.00
Auld Mac, miniature, 2¼" h. 40.00
Bacchus, small, 3½" h. 38.00
Bacchus, large, 6" h. . . . . . . .75.00 to 100.00
Beefeater, large, w/GR on han-
dle . . . . .100.00 to 150.00
Blacksmith, miniature, 2¼" h. 55.00
Blacksmith, small, 3½" h. 60.00
Bootmaker, small, 3½" h. 60.00
(Sergeant) Buz Fuz, "A" mark,
small, 3½" h. 92.00
Cap'n Cuttle, "A" mark, small,
3½" h. 86.00
Capt. Ahab, large 70.00
Captain Henry Morgan, small,
3½" h. 40.00
Captain Hook, miniature, 2¼" h. . . . 365.00

Captain Hook, small, 3½" h. (ILLUS. right) 425.00
Captain Hook, large, 6" h. (ILLUS. left)............................ 425.00
Cardinal, small, 3½" h............. 95.00
Cardinal, "A" mark, large, 6½" h.................150.00 to 175.00
Cliff Cornell, brown, large 225.00
Clown w/red hair, large, 6" h......3,250.00

Clown with White Hair Jug

Clown w/white hair, large, 6" h. (ILLUS.) ....950.00 to 1,100.00
Dick Turpin, mask on face, horse handle, small, 3½" h. 58.00
Dick Turpin, mask on hat, gun handle, large, 6" h. ....125.00 to 150.00
Drake, "A" mark, large, 5 5/8" h. .. 135.00
Fat Boy, miniature, 2¼" h.......... 75.00
Fortune Teller, large, 6" h.......... 500.00
Friar Tuck, large, 6" h. ....325.00 to 350.00
Gaoler, miniature, 1¼" h. 55.00
Gardener, miniature, 2¼" h....... 75.00
Gardener, small, 3½" h............ 85.00
Gladiator, small, 3½" h....275.00 to 300.00
Gladiator, large, 6" h.............. 500.00
Gondolier, miniature, 2¼" h. 475.00
Gone Away, miniature, 2¼" h...... 50.00
Gone Away, small, 3½" h.......... 60.00
Gone Away, large 90.00
Guardsman, miniature, 2¼" h. 55.00
Guardsman, large, 6" h. 80.00
Gunsmith, large, 6" h. 75.00
Hamlet, large..................... 90.00
Jarge, small, 3½" h. 225.00
Jockey, large, 6" h. ....275.00 to 300.00
John Barleycorn, "A" mark, miniature, 2¼" h..................... 50.00
Johnny Appleseed, large, 6" h....................250.00 to 275.00
John Peel, "A" mark, miniature, 2¼" h.......................... 85.00
John Peel, small, 3½" h. 78.00
John Peel, large, 6" h. ....125.00 to 135.00
John Peel, "A" mark, large, 6" h.... 175.00
Lumberjack, large, 6" h........... 89.00
Mad Hatter, miniature, 2¼" h. 90.00
Mad Hatter, small, 3½" h. ..75.00 to 100.00
Mephistopheles, small, 3½" h......1,200.00

Mephistopheles, large, 6" h.......2,200.00
Mikado, miniature, 2¼" h. 300.00
Mikado, small, 3½" h............. 270.00
Mr. Micawber, tiny, 1¼" h. 94.00
Mr. Micawber, miniature, 2¼" h. 85.00
Mr. Pickwick, "A" mark, large, 6" h. 150.00
Night Watchman, miniature, 2¼" h.......................... 55.00
Night Watchman, large, 6" h. 70.00
Old Charley, tiny, 1¼" h. ..100.00 to 125.00
Old Charley, miniature, 2¼" h...... 30.00
Old Charley, "A" mark, miniature, 2¼" h.......................... 55.00
Old Charley, large, 6" h............ 85.00
Old King Cole, tiny, 1¼" h. 75.00
Old King Cole, small, 3½" h..................100.00 to 125.00
Paddy, "A" mark, miniature, 2½" h.......................... 45.00
Paddy, "A" mark, large, 6" h...................100.00 to 125.00
Parson Brown, small, 3½" h........ 75.00
Parson Brown, large, 6" h. 120.00
Pied Piper, miniature, 2¼" h. 40.00
Pied Piper, large 95.00
Punch & Judy Man, large, 6" h. 550.00
Regency Beau, small, 3½" h........ 550.00
Regency Beau, large, 6" h. ....850.00 to 1,000.00
Robin Hood, "A" mark, miniature, 2¼" h.......................... 60.00
Robin Hood, large, 6" h. 150.00
Robinson Crusoe, small, 3½" h. 60.00
Robinson Crusoe, large, 6" h. 70.00
St. George, small, 3½" h. 100.00
Sairey Gamp, tiny, 1¼" h. 90.00
Sairey Gamp, miniature, 2¼" h..... 50.00
Sairey Gamp, small, 3½" h. 60.00
Sairey Gamp, "A" mark, large 75.00
Sam Johnson, small, 3½" h. 225.00
Sam Johnson, large, 6" h........... 275.00
Sam Weller, miniature, 2¼" h. 55.00
Sam Weller, small, 3½" h. 80.00
Sancho Panza, small, 3½" h. 60.00
Simon the Cellarer, small, 3½" h. .. 65.00
Simon the Cellarer, "A" mark, large, 6" h...................... 145.00
Smuggler, large 80.00
Toby Philpots, small, 3½" h. 55.00
Tony Weller, "A" mark, miniature, 2¼" h.......................... 50.00
Tony Weller, small, 3½" h. 75.00
Tony Weller, large, 6" h............ 130.00
Tony Weller, "A" mark, extra large........................... 200.00
Ugly Duchess, small, 3½" h..................275.00 to 300.00
Ugly Duchess, large, 6" h....................450.00 to 495.00
Veteran Motorist, miniature, 2¼" h.......................... 60.00
Veteran Motorist, large, 6" h. 92.00

Vicar of Bray Jug

Vicar of Bray, large, 6" h.
(ILLUS.) .... 150.00 to 170.00
Walrus & Carpenter, miniature,
2¼" h. 50.00

DICKENSWARE

Bowl, 7" d., Fagin scene 125.00
Charger, Fagin, 13" d. 150.00
Dish, rectangular, Tony Weller
scene 125.00
Napkin ring, Mr. Pickwick 460.00
Pitcher, 3" h., Sam Weller
scene 125.00
Pitcher, 6" h., Old Curiosity Shop ... 120.00
Pitcher, milk, embossed w/Mr. Pick-
wick scene 180.00
Plate, 7½" sq., Tony Weller, signed
"Noke"........................ 125.00
Plate, 10¼" d., Sam Weller 85.00
Plate, 10¼" d., Sergeant Buz Fuz ... 85.00
Plate, chop, 13½" d., Tony Weller .. 165.00
Platter, 18" oval, Dick Swiveller 175.00
Toothpick holder, bust of David
Copperfield 200.00
Vase, 6" h., Sairey Gamp scene 250.00

FIGURINES

Autumn Breezes

Abdullah, HN 2104, yellow chair, orange turban, 1953-62 .... 434.00
A 'Courting, HN 2004, 1947-53 ...... 490.00

Afternoon Tea, HN 1747, pink dress,
1935-82........................ 300.00
Alexandra, HN 2398, 1970-76 .... 188.00
Alice, HN 2158, 1960-80 .... 160.00
Anna, HN 2802, 1976-82 .... 119.00
Annabella, HN 1875, red dress,
1938-49....................... 920.00
Aragorn, HN 2916, tan costume,
1981-84....................... 90.00
At Ease, HN 2473, 1973-79 .... 184.00
Autumn, HN 2087, red dress,
1952-59....................... 575.00
Autumn Breezes, HN 1911, peach
dress, green jacket, 1939-76
(ILLUS.)...................... 250.00
Autumn Breezes, HN 2147, white
dress, black jacket, 1955-71 ..... 325.00
Baby Bunting, HN 2108,
1953-59 ....250.00 to 275.00
Bachelor (The), HN 2319, 1964-75 ... 200.00
Ballerina, HN 2116,
1953-73 ....225.00 to 250.00
Barliman Butterbur, HN 2923,
1982-84....................... 300.00
Beat You To It, HN 2871, 1980-87 ... 395.00
Bess, HN 2002, red cloak,
1947-69 ....250.00 to 275.00
Bilbo, HN 2914, 1980-84 .... 85.00
Blacksmith of Williamsburg,
HN 2240, white shirt, brown hat,
1960-83....................... 225.00
Boatman (The), HN 2417, 1971-87 ... 125.00
Boromir, HN 2918, 1981-84 .... 225.00

The Bride

Bride (The), HN 2166, pale pink
dress, 1956-76 (ILLUS.) 210.00
Bridesmaid (The), HN 2148, cream
dress, 1955-59 .... 195.00
Bridesmaid (The Little), HN 1433,
pale yellow dress, 1930-51 .... 155.00
Bridget, HN 2070, 1951-73 ..225.00 to 250.00
Broken Lance (The), HN 2041,
1949-75 ....375.00 to 400.00
Carolyn, HN 2112, 1953-59 (ILLUS.
top next column).......225.00 to 250.00
Celeste, HN 2237, 1959-71.......... 225.00
Cellist (The), HN 2226, 1960-67 ..... 325.00

Carolyn

Charlotte, HN 2421, 1972-86 . . . . 205.00
Christmas Time, HN 2110,
 1953-67 . . . . 350.00 to 375.00
Clown (The), HN 2890,
 1979-88 . . . . 200.00 to 215.00
Cobbler (The), HN 542, yellow shirt,
 dark green robe, 1922-39 . . . . 550.00
Cobbler (The), HN 1706, green &
 blue striped shirt & hat w/yellow,
 1935-69 . . . . 290.00
Coralie, HN 2307, yellow dress,
 1964-88 . . . . 185.00
Crinoline Lady, HN 650, green &
 white, 1924-38 . . . . 1,000.00
Darling, HN 1319, black base,
 1929-59 . . . . 165.00
Daydreams, HN 1732, light blue
 dress, pink trim, 1935-49 . . . . 920.00

Delphine

Delphine, HN 2136, 1954-67
 (ILLUS.) . . . . 250.00 to 275.00
Easter Day, HN 2039, 1949-69 . . . . 440.00
Elfreda, HN 2078, 1951-55 . . . . 665.00
Eliza, HN 2543, 1974-79 . . . . 275.00 to 300.00
Fat Boy (The), HN 555, blue jacket,
 white scarf, 1923-52 . . . . . 550.00 to 600.00
Frodo, HN 2912, 1980-84 . . . . 90.00
Galadriel, HN 2915, 1981-84 . . . . 90.00
Gandalf, HN 2911, 1980-84 . . . . 225.00

Gentleman from Williamsburg,
 HN 2227, 1960-83 . . . . 160.00
Gimli, HN 2922, 1981-84 . . . . 175.00
Gollum, HN 2913, brown,
 1980-84 . . . . 75.00 to 100.00
Gossips, HN 1429, red dress, white
 dress, 1930-49 . . . . 1,250.00
He Loves Me, HN 2046, 1949-62 . . . . . 135.00
Honey, HN 1909, pink dress,
 1939-49 . . . . 350.00 to 400.00
Innocence, HN 2842, 1979-83 . . . . 135.00
Irene, HN 1621, pale yellow dress,
 1934-51 . . . . 225.00
Jack, HN 2060, 1950-71 . . . . 125.00
Jane, HN 2806, 1983-86 . . . . 250.00
Janice, HN 2022, green dress,
 1949-55 . . . . 394.00
Jill, HN 2061, 1950-71 . . . . 125.00
Karen, HN 1994, red dress,
 1947-55 . . . . 450.00
Kate, HN 2789, white dress,
 1978-87 . . . . 225.00

Lady April

Lady April, HN 1958, red dress,
 1940-59 (ILLUS.) . . . . 275.00 to 300.00
Lady Charmian, HN 1948, green
 dress, red shawl, 1940-73 . . . . 195.00
Lady from Williamsburg, HN 2228,
 1960-83 . . . . 160.00
Lady of the Georgian Period (A),
 HN 41, gold & blue, 10¼" h.,
 1914-38 . . . . 1,250.00
Lambing Time, HN 1890, 1938-80 . . . . 180.00
Leading Lady, HN 2269, 1965-76 . . . . 189.00
Legolas, HN 2917, 1981-84 . . . . 60.00
Lights Out, HN 2662, blue trousers &
 yellow spotted shirt, 1965-69 . . . . . 276.00
Lilac Time, HN 2137,
 1954-69 . . . . 225.00 to 250.00
Lily, HN 1798, white shawl, pink
 dress, 1936-49 . . . . 125.00 to 150.00
Lisa, HN 2310, violet & white dress,
 1969-82 . . . . 120.00
Little Boy Blue, HN 2062,
 1950-73 . . . . 200.00 to 225.00
Loretta, HN 2337, rose-red dress,
 yellow shawl, 1966-80 . . . 125.00 to 150.00

Lorna, HN 2311, green dress, apricot
    shawl, 1965-85 .... 125.00
Lucy Ann, HN 1502, red gown,
    1932-51 .... 150.00
Lucy Locket, HN 524, yellow dress,
    1921-49 .... 425.00
Madonna of the Square, HN 2034,
    light green-blue costume,
    1949-51 .... 650.00
Margaret, HN 1989,
    1947-59 ....350.00 to 375.00
Marguerite, HN 1928, pink dress,
    1940-59 ....350.00 to 400.00
Marietta, HN 1341, black costume,
    red cape, 1929-49 .... 795.00
Marjorie, HN 2788, blue & white
    dress, 1980-84 .... 225.00
Mary Mary, HN 2044, 1949-73 ...... 125.00
Mayor (The), HN 2280,
    1963-71 ....400.00 to 450.00
Melody, HN 2202, 1957-62 .... 195.00
Miss Muffet, HN 1936, red coat,
    1940-67 ....200.00 to 225.00
Mr. Pickwick, HN 1894, 1938-42 .... 195.00
Mrs. Fitzherbert, HN 2007, 1948-53 .. 725.00
Noelle, HN 2179, 1957-67 .... 365.00
Olga, HN 2463, 1972-75 .... 179.00
Omar Khayyam, HN 2247, 1965-83 .. 140.00
Once Upon a Time, HN 2047, pink
    dotted dress, 1949-55 .... 330.00
Orange Vendor (An), HN 1966,
    purple cloak, 6¼" h., 1941-49 .... 800.00
Paisley Shawl, HN 1392, white
    dress, red shawl, 1930-49 .... 485.00
Paisley Shawl, HN 1987, cream
    dress, red shawl, 1946-59 .... 190.00
Pearly Boy, HN 1482, red jacket,
    1931-49 .... 275.00
Pearly Boy, HN 2035, red jacket,
    w/hands clasped, 1949-59 .... 150.00
Pearly Girl, HN 1483, red jacket,
    1931-49 .... 275.00
Peggy, HN 2038, red dress, green
    trim, 1949-79 .... 95.00
Pensive Moments, HN 2704, blue
    dress, 1975-81 .... 175.00
Pied Piper (The), HN 2102, brown
    cloak, grey hat & boots, 1953-76 .. 275.00
Polka (The), HN 2156, pale pink
    dress, 1955-69 ....200.00 to 250.00
Polly Peachum, HN 550, red dress,
    1922-49 .... 350.00
Regal Lady, HN 2709, 1975-83 ...... 150.00
Royal Governor's Cook, HN 2233,
    black dress, white apron,
    1960-83 .... 400.00
St. George, HN 2067, purple, red &
    orange blanket, 1950-76 (ILLUS.
    top next column) 3,150.00
Sairey Gamp, HN 2100, white dress,
    green cape, 1952-67 .... 275.00
Samwise, HN 2925, 1982-84 .... 425.00

St. George

Silversmith of Williamsburg,
    HN 2208, green jerkin,
    1960-83 ....125.00 to 150.00
Skater (The), HN 2117, red & white
    dress, 1953-71 .... 325.00
Soiree, HN 2312, white dress, green
    overskirt, 1967-84 ....150.00 to 175.00
Spring Flower, HN 1807, green skirt,
    grey-blue overskirt, 1937-59 ..... 275.00
Stitch in Time (A), HN 2352,
    1966-80 .... 125.00
Summer, HN 2086, red gown,
    1952-59 .... 350.00

Summer's Day

Summer's Day, HN 2181, 1957-62
    (ILLUS.) 275.00
Suzette, HN 2026, 1949-59 .... 290.00
Sweeting, HN 1935, pink dress,
    1940-73 .... 115.00
Thanksgiving, HN 2446, blue over-
    alls, 1972-76 .... 250.00
Top O' the Hill, HN 1833, green
    dress, 1937-71 .... 190.00
Toymaker (The), HN 2250, 1959-73 .. 265.00
Uriah Heep, HN 554, black jacket &
    trousers, 1923-39 .... 600.00
Victorian Lady (A), HN 728,
    red skirt, purple shawl,
    1925-52 ....275.00 to 300.00
Virginia, HN 1693, yellow dress,
    1935-49 .... 500.00

Votes For Women, HN 2816,
1978-81 . . . . 140.00
Winsome, HN 2220, red dress,
1960-85 . . . . 165.00
Winter, HN 2088, shaded blue skirt,
1952-59 . . . . 335.00

MISCELLANEOUS

Royal Doulton Demitasse Service

Ashpot, figural bust, Old Charley . . . 135.00
Ashpot, figural bust, Parson
Brown 135.00
Ashpot, figural bust, Sairey Gamp . . 135.00
Bowl, 5¾" d., Coaching Days
series 49.50
Bowl, cereal, 6" d., Nursery Rhymes
series, "Simple Simon" 79.50
Bowl, 8" d., 3¾" h., Nautical Histo-
ry series, colorful blue sea battle
scenes inside & out, titled "Battle
of the Nile" 225.00
Bowl, 9" d., Shakespeare Characters
series, "Romeo" 125.00
Bowl, fruit, 11" d., footed, scalloped
rim, decorated w/cottage & wood-
land scene, ca. 1930 . . . . 275.00
Candlestick, Dutch series, haystack
scene, ca. 1906, 6" h. 115.00
Cigarette lighter, table model, Long
John Silver 207.00
Creamer, Gondoliers series 70.00
Demitasse service: cov. coffeepot,
large footed creamer, smaller
footed creamer, sugar bowl,
twelve tea cups & saucers, six
demitasse cups & saucers, twelve
dessert plates & two serving
plates; DeLuxe patt., Art Deco designs on the ovoid bodies, each
piece divided into a mint green &
cream half by a black & platinum
stripe, marked & numbered, ca.
1932, coffeepot 8¼" h., 54 pcs.
(ILLUS. of part) 3,080.00
Jar, cov., Coaching Days series,
5¾" h. 200.00
Jardiniere, light yellow enameled
snowflake hearts, Slater's patent,
ca. 1891-1901, 6½" d., 10" h. 250.00
Loving cup, stoneware, cylindrical,
molded tavern scenes around the

sides, three small 'hound' handles, a two-tone glaze w/a dark
brown rim band above the
tan body, Doulton - Lambeth,
5½" h. 159.50
Pitcher, 7" h., jug-type, English Old
Scenes series, "The Gleaners" 195.00
Pitcher, 7¾" h., stoneware, the tall
ovoid body w/a narrow line-
incised neck, the sides w/relief-
molded reserves bordered
w/scrolls, the front reserve showing the H.M. Stanley Memorial, a
dark brown band of glaze around
the neck & shoulder above a light
tan body, Doulton - Lambeth
marks, late 19th c. (minor letter-
ing damage) 253.00
Pitcher, 8" h., Coaching Days series,
"An Old Jarvey," picture of a
coachman, No. D 3188 . . . . 120.00
Pitcher, 8" h., milk, Gondoliers
series 95.00
Pitcher, 8" h., stoneware, a bulbous
ovoid body below a tall cylindrical
neck w/wide pinched spout &
decorated w/a wide sterling silver
rim band, the body w/relief-
molded tavern scenes, the neck &
shoulder w/a dark brown glaze
above a light tan body, silver rim
w/London hallmarks for 1888-89,
the body w/Doulton - Lambeth
marks 132.00
Pitcher, 9" h., Shakespeare Plays
series, Dogberry's Watch scene,
signed "Noke" 185.00
Pitcher, 9" h., stoneware, a com-
memorative of Columbus' 400th
Anniversary, the tall slightly
tapering cylindrical body molded
w/ring bands around the bottom
& the base of the neck, the body
molded w/crisscross banners & an
oval reserve w/a bust of Columbus, dark brown bands & molded
decoration on a tan ground, ca.
1892, Doulton - Lambeth marks . . . 225.50
Pitcher & bowl set, Blue Willow
patt., 2 pcs. 650.00
Pitcher & bowl set, each decorated
w/a wide continuous landscape
scene around the upper rim,
2 pcs. (ILLUS.) 190.00
Plate, 7" d., Nursery Rhymes series,
"Simple Simon," ca. 1920 . . . . 79.50
Plate, 8" d., Coaching Days series,
scalloped edge 78.00
Plate, 9" d., Desert Scenes series,
D 3192 . . . . 55.00
Plate, 9¼" d., openwork rim, deco-
rated w/yellow daisies outlined in
heavy gold, Doulton - Burslem
mark 175.00

Doulton Pitcher & Bowl Set

Plate, 10" d., Countryside series 55.00
Plate, 10" d., Golfers series, scene
  of a caddy blowing on the ball . . . 325.00
Plate, 10" d., King Arthur's Knights
  series, D 2961 . . . . 110.00
Plate, 10" d., rack-type, "The Ad-
  miral". . . . . .75.00 to 95.00
Plate, 10" d., rack-type, "The
  Cobbler" 68.00
Plate, 10" d., rack-type, "Samuel de
  Champlain" 80.00
Plate, 10" d., rack-type, "The
  Doctor" 65.00
Plate, 10" d., rack-type, "The
  Falconer" 90.00
Plate, 10" d., rack-type, "The
  Parson" 65.00
Plate, 10" d., rack-type, "Shake-
  speare" 110.00
Plate, 10" d., Shakespeare Charac-
  ters series, "Romeo," dated
  "1911" 97.50
Plates, dinner, 10" d., cream bor-
  der, gilt floral decoration,
  stamped mark, set of 12 . . . . 880.00
Plate, 10½" d., Castles and
  Churches series, Hurtsmonceaux
  Castle 49.50
Plate, 10½" d., Castles and
  Churches series, Pembroke
  Castle 92.00
Plate, 10½" d., English Old Scenes
  series, "Gipsies," ca. 1914 . . . . 79.00
Plate, 10½" d., Jackdaw of Rhiems
  series, scene of cardinal & monks
  & jackdaw, titled "And they
  served the Lord Primate on bend-
  ed knee," ca. 1906 . . . . 60.00 to 80.00
Plate, 10½" d., flow blue, Shake-
  speare Plays series, scene with
  Shylock & Portia, floral decoration
  on edge 65.00
Plate, 10½" d., Skating series 135.00
Plate, 11¾" d., round w/sterling sil-
  ver rim band, the center w/a
  polychrome bust portrait titled
  "The Hunting Man," polychrome
  hunt scenes around the edge, the

silver rim engraved "C.F.M." &
  marked "Shreve & Co. Sterling,"
  early 20th c. (some rim batter-
  ing) 60.00
Plate, chop, 13¼" d., Historic Eng-
  land series, "Dr. Johnson at the
  Cheshire Cheese," colorful scene
  of Dr. Johnson sitting at a table . . 245.00
Plate, chop, 13½" d., Robin Hood
  series (Under the Greenwood
  Tree), scene of Maid Marian &
  Friar Tuck 300.00
Salt dip, raised blue tulip decoration
  on blue & green glossy ground,
  green interior, ca. 1910, 2¾" d.,
  1½" h. 125.00
Sandwich tray, Athens series 165.00
Sandwich tray, English Old Scenes
  series, "The Gleaners," 6 x 12" . . . 135.00
Service plates, each painted
  w/colorful birds centered by a
  powder blue border w/floral re-
  serves, 10½" d., set of 12 . . . . . . 275.00
Teapot, cov., ovoid body, Dutch se-
  ries, decorated w/a Dutch harbor
  scene, windmill finial, signed
  "Noke," 9½" l., 5¾" h. 210.00
Teapot, cov., Gondoliers series 145.00
Teapot, cov., Kingsware, Mr. & Mrs.
  Micawber 875.00
Tobacco humidor, cov., stoneware,
  "Tobacco" in relief on one side,
  reverse w/monkey holding pipe,
  in shades of beige w/dark
  brown relief, Doulton - Lam-
  beth mark . . . . .150.00 to 175.00
Toothpick holder, bust of Sairey
  Gamp 295.00
Vase, 3" h., flow blue, Babes in the
  Woods series 225.00
Vase, 5½" h., 2½" d., stoneware,
  slender waisted cylindrical body
  w/flared rim, incised scene of
  twin boys in orange, blue & black,
  titled "The Twins" on the reverse,
  tan ground w/brown trim 175.00
Vase, 6" h., Sung Flambe' glaze,
  collared bulbous neck tapering to
  smaller base, signed "Noke" 350.00
Vase, 7" h., Rouge Flambe' glaze,
  house w/woodland scene 175.00
Vase, 7 3/8" h., stoneware, the bulbous ovoid body below a tall slender neck widely flaring at the rim,
  an incised overall leafy vine & floral design against a background
  of dots all in polychrome against
  a tan ground, dark & light colored
  bands around the neck, marked
  "Art Union of London" & w/Doul-
  ton - Lambeth marks 247.50
Vase, 8" h., flow blue, Babes in the
  Woods series, scene of girl hold-
  ing doll 565.00

Vase, 10 1/8" h., stoneware, the wide ovoid body w/a short cylindrical neck, the body incised w/tall pointed arches each w/a large daisy-like blossom framed by scrolls, scrolls on the shoulder & neck, polychrome decoration w/gilt trim, artist-initialed on base, Doulton - Lambeth marks... 330.00

Vase, 10¼" h., stoneware, a tall ovoid body w/a short flaring neck, the upper half incised w/a beaded swag band below a row of large polychrome flower-filled urns, scattered dots around the lower half, a mottled glaze shading from light greyish blue at the top to dark blue around the lower half, Doulton - Lambeth marks, late 19th c. 258.50

Vases, 10 1/8" h., 3¾" d., stoneware, slightly swelled cylindrical body tapering slightly to a wide cylindrical neck, tapestry-like design of stylized white & aqua flowers w/gold trim on a beige tapestry ground, mottled grey neck & shoulder, late 19th c., pr. 245.00

Vases, 15½" h., pottery, baluster-shaped, decorated w/conventionalized floral decoration at the shoulder in pink & purple against a mottled blue ground, the neck glazed greyish green, impressed company marks & artist's initials, pr. 880.00

Vases, 16" h., "lace body" type, footed ovoid body w/a trumpet neck, the lower body w/a trumpet neck, the lower body w/lace design, the shoulder & neck in green w/green & white scattered blossoms, impressed marks, pr. 143.00

DRESDEN

Dresden-type porcelain evolved from wares made at the nearby Meissen Porcelain Works early in the 18th century. "Dresden" and "Meissen" are often used interchangeably for later wares. "Dresden" has become a generic name for the kind of porcelains produced in Dresden and certain other areas of Germany but perhaps should be confined to the wares made in the city of Dresden.

Basket, oblong ruffled reticulated body w/applied blue & pink flowers, large loop handle w/applied flowers, four scroll feet, 4½ x 7½" $125.00

Bowl, 10½" d., open handled, footed, reticulated sides w/applied flowers 125.00

Candelabra, three-light, two cupids hold floral branches, multicolored applied flowers, marked "Unterweissbach, Thuringer," 11½" h., pr. 695.00

Compote, open, 14 3/8" h., deep round bowl w/scroll-molded reticulated sides w/applied blossoms, on a columnar pedestal base surrounded by four children in peasant costume playing Ring Around the Rosie, on a scroll-molded round base w/applied blossoms, made by Von Schierholz, ca. 1915-30 (minor floral chips) 245.00

Cup & saucer, h.p. cupids, lambs & rabbits, trimmed w/a gold & cobalt blue beading 165.00

Demitasse set: cov. demitasse pot, sugar bowl, creamer w/underplate, tray & 10 cups & saucers; scenic decoration in gold on creamy white ground, marked "Dresden 369W," 25 pcs. 2,400.00

Figure of a Victorian girl, standing wearing a yellow bonnet & crinoline dress in red w/tiers of applied white lace, trimmed w/white & pink flowers, 8" h. 290.00

Figure group, a lady in a lace dress seated w/a dog on a sofa pillow at her feet, early 20th c., 7½" h. 80.00

Model of a watering can w/a baroque floral loop double handle & fancy spout, applied pink & blue flowers centering a baroque floral panel, 10 x 10½" 160.00

Plaque, rectangular, decorated w/a scene of a pair of lovers in a forest, the man carving his lover's initials into a tree, artist-signed, framed, 5 1/8 x 7½" 550.00

Plates, luncheon, 10" d., reticulated rim, light blue border & gilt floral details, stamped mark, set of 10 .... 1,210.00

Wall pockets, semi-reclining cupid supporting a container w/flared sides & a pointed crest pierced for hanging, overall h.p. floral decoration, 7" w., 9" h., pr. 495.00

FIESTA

Fiesta dinnerware was made by the Homer Laughlin China Company of Newell, West Virginia, from the 1930's until the early 1970's. The brilliant colors of this inexpensive pottery have attracted numerous collectors. On February 28, 1986, Laughlin reintroduced the popular Fiesta line with minor changes in the shapes of a few pieces and a contemporary color range. The effect of this new production on the Fiesta collecting market is yet to be determined.

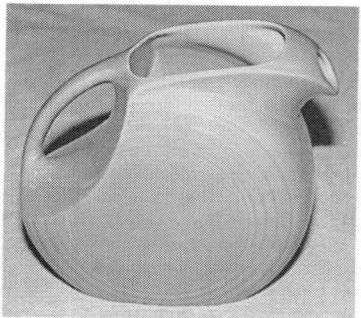

Fiesta Disc-Type Pitcher

Ashtray, forest green	$52.00
Ashtray, grey	65.00
Ashtray, medium green	124.00
Ashtray, rose	52.00
Bowl, individual fruit, 4¾" d., grey	22.00
Bowl, individual fruit, 4¾" d., medium green	318.00
Bowl, individual fruit, 4¾" d., yellow	16.00
Bowl, individual fruit, 5½" d., chartreuse	24.50
Bowl, individual fruit, 5½" d., medium green	56.00
Bowl, individual fruit, 5½" d., red	24.50
Bowl, individual fruit, 5½" d., turquoise	17.50
Bowl, dessert, 6" d., forest green	35.00
Bowl, dessert, 6" d., grey	37.50
Bowl, dessert, 6" d., red	38.00
Bowl, dessert, 6" d., turquoise	30.00
Bowl, individual salad, 7½" d., medium green	73.00
Bowl, individual salad, 7½" d., red	58.00
Bowl, nappy, 8½" d., cobalt blue	31.00
Bowl, nappy, 8½" d., forest green	34.00
Bowl, nappy, 8½" d., ivory	25.50
Bowl, nappy, 8½" d., yellow	24.00
Bowl, nappy, 9½" d., ivory	42.50
Bowl, nappy, 9½" d., light green	33.00
Bowl, nappy, 9½" d., grey	40.00
Bowl, salad, 9½" d., cobalt blue	40.00
Bowl, salad, 9½" d., light green	28.00
Bowl, fruit, 11¾" d., ivory	110.00
Bowl, fruit, 11¾" d., red	141.00
Bowl, cream soup, chartreuse	47.00
Bowl, cream soup, cobalt blue	38.00
Bowl, cream soup, rose	53.00
Bowl, cream soup, yellow	26.00

Bowl, salad, large, footed, cobalt blue	260.00
Bowl, salad, large, footed, light green	212.00
Bowl, salad, large, footed, turquoise	245.00
Cake plate, 10" d., cobalt blue	525.00
Candleholders, bulb-type, cobalt blue, pr.	62.00
Candleholders, bulb-type, ivory, pr.	48.50
Candleholders, bulb-type, turquoise, pr.	53.00
Candleholders, bulb-type, yellow, pr.	55.00
Candleholders, tripod-type, red, pr.	350.00
Candleholders, tripod-type, turquoise, pr.	336.00
Carafe, cov., cobalt blue	153.00
Carafe, cov., red	174.00
Casserole, cov., two-handled, cobalt blue, 10" d.	125.00
Casserole, cov., two-handled, grey, 10" d.	240.00
Casserole, cov., two-handled, ivory, 10" d.	105.00
Casserole, cov., two-handled, red, 10" d.	133.00
Casserole, cov., two-handled, rose, 10" d.	174.00
Casserole, cov., two-handled, yellow, 10" d.	82.00
Coffeepot, cov., demitasse, stick handle, ivory	285.00
Coffeepot, cov., demitasse, stick handle, turquoise	280.00
Coffeepot, cov., demitasse, stick handle, yellow	200.00
Coffeepot, cov., chartreuse	225.00
Coffeepot, cov., light green	128.00
Coffeepot, cov., red	145.00
Coffeepot, cov., rose	350.00
Coffeepot, cov., turquoise	100.00
Compote, 12" d., low, footed, ivory	72.00
Compote, 12" d., low, footed, light green	80.00
Compote, 12" d., low, footed, yellow	85.00
Compote, sweetmeat, high stand, cobalt blue	42.00
Compote, sweetmeat, high stand, ivory	40.00
Compote, sweetmeat, high stand, turquoise	38.00
Creamer, individual size, light green	40.00
Creamer, individual size, yellow	50.00
Creamer, stick handle, cobalt blue	28.00
Creamer, stick handle, red	27.00
Creamer, cobalt blue	13.00
Creamer, forest green	24.00
Creamer, turquoise	16.00

Cup & saucer, demitasse, stick handle, chartreuse.................. 200.00
Cup & saucer, demitasse, stick handle, forest green 195.00
Cup & saucer, demitasse, stick handle, light green 44.00
Cup & saucer, demitasse, stick handle, red 56.00
Cup & saucer, demitasse, stick handle, rose 266.00
Cup & saucer, demitasse, stick handle, yellow 41.00
Cup & saucer, ring handle, cobalt blue 30.00
Cup & saucer, ring handle, ivory 22.00
Cup & saucer, ring handle, light green 21.00
Cup & saucer, ring handle, rose 32.00
Egg cup, chartreuse 112.00
Egg cup, grey.................... 122.00
Egg cup, ivory 34.00
Egg cup, turquoise 29.00
Fork, cobalt blue (Kitchen Kraft) 92.50
Fork, light green (Kitchen Kraft) 59.00
Fork, yellow (Kitchen Kraft) 78.00
Gravy boat, forest green 45.00
Gravy boat, medium green 135.00
Gravy boat, red 45.00
Gravy boat, turquoise 25.00
Marmalade jar, cov., light green ... 150.00
Marmalade jar, cov., turquoise 127.00
Mixing bowl, nest-type, red, size No. 1, 5" d. 103.00
Mixing bowl, nest-type, yellow, size No. 1, 5" d. 55.00
Mixing bowl, nest-type, ivory, size No. 2, 6" d. 47.50
Mixing bowl, nest-type, yellow, size No. 2, 6" d. 42.00
Mixing bowl, nest-type, red, size No. 3, 7" d. 58.00
Mixing bowl, nest-type, yellow, size No. 3, 7" d. 40.50
Mixing bowl, nest-type, cobalt blue, size No. 4, 8" d. 62.50
Mixing bowl, nest-type, ivory, size No. 5, 9" d. 100.00
Mixing bowl, nest-type, red, size No. 5, 9" d. 63.00
Mixing bowl, nest-type, light green, size No. 6, 10" d. 82.50
Mixing bowl, nest-type, red, size No. 6, 10" d. 122.00
Mixing bowl, nest-type, cobalt blue, size No. 7, 11½" d. 295.00
Mixing bowl, nest-type, light green, size No. 7, 11½" d. 143.00
Mixing bowl, nest-type, red, size No. 7, 11½" d. 185.00
Mug, cobalt blue 53.00
Mug, ivory...................... 49.00
Mug, medium green 78.00
Mug, turquoise................... 40.00
Mug, yellow 42.00

Mug, Tom & Jerry style, grey 53.00
Mug, Tom & Jerry style, ivory/gold 33.00
Mug, Tom & Jerry style, turquoise .. 46.00
Mustard jar, cov., cobalt blue 146.00
Mustard jar, cov., ivory 122.00
Mustard jar, cov., light green 117.00
Onion soup bowl, cov., cobalt blue 335.00
Onion soup bowl, cov., ivory ....400.00 to 425.00
Pie server, cobalt blue (Kitchen Kraft) 59.00
Pie server, red.................... 53.00
Pitcher, jug-type, chartreuse, 2 pt... 86.00
Pitcher, jug-type, grey, 2 pt. 83.00
Pitcher, jug-type, rose, 2 pt. 84.00
Pitcher, jug-type, turquoise, 2 pt. .. 38.00
Pitcher, juice, disc-type, chartreuse, 30 oz............................ 100.00
Pitcher, juice, disc-type, grey, 30 oz............................ 130.00
Pitcher, juice, disc-type, red, 30 oz............................ 275.00
Pitcher, juice, disc-type, yellow, 30 oz............................ 30.00
Pitcher, water, disc-type, grey 171.00
Pitcher, water, disc-type, ivory 70.00
Pitcher, water, disc-type, light green 59.00
Pitcher, water, disc-type, red (ILLUS.)........................ 105.00
Pitcher, w/ice lip, globular, cobalt blue, 2 qt. 100.00
Pitcher, w/ice lip, globular, ivory, 2 qt. 95.00
Pitcher, w/ice lip, globular, red, 2 qt. 110.00
Pitcher, w/ice lip, globular, yellow, 2 qt. 76.00
Plate, 6" d., chartreuse 5.00
Plate, 6" d., grey 5.50
Plate, 6" d., ivory 4.00
Plate, 6" d., medium green 12.00
Plate, 6" d., turquoise 3.50
Plate, 7" d., cobalt blue 8.00
Plate, 7" d., ivory 6.50
Plate, 7" d., light green........... 7.50
Plate, 7" d., rose................ 8.50
Plate, 9" d., forest green 11.00
Plate, 9" d., ivory 8.00
Plate, 9" d., light green 7.50
Plate, 9" d., medium green 34.00
Plate, 9" d., red 14.00
Plate, 9" d., yellow.............. 7.50
Plate, 10" d., chartreuse 28.50
Plate, 10" d., forest green 27.50
Plate, 10" d., grey 34.00
Plate, 10" d., rose............... 33.00
Plate, 10" d., yellow 19.00
Plate, 10" d., calendar, ivory (1955) 28.00
Plate, grill, 10½" d., chartreuse 35.00
Plate, grill, 10½" d., ivory 25.00

Plate, grill, 10½" d., light green.... 23.00
Plate, grill, 11½" d., yellow........ 40.00
Plate, chop, 13" d., chartreuse 32.00
Plate, chop, 13" d., forest green.... 56.00
Plate, chop, 13" d., ivory 23.00
Plate, chop, 13" d., red 24.00
Plate, chop, 13" d., rose 52.00
Plate, chop, 15" d., grey 125.00
Plate, chop, 15" d., light green 30.00
Plate, chop, 15" d., red 51.00
Plate, chop, 15" d., turquoise 32.00
Platter, 12" oval, cobalt blue 24.00
Platter, 12" oval, forest green 26.00
Platter, 12" oval, light green 20.00
Platter, 12" oval, turquoise......... 18.00
Relish tray w/five inserts, cobalt
  blue ....250.00 to 275.00
Relish tray w/five inserts, light
  green 113.00
Relish tray w/five inserts, multi-
  colored.............. 127.00
Salt & pepper shakers, chartreuse,
  pr............................... 25.00
Salt & pepper shakers, forest green,
  pr............................... 32.00
Salt & pepper shakers, rose, pr..... 34.00
Salt & pepper shakers, yellow, pr. .. 15.00
Soup plate w/flange rim, char-
  treuse, 8" d..................... 32.00
Soup plate w/flange rim, forest
  green, 8" d. 34.00
Soup plate w/flange rim, light
  green, 8" d. 26.00
Soup plate w/flange rim, medium
  green, 8" d. 67.00
Soup plate w/flange rim, red,
  8" d............................ 29.00
Soup plate w/flange rim, yellow,
  8" d............................ 23.00
Spoon, cobalt blue (Kitchen Kraft) .. 80.00
Spoon, red (Kitchen Kraft) 62.00
Sugar bowl, cov., chartreuse 34.00
Sugar bowl, cov., cobalt blue....... 25.00
Sugar bowl, cov., red.............. 34.00
Sugar bowl, cov., yellow 24.00
Syrup pitcher w/original lid, ivory .. 200.00
Syrup pitcher w/original lid, light
  green 192.00
Syrup pitcher w/original lid,
  yellow 182.00
Teapot, cov., forest green, medium
  size (6 cup) 210.00
Teapot, cov., light green, medium
  size (6 cups) 95.00
Teapot, cov., red, medium size
  (6 cup) 132.00
Teapot, cov., rose, medium size
  (6 cup) 214.00
Teapot, cov., cobalt blue, large size
  (8 cup) 150.00
Teapot, cov., turquoise, large size
  (8 cup) 96.00
Tray, Figure 8, turquoise........... 193.00
Tumbler, juice, cobalt blue, 5 oz. ... 27.00

Tumbler, juice, light green, 5 oz. ... 18.00
Tumbler, juice, rose, 5 oz. 30.00
Tumbler, juice, yellow, 5 oz. 17.00
Tumbler, water, cobalt blue,
  10 oz........................... 43.00
Tumbler, water, light green,
  10 oz........................... 38.00
Tumbler, water, turquoise, 10 oz.... 38.50
Tumbler, water, yellow, 10 oz. 35.00
Utility tray, cobalt blue 34.00
Utility tray, red 28.00
Utility tray, yellow 22.00
Vase, bud, 6½" h., cobalt blue 65.00
Vase, bud, 6½" h., light green 42.00
Vase, 8" h., ivory 334.00
Vase, 8" h., yellow 314.00
Vase, 10" h., cobalt blue.......... 462.00
Vase, 10" h., ivory 428.00
Vase, 10" h., red................ 500.00
Vase, 12" h., light green.......... 507.00

FLOW BLUE

Flowing Blue wares, usually shortened to Flow Blue, were made at numerous potteries in Staffordshire, England and elsewhere. They are decorated with a blue that smudged lightly or ran in the firing. The same type of color flow is also found in certain wares decorated in green, purple and sepia. Patterns were given specific names, which accompany the listings here.

ALASKA (W. H. Grindley, ca. 1891)
Butter pat $34.50
Dinner service for 12 w/serving
  pieces, 95 pcs. 3,900.00
Plate, 7¾" d.................... 35.00
Plate, 9" d..................... 55.00
Plate, 10" d.................... 65.00
Platter, 14" l. oval 135.00
Soup plate w/flanged rim,
  9" d...................55.00 to 65.00
Vegetable bowl, open,
  7½ x 10¼" d................. 80.00

ALBANY (W. H. Grindley, ca. 1899)
Cup & saucer 75.00
Gravy boat 75.00
Plate, 8¾" d................... 45.00
Platter, 11¾" l................. 125.00
Sugar bowl, cov. 165.00

AMOY (Davenport, dated 1844)
Creamer 475.00
Plate, 7¼" d.............75.00 to 85.00
Plate, 8¼" d.................. 105.00
Plate, 9½ to 10½" d. .....125.00 to 135.00
Platter, 10 x 16" 400.00
Sauce dish, 5" d. 72.50
Saucer 40.00

Teapot, cov., 10" h. 375.00
Vegetable bowl, open, 8¼" d. 250.00
Waste bowl, 7" d., 3½" h. 145.00

ARABESQUE (T. J. & J. Mayer, ca. 1845)
Plate, 7½" d. 60.00
Plate, 10¾" d. 125.00
Platter, 10¼ x 13 3/8". 275.00

ARGYLE (W. H. Grindley, ca. 1896)

Argyle Cup & Saucer

Butter pat 42.50
Cup & saucer (ILLUS.) 65.00
Plate, 8" d. 45.00
Plate, 9" d. 65.00
Platter, 7¾ x 11¼" 145.00
Platter, 15" l. 205.00
Platter, 17" l. . . . . 225.00 to 250.00
Sauce dish. 33.00
Sauce tureen, cov. 250.00
Soup plate w/flanged rim, 8¾" d. . . . 77.00

ASHBURTON (W. H. Grindley, ca. 1891)
Butter pat 22.50
Creamer 120.00
Gravy boat 95.00
Plate, 10" d. . . . . 75.00 to 85.00
Vegetable bowl, cov. 275.00

BEAUFORT (W. H. Grindley, ca. 1903)
Bone dish 65.00
Platter, 7¼ x 10" 110.00
Platter, 10 x 14" 150.00
Platter, 11¼ x 16¼" 175.00
Soup plate w/flanged rim, 10" d. . . . 55.00
Vegetable bowl, open, 10" d. 115.00

BEAUTIES OF CHINA (Mellor, Venables & Co., ca. 1845)
Pitcher, 2 qt. 750.00
Plate, 9½" d. 80.00
Platter, 14¾" d. 395.00
Soup plate w/flanged rim, 11" d. . . . 130.00

BELMONT (Alfred Meakin, ca. 1891)
Bone dish, 4½ x 6". 52.50

Creamer & sugar bowl, pr. 275.00
Shaving mug. 185.00

BENTICK (Cauldon, ca. 1905)

Bentick Plate

Compote, 9½" d., two-handled 250.00
Cup & saucer, demitasse 45.00
Plate, 6½" d. . . . . 30.00 to 40.00
Plate, 10" d. (ILLUS.) 65.00
Waste bowl 125.00

BLUE ROSE (W. H. Grindley, ca. 1900)
Bowl, 5" d. 35.00
Bowl, cereal, 6½" d. 40.00
Plate, 6" d. 35.00
Plate, 8" d. 42.50
Sauce dish 32.00

BOLINGBROKE, THE (Ridgways, ca. 1909)
Bone dish 45.00
Creamer, 4" h. 135.00
Plate, 10" d. 75.00

BROOKLYN (Johnson Bros., ca. 1900)
Butter pat 30.00
Cup & saucer 67.00
Plate, 10" d. 68.00

BURLEIGH (Burgess & Leigh, ca. 1903)
Sauce dish 30.00
Sauce tureen 190.00
Soup plate w/flanged rim 75.00

CANDIA (Cauldon Ltd., ca. 1910)
Plate, 10" d. 80.00
Platter, 8¾" l. 135.00
Soup plate w/flanged rim,
    10½" d. 100.00

CANTON (John Maddock, ca. 1850)
Creamer 295.00
Plate, 11" d. 95.00
Platter, 13½ x 18" 595.00

CASHMERE (Ridgway & Morley, G.L. Ashworth, et al., 1840's on)
Plate, 8" d. 125.00

Plate, 9¾" d. 140.00
Platter, 10 x 13" 450.00

CELTIC (W. H. Grindley, ca. 1897)
Cup & saucer 82.50
Pitcher, 7½" h. 250.00
Plate, 9" d. 67.00

CHAPOO (John Wedge Wood, ca. 1850)
Cup & saucer 165.00
Plate, 9 3/8" d. 138.00
Platter, 8¼ x 11", octagonal 235.00
Sugar bowl, cov. 375.00
Toddy plate 55.00

CLAREMONT (Johnson Bros., ca. 1891)
Cup & saucer, handleless 95.00
Gravy boat 115.00
Plate, 7¾" d. 55.00

CLARISSA (Johnson Bros., ca. 1900)

Clarissa Covered Tureen

Cup & saucer, demitasse 95.00
Soup plate w/flanged rim, 9" d. 45.00
Tureen, cov. (ILLUS.) 195.00

CLAYTON (Johnson Bros., ca. 1902)
Bowl, soup 35.00
Butter pat 25.00
Creamer 135.00
Cup & saucer 75.00
Gravy boat w/underplate 135.00
Oyster bowl 100.00
Plate, 8" d. 38.00
Plate, 9" d. 48.00
Plate, 10" d. 60.00
Sauce dish 32.50
Vegetable bowl, cov. 225.00
Vegetable bowl, open, 9½" d. 110.00
Vegetable bowl, open, 7¼ x 9½" . . 75.00

COLONIAL (J. & G. Meakin, ca. 1891)
Plate, 9" d. 65.00
Soup tureen, cov. 395.00
Teapot, cov. 350.00
Vegetable bowl, cov. 225.00

CONWAY (New Wharf Pottery, ca. 1891)
Bowl, 9¼" d. 87.50
Platter, 10¾" l. 125.00
Sauce dish 32.50
Vegetable bowl, open, round 87.50

DAVENPORT (Wood & Sons, ca. 1907)
Butter pat 20.00
Plate, 7" d. 45.00
Plate, 9" d. 65.00

DELAMERE (Henry Alcock, ca. 1900)
Cup & saucer 75.00
Plate, 7" d. 40.00
Platter, 16" l. 250.00
Vegetable bowl, cov. 210.00

DOREEN (W. H. Grindley, ca. 1891)
Chamber pot, cov. 225.00
Pitcher, 7½" h. 190.00
Shaving mug 70.00
Toothbrush holder (small hairline on
 inside of lip) 120.00
Vegetable bowl, cov., hexagonal . . . 160.00

DUCHESS (W. H. Grindley, ca. 1891)
Butter pat 32.00
Creamer & sugar bowl, pr. 225.00
Cup & saucer 85.00
Plate, 8" to 9" d. . . . . 40.00 to 45.00
Plate, 10" d. 65.00
Sauce dish 40.00
Vegetable bowl, cov., oval 195.00

ECLIPSE (Johnson Bros., ca. 1891)
Plate, 9" d. 50.00
Platter, 10¾ x 14¼" 210.00
Vegetable bowl, cov. 210.00

EXCELSIOR (Thomas Fell, ca. 1850)

Excelsior Plate

Cup plate 100.00
Plate, 10" d. (ILLUS.) . . . . 95.00 to 115.00
Soup tureen, cov., large 2,500.00

FAIRY VILLAS - 3 Styles (W. Adams, ca. 1891)
Bowl, soup 62.00
Cup & saucer 70.00
Plate, 7" to 8" d. . . . . 39.00 to 45.00
Platter, 11¾" l. 165.00
Vegetable dish, cov., 10 x 12",
 7½" h. 350.00

FORMOSA (Thos., John & Joseph Mayer, ca. 1850)
Bowl, potato, 11" d. 415.00
Honey dish 60.00
Plate, 9¾" d. 120.00
Platter, 8 x 10 5/8". 275.00
Vegetable bowl, 10½" l. 385.00

GAINSBOROUGH (Ridgways, ca. 1905)
Bowl, 9½" d. .110.00
Butter pat 34.00
Plate, 9" d. 85.00
Platter, 12 x 16" 135.00
Tureen, cov., octagonal 325.00

GENEVA (Royal Doulton, 1906 & 1907)
Cup & saucer 65.00
Pitcher & bowl set, 2 pcs. 1,000.00
Plate, 7½" d. 38.00
Plate, 10½" d. 65.00
Soup plate w/flanged rim 140.00
Soup tureen, cov. 395.00
Vases, 5½" h., pr. 350.00

GIRONDE (W.H. Grindley, ca. 1891)

Gironde Cup & Saucer
Bone dish 45.00
Bowl, berry, 5" d. 35.00
Bowl, soup, 7¾" d. 40.00
Cup & saucer (ILLUS.) 70.00
Gravy boat & undertray, 2 pcs. 145.00
Pitcher, milk. 225.00
Plate, 6½" d. 35.00
Plate, 8" d. 45.00
Plate, 9" d. 55.00
Plate, 10" d. 70.00
Platter, 10¾ x 15¼" 150.00
Platter, 12 x 17" 265.00
Sauce dish 30.00
Vegetable bowl, open, 9" d. 85.00

GRACE (W.H. Grindley, ca. 1897)
Bowl, 6¼" d. 36.00
Butter pat 35.00
Gravy boat 95.00
Plate, 8" d. 45.00
Sauce dish, 5 3/8" d. 30.00

Tureen, cover & underplate, oval,
the set 150.00
Vegetable bowl, open,
7¾ x 10 1/8" 125.00
Vegetable bowl, open, 10½" d. 110.00

GRENADA (Henry Alcock & Co., ca. 1891)
Butter pat 35.00
Cup & saucer 70.00
Platter, 12 x 17" 125.00

HAMILTON (John Maddock & Sons, ca. 1896)
Pitcher, 6½" h. 225.00
Platter, 12½" l. 110.00
Platter, 17" l. 150.00
Sauce tureen w/undertray 225.00

HINDUSTAN (John Maddock, ca. 1855)
Bowl, 9½" d. 195.00
Plate, 6¼" d. 55.00
Plate, 10¾" d. 135.00
Platter, 7¾" l. 195.00
Platter, 13½" l. 325.00

HOLLAND (Johnson Bros., ca. 1891)

Holland Plate
Bowl, berry, 4¾" d. 35.00
Creamer & cov. sugar bowl, pr. 300.00
Gravy boat 97.50
Plate, 6½" d. 35.00
Plate, 9" d. 47.00
Plate, 10" d. (ILLUS.) 78.00
Soup tureen, cov. 395.00
Vegetable bowl, open, 8½" d. 95.00

INDIAN (possibly F. & R. Pratt, ca. 1840)
Creamer 400.00
Cup & saucer, handled. 125.00
Cup & saucer, handleless 130.00
Plate, 7" d. 40.00
Plate, 8¼" d. 78.00
Plate, 9¾" d. 110.00
Platter, 11¾ x 15" 300.00
Relish 175.00
Sauce dish. 55.00

INDIAN STONE (E. Walley, ca. 1850)
Plate, 7½" d. 70.00

Plate, 10½" d. 125.00
Vegetable bowl, cov. 450.00

IRIS (Arthur Wilkinson - Royal Staffordshire Potteries, ca. 1907)
Bowl, soup, 8" d. 30.00
Cup & saucer 65.00
Egg cup 75.00
Teacup & saucer 60.00

JANETTE (W.H. Grindley, ca. 1897)

Janette Sugar Bowl

Butter pat 30.00
Plate, 8¾" d. 45.00
Sugar bowl, cov., 6½" h. (ILLUS.) . . . 130.00
Vegetable tureen, cov. 225.00

KELVIN (Alfred Meakin, ca. 1891)
Butter pat 32.50
Creamer 175.00
Soup tureen, cover & undertray, the
    set. 550.00

LA BELLE (Wheeling Pottery, ca. 1900)

La Belle Chop Plate

Bowl, 9" sq., 2" h. 125.00
Bowl, 13½" d., helmet-shaped 395.00
Butter pat 45.00
Celery dish 80.00
Charger, 12¾" d. 295.00
Pitcher, 7" h. 450.00
Plate, chop, 11½" d. (ILLUS.) 135.00
Sauce dish 30.00
Syrup pitcher & underplate, 2 pcs. . . 325.00

Vegetable bowl, open, leaf-shaped,
    9" d. 195.00

LADAS (Ridgways, ca. 1905)
Gravy boat w/underplate 150.00
Plates, 8" d., set of 6 . . . . 300.00
Plates, 9" d., set of 9 . . . . 540.00
Platter, 12 x 16" 225.00
Soup plates w/flanged rim, 9" d.,
    set of 12 . . . . 720.00
Vegetable bowl, cov., oval 225.00

LANCASTER (New Wharf Pottery, ca. 1891)
Cup & saucer 75.00
Pitcher, 5" h. 175.00
Plate, 9" d. 55.00

LINDA (John Maddock & Sons Ltd., ca. 1896)
Bone dish 55.00
Creamer, 5¼" h. 125.00
Cup & saucer, demitasse 60.00
Gravy boat 95.00
Pitcher, 5½" h. 195.00
Plate, 6" d. 35.00
Plate, 8" d. 40.00
Plate, 9½" to 10" d. 65.00
Platter, 9¼ x 13" 66.00
Punch cup 55.00
Vegetable bowl, cov. 190.00

LORNE (W.H. Grindley, ca. 1900)
Butter pat 38.00
Plate, 6½" d. 25.00
Plate, 10" d. 70.00
Platter, 11½ x 16 1/8" 185.00
Tureen, cov. 200.00
Vegetable bowl, open, 7 x 9¾" 95.00
Waste bowl 55.00

LORRAINE (Ridgways, ca. 1905)
Bone dish 30.00
Butter pat 25.00
Plate, 9¾" d. 45.00
Waste bowl 75.00

MADRAS (Doulton & Co., ca. 1900)
Cup & saucer 75.00
Dinner service: six 10½" d. plates,
    six 9½" d. plates, six 7½"
    plates, 13 x 15¼" platter, 10" d.
    open vegetable bowl, oblong cov.
    vegetable bowl, round cov. vege-
    table bowl & two 9" d. cookie
    plates, 24 pcs. 1,500.00
Pitcher, 7" h. 195.00
Plate, 5¾" d. 45.00
Plate, 9½" d. 78.00
Plate, 10½" d. 85.00
Platter, 12½ x 15 1/8" 220.00
Sauce dish, 4¾" d. 35.00
Vegetable bowl, cov., round 215.00

MANILLA (Podmore, Walker & Co., ca. 1845)
Bowl, soup 195.00
Plate, 8½" d. 87.50
Plate, 9¾" d. 95.00
Platter, 16" l. 695.00

MARIE (W.H. Grindley, ca. 1891)
Butter dish, cov. 290.00
Creamer 165.00
Gravy boat & underplate, 2 pcs. 145.00
Vegetable bowl, cov. 230.00

MELROSE (Doulton, ca. 1891)
Creamer, 4" h. 105.00
Platter, 8 x 11" 120.00
Platters, nested, 8½ x 12", 10 x 14",
   12 x 16" & 13 x 18", set of 4 ..... 650.00
Sauce tureen & underplate, 2 pcs. ... 395.00
Vegetable bowl, cov. 175.00

MILAN (W.H. Grindley, ca. 1893)
Plate, 8" d. 40.00
Plate, 9" d. 45.00
Plate, 10" d. 65.00
Sauce dish 32.00
Soup plate w/flanged rim, 8¾" d. ... 40.00

MURIEL (Upper Hanley Potteries, ca. 1895)
Creamer 115.00
Gravy boat 95.00
Plate, 10" d. 75.00
Vegetable bowl, open, 10" d. 115.00

NEOPOLITAN (Johnson Bros., ca. 1900)
Bone dish 35.00
Butter pat 30.00
Dinner service: eight each 10", 9" &
   7" d. plates, butter pats, bone
   dishes & cups & saucers, seven
   sauce dishes & one each cov. butter dish w/drain insert, round
   cov. vegetable bowl, oval cov.
   vegetable bowl, 9" d. open
   vegetable bowl, cov. sauce tureen
   w/underplate, relish dish,
   8 x 10½" platter, 9 x 12¼"
   platter & 11 x 14¼" platter, the
   set 2,975.00
Plate, 10" d. 70.00
Platter, 10½ x 14" 150.00

NON PAREIL (Burgess & Leigh, ca. 1891)
Bowl, 6½" d. 45.00
Cup & saucer 105.00
Egg cup 195.00
Plate, 7¾" d. 51.00
Plate, 9¾" d. 90.00
Plate, 11" d., two-handled 210.00
Platter, 12¼ x 15½" 370.00
Platter, 15¾" l. 350.00
Sauce ladle 475.00
Vegetable bowl, open, 8½" d. 95.00
Waste bowl 110.00

NORMANDY (Johnson Bros., ca. 1900)
Butter pat 35.00
Creamer & cov. sugar bowl, pr.
   (very minor chip on inside rim of
   creamer) 300.00
Cup & saucer 72.00
Plate, 6" d. 30.00
Platter, 9½ x 12½" 125.00
Sauce dish 25.00
Vegetable bowl, cov., oval 315.00

OAKLAND (John Maddock & Sons, ca. 1895)
Butter pat 25.00
Sauce dish, 6" sq. 25.00
Soup plate, w/flanged rim,
   8¾" d. 35.00

OREGON (T.J. & J. Mayer, ca. 1845)
Plate, 5" to 6" d. 100.00
Platter, 12 x 16" 350.00
Soup plate w/flanged rim,
   10½" d. 185.00
Vegetable bowl, cov. 995.00

ORIENTAL (Ridgways, ca. 1891)
Charger, 12½" d. 125.00
Cup & saucer 60.00
Plate, 7¾" d. 50.00
Plate, 8¾" d. 60.00
Sugar bowl, cov. 165.00
Waste bowl 95.00

ORMONDE (Alfred Meakin, ca. 1891)
Platter, 11 1/8" l. 140.00
Platter, 14 1/8" l. 180.00
Sauce dish, oblong 30.00
Soup plate w/flanged rim 65.00

OSBORNE (W.H. Grindley, ca. 1900)
Bone dish 45.00
Bouillon cup & saucer 85.00
Butter pat 32.00
Cup & saucer 85.00
Gravy boat & underplate 125.00
Platter, 10½" l. 55.00
Platter, 12½" l. 90.00
Platter, 13½ x 18" 395.00
Vegetable bowl, cov. 200.00
Vegetable bowl, open, 8¼" oval ... 60.00
Vegetable bowl, open, 10" oval 48.00

OSBORNE (Ridgways, ca. 1905)
Bone dish 40.00
Bouillon cup & saucer 85.00
Butter pat 45.00
Plate, 9½" d. 60.00
Relish dish, 9" oval 95.00
Soup plate w/flanged rim, 9" d. 50.00
Soup tureen, cov. 450.00
Vegetable bowl, cov., clover-
   shaped 240.00
Vegetable bowl, open, 8¼" oval ... 72.00

OVANDO (Alfred Meakin, ca. 1891)

Dinner service: six each 8" & 6¾" d. plates, 5" d. bowls, butter pats & cups & saucers, five 9" d. plates, three each 6¼" d. bowls, bone dishes, 9" d. soup plates & 6" d. waste bowls, plus oval cov. vegetable bowl, 14" oval platter, round open vegetable bowl & cov. teapot, the set 2,900.00

OXFORD (Johnson Bros., ca. 1900)

Butter pat	35.00
Gravy boat	65.00
Plate, 6¼" d.	35.00
Plate, 10" d.	72.00
Sauce dish, 5 3/8" d.	45.00

PARIS (New Wharf Pottery and Stanley Pottery Co., ca. 1891)

Butter pat 35.00
Dinner service: eight each 9", 8" & 7" d. plates, cups & saucers & sauce dishes plus cov. butter dish w/drain insert, 9" d. open vegetable bowl, 9" oval open vegetable bowl & an 8 x 10½" platter, 52 pcs. 2,395.00

PEKING (Podmore, Walker & Co., ca. 1850)

Tea set, cov. teapot, cov. sugar bowl & creamer, 3 pcs.	850.00
Waste bowl......................	295.00

PERSIAN MOSS (Utzchneider & Co., ca. 1891)

Celery tray	65.00
Platter, 10¾ x 16½"	155.00
Vegetable bowl, cov.	165.00
Vegetable bowl, open, 8¼" d.	50.00

PORTMAN (W.H. Grindley, ca. 1891)

Butter pat	30.00
Gravy boat	110.00
Plate, 6¾" d.	25.00
Relish dish.....................	38.00

PROGRESS (W.H. Grindley, ca. 1894)

Cup & saucer 75.00
Dinner service: child's, six each 4" & 3" d. plates plus cov. vegetable bowl, gravy boat, 3 x 4" platter & 3¾ x 5" platter, 16 pcs. 750.00
Vegetable dish, divided, individual size, 5½" oval 40.00

RHODA GARDENS (Hackwood, ca. 1850)

Cup & saucer, handleless	165.00
Soup plate w/flanged rim, 9¼" d. ...	95.00

ROSE (W.H. Grindley, ca. 1893)

Butter dish, cov.	140.00
Platter, 11 x 15¾" d.	135.00

Soup plate w/flanged rim, 8¾" d. . . .	35.00
Vegetable bowl, open, 8" d.	45.00

ROSEVILLE (John Maddock & Sons, ca. 1891)

Bowl, 9¾" d.	90.00
Butter pat	20.00
Chocolate pot, cov...............	575.00
Vegetable bowl, cov., 11" l........	260.00

SABRAON (Unknown, probably English, ca. 1845)

Pitcher, milk	575.00
Plate, 9¼" d.	95.00
Plate, 10½" d.	170.00
Platter, 16" l.	425.00
Platter, 18¼" l.	750.00

SAVOY (Johnson Bros., ca. 1900)

Savoy Plate

Butter pat	35.00
Creamer	175.00
Cup & saucer	70.00
Plate, 7" d.	35.00
Plate, 9" d. (ILLUS.)	55.00
Platter, 12¼ x 16"	155.00
Sauce dish.....................	30.00

SCINDE (J. & G. Alcock, ca. 1840 and Thomas Walker, ca. 1847)

Scinde Plate

Bowl, 10½" d.	200.00
Cake plate, scalloped rim, 10½" d.	70.00

Cup & saucer, handleless 185.00
Plate, 9" d. 85.00
Plate, 10½" d. (ILLUS.) 200.00
Platter, 11" l. 395.00
Platter, 16" l. 700.00
Sauce tureen, cov. 895.00
Sugar bowl, cov. ....600.00 to 650.00
Teapot, cov. 985.00
Vegetable bowl, cov. 775.00

SEVILLE (New Wharf Pottery, ca. 1891 and Wood & Son)
Butter pat 35.00
Casserole dish, cov. 250.00
Creamer 180.00
Plate, 7" d. 60.00
Soup plate w/flanged rim 85.00

SHANGHAE (J. Furnival, ca. 1860)
Cup, handleless 52.00
Platter, 20" l. 750.00
Teapot, cov. 795.00

SHELL (Wood & Challinor, ca. 1840; E. Challinor, ca. 1860)
Cup & saucer, handleless 165.00
Gravy boat 175.00
Plate, 8½" d. 75.00
Sugar bowl, cov. 325.00

SHUSAN (F. & R. Pratt & Co., ca. 1855)
Creamer 395.00
Gravy boat 275.00
Platter, 16" l. 495.00

SPINACH (Libertas, ca. 1900, brush-painted)

Spinach Bowl

Bowl, 8" d. (ILLUS.) 65.00
Cup & saucer 75.00
Plate, 7¾" d. 55.00
Sauce dish......................... 40.00
Waste bowl........................ 150.00

TIVOLI (Thomas Furnival, ca. 1845)
Cup & saucer 90.00
Cup & saucer, handleless 100.00
Gravy boat 150.00
Platter, 12½ x 16" 250.00

TONQUIN (W. Adams & Son, ca. 1845)
Plate, 7½" to 8½" d. 75.00
Plate, 9½" d. 90.00
Waste bowl........................ 150.00

TOURAINE (Henry Alcock, ca. 1898 and Stanley Pottery, ca. 1898)

Touraine Plate

Bone dish 84.00
Butter dish, cov. 515.00
Butter pat 47.00
Creamer & cov. sugar bowl, pr. 480.00
Cup & saucer ....85.00 to 100.00
Pitcher, 6" h. 395.00
Pitcher, 8" h. 750.00
Plate, 8¾" d. (ILLUS.) 60.00
Platter, 14¾" l. 150.00
Sauce dish, 6¼" d. 52.00
Sugar bowl, cov. 275.00
Vegetable bowl, cov. 315.00
Vegetable bowl, open, 9" d. 100.00
Waste bowl........................ 175.00

TRILBY (Wood & Sons, ca. 1891)
Cake plate, open handled,
    10½" d. 95.00
Toothbrush holder 165.00
Vegetable bowl, open, 9½" d. 70.00
Wash bowl, large 350.00

VERMONT (Burgess & Leigh, ca. 1895)
Bone dish 30.00
Butter pat 35.00
Dinner service: eight each 9" & 8"
    plates, 5" d. bowls, 9" d. soup
    plates, cups & saucers & butter
    pats, plus 6½ x 9" & 7 x 9¼"
    open vegetable bowls, 7 x 10½"
    cov. vegetable bowl, 7½ x 10",
    8½ x 11½" & 11¾ x 16" (small
    chip) platters, 5 x 8" relish
    dish, gravy boat & 4" h. pitcher,
    65 pcs. 2,800.00
Pitcher, 5¼" h. 125.00
Plate, 10" d. 79.00
Platter, 12¼ x 16½" 185.00
Sauce tureen w/underplate 300.00

Vegetable bowl, cov.	175.00
Vegetable bowl, open, 7½ x 10"	110.00

VINRANKA, PERCY (Cefle, Upsala, Ekeby, Sweden, ca. 1968)

Cup & saucer	48.00
Plate, 7½" d.	20.00
Plate, 10¼" d.	45.00
Platter, 11¼" l.	60.00
Sauce dish, 5" d.	15.00
Soup plate w/flanged rim, 9½" d.	45.00
Vegetable bowl, 9¼" oval	60.00

WALDORF (New Wharf Pottery, ca. 1892)

Waldorf Plate

Bacon platter, oval	135.00
Bowl, 9" d.	78.00
Plate, 9" d. (ILLUS.)	70.00
Soup plate w/flanged rim	110.00

WARWICK (Podmore Walker & Co., ca. 1850)

Plate, 8½" d.	58.00
Sauce dish	30.00
Teapot, cov.	450.00

WATTEAU (Doulton & Co., ca. 1900)

Bowl, cereal	35.00
Butter pat	25.00
Egg cup	100.00
Ewer, 12½" h.	500.00
Plate, 9½" d.	50.00
Platter, 14 x 17½"	375.00
Soup plate w/flanged rim	75.00

WAVERLY (W.H. Grindley, ca. 1891)

Creamer	125.00
Plate, 6¾" d.	30.00
Vegetable bowl, open, 10" d.	125.00

(End of Flow Blue Section)

FRANCISCAN WARE

A product of Gladding, McBean & Company of Glendale and Los Angeles, California,

Franciscan Ware was one of a number of lines produced by that firm over its long history. Introduced in 1934 as a pottery dinnerware, Franciscan Ware was produced in many patterns including "Desert Rose," introduced in 1941 and reportedly the most popular dinnerware pattern ever made in this country. Beginning in 1942 some vitrified china patterns were produced under the Franciscan name also.

After a merger in 1963 the company name was changed to Interpace Corporation and in 1979 Josiah Wedgwood & Sons purchased the Gladding, McBean & Co. plant from Interpace. American production ceased in 1984.

Bowl, fruit, 5¼" d., Desert Rose patt., ca. 1941	$8.00
Bowl, soup, 5½" d., 2¼" h., footed, Desert Rose patt., ca. 1941	21.00
Bowl, cereal or soup, 6" d., Cafe Royal patt.	15.00
Bowl, cereal or soup, 6" d., Desert Rose patt., ca. 1941	10.00
Bowl, 7" d., Madeira patt., ca. 1967	6.00
Bowl, 7¾" d., Coronado Table Ware, ivory glaze, 1936-56	9.00
Bowl, salad, 4½ x 8", crescent-shaped, Apple patt., ca. 1940	22.00
Bowl, salad, 10" d., 3¼" h., Desert Rose patt., ca. 1941	65.00
Bowl, cereal, El Patio Table Ware, 1934-54	10.00
Bowl, cereal, Hacienda patt., green glaze, ca. 1964	5.00
Butter dish, cov., Apple patt., ca. 1940, ¼ lb.	35.00
Butter dish, cov., Cafe Royal patt., ¼ lb.	35.00
Butter dish, cov., Coronado Table Ware, ivory glaze, 1936-56	65.00
Butter dish, cov., El Patio Table Ware, 1934-54	45.00
Butter dish, cov., Ivy patt., ca. 1948, ¼ lb.	40.00
Candleholders, Desert Rose patt., ca. 1941, 3" h., pr.	76.00
Casserole, cov., round, handled, Apple patt., ca. 1940, 1½ qt., 6¾" d., 3" h.	75.00
Casserole, cov., round, handled, Ivy patt., ca. 1948, 1½ qt., 8" d., 4" h.	110.00
Coffeepot, cov., demitasse, Coronado Table Ware, ivory glaze, 1936-56	125.00
Coffeepot, cov., Apple patt., ca. 1940, 7½" h.	110.00
Cookie jar, cov., Apple patt., ca. 1940, 9¼" h.	150.00 to 200.00
Cookie jar, cov., Desert Rose patt., ca. 1941, 9¼" h.	200.00 to 250.00
Creamer, Coronado Table Ware,	

golden glow satin glaze, 1936-56 .... 12.50

Creamer, El Patio Table Ware, redwood brown glaze, 1934-54 ...... 8.00

Creamer, Ivy patt., ca. 1948, 4" h. .. 15.00

Cup & saucer, demitasse, El Patio Table Ware, 1934-54 .... 25.00

Cup & saucer, Apple patt., ca. 1940 .... 12.00

Cup & saucer, Cafe Royal patt. 18.00

Cup & saucer, Desert Rose patt., ca. 1941 .... 14.00

Cup & saucer, Oasis patt., ca. 1954 .... 7.50

Egg cup, Apple patt., ca. 1940, 3¾" h. 15.00

Egg cup, Desert Rose patt., ca. 1941, 3¾" h. 20.00

Gravy boat, footed, El Patio Table Ware, golden glow gloss glaze, 1934-54 .... 20.00

Gravy boat w/attached undertray, Ivy patt., ca. 1948, 9" l., 5" h. 35.00

Gravy boat w/attached undertray, Starburst patt., ca. 1954 .... 25.00

Ladle, Apple patt., ca. 1940, 10" l... 20.00

Mixing bowl, Apple patt., ca. 1940, 7½" d., 4¼" h. 22.00

Mug, Apple patt., ca. 1940, 12 oz., 4¼" h. 35.00

Napkin ring, Desert Rose patt., ca. 1941, 1½" h. 25.00

Pitcher, milk, 6½" h., Apple patt., ca. 1940, 1 qt. 85.00

Pitcher, syrup, 6¼" h., Desert Rose patt., ca. 1941, 1 pt. 65.00

Pitcher, water, 8¾" h., Desert Rose patt., ca. 1941, 2½ qt. 125.00

Plate, 6¼" d., Coronado Table Ware, ivory glaze, 1936-56 .... 3.00

Plate, bread & butter, 6¼" d., Ivy patt., ca. 1948 .... 8.00

Plate, bread & butter, 6½" d., Apple patt., ca. 1940 .... 10.00

Plate, 7", Oasis patt., ca. 1954 ... 6.00

Plate, salad, 4½ x 8", crescent-shaped, Desert Rose patt., ca. 1941 .... 24.00

Plate, 8¼" d., El Patio Table Ware, coral satin glaze, 1934-54 .... 6.00

Plate, salad, 8½" d., Apple patt., ca. 1940 .... 7.50

Plate, salad, 8½" d., Cafe Royal patt. 14.00

Plate, luncheon, 9¼" d., Ivy patt., ca. 1948 .... 16.00

Plate, luncheon, 9½" d., Apple patt., ca. 1940 .... 8.00

Plate, luncheon, 9½" d., Desert Rose patt., ca. 1941 .... 10.00

Plate, 9½" d., Coronado Table Ware, maroon gloss glaze, 1936-56 .... 8.00

Plate, dinner, 10½" d., Apple patt., ca. 1940 .... 16.50

Plate, dinner, 10½" d., Cafe Royal patt. 20.00

Plate, dinner, 10½" d., Desert Rose patt., ca. 1941 .... 12.50

Plate, dinner, 10½" d., El Patio Table Ware, coral satin glaze, 1934-54 .... 9.00

Plate, buffet, 11" d., Ivy patt., ca. 1948 .... 24.50

Plate, chop, 12" d., Apple patt., ca. 1940 .... 55.00

Plate, chop, 12" d., Cafe Royal patt. 40.00

Plate, cake, 13" d., Ivy patt., ca. 1948 .... 35.00

Plate, chop, 14" d., Apple patt., ca. 1940 .... 125.00

Plate, chop, 14" d., Ivy patt., ca. 1948 .... 125.00

Platter, 11" l., oval, coupe steak, Desert Rose patt., ca. 1941 ...... 42.00

Platter, 11¼" l., oval, Ivy patt., ca. 1948 .... 35.00

Platter, 8½ x 12¾" oval, Apple patt., ca. 1940 .... 30.00

Platter, 13" l., oval, Coronado Table Ware, ivory satin glaze, 1936-56 .. 16.50

Platter, 13" l., oval, El Patio Table Ware, 1934-54 .... 18.00

Platter, 10¼ x 14" oval, Apple patt., ca. 1940 .... 30.00

Platter, 10¼ x 14" oval, Cafe Royal patt. 45.00

Relish dish, oblong, three-part, Apple patt., ca. 1940, 11¾" l. 30.00

Relish dish, oblong w/end handle, Coronado Table Ware, ivory glaze, 1936-56, 9" l. 15.00

Relish dish, oval, three-part, Desert Rose patt., ca. 1941, 12" l. 60.00

Salt & pepper shakers, Apple patt., ca. 1940, tall, 6¼" h., pr. 45.00

Salt & pepper shakers, Desert Rose patt., ca. 1941, tall, 6¼" h., pr. .. 35.00

Salt & pepper shakers, Madeira patt., ca. 1967, pr. 10.00

Soup plate w/flanged rim, Ivy patt., ca. 1948, 8½" d. 21.00

Soup tureen, cov., three-footed, Apple patt., ca. 1940, 7½" d., 5¼" h. 325.00

Sugar bowl, cov., Coronado Table Ware, yellow glaze, 1936-56 ...... 15.00

Sugar bowl, cov., El Patio Table Ware, maroon gloss glaze, 1934-54 .... 18.00

Sugar bowl, open, individual, Desert Rose patt., ca. 1941, 2" h. 21.00

Teapot, cov., Apple patt., ca. 1940, 4¾" h. 85.00

Tidbit tray, two-tier, Ivy patt., ca. 1948 .... 75.00

Tumbler, water, Apple patt., ca.
1940, 10 oz., 5¼" h. 25.00
Tumbler, Ivy patt., ca. 1948, 10 oz.,
5¼" h. 28.00
Vase, bud, 6" h., Cafe Royal patt.,
w/original box 95.00
Vegetable bowl, open, round, Apple
patt., ca. 1940, 7¾" d., 2" h. 40.00
Vegetable bowl, open, oval, divided, Cafe Royal patt., 7 x 10¾" ... 40.00
Vegetable bowl, open, round, Desert Rose patt., ca. 1941, 8" d.,
2¼" h. 20.00
Vegetable bowl, open, round, El
Patio Table Ware, lettuce green
gloss glaze, 1934-54, 8½" d. 20.00
Vegetable bowl, open, oval, divided, Ivy patt., ca. 1948, 12" l. 60.00
Vegetable bowl, oval, Starburst
patt., ca. 1954 .... 15.00

FRANKOMA

*John Frank began producing and selling
pottery on a part-time basis during the summer of 1933 while he was still teaching art and
pottery classes at the University of Oklahoma. In 1934, Frankoma Pottery became an incorporated business that was successful
enough to allow him to leave his teaching position in 1936 to devote full time to its growth.
The pottery was moved to Sapulpa, Oklahoma in 1938 and a full range of art pottery and
dinnerwares were eventually offered. Since
John Frank's death in 1973, the pottery has
been directed by his daughter, Joniece. In early 1991 Richard Bernstein became owner and
president of Frankoma Pottery which was re-
named Frankoma Industries. Joniece Frank
serves as vice president and general manager. The early wares and limited editions are
becoming increasingly popular with collectors
today.*

Ashtray, advertising, "Can-Tex In-
dustries," green & brown glaze,
7½" l. $24.00
Book ends, model of an Irish Setter,
No. 430, 1942-60, Prairie Green
glaze, Ada clay, 6½" h., pr. 165.00
Bottle-vase, No. V-4, 1972, black &
terra cotta glaze, 12" h. 60.00
Bottle-vase, No. V-5, 1973, Flame
Red glaze w/white interior &
black base, 12" h. 60.00
Candleholders, No. 307, terra cotta
glaze, 3" h., pr. 50.00
Christmas card, 1958 .... 50.00
Cider set: 68 oz. pitcher & four
12 oz. mugs; green glaze, black
ink mark "Frank Potteries, Norman, Oklahoma," 5 pcs. 750.00

Figure, Dreamer Girl, No. 427,
1938-54, Prairie Green glaze, Ada
clay, 5 3/8" h. 190.00
Honey pot, beehive-shaped, Flame
Red glaze 10.00
Model of a Swan, miniature,
No. 168, Prairie Green glaze 35.00
Mug, 1968 (Republican) elephant,
white glaze 59.00
Mug, 1976 (Democratic) donkey,
Centennial Red glaze 20.00
Pitcher, 7" h., Wagon Wheel patt.,
Prairie Green glaze 40.00
Teapot, cov., Wagon Wheel patt.,
Desert Gold glaze 22.00
Toby mug, 1976, Uncle Sam, blue
glaze 7.50
Trivet, Cherokee Indian alphabet ... 35.00
Trivet, Sweet Adelines patt., 1978,
white glaze 25.00
Tumbler, Plainsman patt., Woodland
Moss glaze 10.00
Vase, 6" h., 1936, royal blue glaze.. 125.00
Wall mask, bust of Oriental Man,
No. 134, 1936-38, Osage Brown
glaze, 5½" h. 150.00
Wall mask, Indian bust, miniature,
No. 135, 1973-75, Flat Black glaze,
3¾" h. 45.00
Wall mask, bust of Peter Pan,
No. 100, Ada clay, 6" h. 45.00
Wall masks, busts of Indian Chief &
Indian Maiden, Onyx Black glaze,
Nos. 131 & 132, 1936-38, 5" &
4 1/8" h., pr. 85.00

FULPER

Fulper Ale Set

*The Fulper Pottery was founded in
Flemington, New Jersey, in 1805 and operated until 1935, although operations were curtailed in 1929 when its main plant was
destroyed by fire. The name was changed in
1929 to Stangl Pottery, which continued in
operation until July of 1978, when Pfaltzgraff, a division of Susquehanna Broadcast-
ing Company of York, Pennsylvania, pur-*

chased the assets of the Stangl Pottery, including the name.

Ale set: tankard pitcher & six mugs; the pitcher w/a tall cylindrical neck & long angled handle above the flaring conical base, matching mugs, each w/a caramel & green flambe' glaze w/crystals, five w/incised mark, one w/vertical ink mark, one unmarked, the set (ILLUS.) $467.50

Bowl, 11" d., 7½" h., effigy-type, the wide shallow bowl w/inverted sides supported by three primitive figures resting on a circular base, blue-grey flambe' glaze, vertical ink stamp mark, early 20th c. (small glaze chip on inner rim) . . . 330.00

Bowl, 13½" d., 3¼" h., shallow in-curved sides, an apple green & blue flambe' interior glaze, the outside w/a molded loop & tab geometric design covered in a green, grey & lavender matte glaze, vertical ink mark 357.50

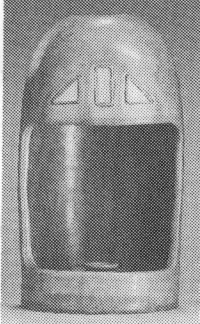

Fulper Candleholder

Candleholder, shield-back type, ovoid bullet-form body w/a large rectangular front opening & round hole at the top, inset candle sock-et, w/a semi-matte moss green glaze, inset above the opening w/a blue rectangular glass piece flanked by two triangular yel-low glass pieces, stamped mark, 10½" h. (ILLUS.) 990.00

Candlestick, tall slender round shaft on a stepped & domed round foot, topped by a flaring inverted bell-form candle socket, brown to mauve glossy flambe' glaze over a matte deep green base, vertical ink mark, 5¼" d., 15½" h. 357.50

Center bowl, shallow wide body w/inverted edge mounted w/three stylized figural birds w/wings spread around the ex-

terior, their feet forming the feet of the bowl, blue-green & flambe' brown interior glaze, mustard brown matte exterior glaze, in-distinct mark, 11" d., 5½" h. 660.00

Dresser box, cov., figural Art Deco lady w/blonde hair 245.00

Ewer, the wide ovoid body tapering toward the foot & to a wide up-right spout rim, rope-twist applied handle, curdled cream, brown & green drippy glaze, early incised mark, 7¼" d., 10½" h. 440.00

Flower frog, Art Deco style, figural nude lady sitting on a base mold-ed w/grass & yellow blossoms, No. 379 . . . . 120.00

Jug, wide ovoid body w/a wide shoulder to the short cylindrical neck, a high arched loop handle on the shoulder, copperdust glaze, raised vertical mark & pa-per label, 7¾" d., 12¼" h. 2,310.00

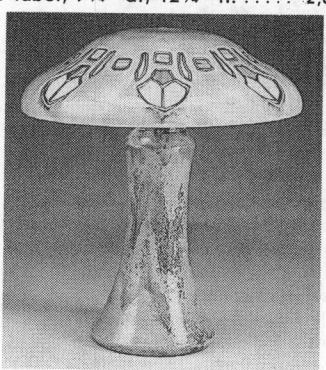

Fulper Pottery Lamp

Lamp, table model, 14" d. pottery mushroom-shaped shade in soft olive green & pierced w/heraldic-form openings filled w/colored leaded glass, on a tall waisted trumpet-form pottery base, print-ed company logo & "Fulper Pa-tents Pending in United States and Canada, England, France and Ger-many," w/numbers, overall 16" h. (ILLUS.) 11,000.00

Model of a bulldog, seated animal w/well-defined detailing, matte ochre & glossy grey & brown flam-be' glaze, unmarked, 10¼" w., 8" h. (restoration to one leg) 770.00

Vase, 6¼" h., 7¼" d., spherical footed body w/a wide shoulder to the short wide neck, three small loop handles from the neck to the shoulder, black mirrored glaze, incised horizontal mark 165.00

Vase, 7½" h., 6¾" d., eight-paneled ovoid form, short neck

w/relief rectangular design, green crystalline & cream flambe' glaze, incised vertical mark 412.50

Vase, 8" h., 5¾" d., a squatty narrow bulbous footed base narrowing to a cylindrical body w/four molded buttress handles down the sides, mirrored black & apple green flambe' glaze, vertical box ink mark 330.00

Vase, 9" h., 10½" d., wide squatty bulbous body on a small footring, a thin stepped shoulder to a short flaring neck, smooth gun-metal black glaze, raised vertical mark 1,650.00

Vase, 9½" h., 7¼" d., bulbous base below a conical body tapering to a small, flat mouth, long pierced angled handles from the rim to the top of the shoulders, fine copperdust glaze over a glossy apple green base, incised mark .. 357.50

Vase, 10" h., 8" d., compressed bulbous base w/a thick foot, tapering to a wide short cylindrical banded neck w/a flaring rim, crystallized gun-metal grey glaze over a tiger's-eye base, vertical ink mark 1,650.00

Vase, 10¾" h., 6½" d., trumpet-type w/compressed globular base, mirrored black to caramel tiger's eye glaze, vertical ink mark...... 412.50

Vase, 11¼" h., 4¾" d., slightly tapering cylindrical body w/low angled handles from the rim down the sides, each w/a narrow rectangular cut-out, crystalline celadon glaze, vertical ink mark .. 302.50

Vase, 12" h., 11½" d., wide bulbous footed body w/a very short wide cylindrical neck & heavy rolled rim, molded loop handles on each side of the shoulder, unusual crystalline celadon & dusty pink glaze, incised vertical mark........................ 880.00

Vase, 15" h., 7" d., amphora-type, closed handles at shoulder, mirrored black to copperdust glaze, vertical ink mark 1,210.00

Vase, 17" h., 9" d., tall footed ovoid body tapering to a flared rim, mahogany brown, cream & gun-metal flambe' glaze, raised vertical mark 1,760.00

Vase, 17½" h., 7" d., floor-type, tall ovoid body tapering to a wide, flat mouth, gold & light blue crystalline flambe' glaze, early vertical incised mark 990.00

Vase, 18½" h., 6¼" d., bottle-shaped, footed ovoid body tapering to a very tall slender neck, set upon a separate round base w/four curled feet, mottled ashes-of-roses glaze on vase, green dripping glaze on base, each piece w/raised mark, vase w/"#176," 2 pcs. (restoration to neck)........................ 1,320.00

Vases, 7" h., 5½" d., baluster-form w/wide flat base, three angled C-scroll handles around the sides, horizontal ribbing up the sides, caramel, blue & mahogany flambe' glaze, vertical ink mark, pr............................. 385.00

Vases, 11¾" h., wide bulbous footed ovoid body w/a short neck flanked by high arched handles w/molded cabochons, bluish green crystalline glaze, original paper label reading "FULPER 515 - vase copper green" & "PANAMA PACIFIC INTERNATIONAL EXPOSITION - SAN FRANCISCO - 1915 - HIGHEST AWARD - TO - FULPER POTTERY," pr.................. 3,300.00

Vases, 13" h., 6½" d., simple baluster-form body tapering to a short flaring neck, semi-matte purple glaze, vertical ink mark, pr............................. 990.00

GAUDY DUTCH

This name is applied to English earthenware with designs copied from Oriental patterns. Production began in the 18th century. These copies flooded into this country in the early 19th century. The incorporation of the word "Dutch" derives from the fact that it was the Dutch who first brought the Oriental wares into Europe. The ware was not, as often erroneously reported, made specifically for the Pennsylvania Dutch.

Cup & saucer, handleless, Carnation patt. (pinpoint flakes, hairlines in cup) $357.50

Cup & saucer, handleless, Single Rose patt. (minor wear & small flake on table ring of cup) 330.00

Plate, 8¼" d., Grape patt. (rim hairline, minor flakes) 407.00

Sugar bowl, cov., footed bulbous oblong body tapering up to a flared closed rim w/end tabs on inside edge, inset conical cover w/blossom finial, short curved table handles at ends of body, Double Rose patt., 5¼" h. (stains, small flakes, cover chipped on interior flange) 550.00

Teapot, cov., footed bulbous oblong
body tapering to a flaring curved
closed rim, stepped domed cover
w/scroll loop finial, swan's-neck
spout & C-scroll handle, Grape
patt., 6¼" h. (old yellowed
repairs) 550.00

GAUDY WELSH

*This is a name for wares made in England
for the American market about 1830 to 1860,
with some examples dating much later, Decorated with Imari-style flower patterns, often
highlighted with copper lustre, it should not
be confused with Gaudy Dutch wares whose
colors differ somewhat.*

Cup & saucer, Floret patt........... $69.00
Cup & saucer, Rhondda patt. 69.00
Cup & saucer, Tulip patt............ 80.00
Loving cup, cylindrical body
w/scrolled loop handles, Oyster
patt., 4" h. 247.50
Pitcher, 7½" h., octagonal paneled
bottom below a curved shoulder
to the high arched spout, angled
handle, Geranium patt. variant,
the bottom panels alternating
w/small round closed blossoms &
large half-blossoms, large half-
blossoms around shoulder & neck
w/a full blossom below the spout,
ca. 1840 (flakes, short rim hairline) 440.00
Pitcher & bowl, miniature, Tulip
patt., 4 3/8" d., 3½" h., the set
(minor wear) 300.00
Tea set: cov. teapot, cov. sugar
bowl, creamer, waste bowl, two
cake plates, twelve cups & saucers & twelve plates; Tulip patt.,
19th c., the set 1,045.00

GOLDSCHEIDER

*The Goldscheider firm, manufacturers of
porcelain and faience in Austria between 1885
and the present, was founded by Friedrich
Goldscheider and carried on by his widow.
The firm came under the control of his sons,
Walter and Marcell, in 1920. Fleeing their native Austria at the time of World War II, the
Goldscheiders set up an operation in the United States. They were listed in the Trenton,
New Jersey, City Directory from 1943
through 1950 and their main production
seems to have been art pottery figurines.*

Goldscheider Figure of a Lady

Book end, figural, cast as the head
of a modern 'Eve' holding an apple, in tans, red, yellow & blue
on a black base, printed factory
mark "MADE IN ENGLAND - by
Goldscheider - WITH MYOTT SON
& CO. - STAFFORDSHIRE," ca.
1925, 8¼" h. $440.00
Figure of a girl w/guitar, the stylish
maiden w/her hand on her hip &
leaning back, wearing a halter
top continuing to a slit skirt patterned w/stylized flowers in maroon & black, impressed factory
marks "Goldscheider - Wien -
MADE IN AUSTRIA - Dakon" &
numbered, ca. 1925, 17½" h. 2,200.00
Figure of "Juliet with Doves,"
12¼" h. 235.00
Figure of a lady wearing a pink
dress & carrying a basket of flowers, 7½" h...................... 95.00
Figure of a lady, the sophisticated
grey-haired matron wearing
a long red fur-trimmed coat
w/matching muff & hat, glazed
in red, white, grey & black, impressed factory marks, ca. 1925,
15¼" h. (ILLUS.) 3,575.00
Figure of a man, dressed in fancy
cloak & top hat, marked, 9" h. 75.00
Figure of "Rose," depicted as a
beautiful maiden wearing a decorated bandeau above a volumi-
nous skirt w/a jeweled girdle at
her hips, the skirt held up from
the hem in her outstretched
hands, stepping forward w/bas-
kets of roses flanking, on a
shaped triangular molded base,
ca. 1925, 21½" h. (several minor
chips to base) 2,750.00
Figure of a Spanish dancer, the
dramatic-looking senorita dressed
in an elaborate lacy costume,
holding a fan in her right hand,
w/a mantilla covering her dark
hair, glazed in rose, black, yellow

& cream, incised factory marks,
ca. 1925, 16" h. 1,375.00
Figure of a young woman, standing
w/head turned & gazing over her
bare shoulder, dressed in an elegant patterned evening dress,
glazed in cobalt blue, grey, white
& cream heightened w/gilding,
after a model by Lorenzel, impressed factory marks, ca. 1925,
11¾" h. 3,300.00
Figure group, modeled as Pierrot in
black-trimmed white costume
kissing his companion in a pink
dress w/flowered underskirt as
she plays a mandolin, stamped
company mark & artist's initials,
18¼" h. 1,760.00
Model of a dog, Collie, No. 856 . . . . 120.00
Model of a dog, German Shepherd
seated, 7½" h. 75.00
Model of a dog, German Shepherd
reclining, 17" l. 145.00
Model of a dog, Spaniel, No. 680 . . . 105.00
Model of a dog, Springer Spaniel,
in seated position, U.S.A. mark,
4½ x 4½" 55.00

GOUDA

Gouda Plaque & Vase

*While tin-enameled earthenware has been
made in Gouda, Holland since the early
1600's, the productions of modern factories
are attracting increasing collector attention.
The art pottery of Gouda is easily recognized
by its brightly colored peasant-style decoration with some types having achieved a
"cloisonne" effect. Pottery workshops located in, or near, Gouda include Regina, Zenith,
Plazuid, Schoonhoven, Arnhem and others.
Their wide range of production included
utilitarian wares, as well as vases, miniatures
and large outdoor garden ornaments.*

Candleholder, shield-back type, Art
Nouveau designs in dark colors . . $67.00

Humidor, cov., colorful designs in
cobalt blue, beige, yellow & or-
ange, artist-signed, 5" h. 265.00
Lamp, blue & rust stylized leaves on
black ground, base 12" h. 195.00
Pitcher, 5" h., stylized tulip blossom
& foliage against an off-white
ground, Royal Zuid mark & paper
label 39.00
Plaque, rectangular, polychrome en-
amel decoration of a village harbor scene, mounted in a wide oak
frame, artist-signed, house symbol for Zuid, plaque 12¼ x 16¼"
(ILLUS. left) 770.00
Vase, 4" h., 6" d., decorated w/pea-
cock feathers on a black satin
ground, house mark, "Zwaro" 90.00
Vase, 5" h., bulbous-form, decorated w/Art Nouveau florals & a
scene w/windmill & sailboat in
lake on an eggshell ground,
marked 50.00
Vase, 13" h., two-handled, Art Nou-
veau-style glossy multicolored
stylized iris decoration, Zuid-
Holland house mark 450.00
Vases, 15½" h., tall baluster-form,
decorated w/flowers & vines in
purple, blue, green & gold on a
white ground, painted factory
marks "Holland Gouda N.P. S8"
for New Porcelain, Zuid, ca. 1910,
pr. (ILLUS. of one, right) 1,320.00
Vase, 17" h., tall ovoid body taper-
ing to a slender trumpet-form
neck flanked by slender round
loop handles, deep umber ground
decorated w/stylized blossoms,
stems & foliage in violet, yellow,
blue & green, painted mark "213
B.O. GOUDA HOLLAND," & in-
cised "213" 1,100.00
Vase, 20½" h., 9¾" d., floor-type,
the tall ovoid body tapering to a
short wide neck, decorated
around the body w/long panels
alternating w/stylized daisies &
slender scrolls, bands of rounded
arches around the base & shoulder & a scalloped band of half
sunbursts at the top, plain dark
bands at the very base & rim, in
polychrome, marked "106 - Daisy
- Z. Holland - Gouda," early
20th c. 1,210.00

GRUEBY

*Some fine art pottery was produced by the
Grueby Faience and Tile Company, established in Boston in 1891. Choice pieces were*

*created with molded designs on a semi-
porcelain body. The ware is marked and often bears the initials of the decorators. The
pottery closed in 1907.*

Grueby Lamp Base

Bowl, 2" d., 3" h., gently rounded
sides decorated w/tooled & applied leaves, rich matte green
glaze exterior w/a contrasting
light green interior, artist-signed,
impressed mark.................$605.00
Bowl, 5" d., 3¼" h., squatty spherical body on a small footring,
tooled & applied wide overlapping
leaves around the sides, matte
green "elephant skin" glaze,
by Wilhelmina Post, impressed
mark.............................. 990.00
Candlestick, cylindrical shaft flaring
toward the base & w/a large
swelled knop below the flaring
rim, long molded leaves, matte
blue glaze, unmarked, 8¾" h..... 467.50
Lamp base, flaring squatty base
tapering to a tall cylindrical body,
decorated w/molded green-
centered five-petaled flowers on
trailing stems, blue glaze over
bisque w/glaze skips, marked, initialed by Wilhelmina Post, drilled
& fitted w/lamp hardware, 8" d.,
14" h. (ILLUS.) 2,475.00
Paperweight, figural, model of a
large scarab beetle, organic matte
light brown glaze, impressed
mark & remnant of a paper label,
4" l. 330.00
Pitcher, 6" h., 5½" d., wide ovoid
body tapering to a short narrow
neck w/pinched spout, angled
strap handle, thick organic matte
green glaze, impressed mark 440.00
Vase, 3" h., 3" d., footed & shouldered spherical body tapering to
a short flared neck, incised thin
blades of grass around the sides,
deep matte green glaze, incised
mark & "PW" 412.50

Vase, 4½" h., 5" d., squatty bulbous
body tapering to a short wide
mouth, embossed around the lower half w/a band of wide leaves
alternating w/thin stems supporting yellow blossoms around the
neck, matte green glaze, by Wilhelmina Post, impressed com-
pany mark & artist's initials.....3,575.00
Vase, 7" h., 4¼" d., slightly ovoid
cylindrical body w/a pinched
three-lobe mouth, the sides tooled
& applied w/three flaring leaves
interspersed w/buds on tall thin
stems, rich matte green glaze, impressed mark (tight hairline) 770.00
Vase, 10" h., tall ovoid body molded
w/five wide leaves alternating
w/four scrolled handles, white
clay glazed in "oatmeal" yellow w/some separation, circular
"Faience" mark & initialed by Wilhelmina Post, one handle edge
chipped.........................4,125.00
Vase, 19½" h., 10" d., floor-type,
bulbous base below a tall cylindrical neck w/flared rim, decorated w/stacked, tooled & applied leaves, fine organic matte
green glaze, decorated by Wilhelmina Post, impressed mark &
"WP -180"......................9,900.00

HALL

*Founded in 1903 in East Liverpool, Ohio,
this still-operating company at first produced
mostly utilitarian wares. It was in 1911 that
Robert T. Hall, son of the company founder,
developed a special single-fire, lead-free glaze
which proved to be strong, hard and non-
porous. In the 1920's the firm became well
known for their extensive line of teapots (still
a major product) and in 1932 they introduced
kitchenwares followed by dinnerwares in 1936
and refrigerator wares in 1938.*

*The imaginative designs and wide range of
glaze colors and decal decorations have led
to the growing appeal of Hall wares with collectors, especially people who like Art Deco
and Art Moderne design. One of the firm's
most famous patterns was the "Autumn
Leaf" line, produced as premiums for the Jewel Tea Company. For listings of this ware see
"Jewel Tea Autumn Leaf."*

Ashtray, Blue Bouquet patt. $6.00
Baker, Blue Bouquet patt. 18.00
Baker, French-style, Red Poppy
   patt. 16.00

Batter pitcher, Sundial shape, Blue
Garden patt. 185.00
Bean pot, cov., tab-handled, Rose
Parade patt. 45.00
Bowl, 5¼" d., Mount Vernon
patt. 4.50
Bowl, fruit, 5½" d., Blue Bouquet
patt. 7.00
Bowl, cereal, 6" d., Orange Poppy
patt. 18.00
Bowl, 7½" d., Radiance shape, Red
Poppy patt. 14.00
Bowl, 7½" d., Rose Parade patt. . . . 30.00
Bowl, flat soup, 8" d., Mount Ver-
non patt. 9.50
Bowl, 8" d., straight-sided, Sil-
houette (Taverne) patt. 15.00
Bowl, salad, 9" d., Orange Poppy
patt. 12.00
Butter dish, cov., Blue Blossom
patt., 1 lb. 400.00
Butter dish, cov., Blue Bouquet
patt. 50.00
Butter dish, cov., Zephyr shape,
Chinese Red 65.00
Casserole, cov., tab-handled, Rose
Parade patt. 50.00
Casserole, cov., Sundial shape,
No. 4, cobalt blue, 8" d. 25.00
Coffeepot, cov., Drip-o-later, Mount
Vernon patt., all china 85.00
Coffeepot, cov., Orange Poppy
patt. 40.00
Coffeepot, cov., Orange Poppy
patt., "Great American"
marking 75.00
Coffeepot, cov., S-Lid style, Wildfire
patt. 45.00
Cookie jar, cov., Gold Dot patt. 65.00
Cookie jar, cov., Star patt., blue &
gold 50.00
Creamer & cov. sugar bowl, Orange
Poppy patt., pr. 45.00
Creamer & cov. sugar bowl, Rose
Parade patt., pr. 225.00
Creamer & cov. sugar bowl, Sil-
houette (Taverne) patt., pr. 35.00
Cup & saucer, Orange Poppy patt. . . 30.00
Cups & saucers, Silhouette (Taverne)
patt., set of 6 . . . . 72.00
Custard cup, Red Poppy patt. 15.00
Custard cup, Wildfire patt. 13.50
Gravy boat, Wildfire patt. 35.00
Mixing bowls, nest-type, Red Poppy
patt., set of 3 . . . . 40.00
Mixing bowls, nest-type, Silhouette
(Taverne) patt., set of 3 . . . . 50.00
Pie baker, Orange Poppy patt. 25.00
Pitcher, ball-type, Blue Bouquet
patt. 45.00
Pitcher, ball-type, Crocus
patt. . . . . 50.00 to 75.00
Pitcher, Daniel shape, Red Poppy
patt. 40.00

Pitcher, 6½" h., Pert shape, Rose
Parade patt. 23.00
Pitcher, 7½" h., Pert shape, Rose
Parade patt. 37.50
Pitcher, Radiance shape, Orange
Poppy patt., No. 5 . . . . 30.00
Plate, 6" d., Orange Poppy patt. 7.00
Plate, 8" d., Crocus patt. 15.00
Plate, 9" d., Orange Poppy patt. 15.00
Plate, 9" d., Red Poppy patt. 10.00
Plate, 9" d., Wildfire patt. 11.50
Platter, 13¼" l., oval, Orange Pop-
py patt. 25.00
Pretzel jar, cov., Crocus patt. 90.00
Pretzel jar, cov., Morning Glory
patt. 55.00
Pretzel jar, cov., Orange Poppy
patt. 90.00
Refrigerator dish, cov., Westing-
house line, Hercules (Aristocrat)
shape, tan 15.00
Salt & pepper shakers, teardrop-
shaped, Blue Bouquet patt., pr. . . . 80.00
Salt & pepper shakers, Medallion
(Colonial) patt., pr. 75.00
Salt & pepper shakers, handled,
Pert shape, Rose Parade patt.,
5" h., pr. 50.00
Salt & pepper shakers, handled,
Wildfire patt., pr. 45.00
Sugar bowl, cov., Orange Poppy
patt. 12.00
Syrup pitcher, cov., Five Band
shape, Chinese Red 85.00
Teapot, cov., Airflow shape, yellow
w/gold, 8-cup size 25.00
Teapot, cov., Aladdin shape, Golden
Glo, 1940's, w/infuser 30.00
Teapot, cov., Aladdin shape, ma-
roon & gold 35.00
Teapot, cov., Albany shape, ma-
hogany & gold, 6-cup size 45.00
Teapot, cov., Doughnut shape, Or-
ange Poppy patt. 400.00
Teapot, cov., Globe shape, no-drip
spout, cobalt blue 65.00
Teapot, cov., Hollywood shape, Chi-
nese Red 75.00
Teapot, cov., Hollywood shape, Kel-
ly green w/gold 35.00
Teapot, cov., Los Angeles shape,
green 28.00
Teapot, cov., McCormick shape,
brown 45.00
Teapot, cov., New York shape, light
blue 17.00
Teapot, cov., New York shape,
Orange Poppy patt., w/gold trim,
6-cup size 175.00
Teapot, cov., Parade shape, canary
yellow w/gold trim 32.00
Teapot, cov., Plume shape, Victorian
line, pink 28.00

Teapot, cov., Streamline shape, canary yellow 23.00
Teapot, cov., Windshield shape, camellia decal 28.00
Vegetable bowl, open, oval, Mount Vernon patt., 9¼" l. 14.00

HAMPSHIRE POTTERY

Lamp Designed by Robertson

Hampshire Pottery was made in Keene, New Hampshire, where several potteries operated as far back as the late 18th century. The pottery now known as Hampshire Pottery was established by J.S. Taft shortly after 1870. Various types of wares, including Art Pottery, were produced through the years. Taft's brother-in-law, Cadmon Robertson, joined the firm in 1904 and was responsible for developing over 900 glaze formulas while in charge of all manufacturing. His death in 1914 created problems for the firm and Taft sold out to George Morton in 1916. Closed during part of World War I, the pottery was later reopened by Morton for a short time and manufactured white hotel china. From 1919 to 1921, mosaic floor tiles became the main production. All production ceased in 1923.

Bowl, 5" d., 3" h., squatty bulbous form molded overall w/artichoke leaves, veined green matte glaze, unmarked $192.50
Ewer, the wide squatty bulbous footed base w/a wide shoulder tapering to a cylindrical neck flaring to a long arched spout & incurved tab attached to the top of the slender S-scroll handle, matte green glaze, marked "J.S.T. & Co. - KEENE, N.H.," 9½" d., 9½" h. .. 247.50
Inkwell, low cylindrical form, the flat top pierced w/pen holes centering the small domed cap w/button finial, ceramic liner, smooth matte green glaze,

marked & numbered "26," 4¼" d., 3½" h. 165.00
Lamp, table model, lobed compressed globular base, matte green glaze, designed by Cadmon Robertson, w/bent panel green slag glass shade, impressed "006," overall 19" h. (ILLUS.) 605.00
Pitcher, tankard, 11¾" h., 6¼" d., tall cylindrical body flared at the base w/a molded panel band at rim & base, angled handle w/scrolled tips, feathered matte green glaze, impressed mark "44" (hairline in base) 88.00
Vase, 6¾" h., 4" d., expanding cylinder w/rounded shoulder, relief-molded leaf decoration, rich curdled & marbleized bluish green matte glaze, marked "33, Hampshire Pottery" 412.50
Vase, 9" h., 4½" d., ovoid, relief-molded elongated oval leaves, matte veined taupe glaze, marked "Hampshire Pottery" 302.50
Vases, 9½" h., 7" d., compressed globular base & long neck w/flaring rim, base decorated w/relief-molded leaves, matte dark blue glaze, marked "124, Hampshire Pottery, M," pr. 770.00
Vase, 15" h., 5" d., tall ovoid body tapering to a narrow short neck w/a widely flaring rim, small loop handles from rim to shoulder, matte green glaze, marked "J.S.T. & Co." 495.00

HARLEQUIN

The Homer Laughlin China Company, makers of the popular "Fiesta" pottery line, also introduced in 1938 a less expensive and thinner ware which was sold under the "Harlequin" name. It did not carry the maker's trade-mark and was marketed exclusively through F.W. Woolworth Company. It was produced in a wide range of dinnerwares in assorted colors until 1964. Out of production for a number of years, in 1979 Woolworth requested the line be reintroduced using an ironstone body and with a limited range of pieces and colors offered. Collectors also seek out a series of miniature animal figures produced in the Harlequin line in the 1930's and 1940's.

Ashtray, basketweave, red $25.00
Ashtray, saucer-type, spruce green 53.00
Bowl, 36s, 4½" d., medium green .. 30.00
Bowl, fruit, 5½" d., maroon 6.50

Bowl, individual salad, 7" d.,
chartreuse 20.00
Butter dish, cov., spruce green 95.00
Butter dish, cov., yellow 55.00
Candleholders, red, pr. 185.00
Creamer, red 10.00
Cup, medium green 16.00
Cup & saucer, demitasse, rose 25.00
Egg cup, single, light green 8.00
Egg cup, single, red 20.00
Egg cup, single, yellow 14.00
Egg cup, double, maroon or rose,
each 27.50
Gravy boat, spruce green 22.00
Pitcher, 9" h., ball-shaped w/ice lip,
chartreuse 47.50
Pitcher, 9" h., ball-shaped w/ice lip,
grey 45.00
Plate, 9" d., chartreuse 9.00
Plate, 9" d., rose 10.00
Platter, 11" l., oval, grey 6.00
Sugar bowl, cov., maroon 19.00
Tea set: cov. teapot, creamer & cov.
sugar bowl; red, 3 pcs. 95.00

HARLEQUIN ANIMALS

Model of a cat, spruce green 110.00
Model of a fish, spruce green 95.00
Salt & pepper shakers, figural lamb,
gold, pr. 40.00
Salt & pepper shakers, figural
"maverick" duck, pr. 45.00

HAVILAND

Haviland porcelain was originated by Americans in Limoges, France, shortly before the mid-19th century and continues in production. Some Haviland was made by Theodore Haviland in the United States during the last World War. Numerous other factories also made china in Limoges, which see.

Bouillon cup & saucer, Clover patt.,
No. 98, Blank No. 1, trim 24 . . . . . $39.00
Bouillon cup & saucer, Paradise
patt. 40.00
Butter dish, cov., Rosalinde patt.,
Blank No. 3, no gold 45.00
Butter pat, Moss Rose patt. 15.00
Cake set: 10 x 16" platter & ten
7¾" d. scalloped plates w/gold
rim; birds & pink florals decora-
tion, the set 355.00
Chocolate pot, cov., decorated over-
all w/gold ribbons & dainty blue &
green sprays of flowers, scalloped
base w/gold trim, marked "H.C.-
L.," 10" h. 195.00
Chocolate pot, cov., wide scalloped
base & ornate, decorated handle,
covered w/decoration of black &

red raspberries & blossoms, gold
trim 129.00
Chocolate set: cov. chocolate pot &
six cups & saucers; each w/a
brownish ground decorated w/yel-
low roses, artist-signed & dated
1912, the set 225.00
Coffeepot, cov., Mignonette patt.,
8" h. 95.00
Creamer, Noinville patt. 30.00
Creamer, Rosalinde patt., Blank
No. 3, no gold 28.00
Creamer & cov. sugar bowl, Dela-
ware patt., pr. 95.00
Creamer & cov. sugar bowl, Pink
Spray patt., pr. 75.00
Cup & saucer, demitasse, grey-
ish pink & yellow roses, Blank
No. 266B 22.00
Cup & saucer, demitasse, No. 1 Ran-
son blank 28.00
Cup & saucer, Apple Blossom
patt. 30.00
Cup & saucer, Autumn Leaf patt. . . . 15.00
Cup & saucer, Mignonette patt. 30.00
Cup & saucer, Moss Rose patt. 20.00
Cup & saucer, Rosalinde patt. 36.00
Cup & saucer, Silver Anniversary
patt. 24.00
Cup & saucer, Wedding Ring patt. . . 40.00
Dessert plates, Baltimore Rose patt.,
Blank No. 8, Haviland & Co., set
of 8 . . . . 160.00
Dinner service: 10 dinner plates,
9 salad plates, 8 bread & butter
plates, 9 cups & saucers plus
gravy boat, open oval bowl &
medium-sized platter; Autumn
Leaf patt., 48 pcs. 875.00
Gravy boat w/attached undertray,
Silver Anniversary patt. 95.00
Mustache cup & saucer, factory-
decorated w/old fashioned floral
design 95.00
Oyster plate, decorated w/tiny gold
sprays, 7½" d. 70.00
Plate, bread & butter, 5" d., Ran-
son blank 12.50
Plate, dessert, 6" d., coupe-shaped,
Clover Leaf patt. 10.00
Plate, salad, 7½" d., Pasadena
patt. 16.00
Plate, salad, 7½" d., Rosalinde
patt. 22.00
Plate, luncheon, 8½" d., decorated
w/daffodils & gold trim 15.00
Plate, luncheon, 8½" d., No. 1 Ran-
son blank 16.00
Plate, dinner, 9½" d., Charonne
patt. 20.00
Plate, dinner, 9½" d., Drop Rose
patt. 90.00
Plate, dinner, 9½" d., Silver An-
niversary patt. 16.00

Plate, 12½" d., salmon & white asters on cream to pale green shaded ground, rococo scroll rim w/gilt design 165.00

Platter, 11" l., Chambord patt. 50.00

Soup plate w/flanged rim, Monocco patt. 16.00

Sugar bowl, cov., Silver Anniversary patt. 49.00

Teapot, cov., Springtime patt. 135.00

Tea set: cov. teapot & four cups & saucers; Silver Anniversary patt., 9 pcs. 175.00

Vase, 5½" h., 3¾" d., wide cylindrical shouldered body on a small footring, wide low neck w/rolled rim, decorated w/tan bands at the shoulder & base above floral bands flanking oval reserves w/figures of turn-of-the-century ladies dressed in rose-hued dresses & wearing large hats, these panels alternating w/panels of flowers & floral garlands, artist-signed 295.00

Vase, 8¼" h., baluster-form w/three applied scrolled handles, decorated w/stylized chrysanthemums in fuchsia & purple over a white ground, designed by Georges de Feure, ca. 1930's, stamped firm mark 528.00

Vase, 18 7/8" h., Art Nouveau style, tall ovoid body molded at the rim w/swirled blossoms & four looped handles, the body decorated w/dragonflies amid daffodils, printed factory mark surrounded by an etched inscription "Fait specialement par... pour," early 20th c. 1,610.00

Vegetable dish, cov., oval, Old Blackberry patt................. 100.00

Vegetable dish, open, oval, Autumn Leaf patt..................... 40.00

HISTORICAL & COMMEMORATIVE

Numerous potteries, especially in England and the United States, made various porcelain and earthenware pieces to commemorate people, places and events. Scarce English historical wares with American views command highest prices. Objects are listed here alphabetically by title of view.

Alaska-Yukon-Pacific Exposition souvenir plate, scene of three Oriental ladies, dark blue, dated 1909 (Rowland & Marsellus) $125.00

The Baltimore & Ohio Railroad (Lev-

el) plate, shell border, circular center w/trailing vines around outer edge of center, dark blue, 10" d. (Wood).................. 750.00

Bank of the United States Philadelphia plate, spread eagles amid flowers & scrolls border, dark blue, 10" d. (Stubbs)............ 500.00

Boston Mails plate, medallions of steamships border, purple, 9¼" d. (James & Thomas Edwards) 225.00

Boston State House pitcher, reverse w/City Hall, New York, rose border, dark blue, 7½" h., Stubbs (hairlines in base) 675.00

Boston State House pitcher, floral border, dark blue, 8½" h. (John Rogers & Son).................. 660.00

Boston State House plate, flowers & leaves border, medium blue, 10" d. (Rogers)................. 200.00

Cadmus plate, shell border w/irregular center, dark blue, 10" d. (Wood) 412.50

The Castle Fleurs in Roxburghshire, Scotland platter, flowers border, dark blue, 16" l. (W. Adams) 385.00

Chesapeake & Shannon Naval Battle scene platter, shell & seaweed border, medium blue, 19½" l. (John Rogers & Son) 575.00

Chesapeake & Shannon Naval Battle scene platter, shell & seaweed border, medium blue, 21½" l., John Rogers & Son (minor edge flakes & stains) 925.00

Chiswick on the Thames (England) sauceboat undertray, oval, shell border, dark blue, 8" l. (Enoch Wood & Sons)................... 350.00

City Hall, New York handleless cup & saucer, rose border, medium blue (Stubbs) 275.00

City Hall, New York plate, long-stemmed roses border, brown, 10½" d., Jackson (minor edge flakes) 130.00

City of Albany - State of New York plate, shell border, dark blue, 10" d. (Enoch Wood) 800.00

Deaf and Dumb Asylum, Hartford, Connecticut pitcher & bowl set, bowl w/Lawrence Mansion, Boston, vining leaf border, dark blue, bowl 14" d., pitcher 10" h., the set (R. Stevenson) 3,740.00

Elm at Cambridge, Mass. plate, fruits & flowers border, dark blue, 10" d. (Rowland & Marsellus) 85.00

Fair Mount Near Philadelphia soup plate, spread eagles amid flowers & scrolls border, dark blue, 10" d. (Stubbs) 275.00

Lafayette at Franklin's Tomb cream-

er, floral border, dark blue, 4" h.,
Wood (chip on spout) 425.00
Lafayette at Franklin's Tomb handle-
less cup & saucer, floral border,
dark blue, Wood (close mis-
match) 275.00
LaGrange, the Residence of the
Marquis Lafayette plate, flowers,
grapes & leaves border, dark
blue, 10" d., Wood (minor
stains) 300.00
Landing of General Lafayette at
Castle Garden, New York, 16 August, 1824 plate, floral & vine border, dark blue, 7 7/8" d., Clews
(pinpoint edge flake) 275.00
Landing of General Lafayette at
Castle Garden, New York, 16 August, 1824 platter, floral & vine
border, dark blue, 15¼" l.,
Clews (minor wear, edge glaze
flakes) 1,100.00
Landing of the Fathers at Plymouth,
Dec. 22, 1620 plate, pairs of birds
& scrolls & four medallions
w/ships & inscriptions border,
medium blue, 8½" d. (Wood) 250.00
Mohammedan's Mosque & Tomb
plate, dark blue, 10" d. (Hall) 225.00
Peace & Plenty plate, standing figure w/shield in center, flower
& scroll border, dark blue,
6 7/8" d., Clews (short rim hair-
line, edge chips) 200.00
Philadelphia - Cities Series plate,
floral border, dark blue, 5½" d.
(Clews) 375.00
Pine Orchard House, Catskill Moun-
tains plate, shell border, dark
blue, 10" d. 550.00

Sancho Panza & Horse Plate

Sancho Panza & Horse plate, floral
border, dark blue, 5½" d., Clews
(ILLUS.) 275.00
States series oval dish, castle
w/flag, boats in foreground
scene, border w/names of fifteen
states in festoons separated by

five-point stars, dark blue, 11" l.,
Clews (hairlines, one w/old re-
pair) 825.00
States series plate, two-story build-
ing w/curved drive, names of
states in festoons separated by
five-point stars border, dark blue,
7¾" d., Clews (edge wear, pin-
point flakes) 275.00
States series plate, three-story
building & observatory, names of
states in festoons separated by
five-point stars border, dark blue,
10½" d. (Clews) 467.50
States series platter, mansion
w/winding drive, border w/names
of fifteen states in festoons separated by five-point stars, dark
blue, 9½" l. 425.00
Table Rock, Niagara plate, shell
border, circular center w/trailing
vines around outer edge of cen-
ter, dark blue, 10" d. (Wood) 600.00
Texian Campaigne - Battle of Buena
Vista plate, symbols of war & a
"goddess-type" seated border,
blue, 8" d. (Shaw) 357.50
Texian Campaigne - Battle of
Chapultepec plate, symbols of war
& a "goddess-type" seated border,
blue, 9½" d. (Shaw) 495.00
Texian Campaigne - Battle of Palo
Alto plate, symbols of war & a
"goddess-type" seated border,
blue, 10½" d. (Shaw) 440.00
View of Trenton Falls - Three people
on rock plate, shell border, circular center w/trailing vine around
outer edge of center, dark blue,
7½" d. (Wood) 400.00
Walsingham Priory, Norfolk (Eng-
land) platter, floral border, medium dark blue, 18¾" l., Stevenson
(surface scratches) 335.00
Washington's Headquarters plate,
blue, 10" d. (Rowland & Marsel-
lus) 65.00
Washington Standing at his tomb
(scroll in hand) teapot, floral border, dark blue, 7" h., Enoch Wood
(crow's foot in bottom, stains,
small flakes on inner lid flange) . . 770.00
The Water Works, Philadelphia
plate, long-stemmed roses border,
black, 9 1/8" d. (Jackson) 75.00

HOUND-HANDLED PITCHERS

*Pitchers and jugs with handles formed as
hunting hounds comprise a unique collecting
category. For the most part, these pitchers*

had a hunting scene molded in relief on the body. Listed below by maker or type of glaze, these pitchers usually command a high price.

American Pottery Company, ovoid body tapering to a cylindrical neck w/high, arched spout, slender hound w/head & neck molded to top paws, the body molded w/a continuous hunting scene, vintage grape design around neck, mottled dark brown Rockingham glaze, impressed "American Pottery Co., Jersey City, N.J.," 19th c., 9¾" h. (stains, chip on bottom edge) $1,100.00

Bromley Pottery, bulbous, footed body w/a rounded shoulder to a wide, cylindrical neck & arched spout, slender molded hound w/the head & neck molded into the top legs, the body embossed w/a continuous hunt scene & the neck w/vintage grapevines, mottled dark brown Rockingham glaze, w/the eagle mark of William Bromley, Zanesville, Ohio, 19th c., 11" h. (minor chips) 1,700.00

Ohio, probably Vance Faience Pottery Co., Tiltonville, bulbous body embossed w/a continuous hunt scene below a cylindrical neck & high, arched spout, green matte glaze, 10" h. 200.00

Parian, tall footed ovoid body molded w/hanging game, wide arched spout, the hound handle w/long legs & the arched neck & head well above the top paws, England, 19th c., 10¾" h. 200.00

Rockingham-glazed, footed baluster-form body w/wide, arched spout, arched hound w/head away from top paws, body molded overall w/hanging game, mottled brown glaze, 7 3/8" h. 350.00

Rockingham-glazed, footed baluster-form body w/wide, arched spout, arched hound w/head away from top paws, body molded overall w/hanging game, mottled brown glaze, 8 7/8" h. 300.00

Rockingham-glazed, the body molded w/a continuous hunting scene, w/a mask spout, America, 19th c., 10½" h. (chips) 165.00

Rockingham-glazed, bulbous footed body w/a slanted shoulder to the cylindrical neck & high, arched spout, the hound handle w/a high, arched neck, the sides of the body embossed w/hunting scenes, mottled light brown glaze, 10¾" h. (bottom repair) 650.00

HULL

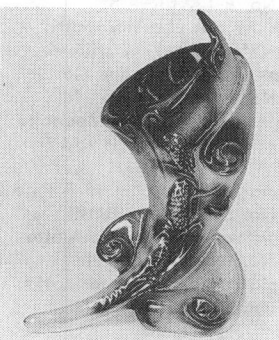

Parchment & Pine Cornucopia-vase

This pottery was made by the Hull Pottery Company, Crooksville, Ohio, beginning in 1905. Art Pottery was made until 1950 when the company was converted to utilitarian wares. All production ceased in 1986.

Ashtray, figural mermaid to one side, Ebb Tide patt., No. E-8 ..... $95.00

Bank, figural pig, sitting, Mirror Brown finish, No. 196, 6" h. 60.00

Basket, Continental patt., persimmon glossy glaze, No. C55, 12½" h. 70.00

Basket, Sunglow patt., yellow, No. 84, 6½" h. 40.00

Basket, Tokay patt., round "Moon" basket, green & white, No. 11, 10½" h. ....60.00 to 75.00

Basket, Wildflower patt., No. 65-7", 7" h. 375.00

Basket, Woodland Gloss patt., No. W22-10½", 10½" h. 110.00

Bottle, figural pink elephant, "Leeds," 7¾" h. 80.00

Candleholder, Woodland patt., No. W30, 3½" h. 15.00

Candleholders, Open Rose patt., model of a dove, No. 117-6½", 6½" h., pr. 150.00

Canister, cov., "Flour," Little Red Riding Hood patt. ....575.00 to 650.00

Casserole, cov., Sunglow patt., No. 51-7½", 7½" d. 20.00

Console bowl, Blossom Flite patt., gold decoration, No. T10, 16½" l. 50.00

Console bowl, Parchment & Pine patt., green, No. S-9, 16" l. 42.50

Console set: console bowl & pair of candleholders; Butterfly patt., bowl No. B21, candleholders No. B22, 3 pcs. 135.00

Cookie jar, cov., Barefoot Boy, made for Hull by Gem Refractories, 13" h. ....315.00 to 350.00

Cornucopia-vase, Bow Knot patt., No. B-5, 7½" h. 98.00

Cornucopia-vase, double, Bow Knot
patt., No. B-13, 13½" h. 165.00
Cornucopia-vase, Ebb Tide patt.,
maroon, No. E-9, 11¾" h. 135.00
Cornucopia-vase, Magnolia Gloss
patt., No. H-10-8½", 8½" h. 49.00
Cornucopia-vase, double, Magnolia
Gloss patt., blue, No. H-15-12",
12" h. 60.00
Cornucopia-vase, Parchment & Pine
patt., No. S-6, 12" h. (ILLUS.) 60.00
Cornucopia-vase, Woodland Matte
patt., No. W5-6½", 6½" h. 35.00
Cornucopia-vase, Woodland Matte
patt., yellow & green,
No. W10-11", 11" h. 55.00
Creamer, Blossom Flite patt., blue &
pink, No. T-15 . . . . 12.50
Creamer, tab-handled, Little Red
Riding Hood patt. 200.00
Creamer, Woodland Gloss patt.,
pink & green, No. W-27, 3½" h. . . 25.00
Creamer & cov. sugar bowl, Little
Red Riding Hood patt., head pour
creamer, pr. 595.00
Dish, leaf-shaped, Imperial patt.,
No. 63, 14" l. 17.00
Dish, leaf-shaped, Tokay patt.,
No. 19, 15" l. 50.00
Ewer, Bow Knot patt., No. B-1-5½",
5½" h. 65.00
Ewer, Bow Knot patt., pink & blue,
No. B-15-13½", 13½" h. 995.00
Ewer, Magnolia Matte patt., yellow
& rose, No. 18-13½", 13½" h. 160.00
Ewer, Woodland Matte patt.,
No. W24-13½", 13½" h. 150.00
Ewer-bud vase, Butterfly patt., white
& blue, No. B1, 6½" h. 35.00
Flowerpot w/attached saucer, Bow
Knot patt., No. B-6-6½", 6½" h. . . . 82.00
Jardiniere, Sueno Tulip patt.,
No. 115-33-7", 7" h. 130.00
Lamp, Little Red Riding Hood
patt. 1,485.00
Mug, Serenade patt., No. S22,
8 oz. 35.00
Mug, chocolate, Little Red Riding
Hood patt. 2,750.00
Pitcher, milk, 8" h., House 'n Gar-
den Ware 10.00
Planter, model of a pink poodle
standing on hind legs w/green fo-
liage to the back, Novelty line,
No. 114, 8" h. 45.00
Planter, model of a swan, yellow
glossy glaze, Imperial line,
No. 69, 8½ x 8½ x 10½" (ILLUS.
top next column) 25.00
Planter, model of two swans, green,
brown & white, "609 USA" in re-
lief, 8½" h. 20.00
Planter, model of twin geese, Nov-
elty line, No. 95, 7¼" h. 30.00

Hull Swan Planter

Planter, single ornate handle at one
end, Blossom Flite patt., No. T-12,
10½" l. 35.00
Plate, dinner, 10¼" d., House 'n
Garden Ware 6.00
Salt & pepper shakers, Little Red
Riding Hood patt., small, 3¼" h.,
pr. 45.00
Spice jar, cov., "Ginger," Little Red
Riding Hood patt. 495.00
String holder, Little Red Riding Hood
patt., 9" h. 1,900.00
Sugar bowl, cov., Little Red Riding
Hood patt. 215.00
Teapot, cov., Butterfly patt.,
No. B18 . . . . 70.00
Teapot, cov., Open Rose patt., pink,
No. 110-8½" 295.00
Teapot, cov., Parchment & Pine
patt., green, No. S-11, 6" 95.00
Tea set: cov. teapot, creamer & cov.
sugar bowl; Magnolia Gloss patt.,
pink & blue glaze, gold trim,
3 pcs. 110.00
Vases, 4¾" h., Dogwood patt.,
No. 516-4¾", pr. 70.00
Vase, 5½" h., Wildflower patt., pink
& blue, No. W-1-5½" 28.00
Vase, 6" h., Orchid patt.,
No. 302-6" 40.00
Vase, bud, 7" h., Open Rose patt.,
No. 129-7" 50.00
Vase, 8" h., Sueno Tulip patt.,
No. 100-33-8" 89.50
Vase, 8½" h., Iris patt., peach,
No. 403-8½" 75.00
Vase, 9½" h., Wildflower patt.,
No. W-12 . . . . 65.00
Vase, 10" h., Parchment & Pine
patt., No. S-4-10" 50.00
Vase, 10½" h., Butterfly patt.,
No. B14 . . . . 45.00
Vases, 10½" h., embossed peacock,
Novelty line, No. 73, pr. 80.00
Vase, 10½" h., Magnolia Matte
patt., No. 8-10½" 110.00

Vase, 10¾" h., Royal Ebb Tide patt.,
  figural fish base, pink, W18 . . . . . . 38.00
Vase, 14" h., Serenade patt., yel-
  low, No. S12 . . . . 75.00
Vase, 14½" h., Continental patt.,
  No. 57 . . . . 65.00
Vase, 16" h., Iris patt.,
  No. 414-16" 435.00
Wall pocket, Bow Knot patt., model
  of a cup & saucer, pink & blue,
  No. B-24-6", 6" h. 145.00
Wall pocket, Sunglow patt., model
  of a sad iron, No. 83, 6" h. 35.00

HUMMEL FIGURINES & COLLECTIBLES

"Boy with Toothache"

The Goebel Company of Oeslau, Germany, first produced these porcelain figurines in 1934 having obtained the rights to adapt the beautiful pastel sketches of children by Sister Maria Innocentia (Berta) Hummel. Every design by the Goebel artisans was approved by the nun until her death in 1946. Though not antique, these figurines with the "M.I. Hummel" signature, especially those bearing the Goebel Company factory mark used from 1934 and into the early 1940's, are being sought by collectors though interest may have peaked about 1980.

Accordion Boy, crown mark,
  1934-49, 5" h. $450.00
Accordion Boy, three line mark,
  1963-71, 5" h. 65.00
Accordion Boy, last bee mark,
  1972-79, 5" h. 95.00
Angel at Prayer font, full bee mark,
  1940-57, 4¾" h. 250.00
Angel Cloud font, 1934-49,
  2¼ x 4¾" 200.00
Angel Duet candleholder, 1972-79,
  5" h. 95.00
Angelic Sleep candleholder, crown
  mark, 1934-49, 3½ x 5" 325.00

Angelic Song, 1940-57,
  4" h. . . . . .125.00 to 150.00
Angel Serenade, 1940-57, 5½" h. . . . 375.00
Angel Shrine font, stylized bee
  mark, 1956-68, 3 x 5" 56.00
Angel with Accordion, 1940-57,
  2¼" h. 55.00
Angel with Accordion, 1956-68,
  2¼" h. 45.00
Angel with Accordion, 1972-79,
  2¼" h. 31.50
Angel with Birds font, 1934-49,
  3½" h. 300.00
Angel with Lute, 1940-57, 2¼" h. . . . 100.00
Angel with Lute, 1956-68, 2¼" h. . . . 39.00
Apple Tree Boy, 1940-57, 4" h. 150.00
Apple Tree Boy, crown mark,
  1934-49, 6" h. . . . . .500.00 to 600.00
Apple Tree Boy, 1940-57, 6" h. 225.00
Apple Tree Boy, 1956-68,
  6" h. . . . . .150.00 to 170.00
Apple Tree Boy, 1972-79,
  10" h. . . . . .500.00 to 600.00
Apple Tree Girl, 1940-57,
  4" h. . . . . .150.00 to 200.00
Apple Tree Girl, 1956-68, 4" h. 86.00
Apple Tree Girl, 1963-71, 4" h. 65.00
Apple Tree Girl, 1972-79, 6" h. 116.00
Artist (The), 1956-68, 5½" h. 160.00
Auf Wiedersehen, 1940-57,
  5" h. . . . . .400.00 to 500.00
Auf Wiedersehen, 1956-68,
  5" h. . . . . .130.00 to 150.00
Auf Wiedersehen, 1934-49, 7" h. . . .1,075.00
Ba-Bee Ring plaque, boy, 1934-49,
  5" d. 125.00
Baker, 1940-57, 4¾" h. . . . .150.00 to 200.00
Band Leader, crown mark, 1934-49,
  5" h. 512.00
Band Leader, 1940-57,
  5" h. . . . . .200.00 to 250.00
Band Leader, 1956-68,
  5" h. . . . . .150.00 to 175.00
Barnyard Hero, 1956-68, 4" h. 105.00
Barnyard Hero, three line mark,
  1963-71, 4" h. 90.00
Barnyard Hero, 1972-79, 4" h. 85.00
Barnyard Hero, 1940-57,
  5½" h. . . . . .425.00 to 450.00
Bashful, 1956-68, 4¾" h. 225.00
Bashful, 1972-79, 4¾" h. . . . .75.00 to 100.00
Begging His Share, 1934-49,
  5½" h. . . . . .450.00 to 550.00
Be Patient, 1963-71,
  6¼" h. . . . . .125.00 to 150.00
Big Housecleaning, 1972-79,
  4" h. . . . . .150.00 to 175.00
Bird Duet, 1963-71, 4" h. 80.00
Birthday Serenade, reverse mold,
  1956-68, 4¼" h. . . . . .350.00 to 400.00
Birthday Serenade, three line mark,
  1963-71, 4¼" h. 210.00
Birthday Serenade, reverse mold,
  1963-71, 4¼" h. 295.00

Birthday Serenade, reverse mold,
1972-79, 5¼" h. 95.00
Birthday Serenade table lamp,
1940-57, 7½" h. 1,000.00
Book Worm, 1940-57,
4" h. . . . . .220.00 to 260.00
Book Worm, 1940-57, 9" h. 760.00
Book Worm, 1956-68, 9" h. 1,350.00
Book Worm book end, 1940-57,
5½" h. 250.00
Book Worm book ends, 1956-68,
5½" h., pr. . . . . 250.00 to 275.00
Boots, crown mark, 1934-49,
6½" h. 565.00
Boots, 1940-57, 6½" h. . . . .300.00 to 400.00
Boots, stylized bee mark, 1956-68,
6½" h. . . . . .175.00 to 225.00
Boots, 1972-79, 6½" h. 70.00
Boy with Bird ashtray, 1934-49,
6½" h. 275.00
Boy with Bird ashtray, 1940-57,
6½" h. 185.00
Boy with Bird ashtray, 1956-68,
6½" h. 90.00
Boy with Toothache, 1940-57, 5½" h.
(ILLUS.) . . . . .225.00 to 250.00
Builder, 1972-79, 5½" h. 110.00
Busy Student, 1972-79, 4¼" h. 135.00
Celestial Musician, 1940-57,
7" h. . . . . .300.00 to 350.00
Chef, Hello, 1956-68,
6¼" h. . . . . .100.00 to 150.00
Chick Girl, 1940-57,
3½" h. . . . . .150.00 to 175.00

"Chick Girl"

Chick Girl, 1956-68, 3½" h.
(ILLUS.) 110.00
Chick Girl, 1956-68, 4¼" h. 175.00
Chick Girl, 1972-79, 4¼" h. 115.00
Chick Girl candy dish, 1956-68,
5¼" h. 275.00
Child in Bed plaque, 1940-57,
2¾" d. 120.00
Chimney Sweep, 1940-57,
4" h. . . . . .100.00 to 150.00
Chimney Sweep, 1940-57,
5½" h. . . . . .200.00 to 225.00
Chimney Sweep, 1956-68, 5½" h. . . . 110.00
Chimney Sweep, 1972-79, 5½" h. . . . 100.00
Confidentially, 1972-79, 5½" h. 150.00

Congratulations (no socks), 1940-57,
6" h. 190.00
Congratulations (w/socks), 1972-79,
6" h. 95.00
Coquettes, 1940-57, 5" h. . .225.00 to 250.00
Coquettes, 1956-68, 5" h. . .125.00 to 150.00
Culprits, 1934-49, 6¼" h. . .450.00 to 550.00
Culprits, 1940-57, 6¼" h. 240.00
Culprits table lamp, 1940-57,
9½" h. 300.00
Dealer display plaque, full bee
mark, 1940-57, 3¾" 425.00
Doctor, crown mark, 1934-49,
4¾" h. 365.00
Duet, stylized bee mark, 1956-68,
5" h. 170.00
Easter Greetings, last bee mark
used, 1972-79, 5½" h. 95.00
Farm Boy & Goose Girl book ends,
1956-68, overall 6" h., pr. 295.00
Farm Boy & Goose Girl book ends,
1972-79, overall 6" h., pr. 145.00
Feathered Friends, 1972-79,
4¾" h. 115.00
Feeding Time, 1940-57, 4¼" h. 325.00
Feeding Time, 1956-68, 5½" h. 180.00
Festival Harmony, w/flute, 1972-79,
10¼" h. 150.00
Flower Madonna, white, 1934-49,
9½" h. 690.00
Flower Madonna, white, 1956-68,
9½" h. 170.00
Flower Madonna, w/color, 1940-57,
open halo, 9½" h. 350.00
For Father, 1956-68, 5½" h. 130.00
For Mother, 1972-79, 5¼" h. 100.00
For Mother, three line mark,
1963-71, 5" h. 90.00
Friends, 1940-57, 5" h. 375.00
Friends, 1956-68, 5" h. 135.00
Friends, 1963-71, 5" h. 72.50
Going to Grandma's, 1956-68,
4¾" h. 300.00
Going to Grandma's, 1972-79,
4¾" h. 210.00
Going to Grandma's, 1934-49,
6" h. 725.00
Good Friends, 1972-79, 4" h. 90.00
Good Friends table lamp, 1956-68,
7½" h. 245.00
Good Night (angel standing),
1940-57, 3½" h. 51.00
Good Shepherd, 1972-79, 6¼" h. . . . 160.00
Good Shepherd font, 1940-57,
2¼ x 4¾" 77.00
Goose Girl, 1940-57, 4" h. 190.00
Goose Girl, 1972-79, 4¾" h. 108.00
Goose Girl, 1972-79, 7½" h. 250.00
Happiness, 1956-68, 4¾" h. 88.50
Happy Birthday, 1972-79, 5½" h. 125.00
Happy Days table lamp, 1963-71,
7¾" h. 475.00
Happy Pastime ashtray, 1956-68,
3½ x 6¼" 175.00

Happy Traveler, 1963-71, 5" h. 175.00
Happy Traveler, 1972-79, 5" h. 66.00

"Hear Ye, Hear Ye"

Hear Ye, Hear Ye, 1940-57, 6" h.
(ILLUS.) 175.00
Heavenly Angel font, 1956-68,
2 x 4¾" 45.00
Heavenly Protection, 1963-71,
6¾" h. 325.00
Herald Angels candleholder,
1934-49, 2¼ x 4" 450.00
Holy Child, 1972-79, 6¾" h. 100.00
Holy Child, 1940-57, 7½" h. 275.00
Holy Child, 1956-68, 7½" h. 100.00

"Home From Market"

Home From Market, 1972-79, 5¾" h.
(ILLUS.) 105.00
Infant of Krumbad, 1956-68, 10" h. . . 145.00
Joyful, 1940-57, 4" h. 115.00
Joyful, 1972-79, 4" h. 65.00
Joyous News, Angel with horn
candleholder, 1956-68,
2¾" h. . . . . 125.00 to 150.00
Just Resting, 1963-71, 3¾" h. 82.00
Just Resting, 1934-49, 5" h. 440.00
Just Resting, 1940-57, 5" h. 250.00
Just Resting, 1956-68, 5" h. 135.00
Kiss Me, w/socks, 1956-68, 6" h. 450.00
Knitting Lesson, 1972-79, 7½" h. 210.00
Let's Sing, 1940-57, 3¼" h. 150.00
Let's Sing, 1956-68, 3¼" h. 79.00

Little Band candleholder music box,
1956-68, 4¾ x 5" 295.00
Little Bookkeeper, 1963-71,
4¾" h. 180.00
Little Cellist, 1972-79, 6" h. 100.00
Little Drummer, 1972-79, 4¼" h. 75.00
Little Fiddler, 1956-68, 4¾" h. 115.00

"Little Fiddler"

Little Fiddler, 1972-79, 4¾" h.
(ILLUS.) 85.00
Little Fiddler, 1972-79, 6" h. 95.00
Little Fiddler, 1972-79, 7½" h. 185.00
Little Gardener, 1972-79, 4" h. 65.00
Little Goat Herder, 1956-68,
4½" h. 120.00
Little Goat Herder, 1940-57,
4¾" h. 250.00
Little Goat Herder, 1956-68,
4¾" h. 155.00
Little Helper, 1972-79, 4¼" h. 70.00
Little Hiker, 1940-57, 4¼" h. 102.00
Little Pharmacist, 1956-68, 6" h. . . . 365.00
Little Pharmacist, 1972-79, 6" h. . . . 185.00
Little Scholar, 1956-68, 5½" h. 125.00
Little Shopper, 1934-49, 4¾" h. 275.00
Little Shopper, 1956-68, 4¾" h. 86.00
Little Sweeper, 1972-79, 4½" h. 78.00
Little Thrifty, 1956-68, 5" h. 125.00
Madonna praying, standing, no
halo, white, 1934-49, 10¼" h. . . . 125.00
Madonna praying, standing, no
halo, 1956-68, 10¼" h. 95.00
Madonna w/child, seated, white,
1972-79, 12" h. 200.00
Madonna plaque, 1934-49, 3 x 4" . . . 200.00
Madonna plaque, 1956-68, 3 x 4" . . . 65.00
Meditation, 1934-49,
5¼" h. . . . . 450.00 to 500.00
Meditation, 1956-68, 5¼" h. 140.00
Merry Wanderer, 1940-57,
6¼" h. . . . . 225.00 to 275.00
Out of Danger, full bee mark,
1940-57, 6¼" h. . . . . 225.00 to 275.00
Out of Danger, 1972-79, 6¼" h. 196.00
Playmates, crown mark, 1934-49,
4" h. 350.00 to 400.00
Playmates, 1940-57, 4" h. 145.00
Playmates, 1956-68, 4" h. 101.00
Playmates, 1956-68,
4¼" h. . . . . 150.00 to 200.00

Postman, 1940-57, 5¼" h 208.00
Prayer Before Battle, 1934-49,
    4¼" h . . . . 400.00 to 500.00
Prayer Before Battle, 1940-57,
    4¼" h 225.00
Puppy Love, 1934-39,
    5" h . . . . 275.00 to 300.00
Puppy Love, 1940-57,
    5" h . . . . 225.00 to 250.00
Retreat to Safety, 1956-68,
    4" h . . . . 50.00 to 100.00
Retreat to Safety, 1963-71,
    4" h . . . . 75.00 to 100.00
Ride into Christmas, 1972-79,
    5¾" h . . . . 325.00 to 350.00
Ring Around the Rosie, 1956-68,
    6¾" h 2,200.00
Ring Around the Rosie, 1972-79,
    6¾" h . . . . 1,700.00 to 2,000.00
School Boy, 1934-49,
    5½" h . . . . 300.00 to 350.00
School Boy, 1956-68, 5½" h 95.00
School Boys, 1934-49, 10¼" h 2,400.00

"School Boys"

School Boys, 1956-68, 10¼" h.
    (ILLUS.) 1,250.00
School Girl, 1940-57,
    4¼" h . . . . 125.00 to 150.00
School Girl, 1956-68, 4¼" h 90.00
School Girl, 1934-49,
    5¼" h . . . . 300.00 to 350.00
Sensitive Hunter, 1934-49, double
    crown mark, 4¾" h 765.00
Sensitive Hunter, 1934-49, 4¾" h 595.00
Sensitive Hunter, 1940-57,
    4¾" h . . . . 200.00 to 225.00
Sensitive Hunter, 1956-68,
    4¾" h . . . . 110.00 to 120.00
Serenade, 1956-68, 7½" h 285.00
Sheep (lying), from large Nativity
    Set, 1963-71, 3¼" h 40.00
She Loves Me, 1934-49,
    4¼" h . . . . 300.00 to 350.00
Shepherd's Boy, 1934-49,
    5¼" h . . . . 400.00 to 450.00
Shepherd's Boy, 1940-57,
    5½" h . . . . 300.00 to 325.00
Shepherd's Boy, 1940-57, 6½" h 250.00

Shining Light, 1972-79, 2¾" h 40.00
Signs of Spring, w/two shoes,
    1940-57, 4" h . . . . 600.00 to 700.00
Silent Night candleholder, 1934-49,
    5½" l., 4¾" h . . . . 500.00 to 550.00
Singing Lesson, 1934-49,
    2¾" h . . . . 300.00 to 350.00
Singing Lesson, 1940-57,
    2¾" h . . . . 100.00 to 125.00
Singing Lesson, 1956-68, 2¾" h 80.00
Sister, 1934-49, 5½" h . . . . 325.00 to 350.00
Sister, 1940-57, 5½" h 125.00

"Sister"

Sister, 1956-68, 5½" h. (ILLUS.) 125.00
Skier, 1934-49, wooden poles,
    5" h 585.00
Skier, 1940-57, 6" h . . . . 150.00 to 200.00
Soloist, 1940-57, 4¾" h . . . 150.00 to 200.00
Soloist, 1956-68, 4¾" h . . . . . 80.00 to 90.00
Soloist, 1972-79, 5½" h 90.00
Spring Cheer, 1934-49, 5" h 286.00
Spring Cheer, 1940-57,
    5" h . . . . 150.00 to 200.00
Spring Cheer, 1956-68, 5" h 150.00
Star Gazer, 1940-57,
    4¾" h . . . . 200.00 to 250.00
Star Gazer, 1972-79, 4¾" h 144.00
Stitch in Time, 1972-79, 6¾" h 140.00
Stormy Weather, 1934-49,
    6¼" h . . . . 750.00 to 950.00
Stormy Weather, 1940-57,
    6¼" h . . . . 550.00 to 600.00
Stormy Weather, 1956-68,
    6¼" h . . . . 250.00 to 275.00
Stormy Weather, 1972-79,
    6¼" h . . . . 200.00 to 250.00
Street Singer, 1934-49, 5" h 300.00
Street Singer, 1940-57,
    5" h . . . . 125.00 to 150.00
Street Singer, 1956-68,
    5" h . . . . 100.00 to 125.00
Strolling Along, 1940-57,
    4¾" h . . . . 250.00 to 300.00
Strolling Along, 1956-68, 4¾" h 130.00
Strolling Along, 1972-79, 4¾" h 108.00
Sweet Music, striped socks, 1934-49,
    5¼" h . . . . 1,450.00 to 1,500.00
Sweet Music, 1956-68,
    5¼" h . . . . 100.00 to 120.00

Telling Her Secret, 1940-57,
5" h. . . . . .225.00 to 250.00
Telling Her Secret, 1956-68,
5" h. . . . . .175.00 to 200.00
Telling Her Secret, 1972-79,
6½" h. 179.00
To Market, 1940-57, 4" h. . . .125.00 to 150.00
To Market, 1956-68, 4" h. . . .100.00 to 125.00
To Market, 1934-49, 5½" h. 450.00
To Market, 1940-57,
5½" h. . . . . .200.00 to 225.00
Trumpet Boy, 1940-57,
4¾" h. . . . . .75.00 to 100.00
Umbrella Boy, 1963-71, 4¾" h. 550.00
Umbrella Boy, 1940-57,
8" h. . . . . .775.00 to 800.00
Umbrella Boy, 1972-79, 8" h. 650.00
Umbrella Girl, 1963-71,
4¾" h. . . . . .300.00 to 350.00
Umbrella Girl, 1940-57, 8" h. 850.00
Umbrella Girl, 1956-68, 8" h. 800.00
Umbrella Girl, 1963-71,
8" h. . . . . .625.00 to 650.00
Vacation Time plaque, w/six posts,
1940-57, 4 x 4¾". 250.00
Village Boy, 1956-68, 4" h. . .75.00 to 100.00
Village Boy, 1972-79, 4" h. . .50.00 to 75.00
Village Boy, 1963-71, 5" h. 50.00
Village Boy, 1934-49,
6" h. . . . . .300.00 to 325.00
Village Boy, 1940-57,
6" h. . . . . .200.00 to 250.00
Village Boy, 1956-68,
6" h. . . . . .125.00 to 150.00
Volunteers, 1934-49,
5½" h. . . . . .750.00 to 800.00
Volunteers, 1956-68, 6½" h. 300.00
Waiter, 1934-49, 6" h. 525.00
Waiter, 1940-57, 6" h. . . . .325.00 to 350.00
Waiter, 1956-68, 6" h. . . . .125.00 to 150.00

"Wash Day"

Wash Day, 1972-79, 6" h. (ILLUS.) . . . 100.00
Watchful Angel, 1940-57, 6½" h. . . . 400.00
Wayside Devotion, 1940-57,
7½" h. 350.00
Wayside Devotion, 1956-68,
8¾" h. . . . . .250.00 to 300.00

Wayside Harmony, 1956-68,
3¾" h. 96.00
Wayside Harmony, 1940-57,
5" h. . . . . .225.00 to 250.00
Wayside Harmony, 1956-68, 5" h. . . . 125.00
Which Hand?, 1963-71, 5½" h. 95.00
Which Hand?, 1972-79, 5½" h. 80.00
Worship, 1956-68, 5" h. 150.00

HUTSCHENREUTHER

The Hutschenreuther family name is associated with fine German porcelains. Carl Magnus Hutschenreuther established a factory at Hohenberg, Bavaria and was succeeded in this business by his widow and sons, Christian and Lorenz. Lorenz later established a factory in Selb, Bavaria (1857) which was managed by Christian and his son, Albert. The family later purchased factories near Carlsbad (1909), Altwasser, Silesia (1918) and Arzberg, Bavaria and, between 1917 and 1927, acquired at least two additional factories. The firm, noted for the fine quality wares produced, united all these branches in 1969 and continues in production today.

Celery tray, oval, decorated w/h.p.
blackberries, blossoms & leaves,
gold trim, artist-signed, ca. 1912,
12½" l. $58.00
Dresser set: tray, two cov. boxes &
two candleholders; decorated
w/green, gold & pink roses,
marked "Hutschenreuther, Bavar-
ia," 5 pcs. 225.00
Figure of a beautiful young girl in
rocking chair, h.p., pale peach &
green, artist-signed, 7½" h. 165.00
Figure of a nude woman seated &
holding bouquet of pastel flowers,
graceful fawn behind her, artist-
signed, 9" h. 495.00
Figure of a woman seated on chair
w/open book in her lap, 6" h. 165.00
Figure group, three cherubs holding
hands & dancing, artist-signed,
6¾" h. 300.00
Plates, dinner, 10¾" d., decorated
w/an etched gilt border & ruby
band, marked, set of 12 . . . . 605.00

IRONSTONE

The first successful ironstone was patented in 1813 by C.J. Mason in England. The body contains iron slag incorporated with the clay. Other potters imitated Mason's ware and today much hard, thick ware is lumped under the term ironstone. Earlier it was called by various names, including graniteware. Both plain white and decorated wares were made throughout the 19th century. We include the Tea Leaf pattern and its variants here.

TEA LEAF

Tea Leaf Platter & Coffeepot

Baker, rectangular, Mellor, Taylor & Co., 5¾ x 17½", 2" h............ $25.00
Bone dish, crescent-shaped, Mayer China Co., Beaver Falls, Pennsylvania 35.00
Bone dish, scalloped, Wilkinson 65.00
Bowl, 6 1/8" d., 3½" h., Homer Laughlin "Kitchen Kraft" line, ca. 1930's (slight wear)............. 55.00
Bowl, 9½" l., rectangular, Wedgwood & Co..................... 40.00
Bowl, 9½" d., Micratex by Adams, ca. 1960's................. 18.00
Bowl, 9¾" w., square, ribbed, Wedgwood & Co................. 65.00
Bowl, 10¾" d., deep rounded sides, Homer Laughlin "Kitchen Kraft" line, ca. 1930's 55.00
Butter dish, cov., Bamboo patt., Grindley & Co................... 60.00
Butter dish, cov., Sunburst patt., Arthur Wilkinson (some wear) 55.00
Butter dish, cover & liner, Chelsea patt., Wedgwood & Co. (slight rim chips) 160.00
Butter dish, cov., square, Mellor, Taylor & Co. 75.00
Butter pat, Anthony Shaw.......... 12.00
Butter pat, square, Wedgwood & Co. 12.00
Cake plate, round, Mayer China Co., Beaver Falls, Pennsylvania (some wear) 55.00
Chamber pot, open, Chelsea patt., Johnson Brothers (slight wear) ... 120.00
Coffeepot, cov., Bamboo patt., Alfred Meakin, 9" h. (ILLUS. left)............................. 225.00
Compote, open, 9½" d., 3½" h., fluted sides, Anthony Shaw 245.00
Compote, open, 10" w., square, footed, Henry Burgess 190.00

Creamer, Bamboo patt., Alfred Meakin.......................... 145.00
Creamer, Chelsea patt., Alfred Meakin (slight wear) 130.00
Creamer, Embossed patt., gold lustre, Powell & Bishop, 5½" h. (slight wear).................. 85.00
Creamer, Empress patt., Micratex by Adams, ca. 1960's 60.00
Creamer, Lily of the Valley patt., Anthony Shaw (slight wear) 290.00
Creamer, plain round, Alfred Meakin, 5¾" d. 135.00
Cup & saucer, handled, child's, gold lustre, Mellor, Taylor (some lustre wear) 110.00
Cup & saucer, handled, Square Ridged patt., Wedgwood & Co. 85.00
Cup & saucer, handled, squatty form, Alfred Meakin, large (some wear) 55.00
Cup & saucer, handled, tapered cylinder, Wedgwood & Co. 55.00
Gravy boat, Bamboo patt., Alfred Meakin (slight wear) 55.00
Gravy boat, Cable patt., Anthony Shaw (slight wear) 55.00
Gravy boat, Fig Cousin patt., pink lustre trim, Davenport (some discoloration).................... 230.00
Gravy boat, Square Ridged patt., gold lustre, Bishop & Stonier (lustre wear) 35.00
Mug, octagonal, Henry Burgess..... 220.00
Mush bowl, round, Mellor, Taylor... 60.00
Mush bowl, round, Anthony Shaw .. 90.00
Pitcher, 6" h., Bamboo patt., Alfred Meakin........................ 165.00
Pitcher, 6" h., Empress patt., Micratex by Adams, ca. 1960's 90.00
Plate, 7" d., gold lustre, Bridgewood 10.00

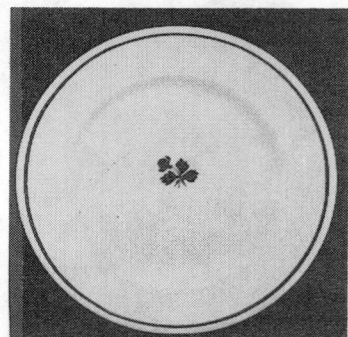

Tea Leaf Plate

Plate, 7" d., Alfred Meakin (ILLUS.)......................... 10.00
Plate, 7 7/8" d., Chinese patt., Anthony Shaw.................... 15.00
Plate, 8" d., Alfred Meakin 12.00

Plate, 9" d., Lily of the Valley patt.,
  Anthony Shaw 22.00
Plate, 9¼" d., Arthur Wilkinson 20.00
Plate, 9¾" d., Wedgwood & Co. 22.00
Plate, 10" d., Red Cliff Company,
  Chicago, ca. 1960's 35.00
Platter, 7½ x 11", rectangular,
  Alfred Meakin 35.00
Platter, 10 x 14", Chinese patt., An-
  thony Shaw 85.00
Platter, 10 x 14", rectangular, Alfred
  Meakin (ILLUS. right) 45.00
Possett cup, handled, footed, Chi-
  nese patt., Anthony Shaw (some
  wear) 300.00
Sauce dish, square, Alfred Meakin,
  4¼" 12.00
Sauce tureen, cover, underplate &
  ladle, Empress patt., Micratex by
  Adams, ca. 1960's, the set 280.00
Shaving mug, Chinese patt., Antho-
  ny Shaw 155.00
Shaving mug, Alfred Meakin,
  3½" d., 3¼" h. 225.00
Soup tureen, cover & ladle, Brocade
  patt., Alfred Meakin, 16" l. 1,700.00
Sugar bowl, cov., Bamboo patt.,
  Alfred Meakin (slight wear) 100.00
Sugar bowl, cov., Cable patt., An-
  thony Shaw 120.00
Teapot, Chinese patt., Anthony
  Shaw, 10" h. 375.00
Toothbrush holder, footed flaring
  cylindrical body w/rolled rim,
  Alfred Meakin (repaired lip
  chip) 200.00
Toothbrush holder, square, Grindley
  & Co. 140.00
Undertray, rectangular, Fish Hook
  patt., Alfred Meakin, 8 x 12" 50.00
Vegetable dish, cov., oblong, Chel-
  sea patt., Alfred Meakin, 10" l. .. 120.00
Vegetable dish, cov., square, Fish
  Hook patt., Alfred Meakin, 9" w.
  (slight wear) 100.00
Vegetable dish, cov., rectangular,
  bracket-footed, Fish Hook patt.,
  Alfred Meakin, 7 x 11" 145.00
Vegetable dish, cov., Gentle Square
  patt., Thomas Furnival & Sons,
  10" w. 120.00
Vegetable dish, cov., Square Ridged
  patt., gold lustre, Powell & Bishop, 7¼" w. 60.00
Vegetable dish, open, oblong, Empress patt., Micratex by Adams,
  ca. 1960's, 8" l. 30.00
Wash set: wash bowl & pitcher,
  shaving mug, cov. toothbrush
  holder, soap dish, cover & liner;
  Lily of the Valley patt., Anthony
  Shaw, the set (ILLUS. of pitcher &
  bowl) 1,195.00

Lily of the Valley Wash Bowl & Pitcher

Waste bowl, round, Square Ridged
  patt., Mellor, Taylor, 6" d. 85.00

TEA LEAF VARIANTS

Baker, oval, Morning Glory patt.,
  Wileman & Co., 6 x 8" 90.00
Butter dish, cover & liner, Teaberry
  patt., J. Clementson 375.00
Creamer, porcelain, footed, Clover-
  leaf patt., gold lustre 30.00
Creamer, Morning Glory patt., Els-
  more & Forster 265.00
Creamer, Teaberry patt., Heavy
  Square shape, J. Clementson,
  5 1/8" h. (some wear) 100.00
Cup & saucer, handled, child's, Tea-
  berry patt., J. Clementson 325.00
Cup & saucer, handleless, Morning
  Glory patt., Portland shape, Els-
  more & Forster (some wear) 55.00
Cup & saucer, handleless, paneled,
  Teaberry patt., J. Clementson 140.00
Cup & saucer, handleless, Tobacco
  Leaf patt., No. 2 blank, Elsmore &
  Forster 65.00
Cup & saucer, handleless, Teaberry
  patt., Ring O'Hearts shape (tiny
  rim pit on cup) 110.00
Cup plate, Laurel Wreath patt., lus-
  tre band trim, Elsmore & Forster .. 75.00
Pitcher & bowl, miniature, h.p. lus-
  tre leaves & berries on white,
  Gray's Pottery, ca. 1935-60 ...... 75.00
Plate, 6 7/8" d., Morning Glory
  patt., Portland shape, Elsmore &
  Forster 35.00
Plate, 8" w., ten-sided, Pinwheel
  patt. (some wear) 27.50
Plates, 7¾" d., Teaberry patt., New
  York shape, J. Clementson, set
  of 4 .... 70.00
Sugar bowl, cov., Morning Glory
  patt. 230.00
Sugar bowl, cov., Pepper Leaf patt.,
  plain round shape w/loop han-
  dles 90.00

Sugar bowl, cov., Teaberry patt.,
plain round shape, J. Clement-
son 165.00

Vegetable dish, cov., oval, loop
handles, Pepper Leaf patt., 10" l.
(slight wear) 130.00

Vegetable dish, cov., oblong octagonal, lustre band trim, Livesley
& Powell, 10" l. (slight wear) 230.00

GENERAL

Mason's Ironstone Dinner Set

Bowl, 13½" d., Sydenham patt., all
white 55.00

Butter dish, cov., President patt., all
white 250.00

Butter dish, cover & liner, Sharon
Arch patt., all white, 3 pcs. 195.00

Chamber pot, cov., Corn & Oats
patt., all white 130.00

Compote, open, reticulated octagonal bowl on pedestal base,
all white, Mellor, Venables & Co.,
ca. 1849 . . . . 235.00

Creamer, Grand Loops patt., all
white 35.00

Cup & saucer, handleless, Columbia
patt., all white 30.00

Cup & saucer, handleless, Lily of the
Valley w/Thumbprints patt., all
white 30.00

Cup & saucer, handleless, Laurel
Wreath patt., all white 40.00

Cups & saucers, handleless, Sydenham patt., all white w/copper lustre bands on inside of cups,
4 sets, 16 pcs. 80.00

Cup plate, "gaudy," Urn patt.,
4 1/8" d. 60.50

Dinner set: 22 - 9½" d. dinner
plates, 19 salad plates, eight
bread & butter plates, 11 soup
plates, 3 graduated lozenge-form
bowls, two lozenge-form platters,
large lozenge-form platter & pair
of sq. cov. vegetable dishes;
underglaze-blue lappet border enclosing a brilliantly enameled
chinoiserie garden scene within a
famille rose border of trailing foliage & fruit, Mason's Patent Iron-

stone mark, mid-19th c., the set
(ILLUS of part) 6,600.00

Pitcher, 8" h., leaves & berries de-
sign, all white, Hughes 55.00

Pitcher, 13" h., rope pattern handle,
all white, Alfred Meakin 80.00

Pitcher, 13" h., round, Corn & Oats
patt., all white 85.00

Plate, 8½" d., fourteen-sided,
"gaudy," Strawberry patt. 78.00

Plate, 8½" d., Wrapped Sydenham
patt., all white, Edward Walley . . . 14.00

Plate, 9" d., Lily of the Valley
w/Thumbprints patt., all white . . . 18.00

Plates, 9" d., transfer-printed w/a
bold blue Imari-style design
trimmed w/red enameling,
marked "Amherst - Japan," set
of 3 . . . . 135.00

Plate, 9 3/8" w., paneled sides,
"gaudy," Urn & Flowers patt. (mi-
nor enamel flaking) 165.00

Plate, 9½" d., Niagara patt., all
white, Edward Walley 16.00

Plate, 9 5/8" w., paneled sides,
"gaudy," Urn & Flowers patt. (mi-
nor enamel flaking) 247.50

Plate, 10" d., Lily of the Valley
w/Thumbprints patt., all white . . . 22.00

Plate, 10½" d., Sydenham patt.,
T. & R. Boote 35.00

Plates, 10" d., gently scalloped rim,
"gaudy" Imari decoration in cobalt
blue, reddish orange & gold on
white, 19th c., set of 4 . . . . 594.00

Platter, 13¼" l., "gaudy" rose decoration in red, blue, green & black,
marked "England" 137.50

Relish dish, Gothic Cameo patt., all
white 25.00

Relish dish, Grenade patt., all
white, Cockson & Chetwyng 17.00

Relish dish, leaf & vine design, all
white, 8" l. 50.00

Relish dish, mitten-shaped, Wheat &
Clover patt., all white 36.00

Relish dish, Vineyard patt., all
white, Davenport 50.00

Sauce tureen, cov., Vintage patt.,
all white, Adams 75.00

Soup plate w/flanged rim, Fan
patt., all white, Anthony Shaw,
9½" d. 10.00

Soup tureen, cover & undertray, bulbous squatty footed body w/mold-
ed lion mask handles, domed
cover w/scroll finial, decorated
w/colorful transfer-printed design
of exotic Oriental style trees &
flowers w/birds, Mason's, third
quarter 19th c., matching oblong
undertray 15" l., the set 1,540.00

Sugar bowl, cov., Victor patt., all
white 65.00

Teapot, cov., Wheat & Clover patt.,
all white, Pierson 155.00

Large Ironstone Tub

Tub, two-part, oval, the deep top
section horizontally ribbed &
transfer-printed in underglaze-
blue w/two wide borders of Oriental vases of flowers alternating
w/stands of bamboo & other
flowering plants between narrower floral & foliate-scroll borders &
trellis diaper bands repeated
around the interior rim, the ends
w/blue dolphin-mask handles, the
top section inset into a very deep
conforming base section w/a
matching decoration & the bottom
of the interior w/the exterior
print within an oval panel, "Semi-
China" octagonal mark in underglaze-blue, abrasions at handles
w/one chipped, the other bolted
on, one side of base cracked, a
chip on the footrim, ca. 1825-35,
23 7/8" l., 23¾" h. (ILLUS.) 4,675.00
Tureen, cov., oblong octagonal footed body w/scrolled end handles,
matching domed cover w/blossom
finial, "gaudy," Urn & Flowers
patt., 9½" l., 7¾" h. (minor
wear) 770.00
Undertrays, rounded rectangular
form w/molded end handles,
transfer-printed w/a bold blue
Imari-style design trimmed w/red
enameling, marked "Amherst -
Japan," 8¾ x 11", pr. 160.00
Vegetable bowl, cov., footed, Cable
patt., all white, Alfred Meakin,
12" l. 45.00
Vegetable bowl, cov., Corn & Oats
patt., all white, 9" d. 80.00
Vegetable bowl, cov., Fig patt., all
white, Wedgwood & Co. 175.00
Vegetable bowl, cov., Octagon
patt., all white, T. & R. Boote 135.00
Vegetable bowl, cov., Prize Bloom
patt., all white, T.J. & J. Mayer .. 195.00

Vegetable bowl, cov., Sydenham
patt., all white, T. & R. Boote,
large......................... 250.00
Vegetable bowl, cov., Washington
patt., all white, ca. 1863 .... 125.00
Vegetable tureen, cov., oval, Blackberry patt., all white, Challinor,
ca. 1862, 6 x 8 x 11½" 110.00
Wash bowl & pitcher, Grape Octagon patt. w/copper lustre trim,
Livesey & Powell, the set 475.00
Wash bowl & pitcher, Sydenham
patt., T. & R. Boote, the set 450.00
Waste bowl, Prize Bloom patt., all
white, T.J. & J. Mayer 40.00

JASPER WARE (Non-Wedgwood)

*Jasper ware is fine-grained exceedingly
hard stoneware made by including barium
sulphate in the clay and was first devised by
Josiah Wedgwood, who utilized it for the
body of many of his fine cameo blue-and-white
and green-and-white pieces. It was subsequently produced by other potters in England
and Germany, notably William Adams &
Sons, and is in production at the present. Also
see WEDGWOOD - JASPER.*

Cheese dish, cov., high domed blue
cover w/white relief figures of
classical ladies in panels, rolled
rim on base w/white relief flower
& leaf band, acorn finial on cover,
Dudson Bros., England, 11" d.,
11¼" h. $550.00
Pitcher, jug-type, 4 7/8" h.,
4 3/8" d., white relief hunting
scene w/men on horses w/dogs
& a stag on a blue ground,
white relief rim band, Copeland,
19th c. 75.00
Pitcher, 6 7/8" h., 4 1/8" d., cylindrical body w/white relief classical ladies in panels around the
dark green sides, a greyish green
rim band w/white relief leaf
band, Dudson Bros., England,
19th c. 110.00
Pitcher, 7 7/8" h., 5" d., cylindrical
body w/a band of small white relief classical figures around the
base & a band of white relief floral swags around the rim all on
the dark blue ground, angled
white handle, Copeland, 19th c. .. 110.00
Plaque, pierced to hang, white relief bust of an Indian in full headdress on green, reads "Painted
Horse Chief Galalla," owl decoration on border, 4¾" d. 125.00
Plaque, pierced to hang, "Lohen-

grin," heavy white relief figure of the swan prince & the fair Elaine on blue ground, molded white relief floral border, Germany, 5¾" d. 95.00

Plaque, pierced to hang, white relief figure of an angel beside two children on a sage green ground, white relief floral border, Germany, late 19th - early 20th c., 5¾" d. 75.00

Plaque, pierced to hang, white relief angel holding baby w/a cupid beside her on a sage green ground, white relief floral border, Germany, late 19th - early 20th c., 5 7/8" d. 75.00

Plaque, pierced to hang, white relief figure of a fisherman w/net & girl w/water jug on sage green ground, white relief floral border, Germany, 6" d. 85.00

Plaque, pierced to hang, white relief figure of Cupid kissing a bust of a lady on a sage green ground, white relief floral border, Germany, 6" d. 75.00

Plaque, pierced to hang, white relief scene of Cupid shooting an arrow at a seated lady on a sage green ground, Germany, 6 1/8" d. 75.00

Plaque, pierced to hang, white relief figure of a fisherman being embraced by a young lady as he steps into a small rowboat on a blue ground, white relief floral border, Germany, 6 3/8 x 7 7/8" oval 125.00

Tea set: 5¾" h. cov. teapot, 4¾" h. cov. teapot, cylindrical hot water pitcher w/metal lid, open sugar & cylindrical creamer; bulbous spherical bodies on pots, each w/white relief bands of classical dancing figures on a dark blue ground, garland bands around tops, Copeland-Spode, the set 245.00

Vase, 6½" h., tall slender waisted ovoid body w/curved leafy loop handles down the sides, white relief figure of a classical lady on a green ground, white relief floral trim, Germany 48.00

JEWEL TEA AUTUMN LEAF

Though not antique, this ware has a devoted following. The Hall China Company of East Liverpool, Ohio, made the first pieces of Autumn Leaf pattern ware to be given as premiums by the Jewel Tea Company in 1933.

The premiums were an immediate success and thousands of new customers, all eager to acquire a piece of the durable Autumn Leaf pattern ware, began purchasing Jewel Tea products. Though the pattern was eventually used to decorate linens, glasswares and tinwares, we include only the Hall China Company items in our listing.

Bean pot, two-handled........... $120.00
Bowl, fruit, 5½" d. 5.50
Bowl, soup, 8¼" d. 12.50
Butter dish, cov., ¼ lb. 180.00

Rare Version of ¼ lb. Butter Dish

Butter dish, cov., 'butterfly' or 'wings' finial, ¼ lb. (ILLUS.) 1,450.00
Cake plate w/"Goldenray" metal base 135.00
Candy dish w/"Goldenray" metal base ....425.00 to 525.00
Casserole, open, swirled souffle', 2 pt. 100.00
Casserole, open, swirled souffle', 3 pt. 12.50
Coffeepot, cov., eight cup, 10" h. 38.00
Coffeepot (or casserole) warmer, oval 165.00
Coffeepot (or casserole) warmer, round 125.00
Creamer & cov. sugar bowl, new style, pr. 25.00
Cup & saucer 8.50
Cup & saucer, St. Denis style 30.00
Custard cup.................. 7.00
Grease jar, cov. 15.00
Irish coffee mug 95.00
Pickle dish, oval, 9" l. 17.00
Pie baker, 9½" d.............. 22.50
Pitcher, utility, 2½ pt. 18.00
Plate, bread & butter, 6" d. 6.00
Plate, salad, 7¼" d............... 6.50
Plate, pie, 8" d............... 21.00
Plate, 9" d................... 7.50
Plate, dinner, 10" d............. 11.00
Salt & pepper shakers, bell-shaped, small, pr........................ 16.00
Teapot, cov., long spout 55.00
Teapot, cov., Newport style 125.00
Tidbit tray, three-tier 59.00
Vase, bud ....150.00 to 175.00
Vegetable bowl, cov., oval, 10" 40.00
Vegetable bowl, open, 9" d. 60.00
Vegetable bowl, open, oval, 10½".. 18.00
Vegetable bowl, open, divided, oval, 10½" l. 70.00

JUGTOWN

This pottery was established by Jacques and Juliana Busbee in Jugtown, North Carolina, in the early 1920's in an attempt to revive the skills of the diminishing North Carolina potter's art as Prohibition ended the need for locally crafted stoneware whiskey jugs. During the early years, Juliana Busbee opened a shop in Greenwich Village in New York City to promote the North Carolina wares that her husband, Jacques, was designing and a local youth, Ben Owen, was producing under his direction. Owen continued to work with Busbee from 1922 until Busbee's death in 1947 at which time Juliana took over management of the pottery for the next decade until her illness (or mental fatigue) caused the pottery to be closed in 1958. At that time, Owen opened his own pottery a few miles away, marking his wares "Ben Owen - Master Potter." The pottery begun by the Busbee's was reopened in 1960, under new management, and still operates today using the identical impressed mark of the early Jugtown pottery the Busbee's managed from 1922 until 1958.

Bowl, 7¼" d., 4" h., deep rounded body on thick footring & w/a flat molded rim, fine Chinese Blue (mottled turquoise blue & deep red) glaze, turquoise blue interior, circular mark $330.00

Bowl, 11" d., 4¾" h., deep angled sides w/an upright banded rim & tapering to a small, thick footring, light grey mottled glaze, circular mark 165.00

Vase, 4½" h., ovoid body, Chinese Blue glaze splashed w/red 195.00

Vase, 5½" h., 6¾" d., bulbous ovoid body below a gently sloping wide shoulder to a short, wide neck, deep red mottled glaze w/turquoise blue spots, circular mark (bruise to rim) 412.50

Vase, 6" h., 5" d., bulbous ovoid body tapering to a short, wide cylindrical neck flanked by small loop handles, alligatored Chinese Blue (mottled turquoise & red) glaze, circular mark 275.00

Vase, 7" h., 3¼" d., cylindrical lower body tapering very slightly to a wide cylindrical neck w/flared rim, two small applied medallions at the shoulder, Chinese Translation-type, a Chinese Blue glaze of mottled *sang-de-boeuf*, green, white & turquoise over a grey clay body, die-stamped circular mark . . 550.00

Vase, 7¾" h., 3¾" d., cylindrical waisted body on a low footring &

tapering to a short, cylindrical neck, Chinese Translation-type, the neck & shoulder covered in a Chinese Blue glaze mottled turquoise & red, the lower body w/a clear glaze over a beige clay body, circular mark 385.00

Vase, 9" h., 6¼" d., bulbous baluster-form body, overall mottled deep red glaze w/blue specks, circular mark 935.00

Vase, 11" h., 7¾" d., footed bulbous ovoid body tapering to a flaring neck, Chinese Translation-type, covered w/a Chinese Blue glaze of mottled turquoise & deep red, circular mark 825.00

LEEDS

The Leeds Pottery in Yorkshire, England, began production about 1758. It made, among other things, creamware that was highly competitive with Wedgwood's. In the 1780's it began production of reticulated and punched wares. Little of its production was marked. Most readily available Leeds ware is that of the 19th century during which time the pottery was operated by several firms.

Model of a stallion, the alert standing animal w/a cream-colored body, rose-outlined mouth & nostrils & brown-glazed mane, tail, ears (repaired), hooves & eyes, wearing a tan harness & standing on a green-glazed chamfered rectangular base molded on the top w/a foliate border & around the footrim w/an ogee-shaped edge, both picked out in brown, early 19th c., 16" l., 17" h. (minor chips beneath base, repaired ankles & neck) $3,300.00

Pitcher, 8½" h., pearlware, ovoid body w/pointed spout & strap handle, h.p. in blue w/a large three-leaf sprig surrounded by small stylized flowers & leaf sprigs, early 19th c. (very minor edge flakes) . . . . '. 715.00

Pitcher, 9 3/8" h., pearlware, ovoid body below a wide & short cylindrical neck w/pointed spout, strap handle, five-color decoration of stylized flowers, sheaf of wheat & farm implements in a landscape w/buildings, inscribed "William Wane, Nottingham 1803" (minor wear & scratches, crow's foot in bottom) 2,172.50

Plate, 8¼" w., pearlware, octagonal, blue feather-edged design w/a h.p. polychrome spread-
winged American eagle & shield
in the center (wear, scratches,
small flakes) 660.00
Sugar bowl, cov., pearlware, wide
gently rounded footed base w/low
domed cover & pointed finial, h.p.
w/a large stylized tulip blossom &
leaves in yellow, green, brown &
orange, early 19th c., 4¼" d.,
4¾" h. (minor flakes on base,
small chips on cover) 412.50
Tea caddy, cov., pearlware, deep
rectangular body raised on short
block feet, the low domed cover
w/center loop handle, h.p. on the
sides w/a bouquet of stylized
flowers in green, dark brown &
yellow ochre, thin band edge
trim, 5¼" h. (hairline on interior
baffle, minor edge wear, small
flake on cover flange) 1,017.50

LENOX

*The Ceramic Art Company was established
at Trenton, New Jersey, in 1889 by Jonathan
Coxon and Walter Scott Lenox. In addition
to true porcelain, it also made a Belleek-type
ware. Re-named Lenox Company in 1906, it
is still in operation today.*

Book end, model of a stylized Trojan
horse head, white glaze, incised
"ABCO '37 L," marked, 7" h. (single) $250.00
Box, cov., raised floral design in
white on pink ground, green
Wreath mark, 2½ x 5" 70.00
Bust of a lady w/cascading hair,
white glaze, green Wreath mark,
8½" h. 325.00
Cake plate, handled, Lenox Rose
patt., green Wreath mark,
11" d. 55.00
Creamer & cov. sugar bowl, Belvi-
dere patt., gold mark, pr. 55.00
Cups & saucers, demitasse, gold
embossed band on lip of cup &
on edge of saucer, artist-signed,
6 sets 150.00
Dresser box, cov., kidney-shaped,
decorated w/violets & butter-
cups 65.00
Jar, cov., ribbed body, pink
w/white-painted finial, 6" h. 225.00
Lamp, table model, green w/double
white bird handles, original hard-
wares & finial, green Wreath
mark 95.00

Model of a penguin, coral glaze,
4¾" h. 185.00
Model of a swan, ivory glaze, green
Wreath mark, 12" l. 55.00
Pitcher, 5" h., pink body w/white
handle, green Wreath mark 45.00
Pitcher, 7" h., stylized bird of paradise design, blue Wreath mark ... 34.00
Salt shaker, pearlized background
decorated w/colorful roses, Palette mark 75.00
Tea set: cov. teapot, sugar bowl &
creamer, six cups & saucers, six
ice cream bowls, six cake plates;
Mandarin patt., 27 pcs. 650.00
Vase, 7" l., basket-form, an upturned cylinder w/open ends, a
round loop handle at the center,
decorated w/silver bands down
the center & around the rims &
handle, ca. 1930 .... 95.00

Lenox Vase with Silver Overlay

Vase, 9¾" h., cylindrical body
w/rounded shoulder to the short
rolled neck, cobalt blue ground
almost completely overlaid w/sil-
ver w/small pierced scrolls
(ILLUS.) 632.50
Vase, 14½" h., tall ovoid body
tapering to a narrow short flared
neck, cobalt blue ground overlaid
w/stylized Art Nouveau style silver lily blossoms & whiplash devices, printed factory mark, mi-
nor losses to overlay, ca. 1920 ... 1,210.00

LIMOGES

*Numerous factories produced china in
Limoges, France, with major production in
the 19th century. Some pieces listed below are
identified by the name of the maker or the
mark of the factory. Although the famed
Haviland Company was located in Limoges,*

wares bearing their marks are not included in this listing. Also see HAVILAND.

Limoges Game Plate

Bowl, 6" d., shell-shaped w/scalloped rim, h.p. gold & rust floral decoration $18.00

Bowl, 9½" d., gold base & gold rococo rim, lavishly decorated inside & out w/red & rust cherries, artist-signed, ca. 1912, T & V (Tresseman & Vogt) 165.00

Box, cov., square, pate-sur-pate, blue ground w/white relief cherubs on cover, ca. 1890, 4¼" w. 195.00

Cake plate, open-handled, decorated w/purple florals & gold trim, 10" d., GDA (Gerard, Dufraisseix & Abbot) 40.00

Candlesticks, four-footed w/gold decoration on cream background & scalloped rims, 6½" h., pr. 65.00

Chamberstick, ring-handled, raised gold overlay on a pink ground w/purple violets, W.G. (William Guerin) 110.00

Charger, pierced to hang, h.p. decoration of two quail on pastel natural background, heavy gold rococo edge, artist-signed, 12" d. 295.00

Charger, decorated w/a lovely color American Indian bust portrait, 13" d. 475.00

Chocolate pot, cov., decorated w/purple floral sprays & gold trim, 9" h., GDA 95.00

Chocolate set: 10" h. cov. pot & four cups & saucers; floral border design w/gold handles & trim, Coronet (George Borgfeldt), 9 pcs. 325.00

Cracker jar, cov., h.p. coral, yellow & white flowers on gold & white ground, artist-signed & dated 1894, 7½" h. 200.00

Creamer & cov. sugar bowl, decorated w/purple florals & gold trim, large, GDA, pr. 70.00

Cup & saucer, demitasse, decorated w/blue forget-me-nots, Lanternier - France 25.00

Cup & saucer, demitasse, pink roses decoration, etched gold rims 25.00

Dinner service: ten each of dinner plates, soup plates, berry bowls & nine dessert plates & cups & saucers plus three serving pieces; decorated w/pink flowers & white daisies, Elite - France, the set 395.00

Dish, three-lobed form w/gold scrolled center handle, irregular edge w/lavish gold trim, each section decorated w/pink roses & green leaves, all w/gold outlining against white background, 13" w., 5" h. 185.00

Dresser set: cov. pin box, candlestick, cov. powder box, cov. hair receiver & cov. trinket box on rectangular tray; each piece decorated w/dark blue flowers & a gold monogrammed medallion & dark blue borders, 6 pcs. 395.00

Dresser tray, h.p. roses on green background, scalloped edges, artist-signed, 12" oval 110.00

Ewer, decorated w/h.p. red, pink & yellow roses, gold spout & handle, artist-signed, 7½" d., 5" h., J.P.L. (Jean Pouyat, Limoges) 195.00

Fish plate, h.p. fish w/large yellow roses, artist-signed, 10" d. 65.00

Fish plates, each h.p. w/a different elegant fish, mollusk & seaplant design, gold border band, 8½" d., set of 12 . . . . 350.00

Fish platter, rectangular w/a scalloped rim, an ivory ground decorated w/a scene of three fish swimming amid kelp & seaweed, gilt border band, 22" l. 302.50

Game plate, h.p. turkey in a landscape, wide deep red scrolling border w/gilt trim, artist-signed, 9" d., L.R. & L. - Limoges - France (Lazeyras, Rosenfeld & Lehman) . . 125.00

Game plates, pierced to hang, h.p. colorful pheasants on one & a pair of quail on the other, w/pastel green & gold background, scalloped edges w/gilt band, artist-signed, 11¾" d., pr. (ILLUS. of one) 395.00

Game plates, each w/a different h.p. game bird, heavy gold rococo border, ca. 1900, 8½" d., set of 12 . . . . 1,200.00

Humidor, cov., round, h.p. lavender & pink floral decoration, gold pipe finial, artist-signed 120.00

Mustache cup & saucer, gold handle, ruffled rim & base, lavender

floral decoration & gold trim, ca.
1908 .... 65.00
Oyster plate, green w/white floral
decoration, Emile Coiffe 175.00
Pitcher, cider, 5½" h., 6½" d.,
squatty bulbous body w/angled
handle, h.p. red cherries & green
leaves against pastel ground, gold
handle & trim, artist-signed 165.00
Pitcher, tankard, 10¾" h., h.p.
w/gooseberry decoration 198.00
Pitcher, tankard, 11" h., figural
dragon handle, mask spout, varied pastel shading w/small fruits,
ca. 1904, J.P.L. (Jean Pouyat,
Limoges) 235.00
Pitcher, tankard, 14½" h., decorated w/the portrait of a monk in a
wine cellar, wearing a white habit
& holding a candle, artist-signed.. 400.00
Pitcher, tankard, 17" h., h.p. floral
decoration, T & V - Limoges -
France (Tressemann & Vogt) 280.00

Limoges Plaque

Plaque, rectangular, h.p. w/a scene
of gleaners, based on the Millet
painting, 19th c., 6 x 9" (ILLUS.) .. 522.50
Plaque, pierced to hang, h.p.
woodland scene w/cabin & pond,
4 x 10½", T & V 650.00
Plaque, h.p. Oriental poppies on
green ground w/heavy gold rococo scroll border, artist-signed,
12¼" d..................250.00 to 275.00
Plaque, scene of Venus & cherubs
reclining above waves, printed
marks, 19th c., framed, 16" w.,
12" h....................... 440.00
Plate, 8" d., violets & leaves decoration w/gold border, T & V -
France 20.00
Plate, 8½" d., seashell decoration
w/gold trim, artist-signed 40.00
Plate, 9" d., decorated w/h.p. fruit,
scalloped border, artist-signed,
ca. 1908 .... 47.50
Plates, 7" d., each decorated
w/different flowers, pansies,
asters, etc., set of 6 .... 165.00
Plates, dessert, 9" d., scalloped rim,

professionally decorated w/a variety of flowers on pink & white,
Elite - France (Bawo & Dotter), set
of 6 .... 245.00
Punch bowl, the exterior decorated
w/deep purple & transparent
green grapes, the interior
w/groupings of putti amid grapevines in pastel clouds on gilt,
14" d........................ 632.50
Ramekin, gold decor on white, ca.
1875, A & D - Limoges, France.... 15.00
Relish tray, decorated w/blue flowers, w/ornate edge, 6 x 12"...... 35.00
Relish tray, shaped oblong form,
decorated w/poppies & other
colorful flowers within gilt borders, 17" l. 220.00
Serving dish, long oval scroll- and
leaf-embossed sides mounted on
a footed gilt-metal base w/a
figural bird & branch handle at
the top edge, decorated w/h.p.
red flowers w/a blue ribbon
against a shaded pink background, artist-signed, marked
"Limoges - France" in green,
12" l. 425.00
Tray, large flowers on deep colored
background, gold trim, artist-
signed, 8 x 12", T & V - France ... 120.00
Tray, gold handles, h.p. roses decoration on gold & white background, gold rim band, artist-
signed, 12½ x 18" 275.00
Tray, rectangular, intricate h.p. geometric design, 15½" l., P.P. -
Limoges - France (Paroutaud
Freres) 235.00
Vase, 6¾" h., two-handled, decorated w/h.p. pink roses, J.P.L....... 165.00
Vase, 11" h., handled, h.p. mums
decoration, lavish gold, T & V -
Limoges 135.00
Vase, 18" h., red & pink roses on
green background w/gold nipple
top 275.00
Vase, 18" h., trumpet-form, h.p. red
& pink roses & gold trim on top,
artist-signed, ca. 1916 .... 275.00
Vegetable dish, cov., oblong, deco-
rated w/small blue flowers, D &
Co. (R. Delinieres).............. 35.00

LIVERPOOL

Liverpool is most often used as a generic term for fine earthenware products, usually of creamware or pearlware, produced at numerous potteries in this English city during the late 18th and early 19th centuries. Many examples, especially pitchers, were decorated with transfer-printed patriotic designs aimed specifically at the American buying public.

Early 19th Century Liverpool Pitcher

Mug, cylindrical, a sepia transfer-printed design of a central oval reserve w/inscription below crossed flags centered by a Liberty cap & above a banner inscribed "Independence," early 19th c., 5" h. (flakes on base) $1,540.00

Pitcher, jug-type, 7 5/8" h., cream-ware, black transfer-printed & enamel-trimmed portraits of "proscribed patriots" Samuel Adams & John Hancock, the reverse w/a three-masted sailing ship & "Success to Trade," under the spout an American eagle & the date "1802," trimmed in blue, red, yellow & green enamel, early 19th c. (repaired spout & minor imperfections) 2,750.00

Pitcher, jug-type, 8" h., one side w/a black transfer-printed oval medallion enclosing a bust of Washington flanked by figures of Justice, Liberty & Victory, the other side w/a large oval medallion w/an inscription to Washington below crossed banners & a Liberty cap & w/a banner reading "Independence" below, an American eagle under the spout, ca. 1800..1,650.00

Pitcher, jug-type, 10" h., black transfer-printed scene entitled "Defense of Stonington, Connecticut," the reverse w/"American Eagle" & cypher "GLP," a wreath beneath the spout, old repair, break to spout, flakes & spider cracks, early 19th c. (ILLUS.) 7,700.00

Pitcher, jug-type, 10½" h., cream-ware, black transfer-printed & enamel-decorated design of the three-masted sailing ship "Car-

penter" flying an American flag & trimmed in red, blue, green, brown & yellow, the reverse w/an oval panel showing a memorial to George Washington, under the spout an American eagle & a foliate monogram, early 19th c. (hairlines, chips at rim & spout) 1,870.00

Pitcher, jug-type, 11" h., cream-ware, black transfer-printed monument to George Washington in a landscape, the reverse w/"Peace, Plenty and Independence," under the handle the inscription "A man without example - a patriot without reproach," the rim & spout w/floral swags, all trimmed w/gold, early 19th c. (discoloration, flakes on base) ...2,200.00

Teapot, cov., slightly ovoid body painted in shades of rose, blue, iron-red, purple & green on either side w/an Oriental-style floral spray & scattered sprigs beneath an iron-red scalloped line around the neck repeated on the cover rim beneath further floral sprays & sprigs, the spout rim & knop dashed in iron-red, Pennington's factory, ca. 1780, 6 5/8" h. (small footrim chip, small hairlines & chips in cover flange) 345.00

LLADRO

Spain's famed Lladro porcelain manufactory creates both limited and non-limited edition figurines as well as other porcelains. The classic simple beauty of the figures and their subdued coloring makes them readily recognizable and they have an enthusiastic following of collectors.

Ballerina, sitting, "Shelley," No. 1357, 6½" h. $185.00
Ballerina, lying down, "Heather," No. 1359, 9¼" l. 185.00
Clown, lying on stomach, No. 4618, 6" l. 300.00
Embroiderer, No. 4865, 10¾" h. 325.00
Girl seated before a scale weighing her cat, No. 5474, 6½" h.........175.00
Girl sleeping in rocker holding her doll, No. 5448, 4½" h...........120.00
Hebrew Student, No. 4684, 10¾" h. 375.00
Little Pals, No. S-7600 ....2,950.00
Little Traveler, No. S-7602 ....850.00 to 900.00
My Buddy, No. S-7609 ....300.00
My Dog, standing lady holding a

Pomeranian, No. 4893, unglazed,
14¾" h. 100.00
School Days, No. S-7604 . . .400.00 to 450.00
Spring Bouquets,
No. S-7603 . . . . .450.00 to 500.00
Star Gazing, No. 1477, 7½" h. 100.00
Wishing on a Star, No. 1475,
6½" h. 100.00

LONGWY

Unusual Longwy Vase

*This faience factory was established in 1798
in the town of Longwy, France and is noted
for its enameled pottery which resembles
cloisonne. Utilitarian wares were the first
production here but by the 1870's an Oriental style art pottery that imitated "cloisonne"
was created through the use of heavy enamels
in relief. By 1912, a modern Art Deco style
became part of Longwy's production and
these wares, together with the Oriental style
pieces, have made this art pottery popular
with collectors today. As interest in Art Deco
has soared in recent years, values of
Longwy's modern style wares have risen
sharply.*

Bowl, 14¾" d., round flaring sides,
white crackled glaze decorated
w/Cubist stylized vine in blue,
green, yellow & grey, the exterior
glazed in blue, stamped "PRIMA-
VERA LONGWY FRANCE" & art-
ist's signature, ca. 1920's $528.00
Box, cov., footed, decorated
w/colorful enameled flowers &
gold trim, 5" sq. 125.00
Charger, the shallow circular dish
molded in low-relief w/stylized
black & white nude ladies in a
tropical beach landscape in eggplant, mustard yellow & shades
of blue, stamped "PRIMAVERA
LONGWY FRANCE," 14½" d. 1,650.00
Charger, circular, painted w/a white
stork surrounded by yellow, pink
& salmon blossoms against a blue

& green ground, decorated by R.
Rizzi, stamped company mark &
"DECOR de R. Rizzi," numbered
"33/60," ca. 1920's, 14¾" 660.00
Plaque w/hanger, cloisonne'-style
enamel decoration of a spread-
winged parrot on colorful blossoming branches against a blue
ground, 9" d. 275.00
Vase, 9" h., tubular shape, enam-
eled florals in blue, yellow &
red 300.00
Vase, 10 7/8" h., footed cylinder
w/everted rim, decorated w/a
Cubist landscape in rust, grey &
moss green over a crackled glaze,
enhanced w/black, stamped
"Atelier primavera LONGWY
FRANCE" & w/artist's signature,
ca. 1920's (some restoration at
rim). 605.00
Vase, 11½" h., gourd-shaped, deco-
rated w/stylized naked women on
a waterside among stylized vegetation, in various tones of blue
trimmed w/green & black,
stamped "PRIMAVERA LONGWY
FRANCE," ca. 1920's 2,640.00
Vase, 13 3/8" h., bell-shaped, a
band of stylized flowers & fruits in
mustard & cherry around the lower portion, the octagonal upper
portion w/defined ribbing ascending to rim, over a crackled glaze,
stamped "SOCIETE DES FAIENCER-
IES LONGWY FRANCE" w/compa-
ny logo (ILLUS.) 935.00

LUSTRE WARES

*Lustred wares in imitation of copper, gold,
silver and other colors were produced in England in the early 19th century and onward.
Gold, copper or platinum oxides were painted on glazed objects which were then fired,
giving them a lustred effect. Various forms
of lustre wares include plain lustre — with the
entire object coated to obtain a metallic effect, bands of lustre decoration and painted
lustre designs. Particularly appealing is the
pink or purple "splash lustre" sometimes referred to as "Sunderland" lustre in the mistaken belief it was confined to the production
of Sunderland area potteries. Objects decorated in silver lustre by the "resist" process,
wherein parts of the objects to be left free
from lustre decoration were treated with wax,
are referred to as "silver resist."*

*Wares formerly called "Canary Yellow Lus-
tre" are now referred to as "Yellow-Glazed
Earthenwares."*

COPPER

Pitcher, 5¾" h., globular lower section, wide neck, C-scroll handle, overall polychrome floral decoration (minor wear) $71.50

Pitcher, 6½" h., commemorative, footed bulbous body w/a flaring cylindrical neck w/long spout, C-scroll handle, a wide canary yellow middle band w/white oval reserves printed in black, one w/"LaFayette," the other w/"Cornwallis," early 19th c. (spout chip).................... 385.00

Pitcher, 6¾" h., jug-type, tapered body on a short foot, a raised beaded band around the rim, squared handle, a wide yellow band around the middle decorated w/a black transfer-printed bust portrait of Andrew Jackson on both sides, titled "General Jackson - The Hero of New Orleans"......................1,100.00

Pitcher, 7¼" h., cylindrical w/narrow neck & flaring top, decorated w/polychrome floral enameling (some wear) 137.50

SILVER & SILVER RESIST

Bowl, 9¼" d., 4¼" h., deep rounded sides on thick footring, silver lustre resist w/large grape clusters & leaves spaced along wavy band, early 19th c. (wear, hairlines in foot) 165.00

Creamer, wide ovoid body w/a short wide cylindrical rim & angled handle, silver resist decoration of a large bird in a tree, 4 5/8" h. (wear) 132.00

Pitcher, 5½" h., jug-type, bulbous ovoid body tapering to a flat rim w/pinched spout, angled handle, silver lustre resist w/a neck band of grapevines, the body w/a large "farmer's arms" design (wear).... 137.50

SUNDERLAND PINK & OTHERS

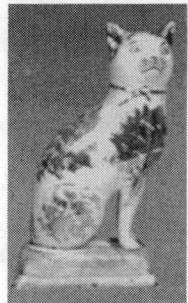

Cat Figure with Pink Lustre

Butter tub w/attached undertray, cov., wide & low cylindrical body, the sides & edge of undertray w/wide white bands between thin pink lustre bands, lavish gold florals & trim, scalloped rim, marked "C.T." w/an eagle in blue, Germany, 6½" d., 4½" h. ... 125.00

Models of cats, seated white animal decorated w/splotches of pink lustre, England, 19th c., 7" h., pr. (ILLUS. of one) 467.50

Pitcher, 4½" h., jug-type, wide bulbous body w/a wide cylindrical neck & angled handle, pink lustre resist w/a vintage grape design & blue rim & base stripes (chips) ... 220.00

Pitcher, 7 1/8" h., jug-type, commemorative, wide ovoid body w/a short cylindrical neck, simple "C" handle, each side w/a large oval reserve transfer-printed in dark brown, one w/"Iron Bridge at Sunderland," the other w/a scene of two sailors drinking, the scenes trimmed in polychrome, the background w/splashed pink lustre, early 19th c. (wear, hairlines & small chips)..................... 385.00

Pitcher, 11½" h., black transfer-print of "Ship Caroline" on one side & "The Shipwright Arms" the other, pink lustre trim 137.50

Plaque, pierced to hang, scroll-molded shaped rim w/pink lustre trim forming a shadow box effect & framing a black transfer scene highlighted w/polychrome enameling, marked "Waverley, S. Moore & Co, Sunderland," 7 7/8 x 8½" 255.00

MAJOLICA

Majolica, a tin-enameled glazed pottery, has been produced for centuries. It originally took its name from the island of Majorca, a source of figuline (potter's clay). Subsequently it was widely produced in England, Europe and the United States. Etruscan majolica, now avidly sought, was made by Griffen, Smith & Hill, Phoenixville, Pa., in the last quarter of the 19th century. Most majolica advertised today is 19th or 20th century. Once scorned by most collectors, interest in this colorful ware so popular during the Victorian era has now revived and prices have risen dramatically in the past few years. Also see MINTON and WEDGWOOD.

ETRUSCAN

Bread tray, Oak Leaf patt. $225.00

Butter dish, cov., Bamboo patt...... 250.00

Coffeepot, cov., Shell & Seaweed
  patt. 695.00
Creamer, Sunflower patt. 290.00
Creamer & cov. sugar bowl, Wild
  Rose patt., cream ground, pr. 100.00
Cup & saucer, Shell & Seaweed
  patt. 230.00

Begonia Leaf Dish

Dish, Begonia Leaf patt., yellow,
  pink & green glaze, 6½ x 8½"
  (ILLUS.) 45.00
Mug, Pineapple patt. 195.00
Pitcher, 5½" h., Wild Rose patt., co-
  balt blue ground 185.00
Pitcher, 8" h., Wild Rose w/Butterfly
  Lip patt. 225.00
Plate, 9" d., apples & strawberries
  on basketweave background 100.00
Plate, 9" d., Cauliflower patt., dark
  rose border . . . . 200.00 to 225.00

Etruscan Morning Glory Plate

Plate, 9" d., Morning Glory patt.,
  red ground, pale yellow blossoms
  (ILLUS.) 325.00
Plate, 13" d., Oak Leaf patt. 180.00
Syrup pitcher w/metal lid, Sunflower
  patt., white w/blue trim 550.00
Tray, serving, oblong w/looped
  branch end handles, Geranium
  patt. 325.00
Trivet, Daisy patt. 295.00
Underplate, Sunflower patt., pink
  glaze, 5" d. 150.00

GENERAL

Bowl, 3¾" d., 2½" h., decorated
  with three groups of yellow

daisies & leaves on basketweave
  designed medium green ground . . 80.00
Bowl, 10" l., oval, handled, openwork edge, h.p. flowers, Italy 80.00
Bowl, 13" l., oval, Wheat patt.,
  American-made, ca. 1890 . . . . 150.00
Bust of a blackamoor, wearing a
  feathered turban & buttoned
  collarless jacket, the face w/a
  matte glaze, the clothing w/a
  glossy glaze in white w/yellow &
  green detailing, Europe, 19th c.,
  24" h. 660.00
Cake dishes, birds, grapes & leaves
  on a blue ground, West Germany,
  6" d., set of 4 . . . . 100.00
Cake plate, birds, grapes & leaves
  on a blue ground, West Germany,
  9¼" d., 3¼" h. 175.00
Center bowl, deep oblong bowl
  w/shaped rim & flower-molded
  loop end handles, the front
  w/molded flower & berry panels,
  the back w/a landscape scene
  w/trees & mountains, all on a red
  ground, France, 6 x 12" 325.00
Centerpiece, ovoid form w/shaped
  lip & bulbous sides, applied &
  molded w/cherubic figures, floral
  garlands & leaf scrolls in relief,
  on a blue ground, each end w/a
  cherubic handle, raised on a
  shaped foot w/similar applied &
  molded decorations including dolphins, scallop shells & leaf scrolls,
  all in pale green, olive green &
  brown, England, 19th c., 17" l.,
  11½" h. 467.50

Ornate Majolica Centerpiece

Centerpiece, the wide shallow bowl
  w/a flattened wide rim above the
  sides w/a band of pierced interwoven rings supported by a center stem flanked by sea nymphs
  w/a helmet at the bottom &
  raised on a round base w/four
  scroll feet, overall polychrome

decoration, impressed marks of Sarreguemines, France, ca. 1875, chips, restorations, 14¾" d., 14¾" h. (ILLUS.) 880.00

Compote, open, 9" d., 3½" h., large red poppies & green leaves on a yellow basketweave ground, Germany 45.00

Compote, open, 9" d., 6" h., Shell patt., Morley 350.00

Compote, open, 9" h., pedestal base, Sunflower patt., Samuel Lear, England 450.00

Compote, open, 9½" h., Strawberry patt., turquoise interior, Wedgwood 395.00

Creamer, Corn patt. 75.00

Creamer, Water Lily patt. 45.00

Majolica Blackamoor Figure

Figure of a Blackamoor, exotically dressed w/a turban, jacket & striped shorts, hands extended to hold a tray, Italy, ca. 1900, 39" h. (ILLUS.) 2,200.00

Flower bowl, boat-shaped w/deep rounded sides & scalloped rim, molded w/panels of pink lily flowers & green leaves against a tan & brown ground, blue interior, England, 10" l., 5½" h. 180.00

Flower bowl, boat-shaped w/two floral handles, red background, the front decorated w/molded flowers, berry reserves & a five-color tree & grassland scene, the reverse decorated w/mountains & shrubs, 6" w., 12" l. 325.00

Garden seat, figural, model of a crouching monkey on a yellow woven rush-style base & holding a yellow pomegranate w/green leaves in one hand, supporting on his head a thin dark blue cushion w/yellow buttons & tassels & green corded trim, Europe, late

19th c., 19" h. (slight firing crack in left wrist & one tassel) 11,000.00

Jardiniere, deep cylindrical sides w/a rounded base & flat everted rim molded w/egg-and-dart design, the cobalt blue body decorated w/colored flowering vines, flanked by lion mask handles, Europe, late 19th c., 13¼" h. (chips) 3,575.00

Jardiniere, model of a large scrolled seashell in white & gold supported on a cluster of coral on a rockwork base, impressed "MINTON" & w/date letter for 1870, 26½" h. 12,100.00

Jardinieres, wide tapering ovoid body w/wide swirled ribbing & a flat everted rim w/egg-and-dart design, the pale blue body w/figural goat head handles joined by large leafy swags w/pink ribbon at the center, similar leaf band around the foot, impressed "Minton," & w/various model numbers, date mark for 1865, 15" h., pr. 7,700.00

Mug, Pond Lily patt., J. Holdcroft, England 165.00

Mug, Sunflower patt., cobalt blue ground, possibly Wedgwood...... 135.00

Mustard pot on attached underplate, cov., Peony patt., peony blossom finial, shades of pink, green & yellow, pink interior............. 225.00

Pitcher, 4 7/8" h., Raspberry patt., Avalon Faience line, Haynes & Co., Baltimore 75.00

Pitcher, 6¾" h., Strawberry patt., Avalon Faience line, Haynes & Co., Baltimore 150.00

Pitcher, 7¼" h., gold floral decoration on white, Florilar line, Haynes & Co., Baltimore 85.00

Pitcher, 7¼" h., model of a yellow ear of corn w/long green leaves 195.00

Pitcher, cov., 7½" h., red poppy w/bluish green leaves on white, possibly Haynes & Co., Baltimore............................ 125.00

Pitcher, 8" h., Wild Rose patt., tree bark background 165.00

Pitcher, 8½" h., cylindrical body w/angled handle, a large pointed leaf w/a fern sprig against a brown tree bark ground 145.00

Pitcher, 9" h., motto-type, cylindrical body w/looped branch handle, molded w/four narrow bands around the body each w/an incised motto alternating w/three wider bands of large green cabo-

chons, tan & brown ground, green
interior, Wedgwood, 19th c. 395.00
Pitcher, 10½" h., figural Pug dog in
an upright seated position, open
mouth w/carved teeth serves as
pouring spout, possibly America . . 495.00
Planter, rectangular, molded on the
side w/a cockatoo on a limb
w/cobalt blue flowers, against a
dark grey patterned ground, pink
interior, English diamond registry
mark, 4¼ x 4¼ x 6½" 350.00
Plate, 7½" d., reticulated border,
relief-molded decoration w/pur-
ple, white & blue flowers & green
leaves 95.00
Plate, dessert, 8" d., light blue
w/strawberry, flower & leaf decoration, Germany 20.00
Plate, 8" d., pink florals & green foliage against a dark grey to green
ground, scalloped rim, Germany . . 35.00
Plate, 8¼" l., Begonia Leaf patt.,
pink & green 65.00
Plate, 8½" d., decorated w/molded
purple grapes & green leaves, St.
Clemens, France mark 55.00
Plate, 8½" d., Strawberry patt.,
Choisy-le-Roi, France 125.00
Plate, 9" d., Water Lily patt., Zell,
Germany 40.00
Plate, 10" d., Blackberry patt. 105.00
Plates, 8" w., grape leaf-shaped,
dark green glaze, marked "Wedg-
wood," set of 8 (minor edge
flakes) 200.00
Sardine box, cov., Sardinia patt.,
Wedgwood 895.00

Sardine Box in Cobalt Blue

Sardine box, cov., rectangular box
on attached undertray, cobalt blue
ground w/a floral vine on the
sides & figural fish on the cover,
rope borders (ILLUS.) 800.00
Sugar bowl, cov., Bamboo patt. 175.00
Sugar bowl, cov., Bird & Fan patt. . . 95.00
Tea set: cov. teapot, cov. sugar
bowl & creamer; flat, rounded
"moon-shaped" bodies w/arched
bases, branch handles, cobalt
blue ground molded w/colorful
flowers & leaves, 3 pcs. (ILLUS.
top next column) 950.00
Toothbrush holder, molded floral

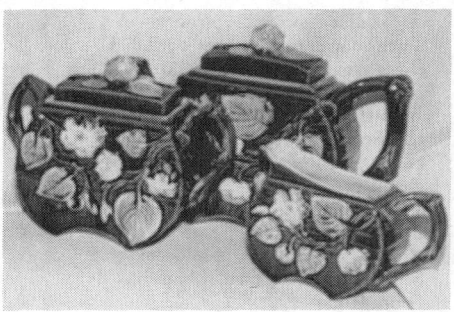

Majolica Tea Set

decoration on white, probably
Haynes & Co., Baltimore, 5" h. . . . 65.00
Tray, diamond-shaped, fans, insects
& bird decoration, 16" l., 11" w. . . 125.00
Vase, 5¾" h., Chrysanthemum
patt., decorated w/dark pink
flowers, Avalon line, Haynes &
Co., Baltimore 85.00
Vase, 9½" h., model of a fish,
Shorter, England 200.00
Vase, 13" h., 7" w., raised butterfly,
bird & leaves on a turquoise
ground, Holdcroft, England, ca.
1873 .... 850.00
Vase, 17" h., baluster-form, supported by three sea sprites, blue, late
19th c. 880.00

Figural Majolica Vases

Vase, figural, modeled as a stork
standing on one leg, a small
snake wrapped around its beak,
white body w/black wing tips,
yellow legs & beak, green rushes
& grey stonework on oval base,
Holdcroft, England, w/repairs
(ILLUS. left) 1,200.00
Vase, figural, modeled as a heron
holding a fish in its beak, standing on one leg, dark green wings
& maroon breast w/white neck &
thighs, brown legs, green rushes
& grey stonework on oval base,

Holdcroft, England, w/repairs
(ILLUS. right) 1,400.00

MARBLEHEAD

Marblehead Cider Set

This pottery was organized in 1904 by Dr. Herbert J. Hall as a therapeutic aid to patients in a sanitarium he ran in Marblehead, Massachusetts. It was later separated from the sanitarium and directed by Arthur E. Baggs, a fine artist and designer, who bought out the factory in 1916 and operated it until its closing in 1936. Most wares were hand-thrown and decorated and carry the company mark of a stylized sailing vessel flanked by the letters "M" and "P."

Bowl, 3½" d., 1½" h., gently rounded sides, speckled mustard yellow ground decorated w/a band of stylized leaves, impressed mark (stilt pull at base) $495.00

Bowl, 6¼" d., 2½" h., shallow sides w/a rounded base below a slightly incurved upright edge, banded decoration of holly in green & red against a matte blue ground, impressed mark 1,320.00

Candlesticks, medium blue, 4¼" h., pr............................ 250.00

Cider set: pitcher & six mugs; ovoid w/angled handles, each glazed in dark green w/subtle darker grey-brown rim & handle, impressed mark, pitcher initialed by Arthur Baggs, mugs 3½" h., pitcher 8" h., the set (ILLUS. of part) 1,760.00

Plaque, rectangular, incised w/a landscape showing a copse of trees, in matte glazes of light brown, blue & grey, impressed twice w/firm's mark, in a wide flat oak frame, plaque 6 1/8 x 9¾" 2,420.00

Plate, 9¼" d., smooth matte green glaze decorated w/a band of short & long brown lines forming

an abstract design around the rim 412.50

Vase, 3½" h., wide ovoid body tapering gradually to a wide, rolled flat rim, decorated w/five oval medallions depicting grape clusters & leaves in blue & green on a greyish-white ground, by Arthur Irwin Hennessey, impressed mark & artist-initialed, ca. 1907 ..1,100.00

Vase, 5½" h., oval, blue body w/repeating border design of modeled green leaves & red berries, green band at top rim, impressed ship mark 660.00

Vase, 6" h., 3¼" d., cylindrical, decorated w/incised Greek key-type designs around the top continuing to bands forming panels around the sides, green bands against a smooth matte blue speckled ground, incised ship mark & "H" 935.00

Vase, 6½" h., 4" d., tall ovoid body w/wide flat mouth, decorated w/a band of tall stylized leafy trees w/blue berries against an ochre ground, smooth matte speckled glaze, impressed mark, remnant of paper label, initialed "H.T." 3,520.00

Vase, 7¼" h., tall ovoid body w/wide, flat mouth, decorated w/a band of stylized trees around the top w/their slender trunks down the body, trees in navy blue wash against a stippled green ground, by Hannah Tutt, impressed mark & artist-initialed, ca. 1910 ....1,100.00

Vase, 9½" h., 5" d., tall cylindrical body w/a flat inverted rim, decorated w/incised blossoms around the rim on tall stems forming panels around the sides, blue & brown against a speckled grey ground, incised mark (restoration to rim, small glaze bubbles) 1,980.00

MARTIN BROTHERS POTTERY

Martinware, the term used for this pottery, dates from 1873 and is the product of the Martin brothers - Robert, Wallace, Edwin, Walter and Charles - often considered the first British studio potters. From first to final stages, their hand-thrown pottery was completely the work of the team. The early wares may be simple and conventional, but the Martin brothers built up their reputation by producing ornately engraved, incised or carved designs as well as rather bizarre figural wares.

The amusing face-jugs are considered some of their finest work. After 1910, the work of the pottery declined and can be considered finished by 1915, though some attempts were made to fire pottery as late as the 1920's.

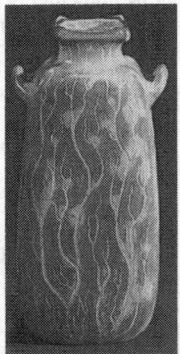

Martin Brothers Vase

Jar, cov., modeled as a grotesque bird, the head w/closed eyes & a laughing expression to the open beak, glazed in browns, beige & deep blues, signed & dated "7-1892" (head) & "10-1891" (body), 4¼" w., 10½" h. (minor nick on beak)......................$6,875.00

Jar, cov., modeled as a strange bird, the cover formed by the head, naturalistic coloring, the base & cover incised "Martin Bros. London Southall RW," & base "71890," & cover "7V890," 15" h. (beak restored)................7,475.00

Model of a grotesque bird, standing w/molded wings & feathers, blue & brown glaze, artist-signed, dated 1893 (or 98), 3" h............ 715.00

Pitcher, 8 1/8" h., jug-type, bulbous ovoid body w/short neck, pulled spout & applied handle, molded in low-relief w/a smiling grotesque face & incised w/clusters of grapes pendent from leafy vines, further decorated in black, chrome green & iron slips under a rich textured salt glaze, inscribed "Martin Bros - London & Southall - 2-1892," dated 1892.............3,575.00

Vase, 5¼" h., 3½" d., ovoid lobed body w/a short, molded neck, overall semi-gloss speckled brown glaze, marked "Martin Bro. - London & Southall - 1X2 - 1 - 1901" .. 412.50

Vase, 6¾" h., 3¼" d., bulbous footed base below a tall, slender cylindrical neck w/flared rim, the base w/looped panels decorated w/stylized 'faces' in light & dark blue against a beige ground, the

tall neck w/stylized palm leaves in the same colors, marked "R.W. Martin - London - 15"............ 770.00

Vase, 9" h., 4" d., slightly tapering cylindrical body w/a short neck w/squared rim, upturned loop handles at the shoulder, decorated w/coral-like branches in sgraffito on a brown ground, script mark & "N5 - 7-1903" (ILLUS.) 1,210.00

MC COY

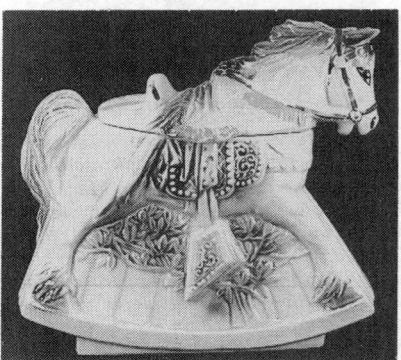

Hobby Horse Cookie Jar

Collectors are now beginning to seek the art wares of two McCoy potteries. One was founded in Roseville, Ohio, in the late 19th century as the J.W. McCoy Pottery, subsequently becoming Brush-McCoy Pottery Co., later Brush Pottery. The other was founded also in Roseville in 1910 as Nelson McCoy Sanitary Stoneware Co., later becoming Nelson McCoy Pottery. In 1967 the pottery was sold to D.T. Chase of the Mount Clemens Pottery Co. who sold his interest to the Lancaster Colony Corp. in 1974. The pottery shop closed in 1985. A different pottery is now operating in the McCoy plant but not using the McCoy mark nor making wares at all like old McCoy.

Coffee server, cov., El Rancho Bar-B-Que.......................... $65.00

Cookie jar, Barn, red, 1963......... 300.00

Cookie jar, Barnum's Animals (Nabisco Wagon), 1972-74 ....200.00 to 225.00

Cookie jar, Bear (Hamm's Bear), 1972 .... 200.00

Cookie jar, Bugs Bunny, cylinder w/decal, 1971-72 .... 65.00

Cookie jar, Bunch of Bananas, 1948-52......................... 80.00

Cookie jar, Caboose, 1961 .... 135.00

Cookie jar, Chairman of the Board, 1985 .... 525.00

Cookie jar, Chinese Lantern ("Fortune Cookies"), 1967 .... 42.00

Cookie jar, Christmas Tree, 1959 ... 425.00

Cookie jar, Circus Horse, black, 1961 .... 155.00

Cookie jar, Clown in Barrel, 1953-56......................... 62.00

Cookie jar, Coalby Cat, 1967-68..... 265.00

Cookie jar, Cookie Jug, two-handled, 1965-68 .... 25.00

Cookie jar, Corn (Ear of Corn), 1958-59......................... 115.00

Cookie jar, Country Stove (Pot Belly Stove), white, 1970-72 .... 40.00

Cookie jar, Covered Wagon (Cookie Wagon), 1959-62 .... 70.00

Cookie jar, Davy Crockett, 1957 .... 450.00

Cookie jar, Duck, 1964............. 58.00

Cookie jar, Dutch Treat Barn, 1968-73........................ 42.00

Cookie jar, Engine, yellow, 1962-64........................ 90.00

Cookie jar, Frog on Stump, 1971 .... 80.00

Cookie jar, Garbage Can, 1978-87 .. 27.00

Cookie jar, Globe, 1960............ 140.00

Cookie jar, Grandfather Clock, 1962-64........................ 75.00

Cookie jar, Grandma, w/red skirt, 1972-73....................... 115.00

Cookie jar, Hen on Nest, 1958-59 ... 70.00

Cookie jar, Hobby Horse, 1948-53 (ILLUS.)....................... 95.00

Cookie jar, Kettle, hammered bronze finish, 1961-67 .... 30.00

Cookie jar, Kitten on Basketweave, 1956-69........................ 45.00

Cookie jar, Kitten on a Coal Bucket, 1983 .... 125.00

Cookie jar, Koala Bear, 1960-77 .... 75.00

Cookie jar, Lunch Bucket, 1978-87 .. 40.00

Cookie jar, Mammy with Cauliflower, 1939 .... 900.00

Cookie jar, Mother Goose, white, 1948-52........................ 90.00

Cookie jar, Mushrooms on Stump, 1972 .... 45.00

Cookie jar, Nabisco, red & tan, 1974 .... 55.00

Cookie jar, Orange, 1970 .... 65.00

Cookie jar, Owl, brown, 1978-79.... 25.00

Cookie jar, Picnic Basket, 1962-63... 40.00

Cookie jar, Pumpkin (Jack-O-Lantern), 1955 ....450.00 to 500.00

Cookie jar, Puppy (holding cookie sign) 65.00

Cookie jar, Rooster, yellow & brown, 1956-58................. 75.00

Cookie jar, Sad Clown, 1970-71 ..... 75.00

Cookie jar, Spaceship (Friendship 7), 1962-63........................ 125.00

Cookie jar, Timmy Tortoise, 1977-80........................ 32.00

Cookie jar, Tugboat (S.S. Cookie), 1985 .... 32.00

Cookie jar, Windmill (Dutch Windmill), 1961 .... 40.00

Cookie jar, Winking Pig, 1972 ...... 260.00

Cookie jar, Yosemite Sam, cylinder w/decal, 1971-72 .... 80.00

Cuspidor, Loy-Nel-Art Line, floral decoration against a dark brown ground, early 20th c. 65.00

Flower bowl, oblong w/folded sides & large applied purple grape cluster at one end, a spattered purple border band on the grey body, ca. 1954, 6 x 9" 28.00

Jardiniere, Onyx Line, floral embossed band above vertical ribbed paneling, mottled black, brown & blue glaze, ca. 1932-38, 7 x 8".... 35.00

Jardiniere, Florastone Line, ca. 1923, 12" h. 95.00

Mug, figural bust of W.C. Fields, produced for Turtle Bay 60.00

Pitcher, tankard, Buccaneer patt., waisted cylindrical body w/relief-molded pirate figure 55.00

Planter, Pine Cone patt., 7" h. 65.00

Bird Dog Planter

Planter, model of a bird dog standing in front of a fence, ca. 1954, 7½ x 12" (ILLUS.) 55.00

Planter, model of an old mill, lettered "Down by the old mill stream," gold lettering & trim 17.50

Planter, model of a wishing well, brown & green glaze, 7" h. 12.50

Soup tureen, cov., model of a sombrero, El Rancho patt., 5 qt....... 55.00

Teapot, cov., Pine Cone patt........ 25.00

Tea set: cov. teapot, open sugar bowl & creamer; Daisy patt., shaded pink & green glaze, ca. 1942, 3 pcs..................... 60.00

Vase, 7" h., model of three white lilies above green leaves on a brown block base, ca. 1950 ...... 20.00

Vase, 8" h., model of double tulips on brownish green leaves, ca. 1948 .... 47.50

Wall pocket, fan-shaped, pink glaze 25.00

Mailbox Wall Pocket

Wall pocket, model of a mailbox
(ILLUS.). 45.00

MEISSEN

Early Meissen Coffeepot

*The secret of true hard paste porcelain,
known long before to the Chinese, was "discovered" accidentally in Meissen, Germany,
by J.F. Bottger, an alchemist working with
E.W. Tschirnhausen. The first European true
porcelain was made in the Meissen Porcelain
Works, organized about 1709. Meissen marks
have been widely copied by other factories.
Some pieces listed here are recent.*

Bouillon cup, Blue Onion patt. $45.00
Bowl, cover & stand, 7" h., decorat-
ed w/panels of flowers alternating w/orange ground, first quar-
ter 19th c., the set 770.00
Bowl, 10 x 14¼" oval, reticulated
sides encrusted w/gold decoration
& yellow accents, blue crossed
swords mark. 375.00
Centerpiece, the oval bowl molded
w/panels of gilt scrollwork on a
grey ground & w/two flower-
encrusted medallions painted
w/summer flowers below a gilt &
colored pierced scroll rim, the
ends w/large demi-putti & scroll

handles draped w/flower swags,
on four scroll feet, underglaze-
blue crossed swords mark, ca.
1860-70, 24" h. 14,355.00
Chocolate pot, cov., Blue Onion
patt., blue crossed swords mark,
early 20th c. 270.00
Clock, tall ornate rococo style case,
the domed reticulated top w/ap-
plied flowers above the waisted
scroll-molded body w/applied
figures at each side & ornate applied blossoms around the round
metal dial w/Roman numerals &
w/a h.p. scene of lovers on the
lower section, raised on an ornate
scroll-molded footed base w/h.p.
florals & applied flowers at each
corner, 19th c., restoration 1,925.00
Coffeepot, cov., footed tall ovoid
body w/a scroll-molded spout, angled scroll handle & domed cover
w/blossom finial, colorfully decorated on each side w/a cluster of
fruit & flowers surrounded by insects & w/smaller fruit sprigs
under the gilt-trimmed spout,
handle, neck & cover, the cover
similarly decorated, underglaze-
blue crossed swords mark, ca.
1755, 9 1/8" h. (ILLUS.) 1,650.00
Coffeepot, cov., Blue Onion patt.,
rose finial, blue crossed swords
mark 395.00

Meissen Cup & Saucer & Plate

Dinner service: twelve dinner
plates, eleven luncheon plates,
twelve soup bowls, eleven tea
cups & saucers, eleven demitasse
cups & saucers, cov. round tureen, cake plate, fruit bowl, open
bordered bowl, round bowl,
square open deep bowl, square
open low bowl, 13 x 19" platter,
10 x 14" platter, relish dish, two
pitchers & two gravy boats; each
piece w/a wide cobalt blue bor-

der & fired-gold inner border,
underglaze-blue crossed swords
mark, the set (ILLUS. of part) 4,675.00

Figure of Bacchus, standing figure
holding bunch of grapes in one
hand & goblet in the other, on a
round base, 9" h. (minor chips) . . . 715.00

Figure of Harlequin playing the bag-
pipes, wearing a gilt-edged iron-
red tricorner hat (small chip on
one corner & black bow), a gilt-
trimmed jacket checked in puce,
turquoise & yellow, a black belt &
gilt-edge black trousers w/iron-
red kneebow repeated on his
grey shoes, playing a cream &
brown bagpipe (lower pipe &
fingers restored), & seated on a
white cairn (left legs & ankle
repaired), modeled by Johann
Kaendler, 1737-40, 4½" h. 3,575.00

Figures of a male & female fish-
monger, 19th c., 6" h., pr. 880.00

Figures, Monkey Orchestra, consisting of twelve musicians in 18th c.
costume, each w/a different musical instrument, blue crossed
swords mark, 19th c., average
5½" h., set of 12 (restorations,
minor chips) 6,050.00

Model of a lady's shoe, slipper-type,
Blue Onion patt., blue crossed
swords mark, ca. 1860, 6" l. 395.00

Model of a lady's shoe, slipper-type,
Tischchen patt., gold shaded,
6" l. 425.00

Mustard pot, cov., barrel-shaped,
painted in iron-red, yellow, puce,
blue, black & shades of green on
the front w/a bowknotted spray
of stylized flowers between a butterfly & a ladybird, the shell-
molded scroll handle w/iron-red
bellflower designs, the gilt-edged
cover (chip at spoon notch) w/two
ladybirds, a fly & a beetle on &
around the ball knop, underglaze-
blue crossed swords mark, impressed number "24," mid-18th c.,
3 15/16" h. 880.00

Plate, 9" d., decorated w/medal-
lions of multicolored flowers
against a cobalt blue ground, further cluster of flowers center,
gold scalloped edge, ca. 1875 . . . . 395.00

Plate, 9½" d., the center painted
w/a scene of a jolly monk, wide
border w/gold design & white
beading on lilac, August Rex
mark 395.00

Plate, 11½" d., Blue Onion patt.,
lattice edge 185.00

Salt shaker, footed, Blue Onion
patt. 85.00

Teapot, cov., chinoiserie-style, bulbous ovoid body w/short angled
spout & D-scroll handle, painted
on either side in underglaze-blue
w/the *Fels und Vogel* patt.
trimmed in gold & further painted
in iron-red, puce, yellow, green &
black w/six Chinese figures at
various pursuits beneath flying insects, additional blossoms on the
flowering plants & an underglaze-
blue & gold scrollwork border
around the rim (two small chips),
the gilt-edged cover (repaired
chip) similarly decorated, the gilt-
edged faceted spout decorated in
underglaze-blue w/a herringbone
pattern, underglaze-blue crossed
swords mark, former's mark of
Johann Daniel Rehschuh, 1730-35,
4 3/8" h. 5,775.00

Tea tile, three-footed, Blue Onion
patt., crossed swords mark,
19th c., 6" 198.00

Thimble case, cov., slightly oval
pear shape, the front, reverse &
cover colorfully painted w/couples
conversing amid shrubbery, the
base painted w/a floral spray, the
rims w/a contemporary chased
copper-gilt hinged mount, ca.
1750, 1 5/16" h. 3,025.00

Meissen Urn

Urns, cov., each w/a figural panel
on opposing sides, the body encrusted w/flowers, fruit & berried
vines fitted w/cherubs, the domed
lids modeled w/a male figure on
one & a female figure on the other, damage, pseudo crossed
swords mark in blue enamel,
28½" h., pr. (ILLUS. of one) 4,313.00

Vase, 10¾" h., pate-sur-pate,
chalice-form w/two scrolled handles, the central oval medallion

decorated in white pate-sur-pate
w/a nymph riding a centaur on a
pink ground, within gilt borders,
reserved on a cobalt blue ground
decorated w/gilt, underglaze-blue
crossed swords mark 5,060.00

METTLACH

Mettlach "Lohengrin" Scene Plaque

*Ceramics with the name Mettlach were
produced by Villeroy & Boch and other potteries in the Mettlach area of Germany. Villeroy and Boch's finest years of production are
thought to be from about 1890 to 1910.
For listings of Mettlach steins, see the
"Steins" category.*

Beaker, PUG, scene of gnomes
drinking, No. 1032, ¼ liter $75.00
Charger, the center incised & decorated w/a profile bust of a young
lady w/long brown hair w/a deep
forest in the background, a border band of stylized flowers on
a white ground, artist-signed,
No. 2547, 15¾" d. 880.00
Charger, decorated w/the incised
bust portrait of a young woman
w/long curling brown hair amid
large pink & brown lilies w/green
leafage & against a bluish grey
ground, matte glaze, artist-
signed, No. 2549, 18" d. 990.00
Pitchers, 12" h., Phanolith, dancing
scene, white on green ground,
No. 7012, pr...................1,800.00
Plaque, pierced to hang, etched
scene depicting cavalier dressed
in blue playing mandolin, brick
color ground, No. 2625, 7½" d.... 295.00
Plaque, pierced to hang, Phanolith,
white relief bust of a lady on
green, No. 7032, ca. 1900,
7½ x 8¾" oval 485.00

Plaque, pierced to hang, etched
scene of man & woman on horseback, jumping fence, signed
"Stocke," No. 2041, 15" d. 800.00
Plaque, pierced to hang, etched
scene of Bismarck on horseback,
No. 2142, 15" d. 950.00
Plaque, pierced to hang, Phanolith, rectangular, decorated
w/white relief-molded figures
in a scene from "The Flying
Dutchman," No. 7046, mate to
No. 7047, artist-initialed "JS,"
ca. 1901, w/original frame,
12 1/16 x 15¼" 1,250.00
Plaque, pierced to hang, Phanolith,
rectangular, decorated w/white
relief-molded figures in a scene
from "The Flying Dutchman,"
No. 7047, w/original frame,
12 3/16 x 15 5/16".............1,250.00
Plaque, pierced to hang, Phanolith,
scene from the opera "Lohengrin,"
signed "Stahl," No. 7026, framed,
12 x 15½" (ILLUS.) 1,045.00
Plaque, pierced to hang, etched
scene of castle above the Rhine
River, gold edge, dated 1895,
No. 1108, 17" d. 1,400.00
Plaque, pierced to hang, etched
castle & river scene, No. 1365,
17" d. 1,400.00
Plaque, pierced to hang, etched design of woman holding flowers,
artist-signed, leather frame,
No. 1488, 11 x 17" 1,750.00
Plaque, pierced to hang, etched design of woman picking grapes,
artist-signed, leather frame,
No. 1489, 11 x 17".............1,750.00
Vase, 7¼" h., Mosaic, footed ovoid
body tapering to a ringed trumpet
neck, the body w/tapering stripes
of stylized blossomhead alternating w/panels of an overall small
diaper design, in shades of brown
& blue, No. 1728 .... 302.50
Vase, 9½" h., Relief, bulbous body
w/flaring mouth, full color geometric design, No. 1829......... 295.00
Vase, 13½" h., tall baluster-form
body w/a cylindrical neck
w/flared rim flanked by long loop
handles from rim to shoulder,
etched large swirled scrolling
leaves in soft colors on a blue
ground, No. 2414................ 385.00
Vase, 18 7/8" h., tall slender
baluster-form body, the tall neck
decorated w/palmettes & looped
band, the body w/a continuous
design of exotic birds in bamboo,
done in shades of blue & beige,
No. 2457 .... 522.50

Vases, 6¾" h., wide ovoid body w/a wide flared neck & raised on a conical foot, a wide body band of stylized florals in a diamond pattern in jewel-like colors on a teal green ground, No. 1573, pr............................. 330.00

Vases, 15" h., 6" d., tall baluster-form body w/a wide shoulder tapering to a short scalloped neck, decorated w/large etched stylized red & gold blossoms on long, flowing stems separated w/dark blue oval reserves w/a red heart at the base, the blossoms on an ivory ground, No. 2909, pr...................1,540.00

MINTON

Minton Pate-Sur-Pate Urn

The Minton factory in England was established by Thomas Minton in 1793. The factory made earthenware, especially the blue-printed variety and Thomas Minton is sometimes credited with invention of the blue "Willow" pattern. For a time majolica and tiles were also an important part of production, but bone china soon became the principal ware. Mintons, Ltd., continues in operation today.

Bowl, 8" d., the interior painted w/a rooster against a lustre ground w/further gold highlights, mounted on a gilt bronze base, marked, ca. 1900......................$495.00

Demitasse set: cov. demitasse pot, sugar bowl, creamer & six cups & saucers; Bird of Paradise patt., signed & dated, the set.......... 425.00

Pedestals, majolica, tall columnar form, the pale blue body modeled w/white drapery swags w/fruit clusters & ribbons above a base w/large molded leaftips in green, on a waisted & wreath-band trimmed socle base & raised on a bracket foot, impressed "Minton" & w/various model numbers & the date letter for 1865, 37½" h., pr. 10,450.00

Plates, dinner, 10" d., cobalt blue border & gilt decoration, stamped mark, set of 8 .... 385.00

Soup plates, pink border decorated w/gold floral designs, gilt rim w/etched decoration, marked, ca. 1920, 9¼" d., set of 12 .... 660.00

Tazza, h.p. roses on a green ground, narrow gold & brown border, 9½" d., 3" h............... 100.00

Urn, pate-sur-pate, the wide ovoid body raised on a short pedestal base, the wide shoulder tapering to a short cylindrical neck w/a wide rolled rim w/an egg-&-dart border, ribbed loop handles at the sides, the front w/a white-relief classical scene of "Cupid The Orator" against a dark olive green ground, ornate gilt trim on the neck, handles, upper & lower body & pedestal base, the design signed "Solon 1877," by Marc Louis Solon for the Paris Exhibition of 1878, 25" h. (ILLUS.) 32,500.00

Vases, 9" h., pate-sur-pate, slightly tapering cylindrical body w/a wide shoulder & molded rim, white-relief classical dancing nymph & cupids on each against a dark blue ground, gilt trim on the shoulder & rim, by Albione Birks, fired-gold Minton globe & crown mark w/"England," 1891-1901, pr. 11,000.00

Vases, 10½" h., pottery, baluster-form, bright yellow painted w/pond lilies & cattails w/gilt ring 'handles,' impressed mark, pr....1,430.00

MOCHA

Mocha Tea Caddy & Mug

Mocha decoration is found on basically utilitarian creamware or yellowware articles and is achieved by a simple chemical reaction.

A color pigment of brown, blue, green or black is given an acid nature by infusion of tobacco or hops. When this acid nature colorant is applied in blobs to an alkaline ground color, it reacts by spreading in feathery seaweed designs. This type of decoration is usually accompanied by horizontal bands of light color slip. Produced in numerous Staffordshire potteries from the late 18th until the late 19th centuries, its name is derived from the similar markings found on mocha quartz. In addition to the seaweed decoration, mocha wares are also seen with Earthworm and Cat's Eye patterns or a marbleized effect.

Bowl, 8½" d., 4" h., deep flaring sides on a wide footring, a wide orangish tan center band decorated w/the Earthworm patt. in pale blue & black, thin black & green stripes around the top & bottom edges (stains, wear, some glaze flaking on rim, two stabilized hairlines) $600.00

Chamber pot, open, miniature, yellowware body decorated w/a white band trimmed w/a bluish seaweed band, 2¼" h. (minor crazing, small flakes on footring) 110.00

Chamber pot, open, applied strap handle, wide white band w/blue seaweed decoration within two narrow brown stripes on yellowware, 9" d. 250.00

Mug, tall cylindrical form, a wide boldly marbleized center band in blue, brown & white flanked by narrow blue & white bands, molded leaftip handle, 4 3/8" h. (minor stains, short rim hairline, minor edge flakes) 675.00

Mug, cylindrical body w/molded base, strap handle w/embossed leaftip end, a wide orangish tan band w/dark green seaweed decoration flanked by thin dark brown stripes & a green embossed rim, hairlines in base, 4¾" h. (ILLUS. right) 350.00

Mug, tall cylindrical body tapering slightly toward rim, strap handle w/embossed leaftip end, embossed rim bands w/stripes of green, black, brown & tan, a wide middle band w/overall roped squiggles in black & white on a blue ground, 5 5/8" h. (hairlines) 800.00

Mug, cylindrical, a wide blue band w/sienna Earthworm patt. flanked by numerous light & dark narrow bands in blue, brown & impressed

green w/blue trim, 19th c., 6¼" h. (hairline) 770.00

Pitcher, 4 7/8" h., ironstone body, tapering cylindrical form w/a wide pale blue center band w/seaweed decoration flanked by narrow white & black stripes, marked "Pint" (minor damage) . . . 125.00

Pitcher, 7" h., jug-type, four alternating light & dark bands around the body, the top band w/Cat's Eye patt., the second & fourth bands w/clusters of small dots & the third band w/Earthworm patt., 19th c. (small spout chip, minor glaze imperfections) 1,540.00

Pitcher, 7" h., jug-type, a wide blue center band decorated in the Earthworm patt. in brown & white, narrow stripes of green & black around the top & bottom, molded leaftip handle (stains, chip on base, pinpoint flakes, rim hairline) 925.00

Pitcher, 7½" h., barrel-shaped, leaftip embossed handle, wide bands of dashed lines in black & white divided by bands in blue, orange & tan (crow's-foot in bottom, chips, minor stains) 1,450.00

Pitcher, 7½" h., wide ovoid body on a footring, stripes & narrow bands of blue separating a wide dark brown band w/three wavy white lines above a wide white band w/a blue & tan leaf sprig band, early 19th c. (wear, stains, rim hairlines, small chips) 2,050.00

Salt dip, a squatty bulbous footed dish, a wide grey band w/black seaweed decoration, a narrow black rim band, 3¼" d. (rim chips) 200.00

Shaker w/domed top, cylindrical body tapering to a pedestal foot & a short neck, wide brown band decorated w/black seaweed design & flanked by narrow black stripes, blue finial & stripe on cover, 5" h. (chips) 725.00

Tea caddy, cov., short cylindrical body w/a tapering neck to a flat rim fitted w/a tall pointed domed cover, bands of thin geometric stripes in black, tan & blue around the body & cover, minor edge damage, yellowed cover repair, 4 7/8" h. (ILLUS. left) 525.00

Waste bowl, deep flaring sides on footring, a wide blue band decoration w/a simple band of Earthworm patt. in black & white, 5" d., 2¾" h. (wear, hairlines in bottom) 175.00

Waste bowl, straight flaring sides,
    narrow blue rim stripes & a wide
    yellow ochre band decorated
    w/scattered black seaweed de-
    sign, 5¼" d., 2 7/8" h. 450.00

MOORCROFT

Pomegranate Pattern Moorcroft Jar

*William Moorcroft became a designer for
James Macintyre & Co. in 1897 and was put
in charge of their art pottery production.
Moorcroft developed a number of popular designs, including* Florian Ware, *while with
Macintyre and continued with that firm until 1913 when they discontinued the production of art pottery.*

*After leaving Macintyre in 1913, Moorcroft
set up his own pottery in Burslem and continued producing the art wares he had
designed earlier as well as introducing new
patterns. After William's death in 1945, the
pottery was operated by his son, Walter.*

Cup & saucer, pansy decoration,
    signed in green, ca. 1913-16. . . . . . $375.00
Jar, cov., Pomegranate patt., wide
    ovoid body w/a domed fitted cov-
    er, decorated on the cover &
    around the upper half w/a band
    of pendent fruits & leafage in
    shades of red, purple, yellow &
    green against a mottled cobalt
    blue ground, base & cover im-
    pressed "Moorcroft - Made in
    England," base signed in blue
    "Moorcroft - July - 1930," 16" h.
    (ILLUS.) 3,575.00
Lamp, table model, tall slightly
    swelled & tapering cylindrical
    base decorated in 'cloisonne' style
    w/large pink, red & purple poppy
    blossoms & green foliage against
    a cobalt blue ground, w/electric
    fittings, bottom drilled, signed
    "Moorcroft - MADE IN ENGLAND,"
    base 6½" d., 14½" h. 825.00

Vase, miniature, 2" h., 1½" d.,
    baluster-form, cloisonne-style,
    decorated w/a red flower against
    a green ground, signed 66.00
Vase, 4¼" h., 3½" d., bulbous
    ovoid body tapering to a short
    flaring neck, Claremont patt.,
    decorated w/large mushrooms in
    yellow, red & purple against a
    clear green shaded to blue
    ground, signed "Moorcroft - Made
    in England 189". 1,540.00
Vase, 6" h., 5½" d., globular body
    w/low flaring mouth, decorated
    w/yellow, red & blue orchids &
    irises against a cobalt blue
    ground, blue signature mark 495.00
Vase, 7¼" h., tapering cylindrical
    body, glazed w/mauve, yellow
    & purple fruit on a deep blue
    ground, mounted on a hammered
    pewter circular foot stamped
    "MADE IN ENGLAND - TUDRIC -
    MOORCROFT - 01358 - MADE BY
    LIBERTY & CO." 550.00

Claremont Pattern Moorcroft Vase

Vase, 13¾" h., tall ovoid body
    tapering to a short neck, Clare-
    mont patt., decorated in red, yel-
    low, blue & green w/toadstools,
    impressed & signature marks & a
    paper label, ca. 1925 (ILLUS.) 3,080.00

MULBERRY

*Mulberry or Flow Mulberry wares were
produced in the Staffordshire district of England in the period between 1835 and 1855 at
many of the same factories which produced
its close "cousin," Flow Blue china. In fact,
some of the early Flow Blue patterns were
also decorated with the purplish mulberry coloration and feature the same heavy smearing
or "flown" effect. Produced on sturdy iron-*

stone bodies, quite a bit of this ware is still to be found and it is becoming increasingly sought-after by collectors although presently its values lag somewhat behind similar Flow Blue pieces. The standard reference to Mulberry wares is Petra Williams' book, Flow Blue China and Mulberry Ware, Similarity and Value Guide.

Bowl, berry, Cypress patt.,
Davenport $20.00
Chamber pot, cov., Jeddo patt.,
Wm. Adams & Sons 255.00
Chamber pot, cov., Vincennes patt.,
Samuel Alcock 250.00
Coffeepot, cov., Corean patt., Podmore, Walker & Co. (repair to finial) 295.00
Coffeepot, cov., Montezuma patt., J. Godwin 295.00
Coffeepot, cov., Washington Vase patt., Podmore, Walker & Co. (finial repair) 295.00
Creamer, Grecian Font patt., Clews 85.00
Creamer, Panama patt., Edward Challinor 150.00
Creamer, Percy patt., Francis Morley 135.00
Creamer, Rhone Scenery patt., Podmore, Walker & Co. 125.00
Cup & saucer, handleless, Athens patt., Charles Meigh 60.00
Cup & saucer, handleless, Cypress patt., Davenport 65.00
Cup & saucer, handleless, Grecian Font patt., Clews 62.00
Cup & saucer, Jeddo patt., Wm. Adams & Sons 55.00
Cup & saucer, Montezuma patt., J. Godwin 75.00
Cup & saucer, Pelew patt., Edward Challinor 65.00
Cup plate, Athens patt., Wm. Adams & Sons 55.00
Cup plate, Cyprus patt., Davenport 50.00
Cup plate, Susa patt., Charles Meigh 55.00
Cup plate, Vincennes patt., Samuel Alcock 60.00
Gravy boat, Jeddo patt., Wm. Adams & Sons 135.00
Pitcher, 8" h., Pelew patt., Edward Challinor 160.00
Plate, 6" d., Tonquin patt. 33.00
Plate, 6¼" d., Athens patt. 20.00
Plate, 7" d., Alleghany patt., Thomas Goodfellow 35.00
Plate, 7" d., Hong patt., Thomas Walker 29.00
Plate, 7½" d., Missouri patt., Broadhurst & Sons 30.00
Plate, 8" d., Temple patt., Podmore, Walker & Co. 45.00

Plate, 8¼" d., Tonquin patt. 40.00
Plate, 8½" d., Cypress patt., Davenport 65.00
Plate, 8½" d., Tonquin patt., T. Heath...................... 45.00
Plate, 9½" d., Pelew patt., Edward Challinor 50.00
Plate, 10" d., Bochara patt., John Edwards...................... 50.00
Plate, 10½" d., Vincennes patt., Samuel Alcock 80.00
Plate, 10 7/8" d., Neva patt., Edward Challinor 65.00
Platter, 7 x 9½", Peruvian patt., John Wedge Wood 75.00
Platter, 10" l., octagonal, Ailanthus patt., C. & W. Harvey, ca. 1845 ... 100.00
Platter, 10¾ x 12", Corean patt., Podmore, Walker & Co. 120.00
Platter, 13¾ x 17½", Bochara patt., John Edwards 300.00
Punch cup, Missouri patt., Bridgett & Bates 75.00
Sauce dish, Bryonia patt., Paul Utzschneider & Co. 5.00
Sauce tureen, cov., Corean patt., Podmore, Walker & Co. (minor repair to lid)..................... 295.00
Soup plate w/flanged rim, Missouri patt., Broadhurst & Sons, 10½" d. 45.00
Sugar bowl, cov., Susa patt., Charles Meigh 175.00
Teapot, cov., Jeddo patt., Wm. Adams & Sons ....350.00 to 375.00
Teapot, cov., Rhone Scenery patt., Podmore, Walker & Co. 350.00
Teapot, cov., Udina patt., J. Clementson 495.00
Toddy plate, Vincennes patt., Samuel Alcock 70.00
Vegetable bowl, cov., Ning Po patt., R. Hall & Co. 350.00
Vegetable bowl, cov., Washington Vase patt., Podmore, Walker & Co. 250.00
Vegetable bowl, open, rectangular, Athens patt., Wm. Adams & Sons, 8 x 10"..................... 150.00
Vegetable dish, open, rectangular, Jeddo patt., Wm. Adams & Sons, 8½ x 9"..................... 130.00

NEWCOMB COLLEGE POTTERY

This pottery was established in the art department of Newcomb College, New Orleans, Louisiana, in 1897. Each piece was hand-thrown and bore the potter's mark and decorator's monogram on the base. It was always a studio business and never operated as a factory and its pieces are therefore scarce, with the early wares being eagerly sought. The pottery closed in 1940.

Newcomb Covered Jar

Bowl, 8¾" d., 3" h., low wide rounded sides on a short footring, the exterior w/an upper band of squirrels & tree branches in pink & green against a dark blue ground, creamy yellow interior, matte glaze, decorated by Henrietta Bailey, impressed company mark & "NW25. 105. HB" $1,870.00

Bowl-vase, bulbous wide ovoid body tapering to a wide flat mouth, decorated w/a landscape of live oak trees hung w/Spanish moss in blues & bluish greens, decorated by C. Longjohn, marked "NC - CL - JM - FR6," 8¼" d., 6½" h. 3,410.00

Chamberstick, flat dished base w/upright rim centered by a short columnar shaft below the cup-form spouted candlesocket w/a wide loop handle at the side, incised around the socket cup & inside the base w/white mistletoe berries & green leaves against a two-tone blue ground, decorated by A. Urquhart, marked "NC - CV83 - AU - W," 5" d., 4" h. 2,200.00

Jar, cov., modeled in low-relief w/naturalistic daffodils & foliage, blue matte glaze, impressed w/potter's cipher, stamped "JM 251 JL '70" & decorator's initials "AFS" for Anna Frances Simpson, w/original paper tag, 6½" h. (ILLUS.) 1,760.00

Mug, conical, decorated around the rim w/a wide band of stylized green & blue fuchsia blossoms w/the blossoms hanging down around the sides, against a light greyish blue ground, dark blue handle, glossy glaze, decorated by Sara B. Levy, marked "NC - SBL - JM - AB3," 5" d., 4¼" h. (small manufacturing flaw) 1,760.00

Plaque, rectangular, decorated w/a tall pine tree w/the moon in the sky behind, in green & blue against a light blue-to-ivory ground, decorated by Henrietta Bailey, incised "NC - HB," & marked in ink "HJ59," remnants of paper label, framed, 5¼ x 9¼" 4,690.00

Plate, 7½" d., decorated w/a lightly molded wide border band of stylized flowers in blue, yellow & green, light blue center, glossy glaze, decorated by Leona Nicholson, impressed company mark & "LN JM W BV17" (light line at rim) 1,320.00

Tile, incised "Paul Morphy - Chess Player" above three rows of three squares each, some w/chess pieces, green & red on an ivory ground, by Leona Nicholson, 4½" sq. 550.00

Trivet, round, incised around the rim w/a wide band of stylized holly berries & leaves in blue & green against a clear greyish blue ground, glossy glaze, decorated by Maria deHoa LeBlanc, marked "NC - MHLB - JM - ss78 - Q.," 6" d. 1,210.00

Vase, miniature, 2½" h., 2" d., ovoid body tapering to a rolled rim, matte green glaze, marked "NC - JM" 165.00

Vase, 3½" h., 4½" d., spherical body tapering toward base & toward wide flat mouth, lightly molded w/white gardenia blossoms & green leaves on a light blue ground, matte glaze, decorated by Sadie Irvine, incised company mark & "SI JM MF93.8" 990.00

Vase, 6" h., 4" d., bulbous footed bottom tapering to a tall cylindrical neck, decorated around the base w/an embossed wreath of white blossoms & pale blue leaves against a deep blue matte-glazed ground, decorated by Henrietta Bailey, marked "NC - JM - HB - PM93 - 174" 1,320.00

Vase, 8¼" h., 6" d., wide ovoid body tapering to a short cylindrical neck w/molded rim, incised & painted w/large white roses on a bluish green ground, decorated by A.F. Mason, marked "NC - EV.60 - JM" 2,090.00

Vase, 9¼" h., 5½" d., baluster-form w/a short wide neck & loop handles on the wide shoulder, incised & decorated w/large stylized blue

grape clusters & green leaves
above blue incised bands forming
very light blue panels, glossy
glaze, decorated by Sara B.
Levy, impressed "NC - SBL -
BF60 - W." 8,800.00
Vase, 13¾" h., 6" d., elongated
ovoid w/wide mouth, decorated
w/a moonlit landscape of tall cypress trees, by Anna Frances
Simpson (short tight rim hairlines) 4,125.00

NILOAK

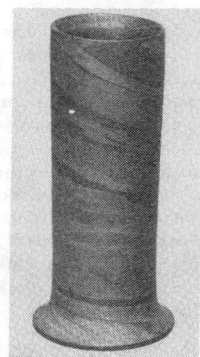

Niloak Mission Ware Vase

*This pottery was made in Benton, Arkan-
sas, and featured hand-thrown vari-colored
swirled clay decoration in objects of classic
forms. Designated Mission Ware, this line is
the most desirable of Niloak's production
which was begun early in this century. Less
expensive to produce, the cast Hywood Line,
finished with either high gloss or semi-matte
glazes, was introduced during the economic
depression of the 1930's. The pottery ceased
operation about 1946.*

Ewer, mauve glaze, 7" h. $25.00
Ewer, matte rose glaze, 7" h. 20.00
Model of a cannon, matte rose
glaze 35.00
Planter, Hywood Line, model of an
elephant, matte maroon glaze.... 35.00
Planter, Hywood Line, model of a
frog, white glaze............... 35.00
Planter, Hywood Line, model of a
pelican...................... 35.00
Planter, Hywood Line, model of a
wishing well, blue glaze, 9" l..... 30.00
Planter, Hywood Line, model of a
wishing well, matte maroon
glaze 35.00
Vase, 4" h., Mission Ware, marbleized shades of brown 75.00
Vase, 10" h., 4½" d., Mission Ware,
tall cylindrical body w/flared

base, swirled marbleized design
in earth tones, impressed mark
(ILLUS.)........................ 110.00
Vase, 14" h., Mission Ware,
baluster-shaped, swirling rust,
brown, grey & blue clays,
stamped mark 605.00
Vase, 18" h., 7" d., Mission Ware,
marbleized swirls 1,400.00

NIPPON

*This colorful porcelain was produced by
numerous factories in Japan late last century and until about 1921. There are numerous
marks on this ware, identifying the producers
or decorating studios. The hand-painted
pieces of good quality have shown a dramatic price increase within recent years.*

Nippon Plaque with Lions

Ashtray, novelty-type, face of a
smiling black man (Rising Sun
mark) $100.00
Basket w/overhead handle, plushy
roses decoration, 7½" h. (green
"M" in Wreath mark) 37.00
Bowl, 6¼" d., handled, scenic decoration w/gold handles (green "M"
in Wreath mark) 90.00
Bowl, fruit, 8" d., 5" h., pedestal
base, gold side handles, decorated w/large pink & red roses &
green leaves on white ground,
gold trim (green "M" in Wreath
mark) 120.00
Bowl, 9" d., footed, relief-molded
squirrel & acorns decoration 650.00
Bowl, 10" d., six pierced handles,
"gaudy" decoration w/raised gold
beading & bright red & yellow
roses 125.00
Bowl, 10" d., pierced handles, scalloped edge, hibiscus decoration
on avocado matte ground,
jeweled & beaded w/gold detail-

ing & outlining (blue Maple Leaf
mark) 275.00

Cake plate, open-handled, pink
roses decoration on cream
ground, gold handles, 10½" d.
(green "M" in Wreath mark) 50.00

Candlestick, blue ground decorated
w/two white doves, 6 1/8" h. 65.00

Candlestick, squared conical shape
w/tapering flared drip tray, mottled dark blue body & heavy gold
overlay top & bottom, 8" h. (green
"M" in Wreath mark) 110.00

Candlestick, cylindrical w/hexagonal
base, landscape scene, 8 1/8" h.
(green "M" in Wreath mark) 85.00

Celery tray, oval, open-handled,
decorated w/pink dogwood, gold
handles, 13¾" l. 75.00

Chamberstick, child's, white ground
delicately enameled w/small
flowers 75.00

Chocolate pot, cov., tall ovoid body
w/short arched rim spout, small
domed cover w/knob finial, C-
scroll handle, decorated w/pink
& peach roses & green leaves
against a white ground, gold handle & finial, 4½" d., 9" h. 88.00

Chocolate set: cov. chocolate pot &
six cups & saucers; scalloped
edges, roses decoration, 13 pcs.
(blue Maple Leaf mark) 295.00

Cider set: pitcher & four cups; h.p.
floral decoration, 5 pcs. 150.00

Compote, open, 6½" d., 3½" h.,
scalloped edge, decorated w/h.p.
swan scene & gold trim (green
"M" in Wreath mark) 115.00

Console bowl, footed, h.p. house in
wood scene, moriage trim, 10" d.
(green "M" in Wreath mark) 250.00

Cracker jar, cov., melon-ribbed,
decorated overall w/roses & foliage w/elaborate gold tracery &
beading, three gold feet (blue
Maple Leaf mark) 175.00

Creamer & cov. sugar bowl, spherical, decorated w/overall moriage
white & yellow dots & medallions
w/multicolored flowers on a soft
green ground, green handles, unmarked, pr. 75.00

Decanter, no stopper, sharply tapering conical body w/an angled
handle, overall heavy 'jeweling'
of small dots & a central round
medallion, 7" h. ("Hand Painted
Nippon" & Crown mark) 200.00

Ewer, ribbed body on pedestal base,
two scalloped handles, moriage
decoration, light green ground
covered w/green & pink in a

snake shape around the body,
7½" h. 215.00

Ewer, wide ovoid melon-lobed body
on a thin scalloped footrim, sides
tapering to a narrow neck w/a
tall, arched leaf-molded spout &
loop twig handle, h.p. w/a scenic
panel & a large bouquet of poppies & leaves against a banded
background, 7½" h. 150.00

Ferner, wide cylindrical body
w/three relief-molded sphinx handles continuing to form small feet,
h.p. stormy seascape around the
sides, jeweled & beaded trim,
8" d. (green "M" in Wreath
mark) 450.00

Hatpin holder, cobalt blue ground
decorated w/roses & gold & green
trim (blue Maple Leaf mark) 75.00

Humidor, cov., decorated w/scene
of deer & doe standing under an
orange tree, cover w/jeweled
moriage trim & decoration of
oranges & green leaves, artist-
signed, 6" h. 265.00

Humidor, cov., cylindrical, slightly
domed cover w/compressed ball
finial, relief-molded & h.p. scene
of camel & rider, 7½" h. (green
"M" in Wreath mark) 795.00

Humidor, cov., decorated w/h.p.
roses & an American flag & eagle,
7¾" h. 550.00

Humidor, cov., h.p. early auto scene
around the sides, brass cover
(green "M" in Wreath mark) 275.00

Humidor, cov., relief-molded stag &
dogs scene (green "M" in Wreath
mark) ....675.00 to 700.00

Mug, two horsemen, silhouetted in
black against a yellow ground.... 95.00

Mug, h.p. violet decoration (Rising
Sun Mark) 30.00

Mustard jar w/attached underplate,
cov., lakeside sunset decoration
w/elaborate raised gold beading
& tracery 75.00

Nappy, lake scene w/forest in distance, moriage trim & beading,
6¼" d. 55.00

Nut set: footed master bowl & six
individual footed dishes; moriage
nuts & leaves decoration, the set
(green "M" in Wreath mark) 160.00

Pitcher, tankard, 11½" h., oval
body, ornate gold band around
rim & base, gold handle, large
full-blown shaded green roses &
foliage against a pale green satin
ground 245.00

Plaque, pierced to hang, h.p. misty
Venetian scene w/gondolier &
bridge, 10" d. (green "M" in
Wreath mark) 155.00

Plaque, pierced to hang, relief-molded scene of two lions in a rocky mountainous landscape, 10½" d., green "M" in Wreath mark (ILLUS.) . . . . .600.00 to 650.00

Plaque, pierced to hang, relief-molded w/an American Indian holding a rifle & riding a running horse, 10½" d. (green "M" in Wreath mark) 650.00

Plaque, pierced to hang, relief-molded scene of a male & female lion in a mountainous setting, 10½" d. (green "M" in Wreath mark) 550.00

Plaque, pierced to hang, center portrait of beautiful young woman, wide border w/ornate gold geometric design, 10½" d. (blue Maple Leaf mark) 160.00

Plaque, pierced to hang, relief-molded stag near a river w/forest in background, 10½" d. (green "M" in Wreath mark) . . . .600.00 to 650.00

Tea set: cov. teapot, creamer, cov. sugar bowl & four cups & saucers; decorated w/Paulownia blossoms w/brown trim & "jewels," 11 pcs. 165.00

Tea set, child's: cov. teapot, creamer, cov. sugar bowl, six plates, six cups & saucers; decorated w/roses & bluebirds on white ground w/green border, 21 pcs. . . . 250.00

Toothpick holder, three-handled, decorated w/black birds 40.00

Urn, "gaudy" style, footed, ornate shoulder handles, decorated w/large red poppies against a cobalt blue ground, heavy gold trim, 10" h. (Royal Nishiki mark) 175.00

Vase, 5½" h., two-handled, scenic landscape w/sky in the background & a lake & bushes in the foreground (green "M" in Wreath mark) 135.00

Vase, 6½" h., high squared handles, relief-molded scene of stag & hunting dogs in a forest setting (green "M" in Wreath mark) 675.00

Vase, 8" h., three-handled, bulbous, h.p. fruit decoration 200.00

Vase, 8½" h., bottle-form, ornate gold handles, "tapestry," river scene depicting a man in a boat w/a woman waiting at the shore, houses & trees in the background (blue Maple Leaf mark) 425.00

Vase, 9" h., handled, decorated w/pink azaleas & green leaves, gold outlining & beading & gold handles 150.00

Vase, 9¾" h., ovoid w/small mouth, relief-molded red strawberries &

green foliage against a shaded green ground (green Maple Leaf mark) 650.00

Vase, 10½" h., slightly tapering cylindrical body w/small mouth, small gold loop handles at shoulder, decorated w/pink roses & gold beading 375.00

Whiskey jug w/original stopper, cylindrical w/wide flat shoulder, short slender neck, decorated w/stylized dragons & ornate jeweling, 6½" h. (green "M" in Wreath mark) 295.00

NORITAKE

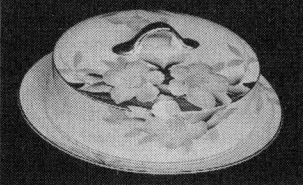

Azalea Butter or Cheese Dish

Noritake china, still in production in Japan, has been exported in large quantities to this country since early in this century. Though the Noritake Company first registered in 1904, it did not use "Noritake" as part of its backstamp until 1918. Interest in Noritake has escalated as collectors now seek out pieces made between the "Nippon" era and World War II (1921-41). The Azalea pattern is also popular with collectors.

Bouillon cup & saucer, Pattern #16034, white w/raised & beaded gold flowers & scrolls on an ivory band $35.00

Bowl, fruit, 5¼" d., Azalea patt., No. 9 . . . . 10.00

Bowl, cereal (oatmeal), 5½" d., Azalea patt., No. 55 . . . . 24.00

Bowl, 11" d., two-handled, detailed landscape scene, elaborate gold trim, cobalt blue rim w/turquoise jeweling (green "M" in Wreath mark) 65.00

Bowl, cream soup & underplate, Sedan patt., No. 11292, 2 pcs. 20.00

Butter (or cheese) dish, cov., Azalea patt., No. 314 (ILLUS.) 115.00

Cake plate, handled, decorated w/exotic birds & flowers, lustre, 10½" d. 85.00

Cake plate, handled, decorated w/a scene of an Art Deco style lady in an orange & black dress smelling a rose, a castle in the background

& a large tree in the foreground,
10½" d. 350.00
Candlestick, Tree in Meadow patt. . . 35.00
Casserole, cov., Azalea patt., pointed gold finial, No. 372, 10¾" l.... 435.00
Celery tray, oval, handled, Pattern
#16034, white w/raised & beaded
gold flowers & scrolls on an ivory
band, 13 3/8" l. 24.00
Compote, 8¼" d., 4¾" h., relief-
molded fruit & nuts decoration in
beautiful colors 110.00
Condiment set: salt & pepper shakers & cov. mustard jar w/spoon
on handled tray; Azalea patt.,
No. 14, the set 56.00
Condiment set: salt & pepper shakers & cov. mustard jar on
shamrock-shaped tray; salt & pepper shakers decorated w/clowns
strumming mandolins, artist-
signed, the set 115.00
Creamer, Acacia patt. 38.00
Creamer & cov. sugar bowl, Azalea
patt., No. 7, pr. 39.00
Creamer & open sugar bowl, demitasse, Azalea patt., No. 123, pr.. 110.00
Creamer & open sugar bowl, individual, Azalea patt., No. 449,
pr. 350.00
Cruet w/original stopper, Azalea
patt., No. 190 .... 163.00
Cup & saucer, Acacia patt. 31.00
Cup & saucer, Azalea patt., No. 2 .. 16.50
Cup & saucer, Lorraine patt., deco-
rated w/small pink roses 20.00
Cup & saucer, Pattern #16034, white
w/raised & beaded gold flowers &
scrolls on an ivory band 8.00
Demitasse pot, cov., Tree-in-
Meadow patt. 145.00
Egg cup, Azalea patt., No. 120 ..... 44.00
Gravy boat w/attached underplate,
Acacia patt. 55.00
Gravy boat w/attached underplate,
Azalea patt., No. 40 .... 49.00
Loving cup, pedestal base, scenic
decoration in front medallion,
enameling & moriage trim 95.00
Napkin ring, Art Deco style, deco-
rated w/a bust portrait of a girl in
red fur-trimmed outfit, blue lustre
ground, 2½" w. 40.00
Napkin ring, Art Deco style, deco-
rated w/a bust portrait of a gen-
tleman in top hat & cape, pale
orange lustre ground, 2¼" w..... 55.00
Pitcher, milk, 5 5/8" h., jug-type,
Azalea patt., No. 100, 1 qt. 100.00
Plaque, pierced to hang, relief-
molded w/three brown & white
dog heads 595.00
Plate, 6" d., Tree in Meadow patt. . . . 9.00
Plate, bread & butter, 6½" d., Azalea patt., No. 8 .... 10.00

Plate, salad, 7½" d., Azalea patt.,
No. 4 .... 10.00
Plate, dinner, 9¾" d., Azalea patt.,
No. 13 .... 26.00
Platter, 10¼ x 14", oval, Azalea
patt., No. 17 .... 60.00
Refreshment set: tray w/cup; Tree
in Meadow patt., 2 pcs. 25.00
Relish dish, oval, Azalea patt.,
No. 18, 8¼" l. 20.00

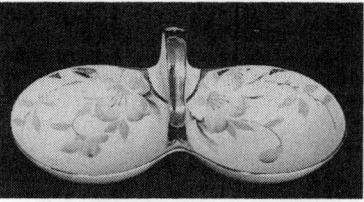

Lobed Azalea Pattern Relish

Relish dish, two-lobed form w/cen-
ter handle, Azalea patt., No. 450,
7½" l. (ILLUS.) 30.00
Soup plate, Azalea patt., No. 19 .... 25.00
Teapot, cov., Tree in Meadow
patt. 90.00
Tea tile, round, Azalea patt.,
No. 169 .... 40.00
Toothpick holder, Tree in Meadow
patt. 65.00
Vase, 5" h., gold lustre ground
decorated w/scarlet birds & flowers in ovals, 1930's 35.00
Vegetable bowl, cov., Azalea patt.,
10½" d., No. 101 .... 60.00
Vegetable bowl, open, oval, handled, Azalea patt., No. 101,
10½" l. 55.00
Wall pocket, floral decoration w/or-
ange & gold lustre background ... 65.00
Wall pocket, wooded scene w/house
near water in a band, blue lustre
ground, 8" h. 75.00

NORTH DAKOTA SCHOOL
OF MINES POTTERY

Bowl with Incised Bird Design

*All pottery produced at the University of
North Dakota School of Mines was made*

from North Dakota clay. In 1910, the University hired Margaret Kelly Cable to teach pottery making and she remained at the school until her retirement. Julia Mattson and Margaret Pachl were other instructors between 1923 and 1970. Designs and glazes varied through the years ranging from the Art Nouveau to modern styles. Pieces were marked "University of North Dakota - Grand Forks, N.D. - Made at School of Mines, N.D." within a circle and also signed by the students until 1963. Since that time, the pieces bear only the students' signatures. Items signed "Huck" are by the artist Flora Huckfield and were made between 1923 and 1949. Pieces were marked with the University name until 1963.

Bowl, 4½ x 5½", Indian-type decoration, artist-signed $395.00
Bowl, 6½" d., 3½" h., squatty bulbous body w/closed rim, molded around the shoulder w/panels decorated w/a scene of an ox pulling a cart, matte green leathery glaze, titled on base "Red River Ox Cart," w/ink stamp mark & "M. Cable - 107" 522.50
Bowl, 7½" d., 4½" h., incised broad band of grotesque birds in green & red flying against a matte ochre ground, incised "Indian Bird" & "Hoffman - HUCKFIELD - 2051" (ILLUS.) 880.00
Ginger jar, cov., burgundy glaze, signed "Middleton," 5" h. 70.00
Pitcher, 6" h., floral decoration 225.00
Tray, leaf-shaped, blues & greens, artist-signed, 6" l. 150.00
Vase, 2¾" h., 3¾" d., squatty bulbous ovoid body tapering to a wide, flat mouth, decorated around the shoulder w/a band of pink flowers & green foliage over a pink body, incised "M Cable," circular mark, 1930 . . . . 495.00
Vase, 3½" h., 3¾" d., spherical body w/closed rim, the upper half w/panels of excised running coyotes alternating w/three bars in glossy cream against an ochre ground, round ink mark & incised "J¼" 522.50
Vase, 8½" h., 6¾" d., wide ovoid body w/a wide shoulder to the short flaring neck, incised overall w/swimming fish in green against a gun-metal ground, incised "Marie," circular ink mark (minute glaze nick on body) 1,430.00
Vase, 9" h., 4¾" d., expanding cylinder w/gently sloping shoulder & short neck, decorated w/dark brown trees against a fading orange ground, artist-initialed, die-stamped mark 935.00

OHR (George) POTTERY

Ohr Mug with Inscription

George Ohr, the eccentric potter of Biloxi, Mississippi, worked from about 1883 to 1906. Some think him to be one of the most expert throwers the craft will ever see. The majority of his works were hand-thrown, exceedingly thin-walled items, some of which have a crushed or folded appearance. He considered himself the foremost potter in the world and declined to sell much of his production, instead accumulating a great horde to leave as a legacy to his children. In 1972 this collection was purchased for resale by an antiques dealer.

Bowl, 3 5/8" h., shouldered inverted cone w/a moss green, pink & blue dappled glaze on the exterior, w/a hematite glaze on the inside, stamped "G.E. OHR Biloxi, Miss." $495.00
Bowl-vase, squatty bulbous footed body below a wider shoulder tapering to a rounded inverted & crumpled short neck, vibrant green glaze speckled w/red & gunmetal drippings, die-stamped mark, 5¼" d., 4½" h. 4,675.00
Chamberstick, wide flaring pedestal base w/molded rim & side strap handle supports a wide candle socket, bright mottled pink & green glaze w/gunmetal spots, mustard yellow interior, script mark, 4" d., 3¼" h. 770.00
Creamer, oblong form w/one end pinched & crumpled, the opposite end forming a wide, rounded spout, clear mottled green glaze on orange clay, early die-stamped mark, 4" l., 2¼" h. 1,980.00
Model of a house, the triangular shelter w/a mottled moss green

glaze, on a highly textured rectangular ground w/a brown glaze,
incised "Biloxi," 6¾" l. 462.00
Mug, footed cylindrical base taper-
ing to a wide flaring neck, strap
handle, the base incised "Here's
to your good health and your family's - and may they all live long
and prosper - J. Jefferson,"
green-over-red glossy glaze, die-
stamped mark & dated "3-18-98
(?)," 4½" d., 4¼" h. (ILLUS.) 1,100.00
Pitcher, 3½" h., 5¼" w., wide
cornucopia-style body w/deeply
pinched spout, double-loop cut-out
handle, black gun-metal glaze,
die-stamped mark 1,650.00
Pitcher, 7¼" h., 5" d., spherical
footed base below a tall cylindrical neck w/pinched spout, applied
strap handle, glazed w/bright
bands of blue in a sponged pattern over a purple ground, orange
interior, die-stamped mark 2,035.00
Teapot, cov., wide footed ovoid
body w/a flared rim & inset flat
cover w/button finial, heavy
swan's neck spout w/forked opening, loop strap handle, green,
dark blue, pink & clear pigeon-
feathered glaze over an orange
clay body, die-stamped mark,
8½" d., 5¾" h. (small chip on
bottom of spout, kiln kiss on
body, new glaze on cover) 1,540.00
Vase, 3" h., 3" d., squatty bulbous
angled base below a wide slightly
flaring cylindrical neck, clear light
green glaze w/gunmetal drips,
die-stamped mark 467.50
Vase, 5¾" h., 5½" d., wide ovoid
body w/a crimped flat rim,
bisque-fired beige clay, script
signature 770.00
Vase, 11¼" h., 3¾" d., bulbous
ovoid body on a flared conical
foot, a flaring trumpet-form neck
w/a deep straight rim section,
mottled brown & green glaze
w/an iridescent sheen, die-
stamped mark 4,675.00

OLD IVORY

*Old Ivory china was produced in Silesia,
Germany, in the late 1800's and takes its
name from the soft white background coloring. A wide range of table pieces was made
with the various patterns usually identified
by a number rather than a name.*

Berry set: master bowl & five sauce
dishes; No. 113, 6 pcs. $250.00

Berry set: 10½" d. master bowl &
six sauce dishes; No. 16, 7 pcs. . . 350.00
Bowl, cereal, 6¼" d., No. 12 . . . . 60.00
Bowl, 9½" d., two-handled, scal-
loped, No. 10 . . . . 110.00
Bowl, master berry, 10" d., No. 78. . 100.00
Bowl, 10" d., No. 84 . . . . 95.00
Butter pat, No. 84 . . . . 180.00
Cake plate, open-handled, No. 10,
9½" d. 95.00
Cake plate, open-handled, No. 7,
10" d. 110.00
Cake plate, open-handled, No. 16,
10" d. 135.00
Cake plate, open-handled, No. 30,
10" d. 50.00
Cake plate, open-handled, No. 84,
10" d. . . . . .75.00 to 100.00
Cake plate, open-handled, No. 75,
10½" d. 135.00
Cake set: 10" open-handled cake
plate & six 6¼" d. plates; No. 16,
7 pcs. 375.00

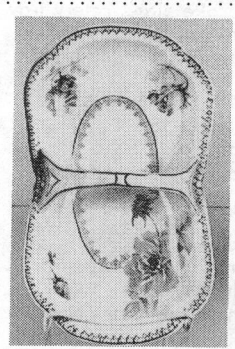

Old Ivory No. 200 Candy Dish

Candy dish, oblong w/pinched sides
& arched center handle, No. 200
(ILLUS.) 147.50
Celery tray, No. 7 . . . . 125.00
Celery tray, No. 15, 11½" l. 145.00
Celery tray, No. 32 . . . . 75.00
Celery tray, No. 122 . . . . 55.00
Celery tray, No. 200, 11½" l. 100.00
Charger, No. 16, 13" d. . . . .200.00 to 300.00
Chocolate cup & saucer, No. 84 . . . . 50.00
Chocolate pot, cov., No. 16, 10" h. . . 245.00
Chocolate pot, cov., No. 84 . . . . 295.00
Chocolate pot, cov., Thistle patt. . . . 180.00
Chocolate set: cov. chocolate pot
& four cups & saucers; No. 28,
9 pcs. 650.00
Chocolate set: cov. chocolate pot
& six cups & saucers; No. 11,
13 pcs. 825.00
Chocolate set: cov. chocolate pot &
six cups & saucers; No. 16,
13 pcs. 825.00
Coffeepot, cov., Alice patt., No. 44,
10" h. 325.00
Cracker jar, cov., No. 10 . . . . 425.00

Cracker jar, cov., No. 11 .... 375.00
Cracker jar, cov., handled, No. 84,
  8" d., 6½" h. 245.00
Creamer & cov. sugar bowl, No. 16,
  pr............................ 155.00
Creamer & cov. sugar bowl, No. 84,
  pr............................ 160.00
Cup & saucer, demitasse, No. 16 ... 125.00
Cup & saucer, No. 7 .... 65.00
Cup & saucer, No. 10 .... 65.00
Cup & saucer, No. 15 .... 67.00
Cup & saucer, No. 84 .... 67.00
Cup & saucer, No. 200 .... 65.00
Cup & saucer, mustache-type,
  No. 84 .... 165.00
Gravy boat on underplate, handled,
  No. 200 .... 150.00
Luncheon set: four place settings
  each w/8½" d. plate, 7¾" d.
  plate, 6" d. plate, sauce dish, cup
  & saucer plus a creamer, sugar
  bowl, large serving bowl, open-
  handled cake plate, celery tray &
  chocolate set; No. 11, the set 1,600.00
Mayonnaise dish w/underplate,
  No. 16, 2 pcs. 290.00
Mustard pot, cov., No. 28 .... 285.00
Pepper shaker, No. 11 .... 35.00
Plate, 6" d., No. 82............... 50.00
Plate, 6" d., No. 200.............. 25.00
Plate, 7½" d., No. 28............. 22.00
Plate, 7½" d., No. 82............. 75.00
Plate, 8" d., No. 16.............. 30.00
Plate, dinner, No. 84 .... 195.00
Relish dish, No. 84, 8½" l. 75.00
Sauce dish, Silesia patt., No. 28,
  5" d. 25.00
Sauce dishes, No. 4, 5½" d., set
  of 6............................ 150.00
Shaving mug, No. 15, pierced soap
  lip 425.00
Soup plate, No. 16 .... 85.00
Spoon holder, No. 200 .... 85.00
Sugar bowl, cov., No. 28.......... 100.00
Sugar bowl, cov., No. 33.......... 65.00
Sugar shaker, No. 11 .... 395.00
Sugar shaker, No. 84 .... 395.00
Tea set: cov. teapot, cov. sugar
  bowl & creamer; No. 16, 3 pcs. ... 875.00
Toothpick holder, No. 16.. 250.00 to 300.00
Toothpick holder, No. 84.......... 275.00
Tray, rectangular w/scalloped rim,
  No. 84, 7 x 12" 165.00
Tray, yellow rose decoration,
  No. 90, 8½ x 11½" 165.00
Vegetable bowl, open, deep sides,
  No. 16, 10" d. 125.00

stoneware and pottery premiums made at the turn of the century first by the Weir Pottery Company and subsequently by Western Stoneware Co., Monmouth, Illinois. On these items the trademark Indian head was signed beneath "Old Sleepy Eye." The colors were Flemish blue on grey. Later pieces by Western Stoneware to 1937 were not made for Sleepy Eye Milling Co. but for other businesses. They bear the same Indian head but "Old Sleepy Eye" does not appear below. They have a reverse design of teepees and trees and may or may not be marked Western Stoneware on the base. These items are usually found in cobalt blue on cream and are rarer in other colors. In 1952, Western Stoneware made a 22 oz. and 40 oz. stein with a chestnut brown glaze. This mold was redesigned in 1968. From 1968 to 1973 a limited number of 40 oz. steins were produced for the Board of Directors of Western Stoneware. These were marked and dated and never sold as production items. Beginning with the first convention of the Old Sleepy Eye Club in 1976, Western Stoneware has made a souvenir which each person attending receives. These items are marked with the convention site and date. It should also be noted that there have been some production items made in recent years.

Old Sleepy Eye Butter Jar

Butter jar, Flemish blue on grey
  stoneware, Weir Pottery Co., 1903
  (ILLUS.).......................$492.00
Pitcher, 5¼" h., cobalt blue on
  white, w/small Indian head on
  handle, Western Stoneware Co.,
  1906-37 (pint) ....215.00 to 250.00
Pitcher, 8½" h., cobalt blue on
  white, w/small Indian head on
  handle, Western Stoneware Co.,
  1906-37 (gallon) ....235.00 to 275.00
Stein, chestnut brown, 1952, 22 oz.
  size 375.00
Vase, 8½" h., Flemish blue on grey
  stoneware, molded Indian, cattails, frog & dragonfly 450.00

OLD SLEEPY EYE

Sleepy Eye, Minnesota, was named after an Indian chief. The Sleepy Eye Milling Co. had

OWENS

Owens pottery is the product of the J.B. Owens Pottery Company, which operated in

Ohio from 1890 to 1929. In 1891 it located in Zanesville and produced art pottery from 1896, introducing "Utopian" wares as its first art pottery. The company switched to tile after 1907. Efforts to rebuild after the factory burned in 1928 failed and the company closed in 1929.

Ewer, Utopian line, floral decoration, shape No. 921, 6" h........$150.00
Jardiniere & pedestal base, Utopian line, floral decoration, dolphins molded on base, two flutes molded on top, matte glaze (professionally restored) 600.00
Mug, Utopian line, decorated w/cherries on a brown ground, artist-signed, 4½" h. 150.00
Plaque, rectangular, decorated w/a raised design in matte glazes of cream-colored ducks waddling toward a blue pond on a mossy green ground, framed, 9 x 11¾" 715.00
Vase, 5½" h., Utopian line, two-handled, pansies decoration, numbered "1115" & artist-initialed "C.B." 145.00
Vase, 10¼" h., 5¼" d., Lotus line, wide ovoid body w/wide flaring rim, decorated w/large peony blossoms in pink, yellow & red against a shaded brown to pink ground, impressed mark & artist-signed, shape No. 1243 .... 605.00

Owens Vase with Dog Portrait

Vase, 15½" h., Utopian line, tall ovoid body tapering to a tiny neck, decorated in slip underglaze w/a portrait of a spaniel-like dog's head, glossy glaze, impressed "Owensart Utopian 1B," normal crazing, ca. 1900 (ILLUS.).. 825.00
Water set: cylindrical 12" h. pitcher & four 5 1/8" h. mugs; Utopian line, the pitcher decorated in a

dark brown glossy glaze painted w/a branch of green leaves & reddish berries & impressed "1 OWENSART UTOPIAN 1015," the mugs similarly decorated & marked, the set 209.00

PARIAN

Parian Figure of John A. Andrews

Parian is unglazed porcelain in the biscuit stage, and takes its name from its resemblance to Parian marble used for statuary. Parian wares were made in this country and abroad through much of the last century and continue to be made. Also see BENNINGTON and COPELAND & SPODE.

Box, cov., molded grape leaves on lid, Victorian, 3½" d. $95.00
Bust of President Garfield, incised "Garfield," 9¼" h. (no base) 150.00
Bust of U.S. Grant, on socle base, 11½" h. 325.00
Bust of Robert E. Lee, inscribed "General Lee," on a socle base, 11¾" h. 575.00
Bust of Abraham Lincoln, on a socle base, 15¾" h. (minor base damage) 600.00
Bust of Sir Walter Scott, on simple socle base, impressed Copeland marks, England, ca. 1860, 15" h. (firing lines) 495.00
Bust of William Shakespeare, atop a simple socle base, impressed "R. Monti S.C. - Crystal Palace Art Union, Copeland, pub. March 18?," Copeland, England, ca. 1860, 13¼" h. (nicks on base) 715.00
Figure of John A. Andrews, standing stocky gentleman wearing a long cloak over his suit, atop a square base w/cut corners, printed verse on the back of the base

impressed marks "M. Milmore
Sc." & "Publishers - J. McD & S
Boston - Copyright," England,
ca. 1867, chips on base, 21" h.
(ILLUS.) 1,210.00
Figure of a peasant girl, a small girl
w/pensive expression, holding
basket of flowers, England, artist-
signed, 11" h................... 95.00
Figure of "Young Columbus,"
modeled as a young man seated
atop a mooring post, waves
splashing at his feet, impressed
title on base, incised on backside
"copyright applied for M.F. Libby,"
England, mid-19th c., 15½" h. (repair to ring on mooring) 495.00
Figure group, "Rock of Ages," young
woman clinging to a giant cross
surrounded by stormy waves, Robinson & Leadbeater, England, ca.
1870 .... 375.00
Pitcher, 8" h., relief-molded thistle
design 148.00
Vase, 10½" h., bulbous base tapering to a slim throat & a flaring
neck, molded grapes & grapevine
decoration.................... 75.00

PARIS & OLD PARIS

Paris Portrait Cup & Saucer

*China known by the generic name of Paris
and Old Paris was made by several Parisian
factories from the 18th through the 19th century; some of it is marked and some is not.
Much of it was handsomely decorated.*

Cup & saucer, cabinet-type, the cup
bearing a portrait of the Duc
d'Orleans within a medallion, the
cup & saucer border gilded, Jac-
ques Lefebre, ca. 1818 (ILLUS.) . .$6,225.00
Figures, an elegant cavalier standing & wearing a feathered hat, a
cloak, a wide ribbon across his
chest & kneebreeches, on a round
base, the facing elegant lady in
18th c. dress on a matching round
base, colorful enamel decoration
in yellow, orange, iron-red &

gold, an interlaced "P" & "L" on
an applied cartouche, 19th c.,
10¾" h., pr. (man lacking
thumb) 192.50
Figures, dwarf musicians, one playing a stringed instrument, the other playing a wind instrument, ca.
1850, 5 3/8" h., pr............... 900.00
Pitcher, 9" h., decorated w/a floral
& gilt neoclassical design,
19th c. 192.50
Urns, a baluster-form body w/a
deeply undulating gilt rim raised
on a pedestal base, a bright blue
ground w/gilt scroll trim surrounding a colorfully painted bouquet on a white center reserve,
applied gilt-trimmed floriform
handles, 19th c., 18" h., pr. 495.00
Vase, 7¼" h., squared-form, flaring
mouth, the leaf-molded body applied w/pink flowers & 'jewels,'
heavy gold trim 125.00
Vases, 11" h., tall cylindrical body
tapering slightly toward the low
foot, applied ribbon handles, the
front decorated w/a large oval
medallion w/putti in a landscape
within cattail & ribbon borders
against a pink ground, 19th c., pr.
(minor gilt & glaze losses) 1,045.00
Vases, 18" h., baluster-form, ornate
gilt handles, painted w/floral bouquets, further decorated w/gilt
detailing, late 19th c., now
mounted as lamps, pr. 1,760.00

PAUL REVERE POTTERY

Paul Revere Pottery Plate

*This pottery was established in Boston,
Massachusetts, in 1906, by a group of philan-
thropists seeking to establish better condi-
tions for underprivileged young girls of the
area. Edith Brown served as supervisor of the
small "Saturday Evening Girls Club" pottery
operation which was moved, in 1912, to a
house close to the Old North Church where*

Paul Revere's signal lanterns had been placed. The wares were mostly hand decorated in mineral colors and both sgraffito and molded decorations were employed. Although it became popular, it was never a profitable operation and always depended on financial contributions to operate. After the death of Edith Brown in 1932, the pottery foundered and finally closed in 1942.

Book ends, sloping blue rectangular blocks decorated w/a multi-colored panel showing a pastoral river landscape, one w/a cottage, impressed circular mark, each marked "F2 24," 4¾" l., 4" h., pr..............................$825.00

Bowl, 9" d., 2 5/8" h., yellow w/stylized Arts & Crafts border of brown & tan tree clusters against white & yellow landscape w/matte black outlines, decorated by Fannie Levine, marked "SEG - FL - 1-23," 1923.....................1,870.00

Breakfast set, child's: bowl, plate & cup; each in navy blue w/light border, each w/a central medallion of a chick in a landscape, inscribed "Mary Phillipa Elwes," mug 3½" h., the set............ 495.00

Creamer, globular, sgraffitoed wild rose border design in white against blue w/grey ground & black outlines, white interior, marked "FR - 255-6-09 - SEG," 2 7/8" h. 357.50

Desk set: 4¾" h. round vase, 4" h. square vase, 3¾" calendar holder-pen tray, 7¾" l. rectangular letter holder, cov. inkwell & cov. stamp box; each glazed in bright royal blue decorated w/turquoise blue band of green leaves w/red berries against light tan & outlined in matte black, each signed "SEG - AM - 12-17," the set 1,100.00

Jar, cov., slightly rounded form, design of purple moths against blue & green stylized band at shoulder all on a white ground, design repeated on cover, signed by Sara Galner & Ida Goldstein & dated 1911, 5" d., 4½" h. 1,540.00

Jardiniere, slightly canted sides, short neck, repeating border of tulips in yellow, green & blue w/matte black outline highlights below shoulder, signed on back "11-26 PRP" w/X-in-circle artist's mark, 5½" d., 4¼" h. 357.50

Pitcher, 4 3/8" h., expanding cylinder, white singing chickens in a wide white & yellow border out-

lined strongly in matte black, yellow w/white interior, marked "SEG - JT - MD - 9-19," 1919..... 275.00

Plate, 12¼" d., the large center scene depicting a quarter moon in star-filled sky above a lakeside cottage w/tall trees & flowering daffodils in the foreground outlined in matte black in the Arts & Crafts style, dark & light shades of blue, green, brown & yellow, signed "SEG - SG - 11-15," dated 1915 (ILLUS.) 11,000.00

Teapot, cov., expanding cylinder, D-shaped handle, straight spout, white w/black outlined repeating yellow crocus design border, pot & cover signed "196-EG - SEG," dated "1912," 5" h. (tiny glaze chip on spout) 192.50

Vase, 4½" h., 3¾" d., small wide ovoid body w/a closed rim, decorated around the rim w/a wide band of stylized lotus blossoms in white against the dark blue ground, dated 1914, ink mark 770.00

Vase, 7¼" h., wide ovoid body tapering to a flat rim, small loop handles at the sides, blue, green, black & white drip glaze over green, impressed circular mark & artist's initials................... 275.00

Vase, 8¼" h., semi-ovoid form, blue accented by a white crocus border beneath a white rim band, matte black outlines, initialed by Sara Galner & dated 1914 .... 880.00

Vase, 9¾" h., tall ovoid body w/molded rim, blue w/a broad band around the top w/green, brown & tan tree clusters outlined in black w/a blue sky above, signed "FM 4-19 SEG" 825.00

PENNSBURY POTTERY

Inspired by the long tradition of Pennsylvania Dutch style pottery in Pennsylvania, Henry and Lee Below founded their pottery near Morrisville in 1950 and named it for the nearby Pennsbury Manor.

Specializing in Pennsylvania Dutch and country-style decoration, Pennsbury Pottery was hand-painted in a variety of colorful designs. Although tablewares were the major products, special commemorative items and a line of bird figures also originated at this pottery until its closure in 1970.

Ashtray, motto-type, round, Amish mother & boy w/"What giffs? - What ouches you?," 5" d. $28.00

Ashtray, round, Amish patt......... 28.00

Ashtray, round, commemorative,
"The Doylestown National Bank
and Trust Co. - Warminster -
1961," w/a building in the center,
1961, 5" d. 25.00
Bowl, fruit, 5" d., Black Rooster
patt.......................... 22.50
Creamer, Amish patt., 2½" h....... 22.00
Creamer, Red Rooster patt.,
2½" h......................... 24.00
Cruets, oil & vinegar, jug-shaped,
the stopper for one in the form of
an Amish woman's head, the other the head of an Amish man,
7" h., pr...............100.00 to 125.00
Cup & saucer, Black Rooster patt.... 22.50
Cup & saucer, Red Rooster patt. 28.00
Desk basket, cylindrical, com-
memorative, "National Exchange
Club," 5" h..................... 30.00
Mother's Day plate, 1972, "Mother
with Child" 17.50
Mug, beer, Gay Nineties patt.,
5" h........................... 30.00
Pie plate, Amish patt., 9" d. 30.00
Pie plate, Amish Family patt., cara-
mel glaze, 9" d................. 26.00
Pitcher, 6¼" h., Amish patt., 1 qt... 65.00
Plaque, rectangular, commemorative
for National Education Associa-
tion, inscribed "Greetings from
P.S.E.A. - N.E.A. Centennial -
1857 - 1957" & a sailing ship over
"Welcome," 5¼ x 7¼" 40.00
Plaque, rectangular, railroad series,
relief-molded early train engine
w/"Pennsylvania R.R. - 1856 - Ti-
ger," 5½ x 7½" ....50.00 to 75.00
Plaque, round, commemorative,
"United States Steel Export Com-
pany" around rim, logo in center,
1954, 8" d. 35.00
Plate, 8" d., Amish patt. 40.00
Plate, 8" d., Hex patt. 30.00
Plate, 8" d., Red Rooster patt...... 20.00
Plate, 10" d., Hex patt. 33.00
Plate, dinner, 10" d., Red Rooster
patt........................... 35.00
Sugar bowl, cov., Red Rooster patt.,
4" h.......................... 26.00
Tray, oblong octagonal, Horses
patt., 3 x 5" 25.00

PETERS & REED

*In 1897 John D. Peters and Adam Reed
formed a partnership to produce flowerpots
in Zanesville, Ohio. Formally incorporated as
Peters and Reed in 1901, this type of production was the mainstay until after 1907 when
they gradually expanded into the art pottery
field. Frank Ferrell, a former designer at the*

*Weller Pottery, developed the "Moss Aztec"
line while associated with Peters and Reed
and other art lines followed. Though unmarked, attribution is not difficult once familiar with the various lines. In 1921, Peters
and Reed became Zane Pottery which continued in production until 1941.*

Peters & Reed Floor Vase

Bowl, 9" d., 3" h., Montene line,
mistletoe decoration, copper
brown iridescent glaze.......... $55.00
Doorstop, model of a cat, yellow
glaze 375.00
Pitcher, tankard, 16" h., grape
design 275.00
Vase, 4" h., jug-type, sprigged on
florals, dark brown ground...... 40.00
Vase, 4" h., squatty shape, Landsun
line 50.00
Vase, 4" h., 5" d., three-legged,
caramel glaze w/flowers........ 65.00
Vase, 5" h., Zane Ware, underglaze
rose decoration 40.00
Vase, 6" h., Moss Aztec line, relief-
molded pansy decoration 48.00
Vase, 7½" h., Landsun line, blended
blue glaze 30.00
Vase, 12" h., Moss Aztec line,
relief-molded grape design...... 55.00
Vase, 22¾" h., 14½" d., floor-type,
olive jar-form w/ridged sides,
matte green glaze, unmarked
(ILLUS.)....................... 495.00
Wall pocket, Moss Aztec line 75.00

PEWABIC

*Mary Chase Perry (Stratton) and Horace J.
Caulkins were partners in this Detroit, Michigan pottery. Established in 1903, Pewabic
Pottery evolved from their Revelation Pottery, "Pewabic" meaning "clay with copper
color" in the language of Michigan's Chippe-
wa Indians. Caulkins attended to the clay formulas and Mary Perry Stratton was the
artistic creator of forms & glaze formulas,*

eventually developing a wide range of colors for her finely textured glazes. The pottery's reputation for fine wares and architectural tiles enabled it to survive the depression years of the 1930's. After Caulkins died in 1923, Mrs. Stratton continued to be active in the pottery until her death, at age ninety-four, in 1961. Her contributions to the art pottery field are numerous.

Ashtray, octagonal, silver & gold iridescent glaze w/Egyptian blue rim, impressed mark $325.00
Bowl, 4¼" d., 2½" h., sharply flaring sides, 'hammered' texture w/an iridescent mauve, gold & orange glaze, paper label....... 192.50
Bowl, 6¼" d., 2¾" h., molded in high-relief w/a repeating leaf design, matte green glaze, impressed mark 1,540.00
Model of a turtle, covered in a burgundy shaded to greyish green iridescent glaze, unmarked, 9½" l., 5½" h. (chip on one foot) 495.00
Plate, 10½" d., decorated w/a border band of running rabbits & trees, outlined in blue against an ivory ground, decorated by M.C. Perry, signed "Perry" (glaze damage on base)..................1,210.00
Trivet, hexagonal, mosaic-type w/multi-colored triangular pieces set in a green iridescent border, unmarked, 10" w. 440.00
Vase, 3¼" h., 2½" d., slightly tapering cylindrical body w/a small molded flat mouth, heavy dripping blue glaze over a dark bisque body, impressed mark 385.00
Vase, 5½" h., 6¼" d., bulbous rounded lower half below a wide conical upper half tapering to a low flaring rim, mottled beige to red iridescent glaze, raised circular mark 770.00
Vase, 6½" h., 4¼" d., wide ovoid body tapering slightly to a short wide neck, dripping iridescent purple, blue & green glaze, impressed mark 715.00
Vase, 7½" h., 4½" d., bulbous footed base w/a tall tapering cylindrical neck, dark iridescent burgundy & green glaze dripping over a matte black body, impressed mark & paper label 1,540.00
Vase, 9½" h., 5¼" d., elongated ovoid, covered in a mottled bright turquoise glaze over a lustered silvery grey to golden mauve base, impressed circular mark "PEWABIC - DETROIT" 4,400.00

PHOENIX BIRD & FLYING TURKEY

The phoenix bird, a symbol of immortality and spiritual rebirth, has been handed down through Egyptian mythology as a bird that consumed itself by fire after 500 years and then rose again, renewed, from its ashes. This bird has been used to decorate Japanese porcelain designed for export for more than 100 years. The pattern incorporates a blue design of the bird, variously known as the "Flying Phoenix," the "Flying Turkey" or the "Ho-o," stamped on a white ground. It became popular with collectors because there was an abundant supply since the ware was produced for a long period of time. Pieces can be found marked with Japanese characters, with a "Nippon" mark, or a "Made in Japan" or "Occupied Japan" mark. Though there are several variations to the pattern and border, we have lumped them together since values seem to be quite comparable. A word of caution to the collectors, Phoenix Bird pattern is still being produced.

Casserole, cov., Phoenix Bird $45.00
Creamer, Phoenix Bird............. 12.50
Egg cup, Phoenix Bird 16.00
Plate, 7" d., Phoenix Bird 12.00
Plate, dinner, 10" d., Phoenix Bird .. 30.00
Sugar bowl, cov., Phoenix Bird 18.50
Teapot, cov., one-cup size, Flying Turkey 35.00

PICKARD

Pickard Portrait Tankard Pitcher

Pickard, Inc., making fine hand-colored china today in Antioch, Illinois, was founded in Chicago in 1894 by Wilder A. Pickard. The company now makes its own blanks but once only decorated those bought from other potteries, primarily from the Havilands and others in Limoges, France.

Berry set: 9¾" d. master bowl & six 5 7/8" d. sauce dishes; decorated w/strawberries, stems, leaves,

scrolls, red tracery & iridescent
trim, artist-signed, ca. 1905, the
set............................$675.00

Bouillon cups & saucers, Maryland
patt., 12 sets 400.00

Bowl, 7¼" d., 1½" h., decorated
w/pale pink & white poppies &
daisies & gilt trim, artist-signed .. 50.00

Bowl, 9½" d., 4" h., three-footed,
decorated w/white lilies & green
leaves, heavy gold trim, artist-
signed 200.00

Bowl, 9¾" d., decorated w/straw-
berries & white flowers, gold scalloped border, artist-signed 185.00

Bowl & underplate, 8" d. & 10" d.,
decorated w/h.p. strawberries inside & out, 2 pcs. 145.00

Cake plate, open-handled, decorated w/fruit w/gold trim, artist-
signed, ca. 1919, 10½" d......... 75.00

Chocolate pot, cov., decorated
w/grapes on a ground of deep
pastel shades of green, red & purple, artist-signed, ca. 1898 ...... 435.00

Coffee set: cov. coffeepot, creamer
& cov. sugar bowl; each decorated w/overall etched gold, the
set........................... 175.00

Compote, open, 5" d., handled, h.p.
white & gold dogwood blossoms,
heavy gold trim, artist-signed 55.00

Creamer & cov. sugar bowl,
diamond-shaped, Bordure Antique
patt., stylized birds w/royal blue
trim over encrusted gold, pr...... 255.00

Cup & saucer, demitasse, Daffodil
patt., artist-signed 85.00

Dish, oval, cut-out gold handles
& gold rim, decorated w/an Italian garden scene, artist-signed,
4½ x 9½"..................... 165.00

Mayonnaise bowl, two-handled,
w/matching underplate, each decorated w/a border of stylized blue
fan-shaped devices & blue corn-
flowers center, lavish gold trim &
handles, artist-initialed, Tresseman & Vogt, Limoges blank, bowl
4 3/8" d., 1¾" h., underplate
7¼" d., 2 pcs. 165.00

Mustard jar, cov., pink enameled
floral decoration, gold trim, artist-
signed 95.00

Pitcher, lemonade, 7" h., decorated
w/stylized chrysanthemums on an
orange ground, gold rim & han-
dle, artist-signed 450.00

Pitcher, tankard, 11" h., tapering
cylindrical body w/lightly molded
ribs, decorated w/orange & pink
carnations, gold rim, S-scroll handle & base, artist-signed 700.00

Pitcher, tankard, 14" h., decorated

w/metallic grapes & grapevines,
heavy gilt trim on rim & handle,
artist-signed 350.00

Pitcher, tankard, 15" h., gilded rim
& handle, decorated w/a portrait
of Falstaff holding a jug of ale
surrounded by grape clusters &
vines, artist-signed (ILLUS.) 1,400.00

Plate, 6" d., blackberries decoration, artist-signed 35.00

Plate, 7¾" d., gooseberries on a
yellow & reddish ground, artist-
signed 70.00

Plate, 8¼" d., scenic decoration of
a meadow landscape w/trees &
flowers, artist-signed 125.00

Plate, 8½" d., scenic, "Yosemite,"
artist signed 195.00

Plate, 9½" d., decorated w/large
daisies, wheat & tendrils, lavish
rococo gold border, artist-signed,
Tresseman & Vogt, Limoges blank,
ca. 1895 .... 90.00

Plate, 9½" d., decorated w/a scene
of a monk at a table peeling a
turnip w/a beer stein nearby, a
wide grapevine border w/a gold
rim band, artist-signed 400.00

Relish tray, h.p. floral decoration,
ca. 1910, 9½" l................. 95.00

Salt & pepper shakers, "Aura Ar-
genta Linear" design, ca. 1910,
pr............................ 49.00

Salt & pepper shakers, individual
size, gold-etched edges, ca. 1930,
pr............................ 45.00

Sauce dish, leaf-shaped w/attached
underplate, decorated w/pink &
maroon flowers emanating from
center gold medallion, graceful
open gold handle & lavish gold
trim, artist-signed, ca. 1910,
3½ x 6½"..................... 225.00

Tea tile, decorated w/apple blossoms, gold trim, artist-signed, ca.
1895, 6¾" d. 225.00

Tray, three compartments w/figural
peacock center handle, etched
gold floral design, unsigned,
10½" d........................ 75.00

Vase, 5¼" h., wide oval w/three
small gold handles at shoulder,
gold up-thrust neck, decorated
w/pastel mums, stems, buds &
scrolls, ca. 1898 .... 405.00

Vase, 7 5/8" h., 3¼" d., tall ovoid
body w/a wide flat mouth, decorated w/yellow blossoms w/green
& maroon leaves in the Art Nouveau style, heavy gold trim,
artist-signed, ca. 1895-98........ 325.00

Vase, 10½" h., baluster form, decorated w/a scene of a stag in a

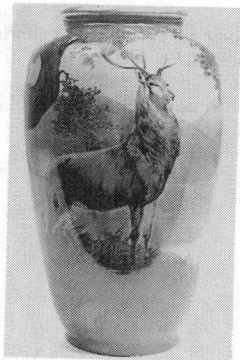

Pickard Scenic Vase
mountainous landscape in tones
of brown & orange, artist-signed
(ILLUS.) 1,300.00
Vase, 10½" h., trumpet-shaped,
decorated w/daisies & carnations,
gilded rim & base, artist-signed .. 425.00

Very Tall Pickard Vase
Vase, 19¾" h., very tall slender
ovoid body w/a flaring gilt scroll-
molded foot & tapering to a tall
slender flaring neck, pierced
scroll gilt handles down the sides,
decorated w/a nude young woman w/long blonde hair followed
by a blackbird, artist-signed
(ILLUS.) 3,400.00

PICTORIAL SOUVENIRS

*These small ceramic wares, expressly made
to be sold as a souvenir of a town or resort,
are decorated with a pictorial scene which is
usually titled. Made in profusion in Germany, Austria, Bavaria, and England, they were
distributed by several American firms including C.E. Wheelock & Co., John H. Roth (Jon-
roth), Jones, McDuffee & Co., Stratton Co.,*
*and others. Because people seldom traveled
in the early years of this century, a small souvenir tray or dish, picturing the resort or a
town scene, afforded an excellent, inexpensive
gift for family or friends when returning from
a vacation trip. Seldom used and carefully
packed away later, there is an abundant supply of these small wares available today at
moderate prices. Their values are likely to
rise.*

Cup,"Hotel Richmond, Richmond,
   Virginia," Germany............. $18.00
Cup, "Schenley High School, Pitts-
   burgh, Pennsylvania," Germany .. 18.00
Dish, "Plymouth Rock, Massachu-
   setts" 10.00
Dish, "Prospect Point, Niagara
   Falls" 10.00
Dish, "Rawlins County Court House,
   Atwood, Kansas"................ 15.00
Mug, "Jackson County Court House,
   Kansas City, Missouri" 10.00
Mug, "Joliet High School, Joliet,
   Illinois" 16.00
Pitcher, 2½" h., "Arkansas State
   Seal"......................... 12.00
Pitcher, 4" h., "Statue of Liberty" ... 20.00
Plate, 6" d., "Court House, Hamil-
   ton, Ohio".................... 12.00
Plate, 7" d., "Carnegie Library,
   Chickasha, Oklahoma," Wheel-
   ock 12.00
Plate, 7" d., "Kankakee State Hospi-
   tal," color scene on cobalt blue
   ground w/gold border, ca. 1915,
   Germany 75.00
Teapot, cov., "Niagara Falls," two
   views of Falls on yellow iridescent
   body, copper lustre neck, white
   spout & handle w/gold tracings,
   Germany 55.00
Teapot, cov., "Lighthouse, Atlantic
   City, New Jersey," cobalt blue
   ground, small.................. 27.50

PISGAH FOREST

*Walter Stephen experimented with making
pottery shortly after 1900 with his parents in
Tennessee. After their deaths in 1910, he eventually moved to the foot of Mt. Pisgah in
North Carolina where he became a partner of
C.P. Ryman. Together they built a kiln and
a shop but this partnership was dissolved in
1916. During 1920 Stephen again began to ex-
periment with pottery and by 1926 had his
own pottery and equipment. Pieces are usually marked and may also be signed "W.
Stephen" and dated. Walter Stephen died in
1961 but work at the pottery still continues,
although on a part-time basis.*

Pisgah Forest Cameo Ware Vase

Creamer & cov. sugar bowl, Cameo ware, bulbous ovoid body tapering to a short flared rim, thick loop handles, white relief covered wagon scene on each on a green ground, both stamped & artist-signed, 1953, sugar bowl 6" w., 3½" h., pr. $385.00

Pitcher, 3½" h., 4¾" d., Cameo ware, a squatty bulbous mottled blue body below a wide, slightly tapering neck band in Wedgwood blue decorated w/a white relief molded covered wagon scene, w/the Stephen mark, 1953 . . . . 247.50

Pitcher, 8" h., 7½" d., Cameo ware, ovoid body tapering slightly to the waisted neck w/pinched spout, decorated w/a white relief band around the neck w/ox-pulled covered wagon on a dark green ground, the lower body in glossy turquoise blue, rose pink interior, raised mark, 1932 . . . . 660.00

Vase, 3" h., 4" d., crackle glaze in turquoise & eggplant, signed "Stephen" 75.00

Vase, 5½" h., 3¾" d., Cameo ware, baluster-form body w/wide mouth, Wedgwood blue decorated w/a white relief pioneer scene depicting an ox-pulled covered wagon, a horse w/two riders & a leaping dog, signed "Stephen" & marked "Pisgah Forest, 19??" (ILLUS.) 770.00

Vase, 7¼" h., 4½" d., ovoid body w/a flaring mouth, lustre glaze in white, blue & bluish green crystals, rose pink interior, raised mark & "Stephen," 1941 . . . . 440.00

Vase, 8¼" h., 5¼" d., ovoid body below a wide flat neck, the neck in green bisque decorated w/cameo-like white relief scene of an Indian on horseback pursuing a buffalo, the base w/a mottled green glossy glaze, raised mark 770.00

Vase, 9½" h., 6½" d., Cameo ware, ovoid body below a wide cylindrical neck, the neck decorated in white relief w/an Indian village scene on a dark green ground, a mottled turquoise blue lower body, raised mark, 1931 . . . . 1,210.00

QUIMPER

This French earthenware pottery has been made in France since the end of the 17th century and is still in production today. Because the colorful decoration on this ware, predominantly of Breton peasant figures, is all hand-painted and each piece is unique, it has become increasingly popular with collectors in recent years. Most pieces offered today date from about the mid-19th century to the present. Modern potteries continue to operate today and contemporary examples are available in gift shops.

Basket, peasant figure decoration, HB - Quimper France, 3 x 4" $95.00

Chamberstick, decorated w/a peasant woman & flowers, marked "Henriot - Quimper - France - 128," 5½" d. 230.00

Inkstand, a high arched scroll-molded back plate w/a pierced crest above a h.p. decoration of rampant lions & shields, the serpentine-shaped base w/molded scrolls fitted w/two round, covered inkwells flanking a center well, on small knob feet, Henriot - Quimper, 13½" l., 6¼" h. 795.00

Pitcher, 5½" h., double-sided, decorated w/a female peasant figure, signed on side "Henriot Q" & "H.H. Ranle" 275.00

Plate, 9½" d., peasant in center w/blue & yellow trim 70.00

Salt & pepper shakers, figural, a seated peasant man & woman, marked "Henriot - France," 2½" h., pr. 185.00

Sweetmeat dish, trefoil-shaped, green handle, French peasant & florals decoration, Henriot - Quimper, 3 x 6" 250.00

REDWARE

Red earthenware pottery was made in the American colonies from the late 1600's. Bowls, crocks and all types of utilitarian wares were turned out in great abundance to supplement the pewter and handmade treen-

ware. *The ready availability of the clay, the same used in making bricks and roof tiles, accounted for the vast production. The lead-glazed redware retained its reddish color though a variety of colors could be obtained by adding various metals to the glaze. Interesting effects occurred accidentally through unsuspected impurities in the clay or uneven temperatures in the firing kiln which sometimes resulted in streaks or mottled splotches.*

Bottle, grotesque figural-type, in the form of a strange humanoid creature w/a round head w/curly hair, incised frowning eyebrows, large eyes, protruding nose & large lips, ovoid body w/realistically modeled hands clutching his belly, unglazed, attributed to the Morganville, New York pottery, late 19th c., 6½" h. $518.00

Creamer, bulbous ovoid body tapering to a flared rim w/pinched spout & strap handle, greenish glaze w/orange spots, 4 7/8" h. (minor glaze flakes) 82.50

Crock, straight sides, eared handles, greenish glaze w/amber spots & brown flecks, impressed "3," Galena pottery, northwestern Illinois, 3 gal., 11¼" h. (chips) 150.00

Cup, low & wide slightly flaring cylindrical sides w/small pinched spout, applied strap handle, dark brown glaze, tooled band, 3½" h. (small flake) 82.50

Dish, oval, deep thick sides, deep green glaze w/orange spots, 11½" l. (wear) 275.00

Figure group, reclining figure of a lion w/mouth open next to a sleeping lamb, oblong base incised w/the inscription "THE Lion ANd lamb Shall Ly DOWn Together," probably Pennsylvania, 19th c., 8" l., 4½" h.............6,600.00

Redware Covered Jar

Jar, cov., ovoid body tapering to a flattened, flaring rim, inset cover w/knob finial, overall dark brown glaze, some wear, 9¼" h. (ILLUS.)..................... 82.50

Jar, cov., cylindrical bottom section below a wider waisted top section w/eared handles & a thick molded rim, tooled bands w/impressed stamp designs & a vining border on the lip, incised label "S.J. Jewett, Monmouth,... 18, 1833," tooled inscription around the base "S.J. Jewitt," New England, 10" h. (cover a bit oversized, wear & edge chips) 1,300.00

Jar, ovoid body w/a wide mouth & thinly molded rim, overall dark reddish glaze w/brown splotches, 5½" h. (small chips) 55.00

Jar, slightly rounded sides, greenish glaze w/amber spots, Galena pottery, northwestern Illinois, 6¾" h. 205.00

Jar, ovoid body tapering to a flaring rim, eared handles, clear glaze w/manganese splotches, 19th c., 9½" h. (imperfections) 522.50

Jar, cylindrical w/slightly flaring mouth, greenish glaze w/amber spots, Galena pottery, northwestern Illinois, 10¾" h......... 150.00

Jug, grotesque face-type, ovoid form w/top neck opening, modeled as a man's head w/round protruding eyes, applied ears, a thick nose & oblong open mouth w/pottery shard teeth, strap handle at the back, w/an overall metallic green glaze, signed "Brown Pottery," Southern U.S., early 20th c., 5½" h.............1,035.00

Jug, wide bulbous ovoid body w/heavy strap handle, dark green glaze w/orange spots, 6" h. (minor wear & small chips)......... 300.00

Jug, ovoid, strap handle, clear glaze w/brown splotches around the top half, 7" h. (wear, chips) 93.50

Milk pan, round w/deep flaring sides & pouring spout, 8" d...... 143.00

Model of a bird, perched on a stump-form base & flanked by short cylinders, incised overall details, Pennsylvania, 19th c., 4" h. 920.00

Models of Spaniels, seated dogs facing the viewer, w/green & brown mottled glaze, Pennsylvania, mid-19th c., 6½" h., matched pr. (minor chips on bases) 2,760.00

Pitcher, 6¼" h., wide ovoid body w/a flat bottom, the low flaring rim w/a pinched spout, small strap handle, green glaze w/orange spots & brown flecks (chips, wear) 75.00

Pitcher, 7¾" h., ovoid body tapering to a wide mouth w/slightly arched pinched spout, small strap handle, light green glaze w/overall small brown splotches (small chips) 247.50

Plate, 10½" d., incised distlefink w/flowers, German inscription & name, dark amber glaze, attributed to Medinger, Pennsylvania, late 19th - early 20th c. 192.50

Preserving jar, cylindrical body below a flat tapering shoulder to the thick molded rim, mottled green & brown glaze, probably Southern, 19th c., 4 5/8" h. 935.00

Preserving jar, cylindrical w/flared lip, dark brown shiny glaze, impressed label "John Bell, Waynesboro," 6¾" h. (minor edge wear) 165.00

Sugar bowl, cov., miniature, footed deep round body w/flaring rim & eared handles, the domed cover w/a pointed ball finial, serrated rims, scattered brown splotches, Pennsylvania, first half 19th c., 3 3/8" d., 3 1/8" h. (old rough spots under base) 1,840.00

Teapot, cov., cylindrical body applied w/diaper panels, scrolling branches, griffins, phoenix & Chinamen, Staffordshire, England, ca. 1750, 6" h. (rim chips to cover, some flaking) 715.00

RED WING

Various potteries operated in Red Wing, Minnesota from 1868, the most successful being the Red Wing Stoneware Co., organized in 1878. Merged with other local potteries through the years, it became known as Red Wing Union Stoneware Co. in 1894, and was one of the largest producers of utilitarian stoneware items in the United States. After a decline in the popularity of stoneware products, an art pottery line was introduced to compensate for the loss and this was reflected in a new name for the company, Red Wing Potteries, Inc., in 1930. Stoneware production ceased entirely in 1947, but vases, planters, cookie jars and dinnerwares of art pottery quality continued in production until 1967 when the pottery ceased operation altogether.

BRUSHED & GLAZED WARES

Ewer, serpent handle, serpents & face around base, matte ivory glaze, 10½" h. $65.00

Vase, bud, 7½" h., yellow speckled w/grey 12.00

Vase, 7¾" h., two-handled, white

exterior w/green interior, No. 763 . . . . 25.00

Vase, 12" h., expanding cylinder w/squared handles rising from narrow shoulder to mouth, Grecian design, No. 155 . . . . 80.00

Vase, 12½" h., squared handles, tapering cylinder, marked w/pre-1936 ink mark, No. 163 . . . . 75.00

DINNERWARES & NOVELTIES

Ashtray, Merrileaf patt. 7.50

Beverage server, cov., Smart Set patt. 95.00

Bowl, 5" d., Magnolia patt. 5.00

Bowl, salad, 6" d., Village Green patt. 8.00

Bowl, 6½" d., Bob White patt. 10.00

Bread tray, Smart Set patt., 24" l. . . 90.00

Butter dish, cov., Merrileaf patt. 16.00

Casserole, cov., Bob White patt., 2 qt. 35.00

Casserole, cov., Round Up patt., 1 qt. 130.00

Celery dish, Midnight Rose patt., 12½" l. 22.00

Cookie jar, cov., King of Tarts 600.00

Creamer, Bob White patt. 15.00

Creamer, Midnight Rose patt., black 10.50

Creamer & cov. sugar bowl, Magnolia patt., pr. 18.50

Cream soup bowl, cov., Lexington Rose patt. 25.00

Cruet set, w/stand, Bob White patt. 150.00

Cup & saucer, Merrileaf patt. 9.00

Cup & saucer, Round Up patt. 40.00

Figure of a tambourine lady, cinnamon glaze, 10" h. 175.00

Gravy boat, cov., Bob White patt. . . 45.00

Mug, cylindrical w/embossed banner reading "Hamm's Krug Klub" over embossed scene of birds & animals in the forest around the body, brown glaze . . . . .55.00 to 65.00

Pitcher, 12" h., Bob White patt., 112 oz. 40.00

Plate, 8" d., Village Green patt. 4.00

Plate, chop, Magnolia patt. 16.00

Platter, 13" l., Lute Song patt. 15.00

Platter, 13½" l., Bob White patt. . . . 27.50

Salt & pepper shakers, Smart Set patt., pr. 35.00

Sugar bowl, cov., Smart Set patt. . . . 30.00

Teapot, cov., Smart Set patt. 275.00

Vegetable bowl, divided, Driftwood patt. 15.00

Vegetable bowl, divided, Merrileaf patt. 12.00

Vegetable bowl, divided, Midnight Rose patt., 13½" d. 28.00

Vegetable bowl, divided, Smart Set patt. 42.00

STONEWARE & UTILITY WARES

Red Wing Stoneware Fruit Jar

Bowl, 6" d., spongeware, green,
  brown & cream daubing 43.00
Bowl, 7" d., Grey Line, stoneware
  w/blue sponge band decoration . . 120.00
Bowl, 7" d., Saffron Ware, rust &
  blue sponging on a creamy
  ground, "Waddington, Geneva,
  Iowa" advertising 125.00
Bowl, 7" d., Saffron Ware w/Min-
  nesota advertising, unmarked 100.00
Bowl, 9" d., Grey Line, stoneware
  w/paneled sides & blue sponge
  band decoration 90.00
Casserole, cov., Saffron Ware,
  9" d. 135.00
Fruit jar w/screw-on zinc lid, "Stone
  Mason Fruit Jar, Union Stoneware
  Co., Red Wing, Minn." printed in
  black (or blue) on stoneware, half
  gal. (ILLUS.) 190.00
Jug, miniature, beehive shape, copy
  of the "little brown jug," symbol
  of football rivalry between Minnesota & Michigan, brown top
  half, grey bottom half printed in
  blue w/"Who Will Win?" 195.00
Pitcher, 8½" h., (so-called Russian
  milk pitcher without pouring
  spout), brown glaze, 1 gal. 75.00

Red Wing "Ko-Rec Feeder"

Poultry feeder (or waterer), stoneware, "Ko-Rec Feeder," half gal.
  (ILLUS.) 125.00
Refrigerator jar w/bail handle,
  white-glazed stoneware w/blue
  bands, No. 5 . . . . 200.00

RIDGWAY

*There were numerous Ridgways among
English potters. The firm J. & W. Ridgway
operated in Shelton from 1814 to 1930 and
produced many pieces with scenes of historical interest. William Ridgway operated in
Shelton from 1830 to 1865. Most wares
marked Ridgway that have been offered in
this country were made by one of these two
firms, or by Ridgway Potteries, Ltd., still in
operation.*

Bouillon cup, Coaching Days & Ways
  series, "Old England Ware," ca.
  1920-50, 5" d. $25.00
Bouillon saucer, Coaching Days &
  Ways series, "Old England Ware,"
  ca. 1920-50 . . . . 15.00
Cracker jar, cov., black transfer-
  printed Coaching Days & Ways
  scene on a brown ground, rattan
  handle, 6½" h. to finial 235.00
Fruit stands, porcelain, lozenge-
  shaped, painted in the center
  (one slightly scratched) in shades
  of yellow, iron-red, purple, green,
  brown & grey w/a cluster of fruit
  within a gilt leaf-and-dot bordered
  oval panel & cobalt blue-ground
  rim bisected by a gold, salmon &
  iron-red-striped band entwined
  w/gold & white leafage issuing
  gold floral sprays, the scalloped
  rim edge lightly molded w/leaves
  within a gilt dentil band interrupted at the ends w/gold & white
  foliate handles, and the conforming foot & underside of rim similarly bordered, pattern number
  "6/2815" in iron-red, ca. 1845-50,
  12 3/16" l., pr. 2,970.00
Mug, cylindrical body tapering at
  the rim, "Coaching Days - Coaching Ways" black transfer-printed
  scene on a shaded brown ground,
  marked, 4¼" h. 35.00
Plaque, Coaching Days & Ways se-
  ries, "In a Snow Drift," yellow,
  12" d. 135.00
Plate, 6" d., Blue Onion patt. 50.00
Plate, 9¼" d., transfer-printed landscape w/buildings, titled on reverse "Catskill Moss, Fairmount
  Gardens," purple, 19th c. 93.50

Plate, 10¼" d., Chinese patt., polychrome decoration 30.00
Tea caddy, cov., black transfer-
printed Coaching Days & Ways
scene on a brown ground,
4½" sq., 5¾" h. 155.00
Tumbler, tall cylindrical form w/dou-
ble loop handles near the rim,
"Coaching Days - Coaching Ways"
black transfer-printed scene on
a shaded brown ground, marked,
6" h. 35.00

ROCKINGHAM

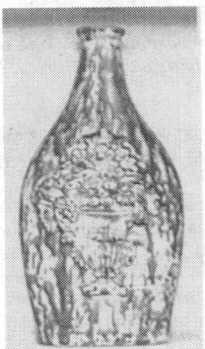

Rockingham-Glazed Bottle

*An earthenware pottery was first estab-
lished on the estate of the Marquis of Rockingham in England's Yorkshire district about
1745 and occupied by a succession of potters.
The famous Rockingham glaze of mottled
brown, somewhat resembling tortoise shell,
was introduced about 1788 by the Brameld
Brothers, and was well received. During the
1820's, porcelain manufacture was added to
the production and fine quality china was
turned out until the pottery closed in 1842.
The popular Rockingham glaze was subsequently produced elsewhere, including Bennington, Vermont, and at numerous other
U.S. potteries. We list herein not only wares
produced at the Rockingham potteries in
England, distinguishing porcelain wares from
the more plentiful earthenware productions,
but also include items from other potteries
with the Rockingham glaze.*

Bank, model of a church, mottled
brown glaze, 3¾" h. $75.00
Bank, model of a two-story house
w/two chimneys, mottled brown
glaze, 4 1/8" h. (small chips) 65.00
Bottle, model of a high-topped
man's shoe, boldly spotted & mottled dark brown glaze, marked
"Ann Reid 1859," 6" h. 247.50

Bottle, ovoid body tapering to a
slender neck w/molded rim,
relief-molded urn of flowers on
each side, runny brown mottled
glaze, 10 3/8" h. (ILLUS.) 352.00
Bowl, 5¼" d., 2½" h., mottled
brown glaze, marked "National" . . 57.00
Bowl, 7 3/8" d., 2 1/8" h., round
w/widely flaring sides, mottled
dark brown glaze 44.00
Bowl, 11½" d., 3½" h., mottled
dark brown glaze 93.50
Cuspidor, flaring scalloped rim, mottled brown & green glaze, bottom
labeled "Steeler, Taylor & Bloor,
Trenton, N.J.," 9¾" d. (profes-
sional repair) 375.00
Jar, cov., cylindrical w/tooled inden-
tation beneath rim, molded handles, acorn finial, mottled brown
glaze, 11¼" h. 145.00

Rockingham-Glazed Lion

Models of lions, standing animal
w/one foot resting on a globe,
mounted on a tiered rectangular
three-step base, tan-glazed coat,
molded curly mane & looped tail
(one repaired), dark brown glaze
on base, one w/cracks in hind
leg, one w/repaired chip, England, mid-19th c., 12¾" l.,
10 1/8" h., pr. (ILLUS. of one) 3,575.00
Mug, waisted body, molded rim
design, mottled brown glaze,
3¾" h. 125.00
Mustache cup, cylindrical body
relief-molded w/a fat Toby Philpot
figure, angled branch handle,
mottled & streaky light brown
glaze, 4¼" h. 104.50
Pie plate, wide bottom w/low flar-
ing sides, mottled dark brown
glaze, 9" d. 71.50
Pitcher, 4¼" h., short wide cylindri-
cal body on footring, short
pinched spout, small strap handle,
mottled brown glaze 45.00
Pitcher, 7½" h., 4¾" d., figural,

modeled as a bust of Wellington raised on a high, shouldered base, his name across the base, early 19th c., mottled dark brown glaze 265.00

Pitcher, 8½" h., molded peacock decoration, mottled dark brown glaze (small spout chip)......... 71.50

Pitcher, 8½" h., low foot, canted sides, branch handle, molded hunt scene & grapevines on sides, mottled brown glaze 175.00

Pitcher, 9 3/8" h., paneled body w/wide horizontal ridges, molded mask spout & serpent handle, mottled brown glaze 565.00

Pitcher, 9 7/8" h., bulbous ovoid body tapering to the wide arched spout, scroll-molded handle, the sides molded w/a large hunting scene w/horseman & hounds in forest, molded leaves under spout, mottled brown glaze, late 19th c. 115.50

Plaque, pierced for hanging, a flaring rectangular shadowbox frame w/rounded corners, molded scrolls along the sides & a flaring scroll crest, the center w/a molded high-relief bust portrait of a man facing right, mottled dark brown glaze, 7½" w., 9" h. (hairline in bust, minor edge damage, small flakes in frame) 385.00

Platter, 15" l. oval, mottled dark brown glaze (chip on back edge of rim) 170.00

ROOKWOOD

Rookwood Porcelain Bowl

Considered America's foremost art pottery, the Rookwood Pottery Company was established in Cincinnati, Ohio in 1880, by Mrs. Maria Longworth Nichols Storer. To accurately record its development, each piece carried the Rookwood insignia, or mark, was dated, and, if individually decorated, was usually signed by the artist. The pottery remained in Cincinnati until 1959 when it was sold to Herschede Hall Clock Company and moved to Starkville, Mississippi, where it continued in operation until 1967.

A private company is now producing a limited variety of pieces using original Rookwood molds.

Basket, rectangular body w/four crimps, braided overhead handle, glossy sage green glaze, No. 213, 1887, artist-signed, 4½ x 5", overall 4" h. $295.00

Book ends, figural, modeled as an elephant w/trunk down on a shaped base, matte deep blue glaze, 1929, 5 x 5¾", pr. 330.00

Book ends, figural, Art Deco style w/a seated Buddha-like figure sitting cross-legged before a stepped backplate, glossy pale blue glaze w/a dark blue headpiece w/a black comb trimmed in red, No. 2362, 1922, William P. MacDonald, 8" h., pr. 825.00

Book ends, model of an owl on book, brown glaze, No. 2655, pr.......................... 225.00

Book ends, model of a penguin, blue matte glaze, 1927, pr....... 225.00

Bowl, 5½" d., 3" h., squatty bulbous form tapering to a wide flat rim, decorated w/pink apple blossoms w/green & brown leafy branches against a white matte ground w/linear borders outlined in blue, No. 1069, 1918, Alice Coven...... 247.50

Bowl, 13¼" d., porcelain, shallow lobed sides w/a scalloped rim, decorated in the center w/a very large six-petal blossom & three-part leaves in blue & brown on a white ground, No. 2813C, 1946, L. Holtkamp (ILLUS.) 275.00

Bowl-vase, squatty bulbous body tapering to a short, wide flat neck, decorated w/a scene of a brown fox fishing in a pond & being observed by three green frogs & attacked by a dark brown lobster, all on a tan ground & bordered around the shoulder w/a lacy impressed gilded band, 1882, Albert R. Valentien, 9 3/8" d.....2,200.00

Bust of a young woman, porcelain, her hair pulled back, rich bluish white glaze, No. 2026, 1956, 7½" w., 8" h................... 192.50

Candlesticks, hexagonal base, magnolia blossom-shaped candle cups, glossy blue trim on matte cream ground, 1927, pr................ 135.00

Charger, round, the center decorated w/a mauve & ochre three-sail galleon against a deep blue ground, the border in a curdled light blue glaze, Matte glaze, 1905, John D. Wareham, 12½" d. 1,430.00

Cider set: pitcher & four mugs; the pitcher w/a wide slightly flaring cylindrical body w/a triple-spout rim & angled handle, the conical mugs w/strap handles; all decorated w/abstract green leaves & burgundy blossoms on a light green ground, Matte glaze, pitcher No. 259BV, mugs No. 587C, 1905, Sallie Coyne, pitcher 9½" d., 8½" h., the set 935.00

Coffeepot, cov., tall slightly tapering cylindrical body w/a short angled spout at the rim, domed cover & C-scroll handle, decorated w/dark teal blue decumbent blossoms, Standard glaze, No. 772, 1898, Amelia B. Sprague, 9" h. 522.50

Ewer, footed bulbous body tapering to a swelled neck w/a high angled spout, applied strap handle, decorated in Limoges-style painting w/black bamboo trees against white clouds & a brown ground, gilded highlights, No. 182, 1883, H. Horton, 5½" d., 7" h. 440.00

Ewer, footed squatty bulbous base tapering to a short neck w/triple-spout rim, loop handle, decorated w/burnt orange maple leaves against a shaded brown, green & orange ground, Standard glaze, No. 718, 1900, Sara Toohey, 6¼" d., 7½" h. 605.00

Ewer, silver overlay, long handle in silver, decorated w/green leaves & narrow yellow flowers, 1893, Laura Fry, 5½" d., 8" h. 4,500.00

Ewer, compressed globular base & long slender neck, decorated w/grapevines against a shaded light brown ground, Standard glaze, 1899, Matthew A. Daly, 13" h. 880.00

Flower bowl, boat-shaped, an elongated form w/incurved rims & one end pulled up into a tall hook, the other end in a lower hook, decorated w/a cluster of pansies, Standard glaze, No. 3745, 1890, Matt A. Daly, 16" l. 880.00

Jug, ovoid body tapering to a small mouth & small loop handle on the shoulder, painted w/golden corn cobs against a shaded dark brown ground w/Standard glaze, ornate pierced & scrolling silver overlay around the base & up the back side w/solid silver on the handle

& neck, No. 512, 1892, Albert R. Valentien, 8¼" h. 3,080.00

Jug, wide ovoid body tapering to a short, narrow neck w/curved strap handle to the shoulder, a bulbous pointed stopper, decorated w/four ears of corn on a dark ground, Standard glaze, No. 512X, 1896, Sallie Toohey, 13" h. 1,210.00

Lamp, kerosene table model, the spherical font decorated w/a Limoges-style design of grey & brown fish & sea grasses against a textured matte grey & smooth ochre ground, gilt accents, Smear glaze, brass footed base & shoulder fittings & burner, No. 95C, 1885, William McDonald, 7" d., 11" h. (base drilled) 770.00

Loving cup, three-handled, cylindrical body decorated w/dark blue gooseberries & green leaves against a shaded brown, green & orange ground, Standard glaze, No. 830E, 1900, C. Lindeman, 6¼" d., 4¾" h. 467.50

Unusual Rookwood Mug

Mug, tapering cylinder, depicting a grotesque frightened man up a tree, Standard glaze, No. 587, Kataro Shirayamadani, 4½" h. (ILLUS.)........................ 935.00

Paperweight, embossed bull on top, on back "Boss, Chas. G. Schmidt, Cincinnati Butchers' Supply Co., Cin., O.," bull & "1888' in small circle, light brown glaze, 1949, 3¼" d., ¾" h. 175.00

Pitcher, 3¼" h., 4¼" d., squatty bulbous footed body below a short wide neck w/pinched spout, round loop handle, Limoges-style decoration of a dragonfly over a pink ground w/gilded trim, 1883, H. Horton 330.00

Pitcher, 7½" h., 7¼" d., ovoid body tapering to a short neck w/pinched spout, applied strap handle, decorated in the Limoges style w/black cranes flying over a lake in white, against a brown ground, some gilding, 1882, A.R. Valentien 660.00

Pitcher, tankard, 14¼" h., 7½" d., a flaring ringed foot below a widely flaring trumpet-form body w/long angled double handles to one side, decorated w/one large ochre lotus blossom & long sinuous stems in green against a shaded dark brown to caramel ground, Standard glaze, No. 292B, 1898, A.M. Valentien 880.00

Rookwood Scenic Vellum Plaque

Plaque, rectangular, decorated w/a mountainous snow-covered landscape in greys w/a distant pale sunset sky, titled "The Top of the Hill," Vellum glaze, 1916, Sara Sax, wide flat frame, plaque 7 3/8 x 9 3/8", frame 13 x 15" (ILLUS.) 4,070.00

Tea set: cov. teapot, cov. sugar bowl & creamer; wide ovoid forms w/inset covers, glossy green overall glaze w/narrow navy blue rim bands, No. 2469, 1919, teapot 5½" h., 3 pcs. (random crazing) .. 330.00

Vase, 4" h., 5" d., bulbous ovoid body w/molded rim, decorated w/large Art Nouveau-style poppies in burnt orange on a dark ground, No. 906E, 1903, J. Swing 440.00

Vase, 4¾" h., 5½" d., canted sides w/flat shoulder & short flaring neck, decorated w/a large fish, a large bird, a seated nude, a face in profile & a large flower in grey & white against a dark blue ground under a thick overglaze, No. 6310, 1943, Jens Jensen 2,310.00

Vase, 5½" h., 5½" d., bulbous ovoid footed body tapering to a wide flared rim, decorated around the shoulder w/a band of burgundy chestnut leaves & blue fruit against a shaded bluish grey to pale green ground, Vellum glaze, pink interior, No. 2831, 1931, Fred Rothenbusch 935.00

Vase, 6½" h., 6" d., 'jeweled' porcelain, trumpet-form w/rolled rim, decorated w/arabesques & curlicues around the lower half in dark blue against a turquoise ground, No. 2240, 1921, Lorinda Epply 605.00

Vase, 7" h., 4¼" d., bottle-shaped w/a footed squatty bulbous base tapering to a tall thin stick neck, decorated w/deep bluish green poplar leaves against a chartreuse green ground, No. 743C, 1896, Artus Van Briggle 1,760.00

Vase, 9½" h., 4¼" d., gently flaring cylindrical shouldered body w/short cylindrical neck w/molded rim, carved around the shoulder w/stylized flowers in green & blue against a bluish green ground, Matte glaze, No. 1920, 1918, C.S. Todd 440.00

Vase, 10" h., 6¾" d., bulbous ovoid body tapering to a short, flared neck, decorated w/large peach dogwood blossoms against a shaded peach & blue ground, Butterfat glaze, No. 6891, 1945, Kataro Shirayamadani 1,760.00

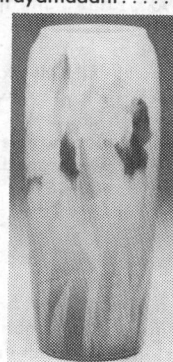

Rookwood Vase with Irises

Vase, 10¼" h., tall cylindrical body decorated w/a tall series of iris blossoms w/shaded lavender, white & grey blossoms & buds & tall leaves & stems, on a similarly shaded ground, Iris glaze, uncrazed, No. 954C, 1905, Lenore Asbury (ILLUS.) 3,300.00

Vase, 10¾" h., 4¼" d., tall cylindrical body tapering slightly to a gently flared rim, decorated around the neck w/a band of polychrome stylized flowers against a red-to-purple matte ground, No. 950C, 1915, Charles Todd 550.00

Vase, 12¼" h., 5¼" d., tall slightly
tapering cylindrical body w/wide
flared rim, decorated around the
top w/a wide band of large red
nasturtium blossoms & brown
leaves against a shaped yellow
'butterfat' ground, Wax Matte
glaze, No. 2790, 1927, L. Abel ...1,210.00

Vase, 15½" h., 7½" d., decorated
w/blue & turquoise peacocks
standing next to brown trees
w/red, brown & blue foliage &
flowers, against a mellow brown
ground, Butterfat glaze, No. 925A,
1925, E.T. Hurley 8,800.00

Vase, 15½" h., tall cylindrical body
tapering slightly to flared rim,
decorated w/a continuous landscape of tall trees beneath a full
moon, in shades of blue, green,
grey & black against a shaded
blue-grey ground, Vellum glaze,
No. 1660A, 1909, Kataro Shirayamadani 2,750.00

Vase, 18" h., 9½" d., wide ovoid
body w/a tapering short cylindrical neck, decorated w/dark violet
& ochre irises w/olive green
leaves against a deep brown
ground, modeled Standard glaze,
No. 905A, 1900, Kataro Shirayamadani 7,975.00

Vase, 21½" h., 9" d., ovoid body
tapering to a wide slightly flaring
cylindrical neck, incised w/two
large peacocks on gnarled
branches in dark blue against a
shaded blue & brown ground,
Matte glaze, No. 308, 1912,
Charles Todd (repair to drill hole
in base) 4,125.00

Vase, 22" h., two-handled, ovoid
body decorated w/berried
branches against a shaded brown
ground, mounted in an elaborate
gilt bronze stand, 1885, Albert
Valentien 1,100.00

Wall pocket, modeled as a large
winged beetle, red & green matte
glaze, No. 1636, 1908, 4¼" w.,
8½" l. 440.00

ROSEMEADE

*Laura Taylor was a ceramic artist who su-
pervised Federal Works Projects in her native North Dakota during the Depression era
and later demonstrated at the potter's wheel
during the 1939 New York World's Fair. In
1940, Laura Taylor and Robert J. Hughes
opened the Rosemeade-Wahpeton Pottery,*
*naming it after the North Dakota county and
town of Wahpeton where it was located.
Rosemeade Pottery was made on a small
scale for only about twelve years with Laura
Taylor designing the items and perfecting
colors. Her animal and bird figures are popular among collectors. Hughes and Taylor married in 1943 and the pottery did a thriving
business until her death in 1959. The pottery
closed in 1961 but stock was sold from the factory salesroom until 1964.*

Ashtray, lettered on top
  "Rosemeade Pottery, Wahpeton,
  N. Dak.," forest green glaze $30.00
Bell, model of an elephant 185.00
Bell, model of a flamingo 145.00
Creamer & sugar bowl, model of a
  turkey, pr................... 130.00
Flower frog, model of a stork 22.50
Model of a kitten, white glaze 15.00
Model of a pheasant, 7" h......... 160.00
Planter, model of a deer & log,
  4" h. 30.00
Planter, model of a kangaroo,
  5" h....................... 55.00
Planter, model of a pony, pink
  glaze 75.00
Salt & pepper shakers, model of a
  bear, black glaze, pr. 75.00
Salt & pepper shakers, model of a
  bell, yellow glaze, pr. 35.00
Salt & pepper shakers, model of a
  bobwhite, pr................. 30.00
Salt & pepper shakers, model of a
  buffalo, pr. 80.00
Salt & pepper shakers, model of a
  chicken, pr................... 20.00
Salt & pepper shakers, model of a
  Chow dog head, brown glaze,
  pr........................ 35.00
Salt & pepper shakers, model of a
  flamingo, pr. 68.00
Salt & pepper shakers, model of a
  gopher, pr................... 50.00
Salt & pepper shakers, model of a
  Greyhound dog head, 2½" h.,
  pr......................... 52.00
Salt & pepper shakers, model of
  mouse, pr. 20.00
Salt & pepper shakers, model of
  Paul Bunyan & Babe the Ox, pr. ... 65.00
Salt & pepper shakers, model of a
  pheasant, cock & hen, paper
  labels, pr. 45.00
Salt & pepper shakers, model of a
  pheasant, large, 5" l., pr........ 100.00
Salt & pepper shakers, model of a
  pig, pr...................... 50.00
Salt & pepper shakers, model of a
  raccoon, pr. 75.00
Salt & pepper shakers, model of a
  Spaniel dog, pr................ 22.00
Spoon holder, Prairie Rose patt. 25.00

ROSE MEDALLION - ROSE CANTON

Rose Medallion Candlesticks

The lovely Chinese ware known as Rose Medallion was made through the past century and into the present one. It features alternating panels of people and flowers or insects with most pieces having four medallions with a central rose or peony medallion. The ware is called Rose Canton if flowers and birds or insects fill all the panels. Unless otherwise noted, our listing is for Rose Medallion ware.

Bowl, 16" d., 6½" h., Rose Mandarin variant, alternating panels of Mandarin figures, 19th c. (minor glaze rubbing)................$1,320.00

Candlesticks, tall slender shaft flaring at the base & w/a flat rim on the candle socket, 19th c., glaze rubbing, 9½" h., pr. (ILLUS.).....1,045.00

Dish, shallow almond-shaped form on a short foot, marked "China," 14¼" l. (wear, chips)........... 250.00

Dishes, Rose Mandarin variant, square, decorated w/a central figural courtyard scene w/floral, bird, butterfly & fruit borders, ca. 1840, 9¼" w., pr. 1,870.00

Jar, cov., bulbous ovoid body tapering to a flat base, the domed cover w/flanged rim & a foo dog finial, gilt animal head bosses around the shoulder, 19th c., 16¾" h. 1,870.00

Jardiniere, 19th c., 14½" d., 12" h. (minor glaze rubbing)........... 770.00

Pitcher, 16" h., heightened w/gilt, 19th c. (base chips) 1,045.00

Platter, 12" l., Rose Canton, w/peacocks & florals 160.00

Platter, 15" l., oval w/shaped rim, decorated w/alternating floral & figural panels, ca. 1860 (gilt rubbing on rim) 990.00

Platter, 16" l. oval, marked "China" 275.00

Punch bowl, deep rounded sides, trimmed w/gilt, 19th c., 11½" d. (gilt rubbing) 715.00

Shrimp dishes, shaped oval, each w/cipher in butterfly reserve & heightened w/gilt, 19th c., 10½" l., pr. (one restored)...... 825.00

Vase, 10" h., cylindrical body tapering slightly to a long neck w/a flared rim, marked "China" 55.00

Vegetable dish, cov., oblong, interior & exterior decorated w/panels of bees, butterflies, flowers & fruit 325.00

ROSENTHAL

Rosenthal Figural Clock

The Rosenthal porcelain manufactory has been in operation since 1880 when it was established by P. Rosenthal in Selb, Bavaria. Tablewares and figure groups are among its specialties.

Clock, figural, the circular drum-form clock cast w/gilt chapter ring, surmounted by a nude female figure w/a length of flowing drapery, flanked on one side by a boy blowing a horn, on the other w/a posy, on a rectangular base w/scrolled ends above an apron cast w/flowers & leafage, on four outward flaring feet, the white body heightened in lime green, lemon yellow, dusty rose, turquoise & gilt, designed by Gustav Oppel, decorated by Kurt Severin, printed factory marks & "Schoenberg" in green enamel, ca. 1925, 14¼" h. (ILLUS.) $2,750.00

Dish, two-handled, decorated w/pale pink roses, artist-signed, 8½" d........................ 45.00

Figure group, princess w/goose & golden egg 325.00

Figure group, Snow White w/dwarf,
9½" h. 375.00

Ginger jar, cov., the tapering hexagonal body w/slightly domed
shoulder & conforming cover,
decorated w/exotic long-billed
birds among highly stylized pendant foliage in shades of orange,
blue, black & mint green, heightened w/gilt, designed by Kurt
Wendler, printed factory mark,
designer's mark, 50th anniversary
printed credit & marked in gilt
"FRANZ," ca. 1920-25, 12¼" h. . . . 1,320.00

Model of a dog, Russian Wolfhound lying down, artist-signed,
7 x 15" 485.00

Model of a dog, Scottie, sitting up &
begging, all white, artist-signed,
10" h. 295.00

Model of a white squirrel on a gold
ball, 3½" h. 45.00

Model of a white swan w/spread
wings, wearing a gold crown,
4" h. 80.00

Plate, 8½" d., overall decoration of
pink bell-shaped flowers & green
leaves, gold trim 48.50

Plate, 10½" d., h.p. Rheinstein Cas-
tle scene 135.00

ROSEVILLE

Roseville Pottery Company operated in Zanesville, Ohio from 1898 to 1954 after having been in business for six years prior to that in Muskingum County, Ohio. Art wares similar to those of Owens and Weller Potteries were produced. Items listed here are by patterns or lines.

APPLE BLOSSOM (1948)

White apple blossoms in relief on blue, green or pink ground; brown tree branch handles.

Basket w/circular handle, pink
ground, No. 309-8", 8" h. $135.00

Bowl, 10" d., pink ground,
No. 329-10" 70.00

Candleholders, squatty, green
ground, No. 351-2", 2" h., pr. 55.00

Console bowl, green or pink
ground, No. 396-12", 12" l.,
each 95.00

Jardiniere & pedestal base,
pink ground, No. 302-8" &
No. 305-8", overall 24½" h.,
2 pcs. (ILLUS. top next col-
umn) . . . . 675.00 to 695.00

Tea set: cov. teapot, creamer & sugar bowl; pink ground, No. 371,
the set 225.00

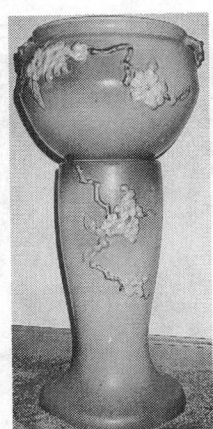

Apple Blossom Jardiniere & Pedestal

Vase, 6" h., two-handled, squatty
base, long cylindrical neck, pink
ground, No. 381-6" 75.00

Vase, 8¼" h., green ground,
No. 385-8" 75.00

Vase, 10" h., base handles, blue
or green ground, No. 388-10",
each . . . . 125.00 to 150.00

Vase, 15½" h., double base handles, short globular base, long
cylindrical neck, green or
pink ground, No. 392-15",
each . . . . 275.00 to 310.00

AZTEC (1915)

Muted earthy tones of beige, grey, brown, teal, olive, azure blue or soft white with slip-trailed geometric decoration in contrasting colors.

Vase, 8" h., tapering cylinder swelling slightly at top, squeeze-bag
decoration of lacy loops & swags
in white against a blue ground . . . 325.00

Vase, 10¼" h., 3¾" d., baluster-
form body w/ringed bands around
the foot & below the flaring rim,
swirled slender stems running up
the sides, each w/a feather blossom in the middle, white blossoms on grey stems against a
matte bluish grey ground, marked
"8" 440.00

Vase, 10¾" h., 3½" d., a flaring
foot tapering to a tall slightly flaring cylindrical body w/a narrow
angled shoulder to a short ring
neck below the wide flat & inverted rim, squeeze-bag decoration of
thin triangular & geometric designs forming a wide band around
the shoulder, done in orange,
white & deep green against a

navy blue ground, unmarked (restoration to base) 165.00
Vase, 11" h., 4½" d., the flaring foot tapering to a tall cylindrical body supporting a bulbous top w/a short tapering neck, squeeze-bag decoration of slender geometric scrolls around the top & foot in white, yellow & grey on a bluish grey ground (minor glaze bubbles at base) 275.00
Vase, 12" h., cylindrical body rising to a short projecting collar beneath a flaring rim, squeeze-bag decoration of stylized heart-shaped devices on thin stems around collar in white & sandy tan against a blue ground 475.00

BANEDA (1933)

Band of embossed pods, blossoms and leaves on green or raspberry pink ground.

Baneda Vase

Bowl, 9" d., 3¾" h., two-handled, raspberry pink ground 195.00
Jardiniere, green ground, 8" h. 750.00
Urn, small rim handles, bulbous, green ground, 5" h. 225.00
Vase, 4" h., tiny handles, green ground, No. 587-4" (ILLUS.) 225.00
Vase, 4½" h., tiny rim handles,
Vase, 5½" h., rounded base w/sharply canted sides w/two handles at rim, raspberry pink ground 180.00
Vase, 9" h., cylindrical w/short collared neck, handles rising from shoulder to beneath rim, raspberry pink ground 275.00

BITTERSWEET (1940)

Orange bittersweet pods and green leaves on a grey blending to rose, yellow with terra cotta, rose with green or solid green bark-textured ground; brown branch handles.

Basket, low overhead handle, shaped rim, green ground, No. 810-10", 10" l. 98.00

Candleholders, handles rising from conical base to midsection of nozzle, grey ground, No. 851-3", 3" h., pr. 70.00
Cornucopia-vase, double, grey ground, No. 858-4", 8½" w., 4" h. 70.00
Vase, double bud, 6" h., green or grey ground, No. 873-6", each ....80.00 to 90.00
Vase, 10" h., handles at midsection, scalloped rim, yellow ground, No. 885-10" 65.00
Wall pocket, curving conical form w/overhead handle continuing to one side, yellow ground, No. 866-7", 7½" h. 110.00

BLACKBERRY (1933)

Band of relief clusters of blackberries with vines and ivory leaves accented in green and terra cotta on a green textured ground.

Console bowl, small pointed end handles, 13" l. 235.00
Jardiniere, two-handled, 10" d., 7" h. 295.00
Vase, 4" h., two-handled, squatty.................185.00 to 210.00
Vase, 12½" h., handles rising from shoulder to rim 635.00
Wall pocket, basket-shaped w/narrow base & flaring rim, 6¾" w. at rim, 8½" h. 375.00

BLEEDING HEART (1938)

Pink blossoms and green leaves on shaded blue, green or pink ground.

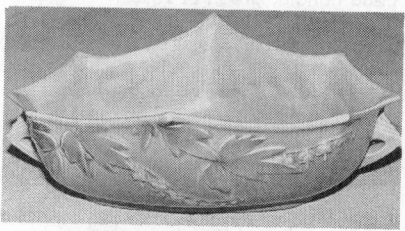

Bleeding Heart Console Bowl

Console bowl, blue ground, No. 382-10", 10" l. (ILLUS.) 135.00
Flower frog, pink ground, No. 40 ... 55.00
Jardiniere & pedestal base, pink ground, jardiniere 8" h., 2 pcs. (handle rub) 875.00
Pitcher, 8" h., asymmetrical w/high arched handle, pink ground, No. 1323 .... 190.00
Vase, 6½" h., base handles, blue ground, No. 964-6" 100.00
Vase, bud, 7" h., green ground, No. 967-7" 95.00

BURMESE (1950's)

Sculptured head of an Oriental-type man or woman. Also included in the line are some plain articles.

Candleholder-book end combination,
woman, black glaze, No. 80B 80.00
Candleholder-book end combination,
woman & man, black or green
glaze, Nos. 80B & 70B, each pr. . .   250.00
Planter, white glaze, No. 92B 37.00
Plaque, pierced to hang, woman,
green glaze, No. 72B, 7½" h. 155.00

BUSHBERRY (1948)

Berries and leaves on blue, green or russet bark-textured ground; brown or green branch handles.

Bushberry Vase

Ashtray, handled, blue ground,
No. 26 . . . .   77.00
Basket w/asymmetrical over-
head handle, green or russet
ground, No. 371-10", 10" h.,
each . . . . 85.00 to 100.00
Beverage set: 8½" h. ice lip pitcher
& four 3½" h. handled mugs; blue
ground, pitcher No. 1325, mugs
No. 1-3½", 5 pcs. 550.00
Candleholders, large flaring han-
dles, green ground, No. 1147,
2" h., pr. 42.00
Console bowl, end handles, russet
ground, No. 385-10", 13" l. 72.50
Cornucopia-vase, double, russet
ground, No. 155-8", 6" h. 73.00
Ewer, cut-out rim, blue ground,
No. 3-15", 15" h. 375.00
Flower frog, blue ground, No. 45 . . .   95.00
Teapot, cov., blue ground, No. 2 . . .   185.00
Umbrella stand, double handles,
blue ground, No. 779-20",
20½" h. . . . . .495.00 to 525.00
Vase, 4" h., conical w/tiny rim
handles, russet ground, No. 28-4"
(ILLUS.) 35.00
Vase, 6" h., asymmetrical side han-

dles, cylindrical w/low foot, blue
ground, No. 29-6" 52.00
Vase, bud, 7½" h., asymmetrical
base handles, cylindrical body,
green ground, No. 152-7" 60.00
Vase, 12½" h., large asymmet-
rical side handles, bulging cylinder w/flaring foot, blue or
russet ground, No. 38-12",
each . . . . .185.00 to 235.00

CAPRI (late line)

Various shapes depicting shells, leaves and overlapping petals. Sandlewood (sic) yellow or cactus green matte finishes and a metallic red semi-matte finish.

Ashtray, shell-shaped, metallic red,
No. 598-9", 9" w. 28.50
Basket w/center overhead branch
handle, molded leaf design at ter-
minal, pointed ends, cactus green,
No. C-1012-10", 10" h. 65.00
Bowl, 15" l., leaf-shaped, cactus
green, No. 532-15" 45.00
Cornucopia-vase, ribbed, metallic
red, No. 556-6", 6" h. 65.00
Window box, flared out at ends,
sandlewood (sic) yellow,
No. 569-10", 3 x 10" 40.00

CARNELIAN I (1910-15)

Matte glaze with a combination of two colors or two shades of the same color with the darker dripping over the lighter tone or heavy and textured glaze with intermingled colors and some running.

Bowl, 11" d., 4" h., deep green &
light green 35.00
Flower holder, fan-shaped w/elab-
orate scrolled handles from rim to
slightly domed base, dark & light
blue, 6" h. 85.00
Vase, 6" h., cylindrical, flaring
slightly at rim, base handles, dark
& light blue 87.50
Vase, 9" h., two-handled, cylindrical
w/wide collared neck, deep green
& light green 85.00
Wall pocket, ornate side handles,
flaring rim, deep green & light
green or dark blue & light blue,
8" h., each . . . . 85.00 to 100.00

CARNELIAN II (1915)

Intermingled colors, some with a drip effect.

Bowl, 6" l., oblong, intermingled
shades of green 50.00
Bowl, 9 x 12½", 5¼" h., rose, tur-
quoise & black 85.00
Vase, 9" h., ovoid w/short collared

mouth, intermingled shades of
red 135.00
Wall pocket, intermingled shades of
green, 8" h. 225.00

CHERRY BLOSSOM (1933)

Sprigs of cherry blossoms, green leaves and twigs with pink fence against a combed blue-green ground or creamy ivory fence against a terra cotta ground shading to dark brown.

Jardiniere, shoulder handles, blue-
green or terra cotta ground, 6" h.,
each ....265.00 to 295.00
Jardiniere, shoulder handles, terra
cotta ground, 8" h. 675.00
Vase, 5" h., two-handled, slightly
globular, terra cotta ground 150.00
Vase, 7" h., jug-type, two-handled,
terra cotta ground 170.00

CLEMANA (1934)

Stylized blossoms with embossed latticework and basketweave on blue, green or tan ground.

Flower frog, low cylindrical base,
central tube surrounded by four
smaller tubes of varying heights,
green ground, No. 23, overall
4" h. 105.00
Jardiniere & pedestal base, green
ground, 2 pcs. 495.00
Urn-vase, small handles at shoulder,
blue ground, 6" h. 175.00
Vase, 8" h., tan ground,
No. 753-8" 395.00

CLEMATIS (1944)

Clematis blossoms and heart-shaped green leaves against a vertically textured ground — white blossoms on blue, rose-pink blossoms on green and ivory blossoms on golden brown.

Console bowl, two-handled, green
ground, No. 460-12", 12" l. 125.00
Creamer, green ground, No. 5 ..... 37.50
Ewer, brown ground, No. 18-15",
15" h. 300.00
Jardiniere, blue ground, No. 667-4",
4" h. 50.00
Vase, double bud, 5" h., two
cylinders joined by a single cle-
matis blossom, brown ground,
No. 194-5" 50.00
Vase, bud, 7" h., angular handles
rising from flared base to slender
neck, blue or brown ground,
No. 187-7", each 40.00
Vase, 15" h., green ground,
No. 114-15" 225.00
Wall pocket, angular side handles, brown ground, No. 1295-8",
8½" h. 85.00

COLUMBINE (1940's)

Columbine blossoms and foliage on shaded ground — yellow blossoms on blue, pink blossoms on pink shaded to green and blue blossoms on tan shaded to green.

Basket w/elaborate handle rising
from midsection, tan ground,
No. 365-7", 7" h. 93.00
Bowl, 12" d., irregular rim form-
ing handles, pink ground,
No. 405-12" 65.00
Cornucopia-vase, pink ground,
No. 149-6", 5½" h. 75.00
Jardiniere, two-handled, blue
ground, No. 655-8", 8" h. 350.00
Rose bowl, two-handled, blue
ground, No. 400-6", 6" d. 100.00
Urn-vase, pink ground, No. 151-8",
8" h. 135.00
Vase, 4" h., pink ground,
No. 12-4" 40.00
Vase, 10" h., two handles at
shoulder, ovoid, pink ground,
No. 23-10" 225.00
Vase, 16" h., floor-type, tan ground,
No. 27-16" 375.00
Wall pocket, blue ground,
No. 1290-8", 8" h. 200.00

CORINTHIAN (1923)

Deeply fluted ivory and green body below a continuous band of molded grapevine, fruit, foliage and florals in naturalistic colors, narrow ivory and green molded border at the rim.

Bowl, 6½" d. 75.00
Compote, 10" d., 5" h. 70.00
Jardiniere, 6" h. 125.00
Vase, double bud, 4½" h., 7" w.,
gate-form 55.00
Vase, 8" h., slightly rounded at
shoulder & base, collared neck ... 60.00
Wall pocket, 8½" h. 145.00

COSMOS (1940)

Embossed blossoms against a wavy horizontal ridged band on a textured ground — ivory band with yellow and orchid blossoms on blue, blue band with white and orchid blossoms on green or tan.

Basket w/pointed overhead handle,
pedestal base, tan ground,
No. 358-12", 12" h. 200.00
Candleholders, loop handles above
flat disc base, slender candle noz-
zle, blue ground, 2½" h., pr...... 70.00
Flowerpot w/saucer, blue ground,
No. 650-5", 5" h. 95.00
Urn-vase, green ground, No. 135-8",
8" h. 125.00
Vase, 4" h., two-handled, globular
base & wide neck, blue ground,
No. 944-4" 52.50

Vase, 10" h., blue or green ground,
 No. 954-10", each ......135.00 to 175.00

Cosmos Vase

Vase, 12½" h., blue ground,
 No. 956-12" (ILLUS.) 200.00
Wall pocket, double, green ground,
 No. 1268-8", 8½" h. 215.00

CREMONA (1927)

*Relief-molded floral motifs including a tall
stem with small blossoms and arrowhead
leaves, wreathed with leaves similar to Velmoss or a web of delicate vines against a
background of light green mottled with pale
blue or pink with creamy ivory.*

Candleholders, squared flaring
 base, baluster-form candle nozzle,
 green ground, No. 1068-4", 4" h.,
 pr............................. 100.00
Console set: console bowl, flower
 frog & pair of candleholders;
 green ground, 4 pcs. 175.00
Urn, green ground, 5" h............ 60.00
Vase, 5" h., fan-shaped, pink
 ground, No. 73-5" 58.00
Vase, 8" h., footed, trumpet-shaped,
 green ground, No. 356-8" 70.00

DAHLROSE (1924-28)

*Band of ivory daisy-like blossoms and green
leaves against a mottled tan ground.*

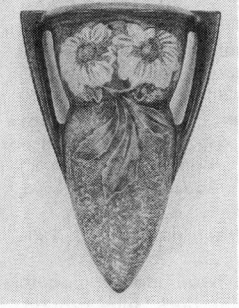

Dahlrose Wall Pocket

Basket, hanging-type, 7½" 140.00
Bowl, 6" d. 98.00
Candleholders, angular handles ris-
 ing from low slightly domed base,
 3½" h., pr...................... 110.00
Jardiniere, tiny rim handles, 6" d.,
 4" h........................... 65.00
Vase, double bud, 6" h., gate-
 form 72.00
Vase, 10" h., two-handled, ovoid
 w/wide flaring rim 145.00
Wall pocket, two-handled, conical,
 10" h. (ILLUS.) 150.00
Window box, 6 x 12½" 245.00

DAWN (1937)

*Incised spidery flowers — green ground with
blue-violet tinted blossoms, pink or yellow
ground with blue-green blossoms, all with yellow centers.*

Ewer, square base, pink ground,
 No. 834-15", 15" h. 450.00
Rose bowl, tab handles at sides,
 square base, yellow ground,
 No. 315-4", 4" d. 55.00
Vase, 6" h., cylindrical w/tab handles below rim, square foot, pink
 or yellow ground, No. 826-6",
 each ....100.00 to 120.00
Vase, 8" h., slender cylinder w/tab
 handles below rim, square foot,
 green or pink ground, No. 828-8",
 each ....135.00 to 155.00

DOGWOOD (1916-18)

*White dogwood blossoms and brown
branches against a textured green ground.*

Basket, hanging-type, w/original
 chains, 7" 175.00
Bowl, 2½" h., bulb-type 60.00
Vase, 9½" h. 95.00
Wall pocket, cone-shaped, 9½" h. ... 140.00

DOGWOOD II (1928)

*White dogwood blossoms & black branches
against a smooth green ground.*

Basket, 10" h. 100.00
Jardiniere, 8" h. 85.00
Planter, tub-shaped w/rim handles,
 7" d., 4" h. 70.00
Wall pocket, two handles in the
 form of blossoming branches,
 No. 1218-10", 10" h. 125.00

DONATELLO (1915)

*Deeply fluted ivory and green body with wide
tan band embossed with cherubs at various
pursuits in pastoral settings.*

Ashtray, 5" d., 3" h.............. 65.00
Basket w/tall pointed overhead han-

dle, cylindrical body, No. 304-12",
12" h. 250.00
Bowl, 6" d., w/flower frog, 2 pcs. . . 85.00
Bowl, fruit, 12" d. 250.00
Candlesticks, single handle at flared
base, cylindrical stem, flared rim,
6½" h., pr. 165.00
Chamberstick, deep saucer base
w/ring handle, No. 1011 . . . . 145.00
Compote, 5" h., bowl w/slightly
curved sides on flared stem 80.00
Flowerpot w/saucer, flaring sides,
5" h. 105.00
Jardiniere & pedestal base, overall
34" h., 2 pcs. . . . . .1,000.00 to 1,500.00
Planter, oval, low, 8" l. 65.00
Umbrella stand 1,000.00

Donatello Double Bud Vase

Vase, double bud, 5" h., gate-form
(ILLUS.). 85.00
Vase, 10" h., baluster-form, grey &
beige trial glaze 295.00

EARLAM (1930)

*Mottled glaze on various simple shapes. The
line includes many crocus or strawberry pots.*

Candlesticks, rectangular canted
base w/flat open handles, mottled
brown & green glaze,
6" h., pr. 85.00
Planter, two-handled, shaped rim,
mottled green & blue glaze,
No. 89-8", 5 x 10½" 130.00
Urn-vase, small rim handles, mot-
tled tan & lavender glaze,
No. 516-4½", 4½" h. 80.00
Vase, 5½" h., two handles rising
from middle of globular base to
rim, mottled tan & lavender glaze,
No. 517-5½" 125.00
Vase, 6" h., two-handled, mottled
tan experimental glaze 150.00

EARLY EMBOSSED PITCHERS (pre-1916)

*Utility pitchers with various embossed
scenes; high gloss glaze.*

The Bridge, 6" h. 85.00
The Cow, 6½" h. . . . . .185.00 to 215.00
The Cow, 7½" h. . . . . .180.00 to 200.00

Goldenrod, 9½" h. 190.00
The Grape, 6" h. 125.00
Holland, No. 2, 9½" h. 80.00
Landscape, 7½" h. 95.00
The Mill, 8" h. 350.00
Owl, 6½" h. 380.00
Poppy, 9" h. 175.00

Tulip Pitcher

Tulip, 7½" h. (ILLUS.). 100.00
Wild Rose, 9½" h. 90.00

EGYPTO (1905)

*Classic shapes resembling those from ancient
Egypt; soft deep green matte glaze.*

Bowl, 7" d., 3½" h., cherub faces at
corners. 225.00
Bowl, 9" d., 3½" h., three-
handled . . . . .115.00 to 135.00
Urn, two-handled, bulbous, 7" h. . . . 450.00
Vase, 6½" h., conical w/bulging
base 395.00
Vase, 12" h. 325.00

FALLINE (1933)

*Curving panels topped by a semi-scallop sepa-
rated by vertical peapod decorations; blended backgrounds of tan shading to green and
blue or tan shading to darker brown.*

Urn, two-handled, tan shading to
blue & green, 6" h. . . . . .400.00 to 450.00
Vase, 6" h., globular w/handles rising from shoulder to rim, tan
shading to blue & green 300.00
Vase, 7½" h., two-handled, slightly
rounded cylinder, tan shading to
blue & green or tan shading to
brown, each . . . . .375.00 to 400.00
Vase, 8" h., two-handled, taper-
ing sides, tan shading to brown,
No. 646-8" 360.00
Vase, 9" h., two-handled, horizon-
tally ribbed lower section, tan
shading to brown 425.00

FERRELLA (1930)

*Impressed shell design alternating with small
cut-outs at top and base; mottled brown or
mottled turquoise and red glaze.*

Bowl, 8" d., sharply canted sides,
low foot, brown glaze,
No. 211-8"...................... 310.00
Compote, 5" d., 4" h., brown glaze,
No. 210-4"...................... 200.00
Flowerpot w/saucer, brown glaze,
No. 620-5", 5" h................. 450.00
Vase, 4" h., squatty base w/exag-
gerated handles & narrow
neck, turquoise & red glaze,
No. 497-4"...................... 245.00
Vase, 9" h., sharply compressed
globular base, large handles rising from midsection to below rim,
brown glaze 325.00
Vase, 10¼" h., 6¼" d., ovoid body
on flaring foot & tapering to a
widely flaring mouth, low angular handles down the sides, the
foot pierced w/a band of small
squares, the mouth pierced w/two
bands of small rectangles, turquoise & red glaze 715.00

FLORANE I (1920's)

*Terra cotta shading to either dark brown or
deep olive green on simple shapes, often from
the Rosecraft line.*

Bowl, 10¼" d., dark brown 65.00
Bowl-vase, two small rim handles,
dark brown, 5" h................ 75.00
Vase, 12" h., slender ovoid form,
dark brown..................... 140.00
Wall pocket, conical w/flaring rim,
dark brown, 9" h................ 110.00
Wall pocket, two-handled, ovoid
w/fan-shaped top, dark brown,
10½" h......................... 140.00

FLORENTINE (1924-28)

*Bark-textured panels alternating with em-
bossed garlands of cascading fruit and florals;
ivory with tan and green, beige with brown
and green or brown with beige and green
glaze.*

Florentine Double Bud Vase

Ashtray, shallow, brown, 5" d. 75.00
Basket, hanging-type, beige,
No. 339-5", 5" 110.00
Bowl, 5½" d., ivory 35.00
Bowl, 7" d., w/flower frog, brown,
2 pcs.......................... 60.00

Bowl, 8" d., 3¾" h., two-handled,
ivory 50.00
Candlestick, flaring base, expanding
cylindrical stem, brown, 8½" h. .. 75.00
Candlesticks, flaring base, baluster-
form stem, brown, 10½" h., pr. .. 210.00
Jardiniere, beige, 8½" h. 126.50
Jardiniere & pedestal base, beige,
29" h., 2 pcs. 490.00
Vase, double bud, 4½" h., 9" w.,
gate-form, brown (ILLUS.) 50.00
Vase, 6" h., ovoid base w/a deeply
cupped rim joined by flat handles,
brown, No. 253-6".............. 79.00

FOXGLOVE (1940's)

*Sprays of pink and white blossoms embossed
against a shaded matte finish ground.*

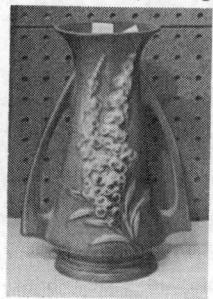

Foxglove Vase

Basket w/circular overhead handle,
blue or pink ground, No. 373-8",
8" h., each 120.00
Basket, hanging-type, green ground,
No. 466-5", 6½" 245.00
Console bowl, blue or pink ground,
No. 422-10", 10", each....85.00 to 100.00
Ewer, blue, green or pink ground,
No. 5-10", 10" h., each ..135.00 to 175.00
Flower frog, cornucopia-form, blue
ground, No. 46, 4" 50.00
Jardiniere, two-handled, blue
ground, No. 659-8", 8" h. 375.00
Tray, single open handle, leaf-
shaped, green ground, 8½" w. 125.00
Vase, double bud, 4½" h., gate-
form, blue ground, No. 160-4".... 60.00
Vase, 6½" h., two-handled, pink
ground, No. 44-6" 68.00
Vase, 10" h., angular handles rising
from base to below flaring rim,
pink ground, No. 51-10" (ILLUS.) .. 185.00
Vase, 16" h., two-handled, green or
pink ground, No. 55-16", each.... 350.00

FREESIA (1945)

*Trumpet-shaped blossoms and long slender
green leaves against wavy impressed lines -
white and lavender blossoms on blended*

green; white and yellow blossoms on shaded blue or terra cotta and brown.

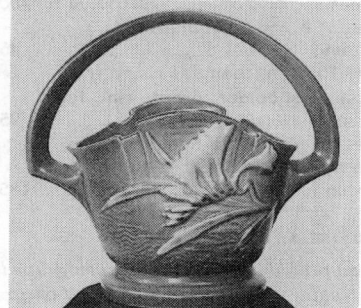

Freesia Basket

Basket w/overhead handle, blue
  ground, No. 391-8", 8" h.
  (ILLUS.) 100.00
Basket, hanging-type, blue ground,
  No. 471-5", 5" 170.00
Bowl, 11" d., two-handled, terra cot-
  ta ground, No. 465-8" 55.00
Cornucopia-vase, terra cotta ground,
  No. 198-8", 8" h. 65.00
Ewer, terra cotta ground,
  No. 21-15", 15" h. 265.00
Flowerpot w/attached saucer, green
  or terra cotta ground, No. 670-5",
  5½" h., each . . . . 75.00 to 85.00
Teapot, cov., terra cotta ground,
  No. 6-T. 195.00
Urn-vase, two-handled, terra cotta
  ground, No. 463-5", 5" h. 75.00
Vase, 9½" h., pointed handles
  at midsection, blue, green or
  terra cotta ground, No. 123-9",
  each . . . . 75.00 to 85.00
Vase, 12" h., two-handled, blue
  ground, No. 127-12" 145.00
Vase, 18" h., green or terra
  cotta ground, No. 129-18",
  each . . . . 350.00 to 365.00
Wall pocket, angular handles,
  blue, green or terra cotta
  ground, No. 1296-8", 8½" h.,
  each . . . . 100.00 to 125.00

FUCHSIA (1939)

Coral pink fuchsia blossoms and green leaves against a background of blue shading to yellow, green shading to terra cotta or terra cotta shading to gold.

Basket w/rounded overhead handle
  & flower frog, blue or green
  ground, No. 350-8", 8" h.,
  each . . . . 250.00 to 285.00
Bowl, 5" d., two-handled, green
  ground, No. 348-5" 95.00
Candleholders, two handles rising
  from disc base, terra cotta
  ground, No. 1132, 2" h., pr. 75.00

Console bowl, two-handled,
  green or terra cotta ground,
  No. 351-10", 12½" l., 3½" h.,
  each . . . . 150.00 to 200.00
Flower frog, blue or terra cotta
  ground, No. 37, each . . . . 110.00 to 135.00

Fuchsia Jardiniere & Pedestal

Jardiniere & pedestal base, blue
  ground, overall 24" h., 2 pcs.
  (ILLUS.) 950.00
Pitcher w/ice lip, 8" h., terra cotta
  ground, No. 1322-8" 255.00
Rose bowl, terra cotta ground,
  No. 347-6", 6" h. 75.00
Urn, two-handled, blue or green
  ground, No. 346-4", 4" h.,
  each . . . . 90.00 to 105.00
Vase, 6" h., two handles rising from
  bulbous base to neck, blue
  ground, No. 891-6" 120.00
Vase, 8" h., handles rising from flat
  base to shoulder, blue ground,
  No. 897-8" 160.00
Vase, 15" h., blue or terra
  cotta ground, No. 904-15",
  each . . . . 385.00 to 435.00
Wall pocket, two-handled, terra cot-
  ta ground, No. 1282-8", 8½" h. 350.00

FUTURA (1928)

Varied line with shapes ranging from Art Deco geometrics to futuristic. Matte glaze is typical although an occasional piece may be high gloss.

Bowl, 8" d., collared base, shaped
  flaring sides w/relief decoration,
  rose glaze, No. 187-8" 240.00
Console bowl w/flower frog, cut-out
  base, sharply canted sides w/em-
  bossed stylized design, No. 196,
  3½ x 5 x 12" 300.00
Jardiniere & pedestal base, brown
  ground, jardiniere 10" h.,
  2 pcs. 1,950.00
Planter, square w/low flat base,
  sides decorated w/relief stylized
  tree w/sparse foliage, cream

w/green highlights, No. 191-8",
7" sq. 375.00

Vase, 4½" h., 6½" w., straight handles rising from sharply canted
low base to rim, upper portion
square w/cut corners & canted
sides, low-relief curving design
on sides & base, terra cotta,
No. 85-4" 250.00

Vase, 6" h., flat flaring body in a
mottled blue over orange glaze
w/a green geometric pattern on
the shoulders, low rectangular
mouth, No. 82-6" 300.00

Vase, 7" h., 5½" d., high domed &
stepped beehive-form body below
a wide & flaring neck joined by
two short strap handles to the
shoulder, shaded cream to blue
body w/green leaves around the
body, unmarked, No. 403-7" 935.00

Vase, 9¼" h., 5¼" d., angular handles raising from bulbous base
to rim, sharply stepped neck,
shaded dark to light green high-
gloss glaze, w/paper label,
No. 389-9" 585.00

Vase, bud, 10" h., stacked conical
form w/gold, green & purple scattered design against a cobalt blue
ground, No. 390-10" 825.00

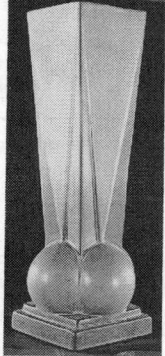

Futura Vase

Vase, 12¼" h., 5½" d., tall flaring
column rising from four spheres &
resting on a square base, grey &
peach, No. 393-12" (ILLUS.)....... 625.00

GARDENIA (1940's)

*Large white gardenia blossoms and green
leaves over a textured impressed band on a
shaded green, grey or tan ground.*

Basket, hanging-type, tan ground,
6" 150.00

Console bowl, grey ground,
No. 632-14", 14" l. 95.00

Ewer, tan ground, No. 618-15",
15" h. 200.00

Jardiniere & pedestal base,
green ground, No. 600-10",
2 pcs. .... 650.00 to 700.00

Vase, 6" h., two-handled, grey
ground, No. 681-6" 45.00

Vase, 10½" h., handles rising from
base to shoulder, ornate rim, tan
ground, No. 686-10" 95.00

Vase, 14½" h., two handles rising
from midsection to below rim, tan
ground, No. 689-14" 185.00

IMPERIAL I (1924)

*Brown pretzel-twisted vine, green grape leaf
and cluster of blue grapes in relief on green
and brown bark-textured ground.*

Basket w/asymmetrical overhead
handle, low sides, No. 291-7",
7" h. 75.00

Bulb bowl, open end handles, low
rounded sides, No. 71-7", 7" d. ... 55.00

Jardiniere, 8" h. 150.00

Planter, open-handled, 10" l.,
3" h. 235.00

Wall pocket, peanut-shaped,
10" h. 145.00

IMPERIAL II (1924)

*Varied line with no common characteristics.
Many of the pieces are heavily glazed with
colors that run and blend.*

Ashtray, blue glaze 195.00

Bowl, 12" d., 8" h., sharply canted &
horizontally ribbed sides, flaring
rim, mottled blue, No. 207 ...... 325.00

Vase, 5½" h., tapering cylinder
w/horizontal ribbing above
base, mottled green ground,
No. 468-5" 145.00

Vase, 7" h., cylindrical w/gently
sloping shoulders, ivory, grey &
gold glossy glaze on matte blue,
No. 472-7" 325.00

Wall pocket, rounded form, relief-
molded wavy horizontal lines,
red over grey glaze, No. 1262,
6½" h. 395.00

Wall pocket, canted sides w/round-
ed bottom, horizontal wide ribbing at base & narrow ribbing at
midsection, green over copper
glaze, No. 1263, 6½" h. 295.00

IRIS (1938)

*White or yellow blossoms and green leaves
on rose blending with green, light blue
deepening to a darker blue or tan shading to
green or brown.*

Basket w/semicircular overhead
handle, rose ground, No. 355-10",
9½" h. 250.00

Console bowl w/flower frog, tan
ground, bowl No. 361-8", 10" l.,
3" h., 2 pcs. 175.00
Cornucopia, rose ground,
No. 131-6", 6" 95.00
Jardiniere, two-handled, blue
ground, No. 647-5", 5" h. 145.00
Urn-vase, rose ground, No. 130-4",
4" h. 75.00

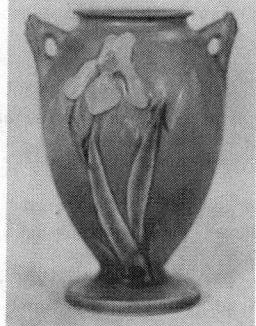

Iris Vase

Vase, 5" h., ovoid body on flat circular base, rim handles, rose
ground, No. 915-5" (ILLUS.) 48.00
Vase, bud, 7" h., two-handled, blue,
rose or tan ground, No. 918-7",
each .... 85.00 to 95.00
Wall pocket, two handles rising
from base to below flaring rim,
tan ground, No. 1284-8", 8" h. 345.00

IXIA (1930's)

*Embossed spray of tiny bell-shaped flowers
and slender leaves - white blossoms on pink
ground; lavender blossoms on green or yellow ground.*

Candleholders, closed pointed handles rising from flat circular base
to rim of candle nozzle, pink
ground, No. 1125-2", 2" h., pr. ... 75.00
Console bowl, green ground,
No. 330-7", 10½" l., 3½" h. 115.00
Flower frog, green ground, No. 34 .. 35.00
Jardiniere, large handles at base,
yellow ground, No. 640-10",
10" h. 375.00
Vase, 6" h., elongated closed handles at shoulders, ovoid body,
pink ground, No. 853-6" 75.00
Vase, 7" h., closed handles rising
from midsection to rim, expanding
cylindrical body, pink ground,
No. 854-7" 95.00
Vase, 8½" h., closed handles at
midsection, globular w/long wide
neck, green ground, No. 857-8" .. 90.00
Vase, 10" h., two-handled, green
ground, No. 861-10" 80.00

JONQUIL (1931)

*White jonquil blossoms and green leaves in
relief against textured tan ground; green
lining.*

Basket w/pointed overhead handle
rising from shoulder, 9" h. 325.00
Bowl, 6 x 10" oval, 3½" h., two-
handled, No. 220 .... 185.00
Bowl-vase, down-turned handles,
globular, No. 524-4", 4" h. 80.00
Jardiniere, two-handled, No. 621-9",
9" h. 275.00
Vase, 7" h., base handles 125.00
Vase, 8" h., tapering cylinder
w/elongated side handles 155.00

JUVENILE (1916 on)

*Transfer-printed and painted on creamware
with nursery rhyme characters, cute animals
and other motifs appealing to children.*

Bowl, 6" d., 1½" h., chicks 95.00
Cup & saucer, chicks, saucer
5½" d., cup 2" h. 220.00
Dinner set: six plates, six cups
& saucers; sunbonnet girl,
18 pcs. 1,200.00
Feeding dish w/rolled edge, duck
w/hat, 8" d. 90.00
Feeding dish w/rolled edge, nursery
rhyme, "Little Jack Horner,"
8" d. 100.00
Mug, chicks, 3" h. 70.00
Mug, standing rabbit, 3" h. 65.00
Pitcher, 3" h., chicks, matte glaze .. 95.00
Plate, 7" d., chicks 75.00
Plate, 8" d., sitting dog 79.00
Plate, 8" d., sunbonnet girl 70.00

LAUREL (1934)

*Laurel branch and berries in low-relief with
reeded panels at the sides. Glazed in deep yellow, green shading to cream or terra cotta.*

Bowl, 6" d., 3½" h., green 125.00
Urn, closed angular handles at
shoulder, No. 250-6", 6¼" h. 190.00
Vase, 6" h., tapering cylinder
w/wide mouth, closed angular
handles at shoulder, deep yellow or terra cotta, No. 667-6",
each .... 110.00 to 135.00
Vase, 7¼" h., tapering cylinder
w/pierced angular handles
at midsection, terra cotta,
No. 671-7¼" 210.00
Vase, 9" h., short cylindrical bottom
w/wide slightly flaring neck,
closed handles at midsection,
deep yellow or terra cotta,
No. 675-9", each 200.00

MAGNOLIA (1943)

Large white blossoms with rose centers and black stems in relief against a blue, green or tan textured ground.

Magnolia Floor Vase

Basket, hanging-type, tan ground,
   No. 469-5" . . . . 125.00 to 150.00
Bowl, 8" d., two-handled, blue or
   green ground, No. 448-8", each . .   65.00
Candleholders, exaggerated angu-
   lar side handles rising from circu-
   lar base to rim, blue ground,
   No. 1156-2½", 2½" h., pr. 80.00
Cornucopia-vase, blue ground,
   No. 184-6", 6" h. 60.00
Ewer, blue ground, No. 15-15",
   15" h. . . . . .275.00 to 300.00
Flowerpot w/saucer, blue ground,
   No. 666-5" 65.00
Jardiniere, two-handled, tan
   ground, No. 665-6", 6" h. 75.00
Model of a conch shell, green
   ground, No. 453-6", 6½" w. 95.00
Pitcher, cider, 7" h., green ground,
   No. 1327 . . . . .150.00 to 185.00
Vase, 4" h., ovoid w/angular
   handles at rim, green ground,
   No. 86-4" 70.00
Vase, bud, 7" h., tan ground,
   No. 179-7" 65.00
Vase, 8" h., globular w/large
   angular handles, blue ground,
   No. 91-8" 100.00
Vase, 16" h., floor-type, blue
   ground, No. 99-16" (ILLUS.) 295.00
Vase, 18" h., floor-type, blue
   ground, No. 100-18" . . . .:. .   475.00

MATT COLOR (1920's)

No distinguishing characteristics in shape or design, but all have a smooth satin solid color matt finish.

Bowl, 4" d., compressed globular
   form w/handles at shoulder,
low foot, aqua matt finish,
   No. 550-4" 40.00
Flower pot, incised geometric de-
   sign, blue matt finish, No. 549-4",
   4" h. 30.00
Pot, scrolled handles at rim, wide
   paneled sides, aqua matt finish,
   No. 548-4", 4" h. 35.00
Vase, 4" h., slightly canted ribbed
   sides, plain color under rim
   w/four raised squares, turquoise
   matt finish, No. 624-4" 20.00

MAYFAIR (late 1940's)

Utilitarian line with various embossed de-signs; high-gloss glaze.

Bowl, 9" w., model of a shell,
   brown & tan glaze, No. 1119-9" . . .   70.00
Candleholders, shell-form, beige
   glaze, No. 115-1, 4½", pr. 35.00
Pitcher, tankard, 12" h., ornate han-
   dle, low foot, embossed feathery
   foliage & blossoms, green glaze,
   No. 1107-12" 90.00
Teapot, cov., straight sides, short
   spout, brown glaze, No. 1121-5",
   5" h. 45.00
Vase, 7" h., stylized lily-form
   w/stalk of leaves to one side, on
   asymmetrical base, beige glaze,
   No. 1104-9 . . . .   75.00

MING TREE (1949)

Embossed twisted bonsai tree topped with puffy foliage—pink-topped trees on mint green ground, green tops on white ground and white tops on blue ground; handles in the form of gnarled branches.

Ming Tree Vase

Ashtray, shaped square w/indented
   rest at each corner, blue ground,
   No. 599, 6" 65.00
Basket, hanging-type, white ground,
   6" 135.00
Model of a conch shell, white
   ground, No. 563, 8½" w. 165.00
Vase, 6" h., cylindrical w/asym-
   metrical branch handles, blue
   ground, No. 581-6" (ILLUS.) 85.00

Vase, 10½" h., cylindrical w/nar-
row shoulder, asymmetrical
branch handles, white ground,
No. 583-10" 115.00
Vase, 14½" h., waisted form
w/wide flaring mouth, asymmetrical branch handles, green ground,
No. 510-14" 225.00
Wall pocket, overhead branch
handle, green or white
ground, No. 566-8", 8½" h.,
each . . . . 250.00 to 300.00

MOCK ORANGE (1950)

*Small cluster of white flowers and green
leaves against a mint green, pink or yellow
ground.*

Basket w/overhead handle, footed,
yellow ground, 10 x 10" 250.00
Bowl, 6" d., pink ground 85.00
Jardiniere, green ground, 8" h. 195.00
Vase, 10½" h., green ground 75.00
Window box, shaped rim, four low
feet, yellow ground, No. 956-8",
4½ x 8½" 45.00

MODERNE (1930's)

*Art Deco style rounded and angular shapes
trimmed with an embossed panel of vertical
lines and modified swirls and circles - white
trimmed with terra cotta, medium blue with
white and turquoise with a burnished antique
gold.*

Bowl, 6" d., low foot, rounded
sides, white, No. 296-6" 95.00
Bowl-vase, low foot, compressed
ball-form, blue, No. 299-6",
6½" h. 115.00
Compote, 6" h., rounded bowl on in-
verted trumpet-form base flanked
by columns, blue, No. 297-6" 90.00
Vase, 6½" h., urn-form w/slen-
der handles, blue or white,
No. 787-6", each . . . . 75.00 to 85.00
Vase, bud, 7" h., two-handled,
white, No. 790-7" 85.00

MONTACELLO (1931)

*White stylized trumpet flowers with black ac-
cents on a terra cotta band — light terra cotta mottled in blue or light green mottled and
blended with blue backgrounds.*

Basket w/pointed overhead handle,
tall collared neck, green or terra
cotta ground, No. 332-6", 6½" h.,
each . . . . 350.00 to 400.00
Console bowl, two-handled, terra
cotta ground, No. 225-9", 9" l. 200.00
Jardiniere, two-handled, terra cotta
ground, No. 559-5", 5" h. 200.00

Vase, 4" h., sharply compressed
globular base, handles rising from
shoulder to rim, terra cotta
ground, No. 555-4" 135.00

Montacello Vase

Vase, 7" h., two-handled, slightly
ovoid, wide mouth, terra cotta
ground, No. 561-7" (ILLUS.) 225.00
Vase, 10½" h., expanding cylinder
w/small base handles, terra cotta
ground, No. 565-10" 475.00

MORNING GLORY (1935)

*Stylized pastel morning glory blossoms and
twining vines in low relief against a white or
green ground.*

Basket w/high pointed overhead
handle, globular body, green
ground, 10½" h. 550.00
Console bowl, small pointed
end handles, green ground,
4½ x 11½" . . . . 300.00 to 350.00
Pot, small angular handles at mid-
section, flaring rim, white ground,
No. 5-5", 5" h. 220.00
Vase, 7" h., tapering sides, base
handles, green or white ground,
each 235.00

MOSS (1930's)

*Spanish moss draped over a brown branch
with green leaves against a background of
ivory, pink or tan shading to blue.*

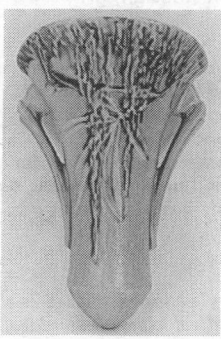

Moss Wall Pocket

Bowl, 7" d., pink ground,
No. 291-7" 100.00
Candlesticks, angular handles
at midsection, tan ground,
No. 1107-4½", 4½" h., pr. 65.00
Console set: 8" d. bowl & pair of
2" h. candleholders; pink ground,
Nos. 292-8" & 1109-2", the set 325.00
Jardiniere, pink ground, No. 635-4",
4" h. 75.00
Vase, 14" h., pink ground,
No. 786-14" 650.00
Wall pocket, elongated side han-
dles, flaring rim, pink ground,
No. 1278-8", 8" h. (ILLUS.) 225.00

MOSTIQUE (1915)

*Incised Indian-type design of stylized flow-
ers, leaves or geometric shapes glazed in
bright high-gloss colors against a heavy, peb-
bled ground.*

Mostique Jardiniere

Bowl, 9" d., 3½" h., handled, glossy
grey glaze 85.00
Flowerpot, stylized floral design,
grey ground, 8" h. 85.00
Jardiniere, geometric design, grey
ground, 9" h. (ILLUS.) 75.00
Jardiniere & pedestal base, arrow-
head leaves design, grey
ground, overall 29" h.,
2 pcs. . . . . 650.00 to 675.00
Vase, 6" h., corset-shaped, arrow-
head leaves design, grey
ground 55.00
Vase, 8" h., waisted cylinder
w/wide flaring mouth, large handles rising from above base to
midsection, geometric design,
grey ground, No. 532-8" 75.00
Vase, 10" h., expanding cylinder,
short ridged neck, geometric de-
sign, sandy beige ground 110.00

ORIAN (1935)

*Art Deco-style shapes, bladelike slender leaf-
shaped handles; high-gloss glaze, often in a
two-tone color combination.*

Candleholder, yellow, 4½" h. 50.00
Compote, 10½" d., 4½" h., glossy
turquoise w/tan lining 85.00
Vase, 7½" h., slender handles ris-
ing from shoulder of squatty
ringed base to rim of short wide
neck, glossy burgundy w/tur-
quoise lining 160.00
Vase, 8" h., two handles rising from
semi-globular base to middle of
tapering cylindrical neck, blue or
tan, each 100.00
Vase, 9" h., slender handles rising
from compressed ringed base to
middle of long wide neck, glossy
blue, small silver label 95.00
Vase, 14" h., red, No. 743-14" 400.00
Wall pocket, double, yellow 595.00

PANEL (1920)

*Recessed panels decorated with embossed
naturalistic or stylized florals or female
nudes.*

Candleholders, flat disc base, stylized florals, dark green ground,
2½" h., pr. 75.00
Jar, cov., stylized florals, dark
brown ground, 10" h. 250.00
Lamp base, ovoid body on low
foot, collared neck w/small
squared handles, female nudes,
butterscotch ground, No. X1F8,
10" h. 1,000.00
Urn, slightly canted sides, styl-
ized florals, dark green ground,
4" h. 90.00
Vase, double bud, 5½" h., waisted
cylinders joined by floral panel,
dark brown or dark green ground,
each . . . . 65.00 to 75.00
Vase, 9" h., wide expanding cylin-
drical body w/narrow shoulder &
low rim, stylized florals, dark
brown ground 150.00
Wall pocket, straight sides, rounded
bottom, slightly flared rim, stylized florals, dark green ground,
9" h. 195.00

PEONY (1942)

*Peony blossoms in relief against a textured
swirling ground — yellow blossoms against
rose shading to green, brown shading to gold
or gold with green; white blossoms against
green.*

Basket w/overhead handle, gold
ground, No. 377-8", 8" h. 85.00
Candleholders, double, green
ground, No. 1153, 5" h., pr.
(ILLUS. top next column) 55.00
Cornucopia-vase, rose ground,
No. 171-8", 8" h. 52.00

Peony Candleholders

Ewer, gold ground, No. 9-15",
15" h. 295.00
Jardiniere & pedestal base, rose
ground, overall 30" h., 2 pcs. 725.00
Planter, rectangular w/angular end
handles, slightly canted sides,
green ground, No. 387-8", 10" l. . . 85.00
Rose bowl, two-handled, gold
ground, No. 427-6", 6" d. 135.00
Teapot, cov., gold ground, No. 3 . . . 135.00
Vase, 8" h., urn-form, rose ground,
No. 169-8". 100.00
Vase, 14" h., angular handles
at midsection, rose ground,
No. 68-14". 235.00
Water set: ice lip pitcher & 4 mugs;
green ground, No. 1326-7½ &
No. 2-3½, 5 pcs. 275.00

PERSIAN (1916)

*Geometric shapes and angular floral designs
in bright colors against creamware.*

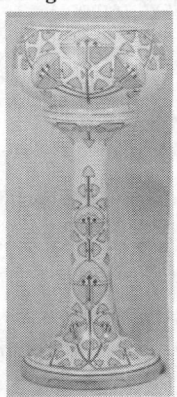

Persian Jardiniere & Pedestal

Jardiniere, wide ovoid body w/in-
curved wide mouth, on thin molded feet, decorated w/h.p. stylized
three-petal purple flowers & whiplash leaves around the top half on
a creamy white ground, 10½" d.,
9¼" h. 275.00
Jardiniere & pedestal base, overall
colorful geometric design, 13" jardiniere, overall 30½" h., 2 pcs.
(ILLUS.). 715.00
Tea & coffee service: cov. teapot,
cov. coffeepot, cov. sugar bowl &
creamer; squared form w/in-

curved tapering sides, angular
handles, decorated w/purple &
green arabesques on a white
ground, 4 pcs. (very minor chip-
ping to coffeepot) 550.00

PINE CONE (1931)

*Realistic embossed brown pine cones and
green pine needles on shaded blue, brown or
green ground. (Pink extremely rare.)*

Pine Cone Bowl

Basket w/overhead branch handle,
blue or brown ground, No. 409-8",
8" h., each . . . . .375.00 to 425.00
Bowl, 6¼ x 9½", 4" h., oval
w/pleated ends, twig handles,
green ground, No. 279-9"
(ILLUS.). 125.00
Candleholders, flat disc base sup-
porting candle nozzle in the form
of a pine cone flanked by needles
on one side & branch handle on
the other, blue ground, No. 1123,
2½" h., pr. 235.00
Cornucopia-vase, blue ground,
No. 126-6", 6" h. 100.00
Ewer, brown ground, No. 851-15",
15" h. 500.00
Jardiniere, two-handled, globular,
blue or green ground, No. 632-5",
5" h., each . . . . .325.00 to 350.00
Pedestal, blue ground,
No. 406-10". 800.00
Planter, single side handle rising
from base, blue or brown ground,
No. 124-5", 5" h., each . . .80.00 to 100.00
Rose bowl, blue ground, No. 261-6",
6" d. 395.00
Vase, 7" h., spherical body w/flat
mouth, raised on a small square
foot, small loop twig handles,
green ground, No. 745-7" 165.00
Vase, 15" h., two-handled, ovoid
w/waisted neck & flaring mouth,
brown ground, No. 807-15". 675.00
Vase, 18½" h., floor-type, two-
handled, low foot, ovoid w/short
neck & flaring rim, No. 913-18" . . . 660.00
Wall pocket, triple, green ground,
No. 466-8½", 8½" w. 350.00

POPPY (1930)

*Embossed full-blown poppy blossoms, buds
and foliage — yellow blossoms on green,*

white blossoms on blue or soft pink blossoms
on a deeper pink.

Basket w/pointed overhead handle,
  slender ovoid body on disc base,
  green ground, No. 348-12",
  12½" h. 215.00
Bowl, 8" d., two-handled, irregular
  rim, blue ground, No. 337-8" 100.00
Ewer, ornate cut-out lip, pink or
  green ground, No. 876-10", 10" h.,
  each . . . . .150.00 to 175.00
Jardiniere & pedestal base, green
  ground, 8" h. jardiniere, 2 pcs. . . . 825.00
Vase, 7½" h., two-handled, expand-
  ing cylinder w/slightly waisted
  neck & wide mouth, green
  ground, No. 868-7" 65.00
Vase, 10" h., two-handled, semi-
  ovoid, cut-out rim, green ground,
  No. 875-10" 225.00
Wall pocket, triple, tapering center
  section flanked by small tapering
  cylinders, green ground,
  No. 1281-8", 8½" h. 310.00

PRIMROSE (1932)

Cluster of long-stemmed blossoms and pod-
like leaves in relief on blue, pink or tan
ground.

Basket, hanging-type, two-handled,
  globular, tan ground, No. 354-5". . 185.00
Jardiniere & pedestal base, pink
  ground, No. 634-10", 2 pcs. 1,500.00
Vase, 7" h., two-handled, blue
  ground, No. 762-7" 75.00
Vase, 10" h., shoulder handles, pink
  or tan ground, No. 770-10",
  each . . . . .150.00 to 175.00

RAYMOR (1952)

Modernistic design oven-proof dinnerware.

Bean pot, cov., individual size, Contemporary white, No. 195 . . . . 35.00
Bowl, soup, lug-type, Autumn
  brown, No. 155 . . . . 18.00
Corn servers, individual size, long
  slender form w/section for butter,
  one each Autumn brown, Avocado
  green, Terra Cotta, Beach gray &
  Contemporary white, 12½" l., set
  of 5 . . . . 200.00
Cup & saucer, Beach gray, Nos. 150
  & 151, set 25.00
Plate, salad, Beach gray or Terra
  Cotta, No. 154, each 15.00
Platter, rectangular, Avocado green,
  No. 163 . . . . 50.00
Teapot, cov., black, No. 174 . . . . 125.00

ROSECRAFT HEXAGON (1924)

Six-sided form decorated with a simple impressed circular medallion enclosing an elongated stylized flower.

Bowl, 7½" d., sharply compressed
  sides, brown 150.00
Pin tray, green 115.00
Vase, 4" h., brown 250.00
Vase, double bud, 5" h., gate-form,
  dark green 200.00
Wall pocket, slender w/flaring rim,
  brown, 8½" h. 195.00

ROSECRAFT VINTAGE (1924)

Curving band of brown and yellow grapevine
with fruit and foliage at top, usually on a dark
brown ground.

Rosecraft Vintage Vase

Bowl, 6" d., low, compressed
  sides 40.00
Candlesticks, circular flaring base,
  expanding cylindrical stem, 8" h.,
  pr. 175.00
Jardiniere, 6" h. 140.00
Vase, 5" h., expanding cylinder
  (ILLUS.) 65.00
Vase, 8½" h., small rim handles,
  expanding cylinder 145.00
Wall pocket, two-handled, conical
  w/shaped rim 185.00

ROZANE (early 1900's)

Underglaze slip-painted decoration on dark
blended backgrounds.

Jardiniere, squeeze bag decoration
  of flying geese & stylized trees,
  artist-signed, 10" d., 6" h. 605.00
Vase, 8¼" h., 5" d., tall ovoid body,
  decorated w/burnt orange poppies on green stems & w/green
  leaves in a glossy glaze against a
  creamy bisque ground, glossy-
  glazed interior 1,540.00
Vase, 10¼" h., 6¼" d., a wide
  domed base on tab feet tapering
  sharply to a bulbous knob at the
  base of the tall slender cylindrical
  neck w/a widely flaring rim, slender straight handles running from
  rim to top of knob, squeeze-bag

decoration w/dark bands trimmed in delicate scrolls around the base & on the knob, the base further decorated w/a large cluster of chestnuts & leaves in bluish grey & brown against a light ground, artist-signed (two tight horizontal hairlines in handles) 1,320.00

Vase, 13" h., 6" d., tall footed ovoid body tapering to a short wide slightly flaring neck, decorated w/a bust portrait of an Indian warrior against a dark shaded ground, artist-signed & die-stamped "A (?) PPC - D" 660.00

Vase, 21¼" h., 12" d., floor-type, tall footed ovoid body tapering to a short narrow neck w/flared rim, golden & brown irises on a dark brown ground, artist-signed (very minor rim chip). 1,320.00

ROZANE (1917)

Clusters of delicately tinted roses and green leaves against a honeycomb background in blue, ivory, light green, pink or yellow.

Basket w/overhead handle, ivory ground, 7" h. 60.00

Bowl-vase, ivory ground, 9" d. 60.00

Compote, 6½" h., ivory ground. 75.00

Wall pocket, semi-ovoid, 7½" h.. . . . 100.00

RUSSCO (1930's)

Narrow perpendicular panel front and back, stacked handles and octagonal rim openings; solid matte glaze or matte glaze with crystalline overglaze.

Russco Lamp Base

Jardiniere, brown glaze, 6" h. 155.00

Lamp base, urn-shaped, two slender elongated handles, crystalline orange glaze, 10½" h. (ILLUS.) 220.00

Vase, 8¼" h., 6¾" d., urn-shaped, the bulbous base w/small molded buttress handles below the wide slightly tapering octagonal upper

section w/a flared rim, raised on a flaring pedestal base, gold glaze 110.00

Vase, double bud, 8½" h., tall slender cylinder attached by a narrow strip to a shorter & wider cylinder, octagonal base, tan glaze . . . 65.00

Vase, 12½" h., low foot, slightly bulbous base, closed handles at midsection, blue glaze 115.00

SILHOUETTE (1952)

Recessed shaped panels decorated with floral designs or exotic female nudes against a combed background.

Ashtray, square w/indentations at corners, rose, No. 799 . . . . 45.00

Basket w/curved rim & asymmetrical handle, florals, white w/turquoise blue panel, No. 710-10", 10" h. . . . 125.00

Basket, hanging-type, florals, turquoise blue. . . . . .80.00 to 100.00

Bowl, 12" l., florals, tan, No. 729-12" 75.00

Ewer, sharply canted sides, florals, rose, No. 717-10", 10" h. 80.00

Planter, florals, turquoise blue, No. 769-9", 9" l. 80.00

Rose bowl, female nudes, turquoise blue, No. 742-6", 6" h. 230.00

Vase, 6" h., small angular handles between compressed globular base & tall wide neck, turquoise blue, No. 780-6" 275.00

Vase, 8" h., urn-form, tapering ovoid body raised on four angled feet on a round disc base, wide slightly flaring mouth, turquoise blue, No. 763-8" 330.00

Vase, 9" h., double, base w/canted sides supporting two square vases w/sloping rims, joined by a stylized branch-form center post, florals, rose, No. 757-9" 85.00

Wall pocket, bullet-shaped w/angular pierced handles, white w/turquoise blue panel, No. 766-8", 8" h. 120.00

SNOWBERRY (1946)

Clusters of white berries on brown stems with green foliage over oblique scalloping, against a blue, green or rose background.

Basket w/low pointed overhead handle, shaded ground, No. 1BK7", 7" h. 115.00

Book ends, shaded blue or rose ground, No. 1BE, each pr.. . . . . .145.00 to 175.00

Candlesticks, angular side handles, shaded rose ground, No. 1CS2-4½", 4½" h., pr. 50.00

Cornucopia-vase, shaded green or
rose ground, No. 1CC-6", 6" h.,
each 45.00
Creamer & sugar bowl, angular side
handles, shaded blue ground,
Nos. 1C & 1S, pr. 95.00
Ewer, sharply compressed base
w/long conical neck, shaded blue
ground, No. 1TK-10", 10" h. 125.00
Ewer, flaring base, oval body,
shaded green or rose ground,
No. 1TK-15", 16" h.,
each . . . . .250.00 to 300.00
Jardiniere & pedestal base, shaded
blue ground, 2 pcs. 600.00

Snowberry Vase

Vase, 6½" h., pillow-type, shaded
green ground, No. 1FH-6"
(ILLUS.). 52.00
Vase, 18" h., shaded blue ground,
No. 1V-18" 575.00
Window box, shaded rose ground,
No. 1WX-8", 8" l. 70.00

SUNFLOWER (1930)

*Long-stemmed yellow sunflower blossoms
framed in green leaves against a mottled
green textured ground.*

Sunflower Vase

Candlestick, 4" h. 250.00
Urn, globular w/small rim handles,
4" h. 210.00

Urn, straight sided, 5" h. 280.00
Vase, 5" h., two-handled, bulbous
(ILLUS.). 240.00
Vase, 6" h., cylindrical w/tiny rim
handles 235.00
Wall pocket, curved openwork doub-
le handle, 7½" h. 600.00

TEASEL (1936)

*Gracefully curving long stems and delicate
pods.*

Basket w/low overhead handle, cut-
out rim, pale blue, No. 349-10",
10" h. 85.00
Rose bowl, beige shading to tan,
No. 342-4", 4" h. 52.50
Vase, 6" h., closed handles at mid-
section, cut-out rim, beige shad-
ing to tan, No. 881-6" 45.00

THORN APPLE (1930's)

*White trumpet flower and foliage one side,
reverse with thorny pod and foliage against
shaded blue, brown or pink ground.*

Basket w/pointed overhead handle,
conical w/low foot, shaded brown
ground, No. 342-10", 10" h. 135.00
Basket, hanging-type, shaded brown
ground, No. 355-5", 7" d. 150.00
Jardiniere, shaded blue ground,
No. 638-5", 5" h. 55.00
Vase, 6" h., shaded blue ground,
No. 810-6".   70.00
Vase, 8½" h., semi-ovoid body
flanked by slender columns, on
low disc base, shaded pink
ground, No. 816-8" . . . . . .115.00 to 135.00
Vase, 12" h., shaded pink ground,
No. 823-12" 250.00
Vase, 15", floor-type, shaded pink
ground, No. 824-15" 350.00
Wall pocket, triple, shaded blue or
brown ground, No. 1280-8", 8" h.,
each . . . . .275.00 to 300.00

TOPEO (1934)

*Four evenly spaced vertical garlands begin-
ning near the top and tapering gently down
the sides.*

Bowl, 11½" d., 3" h., wide low
sides w/angled flat shoulder to a
wide, low rim, molded around the
shoulder w/four small "snails" in
pink & blue on a mottled matte
blue ground 165.00
Console set: 13" l. bowl & pair of
5" h., double candlesticks; green
crystalline glaze shading to blue,
the set 575.00

Vase, 7" h., slightly bulbous base & straight tapering sides, short collared mouth, glossy deep red glaze 185.00

Vase, 7" h., globular base & flaring mouth, green crystalline glaze shading to blue 240.00

TOURMALINE (1933)

Produced in various simple shapes and a wide variety of glazes including rose and grey, blue-green, brown or azure blue with green and gold, and terra cotta with yellow.

Bowl, 8" d., mottled blue 70.00

Console bowl w/flower frog, mottled blue, No. 241-12", 12" l. 175.00

Cornucopia-vase, semi-gloss medium blue glaze, No. 106-7", 7" h. 45.00

Urn, compressed globular base w/short collared neck, mottled turquoise, No. A-200-4", 4½" h. . . 70.00

Vase, 5½" h., globular w/loop handles rising from midsection to rim, mottled turquoise blue, No. A-517-6" 72.00

Vase, 10 3/8" h., hexagonal body tapering toward the base, four sides molded w/diminishing circular designs, glazed in striated & streaked blue over pale green & blue, No. 616-10" 132.00

TUSCANY (1927)

Gently curving handles terminating in blue grape clusters and green leaves.

Flower arranger, pedestal base, flaring body, open handles, mottled pink, 5" h. 80.00

Flower frog, mottled pink, 3" h. 32.50

Urn-vase, mottled grey or mottled pink, 5" h., each . . . . 60.00 to 75.00

Vase, 8" h., two-handled, mottled grey 135.00

Vase, 10" h., shoulder handles, bulbous, mottled pink 100.00

VELMOSS (1935)

Embossed clusters of long slender green leaves extending down from the top and crossing three wavy horizontal lines. Some pieces reverse the design with the leaves rising from the base.

Urn-vase, angular pointed side handles, mottled pink, No. 265-6", 6" h. 175.00

Vase, 5" h., angular handles, mottled green 65.00

Vase, 7" h., angular side handles at midsection, cylindrical w/low foot, mottled blue or raspberry red, No. 715-7", each . . . . 135.00 to 150.00

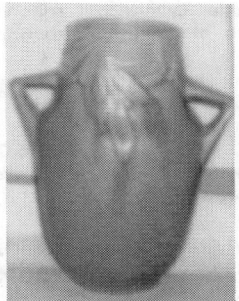

Velmoss Vase

Vase, 9½" h., angular handles, mottled green, No. 719-9" (ILLUS.) 250.00

VISTA (1920's)

Embossed green coconut palm trees and lavender blue pool against grey ground.

Basket, hanging-type, wide low-sided cylindrical form w/three low strap handles along the sides, 8" d., 4" h. (two bruises on the rim) 302.50

Jardiniere, 6½" h. 185.00

Vase, 10" h., cylindrical w/flaring base 265.00

Wall pocket . . . . 450.00 to 500.00

WATER LILY (1940's)

Water lily blossoms and pads against a horizontally ridged ground. White lilies on green lily pads against a blended blue ground, pink lilies on a pink shading to green ground or yellow lilies against a gold shading to brown ground.

Water Lily Cookie Jar

Basket, hanging-type, gold shading to brown ground, No. 468-5", 9" . . 135.00

Cookie jar, cov., angular handles, blended blue ground, No. 1-8", 8" h. (ILLUS.) . . . . 250.00 to 300.00

Ewer, swollen cylindrical form on
flat base, blended blue ground,
No. 12-15", 15" h. 260.00
Flower holder, two-handled,
fan-shaped body, pink shading
to green ground, No. 48,
4½" h. . . . . .45.00 to 50.00
Jardiniere, two-handled, gold shad-
ing to brown ground, No. 663-3",
3" h. 45.00
Model of a conch shell, gold shading
to brown or pink shading to green
ground, No. 438-8", 8" h., each. . . 150.00
Rose bowl, two-handled, gold shading to brown or pink shading to
green ground, No. 437-4", 4" h.,
each .50.00 to 75.00
Vase, 4" h., blended blue ground,
No. 71-4" 47.00
Vase, 8" h., two-handled, blended
blue ground, No. 76-8" 80.00
Vase, 14" h., angular side han-
dles, gold shading to brown or
pink shading to green ground,
No. 82-14", each . . . . .250.00 to 275.00

WHITE ROSE (1940)

*White roses and green leaves against a ver-
tically combed ground of blended blue, brown
shading to green or pink shading to green.*

Basket w/low pointed overhead
handle, blended blue ground,
No. 362-8", 7½" h. 125.00
Basket w/sweeping handle rising
from base to rim at opposite side,
blended blue ground, No. 364-12",
12" h. 190.00
Basket, hanging-type, blended blue
or brown shading to green
ground, No. 463-5", each 150.00
Book ends, blended blue ground,
No. 7, pr. . . . . .135.00 to 165.00
Console set: bowl, pair of candle-
holders & flower frog w/overhead
handle; pink shading to green
ground, No. 392-10", No. 1141 &
No. 41, the set 245.00
Ewer, compressed globular base,
blended blue or pink shading to
green ground, No. 981-6", 6" h.,
each . . . . .65.00 to 75.00
Jardiniere & pedestal base, pink
shading to green ground, 10" h.
jardiniere, 2 pcs. (minor chips). . .1,095.00
Vase, double bud, 4½" h., two
cylinders joined by an arched
bridge, blended blue ground,
No. 148 . . . . 115.00
Vase, 7" h., pink shading to green
ground, No. 983-7" 65.00
Vase, 8" h., base handles, brown
shading to green ground,
No. 984-8" 100.00

Vase, 18" h., two-handled, blended
blue ground, No. 994-18" 465.00
Wall pocket, swirled handle, flaring
rim, pink shading to green
ground, No. 1288-6", 6½" h. 175.00

WINCRAFT (1948)

*Shapes from older lines such as Pine Cone,
Cremona, Primrose and others, vases with an
animal motif, and contemporary shapes. High
gloss glaze in bright shades of blue, tan, yellow, turquoise, apricot and grey.*

Wincraft Ewer

Basket w/low overhead handle,
shaped rim, narcissus-type blossoms & foliage in relief on blue
ground, No. 208-8", 8" h. 105.00
Book ends, yellow, No. 259, 6½" h.,
pr. 60.00
Bowl, 8" d., blue, No. 226-8" 75.00
Candleholders, brown, No. 251,
pr. 92.50
Cigarette box, cov., rectangular,
blue, No. 240, 4½" l. 95.00
Cornucopia-vases, low rectangular
base, relief florals against a mottled blue ground, No. 221-8",
9" l., 5" h., pr. 90.00
Ewer, stepped lower portion & long
slender neck w/flaring mouth,
leaves in relief on shaded lime
green ground, No. 218-18", 18" h.
(ILLUS.). 350.00
Vase, 6" h., asymmetrical fan
shape, pine cones & needles in
relief on shaded brown ground,
No. 272-6" 75.00
Vase, 10" h., cylindrical, tab
handles, black panther &
green palm trees in relief on
shaded lime green ground,
No. 290-10". . . . . .250.00 to 300.00
Vase, 18" h., floor-type, blue,
No. 289-18" 425.00
Wall pocket, horizontally ribbed
square body, shaded brown, No.
266-4, 8½" h. 125.00

WINDSOR (1931)

Stylized florals, foliage, vines and ferns on some, others with repetitive band arrangement of small squares and rectangles, on mottled blue blending into green or terra cotta and light orange blending into brown.

Vase, 6" h., canted sides, handles rising from shoulder to rim, geometric design against mottled terra cotta ground, No. 546-6" 175.00

Vase, 7" h., large handles, globular base, stylized ferns against mottled blue ground, No. 548-7" 320.00

Vase, 9" h., two handles rising from globular base to rim of wide neck, stylized ferns against mottled terra cotta ground 400.00

Vase, 10¼" h., 7" d., ovoid body tapering to a wide conical neck, curved handles from neck to shoulders, orange ground w/lightly molded green leaves at neck, silver paper label 302.50

WISTERIA (1933)

Lavender wisteria blossoms and green vines against a roughly textured brown shading to deep blue ground, rarely found in only brown.

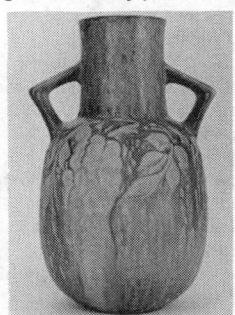

Wisteria Vase

Bowl, 4" h., angular rim handles, brown ground, No. 242-4" 145.00

Planter, rectangular w/angular end handles, brown ground, No. 243, 5 x 9" 225.00

Vase, 6½" h., globular w/angular rim handles, No. 637-6½" 430.00

Vase, 7" h., angular handles at shoulder, brown ground, No. 634-7" 210.00

Vase, 8" h., 6½" d., wide tapering cylindrical body w/small angled handles flanking the flat rim, No. 633-8" 350.00

Vase, 9½" h., cylindrical body w/angular handles rising from shoulder to midsection of slender cylindrical neck, No. 638-9" (ILLUS.) 450.00

Wall pocket, flaring rim, 8" h. 575.00

ZEPHYR LILY (1946)

Deeply embossed day lilies against a swirl-textured ground. White and yellow lilies on a blended blue ground; rose and yellow lilies on a green ground; yellow lilies on terra cotta shading to olive green ground.

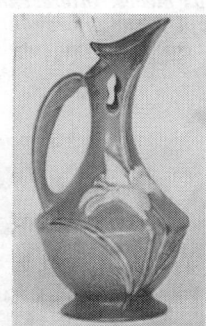

Zephyr Lily Ewer

Basket w/low, wide overhead handle, disc foot, cylindrical body flaring slightly to an ornate cut rim, terra cotta ground, No. 395-10", 10" h. 175.00

Basket, hanging-type, blue, green or terra cotta ground, No. 472-5", 7½", each . . . . .125.00 to 150.00

Book ends, green ground, No. 16, pr. 135.00

Candlesticks, terra cotta ground, No. 1163-4½", 4½" h., pr. .60.00 to 75.00

Console bowl, end handles, terra cotta ground, No. 474-8", 8" l. 80.00

Creamer, terra cotta ground, No. 7-C 60.00

Cornucopia-vase, green or terra cotta ground, No. 204-8", 8½" h., each .65.00 to 75.00

Ewer, terra cotta ground, No. 23-10", 10" h. (ILLUS.) 110.00

Rose bowl, blue ground, No. 471-6", 6" h. 100.00

Teapot, cov., terra cotta ground, No. 7T 190.00

Vase, 8" h., green ground, No. 134-8" 85.00

Vase, 10" h., semi-ovoid base & wide tall cylindrical neck, handles at midsection, green or terra cotta ground, No. 138-10", each . . . . .125.00 to 150.00

Vase, 12" h., conical w/base handles, green ground, No. 139-12" . . 125.00

Vase, 18" h., terra cotta ground, No. 142-17" 350.00

(End of Roseville Section)

ROYAL BAYREUTH

Good china in numerous patterns and designs has been made at the Royal Bayreuth factory in Tettau, Germany, since 1794. Listings below are by the company's lines, plus miscellaneous pieces. Interest in this china remains at a peak and prices continue to rise. Pieces listed carry the company's blue mark except where noted otherwise.

CORINTHIAN

Corinthian Pitcher

Creamer, classical figures on black ground	$50.00
Mug, classical figures, 4¾" h.	55.00
Pitcher, 5½" h., classical figures on orange ground	65.00
Pitcher, 5½" h., classical figures on black ground, yellow bands w/leaf decoration around neck & base (ILLUS.)	75.00
Pitcher, 7 1/8" h., 4 3/8" d., classical figures on black ground	135.00
Vase, 3½" h., classical figures on green ground	125.00

DEVIL & CARDS

Devil & Cards Candy Dish

Ashtray	450.00
Ashtray w/match holder & striker	1,000.00
Candleholder, low	350.00 to 400.00
Candlestick, 8" h.	3,000.00
Candy dish, 7" d. (ILLUS.)	300.00 to 350.00
Creamer, 4" h.	225.00
Dresser tray	500.00 to 600.00
Match holder, wall-type	525.00
Match holder, wall-type, full figure-style	1,800.00
Pitcher, water, 7¼" h.	550.00 to 600.00
Stamp box, cov., 3½" l.	800.00

MOTHER-OF-PEARL FINISH

Bowl, nut, poppy mold, pearlized finish	110.00
Cracker jar, cov., grape cluster mold, pearlized white	425.00 to 450.00
Creamer, grape cluster mold, pearlized finish	145.00
Creamer, poppy mold, lavender pearlized finish	150.00
Cup & saucer, demitasse, Murex Shell patt., pearlized finish	150.00
Gravy boat & underplate, poppy mold, pearlized finish, 2 pcs.	150.00
Hatpin holder, octagonal, scalloped rim w/gold scroll trim, pearlized finish	135.00
Marmalade jar, cov., grape cluster mold, pearlized yellow finish	350.00
Mustard jar, cov., poppy mold, pearlized finish	300.00
Pitcher, 4" h., 2¾ x 6¼", Murex Shell patt., pearlized finish exterior (unmarked)	79.00
Salt dip, open, poppy mold, pearlized finish	150.00
Salt & pepper shakers, grape cluster mold, pearlized red finish, pr.	160.00
Sugar bowl, cov., grape cluster mold, pearlized finish	165.00
Sugar bowl, cov., poppy mold, white pearlized finish	575.00

ROSE TAPESTRY

Rose Tapestry Dresser Tray

Basket, three-color roses, 4½" w., 4" h.	285.00
Basket, footed, drapery chain of buds on base w/handle & base cut-outs, 5½" h.	455.00

Bell w/wooden clapper, pink roses decoration on white background, gold handle 395.00

Box, cov., three-color roses, 2½" sq. 275.00

Box, cov., oval, one-color roses, 4" l. 235.00

Cake plate, three-color roses, free-form fancy rim w/gold beading, 9½" w. 365.00

Cake plate, pierced gold handles, three-color roses, 10½" d. 450.00

Clock, two-color roses, German works (runs) 1,200.00

Creamer, three-color roses, 3¼" h. 175.00

Creamer, pinched spout, two-color roses, 3½" h. 195.00

Creamer, pinched spout, three-color roses, 3½" h. 195.00

Creamer, corset-shaped, three-color roses, 3¾" h. 195.00

Dish, leaf-shaped, three-color roses 195.00

Dresser tray, rectangular, two-color roses, 10" l. 325.00

Dresser tray, rectangular, three-color roses, 8 x 11½" (ILLUS.) 350.00

Hair receiver, cov., three-color roses ....250.00 to 300.00

Match holder, hanging-type, three-color roses 395.00

Pitcher, milk, 4" h., three-color roses 185.00

Rose Tapestry Pinched-Spout Pitcher

Pitcher, 4¼" h., pinched spout, three-color roses (ILLUS.) 285.00

Pitcher, water, 5 7/8" h., pinched spout, three-color roses.......... 610.00

Plate, 6" d., red roses & daisies 125.00

Plate, 6" d., three-color roses 180.00

Sauce dishes, red roses & green & yellow leaves, 5¾" d., pr. 250.00

SAND BABIES

Creamer, spherical body w/narrow, short neck, decorated w/three children running, pastel ground, gold handle, 2¼" d., 3" h. 75.00

Dish, clover-shaped, 4¼" w. 159.00

Dish, diamond-shaped, 4¼" w. 135.00

Feeding dish, 7¼" d. 145.00

Plate 125.00

SNOW BABIES

Candleholder, shield-back, handled ....225.00 to 250.00

Inkwell, cov., w/original paper label 375.00

Nappy, handled, curled-in sides, 3½ x 5"...................... 110.00

Plate, 9" d. 140.00

Teapot, cov. 225.00

SUNBONNET BABIES

Bell, babies cleaning ..... 350.00 to 450.00

Bowl, 6" d., footed, babies mending 175.00

Bowl, 7" d., scalloped edge, babies ironing 310.00

Cake plate w/open handles, babies washing, 8¼" d. 225.00

Candleholder, shield-back, babies sweeping..................... 700.00

Candlestick, babies fishing, 5¼" h. 195.00

Chamberstick, babies sewing, 5" d. 295.00

Creamer, babies cleaning, gold handle, 3" h........................ 245.00

Creamer, babies washing, 4" h. 175.00

Creamer & open sugar bowl, boat-shaped, babies fishing on sugar, babies cleaning on creamer, gold handles, pr. 395.00

Dish, clover leaf-shaped, babies ironing, 4 x 5" 195.00

Mug, babies ironing, 2" h. 110.00

Mug, babies sweeping, 3" h. 395.00

Pitcher, milk, 5" h., pinched spout, babies sweeping 350.00

Plate, 6" d., babies ironing........ 175.00

Plate, 7½" d., babies ironing....... 195.00

Teapot, cov., bulbous, babies cleaning...................... 450.00

Teapot, cov., babies fishing, 3½" h. 500.00

Teapot, cov., babies sewing........ 475.00

Toothpick holder, babies cleaning .. 800.00

Vase, 3½" h., babies sweeping 220.00

TOMATO ITEMS

Tomato Sugar Bowl

Tomato box, cov., 3¾" d........... 51.00

Tomato creamer, cov., large 115.00
Tomato mustard jar, cov. 77.00
Tomato sugar bowl, cov. (ILLUS.) . . . 70.00
Tomato teapot, cov.,
   large . . . . .150.00 to 175.00
Tomato teapot, cov., small 275.00
Tomato tea set: large cov. teapot,
   creamer & cov. sugar bowl; foot-
   ed, 3 pcs. . . . . .325.00 to 375.00

MISCELLANEOUS

Figural Lobster Bowl

Ashtray, figural elk 185.00
Ashtray, decorated w/Japanese
   chrysanthemums, 4¾" sq. 275.00
Ashtray, mountain goat scene,
   brown, tan & grey, unmarked,
   3¾ x 5½", 2¼" h. 165.00
Ashtray, stirrup-shaped w/leather-
   like figural thong handle, buckled
   strap forms holder for cigarettes,
   scene of beagles trapping a
   moose in the water, silver trim all
   around 125.00
Basket, Cavalier Musicians decora-
   tion, 4 x 6½", 6" h. 350.00
Basket, "tapestry," decorated
   w/Japanese chrysanthemums,
   gold rope handle & gold rope trim
   on rim & base, 3¼ x 4¼", 7" h. . . 450.00
Bell, goose girl decoration 165.00
Bell, Jack & Jill decoration 250.00
Bell, Little Boy Blue decoration 195.00
Berry set: master bowl & six sauce
   dishes; figural oak leaf, green,
   the set 1,150.00
Bowl, 6" d., figural rose 850.00
Bowl, 6 7/8" d., 2½" h., footed,
   shallow slightly scalloped sides,
   Cavalier Musicians decoration,
   gold trim on feet 110.00
Bowl, 4¾ x 8", figural red lobster
   (ILLUS.) . . . . .275.00 to 300.00
Bowl, 9½" d., figural
   poppy . . . . .100.00 to 125.00
Bowl, 10" d., scalloped & cut-out
   rim, relief-molded body w/overall
   roses decoration 195.00
Bowl, 10½" d., molded edge w/mul-
   ticolor roses & blue & white shadow leaves decoration . . . .100.00 to 125.00

Bowl, 10½" d., "tapestry," fluted
   edge, decorated w/pink roses &
   white snowballs on turquoise &
   green ground, lavish gold trim . . . 125.00
Box, cov., "tapestry," decorated
   w/violets 425.00
Candleholder, farmer & horses deco-
   ration, 4" h. 120.00
Candleholder, shield-back, Cavalier
   Musicians decoration, 4¾" h. 270.00
Candlestick, elks scene, 4" h. 60.00
Candlestick, figural red poppy 675.00
Candlestick, Jack & Jill decoration,
   4¼" h. 150.00
Charger, donkey boy decoration,
   13" d. 325.00
Chocolate pot, cov., "tapestry,"
   man tending turkeys decoration,
   8½" h. 1,000.00
Creamer, Arab scene decoration . . . 85.00
Creamer, beige body w/figural
   black cat handle 425.00
Creamer, Brittany Girls decoration . . 75.00
Creamer, decorated w/scene of man
   lighting pipe, 3¾" h. 75.00
Creamer, donkey boy decoration,
   4½" h. 200.00
Creamer, Cavalier Musicians decora-
   tion, 5" h. 80.00
Cup, demitasse, figural pear,
   unmarked 200.00
Cup & saucer, demitasse, figural
   green lettuce leaf, red lobster
   claw handle 65.00
Cup & saucer, demitasse, pedestal
   base, h.p. roses decoration
   w/heavy gold trim 40.00
Demitasse pot, cov., stork
   decoration 255.00
Dresser tray, man w/horses decora-
   tion, 11½" l. 325.00
Dresser tray, goose girl decora-
   tion 260.00
Feeding dish, child's, Little Bo Peep
   decoration w/full nursery rhyme,
   8" d. (minor paint wear) 250.00
Feeding dish, child's, Little Miss
   Muffet decoration, 8" d. 225.00
Ferner, "tapestry," cows grazing
   scene . . . . .225.00 to 275.00
Ferner w/insert, Jack & Jill decora-
   tion, 2 pcs. 225.00
Hair receiver, cov., cylindrical, hunt-
   ing scene decoration 110.00
Hair receiver, cov., footed, lady &
   turkeys decoration, 3" h. 110.00
Hair receiver, cov., "tapestry,"
   courting couple decoration on top,
   delicate rainbow-colored base 550.00
Hatpin holder, figural penguin, red,
   5" h. (ILLUS. top next column) 600.00
Hatpin holder, figural poppy, red . . . 650.00

Figural Penguin Hatpin Holder

Hatpin holder, goose girl decoration, unmarked 495.00
Hatpin holder, bell-shaped, scene of lady riding sidesaddle & couple w/croquet mallet, 5" h. 150.00
Hatpin holder, saucer base, decorated w/scene of a man tending turkeys 250.00
Hatpin holder, "tapestry," goats grazing decoration 325.00
Humidor, cov., figural chimpanzee . . . . 1,700.00 to 1,900.00
Humidor, cov., figural clown 1,700.00
Humidor, cov., figural eagle 1,495.00
Match holder, ball-shaped w/striker on rim, Hunt scene w/horseman & dogs, 3" l., 2½" h. 110.00
Match holder, hanging-type, figural red clown . . . . 300.00 to 325.00
Match holder w/striker, figural Santa Claus (slight damage) 2,200.00
Match holder, hanging-type, figural stork 260.00
Match holder, hanging-type, man working w/two horses scene on cup, cottage scene background . . . 150.00
Match holder, hanging-type, nursery rhyme scene & verse w/Little Miss Muffet 325.00
Match holder, hanging-type, "tapestry," Cavalier Musicians scene 345.00
Mayonnaise dish, cover & underplate, figural red poppy, the set . . 525.00
Model of a lady's shoe, "tapestry," courting couple scene decoration 600.00
Model of a lady's shoe, "tapestry," decorated w/violets, original shoe lace 750.00
Mug, beer, figural elk, 5¾" h. 650.00
Mug, nursery rhyme scene w/Jack & Jill, 3" h. 150.00
Mug, peacock in foliage decoration, 3½" h. 75.00
Mustard jar, cov., figural lobster . . . 165.00
Mustard jar, cov., figural pansy 250.00
Mustard jar, cov., figural shell 145.00

Nappy, handled, spade-shaped, nursery rhyme scene w/Little Jack Horner 135.00
Pin dish, figural turtle 500.00
Pin tray, rectangular w/cut corners, Hunt scene w/rider & hounds, 3½ x 5" 50.00
Pipe holder, figural Basset Hound . . . 495.00
Pitcher, 4" h., boy & donkeys scene 150.00
Pitcher, 4" h., Brittany Girl decoration 95.00
Pitcher, 4" h., decorated w/a scene of fisherman in boat 135.00
Pitcher, milk, 4" h., figural owl . . . . 275.00 to 300.00
Pitcher, milk, 4½" h., figural clown, yellow 575.00
Pitcher, milk, 4¾" h., figural oak leaf 295.00
Pitcher, milk, 5" h., figural elk . . . . 150.00 to 175.00

Rare Santa Claus Milk Pitcher

Pitcher, milk, 5¼" h., figural Santa Claus (ILLUS.) 3,500.00
Pitcher, milk, 5½" h., figural fish head 185.00
Pitcher, 5½" h., stork decoration on yellow ground 75.00
Pitcher, water, 6" h., figural apple . . 875.00
Pitcher, water, 6½" h., figural poppy 795.00
Pitcher, 7" h., fighting cocks scene decoration 90.00
Pitcher, water, 7" h., Jester pictured & "Never say die - Up man and try" 375.00
Pitcher, water, 7" h., figural elk . . . . 400.00 to 450.00
Pitcher, water, 7" h., figural orange 500.00
Pitcher, water, 7" h., figural Santa Claus 3,100.00
Pitcher, lemonade, 7¾" h., figural lemon 395.00
Pitcher, 8" h., pinched spout, Hunt scene decoration w/rider & hounds 110.00

Plate, 4½" d., full figure red devil
against a black clock face........ 575.00
Plate, 4½" d., full figure red devil
against a white clock face
w/black Roman numerals 575.00
Plate, 6½" d., nursery rhyme scene
w/Little Bo Peep & rhyme........ 125.00
Plate, 7½" d., figural purple
pansy 225.00
Plate, 8" d., nursery rhyme scene
w/Jack & Jill 135.00
Salt & pepper shakers, figural lobster, pr.......................... 110.00
Salt & pepper shakers, figural rad-
ish, pr.......................... 185.00
Salt & pepper shakers, figural seashell, multi-colored glaze, pr. 170.00
Salt dip, figural pansy 100.00
Salt shaker, figural bellringer (un-
marked)......................... 250.00
Salt shaker, figural lemon (un-
marked)......................... 85.00
Shaving mug, figural elk ...450.00 to 550.00

Rooster Head String Holder

String holder, hanging-type, figural
rooster head (ILLUS.) 350.00
Sugar bowl, cov., figural lobster 75.00
Sugar bowl, cov., figural pansy 235.00
Sugar bowl, cov., figural strawberry
(unmarked) 95.00
Table set: creamer, cov. sugar bowl,
salt & pepper shakers; figural
grape cluster, purple, artist-
signed, 4 pcs.................... 325.00
Teapot, cov., "tapestry," Arab &
horses scene, blue ground,
5" h............................. 149.00
Tea strainer, figural poppy, red (unmarked)......................... 300.00
Toothpick holder, dice-shaped, table
tennis scenes on sides, 2½" h. 950.00
Toothpick holder, figural bell ringer,
3" h............................. 425.00
Toothpick holder, Goose Girl decoration (unmarked)............... 125.00
Toothpick holder, three-footed, jest-

er pictured & "More than enough
is too much" (unmarked)........ 600.00
Toothpick holder, three-handled,
Goose Girl decoration 145.00
Toothpick holder, pedestal base,
decorated w/lavender roses &
butterflies 145.00
Toothpick holder, three-handled,
moose & dogs scene decoration .. 300.00
Toothpick holder, three-handled,
Hunt scene w/rider & hounds 78.00
Tumbler, "tapestry," castle by the
lake scene, 3¾" h............... 200.00
Tumbler, "tapestry," wooded scene
w/deer in stream & gazebo in
background...................... 225.00
Vase, 3½" h., 2" d., conical body
w/flared rim issuing four small
loop handles, Hunt scene w/rider
& hounds (unmarked)............ 45.00
Vase, 3½" h., 4¼" d., ring-handled,
ruffled rim, nursery rhyme scene
w/Little Miss Muffet 165.00
Vase, 4¼" h., scenic decoration of
man w/dog hunting ducks 225.00
Vase, 6" h., handled, "tapestry,"
castle scene decoration 310.00
Wall pocket, figural grape cluster,
pink 175.00
Wall pocket, pictures a jester &
"Penny in Pocket," 9" h. 550.00

ROYAL BONN & BONN

*Bonn and subsequently Royal Bonn china
were produced in Bonn, Germany, in a
manufactory established in 1755. Later wares
made there are often marked Mehlem or bear
the initials FM or a castle mark. Most wares
were of the hand-painted type. Clock cases
were also made in Bonn.*

Charger, decorated w/a floral bouquet, impressed marks, 19th c.,
20" d. $165.00
Plaque, round, Delft-type decoration w/portrait of Rembrandt, late
19th c., 18" d. 100.00
Plaque, round, Delft-type decoration
w/portrait of Franz Liszt, late 19th
- early 20th c., 19 7/8" d. 100.00
Vase, 5½" h., 6¾" d., squatty conical shape tapering to a flaring
rim, wide center band of gold &
gold foliage w/yellow, pink & red
roses, green top & bottom bands,
fancy gold trim, late 19th c. 125.00
Vase, 8" h., 3" d., cylindrical
w/rounded shoulder & short tiny
neck w/slightly flared rim, decorated w/yellow, white & pink
roses on a pastel pink, blue &

yellow background, Royal Bonn
mark......................... 88.00
Vase, 10¾" h., 4 5/8" d., footed
ovoid body tapering to a flaring
scalloped neck, small gold scroll
handles on shoulders, h.p. w/the
bust portrait of a dark blonde-
haired lady wearing a blue dress
& hat against a shaded gold &
brown ground, gold neck & trim,
artist-signed, late 19th c. 450.00
Vase, 14" h., pear-shaped body
w/short cylindrical neck & pointed
bottom suspended by two slender
side handles continuing down to
tripod feet on a round base, the
handles terminate w/ogre heads,
decorated w/roses & leaves on a
cream ground, signed "FM" (Franz
Mehlem) 350.00
Vase, 17½" h., Art Nouveau style,
the baluster-form body applied
w/elaborate handles in gilt,
raised on a squared base w/C-
scrolled feet, the cream glazed
ground decorated w/bright floral
sprays of chrysanthemums & wildflowers in purple, red, yellow,
blue & green 385.00

ROYAL COPENHAGEN

*This porcelain has been made in Copenha-
gen, Denmark, since 1715. The ware is
hardpaste.*

Figure of a boy on a barrel,
No. 3647 ....$100.00
Figure of a boy w/ball, No. 3542 ... 145.00
Figure of a girl w/her doll,
No. 1938, ca. 1952 .... 185.00
Figure of Greenland Girl,
No. 12415 .... 395.00
Model of a bear cub, white,
No. 729, 4" l. 85.00
Model of a cat in seated position,
grey striped coat w/white chest,
No. 1803, 5½" h. 85.00
Model of a dog, Dachshund,
No. 856 ....250.00 to 275.00
Model of a dog, Pug, No. 3169 ..... 90.00
Model of a dog, Terrier, No. 3020,
5½ x 6½"...................... 150.00
Model of a dog, Wire-haired Terrier,
No. 3170, 3" h. 45.00
Model of a penguin, No. 1283,
4" h.......................... 46.00
Plate, 5½" d., Flora Danica patt.,
decorated w/violets & gold edge,
signed 450.00
Vase, 21" h., tall cylindrical body
swelling at the shoulder then

tapering to a flat rim, seafoam
green & pale blue ground decorated w/swimming pale salmon-
colored fish, signed twice "Jenny
Meyer," painted company mark &
"22/11 1920" 2,200.00

ROYAL DUX

Ornate Royal Dux Bust

Bust of a young woman, smiling &
facing left, cymbidium orchids &
leaves in her flowing blonde hair
& down her bodice, decorated in
naturalistic pastel shades, impressed factory marks, ca. 1900,
minor losses, overall 20¾" h.
(ILLUS.) $2,475.00
Centerpiece, figural, modeled as
two maidens in flowing gowns
flanking a large stem, their arms
upraised & supporting a large
blossom-form vessel, glazed in
shades of pale green, pink & tan,
the whole heightened in gilt, impressed factory marks & numbers,
ca. 1900, 19" h. 1,925.00
Figure of a young woman seated on
a rock reading a book, her dress
decorated in green w/gold over-
lays, 14" h. 330.00
Figure of a nude young woman,
shown seated on a pedestal rockwork base, her hair pulled back
into a bun, looking down while
drying her foot w/a drapery in
her lap, natural coloration,
19th c., 21½" h. 880.00
Figure of a lady dancing, long brunette hair, wearing a long-sleeved
blouse w/bare midriff & a long
flower-decorated skirt, on a round
base, artist-signed & stamped
"Royal Dux - Czechoslovakia," ca.
1920's, 22¾" h.................1,320.00
Figure group, Dutch girl wearing a
greenish gold dress & pink apron

& standing beside a large basket, two white geese in front, pink triangle mark, 10" h. 595.00

Figure group, two bearded fisherman wearing sou'westers, crouching & straining to pull in a net full of fish, trimmed in pastel shades, 15" h. 385.00

Figural Royal Dux Mirror

Mirror, table model, figural, the upright oval mirror plate supported at one side by the curved figure of an Art Nouveau maiden issuing from a large flowering lotus plant continuing down across the base, raised on a rectangular base molded w/leaves, pink triangle mark, overall 23 5/8" h. (ILLUS.) 1,540.00

Vases, 36" h., figural, the vase molded as a leafy fruiting palm tree, one mounted w/the figure of an Arab man playing a lute, the other w/an Arab girl standing beside a tall jug, each on a round base, naturalistic colors, late 19th c., restoration, one w/a base hairline, pr. 715.00

ROYAL RUDOLSTADT

This factory began as a faience pottery established in 1720. E. Bohne made hard paste porcelain wares from 1852 to 1920, when the factory became a branch of Heubach Brothers. The factory is still producing in what was East Germany.

Chocolate pot, cov., cylindrical body w/pulled & pointed rim spout, curved shoulder to inset domed cover w/loop handle, angled side handle, decorated w/yellow roses

against a pastel ground, gold handle & finial, 4" d., 9½" h. $88.00

Ginger jar, cov., decorated w/gold florals, 7¼" h. 85.00

Smoking set, bisque, figural, modeled as a brown & white cat standing on a fence above a barking grey dog below, green grass & pink flowers on the base, openings in the rear for cigars, fresh matches & used matches, late 19th c., 6½" w., 6" h. 165.00

Urn, cov., the front medallion decorated w/a scene of a lovely young woman in a wooded landscape, gold outlining & gold handles, shield & crown "RW" mark 60.00

Vase, 8" h., handled, roses on a cream ground, gold handles 115.00

Vase, 14" h., 9" d., handles modeled in the form of semi-nude maidens, flaring gold rim, body decorated w/baroque panels of multicolored florals against a creamy white ground, overall gold trim 450.00

ROYAL VIENNA

Royal Vienna Demitasse Set

The second factory in Europe to make hard-paste porcelain was established in Vienna in 1719 by Claud Innocentius de Paquier. The factory underwent various changes of administration through the years and finally closed in 1865. Since then, however, the porcelain has been reproduced by various factories in Austria and Germany, many of which have reproduced also the early beehive mark. Early pieces, naturally, bring far higher prices than the later ones or the reproductions.

Demitasse set: cov. coffeepot, cov. sugar bowl, twelve cups & saucers & a rectangular serving tray; each w/a cobalt blue ground decorated w/round panels featuring classical figures, scattered gilt blossoms on the blue ground, beehive shield & "Made in Austria" markings, w/a

carrying case, tray 15¼" l., the
set (ILLUS.).....................$1,540.00
Dresser tray, decorated w/a portrait
of a Victorian lady, green &
red background, beehive mark,
8 x 15"..........................300.00
Plaque, rectangular, decorated w/a
scene of a young fisherman on a
rocky beach pulling a large fish
from the waves while a mermaid
emerges from the waves to save
it, titled on the reverse "Der
Fischer," artist-signed, blue beehive mark, within an ornate
scroll-molded giltwood frame,
5½ x 9"........................1,430.00
Plate, 9½" d., decorated in the center w/a color scene of a seated
boy in a toga decorating a classical pottery vase while a standing
young lady looks on, a wide dark
blue rim band decorated w/ornate
gilt scrolling, titled on the reverse
"Kunst Bringt Grust"............ 550.00
Side table, giltwood & porcelain, the
round top mounted around the
edge w/thirteen small porcelain
portrait plaques centering a large
central portrait plaque of Queen
Louise, all plaques feature lovely
young ladies, central plaque
artist-signed, the giltwood frame
w/a pierced scrolling apron &
scroll-carved cabriole legs joined
by arched cross stretchers, blue
beehive mark on plaques, late
19th c., 21" d.................3,300.00
Vases, cov., 20½" h., tall urn-form
body tapering to a short pedestal
raised on a very high domed flaring base on short block feet, the
shoulder tapering to a short neck
supporting a low conical cover
w/pointed finial, scrolled & angled gilt handles at the sides, the
fronts w/large panels h.p. in color
w/classical scenes reserved between ornate gilt borders on a
lustrous red ground, ornate gilt
trim overall, blue beehive mark,
ca. 1870, artist-signed, pr.......19,140.00

ROYAL WORCESTER

*This porcelain has been made by the Roy-
al Worcester Porcelain Co. at Worcester, England, from 1862 to the present. For earlier porcelain made in Worcester, see WORCESTER
(December - January 1993). Royal Worcester
is distinguished from those wares made at
Worcester between 1751 and 1862 that are referred to as only Worcester by collectors.*

Royal Worcester Melon-Form Pitcher

Basket, molded basketweave design
w/gold trim, center handle, beige
satin finish, dated 1911,
3¼ x 4½", 3" h................$115.00
Candleholders, model of a bamboo
shoot, a curled stalk handle issuing a flaring dished shoot centered by a candle socket, interior
of top decorated w/colorful floral
sprays trimmed w/gilt, gilt leaves
on exterior & gilt handle, 6" l.,
pr............................ 302.50
Cracker jar, cov., slightly swelled
cylindrical body, a beige satin
ground h.p. w/pink, yellow & lavender flowers, silver plate rim,
cover & twisted bail handle,
marked, 5" d., 6¾" h........... 245.00
Cracker jar, cov., cylindrical body
molded as a section of bamboo in
white decorated w/scattered h.p.
blue bamboo leaves, 5¾" d.,
7" h........................... 355.00
Cup & saucer, beige satin ground
decorated w/pink & yellow roses,
gold trim, dated 1906, saucer
5 5/8" d., cup 3 3/8" d., 2½" h... 95.00
Cups & saucers, demitasse, Duchess
patt., set of six................ 200.00
Demitasse set: cov. coffeepot & four
cups & saucers; each in white
w/blue Oriental scenes including
a pagoda, bridge & trees, ca.
1912, the set.................. 255.00
Ewer, tusk-form, the gently curving
cylindrical body w/a scalloped rim
& branch handle, decorated overall w/colorful wildflowers & butterflies on a creamy ground, gilt
bands on neck & base, gilt highlights & handle, crowned circle
mark, 9¾" h.................. 165.00
Ewer, bulbous bottom tapering to
tall, slender neck, gold serpent
handled, decorated w/owl in
branch before a moonlit sky, ca.
1885, 11¼" h................. 930.00
Figure, "Grandmother's Dress,"
No. 3081, designed by F. Doughty,
ca. 1935...................... 195.00

Figure, "Mischief," little girl picking
flowers, No. 2914, designed by F.
Doughty, ca. 1931 ......140.00 to 160.00
Figure, "Saturday's Child," No. 3524,
designed by F. Doughty, ca.
1954 .... 195.00
Figure, "Wednesday's Child,"
No. 3521, designed by F. Doughty,
ca. 1954 .... 175.00
Jar, cov., footed bulbous ovoid body
w/a short wide cylindrical neck
supporting a domed reticulated
cover w/a bulbous lobed finial
w/a pointed tip, the cover & neck
w/a molded basketweave design
& the lower body & foot also
w/molded basketweave, the
shoulder & sides h.p. w/a large
flock of flying swallows & clusters
of colorful wildflowers, gilt trim
on the basketweave section & the
finial, marked, No. 1286, late
19th c., 8¼" d., 11½" h.......... 550.00
Pitcher, 8½" h., melon-form body
w/a wide cylindrical leaf-molded
neck & spout, gilt leaves continuing to vine handle, the body
decorated w/pastel floral
sprigs, No. 1369, ca. 1889
(ILLUS.) ....400.00 to 450.00
Pitcher, ice water, 10" h., tusk-form,
yellow ground w/stylized gilt
florals, No. 1116, ca. 1885 .... 265.00
Plate, 9 1/8" d., h.p. bird decoration
w/red & gold embossed gilded
border, artist-signed, No. W-202,
ca. 1880 .... 75.00
Plate, 10¾" d., h.p. Tewkesbury
village scene, artist-signed, ca.
1953 .... 225.00
Plates, luncheon, 9¼" d., decorated
w/flowers against a pink border,
gilt foliate designs, printed mark,
ca. 1920, set of 12.............. 660.00
Platter, 12½" l., Blue Willow patt. .. 75.00
Spill vase, Japanese-style, square
tapering sides applied w/a model
of a climbing frog & molded w/ivy
vines, No. 499, ca. 1875, 3½" h... 295.00
Teapot, cov., molded melon-form in
the Japanese taste, the lobed
creamy body decorated w/gilt
& iron-red leaf & stalk forms,
6" h. 247.50
Vase, 7¾" h., ovoid body molded
w/a basketweave design & decorated w/applied leafy vines in
gold & iron-red, Crown & Circle
mark........................... 302.50
Vase, 8" h., ovoid body on circular
foot & applied handles, pale blue
w/gilt & iron-red floral decoration, Crown & Circle mark,
No. 1654, ca. 1893 .... 302.50

Vase, 8½" h., 5½" w., figural nautilus shell bowl raised on a coral
branch stem & a round domed
base, glossy cream ground decorated w/heavy gold & bronze
trim, dated 1888 .... 395.00
Vase, 13¾" h., bulbous body supporting a cylindrical neck w/retic-
ulated lip, applied gilt handles,
decorated w/purple & lavender
flowers on gilt branches, Crown &
Circle mark, artist-initialed....... 825.00

Ornate Royal Worcester Vase

Vase, cov., 23" h., footed bottle-
form tapering to a slender reticulated flaring neck w/low domed
cover topped by a scroll-molded
finial, applied angular reticulated
handles down the sides, creamy
body h.p. on both sides w/colorful
wildflowers w/gilt trim, further
silver & bronze trim w/gilt beading, Crowned Circle mark, ca.
1880 (ILLUS.) 2,200.00
Vases, 11½" h., moon flask-shaped
on a flaring foot, small flat angled
handles from the neck to the
shoulder, decorated in the Japanese style w/a flying crane &
leafy branch on one side & a bouquet of blossoms on the other, a
reticulated band around the bottom above the foot, delicate
colors & gold & silver trim, pr. ... 302.50

R.S. PRUSSIA & RELATED WARES

*Ornately decorated china marked "R.S.
Germany" and "R.S. Prussia" continues to
grow in popularity. According to Clifford J.
Schlegelmilch in his book,* Handbook of Erdmann and Reinhold Schlegelmilch — Prussia
— Germany and Oscar Schlegelmilch — Germany, *Erdmann Schlegelmilch established a*

porcelain factory in the Germanic provinces at Suhl, in 1861. Reinhold, his younger brother, worked with him until 1869 when he established another porcelain factory in Tillowitz, upper Silesia. China bearing the name of this town is credited to Reinhold Schlegelmilch. It customarily bears also the phrase "R.S. Germany." Now collectors seek additional marks including E.S. Germany, R.S. Poland and R.S. Suhl. Prices are high and collectors should beware the forgeries that sometimes find their way to the market. Mold names and numbers are taken from Mary Frank Gaston's books on R.S. Prussia.

R.S. GERMANY

Ashtray, clover-shaped w/figural
   pipe handle, decorated w/gilt
   trim, artist-signed $175.00
Bowl, 9½" d., deep rounded sides,
   decorated w/colorful roses 80.00
Bowl, 10¼" d., decorated w/horse
   chestnuts 120.00
Butter dish, cov., decorated w/white
   flowers, 7" d. base, 2" h. 60.00
Cake plate, open-handled, car-
   nations on a lavender ground,
   9¾" d. 30.00
Cake plate, open-handled, decorat-
   ed w/white flowers & foliage,
   gold rim, 11" d. 75.00
Cake stand, pedestal base, decorat-
   ed w/a windmill scene, 9½" d.,
   5" h. 375.00
Chocolate pot, cov., simple tankard
   form w/angled handle & loop finial on the cover, decorated
   w/large white & apricot flowers
   on a shaded ground, 10½" h. 300.00
Coffeepot, cov., Mold 606, inverted
   conical body on flattened flaring
   foot, C-scroll handle, colored floral decoration, pearlized finish,
   10" h. 500.00
Compote, open, 6¼" d., 3½" h.,
   pedestal base, decorated w/car-
   nations & snowball plants, satin
   finish 70.00
Creamer, footed, scalloped rim,
   shaded ground decorated w/vio-
   lets, 3½" h. 45.00
Plate, 11½" l., Leaf mold (Mold 10),
   decorated w/cattails & lavender
   trim 120.00
Teapot, cov., footed, steeple finial
   on cover, decorated w/cabbage
   roses, burnished gold trim,
   8½" h. 125.00
Toothpick holder, cylindrical
   w/three angled gold handles,
   cream ground decorated w/blue
   flowers, 3" d., 2½" h. 75.00
Tray, rectangular, open-handled,

decorated w/a scene of an old
   house, 9½" l. 135.00
Wall pocket, decorated w/an em-
   bossed robin, dated "1928," 4" w.,
   8¼" h. 250.00

R.S. PRUSSIA

Mold 155 Berry Set

Basket, three-handled, Scallop &
   Fan mold (Mold 501), decorated
   w/California poppies, 8½" d. 600.00
Berry set: 11" d. master bowl & five
   sauce dishes; Mold 155, Sheep-
   herder scene decoration, 6 pcs.
   (ILLUS.) 1,300.00
Berry set: 10½" d. master bowl &
   six sauce dishes; Sunflower mold
   (Mold 102), white ground w/pink
   poppies, satin finish, 7 pcs. 1,025.00
Berry set: master bowl & six sauce
   dishes; Mold 156, lily of the valley
   decoration, 7 pcs. 335.00
Bowl, 9¼" d., Lily or Daisy mold
   (Mold 30), poppies on a lavender,
   blue & yellow background, un-
   marked 125.00
Bowl, 9¼" d., Plume or Feather
   mold (Mold 16), Easter lilies
   decoration 250.00
Bowl, 10" d., Carnation mold
   (Mold 28), decorated w/roses 250.00
Bowl, 10" d., Icicle mold (Mold 7),
   Snow Bird scene 2,050.00
Bowl, 10" d., Lettuce mold (Mold
   12), multicolored roses on beige
   shaded ground, satin finish 275.00
Bowl, 10" d., Point & Clover mold
   (Mold 82), pink & yellow florals,
   satin finish 275.00
Bowl, 10¼" d., Lily or Daisy mold
   (Mold 29), Four Seasons portrait
   medallions around the sides, flo-
   ral decoration in the center 2,700.00
Bowl, 10¼" d., Lily or Daisy mold
   (Mold 30), decorated w/pink
   poppies 215.00
Bowl, 10½" d., Carnation mold vari-
   ation (Mold 28A), Lebrun portrait
   decoration, red, pink & gold decoration around the sides (ILLUS.) . .1,450.00

Carnation Mold Bowl

Bowl, 10½" d., Fleur-de-Lis mold
(Mold 9), decorated w/lilacs on a
cobalt blue ground 420.00
Bowl, 10½" d., Icicle mold (Mold 7),
Man in the Mountain scene 700.00
Bowl, 10½" d., Iris mold (Mold 25),
Winter Season scene, white
ground, satin finish, also marked
"Gesetzlich Geschutzt" 2,400.00
Bowl, 10½" d., Lily or Daisy mold
(Mold 30), floral medallions
around the sides & flowers in the
center. 375.00
Bowl, 10½" d., Medallion mold
(Mold 14), Diana the Huntress
decoration 1,800.00
Bowl, 10½" d., Point & Clover mold
(Mold 82), Countess Potocka por-
trait decoration, red & gold
trim 1,850.00
Bowl, 10½" d., Mold 90, decorated
w/pink poppies on a green
ground 180.00
Bowl, 11" d., Carnation mold (Mold
28), pink & white roses & gold-
trimmed carnations 500.00
Bowl, 11" d., Mold 351, decorated
w/California poppies, Tiffany bor-
der & satin finish 1,450.00
Cake plate, open-handled, Plume or
Feather mold (Mold 16), reflecting
poppies, roses & daisies in pinks
& blues w/gold beading, 9¾" d. . . .   195.00
Cake plate, open-handled, Icicle
mold (Mold 7), swan decoration,
unmarked, 10" d. 325.00
Cake plate, open-handled, Swag &
Tassel mold (Mold 155), scene of
swallows, chickens & ducks beside
water w/lilies, 10" d. 1,010.00
Cake plate, open-handled, Icicle
mold (Mold 7), Man in the Moun-
tain scene, 10½" d. 895.00
Cake plate, open-handled, Point &
Clover mold (Mold 82), red &
white roses on a white ground,
satin finish, 11" d. 300.00

Cake plate, open-handled, Plume or
Feather mold (Mold 16), decorated
w/a wicker basket of pink, peach,
maroon & white roses on a shaded brown, gold & cream back-
ground, gold trim, 11" d. 275.00
Celery tray, Iris mold (Mold 25),
decorated w/roses & lavish gold
trim, 9½" l.   185.00
Celery tray, Lily or Daisy mold
(Mold 30), roses on a lavender & white ground, unmarked,
5¾ x 12½" 125.00
Chocolate pot, cov., Medallion mold
(Mold 631), Lebrun portrait medallions at the rim, colored florals on
the front & back & cobalt blue
bands w/gilt trim at the top &
base, 9" h. .2,200.00
Chocolate pot, cov., Icicle mold
(Mold 7), decorated w/roses,
10" h. 350.00
Chocolate pot, cov., Mold 520,
floral-molded handle, Madame
Recamier portrait, Tiffany border
decoration, 12" h. 1,700.00
Demitasse set: cov. coffeepot & six
cups & saucers; Drapery mold,
pink roses on a white ground,
pearlized finish, 7 pcs. 2,700.00
Dresser tray, rectangular, Icicle
mold (Mold 7), Swans decoration,
7¼ x 11¾" 495.00
Letter holder, Mold 856, flying blue-
birds on the inside of the back &
a colored mill scene on the front,
unmarked, 4½" w., 4¾" h. 450.00
Model of a man's slipper, pearlized
lustre finish, Surreal Dogwood
Blossoms patt., four eyelets,
turned-up toe, 2 x 5", 1 5/8" h.
(unmarked) 165.00
Mustard jar, cov., Fleur-de-Lis mold
(Mold 9), decorated w/carna-
tions 145.00

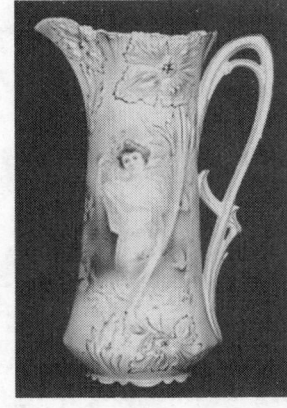

Summer Season Tankard Pitcher

Pitcher, tankard, Carnation mold variation, Summer Season portrait decoration (ILLUS.) 6,500.00

Pitcher, tankard, 11" h., Mold 583, red roses decoration & gold trim on a slate grey shaded to light grey background, satin finish 575.00

Pitcher, tankard, 11½" h. (similar to Mold 520), decorated w/yellow & pink roses (unmarked) 325.00

Unique Bird of Paradise Pitcher

Pitcher, tankard, 12" h., gently lobed body w/scalloped & scroll-molded rim & scalloped foot, Bird of Paradise decoration & gilt trim, white satin ground, only known example (ILLUS.) 16,000.00

Pitcher, tankard, 13" h., Fleur-de-Lis mold (Mold 9), decorated w/colored florals 650.00

Pitcher, tankard, 13" h., Stippled Floral mold (Mold 525), decorated w/a Dutch boy & geese scene & pink florals (unmarked) 2,950.00

Pitcher, tankard, 13" h., Stippled Floral mold (Mold 525), decorated w/pink poppies 700.00

Pitcher, tankard, 14" h., Mold 632, little gold feet, decorated w/pink & yellow roses on an ivory ground further enhanced w/deep rose & pink 850.00

Pitcher, tankard, 18" h., Mold 644, Winter Season portrait decoration 8,500.00

Plaque, pierced to hang, Mold 426, Indian Runner Duck decoration w/pearlized finish, 6" d. 595.00

Plate, 6" d., Ribbon & Jewel mold (Mold 18), Melon Eaters "keyhole" decoration 550.00

Plate, 7½" d., Mold 208, Swans decoration, pearlized finish 140.00

Plate, 8½" d., Mold 152, Spring Season portrait decoration, yellow & green shadings 1,150.00

Plate, 9" d., Icicle mold (Mold 7), Swans decoration 395.00

Poached egg server, Mold 470, a tapering cylindrical handled base & insert cup w/flared rim, decorated w/clusters of small pink roses & green leaves, 2½" h., 2 pcs. 325.00

Spoon holder, narrow oblong shape w/angled gold end handles, decorated w/colored florals & gold trim, 2½ x 7¾" 325.00

Tea set: cov. teapot, cov. sugar bowl & creamer; Mold 577, decorated w/cherubs in narrow leaf medallions & scattered pink rose sprigs on a white ground, satin finish, 3 pcs. 1,250.00

Toothpick holder, two-handled, Plume (or Feather mold, Mold 16), decorated w/roses 300.00

Toothpick holder, two-handled, Mold 644, decorated w/pink & red poppies, gold trim 195.00

R.S. Prussia Covered Urn

Urn, cov., egg-shaped ovoid body flanked by long loop handles & raised on a slender pedestal w/a scalloped foot, pyramidal cover w/pointed finial, Melon Eaters decoration, jeweled trim & satin finish, 12½" h. (ILLUS.) 1,600.00

Vase, bud, 3¼" h., bulbous body tapering to a narrow neck, Ostrich decoration & gold trim 295.00

Vase, 6" h., gently tapering ovoid body w/small angled handles at the rim, Peace Bringing Plenty scene decoration 450.00

Vase, 10" h., portrait of Victorian woman w/blue & green Tiffany iridescence 900.00

OTHER MARKS

Basket, center reserve decoration of woman & child, gold trim & luster finish (Royal Saxe - E.S. Germany) 125.00

Bonbon, handled, robin decoration (E.S. Germany - Prov. Saxe) 40.00

Bowl, 5 3/8" d., 7/8" h., plain round shape w/shallow sides, decorated w/Rembrandt's "Night Watch" scene, colors against a greyish blue ground (R.S. Poland) 145.00

Bowl, 7" d., decorated w/bird on a floral branch (E.S. Germany - Prov. Saxe) 45.00

Bowl, 11" d., decorated w/a Queen Louise portrait & a pink ground w/poppies (O.S. St. Killian) 400.00

Box, cov., Melon Eaters scene, 4" d. (R.S. Tillowitz - Germany) 150.00

Cake plate, open handles, decorated w/a fox hunting scene, 10" d. (E.S. Germany - Prov. Saxe) 275.00

Cake plate, open handles, girl w/seashell decoration w/elaborate gold & iridized trim, 10" d. (E.S. Germany - Prov. Saxe) 275.00

Candlestick-flower holder, a tall slender stem w/a squatty bulbous section pierced w/small holes just below the candle socket, decorated w/a colorful courting scene, 4¾" h. (E.S. Germany - Prov. Saxe) 250.00

Candy dish, Madame Recamier & four portrait medallions decoration, 7" l. (E.S. Germany - Prov. Saxe) 175.00

Egg carrier, a long & wide undulating ribbon-shaped dish w/an arched scrolling ribbon handle in the center, florals on a blue ground, 2¾ x 14¾" (E.S. Germany - Royal Saxe) 575.00

Ewer, short pedestal base, inverted pear-shaped body tapering to a slender neck w/divided rim & high arched spout & ornate gold scrolling handle, bust portrait of a young woman w/daisies in an oval medallion framed by ornate gilt scallops & beading against white, turquoise blue neck & pedestal base w/gilt trim, 12" h. (E.S. Germany - Prov. Saxe) 425.00

Ewers, pedestal base, each decorated w/portraits of different Victorian girls, red & gold trim, 18¾"h., facing pr., E.S. Germany - Prov. Saxe (ILLUS. top next column) ...2,300.00

Game plate, pierced to hang, decorated w/a grouse, 10" d. (E.S. Germany - Prov. Saxe) 140.00

Pitcher, tankard, 14½" h., bulbous base tapering to a scalloped rim, pierced scrolling handle, oval medallion w/colored mythological

E.S. Germany - Prov. Saxe Ewers

scene against a dark green ground w/red stripes & scattered gilt sprigs (O.S. St. Killian) 350.00

Pitcher, tankard, 15" h., bulbous base tapering slightly to a gently scalloped rim, ornate gilt scroll handle, a large oval medallion of red roses against a white ground w/gilt trim, pearlized finish (E.S. Germany - Prov. Saxe) 550.00

Plaque, pierced to hang, flame-shaped w/portrait decoration of the Goddess of Fire, iridescent white & light yellow ground, 10¾ x 16¾" (E.S. Germany - Prov. Saxe) 795.00

Plate, 6¾" d., decorated w/cherubs (E.S. Suhl) 80.00

Plate, 8¾" d., scalloped rim, decorated w/a portrait of American Indian "High Hawk," green edge trim (E.S. Germany - Royal Saxe) 100.00

Tea set: cov. teapot, creamer & cov. sugar bowl; dogwood decoration w/blue & gold trim, the set (R.S. Suhl) 300.00

Tea strainer w/pierced loop handle & tiny holes pierced in the bowl, pink rose swags & gilt scrolls around the rim, 6" d. (E.S. Prussia) 125.00

Vase, miniature, 3" h., cylindrical body tapering to a tiny short neck w/flared rim, decorated w/a portrait framed by heavy gilt trim against a pink & deep red ground, in original wooden box (E.S. Germany - Prov. Saxe) 385.00

Vase, 8¾" h., tapering ovoid body w/a short narrow neck flanked by arching pierced gold handles, four portraits of standing ladies in diaphonous gowns around the sides, each framed by heavy gilt bands (E.S. Germany - Prov. Saxe) 525.00

Vase, 10¾" h., wide ovoid body
w/flared rim, decorated w/an allegorical scene of Peace Bringing
Plenty featuring two classically-
gowned ladies, against a dark
shaded green & brown ground &
w/a deep red gilt-trimmed top
border (R.S. Tillowitz) 1,800.00

E.S. Germany - Prov. Saxe Vases

Vases, 11¼" h., ovoid body tapering to a flared & scalloped neck,
scrolled loop gold handles from
rim to shoulder, one decorated
w/a woman holding flowers, the
other w/a Goddess of the Sea
portrait, pr., E.S. Germany - Prov.
Saxe (ILLUS.) 1,050.00
Vases, 12" h., simple ovoid body
tapering to a short, wide neck
w/flat rim, open angled gold handles at the shoulder, each decorated w/dancing classical ladies in
a woodland landscape, pr. (R.S.
Suhl) 2,400.00

RUSSEL WRIGHT DESIGNS

*The innovative dinnerwares designed by
Russel Wright and produced by various companies beginning in the late 1930's were an
immediate success with a society that was
turning to a more casual and informal
lifestyle. His designs, with their flowing lines
and unconventional shapes, were produced in
many different colors which allowed the hostess to arrange a creative table. Although not
antique, these designs, which we list below
by line and manufacturer, are highly collectible. In addition to dinnerwares, Wright was
also known as a trend-setter in the design of
furniture, glassware, lamps, fabrics and a mul-
titude of other household goods.*

**AMERICAN MODERN (Steubenville Pottery
Company)**
Ashtray, coaster-type, chartreuse ... $10.00

Baker, small, cantaloupe (orange) .. 35.00
Baker, small, white 35.00
Bowl, fruit, lug handle, glacier
blue 20.00
Bowl, soup, lug handle, chutney
(deep brown) 12.00
Bowl, soup, lug handle, glacier
blue 20.00
Carafe w/stopper, chartreuse 40.00
Carafe w/stopper, seafoam blue ... 200.00
Casserole, cov., stick handle,
cantaloupe 65.00
Casserole, cov., stick handle,
seafoam blue 50.00
Celery tray, slender oblong shape
w/asymmetrical incurved sides,
cantaloupe, 13" l. 40.00
Celery tray, slender oblong shape
w/asymmetrical incurved sides,
chartreuse, 13" l. 12.00
Celery tray, slender oblong shape
w/asymmetrical incurved sides,
chutney, 13" l. 18.50
Celery tray, slender oblong shape
w/asymmetrical incurved sides,
white, 13" l. 40.00
Coffeepot, cov., demitasse, granite
grey 65.00
Creamer, cantaloupe 15.00
Creamer, granite grey 10.00
Cup & saucer, demitasse, coral 16.00
Cup & saucer, demitasse, white 18.00
Cup & saucer, cantaloupe 15.00
Cup & saucer, chartreuse 8.00
Cup & saucer, glacier blue 15.00
Cup & saucer, white 10.00
Gravy boat, granite grey 13.00
Pitcher, water, 12" h., cedar
green 95.00
Pitcher, water, 12" h., chutney 60.00
Pitcher, water, 12" h., granite
grey 75.00
Plate, bread & butter, 6¼" d., gran-
ite grey 4.00
Plate, dinner, 10" d., cantaloupe ... 12.50
Plate, dinner, 10" d., granite grey .. 6.00
Plate, chop, 13" w., white 40.00
Platter, 13¾" l., oblong, char-
treuse 25.00
Platter, 13¾" l., oblong, white 40.00
Salt & pepper shakers, bean brown,
pr. 16.00
Salt & pepper shakers, chutney,
pr. 10.00
Salt & pepper shakers, coral, pr. ... 8.50
Sugar bowl, cov., coral 13.00
Teapot, cov., coral 45.00
Tumbler, cedar green............ 55.00
Vegetable bowl, open, oval, char-
treuse, 10" l. 20.00
Vegetable bowl, open, oval,
seafoam blue, 10" l. 25.00
Vegetable dish, divided, seafoam
blue 50.00

CASUAL CHINA (Iroquois China Company)

Bowl, 5" d., cereal, pink sherbet . . .	5.00
Bowl, cereal, restyled, oyster grey . .	15.00
Butter dish, cov., nutmeg brown	110.00
Carafe, cov., parsley green, 10" h.	55.00
Carafe, cov., ripe apricot, 10" h. . . .	75.00
Casserole, cov., divided, nutmeg brown, 1½ qt.	40.00
Casserole, cov., divided, sugar white, 1½ qt.	85.00
Casserole, cov., charcoal, 2 qt.	35.00
Casserole, cov., ice blue, 2 qt.	22.00
Casserole, cov., ice blue, 4 qt.	45.00
Creamer, lettuce green	13.00
Creamer, ripe apricot.	9.00
Creamer, restyled, charcoal	35.00
Creamer & sugar bowl, stack-type, ice blue, pr.	10.00
Cup & saucer, coffee, oyster grey . . .	18.00
Cup & saucer, tea, charcoal	10.00
Cup & saucer, tea, ice blue	8.50
Cup & saucer, tea, ripe apricot	6.00
Gravy boat, cover & underplate, restyled, pink sherbet	75.00
Gumbo soup bowl, handled, ripe apricot	18.00
Mug, nutmeg brown, 13 oz.	35.00
Mug, restyled, ice blue	35.00
Mug, restyled, parsley green	45.00
Pitcher, restyled, lettuce green, 2 qt.	65.00
Plate, bread & butter, 6" d., oyster grey	4.50
Plate, luncheon, 9" d., ice blue	4.00
Plate, luncheon, 9" d., oyster grey . .	7.50
Plate, dinner, 10" d., ice blue	5.50
Platter, 12¾" l., oval, charcoal	22.00
Platter, 12¾" l., oval, lettuce green	30.00
Platter, 12¾" l., oval, pink sherbet	22.00
Platter, 14½" l., oval, pink sherbet	18.00
Salt shaker & pepper mill, ice blue, pr.	100.00
Sugar bowl, cov., restyled, lettuce green	15.00
Teapot, cov., small, ripe apricot, 4½" h.	70.00
Vegetable bowl, open, lettuce green, 8" d.	9.00

SAN ILDEFONSO (Maria) POTTERY

A thin-walled and crudely polished blackware has been made at most Rio Grande Pueblos. Around 1918 a San Ildefonso Pueblo woman, Maria Montoya Martinez and her husband, Julian, began making a thicker walled blackware with a finely polished gunmetal black sheen. It was fired in the tradi-tional manner using manure to smother the firing process and produce the black coloration. The following is a chronology of Maria's varied signatures: Marie, mid to late teens-1934; Marie & Julian, 1934-43; Marie & Santana, 1943-56; Maria & Popovi, 1956-71 and Maria Poveka, used on undecorated wares after 1956. Maria died in July of 1980. Rosalia, Tonita, Blue Corn and other signatures might also be found on pottery made at the San Ildefonso Pueblo. Considered a true artistic achievement, early items signed by Maria, or her contemporaries, command good prices. It should be noted that the strong pottery tradition is being carried on by current potters.

Large San Ildefonso Plate

Bowl, 4¾" d., 1½" h., blackware w/rounded bottom below shallow flat incurved sides, geometric matte & glossy designs, signed "Marie," w/paper label from 1930's world's fair	$797.50
Bowl, 7 3/8" d., 2 3/8" h., blackware w/shallow incurved sides, old 1930's world's fair paper label reading "Exhibit by Marie & Julian," incised signature "Marie" (very minor wear)	687.50
Bowl, 8" d., 4" h., glossy & matte black on black feather design, signed "Florence & Joe" (needs cleaning)	150.00
Jar, squatty bulbous ovoid body, blackware w/geometric design, attributed to Maria, w/1930's exhibit sticker on bottom, 2 1/8" d., 1¾" h.	247.50
Jar, blackware, squatty ovoid body tapering to a flared rim, black gunmetal sheen w/a feather design, signed "Marie & Santana," 4½" d., 3 5/8" h. (pinpoint rim flakes)	522.50
Jar, semi-ovoid, glossy & matte black on black design, signed "Marie & Julian," ca. 1935,	

4½" d., 3¾" h. (some minor
glaze wear) 650.00
Plate, 5¾" d., black on black feath-
er design, gunmetal glaze, signed
"Maria & Popovi" 550.00
Plate, 11 1/5" d., blackware
w/matte & glossy feather design, signed "Maria & Popovi"
(ILLUS.) 2,860.00
Vase-lamp base, wide bulbous base
tapering to a tall cylindrical
neck, signed "Marie & Santana" . . 6,050.00

SATSUMA

Ornate Satsuma Jar

*These decorated wares have been produced
in Japan since the end of the 18th century.
The early pieces are scarce and high-priced.
Later Satsuma wares are plentiful and, with
prices rising, as highly collectible as earlier
pieces.*

Bowl, 6" d. wisteria blossoms & foli-
age decoration $275.00
Bowl, 6" d., footed, sides decorated
w/panels of figural scenes against
a "brocade" ground, signed
"Fuzan," 19th c. 275.00
Box, cov., flattened disc-form, the
slightly domed cover decorated
w/a scene of musicians & a geisha dancing as a samurai
watches, against a pale green ve-
randa under a grey sky, the interior decorated w/auspicious
implements, signed "Yoshigawa,"
4¼" d. 1,650.00
Charger, round, decorated w/three
overlapping reserves, the largest
in a rounded heart-shape filled
w/a landscape scene of ladies &
children in a garden, the second
w/other figures & the third fan-
shaped reserve w/florals & auspi-

cious elements, the border profusely decorated w/small florals,
signed, 8¾" d. 550.00
Jar, cov., miniature, ovoid body
tapering to a small opening w/a
domed cover w/knob finial, decorated around the middle w/panels
of children at play, floral bands
around the top & bottom, signed
"Kizan," Meiji period, 3 3/8" h.
(ILLUS.) 1,320.00
Koro (incense burner), three-legged,
globular, decorated w/reserves
on a chrysanthemum ground,
signed "Denchu sai," 19th c.,
4½" h. 2,090.00
Sake pot, cov., compressed form,
molded in the shape of a chrysanthemum blossom, the lobed sides
decorated in enamels & gilt
w/butterflies fluttering among a
profusion of flowers, supported on
three leaf-form feet, the cover
surmounted by a *kiku*-form finial,
signed "Nihon Yozan," 19th c.,
4¼" h. (overhead handle missing,
one handle base restored) 1,540.00

Satsuma Teabowl

Teabowl, deep rounded & gently
flaring sides, the interior decorated w/Thousand Butterflies patt.,
the exterior w/overall chrysanthemums, signed "Shizan," 3" h.
(ILLUS.) 1,980.00
Teapot, cov., flattened round form
w/arched loops for the swing
handle (missing) & a short spout,
raised on three small knob feet,
the small domed cover molded
w/grapes, the domed top decorated w/panels of samurai on a
ground of flowers, spirals & other
stylized shapes, signed, 4¼" d.
(signature rubbed) 440.00
Vase, 4½" h., a small short pedes-
tal foot supporting a sharply
tapering conical body w/a tiny
flaring mouth, decorated w/gei-
sha strolling in a garden, the un-

derside above the footed base decorated w/waves & kites, signed 330.00

Vase, 4¾" h., slender ovoid form, decorated w/a continuous processional scene winding up the sides, floral & key design at base & shoulder, signed "Kyoto Kinkozan," Meiji period 3,300.00

Vase, 5" h., globular body on a small footring, the tiny short neck w/a flared rim, decorated w/two panels separated by a decorative border, one depicts young ladies w/departing children, the second shows samurai, signed 385.00

Vase, 7" h., tapering cylindrical body w/a squared shoulder & small mouth, decorated w/a parade of samurai, the reverse w/a blooming garden reserved on a green ground decorated w/stylized designs & flowers 3,960.00

Vase, 7½" h., baluster-form w/everted rim, depicting three scholars in relief on a gilt ground w/a white dragon encircling, signed on the base 137.50

Vase, 8¼" h., deeply waisted cylindrical footed form w/a flaring shoulder & base section, tapering to a tiny short neck, decorated overall w/a profusion of flowers on a ground of gilt dots, a central band decorated w/boys & girls engaged in various games, signed 2,750.00

Vase, 9½" h., a squatty rounded base on a flaring foot, the wide shoulder tapering to a tall stick neck w/widely flaring rim, decorated w/reserves of samurai, geishas, a procession & a poetry reading on a ground decorated w/colorful blooming chrysanthemums (small chip on body, minor gilt rubbing) 660.00

Vases, 5½" h., slender tapering footed baluster-form, the sides decorated w/long panels w/samurai & other figures in landscape scenes, incised signature, pr........................ 440.00

Vases, 6" h., footed cylindrical body w/a gently sloping shoulder to the short cylindrical neck, decorated w/a panel depicting a woman & small children, samurai, Immortals & geisha, gilt trim, signed, pr. 357.50

Vases, 9¼" h., spherical body w/a tiny neck fitted w/a pointed metal stopper, decorated w/alternating bands of blue & white floral

scrolls & white chrysanthemums on a ground of gilt dots, pr....... 715.00

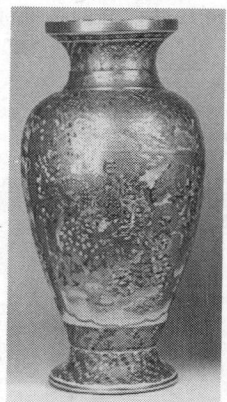

Tall Satsuma Vase

Vases, 29" h., baluster-form, decorated w/panels of figural scenes, 19th c., pr. (ILLUS. of one)......6,600.00

SCHAFER AND VATER

Founded in Rudolstadt, Thuringia, Germany in 1890, the Schafer and Vater Porcelain Factory specialized in decorative pieces of porcelain usually in white or colored bisque. They produced many novelty figural items such as creamers, toothpick holders, boxes and hatpin holders and also produced a line of jasper ware with white relief decoration in imitation of the famous Wedgwood jasper wares. The firm also decorated white ware blanks.

The company ceased production by 1962 and collectors now seek out their charming pieces which may be marked with a crown over a starburst containing the script letter "R."

Ashpot, bisque, figural, bust of a miner, wide-eyed man w/mouth open wide exposing irregular teeth, holds in cap for matches, small miner's light fastened on hat, "How are you off for coals?" on base, natural colors, 3½" d., 3 5/8" h. $185.00

Box, cov., jasper ware, oblong cartouche shape, the cover w/a white relief bust portrait of a lady wearing a poke bonnet in a blue oval ground & flanked by white relief flowers on the sage green cover, sage green base, 2 5/8 x 3½", 1 7/8" h........... 85.00

Figure, bisque, Scotchman w/real
fabric kilt, "Mind Your Own Business" on base, "Of Course I've
Pants ye fool" on underpants un-
der kilt, marked, 3" d., 5½" h. 185.00
Figure, bisque, "Mr. Tenor," tall,
thin, bug-eyed man w/puffy hair-
do, wearing black tuxedo, red
stockings & black shoes, singing,
unmarked, 7 5/8" h. 185.00
Hair receiver, cov., lavender deco-
rated w/multicolored "jewels,"
artist-signed, 3¼" d. 50.00
Hatpin holder, bisque, figural, bust
of a woman w/an ornate tower-
ing headdress, pink 145.00
Match striker, bisque, figure of a
man looking through telescope,
"A very fine view" on front &
back, natural colors, marked,
3" d., 4" h. 185.00
Match striker, bisque, figure group
of black mother cat facing forward w/striker on her back, a kitten facing forward w/"Don't
scratch me, scratch Mother,"
marked, 3¼" d., 4" h. 170.00
Mug, cylindrical, relief-molded elk's
head on each side, realistic coloring, tan & brown satin finished
ground, 3" d., 3¼" h. 75.00
Pitcher, 4" h., figural seated China-
man, grotesque grinning face
w/long nailed fingers holding up
corners of mouth, big feet, artist-
signed, No. 7458 . . . . 150.00
Plaque, pierced to hang, round, jas-
per ware, the center w/a white
relief scene of a standing Cupid
in a landscape, the wide rim
w/white relief flowers & leaves,
all on a dark green ground,
5 3/8" d. 65.00
Salt & pepper shakers, figural smil-
ing apple & smiling pear, multi-
colored, pr. 85.00
Sugar bowl, cov., jasper ware, wide
squatty cylindrical body w/domed
cover & loop handles, white relief
figure of a lady & winged cupids
on blue ground, white handles . . . 95.00
Teapot, cov., figural smiling apple,
multicolored, 1 cup size 105.00
Toothpick holder, figural laughing
man w/holes in tongue, multi-
colored 98.00
Vase, 4¼" h., 5¼" w., figural, Gei-
sha girl kneeling w/arms outstretched in front of a large
fan-shaped vase, blue & white,
marked 145.00
Vase, 7 7/8" h., 2" d., jasper ware,
tall slender cylindrical body on a

cushion foot, tapering slightly to a
narrow cylindrical neck flanked
by straight open handles to the
shoulder, white relief portrait of
a lady & birds on a light blue
ground, signed 85.00

SEVRES & SEVRES-STYLE

Sevres Bisque Figure Group

*Some of the most desirable porcelain ever
produced was made at the Sevres factory,
originally established at Vincennes, France,
and transferred, through permission of Madame de Pompadour, to Sevres as the Royal
Manufactory about the middle of the 18th
century. King Louis XV took sole responsibility for the works in 1759 when production
of hard paste began. Between 1850 and 1900,
many biscuit and soft-paste porcelains were
again made. Fine early pieces are scarce and
high-priced. Many of those available today
are late productions. The various Sevres
marks have been copied and pieces listed as
"Sevres-Style" are similar to actual Sevres
wares, but not necessarily from that factory.*

Cachepots, Sevres-Style, wide waisted body w/flaring rim, decorated
on the side w/an oval panel
depicting a ram or fawn on one
side & a parrot on the other side
all against the turquoise blue
ground, fitted within a gilt-bronze
framework w/egg-and-dart molded rim band flanked by strap handles topped by winged baby sea
nymphs & continuing to the round
molded base raised on a squared
plinth on paw feet, pseudo interlaced "L's" mark in blue, late
19th c., 11¼" h., pr. (replace-
ments) $3,300.00
Charger, a center medallion
w/colorful h.p. peacocks in a
courtyard scene, gold enamelings

& florals, interlaced "L's" mark, ca. 1895, 16" d. 695.00

Creamer & cov. sugar bowl, white ground decorated w/cornflowers, trimmed w/gilt, marked, ca. 1910, sugar 4¾" h., creamer 5½" h., pr. 330.00

Equestrian figure, bisque, depicting Louis XIV, ormolu base, incised mark, 19th c., 16" h. 1,210.00

Figurine, "The Ice Queen," a striding female in icicle headdress & sweeping cream crystalline-glazed gown, her train exposing two chilly putti, Sevres stamp for 1907, 12¾" h. 1,870.00

Figure group, bisque, "La Lanterne Magique," a boy pulling the strings of his peep-show while a young woman holding a basket of eggs kneels to look into the peephole while a small boy clambers for his turn, on a rocky mound base, modeled by Etienne-Maurice Falconet after Francois Boucher, incised heart mark, 1757-65, firing cracks, 6 3/8" h. (ILLUS.) 4,950.00

Figure group, depicting a dancing couple, she in a blue-trimmed floral dress w/yellow floral cape, he in green trousers, floral vest & purple coat, interlaced "L's," 11 x 12" 1,650.00

Sevres-Style Jardiniere

Jardiniere, Sevres-Style, pail-form, gilt bands simulating staves & bands, four square tab handles at the rim mounted w/gilt ram's heads, interlaced "L's" mark, late 19th c., losses (ILLUS.) 4,600.00

Plaque, Sevres-Style, round, depicting a woman & child on a settee, 18" d. 1,100.00

Plates, 9½" d., "Rosso Antico," each w/a brick-red ground reserved & finely painted in the center, one in green, yellow, blue, brown, orange & gold w/two urns & a palm frond, the other painted in brown, green, yellow, orange, purple, blue & tan w/an overturned urn, a ewer & a lizard crawling into a dish of fruit, the rims w/a gold & white grapevine border, crowned "N" marks in iron-red, oval date marks & various other marks, dated 1852 & 1853, pr. 7,150.00

Plates, 9 7/16" to 9¾" d., each colorfully painted w/scattered sprays & sprigs of flowers, the gilt-edged scalloped rim lightly molded w/foliate C-scrolls outlined in blue, interlaced "L's," various painter's & gilder's marks, various incised marks, all but two w/date letters, ca. 1761-82, set of 14 .... 3,025.00

Early Sevres Urn

Urn, the footed body w/a widely flaring neck w/a dark gold ground decorated w/a h.p. color reserve featuring a military battle framed by ornate gilt scrolls, a gilt eagle in wreath on the lower body, black interior & black swan's head handles at the shoulders, raised on a square molded black base w/paw feet, early 19th c., 12" d., 23" h. (ILLUS.) 3,250.00

Urns, cov., Sevres-Style, the large cylindrical body w/a rounded bottom supports a waisted domed cover w/large pineapple finial, the body w/a pierced gilt-bronze scroll band around the rim flanked by gilt-bronze handles headed by classical lady busts, the dark blue ground decorated w/a colorful panel of lovers in 18th c. attire, the panel framed by an ornate gilt scroll border, the body raised on a gilt-bronze disc above the domed porcelain base raised on a square gilt-bronze foot w/canted corners, the panel artist-signed, interlaced "L's" mark, late 19th c., 22" h........7,150.00

Vase, 4 3/8" h., small ovoid body w/elongated flaring neck, pale lavender & blue crystalline glaze, designed by Taxile Doat, signed "T DOAT - Sevres," ca. 1900...... 770.00

Vase, cov., 30" h., Sevres-Style, tall baluster-form body raised on a very slender ringed pedestal w/domed base w/footed cartouche-form foot, domed cover w/flame finial, the body decorated w/an oblong reserve painted w/a bust portrait of a semi-clad young woman w/long, dark flowing hair, against a celeste blue lustre ground heavily trimmed w/gilt irises & wide leaves, gilt-bronze mounts, interlaced "L's" mark, late 19th c. 5,170.00

Vases, 8" h., Sevres-Style, baluster-form body raised on a pedestal base w/central shaft & three open legs w/hoof feet, decorated w/a colorful floral reserve on an apple green ground, trimmed w/gilt, 19th c., pr. 302.50

Vases, cov., 15½" h., the tall gently tapering cylindrical body raised on a slender short pedestal on footed, domed base, the front of the body w/a large oblong reserve decorated w/semi-clad nymphs & cherubs, the reverse w/colorful floral sprays, all on a cobalt blue ground trimmed w/gilt scrolls, the domed cover w/a pine cone finial & gilt lappets on cobalt blue, gilt-bronze female mask handles at the gilt-bronze scalloped rim band, artist-signed, interlaced "L's" mark & "Chateau de Tuileries" stamp, mid-19th c., pr.......2,860.00

SHAWNEE

The Shawnee Pottery operated in Zanesville, Ohio, from 1937 until 1961. Much of the early production was sold to chain stores and mail-order houses including Sears Roebuck, Woolworth and others. Planters, cookie jars and vases, along with the popular "Corn King" oven ware line, are among the collectible items which are plentiful and still reasonably priced. Reference numbers used here are taken from Mark E. Supnick's book, Collecting Shawnee Pottery *and* The Collector's Guide to Shawnee Pottery *by Duane and Janice Vanderbilt.*

Bank, figural Howdy Doody riding a pig $425.00

Butter dish, cov., "Corn Queen" line, No. 72.................... 30.00

Casserole, individual size, "Corn King" line, No. 73, 9 oz. 45.00

Cookie jar, Basket of Fruit, No. 84 .. 82.50

Shawnee Clown Cookie Jar

Cookie jar, figural Clown w/seal & ball, No. 12 (ILLUS.) .....200.00 to 225.00

Cookie jar, Drummer Boy, model of a drum w/boy finial on lid, No. 10 ....250.00 to 275.00

Cookie jar, figural Dutch Boy w/blue patches & gold trim .....200.00 to 225.00

Cookie jar, figural Elephant, pink, No. 60 ....100.00 to 125.00

Cookie jar, figural Mugsey Dog, w/blue bow ....200.00 to 250.00

Cookie jar, figural Smiley Pig, clover leaf decoration ....150.00 to 200.00

Cookie jar, figural Winnie Pig, blue collar & flowers........200.00 to 225.00

Creamer, figural Elephant.......... 25.00

Creamer, figural Puss 'n Boots, gold trim........................ 150.00

Cup & saucer, "Corn King" line, Nos. 90 & 91 .... 40.00

French casserole, cov., Lobster Ware, Kenwood Line, black base w/stick handle, domed white cover w/red lobster finial, No. 902, 16 oz. 30.00

French casseroles, Lobster Ware, Kenwood Line, black base w/stick handle, white domed cover w/red lobster handle, No. 901, 10 oz., set of 4 .... 48.00

Lamp bracket, small urn-form font molded w/flowers extends from leaf-molded round wall mount, patented in 1947 .... 145.00

Mixing bowl, "Corn King" line, No. 8, 8" d. 27.00

Mug, "Corn Queen" line, No. 69, 8 oz. 40.00

Pitcher, ball-type, Pennsylvania Dutch patt. 65.00

Pitcher, ball-type, Sunflower patt. ... 55.00

Pitcher, figural Chanticleer
  Rooster 60.00
Pitcher, figural Little Bo Peep, blue
  bonnet 90.00
Pitcher, figural Smiley Pig, peach,
  blue & gold flowers 165.00
Planter, figural Dutch children at
  well, No. 710 .... 20.00
Planter, figural man pulling rick-
  shaw, No. 539 .... 6.00
Planter, model of an antique open
  car, w/gold trim, No. 506 .... 20.00
Planter, model of a covered wagon,
  large, No. 733 .... 40.00
Planter, model of a doe & fawn in
  front of a curved trough, No. 669,
  6¼" l., 5¾" h. 20.00
Planter, model of a fawn standing
  in front of scrolling leaves,
  No. 737 .... 22.50
Planter, model of four birds on a
  branch, No. 502 .... 40.00
Planter, model of a tractor trailer,
  w/truck cab & trailer, No. 681,
  2 pcs. 20.00
Plate, salad, 9" oval, "Corn King"
  line, No. 93 .... 39.00
Plate, 10" oval, "Corn Queen" line,
  No. 68 .... 30.00
Range set: cov. waste jar & figural
  lobster claw salt & pepper shak-
  ers; Lobster Ware, Kenwood Line,
  No. 906, the set 45.00
Salt & pepper shakers, figural Chef,
  w/bodies in shape of "S" & "P",
  gold trim, pr. 23.00
Salt & pepper shakers, figural
  flowerpot, pr. 12.00
Salt & pepper shakers, figural milk
  can, pr. 15.00
Salt & pepper shakers, figural Puss
  'n Boots, small, pr. 22.50
Salt & pepper shakers, figural
  Smiley Pig, clover leaf decoration,
  large, pr. 60.00
Salt & pepper shakers, Sunflower
  patt., large, 5" h., pr. 39.00
Salt & pepper shakers, figural
  watering can, large, pr. 13.00
Sugar bowl, cov., "Corn King" line,
  No. 78 .... 28.00
Teapot, cov., "Corn King" line,
  individual size, No. 65,
  10 oz. ....50.00 to 75.00
Teapot, cov., "Corn Queen" line, in-
  dividual size, No. 65, 10 oz. 100.00
Teapot, cov., figural elephant, blue
  glaze 135.00
Teapot, cov., figural Tom, Tom the
  Piper's Son, No. 44 (ILLUS. top
  next column) 70.00
Vase, bud, figural boy at cornuco-
  pia, No. 1265 .... 12.00

Shawnee Tom, Tom Teapot

Wall pocket, figural girl head w/rag
  doll, No. 810................... 15.00
Wall pocket, Little Jack Horner
  design within circle on a square,
  No. 585 .... 12.00
Wall pocket, model of a grandfather
  clock, No. 1261 .... 20.00

SHELLEY

Members of the Shelley family were in the pottery business in England as early as the 18th century. In 1872 Joseph Shelley formed a partnership with James Wileman of Wileman & Co. who operated the Foley China Works. The Wileman & Co. name was used for the firm for the next fifty years, and between 1890 and 1910 the words "The Foley" appeared above conjoined "WC" initials.

Beginning in 1910 the Shelley family name in a shield appeared on wares, although the firm's official name was still Wileman & Co. The company's name was finally changed to Shelley in 1925 and then Shelley China Ltd. after 1965. The firm changed hands in the 1960's and became part of the Doulton Group in 1971.

At first only average quality earthenwares were produced but in the late 1890's new shapes and better quality decorations were used.

Bone china was introduced at Shelley before World War I and these fine dinnerwares became very popular in the United States and are increasingly popular today with collectors. Thin "eggshell china" teawares, miniatures and souvenir items were widely marketed during the 1920's and 1930's and are sought-after today.

Ashtray w/holder, White Horse
  patt. $97.50
Butter dish, cov., Blue Rock patt.,
  Dainty shape 100.00
Cake plate, footed, Rosebud patt. .. 195.00
Chocolate cup & saucer, Regency
  patt. 30.00

Chocolate pot, cov., Phlox patt., Eve shape	135.00
Chocolate pot, cov., Versailles patt., Court shape	135.00
Coffeepot, cov., Bridal Rose patt., Dainty shape	130.00
Coffeepot, cov., Regency patt.	118.00
Creamer, Blue Rock patt., Dainty shape	25.00
Creamer & sugar bowl, Dainty Blue patt., pr.	75.00
Creamer & open sugar bowl, Regency patt., pr.	65.00
Creamer & sugar bowl, Sunrise patt., pr.	70.00
Creamer, sugar bowl & tray, Bridal Rose patt., the set	75.00
Cup & saucer, demitasse, Regency patt.	45.00
Cup & saucer, demitasse, Rock Garden patt.	45.00
Cup & saucer, demitasse, Woodland patt.	34.00
Cup & saucer, Begonia patt., six-flute shape	42.50
Cup & saucer, Blue Rock patt., six-flute shape	38.00
Cup & saucer, Heather patt.	25.00
Cup & saucer, Orchid patt., fluted shape	40.00
Cup & saucer, Wild Anemone patt.	65.00
Dish, gold handle, Regency patt., 4½ x 6"	30.00
Egg cup, double, Blue Rock patt., Dainty shape	35.00
Egg cup, Dainty Blue patt.	60.00
Egg cup, Lily of the Valley patt.	55.00
Muffin dish, cov., Dainty Blue patt.	200.00
Plate, 6" d., Rosebud patt., fluted shape	20.00
Plates, 6" d., Indian Peony patt., set of 6	95.00
Plate, 6¼" d., Blue Iris patt., Queen Anne shape	25.00
Plate, 7" d., Dainty Blue patt.	25.00
Plate, 7" d., Phlox patt.	37.50
Plate, 8" d., Begonia patt., six-flute shape	22.50
Plate, 8" d., Dainty Blue patt., six-flute shape	35.00
Plate, 8" d., Regency patt.	20.00
Plate, 10" d., Hunt Scene patt.	45.00
Plate, dinner, 10¾" d., Sheraton patt.	45.00
Plate, 11" d., Dainty Blue patt., six-flute shape	65.00
Plate, chop, 13" d., Dainty Blue patt.	150.00
Sugar bowl, cov., Blue Rock patt., Dainty shape	25.00
Sugar bowl, cov., Lily of the Valley patt.	25.00

Teapot, cov., Dainty Blue patt., six-flute shape, 6" h.	200.00
Teapot, cover & trivet, Queen Anne patt., pink & green, the set	400.00
Vegetable dish, cov., Georgian patt., 8" d.	95.00
Vegetable bowl, open, oval, Dainty Blue patt.	170.00

SHENANDOAH VALLEY POTTERY

J. Bell Covered Pitcher

The potters of the Shenandoah Valley in Maryland and Virginia turned out an earthenware pottery of a distinctive type. It was the first earthenware pottery made in America with a varied, brightly colored glaze. The most notable of these potters, Peter Bell, Jr., operated a pottery at Hagerstown, Maryland and later at Winchester, Virginia, from about 1800 until 1845. His sons and grandsons carried on the tradition. One son, John Bell, established a pottery at Waynesboro, Pennsylvania in 1833, working until his death in 1880, along with his sons who subsequently operated the pottery a few years longer. Two other sons of Peter Bell, Jr., Solomon and Samuel, operated a pottery in Strasburg, Virginia, a town sometimes referred to as "pot town" for six potteries were in operation there in the 1880's. Their work was also continued by descendants. Shenandoah Valley redware pottery, with its colorful glazes in green, yellow, brown and other colors, and the stoneware pottery produced in the area, are eagerly sought by collectors. Some of the more unique forms can be considered true American folk art and will fetch fantastic prices.

Dish, oval tub-form w/molded lines & applied small rope handles at the top edge of the ends, white slip w/mottled green & brown, impressed "J. Bell & Sons, Strasburg, Va.," 8" l. (rim glaze chips) $2,310.00
Food mold, redware, sides w/light horizontal lines, conical center stem, coggled rim, creamy white slip w/green & clear glaze, im-

pressed "Solomon Bell, Strasburg, Va.," 7¾" d., 3½" h. (wear & glaze flakes) 1,200.00

Food mold, Turk's turban-style, sponged green & brown glaze, impressed "Upton M. Bell, Waynesboro, Pa.," 5¾" d. (rim chip) 330.00

Jar, ovoid w/molded rim, brown sponged glaze, impressed label "John W. Bell, Waynesboro, Pa.," 6½" h. (chips) 400.00

Model of a dog, Whippet in reclining position on an oblong base, overall reddish tan glaze w/brown highlights, inside lip of base incised "S.B. Anno 1878, by F.C. 150," 9" l. 445.50

Pitcher, cov., 9" h., redware, spherical footed body tapering to a wide cylindrical neck, thick strap handle, domed cover w/button finial, overall finely spattered green & blue on a cream-glazed ground, stamped "J. Bell" twice, ca. 1860 (ILLUS.) 7,150.00

Pitcher, 9¾" h., redware, cylindrical body, squared rim w/pinched spout, white slip w/green & brown glaze, impressed "S. Bell & Son, Strasburg," wear, chips & glaze flakes................... 3,350.00

SLIPWARE

Rare Slipware Charger

This term refers to ceramics, primarily redware, decorated by the application of slip, or semi-liquid paste made of clay. Such wares were made for decades in England and Germany and elsewhere on the Continent, and in the Pennsylvania Dutch country and elsewhere in the United States. Today, contemporary copies of early Slipware items are featured in numerous decorator magazines and offered for sale in gift catalogs.

Beer cask, barrel-shaped, overall brown glaze w/yellow slip wide bands at the ends & incised &

trimmed in slip "TW" & dated "1774," small top protrusion w/small opening & holes for a hanging strap, Staffordshire, England, 9" h. (chips, some glaze losses) $990.00

Charger, circular w/crimped rim, interior w/yellow slip inscription "G.W. Rhoads Dealer in Dry Goods Groceries & cc. also Schwitzer Kase," Pennsylvania, 19th c., 13½" d. (ILLUS.) 3,738.00

Charger, coggled edge, squiggly line decoration on redware, 14½" d. (old chips, wear & hairlines) 286.00

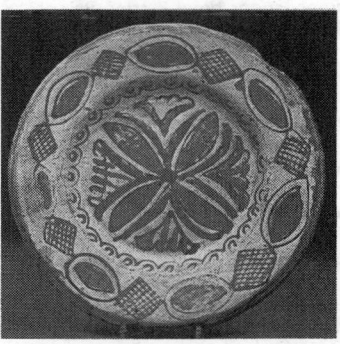

Staffordshire Slipware Dish

Dish, round, the center decorated w/a four-petaled brown flower w/blue edging within iron-red circlets & a wide border band of blue & brown ovals alternating w/brown diaper diamonds, rim restored & chipped, Staffordshire, England, second quarter 18th c., 15¾" d. (ILLUS.) 11,000.00

Flowerpot, wide slightly flaring cylindrical form w/a molded rim, a yellow slip band around the top scratched through & inscribed "Success to the British Navy and God save the King 1799," below this a yellow slip script inscription of "SB - 1799" & rows of slip dots, England, 8¼" h. (rim chip, crack) 935.00

Loaf dish, oval w/gently curved edges & a crimped rim, the interior decorated w/two angled rows of triple-line S-curves in yellow slip flanking a long center tripleline slip band, Pennsylvania, first half 19th c., 16½" l. (minor flakes on rim) 2,070.00

Pie plate, redware w/coggled rim, clear amberish glaze w/two triangular grape cluster-type designs in brown & green slip, 8½" d. (minor wear & old chips) 1,200.00

Pie plate, coggled rim, an irregularly undulating three-line yellow slip band across the middle, a smaller S-form triple yellow slip band flanking it, 9" d. (old edge chips) 467.50

Plate, 11" d., notched rim, yellow slip decoration of a pair of double loops w/long tails ending in three dashes, 19th c. (chips) 880.00

Tray, rectangular w/rounded corners, deeply notched rim, redware covered in a dark brown glaze slip-decorated w/overall wide squiggles in white, early 19th c., probably England, 14¾ x 17" (some chips on bottom) 880.00

Trencher, rectangular w/sloped sides & coggled edge, interior inscribed "Money Wanted" in yellow slip script, Pennsylvania, 19th c., 10½ x 14½" (small chip to one end) 7,150.00

SPATTERWARE

This ceramic ware takes its name from the "spattered" decoration, in various colors, generally used to trim pieces hand-painted with rustic center designs of flowers, birds, houses, etc. Popular in the early 19th century, most was imported from England.

Related wares, called "stick spatter," had free-hand designs applied with pieces of cut sponge attached to sticks, hence the name. Examples date from the 19th and early 20th century and were produced in England, Europe and America.

Creamer, tapering octagonal body w/arched spout & angled handle, Fort patt., free-hand building in green, black & red, blue spatter background, 6" h. (small chips) ... $336.00

Cup & saucer, handleless, miniature, Peafowl patt., free-hand bird in blue, red, black & yellow, green spatter blotches around the sides 280.50

Cup & saucer, handleless, Flower patt., free-hand four-petal starflower in blue, black & red in the center of saucer & on side of cup, brown spatter background (chip on cup table ring) 467.50

Cup & saucer, handleless, free-hand central cluster of four buds in red & green, red & blue spatter borders, impressed mark "Harvey" .. 220.00

Cup & saucer, handleless, Rainbow patt., spatter bands in red, blue &

green, impressed "Adams" (small flakes on table ring of saucer) ... 522.50

Cup & saucer, handleless, Rose patt., free-hand blossom & leaves in red, green & black, a narrow band of purple spatter at the rim of the cup & saucer (pinpoint flake on saucer footring) 258.50

Cups & saucers, handleless, Tick-Tack-Toe Crosses design forms a border band in red & green spatter, set of 6 (minor table ring flake on one) 726.00

Pitcher, 7½" h., bulbous footed body tapering to a wide paneled neck w/scalloped rim & wide arched spout, S-scroll handle, Rainbow patt., slightly swirling stripes down the sides in red, blue, green, yellow & black spatter (stains, hairlines, spout & rim chips) 577.50

Plate, 7½" d., Rose patt., free-hand flower in red w/green leaves & black trim, blue spatter border band 330.00

Plate, 8¼" d., Acorn & Oak Leaf patt., free-hand center design in greens, black & yellow w/a blue spatter border (hairline) 660.00

Plate, 8¼" d., Peafowl patt., free-hand bird in blue, yellow, green & black, red spatter background (stains, crazing, small repaired rim chips) 247.50

Plate, 8¼" d., Star patt., free-hand six-point star in red, green & yellow, blue banded spatter rim 605.00

Plate, 8¼" d., Tulip patt., free-hand colorful flower, purple spatter border 275.00

Plate, 8½" w., lightly paneled sides, Rose patt., free-hand flower in red, green, blue & black, red spatter border 247.50

Plate, 8 5/8" d., Pomegranate patt., free-hand fruit in red, green, blue, black & yellow, blue spatter border (minor wear & stains) 330.00

Plate, 8¾" d., Dahlia patt., free-hand five-point starflower in blue, green & black, yellow spatter rim band (stains, damage on blue) ... 1,017.50

Plate, 9" w., twelve-sided, Bull's-eye patt., purple spatter bull's-eye, inner rim band & outer swag band (rim flakes, stains) 423.50

Plate, 9 5/8" d., scalloped rim, Rainbow patt., rim bands in red, blue & green spatter 467.50

Teapot, cov., tall tapering octagonal body w/domed cover & pointed finial, angled handle & swan's-neck spout, Acorn patt., free-hand

green, black, teal & yellow ochre
acorn sprig, overall red spatter
ground, 8¼" h. (professional repair) 550.00

STICK OR CUT-SPONGE SPATTER

Bouillon cup, two-handled, free-
hand red flowers & green leaves
w/small blue cut-sponge flowers 46.00

Cup & saucer, handleless, each
piece w/two bands of purple cut-
sponge design separated by a
green stripe 93.50

Cup & saucer, handleless, three
bands of cut-sponge stylized geometric designs in red, green &
black 82.50

Plate, 6½" d., red & green free-
hand flowers center decoration,
blue cut-sponge border 72.00

Plate, 6 5/8" d., the center w/h.p.
columbine blossom w/rose bud &
thistle in red, blue, green & purple, a wide border band of purple
cut-sponge daisy-like blossoms
(minor glaze imperfections) 121.00

Plate, 8½" d., decorated w/free-
hand green leaf sprays & clusters
of red cut-sponge cherries, Maas-
tricht, Holland 58.00

Plate, 9 1/8" d., Rabbit patt.,
transfer-printed rabbit in center,
h.p. stylized leafy vines & cut-
sponge blossoms around border in
polychrome enamels............. 330.00

Plate, 10 1/8" d., a wide border
band of cut-sponge scalloped
flowerheads in green, an inner
band of smaller red flowerheads
(minor wear & pinpoint flakes) ... 126.50

Plates, 9" d., a wide free-hand border band of large red blossoms &
green leaves w/scattered small
blue cut-sponge flowerhead
clusters, Baker & Co., England,
late 19th - early 20th c., set
of 6......................... 330.00

SPONGEWARE

*Spongeware's designs were spattered,
sponged or daubed on in colors, sometimes
with a piece of cloth. Blue on white was the
most common type, but mottled tans, browns
and greens on yellowware were also popular.
Spongeware generally has an overall pattern
with a coarser look than Spatterwares, to
which it is loosely related. These wares were
extensively produced in England and America well into the 20th century.*

Bowl, 5" d., 2" h., tan & brown..... $45.00
Bowl, 5" d., brown on yellowware .. 15.00
Bowl, 6" d., blue & rust on cream,
"Rockwell City, Iowa" advertising 95.00
Bowl, 9¾" d., blue & rust, w/adver-
tising, "Mix with Us, Farmers
Grain & Mercantile Co., Round
Lake, MN".................... 250.00
Bowl, 10" d., blue on white 165.00
Pitcher, 8¼" h., bulbous base tapering to a narrow flared spout, high
arched handle, blue on white
w/narrow blue stripes flanking a
wide central band 220.00
Pitcher, 9" h., cylindrical body
w/small pinched spout, vertical
bands of stylized paired leaves in
blue alternating w/white bands
(hairline) 275.00
Pitcher & bowl set, blue on white
w/solid band between white
bands decoration, bowl 14¼" d.,
pitcher 11 3/8" h., the set 310.00
Plate, 9" d., blue on white 85.00
Platter, 7¾ x 11", slightly scalloped
rim, the interior & exterior
w/mottled blue on white 275.00
Teapot, cov., footed, bulbous body
w/straight sides, domed cover, olive green on white, 7¼" h. (chips
on lid) 291.50

Spongeware Water Cooler

Water cooler, cov., barrel-shaped,
slightly domed cover w/indented
knob finial, white w/overall blue
sponging & blue banding, metal
spigot at the front bottom, late
19th c., some flakes, handle on
spigot broken, 16½" h. (ILLUS.)... 495.00

STAFFORDSHIRE FIGURES

*Small figures and groups made of pottery
were produced by the majority of the
Staffordshire, England potters in the 19th*

century and were used as mantel decorations or "chimney ornaments," as they were sometimes called. Pairs of dogs were favorites and were turned out by the carload, and 19th century pieces are still available. Well-painted reproductions also abound and collectors are urged to exercise caution before investing.

Staffordshire Spaniel

Bust of Milton, attributed to R.A. Wood, on a socle base, white w/some polychrome trim, early 19th c., 9¼" h. $192.50

Dog, miniature, Spaniel in seated position, porcelain, white w/black spots, molded collar, painted facial features, 2 7/8" h. 85.00

Dog, miniature, Spaniel in seated position, white w/large reddish spots, painted facial features, molded & painted collar, 3 5/8" h. (minor wear) 125.00

Dog, Spaniel in seated position, well-molded fur & detailing, white w/shaded reddish spots, well-painted facial features, molded & painted collar w/locket, 4½" h. (wear & minor damage) 225.00

Dog, Spaniel in seated position, molded fur, white w/rust red spots & ears, painted facial details, 19th c., 5 5/8" h. (some wear) 214.50

Dog, Spaniel in seated position, a slender well-molded body & head w/delicate fur in white w/heavy black spotting, well-painted facial details, molded & painted collar & locket, 6 7/8" h. (minor wear, chip on base) 275.00

Dog, miniature, Whippet in seated position, porcelain, white w/brown shading, on a green molded base, 2½" h. 85.00

Dog, miniature, Whippet in recumbent position on an oval mound base, white w/green, brown & blue trim, 3" l. (small chips) 264.00

Dogs, Poodle in seated position, white w/heavy "coleslaw" trim on ears, shoulders & tail, well-

painted facial features, molded & painted collar, 5½" h., facing pr. (crazed) 600.00

Dogs, Poodle in seated position, white w/reddish spots, gold trim, 10½" h., pr. 360.00

Dogs, miniature, Spaniel in seated position, white w/rust red spots, 19th c., 2 7/8" h., pr. (chips) 165.00

Dogs, Spaniel in seated position, white w/greenish copper lustre spots, molded & painted collar & long chain draped over his back, painted facial features, 19th c., 9¼" h., pr. (minor hairlines) 350.00

Dogs, Spaniel in seated position, white w/lightly molded fur & bushy tail, long molded chain down the sides, painted facial features & gilt trim on the body, 13½" h., pr. (ILLUS. of one) 275.00

Equestrian figure, entitled "Duchess," a woman on horseback, riding sidesaddle on a white prancing animal, polychrome clothing, rectangular base, late 19th - early 20th c., 5 7/8" h. 137.50

Equestrian figure, Scottish laird on horseback, mid-19th c., 14 3/8" h. 175.00

Equestrian group, miniature, huntsman on horseback w/hound beside them, polychrome enamel trim, 19th c., 4¼" h. (minor wear) 75.00

Figure of a dandy holding a dove, w/a viola by his side, 9" h. 110.00

Figure of a gentleman, creamware, standing & wearing a cape over his left shoulder & in a kilt, splashed in dark grey & ochre on a green mound base, ca. 1765, 3¾" h. (base chip) 330.00

Figure of Gladstone, elderly man standing w/one arm leaning on a tree stump, on oval base marked "Gladstone," third quarter 19th c., 17" h. 1,045.00

Figure of The Lion Slayer, man in Scots outfit holding a dead lion by one rear paw, oval base w/title molded, late 19th c., 17" h. 330.00

Figure of a Scottish lass, mid-19th c., 7¼" h. 100.00

Figure of Shakespeare, standing & leaning on square column piled w/books, oval base w/"Shakespeare," 19th c., 17" h. 522.50

Figure of Sir Charles Napier, in military dress standing beside a cannon & ammunition, 19th c., 16" h. 220.00

Figure group, miniature, a standing man & woman, probably repre-

senting Queen Victoria & Prince
Albert, polychrome trim, 4 3/8" h.
(small edge chips & short hairlines) 105.00

Figure group of Eva & Uncle Tom,
modeled as Uncle Tom seated
wearing a yellow jacket & flowers
around his neck & holding a Bible
in his left hand, Eva standing
on his right knee, inscribed on
the rockwork base w/a quote,
19th c., 7¾" h. 528.00

Figure group, a seated dark-haired
young girl wearing a red cape
w/a small dog reclining next to
her, polychrome enamel trim,
8" h. (flake on base) 412.50

Figure group, pearlware, lady &
man in 18th c. peasant costume
seated on raised rockwork w/a
small tree behind, on rectangular
plinth base marked "Rural Pas-
time," early 19th c., 7" h. 715.00

Figure group, creamware, "The Lost
Sheep," modeled as a standing
shepherd wearing a black tricorn
hat, green coat & breeches & grey
waistcoat & carrying a lamb over
his right shoulder, on a rocky
base w/tree stump splashed
in brown & green, ca. 1780,
8 5/8" h. (his neck & one ear on
lamb restored, chips to base) 990.00

Figure group, Scottish man & lady,
standing wearing costumes, he
wearing a large tam, she carrying
a large bundle on her head
balanced w/one hand, polychrome & worn gilt trim, 19th c.,
12¾" h. (crazing, minor hairlines) 247.50

Figure group, figure of a young
seated girl flanked by a pair of
sheep, mid-19th c., 8" h. 70.00

Figure group of "John Brown," the
bearded man modeled standing
w/two black children at his side,
on an oval base w/the title,
19th c., 10¾" h. 660.00

Figure group of "Topsy & Eva," each
girl modeled kneeling, Topsy in a
striped tunic & pink skirt, Eva in a
white dress w/orange sash, on a
shaped oval base w/the title in
gilt, 19th c., 8¾" h. 528.00

Hen in setting position, on a low
oval base molded w/small leaves,
creamware splashed w/green &
brown, ca. 1760, 2½" h. (chip) ... 330.00

Hen on nest, polychrome body &
head on a colored basketweave
base, 5¼" l. 225.00

Hen on nest, white bisque hen
w/red comb on green grass & a

brown basket base, 5 x 6¾",
6¾" h. 245.00

Hen on nest, white bisque body
w/polychrome trim on head, colored basketweave base, 6¾" l. ... 275.00

Lamb, miniature, standing animal
w/white sanded coat, on an oblong base, 19th c., 2½" h. (wear,
chips) 104.50

Lamb, miniature, recumbent animal
on an oval base, white sanded
coat, polychrome facial features,
3 3/8" l. 192.50

Lion, miniature, seated on a round
base, worn polychrome trim,
2 3/8" h. 80.00

Early Staffordshire Animals

Lion, miniature, creamware, crudely
modeled animal w/a shaggy
mane, an open mouth w/teeth
& tongue & a long tail curled
around his belly & back, seated
on a low rectangular mound base
w/his left foreleg on a small tree
stump, the base & stump dimpled,
splashed overall w/brown, green
& blue, ca. 1765, minor chipping,
3 7/16" h. (ILLUS. right) 2,013.00

Peacock, creamware, his head
turned slightly to the right, the
tail feathers displayed, perched
on a dimpled mound base, spattered overall in dark bluish green,
ca. 1765-75, some tiny chips,
3 3/8" h. (ILLUS. left) 1,495.00

Rooster, miniature, pearlware,
realistically modeled standing
bird on a thin round base, polychrome enamel decoration,
3¼" h. (small flakes around base,
minor wear) 247.50

Squirrel, creamware, the seated animal w/pointed ears, a bushy upright tail & holding its paws to its
mouth, incised coat & tail, wearing a collar & chain, on a mound
base, splashed overall w/a dark
grey glaze, Staffordshire, England,
ca. 1780, 7 1/8" h. (restored ears,
chips on base).................1,380.00

Swan swimming, creamware, the
body w/molded details splashed

w/blue & w/a brown beak &
feather tips, ca. 1800, 3½" h.
(cracked, chipped at base) 660.00
Tiger, miniature, standing animal
w/closed legs on an oval base,
yellow w/black stripes, 3¼" h.
(minor wear) 154.00
Vase, 4 3/8" h., figural, shepherd
boy, girl & goat standing in front
of a tall tree stump vase, polychrome enamel trim 236.50
Vase, 4 5/8" h., figural, two sleeping children seated against vase,
polychrome enamel trim (wear to
paint) 302.50
Vase, 5 1/8" h., figural, ram
w/sanded coat standing w/head
turned to left, in front of a slender low tree stump vase, on a
grassy mound base, polychrome
enamel trim 357.50

Figural Staffordshire Vase

Vase, 16½" h., figural, a standing
Scottish hunter beside a tall tree
trunk vase, a spotted seated setter dog in front of the stump,
polychrome trim, 19th c. (ILLUS.).. 220.00

STAFFORDSHIRE TRANSFER WARES

Rural Scenery Pattern Soup Tureen

*The process of transfer-printing designs on
earthenwares developed in England in the*
*late 18th century and by the mid-19th centu-
ry most common ceramic wares were decorated in this manner, most often with romantic
European or Oriental landscape scenes,
animals or flowers. The earliest such wares
were printed in dark blue but a little later
light blue, pink, purple, red, black, green and
brown were used. A majority of these wares
were produced at various English potteries
right up till the turn of the century but French
and other European firms also made similar
pieces and all are quite collectible. The best
reference on this area is Petra Williams' book
Staffordshire Romantic Transfer Patterns -
Cup Plates and Early Victorian China (Fountain House East, 1978). Also see ADAMS and
HISTORICAL & COMMEMORATIVE
wares, under Ceramics.*

Cake plate, footed, Alhambra patt.,
brown, ca. 1880 .... $75.00
Cake plate, handled, Phileau patt.,
brown, G.W. Turner, ca. 1880,
10" d. 30.00
Creamer, decorated w/a portrait of
"Sir Garnet Wolsey - England's
Hero," mauve, Cochran & Co.,
Glasgow, Scotland, late 19th c.,
6" h. 40.00
Creamer, Washington Vase patt.,
purple, Podmore, Walker & Co.,
ca. 1850 .... 110.00
Cup & saucer, handleless, Tyrolean
patt., brown, Wm. Ridgway, ca.
1845 .... 40.00
Cup & saucer, handleless, Warwick
patt., brown, Podmore, Walker &
Company 42.00
Cup plate, Union patt., blue,
Venables 75.00
Mug, cylindrical, scene of a lady
walking in a landscape carrying
a water yoke, black, ca. 1840,
2 7/8" h. 85.00
Mug, scene entitled "The Husband-
man's Diligence Provides Bread,"
black w/polychrome enameling,
3 7/8" h. 121.00
Pitcher, 6¾" h., "The Pawtucket
Falls", scene showing bridge,
buildings w/reverse scene of "The
Old Jones School House," brown,
Carpenter & Co................. 75.00
Pitcher, 9" h., bulbous ovoid footed
body tapering to a scalloped rim,
high arched S-scroll handle, decorated w/large panels of European scenery, purple, ca. 1840
(stains)...................... 125.00
Pitcher, 10½" h., footed bulbous
paneled body tapering to a scalloped rim & wide spout, S-scroll
handle, Good Samaritan patt.,
red, Clews, ca. 1830's 412.50

Pitcher & bowl set, the pitcher w/a bulbous body raised on a flaring foot & tapering to a very wide & highly arched spout, double-scroll handle, the widely flaring bowl w/scalloped rim, Arabian Pedlar (sic) patt., black, marked "Adams," ca. 1830-40, traces of silver paint on pitcher, bowl 13½" d., pitcher 11¼" h., the set (minor edge damage & chip on thumbpiece of pitcher) 325.00

Plate, 6½" d., Excelsior patt., purple w/polychrome trim, G. Woolliscroft, ca. 1850 . . . . 30.00

Plate, 6 5/8" d., embossed daisy rim band, the center w/a brown design of a knight on horseback trimmed in polychrome enamels . . 25.00

Plate, 8" d., motto-type, a black center landscape scene surrounded by the motto "Make Hay While the Sun Shines," an embossed rim w/a red edge stripe (wear, stains) 85.00

Plate, 9" d., center scene of hunters & dogs in a landscape, flowering vine border, dark blue, ca. 1830's (minor wear) 125.00

Plate, 9" d., the center w/a river landscape scene framed by a floral border, brown, impressed "Wedgwood" 25.00

Plate, 9" d., Scroll patt., black 35.00

Plate, 9 1/8" d., Clyde Scenery patt., black, Jacksons, ca. 1830's (minor stains & scratches) 35.00

Plate, 10¼" d., Coral patt., black, J. Furnival, ca. 1845 . . . . 40.00

Plate, 10¼" d., Neapolitan patt., red, Dimmock, ca. 1835 . . . . 65.00

Plate, 10¼" d., Quadrupeds series, dark blue, ca. 1830's (stains, wear) 126.50

Plate, 10½" d., Bean & Bird patt., black, B.W. Co., ca. 1880 . . . . 40.00

Plate, 10½" d., Millenium patt., dark brown, Ralph Stevenson & Son, ca. 1830's 67.50

Plate, 10½" d., Rhone Scenery patt., blue, T.J. & J. Mayer 60.00

Platter, 12" l., octagonal, Geneva patt., brown, J. Heath, ca. 1845 . . 80.00

Platter, 13" l., Bosphorus patt., brown, J. Marshall, ca. 1854 . . . . . 89.00

Platter, 13¾" l., oval, Indus patt., brown, Ridgway, ca. 1877 . . . . 80.00

Platter, 17 1/8" l., oval, Parma patt., blue, Wedgwood & Co., mid-19th c. 110.00

Platter, 20¼" l., shaped oblong form w/cut corners, Windsor Ware patt., brown w/polychrome trim, Johnson Bros., early 20th c. 125.00

Platter, 21" l., molded well & tree, grey floral design, Sydenham patt., w/English registry mark (minor wear, flakes on table ring) 115.00

Sauce tureen, cover & undertray, Naples Shield patt., black, 3 pcs. 110.00

Soup plate w/flanged rim, a landscape design featuring a lady in a boat w/others on shore, marked on the back "Lady of the Lake - Careys," blue, Thomas & John Carey, ca. 1823-42, 9 7/8" d. 85.00

Soup tureen, cover, underplate & ladle, Rural Scenery patt., blue, ca. 1840, some chips, overall 11½" h., 4 pcs. (ILLUS.) 1,650.00

Toothbrush holder, cov., Priory patt., blue, John Alcock, ca. 1860 . . . . 95.00

Early Staffordshire Tray

Tray, oval w/openwork chain border, the center w/a large bouquet of flowers in an urn, blue, ca. 1830, 8¾ x 10 5/8" (ILLUS.) 440.00

Vegetable bowl, open, oval, Castle Scenery patt., brown, J. Furnival, ca. 1855, 10¾" l. 50.00

Vegetable bowl, open, oval, Holy Bible - Mt. Lebanon patt., brown, J. & J. Jackson, ca. 1835, 10½" l. 65.00

Vegetable dish, cov., oblong, Elite patt., brown, Henry Alcock, ca. 1890, 11" l. 85.00

Vegetable dish, cov., octagonal, Washington Vase patt., light blue, Podmore, Walker & Co., ca. 1840's 125.00

Vegetable dish, cov., square, Wild Rose patt., blue, J. Meir, ca. 1840 . . . . 325.00

Waste bowl, spread-winged American eagle resting on a large shield, a landscape in the distant background, dark blue, ca. 1830's, 6¼" d., 3½" h. (chips on base & foot) 880.00

STANGL BIRDS

Broadtail Hummingbird

Johann Martin Stangl, who first came to work for the Fulper Pottery in 1910 as a ceramic chemist and plant superintendent, acquired a financial interest and became president of the company in 1926. The name of the firm was changed to Stangl Pottery in 1929 and at that time much of the production was devoted to a high grade dinnerware to enable the company to survive the Depression years. Around 1940 a very limited edition of porcelain birds, patterned after the illustrations in John James Audubon's "Birds of America," was issued. Stangl subsequently began production of less expensive ceramic birds and these proved to be popular during the war years, 1940-46. Each bird was handpainted and each was well marked with impressed, painted or stamped numerals which indicated the species and the size. Collectors are now seeking these ceramic birds which we list below.

Bird of Paradise, No. 3408, 5½" h... $87.50
Blackpoll Warbler, No. 3810 .... 160.00
Bluebird, No. 3276, 5" h............. `85.00
Bluebird (Double), No. 3276-D,
    8½" h...................175.00 to 195.00
Blue Jay, No. 3716, 10¼" 525.00
Broadtail Hummingbird, No. 3626,
    6" h. (ILLUS.) 245.00
Cardinal, No. 3444, 6½" h.......... 82.50
Cerulean Warbler, No. 3456,
    4¼" h........................... 80.00
Cockatoo, No. 3405, 6" h.......... 60.00
Cockatoo, medium, No. 3580,
    8 7/8" h. ....125.00 to 150.00
Grey Cardinal, No. 3596, 4¾" h. ... 75.00
Group of Chickadees, No. 3581,
    5½ x 8½"..............175.00 to 200.00
Hen, No. 3446, 7" h............... 145.00
Hen Pheasant, No. 3491,
    6¼ x 11"..............175.00 to 200.00
Kentucky Warbler, No. 3598, 3" h. .. 45.00
Key West Quail Dove, No. 3454,
    9" h..................200.00 to 225.00
Love Bird, No. 3400, 4" h.......... 48.00
Magnolia Warbler, No. 3925,
    5¼" h. 400.00

Nuthatch, No. 3593, 2½" h. 38.00
Oriole, No. 3402, 3¼" h. 58.00
Pair of Cockatoos, No. 3405-D,
    9½" h..................100.00 to 125.00
Pair of Kingfishers, No. 3406-D,
    5" h....................150.00 to 175.00
Pair of Orioles, No. 3402-D,
    5½" h....................... 90.00
Pair of Redstarts, No. 3490-D,
    9" h....................150.00 to 175.00
Pair of Wrens, No. 3401-D, 8" h..... 98.00
Parula Warbler, No. 3583, 4¼" h. .. 55.00
Pheasants, cock & hen, No. 3491 &
    No. 3492, pr. 425.00
Red-Headed Woodpecker, No. 3751-S,
    6¼" h..................225.00 to 250.00
Rooster, grey, No. 3445, 9" h. 150.00
Titmouse, No. 3592, 2½" h. ..60.00 to 80.00
Wilson Warbler, No. 3597, 3½" h. .. 60.00
Yellow Warbler, No. 3447,
    5" h....................75.00 to 100.00

STONEWARE

Stoneware Butter Crock

Stoneware is essentially a vitreous pottery, impervious to water even in its unglazed state, that has been produced by potteries all over the world for centuries. Utilitarian wares such as crocks, jugs, churns and the like, were ous potteries that sprang into existence in the United States during the 19th century. These items were often enhanced by the application of a cobalt blue oxide decoration. In addition to the coarse, primarily salt-glazed stonewares, there are other categories of stoneware known by such special names as basalt, jasper and others.

Batter jug, slightly ovoid, brushed
    cobalt blue floral decoration, impressed label "Cowden & Wilcox, Harrisburg, Pa.," wire bail handle w/wooden handgrip, late 19th c., 8 5/8" h. (tin lid & spout cap missing, minor short firing hairline in base) $2,050.00
Butter crock, cov., wide short cylindrical form w/relief-molded

grapevine design highlighted in cobalt blue around the sides & on the flat cover, fine hairline in base & cover, two shallow flakes in cover, ca. 1880's, 8" d., 4½" h. (ILLUS.) 137.50

Butter crock, wide short cylindrical form w/molded rim & eared handles, slip-quilled cobalt blue elongated bird around one side, impressed label "D.P. Hobart, Agent 1½ Williamsport, Pa." highlighted in blue, late 19th c., 10¼" d., 5½" h. (minor edge chips) 797.50

Crock, cylindrical w/molded rim & eared handles, slip-quilled cobalt blue large crosshatched blossom on a short stem w/four long, rounded leaves, a "2" below the rim, impressed label "J. Burger, Rochester, N.Y.," 19th c., 2 gal., 9" h. 400.00

Rare Crock with Landscape Scene

Crock, cylindrical w/heavy molded rim & eared handles, brushed cobalt blue landscape of a two-story house w/large trees between two picket fences, stamped "Seymour and Bosworth, Hartford, Conn. No. 3," 1873-90, 3 gal., 10 3/8" h. (ILLUS.) 4,620.00

Crock, cylindrical w/eared handles, cobalt blue slip-quilled inscription running vertically up the side & reading "M.W. Sackett - No. 124 Water St. - Meadville, Pa. 5," 5 gal., 12¾" h. (hairline in back & bottom, minor edge chips) 350.00

Jar, ovoid w/wide flat slightly misshapen rim, eared handles, incised neck bands, incised name "Paul Cushman," Albany, New York, early 19th c., 8½" h. 165.00

Jar, ovoid w/wide flat rim & eared handles, brushed cobalt blue large double leaf design below the impressed mark "C. Boynton &

Co. Troy," New York, 1826-29, 10¾" h. (small chips) 250.00

Jar, ovoid w/applied shoulder handles, incised lines at neck, brushed cobalt blue floral decoration on sides, minor rim flakes, 14½" h. 400.00

Jar, tall cylindrical body tapering to a flat mouth, incised in script "Hanna & Co. - Snuff" & impressed "4," all washed in blue, 4 gal., 15¼" h. 300.00

Jar, ovoid, small molded mouth flanked by loop handles, stenciled cobalt blue label "W.H. Clark, Maker, Swan, O.," impressed "5," 19th c., 5 gal., 17¾" h. 250.00

Jug, ovoid, small molded lip, rounded strap handle on shoulder, 7½" h. 70.00

Jug, slightly ovoid, impressed label "C. Crolius Manufacturer, Manhattan Mills, New York," brushed cobalt blue at label & handle, tooled neck, 11 3/8" h. (firing crack at top of handle) 700.00

Jug, ovoid, impressed label "Thompson & Co., Gardiner," brushed cobalt blue at base of handle, 11½" h. 105.00

Jug, ovoid, simple brushed cobalt blue design, impressed mark "N.White, Utica," New York, 1838-49, 11½" h. (stains, minor chips) 200.00

Jug, ovoid, brushed cobalt blue stylized blossom on a leafy stem, impressed "H.Purdy 2," Mogadore, Ohio, 1838-ca. 1850, 2 gal., 13¼" h. 522.50

Jug, ovoid body tapering sharply to the base & narrow top, brushed cobalt blue "2" at the top, 2 gal., 13¼" h. (long shallow chip on lip) 236.50

Jug, very ovoid body, small arched loop handle at the molded neck, two-tone brown & grey salt glaze w/tooled lines & ribbed handle, impressed "Boston," attributed to Frederick Carpenter, early 19th c., 14½" h. 698.50

Jug, ovoid, impressed mark "C. Boynton" inside stylized urn highlighted in cobalt blue, probably by C. Boynton & Co., Troy, New York, ca. 1860-65, 15½" h. 412.50

Jug, ovoid, brushed cobalt blue cluster of tall-stemmed flowers w/ball-shaped blossoms up the front, impressed mark "W.E. Welding, Brantford 3," Ontario, Canada, 1873-94, 3 gal., 16¼" h. 385.00

"Grotesque" Stoneware Jug

Jug, ovoid w/large loop handles at the shoulder, small mouth, side molded w/grotesque face, impressed mark at base, Burton Craig, Lincoln County, North Carolina, 16½" h. (ILLUS.) 330.00

Jug, semi-ovoid, brushed cobalt blue "1837" within crossed fronds, impressed "New York Stoneware Co., Edward, NY," 4 gal., 19" h. . . 385.00

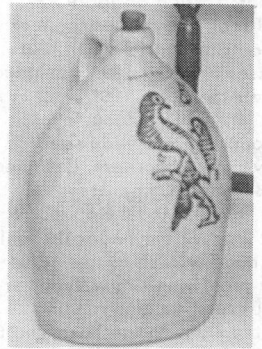

Decorated Stoneware Jug

Jug, semi-ovoid, slip-quilled cobalt blue pair of polka dot birds, perched on a branch one above the other & each looking over its shoulder toward the other, & below a "5," impressed "Penn Yan," New York, minor wear, short hairlines, mid-19th c., 5 gal., 18½" h. (ILLUS.) 2,600.00

Model of a dog, seated Spaniel on an oblong base, molded fur & facial details trimmed w/green & green spots on the body, Ohio, 19th c., 6¼" h. (ILLUS. top next column) 770.00

Pitcher, 8¾" h., slightly bulbous base, collared neck w/pinched spout, brushed cobalt blue floral decoration (chips on base) 600.00

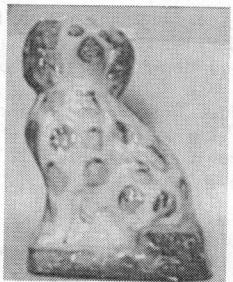

Stoneware Dog

Pitcher, 9" h., globular w/low cylindrical neck & pinched spout, two-tone brown glaze, applied hunt scenes on body, neck w/sgraffito inscription "James N. Wells, 38 Hudson Street" (edge wear & chips, short internal hairline) 1,700.00

Pitcher, 10¼" h., tapering cylindrical body w/pinched rim spout & applied strap handle, brushed cobalt blue wavy stripes down the sides (small edge chips) 2,750.00

Pitcher, 11¼" h., cylindrical base below a waisted midsection & flaring top, impressed label "E. Norton & Co., Bennington, Vt.," dark brown Albany slip 275.00

Pitcher, 13" h., slightly ovoid base w/wide neck w/pinched spout, brushed cobalt blue floral decoration, impressed "2 (slight hairline in rim near handle) 765.00

Preserving jar, semi-ovoid, stenciled cobalt blue marking "Graham & Stone Gen. Merchandise Jackson C.N. W. VA," ca. 1870-90, ½ gal., 7½" h. 198.00

Preserving jar, semi-ovoid, stenciled cobalt blue marking "Bayles McCarthey & Co. Louisville," ca. 1870-80, ½ gal., 7 7/8" h. (old chip on side of lip) 198.00

Preserving jar w/narrow mouth, upright barrel-form w/four molded bands decorated in blue, 8" h. (chip on base) 275.00

Preserving jar, semi-ovoid, stenciled cobalt blue marking "Jas. Benjamin, Wholesale Stoneware Depot No. 14, Water St. Cincinnati, O.," ca. 1870-90, ½ gal., 8 1/8" h. 220.00

Preserving jar, cylindrical, stenciled cobalt blue marking "Excelsior Works, Isaac Hewitt, Jr., Rices Landing, PA," ca. 1870-90, ½ gal., 8 3/8" h. 495.00

Preserving jar, straight sides, eared handles, brushed cobalt blue floral decoration, impressed label "Cowden & Wilcox, Harrisburg, Pa.," 9½" h. (small chips) 250.00

Preserving jar, slightly ovoid, rolled
rim, cobalt blue stenciled label
"Jas. Hamilton & Co, Greensboro,
Pa." w/rose, 10" h. 225.00
String holder, hollow beehive shape,
hole in side near bottom for string
exit, brown Albany glaze, 4¾" d.
at base, 6½" h. 130.00

TECO POTTERY

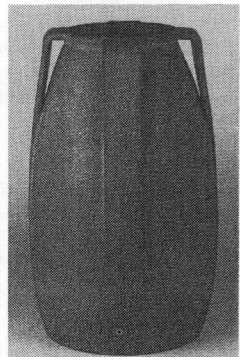

Large Teco Vase

*Teco Pottery was actually the line of art
pottery introduced by the American Terra
Cotta and Ceramic Company of Terra Cotta
(Crystal Lake), Illinois in 1902. Founded by
William D. Gates in 1881, American Terra
Cotta originally produced only bricks and
drain tile. Because of superior facilities for experimentation, including a chemical laboratory, the company was able to develop an art
pottery line, favoring a matte green glaze in
the earlier years but eventually achieving a
wide range of colors including a metallic lustre glaze and a crystalline glaze. Though some
hand-thrown pottery was made, Gates favored a molded ware because it was less expensive to produce. By 1923, Teco Pottery
was no longer being made and in 1930 American Terra Cotta and Ceramic Company was
sold. A recently published book on the topic
is* Teco: Art Pottery of the Prairie School, *by
Sharon S. Darling (Erie Art Museum, 1990).*

Bowl, 7" d., 2½" h., squatty
w/rolled rim, smooth matte
green glaze, die-stamped mark,
No. 80 . . . . $440.00
Coaster, Chicago Cubs "C" within a
circle logo against an oatmeal
ground, impressed mark,
4¼" d. 137.50
Stein, slightly tapering cylindrical
form w/heavy molded bands &
stylized cattails around the
sides, heavy strap handle, smooth

matte green glaze, die-stamped
mark, Model No. 298, 5" d., 6" h.
(manufacturing line through
length of handle) 247.50
Vase, 3½" h., 3¾" d., squatty bul-
bous body raised on three small
curved pad feet, tapering to a
wide, low neck, Aventurine glaze
in black, orange & yellow crystal-
line, die-stamped mark 137.50
Vase, 5" h., 3" d., simple ovoid
body w/small molded mouth, unusual smooth matte brown glaze,
die-stamped mark 275.00
Vase, 5¼" h., 3" d., ovoid body
tapering to a short cylindrical
neck flanked by angled handles
continuing down to form buttresses, smooth matte green glaze,
die-stamped mark 495.00
Vase, 5¾" h., 3" d., tall ovoid body
divided into four sections by
squared buttresses up the sides,
smooth green glaze, numbered
"428," faint mark 825.00
Vase, 9" h., gourd-like body
w/three bulbous protrusions &
three openwork clover-shaped
openings, resting on three extended feet, the cylindrical neck
w/trefoil rim, matte green glaze,
impressed "TECO - 115," designed
by Fritz Albert, ca. 1901 . . . . 880.00
Vase, 11" h., wide bulbous ovoid
base tapering to a wide squared
neck w/peaked corners, designed
by W.B. Mundie, impressed
"TECO" twice, Model No. 268 . . . .2,420.00
Vase, 12" h., wide cylindrical shouldered body w/a short neck &
widely projecting rim w/four vertical buttress handles running
down the sides to the base, matte
green glaze, impressed "265
TECO" twice, designed by Max
Dunning 3,300.00
Vase, 14" h., bottle-form w/tall
slender neck w/an everted
quatrefoil rim, w/four long leaf-
form handles from the neck down
the sides to the base, pale matte
green glaze, designed by Fritz Albert, impressed "220 TECO" 3,850.00
Vase, floor-type, 20 5/8" h.,
8 5/8" d., tall elongated ovoid
body w/thin rolled rim continuing
into four squared strap handles
down the sides, matte green
glaze, impressed mark, ca. 1906,
minor handle nicks, unobtrusive
base chip (ILLUS.) 7,150.00
Wall pocket, flattened & squared
top section w/molded roundels
above a round, swelled bottom

Teco Wall Pocket

section w/a molded swastika design, matte green glaze, impressed mark, 5¼" w., 6½" h. (ILLUS.) 385.00

TEPLITZ - AMPHORA

Teplitz Wall Plaque

These wares were produced in numerous potteries in the vicinity of Teplitz in the Bohemian area of what is now Czechoslovakia during the late 19th and into the 20th century. Vases and figures, of varying quality, were the primary products of such firms as Riessner & Kessel (Amphora), Ernst Wahliss and Alfred Stellmacher. Although originally rather low-priced items, today collectors are searching out the best marked examples and prices are soaring.

Basket, two arched handles trimmed w/blue "jewels" meet at the top above the squatty bulbous body molded w/green leaves & applied w/four clusters of burnished gold grapes, heavy gold trim on a cobalt blue ground, iridized finish, Amphora mark, 7¾" h. $475.00

Centerpiece, figural, designed as three children w/baskets deco-

rated in soft green & brown tones, impressed Amphora marks, 9" h. 605.00

Ewer, Art Nouveau style w/flower-form neck & double-loop handle, cream ground decorated w/green leaves & gold iridescence, Amphora mark, 14" h. 495.00

Plaque, wall-type, rectangular w/'eared' upper corners & rounded lower corners, a molded framework around a bisque low-relief panel w/portraits of a young couple holding a musical score & decorated in earthtones, impressed "Made in Austria - Ernst Wahliss - Turn - Wien - 224," 18 x 21" (ILLUS.) 2,420.00

Vase, 5" h., Symbolist style, bulbous ovoid body w/molded whiplash handles, decorated w/a female portrait on one side w/a forest background above a lower border of blossoms, in shades of pale blue, purple, mauve & green trimmed in gilt & raised gold, impressed & printed Amphora marks, ca. 1900 . . . . 1,540.00

Vase, 6 1/8" h., ovoid body w/short pierced neck & handles, decorated w/the bust of a maiden within a bower of stylized blossoms & leafage w/a misty forest scene in the distance, in shades of pink, green, purple & blue, heightened in gilt, printed factory marks, ca. 1900 . . . . 3,190.00

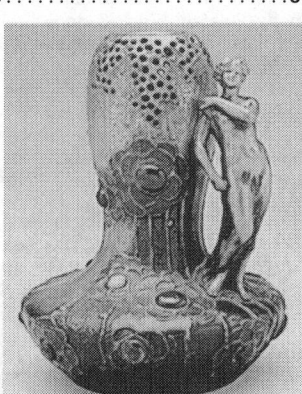

Figural Amphora Vase

Vase, 10½" h., figural, the squatty bulbous base below a wide shoulder to the tall swelling cylindrical neck w/a full figural young maiden standing beside it, molded blossoms & vines w/jeweled trim, marked "Amphora - Austria - 8168" (ILLUS.) 880.00

Vase, 10 7/8" h., cylindrical body expanding to bulbous shoulders molded w/integral handles, decorated w/a bust of a maiden in exotic costume within a mystical forest, in shades of purple, green, blue, rose & brown, heightened in gilt, printed factory marks, ca. 1900 . . . . .3,575.00

TERRA COTTA

Terra Cotta Figure Group

This is redware or reddish stoneware, usually unglazed. All kinds of utilitarian objects have been made for centuries as have statuettes and large architectural pieces.

Amphora, Attic-Style, the baluster-form body painted black & decorated in orange & black on the front w/a classically draped seated maiden tending a group of frolicking putti, the scene beneath a leaf & berried vine & a border of palmettes around the shoulder & above a Greek key band & wide border of vertical lappets around the lower body, the sides decorated w/large anthemion designs below loop handles, the trumpet-shaped neck w/a wide mouth painted w/a tongue-and-dart band & affixed at each side w/a loop handle, impressed "P.Ipsen kjobenhave Eneret" & numeral "91," ca. 1875, 14 1/16" h. (some wear on mouth) $3,025.00

Bust of the young Charles X, depicted when he was the Comte D'Artois, inscribed "Comte D'Artois," signed "Fernand...," Joseph Fernande, France, 19th c., 10" h. . . .1,320.00

Figure group, modeled in the 18th century taste as two Oriental children, the boy standing & about to beat the drum, the girl seated & also holding a drumstick, end of one stick missing, on a circular base, France, 13¾" h. (ILLUS.) . . .4,125.00

Model of a Bulldog, original polychrome paint, glass eyes, 10" 150.00

Urns on stands, leaf- and pear-carved rim above a floral & foliate swagged body, ending in a leaf tipped & masked base, flanked by scrolled & rope-like ringed handles, base further decorated w/foliate swags & masks, inscribed "RAFFAELLO AGRESTI ITALIA," 37" h., pr. 12,100.00

TIFFANY POTTERY

Tiffany Pottery Vases

In 1902 Louis C. Tiffany expanded Tiffany Studios to include ceramics, enamels, gold, silver and gemstones. Tiffany pottery was usually molded rather than wheel-thrown, but it was carefully finished by hand. A limited amount was produced until about 1914. It is scarce.

Bowl-vase, squatty bulbous body on a narrow footring, tapering at the top to a molded ring neck w/flat rim, decorated w/a raised white dot pattern of fanciful rampant lions & stylized sunflowers between geometric borders on a shaded dark green & blue ground, ca. 1910, incised "LCT," 6½" h. (ILLUS. left) $2,200.00

Compote, open, 6¾" h., the circular base modeled as lily pads supporting stems w/climbing frogs, the bowl formed by flowering lotus blossoms, all w/a mottled caramel & white glaze, incised w/the "LCT" monogram 11,000.00

Pitcher, 10½" h., 5" d., cylindrical w/flat disc base, embossed w/a fruit design, clear green glaze, marked "LCT" (restoration to foot) 522.50

Squatty Tiffany Vase

Vase, 7" h., squatty ovoid body on a wide footring, the sides tapering to a wide flat rim, molded w/ribs of stylized vegetal designs, glazed in cream & deep olive green, incised "LCT" (ILLUS.) 2,420.00

Vase, 8¼" h., irregular ovoid body molded as a cluster of milkweed pods, the stems incurving & pierced at the top, glazed in matte pale yellowish green, inscribed "LCT," ca. 1910 (chip at base)........................4,400.00

Vase, 9¾" h., cylindrical w/swelled upper section w/a wide, flat rim, molded in low-relief w/clusters of magnolia blossoms & leafage in green & black against a mottled brown ground, inscribed "LCT" & "P1217 L.C.T. - L.C.Tiffany Favrile Pottery" & in oxide "EL," three hairlines at rim (ILLUS. right) 1,430.00

Vase, 14½" h., flaring cylindrical body, mottled dark blue & mustard glaze, base inscribed "P1077 L.C. Tiffany - Favrile Pottery" & incised interlaced initials "LCT" 1,870.00

TILES

Tiles have been made by potteries in the United States and abroad for many years. Apart from small tea tiles used on tables, there are also decorative tiles for fireplaces, floors and walls and this is where present collector interest lies, especially in the late 19th century American-made art pottery tiles.

American Encaustic Tiling Company (Zanesville, Ohio), decorated w/a photograph-like bust portrait of President Grant, clear peacock green glaze, framed, tile 6" sq. (small chips to corners) $302.50

American Encaustic Tiling Company,

a harvest scene w/a Grecian youth, nude but for a lap drapery, seated on the left w/his dog & holding a bowl in one hand, two putti picking & carrying fruits on the right, light green glossy glaze, artist-signed, marked, framed, 11½ x 17½" (shallow scratch across lower corner) 1,540.00

Arts & Crafts style, grotesque-type, molded in relief w/a stylized grinning satyr mask, heavily curdled matte brown & green glaze, attributed to Wheatley Pottery Company, Cincinnati, Ohio, 8" sq. (minor nick on front) 330.00

Barratt Portrait Tile

Barratt (J.H.) & Co. (Staffordshire, England), lifelike bust portrait of Theodore Roosevelt in tones of grey, black & white, by George Cartlidge, signed & marked, in wide, flat oak frame, 5¾ x 8¾" (ILLUS.)...................... 385.00

Batchelder, Ernest A. (Los Angeles, California), decorated w/an incised landscape of a large tree beside a river, dead-matte blue glaze over a bisque body, die-stamped & ink marks, 8" sq. 220.00

Beaver Falls Art Tile Company (Beaver Falls, Pennsylvania), a bust portrait of George Washington & a facing one of Martha Washington, clear taupe glaze, by Isaac Broome, impressed mark, pair framed together, each 6" sq. 715.00

California Faience Company, cloisonne'-style decoration of a three-masted galleon w/unfurled sails, glossy & matte glazes in blues & browns, marked, 5½" sq. 275.00

DeMorgan, William, fifteen-tile frieze, depicts an ancient warship under sail in mineral tones of Persian blue, yellow & black, back w/raised mark "Poole - Dorsett," framed, tiles 8 x 20"...........1,430.00

Fine Art Ceramic Company (Indianapolis, Indiana), decorated w/a lifelike bust portrait of Abraham Lincoln in black & white, designed by George Cartlidge, die-stamped & artist-signed, framed, overall 5½ x 8¾".................... 385.00

Grueby Faience & Tile Company, cloisonne'-style decoration of a brown & ochre turtle below a band of spade-shaped green leaves all on a mottled brown ground, signed, framed, 6" sq. ... 605.00

Grueby Faience Scenic Tile

Grueby Faience & Tile Company, scene of La Belle Chocolatiere, the Baker's Chocolate lady, carrying a serving tray, glazed in blue, white, yellow, green & lavender against a tan ground, artist-initialed "A.F." & impressed "Grueby Tile Boston," chip at side, 6¼" sq. (ILLUS.) 357.50

Low (J. & G.) Art Tile Works (Chelsea, Massachusetts), bust portrait of Gallileo wearing a hat & pointing skyward, impressed along the top "Vox Stellarum," framed, marked, 6" sq................... 220.00

Low (J. & G.) Art Tile Works, relief molded design of a standing monk looking to the side & holding a rosary, titled at the top "Ave Maria," glossy peacock blue glaze, artist-signed, marked, framed, 6¾ x 17¼" 990.00

Marblehead Pottery (Marblehead, Massachusetts), a deep brown border of long dashes on the green ground, a solid dark brown edge band, matte glaze, impressed mark, 6" sq. (minor nicks) 660.00

Mintons China Works (Stoke-on-Trent, Staffordshire, England), decorated w/a brown & pale blue transfer-printed scene of cows, signed, framed, tile 8" sq. 60.50

North Dakota School of Mines (Grand Forks, North Dakota), incised w/a scene of oxen pulling a covered wagon, matte green & brown glaze, Flora Huckfield, stamped mark & incised artist's mark, 5" d..................... 247.50

Pardee Works (Perth Amboy, New Jersey), impressed design of a stylized cat & leaf sprig in beige against a blue ground, marked, 4¼" sq. (minor corner nick) 220.00

Paul Revere Pottery (Boston, Massachusetts), decorated w/an incised Boston street scene in pink, blue, brown, white & grey w/black outlines, a large building in foreground, inscribed "Corner North Bennet & Salem Streets," signed "51.5.11. SEG RB," 3¾" sq. 385.00

Pilkington's Tiles, Ltd. (England), incised & decorated w/the figure of a kneeling Middle Eastern princess in blue & red against a green floral ground, wide black wood frame, oval mark, 5½ x 11½" ... 467.50

Rookwood Pottery Company (Cincinnati, Ohio), two rectangular tiles painted w/rooks perched & alighting on pine boughs, in black, grey & green against a yellow ochre ground, decorated by Albert Valentien, dated 1901, framed, each 8¾ x 10½", pr. 6,600.00

Rozenberg Den Haag (Holland), canal scene, The Hague, the picture composed of six tiles, each signed verso, image signed "F. Klinkeobern(?)," framed, late 19th c., image 12 x 18".................. 660.00

Salvador Dali-designed, each w/modernistic colorful designs representing "Life," "Death," "Love," "Music," "War" & "Peace," accompanied by informative papers, each 7½" sq., set of 6 ... 495.00

Trent Tile Company (Trenton, New Jersey), profile head portrait of a young woman wearing a low-brimmed hat, clear caramel glaze, marked, artist-signed, framed, tile 4¼" sq. (minor nicks to high points) 110.00

Wedgwood, Josiah (England), "Fairyland Lustre," a fantastical landscape scene of nymphs & gnomes by the banks of a river in a forest, polychrome w/gilt trim, framed, 4¼ x 10" 2,640.00

Weller Pottery (Zanesville, Ohio), four-tile landscape scene w/elephants in a river w/jungle in the background, heavy polychrome slip-glazing, decorated by Mae Timberlake, framed, ca. 1925, 8½" sq. (few edge nicks) ..3,080.00

TOBY MUGS & JUGS

Ralph Wood-Type Toby

The Toby is a figural jug or mug usually delineating a robust, genial drinking man. The name has been used in England since the mid-18th century. Copies of the English mugs and jugs were made in America.

For listings of related Character Jugs see DOULTON & ROYAL DOULTON, under Ceramics.

Evans (Alfred) Toby, Napoleon, white background w/colored decoration, marked "Napoleon Jug - Alfred Evans, Phila. Pa.," 9¾" h. (some wear & crazing) $247.50

Melba Ware Toby, Henry VIII seated, H. Wains & Sons, Ltd., England, after 1951 . . . . 99.00

Prattware Toby, seated Mr. Toby wearing a brown tricorn hat above his brown hair & eyebrows, a streaky teal blue coat, blue waistcoat, ochre breeches & brown shoes, supporting on his lap a blue-spotted jug & seated on a brown chair w/a fishscale patterned handle, a pipe between his feet on the stepped & chamfered rectangular base, the whole covered in a speckly blue glaze, England, 1790-1800, 7 9/16" h. 460.00

Staffordshire creamware Toby, seated Mr. Toby wearing a brown tricorn hat over his light brown hair & face, a blue coat, white waistcoat, yellow breeches & brown shoes, holding in his right hand a beaker, in his left a light brown jug of ale, seated on a brown chair above a brown chamfered rectangular base, England, ca. 1780, 6 3/8" h. (hat & right wrist repaired, small chips on base) 575.00

Staffordshire creamware Toby, seated Mr. Toby wearing a brown tricorn hat on his grey hair, a green-washed coat, very pale green waistcoat & breeches & brown shoes, holding a pale manganese jug in his left hand, raising a beaker in his right, seated on a pale manganese chair above a chamfered rectangular base, England, ca. 1780, 6 7/16" h. (right hand restored) 575.00

Staffordshire creamware Toby, Ralph Wood-type, seated Mr. Toby wearing a black tricorn hat, dark blue coat & yellow breeches, holding a frothing jug of ale & a beaker, a pipe between his feet, ca. 1780, pipe stem broken, 9¼" h. (ILLUS.) 1,100.00

Early Creamware Toby

Staffordshire creamware Toby, seated Mr. Toby wearing a dark brown tricorn, amber coat & shoes & mustard yellow breeches, holding a foaming jug of ale, seated on a scroll-footed chair above a rectangular base w/cut corners, ca. 1820, restored hat chips, shallow chip & star crack on base, 9½" h. (ILLUS.) 345.00

Staffordshire creamware "Thin Man" Toby, seated man wearing a brown tricorn hat on his long brown hair, a white coat w/green cuffs & sprinkles of brown on his sleeves, a green waistcoat & brown breeches, smoking a pipe & holding a brown slip-glazed jug, seated on a green-washed & brown-sprinkled chair, brown-shod feet, on a brown-fronted base, England, ca. 1780, 9 5/8" h. (hat restored, star crack in back, various repairs, cracks & regluing) 690.00

Staffordshire pearlware "Rodney's Sailor" or "Planter" Toby, the seated man wearing a brown flattened tricorn hat on his grey hair, a green waistcoat, manganese brown jacket, trousers & shoes,

holding a beaker in his right hand
& a green jug in his left supported
on a manganese chest beneath
his green chair, a loop handle issuing from its back, on a green-
washed base molded w/rocks
& grasses, England 1775-85,
11 11/16" h. (repaired hat, abrasions, chip on back edge) 805.00
Staffordshire pearlware "Squire"
Toby, seated man wearing a
brown tricorn hat on his long
brown hair, a blue coat over a
white waistcoat & breeches &
blue-tied brown shoes, holding a
foaming brown jug in his right
hand, smoking a long-stemmed
brown pipe in his left hand, seated on a green-washed corner
chair issuing an ear-shaped handle up to the back of his head, inscribed on back "I.Hardin," the
arrowhead-shaped base w/an
underglaze-blue trellis diaper border, England, 1790-1800, 11" h.
(repaired chips, tips of finger &
jug handle repaired, repaired pipe
& back handle, base w/hairline
crack, chips & reduced) 805.00
Staffordshire pearlware Toby, miniature, seated rotund man wearing
tricorn, polychrome enamel,
3¾" h. (chips on hat rim) 165.00
Staffordshire Toby, seated Mr. Toby
wearing tricornered hat, decorated in underglaze blue & poly-
chrome enamel, 8½" h. 440.00
Staffordshire Toby, seated Mr.
Toby holding a pitcher & cup &
decorated w/orange, yellow,
black & grey, unmarked, 19th c.,
9½" h. 330.00
Staffordshire yellowware Toby, seat-
ed man holding a jug in one
hand, white slip decorated in
black, tan, brown & blue glaze,
10¼" h. (old professional re-
pair) 385.00
Syracuse China Toby, Herbert
Hoover, ca. 1928 . . . . 115.00

VAN BRIGGLE

*The Van Briggle Pottery was established
by Artus Van Briggle, who formerly worked
for Rookwood Pottery, in Colorado Springs,
Colorado, at the turn of the century. He died
in 1904 but the pottery was carried on by his
widow and others. From 1900 until 1920, the
pieces were dated. It remains in production
today, specializing in Art Pottery.*

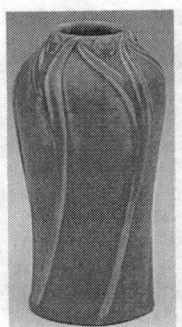

Van Briggle Vase

Book ends, model of an owl,
spread-winged stylized bird
w/bluish green glaze, impressed
mark, 5" h., pr. $247.50
Book ends, model of a peacock,
Persian Rose glaze, ca. 1920,
pr. 150.00
Book ends, model of a polar bear,
Persian Rose glaze, 5½" w.,
5" h., pr. 275.00
Bowl, 7" d., 3½" h., rounded base,
flat shoulder decorated w/stylized
leaves, Shape No. 84, mottled
robin's-egg blue glaze, dated
1906 . . . . 330.00
Bowl, 8" d., 3½" h., squatty bulbous
shape tapering to a closed rim,
molded around the rim w/scroll-
ing stylized leaves, each centering
a cabochon, Shape No. 22, matte
green glaze, incised mark, 1902. .1,375.00
Candlestick, hexagonal, dark purple
glaze, ca. late 1920's, 10" h. 125.00
Console bowl & flower frog, the
wide shell-shaped bowl on flattened knobby feet, the rim of the
bowl molded w/the large figure
of a reclining mermaid, the opposite inside rim molded w/swim-
ming fish, a shell-shaped flower
frog in the center, matte burgundy & green glaze, marked "VAN
BRIGGLE - Colo Spgs - 25," ca.
1925, 8 x 14½", 2 pcs. 715.00
Figure of a nude seated girl holding
a large seashell in her lap, on a
rounded base, Persian Rose glaze,
incised mark, 7" h. 247.50
Flower frog, model of a scarab,
dark blue & turquoise glaze 75.00
Incense burner, figural, a teardrop-
form molded in relief at the front
w/the seated figure of a grotesque gnome, his arms wrapped
around his legs pulled up to his
body, his small mouth forming the
smoke opening, light & dark blue
matte glaze, beige clay showing

through, unmarked, ca. 1914,
4½" w., 4¼" h. 247.50
Model of a conch shell, Turquoise
Ming glaze, 5¾ x 12" 105.00
Mug, slightly rounded cylindrical
body w/angled handle, smooth
matte green glaze, Shape
No. 27B, 1902, 5¼" d., 5" h. 302.50
Night light, model of a large owl
w/the lower body hollowed out to
hold a bulb, small loop handle at
the back, light refracting glass
eyes, turquoise blue matte glaze,
unsigned, 8½" h. 412.50
Plate, 8¼" d., molded w/swirled
poppy blossoms & leaves, organic
matte blue glaze against a dark
burgundy ground, Shape No. 12,
1908-11 . . . . 440.00
Plates, 6" d., each molded around
the rim w/a band of elongated
heart-shaped leaves, matte glaze,
four in deep green, one in brown,
Shape No. 13, 1907-11, set of 5 . . . 825.00
Vase, 3¾" h., 4¾" d., squatty bulbous form tapering to a flat molded mouth, decorated w/molded
crocus blossoms in a band around
the shoulder, the slender stems
going down the sides, matte
ochre glaze, Shape No. 145, in-
cised mark & "1903 - 145 - III" 880.00
Vase, 5½" h., 6" d., bulbous spherical body tapering to a short, flat
neck, molded around the lower
half w/a band of stylized lotus
blossoms on slender stems, matte
deep bluish green glaze, Shape
No. 829, incised mark, dated
1914 . . . . 522.50
Vase, 6" h., expanding cylindrical
body molded w/five stylized flowers at the shoulder, caramel glaze
w/moss green mottling, Shape
No. 836, incised mark, dated 1913
(ILLUS.) 467.50
Vase, 6¾" h., 3¼" d., ovoid body
tapering to a tall cylindrical
neck, molded around the middle
w/paired crescent-shaped leaves
on slender stems continuing up to
small daisy-like blossoms around
the rim, robin's-egg blue glaze,
ink mark, Shape No. 921,
1908-11 . . . . 467.50
Vase, 7" h., 3¾" d., ovoid body
tapering to a short neck molded
on each side w/a dragonfly, a
slender band dividing the sides
into two segments, light blue
glaze, Shape No. 489, incised
mark, dated 1907 . . . . 660.00
Vase, 9½" h., "Lorelei," ovoid body
modeled w/the figure of a wom-

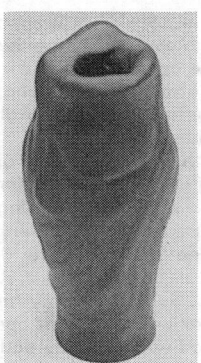

Van Briggle "Lorelei" Vase

an, Persian Rose glaze, impressed
"AA - Van Briggle - Colo. Spgs."
(ILLUS.) 467.50
Vase, 9½" h., 9¾" d., bulbous
spherical body, the rounded
shoulder tapering to a short,
closed neck, molded around the
sides w/large brown-eyed Susans
& leaves, peacock green against
burgundy glaze, Shape No. 754 . . . 385.00
Vase, 10" h., 5¼" d., bottle-shaped
w/short neck, the bulbous base &
body molded around the sides
w/large fanned leaves & slender
stems rising up the sides to the
neck, mottled matte green glaze,
Shape No. 202, incised mark &
"1903 - 202 - X" 1,870.00
Vase, 11¼" h., 4" d., embossed
peacock feather design, Shape
No. 174, matte peacock green-
blue glaze, dated 1904 . . . . 1,870.00

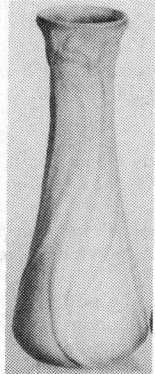

Tall Van Briggle Vase

Vase, 12" h., 4½" d., tall tapering
cylindrical body w/a slightly flaring rim, molded w/stylized blossoms on long swirling leafy
stems, Shape No. 786, Turquoise
Ming glaze, dated 1914 (ILLUS.) . . . 440.00

Vase, 13½" h., 6½" d., "Despondency," the ovoid body molded around the opening w/the curled-up figure of a reclining young man, mountain craig brown glaze, incised mark, 1926 . . . . 1,430.00

Vase, 14½" h., 10" d., a wide ovoid body tapering to a slightly flaring foot & to a small, short flaring neck, Shape No. 378, feathered matte green & purple glaze, dated 1905 . . . . 1,100.00

Vase, 15" h., 5½" d., slightly tapering cylinder w/a small flat opening, molded w/oblong lily pads around the top above long, slender vines down the sides, Shape No. 106, a feathery deep purple matte glaze, dated 1903 . . . . 2,970.00

VERNON KILNS

The story of Vernon Kilns Pottery begins with the purchase by Mr. Faye Bennison of the Poxon China Company (Vernon Potteries) in July 1931. The Poxon family had run the pottery for a number of years in Vernon, California, but with the founding of Vernon Kilns the product lines were greatly expanded.

Many innovative dinnerware lines and patterns were introduced during the 1930's, including designs by such noted American artists as Rockwell Kent and Don Blanding. In the early 1940's items were designed to tie in with Walt Disney's animated features "Fantasia" and "Dumbo." Various commemorative plates, including the popular "Bits" series, were also produced over a long period of time. Vernon Kilns was taken over by Metlox Potteries in 1958 and completely ceased production in 1960.

DINNERWARES

Bowl, 9" d., May Flower patt. $12.00
Butter dish, cov., May Flower patt., ½ lb. 45.00
Carafe & stopper, Homespun patt. . . 28.00
Casserole, cov., individual size, Organdie patt. 20.00
Creamer, Organdie patt. 5.50
Cup & saucer, Gingham patt. 5.00
Cup & saucer, Organdie patt. 7.50
Cup & saucer, Raffia patt., green & brown 5.50
Egg cup, Early California patt., cobalt blue 14.00
Egg cup, Early California patt., tan . . 12.00
Egg cup, Frontier Days (Winchester 73) patt. 35.00
Egg cup, double, Organdie patt. 8.00

Pitcher, 8½" h., Homespun patt. . . . 18.00
Pitcher, 9" h., streamlined style, Gingham patt. 45.00
Pitcher, beverage-type, Tam O'Shanter patt. 15.00
Pitcher, water, Tam O'Shanter patt. 35.00
Plate, bread & butter, 6½" d., Organdie patt. 3.00
Plate, 7" d., Organdie patt. 2.50
Plate, dinner, 10" d., Chintz patt. . . . 9.00
Plate, dinner, 10" d., Tickled Pink patt. 6.00
Plate, dinner, 10¼" d., Dolores patt. 14.00
Plate, dinner, 10¼" d., Frontier Days (Winchester 73) patt. 55.00
Plate, dinner, 10½" d., Gingham patt. 8.00
Plate, dinner, 10½" d., Organdie patt. 4.00
Plate, dinner, 10½" d., Tam O'Shanter patt. 5.00
Platter, 14" l., oval, May Flower patt. 22.50
Platter, 14" d., Frontier Days (Winchester 73) patt. 95.00
Salt & pepper shakers, Frontier Days (Winchester 73) patt., pr. 38.50
Soup bowl w/flanged rim, Gingham patt. 7.00
Sugar bowl, cov., Organdie patt. . . . 9.50
Sugar bowl, cov., Raffia patt., green & brown 8.00
Syrup pitcher, Gingham patt. 49.00
Teapot, cov., Bel Air patt. 35.00
Teapot, cov., Brown Eyed Susan patt. 45.00
Teapot, cov., Gingham patt. 24.00
Teapot, cov., Organdie patt. 22.00
Teapot, cov., Tam O'Shanter patt. . . 42.50
Tumbler, Brown Eyed Susan patt., 5½" h. 17.00
Tureen, cover & underplate, Hibiscus patt., large, 3 pcs. 325.00
Vegetable bowl, open, divided, Organdie patt., 11½" oval 15.00

"BITS" SERIES

Plate, 8½" d. Bits of Old New England, "The Cove" 21.00
Plate, 8½" d., Bits of Old New England, "Haying" 20.00
Plate, 8½" d., Bits of the Old South, "Cypress Swamp" 25.00

CITIES SERIES - 10½" d.

Plate, "Albuquerque, New Mexico," Maisel's Trading Post 20.00
Plate, "Honolulu, Hawaii," brown . . . 15.00
Plate, "Lincoln, Nebraska" 15.00
Plate, "Long Beach, California" 9.00
Plate, "Los Angeles, California" 9.00
Plate, "Reno, Nevada" 9.50

Plate, "Washington, D.C." 14.00
Plate, "Yakima, Washington,"
   blue 10.00

DISNEY "FANTASIA" & OTHER ITEMS

Bowl, 7 x 12" rectangle, Mushroom
   design, pink, No. 120 . . . . 400.00 to 500.00
Bowl, 10½" d. 3" h., Sprite design,
   light green, No. 125 . . . . 350.00
Bowl, 12" base d., 2½" h., Winged
   Nymph design, pistachio,
   No. 122 . . . . 250.00
Figure of Baby Weems, 6" h. 495.00
Plate, 9½" d., Nutcracker patt. 150.00
Salt & pepper shakers, model of a
   mushroom, tan glaze, 3½" h.,
   pr. . . . . 175.00 to 200.00
Vase, 5½" h., 8" w., Goldfish patt.,
   pink ground, marked & copyright-
   ed 1940 . . . . 195.00

DON BLANDING DINNERWARES

Plate, 7" d., Hawaiian Flowers patt.,
   maroon 12.00
Plate, 8" d., Hawaiian Flowers patt.,
   maroon 18.00
Plate, 9" d., Hawaiian Flowers patt.,
   maroon 20.00
Plate, 9" d., Leilani patt. 20.00
Plate, luncheon, 9½" d., Hawaiian
   Flowers patt., maroon 18.00
Plate, chop, 13" d., Leilani patt.,
   maroon 75.00
Plate, chop, 14" d., Hawaiian Flow-
   ers patt., maroon 65.00
Sugar bowl, cov., Hawaiian Flowers
   patt., maroon 22.00
Tureen, cov., Hawaiian Flowers
   patt., maroon 75.00

ROCKWELL KENT DESIGNS

Charger, "Our America" series,
   16½" d. 225.00
Creamer, Salamina patt., regular
   size 58.00
Plate, 7½" d., Salamina patt. 40.00
Plate, 9½" d., Salamina
   patt. . . . . 75.00 to 100.00
Plate, dinner, 10" d., Moby Dick
   patt. 58.00
Plate, 12" d., "Our America" series,
   brown 58.00
Saucer, Moby Dick patt. 9.00
Server w/handle, "Our America"
   series, 14" d. 125.00
Soup bowl, lug handle, Salamina
   patt. 40.00

STATES SERIES - 10½" d.

Plate, "California" 12.50
Plate, "Indiana" 11.00
Plate, "Kentucky" 14.00
Plate, "Louisiana," blue 30.00
Plate, "Massachusetts" 14.00

Plate, "Montana" 11.00
Plate, "South Dakota" 11.00
Plate, "Tennessee" 9.00
Plate, "Utah" 14.00
Plate, "Vermont - The Green Moun-
   tain State," blue 30.00
Plate, "Washington - The Evergreen
   State," blue 15.00

MISCELLANEOUS COMMEMORATIVES

Ashtray, "Connecticut" 12.00
Ashtray, "Kentucky," 5¾" d. 25.00
Coaster, "Texas," 4½" d. 20.00
Cup & saucer, demitasse, "Salinas -
   Home of the California Rodeo" . . . 28.00
Cup & saucer, "Statue of Liberty" . . . 38.00
Plate, 10½" d., "Baker's Chocolate,"
   1st edition, 1940 . . . . 25.00
Plate, 10½" d., "California Centen-
   nial," w/El Camino Real 12.00
Plate, 10½" d., "California Missions"
   design, 25 missions along El Cami-
   no Real shown 40.00
Plate, 10½" d., "Monticello," vari-
   ous scenes around the border,
   blue 25.00
Plate, "New Hampshire Aerial
   Tram" 9.00

WARWICK

Numerous collectors have turned their attention to the productions of the Warwick China Manufacturing Company that operated in Wheeling, West Virginia, from 1887 until 1951. Prime interest would seem to lie in items produced before 1914 that were decorated with decal portraits of beautiful women, monks and Indians. Fraternal Order items, as well as floral and fruit decorated items, are also popular with collectors.

Dresser tray, rectangular, fluted
   rim, small blue & yellow flowers
   on a blue & yellow ground, black
   "Warwick China" mark, 6 x 10" . . . $30.00
Ewer, decorated w/a colorful hibis-
   cus blossom, 8" h. 125.00
Lemonade set: 10½" h. pitcher & six
   4½" h. mugs; monk decoration,
   IOGA marks, the set (one mug
   w/small chip) 450.00
Mug, bust portrait of a laughing
   monk, IOGA mark, 4½" h. 75.00
Pitcher, 6" h., 5" d., pinched spout,
   green shaded ground decorated
   w/large red & pink roses, gold
   trim on rim, IOGA mark 75.00
Pitcher, 9½" h., poppies decoration,
   IOGA mark 120.00
Plate, 10" d., full-color coaching
   scene, yellow & gold banding 95.00

Vase, bud, 8¾" h., bulbous base below a tall, slender trumpet neck, decorated w/roses 125.00

Vase, 10½" h., cylindrical w/small twig handles & a scalloped rim, decorated w/cranes against a white ground 195.00

Vase, 10½" h., cylindrical w/small twig handles & a scalloped rim, decorated w/a bust portrait of a gypsy girl w/long hair & a blue ribbon, against a brown ground . . 155.00

Vase, 10½" h., cylindrical w/small twig handles & a scalloped rim, decorated w/hibiscus blossoms on a shaded brown ground, IOGA mark 110.00

Vase, 10½" h., cylindrical w/small twig handles & a scalloped rim, decorated w/a portrait of a mother & child embracing 195.00

WATT POTTERY

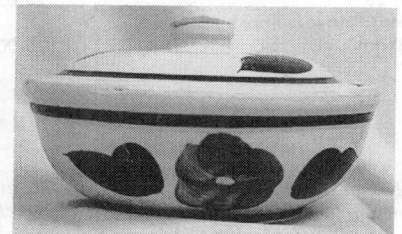

Posey Pattern Casserole

Founded in 1922, in Crooksville, Ohio, this pottery continued in operation until the factory was destroyed by fire in 1965. Although stoneware crocks and jugs were the first wares produced, by 1935 sturdy kitchen items in yellowware were the mainstay of production. Attractive lines like Kitch-N-Queen (banded) wares and the hand-painted Red Apple, Cherry and Pennsylvania Dutch (tulip) patterns were popular throughout the country. Today these hand-painted utilitarian wares are "hot" with collectors.

Bean pot, cov., Eagle patt., No. 76 . . $145.00

Bean pot, cov., Red Apple patt., No. 76 . . . . 68.00

Bowl, 5¼" d., Bleeding Heart patt., No. 5 . . . . 15.00

Bowl, 5¼" d., Pennsylvania Dutch (tulip) patt., No. 5 . . . . 55.00

Bowl, 6" d., Rooster patt. 20.00

Bowl, 6¼" d., Red Apple patt., No. 6 . . . . 45.00

Bowl, 6½" d., Red Apple patt., w/advertising 39.00

Bowl, 7¼" d., Autumn Foliage patt., No. 7 . . . . 30.00

Bowl, 7¼" d., Bleeding Heart patt., No. 7 . . . . 17.00

Bowl, 7¼" d., Red Apple patt., No. 7 . . . . 35.00

Bowl, 7¼" d., Rooster patt., w/advertising, No. 7 . . . . 65.00

Bowl, 7¼" d., Star Flower (Poinsettia) patt., w/advertising, No. 7 . . . 25.00

Bowl, 7½" d., Tulip patt. 65.00

Bowl, 8" d., Autumn Foliage patt., No. 8 . . . . 15.00

Bowl, 8" d., Red Apple patt., No. 8 . . . . 45.00

Bowl, 8" d., Star Flower patt., w/advertising, No. 8 . . . . 30.00

Bowl, 8" d., waffle design, green, No. 8 . . . . 20.00

Bowl, 9" d., Red Apple patt., No. 9 . . . . 52.00

Bowl, 11¾" d., Red Apple patt., No. 55 . . . . 65.00

Bowl, cov., Cherry patt., No. 52 . . . . 45.00

Bowl, Autumn Foliage patt., No. 120 . . . . 10.00

Bowl, Pennsylvania Dutch (tulip) patt., No. 65 . . . . 115.00

Bowl, cereal, Red Apple patt., No. 74 . . . . 25.00

Canister, cov., "Flour," Red Apple patt., No. 81 . . . . 400.00

Casserole, cov., Posey (or Pansy) patt. (ILLUS.) . . . . 50.00 to 60.00

Casserole, cov., Rooster patt. 125.00

Cookie jar, cov., Pennsylvania Dutch (tulip) patt., No. 503 . . . . 185.00

Cookie jar, cov., Red Apple patt., No. 21 . . . . 175.00 to 225.00

Cookie jar, cov., Tulip patt., red & blue, No. 62 . . . . 55.00

Creamer, Cherry patt., No. 62 . . . . . . 65.00

Creamer, Pennsylvania Dutch (tulip) patt., No. 62 . . . . 85.00

Creamer, Red Apple patt., No. 62 . . . . 50.00 to 60.00

Creamer, Star Flower patt., No. 62 . . . . 65.00

Custard cup, Star Flower patt. 22.00

Loaf dish, rectangular, Rooster patt. 250.00

Mug, Autumn Foliage patt., No. 121 . . . . 175.00

Mug, Red Apple patt., No. 121 . . . . 175.00 to 250.00

Pepper shaker, Red Apple patt. 75.00

Pie plate, Red Apple patt. 80.00

Pitcher, Autumn Foliage patt., No. 16 . . . . 35.00

Pitcher, square, Bleeding Heart patt., No. 69 . . . . 175.00

Pitcher, hourglass shape, brown bands decoration, No. 115 . . . . 60.00

Pitcher, Cherry patt., No. 15 . . . . 55.00

Pitcher, embossed Morning Glory patt., No. 97 . . . . 90.00

Pitcher w/ice lip, Red Apple patt.,
No. 17 . . . . .250.00 to 275.00
Pitcher, square, Rooster patt.,
No. 69 . . . . 225.00
Pitcher, 5½" h., Tulip patt., blue &
red, No. 15 . . . . 55.00
Pitcher, Tulip patt., No. 16 . .80.00 to 100.00
Plate, dinner, 9¾" d., Posey (Pansy)
patt. 55.00
Plate, dinner, 9¾" d., Red Apple
patt., w/advertising 500.00
Salt shaker, straight-sided, Red Ap-
ple patt. 85.00
Salt shaker, Star Flower patt. 65.00
Soup bowl, cov., lug-handled, Red
Apple patt., No. 18 . . . . 35.00
Spaghetti bowl, Cherry patt. 105.00
Sugar bowl, cov., brown band deco-
ration, No. 98 . . . . 140.00
Sugar bowl, cov., Red Apple patt.,
w/advertising 250.00
Sugar bowl, cov., Rooster patt.,
w/advertising, No. 98 . . . . 115.00
Sugar bowl, cov., Star Flower patt.,
green & white 25.00

WEDGWOOD

Reference here is to the famous pottery es-
tablished by Josiah Wedgwood in 1759 in
England. Numerous types of wares have been
produced through the years to the present.

BASALT

Basalt Figure of a Nymph

Cups & saucers, wide rounded cups,
deep saucers, each decorated w/a
gilt anthemion border, upper-
lower case marks, ca. 1790, saucer 4¾" d., 2 sets (minor wear) . .$522.50
Figure of a 'Nymph at Well,'
modeled as a scantily clad female
figure seated looking down &
holding a shell in one hand, on a
molded oval base, inscribed w/ti-
tle & impressed mark, ca. 1840,
11" h. (ILLUS.) 1,045.00

Figure of a 'Sleeping Boy,' modeled
lying on his back upon a drapery
& a rockwork mound base, impressed "WEDGWOOD," late 18th
- early 19th c., 5" l. 1,980.00
Inkwell, applied w/rosso antico de-
signs in the Egyptian manner,
mounted atop a square flat
base, removable ink pot insert,
impressed mark, late 18th c.,
2 5/8" h. (nick to applied relief) . . 605.00
Model of an elephant, shown walk-
ing, its trunk down, glass eyes,
impressed mark, ca. 1916,
3½" h. 302.50

Early Basalt Vase

Vase, 4¼" h., naturalistically
modeled as four short bamboo
stalks (one w/rim chip), mounted
on a mound base (hairline crack)
modeled w/moss, florettes &
leaves, the interiors glazed, impressed mark "Wedgwood & Bent-
ley," ca. 1778 (ILLUS.) 1,540.00

CREAMWARE

Model of a polar bear in a sitting
position, artist-signed "J. Skeap-
ing," ca. 1927, 4 1/8 x 10",
7" h. 395.00
Plate, 9 1/8" d., "Anticipation is
Rather Dangerous," h.p. scene of
girl sitting on stool by kettle, gold
border, artist-signed "E. Lessore,"
date mark of 1863 . . . . 395.00
Plate, 9 1/8" d., "Buns! Buns!
Buns!," man selling buns to lady
& child h.p. center scene, gold
border, artist-signed "E. Lessore,"
date mark of 1863 . . . . 395.00
Veilleuse (night light/kettle warm-
er), a cylindrical canister w/large
opening at the front base below a
delicate pierced design & loop
handles at the sides, supporting a
small spherical teapot w/long
spout & fixed bail handle, early
19th c., overall 10½" h., 2 pcs.
(minor rim nick) 825.00

JASPER WARE

Cracker jar, cov., barrel-shaped, white relief classical figures on dark blue, silver plate rim, cover & bail handle, marked "Wedgwood" only, 5" d., 6" h. 225.00

Cracker jar, cov., cylindrical, white relief classical ladies & cupids on dark blue, replated silver cover, ball-footed base & bail handle, marked "Wedgwood" only, 5½" d., 6 5/8" h. 225.00

Cracker jar, cov., cylindrical, white relief classical ladies on sage green, replated silver cover, ball-footed base & bail handle, marked "Wedgwood" only, 5½" d., 6¾" h. 250.00

Cracker jar, cov., cylindrical, white relief classical ladies & cupids on a salmon ground, replated silver cover, ball-footed base & bail handle, marked "Wedgwood - England," 5 3/8" d., 7" h. 395.00

Cracker jar, cov., bulbous, footed, three-color w/yellow bands at top & bottom, white relief classical figures around center w/white relief acanthus leaf trim on black, silver plate lid, rim & bail handle, 9½" h. to top of handle 815.00

Mug, three-handled, white relief classical figures in an oval vignette on blue, late 19th c., 4½" h. 325.00

Pitcher w/pewter cov., 9" h., jug-type, white relief classical figures on blue, white relief scene of "Sacrifice to Love" on the front, late 19th c. 180.00

Plaque, rectangular, solid green body decorated in white-relief w/a scene of Bacchus (hairline through his body) seated in a chariot drawn by two horses, Silenus by his side, a trumpeter & a draped figure w/raised arms before him, the reverse w/twenty firing holes, impressed "WEDGWOOD & BENTLEY," modeled by William Hackwood, 1776-80, 6¼ x 13" (two firing cracks in the relief & three small patches of 'bleeding') 12,100.00

Tray, oval, white relief classical figures on a crimson ground, 6 3/8" w., 9¼" l. 975.00

Tray, octagonal, white relief classical figures on a blue ground, early 20th c., 10½" w. 225.00

MISCELLANEOUS

Bowl, 9" w., octagonal, Dragon Lustre, orange exterior, purple w/blue mottled interior, No. Z4825, printed mark, ca. 1925 (interior wear) 330.00

Wedgwood Fairyland Lustre Bowl

Bowl, 9 5/8" w., octagonal, Fairyland Lustre, printed in gold & painted in Daylight Fairyland tones, the paneled exterior w/'Dana - Castle on a Road' w/'Cobble' bead borders, the interior w/'Fairy in a Cage' & a central roundel decorated in gold w/flying elves within a 'Cobble' bead border on a crimson ground shading to mother-of-pearl at the edges, pattern No. Z5125, Portland Vase mark, ca. 1917-41 (ILLUS.) 3,190.00

Bust of John Milton, parian, designed by E.W. Wyon, bolted to socle base, marked "Wedgwood" only, 8" d., 14" h. 895.00

Cup & saucer, Patricia patt. 25.00

Demitasse set: cov. demitasse pot & six cups & saucers; Florentine patt., 13 pcs. 285.00

Wedgwood Majolica Game Dish

Game dish, cov., wide round cylindrical base w/molded fern vines & hanging game birds in brown & green against a pale blue ground, the low domed cover w/molded game birds finial, 19th c. (ILLUS.) 1,700.00

Plaque, rectangular, Fairyland Lustre, decorated w/a fantasy

fairyland scene in pale colors &
gilt trim on a black ground, wide
border band of dark blue w/over-
all fine gold dot design, black
wood frame, marked, No. Z5288,
7¼ x 10½" 4,125.00

Plate, 8" d., majolica, geranium leaf
design 110.00

Plate, 9¼" d., commemorative, "The
Boston Tea Party," blue transfer
on white, dated 1899 .... 42.00

Plate, 9¼" d., commemorative,
"Marietta College," blue transfer
on white, ca. 1960 .... 20.00

Plate, 10½" d., commemorative,
"Newark, New Jersey," blue
transfer on white, ca. 1929 ...... 20.00

Plate, 10½" d., commemorative,
"U.S. Naval Academy," rose transfer on white 20.00

Plate, flow blue, Ivanhoe series,
"Rebecca Repelling the Tem-
plar" 85.00

Toothpick holder, Butterfly Lustre,
gold & orange, 3" h............. 350.00

Wedgwood Fairyland Lustre Vases

Vases, 8" h., Fairyland Lustre,
baluster-form, each printed in
gold & painted on the exterior in
copper-bronze lustre w/"Jeweled
Tree" patt. framing three 'Flame
Fairyland' panels depicting "Feng
Huang," "Bridge" & "Ship and
Tree," the mother-of-pearl lustre
interior w/a copper-bronze "Beo-
wulf" bead border above a green
'Pebble and Grass' band, printed
Portland Vase mark, shape
No. 3150, pattern No. Z5360, pr.
(ILLUS.) 4,950.00

Vase, cov., 9 3/8" h., Fairyland Lustre, tall ovoid body w/fitted
domed cover, printed in gold &
painted on the exterior in black
Fairyland tones w/the "Sycamore
Tree" patt. framing three panels
depicting the "Feng Huang,"
"Bridge" & "Ship & Tree" patterns

between "Roseberry" bead bor-
ders at the base & neck, the cov-
er w/a Leafy Fairy above a Drag-
on bead border on the exterior,
"Elves on a Branch" patt. within a
'Pan Fei' border on the mother-of-
pearl ground interior, printed
Portland Vase mark & "WEDG-
WOOD ENGLAND - MADE
IN...," shape No. 2410, pattern
No. Z4968, 1916-41.............6,600.00

WELLER

*This pottery was made from 1872 to 1945
at a pottery established originally by Samuel
A. Weller at Fultonham, Ohio, and moved in
1882 to Zanesville. Numerous lines were
produced and listings below are by the pattern or lines.*

ALVIN (1928)

*Various shapes with molded fruits, branches
or vines with a matte glaze.*

Vase, double bud, 6" h. $62.50
Vase, bud, 7½" h. 30.00
Vase, double bud, 8" h. 95.00
Vase, bud, 8½" h. 45.00

ARDSLEY (1928)

*Various shapes molded as cattails among
rushes with water lilies at the bottom. Matte
glaze.*

Ardsley Console Bowl

Candlesticks, blossom-shaped, 3" h.,
pr. 65.00

Console bowl, molded rushes
around the sides w/four blossoms
in the center bottom, 12" d.
(ILLUS.)...................... 40.00

Console set, oblong irregular console bowl & pair of 3" h. candleholders, 3 pcs. 130.00

Vase, double bud, 10" h. ...75.00 to 100.00

AURELIAN (1898-1910)

*Similar to Louwelsa line but brighter colors
and a glossy glaze.*

Vase, 9½" h., decorated w/jonquils,
artist-signed 300.00
Vase, 10½" h., blackberries & flo-
ral decoration on a dark
ground . . . . .350.00 to 395.00

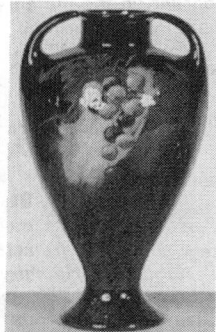

Aurelian Vase with Cherries

Vase, 11" h., tall ovoid body tapering to a flaring foot, short cylindrical neck joined to the shoulder
w/loop handles, decorated
w/cherries & leaves on a dark
ground (ILLUS.) . . . . .400.00 to 425.00

BALDIN (about 1915-20)

*Rustic designs with relief-molded apples and
leaves on branches wrapped around each
piece.*

Jardiniere & pedestal, 34" h.,
2 pcs. 450.00
Lamp base, factory-drilled, 12½" h.
(no fittings) 200.00
Vase, 6" h., bulbous base 42.50
Vase, 7" h., bulbous base, glossy
glaze, experimental 75.00
Vase, 13" h., dark blue ground 795.00

BONITO (1927-33)

*Hand-painted florals and foliage in soft tones
on cream ground.*

Vase, 4" h., ovoid body w/small tab
handles at flat rim 50.00
Vase, 5" h., ovoid body on flared
foot, shaped rim w/arched
C-scroll handles 75.00
Vase, 6" h., bulbous ovoid body
w/ruffled rim, small hook handles
at the center sides, decorated
w/pansies 95.00
Vase, 7½" h., two-handled, tall cyl-
inder flaring toward base & then
tapering to round foot, two slender scrolled handles down sides . . 120.00
Vase, 9¼" h., decorated w/small
h.p. blue & lavender flowers 160.00
Vase, 9¼" h., h.p. orange tiger lily
decoration 160.00

Vase, 10" h., slightly tapering cylindrical body w/flaring foot & rim,
small scroll loop handles at rim,
artist-signed 180.00
Vase, 10¼" h., h.p. bluebell
decoration 185.00

BRIGHTON (1915)

*Various bird or butterfly figurals colorfully
decorated and with glossy glazes.*

Butterfly, brown, 2" w. 115.00
Canaries (2) flower frog, 4" h. 200.00
Kingfisher flower frog, 9" h. 375.00
Parrot, multicolored,
7½" h. . . . . .650.00 to 750.00
Swans (2) flower frog 395.00

BRONZE WARE (before 1920)

*Metal-clad pottery pieces done by Charles
Clewell. Generally simple shapes.*

Vase, 10" h. . . . . .150.00 to 175.00
Vase, 11½" h., tall footed ovoid
form 200.00
Vase, 15" h., metallic purple
finish 400.00

CACTUS (early 1930's)

*Various humorous stylized animal figures
with a reddish brown, blue-green or golden
glaze.*

Model of a camel, kneeling, blue-
green glaze. 60.00
Model of a Dachshund dog, blue-
green glaze, 6" l. . . . . .50.00 to 75.00
Model of a duck, blue-green glaze,
4½" h. 55.00
Model of an elephant, reddish
brown glaze 75.00
Model of a snail, golden glaze,
3½" h. 62.50

CHENGTU (1925-36)

*Simple graceful shapes covered with an over-
all deep Chinese red glaze.*

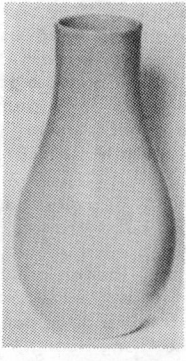

Tall Chengtu Vase

Vase, 6" h.   45.00
Vase, 8" h., stamped "Weller". 55.00
Vase, 11¼" h., tall ovoid body
    tapering to a flat rim (ILLUS.) 125.00
Vase, 13" h., 5" d., tall baluster-
    form body w/flared rim, matte
    vermillion glaze, ink stamped
    mark. 137.50

CLARMONT (ca. 1920)

*Generally rounded forms molded with
horizontal ribbing or wide bands often molded with abstract florals. Decorated with an
overall dark brown glaze.*

Candlesticks, w/side handles, 8" h.,
    pr. 175.00
Vase, 5" h. 40.00
Vase, 6¾" h., three-loop handles. . .   125.00

CLAYWOOD (ca. 1910)

*Etched designs against a light tan ground,
divided by dark brown bands. Matte glaze.*

Basket, hanging-type, 10½" h. 75.00
Bulb bowl, 8" d. 55.00
Ferner, etched decoration of winged
    lion-like creatures, 4 x 8". 120.00
Vase, 3" h., 4½" d. 35.00

CLINTON IVORY (before 1914)

*Various molded designs on a cream-colored
ground with rubbed brown trim. Matte glaze.*

Ewer, 10" h. 76.00
Jardiniere, 8" h. 85.00
Vase, 10" h., cylindrical body 48.00

CLOUDBURST (1921)

*Overall crackle glaze with a lustre finish on
simple rounded shapes.*

Vase, 5½" h., 7" d., two-handled. . .   85.00
Vase, 6" h., orange lustre 30.00
Vase, 10" h., gold lustre 200.00
Vase, 10" h., yellow lustre 80.00

COPPERTONE (late 1920's)

*Various shapes with an overall mottled green
glaze. Some pieces with figural frog or fish
handles. Models of frogs also included.*

Ashtray, low rounded form w/model
    of a frog seated on the rim,
    6½" d. 125.00
Bowl, 5½ x 10¼", irregularly
    shaped flattened rim on deep
    tapering sides, molded on the ex-
    terior w/three large fish, a life-
    sized figural frog sitting on the
    rim, mottled matte green glaze,
    marked "Weller Pottery - #2". 495.00

Candleholder, model of a turtle
    w/lily blossom, 3" h. 200.00
Cigarette stand, model of a frog,
    5" h. 150.00
Flower frog, model of a lily pad
    bloom w/seated frog, 4½" h. 75.00
Model of a frog, 2" h. 85.00
Pitcher, 7½" h., wide ovoid body
    composed of molded lily pad
    leaves tapering to the shaped
    rim, large figural fish handle, ink-
    stamped mark & "MD - 19" 1,100.00
Vase, 7¼" h., 7¼" d., wide ovoid
    body w/closed rim, molded on the
    exterior w/large lily pads, a
    figural frog at one side of the
    rim, mottled matte green over
    brown glaze 495.00
Vase, 8" h., model of a water lily
    pad 150.00

DICKENSWARE 2nd LINE (1900-05)

*Various incised "sgraffito" designs usually
with a matte glaze.*

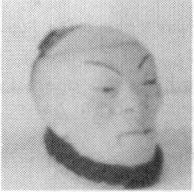

Chinese Man's Head Tobacco Jar

Jug, two-handled, portrait of an In-
    dian, "Blue Hawk," artist-signed,
    7" h. 1,000.00
Mug, bust portrait of American Indi-
    an "Blue Hawk," 6¾" h. 525.00
Mug, BPOE elk head, 5¾" h. 265.00
Mug, monk drinking ale scene,
    5½" h. 295.00
Pitcher, 5" h., incised grotesque
    fish 325.00
Tobacco jar, cov., model of a Chi-
    nese man's head, 6" h. (ILLUS.) . . .   850.00
Umbrella stand, decorated w/a
    scene of an elk in a lake, in
    shades of green & yellow, glossy
    glaze, unmarked 2,200.00
Vase, 4½" h., two-handled, incised
    grotesque fish, artist-signed 325.00
Vase, 5½" h., clover & grass
    decoration. 125.00
Vase, 10" h., bulbous body, monk
    portrait decoration 525.00
Vase, 10" h., 4" d., tall ovoid body
    tapering to a short neck w/widely
    flared rim, incised w/a design of
    mythical dancing cherubs & god-
    dess in a landscape of tall trees,
    semi-gloss glaze, die-stamped
    mark. 495.00

Vase, 11½" h., 4½" d., waisted cylinder w/twisted effect, incised
Northwestern landscape w/cari-
bou, artist-signed (repair to small
chip inside rim) 440.00
Vase, 13" h., etched dragon decoration on blue ground 1,000.00

EOCEAN (1898-1918)

*Early art line with various hand-painted flow-
ers on shaded grounds, usually with a glossy
glaze.*

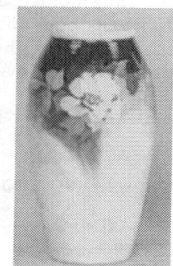

Eocean Vase with Flowers

Jardiniere & pedestal base, dark red
poppy-type blossoms against a
dark green shading to grey
ground, 2 pcs. 675.00
Mug, mushrooms decoration,
5¾" h. 145.00
Vase, 7½" h., ovoid body decorated
with swirling pink blossoms on a
shaded dark to light blue ground,
signed (ILLUS.) 220.00
Vase, 8½" h., 4" d., tall slightly
ovoid cylindrical form, decorated
w/yellow roses against a black,
pink, yellow & mauve ground,
artist-initialed (minor stilt pull at
base) 302.50
Vase, 9" h., 4" d., slightly waisted
ovoid body tapering to a small
molded mouth, decorated w/an
owl perched on a pine branch, a
big full moon behind, against a
shaded black to white ground, incised mark & artist-signed, numbered "X466" 935.00
Vase, 11¼" h., 4" d., tall cylindrical
body swelling slightly toward the
rounded shoulder & tapering to
the short, rolled neck, shaded
greyish green ground decorated
w/purple & pink irises, die-
stamped mark 467.50

ETCHED & MODELED MATT (ca. 1905)

*Incised or molded designs against a light
ground and using a light clay. Comparable to
2nd Line Dickensware.*

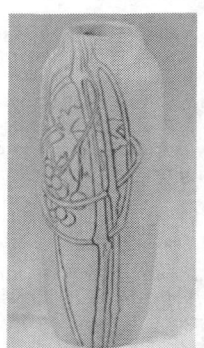

Etched Matt Vase with Grapes

Vase, 9¼" h., 3¾" d., slender
baluster-form body, decorated
w/a stem w/a large yellow rose &
green leaves running up the side
against an orange ground, die-
stamped mark 247.50
Vase, 10½" h., 4" d., tall slender
waisted shape w/a molded rim,
decorated w/long slender stems
w/white berry clusters & green
leaves against a yellow ground
running up the sides, die-stamped
mark 247.50
Vase, 13" h., 4½" d., tall slender
slightly swelling cylindrical body
tapering to a flat mouth, incised
grapevine in green & yellow on
an orange ground, ink mark
(ILLUS.) 522.50

ETHEL (ca. 1915)

*Cream-colored bodies with most pieces featur-
ing an oval reserve with a profile bust of Ethel
Weller sniffing a rose; vertical bands of stylized blossoms around the sides and diamond
trellis bands at the top and bottom.*

Vase, bud, 8½" h., square shape
w/square handles at top 95.00
Vase, 10½" h., slightly flaring cylindrical body w/a wide flat mouth,
molded ring handles, round base
w/small feet 165.00

ETNA (1906)

*Similar to Eocean line but designs are mold-
ed in low-relief and colored.*

Jardiniere, slip-painted roses,
8 x 10" 250.00
Pitcher, 6¼" h., 3¾" d., ovoid body
tapering to a bulbous rim
w/pinched spout, simple strap
handle, decorated w/one blue
pansy against a shaded grey to
pink ground, etched mark 110.00
Pitcher, tankard, 10½" h., 5½" d.,

slightly tapering cylindrical body w/a long angled handle, decorated w/lavender hydrangea blossoms against a fading grey ground, etched mark 165.00

Pitcher, tankard, 13½" h., grape & floral decoration 350.00

Vase, 5" h., 7" d., slip-painted pink florals on a greyish blue ground . . 125.00

Vase, 14" h., 5" d., cylindrical w/shallow shoulder & wide mouth, decorated w/embossed pink roses against a shaded bluish grey ground, marked "WELLER ETNA" 220.00

FLORAL (late 1930's)

White flowers on a lightly paneled background in pastel colors. Semigloss finish.

Candlesticks, double, light green, No. F12, pr. 60.00

Console bowl, light green, No. F9 . . 50.00

Wall pocket. 55.00

FOREST (mid-Teens-1928)

Realistically molded and painted forest scene.

Jardiniere, full kiln mark, 5½" h. . . . 150.00

Pitcher, 5" h., cylindrical, glossy glaze 150.00

Teapot, cov., glossy glaze, 4½" h. . . 250.00

Umbrella stand, cylindrical, No. 609, 10½" d., 19½" h. (small repaired chip on body) 605.00

Vase, 8" h., 4" d., cylindrical 75.00

Vase, 8" h., waisted cylinder w/flaring rim 125.00

Vase, 12" h., waisted cylindrical form 225.00

FRUITONE (Before 1920)

Upright streaks of color, shaded like a piece of fruit.

Bowl, 8" d., apple green & cherry red 80.00

Jardiniere, 8" h. 195.00

Vase, 5" h., handled 65.00

GLENDALE (early to late 1920's)

Various relief-molded birds in their natural habitats, life-like coloring.

Candleholders, birds w/nest, 5½" d., 2" h., pr. 195.00

Flower frog, molded nest w/eggs . . . . 125.00 to 150.00

Vase, 8½" h., two yellow birds w/nest 375.00

Wall pocket, bird w/chicks in nest, long conical form w/curved & pointed base, 12½" h. 425.00

HUDSON (1917-34)

Underglaze slip-painted decoration.

Vase, bud, 5¼" h., tall slender tapering stick-form, blue & pink floral decoration on shaded grey blue ground 145.00

Vase, 5¾" h., 5" d., iris decoration 255.00

Vase, 6" h., handled, dogwood floral decoration, blue ground 310.00

Vase, 7½" h., swelled cylindrical body, pink & yellow blossoms between narrow yellow bands at the top, on an overall navy blue ground 235.00

Vase, 10" h., 5½" d., slightly tapering cylindrical shouldered form w/a raised, flat mouth, decorated w/pink & white nasturtium blossoms & green leaves on a shaded ground, artist-signed, paper label 605.00

Vase, 12" h., 4¾" d., tall body w/flaring neck, decorated w/sprigs of white & mauve lilacs against a shaded blue ground, artist-signed 522.50

Vase, 12" h., 6½" d., ovoid w/flaring mouth, decorated w/a continuous scene of Juliet at her balcony, surrounded by palm trees & flowers, overlooking Venice's Grand Canal w/floating gondolas, after J.M.W. Turner, artist-signed, incised "WELLER" . . . 4,400.00

Vase, 13" h., 4¼" d., tall tapering body, decorated w/a large sprig of white lilacs against a shaded lavender, green & blue ground, artist-signed 495.00

JAP BIRDIMAL (1904)

Stylized Japanese-inspired figural, bird or animal designs on various solid colored grounds.

Lamp base, a wide baluster-form body w/a short wide neck & molded flat rim, decorated in squeeze-bag technique w/the figure of a kimono-clad Japanese woman holding a parasol & surrounded by butterflies, in polychrome over deep green, designed by F.H. Rhead, incised Weller mark & "Rhead Faience," 8¼" d., 12¼" h. 1,045.00

Vase, 5½" h., 5¾" w., pillow-type, decorated w/a black & yellow Viking ship against a bluish grey ground, marked "WELLER, X, 352" 302.50

Vase, 10" h., 7¼" d., a wide tapering ovoid body w/a wide, flat

mouth, squeeze-bag decoration of
a geisha in costume walking under green trees, on a burnt orange ground, designed by Frederick Rhead, marked "Weller
Rhead Faience - X486," early
20th c. 1,650.00

L'ART NOUVEAU (1903-04)

*Various figural and floral-embossed Art Nou-
veau designs.*

Tall L'Art Nouveau Vase

Vase, 8¾" h., 7" w., two-handled,
flattened body w/undulating rim,
embossed w/the swirling figure of
a woman, green matte finish,
marked 495.00
Vase, 12" h., waisted tall body
swelled at the top below a low,
scalloped neck, embossed cameos
of a lady's face around the top . . . 375.00
Vase, 14¾" h., 4½" w., tall tapering square body w/four swelled
embossed poppy blossoms at the
rim w/the stems & leaves forming
the corners, each panel embossed
w/a sensuous Art Nouveau lady
figure, h.p. salmon pink over a
celadon green ground, circular
mark (ILLUS.) 440.00

LASA (1920-25)

*Various landscapes on a banded reddish and
gold iridescent ground.*

Vase, bud, 6" h., slender tapering
stick-form . . . . .225.00 to 250.00
Vase, 6¾" h., 3¼" d., slender ovoid
body w/a molded rim, decorated
w/a landscape of bare trees,
signed at side of base (ILLUS. top
next column) 220.00
Vase, 11" h., 7" d., ovoid body
tapering to a short collared
mouth, decorated w/a lake &

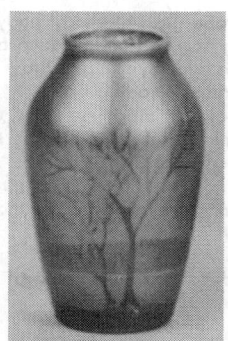

Lasa Vase with Bare Trees

mountain landscape in gold, purple, red & green iridescence,
marked "Weller La Sa" on side . . . 880.00

LOUWELSA (1896-1924)

*Hand-painted underglaze slip decoration on
dark brown shading to yellow ground; glossy
glaze.*

Bowl, 7¼" d., 3" h., yellow floral
decoration on shaded brown
ground, artist-signed 175.00
Ewer, squat bulbous base tapering
to a short neck w/tricornered
ruffled rim, yellow daffodils &
green leaves decoration, 7½" d.,
6" h. . . . . .150.00 to 175.00
Ewer, footed bulbous ovoid body
tapering to a tall slender neck
w/flaring rim w/pinched spout,
S-form strap handle, decorated
w/yellow, red & black berries
against a rich reddish brown
ground, artist-signed, stamped
mark, 5" d., 10½" h. 220.00
Jug, currants decoration, artist-
signed, 6¼" h. 175.00
Lamp base, ovoid, decorated
w/tulips, artist-signed, w/glass
shade, overall 11" h. . . . .350.00 to 375.00
Mug, tapering sides, decorated
w/the portrait of a monk in profile, in shades of brown against a
dark brown ground, glossy glaze,
marked "LOUWELSA WELLER, S,
582, 1," 5½" d., 5¾" h. 165.00
Mug, tapering sides, decorated
w/large dark purple grapes &
green grape leaves, artist-signed,
6" h. 195.00
Pedestal, decorated w/tulips,
15" h. 295.00
Vase, 2¼" h., 2 5/8 x 4¼", squatty
oblong body tapering to a short
center neck, loop handles extending to the neck from the ends,
decorated w/green leaves on the

shaded deep green & brown
ground, marked 75.00
Vase, 9½" h., ruffled edge, floral
decoration on dark brown ground,
stamped "No. 159" 200.00

MAMMY LINE (1935)

Figural black mammy pieces or pieces with figural black children as handles.

Cookie jar, 11" h. 3,400.00
Kitchen set, cov. cookie jar, cov.
teapot, batter bowl, syrup pitcher,
creamer & sugar bowl, 6 pcs. 8,500.00
Syrup pitcher, cov., 6" h. . .600.00 to 750.00

MARVO (mid-1920's-33)

Molded overall fern and leaf design on various matte background colors.

Marvo Wall Pocket

Pedestal, green, 22½" h. 250.00
Umbrella stand, green, 19½" h. 350.00
Vase, double bud, 4½" h., cylindri-
cal vases joined by openwork lat-
tice bars . . . . .50.00 to 75.00
Wall pocket, conical, green, 8½" h.
(ILLUS.) 78.00

MUSKOTA (1915-late 1920's)

Figural pieces with human figures, birds, animals or frogs. Matte glaze.

Flower frog, figural frog half im-
mersed in water lily, 4½" h. 110.00
Flower frog, model of a kingfisher,
9" h. 375.00
Flower frog, model of a lizard on a
rock 100.00

OAK LEAF (before 1936)

Molded oak leaves on one side and acorns on the other; various background colors. Matte glaze.

Basket-vase, four-part handle, green
leaves on a blue ground, 9" h. . . . 55.00
Ewer, footed cylinder w/indented
rim & angled handle, green
leaves on a blue ground,
8½" h. 50.00

Vase, 8" h., tall footed ovoid body
w/small double loop handle on
one side, brown ground 35.00
Wall pocket, conical, blue ground,
8½" h. 67.00

PEARL (1917-19)

Cream-colored ground with embossed pale colored swags of pearl-like beading between red flowerheads.

Basket, ovoid footed body w/high
center handle, 6½" h. 135.00
Bowl, 7" d., 4" h. 65.00
Jardiniere, wide ovoid-form, 7" h. . . 168.00
Vase, 10" h., tall ovoid body
w/small loop handles around the
top 225.00

PERFECTO or LOUWELSA PERFECTO (1903-04)

Early art line featuring pale ground usually of shaded greens or green to pink with hand-painted designs of fruits, flowers, animals or portraits in pastel shades; matte or unglazed finish.

Vase, 7" h., pine cone decoration on
shaded brown & gold ground,
artist-signed 325.00
Vase, 16" h., water lily decora-
tion 1,100.00

ROMA (1912-late 1920's)

Cream-colored ground decorated with embossed floral swags, bands or fruit clusters.

Console bowl, deep flaring oval
body w/scalloped rim, on four
small shell feet, red rose clusters
& green leaves around the rim,
10½" l., 4½" h. 135.00
Vase, double bud, 8" h., two slen-
der square vases flaring out from
a footed round base & joined at
the top by an open oval ring 80.00
Wall pocket, conical, decorated
w/floral basket & swags in
Dupont motif, 10" h. 125.00

SABRINIAN (late 1920's)

Pieces modeled as seashells with sea plant trim and figural sea horse handles. In pastel shades of violet, blue, green and brown.

Candleholder, low shell-shape
w/cylindrical center socket,
2" d. 95.00
Wall pocket, conical, 8½" h. 300.00

SICARDO (1902-07)

Various shapes with iridescent glaze of metallic shadings in greens, blues, crimson, purple or coppertones decorated with vines, flowers, stars or free-form geometric lines.

Fine Sicardo Vases

Planter, a square oak framework w/a wide, flat rim supports four pottery side panels each decorated w/different flowers in the Art Nouveau style, in a gold, green & purple mottled iridescent glaze, lined w/metal, unmarked, 12 x 13" .1,540.00

Vase, 4" h., 2¾" d., pear-shaped body decorated w/arabesques in a gold & burgundy lustred glaze, signed 302.50

Vase, 6" h., waisted cylindrical body w/a swelled shoulder tapering to a small mouth, iridescent tall, slightly swirled leaves, stems & flowers on a lavender lustre ground, signed. 450.00

Vase, 7½" h., 3½" d., trumpet-form w/widely flaring footed base, decorated w/stylized plants w/whiplash peacock feathers in an iridescent green & burgundy glaze, signed, incised "X 368" 715.00

Vase, 9" h., wide bulbous tapering body w/a thin molded rim, incurved loop handles at the sides, purple lustre glaze decorated w/gold daisies & petals blowing in the wind, impressed marks (ILLUS. left) 1,650.00

Vase, 9 1/8" h., cylindrical body w/rounded shoulder to a short, flared neck, purple lustre glaze w/gold decoration of stylized snails & their iridescent trails, painted mark & impressed numbers (ILLUS. right) 1,320.00

Vase, 11" h., 7" d., ovoid lobed body tapering to a bulbous lobed & incurved scalloped rim, iridescent design of dandelions in purple, green & crimson, impressed "WELLER #39" 1,870.00

Vase, 11" h., 7½" d., wide cylindrical body w/a flat shoulder to a short tapering neck, decorated w/iridescent arabesques against

a burgundy-to-green ground, signed 1,760.00

Vase, 15½" h., 10" d., bulbous ovoid footed body w/a short flaring neck w/closed rim, decorated w/stylized dandelions in an iridescent green glaze against a burgundy ground, from Samuel Weller's home, signed (restoration to base hole) 3,960.00

Vase, 15¾" h., tall slightly tapering cylindrical body w/three long angular handles from the rim down the sides, dark purple lustre glaze decorated w/gold & silvery blue foliage & flowers ascending from the base, molded signature "14 WELLER" .1,320.00

WILD ROSE (early to mid-1930's)

An open white rose on a light tan or green background. Matte glaze.

Basket, round bulbous footed body w/sides continuing to form strap handle across top, this handle topped by second smaller arched handle, green ground, 5½" h. 45.00

Vase, 6" h., double, two cylinders angle up from arched feet, joined at top by arched handle, green ground 45.00

Vase, 6½" h., footed baluster-form, slender loop handles near the rim 28.00

Vase, 8" h., footed cylinder tapering slightly toward flat rim, angled handles at rim 42.00

WOODCRAFT (1917)

Rustic designs simulating the appearance of stumps, logs and tree trunks. Some pieces are adorned with owls, squirrels, dogs and other animals.

Woodcraft Planter with Foxes

Basket, hanging-type, round tree trunk-form w/an owl peeking out of a round hole, 10" d., 5½" h. . . 325.00

Bowl, 6" d., 3½" h., molded w/design of a seated squirrel amid tree branches. . . . . .100.00 to 125.00

Console bowl, low rounded sides,
11" d. 145.00
Lamp, narrow tree trunk base sup-
ports leafy cluster topped by four-
sided owl figure, owl-decorated
shade, base 12½" h. 450.00
Planter, cylindrical tree trunk form
w/three small foxes peeking out
at side, 4½" h. (ILLUS.) 135.00
Vase, 7" h., cylindrical tree trunk
form molded w/a full figural owl
sitting on branch 350.00
Vase, 12" h., smooth tree trunk
form w/molded leafy branch
around rim & down sides w/hang-
ing purple plums 150.00
Vase, 13¼" h., 5½" d., tall tree
trunk form w/pierced branch handles around the rim above an owl
peeking out of a hole, marked . . . 605.00

WOODROSE (pre-1920)

*Rustic oaken bucket forms with rose clusters
or berries near the rim. Matte glaze.*

Basket, hanging-type 110.00
Candlestick, handled, molded blue-
berries 55.00
Jardiniere, bucket-form w/tab rim
handles, 7" h. 135.00

ZONA (about 1920)

*Red apples and green leaves on brown
branches all on a cream-colored ground; some
pieces with molded florals or birds with various glazes.*

*A line of children's dishes was also
produced featuring hand-painted or molded
animals. This is referred to as the "Zona Baby
Line."*

Creamer, ovoid body w/twig han-
dle, dinnerware line, 3½" h. 35.00
Pitcher, 7" h., cylindrical body,
paneled splashing duck decora-
tion 155.00
Pitcher, 8" h., cylindrical, paneled
colored kingfisher decoration on a
cream ground, brown branch
handle 220.00
Pitcher, 8" h., cylindrical, paneled
kingfisher decoration w/overall
dark green glaze 125.00
Pitcher, 8" h., cylindrical body,
paneled kingfisher decoration
w/overall dark pink glaze, branch
handle 145.00
Umbrella stand, cylindrical, decorat-
ed w/a row of tall, standing
maidens in long dresses holding a
continuous garland of pink roses,
green ivy vines around the top,
all on a cream ground, glossy
glaze, 20½" h. 1,400.00

(End of Weller Section)

WHIELDON-TYPE WARES

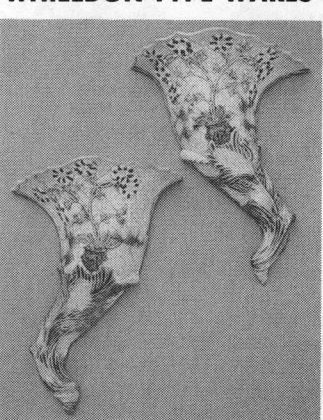

Whieldon-Type Wall Pockets

*The Staffordshire potter, Thomas Whiel-
don, first established a pottery at Fenton in
1740. Though he made all types of wares
generally in production in the 18th century,
he is best known for his attractive, warm-
colored green, yellow and brown mottled
wares molded in the form of vegetables, fruit
and leaves. He employed Josiah Spode as an
apprentice and was briefly in partnership
with Josiah Wedgwood. The term Whieldon
ware is, however, a generic one since his
wares were unmarked and are virtually in-
distinguishable from other similar wares
produced by other potters during the same
period.*

Basket & undertray, oval basket
w/end loop handles & flaring
reticulated sides splashed in mottled blue, green & ochre glaze
on a brown ground, the matching
undertray w/a reticulated border band, ca. 1760, undertray
9 5/8" l., 2 pcs. (one handle
reglued) $6,050.00
Plate, 9" d., commemorative-type,
the scalloped wide rim molded
w/a diaper pattern & reserved
w/panels inscribed "Success to
the - King of Prussia - And His
Forces," his portrait, martial
trophies & an eagle, splashed
overall w/a mottled green, ochre,
blue, brown & grey glaze, ca.
1770 . . . . 2,640.00
Plate, 9 5/8" d., scalloped rim mold-
ed w/a narrow beaded band,
mottled tortoiseshell glaze in
black, green, blue & brown (minor
wear & scratches) 214.50
Plates, 8 5/8" w., octagonal,
splashed overall w/mottled green
& yellow on a grey ground within

a reeded rim band, ca. 1770, set
of 4 . . . . .3,080.00
Platter, 18" l., oval w/scalloped
wide rim molded w/a diaper,
basketweave & scroll design &
splashed overall w/a mottled
green, ochre, grey & brown
glaze, ca. 1770 . . . . .7,700.00
Soup plates w/flanged rims, the
scalloped wide rim molded
w/paneled ermine borders,
splashed overall w/mottled ochre,
brown, grey & green, ca. 1770,
8¾" d., pr. (rim chips) 3,850.00
Teapot, cov., spherical body w/inset
cover w/knob finial, swan's-neck
spout & loop handle w/thumb tab,
overall mottled brown, yellow &
green tortoiseshell glaze, Little
Fenton, England, mid-18th c.,
5¼" h. 385.00
Vase, 6½" h., ovoid tapering body
w/a short cylindrical neck,
splashed overall w/a mottled
brown, blue & grey glaze, ca.
1770 (rim chip) 3,520.00
Wall pockets, creamware, cornu-
copia-form, molded on the front
w/a pot of ochre & brown flowers
w/green trailing leaves on the
diaper-molded ground above a
scrolling leaf-molded base in yellow & green, ca. 1765, some
restoration to both, 9½" h., pr.
(ILLUS.) 7,700.00

WILLOW WARES

*This pseudo-Chinese pattern has been used
by numerous firms throughout the years. The
original design is attributed to Thomas Minton about 1780 and Thomas Turner is be-
lieved to have first produced the ware during
his tenure at the Caughley works. The blue
underglaze transfer print pattern has never
been out of production since that time. An
Oriental landscape incorporating a bridge,
pagoda, trees, figures and birds, supposedly
tells the story of lovers fleeing a cruel father
who wished to prevent their marriage. The
gods, having pity on them, changed them into
birds enabling them to fly away and seek
their happiness together.*

*Also see BUFFALO POTTERY and
CHILDREN'S DISHES.*

BLUE

Basket, decorated, 10" d., 10" h. $27.50
Bone dish, large 60.00
Bowl, 5 3/8" d., Ridgway 15.00
Bowl, 5½" d., Royal China 4.00

Bowl, 5¾" d., Steventon & Sons 37.50
Bowl, cereal, 5 7/8" d., crown mark,
England 15.00
Bowl, 5 7/8" d., Ridgway 10.00
Bowl, 6½" d., Alfred Meakin 13.00
Bowl, 8¼" d., Wood's Ware 25.00
Bowl, 9½" d., Japan 22.50
Butter dish, cov., England, ¼ lb. . . .   55.00
Butter pat, Allerton, England 12.00
Butter warmer, stick-handled cup
w/spout fitted into a wire stand,
Japan 150.00
Canister, cov., tall ovoid body
marked "Instant Coffee," Japan . .   95.00
Carafe w/stopper & warmer, Japan,
overall 10" h., 2 pcs. 195.00
Casserole, cov., Allerton, England,
ca. 1932 . . . . 155.00
Casserole, cov., Gibson, England,
1912-30 . . . . 130.00
Chambersticks, scalloped saucer
base, gold trim, Gibson & Sons,
England, 5" d., pr. 95.00
Cheese dish, cov., England 150.00
Child's dinner set, cov. teapot, cov.
sugar bowl, creamer, six dinner
plates, six cups & saucers, large
cov. casserole, 7" l. platter, two
small serving plates & a footed
vase, 26 pcs. 325.00
Coffeepot, cov., footed cylindrical
body, Japan, 7" h. 110.00
Cracker jar, cov., cylindrical body
w/china cover, wicker bail han-
dle, Japan 125.00
Cracker jar w/silver plate cover, rim
& bail handle, Mintons, England . . 189.00
Creamer, Barratt's of Staffordshire,
England, ca. 1946 . . . .   35.00
Creamer, child's, 1½" h. 6.00
Creamer, Ridgway, England,
3¼" h. 35.00
Creamer & cov. sugar bowl, oval,
Japan, pr. 20.00
Creamer & cov. sugar bowl, Steven-
ton, England, large, pr. 35.00
Cup & saucer, demitasse, J. Wedg-
wood, ca. 1892 . . . .   38.00
Cup & saucer, Booth's, England 28.00
Cup & saucer, Ridgway 15.00
Cup & saucer, Royal Albert 16.00
Cup & saucer, Wood & Sons 14.00
Egg cup, single, Alfred Meakin,
England 20.00
Egg cup, double, Burleigh, Eng-
land 10.00
Egg cup, double, Japan 13.50
Gravy boat, Bakewell Bros., Ltd.,
England, 1927-43 . . . . 125.00
Gravy boat, Ridgway, England 35.00
Gravy dish, round, spout on either
side, "Gravy" and "Lean" printed
inside dish, 6" d. 75.00

Lamp, kerosene wall-type w/reflec-
tor, Japan, 8" h. 85.00
Pitcher, 5½" h., Ridgway, England . . 45.00
Pitcher, 6½" h., Japan 35.00
Pitcher, water, 11" h., octag-
onal, Mason's Ironstone,
19th c. . . . . 425.00 to 475.00
Pitcher, milk, Woods Ware, England,
ca. 1920 . . . . 75.00
Plate, child's, 3¼" d. 8.00
Plate, 5¾" d., Stevenson & Sons,
England, ca. 1920's 30.00
Plate, 6" d., Allerton, England 12.00
Plate, 6" d., Occupied Japan 10.00
Plate, 7" d., Ridgway, England 8.00
Plate, 8¾" d., Occupied Japan 25.00
Plate, 9" d., Wm. Adams, England . . 15.00
Plate, 9" d., Homer Laughlin 8.00
Plate, 9" d., Ridgways, England,
bow & quiver mark 20.00
Plate, 9¾" d., smooth edge, Aller-
ton, England 12.00
Plate, dinner, 10" d., Allerton,
England 22.00
Plate, dinner, 10" d., Barker Bros.,
England 10.00
Plate, dinner, 10" d., Brittania Pot-
tery Co., England, ca. 1930 . . . . . . 10.00
Plate, grill, 10¼" d., Japan 14.00
Platter, child's, 6¼" l., Japan 19.00
Platter, 9¼" l., Ridgway, England . . . 60.00
Platter, 12" l., Occupied Japan 32.00
Platter, 13½" l., Homer Laughlin . . . 20.00
Platter, 17½" l., Ridgway, England . . 175.00
Soup plates w/flanged rims,
10½" d., pr. 50.00
Sugar bowl, cov., child's 10.00
Sugar bowl, cov., Ridgway, England,
5" h. 45.00
Sugar bowl, cov., Japan 40.00
Teapot, cov., child's, 2½" h. 30.00
Teapot, cov., Allerton, England 125.00
Teapot, cov., individual size, Sadler
& Sons, England 30.00
Teapot, cov., reeded handle, w/in-
fuser, Japan 35.00
Vegetable bowl, cov., Burleigh
Ware, Burgess & Leigh, England,
ca. 1930 . . . . 165.00
Vegetable bowl, cov., handled,
Ridgway, England, 9" d. 65.00
Vegetable bowl, open, Royal China,
E. Hughes & Co., ca. 1920-40,
9" l. 15.00

WORCESTER

*The famed English Worcester factory was
established in 1751 and produced porcelains.
Earthenwares were made in the 19th century. Its first period is known as the "Dr. Wall"*
*period; that from 1783 to 1792 as the "Flight"
period; that from 1792 to 1807 as the "Barr
and Flight & Barr" period. The firm became
Barr, Flight & Barr from 1807 to 1813; Flight,
Barr & Barr from 1813 to 1840; Chamberlain
& Co. from 1840 to 1852, and Kerr and Binns
from 1852 to 1862. After 1862, the company
became the Worcester Royal Porcelain Company, Ltd., known familiarly as Royal
Worcester, which see. Also included in the following listing are examples of wares from the
early Chamberlains and early Grainger factories in Worcester.*

Early Worcester Pitcher

Basket, shallow oval form w/reticu-
lated sides studded w/florettes,
rope-twist end handles terminating in clusters of blossoms, decorated w/blue transfer-printed
"Pine Cone" patt. w/a central
cluster of flowers, fruit & pine
cones, the openwork border
w/blue interlocking circlets
w/scrolls & pendants & blue-
centered florettes, hatched Crescent mark in underglaze-blue, ca.
1775, 11 1/16" l. (some small
chips) $920.00
Caudle cups, covers & underplates,
each finely transfer-printed after
Robert Hancock in black on the
front of the ogee-shaped cups &
covers & in the center of the deep
plates w/the The Tea Party, No. 2
patt. depicting a small spaniel
romping at the feet of a couple
seated on a bench before a tea
table in a garden, the reverse of
the cups & covers w/the Maid &
Page, No. 1 patt. depicting a boy
or young blackamoor carrying a
kettle & walking beside a lady in
a garden, the cover sides decorated w/sprays of roses or other
flowers, cups w/pairs of scroll
side handles, each w/a black enamel line edging of the scalloped

& barbed rim, ca. 1765, underplates 5 13/16" d., 4¾" h., 2 sets
(minor knop chips) 2,875.00

Coffeepot, cov., pear-shaped,
transfer-printed in black &
enameled in green, blue, iron-
red, yellow, white, black, rose &
gold on either side w/a chinoiserie design of a Mandarin gentleman seated at a marbleized
table & holding a tea bowl & surrounded by three admiring ladies
& a child beneath an iron-red &
gilt scallop-and-dot border around
the rim, the cover similarly decorated, the gilt-edged spout decorated w/a vase of flowers,
1770-75, 8 7/8" h. (small spout
chip, some grittiness around
base) 920.00

Dishes, leaf-shaped, modeled as
overlapping vine leaves w/grey
veins, brown branch handle &
shaded yellow & green edges
painted in colors w/bouquets &
scattered sprigs, ca. 1760, 7¾" l.,
pr. (one w/rim chip & small hair-
line) 4,400.00

Junket dish, round shallow sides
w/scalloped & barbed rim, the interior molded w/an underglaze-
blue-trimmed flowerhead encircled by six scallop shells painted
alternately w/floral sprigs or bouquets & interrupting an underglaze-blue cell diaper border at
the rim, Open Crescent underglaze-blue mark, ca. 1770,
9¾" d. 805.00

Mug, cylindrical, transfer-printed in
underglaze-blue on either side
w/a floral spray from The Natural
Sprays Group, the reverse w/a
concave strap handle, underglaze-
blue hatched Crescent mark, ca.
1770, 3¼" h. 385.00

Pitcher, 6¾" h., jug-type, footed
baluster-form body w/S-scroll
handle, painted w/the Beckoning
Chinaman patt. featuring a
purple-robed Chinese man beckoning to a young boy wearing a
blue & yellow costume w/an iron-
red collar & cuffs, running by a
purple, green & iron-red stylized
rock on a green & turquoise lawn,
the back w/a *famille rose* palette
flowering branch, ca. 1758, two
small chips on spout lip (ILLUS.) . .3,630.00

Plate, dessert, 8 1/8" d., finely
painted in the center w/a full-
blown pink rose, three buds &
shaded green leaves against a
brown ground within a gilt-edged

roundel reserved on a gilt ver-
miculated ground, impressed
crowned "BFB" mark & crown &
Prince of Wales feathers above
"BARR FLIGHT & BARR Royal Por-
celain Works WORCESTER -
London-House FLIGHT & BARR
Coventry Street," ca. 1810 . . . . 575.00

Platter, 15" l., rectangular w/cut &
notched corners, Phoenix patt.,
painted in an expanded Kakiemon
palette of iron-red, green, blue,
yellow, rose, black & gold w/a
phoenix & insects in flight above
another phoenix perched amid
flowering branches & wheat
sheaves, the rim w/floral sprigs &
sprays within a border of iron-
red foliate scrolls alternating
w/gilt scroll-edged panels of iron-
red & gold trellis diaperwork at
the slightly upturned edge, painted probably in the atelier of
James Giles, ca. 1770 . . . . .2,013.00

Spill vase, footed cylindrical body
w/flared rim & gilt eagle's-mask-
and-ring handles, the body reserved on the front w/a gilt-
edged panel painted in shades of
rose, purple, yellow, green &
iron-red w/a basket of flowers on
a ledge against a shaded brown
ground, a border of applied white
beading under the flared rim, the
rim interior w/a gilt-stippled border edged in scrolls & foliate
sprays, the gilt-stippled square
foot w/gilt & bronze bands, unmarked Flight, Barr & Barr, ca.
1820, 4¼" h. 2,013.00

Teacup & saucer, each transfer-
printed after Robert Hancock in
purple & enameled in iron-red,
brown, green, yellow & gold, the
saucer also in blue, decorated
w/a scene of figures before classical ruins in an Italianate landscape, the reverse & interior of
the cup w/landscape vignettes
lacking figures & the rim edged in
gilt, underglaze-blue Crossed
Swords mark & "9," ca. 1770, saucer 5 1/8" d. (gilt slightly worn on
cup) 403.00

Vase, 6" h., footed trumpet-form
body, decorated on the front in
shades of green, yellow, brown,
blue, purple & salmon w/three
cows grazing or resting in a landscape at dusk before a distant
town, within gilt vine-edged oval
panel interrupting a gilt horizontal
foliate band & a narrow gilt bead-
and-reel band repeated around

the ankle, the sides w/molded
gilt ring handles, gilt rim bands,
mark of Flight & Barr in purple
script, ca. 1795 (slight rim wear). . 920.00

YELLOWWARE

Yellowware Mug

Yellowware is a form of utilitarian pottery produced in the United States and England from the early 19th century onward. Its body texture is less dense and vitreous (impervious to water) than stoneware. Most, but not all, yellowware is unmarked and its color varies from deep yellow to pale buff. In the late 19th and early 20th centuries bowls in graduated sizes were widely advertised. Still in production, yellowware is plentiful and still reasonably priced.

Bowl, 14" d., 3¾" h., widely flaring
sides, molded rim, marked on
base "Sharpes Warranted fire
proof," England, late 19th c. $85.00
Butter crock, cov., brown & white
stripes, 7½" d., 4" h. 125.00
Chamberpot, open, miniature, bulbous footed form, white band
around the middle, 1¾" h. (pinpoint flakes on foot) 49.50
Mixing bowl, deep rounded sides &
molded rim, a band of thin white
stripes under the rim, 13½" d.,
5¾" h. 55.00
Mixing bowl, deep slightly rounded
tapering sides to footring, wide
molded rim, a band w/thin brown
stripes flanking thin white stripes
under the rim, 13½" d., 6½" h. . . 65.00
Model of a dog, Spaniel-like animal
crudely modeled in a seated position holding a small basket in its
mouth, spotted coat, clear greenish glaze, 5" h. 225.00
Mug, cylindrical w/molded base,
C-scroll handle, a wide white middle band flanked by narrow
brown stripes, 3¾" h. (ILLUS.) 105.00
Preserving jar, cylindrical w/slightly
flaring lip, 8¼" h. (ILLUS. top next
column) 120.00
Shaker, footed baluster shape
w/domed cover, narrow bands of
blue, brown & white around the

Yellowware Preserving Jar

middle & the edge of the cover,
4 3/8" h. (small flakes) 385.00

ZSOLNAY

Zsolnay Figural Jardiniere

This pottery was made in Pecs, Hungary, in a factory founded in 1855 by Vilmos Zsolnay. Currently Zsolnay pieces are being made in a new factory.

Jardiniere, low squatty bulbous
body w/curved & tapering sides,
cast on the upper half w/two fancy pheasants, their long tails
arched & forming handles, glazed
in purple, silvery white, turquoise
& violet iridescence, signed in
overglaze "ZSOLNAY - PECS" &
"MADE IN - HUNGARY" w/other
impressed marks, several minor
chips, ca. 1900-20, 15½" d.,
7 5/8" h. (ILLUS.) $3,575.00
Vase, 5" h., 3½" d., short bulbous
body on a flaring foot & tapering
to a widely flaring rim, decorated
w/a bright iridescent glaze in red,
gold & green forming random
"bubbles" against a red, purple &
gold ground, marked "Zsolnay
Pecs" 440.00
Vase, 6 7/8" h., double gourd-shape
w/four handles, red & mustard
iridescent glaze, the upper section
decorated w/four mice, impressed
mark & "6020" 990.00
Vase, 8 1/8" h., double gourd-form,
decorated w/a forest landscape
w/leafy trees in the foreground,
glazed in purple, green, red, blue

& amber iridescence, raised & incised factory marks, ca. 1900 ....2,475.00

Vase, 10" h., tall baluster-form footed body tapering slightly to a
wide cylindrical neck, overall
swirled peacock blue iridescent
glaze, five-towered circular company mark...................... 660.00

Vase, 15 7/8" h., figural, the fanned
ovoid body cast at the front in
full-relief w/the figure of a standing nude maiden within a niche
w/her arms overhead holding a
furling length of drapery, three
tulip blossoms range overhead,
the background of the body cast
in low-relief w/whiplash designs,
glazed in iridescent lustre shading
from deep purple to golden green
& copper, impressed factory mark
& number "6235," ca. 1900 (repaired) 2,530.00

(End of Ceramics Section)

CHALKWARE

Chalkware Figure of a Girl Reading

*So-called chalkware available today is ac-
tually made of plaster of Paris, much of it
decorated in color and primarily in the form
of busts, figurines and ornaments. It was
produced through most of the 19th century
and the majority of pieces were originally
quite inexpensive when made. Today even
20th century "carnival" pieces are collectible.*

Bank, figural toddler, carnival prize,
  12" h......................... $60.00

Bank, figure of a redheaded clown
  riding a spotted pig, carnival
  prize, artist-signed, dated 1949,
  8 x 11"........................ 46.00

Bank, model of a cat, seated
  w/black & red ribbon collar &
  pipe, Pennsylvania, 19th century,
  10½" h....................... 198.00

Figure of a boy w/dog, carnival
  prize, 9 x 10".................. 65.00

Figure of a girl seated reading,
  polychrome paint, some paint
  wear, 19th c., 18½" h. (ILLUS.) ... 550.00

Figure of a young boy reading,
  decorated in mustard, red &
  brown, possibly Pennsylvania,
  19th c., 16½" h. (minor wear) ...1,320.00

Model of a cat, seated animal
  w/body molded as part of the
  base, the head turned facing the
  viewer, painted w/dark spots
  & polychrome trim, 19th c.,
  7½" h........................ 440.00

Model of a dog, Rin Tin Tin, carnival
  prize, 19" h.................... 50.00

Model of love birds, facing w/beaks
  touching, worn original polychrome paint, 3 1/8" h. (some
  surface wear & damage)........ 250.00

Model of a rooster, standing bird
  w/polychrome stripes on wings &
  tail, 19th c., 7¼" h. (black may
  be later, hole in tail) 800.00

Model of a squirrel, seated animal
  nibbling on a nut held in front
  paws, solid cast body w/old
  yellow-tinted varnish finish, 8" h.
  (wear & old chips)............. 65.00

Models of doves, large white bird
  on a thick squared base molded
  w/leaves & berries, worn polychrome trim, early 19th c., 11" h.,
  pr. (one w/base hairline) 750.00

CHARACTER COLLECTIBLES

Betty Boop Figure

*Numerous objects made in the likeness of
or named after movie, radio, television, comic strip and comic book personalities or*

characters abounded from the 1920's to the present. Scores of these are now being eagerly collected and prices still vary widely. Also see ADVERTISING ITEMS, BIG LITTLE BOOKS, DISNEY COLLECTIBLES, GAMES & GAME BOARDS and MOVIE MEMORABILIA.

Addams Family (TV) bank, "Thing," w/original box $115.00
Addams Family (TV) 'Thing's Box,' the wooden hinged box w/gold brocade fabric adhered w/brass studs, the inside painted gold w/a knob attached to open the box from the inside, together w/four photographs of Jackie Coogan & Ted Cassidy as Uncle Fester & Lurch, & a letter from Mrs. Jackie Coogan, 1964-66, the group 22,000.00
All in the Family card game, Milton Bradley, 1972 .... 7.00
Amos & Andy booklet, "Joy of a Nation," Edison Mfg. Co. 15.00
Amos & Andy figures, metal, 5" h., pr............................ 55.00
Amos & Andy paperweight, metal, Andy standing next to seated Amos, base signed "Amos & Andy, I won't do it - Shut up" 195.00
Andy Gump toy, car, Tootsietoy 275.00
Barbie, Midge & Skipper thermos, 1965 .... 35.00
Barnacle Bill (Popeye) toy, windup tin, featuring a springless rubber band windup motor causing a lithographed sailor to row his boat w/his oars, Emmert-Hammes, ca. 1925, in original box, 9½" l.................... 550.00
Barney Google figure, pressed wood, Multi Products of Chicago, 4" h.............................. 85.00
Batman mug, milk white glass, 1960's, near mint condition 15.00
Batman puppet, hand-type, 1965, mint on card 50.00
Batman & Robin paper plates, Batman & Robin pictured, 1966, package of 8....................... 6.00
Batman & Robin pillow, 1966, near mint condition 45.00
Bat Masterson (TV) game, board-type, "Bat Masterson Game," by Lowell Toys, 1958 .... 85.00
Beatles bath towel, pictures the four Beatles & their signatures, Nems, 1964 copyright 175.00
Beatles blanket, wool, Whitney, 45 x 72", mint condition 400.00
Beatles book, "The Beatles Illustrated Lyrics," by Alan Aldridge, w/dust jacket................. 20.00

Beatles buttons, model of the Yellow Submarine, set of 4 .... 15.00
Beatles figure set, hard plastic body, soft vinyl head & rooted hair, each figure holds a removable die-cut plastic instrument w/his name in facsimile signature in gold, back of each marked "The Beatles © 1964," Remco Plastics, 4½" h., set of 4 .... 250.00
Beatles game, card-type, "Dear Diary"......................... 50.00
Beatles guitar, Mexican-type, wood, inscribed by all four members of the group w/"Love from Paul McCartney xxx - George Harrison - Ringo Starr xxx - John Lennon," w/guitar case, ca. 1965, 2 pcs. (missing the strings) 11,000.00
Beatles lobby cards, from the movie "Hard Day's Night," set of 8 ...... 480.00
Betty Boop cookie jar, ceramic, Vandor....................... 105.00
Betty Boop figure, wood-jointed, oversized head w/bee-stung lips & enormous eyes, short black dress, w/"Betty Boop" heart-shaped label, ca. 1935, 13" h. (ILLUS.) 935.00
Betty Boop salt & pepper shakers, ceramic, Vandor, pr............. 20.00
Billie Holiday passport, official United States passport, issued to "Eleanor G. McKay Known as Billie Holiday, a citizen of the United States...," dated December 23, 1953, used extensively in 1954, 3¾ x 6" 2,750.00
Bimbo (Betty Boop's dog) figure, wood-jointed, depicted w/large head, big feet & enormous eyes, wearing a green sweater, colorfully painted, America, ca. 1935, 9" h. 462.00
Blondie game, card-type 15.00
Blondie Halloween costume, boxed.......................... 18.00
Blondie "hingees," paper assembly toy by King, Larson, McMahon of Chicago, unused in original envelope, 1944 .... 30.00
Blondie, Dagwood, Alexander & Cookie figures, wood, Multi Products of Chicago, 5" h., set of 4 .... 395.00
Bob Hope book, "I Never Left Home," 1944 .... 20.00
Bonanza coloring set, "Foto Fantasticks," 1966, in original box ... 75.00
Buck Jones badge, "Rangers' Club Member" 45.00
Buck Rogers book, pop-up type, "Buck Rogers in A Dangerous Mission"...................... 155.00

Buck Rogers Christmas light covers,
in original box, the set 130.00

Buck Rogers figures, cast metal, includes figures of Buck Rogers,
Wilma, Dr. Huer, Ardela & two
robots, made by Britains, Ltd. of
England for John Dille Company in
the U.S.A., each colorfully painted, ca. 1935, all fastened in original box, Cream of Wheat radio
premium, approximately 2¼" h.,
set of 6 .... 3,740.00

Buck Rogers thermos, Aladdin Industries, 1979 .... 12.50

Buck Rogers toy, "Flash Blast Attack
Ship," Tootsietoy, 1930's 105.00

Buddy Holly stage suit, white linen,
jacket & pleated pants, "Buddy
Holly" printed inside the right
pocket of the pants, ca. 1958 .... 1,870.00

Bugs Bunny book, "Bugs Bunny -
Stories for Children," 1947 ...... 14.00

Bullwinkle construction set, 1969,
mint on card 30.00

Bullwinkle game, "Bullwinkle's Table
Tennis," 1969, mint on card 18.00

Bullwinkle wrist watch, 1970, mint
condition 175.00

Captain Kangaroo (TV) playing
cards 6.00

Captain Marvel belt buckle w/secret
gumball dispenser, mint w/gum-
balls & original display card 45.00

Captain Marvel coloring book,
1941 .... 65.00

Captain Marvel puzzle, jigsaw-type,
1941, w/original box 47.00

Captain Marvel toy, "Balloon Flute,"
1947-48 .... 45.00

Captain Midnight decoder, 1940,
"Code-O-Graph," Ovaltine
premium 110.00

Captain Midnight decoder manual,
1957, mint condition 250.00

Captain Midnight patch, iron-on
type, 1940's, w/original envelope 150.00

Captain Video press book, pictures
toys, merchandise & poster 75.00

Casper, the Friendly Ghost (TV)
cookie jar, ceramic, American
Bisque (ILLUS. top next col-
umn) .... 850.00 to 1,000.00

Casper, the Friendly Ghost figure,
pressed wood, Multi Products of
Chicago, 4¾" h. 65.00

Casper, the Friendly Ghost lamp
shade, pictures Casper & friends
on a merry-go-round, near mint .. 28.00

Charlie Brown & Lucy figures, "bob-
bing head" type, Charlie wearing
a baseball cap & Lucy wearing a
red dress, 5½" h., pr. 185.00

Charlie Chaplin comic book,

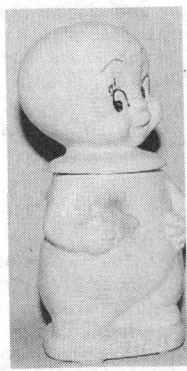

Casper the Ghost Cookie Jar

M.A. Donohue & Co., ca. 1917,
9¾ x 16" 80.00

Charlie Chaplin glove box, wooden
w/pyrographic decoration 100.00

Charlie Chaplin marionette, Hazelle,
mint in box 125.00

Charlie Chaplin toy, windup tin,
Charlie carries his cane & swings
his body from side to side at the
hip as he shuffles along, Gunther-
mann, ca. 1920, 9" h. 1,100.00

Charlie Chaplin w/Sunbonnet Babies
Easter egg decals, "Paas Dye
Co." 50.00

Charlie McCarthy card, greeting-
type, pictures Charlie & actress
Andrea Leeds, 1938 .... 28.00

Charlie McCarthy egg cup, porcelain, 1930's, excellent condition... 160.00

Charlie McCarthy match box w/six
match books, pictures Charlie &
Edgar, commemorates Tourna-
ment of Roses, 1957 .... 75.00

Charlie McCarthy soap figure, mint
in box........................ 85.00

Charlie McCarthy ventriloquist dum-
my, composition head, hands &
feet, straw-stuffed body, original
suit & monocle, marked "K & S,"
1930's, 32" h. 200.00

Chewbacca (Star Wars) figure,
w/cross bow laser rifle, Kenner
Products, Cincinnati, Ohio,
15" h. 125.00

Cheyenne (TV) play set, includes
plastic Indians, cavalry soldiers &
horses w/a vinyl & cardboard
case that opens up to a fort &
raised teepees village, Ideal Toy
Co., the set................... 75.00

Chilly Willy (Woody Woodpecker
Show, TV) tumbler, clear glass
w/black lettering, Pepsi-Cola
Walter Lantz series, 12 oz. (ILLUS.
top next column) 12.00

Chipmunks lunch box, vinyl 375.00

Chilly Willy Tumbler

Cisco Kid (TV) decal, star-shaped, pictures Duncan Renaldo, 1952, in original envelope 20.00

Cisco Kid lariat, paper, humming-type, ca. 1953.................. 38.00

Clarabell (Howdy Doody) ring, w/replica of horn on top, near mint condition 375.00

Daddy Warbucks pinback button, Kellogg's Pep Cereal premium.... 10.00

Daffy Duck cartoon cel, from "Kiss Me Cat," gouache on celluloid, applied to a gouache production background, the multi-cel setup depicting Daffy dressed in a chef's hat & apron in a kitchen, 1953, framed, 8½ x 10½" 1,980.00

Dagwood ring, metal, Post Toasties premium, ca. 1949 .... 20.00

Dale Evans book, "Danger in Crooked Canyon," 1958 .... 12.00

Dale Evans necklace, on original card 85.00

Dale Evans wrist watch, Ingraham, 1951 ....145.00 to 165.00

Daniel Boone (Fess Parker) shoes, high-top type, leather, size 6, mint in box picturing Daniel w/musket & horn 90.00

Dennis the Menace gun, squirt-type, ca. 1954, mint w/original box 60.00

Dennis the Menace napkins & coasters, 1950's, mint in box 45.00

Dennis the Menace paint set, 1958, mint in box.................. 125.00

Dick Tracy book, pop-up type, "The Capture of Boris Arson," 1935, published by Pleasure Books, Inc. 250.00

Dick Tracy camera, "Dick Tracy Candid Camera," w/50mm lens, plastic carrying case & uses 127 film, Seymour Sales Co., Chicago, Illinois, w/original 3 x 3 x 5¼" box (ILLUS. top next column) 195.00

Dick Tracy card game, "Super Detective Mystery Card Game," 35

Dick Tracy Candid Camera

cards, magnifying glass, boxed, 1941 .... 65.00

Dick Tracy comic book, "Dick Tracy - The Detective," first & rarest Dick Tracy comic book, David McKay Publications, May 1937, 100 pp. ...3,025.00

Dick Tracy Halloween costume, w/booklet, Motorola premium.... 45.00

Dick Tracy hat, fedora, "Dick Tracy Junior Crimestoppers Club," near mint 95.00

Dick Tracy pocket knife, 1940's 75.00

Dick Tracy poster, movie serial, "Dick Tracy vs. Crime Inc.," Chapter 1" 250.00

Dick Tracy puzzle, jigsaw-type, Jaymar Co., 14 x 22", w/original box 30.00

Dick Tracy ring, enameled bust portrait of Dick Tracy, radio premium 195.00

Dick Tracy submachine gun, green plastic, 1948, w/original box 200.00

Dick Tracy suspenders, from Detective set, boxed............... 48.00

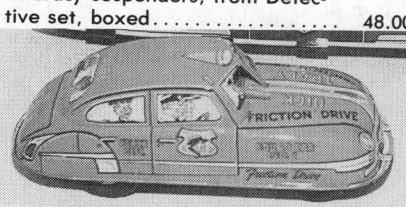

Dick Tracy Squad Car No. 1

Dick Tracy toy, "Squad Car No. 1," lithographed tin, friction drive, green, Marx, ca. 1949, 6½" l. (ILLUS.)........................ 125.00

Dionne Quintuplets blotter, 1935.... 22.00

Dionne Quintuplets book, "Going On Three," 1936 ....40.00 to 50.00

Dionne Quintuplets book, "Story of Dionne Quintuplets," 1935, 40 pp., mint condition 98.00

Dionne Quintuplets book, "We're Two Years Old," Whitman Publishing Co., 1936, illustrated, 50 pp.................40.00 to 50.00

Dionne Quintuplets calendar, 1953, "Dionne Quintette" 20.00

Dionne Quintuplets handkerchief, pictures the Quints 24.00

Dionne Quintuplets magazine cover, "Life," September 2, 1940, pictures the Quintuplets receiving First Communion................... 15.00

Don McNeill (radio) Breakfast Club
  yearbook, 1948 . . . .   11.00
Dudley Do-Right (Bullwinkle - TV)
  tumbler, pictures him in a canoe,
  clear glass, Pepsi collection se-
  ries, 12 oz.   10.00
Elvis Presley book, "Top Pop Stars,"
  includes Elvis' story, hardcover,
  1963 . . . .   45.00
Elvis Presley dog tag anklet, on
  original card, dated 1956 . . 40.00 to 50.00
Elvis Presley earrings, gold-plated,
  1956, mint in original package. . . .   40.00
Elvis Presley flicker button, "Love
  Me Tender" changes to a perform-
  ing pose, 1956, 2½" d. 22.00
Elvis Presley necklace, "Love
  Me Tender," on original
  card . . . . 200.00 to 225.00
Elvis Presley record album cover,
  "Elvis Presley in Kid Galahad,"
  autographed by Elvis, framed
  w/plaque reading "Elvis Presley -
  1935-1977 - The King of Rock and
  Roll," frame 12½ x 15¼" 330.00
Felix the Cat baby bottle, clear
  glass, embossed illustration of Fe-
  lix, ca. 1930 . . . .   75.00
Felix the Cat figure, jointed wood
  body, Schoenhut, dated 1924,
  4" h. . . . . 100.00 to 125.00
Felix the Cat game, board-type, ca.
  1960, near mint 60.00
Flash Gordon coloring book, 1953. . .   18.50
Flash Gordon play set, "Flash Gor-
  don Solar Commando Space Set,"
  w/plastic spaceships & space
  man, Premier Products, 1952, near
  mint on card. 65.00

Flash Gordon Ring

Flash Gordon ring, metal, premium
  from Post Toasties cereal, 1949
  (ILLUS.). 20.00
Flintstones (TV) ashtray, pottery,
  scene w/Barney, 1961 . . . .   95.00
Flintstones (TV) bubble pipe, pictures
  Pebbles, on original card . . 20.00 to 30.00
Flintstones (TV) card game, "Animal
  Rummy," 1961, complete in origi-
  nal box 45.00
Flintstones (TV) cartoon cel, scene
  of Fred, Barney, Wilma & Betty in
  Barney's "car" heading for a night
  on the town, multi-cel setup applied to a water-color production
  background, Hanna-Barbera Stu-
  dios, ca. 1960's, 7½ x 9½" 990.00

Flintstones Cookie Jar

Flintstones (TV) cookie jar, cover
  w/Dino finial, pictures Fred &
  "Flintstones" impressed on upper
  part of jar, American Bisque
  Company, base marked "USA"
  (ILLUS.) 1,400.00
Flintstones (TV) cookie jar, cov.,
  Wilma sitting in a chair talking on
  the telephone, "Flintstones" on
  chair arm, American Bisque Com-
  pany, base marked "USA" 1,600.00
Flintstones game, "Stone Age
  Tiddlywinks," 1961, original
  package 40.00
Flintstones Halloween costume,
  Fred, w/original box 25.00
Flintstones play set, "The Flintstones
  Bedrock Express," includes a plas-
  tic & metal windup handcar, train
  track & a three-dimensional plas-
  tic Bedrock community, Louis
  Marx & Co., New York, New
  York, 1962, mint in original box . .   100.00
Flintstones toy, battery-operated,
  "Fred Flintstone and Dino the
  Dinosaur," Marx, ca. 1960,
  22" l. . . . . 425.00 to 475.00
Gene Autry bicycle horn, in original
  box 95.00
Gene Autry book, "Gene Autry &
  the Thief River Outlaws," 1944 . . .   20.00
Gene Autry book, "Gene Autry
  Book of Adventures," hard cover,
  illustrated, England, 1958 . . . .   65.00
Gene Autry boots, rubber,
  w/box . . . . 125.00 to 150.00
Gene Autry coloring book, 1957,
  unused 10.00
Gene Autry flashlight, pictures
  Gene w/lariat, in original box. . . .   135.00
Gene Autry game, board-type,
  "Dude Ranch" 40.00
Gene Autry guitar, cardboard
  w/leather-like design, Emenee,
  w/original box. . . . . 175.00 to 200.00
Gene Autry phonograph record,
  "Frosty the Snowman," 78 rpm,
  w/decorative jacket 36.00

Gene Autry sheet music, "Red River Valley," 1935 .... 22.00

Gene Autry wrist watch, his gun indicating seconds, back die-bossed "Always Your Pal, Gene Autry," green radium hands, brown leather band, Wilane copyright 1948, mint in box .... 350.00 to 400.00

Green Hornet kite, colorfully illustrated, ca. 1950, in unopened package 35.00

Green Hornet (TV) lunch box w/thermos bottle, King Seeley, 1967 .... 150.00 to 175.00

Gunsmoke (TV) game, board-type, "Gunsmoke," by Lowell Toy, late 1950's 40.00

Gunsmoke (TV) sign, cardboard, pictures Matt Dillon & Miss Kitty, promotion from "L & M Cigarettes," early 1960's, 21 x 22" 40.00

Hogan's Heroes (TV) jeep, 1968, mint in box 95.00

Hopalong Cassidy badge, "Savings Club Teller" 30.00

Hopalong Cassidy bedroom set: bedspread, drapes & rug; colorfully illustrated w/Hoppy & Topper, 3 pcs. 625.00

Hopalong Cassidy belt buckle, heavily embossed Hopalong face between buckles, marked "EACO," 1950 .... 28.00

Hopalong Cassidy bicycle, girl's, fully restored, including new Hoppy guns, 20" 3,750.00

Hopalong Cassidy book, pop-up type, "Hopalong Cassidy and Lucky at Copper Gulch," 1950's ... 70.00

Hopalong Cassidy "Pop-Up" Book

Hopalong Cassidy book, pop-up type, "Hopalong Cassidy and Lucky at the Double X Ranch," Garden City Publishing Company, 1950, 8½ x 11" (ILLUS.) 75.00

Hopalong Cassidy briefcase, illustration of Hoppy & Topper on front, mint condition 195.00

Hopalong Cassidy Camera

Hopalong Cassidy camera, Galter Products Co., 1940, original box (ILLUS.) 250.00

Hopalong Cassidy cap guns & holster set, black leather holster, Wyandotte Toys (Wyandotte, Michigan), 1950, the set .... 550.00 to 650.00

Hopalong Cassidy cap guns & holster set, white grips w/black embossed Hopalong bust, made by Geo. Schmidt, 1950, the set 695.00

Hopalong Cassidy counter display, yellow & black easel-type, special promotion from "Wonder Bread" to promote guests on the TV show, 11 x 14½" 175.00

Hopalong Cassidy cowgirl outfit, Iskin, size 10, 1950, in original box, 4 pcs. .... 250.00 to 275.00

Hopalong Cassidy game, "Ring Toss Lasso," figural Hopalong on Topper, two posts & rings, w/box 250.00

Hopalong Cassidy ice cream carton, "Weber's Ice Cream - My Favorite Kind," cardboard, pictures Hopalong, ½ gal. 38.00

Hopalong Cassidy key chain, on original card 125.00

Hopalong Cassidy magazine cover story, "Life," June, 1950 .... 35.00

Hopalong Cassidy milk bottle, black & red graphics, Dairy-Lee Milk, qt. .... 50.00 to 75.00

Hopalong Cassidy napkins, paper, set of 50, in original package 65.00

Hopalong Cassidy neckerchief & steer head neckerchief slide, red neckerchief, 2 pcs. 80.00

Hopalong Cassidy plate, milk white glass w/black decal of Hoppy & Topper, Anchor Hocking, 7" d. (ILLUS. top next page) 62.50

Hopalong Cassidy Plate

Hopalong Cassidy postcard, advertising Chrysler-Plymouth, 1942 .... 9.00

Hopalong Cassidy Movie Poster

Hopalong Cassidy poster, for the movie "Riders of the Deadline," ca. 1945, 28 x 44½" (ILLUS.) 121.00

Hopalong Cassidy puzzle, color frame tray, inlay picture puzzle w/sleeve, 1950 .... 55.00

Hopalong Cassidy record, "Hopalong Cassidy Happy Birthday," w/original colorful record sleeve, 78 rpm 45.00

Hopalong Cassidy rug, chenille, horsehead & fence, 2 x 4' ....150.00 to 175.00

Hopalong Cassidy wrist watch, picture of Hoppy on face, black strap, die-bossed "Good Luck from Hoppy," U.S. Time, 1950-67, w/box ....250.00 to 300.00

Hoss (Bonanza, TV) figure w/horse, distributed by Sears, Roebuck & Co. exclusively, in original stable-like display box 250.00

Howdy Doody bank, ceramic, a figure of Howdy astride a small, smiling pig, 7" h. 285.00

Howdy Doody camera, "Sun Ray," mint in original package 65.00

Howdy Doody clock, "Time Teacher," in original package, 18" 30.00

Howdy Doody coloring book, Poll Parrot Shoes premium 40.00

Howdy Doody "Cookie-Go-Round" container, tin, pictures Howdy & friends riding carousel, 1950's, large ....200.00 to 250.00

Howdy Doody cookie jar, cov., head of Howdy w/winking eye, Vandor ....350.00 to 450.00

Howdy Doody figure, wood-jointed push-up type, Howdy shown in front of an N.B.C. mike, w/rare original box ....200.00 to 250.00

Howdy Doody handkerchief, colorful, pictures Howdy, 8 x 8¼" 30.00

Howdy Doody ice cream cup, pictures five main characters, Kagran (no lid) 65.00

Howdy Doody light fixture, glass, pictures Howdy sitting on a chimney w/Santa standing next to him, w/original box .....250.00 to 300.00

Howdy Doody marionette, composition hands, head & feet, dressed in original cowboy outfit, 16" h. .. 175.00

Howdy Doody paint-by-number set, w/original oil paints, in original box ....40.00 to 60.00

Howdy Doody record, "Christmas Carol," 45 rpm, in original colorful sleeve 20.00

Howdy Doody record player, "Phono Doodle," 1950's, w/original box ....200.00 to 250.00

Howdy Doody ring, flashlight-type w/a molded Howdy face mask on a metal ring ....125.00 to 175.00

Howdy Doody shake-up mug, Ovaltine premium, Bob Smith copyright 120.00

Howdy Doody Toy Figure

Howdy Doody toy, plastic figure of Howdy w/a movable mouth, w/box marked "Howdy Doody - a Tee Vee Toy" on top, ca. 1950's, 4" h. (ILLUS.) 46.00

Howdy Doody tumbler, glass, "Howdy Doody & Dilly Dally," Welch's, 1953, 4" h. 55.00

Howdy Doody ukulele, "Howdy Doody Uke," Emenee Mfg., marked "Copyright Kagran," ca. 1950, 17" l., mint in box ..... 225.00 to 250.00

Howdy Doody characters ceiling fixture, glass, pictures Howdy, Clarabell, Flub-a-dub & Mr. Bluster, 11 x 11" sq. 175.00

Howdy Doody characters puppets, hard plastic, includes Howdy, Clarabell, Dilly Dally, Princess Summerfall-Winterspring & Mr. Bluster, figures each w/a movable mouth operated by a small lever in back of the head, each figure w/a "Tee Vee" and each dressed in pink accented by reds & blues, box designed to serve as a small theatre, each figure about 4" h., the set, mint in box 125.00

Huckleberry Hound (TV) bank, hard plastic, figural w/top hat, top hat has coin slot & head is removable, red w/tan & black accents, Knickerbocker Toys, ca. 1960, 10" h. ... 25.00

Huckleberry Hound puppet, handtype, Ka-Klar Toys.............. 23.00

Huckleberry Hound TV tray, metal w/folding legs, colorful lithographed cartoon scene showing Huckleberry & friends, 13 x 18"... 35.00

I Love Lucy magazine, "TV Guide," April 3, 1953, Volume 1, No. 1, cover pictures Lucy & Desi's newborn son & a small picture of Lucy in the upper left hand corner, cover article is titled "Lucy's $50,000,000 Baby," w/color pictures of the new parents in the article & scenes from "I Love Lucy" 400.00

Jack Armstrong booklet, entitled "Jack Armstrong Treasure Hunter," Wheaties premium 6.00

Jackie Coogan pencil box, tin, 1920's, 2 x 7¾" (ILLUS. top next column) 45.00

Jetsons coloring book, produced by Hanna-Barbera Productions, unused 30.00

Jiggs pinback button, Kellogg's Pep Cereal premium................ 25.00

Jimi Hendrix shawl, pale green silk embroidered w/pink & white floral designs & green fringe, ca.

Jackie Coogan Pencil Box

1969, 55" sq. (some tears & stains)........................1,760.00

Joe Palooka (comics) comic book, "Joe Palooka's Toughest Fight," 1947, framed 22.00

Joe Palooka comic book, entitled "School Bus Safety Tips," premium from "Superior Coach Corporation," 1950.................... 20.00

John Lennon (Beatles) guitar, Hofner Compensator steel-string acoustic "Senator" model, No. 4697, w/simulated tortoiseshell fingerplate, mother-of-pearl inlaid fret markers, five steel strings, w/letter of authenticity signed by George Harrison, w/carrying case, early 1960's, the group ...33,000.00

Kojak (TV) handcuff set, mint on original card.................... 20.00

Krazy Kat original cartoon strip art, pen & ink on cardboard, depicting antics of Krazy Kat, Ignatz Mouse & Officer Pup, by George Herriman, unframed, 17" w., 25" h....5,500.00

Li'l Abner ashtray, ceramic, 1960's .. 95.00

Li'l Abner paint set, ca. 1940, mint in original box..........100.00 to 120.00

Li'l Abner stickers, premium from "Orange Crush," colorful, set of 8........................ 15.00

Li'l Abner toy, windup tin, "Li'l Abner & His Dogpatch Band," Unique Art, 1945, w/box............... 660.00

Li'l Abner tumbler set: includes illustrations of Daisy Mae, Li'l Abner, Lonesome Polecat, Mammy Yokum, Marryin' Sam/Sadie Hawkins, Pappy Yokum, Shmoos, Unwashable Jones; clear glass, United Features Syndicate, 1949, 4¾" h., set of 8................. 150.00

Little Lulu (comics) book, "Little Lulu & Her Pals," 1939, w/dust jacket........................ 35.00

Little Lulu doll, cloth head w/mask
face, painted black eyes, single
stroke brows, accented nose,
closed smiling mouth, black flannel 'hair' w/black yarn hair
around face, cloth body jointed at
shoulders & hips, dressed in original clothing w/original blue plastic purse, original tag reads "Little
Lulu, Copr. 1944 Marjorie H. Buell;
Little Lulu by Marge, Georgene
Novelties, Inc., New York City,
Exclusive Licensed Manufacturers,
Made in U.S.A.," 14" h. 700.00
Little Lulu original artwork, pen &
ink on illustration board of a comic book page by John Stanley,
from "Little Lulu No. 106," 1950's,
14 x 20" 715.00
Lone Ranger badge, brass, horse-
shoe-shaped, "Lone Ranger Club,"
1930's 15.00
Lone Ranger book, "Lone Ranger
and The Mystery Ranch," 1940's,
published by Grosset & Dunlap,
hard bound, w/dust jacket 25.00

Lone Ranger Bookbag

Lone Ranger bookbag, leatherette,
multicolored picture on tan,
10 x 12" (ILLUS.) 175.00
Lone Ranger cap pistol, cast iron,
Kilgore Mfg. Co. (Westerville,
Ohio), 1938, near mint condition . .   395.00
Lone Ranger coin, premium from
"Merita Bread," inscribed "Peace
Patrol" 35.00
Lone Ranger comic book, Cheerios
premium, 1956, near mint 15.00
Lone Ranger decal, premium from
"Blue Ribbon Bread" 175.00
Lone Ranger game, skill-type, pin-
ball ball-bearing mechanism,
backplate decorated w/a scene
of the Lone Ranger & four men
panning for gold, glass frame,
3½ x 5" 25.00
Lone Ranger play set: plastic gun,
leather holster & leather cuffs;
mint in original box, 4 pcs. 255.00

Lone Ranger play set: belt, jail keys,
badge, bullet keychain & mask;
mint on card, the set 145.00
Lone Ranger play set: "Frontier
Town," includes 56 assembled
houses, four maps & accessories;
Cheerios premium, 1949, the
group 250.00
Lone Ranger pocket watch, New
Haven Clock Co., 1939 . . .350.00 to 375.00
Lone Ranger ring, "Atom Bomb,"
w/instructions . . . . .75.00 to 100.00
Lone Ranger ring, "Six-shooter,"
Cheerios premium,
1940's . . . . .75.00 to 100.00
Lone Ranger tattoo transfers kit, ca.
1940, in original mailer 25.00

Lone Ranger Tumbler

Lone Ranger tumbler, clear glass
w/white enameled Lone Ranger &
Silver, dated 1938 (ILLUS.) 52.50
Lost in Space (TV) lunch box & ther-
mos, dome-top, 1967-68 . . . .   475.00
Lum & Abner (radio) book, "Lum
and Abner's Adventures in
Hollywood and 1938 Family
Almanac" 4.00
Maggie & Jiggs salt & pepper shak-
ers, china, Germany, ca. 1920,
pr. 275.00
Man From U.N.C.L.E. (TV) card
game, 1965, complete in original
box 45.00
McHale's Navy (TV) game, board-
type, pictures Ernest Borgnine on
box 85.00

Mighty Mouse Title Card Artwork

Mighty Mouse (cartoons) original title card artwork, water-color on paper applied to a water-color production background, shows Mighty Mouse flying through a starry sky, ca. 1940's, 8 x 10½" (ILLUS.) 1,760.00

Mighty Mouse record, story-type, "Mighty Mouse & Dinky Duck," 78 rpm, w/original sleeve........ 10.00

Mighty Mouse tambourine, vinyl 30.00

Monkees (TV) ring, flasher-type 25.00

Moon Mullins (comics) figure, bisque, 7" h.................... 95.00

Munsters (TV) card game, 1964 ....35.00 to 45.00

Munsters (The) puppet, figure of Herman Munster, w/working voice box.................. 195.00

Mutt & Jeff (comics) figures, bisque, nodder-type, Germany, each 2¾" h., pr. 125.00

Mutt & Jeff figures, composition, ball-jointed limbs, dressed in original felt clothing, 6" & 8" h., pr............................. 550.00

Nancy (comic strip) doll, stuffed cloth, cloth mask face w/painted black eyes, single stroke brows, closed smiling mouth, black synthetic hair, cloth body jointed at shoulders & hips, wearing original dress, striped socks & yellow shoes part of the legs, 14" h. (played-with condition, wear & soil on face) 110.00

Olive Oyl (Popeye's girlfriend) pen, fountain-type, Bakelite, green 55.00

Olive Oyl pin, enameled metal, 1938 .... 65.00

Olive Oyl pinback button, Kellogg's Pep Cereal premium............. 25.00

Orphan Annie coloring book, "Jr. Commando," 1943 ....35.00 to 45.00

Orphan Annie decoder, 1937, Ovaltine premium ....35.00 to 45.00

Orphan Annie 1938 Decoder

Orphan Annie decoder, "Telematic," 1938, Ovaltine premium (ILLUS.)..................40.00 to 50.00

Orphan Annie decoder manual, 1935, Ovaltine premium 35.00

Orphan Annie decoder, 1936, Ovaltine premium, w/Secret Society manual, 2 pcs................... 80.00

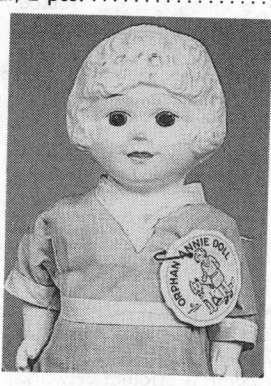

Orphan Annie Doll

Orphan Annie doll, composition shoulder head w/painted blue eyes, closed mouth & molded & painted hair, cloth body w/composition arms, wearing original dress, underwear, shoes & socks, w/original paper tag, 1930's, 15" h. (ILLUS.) 180.00

Orphan Annie game, "Light up the Candles," tin & cardboard, Colmor 50.00

Orphan Annie game, "Treasure Hunt," Ovaltine premium, 1933, Wander Co.................... 56.00

Orphan Annie "Penny" books, in original holder, miniature, 1934, mint condition, set of 6 .... 120.00

Orphan Annie "shake-up" mug, Beetleware, w/orange cover, Ovaltine premium, 1935 ...40.00 to 50.00

Orphan Annie Sheet Music

Orphan Annie sheet music, "Little Orphan Annie's Song," 1931 (ILLUS.)...................... 15.00

Orphan Annie & Sandy plate, china w/lustre finish, Japan, ca. 1920, 4" d. 28.00

Orphan Annie & Sandy toothbrush holder, bisque ....150.00 to 175.00

Our Gang blotter, Majestic radios premium 30.00

Our Gang photograph, autographed by Jean Darling, w/original decorative matt, 1928............ 175.00

Our Gang plate, pictures Jean Darling, Sebring Pottery............. 65.00

Paladin play set, w/Paladin, cowboys, horses, mine camp w/operating pump & sluice, w/original box 295.00

Partridge Family (TV) notebook, unused 15.00

Paul McCartney "Soaky" container, 1964 .... 75.00

Peanuts (comics) original artwork, pen & ink on illustration board for a daily strip featuring Charlie Brown, by Charles Schulz, August 24, 1979, 7 x 23½" 1,540.00

Phantom, The (comics) original artwork, pen & ink on illustration board for a Sunday comic strip, June 6, 1943, 19 x 29" 1,320.00

Planet of the Apes game, board-type 30.00

Planet of the Apes mask, latex, full-head type w/molded hair 125.00

Planet of the Apes play set, "Planet of the Apes Colorforms Adventure Set," 1967, complete in box 45.00

Pogo (comics) original artwork, pen & ink on illustration board of a daily comic strip, by Walt Kelly, December 20, 1956, 6 x 17".......1,210.00

Popeye bank, "Daily Quarter Bank," lithographed metal, 3 x 4 x 4½".. 225.00

Popeye belt buckle, etched "Popeye says 'Strength Thru Spinach'," 3" d. 29.00

Popeye book, "Popeye & the Gold Mine Thieves," 1935 .... 40.00

bust of Popeye, American Bisque Co., marked "USA" (ILLUS.) 725.00

Popeye cookie jar, cov., ceramic, white cylinder decorated w/a colorful decal, McCoy, 1971-72.... 155.00

Popeye game, "Popeye Pick-Up Sticks," 1957, complete in can 30.00

Popeye halloween costume, Collegeville, ca. 1950, w/original box 48.00

Popeye original artwork, pen & ink on illustration board for daily strip featuring Popeye in the "Land of the Goons," December 28, 1937, by E.C. Segar, 5 x 22"...........1,320.00

Popeye pinback button, "Penney's Back to School Days," w/picture of Popeye, 1935, 7/8" d. 60.00

Popeye toy, pop-up type, "Popeye Spinach" can, plastic & metal, Popeye's head comes up when the can is opened................... 95.00

Princess SummerFall/WinterSpring (Howdy Doody, TV) scarf, silk, 17" sq. 60.00

Quick Draw McGraw (TV) game, target-type, "Pop a Dart," Knickerbocker, 1960, mint in near mint box 70.00

Ringo Starr doll, vinyl, inflatable-type, 16" h. 17.50

Rin Tin Tin (TV) cap gun 45.00

Rin Tin Tin coloring book.......... 35.00

Rin Tin Tin toy, "Wonder Scope" 115.00

Rin Tin Tin & Rusty toy, play set, includes bronze-tone gun, holster, telescope & cartridge clip, the set................................. 150.00

Rootie Kazootie (TV) card game, 1953, in original box 30.00

'Flying Fickle Finger of Fate' Award

Rowan and Martin's "Laugh-In" (TV) prop, the "Flying Fickle Finger of Fate Award," plaster & wood w/gold & faux wood finish, a large pointing hand w/tin wings

Popeye Cookie Jar

Popeye cookie jar, cov., ceramic,

on pointer finger, raised on a square platform base w/the inscription "The Rowan-Martin Laugh-In Flying Fickle Finger of Fate Award," presented each week on the program, 1968-73 (ILLUS.) 2,860.00

Roy Acuff book, "The Smokey Mountain Boy" 25.00

Roy Rogers birthday napkins, 1950's, unopened package 18.00

Roy Rogers book, "Roy Rogers & The Outlaws of Sundown Valley," 1950 .... 12.00

Roy Rogers calendar, 1959, w/complete pad 195.00

Roy Rogers lariat, rodeo-type, mint on original card 175.00

Roy Rogers pencil, embossed "King of the Cowboys" 3.00

Roy Rogers & Dale Evans paper dolls, "Roy Rogers and Dale Evans Cut-out Dolls," cardboard folder w/inside pockets holding stiff cardboard stand-up Roy & Dale dolls, w/paper sheets of clothing for each, Whitman, 1954, uncut ... 120.00

Saturday Night Live (TV) skit prop, pair of "Killer Bee" antennae, black plastic headband w/yellow painted coils & glitter attached to resemble antennae, used by John Belushi, ca. 1980's 385.00

Sergeant Preston distance finder, 1955 .... 50.00

Sergeant Preston land deed, "Klondike Big Inch Land Co., Inc.," certificate citing legal terms & authorizing bearer to a single square inch of territory in the Yukon, printed on both sides, Quaker Cereal premium, 1955, 5 x 8".. 65.00

Shari Lewis play set, "Lamb Chop Stuff & Lace," mint in box 125.00

Shirley Temple doll carriage, wooden body w/Shirley Temple decals on sides, metal frame & handle, oilcloth hood, rubber tires, "Shirley Temple" on hub caps & hood knobs, labeled "Genuine Shirley Temple, 20th Century Fox Film Star, Whitney-Ideal, Doll Carriage," 25" h. (metal somewhat rusted, oilcloth finish is cracking) 400.00

Shirley Temple handkerchief, pictures Shirley in costume from "Little Colonel," mint in box 60.00

Shirley Temple paper doll book, No. 1761, Saalfield, 1937, uncut .. 275.00

Shirley Temple pencil kit, green taffeta, "Little Shirley" in gold lettering on the cover & "Onward" on a bottom corner, handle, fold over closure snaps & corner protectors, mint condition 125.00

Shirley Temple photograph, pictures Shirley drinking a glass of milk, signed "Drink Milk Daily - Shirley Temple," publicity photo provided by 20th Century-Fox, 1938, 8 x 10" 23.00

Shirley Temple playing cards, bridge-type, pictures Shirley wearing a bonnet, w/original box 50.00

Shirley Temple scarf clasp, enameled w/"Shirley Temple's Pet 'Howdy'," & an illustration of the dog 65.00

Shirley Temple sheet music, "Laugh You Son of a Gun" 65.00

Shirley Temple theatre ticket for Hollywood world premiere of "The Bluebird," unused 45.00

Skeezix (comics) doll, oilcloth w/cotton stuffing, 1924, 14" h. 125.00

Smokey the Bear pocket watch, mint in box 175.00

Snoopy apron, bib-type, pictures Snoopy on top of his doghouse & "Home is where the supper dish is," 19 x 28½" 12.50

Snoopy hot water bottle 35.00

Snoopy night light, Snoopy dressed as a W.W. I flying ace 15.00

Snoopy paperweight, ceramic, Snoopy lying on his tummy 18.00

Snoopy postcards, depicts Snoopy w/"Snoopy for President" caption, different scene on each, set of 5 .... 35.00

Snoopy & Peanuts characters megaphone, metal, J. Chein & Co., New York, New York 25.00

Spider-Man radio, figural, 1973 ..... 45.00

Spider-Man telephone, 1984, excellent condition 150.00

Spider-Man water gun, 1975, mint on original card 12.50

Spike Jones drum set, mint condition 650.00

Star Trek (TV) lunch box & thermos, starship Enterprise on front, Captain Kirk & Mr. Spock on the back, Aladdin Industries, 1968, 2 pcs. 1,320.00

Star Trek pinball machine, Bally Mfg. Co., ca. 1978, w/service & instruction books 1,750.00

Star Trek puzzle, jigsaw-type, 1976, 150 pcs. 15.00

Star Trek tunic, red & black zippered nylon tunic, worn by an "Engineering and Support Services" crewman on the starship Enterprise, 1960's (ILLUS. top next page) 1,650.00

Star Trek Crewman's Tunic

Superman bandages, "Curad Bandages by Colgate-Palmolive," in colorful box 20.00

Superman book, "Superman," by George Lowther, 1942, Random House Press, first full-length novel describing the origin & story of Superman 209.00

Superman hairbrush, black w/two red, white & blue decals, 4" l 150.00

Superman Movie Cel

Superman movie cel, gouache on celluloid, full-figure depiction of Superman standing w/hands on hips, Fleischer Studios, 1941, together w/letter of authenticity, 6¾ x 11", 2 pcs. (ILLUS.) 3,300.00

Superman paint by number book, 1966 . . . .   55.00

Superman photograph, pictures Kirk Allen as Superman, black & white w/sepia tone highlights, Columbia Pictures Serial, 5 x 7" 135.00

Superman slippers, sock-type, 1973 . . . .   18.00

Superman toy, "Krypton Rocket & Launcher," plastic, Kellogg's premium, 1950-59, w/box 500.00

Tarzan book, pop-up type, Blue Ribbon, 1934 . . . . 200.00

Tarzan comic strip artwork, pen & ink on illustration board of a full Sunday page strip No. 903, by Burne Hogarth, June 20, 1948, 21 x 28" 1,540.00

Three Stooges carpenter's apron, "Cooper Tools" premium 35.00

Three Stooges fan club kit, 1959 . . . .   85.00

Tom & Jerry (TV) mug, illustrates the two characters in combat, Staffordshire Potteries, England, 1970, 3¼" h. 35.00

Tom Corbett, Space Cadet, bedspread & drapes set, near mint condition 225.00

Tom Corbett, Space Cadet, book, "The Robot Rocket," w/dust jacket, 1956 . . . .   25.00

Tom Corbett, Space Cadet, coloring & cut-out book, 1952 . . . .   95.00

Tom Mix belt buckle w/decoder & secret compartment, Ralston premium, 1946 . . . .   85.00

Tom Mix decoder badge, "Six Gun Decoder," 1941 . . . .   52.00

Tom Mix lobby cards, from the movie "Deadwood Coach," pr. 100.00

Tom Mix manual, "Life Of Tom Mix and the Ralston Straight Shooters Manual," 1933, w/original mailer 110.00

Tom Mix ring, "Look Around," 1946 . . . . 110.00

Tom Mix toy, "Rocket Parachute," in original mailer, 1936 . . . . 175.00

Tonto egg cup, cream-colored porcelain, pictures Tonto, ca. 1950 . . .   35.00

Tweety Bird (TV) tumbler, clear glass w/illustration & "Tweety Bird" on both sides, Warner Brothers Collector Series, Pepsi-Cola premium, 1973 . . . .   7.00

Voyage to the Bottom of the Sea (TV) game, board-type 135.00

Wanted: Dead or Alive (TV) cap gun, mint on card 125.00

Wild Bill Hickok, The Adventures of (TV) holster & double gun set 235.00

Wimpy (Popeye's friend) ring, Post Toasties premium, mint in package 18.00

Wizard of Oz tumbler, Cowardly Lion, glass, Swift's Peanut Butter container, 1950 (ILLUS. top next column) 182.00

Wizard of Oz valentine card, Scarecrow, licensed by Loew, 3 x 5" . . .   60.00

Woody Woodpecker cookie jar, cov., ceramic, bust of Woody, base marked "© 1967 Walter Lantz," 14¼" h. 875.00

Woody Woodpecker puppet, handtype, w/talking mechanism, Mat-

Wizard of Oz Tumbler

tel, Inc. (Hawthorne, California), 1963 .... 60.00

Woody Woodpecker tumbler, shows Woody chasing butterflies, clear glass, Pepsi-Cola collection series, 12 oz. 10.00

Wyatt Earp gun & holster set, "Junior Wyatt Earp," cowhide leather holster & belt w/matched pair of silvered metal pistols, mint in box, the set 255.00

Yellow Submarine (Beatles' movie) lunch box & thermos, cartoon scenes, King Seeley Thermos, 1969, 2 pcs. (near mint)......... 528.00

Yogi Bear game, "Score-A-Matic Ball Toss Game with Automatic Ball Return," hard plastic bust of Yogi w/mouth open, includes plastic balls which are thrown into the mouth for the score, score dial on bust, Transogram, © 1960, in box 65.00

Yogi Bear slippers, in original box .. 85.00

CHILDREN'S BOOKS

The most collectible children's books today tend to be those printed after the 1850's and, while age is not completely irrelevant, illustrations play a far more important role in determining values. While first editions are highly esteemed, it is the beautiful illustrated books that most collectors seek. The following books, all in good to fine condition, are listed alphabetically.

"A Child's Garden of Verses," by Robert Louis Stevenson, 1905, w/12 full color pen & ink illustrations by Jessie Willcox Smith $85.00

"A Cup of Tea," by E.S. Tucker, 1892, Worthington Co., New York, book of dolls & verse, 8 x 11", hard cover.................... 45.00

"Adventures of Unc' Billy Possum," by Thornton Burgess, 1919 .... 15.00

"Animated Antics in Playland," by Julian Wehr, 1946 .... 55.00

"Billy Whiskers Twins," by Frances Montgomery, 1911, Saalfield 16.00

"Bonny Bairns," by Ida Waugh, 1888, many full page color illustrations of children, 48 pp. 250.00

"Dick Hamilton's Steam Yacht," by Goris, 1913 .... 5.00

"Hans Brinker or The Silver Skates," by Mary Mapes Dodge, 1931, color illustrations by Alice Carsey ... 30.00

"Jack & the Beanstalk and Other Stories," illustrated by John Neill, 1908 .... 15.00

"Little Mr. Thimblefinger," by Joel Chandler Harris, 1922 .... 18.00

"Little Red Riding Hood," illustrated by Sharon Koester, 1959, Little Golden Book No. A34, w/uncut paper dolls 38.00

"Nice Puppy!," by Martha Paulsen, 1943, color illustrations by Mabel Hatt, Saalfield 35.00

"Old Mr. Toad," by Thornton Burgess, 1919, Boston, illustrated, w/dust jacket................. 23.50

"Pets," published by Saalfield, 1917, 8½ x 10", linen cover 25.00

"Pinocchio," by C. Collodi, 1916, Whitman, color illustrations by Alice Carsey 35.00

"Raggedy Ann & Andy and the Camel with the Wrinkled Knees," by Johnny Gruelle, 1924 .... 25.00

"Sunny Rhymes for Happy Children," by Olive Beaupre Miller, 1917, B.F. Volland Co., illustrated by Carmen L. Browne 25.00

"Tale of Paddy Muskrat," by Bailey, 1916 .... 9.00

"The Book of Bow Wows," by Elizabeth Gordon, 1913 .... 25.00

"The Hole Book," by Peter Newell, 1908 .... 85.00

"The Little Postcard Painter," published by McLaughlin Bros., 1904, 16 postcards to paint, 7 x 11", soft cover 45.00

"The Little Red Hen," illustrated by Rudolf Freund, 1942, Little Golden Book, No. 0060 .... 15.00

"The Magic Aeroplane," illustrated by Emile Nelson w/Christmas & winter scenes, 1911 .... 125.00

"The Magical Monarch of Mo," by L. Frank Baum, 1915, Chicago, eight color illustrations, blue cloth covers (back cover stain) 75.00

"The Rover Boys In The Air," by Winfield, 1912 .... 5.00

"Twilight Tales," by Beard, 1934 .... 20.00

"Two Little Travelers," by Frances Humphrey, 1883 . . . . 15.00

"Wooden Willie," by Johnny Gruelle, 1927 . . . . 40.00

CHILDREN'S DISHES

Drum Pattern Creamer

During the reign of Queen Victoria, doll-houses and accessories became more popular and as the century progressed, there was greater demand for toys which would subtly train a little girl in the art of homemaking. Also see DEPRESSION and PATTERN GLASS and WILLOW WARES in Ceramics.

Banana dish, pressed glass, Fine Cut Star & Fan patt., clear $32.00

Berry bowl, individual, pressed glass, Oval Star patt., clear 10.00

Berry set: master bowl & five sauce dishes; pressed glass, Oval Star patt., clear, 6 pcs. 75.00

Berry set: master bowl & six sauce dishes; pressed glass, Nursery Rhyme patt., clear, 7 pcs. 150.00

Bowl, master berry, pressed glass, Wheat Sheaf patt., Cambridge, clear 50.00

Butter dish, cov., pressed glass, Bead & Scroll patt., clear 75.00

Butter dish, cov., pressed glass, Button Panel patt., clear 120.00

Butter dish, cov., pressed glass, Diamond Panels patt., clear 25.00

Butter dish, cov., pressed glass, Hobnail w/Thumbprint patt., blue 85.00

Cake stand, pressed glass, Palm Leaf patt., clear 30.00

Canister set, tin w/white porcelain knobs, Dutch design in blue & cream, 8 pcs. 225.00

Coffeepot, cov., china, Blue Willow patt., Japan 42.50

Coffeepot, cov., dripolater-type, aluminum, red wooden knob & bar

handle, embossed picture of Cinderella, ca. 1940's 20.00

Compote, open, footed, white porcelain decorated w/lavender & pink buds & shaded green leaves, probably Germany, 4" d., 1 3/8" h. 45.00

Compote, fruit, porcelain, openwork lattice sides w/pointed scallops on rim, on a square pedestal base, white ground decorated w/lavender & pink buds & shaded green leaves, probably Germany, 3" d., 3" h. 75.00

Creamer, pressed glass, Acorn patt., clear 110.00

Creamer, pressed glass, Buzz Star patt., clear 25.00

Creamer, pressed glass, Colonial patt., Cambridge, clear 20.00

Creamer, pressed glass, Drum patt., clear (ILLUS.) 50.00

Creamer, pressed glass, Ear of Corn patt., milk white w/green-painted leaves, 3¼" h. 35.00

Creamer, pressed glass, Horizontal Thread patt., clear 22.00

Creamer, pressed glass, Liberty Bell patt., clear 120.00

Creamer, pressed glass, Sultan patt., frosted clear 65.00

Creamer, pressed glass, Wee Branches patt., clear 40.00

Creamer, pressed glass, Whirligig patt., clear 15.00

Creamer & cov. sugar bowl, pressed glass, Star & Bar patt., amber, pr. 40.00

Cup, pressed glass, Prism & Pinwheel patt., clear 28.00

Cup & saucer, pressed glass, Basketweave patt., vaseline 30.00

Dinner set, service for six w/serving pieces, china, Bluebird patt., Noritake, the set 350.00

Dish, rectangular, pressed glass, decorated w/embossed dancing children scene, clear, Sowerby, England 55.00

Fork & spoon set, orange plastic handles w/inset creamy white cats, 1950's, 5" l., 2 pcs. 40.00

Mug, pressed glass, Acanthus Leaves patt., cobalt blue 25.00

Mug, pressed glass, Gooseberry patt., blue opaque 25.00

Mug, pressed glass, Grapevine patt., cobalt blue 20.00

Mug, pressed glass, Liberty Bell patt., clear 95.00

Pitcher, water, pressed glass, Fancy Cut patt., clear 75.00

Pitcher, water, pressed glass, Oval Star patt., clear 80.00

Pitcher, pressed glass, Pattee Cross
patt., clear 35.00
Plate, china, depicts two children,
dog & doll w/earphones listening
to a three-tube wireless radio,
Bavaria, 7" d. 35.00
Plate, pressed glass, Little Bo Peep
patt., w/incised bear border,
clear 40.00
Platter, porcelain, oval, white deco-
rated w/lavender & pink buds &
shaded green leaves, probably
Germany, 4 x 5½" 25.00
Punch bowl, pressed glass, Oval
Star patt., clear 50.00
Punch bowl, pressed glass, Wheat
Sheaf patt., Cambridge, clear 30.00
Punch bowl, pressed glass, Whirligig
patt., clear 20.00
Punch cup, pressed glass, Buzz Star
patt., clear 8.00
Punch set: punch bowl & six
cups; pressed glass, Nursery
Rhyme patt., milk white,
7 pcs. ....350.00 to 400.00
Punch set: punch bowl & six cups;
pressed glass, Wild Rose patt.,
clear, 7 pcs. 150.00
Spooner, pressed glass, Button
Panels patt., clear.............. 30.00
Spooner, pressed glass, Colonial
patt., Cambridge, cobalt blue 28.00
Spooner, pressed glass, Diamond &
Panels patt., clear.............. 20.00
Spooner, pressed glass, Euclid patt.,
clear 23.00

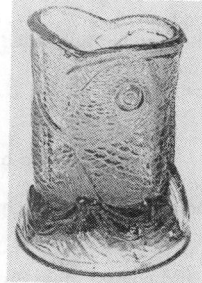

Menagerie Pattern 'Fish' Spooner

Spooner, pressed glass, Menagerie
patt., fish, blue (ILLUS.) 140.00
Spooner, pressed glass, Michigan
patt., clear w/gold 40.00
Spooner, pressed glass, Rooster
patt., clear 65.00
Sugar bowl, cov., porcelain, deco-
rated w/three cats, 2½" h. 40.00
Sugar bowl, cov., pressed glass,
Acorn patt., clear 175.00
Sugar bowl, cov., pressed glass,
Button Panels patt., clear 65.00
Sugar bowl, cov., pressed glass,
Drum patt., clear............... 110.00

Sugar bowl, cov., pressed glass,
Lion patt., clear................ 105.00
Sugar bowl, cov., pressed glass,
Nursery Rhyme patt., clear...... 85.00
Sugar bowl, cov., pressed glass,
Sawtooth Band patt., Heisey,
clear........................ 110.00
Table set: cov. butter dish, creamer
& cov. sugar bowl; pressed glass,
Tappan patt., amber, 3 pcs. 130.00
Table set: cov. butter dish, creamer,
cov. sugar bowl & spooner;
pressed glass, Fernland patt.,
green, 4 pcs. 90.00
Table set, pressed glass, Sawtooth
Band patt., Heisey, clear, 4 pcs. ... 250.00
Tea set: cov. teapot, cov. sugar
bowl, creamer & two cups & saucers; Royal Bayreuth, Nursery
Rhyme patt., each piece w/differ-
ent picture & rhyme, 7 pcs. 295.00
Tea set: cov. teapot, cov. sugar
bowl, creamer & six cups & saucers; bulbous pearlware bodies
h.p. w/small colored sprigs, impressed "Davenport," ca. 1830,
15 pcs. (some minor damage & a
little repair) 400.00
Tea set: cov. teapot, cov. sugar
bowl, creamer, waste bowl, four
cups & saucers, four tea plates;
china, delicate blue florals,
Knowles, Taylor, Knowles, signed
"KTK," ca. 1890, 16 pcs.......... 225.00
Tea set: cov. teapot, creamer, cov.
sugar bowl, six cups & saucers &
six plates; china, decoration of
boy giving girl a bouquet while
playing w/bunnies, colorful,
marked "Germany," ca. 1900,
21 pcs. (chip in one cup) 325.00
Tray, pressed glass, Hobnail &
Thumbprint patt., amber 40.00
Tumbler, pressed glass, Flattened
Diamond & Sunburst patt., clear .. 10.00
Tumbler, pressed glass, Pattee
Cross patt., clear.............. 13.50
Water set: pitcher & three tumblers;
pressed glass, Beaded Swirl patt.,
clear, 4 pcs. 120.00
Water set: pitcher & four tumblers;
pressed glass, Pattee Cross patt.,
clear, 5 pcs. 135.00
Water set: pitcher & six tumblers;
pressed glass, Nursery Rhyme
patt., clear, 7 pcs. 300.00

CHILDREN'S MUGS

*The small sized mugs used by children first
attempting to drink from a cup appeal to
many collectors. Because they were made of*

such diverse materials as china, glass, pottery, graniteware, plated silver and sterling silver, the collector can assemble a diversified collection or single out a particular type around which to base a collection. Also see CHILDREN'S DISHES and PATTERN GLASS.

China, colored transfer scene of "Little Miss Muffet" & the nursery rhyme $45.00

China, lilac & blue transfer-printed banners lettered "Universal Brotherhood - Freedom of Commerce," etc., 2½" h. 85.00

China, "Souvenir of Winnipeg," bird whistle on handle, marked "Germany," 2¾" h. 35.00

Porcelain, floral decoration w/blue lustre trim, lettered "Present," marked "Saxony," 2 5/8" h. 30.00

Pressed glass, Beads in Relief patt., milk white, 3¼" h. 22.00

Pressed glass, Begging Dog patt., blue 70.00

Pressed glass, Bird & Harp patt., clear, 3" h. 40.00

Pressed glass, Bird in Nest with Flowers patt., clear, 3½" h. 45.00

Pressed glass, Bird on Branch patt., blue, 3½" h. 50.00

Pressed glass, Double Eye patt., amber, 3" h. 25.00

Pressed glass, Heron & Peacock patt., vaseline 40.00

Pressed glass, Humpty Dumpty patt., amber 45.00

Pressed glass, Log & Star patt., amber, 3" h. 25.00

Pressed glass, Monkey & Vines patt., clear, 2½" d., 2½" h. 55.00

Pressed glass, Song Bird patt., amber 18.50

Silver plate, "Ring Around the Rosie," engraved scene w/ten children 55.00

Staffordshire pottery, cylindrical, purple transfer-printed scene w/a Franklin Maxim reading "Creditors have better memories than debtors," 2 5/8" h. 192.50

Staffordshire pottery, cylindrical, black transfer-printed design of a woman & children w/polychrome enamel trim, 2¾" h. (minor pinpoints) 110.00

Tin, yellow-painted alphabet & "For A Good Boy" 65.00

Yellow-glazed earthenware, brown transfer-printed scene of "Boys Balancing," leaf-tip handle, early 19th c., 2¼" h. (pinpoint edge flakes) 225.00

Yellow-glazed earthenware, black transfer-printed scene of children at play, 2 5/8" h. (wear, rim glaze chips) 235.00

CHRISTMAS TREE LIGHTS

Along with a host of other Christmas-related items, early Christmas tree lights are attracting a growing number of collectors. Comic characters seem to be the most popular form among the wide variety of figural lights available, most of which were manufactured between 1920 and World War II in Germany, Japan and the United States. Figural bulbs are generally painted clear or milk white glass unless otherwise noted.

BULBS

Andy Gump $60.00
Bell 20.00
Boy holding a carrot, celluloid 100.00
Cat, begging, purple 35.00
Cat w/banjo 50.00
Cottage 15.00
Dick Tracy .... 110.00 to 140.00
Grape cluster 21.00
Japanese lantern 15.00
Kayo 75.00
Lantern, standard base, Germany, 4¾" h. (works) 33.00
Monkey 50.00
Moon Mullins .... 100.00 to 125.00
Mushroom 22.00
Pear 16.00
Red Riding Hood, oval 50.00
Santa Claus, full-figure, two-sided .. 42.00
Santa's head, two-faced 22.00
Zeppelin, colorful 35.00

SETS

Figural, milk white glass, string of eight, including watch, girl w/doll, cobalt blue dogs, fire hydrant, etc., the set 90.00

Figural, assorted small & fancy lanterns, assorted colors, made in Occupied Japan, in original box, the set 70.00

Mazda Popeye set, ca. 1930's, mint in box 295.00

NOMA bubble lights, set of 9, in original box w/two extra bulbs, the set 70.00

CHRISTMAS TREE ORNAMENTS

The German blown glass Christmas tree ornaments and other commercially-made orna-

ments of wax, cardboard and cotton batting were popular from the time they were first offered for sale in the United States in the 1870's. Prior to that time, Christmas trees had been decorated with homemade ornaments that usually were edible. Now nostalgic collectors who seek out ornaments that sold for pennies in stores across the country in the early years of this century are willing to pay some rather hefty prices for unusual or early ornaments.

Acorn, blown glass, gold w/frosted top $10.00
Angel, wax w/spun glass wings, blonde curly hair 55.00
Balloon-shaped, blown glass, w/applied tinsel wrap & scrap angel, Victorian, 5½" h. 60.00
Basket of flowers, blown glass, silver & pink, 2" h. 50.00
Basket w/six bottles, Dresden-type cardboard 198.00
Boy fishing, blown glass, Germany, ca. 1900 .... 75.00
Boy riding lion, Dresden-type cardboard 330.00
Boy w/cap, blown glass, standing figure w/oversized head w/side-glancing eyes & smiling mouth & wearing a peaked cap, arms to his side, painted in pastel colors, 5" h. 49.50
Brown bear, Dresden-type cardboard 255.00
Cannon, Dresden-type cardboard ... 300.00
Carousel horse, Dresden-type cardboard 120.00
Christ child's head, blown glass 69.00
Christmas tree, tin w/punchwork decoration, ca. 1930's 45.00
Clown, blown glass, silver, 3½" h. 65.00
Cow, Dresden-type cardboard 260.00
Dwarf in flying position, papier-mache', the round-bodied figure w/half-round knob feet & rounded arms flared out from the body, round head w/a pointed cap, painted & trimmed w/glitter, 4¾" h. 10.00
Fish, blown glass, green, pink & gold, Germany 25.00
Girl on a swing, Dresden-type cardboard 295.00
Grape cluster, blown glass, cobalt blue, brass hanger, 6" l. 165.00
Grape cluster, blown glass, light green, brass hanger, 3¼" l. 135.00
Icicles, blown glass, silver & aqua, frosted at top, Germany, 6½" l. ... 50.00
Jockey on horse, Dresden-type cardboard 350.00
Kugel, gold, 3" d. 50.00

Kugel, light green, brass hanger, 3¼" d. 55.00
Kugel, silver, w/brass hanger, 5" d. 135.00
Lady's shoe, Dresden-type cardboard 120.00
Moon face, blown glass, gold & white 12.00
Owl, blown glass, Germany, 3½" h. 30.00
Pine cone, blown glass, pink, gold & blue, frosted, West Germany, 4½" h. 35.00
Pistol, Dresden-type cardboard 210.00
Rhinoceros, Dresden-type cardboard 340.00
Santa Claus, blown glass, standing position 15.00
Star, thin white opaque glass beads, beaded circle inside, Czechoslovakia, 3½" 52.00
Stork, blown glass 50.00
Sun god, Dresden-type cardboard ... 320.00
Violin, blown glass, red 8.00

HALLMARK KEEPSAKE ORNAMENTS

Note: These must be "Mint in box" to bring top prices.

A Cool Yule, "Frosty Friends" series, first edition, 1980 .... 430.00
Angel, "Bellringer" series, fourth edition, 1982 .... 75.00
Baby's First Christmas - Stroller, "Commemorative" ornaments, 1985 .... 20.00
Baroque Angel, "Handcrafted" ornaments, 1982 .... 125.00
Bell, "Colors of Christmas" ornaments, 1977 .... 40.00
Betsey Clark, "Christmas Spirit" ball ornament, "Property" ornaments, sixth edition, 1978 .... 40.00
Cardinalis, Cardinalis, "Holiday Wildlife" series, first edition, 1982 .... 225.00
Christmas Kitten, "Little Trimmers" ornaments, 1982 .... 15.00
Christmas Owl, "Holiday Highlights" ornaments, 1980 .... 16.00
Cinnamon Teddy, "Porcelain Bear" series, first edition, 1983 .... 55.00
Currier & Ives, "Keepsake" ornaments, 1974, 2 pcs. 12.00
Do Not Disturb Bear, "Holiday Humor" ornaments, 1985 .... 20.00
Dress Rehearsal, "Norman Rockwell" series, fourth edition, 1983 .... 27.50
Drummer boy, "Little Trimmers" ornaments, 1978 .... 35.00
Elfin Artist, "Handcrafted" ornaments, 1982 .... 40.00

Fine Porcelain, "Miniature Creche"
series, second edition, 1986 . . . . . .   50.00
Frosty Friends, "Frosty Friends" se-
ries, fourth edition, 1983 . . . .   165.00
Heavenly Trumpeter, "Limited Edi-
tion" ornaments, 1985 . . . .   40.00
Holiday Scrimshaw, "Handcrafted"
ornaments, 1979 . . . .   130.00
House, "Yesteryears" collection,
1977 . . . .   80.00
Joyful Carolers, "Christmas Medley"
collection, 1986 . . . .   17.00
Mele Kalikimaka, "Windows of the
World" series, third edition,
1987 . . . .   18.00
Nativity, "Nostalgia Collection" or-
nament, 1977 . . . .   100.00
Nutcracker Ballet, "Christmas Clas-
sics" series, 1986 . . . .   65.00
Partridge in a Pear Tree, "Twelve
Days of Christmas" series, first
edition, 1984 . . . .   190.00
Raggedy Ann, "Adorable Adorn-
ments" ornaments, 1975 . . . .   180.00
Ready for Christmas, "Handcrafted"
ornaments, 1979 . . . .   65.00
Rocking Horse, Black, "Rocking
Horse" series, second edition,
1982 . . . .   185.00
Santa and Friends, "Carrousel"
series, sixth edition, 1983 . . . .   85.00
Santa Express, "Here Comes Santa"
series, fifth edition, 1983 . . . .   145.00
Santa Pipe, "Traditional" ornaments,
1985 . . . .   30.00
Santa's Woody, "Here Comes Santa"
ornaments, ninth edition, 1987 . . .   35.00
Scottish Highlander, "Clothespin
Soldiers Collectibles" series,
1985 . . . .   22.00
Spencer Sparrow, "Property" orna-
ments, 1979 . . . .   30.00
Star, "Holiday Highlights" collection,
1977 . . . .   40.00
Star over Bethlehem, "Colors of
Christmas" ornaments, 1979 . . . . . .   15.00
Thimble Angel, "Thimble" series,
fourth edition, 1981 . . . .   75.00
Tin Locomotive, "Tin Locomotive" se-
ries, second edition, 1983 . . . .   160.00
Tin Locomotive, "Tin Locomotive" se-
ries, sixth edition, 1987 . . . .   60.00
Wee Chimney Sweep, "Artists'
Favorites" ornaments, 1987 . . . . . .   15.00
Wynken, Blynken & Nod, "Holiday
Humor" ornaments, 1986 . . . .   32.00
Yarn Soldier, "Handcrafted" orna-
ments, 1973 . . . .   15.00
Yesteryears Train, "Handcrafted" or-
naments, 1976 . . . .   95.00

CIGAR & CIGARETTE CASES, HOLDERS & LIGHTERS

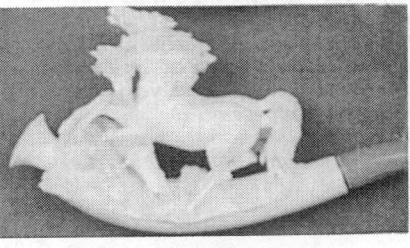

Meerschaum Cheroot Holder

Cheroot holder, meerschaum,
carved to depict Cupid & Venus,
amber stem, w/fitted case,
6 1/8" l. $137.50
Cheroot holder, meerschaum,
carved to depict two galloping
horses, amber stem, damages,
w/fitted case, 7 1/8" l. (ILLUS.) . . .   357.50
Cigar box, Arts & Crafts style, hand-
hammered copper, rectangular
w/flared base band, the overhanging domed cover w/a round
twist strap handle, panel construction w/interior fitted w/Spanish
cedar, branded & impressed
marks of Gustav Stickley, Model
No. 268, ca. 1912, 5½ x 7¼",
3½" h. 715.00
Cigarette box, silver-gilt, reeded de-
sign w/monogram on lid, highlighted by a ruby cabochon &
bezel-set diamond, interior
w/compartments for cigarettes
& matches, Russian maker's
marks 275.00
Cigarette case, Art Deco style, black
enamel & chrome, Ronson, ca.
1930 . . . .   65.00
Cigarette case, gold, alternating
stripes of red & green gold, further decorated w/an engraved
overall diamond design, w/cabo-
chon sapphire thumbpiece, Khlebnikov, Moscow, Russia, ca. 1910,
4¼" l. 3,850.00
Cigarette case, silver, shaped &
decorated to depict a bird of prey
w/*basse taille* enamel eye & lavender beak, G.A.S., Vienna, Austria, ca. 1900, 900 fine, 2 3/8" w.,
3 1/8" l. 550.00
Cigarette case, silver, in the form
of a silver basketweave suitcase w/gold ends & clasp, 950
fine, Madrid, Spain, 20th c.,
15/16 x 2 5/8", 3 5/8" l. (dents) . .   165.00
Cigarette case, silver & enamel,
both sides enameled w/a large
central rectangle w/incurved sides

in translucent strawberry red over a ground engraved w/foliage, the borders enameled w/blue scrolling foliage on a stippled ground, Grachev, St. Petersburg, Russia, ca. 1900, 3 7/8" l. 2,200.00

Cigarette case, steel, applied on one side w/an enameled coat-of-arms, the other side applied w/a gold & enamel miniature shoulder board of a Major General of the Czar's First Grenadier Division, unmarked, probably by Faberge', Russia, ca. 1915, 4" l. 4,675.00

Art Deco Silver Cigarette Case

Cigarette case, sterling silver, Art Deco style, rectangular, stamped w/a stylized leaping doe & stag surrounded by leafy foliage, stamped in the design "C.H.," Evans & Co., New York, 3 1/8 x 5 3/8" (ILLUS.) 495.00

Cigarette lighter, advertising, "Ford Falcon" plant, w/logo, chrome, 2¼" l. 20.00

Cigarette lighter, advertising, "Metropolitan Life Insurance," metal, shaped like lipstick case . .   20.00

Cigarette lighter, advertising, "R.C. Cola," metal, bottle-shaped 25.00

Cigarette lighter, "Dunhill Silent Flame," chrome-plated nude atop Bakelite base, in original box 65.00

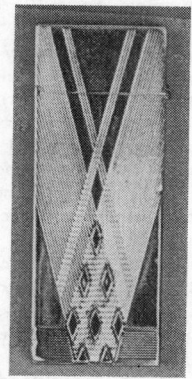

Van Cleef & Arpels Lighter

Cigarette lighter, engine-turned metal, the long rectangular case w/intersecting lines, gold accents & navette-shaped blue stones, stamped "Styptor," from Van Cleef & Arpels, ca. 1940 (ILLUS.) . .   302.50

Cigarette lighter, 14k gold-plated, "Frostie," mint in box 48.00

Cigarette lighter, gold (14k), cylindrical, engine-turned polka dot designs, cap accented by a cabochon sapphire, marked "Cartier 14ct 5998" 247.50

Cigarette lighter, gold (14k yellow), polished case, engraved w/initials "R.S.C.," Dunhill 192.50

Cigarette lighter, silvertone metal, "Ronson Maximus," in maroon celluloid box w/gold writing, ca. 1940's, mint in box, box 1¼ x 3¾ x 6 1/8", lighter 5/8 x 1¾ x 2 1/8" 65.00

Cigarette lighter, table model, enamel & chromium-plated metal, designed as a streamlined locomotive, quarter-square shape enameled in black, impressed "RONSON TOUCH-TIP U.S. PAT. 1986.754" w/further information on other patents, 3¾" h. 220.00

Cigarette lighter, table model, silvertone metal, football-shape on pedestal, Occupied Japan, ca. 1940's, 1 5/8 x 3" 45.00

Cigarette lighter, Zippo "Lady Bradford," w/original box 22.00

CIRCUS COLLECTIBLES

The romance of the "Big Top," stirred by memories of sawdust, spangles, thrills and chills, has captured the imagination of the American public for over 100 years. Though the heyday of the traveling circus is now past, dedicated collectors and fans of all ages eagerly seek out choice memorabilia from the late 19th and early 20th centuries, the "golden age" of circuses.

Broadside, "The New York Circus," pictures acrobats, golden chariot, etc., ca. 1870, 26" l. $135.00

Pony harness, complete w/fancy red, blue & yellow feathers, straps covered w/little bells & mirrors, small. 450.00

Poster, "Clyde Beatty - Cole Bros. Combined Circus," color scene of lion tamer & rearing lion w/"Clyde Beatty in Person" at the bottom, printed red, blue, yellow,

grey, white & flesh tones, ca.
1940, 21 x 28" (edge wear)...... 88.00

Poster, "Cole Bros. Circus," shows
Edmida Loyal, Champion Eques-
trienne of Continental Europe,
full-color, ca. 1940, 21 x 28"..... 27.50

Poster, "Cristiani Bros. Circus," full-
color scene w/animals, wagons &
people, word "Cristiani" pasted
over "King," ca. 1940, 21 x 28" ... 82.50

Poster, "King Bros. & Cristiani Combined Circus," full-color scene
showing monkeys walking on
tightrope, playing a drum or playing cymbals, ca. 1950, 21 x 28"
(very light creases)............. 27.50

Poster, "Ringling Bros. and Barnum
& Bailey," full-color scene showing
five rings full of action, ca. 1945,
16 x 28"...................... 143.00

Colorful Circus Poster

Poster, "Ringling Bros. and Barnum
& Bailey," color scene of four
giraffes w/"The Greatest Show on
Earth" in lower left corner, ca.
1944, some light creases, 21 x 28"
(ILLUS.)...................... 33.00

Poster, "Ringling Bros. and Barnum
& Bailey," color scene of mother &
baby hippos in water, printed in
red, yellow, green, black & blue,
ca. 1945, 21 x 28"............. 33.00

Poster, "Wallace Bros. - World's
Largest Circus," color portrait of
clowns, printed in yellow, dark
green, grey, blue, pink & flesh
tones, ca. 1945, 21 x 28" (4" tear
in top) 49.50

Program, "Barnum & Bailey," 1893,
Columbus pageant, side show, il-
lusions, menagerie, etc. 110.00

Program, "Ringling Bros. and Barnum & Bailey Circus," 1955,
76 pp......................... 20.00

CLOCKS

Acorn shelf clock, The Forestville
Mfg. Co., Bristol, Connecticut,

Early Acorn Shelf Clock

laminated rosewood case w/an
inverted acorn top section framing
an arched panel w/a round dial
w/Roman numerals & floral spandrels above the sharply waisted
lower case framing a painted panel depicting a house & inscribed
"Residence of J.C. Brown, Esq.,
Bristol, CT...," serpentine brackets
w/acorn finials flank the case &
support it on a stepped base, two-
train movement w/brass fusees,
mounted on an iron block, ca.
1845, 5¼ x 14¾", 24½" h.
(ILLUS.) $6,600.00

Animated, Lux Clock Company, Waterbury, Connecticut, figural Scottie dog 300.00

Banjo, Aaron Willard, Boston, Federal mahogany case, the circular
white-painted dial w/Roman chapter ring inscribed "Aaron Willard,
Boston" over a throat filled w/a
verre eglomise' panel decorated
w/an urn issuing gilt foliage within a leafy border flanked by
pierced brass scrolls above a box
base w/panel painted w/a scene
of a naval engagement beneath
an American shield, ca. 1810,
30" h. (painting reinforced) 3,850.00

Black Forest shelf clock, ornately
carved case from a single block of
wood, carved at the top w/a running deer beneath a tree on rockwork, carved below the round
dial w/running hounds on a rockwork base, windup clock mechanism w/chimes, slight age crack
in deer's body, one deer leg
repaired, Germany, late 19th c.,
10 x 18", 30" h. (ILLUS. top next
column)....................1,100.00

Calendar clock, wall-type, double
dial, Welch, Spring & Co., Forestville, Connecticut, rosewood
veneer case w/a large circular

Ornately Carved Black Forest Clock

Victorian Calendar Clock

frame at the top framing the round dial w/Roman numerals & days of the week in the middle, the lower rectangular case w/a circular molded bezel set w/a subsidiary painted dial indicating the date & month, weight-driven movement w/anchor escapement, ca. 1880, 34½" h. (ILLUS.) 770.00

Carriage, silver-gilt & enamel, an upright rectangular case w/the sides enameled w/allegorical scenes, the corners w/silver-gilt caryatids, an ornate scrolling openwork silver-gilt base on four feet & a silver-gilt frame around the top supporting an ornate silver-gilt carrying handle, Vienna, Austria, ca. 1885, 4" h. 1,980.00

Dwarf Grandfather, Joshua Wilder, Hingham, Massachusetts, Federal style mahogany case, the hood w/turned finials centering scrolling pierced fretwork above an arched molded cornice & conforming glazed door opening to a white-painted dial w/Roman

numerals, the spandrels painted w/gilt ornaments amid scrolling foliage beneath an urn flanked by flower-filled cornucopia & drapery swags, signed "J. WILDER, HINGHAM," flanked by spirally-turned & foliate-carved colonettes above a waisted case w/rectangular door flanked by lozenge-carved quarter columns over a box base w/shaped apron, on bracket feet, 1825-35, 7 x 13¼", 4' 4¾" h. (later crossbanding to door) 10,450.00

Grandfather, William Claggett, Newport, Rhode Island, Queen Anne style mahogany case, small platform on the domed top above the flared & stepped cornice set w/small blocks & brass ball finials at the front corners above a glazed door flanked by colonettes opening to the brass dial w/Roman numerals, seconds indicator & calendar aperture, dial engraved "Will Claggett - Newport," the tall waisted case w/a single tall door on a stepped-out block base w/molded flat apron, old refinish, ca. 1725-40, 7' 4¼" h. (imperfections) 25,300.00

Grandfather, Thomas Harland, Norwich, Connecticut, Federal style cherry case, the hood w/scroll-carved cresting centering three urn-and-flame finials above an arched glazed door opening to a silvered brass dial engraved "Thos. Harland Norwich," w/a seconds dial & a calendar aperture, stop-fluted colonettes flanking, the waisted case w/long solid shaped door, high base on ogee bracket feet, eight-day brass movement, ca. 1775, 7' 9" h. (refinished, imperfections) 42,900.00

Ansonia Figural Clock

Shelf, or mantel, Ansonia Clock Co., New York, figural spelter case, the oblong cast spelter platform base decorated w/leafy scrolls &

a central scroll crest, fitted w/a large spelter figure of a seated gypsy girl playing a mandolin beside an ornate upright case fitted w/three finials above a scroll-molded crest flanking the brass bezel & porcelain dial w/Roman numerals & open escapement, the lower case w/colonettes flanking a silvered metal panel w/a scene of Renaissance-style figures, late 19th c., 23½" l., 22½" h. (ILLUS.) 1,300.00

Shelf, or mantel, Ansonia Clock Co., New York, molded china case, "La Rambler" model, top portion of case rose-colored, the lower half in shades of green decorated w/pink & white flowers, ca. 1900 . . . . 525.00

Shelf, or mantel, Art Nouveau style, carved sycamore & brass case, tall flattened ovoid outline flaring at the base, carved & inset on the front w/three brass panels w/stylized interlaced stems around a circular brass dial cast w/Arabic numerals, designed by Maurice Dufrene for Maison Moderne, ca. 1900, 15¼" h. 1,980.00

Shelf, or mantel, Birge & Ives, Bristol, Connecticut, late Federal style carved mahogany case, the pediment w/elaborately carved spreadwinged eagle flanked by bull's-eye carved plinths above a hinged square glazed door opening to a white-painted dial w/Roman numerals, the spandrels embellished w/gilt C-scrolls above a *verre eglomise'* panel flanked by waterleaf-carved supports over a hinged rectangular door w/*verre eglomise'* panel above a rectangular base, on four ball feet, 1832-34, 5 1/8 x 17", 37 3/8" h. 1,650.00

Shelf, or mantel, Ephraim Downes, Bristol, Connecticut, Pillar & Scroll mahogany case, swan's neck pediment centering three brass ball finials above a glazed door opening to a white-painted dial w/Roman numerals over an eglomise' panel depicting a landscape w/a house in the distance, flanked by free-standing colonettes over a shaped apron on bracket feet, thirty-hour wooden weight-driven movement, ca. 1825, 29½" h. (imperfections) 1,210.00

Shelf, or mantel, Gilbert Clock Co., Winsted, Connecticut, molded china case, Model No. 427, rose-

colored ground decorated w/purple flowers, eight-day time & strike movement, ca. 1900 . . . . . . 325.00

Shelf, or mantel, L. & J.G. Stickley, Mission-style oak case, the thin rectangular top widely overhanging the tapered rectangular case on a beveled rectangular foot, the round wooden dial w/Arabic numerals near the top front, a small rectangular open window exposing the pendulum below, the maker's red decal mark, Model No. 85, ca. 1912, 8 x 16", 22" h. 13,200.00

Seth Thomas Violin Clock

Shelf, or mantel, Seth Thomas Company, Thomaston, Connecticut, carved walnut violin-shaped case, carved w/leafy scrolls framing the rectangular glazed door w/gilt musical designs over the white-painted dial w/Roman numerals & the pendulum, raised on a rectangular molded base w/small ogee bracket feet, 19th c., 4¾ x 13¾", 29" h. (ILLUS.) 4,180.00

Shelf, or mantel, Waterbury Clock Company, Waterbury, Connecticut, molded china case, decorated w/floral garlands & gilt trim, No. 80 movement, patented January 13, 1891, 11" h. 220.00

Waterbury China Case Clock

Shelf, or mantel, Waterbury Clock
Company, Waterbury, Connecticut,
molded china case, arched leafy
scroll-molded top & molded short
colonettes & scrolls & blossoms
down the sides & across the bottom, the round dial w/a brass
bezel & Arabic numerals, green &
gold trim on the molded work & a
transfer-printed cluster of pink &
yellow flowers below the dial,
late 19th c. (ILLUS.) 300.00

Ornate Ansonia Wall Clock

Wall, Ansonia Clock Co., New
York, ormolu-mounted walnut
case, the crest w/a large triangular pediment framing an ormolu
figural mount of a seated classical
lady & two putti & flanked by a
pair of urn-form finials, all above
a frieze band w/a figural ormolu
band above a pair of ormolu-
mounted pilasters flanking the
embossed ormolu dial w/enam-
eled Roman numerals, another
ormolu frieze band below the dial
& above the stepped-back open
case w/curved & reeded pilasters
flanking the ornate ormolu pendulum, the lower case backed by a
carved arch framing a figural ormolu mount, a further ormolu
frieze band & scroll mounts at
the scalloped base drop, 19th c.
(ILLUS.) 3,190.00
Wall, Vienna Regulator, walnut &
burl walnut case, the arched crestrail topped by a palmette-carved
finial above a scroll-carved frieze
band over a pair of long carved
& ball-turned colonettes flanking
the arched glazed panel over the
round dial w/Roman numerals,
the three brass weights & long

Vienna Regulator Wall Clock

brass pendulum, the lower case
w/carved panels & an arched
base drop w/turned finials, late
19th c. (ILLUS.) 1,250.00

CLOISONNE & RELATED WARES

*Cloisonne' work features enameled designs
on a metal ground. There are several types
of this work, the best-known utilizing cells of
wire on the body of the object into which the
enamel is placed. In the plique-a-jour form of
cloisonne', the base is removed leaving translucent enamel windows. The champleve' technique entails filling in, with enamels, a design
which is cast or carved in the base. "Pigeon
Blood" (akasuke) cloisonne' includes a type
where foil is enclosed within colored enamel
walls. Cloisonne' is said to have been invented by the Chinese and brought to perfection
by the Japanese.*

CLOISONNE

Chinese Cloisonne Brush Pot

Basin, deep slightly flaring cylindrical sides w/a flat bottom & a

molded rim, colorfully decorated around the exterior w/a continuous landscape scene w/numerous deer & cranes in varying poses amid a rocky landscape w/a water cascade & including fruiting peach, finger citron, pomegranate, prunus, bamboo, pine & magnolia, the interior w/a central large carp encircled by four other large carp on the well, all swimming amid numerous other smaller fish, crustaceans, water beetles, spotted amphibians & aquatic plants, the underside w/plum blossoms on a 'cracked ice' ground, China, late 18th c., 24½" d., 10½" h. (typical pitting & losses).....................$27,500.00

Brush pots, cylindrical, each decorated on the exterior w/sprays of peony, prunus, chrysanthemum & lotus, also a bird, butterfly or dragonfly, on a turquoise diaper ground, China, Jiaqing period, 6¼" h., pr. (ILLUS. of one) 2,475.00

Ice chest, cov., square w/outward tapering sides, the top pierced w/six cash symbols, enameled in the center w/a stylized flowerhead on a ground of blue feathery leaves among dense green foliage, the sides w/swing carrying handles & decorated w/panels of lotus blossoms & bat motifs, China, 31½" sq., 20¾" h. 11,500.00

Model of a peacock, standing w/its head turned over its back, the folded wing section enclosing a plain interior, the long tail feathers enameled in shades of green, blue & russet, China, 18th c., 17¾" l. 5,500.00

Teapot, cov., miniature, spherical body, four rounded panels in green, turquoise & two in royal blue foil w/colorful flowers & butterfly, panels surrounded by black, navy & dark green, Japan, 3" d., 4" h. 125.00

Vase, garlic head-form, a squatty bulbous body raised on a flaring foot & tapering to a slender tall neck swelled at the top, finely decorated around the sides in alternating register w/eight large lotus blooms borne on & encircled by continuous foliate vines bearing further smaller blooms, the tall neck & footring w/matching decoration, the underside w/a cast four-character mark, Qianlong Dynasty, China, 15" h. (typi-

cal pitting, chips, minor restoration).........................4,620.00

Vases, double-gourd form, elaborately decorated overall w/a dense pattern of exotic floral blooms, sashed around the waist w/a blue-ground ribbon in relief forming two large bows, the ends trailing elegantly down the sides, the underside cast w/a four-character mark, Qianlong Dynasty, China, 14¾" h., pr. (drilled in base, typical pitting).........16,500.00

RELATED WARES

Champleve Candlestick

Champleve candlesticks, squared & shaped standard raised on a squared foot, decorated w/stylized scroll designs in red, blue, green & yellow, 8" h., pr. (ILLUS. of one)........................ 440.00

Champleve Vase

Champleve vases, each w/a slightly tapering cylindrical body below a flaring gilt-bronze rim, flanked by gilt-bronze branch & blossom handles & raised on scrolled blossom feet, the body w/multi-colored stylized flowers in shaped panels against a light blue ground, France, 19th c., 13½" h., pr. (ILLUS. of one) 4,125.00

Plique-a-jour bowl, the lobed silver-gilt body w/ring foot decorated w/wide panels of translucent stylized foliage in brilliant tones of red, blue & green, Khlebnikov, Moscow, Russia, ca. 1910, 3¾" d. 3,300.00

Plique-a-jour napkin ring, oval, silver-gilt, decorated w/translucent stylized flowers & foliage in tones of blue, red & green all within a stippled surround, beaded borders, Ivan Saltykov, Moscow, Russia, ca. 1900, 2" l. 2,090.00

CLOTHING

Late Victorian Dolman Cape

Recent interest in period clothing, uniforms and accessories from the 18th, 19th and through the 20th century compels us to include this category in our compilation. While style and fabric play an important role in the values of older garments of previous centuries, designer dresses of the 1920's and 30's, especially evening gowns, are enhanced by the original label of a noted couturier such as Worth, or Adrian. Prices vary widely for these garments which we list by type, with infant's and children's apparel so designated.

Apron, white, hemstitch & handmade lace, long................ $28.00

Bathing boots, above the ankle laced style, bright green satin w/white trim & white rubber soles, soles molded "Hood Seaview Bathing Made in U.S.A.," ca. 1910, size 4½, pr. (rubber

cracking slightly on the toe tips) 1,540.00

Bathrobe, lady's, floral print, Beacon, 1940's 45.00

Belt, snake-form, gilt sterling silver highlighted by blue, white, orange & green enamel, adjustable 2,090.00

Blouse, lady's, cotton batiste, ca. 1900 .... 45.00

Blouse & skirt, overall print of circus ringmaster & horses, blouse w/padded shoulders, peplum & yellow sash, skirt w/front vent, Adrian, America, ca. 1940, 2 pcs. 935.00

Bodice, lady's, green w/white velvet trim, Civil War era 45.00

Bush jacket, white cotton twill, bellow pockets, full belt, never worn, ca. 1940 .... 13.00

Cape, lady's, beige cotton velour, mid-calf length, ca. 1920's 45.00

Cape, lady's, black seal, ca. 1920's 40.00

Cape, lady's, black velour, ca. 1900 .... 75.00

Cape, lady's, Dolman-type, scarlet, the front panels fastened by hook & eye, the slashed sleeves which are inset at the back forming a cape effect over this, the whole cape embroidered in Turkish Moresque patterns w/coral, scarlet & gold thread, black & scarlet woven label for "Au Louvre," Paris, & numbered "58030," France, ca. 1895, one small hole to bottom of right sleeve, some discoloration to lining (ILLUS.) ...2,200.00

Christening dress, tucked lawn cloth, eyelet, lace, ca. 1860, 44" l. 90.00

Coat, lady's, black seal w/mink cuffs & shawl collar, 1920's 125.00

Coat, lady's, black virgin wool, w/big collar, Forstmann, ca. 1960's 40.00

Coat, lady's, blue velvet, w/Art Deco-style silk lining, ca. 1920's .. 135.00

Coat, lady's, brown muskrat fur, ca. 1940 .... 90.00

Coat, lady's, brown striped wool, long ulster-style, ca. 1870's 75.00

Coat, lady's, shantung, full-length, black w/brown velvet collar, L.C. Mae, California, ca. 1950 .... 50.00

Coat, lady's, stenciled velvet, steel grey velvet stenciled w/a voluptuous Renaissance-inspired pomegranate & pineapple design, no fastenings, fabric designed by Fortuny, labeled "Caroline, 64 Rue Laboetie, Paris," France, early 1920's 1,430.00

Coat, man's, bearskin, w/matching gauntlet-style gloves, "Hubley," the set 419.00

Dinner dress, navy blue silk taffeta, cross-over bodice, deep flounce to the hem, w/matching ballooning waist sash, labeled "Balenciaga," & numbered "11020," France, 1951 (zipper replaced, a hole & a repair at underarms) 1,760.00

Dress, Adrian's 'Gothic Period' morning-style, quilted black & white print cotton, floor-length w/front zipper fastening, slim floor-length sleeves which taper to points w/fringed loops, full skirt w/kick pleat to hem border, w/unusual matching wired bustle, labeled "Adrian," America, 1940's 3,575.00

Dress, baby's, black & white stripes, long sleeves, lace around yoke, long skirt, ca. early 1900's 25.00

Dress, baby's, strawberry colored print, very long lace around yoke, long sleeves, ca. early 1900's..... 25.00

Dress, black net w/beadwork & embroidery, size 7, ca. Teens (needs minor repairs) 60.00

Dress, child's, Amish, dark blue, long sleeves, gathered yoke topped w/white lawn pinafore, 17½" l. 25.00

Dress, child's, fine batiste & lace, size 6-7, ca. early 20th c. 50.00

Dress, child's, fine corded cotton, lavish lace trim, size 3-4, ca. 1880 .... 75.00

Dress, cocktail-type, black silk, ca. 1950's 30.00

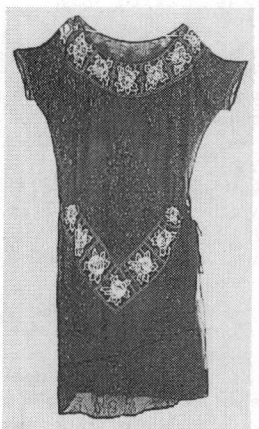

Black Beaded Flapper Dress

Dress, flapper era, black beaded chiffon, the neck & hip detail in pink, blue & purple floral bands, overall black & gold beaded trim,

size 12-14, 1920's, minor wear (ILLUS.)........................ 412.50

Dress, flapper era, gold- and pink-beaded, the cloth of gold ground, the skirt cornered in pink & gold bugle beaded fringe, in elliptical designs, ca. 1926-27, France .. 495.00

Dress, flapper era, winter-weight, heavy material w/fantastic design, brown w/ecru lace inserts, scallops, pleats, ca. 1920's 45.00

Dress, girl's, Glengarry, Shirley Temple model w/original tag..... 24.00

Dress, girl's, lace & organdy embroidery, size 10, ca. 1910 .... 65.00

Dress, mid-calf length, deep red ombre' silk, long sleeves, "V" neck, the seams run from an upturned "V" on the shoulders down the front hips to the gently flaring skirt, w/matching slip, blue on ivory printed silk Madeleine Vionnet label, numbered "38136," France, ca. 1930 ....3,850.00

Dress, party-type, black crepe w/beadwork, size 14, ca. 1940's .. 35.00

Dress, royal blue & black striped, smocked, draped bustle, Victorian.............................. 235.00

Dress, silk brocade w/velvet & bead trim, grey tones, Victorian, two-piece 250.00

Dress, teenager's, white w/tiny embroidered tucks, w/French lace inserts, Victorian 135.00

Evening dress, ankle-length, shot green & gold tussah silk, the boned bodice w/diagonal neckline, a pleat of bodice silk forming a swathed strap, complete w/a fringed girdle covering the entire skirt from hip to hemline, studded w/brass & pearlized beads, Mainbocher, America, late 1940's - early 1950's (zipper replaced, one bodice dart slightly let out)........................ 550.00

Evening dress, mauve pink faille, boned, strapless bodice & crinoline skirt overlaid w/crushed folds of fabric which culminate in a large sash tying at the back, white lace ruffled flounce to the hem, labeled "Balenciaga" & numbered "51783," France, 1955 (wired crinoline under-pinning, slight underarm discoloration, light stains to skirt front).......4,950.00

Evening jacket, the floral brocade in shades of pink & grey contrasted w/gold thread foliage, peppermint green velvet lining, labeled "Liberty & Co., Regent St, London," England, 1920's 770.00

Gloves, lady's, white leather, above the elbow, w/three pearl buttons at the wrist 35.00

Gown, Medieval-style, brown velvet, the long-sleeved gown stamped in gilt w/elaborate geometric designs, the sides inset w/pleated rose silk, lined in champagne-colored silk, the sides & sleeves strung w/striped Venetian glass beads, probably Fortuny, Italy (small holes in silk insets) 1,870.00

Gym suit, college girl's, bloomer-type, ca. 1914, 1 pc. 10.00

Hat, lady's, felt cloche trimmed w/sequins & beading 20.00

Hat, man's, derby, black, Red Seal brand 25.00

Jacket, lady's, blue silk, stamped in a gold floral decorative design, the neckline trimmed in cord ending in single Venetian beads, the hemline decorated w/Venetian beads, labeled "Made in Italy - Fabrique en Italie - Fortuny Depose' " (some staining at neckline) 990.00

Morning dress, pink velvet & wool cutwork, w/a pink moire' taffeta collar & inner bodice front panels, deep velvet collar over the shoulders, wide rounded lapels, pale pink cutwork overlay of fruits & blooms w/embroidered raised centers, gently flared wool skirt, the whole lined in taffeta, Worth, France, ca. 1890-1900 (lining torn) 1,100.00

Mounted Police uniform, boy's, Yankiboy, size 6 .... 105.00

Muff, monkey fur, ca. 1930's, 12 x 14" 35.00

Opera cape, lady's, sea green velvet stenciled in a bold 15th c. inspired design in varying shades of gold, the raised collar consists of nine separately applied panels of velvet each edged w/crimped green chiffon, the pieces overlapping to form a highly structured sculptural effect by means of prestuds, six green glass beads on silk thongs fasten the neck, the blue chiffon lining stenciled w/gold palmettos, Maria Gallenga, France, ca. 1910-20, chiffon lining bears remains of stenciled signature (chiffon snagged a bit at shoulders, chiffon at collar torn) .. 990.00

Parasol, child's, folding ivory handle, metal piece slides over hinge in middle of handle, silk exterior & silk lining, original heavy fringe, 22" (silk very fragile) 95.00

Parasol, lady's, black lace, ca. 1890's 85.00

Petticoat, white batiste w/lavish lace trim 75.00

Sacque, infant's, white cotton w/lace trim, Peter Pan collar, 20" l. 15.00

Shawl, Kashmir, twill tapestry technique w/an intertwining boteh design, square cream-colored center, mid-19th c., 76" sq. 1,100.00

Shoes, baby's, leather w/fur trim, ca. 1940's, mint in box, pr....... 40.00

Shoes, baby's, white leather w/ankle strap, pr. 65.00

Shoes, child's, "Culver Cubs," in suitcase box depicting little girl walking w/Teddy bear, ca. 1940's, pr. 35.00

Shoes, lady's, black moire' taffeta, heels decorated w/gilt & rhinestones, Paris, 1920 .... 65.00

Slippers, child's, w/beading & fur trim, ca. 1940's, size 4 .... 8.00

Stockings, child's, Red Riding Hood decoration, Durham Hosiery Mills, mint condition w/original tags, 1917, pr. 35.00

Stockings, lady's, silky white rayon, four pair in original box marked "Valor Hosiery," ca. 1940's 12.00

Suit, lady's, grey tweed, double-breasted w/six chunky buttons, below-knee skirt, probably Dior, France, ca. 1963, 2 pcs.......... 110.00

Suit, man's, blue, lined, size 36-38, ca. 1940's..................... 40.00

Underwear, boy's, BVD-style, original box portrait, "Honest As The Man It's Named For," Franklin-Athletic Underwear, 2 pr........ 28.00

Uniform, lady's, Red Cross, w/hat, jacket, skirt & insignia, ca. 1940's 95.00

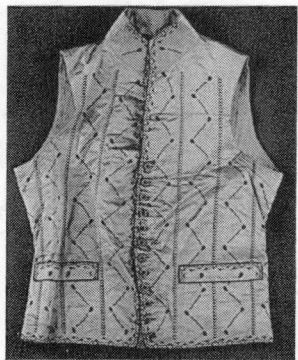

Gentleman's Silk Waistcoat

Waistcoat, satin-weave silk, embroidered w/silk & metallic threads

& heightened w/spangles, some
fiber loss & minor discoloration,
late 18th c. (ILLUS.) 605.00
Walking suit, saffron yellow silk
gauze, the jacket cleverly cut
w/swallow-tail overlap to collar
& similar shaping to hem, both
applied w/two brown & ivory
buttons, the waist & sleeves
w/V-shaped bands of stitching,
the curved skirt pockets similarly
finished, ca. 1916-18, 2 pcs. (tear
at shoulder) 110.00
Wedding dress w/petticoat, white
lawn, handmade, dress gathered
at waist w/full skirt, decorated
w/smocking, hem-stitching & tiny
tucks overall, tiny snaps on back,
cotton petticoat, very ornate
w/gathered tiers, rows of tucking
& lace, silk ribbon straps w/but-
terflies, tiny snaps closure, ca.
early 1900's, 2 pcs. 210.00

COCA-COLA ITEMS

1951 Coca-Cola Blotter

*Coca-Cola promotion has been achieved
through the issuance of scores of small objects through the years. These, together with
trays, signs, and other articles bearing the
name of this soft drink, are now sought by
many collectors.*

Advertisement, lithographed in color
on paper, a delicate portrait of a
seated young woman wearing a
classically draped robe & holding
one knee, printed w/"1915" above
the portrait & in the lower left-
hand corner "Drink Bottled Coca-
Cola - Order it by the case,"
framed, 13½ x 18½" $159.50
Ashtray set, ruby glass, each in the
form of a suit (diamond, heart,
spade & club), 1950's, set of 4 . . . . 590.00
Ball bat, "Knoxall, Drink Coca-Cola
in Bottles," wood, 1930's 225.00
Bank, model of Coca-Cola vending
machine, red-painted metal,
1950's, 5½" h. 125.00
Billfold, pigskin, 1940's, in original
box 37.50

Blotter, 1938, pictures a policeman,
"Stop for a pause - Go refreshed"
& "Drink Coca-Cola" 15.00
Blotter, 1940, pictures a clown, "The
greatest pause on earth" & "Drink
Coca-Cola - Delicious and Refresh-
ing" 55.00
Blotter, 1951, Sprite Boy behind bot-
tle, "Delicious and Refreshing"
(ILLUS.) 7.50
Blotter, 1953, Sprite Boy w/bottle,
"Good" 10.00
Book, "Alphabet Book of Coca-
Cola," 1928 . . . . 35.00
Booklet, "Our America," 1940 . . . . . . 10.00
Booklet, "The Planned Call," illus-
trated training guide for Coca-
Cola sales people 30.00
Booklet, "The Truth about Coca-
Cola," 1912 . . . . 30.00
Booklets, "Flower Arranging,"
Vols. 1 & 2, 1940's, pr. 20.00
Bookmark, 1906, celluloid, owl hold-
ing book, 1 x 3½" . . . . . . 600.00 to 700.00
Bottle carrier, aluminum, 1950's,
6-pack 28.00
Bottle carrier, wooden w/wooden
slat handle, 1940's . . . . 40.00 to 60.00
Bottle carton-carrier, cardboard,
1937, 6-pack 35.00
Bottle holder for automobile, card-
board, ca. 1950 . . . . 18.00
Bowl, pretzel, aluminum, three
bottle-shaped legs, 1936,
8¼" d. . . . . 150.00 to 175.00

1908 Coca-Cola Calendar

Calendar, 1908, pretty young lady
wearing large feathered hat sitting & drinking a glass of Coca-
Cola, reads "Drink Coca-Cola -
Relieves Fatigue" across the top,
full pad, matted & framed, some
tears (ILLUS.) 3,300.00
Calendar, 1935, boy & dog fishing
from stump, Norman Rockwell il-
lustration, full pad 475.00

Calendar, 1938, pretty girl in summer dress & hat holding a bottle of Coca-Cola, full pad 625.00

Calendar, 1947, girl w/skis, matted & framed 125.00

Calendar, 1951, beautiful girl holding bottle of Coca-Cola, full pad .. 55.00

Calendar, 1955, beautiful girls w/bottles of Coca-Cola, full pad .. 55.00

Calendar, 1959, a group of teenagers at a basketball game, full pad 40.00

Calendar, 1960, ski couple 25.00

Calendar, 1962, Audubon "Birds of America" 17.00

Cigarette lighter, figural bottle, 1950's, 2½" h., mint in box 50.00

Cigarette lighter, musical-type, red & white, "Drink Coca-Cola," 1963, mint in box 150.00

Cigarette lighters w/miniature wooden bottle case, includes nine miniature bottle-shaped lighters, 1950's, 10 pcs. 225.00

Clock, wall-type, electric, rectangular, plastic, "Drink Coca-Cola" at bottom, 1960's 50.00

Clock, wall-type, electric, round, red metal frame, "Drink Coca-Cola" printed in the center, ca. 1939-41 ....450.00 to 480.00

Clock, wall-type, electric, round, wide silver metal outer edge w/numbers, "Drink Coca-Cola" printed in the center, 1951, 17½" d.................125.00 to 175.00

1960's Coca-Cola Clock

Clock, wall-type, electric, square, pale green ground w/red numbers & "Drink Coca-Cola" printed in red in the center, 1960's, slight damage at corners of the dial (ILLUS.)......................... 44.00

Coupon, w/magazine ad illustrating Lillian Nordica, 1905 .... 150.00

Delivery man's jacket, 1940's 45.00

Door push plate, porcelain, red & white, "Ice Cold Coca-Cola in Bottles," 1950's, 4 x 30" ....150.00 to 175.00

Game, Chinese Checkers, wood & heavy paperboard playing board, 1940's 60.00

Game, "Darts," box marked "3 Darts - Compliments of the Coca-Cola Bottling Company," 1950's, the set 85.00

Marbles, glass swirls in plastic bag, "Free with every carton," 1950 ... 25.00

Match strike plate, porcelain, "Drink Coca-Cola" over "Strike Matches Here" lower rough surface, pierced to hang, 4½" sq. 325.00

Mirror, pocket-type, 1911, Coca-Cola Girl, "The Whitehead & Hoag Co." etc. on rim, oval ....350.00 to 375.00

Mirror, pocket-type, 1916, Garden Girl, "Whitehead & Hoag Co." etc. on rim, oval 325.00

Neckerchief, Kit Carson, printed cotton, red, white & black, 1950..... 48.00

Notebook, simulated alligator skin cover, stamped in gold "Compliments - The Coca-Cola Co.," ca. 1905 .... 225.00

Pencil, mechanical-type, w/mini bottle inside clear plastic top, 1950's 40.00

Pencil box, 75th Anniversary 75.00

Playing cards, 1943 World War II service woman, mint ......70.00 to 90.00

Playing cards, 1943, Autumn Girl, original box 55.00

Playing cards, 1956, Ice Skating Girl 56.00

Radio, model of a cooler, red Bakelite case, 1949-53, 7 x 9½ x 12" .... 1,000.00 to 1,200.00

Rodeo program, front cover pictures a bronc buster, bull rider & bull-doger, back cover illustrated w/bottles of Coca-Cola & a Coca-Cola button 12.00

Sewing kit, World War II, gold "US Army" & American Eagle on khaki-colored leatherette kit, w/thread, buttons & needles, 1940's ....25.00 to 30.00

Sign, cardboard, rectangular, colorful illustration of a pretty lady carrying a carton of Coke, "Take Home A Carton" above, "Drink Coca-Cola" within a circle above lady's shoulder & "Easy to carry" at the bottom, matted & framed, ca. 1937, 14 x 31½" (near mint condition) 1,825.00

Sign, porcelain, button-type, "Drink Coca-Cola in Bottles," 1950's, 12" d. 250.00

Sign, porcelain, rectangular, "Coca-Cola - Sold Here Ice Cold," red & white w/green border, 12 x 29", 1940's 425.00

Sign, porcelain, rectangular, "Drink Coca-Cola - Fountain Service," 1930's, 48 x 60" 550.00

Sign, lithographed tin, rectangular w/"Drink Ice Cold Coca-Cola in Bottles" spaced on three lines on a white ground, letters in red except "Ice Cold" in yellow, 1940's, 11 x 24" 115.00

Early Coca-Cola Sidewalk Sign

Sign, lithographed tin, sidewalk-type, rectangular, reads "For Headache and Exhaustion - Drink Coca-Cola - 5c A Glass - Delicious & Refreshing" w/a hand holding a glass in a metal holder, early 20th c., edge wear, 20 x 32" (ILLUS.) 4,400.00

Sign, lithographed tin, rectangular w/"Drink Coca-Cola Delicious & Refreshing" spaced on four lines & pictures of a pretty girl drinking Coke, 1941, 19 x 54" . . . .250.00 to 275.00

Sign, tin, rectangular, green, red & white w/black outlining, three sections, top reads "Delicious - Refreshing," the center "Drink - Coca-Cola" & bottom section w/"5c" on each side & "At All - Soda Fountains," wood frame, ca. 1899, 19½ x 27" 6,790.00

Sign, tin, rectangular, "Curb Service - Coca-Cola - Sold Here - Ice Cold," red, yellow, green & white, ca. 1934, 19 x 28" 550.00

Sign, tin, rectangular, "Serve Coke at Home," in green letters, shows six-pack of Coke, 1948, 16 x 40" . . 250.00

Sign, school crossing-type, metal, figure of a policeman holding a shield w/"SLOW School Zone," on a round cast-iron base marked "Drink Coca-Cola," 1950's . . . . .650.00 to 850.00

Sign, wooden shield-shaped w/met-

al leaf-like scrolling at top, pierced for hanging, pictures two Coke glasses above "Drink Coca-Cola," 1930's, 9 x 11" . . . . .725.00 to 800.00

Syrup bottle, clear glass, "Drink Coca-Cola" within wreath, 1910 .425.00 to 500.00

Syrup dispenser knob for push handle, porcelain, "Enjoy Coca-Cola Here," 1950's 95.00

Thermometer, metal w/glass front, round, "Drink Coca-Cola," early 1950's 125.00

Thermometer, tin, bullet-shaped, w/silhouette portrait of girl drinking from bottle at bottom, 1939, 6½" w., 16" h. . . .150.00 to 200.00

Thermometer, tin, shaped oblong form w/two small bottles above "Drink Coca-Cola," 1941, 7" w., 16" h. 150.00

Thermometer, tin, bottle-shaped, 1950's, 17" h. . . . . .75.00 to 100.00

Thermometer, tin, embossed bottle shape, ca. 1958, 8½" w., 30" h. . . 75.00

Thimble, aluminum, dated 1920 . . . . . 35.00

Toy truck, "Buddy L," yellow metal, 1960, 10½" l. 120.00

Toy truck, "Marx," yellow plastic, w/six cases, ca. 1948, w/box 450.00

Toy truck, "Matchbox," Lesney Product, ca. 1960 . . . . 65.00

Toy truck, wood & red metal, wood & wire sides, metal cab, w/six original wood blocks, made by Smith-Miller, 1940's, w/original box 1,095.00

Toy trucks set, plastic & metal, 50th Anniversary trucks for the Panama Bottling Co., set of 6 (all different models) 750.00

Toy van, printed metal, long Volkswagen van, 1950's 225.00

Trade card, illustration of well-dressed Victorian lady sitting at a soda fountain, promotional advertising on the reverse side, early 1890's, 3½ x 5½" (one spot on middle left has top layer of paper peeled off approximately ½ x 1½") 2,200.00

Trade card, 1901, Hilda Clark w/flowers, free Coca-Cola coupon on reverse side, 2½ x 3 7/8" (minor scratch just to the lower right of Hilda) 1,100.00

Tray, change, 1900, Hilda Clark seated at a table, 6" d. (a few chips in background & some rim chips) 5,100.00

Tray, change, 1907, young lady holding up a glass w/"Relieves Fatigue," 4½ x 6¼" oval 325.00

Tray, change, ca. 1907, glass receiver, bold scrolls & "Drink Coca-Cola 5c," 8" d. . . . . .800.00 to 850.00

Tray, change, 1910, Hamilton King Girl, 6" oval 400.00

Tray, change, 1913, Hamilton King Girl in a picture hat holding a glass, 4¼ x 6" oval 300.00

Tray, change, 1914, Betty, 4¼ x 6" oval . . . . .250.00 to 300.00

Tray, change, 1916, girl under tree holding glass, 4¼ x 6" oval . . . . .130.00 to 160.00

Tray, change, 1920, Garden Girl, 4¼ x 6" oval . . . . .300.00 to 350.00

Tray, 1901, Hilda Clark w/flowers, 9¼" d. (good condition) 1,850.00

Tray, 1913, Hamilton King Girl, 12½ x 15¼" oval (near mint w/minor rim chips & scratches) . .2,450.00

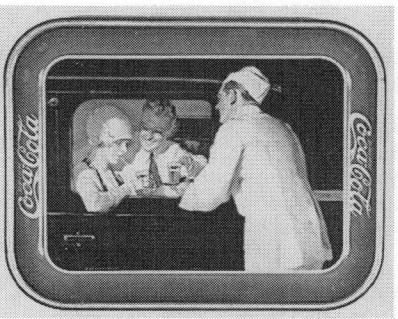

1927 "Curb Service" Tray

Tray, 1927, Curb Service, 10½ x 13¼" rectangle, near mint, minor rim wear & tiny rim dents (ILLUS.) . . .1,460.00

Tray, 1928, girl sipping a bottle of Coke, 10½ x 13¼" rectangle (minor rubs & chips) 890.00

1921 "Summer Girl" Tray

Tray, 1921, Summer Girl, 10½ x 13¼" rectangle, light scratches & corner rim flaking (ILLUS.) 962.00

Tray, 1923, Flapper Girl, 10½ x 13¼" rectangle . .300.00 to 350.00

1928 "Soda Fountain Clerk" Tray

Tray, 1928, Soda Fountain Clerk, 10½ x 13¼" rectangle, some minor rim chips (ILLUS.) 733.00

Tray, 1929, Girl in Yellow Swimsuit holding bottle, red border, 10½ x 13¼" rectangle . .300.00 to 325.00

Tray, 1930, Girl w/Telephone, 10½ x 13¼" rectangle . .250.00 to 300.00

Tray, 1933, Francis Dee, 10½ x 13¼" rectangle (very minor rim scratches & chips) 1,437.00

Tray, 1934, Johnny Weismuller & Maureen O'Sullivan (Tarzan & Jane), 10½ x 13¼" rectangle (minor rim chips & scratches) 1,400.00

Tray, 1935, Madge Evans, 10½ x 13¼" rectangle . .250.00 to 300.00

Tray, 1936, Hostess, 10½ x 13¼" rectangle . . . . .200.00 to 225.00

Tray, 1938, Girl in the Afternoon, 10½ x 13¼" rectangle . .100.00 to 125.00

Tray, 1940, Girl Fishing, 10½ x 13¼" rectangle 175.00

Tray, 1942, Two Girls at Car, 10½ x 13¼" rectangle 145.00

1926 "Golfer & Lady" Tray

Tray, 1926, Golfer & pretty lady, 10½ x 13¼" rectangle, minor rim chips, rim scrape & two tiny rim dents (ILLUS.) 1,346.00

Tray, 1950-52, Girl w/Bottle
of Coke, 10½ x 13¼" rec-
tangle....................50.00 to 65.00
Tumbler, bell-shaped, pewter, ca.
1930's, w/leather pouch 500.00
Vending machine, "Cavalier 33,"
office-type..................... 750.00
Watch fob, brass, rectangular, front
w/relief bust portrait of a young
lady w/a glass & "Relieves Fatigue," reverse w/advertising, ca.
1907 .... 125.00
Window display, folding cardboard,
three-fold theatre stage design,
lithographed in deep blue, greens
& red, the center stage section
w/a cameo illustration of a pretty
lady flanked by theatre side curtain side panels each printed
w/"Drink Coca-Cola" in an oval,
early 20th c. (some stains, minor edge wear & separated at
folds)........................4,400.00

Lap-type, poplar dovetailed case
w/nailed drawer, brass hopper
w/decorative detail, turned wood
handle, old cherry-colored finish,
10¼" h. 150.00
Lap-type, poplar & pewter, a round
pewter cup at the top w/an iron
turn handle w/wooden knob grip,
the dovetailed square wooden
base w/a single drawer, old soft
finish, 9¼" h.................... 126.50
Store counter model, side crank
handle, cast iron, "Enterprise
No. 1," w/original stenciling,
overall 12" h. 250.00
Store counter model, two-wheel,
cast iron, "Enterprise No. 2," 8" d.
wheels, original paint & decals ... 575.00
Store counter model, two-wheel,
cast iron, "Enterprise No. 5" 350.00
Store counter model, two-wheel,
cast iron, "Landers, Frary & Clark
No. 10," excellent original condition 850.00

COFFEE GRINDERS

Imperial No. 705 Coffee Grinder

*Most coffee grinders collected are lap or ta-
ble and wall types used in many homes in the
late 19th and early 20th centuries. However,
large store-sized grinders have recently been
traded.*

Lap-type, "Imperial No. 705," cast
iron & wood, a long iron crank
handle above the domed cast-iron
top w/molded scrolls above the
dovetailed wooden case w/a
small drawer & remnants of the
label above the drawer, 6" sq.,
overall 11" h. (ILLUS.) $50.00
Lap-type, pine box w/fingered
joints, one drawer w/iron pull,
iron top cup w/iron handle &
wooden knob, ca. 1880, 5¾" sq.,
6" h. 85.00

Simmons Koffee Krusher

Store counter model, two-wheel,
cast iron, "Simmons Koffee Krush-
er," original dark blue paint
w/gilt stenciling, marked "KK 13"
on the front of the drawer
(ILLUS.) 1,150.00
Wall-type, cast iron & glass, "Arcade No. 25," clear glass jar &
lid 60.00
Wall-type, tin & iron, "Parker
No. 50," on original mounting
board 68.00
Wall-type, coppered-iron, "Parker &
Co. No. 360," patented April 4,
1876, ornate cast scroll designs... 125.00

COMIC BOOKS

First The Amazing Spider-Man Comic

Comic books, especially first, or early issues of a series, are avidly collected today. Prices for some of the scarce ones have reached extremely high levels. Prices listed below are for copies in fine to mint condition.

Aces High, No. 3, 1955 . . . . $15.00

Action Comics, No. 1, June 1938, D.C. Comics, first appearance of "Superman" (very fine) 29,700.00

Al Capp's Shmoo, No. 3, 1949 . . . . . . 15.00

All-American Comics, National Periodical Publications No. 44, November 1942 . . . . 462.00

All New Short Story Comics, Family Comics No. 1, January 1943 . . . . . . 660.00

All Star Comics, Periodical Publications No. 3, Winter 1940, origin & first appearance of the Justice Society of America 2,640.00

Amazing Fantasy, Marvel Comics No. 15, August 1962, origin & debut appearance of Spider-Man by Ditko (coupon page replaced) 1,980.00

Amazing Spider-Man (The), Marvel Comics No. 1, March 1963, debut of Spider-Man, mint condition (ILLUS.) 8,250.00

Archie, MLJ No. 1, Winter 1942, first teenage comic book 1,430.00

The Avengers, Gold Key No. 1, 1968, based on the TV series, file copy 132.00

Batman, D.C. Publications No. 1, Spring 1940, origin of Batman retold, first appearance of "Joker" & "Catwoman" (very slight restoration, interior pages acid-neutralized) 15,400.00

Batman, National Periodical Publications No. 3, featuring first Catwoman in costume 1,650.00

Bill Elliott, Dell Publishing Co. No. 278, May 1950 . . . . 15.00

Bonanza, Dell-Gold Key No. 1283, 1962 . . . . 30.00

Boy Explorers Comics, Family Comics No. 1, May-June 1946, Simon & Kirby's first work after World War II 935.00

Brave and The Bold, National Periodical Publications No. 28, February-March 1960, introduction of the Justice League 1,320.00

Bulletman, Fawcett Publications No. 1, Summer 1941 (color touchup on spine) 1,430.00

Captain Marvel Adventures, No. 1, January 2, 1941, Fawcett Publications (slight restoration) 3,850.00

Classics Illustrated, No. 39, Jane Eyre, July 1947 . . . . 50.00

Daredevil Comics, Lev Gleason Publications Nos. 1-2, 1941, No. 1 w/photographic Hitler cover, pr. (near mint) 12,100.00

Detective Comics, National Publications/D.C. Comics No. 1, March 1937 (moderate restoration w/tan pages) 7,700.00

Detective Comics No. 27

Detective Comics, National Publications/D.C. Comics No. 27, May 1939, first appearance of Batman, very fine condition (ILLUS.) 38,500.00

Detective Comics, National Publications/D.C. Comics No. 29, July 1939 (light restoration) 4,180.00

Donald Duck, Walt Disney Comics Vol. 1, No. 3, December 1940 . . . . 300.00

Exciting Comics, Better Publications Nos. 1 & 2, April 1940, 2 pcs. 1,650.00

Fantastic Four, Marvel Comics No. 1, November 1961, first appearance of the Fantastic Four . . .3,520.00

Funnies on Parade, 1933, Eastern Printing Company, the first modern format comic book, reprinting Sunday funnies (slight restoration to spine, cleaned) 4,675.00

Green Lantern, National Periodical
  Publications No. 1, Fall 1941, ori-
  gins of Green Lantern retold.....5,280.00
Gunsmoke, Dell-Gold Key No. 8,
  1958 ....   28.00
Li'l Abner, Harvey Publishing
  No. 65, August 1947 ....   20.00
Lone Ranger (The), Dell No. 1,
  January-February 1948
  (mint) 1,045.00
Marvel Comics, Timely Publications
  No. 1, November 1939, The Hu-
  man Torch on the cover (very
  fine)........................28,600.00
Marvel Mystery Comics, Timely Pub-
  lications No. 2, December 1939
  (very fine) 4,950.00
Marvel Mystery, Timely Publications
  No. 4, 1940, w/the introduction of
  Electro 440.00
Master Comics, Fawcett Publications
  No. 22, January 1942 .... 880.00
More Fun Comics, National Periodi-
  cal Publications No. 9, March
  1936........................2,200.00

Our Fighting Forces No. 1

Our Fighting Forces, National Peri-
  odical Publications/D.C. Comics
  No. 1, October-November 1954,
  near mint (ILLUS.) 605.00
Pogo Possom, Dell Publishing
  No. 11, 1950 ....   50.00
Science Comics, Fox Features No. 1,
  February 1940 (spine split).......1,650.00
Sensation Comics, National Periodi-
  cal Publications/D.C. Comics
  No. 1, January 1942, origin of
  "Wonder Woman" continued
  from *All-Star Comics*
  No. 8 ....2,750.00 to 3,000.00
Shock Illustrated, E.C. Comics No. 3,
  Spring 1956, file copy 1,100.00
Star Ranger, Ultem Publications
  No. 1, February 1937, first comic
  book w/a Western theme 1,760.00

Superboy, National Periodical Publi-
  cations No. 1, March-April 1949 ..2,640.00
Thunda, Magazine Enterprises No. 1,
  1952, only comic book done en-
  tirely by Frank Frazetta 1,320.00
USA Comics, Timely Comics No. 1,
  August 1941 .... 770.00
Weird Fantasy, E.C. Publications
  No. 13 (No. 1), May-June 1950 ... 275.00
Weird Science-Fantasy Annual, E.C.
  Comics, 1953................... 715.00
Western Round-Up, Dell Giant
  Comics No. 13, 1956............   30.00
Whiz Comics, No. 2 (No. 1), January
  1940, Fawcett Publications, origin
  & first newstand appearance of
  "Captain Marvel" (fine plus) 9,900.00

COMMEMORATIVE PLATES

*Limited edition commemorative and collec-
tor plates rank high on the list of collectible
items. The oldest and best-known of these
plates, those of Bing & Grondahl and Royal
Copenhagen, retain leadership in the field, but
other companies are turning out a variety of
designs, some of which have been widely embraced by the growing numbers who have
made plate collecting a hobby. Plates listed
below are a representative selection of fine
porcelain, glass and other plates available to
collectors.*

ANRI

Christmas
1971, St. Jakob in Groden.......... $45.00
1972, Pipers at Alberobello 48.00
1973, Alpine Horn 348.00
1974, Young Man & Girl 68.00
1975, Christmas in Ireland 70.00
1976, Alpine Christmas 95.00
1977, Legend of Heiligenblut 83.00
1978, The Klockler Singers 83.00
1979, The Moss Gatherers of Vill-
  noess 62.00
1980, Wintry Church-going in Santa
  Christina 80.00
1981, Santa Claus in Tyrol.......... 105.00
1982, Star Singers 116.00
1983, Unto Us a Child Is Born....... 171.00
1984, Yuletide in the Valley 76.00
1985, Good Morning, Good Cheer .. 130.00

BAREUTHER

Christmas
1967, Stiftskirche 77.00
1968, Kappl......................   13.50
1969, Christkindlesmarkt 12.00
1970, Chapel in Oberndorf 11.00

1971, Toys for Sale	10.00
1972, Christmas in Munich	18.50
1973, Christmas Sleigh Ride	8.50
1974, Church in the Black Forest	13.00
1975, Snowman	22.00
1976, Chapel in the Hills	13.50
1977, Story Time	17.00
1978, Mittenwald	13.50
1979, Winter Day	17.00
1980, Miltenberg	21.00
1981, Walk in the Forest	16.00
1982, Bad Wimpfen	25.00
1983, The Night Before Christmas . . .	25.50
1984, Zeil on the River Main	24.50
1985, Winter Wonderland	27.50
1986, Market Place in Forchheim . . .	26.50

Father's Day

1970 Bareuther Father's Day Plate

1969, Castle Neuschwanstein	17.00
1970, Castle Pfalz (ILLUS.)	9.00
1971, Castle Heidelberg	13.00
1972, Castle Hohenschwangau	11.50
1973, Castle Katz	10.50
1974, Wurzburg Castle	16.00
1975, Castle Lichtenstein	21.00
1976, Castle Hohenzollern	27.00
1977, Castle Eltz	27.00
1978, Castle Falkenstein	30.00
1979, Castle Rheinstein	25.00
1980, Castle Cochem	22.00
1981, Castle Gutenfels	35.50
1982, Castle Zwingenberg	25.50
1983, Castle Lauenstein	25.50
1984, Castle Neuenstein	19.00
1985, Castle Wartburg Near	
Eisenach	30.50
1986, Castle Hardegg	29.50
1987, Castle Buerresheim	20.00

Mother's Day

1969, Dancing	21.00
1970, Mother & Children	9.00
1971, Doing the Laundry	11.50

1972, Baby's First Step	10.00
1973, Mother Kissing Baby	18.50
1974, Musical Children	13.00
1975, Spring Outing	9.50
1976, Rocking Cradle	13.00
1977, Noon Feeding	15.00
1978, Blind Man's Bluff	20.00
1979, Mother's Love	13.00
1980, First Cherries	15.00
1981, Playtime	15.50
1982, Suppertime	16.50
1983, On Farm	16.00
1984, Village Children	25.00
1985, Sunrise	21.00
1986, Playtime	32.50
1987, Pets	19.00

BING & GRONDAHL

Christmas

1916 Bing & Grondahl Christmas Plate

1895	5,595.00
1896	1,627.00
1897	1,585.00
1898	618.00
1899	1,040.00
1900	821.00
1901	343.00
1902	271.00
1903	245.00
1904	114.00
1905	113.00
1906	76.00
1907	83.00
1908	59.00
1909	79.50
1910	70.00
1911	64.00
1912	69.00
1913	55.00
1914	58.00
1915	100.00
1916 (ILLUS.)	53.00
1917	52.50
1918	53.00
1919	44.00
1920	61.00

1921	51.00
1922	48.00
1923	45.00
1924	51.00
1925	58.00
1926	57.00
1927	68.00
1928	46.00
1929	50.00
1930	69.00
1931	55.00
1932	59.00
1933	51.00
1934	49.50
1935	48.50
1936	48.00
1937	52.00
1938	101.00
1939	118.00
1940	121.00
1941	192.00
1942	128.00
1943	128.00
1944	72.50
1945	94.00
1946	50.00
1947	71.00
1948	62.50
1949	51.00
1950	80.00
1951	68.50
1952	66.00
1953	58.00
1954	57.00
1955	74.00
1956	90.00
1957	94.00
1958	60.00
1959	79.00
1960	102.00
1961	81.00
1962	42.00
1963	61.00
1964	23.00
1965	24.00
1966	21.00
1967	23.00
1968	22.00
1969	12.50
1970	11.00
1971	10.00
1972	10.00
1973	11.50
1974	11.50
1975	13.00
1976	12.50
1977	14.00
1978	16.00
1979	14.50
1980	17.50
1981	19.50
1982	29.00
1983	28.00
1984	22.50

1985	21.00

Mother's Day

1969, Dog & Puppies	293.00
1970, Birds & Chicks	12.50
1971, Cat & Kitten	9.00
1972, Mare & Foal	11.00
1973, Duck & Ducklings	9.00
1974, Bear & Cubs	10.00
1975, Doe & Fawns	11.50
1976, Swan Family	11.00
1977, Squirrel & Young	11.00
1978, Heron	12.50
1979, Fox & Cubs	15.00
1980, Woodpecker & Young	18.00
1981, Hare & Young	20.00
1982, Lioness & Cubs	20.00
1983, Raccoon & Young	22.00
1984, Stork & Nestlings	21.00
1985, Bear with Cubs	25.00
1986, Elephant with Calf	28.00
1987, Sheep with Lambs	49.00

Jubilee

1915, Frozen Window	114.00
1920, Church Bells	52.50
1925, Dog Outside Window	90.00
1930, The Old Organist	109.00
1935, Little Match Girl	568.00
1940, Three Wise Men	1,525.00
1945, Royal Guard Amalienborg Castle	117.00
1950, Eskimos	124.00
1955, Dybbol Mill	124.00
1960, Kronborg Castle	79.00
1965, Churchgoers	44.00
1970, Amalienborg Castle	19.50
1975, Horses Enjoying Meal	31.00
1980, Happiness over Yule Tree	15.50

FENTON (Glass)

Christmas

1971 Fenton Carnival Glass Plate

1970, Little Brown Church, blue satin	17.00
1970, Little Brown Church, carnival	20.00

1971, Old Brick Church, blue satin .. 16.00
1971, Old Brick Church, carnival
(ILLUS.)......................... 22.00
1972, Two Horned Church, carnival............................. 20.00
1972, Two Horned Church, white
satin 30.00
1973, St. Mary's, carnival 22.50
1974, Nation's Church, carnival 23.00
1974, Nation's Church, white satin .. 12.50
1975, Birthplace of Liberty, blue
satin 24.50
1975, Birthplace of Liberty, carnival............................. 19.00
1975, Birthplace of Liberty, white
satin 14.50
1976, Old North Church, carnival ... 17.50
1977, San Carlos Borromeo, carnival............................. 15.00
1977, San Carlos Borromeo, white
satin 14.50
1978, Church of Holy Trinity, blue
satin 15.00
1978, Church of Holy Trinity,
carnival 15.00
1978, Church of Holy Trinity, white
satin 14.50
1979, San Jose y Miguel de Aguayo,
blue satin 15.00
1979, San Jose y Miguel de Aguayo,
carnival 12.50
1979, San Jose y Miguel de Aguayo,
white satin 9.00
1980, Christ Church, carnival 15.00
1981, Mission of San Xavier del Bac,
carnival 16.00

Mother's Day
1971, Madonna with Sleeping Child,
blue satin 17.00
1971, Madonna with Sleeping Child,
carnival 16.50
1972, Madonna of the Goldfinch,
blue satin 13.50
1972, Madonna of the Goldfinch,
carnival 8.00
1972, Madonna of the Goldfinch,
white satin 20.00
1973, Cowper Madonna, blue satin.. 60.00
1973, Cowper Madonna, carnival ... 10.50
1974, Madonna of the Grotto, blue
satin 12.00
1974, Madonna of the Grotto,
carnival 8.00
1974, Madonna of the Grotto, white
satin 14.50
1975, Taddei Madonna, blue satin .. 60.00
1975, Taddei Madonna, carnival 15.00
1976, Holy Night, carnival 11.50
1977, Madonna & Child, blue satin .. 17.00
1977, Madonna & Child, carnival 12.50
1978, Madonnina, carnival 9.50
1978, Madonnina, white satin 15.00

1979, Madonna of the Rose Hedge,
carnival 12.00

FERRANDIZ, JUAN

Christmas - Anri (Wood)
1972, Christ in Manger 139.00
1973, Boy with Lamb 70.00
1974, Nativity 169.00
1975, Flight into Egypt 75.00
1976, Mary & Joseph Pray......... 127.00
1977, Girl with Tree 45.00
1978, Leading the Way............ 65.00
1979, Drummer Boy 86.00
1980, Rejoice 95.00
1981, Spreading Word 73.50
1982, Shepherd Family 75.00
1983, Peace Attend Thee........... 80.00

Mother & Child - Schmid (Porcelain)
1977, Orchard Mother 37.50
1978, Pastoral Mother 31.00
1979, Floral Mother.............. 39.50
1980, Avian Mother 42.50

Mother's Day - Anri (Wood)
1972, Mother Sewing 112.00
1973, Mother & Child 62.00
1974, Mother & Child 79.00
1975, Mother Holding Dove 79.00
1976, Mother & Child ....50.00 to 75.00
1977, Girl with Flowers 59.00
1978, Beginning 65.00
1979, All Hearts................. 80.00
1980, Spring Arrivals 101.00
1981, Harmony 77.00
1982, With Love 75.00

FRANKLIN MINT (STERLING SILVER)

Norman Rockwell Christmas Series
1970, Bringing Home the Tree 183.00
1971, Under the Mistletoe......... 100.00
1972, The Carolers 80.00
1973, Trimming the Tree 80.00
1974, Hanging the Wreath 108.00
1975, Home for Christmas......... 136.00

FRANKOMA

Christmas
1965, Goodwill Toward Men........ 207.00
1966, Bethlehem Shepherds 89.00
1967, Gifts for the Christ Child 60.00
1968, Flight into Egypt 26.50
1969, Laid in a Manger (ILLUS. top
next page) 16.00
1970, King of Kings 20.00
1971, No Room in the Inn 11.00
1972, Seeking the Christ Child 15.00
1973, The Annunciation 9.50
1974, She Loved & Cared.......... 16.00
1975, Peace on Earth 17.50

1969 Frankoma Christmas Plate

1976, Gift of Love 18.00
1977, Birth of Eternal Life 18.50
1978, All Nature Rejoiced 22.50
1979, Star of Hope 15.00
1980, Unto Us a Child Is Born. 12.50
1981, O Come Let Us Adore Him. . . .   15.00
1982, Wise Men Rejoice. 13.00
1983, Wise Men Bring Gifts 14.00
1984, Faith, Hope & Love. 13.00
1985, The Angels Watched 13.50

FURSTENBERG

Christmas
1971, Rabbits 19.00
1972, Snowy Village 19.00
1973, Christmas Eve 23.50
1975, Deer Family 12.00
1976, Winter Birds. 22.00

Mother's Day
1972, Hummingbird. 21.00
1973, Hedgehogs 12.00
1974, Doe with Fawn 14.00
1975, Swan Family 13.50
1976, Koala Bear 21.00

GORHAM - NORMAN ROCKWELL

Christmas
1974, Tiny Tim 24.00
1975, Good Deeds. 24.00
1976, Christmas Trio 19.00
1978, Planning Christmas Visits 18.50
1979, Santa's Helpers 15.00
1980, Letter to Santa 22.50
1981, Santa Plans His Visit 19.00
1982, The Jolly Coachman 19.50
1983, Christmas Dancers 28.00
1984, Christmas Medley 28.00
1985, Home for the Holidays 25.00
1987, The Homecoming 25.00

Four Seasons
1971, A Boy & His Dog, set of 4 . . . .   206.00
1972, Young Love, set of 4 . . . .   106.00
1973, The Ages of Love, set of 4. . . .   167.00
1974, Grandpa & Me, set of 4 . . . . . .   91.00
1975, Me & My Pal, set of 4 . . . .   132.00
1976, Grand Pals, set of 4 . . . .   122.00
1977, Going on Sixteen, set of 4. . . .   71.00
1978, The Tender Years, set of 4. . . .   63.00
1979, A Helping Hand, set of 4 . . . . .   59.50
1980, Dad's Boy, set of 4 . . . .   111.00
1980, Landscape Series, set of 4 . . . .   95.00
1981, Old Timers, set of 4. . . . .   72.00
1982, Life with Father, set of 4 . . . . .   61.00
1983, Old Buddies, set of 4 . . . .   75.00

HAVILAND & CO.

Christmas
1970, A Partridge in a Pear Tree. . . .   50.00
1971, Two Turtle Doves 26.00
1972, Three French Hens 17.00
1973, Four Colly Birds 18.00
1974, Five Golden Rings 15.50
1975, Six Geese A'Laying 19.00
1976, Seven Swans A'Swimming 24.00
1977, Eight Maids A'Milking 25.00
1978, Nine Ladies Dancing 43.00
1979, Ten Lords A'Leaping 32.00
1980, Eleven Pipers Piping 45.50
1981, Twelve Drummers Drum-
  ming 42.00

HAVILAND & PARLON

Christmas
1972, Madonna & Child (Raphael) . . .   53.00
1973, Madonnina (Feruzzi) 49.00
1974, Cowper Madonna & Child
  (Raphael). 35.00
1975, Madonna & Child (Murillo) 34.50
1976, Madonna & Child (Botticelli) . .   32.50
1977, Madonna & Child (Bellini). 24.50
1978, Madonna & Child (Fra Filippo
  Lippi) 25.00
1979, Madonna of the Eucharist (Bot-
  ticelli). 90.00

Mother's Day
1975, Laura & Child. 15.00
1976, Pinky & Baby 9.50
1977, Amy & Snoopy. 10.00

Tapestry Series
1971, The Unicorn in Captivity 62.00
1972, Start of the Hunt. 26.00
1973, Chase of the Unicorn. 53.00
1974, End of the Hunt. 51.50
1975, The Unicorn Surrounded 43.50
1976, The Unicorn is Brought to the
  Castle. 30.00

The Lady & The Unicorn
1977, To My Only Desire 18.00
1978, Sight 23.00
1979, Sound 26.00
1980, Touch. 27.00

1981, Scent 26.00
1982, Taste 28.50

HUMMEL (GOEBEL WORKS)

Annual
1971, Heavenly Angel 470.00
1972, Hear Ye, Hear Ye 39.00
1973, Globe Trotter 83.00
1974, Goose Girl 45.00
1975, Ride into Christmas 44.00
1976, Apple Tree Girl 42.00
1977, Apple Tree Boy 51.00
1978, Happy Pastime 40.00
1979, Singing Lesson 28.00
1980, School Girl 41.00
1981, Umbrella Boy 47.00
1982, Umbrella Girl 86.00
1983, The Postman 137.00
1984, Little Helper 43.00
1985, Chick Girl 71.00
1986, Playmates 97.00
1987, Feeding Time 186.00

Anniversary
1975, Stormy Weather 68.50
1980, Spring Dance 51.00
1985, Auf Wiedersehen 140.00

LALIQUE (GLASS)

Annual

1971 Lalique Plate

1965, Deux Oiseaux (Two Birds) 900.00
1966, Rose de Songerie (Dream
Rose) 115.00
1967, Ballet de Poisson (Fish
Ballet) 94.00
1968, Gazelle Fantaisie (Gazelle
Fantasy) 77.00
1969, Papillon (Butterfly) 88.00
1970, Paon (Peacock) 75.50
1971, Hibou (Owl) [ILLUS.] 60.00
1972, Coquillage (Shell) 50.00
1973, Petit Geai (Jayling) 91.00
1974, Sous d'Argent (Silver Pen-
nies) 75.00

1975, Duo de Poisson (Fish Duet) . . . 105.00
1976, Aigle (Eagle) 81.00

LENOX

Boehm Bird Series
1970, Wood Thrush 140.00
1971, Goldfinch 73.00
1972, Mountain Bluebird 32.00
1973, Meadowlark 29.50
1974, Rufous Hummingbird 39.00
1975, American Redstart 33.50
1976, Cardinals 43.00
1977, Robins 47.00
1978, Mockingbirds 56.50
1979, Golden-Crowned Kinglets 77.00
1980, Black-Throated Blue War-
blers 82.50
1981, Eastern Phoebes 71.50

Boehm Woodland Wildlife Series
1973, Raccoons 46.50
1974, Red Foxes 48.00
1975, Cottontail Rabbits 44.00
1976, Eastern Chipmunks 48.00
1977, Beaver 55.00
1978, Whitetail Deer 46.00
1979, Squirrels 72.50
1980, Bobcats 68.50
1981, Martens 88.50
1982, Otters 103.00

LIHS-LINDNER

Christmas
1972, Little Drummer Boy 15.50
1973, Little Carolers 9.00
1974, Peace on Earth 9.00
1975, Christmas Cheer 9.00
1976, Joy of Christmas 11.00
1977, Holly-jolly Christmas 19.00
1978, Holy Night 10.00

ORREFORS (GLASS)

Annual Cathedral Series
1970, Notre Dame Cathedral 20.00
1971, Westminster Abbey 30.00
1972, Basilica di San Marco 25.00
1973, Cologne Cathedral 61.00
1974, Temple Rue de la Victoire,
Paris 49.00
1975, Basilica di San Pietro, Rome . . 36.00
1976, Christ Church, Philadelphia . . . 36.00
1977, Masjid-E-Shah 81.00
1978, Santiago de Compostela 56.50

Mother's Day
1971, Flowers for Mother 17.50
1972, Mother & Children 17.00
1973, Mother & Child 16.00
1974, Mother & Child 15.00
1975, Child's First Steps 45.50
1976, Children & Puppy 17.50

1977, Child & Dove 17.50
1978, Mother & Child 17.50

PICKARD

Lockhart Wildlife Series

1970, Woodcock & Ruffed Grouse,
 pr....................200.00 to 225.00
1971, Green-Winged Teal & Mallard,
 pr....................150.00 to 175.00
1972, Mockingbird & Cardinal, pr.... 125.00
1973, Wild Turkey & Ring-Necked
 Pheasant, pr. 179.00
1974, American Bald Eagle 600.00
1975, White-Tailed Deer 100.00
1976, American Buffalo 97.00
1977, Great Horned Owl 93.00
1978, American Panther 129.00
1979, Red Fox..................... 68.00
1980, Trumpeter Swan 150.00

PORSGRUND

Christmas

1970 Porsgrund Christmas Plate

1968, Church Scene................ 100.00
1969, Three Kings 9.00
1970, Road to Bethlehem (ILLUS.) ... 9.00
1971, A Child is Born 9.50
1972, Hark, the Herald Angels
 Sing 10.00
1973, Promise of the Savior 14.50
1974, The Shepherds............... 23.00
1975, Jesus on the Road to the
 Temple........................ 14.00
1976, Jesus & the Elders 13.00
1977, Draught of the Fish 14.50

Traditional Norwegian Christmas

1978, Guests Are Coming 15.00
1979, Home for Christmas.......... 17.00
1980, Preparing for Christmas 18.50
1981, Christmas Skating............ 22.50
1982, White Christmas 20.00

Father's Day

1971, Fishing..................... 10.50
1972, Cookout 10.00
1973, Sledding 6.00

1974, Father & Son 5.00
1975, Skating 10.00
1976, Skiing 6.00
1977, Soccer 8.50
1978, Canoeing 8.50
1979, Father & Daughter 11.50
1980, Sailing 6.50

Mother's Day

1970, Mare & Foal................. 8.50
1971, Boy & Geese 9.00
1972, Doe & Fawn 9.00
1973, Cat & Kittens 5.00
1974, Boy & Goats................. 9.00
1975, Dog & Puppies............... 8.50
1976, Girl & Calf 11.00
1977, Boy & Chickens 7.50
1978, Girl & Pigs 9.00
1979, Boy & Reindeer 10.00
1980, Girl & Lambs 10.00
1981, Boy & Birds 10.00
1982, Girl & Rabbits 12.00

RORSTRAND
Christmas

1970 Rorstrand Christmas Plate

1968, Bringing Home the Tree 374.00
1969, Fisherman Sailing Home 16.00
1970, Nils with His Geese (ILLUS.) .. 11.00
1971, Nils in Lapland 24.00
1972, Dalecarlian Fiddler.......... 9.00
1973, Farm in Smaland 50.00
1974, Vadstena 40.00
1975, Nils in Vastmanland 16.00
1976, Nils in Uppland 19.00
1977, Nils in Varmland 16.00
1978, Nils in Fjallbacka 22.00
1979, Nils in Vaestergoetland 25.00
1980, Nils in Halland 30.00
1981, Nils in Gotland 28.00
1982, Nils at Skansen in Stock-
 holm......................... 33.00
1983, Nils in Oland 32.00
1984, Nils in Angermanland 37.00
1985, Nils in Jamtland 40.00

Father's Day

1971, Father & Child 9.50
1972, Meal at Home 6.50

1973, Tilling Fields	6.50
1974, Fishing	7.00
1975, Painting	6.50
1976, Plowing	6.00
1977, Sawing	7.00
1978, Self-Portrait	15.00
1979, Bridge	15.50
1980, My Etch-Nook	15.00

ROSENTHAL
Christmas

1910	370.00
1911	160.00
1915	118.00
1916	160.00
1923	95.00
1926	115.00
1927	95.00
1928	110.00
1929	135.00
1930	69.00
1931	168.00
1933	145.00
1934	145.00
1935	131.00
1936	120.00
1937	110.00
1938	100.00
1939	90.00
1942	200.00
1944	173.00
1945	240.00
1946	157.00
1949	110.00
1950	110.00
1951	250.00
1952	115.00
1953	125.00
1954	125.00
1955	120.00
1956	133.00
1957	115.00
1958	115.00
1959	105.00
1960	115.00
1961	99.00
1962	87.00
1963	105.00
1964	101.00
1965	89.00
1966	123.00
1967	120.00
1968	117.00
1969	133.00
1970	86.00
1971	64.00
1972	63.00
1973	57.00
1974	47.00
1975	54.00

Wiinblad Christmas

1971, Maria & Child	600.00
1972, King Caspar	215.00
1973, King Melchior	186.00
1974, King Balthazar	258.00
1975, The Annunciation	138.00
1976, Angel with Trumpet	118.00
1977, Adoration of the Shepherds	132.00
1978, Angel with Harp	123.00
1979, Exodus from Egypt	129.00
1980, Angel with Glockenspiel	131.00
1981, Christ Child Visits Temple	148.00
1982, Christening of Christ	143.00

Hibel Nobility of Children Series

1976, La Contessa Isabella	78.00
1977, La Marquis Maurice-Pierre	78.00
1978, Baronesse Johanna-Maryke Van Vollendam Tot Marken	95.00
1979, Chief Red Feather	101.00

ROYAL BAYREUTH

Christmas

1972, Carriage in the Village	31.00
1973, Snow Scene	12.00
1974, Old Mill	10.00
1975, Forest Chalet "Serenity"	8.50
1976, Christmas in the Country	9.50
1977, Peace on Earth	8.00
1978, Peaceful Interlude	25.00
1979, Homeward Bound	17.50

Mother's Day

1973, Consolation	21.50
1974, Young Americans	79.00
1975, Young Americans II	24.00
1976, Young Americans III	41.00
1977, Young Americans IV	25.00
1978, Young Americans V	16.00
1979, Young Americans VI	30.00
1980, Young Americans VII	33.00
1981, Young Americans VIII	22.50
1982, Young Americans IX	27.00

ROYAL COPENHAGEN

Christmas

1920 Royal Copenhagen Christmas Plate

1908	3,650.00
1909	116.00

1910	95.00
1911	114.00
1912	120.00
1913	97.00
1914	110.00
1915	108.00
1916	70.00
1917	67.00
1918	69.00
1919	68.00
1920 (ILLUS.)	70.00
1921	63.00
1922	57.50
1923	54.50
1924	76.00
1925	61.00
1926	65.00
1927	116.50
1928	66.00
1929	68.00
1930	83.00
1931	80.00
1932	82.00
1933	110.00
1934	99.00
1935	160.00
1936	128.00
1937	168.00
1938	215.00
1939	266.00
1940	316.00
1941	251.00
1942	289.00
1943	376.00
1944	166.00
1945	307.00
1946	125.00
1947	189.00
1948	155.00
1949	159.00
1950	170.00
1951	272.00
1952	92.50
1953	99.00
1954	95.00
1955	130.00
1956	132.00
1957	66.00
1958	101.00
1959	88.00
1960	105.00
1961	120.00
1962	146.00
1963	59.00
1964	40.00
1965	39.00
1966	21.00
1967	22.00
1968	19.00
1969	20.00
1970	22.00
1971	12.50
1972	15.00
1973	15.00

1974	18.00
1975	13.50
1976	16.50
1977	16.50
1978	18.00
1979	26.00
1980	48.50
1981	22.00
1982	33.00
1983	32.00
1984	33.00
1985	41.00

Mother's Day

1971, American Mother	11.00
1972, Oriental Mother	8.00
1973, Danish Mother	8.00
1974, Greenland Mother	8.00
1975, Bird in Nest	8.00
1976, Mermaids	7.50
1977, The Twins	6.50
1978, Mother & Child	6.50
1979, A Loving Mother	8.00
1980, An Outing with Mother	14.00
1981, Reunion	14.50
1982, Children's Hour	13.50

Motherhood Series

1982, Mother Robin & Her Young Ones	18.00
1983, Mother Cat & Kitten	20.00
1984, Mare with Foal	17.00
1985, Mother Rabbit with Bunny	23.00
1986, Dog & Puppies	26.00
1987, Goat & Kid	33.00

ROYAL DOULTON
Beswick Christmas Series

1972, Christmas in England	25.00
1973, Christmas in Mexico	22.50
1974, Christmas in Bulgaria	35.00
1975, Christmas in Norway	45.00
1976, Christmas in Holland	46.00
1977, Christmas in Poland	38.50
1978, Christmas in America	27.00

Victorian Christmas

1977, Skater	13.00
1978, Victorian Girl	11.50
1979, Sleigh Ride	13.00
1980, Santa's Visit	15.50
1981, Carolers	16.50
1982, Santa's Visit	17.00

Mother & Child Series

1973, Colette & Child	278.00
1974, Sayuri & Child	92.00
1975, Kristina & Child	40.00
1976, Marilyn & Child	50.00
1977, Lucia & Child	43.00
1978, Kathleen & Child	39.00

SCHMID HUMMEL
Christmas

1971, Angel	15.00

1972 Schmid Hummel Christmas Plate

1972, Angel with Flute (ILLUS.)	11.50
1973, The Nativity	57.00
1974, The Guardian Angel	11.00
1975, Christmas Child..............	15.50
1976, Sacred Journey	13.00
1977, Herald Angel	14.00
1978, Heavenly Trio	12.00
1979, Starlight Angel	11.00
1980, Parade into Toyland..........	22.00
1981, A Time to Remember	17.00
1982, Angelic Procession	16.50
1983, Angelic Messenger..........	21.50
1984, A Gift from Heaven	27.00
1985, Heavenly Light	22.50

Mother's Day

1972, Playing Hooky	11.00
1973, Little Fisherman	38.00
1974, Bumblebee	10.50
1975, Message of Love............	17.00
1976, Devotion for Mother	12.00
1977, Moonlight Return	15.50
1978, Afternoon Stroll	15.00
1979, Cherub's Gift	15.00
1980, Mother's Little Helpers	17.00
1981, Playtime	11.00
1982, The Flower Basket	16.00
1983, Spring Bouquet	20.00
1984, A Joy to Share	23.00
1985, A Mother's Journey	20.00

SPODE

Christmas

1970, Partridge in a Pear Tree......	20.00
1971, In Heaven the Angels Sing- ing	12.50
1972, We Saw Three Ships A'Sail- ing	18.00
1973, We Three Kings of Orient Are	32.50
1974, Deck the Halls..............	29.00
1975, Christbaum	34.50
1976, Good King Wenceslas	16.50
1977, The Holly & the Ivy	21.00
1978, While Shepherds Watched	24.50
1979, Away in a Manger	21.00

1980, Bringing in the Boar's Head ...	25.00
1981, Make We Merry	47.00

WEDGWOOD

Christmas

1969, Windsor Castle	107.00
1970, Christmas in Trafalgar Square	20.00
1971, Picadilly Circus, London	22.50
1972, St. Paul's Cathedral	21.00
1973, Tower of London.............	44.00
1974, Houses of Parliament	24.00
1975, Tower Bridge...............	28.50
1976, Hampton Court	26.00
1977, Westminster Abbey	37.00
1978, Horse Guards	24.00
1979, Buckingham Palace	32.00
1980, St. James Palace	30.00
1981, Marble Arch................	40.00
1982, Lambeth Palace.............	59.00
1983, All Souls, Langham Palace....	55.00
1984, Constitution Hill	45.00
1985, The Tate Gallery.............	53.00
1986, Albert Memorial	51.00
1987, Guildhall..................	75.00
1988, The Observatory, Greenwich..	70.00

Mother's Day

1971, Sportive Love...............	10.00
1972, Sewing Lesson..............	10.00
1973, Baptism of Achilles	12.50
1974, Domestic Employment	21.00
1975, Mother & Child	19.50
1976, The Spinner	13.00
1977, Leisure Time	24.00
1978, Swan & Cygnets	19.00
1979, Deer & Fawn	28.00
1980, Birds	28.50
1981, Mare & Foal................	30.00
1982, Cherubs with Swing	20.50
1983, Cupid & Butterfly	19.00
1984, Cupid & Music	23.00
1985, Cupid & Doves..............	30.50

COMPACTS & VANITY CASES

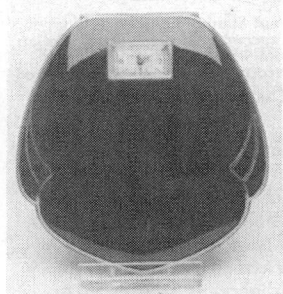

Art Deco Compact with Watch

Brass compact, elephants decoration, "Marinello" $35.00

Brass compact, octagonal, pumpkin decoration, "Damee Inc." 35.00

Brushed silvered metal compact, floral engraving, faux amethyst catch 75.00

Celluloid compact, raised rose on round lid, interior fitted w/mirror & powder on one side, the other w/two mirrors & rouge, lipstick in handle 125.00

Confetti Lucite compact, square, "Zell," w/original box 40.00

Damascened metal compact, inlaid w/gold & silver view of Mt. Fuji on black matte ground, musical, ca. 1920's...................... 195.00

Enameled compact, Art Deco shell shape, black enamel w/gold trim, the top fitted w/a rectangular watch marked "Weldwood," case marked "Illinois Watch Case Co.," 1930's, 3½" l. (ILLUS.) 467.50

Enameled compact, green, model of a suitcase w/travel stickers, detailed, ca. 1930, unused 120.00

Enameled compact, w/rhinestones in crown at center, "de Markoff," w/original box, 3¾" sq. 65.00

Enameled compact, double vanity-type, silver & blue horse & carriage design on gold ground w/six blue dots on top, "Evening in Paris" by Bourjois, New York, w/rouge & face powder, w/sample packs of Rose Indian & Brilliant, mint in box, ca. 1930's-40's, 5/8 x 2 5/8 x 3½" 100.00

German silver compact, round, decorated w/Victorian lady w/embossed flowers, w/old English initials, "L'Ame" by La May, patented 4/21/25, ½ x 2 1/8" 35.00

Gold (14k) compact, square case w/reeded design centering a diamond-lettered monogram & flanked by a dentiled-effect line design, Cartier, Model No. 3375, in red leather slip-case, 2¾" sq. 770.00

Gold (14k yellow) compact, circular w/an engine-turned design on the cover, Cartier, Model No. 4133, in original suede case............. 605.00

Gold & diamond case w/timepiece, the interior fitted w/a mirror & money clip, two spring-loaded change holders, two covered compartments including one for powder, the case engraved w/intersecting diagonals & fitted w/a watch w/silvered matte dial &

rose-cut diamond-set bezel, ca. 1915, 8.6 cm l. 2,475.00

Goldtone compact, w/engraved rays & square cluster of rhinestones, "Volupte' " 38.00

Goldtone compact, 1½" d. rhinestone cluster in center, "Elizabeth Arden," 4" d. 59.00

Goldtone compact, rounded rectangular form w/engraved floral design, "Elgin American".......... 36.00

Goldtone compact, round, shadow rose design, "Melissa" 45.00

Jade, diamond & enamel vanity case, Art Deco style, the rectangular case w/black enamel borders, jade corners, central panel of carved & pierced jade, pave' diamond thumbpiece, the interior fitted w/mirror, lipstick & powder compartments, marked "Cartier, Paris, Londres, New York, Made in France, 0772" 9,350.00

Leather compact, round, handtooled grape vines decoration, "Rex of 5th Avenue," 4½" d...... 75.00

Lucite compact, blue mirror lid, "Bellayre" 69.00

Mother-of-pearl compact, square, "Rex of 5th Avenue" 60.00

Red Lucite compact, w/sterling silver doves design, marked "Jensen," 2 7/8" sq. 125.00

Rhinestone compact, rhinestone scenes from courtship to marriage to baby, "Love & Marriage" by Zell 185.00

Silver compact, w/miniature painting on ivory of Princess de Lamballe, front pierced w/florals & back engraved w/plumes, 3 x 3"...................... 198.00

Gem-encrusted Compact

Silver-gilt encrusted w/gems compact, rectangular, a border of sixty emerald-cut sapphires, the center w/a pierced floral panel set w/natural & synthetic colored stones & approximately thirty-three rose-cut diamonds, engraved case, Italy, two stones missing (ILLUS.) 990.00

Silver-plated compact, nymphs decoration, "Djer Kiss," patent dated '5/19/25' 125.00

Silvertone compact, basketweave design, "Pilcher," w/box 34.00

Sterling silver vanity case, cobalt blue enameled ground w/foliate engraving, containing a watch, lipstick, powder & mirror, Austria 357.50

Wood & imitation leather compact, wooden top w/cowboy decoration, bottom of imitation leather, 2¾" d. 15.00

COOKBOOKS

Cookbook collectors are usually good cooks and will buy important new cookbooks as well as seek out notable older ones. Many early cookbooks were published and given away as advertising premiums for various products used extensively in cooking. While some rare, scarce first edition cookbooks can be very expensive, most collectible cookbooks are reasonably priced. We list our advertising cookbooks alphabetically by the names of the companies which produced them.

Advertising, "Alaga Syrup," 15 pp., 1920's $5.00

Advertising, "Aunt Jemima - New Temptilatin' Recipes," 18 pp., 1949, 4 x 6" 25.00

Advertising, "Betty Crocker's Children's Cookbook," spiral-bound, 156 pp. 15.00

Advertising, "Betty Crocker Party Book," spiral-bound, 1960 .... 8.00

Advertising, Bisquick, "Let the Stars Show You," features Clark Gable, Joan Crawford & others, 1935 .... 9.00

Advertising, "Carnation Milk," 32 pp., 1915 .... 10.00

Advertising, Crisco, "A Calendar of Dinners - The Story of Crisco," 1925 .... 15.00

Advertising, "Maxwell House Coffee," 22 pp., 1927 .... 7.00

Advertising, "Nucoa Oleo (Best Foods) - Round-the-World," by Ida Bailey Allen, 1934 .... 10.00

Advertising, "Pillsbury's 13th Grand National Bake-Off," 1961 .... 10.00

Advertising, "Prudential Cookbook," 1909 .... 25.00

Advertising, "Ralston Recipe Book," w/nursery rhyme illustrations by Crosby Buck, 23 pp., 1923 .... 18.00

Advertising, "Walter Baker Best Chocolate & Cocoa Recipes," 1931 .... 14.00

"The American Woman Cookbook," published by Butterick Publishing Company, 700 pp., indexed, w/dust jacket, 1939 .... 20.00

"Calendar of Sandwiches, Salads & Cakes," 365 daily recipes, three volumes, ca. 1920's 30.00

"Dainty Desserts," by Ida Bailey Allen, Buzza Co., 1925 .... 5.00

"The Four Seasons Cookbook," by Charlotte Adams, big pictures & photographs, in color, w/dust cover, 319 pp., 1971, 8½ x 12" 30.00

"Good Meals & How to Prepare Them," by Good Housekeeping, 1927 .... 10.00

"Heinrich's House Companion Cookbook," by Dr. Book, Minneapolis, Minnesota, 1920 .... 20.00

"Kitchen of Nations," from 1st Annual Food & Appliances Exposition in Chicago by Illinois Girls' Club, ca. 1930 .... 20.00

"Miss Parloa's Cookbook," illustrated, 1882 .... 32.00

"The Settlement Cookbook," by Kander, Milwaukee, 662 pp., 1943 .... 10.00

"Sloan's Hints & Up-to-date Cookbook," 1901 .... 15.00

"The White House Cookbook," 1926 edition 25.00

COOKIE CUTTERS

Horse Cookie Cutter

Recently there has been an accelerated interest in old tin cookie cutters. For the most part, these were made by tinsmiths who shaped primitive designs of tin strips and then soldered them to a backplate, pierced to allow air to enter and prevent a suction from holding the rolled cookie dough in the form. Sometimes an additional handle was soldered to the back. Cookie cutters were also manufactured in great quantities in an outline form that could depict animals, birds, star and other forms, including the plain round that sometimes carried embossed advertising for flour or other products on the handle. Aluminum cookie cutters were made after 1920. All cutters listed are tin unless otherwise noted.

Hand, flat backplate pierced w/five
  holes, 4½" l. $170.00
Horse, flat backplate pierced
  w/three holes, 5¼" l. 50.00
Horse, stylized bobtailed figure, flat
  backplate w/center hole, 6½" l... 40.00
Horse, standing animal w/bobtail &
  rounded features, flat backplate
  pierced w/three holes, 7½" l.
  (ILLUS.)......................... 82.50
Horse & rider, large primitive design, 9" h. (somewhat battered,
  soldered repair)................. 180.00
Multiple design, a thin ring surrounding five different cutters,
  three in the form of stylized
  hearts, one a crescent moon & the
  other a five-point star, 6" d. 93.50
Scottie dog, strap handle, animal
  w/upright tail, dark patina,
  3 x 4"........................... 35.00
Turkey, flat backplate pierced
  w/single hole, 4 7/8" h. (some
  battering, loose seams) 235.00

COOKIE JARS

*All sorts of charming and whimsical cook-
ie jars have been produced in recent decades
and these are increasingly collectible today.
Many well known American potteries such
as McCoy, Hull and Abingdon, produced
cookie jars and their products are included
in those listings in our "Ceramics" section.
Below we are listing cookie jars, mainly ceramic, produced by other, lesser known companies. A recent book,* The Collector's
Encyclopedia of Cookie Jars, *by Fred and
Joyce Roerig (Collector Books, 1991), will
prove of help to many collectors.*

AMERICAN BISQUE
After School Cookies $40.00
Bear with Honey, flasher ..200.00 to 250.00
Bow Bear........................ 75.00
Boy Bear, w/blue pants........... 62.50
Carousel 37.00
Cat w/Tail Finial 145.00
Chick w/Indented Dots 89.00
Churn Boy 201.00
Davy Crockett, standing in the
  woods 1,100.00
Feed Bag 90.00
Magic Bunny 85.00
Mr. Rabbit 150.00
Pennsylvania Dutch Girl 235.00
Sailor Elephant.................. 95.00
Spaceship, w/"Cookies Out of This
  World" 185.00

BRUSH - MC COY
Cow w/Cat Finial, purple & white... 500.00
Crock w/Duck Finial 45.00

Dog w/Basket 325.00
Elephant w/Ice Cream Cone, wear-
  ing baby hat 340.00
Happy Bunny 202.00
Lantern 75.00

Peter Pan by Brush-McCoy

Peter Pan, large (ILLUS.)...450.00 to 550.00
Peter Pumpkin Eater (Pumpkin
  w/Lock on Door)........250.00 to 300.00
Sitting Hippo, w/hat, green glaze... 400.00
Squirrel on Log 52.00
Teddy Bear, feet apart ....150.00 to 175.00

CALIFORNIA ORIGINALS
Big Bird on Nest 45.00
Circus Wagon, lion on lid 55.00
Clock, "Cookie Time" 40.00
The Count 400.00
Dog, No. 458 .... 25.00
Gumball Machine 65.00
Li'l Ole School House 120.00
Oscar the Grouch, No. 972 .... 68.00
Rabbit on Stump, No. 2620 .... 40.00
Scarecrow, No. 871............... 90.00
Superman, w/phone
  booth ....250.00 to 300.00

CARDINAL
French Chef, bust 85.00
Garage, "Free Parking For
  Cookies" 42.50
Sack of Cookies................. 50.00
Smart Cookie, bust of
  boy ....100.00 to 125.00

DORANNE OF CALIFORNIA
Cow Jumped Over the
  Moon ....150.00 to 175.00
Fire Hydrant, yellow glaze 60.00
Hound Dog 50.00
Old Woman in the Shoe 75.00

METLOX (Poppytrail)
Barrel of Apples 59.00
Bluebird on Pine Cone 60.00
Calf's Head 250.00
Mrs. Rabbit, w/carrot............. 70.00
Orange 50.00
Pinocchio, bust ....400.00 to 450.00

Rabbit on Cabbage 88.00
Scottie Dog, black 160.00
Sheaf of Wheat 50.00

POTTERY GUILD

Elsie the Cow Cookie Jar

Dutch Girl .... 50.00 to 75.00
Elsie the Cow (ILLUS.) ..... 225.00 to 275.00
Little Red Riding Hood 125.00

REGAL CHINA

French Chef 200.00
Humpty Dumpty .... 200.00 to 250.00
Majorette, bust .... 300.00 to 350.00
Pig in Diaper .... 300.00 to 350.00

ROBINSON RANSBOTTOM (RRP)

Ol' King Cole Cookie Jar

Cop 95.00
Dutch Girl .... 175.00 to 225.00
Jocko the Monkey .... 300.00 to 375.00
Ol' King Cole (ILLUS.) 295.00
Oscar, bust 120.00
Sheriff Pig 100.00

TREASURE CRAFT

Adobe House 35.00
Bear with Red Heart 32.00
Cactus with Flower 35.00
Hobo 80.00
Ice Wagon 50.00
Victorian House 49.00

TWIN WINTON

Bear on Stump 45.00
Cookie Elf 50.00
Cookie Sack, gold label 48.00
Dutch Girl 50.00
Friar Tuck 40.00
Ranger Bear 38.00

WISECARVER

Black Chef Head 125.00
Little Red Riding Hood 200.00
Oriental Man, w/original label 125.00
Teepee 125.00

COUNTRY STORE COLLECTIBLES

Country store museums have opened across the country in an effort to recreate those slower-paced days of the late 19th and early 20th centuries when the general store served as the local meeting place for much of rural America. Here one not only purchased necessary supplies for upcoming weeks, but caught up on important news events and local gossip. With strong interest in colorful tin cans during the early 1960's came the realization that these stores and neighborhood groceries were fast disappearing, replaced by the so-called supermarkets, and collectors began buying all items associated with these early stores. Also see CANS & CONTAINERS and CASH REGISTERS.

Cabinet, counter-type, button, "Banasch's Sewing Supplies," Cincinnati, Ohio, inside door display of almost 400 various mounted buttons, 40 drawers w/buttons, as on door, 13 x 18", 24" h......... $250.00
Cabinet, counter-type, sewing thread, "Star 6 Cord," metal, two drawers 225.00
Cabinet, counter-type, spool, "Lister's," swivels on pedestal, much stenciling, vertical columns of spools behind glass on four sides 375.00
Cabinet, counter-type, spool, "Willimantic Six Cord Star Thread," Star trademark & gold leaf lettering retained, original solid brass drawer pulls & inkwell w/lid, four drawers w/spool compartments (refinished, canvas on top replaced) 450.00
Display case, counter-type, crochet hooks, "Boye Crochet Hooks," dovetailed wood w/glass front, excellent finish & lettering, complete w/crochet hooks 275.00
Display case, counter-type, needles,

"Boye," wood & glass w/metal inserts, w/decals, 7 x 12", 11" h.... 225.00
Display rack, counter-type, tin, "St. Joseph Aspirin" 78.00
Door push bar, "Pepsi," wrought iron, ca. 1960's 95.00
Scale, "Wrigley's Spearmint Pepsin Gum" embossed on brass face, small (restored) 300.00
Seed box, "Websters Seeds" on interior lid, dovetailed construction 85.00
Seed box, "Wood's Tested," w/stand 250.00
Wrapping paper holder, "Keen Kutter" 95.00

CURRIER & IVES

American National Game of Base Ball

This lithographic firm was founded in 1835 by Nathaniel Currier with James M. Ives becoming a partner in 1857. Current events of the day were portrayed in the early days and the prints were hand-colored. Landscapes, vessels, sport, and hunting scenes of the West all became popular subjects. The firm was in existence until 1906. All prints listed are hand-colored unless otherwise noted.

American Country Life, May Morning, after F.F. Palmer, N. Currier, large folio, 1855, framed $660.00
American Field Sports, "On A Point," after A.F. Tait, large folio, 1857, framed (tear in upper margin, slight discoloration & foxing) 3,025.00
American Fruit Piece, small folio, undated, in an old molded frame w/gilt liner 165.00
American Jockey Club Races: Jerome Park..., large folio, 1873, framed (slight mat stain & foxing, colors possibly renewed, laid down) 880.00
American National Game of Base Ball (The), large folio, 1866, light foxing & stains, laid down, framed, overall 19¾ x 29¾" (ILLUS.) 16,500.00
American Winter Scenes, Evening, after F.F. Palmer, large folio, N. Currier, 1854 (somewhat discolored, water stains in margins, few nicks, scuffs & short tears) ..3,410.00
An Increase of Family, medium folio, 1863, framed (minor stains)... 145.00
Art of Making Money (The), Plenty... by Doctor Franklin, N. Currier, small folio, 1845, framed (stained, tear in left margin, few creases, foxed) 990.00
Autumn Fruits, medium folio, 1861 (few nicks, small losses & margin stains, discoloration, lower right edge retouched) 605.00
Battle of the Giants - Buffalo Bulls of the American Prairies, small folio, undated (small tears, minor staining & paper loss to margins) 495.00
Buffalo Hunt (The) - Surrounding the Herd, after George Catlin, medium folio, undated (pale light-staining, small paper losses at margin, pale soiling & staining on margins) 605.00
Cedars of Lebanon (The), small folio, undated (minor edge damage to margins) 125.00
Celebrated Trotting Horse Hopeful... (The), large folio, 1881 (skinning & traces of glue on verso, few edge nicks, slight discoloration) 1,650.00
Celebrated Trotting Horse Trustee... (The), N. Currier, large folio, 1848, framed 1,100.00

Champion Pacer Johnston...

Champion Pacer Johnston... (The), large folio, 1884, several skinned spots, one repaired, some discoloration & soiling on verso (ILLUS)..1,210.00
Champion Stallion "George Wilkes" (The), large folio, 1888, framed (professionally repaired tears in margins) 500.00
City of New York, N. Currier, large folio, 1856 (pale foxing & staining, remains of old paper tape on reverse) 6,050.00

Clipper Ship "Comet" of New York, after C. Parsons, large folio, 1855 (stains, foxing, some scrapes, tiny pinhole) 3,300.00

Fiend of the Road (The), large folio, 1881, framed (no glass, toning & soiling in margins, tear in upper margin) 357.50

Flora Temple & Lancet - In their great match...," large folio, N. Currier, 1856, framed (slight staining & cockling) 1,100.00

Frolicksome Pets, small folio, undated, in bird's-eye maple veneer frame, 17¼" w., 13¼" h. 110.00

Fruits of the Season, small folio, 1870, framed 185.00

Going to Pasture, small folio, undated, framed 105.00

Great Ocean Yacht Race (The), Between the Henrietta, Fleetwing and Vesta..., large folio, 1867, framed 2,750.00

Lady Thorn and Mountain Boy..., large folio, 1867 (restored skinned spot, repaired tears, faint discoloration & some soiling) 1,320.00

Lake Lugano, Italy, large folio, undated (minor surface soiling, small paper loss at margin corner)...................... 110.00

Little Brother and Sister, small folio, 1863, matted & framed 93.50

Little White Kitties - Into Mischief, small folio, 1871, matted (minor edge repair) 150.00

Midnight Race on the Mississippi (A), after F.F. Palmer, large folio, 1860, framed (minor soiling & repaired tears & nicks at edges)..................... 4,600.00

Mount Washington and The White Mountains, From the Valley of Conway, after F.F. Palmer, large folio, 1860, unframed (pale water staining, a few abrasions, crease in lower left) 2,645.00

New York Bay - From Bay Ridge, L.I., after F.F. Palmer, medium folio, 1860, framed (discoloring in margin, faint light stains) 1,650.00

Pigeon Shooting - "Playing the Decoy," after A.F. Tait, large folio, 1862, framed (discoloration & soiling in margin, repaired tear in margin, filled-in loss & abraded area, small tear in inscription) ...2,875.00

Road (The) - Winter, large folio, N. Currier, 1853, framed, faint foxing, slight scuff in margin (ILLUS. top next column) 34,500.00

Rosebud and Eglantine (portraits), small folio, undated, hand-carved walnut frame 125.00

The Road - Winter

Scenery on the Upper Mississippi - An Indian Village, small folio, undated, in a beveled mahogany veneer frame (minor surface damage) 313.50

Scholar's Rewards, small folio, 1874, in beveled mahogany veneer frame (margins slightly trimmed) 49.50

Shooting on the Beach, small folio, undated, framed (paper tone discolored, small tears & soiling in margins, tiny scuffs & foxing, backboard stain on verso) 1,150.00

Through to the Pacific, small folio, 1870, old walnut criss-cross frame (short edge tears, trimmed) 687.50

Tobogganing on Darktown Hill - Getting a Hist..., small folio, 1890, matted, unframed (minor edge damage, small corner repair) 302.50

Two Souls With But A Single Thought (black comic), small folio, 1889, unframed (small edge repairs) 247.50

U.S. Mail Steamship Adriatic..., large folio, N. Currier, 1856, framed (small repaired tears, crease in margin)..............1,380.00

Washington, N. Currier, small folio, undated, the General standing beside his horse, old grained frame w/wavy glass, mid-19th c. (stains)....................... 220.00

Washington Crossing the Delaware..., small folio, 1876, matted, unframed 192.50

Winning "Hands Down," with a Good Second, large folio, 1887, framed (mat stain, slight foxing & soiling, tiny edge nicks, repaired margin loss) 690.00

Wreck of the Steam Ship 'San Francisco' (The), large folio, N. Currier, 1854, framed (minor discoloration in margin & minor edge nicks) 9,488.00

CUSPIDORS

Bennington Shell Cuspidor

The cuspidor, or spittoon, is a bowl-shaped vessel into which tobacco chewers could spit. These containers were a necessity in an era when much of the male population chewed tobacco and even some ladies were known to "take a chew." Made of metal, earthenware pottery, china and glass, they ranged in size from the large barroom floor models to small glass cuspidors designed for the ladies.

Bennington pottery, Shell patt., mottled brown Rockingham glaze, vent hole at side, 10" d., 4" h. (ILLUS.)..........................$200.00
Nickel-plated brass, Arcade Model No. 401, 7½" d. 250.00
Porcelainized cast iron, light grey outside, white inside, marked "Valley R.R.".................... 95.00

DECOYS

Decoys have been utilized for years to lure flying water fowl into target range. They have been made of carved and turned wood, papiermache', canvas and metal, and some are in the category of outstanding folk art and command high prices.

Blackbellied Plover Decoy

Blackbellied Plover, by Elmer Crowell, East Harwich, Massachusetts, carved wood w/original paint (ILLUS.)................$38,500.00

Black Duck Drake, preening, attributed to A.A. (Gus) Wilson, South Portland, Maine, carved wood, inletted head, original paint, first quarter 20th c., 15½" l. (minor paint loss) 4,125.00
Bluebill Drake, carved wood w/good detail, original paint, 13¾" l. (some paint wear & short scars) .. 225.00
Bluebill Drake, attributed to John Auchland, Augres, Michigan, carved wood bobtail version, old working repaint & glass eyes, 14" l. 85.00
Bluebill Drake, carved wood, well-shaped head, tack eyes, old repaint w/traces of original paint, Sandusky-Port Clinton, Ohio area, 19th c., 14 3/8" l. (some bottom damage, chip on tail)............ 335.00
Bluebill Hen, by Thomas Chambers, Canada Club, Ontario, Canada, carved hollow body, glass eyes, old working repaint, ca. 1900, 15¾" l. (paint wear) 525.00
Canada Goose, carved & painted wood, in swimming position, solid cedar construction w/root head & neck, weathered original paint w/remains of leather thong, Maritime Provinces, Canada, early 20th c. (body checks) 825.00
Canvasback Drake, by C. Klopping, Ohio, carved wood, original paint & glass eyes, branded w/maker's name, 13¾" l. (end of bill professionally restored) 550.00
Canvasback Drake, carved wood w/long head & boldly carved wings, old worn paint w/yellowed varnish, glass eyes, marked "W.E. Beck," 18½" l. (minor age cracks & wear) 350.00
Curlew, attributed to Thomas Gilston, Long Island, New York, carved wood, original worn paint, early 20th c., 12½" l. (replaced bill & eyes) 770.00
Fish, "Brook Trout," polychromed wood, w/tin fins, lead-weighted, 5" l. 215.00
Fish, "Muskie," wooden body, tin fins, leather tail & glass eyes, old paint, w/line & weight, 11" l. 175.00
Fish, "Pike," carved wood w/tin fins & leather tail, original polychrome paint & glass eyes, w/line & weight, 10½" l. 185.00
Fish, "Pike," carved wood w/tin fins & tack eyes, worn original polychrome paint, found in Wisconsin, on modern base, 27¾" l. 375.00
Fish, "Sucker," painted wood body w/cast lead fins & aluminum tail,

by the Randall Decoy Co., 11¾" l.
(worn paint) 65.00

Greenwing Teal Drake, by Charles
Moore, carved wood in preener
position, original paint, glass
eyes & metal feet, signed "Chas.
Moore," 7¾" l. 110.00

Mallard Drake, factory-carved, old
paint & glass eyes, 16¾" l. 105.00

Mallard Drake, by Ken Snow, Royal
Oak, Michigan, carved wood,
original paint & glass eyes, un-
signed, 17¼" l. 45.00

Mallard Drake & Mallard Hen, by
Peter Perkins, carved wood
w/original paint & glass eyes,
branded "P," 13" l., pr. 495.00

Mallard Hen, by Charles Perdew,
Illinois, carved body in sleeping
position, original paint 33,000.00

Merganser Drake, primitive carved
wood w/simple relief carving, old
brown paint, rusted tack eyes,
& bristle crest, 16½" l. (some
professional restoration) 440.00

Owl, papier-mache', stick-up confi-
dence-type, original paint & glass
eyes, marked "...Swisher, Pat.
Pend. Decatur, Illinois," 14" h.
(minor edge wear) 100.00

Pintail Drake, by Charles Perdew, Illinois, carved hollow body, original paint & glass eyes, lead
weight w/cast label "Perdew,
Henry, Ill.," 16" l. 450.00

Pintail Drake & Hen Decoys

Pintail Drake & Hen, by Charles
Perdew, Illinois, carved wood
w/original paint, glass eyes, pr.
(ILLUS.) 18,150.00

Redhead Drake, by Frank Schmidt,
Detroit, Michigan, carved wood,
relief-carved wing tips, good
original paint, glass eyes, 15½" l.
(some wear, minor age cracks,
nailed neck break) 200.00

Ruddy Duck, by Lee & Lem Dudley,
Knott's Island, North Carolina,

Ruddy Duck Decoy

carved wood w/original worn
paint, ca. 1900 (ILLUS.) 52,800.00

Swan, by Charles T. Hudson, Talbot
County, Maryland, solid cedar
body & root head, worn white
paint, signed on the bottom
"Chas. T. Hudson Talbot Co. MD,"
1910-15 (age cracks, wear) 1,320.00

Turkey Hen, stick-up type, papier-
mache' w/original paint & glass
eyes, labeled "Hardy's Wild Turkey Decoy, Roanoke, N.C.," con-
temporary, 26½" l. 900.00

Yellowlegs, by Ira Hudson, Chin-
coteague, Virginia, carved body
w/original paint 21,450.00

DISNEY COLLECTIBLES

Alice in Wonderland Movie Cel

*Scores of objects ranging from watches to
dolls have been created showing Walt Disney's copyrighted animated cartoon characters, and an increasing number of collectors
now are seeking these, made primarily by
licensed manufacturers.*

Alice in Wonderland cookie jar,
ceramic, marked "Walt Disney
Productions," Regal China,
1950's . . . .$195.00 to 225.00

Alice in Wonderland movie cel,
trimmed celluloid applied to a
water-color background, Alice in
a garden scene w/chairs set next
to a table prepared for a tea

party, 1951, matted & framed,
10¾ x 14½" (ILLUS.) 47,300.00
Bambi movie cel, full celluloid
depicting Bambi meeting Flower,
gouache on laminated celluloid
applied to a Courvoisier airbrush
& water-color background, un-
framed, 1942, 8½ x 11¼" 4,180.00
Bambi planter, ceramic, butterfly on
the tail, American Pottery 145.00
Bambi wall plaque, Youngstown
Pressed Steel Co. 40.00

Big Bad Wolf Doll

Big Bad Wolf (from "Three Little
Pigs") doll, stuffed cloth, colorfully
dressed in blue felt trousers & a
tall red felt hat, standing w/his
mouth open & tongue hanging
out, about to devour a sandwich
containing one of the pigs,
20½" h. (ILLUS.) 935.00
Briar Rose (Sleeping Beauty) tum-
bler, glass, 1958 . . . . 12.00
Captain Hook (from "Peter Pan")
movie cel, full celluloid w/scene
of Captain Hook peering over the
rocks, applied to a water-color
production background, 1953, un-
framed, 10½ x 13" 6,600.00
Cinderella handkerchief, Walt Dis-
ney Productions, 8½" square 20.00
Cinderella movie poster, one-sheet,
color print w/movie vignettes in
the upper right & lower left corners & the title & credits filling
the center from top left to lower
right, linen-backed, 1949,
27 x 41" 462.00
Cinderella tea set: cov. teapot,
creamer, sugar bowl, tray & six
plates, cups & saucers; tin, Ohio
Art Co., the set 150.00
Davy Crockett bank, embossed
"Davy Crockett Pony Express,"

saddle bag-shaped, mint in
package 45.00
Davy Crockett bedspread, chenille,
pictures Davy fighting a bear 195.00
Davy Crockett billfold, 1955, mint in
box 54.00
Davy Crockett game, "Davy Crockett
to the Rescue" 72.00

Davy Crockett Guitar & Case

Davy Crockett guitar, wood, in original box labeled "Walt Disney's
Official Davy Crockett Guitar"
w/picture of Davy, 25" l., 2 pcs.
(ILLUS.) 66.00
Davy Crockett lamp, composition,
figure of Davy, w/original
shade 125.00
Davy Crockett outfit, coonskin cap,
jacket & socks, the set 60.00
Davy Crockett thermos, 8½" h.,
1955 . . . . 60.00
Davy Crockett tray, tin, lithographed
picture of Davy Crockett & scenes
from Alamo & Congress around
him 55.00
Disney characters book, "The Three
Caballeros," Walt Disney Productions, 1944, excellent condition . . . 40.00
Disney characters cartoon poster,
"Alice the Peacemaker," center
portrait of a blonde-haired girl in
a large heart above a cartoon cat
& mouse, early Disney production
from Winkler Pictures, one-sheet,
1924, paper-backed, 27 x 41" . . . 22,000.00
Disney characters cookie tin, long,
low rectangular metal container
w/a colorfully printed lid featuring a landscape scene full of Disney characters including the Three
Little Pigs, Mickey & Minnie
Mouse, Donald Duck, Goofy &
Snow White, ca. 1940, 12 x 18"
(minor dents & scratches) 77.50
Disney characters hooked rug, scene
including Mickey & Minnie Mouse,
Pluto, Pinocchio, Bambi, the seven
Dwarfs & other characters worked
in red, green, yellow, salmon &
black cotton fabric, America, ca.
1940, 66 x 106" (ILLUS. top next
column) 2,860.00
Disney characters paint set, illustra-

Disney Characters Hooked Rug

tion on box cover shows several Disney characters, Walt Disney Enterprises, 1939 .... 120.00

Disney characters World War II ration book holder w/color graphics of Mickey, Minnie, Pluto & Donald, ca. 1943 .... 33.00

Disneyland game, board-type, "Disneyland," Walt Disney Productions, 1950, mint in box 37.00

Disneyland game, board-type, "Pirates of the Caribbean" 12.00

Disneyland magazine, "Disneyland Holiday," Vol. 1, No. 1 .... 55.00

Disneyland puzzle, jigsaw-type, "Adventureland," Jaymar, 1962 ...... 22.00

Disneyland toy, windup tin, "Disneyland Ferris Wheel," J. Chein & Co., New York, New York, 1939, w/original box 750.00

Donald Duck animation cel, trimmed cel depicting an angry Donald w/clenched fists, applied to an airbrushed background, stamped lower right "WDP," 1940's, matted & framed, 8½" d. 880.00

Donald Duck book, "Donald Duck's Adventure," Little Golden Book, 1950 .... 25.00

Donald Duck book, "Walt Disney Story Books - Donald Duck," Grosset & Dunlap, 1936, full-page illustrations, pictorial covers, 9½ x 10½" (spine & corners chipped, small tears).................... 110.00

Donald Duck candy bar wrapper, "Donald Duck Milk Chocolate," by Comic Candies, Brooklyn, NY, 1940's 45.00

Donald Duck cola bottle, 1953, 7 oz. 14.00

Donald Duck cookie jar, cov., ceramic, cylindrical, California Originals 110.00

Donald Duck figure, bisque, long-billed, 1930's, 4½" h............ 350.00

Donald Duck figure, composition, long-billed Donald w/socket head, black-painted side-glancing eyes, molded & painted blue sailor hat, accented nostrils, one-piece body

w/sailor shirt, wearing original black plush hat & velvet cape, marked "Walt Disney, Knickerbocker Toy Co." on back, 9" h. (general crazing & fine cracks in finish of composition under cape) 925.00

Donald Duck juice can, "Donald Duck Florida Orange Juice," tall cylinder w/a picture of Donald & a large glass of juice, ca. 1950's, 1 qt., 14 fl. oz. (some wear, no lid) 35.00

Donald Duck letter opener, celluloid, 1936 .... 135.00

Donald Duck pencil sharpener, Bakelite, long-billed Donald decal 87.50

Donald Duck playing cards, 1941.... 75.00

Donald Duck projector, plastic, modeled as Donald seated in a train engine, w/original box (box worn) 35.00

Donald Duck sign, tin, "Donald Duck Bread" over picture of Donald & loaf of bread in colorful wrapper over "Oven Fresh Flavor" 275.00

Donald Duck toy, "Donald the Bubble Duck," plastic, squeeze Donald & he blows bubbles, Morris Plastic Corporation 100.00

Donald Duck toy, windup celluloid, Donald Duck carousel, figure of Donald under umbrella suspended w/jointed knobbed bars, on a wheeled base w/the mechanism, rolls forward & revolves carousel when wound, Japan, ca. 1930's, 6½" h. 770.00

Donald Duck toy, windup tin & celluloid, an early winking Donald w/white satin pants & celluloid webbed feet attached to the pedals of his green tricycle w/red & blue wheels, when wound Donald pedals away, a British flag waving off the back of the tricycle, Japan, 6" l. 1,320.00

Donald Duck tumbler, clear glass, Bosco premium 42.00

Donald Duck valentine card, dated 1939, mint condition 25.00

Donald Duck & Mickey Mouse paint box, tin interior w/pictures of Mickey Mouse, Minnie Mouse, Donald Duck, Pluto, Goofy & Dopey, Transogram, Inc., Walt Disney Products................... 55.00

Donald Duck & nephews rug, shows the nephews playing tricks 69.00

Donald Duck & Pluto ceiling globe, Donald chasing butterflies on one side & Pluto chasing butterflies on

the other side, 11" d., mint condition.....................275.00 to 350.00

Dumbo the Elephant book, "Dumbo
of the Circus," 1942 .... 30.00

Dumbo the Elephant cookie jar,
cov., "Dumbo's Greatest Cookies
on Earth," California Originals.... 475.00

Dumbo movie cel, gouache on celluloid, applied to an airbrushed
Courvoisier background, depicting
Dumbo flapping his ears while
taking a bubble bath, stamped
"WPD" & w/remains of Courvoisier Galleries label on the back,
framed, 1941, 7¾ x 9".........3,190.00

Dwarf Bashful movie cel, from
"Snow White and the Seven
Dwarfs," full celluloid depicting
Bashful playing the accordion, applied to a Courvoisier wood-
veneer background, 1937,
6¼ x 8¼" 1,540.00

Dwarf Doc clock, w/moving eyes,
Mi-Ken Company, Japan 95.00

Dwarf Dopey bank, tin, dime register, dated "1939"............... 145.00

Dwarf Dopey movie cel, from "Snow
White and the Seven Dwarfs," applied to a hand-prepared background, depicting Dopey sitting on
a log holding up a feather & surrounded by forest animals, 1937,
framed, 7 x 9¼" 4,400.00

Fantasia magazine cover & story,
"Time," pictures Leopold
Stokowski on cover & pictures
from scenes of the movie in the
article, 1940's 30.00

Fantasia movie cel, from The Sor-
cerer's Apprentice segment, gouache on celluloid applied to an
airbrushed background, showing
Mickey Mouse in costume waving
his right hand, stamped "WDP" at
lower right, w/Courvoisier Galleries label on the back, framed,
1940, 8½ x 9½" 10,450.00

Ferdinand the Bull book, "Ferdinand
the Bull," ca. 1938.............. 25.00

Ferdinand the Bull sheet music, Walt
Disney Productions, 1936......... 25.00

Ferdinand the Bull soap figure...... 70.00

Goofy poster, "A Goofy Lunch Pulls
Your Punch," pictures Goofy try-
ing to stay awake, produced by
Disney for the Food & Nutrition
Committee of California, Disney
copyright, 1942, 12¼ x 19"....... 65.00

Lady & the Tramp apron, colorful
illustration..................... 55.00

Ludwig Von Drake card game,
Walt Disney Productions, 1963,
w/box 10.00

Ludwig Von Drake doll, plush velveteen, Gund, 18" h. 45.00

Ludwig Von Drake salt shaker, ceramic, Walt Disney Productions... 20.00

Maleficent (witch from Sleeping
Beauty) tumbler, clear glass...... 28.00

Mary Poppins paper doll set, includes three magic dolls & a 63
piece wardrobe, in box 35.00

Mickey Mouse alarm clock, shaped
like oversized pocket watch, Bradley, 1979 .... 50.00

Mickey Mouse baby rattle, wood,
pie-cut eyes, ca. 1930 .... 55.00

Mickey Mouse bank, silver plate,
figural Mickey w/large black
nose, made in England & authorized by Walt Disney Productions,
6" h.......................... 60.00

Mickey Mouse blocks, picture-type,
Germany, ca. 1950's, in original
carrying case 110.00

First Mickey Mouse Book

Mickey Mouse book, "Mickey Mouse
Book," cover art by Ub Iwerks,
first appearance of Mickey & Minnie Mouse in a Disney book, published by Bibo and Lang, ca. 1930
(ILLUS.) 4,840.00

Mickey Mouse book, "Mickey Mouse
& the Smugglers," 1935 .... 40.00

"Mickey Mouse in Giantland" Book

Mickey Mouse book, "Mickey Mouse
in Giantland," 1931-34, color
illustrations, hardbound
(ILLUS.) ....100.00 to 150.00
Mickey Mouse book, "Mickey Mouse
Stories," Book No. 2, Mickey &
Pluto on soft cover, Dave Mc-
Kay Publications, 1934, unused,
3/8 x 6¼ x 8½" 95.00
Mickey Mouse book, "Mickey
Mouse's Summer Vacation," Whit-
man Publishing Co., 1948 .... 25.00
Mickey Mouse bowl, cereal,
Beetleware, Post Grape-Nuts
premium, marked "W.D. Ent.,"
ca. 1930's ....40.00 to 50.00
Mickey Mouse camera, "Mick-A-
Matic," ear actuated 40.00
Mickey Mouse cartoon cel, from
"The Band Concert," gouache on
celluloid, applied to a water-color
key production background,
depicting Mickey standing on his
rostrum conducting music from
"The Storm," in a delicate landscape setting, artist Les Clarke,
production information inscribed
along the bottom of background,
1935, framed, 9 x 11" 55,000.00
Mickey Mouse charm, celluloid,
1930's, ¾" l...................... 20.00
Mickey Mouse Christmas card, die-
cut, Walt Disney Enterprises,
1936 .... 50.00
Mickey Mouse clothes brush, silver
& black metal, Disney Enterprises,
ca. 1930's ....50.00 to 60.00
Mickey Mouse comic strip artwork,
pen & ink on board, daily strip
from December 16, 1942, drawn
by Floyd Gottfredson, matted,
5½ x 25" 2,750.00

Mickey Comic Strip Artwork

Mickey Mouse comic strip artwork,
pen & ink on illustration board,
by Floyd Gottfredson, for a Sunday page, January 3, 1937,
18¼ x 28½" (ILLUS. of part) 8,800.00

Mickey Mouse cookie jar, cov.,
Mickey Clock, pictures Mickey &
"Mickey Mouse Cookie Time" on
the clock face of a Big Ben-type
alarm clock, marked "Enesco
WDE-219".................... 280.00
Mickey Mouse creamer, china, gold
& blue lustre finish 70.00
Mickey Mouse decals, "Mickey
Mouse Transfer-O-S for Easter
Eggs," Paas Dye Co., Newark,
N.J., Walt Disney Enterprises, ca.
1930 .... 25.00
Mickey Mouse dollhouse w/battery
powered lights, plastic furniture
including a Mickey crib & a
Donald playpen, also Mickey's car
w/wooden wheels, Louis Marx &
Co. 250.00
Mickey Mouse drawing, pencil on
paper, Mickey about to be tackled
by a huge player, from "Touch-
down Mickey" cartoon, 1932,
5½ x 7¼" 825.00
Mickey Mouse figure, bisque, Mickey holding baseball glove & ball,
ca. 1930, 3¼" h. 75.00
Mickey Mouse figure, bisque, Mickey wearing green shorts, hinged
arms, the base inscribed "Mickey
Mouse" & stamped "Japan,"
1930's, 7¼" h. 440.00
Mickey Mouse figure, papier-
mache', standing Mickey w/one
arm extended & legs wide apart,
painted in bright colors, England,
1950's, 36" h. (slight paint
loss)........................1,386.00
Mickey Mouse game, "Pin the Tail
on Mickey," oilcloth, Louis Marx,
ca. 1935 .... 130.00
Mickey Mouse lamp, table model,
metal base & rod w/bobbin-head
Mickey mounted on base, parch-
ment-type paper shade, three-way
light switch, ca. 1950, overall
19½" h..................... 215.00
Mickey Mouse magazine, Volume 2,
No. 8, May, 1937, illustration of
Mickey & Pluto on the cover 65.00
Mickey Mouse map, "Globetrotters,"
w/original stickers 125.00
Mickey Mouse marionette, composition, dressed in a striped shirt,
shorts & shoes, by Madame Alexander, 1938-39, 9½" h. marionette, overall 21" h............ 950.00
Mickey Mouse movie projector, Keystone Mfg. Co., 1930's 700.00
Mickey Mouse rug, pictures Mickey
riding a donkey, ca. 1949,
21 x 39"...................... 85.00
Mickey Mouse slippers, fleece-lined
sheepskin w/Mickey decals on

front & printed Mickey & Minnie figures on each side, marked "Size 11," children's, pr. 75.00

Mickey Mouse soap figure, "Castile," 1932, w/box, 5" h. 175.00

"Drumming Mickey Mouse" Toy

Mickey Mouse toy, battery-operated, remote control, "Drumming Mickey Mouse," featuring lithographed tin Mickey in cloth outfit, he drums, walks & nods his head as his eyes light up, Line Mar, ca. 1955, w/original box, 11" h. (ILLUS.) . . . . 800.00 to 1,000.00

Mickey Mouse toy, battery-operated, "Mickey Mouse Krazy Car," Marx, mint in box 120.00

Mickey Mouse toy, "Movie Jecktor," by Movie Jecktor Company, New York, New York, 1930's, w/films & original box . . . . 350.00 to 500.00

Mickey Mouse toy, pull-type, "Mickey Mouse Safety Patrol," Fisher-Price, No. 733, ca. 1956 . . . . 150.00 to 175.00

Mickey Mouse tumbler, clear glass w/black figure of Mickey, first dairy series, 1936 . . . . 95.00

Mickey Mouse umbrella, Mickey handle, Disney characters screen-printed on blue silk top . . 100.00 to 125.00

Mickey Mouse & Donald Duck tie rack, child-size, wooden, pictures Mickey & Donald, 1930's, 5 x 9" . . . . 200.00 to 250.00

Mickey Mouse & Donald Duck toy, rubber, Mickey & Donald riding fire truck, Sun Rubber Co., 1940's, 6½" l. 85.00

Mickey Mouse & Horace Horsecollar porringer, silver plate, engraved illustration of Mickey & Horace in the center of the bowl & engraving of Mickey on the handle, International Silver Co., ca. 1930 . . . 250.00

Mickey & Minnie Mouse figures, glazed china, Mickey wearing

long pants & Minnie wearing balloon skirt, ca. 1940, 3" h., pr. 55.00

Mickey & Minnie Mouse platter, china, lustreware glaze, pictures Mickey & Minnie dining, 5" l. 20.00

Mickey & Minnie Mouse & Donald Duck toothbrush holder, bisque, marked "Walt Disney," original paint, 1930's . . . . 200.00 to 250.00

Mickey & Minnie Mouse & Pluto flashlight, lithographed tin, 1936 . . 395.00

Mickey Mouse Club lunch box, w/metal thermos, excellent condition 55.00

Mickey Mouse Club toy, battery-operated type, "Dance a Tune," Jaymar Co., in original box 85.00

Early Minnie Mouse Book

Minnie Mouse book, "pop-up" type, 1933 (ILLUS.) 250.00

Minnie Mouse costume, by Ben Cooper, mint in box 27.00

Minnie Mouse figure, jointed wood, "Fun-e-Flex," 5" h. 225.00

Minnie Mouse toy, windup tin, lithographed Minnie rocks to & fro while "knitting" on a piece of cloth, Line Mar, Japan, w/box, 7" h. . . . . 600.00 to 800.00

Peter Pan book, colorfully illustrated w/24 characters including Tinkerbell, die-cut cover w/plastic sword & feather, Spain, 1944 . . . . 45.00

Peter Pan game, board-type, Hunt Foods premium, 1969 . . . . 16.00

Peter Pan hand puppet, Gund Mfg. Co., Walt Disney Productions 30.00

Peter Pan movie poster, one-sheet, color print showing a large Peter standing to one side w/a band of small characters above & below him, title to the left, linen-backed, 1953, 27 x 41" (ILLUS. top next column) 495.00

Peter Pan wrist watch, on original card w/several Peter Pan characters illustrated, Germany 65.00

Pinocchio book, "Pinocchio," Little Golden Books, Walt Disney Productions, 1948 . . . . 12.00

Peter Pan Movie Poster

Pinocchio coloring & paint book,
1939 .... 45.00
Pinocchio doll, composition, large
features, Steiff, Germany, 1938,
15" h. 475.00
Pinocchio doll, vinyl, Italy, ca. 1960,
10" h. 85.00
Pinocchio doll, wood & composition,
Ideal, 7" h. 175.00
Pinocchio figure, carnival-type
chalkware, 16" h. 95.00
Pinocchio mask, paper, Gillette Blue
Blades advertising premium, uncut, 1939 .... 35.00
Pinocchio movie poster, one-sheet,
color lithographed scene of Pinocchio & Jiminy Cricket above "Walt
Disney's full length Feature
production - Pinocchio - in Mul-
tiplane Technicolor," 1940, linen
backed, 27 x 41" 6,050.00
Pinocchio teaspoon, silver plate,
Duchess Silverplate, ca. 1939 ..... 20.00
Pinocchio character mirror, Pinocchio & other characters from the
movie embossed around the
frame, 20" oval 225.00

Pluto Desk-Table

Pluto child's desk-table, wooden, a
sawhorse-form base w/a cut-out
head of Pluto, mounted w/a
slightly slanted desk unit w/a
Masonite lifting chalkboard top,

some water stains on head,
marked "Copyright - Walt Disney
Productions," 35" l., 26" h.
(ILLUS.)...................... 220.00
Pluto figure, chalkware, 3" h. 30.00
Pluto toy, windup tin, "Rollover,"
plush-covered Pluto runs forward,
rolls over & raises up on his feet
to beg, "Watch Me Roll Over" on
side, Line Mar, in original box,
6½" l. ....250.00 to 275.00

Silly Symphonies Cartoon Cel

Silly Symphonies cartoon cel, from
"Grasshopper & The Ants," gouache on trimmed celluloid applied
to a water-color production background, showing the queen ant
being carried by her soldiers in
her sedan chair, various set-up
notations on the margins, 1934,
framed, 9½ x 11" (ILLUS.) 13,200.00
Sleeping Beauty movie poster, one-
sheet, color print w/vignette
scenes of the movie around the
sides & the title & credits in
the center, linen-backed, 1959,
27 x 41" 495.00
Snow White bank, dime register,
lithographed tin, dated 1939 ..... 160.00
Snow White book, "Edgar Bergan's
Charlie McCarthy Meets Walt Disney's Snow White," Whitman,
1938 .... 55.00
Snow White doll, dressed in original
clothing, Ideal Toy Corp., mint
w/original tags, 16" h. 300.00
Snow White ironing board,
lithographed tin, Ohio Art Co..... 50.00
Snow White jigsaw puzzle, 1973 .... 8.00
Snow White whisk broom, figural
composition Snow White handle,
h.p., England 125.00
Snow White wrist watch, "Magic
Mirror," U.S. Time, 1950, w/box .. 350.00
Snow White & the Seven Dwarfs
candy box, tin, rectangular, illus-
trated overall w/Snow White, the
Dwarfs & forest friends 120.00
Snow White & the Seven Dwarfs
card game, scenes on each card,
England, 1938, boxed 30.00

Snow White & Seven Dwarfs Bracelet

Snow White & the Seven Dwarfs
　　charm bracelet, enameled metal,
　　depicting Snow White & the
　　Dwarfs, each w/a name at the
　　base, on a gold metal chain
　　bracelet (ILLUS. of part)......... 275.00

Snow White & Dwarfs Painting

Snow White & the Seven Dwarfs
　　concept painting, water-color on
　　paper, showing the forest animals
　　crowding around to peer in the
　　window of the dwarf's cottage,
　　1937, 12 x 15½" (ILLUS.) 22,000.00
Snow White & the Seven Dwarfs
　　fabric, Walt Disney Productions,
　　38 x 45"...................... 32.00
Snow White & the Seven Dwarfs ra-
　　dio, plastic, embossed scene of
　　Snow White & the Seven Dwarfs,
　　white background w/colorfully
　　painted figures, Emerson Radio
　　and Phonograph Corporation,
　　Model No. 411, 1938 ....3,000.00
Snow White & Dwarf Dopey maga-
　　zine cover, "Liberty," 1938 .... 25.00
Three Little Pigs doll, cloth, the
　　'Practical Pig,' standing w/his
　　tongue sticking out, dressed in a
　　jacket & red bow tie, original pa-
　　per label tied to his wrist, France,
　　1930's, 17" h. 770.00
Three Little Pigs drum, lithographed
　　tin, Ohio Art Co., 6½".......... 190.00
Thumper (from Bambi) figure, minia-
　　ture, Hagen-Renaker 75.00
Tinkerbell (from Peter Pan) movie
　　cel, gouache on partial celluloid,

Tinkerbell Movie Cel

applied to a water-color produc-
　　tion background, depicting Tinker-
　　bell sitting on top of a bottle
　　& laughing, unframed, 7½ x 9"
　　(ILLUS.) 5,280.00
Tinkerbell pin, flasher-type, sou-
　　venir from Walt Disney World,
　　1972 .... 20.00
Tramp (from Lady and the Tramp)
　　clock, wall-type, eyes move,
　　1960's 95.00
Tramp (from Lady and the Tramp)
　　hand puppet, Walt Disney Produc-
　　tions 20.00
Tweedle Dum & Tweedle Dee salt &
　　pepper shakers, Walt Disney Pro-
　　ductions, 1950's, pr. 150.00
20,000 Leagues Under the Sea color-
　　ing book, 1953 .... 30.00
Wendy (from Peter Pan) hand pup-
　　pet, Gund Mfg Co., Walt Disney
　　Productions 30.00
Winnie-the-Pooh mug, china, illus-
　　trates Winnie & Christopher, Eng-
　　land 65.00
Zorro cap gun & holster........... 125.00
Zorro jigsaw puzzles, set of 4, mint
　　in box........................ 95.00
Zorro pencil case, mint w/original
　　contents 85.00
Zorro play set, "Rub-Ons Magic Pic-
　　ture Transfers," in original box ... 70.00
Zorro toy, "Zorro Magic Erasable
　　Crayon Slate," mint in package ... 65.00

DOLL FURNITURE & ACCESSORIES

Armoire, ornate crest above rectan-
　　gular top w/rounded cornice
　　above two doors, the narrow one
　　w/painted floral scene & the oth-
　　er mounted w/a mirror, each
　　door opening to three shelves,
　　one drawer at bottom over cut-
　　out apron, 19" h................$650.00

Baby bottle, amber glass w/rubber nipple, embossed "Ounces" & "Doll-E-Toys" 9.00

Bed, country rope-style, turned wood, low-post head- & foot-boards w/turned posts w/finials, old varnish finish, w/a mattress, pillow & liner w/crocheted lace trim, 10 x 16", the group 200.00

Bed, Federal-style low poster, rope-type, shaped cherry headboard w/scrolling ears flanked by curly maple turned posts w/ball finials, turned footrail flanked by conforming posts, birch siderails, one post showing dark bark stain, together w/old stained bed linens, 11 x 16", the group............. 175.00

Bed, painted pine & poplar, headboard w/three square slats between square corner posts, wide siderails to slightly lower footboard also w/slats, board slats for mattress support, old red repaint, 12½ x 27" (no mattress) 65.00

Bed, walnut-stained wood, canopy-type w/rope foundation, tall baluster- and ring-turned posts support arched canopy w/lace hangings, 17" l., posts 16" h...... 400.00

Bread tin, hinged dome lid, blue & white Dutch theme decorations, lettered "Bread" across side, bottom embossed "Tindeco," 2¼ x 2½ x 4½" 40.00

Wicker Doll Buggy

Buggy, wicker, deep rounded body w/adjustable hood, metal spring frame on rubber-rimmed metal wheels, natural finish, early 20th c., 24" l., 29" h. (ILLUS.)..... 175.00

Candlesticks, pressed milk white glass, Swirl patt., 3½" h., pr. 32.00

Carriage, decorated wood, three-wheel model, sleigh-form body w/seat, the exterior painted maroon, the interior creamy yellow,

w/a black leather adjustable top, two large back & one smaller wooden-spoked wheels, long wooden handlebar at back, Vermont Novelty Works, ca. 1875, overall 31½" l. 440.00

Carriage, painted wood, rectangular seat platform w/low shaped sides, original varnish & red paint w/yellow striping, black leatherized cloth top w/red fringe, large back wheels & small front wheels, Victorian, 32" l., 28" h. 400.00

Chest of drawers, Victorian country-style, pine, a tall scroll crestboard behind a pair of small hanky drawers on the rectangular top above a case w/three long graduated drawers, scroll-carved apron, 16" w., 19" h. (refinished, repairs, some renailing) 275.00

Clothing, Barbie "American Airline Stewardess" outfit, 1964, complete........................ 40.00

Clothing, Barbie "Sheath Sensation" outfit, 1961-64, complete 17.50

Clothing, Barbie "Stormy Weather" outfit, 1964-65, complete 7.50

Clothing, Barbie "Sweet Dreams" outfit, yellow, 1959-63, complete........................ 15.00

Clothing, Ken (Barbie's boyfriend) "Here Comes the Groom" outfit, 1966 (missing tie tac) 450.00

Coffeepot, black japanned tin, short pedestal base & bulbous body w/side handle, ca. 1840, 2½" h... 39.00

Cookbook, "Barbie's Easy-As-Pie Cookbook," Random House, 1964 .... 75.00

Cradle, painted pine, rectangular w/slightly canted sides, slightly arched headboard & stepped long sides, old brown repaint w/yellow striping & polychrome floral decoration, dovetailed construction, old red paint shows beneath brown, 17½" l. (some edge damage & age cracks) 40.00

Cradle, painted poplar, country-style w/low shaped sides, original red & yellow paint, bottom w/faded pencil inscription & date "1880," 15½" l. (one rocker renailed) 150.00

Cradle, painted poplar, high scalloped headboard, angled sloping sides to flat-topped footboard, on wide rockers, old brownish yellow repaint over old red, 17½" l...... 65.00

Cradle, painted & decorated poplar, slightly curved head- & footboards, high scrolled sideboards tapering down to low sides, yellow striping & floral decoration in red, green & yellow on original black ground (one rocker damaged, nailed repair) 125.00

Desk, drop-front type, walnut, rectangular top over shaped molding above a drop-front lid opening to an interior w/one long drawer & shelf, above a case w/three long drawers, molding at top, bottom & sides, 15½" h. 1,300.00

Dollhouse, lithographed paper on wood, "Wild Rose Cottage," the facade depicts potted geraniums & Little Red Riding Hood at the door, Bliss, 10 x 13", 13" h. 1,100.00

Dollhouse armchair, plastic, "Petite Princess," mint in box 7.00

Dollhouse bed, metal, "Tootsie-toy" 12.50

Dollhouse host chair & 2 side chairs, metal, "Tootsietoy," 3 pcs. 35.00

Dollhouse ladder, cast iron, green, "Kilgore" 40.00

Dollhouse washing machine, plastic, "Renwal" 65.00

Egg beater, "A & J," 6" 15.00

Egg beater, tin, "Baby Bingo," 5½" 12.00

Food grinder, metal, 3" h. 19.00

Parasol, long wooden handle w/metal disc tip, original blue & white cotton covering trimmed w/lace, 15½" l. (fabric slightly soiled) 75.00

Pitcher & bowl set: footed bowl w/flared rim & pitcher w/wide spout & high arched handle; ceramic, lacy blue design on white ground, marked, "P," pitcher 2½" h., bowl 4½" d., 2 pcs. 30.00

Scarf, black ostrich feather, 35" l. . . 25.00

Scrapbook, "Barbie's Snips 'n Scraps" book, by Ponytail Scrapbook, blue. 145.00

Shipping box, wood & cardboard w/cloth strings to tie the doll in, paper label on end reads "Bebe Jumeau - Chemise - Yeux - 10 - Coiffe," circular label on lid reads "United States Lines - W...," late 19th c., 27½" l. (parts of sides & ends missing from lid, one wooden end replaced, one side patched, water damage & warping) 135.00

Sideboard, mirrored backboard w/shelf at top above base w/one drawer & two cupboard doors, scalloped trim, 5 x 11", 13" h. 175.00

Spice set, barrel-shaped covered canisters lettered "Coffee," "Tea," "Barley" & "Flour" in gold, together w/hanging salt box w/wooden

cover & measuring pitcher, the set 125.00

Stroller, wicker & wood, the sides composed of teardrop-shaped panels of natural wicker flanking wooden seat, a turned wooden handle at the back supports a wire suspending a cloth parasol, a scrolled wicker adjustable footrest at the front, curled metal springs & wheels, late 19th - early 20th c., 36" l. (some wicker damage on footrest, metal rod for parasol replaced) 320.00

Stroller, stepped wooden sides decorated w/wicker curlicues, leatherized cloth telescoping hood, single bar handle w/T-bar handhold, footrest w/sides trimmed w/wicker curlicues, two large & two small spoked wheels, painted red, 28" l., 31" h. (some damage) 104.50

Trunk, metal-covered wood w/wood trim, leather end handles, metal fastenings, lined w/plain paper w/decorative border inside top, 18" l., 11½" h. (metal finish worn, inner tray missing) 150.00

Trunk, wardrobe-type, metal, section for hanging clothing w/four drawers to one side, exterior w/travel stickers, 19" h. 50.00

Trunk & Doll Clothing

Trunk & clothing, fabric-covered wooden trunk w/metal trim on edges, wooden bands, paper lining & original tray w/cover, included in the trunk are a checked dress, two-piece white sailor outfit, two-piece outfit w/pants & top, white lace-trimmed half-slip & pants, all clothing sized for a 14-16" doll, trunk 18" l., the group (ILLUS.) 300.00

Waffle iron, cast iron, "Arcade" 125.00

Washboard, clear glass, "Midget Washer," 6 x 8" 28.00

Yard swing, two facing benches, slat floor, 23" h. 55.00

DOLLS

"Alabama Baby" Doll

"Alabama Baby," by Ella Smith, molded head w/finely painted features, cloth body w/original costume (ILLUS.) $3,600.00

Alexander (Madame) Binnie Walker, composition, original dress & shoes, 21" 150.00

Alexander (Madame) Cinderella, hard plastic, blue sleep eyes w/real lashes, closed mouth, floss-type hair, five-piece body, original clothing, 14" (tiny rub on nose, small holes in dress) 475.00

Alexander (Madame) Cissy, hard plastic w/vinyl arms, blue sleep eyes w/real lashes, closed mouth, original synthetic wig, jointed at shoulders, elbows, hips & knees, "high heel" feet, dressed in original slacks & knit top, w/hat, handbag & sun glasses, together w/two marked Alexander hat boxes w/shoes, 19" 330.00

Madame Alexander Coco - Melanie

Alexander (Madame) Coco - Melanie, vinyl head w/blonde hair, jointed vinyl body, original costume, played-with condition (ILLUS.). 850.00

Alexander (Madame) Groom, hard plastic head w/walking mechanism, blue sleep eyes w/molded lashes, single stroke brows, painted lower lashes, synthetic wig, closed mouth, hard plastic child body jointed at shoulders, hips & knees, dressed in original Groom outfit, in original box marked "Madame Alexander, Alexander Doll Company, N.Y., N.Y., 356," 8" (mark on each side from stand) 150.00

Alexander (Madame) Marybel marked "Mme Alexander, 1971," vinyl head, brown sleep eyes w/real lashes, feathered brows, painted lower lashes, rooted synthetic hair, closed mouth, vinyl body jointed at waist, shoulders & hips, dressed in original tagged romper, original shoes, in original case marked "Marybel, the Doll That Gets Well" w/all accessories including gauze, tape, casts, crutches, measles spots, etc., 15" 275.00

Armand Marseille "Googlie-Eyed" Girl

A.M. (Armand Marseille) bisque head girl marked "Germany - 323 - A. O. M.," brown wig, blue glass "googlie" side-glancing eyes, closed mouth, on a toddler wood & composition ball-jointed body, 12" (ILLUS.) 1,540.00

A.M. bisque socket head baby marked "A M Germany, 351/3K," blue sleep eyes, softly blushed brows, painted lashes, accented nostrils, softly blushed hair, open mouth w/two lower teeth, five-piece composition baby body, dressed in contemporary clothing, 15" (torso touched up around neck opening & front seam) 200.00

A.M. bisque socket head child marked "1894, A M 3 DEP," set blue eyes, heavy feathered brows, painted lashes, accented nostrils, blonde mohair wig, open mouth w/four upper teeth, wood & composition jointed French body, dressed in old clothing, 16" (inherent color flaw near crown in front, body repainted) 550.00

A.M. bisque socket head baby marked "A.M. Germany, 351/4.K," brown sleep eyes, softly blushed brows, painted lashes, accented nostrils, softly blushed hair, open mouth w/two lower teeth, composition five-piece baby body, dressed in contemporary baby doll dress, 17" 220.00

Armand Marseille Character Girl

A.M. bisque head character girl No. 590, blonde wig, blue glass eyes, open-closed mouth, jointed composition body, wearing a green checked dress, 18" (ILLUS.) 1,400.00

A.M. bisque socket head baby marked "Germany, G 327B, D.R.G.M. 259, A. 12M," blue sleep eyes, feathered brows, painted upper & lower lashes, synthetic wig, open mouth w/two upper & two lower inset teeth, five-piece composition baby body, dressed in antique baby dress, 21" (body repainted, light wear at joints) ... 375.00

Amberg (Louis) composition socket head girl marked "L.A. & S., 40," blue tin sleep eyes, feathered brows, painted lashes, original blonde mohair wig, open mouth w/four upper teeth, jointed wood & composition body, redressed, 15" (tiny flaw on upper right ear, feet repaired & repainted) 325.00

American Character "Amosandra," w/original layette, character on

Amos & Andy show, original box 500.00

American Character "Collegiate Tony," w/watch & booklet, all original, 10" 65.00

American Character "Teenie Weenie," composition swivel head girl, brown sleep eyes, soft body w/composition lower arms, wearing a christening dress & bonnet, 12" 85.00

Arranbee Bo-Peep Doll

Arranbee composition "Bo-Peep" character girl, molded painted hair, eyes & closed mouth, jointed composition body, wearing original costume w/shepherd's crook & lamb, in original box w/latch & handle, doll 8¾" (ILLUS.) 110.00

Averill (Georgene) bisque head "Bonnie Babe" baby marked "Copr. by - Georgene Averill - 1005 - 3652," molded hair, blue sleep eyes, open mouth w/tongue & two lower inset teeth, cloth body w/celluloid hands, wearing a white cotton christening gown w/copper medal for Madame Hendren Dolls, head circumference 10½" 825.00

Averill (Georgene) all-bisque "Sonny" baby, life-like molded head w/brushed hair & inset glass eyes, jointed arms & legs, wearing a knit jumper, 6" (ILLUS. top next column) 3,000.00

Barbie, "No. 1," black hair, loop earrings, skirt & knit sweater, w/original box, 11½" (ILLUS. next column) 3,500.00

Barbie, "Bubble Cut Barbie," blonde, small pink lip color, pearl earrings, nude, 1964 (lip rub, discoloration on ears)................. 30.00

Barbie, "Bubble Cut Barbie," bru-

Georgene Averill "Sonny"

Original No. 1 Barbie
nette, full coral lips, original
swimsuit, 1964 . . . . 50.00
Barbie, "Scottish Barbie," Interna-
tional Series, 1980, mint in box . . . 100.00
Bisque baby girl marked "Germa-
ny," painted facial features, sculptured hair, jointed hips &
shoulders, bent arms & legs,
dressed in original clothing, 4" . . . 80.00
Bisque black socket head child,
painted black eyes, single stroke
brows, original black mohair wig,
closed mouth, body jointed at
neck, shoulders & hips, dressed in
possibly original crocheted clothing, 2½" (neck opening chipped
front & back, rub on left cheek &
tip of nose) 110.00
Bisque boy, painted blue eyes, sin-
gle stroke brows, molded & painted blond hair, closed mouth,
molded & painted hat, sweater,
knickers, socks & shoes, jointed
at shoulders, 4" (light color wear
on toes) 75.00

Bisque 'bonnet-head' girl, painted
blue eyes, single stroke brows,
molded pink bonnet w/green bow
over molded & painted long
blonde hair, open-closed mouth,
jointed at shoulders & hips, molded & painted socks & shoes,
redressed in pink dress & pants,
5" 85.00

Fine Bru Doll
Bru bisque head girl marked "Bru
Jne - No.3," original kid wig,
brown paperweight eyes, pierced
ears, open-closed mouth, gusseted kid body w/paper label &
bisque lower arms w/kid-over-
wood upper arms, wearing original maroon silk dress trimmed
w/lace & commercial white chemise trimmed w/pink ribbons,
leather shoes marked "3 - Bru Jne
- Paris," 13" (ILLUS.) 17,600.00
Bru bisque head Fashion lady
marked "F," swivel head on
shoulder plate, blue paperweight
eyes, closed smiling mouth,
pierced ears, blonde wig on cork
pate, kid body, wearing a cream-
colored dress w/petticoats & pant-
aloons, 17" 2,860.00
Bru bisque head "Circle Dot" Fash-
ion lady, bisque head w/original
wig, glass eyes & open-closed
mouth, kid body w/bisque lower
arms, wearing original elaborate
silk costume (ILLUS. top next
page). 18,000.00
Buddy Lee, hard plastic boy, jointed
at shoulders, painted black side-
glancing eyes, molded & painted
hair, closed mouth, molded &
painted boots, wearing original
bib overalls marked "Lee," red
bandana & denim shirt, 12" 75.00
Bye-Lo Baby, bisque flange head
marked "Copr. by Grace S. Putnam, Made in Germany, 1373

Rare "Circle Dot" Bru

(rest illegible)," set brown eyes, softly blushed brows, painted lashes, molded & painted hair, closed mouth, cloth body w/"frog" legs & celluloid hands, redressed in period baby dress, 14" (eyes newly set w/no rocker, small flaw on left ear, firing line behind right ear)........................... 350.00

Celluloid Swedish girl marked "Germany" w/turtle mark on shoulder plate, celluloid shoulder head w/brown glass sleep eyes, feathered brows, painted lashes, original blonde mohair wig, open mouth w/four upper teeth, cloth body w/celluloid lower arms, dressed in original Swedish regional outfit, 14" (small spot of color off top lip) 200.00

Celluloid socket head black boy, unmarked, brown set eyes w/real lashes, flocked hair, molded brows, closed mouth, wood & composition jointed body, dressed in blue pants & red checked shirt, 19½" (some lashes missing, minor body wear) 275.00

Chase (Martha) stockinet boy, textured painted blond hair & painted facial features on a cloth body jointed at the shoulders, elbows, hips & knees, stamped on body "Chase Stockinet," 26" 990.00

China head boy, molded & painted short black hair w/brush strokes around face, exposed ears, painted blue eyes w/red accent lines over lids, single stroke brows, pale pink tint, kid body w/gussets at elbows, hips & knees, bisque lower arms, redressed in blue velvet w/cape-style double collar, 20" (very minor wear on hair, fingers on right hand chipped on tips, few minor repairs on body).. 400.00

China head girl, painted blue eyes, single stroke brows, red line over eyes, accented nostrils, closed mouth w/accent line between lips, molded & painted flat-top hair, old cloth body w/kid arms, redressed, 30" (arms patched).... 275.00

China head lady, painted blue eyes, single stroke brows, painted black line over eyes, closed mouth, solid dome head w/original mohair wig w/curls & braids, original cloth body w/red stitching, china lower arms & legs, original clothing, 11" (left foot broken & reglued)....................... 650.00

China head lady, painted blue eyes, single stroke brows, red line over eyes, accented nostrils, molded & painted flat-top hair w/center part, closed mouth, original cloth body w/china lower arms & legs, wearing original dress w/black silk melting, 12" 170.00

Fine China Head Lady

China head lady, finely molded head w/full smiling lips, tinted cheeks & detailed eyes, elaborate molded curly black hair, wearing an ornate period style costume w/bonnet, 48" (ILLUS.) 2,750.00

Cloth doll, boy, printed in colors, blue eyes, heavy brows, printed lashes, nose & open-closed mouth, curly hair, dressed in a printed fancy Victorian-style suit, 12" (spot on knee taped, several mended areas on side seams, some cork stuffing missing) 75.00

Cloth doll, girl, printed face sewed to doll, brown eyes & all features printed on fabric, including hair framing face, back of head & remainder of doll are plain cloth, dressed in original pink plaid

dress & matching bonnet, 14½"
(some color wear on face) 150.00

Composition, General Douglas
MacArthur, paper tag "Gen.
MacArthur, 'The Man of the Hour,'
manufactured by Freundlich Nov.
Corp., New York, N.Y.," painted
black eyes, closed mouth, painted
hair, single stroke brows, molded
& painted Army hat, stiff neck on
composition body, jointed at
shoulders & hips, right arm molded as if saluting, dressed in original Army uniform, 19" (small tear
on front of jacket).............. 175.00

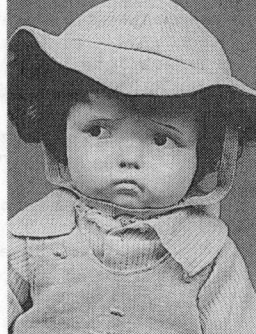

Composition "Baby Grumpy"

Denivelle (Otto) "Baby Grumpy,"
marked "Deco" on back of head,
composition flange head w/blue
intaglio side-glancing eyes, closed
pouty mouth, original brown mohair wig, cloth body w/composi-
tion hands, disc joints at shoulders & hips, wearing original
three-piece outfit w/hat, paint
flaking on right hand, light flaking
on left hand, 11" (ILLUS.) 200.00

Dewees Cochran latex socket head
child marked "© D on C, LL" in
mold, "9" & signature behind left
ear, painted brown eyes w/real
lashes, single stroke brows, h.h.
(human hair) wig, closed smiling mouth, five-piece molded latex child body, dressed in original clothing & underclothing,
10½"......................2,100.00

Dollhouse bisque shoulder plate
lady marked "556 10/0," painted
blue eyes, closed mouth, original
brown mohair wig, bisque arms
strung through shoulder plate,
cloth body w/bisque lower legs,
dressed in original silk wedding
dress & underclothing, 7" (paint
flaw corner of right eye, arms
need restringing, dress "melting")......................... 135.00

Donny & Marie Osmond, Mattel,
1976, w/original boxes, pr. (boxes
worn) 17.50

Dressel (Cuno & Otto) bisque socket
head girl marked "Made in Germany - 1912-6" & "X" on forehead
near crown, brown sleep eyes
w/real lashes, brown mohair wig,
open mouth w/four upper teeth,
jointed wood & composition body,
redressed in red print dress, underclothing, shoes & socks, 24"
(tiny flaw on forehead, tiny flake
on lower right eye lid, slight
roughness at neck opening) 300.00

Eden Bebe bisque head girl marked
"Eden Bebe - Paris - M," cork
pate, brown wig, blue paperweight eyes, pierced ears, closed
mouth, on a five-piece composition body, dressed in period dress
& hat w/large flowers, 23"....... 880.00

Effanbee "American Child" girl,
composition head w/brown sleep
eyes w/real lashes, open mouth
w/four upper teeth, original
brown h.h. wig, composition five-
piece child body marked "Effanbee Anne Shirley" on torso, redressed in period clothing & possibly original underclothing, replaced shoes & socks, 14" (glass-
ene eyes cracked, minor crazing) 245.00

Effanbee "Anne Shirley"

Effanbee "Anne Shirley," composition head w/blue sleep eyes
w/real lashes, multi-stroke brows,
closed mouth, brown h.h. wig,
five-piece composition child body,
wearing original dress, underclothing, socks & shoes, light
general crazing, crack in finish on
right side seam of torso & inside
left leg, 20" (ILLUS.) 150.00

Effanbee "Little Brother" marked
"FanB, Made in U.S.A." on back

of composition head, painted blue eyes, multi-stroke brows, painted lashes, reddish yarn hair, closed mouth, cloth body w/composition hands, wooden neck plug, dressed in original shirt, pants, socks & shoes, 16" (fine light crazing on face) 250.00

Effanbee "Wee Patsy," all-composition, painted blue eyes, single stroke brows, closed rosebud mouth, molded & painted hair w/headband, stiff neck, jointed at shoulders & hips, painted socks & shoes, dressed in original clothing, 6" 340.00

Farnell "Jean Harlow" lady, felt, blonde curly wig, painted facial features, wearing black velvet pants w/white silk insets w/a matching high-waisted jacket, felt dancing shoes decorated w/stones, black velvet evening gloves & a velvet cap decorated w/a feather, label on foot "Farnell's - Alpha toys - Made in England," added Lenci label on clothes, ca. 1930's, 26" 715.00

Felt Puss in Boots character marked "100% Wool - Made in Italy" on tag on bottom of right foot, facial features molded in felt, applied ears & whiskers, wire armature body padded & covered w/felt, wire tail covered w/felt, bright yellow gloves & boots, large orange felt hat, white felt collar, brown felt belt holds felt sword, 11" (tiny moth holes on bottom of left foot) 90.00

Florodora (Armand Marseille) bisque socket head girl marked "Made in Germany, Florodora, A 0½ M," brown sleep eyes, molded & feathered brows, painted lashes, original blonde mohair wig, open mouth w/four upper teeth, crude five-piece composition body w/unfinished torso, dressed in factory original blue dress & hat, both trimmed w/lavish lace & ribbons, 16" (small firing line from crown on left side of forehead becomes hairline, minor rub on nose & right cheek) 175.00

French Fashion, bisque socket head on shoulder plate marked "2," blue threaded paperweight eyes, original blonde mohair wig, closed mouth w/accented lips, pierced ears, rare kid over wood body w/wooden arms jointed at elbows & wrists, bisque lower legs, dressed in two-piece outfit made from old fabric, shoes marked "1 ½," 15½" (minor paint flaking on arms) 2,400.00

Frozen Charlotte, all-china, painted blue eyes, single stroke brows, closed mouth, molded & painted black hair w/molded bow, arms extended to the front, 5" 70.00

Gaultier (F.) bisque head French Fashion lady marked "5," blonde wig on cork pate, blue threaded eyes, pierced ears, closed outlined mouth, gusseted kid body w/jointed wooden arms, wearing a pink silk dress, 18" (small chip on ear lobe, hand repainted) 1,540.00

Handwerck (Heinrich) bisque socket head girl marked "79 - 5n - Germany - Handwerck," blue sleep eyes, open mouth w/accent line on lower lip & four upper teeth, replaced blonde h.h. wig, pierced ears, jointed wood & composition child body, wearing a blue & white cotton & organdy dress, antique underclothing & replaced shoes & socks, 14½" (small flake on left earring hole, hands well repainted) 250.00

Heinrich Handwerck Girl Doll

Handwerck (Heinrich) bisque socket head girl marked "Germany - Heinrich Handwerck - Simon & Halbig - 2 ¼," blue sleep eyes, brown h.h. wig, open mouth w/four upper teeth, pierced ears, jointed wood & composition child body, redressed in old fabrics & w/a straw hat, inherent white spot on side of head, body repainted, 24" (ILLUS.) 625.00

Handwerck (Heinrich) bisque socket head girl marked "119-13 - Handwerck - 5 - Germany," blue sleep eyes, synthetic blonde wig, open mouth w/accented lips & four upper teeth, pierced ears, jointed wood & composition child body, wearing lovely antique dress, underclothing & replaced shoes & socks, 25" (general wear & some surface cracks on body, both little fingers repaired) 800.00

Handwerck (Heinrich) bisque head girl marked "109 15 - DEP - Germany - Handwerck - 6," brown h.h. wig, pierced ears, blue sleep eyes, open mouth w/inset upper teeth, on a wood & composition ball-jointed body, body stamped "Heinrich Handwerck - Germany - 6," 31" (two fingers broken) 990.00

Handwerck (Max) bisque socket head girl marked "283 - 275 - Max. Handwerck - Germany 1," blue sleep eyes, original blonde mohair wig, open mouth w/four upper teeth, jointed wood & composition body, wearing probably original white dress trimmed w/lace & tucks, matching underclothing, pink socks & shoes & lacy bonnet, 21" (tiny rub on left cheek) 450.00

Hertel, Schwab & Co. bisque socket head baby marked "151-10," blue sleep eyes w/real lashes, lightly molded & brush-stroked hair, open-closed mouth w/two upper teeth, five-piece bent-limb composition baby body, dressed in a two-piece knit suit & cap, 15" (minor inherent flaw on right ear, tiny flake at neck opening, ends of fingers chipped) 495.00

Hertel, Schwab & Co. bisque head baby marked "151 - 11," blue sleep eyes, molded & brush-stroked hair, open mouth w/four upper teeth, five-piece bent-limb composition baby body, wearing contemporary long baby dress, 17" (very minor body wear) 625.00

Heubach (Ernst) - Koppelsdorf bisque head East Indian child marked "Heubach Koppelsdorf - 414 - 15/0 - D R - Germany," brown painted head w/brown sleep eyes, painted black hair, open mouth w/two lower teeth, five-piece composition body, wearing original East Indian-style costume w/turban, vest & full pants, 8" (small flakes off back of head, left ear & lower neck) 300.00

Heubach (Gebruder) bisque socket head character girl marked "9573 - 6 - Heubach - Germany," brown "googlie" sleep eyes, closed smiling mouth, blonde mohair wig, five-piece composition body

w/molded & painted socks & shoes, wearing possibly original dress & panties, 7" (small flake off right side of forehead, crude unfinished torso w/wear) 400.00

Heubach (Gebruder) bisque head boy marked "5/0 D 87 - 33 - Germany," blue intaglio eyes, molded & lightly painted hair, closed mouth, crude five-piece papier-mache' body, redressed in boy's clothing, 8" 175.00

Heubach (Gebruder) black bisque shoulder head character baby marked "DEP, Germany" & sunburst, brown intaglio eyes w/molded eyelids, single stroke brows, molded & painted short curly hair, open-closed mouth w/two lower teeth, black cloth body w/composition lower limbs, dressed in possibly original red & yellow clown suit, 13" (lower arms do not match, crazing on lower right arm) 1,100.00

Horsman composition head baby, blue flirty sleep eyes w/real lashes, feathered brows, painted lower lashes, molded & painted hair, closed mouth, cloth body w/composition hands & lower legs, dressed in original pink organdy slip, dress, bonnet, socks & shoes, in box marked "Horsman Doll, Genuine Horsman Art Doll, Made in U.S.A., Trade Mark Reg. U.S. Pat. Office, Horsman Dolls, Inc., Trenton, New Jersey, No. 2448," w/price of $4.98 written on it, 21" (general light crazing on all composition) 275.00

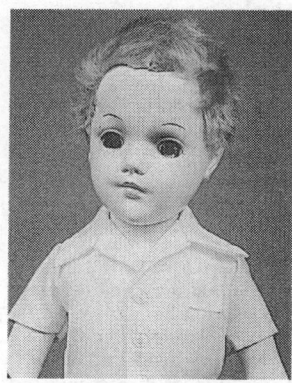

Mary Hoyer Boy Doll

Hoyer (Mary) boy marked "Original - Mary Hoyer - Doll," hard plastic head w/blue eyes w/real lashes, closed mouth, original skin wig, five-piece hard plastic body, redressed as a boy in white shirt, black pants, original shoes & socks, 14" (ILLUS.) 370.00

Ideal Novelty & Toy Co. "Deanna Durbin" marked "Deanna Durbin, Ideal Doll" on head & "Ideal Doll, 25" on torso, composition head, hazel sleep eyes w/real lashes, feathered brows, painted lower lashes, eye shadow, original h.h. wig, open mouth w/eight upper teeth, five-piece composition body, dressed in original clothing w/reproduction pin, 24" (general light crazing, lips touched up, tiny touch-up above left eye, legs touched up).................... 375.00

Ideal 'flexy' boy, composition head marked "Ideal Doll, USA," painted blue eyes, single stroke brows, painted lashes, molded & painted hair, closed smiling mouth, wooden torso & feet, composition hands, wire "flexy" arms & legs, dressed in original clothing, 12" (felt coat a bit faded) 175.00

Jensen (Helen W.) "Gladdie" child, marked "Gladdie - Copyright by Helen W. Jensen," biscaloid flange head w/set brown eyes, feathered brows, open-closed smiling mouth w/four upper teeth, molded & painted hair, cloth body w/composition arms & legs, wearing white baby dress, 16" (rub on hair in front & right cheek, minor cracks in finish) 525.00

Jumeau (E.) bisque head girl marked "Depose - Tete Jumeau - Bte. S.G.D.G. - 6," cork pate, brown h.h. wig, brown paperweight eyes, pierced ears, outlined closed mouth, eight-ball composition ball-jointed body stamped in blue "Jumeau - Medaille d'Or - Paris," w/straight wrists, wearing a white wool sailor costume & leather shoes marked "J - Paris," 16".........3,080.00

Jumeau (E.) bisque head 'long face' girl marked "9," brown paperweight eyes, closed mouth, cork pate w/long brown curled wig, applied pierced ears, jointed composition & wood body stamped in blue "JUMEAU Medaille d'Or Paris," wearing a silk red dress w/ivory lace inset & matching red feathered hat, 20" 15,400.00

Jumeau (E.) bisque head girl marked "Depose E 11 J," brown paperweight eyes, closed mouth, long brown curled wig, applied pierced ears, jointed body

w/straight wrists stamped in blue "JUMEAU Medaille d'Or Paris," wearing an old ivory cotton dress trimmed in lace & light pink ribbon, 24" 5,500.00

Jumeau "Long-Faced" Girl

Jumeau (E.) bisque head "triste" or "long-faced" girl, blue paperweight eyes, closed mouth, brown h.h. wig, pierced ears, wearing an antique silk & taffeta costume, 31" (ILLUS.) 20,000.00

K (star) R (Kammer & Reinhardt) bisque socket head girl marked "192 - 6/0," brown sleep eyes, original blonde mohair wig, open mouth w/three upper teeth, five-piece composition body w/molded & painted shoes & socks, original outfit of pink wool dress, white wool bonnet, underclothing, brown cotton stockings, leather shoes w/ribbon rosettes, 8" 375.00

K (star) R bisque socket head "Marie" character girl marked "K★R 101 - 33," painted blue eyes, replaced brown mohair wig, closed pouty mouth, wood & composition body jointed at shoulders, elbows, wrists, hips & knees, redressed in antique fabrics, 9" (minor wig pulls, repair on right hip joint) 1,800.00

K (star) R bisque socket head character boy marked "K★R 114 - 34," painted blue eyes, original blond mohair wig, closed pouty mouth, jointed wood & composition body, wearing original factory chemise, 13" (tiny inherent line on left side of nose) 3,000.00

K (star) R bisque head character baby marked "K★R 127 - 32," blue sleep eyes, molded & painted hair, open mouth w/two upper teeth & wobble tongue, five-piece bent-limb composition baby body, wearing antique long baby dress, 14" (neck plug in base of head) .. 850.00

K★R "Googlie" Character Girl

K (star) R bisque head character girl marked "131," blonde wig, 'googlie' side-glancing eyes, closed smiling mouth, jointed composition body, wearing a lace-trimmed dress, 15" (ILLUS.) 8,000.00

K (star) R bisque socket head character girl marked "K★R - 114 -43," painted blue eyes w/black accent line, closed pouty mouth, blonde mohair wig, jointed wood & composition body, redressed in antique clothing, underclothing, socks & shoes, 16½" (body repainted)................3,600.00

K (star) R bisque socket head baby marked "K★R - Simon & Halbig - 121 - 62," blue sleep eyes, original blonde mohair wig, open mouth w/two upper teeth & wobble tongue, five-piece bent-limb composition baby body, wearing an antique baby dress, underclothing & a long coat, 23" 1,200.00

Kampes (L.A.) 'Kamkins' boy marked "Kampes - Atlantic City," oil-painted cloth swivel head w/painted blue eyes, closed mouth, brown mohair wig, oil-painted cloth body w/disc joints at shoulders & hips, stitched fingers & applied thumbs, wearing old Buster Brown-type boy's suit in red, socks & shoes, 18" (light color wear on face, light soil to finish) 1,000.00

Ken (Barbie's boyfriend), "Hawaiian Ken," w/surfboard & accessories, 1978, mint in box 17.50

Kestner (J.D.) bisque socket head character boy marked "A Made in Germany 5, 143" on head & "Germany 3/0" on torso, blue sleep eyes, feathered brows, painted

lashes, original blond mohair wig, open mouth w/two upper teeth, jointed wood & composition body, redressed in romper, 12" (very faint rub on nose, light wear & minor repairs at joints on body) .. 750.00

Kestner (J.D.) bisque socket head "Hilda" baby marked "F Made in Germany 10, 237, J.D.K. jr, C Hilda, ges. gesch," blue sleep eyes, feathered brows, painted lashes, original plaster pate & softly curled original skin wig, open mouth w/accented lips & two upper teeth, five-piece composition bent-limb baby body, 12" (tiny inherent line under nose, superficial surface crack on rear torso) 1,850.00

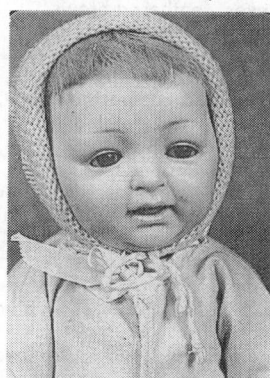

Kestner Baby Doll

Kestner (J.D.) bisque head baby marked "G made in Germany 11, 211, J.D.K," blue sleep eyes, feathered brows, painted lashes, blond h.h. wig, original plaster pate, open-closed mouth w/accented lips, five-piece bent-limb baby body, dressed in contemporary flannel diaper & jacket, knit hat & booties, several small rubs on nose, cheeks & eyebrows, touch-up on hands & toes, tiny kiln speck high on right side of forehead, 15" (ILLUS.) 525.00

Kestner (J.D.) bisque socket head girl marked "B ½ made in Germany 6 ½ - 171," blue sleep eyes w/real lashes, open mouth w/four upper teeth, original auburn mohair wig, jointed wood & composition body, wearing antique white eyelet dress, underclothing, socks & shoes, 17" (light wear on body & hands) 400.00

Kestner (J.D.) bisque socket head child marked "G Made in Germany 11, 143" on head & "Excelsior, D.R.P. No. 70685, Germany, 2"

on rear torso, brown sleep eyes,
feathered brows, painted lashes,
original mohair wig, open mouth
w/two upper teeth, jointed wood
& composition body, redressed,
17½" (minor firing line on seam
above ear, arms repainted) 925.00

Kestner (J.D.) bisque head girl
marked "Made in Germany - 14
JDK - 214," brown sleep eyes,
open mouth w/four teeth, brown
wig, wood & composition jointed
body, wearing a yellow & white
dress & black shoes, 25" (crazing
to left leg) 825.00

Kestner (J.D.) bisque socket head
child marked "M ½ Made in Germany 16½ J.D.K., 214," brown
sleep eyes, feathered brows,
painted lower lashes, original
blonde mohair wig, plaster pate,
open mouth w/four upper teeth,
jointed wood & composition body,
dressed in period clothing,
replaced socks & shoes, 32"
(hands repainted) 1,300.00

Kley & Hahn bisque head character
boy marked "Germany, K & H (in
banner), 138, 1," blue intaglio
eyes, brush-stroked hair, open-
closed mouth, jointed wood &
composition body, dressed in blue
pants & shirt w/white rick-rack
trim, new shoes & socks, 12" (two
small flakes on rim of right ear,
minor wear on body, repair to upper leg joint) 600.00

Kruse (Kathe) boy marked "Kathe
Kruse" on bottom of left foot, incomplete stamp on bottom of
right foot, original paper tag
marked "Original Kathe Kruse
Stoffpuppe - Made in Germany,"
hard plastic head w/painted blue
eyes, closed mouth, synthetic
blond wig, five-piece stockinette
body, wearing original clothing,
underclothing, shoes & socks,
14" 150.00

Kruse (Kathe) girl marked "B" on
bottom of right foot, illegible
mark on left foot, hard plastic
head w/painted brown eyes,
closed mouth & synthetic blonde
wig, cloth body jointed at shoulders & hips, wearing original blue
sailor dress, underclothing &
replaced socks & shoes, 14" (small
rub on end of nose & chin) 125.00

Lenci Mountain Climber boy,
pressed felt head w/painted
brown side-glancing eyes, open-
closed mouth, brown felt hair,
jointed cloth body w/felt arms,

wearing original mountain climber
outfit w/short pants, vest & cap
w/eidelweiss flowers, nails on the
bottom of the shoes, cloth tag
reads "Lenci - Made in Italy," paper tag reads "Lenci - Torino -
Made in Italy," 9" 225.00

Lenci Russian Peasant Doll

Lenci Russian Peasant lady, 'Sonia,'
pressed felt head w/painted blue
side-glancing eyes, smiling open
mouth w/painted teeth, carrot-red
hair, jointed cloth body w/felt
arms, wearing pink felt pinafore
w/appliqued flowers & embroidered stems, blue jacket w/gold
metal thread decoration, white
blouse, yellow headscarf over
cream cap, cotton petticoats & underwear, hoop petticoat & red
boots, some fading & minor moth
damage, late 1920's - early 1930's,
26½" (ILLUS.) 2,530.00

Lanternier (A.) bisque head girl
marked "Lanternier Limoges
'Cherie'," blue glass eyes, brown
human hair (h.h.) wig, open
mouth w/upper teeth, pierced
ears, jointed composition body,
dressed in old red cotton print
dress & underwear, 17" 650.00

'My Sweetheart' bisque socket head
girl marked "101 - 13½ - A.W. -
My Sweetheart - B.J. & Co.," blue
sleep eyes, molded & feathered
brows, synthetic brown wig, open
mouth w/four upper teeth, jointed
wood & composition body, wearing antique dress, underclothing,
shoes & replaced socks, 28"
(ILLUS. top next column) 450.00

Nancy Ann Storybook black girl,
brown bisque head w/stiff neck,
painted black eyes, closed mouth,
original black mohair wig, all-
bisque body jointed at shoulders

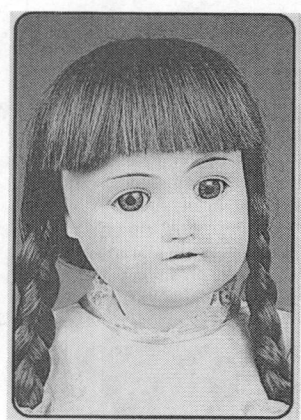

My Sweetheart Bisque Head Doll

& hips, molded & painted two-
button shoes, wearing original red
& white checked dress, panties &
hair ribbons, 5" (right leg w/crack
around lower part) 50.00

Papier-mache' shoulder head baby,
blue glass paperweight eyes,
original blonde mohair wig,
closed mouth w/accented lips, kid
body w/bisque lower arms, gussets at elbows, hips & knees,
wearing possibly original clothing,
underclothing & socks, 17" (tip of
one finger chipped, several tiny
bubbles in paint finish) 245.00

Parian bisque shoulder head lady,
painted blue eyes, blonde hair
molded into tight curls in the front
& braided in back, cloth body &
leather hands, wearing a purple
silk dress w/ecru lace trim, underclothing, shoes & stockings,
17" 575.00

Parian bisque shoulder head girl,
molded & painted short blonde
hair w/soft curls on nape of neck,
painted blue eyes w/red accent
line, open-closed mouth w/accent-
ed lips & four upper teeth, kid
body w/bisque lower arms, gussets at elbows, hips & knees,
wearing a pale yellow dress & antique underclothing, socks &
shoes, 20" (some minor repairs to
gussets) 700.00

Peck (Lucy) poured wax shoulder
head baby faintly stamped "Mrs.
Peck - the Doll's Home - 131 Regent Street - London W - Dolls
and Toys of All - Descriptions
Repaired," blue sleep eyes
w/heavy wax lids, closed pouty
mouth, brown h.h. inserted in
scalp, cloth body w/wax lower
arms & legs, wearing original

eyelet & lace baby dress, bonnet,
cape & underclothing, 26" (stringing hole on top of right arm bro-
ken through) 3,000.00

Queen Louise bisque socket head
girl marked "285 - Germany -
Queen Louise - 6," blue sleep
eyes w/real lashes, old brown
h.h. wig, open mouth w/four upper teeth, jointed wood & composition body, wearing a blue cotton
dress w/lace inserts & trim, antique underclothing, replaced
shoes & socks, 21" 375.00

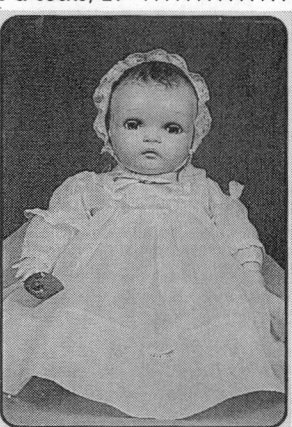

Sayco Baby Ann Doll

Sayco "Baby Ann," composition
flange head w/blue sleep eyes
w/real lashes, closed mouth,
molded & painted hair, cloth body
w/composition hands & lower
legs, wearing original organdy
dress, bonnet, underclothing,
socks & shoes, original paper
wrist tag reads "Baby Ann - Dolls
of Quality - A Sayco Doll," one
small finish break on back of
head, two fingers broken, 21"
(ILLUS.) 200.00

Schmidt (Franz) & Co. bisque head
baby marked "F.S. & C., Simon &
Halbig, Made in Germany, 1296,
24," blue sleep eyes, open mouth
w/two upper teeth & wobble
tongue, synthetic wig, feathered
brows, painted lashes, pierced
nostrils, five-piece composition
baby body, dressed, 9" (body
repainted) 310.00

Schoenau & Hoffmeister bisque
socket head girl marked "16 -
Germany - S PG (in star) H - 1906
- O S," blue sleep eyes, synthetic
blonde wig, open mouth w/four
upper teeth, jointed wood & composition body w/straight wrists,

wearing antique child's dress, underclothing, replaced shoes & socks, 16" (inherent flaw on back of head, small firing lines above left ear) 305.00

Schoenhut character girl, wooden, the head carved w/a bonnet secured w/chin strap, painted wisps of hair, intaglio eyes, spring-jointed wooden body, wearing a later green cotton romper dress, ca. 1910, 14¼" (one hand missing two fingers, paint loss on limbs & head) 1,320.00

Schoenhut boy, wooden, carved hair, intaglio eyes, closed mouth, spring-jointed body, wearing a blue cotton outfit, w/Schoenhut button, 15" (body repainted, some crazing on face) 660.00

Schoenhut toddler, wooden socket head w/painted blue eyes, closed mouth, painted hair, on a spring-jointed wooden body marked "Schoenhut Doll - Pat. Jan. 17th 1911 - U.S.A.," redressed as a clown, 16" (some scuffs & light wear) 350.00

S.F.B.J. (Societe Francaise de Fabrication de Bebes & Jouets) bisque head toddler girl marked "S.F.B.J. 236 Paris," blue glass sleep eyes, open-closed mouth, original brown h.h. wig, jointed composition body, dressed in fuchsia silk dress w/cream collar & belt & matching bonnet w/underclothes, socks & shoes, 17" 1,350.00

S.F.B.J. bisque socket head character boy marked "S.F.B.J. 235 Paris 8," blue 'jewel' eyes, molded & flocked brown hair, open-closed smiling mouth w/two upper teeth, jointed wood & composition French body, redressed in plum silk French boy's dress outfit w/lace cravat & cuffs, 20" (tiny repaired eye chip, minor wear on flocking) 850.00

S.F.B.J. bisque head girl marked "S.F.B.J. - 301 - Paris," blue glass eyes, open mouth, composition jointed body, doll walks & turns her head & throws kisses, dressed, 22" 660.00

S.F.B.J. bisque head girl marked "S.F.B.J. - 230 - Paris" in circle, blue glass sleep eyes, light brown French curled wig, open mouth w/inset upper teeth, jointed French composition body, dressed in maroon silk dress w/ecru lace trim & matching hat, under-

clothes, stockings & old shoes, 23" 1,550.00

Shirley Temple, five-piece composition child body, hazel sleep eyes w/real lashes, painted lower lashes, multi-stroke brows, open mouth w/six upper teeth, accented nostrils, original blonde mohair wig, dressed in original red & white dress w/NRA tag, original underclothing, socks & shoes, 13" (minor crazing on face & body, left side of wig slightly sparse, minor wear at joints) 350.00

Shirley Temple Doll with Trunk

Shirley Temple, marked "13, Shirley Temple, Cop. Ideal N & T Co." on head, "Shirley Temple, 13" on back, five-piece composition child body, hazel sleep eyes w/real lashes, open mouth w/six teeth, original blonde mohair wig, multi-stroke brows, painted lower lashes, accented nostrils, dressed in original tagged organdy Little Colonel dress & underclothing, socks & shoes, original Shirley Temple pin, together w/wooden Shirley Temple trunk w/movie stickers on it, containing original red & white dress & underclothing, blue organdy dress w/matching bonnet, & rollerskates, color wear on lip, 13", the ensemble (ILLUS.) 950.00

Shirley Temple, composition, hazel sleep eyes w/real lashes, original blonde mohair wig in original set, open mouth w/six upper teeth, five-piece composition child body, wearing original tagged blue organdy pleated dress from "Baby Take A Bow," original underclothing, shoes & socks & w/original Shirley Temple button, unplayed-with condition, 16" (eyes cracked,

fine lines around eyes & on torso
& left arm) 600.00
Simon & Halbig bisque head boy
marked "S & H 3/950," fixed
brown eyes, closed mouth,
pierced ears, original curly blond
mohair wig, white kid straight
limb body w/separate wire-
stiffened fingers, wearing original
Scottish plaid kilt, black velvet
jacket, hat & brown leather shoes
marked "CM," 14¾" 825.00
Simon & Halbig bisque head girl
marked "S H4, 950," set brown
eyes, closed mouth, pierced ears,
almost closed dome w/single
small hole, original blonde mohair
wig, feathered brows, painted
lashes, accented nostrils, cloth
body w/bisque lower arms,
dressed in ornate original
regional-type costume, 15½" (tiny
kiln speck left cheek, tiny flaw
side of right cheek) 1,000.00
Simon & Halbig bisque socket head
black girl marked "S 12 H 739
DEP," light brown bisque head
w/brown paperweight eyes, original curly black mohair wig, open
mouth w/four upper teeth,
pierced ears, jointed wood & composition body w/original finish,
wearing original fancy red dress &
matching hat, underclothing,
socks & shoes marked "France"
inside & "12 C.M." on bottom, 22"
(minor chips at earring holes)....3,400.00
Special bisque socket head boy
marked "Special - 65 - Germany,"
blue sleep eyes w/real lashes,
blond h.h. wig, open mouth
w/four upper teeth, jointed wood
& composition child body, redressed w/dark pants, a striped
shirt & a straw hat, 25" (some
touch-up on body) 475.00
Steiner (Jules) bisque socket head
'Le Parisien' lady marked "Le Parisien - A.3.4," fine blue paperweight eyes, original blonde
mohair wig, closed mouth w/ac-
cented lips, pierced ears, composition Steiner body jointed at
shoulders, elbows & hips, left hip
marked "Bebe Le Parisien -
Medaille d'Or - Paris," redressed
in French-style outfit made w/an-
tique fabrics & trim, 10½" 2,700.00
Steiner (Jules) bisque head girl
marked "J. Steiner - Bte S.D.G.D.
- Paris - Fre A 9," cork pate
w/blonde wig, pierced ears, blue
glass eyes, closed mouth, wood &
composition jointed body w/"Le

Petit Parisien 1889" paper label,
wearing original yellow silk dress
& commercial chemise, w/match-
ing bonnet & shoes marked "CM,"
17" 4,950.00
Tiny Terri Lee, hard plastic head
w/inset eyes w/real lashes, original blonde mohair wig, closed
mouth, five-piece hard plastic
body w/walking mechanism,
wearing tagged Girl Scout uniform, panties, socks & shoes, 10"
(panties probably replaced) 95.00
Unis France bisque socket head girl
marked "11 Unis France 14 - 301,"
blue sleep eyes w/real lashes,
brown h.h. wig, open mouth
w/four upper teeth, jointed wood
& composition body, redressed in
pink & white print dress, antique
wool coat & hat, underclothing,
socks & shoes, 23" (tiny fleck at
neck) 600.00

Vogue Uncle Sam & Miss America

Vogue "Toodles" boy & girl, each
w/composition head w/painted
blue side-glancing eyes, closed
mouth & original blond mohair
wigs, on five-piece composition
child body, each dressed in patriotic clothing, the boy as Uncle
Sam, the girl as Miss America,
red & white striped pants & skirt
& blue jackets, each hat w/stripes
& his hat w/a band of white stars
on blue, unplayed-with condition,
craze lines around nose & mouth,
8" h., pr. (ILLUS.) 400.00
Wax head child, blue glass eyes,
closed mouth w/modeled lips, human hair inserted into wax of
scalp, real hair eyebrows inserted
individually into wax, real lashes,
cloth body w/composition arms &
lower legs, redressed in antique
white dress w/leg-of-mutton

sleeves & lace front & lacy white cap, 38" (hair has been cut in back, light discoloration in wax around facial features, cloth torso recovered or replaced, light wear on hands) 800.00

Wax over papier-mache' lady, original brown h.h. wig, dark pupilless sleep eyes, closed smiling mouth, cloth body w/kid lower arms, wearing original white silk dress, silk shawl, bonnet, layers of underclothing, shoes & stockings, 26" (some light discoloration, minor repair on right arm, stockings deteriorating) 700.00

Wax over papier-mache' shoulder head lady, set dark pupilless eyes, original brown h.h. wig, closed smiling mouth, cloth body w/kid lower arms, wearing probably original white dress, underclothing & socks, 26" (some areas of restoration, mended kid attachment at right arm, right leg deteriorated)..................... 250.00

Wooden shoulder head nun doll, blue set glass eyes, no wig, closed mouth w/accent line, kid body w/bisque lower arms, gussets at elbows & knees, rivet joint at hips, cloth lower legs, wearing original black & white habit, slip & socks, 13" (minor wear, ears missing, kid torn & mended on torso, upper arms repaired) 65.00

DOORSTOPS

Victorian Dolphin Doorstop

All doorstops listed are flat-back cast iron unless otherwise noted. Most names are taken from Doorstops - Identification & Values, *by Jeanne Bertoia (Collector Books, 1985).*

Apple Blossoms, in basket, Hubley, 7 5/8" h. $95.00

Cape Cod Cottage, colorful flowers growing up onto two-level roof, two large trees behind, Hubley, No. 444, 7¾" w., 5½" h. 250.00

Cat, reclining kitten, white 225.00

Cat, seated black animal w/large head, ribbon at neck, four white paws, one raised, 4½" w., 7" h... 100.00

Cat, seated w/a bow on the left side of its neck, full figure, old worn black & white repaint, 7½" h. 154.00

Cats, Basket of Kittens (3), original polychrome paint, marked "M.Rosenstein, Copyright 1932, Lancaster, PA USA," 7 x 10" 370.00

Clipper ship, original polychrome paint, 11¼ x 20½" 70.00

Cockatoo, white, beautiful pastel shading, Albany & National Foundry, 5¼" w., 11¾" h. 160.00

Colonial Lawyer, orange jacket & black pants, WS in triangle mark, 9 5/8" h. 400.00

Cottage with Fence, arch of roses over door, further colorful flowers around house, picket fence to back, red roof, National Foundry, No. 32, 8" w., 5¾" h. 165.00

Cottage, w/roses around door, Hubley & National Foundry, 7½" w., 5¾" h................. 160.00

Dog, Cocker Spaniel, full figure, standing black animal, Hubley, 11" l., 6¾" h................... 325.00

Dog, Cocker Spaniel, seated black animal marked "Va Metalcrafters, Waynesboro, Va. WK, Dream Boy 18-7 1949," 7" w., 9" h. 145.00

Dog, German Shepherd, full figure, 9¾ x 13"....................... 165.00

Dog, Russian Wolfhound (large), full figure, standing animal w/head slightly turned, old white paint, 16" l., 9" h...................... 245.00

Dog, St. Bernard, standing animal w/brandy keg at his neck, on long oval base, original metallic brown & black paint, 9¼" l....... 175.00

Dog, Terrier, standing animal on base, polychrome paint, marked "Spencer, Guildford, Conn.," wedge in back, 5¼ x 6" 130.00

Dolphin, stylized creature on a cushion plinth, Victorian, 19th c. (ILLUS.) 6,600.00

Drum Major, full figure, solid bright blue jacket & hat, 13½" h. 375.00

Duck, standing w/head up, old white repaint, 6½" w., 9½" h. ... 250.00

Elephant, full-bodied free-standing walking animal w/trunk curled down between front legs, worn white paint, 7" l................. 82.50

Fisherman in Boat, man in yellow slicker standing at back of small boat, 4" w., 6¾" h. 275.00

French Basket, mixed bouquet in woven basket w/gently curving rim, overhead handle w/large bow, rounded base, Hubley, No. 69, 6¾" w., 11" h. 225.00

Heron, original polychrome paint, Albany Foundry, 7½" h. 145.00

Lilies of the Valley, ribbed basket w/blue bow & base, Hubley, 7½" w., 10½" h. 195.00

Lion rampant, one front paw resting on a tree stump, on a waisted plinth base, unpainted, 15" h. (pitted) 80.00

London Royal Mail Coach, coach w/figures pulled by two horses, original polychrome paint, marked "Pat. Pending," 12" l., 7" h. 110.00

Man in Chair, seated figure in side chair wearing a stocking cap & resting a stein on one knee, England, 5¾" w., 9½" h. 225.00

Monkey, full figure, seated animal w/head resting on one paw, brown paint, 4 5/8" w., 8½" h. 350.00

Narcissus, a variety of narcissus in a low, half-round basket w/striped sides trimmed w/a slender floral swag, Hubley, No. 266, 6¾" w., 7½" h. 300.00

Old Fashioned Lady, light blue dress & hat, Hubley, 4" w., 7¾" h. 550.00

Organ Grinder, man cranking street organ w/monkey crouched at his feet, 5¾" w., 9 7/8" h. 450.00

Oriental Girl, full figure, green & yellow, solid one-piece casting . . . 235.00

Parrot on stump, original polychrome paint, marked "Blodgett Studio, Lake Geneva, WIS, #1010," 4½" w., 12½" h. 650.00

Petunias and Asters, footed, ovoid basketweave vase holding colorful bouquet, Hubley, 6½" w., 9½" h. 175.00

Pied Piper, little elf in red jacket seated atop a large mushroom & playing a horn, 5" w., 7½" h. 285.00

Policeman, holding billy club in one hand, cap down over one eye, marked "Le Mur Lgt Co. PAT," 4" w., 7 7/8" h. 265.00

Poppies and Daisies, globular vase w/overall diamond design holding a colorful floral bouquet, on a stepped base, Hubley, 6" w., 7¼" h. 180.00

Poppy Basket, red poppies in brown basket w/four-sided angular handle, 9½ x 10½" . . . . 250.00 to 300.00

Quail, two birds on grassy, round

base, Hubley, No. 459, 6¼" w., 7¼" h. 400.00

Rabbit Eating Carrot, standing rabbit wearing red sweater, 8 1/8" h. 210.00

Rooster, w/head up, naturalistic paint, browns, yellows & red, 8½" w., 13" h. 600.00

Snow White & the Seven Dwarfs, each painted differently, modeled after the Brothers Grimm fairy tale, Denmark, Snow White 16" h., dwarfs from 10" to 12" h., set of 8 . . . . 4,000.00

Squirrel, seated on tree stump holding nut in paws, grey paint, 6 3/8" w., 9" h. 200.00

Stagecoach, w/driver & pair of horses, Hubley, No. 376, 11¼" w., 5 7/8" h. 170.00

Tulips in Pot, reddish orange blossoms & green leaves in low, cylindrical pot on base w/cut corners, marked "LA-CS 770," 5 7/8" w., 10½" h. 300.00

Woman with Fan, lady wearing bonnet, yellow dress & a shawl, holding a cluster of flowers in her right hand & a fan in her upraised left hand, 9½" h. 250.00

ENAMELS

Early English Enamel Candlesticks

Enamels have been used to decorate a variety of substances, particularly metals. The best-known small enameled wares, such as patch and other small boxes and napkin rings, are the Battersea Enamels made by the Battersea Enamel Works in the last half of the 18th century. However, the term is often loosely applied to other English enamels. Russian enamels, usually on a silver or gold base, are famous and expensive. Early 20th century French enamel on copper wares and those items produced in China at the turn of the century in imitation of the early Russian style are also drawing dealer and collector attention.

Bowl, silver-gilt & shaded enamel, the lobed body enameled w/flowers on alternating grounds of pale blue & brick red, the upper border enameled turquoise between silver filigree scrolls, set w/a band of red hardstone cabochons, the spreading ring foot enameled w/white pales, Nicholai Alexeyev, Moscow, Russia, ca. 1900, 3 7/8" d.......................$2,640.00

Box, cov., model of a large turtle, the body forming the box & enameled inside & out w/oval reserves showing allegorical scenes against a deep pink ground w/further enameled scrolls & flowers, the body raised on four tab-form legs w/blue & black inlay, the top mounted w/a putto holding reins extending from the turtle's head, Hermann Bohm, Vienna, Austria, ca. 1885, 7¼" l.......................2,750.00

Candlesticks, a flaring & lobed rim on the cylindrical candle socket above the ring-turned standard & domed, scalloped foot, decorated w/polychrome floral sprays & floral reserves on a white ground, England, ca. 1760, 13" h., pr. (ILLUS.) 3,135.00

Creamer, spherical footed body w/arched spout & C-scroll handle, silver enameled overall w/colorful flowering foliage, the base w/a border of white beads, Gregori Sbitnev, Moscow, Russia, ca. 1910, 3 3/8" h. 605.00

Plaque, copper enameled w/a scene depicting figures in 18th c. costume playing blind man's bluff, in a giltwood frame, France, 8½" w., 6½" h. 1,430.00

Tea set: cov. teapot, cov. sugar bowl, cream jug & waste bowl; silver-gilt & enamel, chinoiserie style, each piece of tapered octagonal shape w/raised rim surmounted by eight enameled balls, each foot similarly decorated, the bodies finely enameled w/flowers & foliage on grounds of Chinese red & sky blue, the borders enameled w/Chinese-style geometric designs, the teapot & sugar bowl w/hinged covers, Nicholai Alexeyev, Moscow, Russia, ca. 1900, 4 pcs. 18,700.00

Vase, spherical copper body enameled in low- and medium-relief w/sprays of daisies in shades of blue, green, pink & white reserved against a turquoise, yellow & lavender ground, designed by Camille Faure', signed in enamel "Faure' - Limoges, France," ca. 1925, 4¾" h. 1,320.00

Vase, enameled copper, tapering ovoid body decorated overall w/large stylized geometric flowerheads in white, grey & black w/leaves in deep blue & powder blue w/thick applied trailings, by A. Sarlandie, signed in enamel "Sarlandie - Limoges," France, ca. 1925, 11" h....................3,300.00

Vases, inverted pear-shaped body raised on a knopped pedestal & domed foot, w/a slender trumpet-form neck w/wide cupped rim, silver ground enameled overall w/reserves featuring mythological scenes & w/collars enameled w/geometric & scroll designs in color, Hermann Bohn, Vienna, Austria, ca. 1885, 8¼" h., pr.....4,400.00

EPERGNES

Epergnes were popular as centerpieces on tables of last century. Many have receptacles of colored glass for holding sweetmeats, fruit or flowers. Early epergnes were made entirely of metal including silver.

Sterling Silver & Etched Glass Epergne

Amethyst to clear frosted glass, single lily, tall trumpet-form lily w/ruffled rim, lower wide ruffled bowl, bronze-finished domed metal base bolts through bowl, metal center holds lily, 10" d., 16" h. ...$395.00

Blue opalescent glass, single lily, ribbed & ruffled lily & bowl w/blue edges shading to opalescent, ornate nickel-plated four-footed round base bolts through bowl, metal center holds lily, 10¼" d., 15½" h. 245.00

Clear shading to opalescent vaseline glass, three-lily, tall center trumpet vase w/ruffled rim, two smaller lilies in a rusty rose color w/fluted rims & applied clear spiraling on each, set in a 9½" d. fluted bowl w/brass mounts, 16½" h. 575.00

Cranberry glass, single lily, center lily w/flat rim applied w/opaque white threading at the top & applied cranberry band down the sides, wide shallow lower bowl w/applied opaque white threading on the exterior, on applied clear pedestal foot, 11½" d., 15" h. 325.00

Cranberry opalescent shaded to green spatter glass, single lily, ruffled rim on lily & deeply ruffled bowl, raised on an ornately embossed silvered metal domed base, 19th c., bowl 10" d., overall 17" h. 395.00

Cut glass & gilt-metal, four-lily, a matching set of four cranberry cut to clear trumpet-form vases, each w/a wide rounded top cut w/large diamonds & scalloped fans, the slender body cut w/fine diamond point design & the bottom tapering to a pointed knob, each set within the gilt-metal framework composed of slender scrolls, a raised center holder above three lower holders raised on three curved supports on a three-lobed base on three small feet, attributed to Baccarat, overall 10¾" h. 550.00

Shaded peach cased glass, single lily, tall center lily w/lightly molded ribbing & a wide crimped & ruffled rim, matching wide shallow base bowl, each enameled w/white blossoms & green & brown leaves, white lining, ornate embossed & footed plated metal base bolts through bowl, metal center holds lily, 9½" d., 13½" h. 325.00

Silver-gilt, four-basket, the oval undulating base decorated w/trelliswork & scrolls centered by a tapering pedestal supporting a detachable rectangular plateau w/four scrolling arms supporting four pendent swing-handled baskets chased w/flowers, foliage & lattice & scrollwork borders matching the base, Frank W. Smith, Philadelphia, retailed by Bailey, Banks & Biddle, ca. 1900, overall 22¾" l. 5,775.00

Sterling silver & etched glass, four-lily, three small frosted & etched clear glass petal-form bowls raised on entwined grapevine branches framing a taller center branch supporting a large frosted & etched bowl, the branches flanked at the bottom by three classical lady figures standing above a flaring ribbed base on shell feet, late 19th c. (ILLUS.) ...6,600.00

EYE CUPS

Wyeth Solution Bottle & Stopper

The eye cup was an early means of treating an injured or infected eye. The oval cup, filled with a medicated solution, was held over the open eye. With the advent of eye droppers and plastic dropper bottles, the eye cup became obsolete.

Blue glass, "Elder's," w/embossed eye $105.00

Clear glass, bulbous fish bowl-shape, marked "Q6," 2¼" h. 17.50

Clear glass, "E-Z," embossed eyes & "Pat.1-19-37" 60.00

Clear glass, "Glasco" 10.00

Clear glass, paneled, marked "12," 2¼" h. 16.00

Cobalt blue glass, embossed eye, base marked "Elder Flower Lotion Co." 26.50

Cobalt blue glass, paneled, "John Bull" 85.00

Cobalt blue glass, solution bottle
w/eye cup stopper top, "Wyeth
Collyrium" (ILLUS.) 75.00
Milk white glass, "John Bull" 39.00
Porcelain, the gilt-edged cup supported on a pedestal foot
w/domed base, decorated in the
famille rose palette w/scattered
flower twigs including roses,
morning glory, daisies, cornflow-
ers & chrysanthemum, Chinese Export, ca. 1750, 2 3/8" h. (very
slight wear) 1,650.00
White porcelain 92.50

FABERGE'

Faberge' Belt Buckle

*Carl Faberge' (1846-1920) was goldsmith
and jeweler to the Russian Imperial Court
and his creations are recognized as the finest
of their kind. He made a number of enamel
fantasies, including Easter eggs, for the Imperial family and utilized precious metals and
jewels in other work.*

Belt buckle, silver & enamel, shaped
oval form, the border chased
w/scrolls & a flowerhead,
enameled translucent blue over
an engine-turned ground, marked
w/Cyrillic initials of Workmaster
Michael Perchin, Faberge in Cyrillic & 88 standard, St. Petersburg,
ca. 1900, 3 1/8" l. (ILLUS.) $3,300.00
Cups, cylindrical w/angled handle,
the top w/a wide border featuring
spread-winged swans on a matted
ground, the edges w/a Greek key
design, gilded interior, each engraved w/a name, marked K.
Faberge in Cyrillic & w/Imperial
warrant & 84 standard, ca. 1900,
3" h., pr. 2,860.00
Glove box, silver-gilt & enamel, of
elongated rectangular shape,
enameled in violet translucent enamel over a *guilloche'* ground,
the hinged cover set w/the monogram of Empress Alexandra Feo-
dorovna in diamonds, w/beaded
borders, marked K Faberge' in
Cyrillic w/Imperial warrant &

maker's mark only, ca. 1900,
14¾" l. 46,750.00
Model of an elephant, carved obsid-
ian, the standing animal facing
forward w/curled trunk, the eyes
set w/diamonds, St. Petersburg,
Russia, ca. 1890, 2" l. 3,025.00
Model of a terrier, smokey quartz,
carved w/head lowered & front
legs outstretched in a playful pos-
ture, w/realistically carved fur,
the eyes set w/diamonds, in original fitted holly wood box, the interior of the lid lined in silk &
stamped in gold "Faberge', St.
Petersburg, Moscow" in Cyrillic,
1887-90, 1½" l. 39,600.00
Stickpin, carved nephrite, in the
form of two owls perched on a
branch, the eyes set w/red
stones, in gold mounting, marked
w/Cyrillic initials of Workmaster
Alfred Thielemann & 56 standard, St. Petersburg, ca. 1890,
3 5/8" l. 7,150.00
Tumbler, miniature, silver-gilt & enamel, cylindrical, enameled overall in translucent salmon pink
over an engine-turned ground, the
base w/a *plique-a-jour* enamel
leaf, marked Faberge in Cyrillic,
88 standard & unidentified Cyrillic
workmaster's initials "AP," ca.
1900, w/original fitted holly wood
case, 1¾" h. 7,425.00

FANS

Silver & Enamel Chinese Fan

Ivory, the blades carved w/an intricate design of Oriental figures &
a monogram, mounted in a black
lacquer frame, fan 13" l. (very minor damage)...................$450.00
Ivory & h.p. silk, decorated w/a
long central courting scene surrounded by delicate floral scrolls
& flanked by small scroll-framed
reserves of musical instrument
trophies, gilt-ivory sticks, France,
ca. 1880, 9½ x 18" 440.00

Lace & silk, delicate white floral
lace over a white silk backing,
mother-of-pearl blades, sold by
Tiffany & Company, New York,
w/case 467.50

Ostrich feather, fuchsia to pink,
20 x 24" 90.00

Ostrich feather & silk, 5" l. black ostrich feather tips & h.p. black silk
on pierced & carved black
Malayan wood blades, England,
ca. 1880, 12 x 24" 225.00

Ostrich feather & silk, white feather
tips & h.p. cream silk on carved
Malayan wood blades, dated
"1892" & w/the names of wedding
guests on the back, England 250.00

Sterling silver & enamel, the silver
filigree blades enameled in blue,
green & yellow w/a flowing scroll
design, the exterior blades decorated w/chased designs of Chinese figures in a landscape, China
(ILLUS.) 330.00

Tortoiseshell & lacquer, the center
gilt-decorated w/a landscape
scene w/seated Chinese figures,
China, 8" l. (ribbon broken) 231.00

FARM COLLECTIBLES

Rooster Windmill Weight

Bee skep, woven rye straw
w/wooden trim, 15½" h. (some
damage) $451.00

Book, "Diseases of the Horse," by
the U.S.D.A., illustrated, 1923,
630 pp. 17.00

Book, "Rural Science Farm Poultry,"
by George Watson, 1912,
378 pp. 10.00

Book, "Treatise On the Horse & His
Diseases," 1881 . . . . 28.00

Branding iron, letter "T," wooden
handle 12.00

Bull nose ring, copper 12.00

Corn husker, wrist-type, leather &
metal, early 15.00

Corn sheller, cast iron w/original
paint, "F & F Co.," Springfield,
Ohio, patented July 6, 1869 . . . . . 750.00

Corn sheller, clamp-on model, walnut & iron, round disc w/blade &
upright cob holder w/crank handle at top, marked "Pat. Apld. for
Nov. 9, 1869," 9½" d., 13" h. 395.00

Egg carrier, wood w/bail handle &
cardboard dividers, holds one doz-
en, "Star," Elbs, Rochester, New
York 45.00

Implement seat, cast iron, "Buckeye," Aultman & Co. on back 62.50

Implement seat, cast iron, "Duane
H. Nash, Millington, New Jer-
sey" .125.00 to 135.00

Implement seat, cast iron,
"McCormick" 55.00

Implement seat, cast iron, "Mo-
line" 75.00

Implement seat, cast iron,
"Stoddard" 65.00

Implement seat, cast iron, "Walter
Wood" 75.00

Pump, pitcher-style, cast iron, embossed "Chandler, Cedar Rapids
A2" 55.00

Sample box, red leatherette, contains six sample bottles of fertiliz-
er, marked "ANIMAL BONE FER-
TILIZER," Reading, Pennsylvania . . 29.00

Seed bag, "Whitney-Eckstein TIMO-
THY," eagle logo 24.00

Snowshoes, modified bear-paw,
bentwood w/mortised wooden
crosspieces, leather strap on
hinged wooden plate, 11 x 23½",
pr. 125.00

Well pump, copper bottom, "Union,"
patented 1871 . . . . 65.00

Windmill weight, model of a
bull, plain, black, by Fair-
bury . . . . .1,200.00 to 1,800.00

Windmill weight, cast iron, dove on
square plinth, 8½" h. 500.00

Windmill weight, cast iron, dove,
clawed feet on cylindrical plinth,
traces of white paint, 9¾" h. 350.00

Windmill weight, cast iron, model
of a horse, old worn tan paint,
16½" h. 260.00

Windmill weight, cast iron, model of
a rooster facing right, marked on
tail "Hummer - E 184," ca. 1900,
9" h. 660.00

Windmill weight, cast iron, model of
a rooster, white-painted body,
rainbow-colored tail & red comb
& wattle, attributed to Elgin
Wind Power & Pump Company,

Elgin, Illinois, 16" w., 18¾" h.
(repainted) 1,210.00
Windmill weight, cast iron, model of
a full-bodied rooster w/serrated
tail feathers, painted white w/red
comb & wattle, on a C-shaped integral base, attributed to the
Elgin Wind Power & Pump Company, Elgin, Illinois, ca. 1880,
17¾" l., 19½" h. 2,640.00
Windmill weight, cast iron, model of
a rooster, arched & ribbed tail,
worn silver & red paint, attributed
to the Elgin Wind Power & Pump
Company, damaged mounting
bracket (ILLUS.) 900.00

FIREARMS

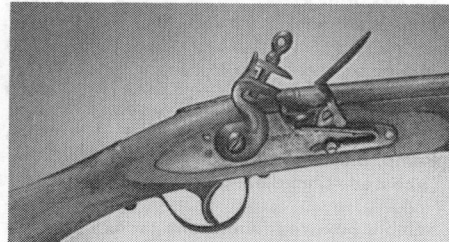

Early Hudson Bay Co. Musket

Musket, Hudson Bay Company trade
model, long scratch-rifled barrel,
iron lock stamped "Cooper, London," wooden full stock & club-
shaped butt, retains nearly all of
the original orange-painted finish,
full brass mounts in the military
style & original wooden ramrod,
England, late 18th c., barrel 52" l.
(ILLUS.)........................$880.00
Pistol, Colt Model 1888, .41 caliber,
side-swing, double action, re-
blued, original grips (chipped),
excellent rifling 795.00
Pistol, Colt 32-20 caliber W.C.F.
model, nickel-plated, last patent
date "July 1905," good rifling,
tight & clean, 5" l. barrel (some
chips on top of barrel) 795.00
Pistol, Flobert saloon parlor model,
ornately carved & fluted stock,
engraved iron furniture, 75%
original bright bluing, ca. 1870-80,
14" l. 365.00
Pistol, Smith & Wesson Model 1½,
five-shot 250.00
Pistols, percussion pocket-style,
marked "DLª," Henry Derringer,
Philadelphia, 1830-68, barrel 3" l.,
pr. 2,090.00

Revolver, Remington-Smoot "bird
head" model, .30 caliber, 98%
original nickel plating, colored
hammer, original hard rubber
grips, ca. 1870-80 .... 225.00
Rifle, flintlock, curly maple stock
w/brass inserts, pre-1860 A.W.
Spies mechanism, octagonal barrel, overall 46" l................ 675.00
Rifle, Kentucky full-stock, curly maple stock w/percussion lock, barrel 41½" l., overall 57" l. (stock
damage & repair) 412.50
Rifle, Kentucky half-stock, curly maple stock, percussion lock marked
"Davidson & Co. Cincinnati," octagonal barrel marked "A.C.
McGirr, Marietta, O.," brass patch
box w/simple engraving, two sil-
ver inlays, overall 55" l..........1,100.00

FIRE FIGHTING COLLECTIBLES

Early Fire Bucket

Badge, fireman's, Strasburg, Virginia, early 20th c. $65.00
Book, "Memories of the Chicago
Fire," by M.E. & E.W. Blatch-
ford, 1921, private printing, soft
cover 35.00
Bucket, painted & decorated leather,
cylindrical w/rounded bottom,
swing strap handle, painted red &
decorated w/a scroll-enclosed cartouche depicting a burning building above the inscription "Charles
W. Eliot," age cracks, paint loss,
19th c., 8½" h. (ILLUS.) 880.00
Cake print, carved wood, double-
sided, rectangular board carved
w/a long almond-shaped reserve
featuring a profile portrait of a
standing fireman w/helmet blowing a horn, smaller fireman, stars,

flowers & other designs around the edges, a scalloped outer border band, "Fire Fire" incised above the large fireman's head in reverse lettering, signed "P E Coon," reverse side w/floral medallions, 19th c., 11" l. 715.00

Certificate of service, hand-colored engraving on paper, a round vignette at the top framed by crossed poles & flags above the inscription, a fire scene across the bottom, presented to Joseph Chadwick by the City of New York, dated 1807, framed, 10¼ x 14" (toning) 357.50

Fire extinguisher, clear glass, "American Fire Extinguisher Co. Hand Grenade," raised diamond lattice design, smooth base, tooled lip, ca. 1880-90, 6 3/8" h. (light inside haze) 198.00

Fire extinguisher, clear glass, "Descours & Co. Fire Watcher - Hand Fire Grenade" on paper label, original blue-colored contents, wire hanger, England, ca. 1900, 5¼" h. 264.00

Fire extinguisher, cobalt blue glass, "Sinclair & Co. Hand Grenade, London" on paper label, "TOOT" on smooth base, barrel-shaped w/two raised bands, metal neck seal, original contents, 80% of label, England, ca. 1900, 7¼" h. . . . 176.00

Fire extinguisher, copper cylinder, "Randolph's Soda - Acid Fire Extinguisher," made by Randolph Laboratories, Chicago, Illinois, early - mid-20th c. (rebuffed & polished) 20.00

Fire extinguisher, turquoise blue glass, "Hayward's Hand Fire Grenade - Patented Aug. 8 1871 - S.F. Hayward 407 Broadway N.Y." embossed in large diamonds on the four rounded sides, paper label on neck w/"Hayward," original contents, ca. 1890, 6¼" h. 350.00

Fire extinguisher, turquoise blue glass, "Star (embossed inside a star on shoulder)" & "Hardens Hand Grenade Fire Extinguisher" on center band, finely ribbed spherical body, "This Bottle Pat May 27 84" on the smooth base, sheared lip, original contents & neck label, ca. 1885-95, 6 5/8" h. 115.50

Fire extinguisher, yellowish green glass, "W.D. Allen - Manufacturing - Company - Chicago - Illinois" & crescent moon logo around the

paneled sides, original contents, ca. 1880, 8" h. 1,000.00

Fireman's belt, leather, black w/red trim & white lettering "South Penn 31," 48" l. (worn) 75.00

Fire Society Meeting Invitation

Invitation, engraved paper, a notice of a meeting of the "Alert Eagle Fire Society," the text enclosed by a frame w/columns & topped by a spread-winged eagle over a seaport vignette & cherubs, further small vignettes along the bottom of the frame, dated "Boston, Feb. 25, 1800," signed in the plate "D. Staniford del" & "S.Hill SC 1800," signed in ink by the Society secretary, hand-colored, small losses at edges, discoloration & foxing, 6½ x 7 5/8" (ILLUS.) 880.00

Parade hat, ceremonial, pressed felt top hat painted w/the figure of an Indian chief wearing a feathered headdress & red cloak standing on a bluff overlooking Niagara Falls, the vignette surrounded by an ornate banderole against a dark bluish green ground, the reverse w/the initials "NHC" in gilt script lettering, the underrim painted red, Niagara Hose Company, initialed "H.J.," probably New York, mid-19th c., 6¾" h. (some minor restoration) 13,750.00

Parade hat, ceremonial, painted leatherboard, top hat w/the top painted w/the figure of a wolf surrounded by laurel wreaths & the initials "A.R.R.," the front w/a wooden fire hydrant & hose in gold flanked by a scrolling banner inscribed "Independence Hose Company," the back w/the initials "I.H." in red & gold on a black ground, probably Pennsylvania, mid-19th c., 7" h. (ILLUS. top next page) 5,750.00

Early Parade Hat

Print, chromolithograph on paper, "Firemen, Past and Present - The Old and the New," lithographed by H.A. Thomas & Wylie Lithography Company, & published by Buchanan & Lyall's Tobacco, 1895, framed, 21 x 27¼" (toning, scattered foxing, minor tear in margin) 605.00

Print, chromolithograph on paper, a design of an early horse-drawn pumper wagon shown in a streetscape, printed inscription under the picture "Hunneman & Co., Builders, Boston, Mass.," printed by L.H. Bradford and Company, ca. 1854-59, in period frame, 22 x 32½" (repaired tears, creases, staining, toning, probably laid down) 440.00

FIREPLACE & HEARTH ITEMS

Figural Dolphin Andirons

Andirons, bell metal & wrought iron, Chippendale, ball finial & vase-form standard, on spurred arched supports ending in claw-and-ball feet, Rhode Island, ca. 1775, 22½" l., 18½" h., pr. $2,200.00

Andirons, brass, Federal style, ball finial above a ring-turned & paneled standard, on spur-arched legs on ball feet, 17½" h., pr..... 500.00

Andirons, brass, Federal style, urn-form top w/pointed knob finial above a columnar shaft on a square plinth raised on the scrolled arched legs on knob feet, iron log bar, New York, ca. 1800, 27½" h., pr. 1,870.00

Andirons, brass & wrought iron, Arts & Crafts style, the circular pierced brass finials cast w/stylized thistle blossoms & scrolling branches emanating from a pineapple base, raised on a shaped standard above an arched base ending in flattened feet, unsigned, England, ca. 1880, 27 3/8" h., pr...................6,050.00

Andirons, brass & wrought iron, Chippendale, spiral-twist lemon-form finial above a faceted ball, the lower shaft vase-form & twisted, on double-spurred arched supports ending in claw-and-ball feet, New York, ca. 1775, 21" l., 24¼" h., pr. 6,050.00

Andirons, bronze, the rectangular tapering shafts w/terminals cast in full-relief w/scrolling cobras, rich brown patina, designed by Edgar Brandt, signed "E. BRANDT," ca. 1925, 17½" h., pr. 35,750.00

Andirons, cast iron, figure of George Washington standing w/cape over shoulder & draped by his feet, on ornate base w/star-type device in center & reeded corners, traces of red paint, 20" h., pr. 220.00

Andirons, gilt brass, cast as a dolphin w/scrolled tail, wrought-iron billet bar, marked "Bradley & Hubbard," 14" h., pr. (ILLUS.) 1,540.00

Bellows, turtle-back type, painted & decorated wood & leather, gilded & painted leafy designs continuing to ring-turned tapering cylindrical mouth, w/label stenciled "by I.M. Johnson, Southington, Con.," mid-19th c., 8" l. 550.00

Bellows, painted & decorated wood, original red & black rosewood graining w/yellow striping & gold & black stenciled border & a basket of stylized fruit & foliage in yellow, green, gold & black, brass nozzle, 17¾" l. (some wear, old releathering) 247.50

Fireboard, oil on canvas, rectangular, decorated w/four oval vignette scenes, one at each side, each joined to the other w/ornate leafy scrolls, the center decorated w/a large floral bouquet & two flying birds, all on a dark ground, the scenes based on Newport scenes, painted ca. 1857-60, framed, 28¼ x 40" 3,575.00

Fireplace fender, brass & wrought iron, Federal style, the serpentine brass rail centering three faceted brass finials above a conforming wire mesh w/meandering vine over a conforming wrought-iron base, America, early 19th c., 43¾" w., 13¼" h. 3,850.00

Arts & Crafts Style Fireplace Screen

Fireplace screen, painted & decorated wood, Arts & Crafts style, three horizontal panels mounted w/block-topped pegs on shaped uprights w/shoe feet, incised & stained golfer portrait, unsigned, color loss, 36¼" w., 42½" h. (ILLUS.)...................... 330.00

Fireplace set: fire fender & set of three tools; brass, Art Nouveau style, the fender w/a low bar front w/stylized double-spade upright terminals at the front corners, matching shovel, poker & tongs w/pointed ball terminals, Europe, ca. 1900, fender 54" l., 12" h., the set 467.50

Fireplace set: andirons & fender; wrought iron, Arts & Crafts style, the andirons w/tapering four-sided shafts decorated w/graduated diamond bosses below a wide diamond-form finial & raised on flaring angular legs, the fender composed of a double band of slender square bars w/square corner blocks, painted black, Bradley

& Hubbard, each piece marked, early 20th c., fender 12¼ x 42½", 6¾" h., andirons 10¾" w., 20½" h., the set 550.00

Hearth toaster, wrought iron, good scrolled & twisted detail, 12½" w., 19" l. handle 275.00

FISHER (Harrison) GIRLS

The Fisher Girl, that chic American girl whose face and figure illustrated numerous magazine covers and books at the turn of the century, was created by Harrison Fisher. A professional artist who had studied in England and was trained by his artist father, he was able to capture an element of refined, cultured elegance in his drawings of beautiful women. They epitomized all that every American girl longed to be and catapulted their creator into the ranks of success. Harrison Fisher, who was born in 1877, worked as a commercial artist full time until his death in 1934. Today collectors seek out magazine covers, prints, books and postcards illustrated with Fisher Girls.

Book, "A Dream of Fair Women," numerous color illustrations by Harrison Fisher, w/original gift box w/illustrated cover, Bobbs-Merrill Co., 1907 ....$175.00

Book, "A Girl's Life & Other Pictures," 16 full page color illustrations including six wedding scenes, Scribners, 1913, 12 3/8 x 17 3/8" (light cover wear) 350.00

Book, "American Beauties," illustrated by Harrison Fisher, 1909, 21 color plates ....200.00 to 250.00

Book, "American Belles," 1911, w/original box 275.00

Book, "A Song of Hiawatha," by Henry Wadsworth Longfellow, color illustrations by Harrison Fisher 135.00

Book, "The Harrison Fisher Book," 1907, w/color & black & white illustrations 48.00

Book, "Jane Cable," by George Barr McCutcheon, novel illustrated by Harrison Fisher, Bobbs-Merrill Co., 1906 .... 35.00

Book, "Love Finds the Way," by Paul Leicester Ford, 1904, first book illustrated by Harrison Fisher, fine condition 75.00

Book, "Truxton King, A Story of Graustark," by George Barr

McCutcheon, 1909, novel illustrated by Harrison Fisher 35.00
Sheet music, "Only A Rose," cover illustration by Harrison Fisher 25.00

FISHING COLLECTIBLES

BOOKS & PAPER ITEMS
Book, "Fish & Fishing of the United States & British Provinces of North America," by F. Forester, 1851, third edition, w/supplement & hand-tinted fly plate $110.00
Book, "Flyfishing For Duffers," by R.D. Peck, 1934, London, illustrated 10.00
Book, "McClane's Fishing Encyclopedia Guide," 1965, illustrated in color, w/dust jacket, 1,059 pp. ... 20.00
Book, "The Standard Book of Fishing," by Bruce Tuttle, 1956, illustrated, 532 pp., w/original box ... 45.00
Book, "Trout Fishing Memories & Morals," by Sheringham, 1920, Boston, Massachusetts 20.00
Catalog, "Abbey & Imbrie," 1910, fishing tackle, 80 pp. 75.00
Catalog, "Creek Chub," 1947 .... 35.00
Catalog, "Kiest Reels," Knox, Indiana 15.00
Catalog, "Richardson Fishing Rods," 1941 .... 14.00

LURES
Arbogast (Fred) Co. "Hula Diver," plastic, 2" l. 5.00
Arbogast (Fred) Co. "Hula Popper," plastic, 2" l. 3.00
Creek Chub Bait Co. "Castrola (The)," No. 3100 series, late 1920's - early '30s, 3 5/8" l. 95.00
Creek Chub Bait Co. "Gar Underwater Minnow (The)," No. 2900 series, 1927-46, 5¼" l. 150.00
Creek Chub Bait Co. "Pikie Minnow (The Famous)," No. 701W, 1919-21, 4½" l. 25.00
Heddon "Crazy Crawler," No. 2100 series, plastic, 2½" l. 20.00
Kautzky Mfg. Co. "Lazy Ike No. 4," Ft. Dodge, Iowa, ca. 1940's, 4" l. 8.00
Lane (Charles W.) "Wagtail Wobbler," wood body, wire leader, dark green scale, patented 3/16/20, Madrid, New York, 2¾" l. (minor flakes) 250.00
Paw Paw Bait Co. "Lippy Joe," No. 1200 series, wooden, ca. 1955, 2¾" l. 10.00

Shakespeare "Wonder Bar," plastic, 2½" l. 10.00
Winchester Repeating Arms Co. "Fluted Bait," No. 9613, new condition, on card 125.00
Wood Mfg. Co. "Dipsy Doodle," wooden, ca. 1947, 1¾" l. 10.00

REELS
Apache Airex spin cast reel, made by The Lionel Train Co. 20.00
Hardy Bros. "The Gem," fly-type, England, ca. 1920's 150.00
Hardy Bros. "The Tenth," fly-type, England 100.00
Humphrey "Denver Model 3A" 85.00
Martin "No. 1 Automatic" 25.00
Meek & Sons (B.F.) "No. 33 Bluegrass N/LW" bait casting reel, Carter's patent, last date 11/28/05, w/red suede sack 300.00
Meisselbach (A.F.) & Co., "No. 630 Okeah LW" bait casting reel, patent 8/3/09, Elyria, Ohio, w/original box & paper 250.00
Meisselbach (A.F.) & Co. "Tripart No. 581" 35.00
Ocean City "Imperial" level-wind reel w/star drag 20.00
Pflueger "Progress No. 1774" fly reel, metal 85.00
Pflueger "Sal Trout No. 1558" 25.00
Pflueger "Summit No. 1993L" 25.00
Pflueger "Supreme No. 1572," in pouch & box 30.00
Shakespeare "Model HG Automatic" fly reel 65.00
South Bend "Model D Automatic" ... 65.00
South Bend "No. 1150" spinning reel, Bakelite 15.00
Winchester Repeating Arms Co. "No. 2726" 95.00

RODS
Orvis "Battenkill" fly rod, bamboo, serial No. 70, 355, one tip, 3 7/8 oz., HDG/6 line, original cloth rod sack & metal rod tube, 7½' l. 750.00
Shapleigh "Diamond Brand" fly rod, split bamboo 55.00
Simmons (E.C.) fly rod, steel 79.00

MISCELLANEOUS
Bait box, "Cole's Wisconsin Bobbet," belt-mounted, revolving-type, "One turn & there's your worm" 25.00
License, button-type, 1945, Pennsylvania, resident, 1½" d. 25.00
Tackle box, mahogany w/brass corners, hardware & screws, two lift-out trays, ca. 1920's, 10 x 12 x 20" 350.00

Tackle box, metal w/leather handle,
Sherman-Klover 25.00

FOOT & BED WARMERS

Bed warmer, brass pan w/engraved
flowers & bird on the cover,
turned cherry handle, 42½" l. (old
repair to pan) $357.50

Bed warmer, brass pan w/tooled
floral & peacock design on cover,
turned wood handle, 43" l 357.50

Bed warmer, brass pan w/pierced
scattered holes & an engraved
rooster on the cover, long turned
cherry handle, 44½" l. 440.00

Bed warmer, brass & wrought iron,
brass pan, the circular lid decorated w/a flower & heart design,
tapering wrought-iron heart-
pierced handle, 43½" l. 715.00

Bed warmer, copper pan w/a brass
lid & a long turned wood handle,
the lid decorated w/a punched
design of a basket of flowers, old
brown graining on the handle,
43½" l. 330.00

Bed warmer, tin pan & cover
w/brass trim, long turned wood-
en handle w/old black paint,
42½" l. 82.50

Foot warmer, mahogany & tin, rectangular wooden frame w/tin top
& sides pierced in a pattern of
hearts & dots, the front similarly
pierced & sliding up to reveal a
metal container for coals, Victori-
an, 19th c., 10½" h. 440.00

Foot warmer, pottery, white embossed w/a leaf design around
the filler hole, overhead bail handle, marked "Goodwill's Bed &
Foot Warmer - and Water Carrier
- Pat. Aug. 20, 1895" 98.00

Foot warmer, tin & wood, butternut
frame w/turned corner posts
w/old worn patina, tin panels
punched w/concentric rings & a
center & corner small diamonds,
branded "W.P.," 19th c., 7½ x 9",
5¾" h. 220.00

Foot warmer, tin & wood, mortised
wooden frame w/turned corner
posts framing the tin sides & top
punched w/diamond & circle designs, old patina, w/interior pan,
large size, 14 x 14", 8" h. 440.00

Foot warmer, tole & wood, a square
flat wooden top above the tole
case w/worn brown japanning & a
gilt-stenciled lyre design, a square

wooden base w/chamfered edges,
19th c., 7½" sq. 93.50

Foot warmer, walnut & tin, mortised
frame w/turned corner posts,
punched tin panels w/hearts &
circles, old finish, 7½ x 9", 6" h.
(wear, old break in one post) 225.00

FOOT & BOOT SCRAPERS

Early Wrought-Iron Boot Scraper

Cast iron, double griffin-form, 13" l.,
9 1/8" h. $275.00

Cast iron, lyre-shaped, on base 60.00

Wrought iron, model of a silhouetted black cat walking on a narrow
rectangular base, long rod tail angled up & curved up near tip,
17¾" l. 302.50

Wrought iron, ram's horn style w/a
wide crossbar w/half-round openings at the ends & along the bottom edge & three smaller holes in
the center, 19th c., 13" w. 275.00

Wrought iron, the sides w/tall tight
double scrolls flanking the curved
wide scraper blade & mounted in
a weathered white stone rectan-
gular block, 15" h. 385.00

Wrought iron, a pair of tall curved
bars terminating in double forked
scrolls, joined near the base w/a
heavy stepped bar, the tips set in
a heavy block base, 23½" w.,
20½" h. (ILLUS.) 770.00

FOX (R. Atkinson) PRINTS

*Robert Atkinson Fox (1860-1935) was an
American artist whose prolific output included romantic landscapes, mountain scenes and
portraits of domestic livestock & wildlife.
Many of his paintings were reproduced as
popular prints early in this century. Today
these prints are increasingly collectible
thanks in great part to the well-researched series of articles written by Rita Mortenson for*

The Antique Trader Weekly *beginning in 1980. This series then led to her 1985 book,* R. Atkinson Fox, His Life and Work *(Wallace-Homestead). The numbers accompanying our listings are those assigned by Mrs. Mortenson in her works.*

CALENDARS
1927, w/print entitled "When Evening Shadows Fall" $150.00
1928, w/print entitled "When the Day is Done," 3½ x 5½" 50.00

PRINTS
"The Artist Supreme," No. 360, framed, 8 x 10" 135.00
"Blooming Time," No. 37, framed, 14 x 18" 95.00
"Blue Lake," No. 5, framed, 14 x 20" 45.00
"By a Waterfall," No. 144, framed, 7 x 10" 40.00
"Dawn," No. 1, framed, 10 x 18" . . .   80.00
"Elysian Fields," No. 70, framed, 16 x 20" 85.00
"English Garden," No. 57, framed, 10 x 14" 35.00
"Fallen Monarch, (A)," No. 98, framed, 9 x 12" 100.00
"Glorious Vista," No. 6, framed, 15½ x 20" 38.00
"Haven of Beauty," No. 204, framed, 18 x 30" 90.00
"Hunter's Paradise," No. 197, framed, 15 x 17" 85.00
"Indian Summer," No. 35, framed, 20½ x 32½" 150.00
"Memories of Childhood Days," No. 305, w/verse, framed, 9 x 12" 74.00
"Midsummer Magic," No. 8, framed, 8 x 12" 40.00
"Promenade," No. 185, framed, 8 x 12" 30.00
"Spirit of Youth," No. 4, framed, 12 x 20" 475.00
"Sunrise," No. 30, framed, 17½ x 22" 95.00
"Venetian Garden," No. 7, framed, 14 x 18" 45.00

FRAKTUR
Fraktur paintings are decorative birth and marriage certificates of the 18th and 19th centuries and also include family registers and similar documents. Illuminated family documents, birth and baptismal certificates, religious texts and rewards of merit, in a particular style, are known as "fraktur" because of the similarity to the 16th century type-face of that name. Gay water-color borders, frequently incorporating stylized birds, angels, animals or flowers, surrounded the hand-lettered documents, which were executed by local ministers, school masters or itinerant penmen. Most are of Pennsylvania Dutch origin.

Early 19th Century Birth Record

Birth & baptism certificate, pen & ink & water-color on wove paper, a large rectangular panel at the bottom below half-round scalloped below arched bands of leafy sprigs w/large flowerheads, a narrow running vine border, in shades of red, yellow, green, blue & black, the panel enclosing the ink inscription "Certificate of Birth and Christening for Samuel Creger, One leg township, Tuscarawas County, 1824," Ohio, unframed, 7½" w., 12½" h. (edge damage, fold lines, center tear at fold, minor wear & water damage) $2,310.00
Birth & baptism certificate for Phebe Beamer, pen & ink & water-color, colorful stylized flowers & vines frame rectangular blocks w/inscriptions, inscribed "Certificate of Birth & Christening... Phebe Beamer, born March 22, 1815 in Tuscarawas County, Ohio," in old molded walnut frame, 10¼ x 15" (some stains & fading, paper creases & tears) 2,100.00
Birth letter for Salome Holtzmann, water-color & pen & ink & graphite on wove paper, angels w/cornucopia of flowers at upper corners, flower filled vases in lower corners, oval wreaths at top, bottom & sides around a central shaped reserve, all containing various inscriptions, signed & dated "Carl Munch A.D. 1810" at center, framed, 15" w., 12½" h. . . . 55,000.00

Birth record for Margaret Green, water-color & pen & ink on wove paper, English script birth statistics flanked by red, yellow & blue stylized stars above a figure of a young woman wearing a red dress, holding a basket & a spray of flowers, her hair fixed w/a tortoise shell comb, flanked by birds & flowers, also in shades of red, yellow & blue, by Reverend Henry Young, Lycoming County, Pennsylvania, ca. 1822, unframed, 8¾ x 10 3/8" (ILLUS.) 7,480.00

Birth record for Jacob Becter, water-color & pen & ink on laid paper, a wide border design composed of blocks w/compass stars & other geometric devices in orange, yellow & olive green, lengthy German inscription in the center, Pennsylvania, 1814, in beveled curly maple frame, 14 x 17¾" (acid ink holes in border). 1,320.00

Book plate, pen & ink & water-color on paper, a large tulip on a tall slender leafy stem flanked by two leafy stems w/small tulip blossoms at one end & petaled blossoms at the other, done in red, blue, green, black & yellow, dated "1827," framed, 5¾ x 8 5/8" (edge damage, tears & stains) . . .1,375.00

Drawing, water-color & pen & ink on brown paper, a pair of facing birds on long-leaved vines w/blossoms, dated "Anno 1793," Pennsylvania, framed, 7 3/8 x 11 5/8" (stains) 880.00

Vorschrift, pen & ink & water-color on paper, rectangular, the top w/a banner & leafy vine beside a pair of facing birds at the center above the large name "Joseph Hahm" above inscriptions in German script, leafy vines & strapwork trim, done in red, yellow & black, by Johann Adam Eyer, Pennsylvania, ca. 1800, framed, 7¾ x 10¾" 2,090.00

FRAMES

Bronze, rectangular, Zodiac patt., impressed "TIFFANY STUDIOS - NEW YORK - 942," 1899-1928, 7 1/8 x 8¼" $880.00

Bronze & glass, wide rectangular border w/mottled green glass overlaid w/a pierced maple leaf design w/a greenish brown pati-na, beaded border band, stamped "TIFFANY STUDIOS NEW YORK" & w/company monogram, early 20th c., 7¼" h. 935.00

Cherry, Empire style, rectangular w/square corner blocks joined by simple ring-turned half-round colonettes along the sides, old red paint, America, ca. 1840, 12¾ x 16½" 423.50

Curly maple, flat rectangular sides w/small corner blocks, old varnish finish, mid-19th c., 7 x 8¾" 275.00

Decorated pine, 1½" w. flat molding decorated w/original brown flame graining, 19th c., 14¾ x 16½", pr. 209.00

Gilded plaster, molded w/acanthus leaf & helix designs surrounded by a ribbed cove & laurel design & w/a lunette-shaped liner, American-made, 19th c., 24¼ x 30½" (minuscule losses) . .1,210.00

Gilded plaster, a laurel leaf design surrounded by lozenges & ribs w/foliate designs, American-made, 19th c., inner dimensions 35½ x 43" (minor losses, regilded) 275.00

Gilded plaster, molded w/grotesque figures, lozenges & ribs against a foliage ground, Europe, 19th c., inside dimensions 40 x 48¾" (scattered losses) 110.00

Early Gilded Plaster Frame

Gilded plaster, molded w/a wide band of acanthus leaves around the ogee outer border, Europe, late 18th - early 19th c., minor losses to gilding & plaster, inner dimensions 34½ x 56¾" (ILLUS. of part) 935.00

Gilded wood, carved at the flaring corners w/scrolled leaves & small blossom clusters, thin beaded out-

Carved & Gilded Frame

er band & thin leaf-carved liner,
American-made, late 19th - early
20th c., minor losses, inner
dimensions 65 x 106" (ILLUS. of
part) 1,100.00
Gilt-bronze & champleve', rectangular, each side decorated w/a rectangular panel of champleve'
enamel, similar roundels at each
corner, 12½" w., 8¾" h. 4,600.00

Art Nouveau Mahogany Frame

Mahogany, Art Nouveau style,
shaped rectangle carved w/un-
dulating whiplash designs, Louis
Majorelle, France, ca. 1900,
33 x 39½" (ILLUS.) 5,500.00
Oak, Modern style, rectangular, the
sides each composed of two slender bars joined by short criss-
cross corners, stained finish,
designed by Gerrit Rietveld, ca.
1920, 32 5/8 x 44½" 7,700.00
Painted & decorated pine, wide
beveled sides w/original red &
black graining & faded yellow
stenciled decoration, 19th c.,
14¼ x 17¼" 137.50

Poplar, rectangular, old black
paint, 1 5/8" w. beveled molding,
14¼ x 18¼"................... 55.00
Walnut, rectangular, old finish, 2" w. beveled molding,
13¾ x 17¼"................... 38.50
Wood marquetry, "marqueterie de
paille" (straw-style) design, rectangular w/wide flat sides & an
angled edge band, overall design
of diamonds & triangles, by Jean-
Michel Frank, early 20th c.,
17½ x 24" 7,475.00
Wrought iron, rectangular, wrought
w/stylized ivy leaves, berries &
scrolling tendrils at the top, raised
on triple ball feet, w/scroll-ended
back support, impressed "E.
BRANDT," Edgar Brandt, ca. 1925,
8 5/8 x 13 3/8"................3,163.00

FRATERNAL ORDER COLLECTIBLES

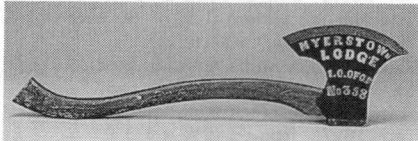

Odd Fellows Fire Ax

B.P.O.E. (Benevolent & Protective
Order of Elks) pillowcase, embroidered elk...................... $15.00
B.P.O.E. pinback button, "Elks Carnival, Fulton, NY, Aug. 1914,"
w/picture of elk on clock dial 22.00
B.P.O.E. watch fob, 1929 membership certificate in sterling silver
case 50.00
Eastern Star ring, gold (10k), emblem in black enamel 56.00
F.O.E. (Fraternal Order of Eagles)
auto radiator badge, enameled
metal, ca. 1920's 35.00
F.O.E. doorstop, cast iron, model of
an eagle, 1917, 8 x 10" 75.00
G.A.R. (Grand Army of the Republic) flask, silver & copper, souvenir of the 26th Grand Annual
Encampment, 1892 .... 275.00
G.A.R. lapel button, brass, ca.
1894 .... 55.00
G.A.R. medal, 34th Annual Encampment, 1900, Gettysburg, two-
piece, heavily embossed copper
w/cannons, battle scene, bust
portrait & portrait of officer on
horseback, on red ribbon 25.00
G.A.R. paperweight, cast iron, model of an officer's hat............ 45.00

I.O.O.F. (Independent Order of Odd
Fellows) book, "Journal of
Proceedings of the Sovern Lodge,"
1925, paperback 22.00

I.O.O.F. book, "Proceedings of the
Grand Lodge of Kansas," 1925,
paperback 10.00

I.O.O.F. fire ax, the handle grain-
painted, the wooden blade painted black w/gilt hand holding a
heart on one side & inscription
"Myerstown Lodge - I.O.O.F. of
No. 358," Myerstown, Pennsylva-
nia, 19th c., 33½" l. (ILLUS.) 1,100.00

I.O.O.F. souvenir spoon, Springfield,
Ohio home in bowl, engraved
monogram & dated "10/27/98" ... 30.00

I.O.O.F. trivet, brass, three circles,
hand & heart in center, 5¼ x 8".. 78.00

Masonic apron, printed silk, signed
"Published by Louis Roberson,
Wethersfield, Vt.," bound in rose
silk ribbon, ca. 1825, 13½ x 16"
(foxing) 192.50

Masonic blanket, orange & gold,
palm tree & camel top & bottom,
emblem in center, 48 x 75" 235.00

Masonic books, "Encyclopedia of
Freemasonry," by Mackey, 1920,
2 vols. 50.00

Masonic collar box, gutta percha,
patent dated 1877 .... 125.00

Coverlet with Masonic Designs

Masonic coverlet, Jacquard-type, the
center w/six large leaf & blossom
clusters alternating w/four-petal
florettes, star clusters above pairs
of eagles flanking Masonic emblems around the border, corner
blocks inscribed "Agriculture &
Manufactures Are The Foundation
of Our Independence - July 4,
1827 - Gnrl. LaFayette," & signed
along ends "McGuernsey," blue &

white, imperfections, 78 x 96"
(ILLUS.)....................... 715.00

Masonic Frame & Certificates

Masonic frame & certificates, the
wooden frame ornately pierce-
carved w/an arched top w/vari-
ous Masonic symbols above an
arched opening flanked by
columns, further carved emblems
across the bottom, gilt liner, holds
Masonic certificates of Amos
Galloupe, 1865, & Elias A. Galloupe, 1872, ca. 1870's, 22 x 31"
(ILLUS.)....................... 935.00

Masonic paperweight, sulphide, emblem against blue background,
late 19th - early 20th c........... 115.00

Masonic sundial, bronze & stone,
bronze dial mounted on an octagonal pedestal carved w/Ma-
sonic & Eastern Star emblems,
29½" h....................... 550.00

Early Masonic Textile

Masonic textile, copper-printed
white linen, printed in red w/a
wide variety of Masonic symbols,
w/paper label describing owners, late 18th - early 19th c.,
22½ x 24" (ILLUS.)............. 2,588.00

Masonic watch, open-face pocket-
type, sterling silver, triangular

case w/embossed chain border, the mother-of-pearl dial w/various symbols in place of numerals & "Love Your Fellow Man, Lend Him A Helping Hand" across the bottom, 15-jewel movement, three adjustments, Tempor W. Co., G. Schwab-Loeille 2,200.00

Masonic watch, open-face pocket-type, 19-jewel, brushed metal dial w/Arabic numerals & subsidiary dial for seconds, Masonic cut-out backplate, Serial No. 547, Dudley Watch Co., Lancaster, Pennsylvania 1,650.00

Masonic watch fob, black w/gold emblem insert 75.00

Shrine champagne, glass, "New Orleans - Syria," alligator on each side, 1910, 4½" h. 85.00

Shrine goblet, clear glass, "Los Angeles," 1907 .... 95.00

Shrine tie tack, gold (14k) w/diamonds 95.00

Shrine tumbler, glass, "Steering Over the Hot Sands to Dallas," 1898 .... 110.00

FRUIT JARS

Excelsior Fruit Jar

Adams & Co. Manufacturers, Pittsburgh, PA., pressed laid-on ring, stopper neck finished for glass stopper, aqua...................$525.00

American Fruit Jar, embossed eagle & flag, ground lip, glass lid & metal screw, light green, qt. 100.00

Atherholt, Fisher & Co., Philada, tapering neck finished for stopper or cork, aqua, qt. 300.00

Atlas E-Z Seal, amber, qt............ 35.00

Ball Ideal on front, Bi-centennial Celebration medallion & "Made in the U.S.A." on the reverse, aqua, qt.................................. 12.00

Ball (The) Pat. Apl'd For, aqua, qt... 300.00

Belle, Pat. Dec. 14th 1869, three raised feet, dome-shaped glass lid, wire bail w/ends fitting into a metal band around the neck of jar, aqua, qt. 750.00

Bloeser Jar, ground lip, glass lid, wire & metal clamp, aqua, qt..... 180.00

Buckeye - 2, deep aqua, ½ gal. 150.00

Burnham (C.) & Co., Manufacturers, PhilaDa, ground lip, iron lid w/gutta percha insert, aqua, pt... 600.00

Champion Syrup & Refining Co. - Indianapolis, ground lip, shoulder seal, aqua, qt. 30.00

Conserve Jar, ground lip, glass lid & wire clamp, clear, pt. 20.00

Dandy (The), clear, qt. 27.00

Dodge Sweeney & Co's, California Butter, ground lip, glass insert & screw band, product jar, aqua, 1½ qt. ....325.00 to 425.00

Excelsior, tapering sides, aqua, qt., 7¼" h. (ILLUS.) 33.00

Excelsior, w/basket of fruit, aqua, qt............................. 575.00

Flaccus Bros. Steers Head Fruit Jar (steer's head), bright green, pt. .. 775.00

Flaccus Bros. Steers Head Fruit Jar (steer's head), milk white, pt.....................200.00 to 245.00

Flaccus (E.C.) Co. - Trade Mark (stag's head), green, pt. 825.00

Flaccus (E.C.) Co. - Trade Mark (stag's head), milk white, pt...... 400.00

Franklin Fruit Jar, ground lip, unlined zinc lid w/two horizontal prongs on top, aqua, midget 220.00

GJCo monogram (Gilchrist Jar Co.), unlined aluminum lid marked "The Keystone Jar," aqua, qt. 20.00

Globe, amber, pt..........85.00 to 125.00

Globe, amber, qt.........50.00 to 60.00

Haine's 3 Patent March 1st 1870, glass lid w/wire clamp, aqua, qt. 80.00

Haller (Mrs. G.E.) Patd. Feb. 25. 73, glass stopper, aqua, pt. 275.00

Hansee's - Palace Home Jar, monogrammed "PH," ground lip, glass straddle-lid top seal, closed by lever w/fulcrum in wire bail, green, pt. 125.00

Howe (The) Jar - Scranton, PA, Pat. Feby,28/88 on glass lid, wire clamp, aqua, qt. ....50.00 to 60.00

Johnson & Johnson, New York, ground lip, smooth base, screw band, cobalt blue, qt. 325.00

Kinney (J.T.) between "Manufactured For" & "Trenton, N.J.," aqua, qt. 145.00

Kline - Patent Oct. 27 1863, glass stopper, aqua, qt. 20.00

Knowlton Vacuum (star) Fruit Jar, glass top & perforated zinc cover, glass insert marked "Knowlton Vacuum Pat'd May 1903," aqua, pt. 34.00

Lafayette in script, glass & metal stopper, aqua, qt. 125.00

Leader (The), glass lid & two-piece wire clamp, amber, ½ gal. 100.00

Lee (J. Ellwood) Co., Conshohocken, PA. U.S.A., ground lip, glass insert & metal screw, amber, qt. ... 120.00

Lightning below arched "Trade Mark," medium olive yellow, pt... 350.00

Lightning Trade Mark Putnam Reg. U.S. Pat. Off. (on base), glass lid & wire clamp, amber, 1½ pt. 85.00

Lightning below arched "Trade Mark," medium olive yellow, qt... 185.00

Lorillard (P.) Co., glass insert & wire clamp, amber, qt. 25.00

Magic (The) Fruit Jar, embossed star, ground lip, metal lid & yoke clamp, aqua, pt. 300.00

Mason's 8 Patent, smooth lip, Mason shoulder seal, aqua, midget pt. ... 175.00

Mason's Fruit Jar (two lines), medium amber, pt. 150.00

Mason's Improved Trade Mark - CFJCo., light yellow green, midget pt. 110.00

Mason's (cross) Patent Nov. 30th 1858, w/zinc lid, amber, qt. ....85.00 to 95.00

Mason's 7 Patent, Nov 30th 1858, ground lip, Mason shoulder seal, unlined zinc lid, aqua, qt. 325.00

Mason's Patent Nov. 30th, 1858, smooth base, ground lip, zinc lid, medium olive green, midget pt...1,150.00

Mason's Patent Nov 30th 1858 - CFJCo, ground lip, Mason shoulder seal, zinc lid, medium yellow green w/deeper color striations throughout, midget pt. 1,400.00

M C Co. 3, groove ring wax sealer, pressed laid-on ring, amber, qt. ... 100.00

McMechens Always the Best Old Virginia, Wheeling, W. V. (in circle), clear, pt. 130.00

Millville Atmospheric Fruit Jar, aqua, ½ gal. 130.00

Mission Mason Jar, embossed bell w/trade name & "Made in California," clear, qt. 12.00

Moore (John M.) & Co. - Manufacturers - Fislerville N.J. - Patented Dec 3d 1861, glass lid & iron yoke clamp w/thumbscrew, aqua, ½ gal. 185.00

Peerless, glass lid & iron yoke clamp, lid marked "Patented Feb. 13, 1863," aqua, qt. 100.00

Peerless Brand Mocha & Java Coffee

- M.S. Ayer & Co. - Wholesale Grocers Boston Mass. U.S.A., zinc screw lid, amber, qt. 45.00

Potter & Bodine, Philadelphia, ground lip, metal lid w/soldered wire clamp, aqua, ½ gal........ 150.00

Protector, paneled, aqua, ½ gal. ... 50.00

Retentive, aqua, qt. 250.00

Royal, base embossed "Pat. Feb. 27, 1877," ground lip, glass insert & screw band, black, qt. 3,250.00

Royal, unmarked glass lid & zinc collar, Pat. June 9 63 stamped into the metal, aqua, qt. 100.00

Royal of 1876, ground lip, glass insert & screw band, clear w/amethyst tint, qt. 180.00

Safety Valve Patd May 21, 1895 w/monogram (on base), glass lid w/metal band clamp, light apple green, ½ gal. 65.00

Star (above star emblem) Pat'd Feb 5 1867 (on base), ground lip, smooth base, zinc insert & screw band, aqua, qt. 300.00

A. Stone Philada, E.T. Whitehead, correct hollow stopper, rather light embossing, aqua, qt.....................650.00 to 675.00

Telephone (The) Jar Trademark Reg. Whitney Glass Works, glass lid w/wire, cornflower blue, pt. 30.00

Van Vliet (The) Jar of 1881, ground lip, glass lid, aqua, qt. 425.00

Wan-eta Cocoa Boston, glass lid w/twin clamps, clear, qt. 25.00

Whitmore's Patent Rochester, N.Y., ground lip, glass lid w/wire bail, ground lip, smooth bottom, aqua, qt. 425.00

B.B. Wilcox Fruit Jar

Wilcox (B.B.) - 8 - (below arched) Pat'd March 26th 1867, ground mouth, aqua green, qt., 8¼" h. (ILLUS.)........................ 49.50

Yeoman's Fruit Bottle, waxed cork closure, aqua, qt. 40.00

Special Focus: Furniture   by Connie Morningstar

Revival Style Furniture
of the Early 20th Century

It was the Golden Age of Furniture—that era between the Great War and the Great Depression. The world was changing around them but on the homefront the newly affluent clung to the traditional.

So it was that their bungalows, Georgians, Tudors, and the award-winning Dutch Colonials were likely to be furnished with 20th-century versions of Elizabethan, pine Puritan, Spanish Renaissance, or Phyfe. Some manufacturers turned out licensed reproductions of museum pieces. A few, notably Wallace Nutting, meticulously copied the originals. Most, however, took great liberties with style, combining and interpreting features to their liking and calling everything "Colonial." Now these mass-produced but well made pieces, some of them pushing eighty, have taken on the patina of age and have moved from thrift shops to antiques galleries where they are modestly priced. Look for them also at estate sales.

While just about every furniture style theretofore known was produced in the early 20th century, most Period reproductions fall into the categories that follow:

Italian Renaissance (1443-1564). This revival of classical Greek and Roman formal styles accentuated architectural lines—heavy, low, and rectangular. The principal wood was walnut. Chairs might have X-shaped bases (Savanarola), curule (Roman), or straight legs ending on runners. Favored upholstery was crimson velvet with gold fringe, tassels, and nails. Leather was used also. By the late 1920's, it was recommended that this furniture be used with restraint and only in homes of Mediterranean architecture.

Spanish Renaissance (1500-1650). Arches, spindles, and scrolls are characteristic of this Moorish-inspired style. Various woods were used including walnut, oak, cedar, and pine. Wrought-iron braces reinforced splay-legged tables and benches. The most distinctive piece was the *vargueno*, a dropfront desk that rested on a chest or trestle stand. High-backed chairs had arched crests and notched finials. Low-backed chairs had upholstered backs and straight tops. Much gold embroidery and gold fringe were used on red or green velvet. Studding with gilt nails was common. Ideal for the popular Spanish style homes of the 1920's, furniture of this persuasion was widely produced at that time.

Elizabethan (1558-1603). Heavy, melon-shaped turnings of legs and supports distinguish this old English style. Stretchers were placed close to the floor just above block or bun feet. Court (French for "short") cupboards were common. Oak was the principal wood and was given only a waxed finish. Dining suites prevailed during the 1920's with the court cupboard serving as a china cabinet. The trestle-base sofa table was introduced.

Jacobean (1660-1689). Originating during the reigns of English monarchs Charles II and James II, this style featured spiral-turned legs and applied decoration of split balusters and geometric moldings. The court cupboard continued to be popular with drawers replacing doors.

William and Mary (1688-1702). Half-Dutch

and half-English, this was a marriage of furniture styles as well as royalty. The style can be recognized by flat, often crossed, stretchers; inverted cup (trumpet) turnings on legs; arched aprons with pendants; and double arched tops on cabinets and settee backs. Marquetry, a Dutch style in floral and seaweed patterns, was brought to England at this time. Walnut was the favored wood; veneering began to be used extensively. High caned-back chairs (India), together with highboys and lowboys, came into general use. The secretary (desk-bookcase) evolved during this period. Its ease in manufacture made the William & Mary style admirably adapted to 20th-century production.

Queen Anne (1702-1714). A 1927 account noted, "No style of furniture has been more popularly used in modern reproductions than the Queen Anne. It is simple, home-like, and liveable with a charm all its own." The style's most distinctive characteristics are cabriole legs without stretchers; pad or slipper feet; solid, fiddle-shaped splats on chair backs; and cockle shell carvings. Walnut was the principal wood used originally; mahogany in reproductions.

Chippendale. Thomas Chippendale (1718-1779), a London cabinetmaker, was the first craftsman whose name became a style. His pattern book, *The Gentleman and Cabinet-Maker's Director*, published in 1754, was the source for the various designs that carry his name. Richly carved cabriole legs ending in ball-and-claw feet are indicative of the style. Pierced back splats always connect with the seatrail. Chinese Chippendale pieces have straight members interlaced or braced with geometric fretwork. Easily carved mahogany was used almost exclusively. Newport, Rhode Island, and Philadelphia were the principal centers for the production of this style during the 18th century in America. Often referred to now as "Centennial Chippendale," the style enjoyed a revival of sorts at the time of the Philadelphia Exhibition in 1876. Always expensive, 20th-century reproductions carried considerable snob appeal.

Hepplewhite. George Hepplewhite, a London cabinetmaker, died in 1786 and is known only for his designs in *The Cabinet-Maker and Upholsterer's Guide*, published posthumously. The style is evidenced by straight legs—squared, tapered, and ending in spade feet. Shield-shaped chair backs are characteristic. Serpentine fronts with convex centers and concave ends identify case pieces. Sideboards, as such, were introduced. Mahogany banded with light wood inlays was used frequently. The small scale of Hepplewhite furniture made reproductions ideal for the smaller rooms of the 20th century.

Sheraton. It is doubtful that Thomas Sheraton, an English designer and entrepreneur, actually made any furniture. His book, *The Cabinet-Maker and Upholsterer's Drawing Book*, published in 1790, inspired interpretations on both sides of the Atlantic. Case pieces with oxbow fronts (the reverse of Hepplewhite's) distinguish the style. Slender legs usually are rounded, reeded, and tapered. Flat arms characteristically curve forward from stile tops to supports, most of which are straight, vase-like forms, fluted or reeded. Drawer pulls often are lions' heads with ring handles. Mahogany was favored, often with light wood inlays.

Duncan Phyfe. Working between 1795 and 1820 in New York City, this Scottish immigrant was the first American cabinetmaker whose name became synonymous with a style. The lyre motif, pedestal tables with concave supports, and cornucopia legs are identifying features. Carving, particularly the acanthus leaf motif, was common. Brass paw mounts and lion head pulls were used extensively. Mahogany was the wood of choice. Beginning in the late 1920's, the style continued to be favored for some twenty years.

Louis XV. Called simply "French style" by manufacturers of this century, the curvy, feminine lines of this style originated during the profligate reign of Louis XV of France, 1715-1774. All lines curve; cabriole legs end in dolphin or peg feet; stretchers are absent. Luxurious fabrics were used for upholstery. Mahogany, walnut, and ebony were popular, often inlaid; and many pieces were lacquered or painted with white, gold, and pastels prevailing. The style was particularly suited for 20th-century bedrooms.

Louis XVI. Small, slender, straight-lined furniture was favored during the reign of this French monarch, 1774-1793. The style can be recognized by its straight, tapered, and fluted legs often flared or ringed at the knee. Feet are merely tapered endings of legs. Moldings are long and narrow; corners often broken. Mahogany was favored; soft woods were painted or gilded. Again, mostly bedroom pieces were reproduced.

And there were more. Windsors, furniture in the Country genre, Victorian and Empire (both French and American) were copied or interpreted, as well, in the 'Twenties and 'Thirties. Being aware of this is a big help in dating a piece. Always look for a label!

Among the more prominent manufacturers of that time were Berkey & Gay, Widdicomb, Johnson-Handley-Johnson, Grand Rapids Chair, Century, and Luce, all of Grand Rapids, Michigan; Baker of Holland, Michigan. In New York state were Kittinger, Buffalo; Elgin A. Simonds, Syracuse; and Erskine-Danforth, Richter, Flint & Horner, and Somma Shops in New York City. Conant-Ball was in Gardner, Massachusetts; Shaw in Cambridge. But the work of Wallace Nutting, alone, is collectible today in its own right. His factory functioned in Framingham, Massachusetts, from about 1917 until 1944. Of interest here is a Connecticut "Sunflower" chest (Jacobean) bearing the Nutting brand that sold at Sotheby's in 1990 for $5,775. Its 1932 catalog price was $375.

(EDITOR'S NOTE: *Connie Morningstar, a free-lance writer based in Salt Lake City, Utah, is the author of three books and numerous articles about American furniture. Her question-and-answer column, "All About Furniture," appears regularly in* The Antique Trader Weekly.)

PRICE LISTINGS:

ELIZABETHAN STYLE

Dining room suite: dining table w/self-stored leaves, two arm-chairs & four side chairs; oak, arched scroll-carved crests over solid veneered splats, upholstered seats, bulbous knobs on turned legs, 7 pcs. (ILLUS. of part) $1,100.00

Dining room suite: dining table, buf-fet, two armchairs & four side

chairs; oak, the chairs w/arched leaf-carved crest above an arched upholstered back, flat shaped arms on ring- and baluster-turned arm supports, upholstered seat, bulbous turned front legs, ca. 1915, 8 pcs. (ILLUS. of an arm-chair) 5,295.00

Dining room suite: dining table w/self-stored leaves, buffet, two armchairs, four side chairs; oak, chairs w/tapestry-upholstered seats & backs, 8 pcs. (Not Illus-trated) 5,295.00

Dining room suite: extension dining table, court cupboard, buffet, one armchair & five side chairs; oak, chairs w/Gothic arch crestrails flanked by scrolled ears over a flat arch-carved splat, upholstered slip seat, bulbous knob-turned front legs, 9 pcs. (ILLUS. of a side chair) 6,295.00

Dining room suite: dining table w/two skirted leaves, buffet, chi-na cabinet, one armchair & five side chairs; oak, the chairs w/arched & pierce-carved crest-rails over pierce-carved vase splats over upholstered seats, bul-

bous knob-turned front legs,
9 pcs. (ILLUS. of part) 3,800.00

JACOBEAN STYLE

Dining table, drop-leaf type, walnut,
a rectangular top flanked by two
wide D-form drop leaves above a
shaped apron, baluster- and ring-
turned legs w/two swing-out gate
legs. 225.00

Library or sofa table, hardwood,
rectangular long top above a
paneled apron w/a long, narrow
center drawer w/brass pulls,
spiral-turned legs joined by spiral-
turned stretchers 225.00

Side cabinet, oak, rectangular top
above a pair of cupboard doors

w/a shaped rectangular panel
over a double arch panel, on bun
feet, paneled sides 2,800.00

Side table, oak, round top w/in-
cised scroll-carved border band,
baluster- and spiral-turned legs
joined by arched stretchers, knob
feet, 20" d., 20" h. 189.00

SPANISH RENAISSANCE STYLE

Desk, oak, flat-top style w/double
pedestal, eight legs joined by
cross stretchers, five drawers,
w/label of Salvador Franco (Not
Illustrated) 475.00

Side chairs, oak, arched & lightly incised crestrail flanked by small
ears over two slender turned
spindles in the raised back, upholstered slip seat, ring- and
baluster-turned front legs,
H-stretcher, labeled by the
Thomasville Chair Co., ca. 1927,
set of 4 (ILLUS. of one) 160.00

WILLIAM & MARY STYLE

Dining room suite: dining table
w/six leaves, one armchair & five
side chairs; hardwood, the chairs
w/shaped crestrails over swelled
back splats & lower back rails,

upholstered slip seat, bulbous knob-turned front legs, labeled by the Abernathy Furniture Co., stripped & refinished, 7 pcs. (ILLUS. of part) 1,750.00

Sideboard, hardwood, a low beaded crestrail on the rectangular top w/molded edges above a pair of paneled cupboard doors flanking two long, deep drawers, all w/teardrop pulls, scalloped apron above four bulbous-turned front legs joined by shaped stretchers, labeled by the Abernathy Furniture Co. (retail price) 749.00

Sideboard, walnut & walnut veneer, low crestrail w/a scroll-carved center crest above the rectangular top w/molded edges over a lappet-carved band above a pair of small drawers over cupboard doors w/arched panels flanking a long narrow drawer over a long deep

drawer, scroll-carved apron on bulbous knob-turned legs joined by scroll-carved stretchers, metal pulls (auction price) 132.00

Side chairs, hardwood, arched crest over a caned back panel flanked by baluster-turned stiles topped by knob finials, upholstered slip seat above block- and baluster-turned legs joined by a turned front stretcher, set of 3 (ILLUS. of one) 175.00

QUEEN ANNE STYLE

Cedar chest, mahogany finish, rectangular lift top opening to a deep well, the front of the case w/four false drawers above a medial molding & a true long drawer, scalloped apron w/shell carved at center, on short cabriole legs ending in pad feet, brass batwing pulls, Lane Company label 150.00

Highboy, maple & tiger stripe maple veneer, bonnet-top style w/a broken arch crest w/urn-turned finials above four long graduated drawers above a medial molding

over a long narrow drawer above
two deep drawers flanking a
shell-carved panel, scroll-cut
apron, simple cabriole front legs
ending in pad feet, brass batwing
pulls, ca. 1920, 30" w., 6' h. 2,985.00

Queen Anne-Style Rocking Chair

Queen Anne-Style Settee

Lowboy, mahogany, rectangular top
w/molded edge above a long
drawer over three deep drawers,
the center one shell-carved,
carved drops in the apron, on
cabriole legs ending in pad feet,
brass batwing pulls, label of the
Bartley Collection, Ltd............ 550.00

Rocking chair without arms, mahogany finish, gently arched crestrail over a simple vase splat
above the seat w/a square caned
panel, simple cabriole front legs
on rockers, H-stretcher, label of
the Stomps-Burkhart Co. (ILLUS.
top next column) 110.00

Settee, walnut, a shaped crestrail
continuing to rounded corners
continuing to shaped sides around
the upholstered back, outswept
arms on S-form arm supports
above the upholstered seat, simple cabriole front legs ending in
pad feet (ILLUS. next column) 1,395.00

Tea table, mahogany, rectangular
rimmed top above apron w/pull-
out end candle shelves, scalloped
border continuing to simple cabriole legs ending in pad feet, made
by Kittinger..................... 335.00

Wingchair, slightly arched crestrail
above outswept wings & arms,
cabriole legs ending in pad feet,

joined by a turned H-stretcher, bold crewel upholstery 485.00

CHIPPENDALE STYLE

Coffee table, mahogany finish, Chinese Chippendale-Style, rectangular top w/narrow rope-carved border above the apron w/beaded edges & pierced corner brackets, flat band-incised chamfered legs w/block feet................... 125.00

Console extension table, mahogany, rectangular top above apron w/false drawer, cabriole front legs w/carved knees & ball-and-webbed claw feet, straight back legs (Not Illustrated) 295.00

Dumbwaiter (two-tier stand), mahogany veneer, two graduated round tops w/dot-and-dash-carved edges joined by a leaf-carved baluster-turned support, on a columnar pedestal w/turned knob above the tripod base w/cabriole legs w/loop-carved knees & leaf-carved snake feet, 22" d., 30" h........................ 225.00

Highboy, mahogany, bonnet-top type w/broken arch top w/carved florette terminals & flame-carved finials above two small drawers flanking a large patera-carved center drawer above four long graduated drawers over a medial molding above a pair of drawers over three small, deep drawers, the center one shell-carved, shaped apron, cabriole legs ending in claw-and-ball feet, batwing brasses 7,800.00

"Rent" table, walnut, round top above an apron w/false drawers, baluster- and knob-turned pedestal above four cabriole legs w/acanthus-carved knees & claw-and-ball feet, 26" h............. 395.00

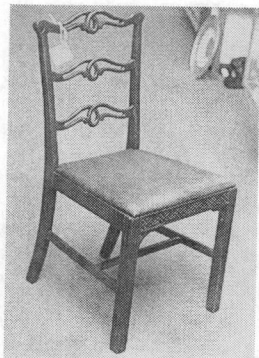

Side chair, ladder-back style, mahogany, three arched "pretzel-carved" slats above the plastic upholstered slip seat, lattice-carved seatrail, square reeded front legs, H-stretcher, label of J.B. Van Sciver Co., Camden, New Jersey 45.00

Side chair, mahogany, shaped crestrail above a pierce-carved splat above the needlepoint-upholstered slip seat, shell-carved front seatrail, cabriole front legs w/shell-carved knees & claw-and-ball feet........................ 295.00

Side table, Chinese Chippendale, mahogany, a rectangular top

w/glass insert above a pierced lattice-carved apron, pierced corner blocks on square paneled legs w/block feet.................... 115.00

HEPPLEWHITE STYLE

Chest of drawers, mahogany, rectangular top w/oxbow front above conforming case w/five long graduated drawers w/stamped brass oval pulls, shaped apron & French feet, label of Hallmark Quality Furniture 398.00

China cabinet, mahogany, the upper section w/two eight-paned cupboard doors opening to three shelves, the lower section w/three drawers w/brass ring pulls, on bracket feet (Not Illustrated) 500.00

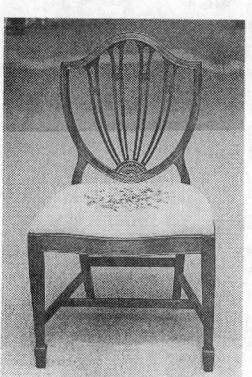

Dining room suite: Phyfe-style drop-leaf dining table, one armchair & five side chairs; mahogany, each chair w/a shield back w/four slender pierced splats above a needlepointed slip seat, square tapering front legs ending in spade feet, H-stretchers, 7 pcs. (ILLUS. of one chair) 1,529.00

Dining room suite: Phyfe-style double-pedestal extension dining table, two armchairs & four side chairs; mahogany, each shield-back chair w/a shaped pierced splat w/a central carved urn, upholstered slip seat, square tapering legs, H-stretchers, 7 pcs. (ILLUS. of one chair) 900.00

Server, mahogany, rectangular top w/three-quarter gallery & gently swelled front above a conforming case w/a long narrow drawer above a double-faced deep drawer for silver, on square tapering legs, round brass pulls & keyhole escutcheons 250.00
Side chair, mahogany, shield-back w/wheat sheaf-carved splat, upholstered slip seat (Not Illustrated) 75.00

SHERATON STYLE

Armchair, mahogany, a square upholstered back, slender square arms on fluted columnar arm supports, upholstered seat on molded seatrail, round tapering fluted legs (ILLUS. top next column) 225.00

Sheraton-Style Armchair

Chairs, mahogany, armchair w/flat line-incised crestrail above a pierced lattice slat flanked by gently curved reeded stiles, S-curved reeded arms on turned urn-form arm supports, upholstered seat, rod- and ring-turned tapering front legs, one armchair & four side chairs, 5 pcs. (ILLUS. of armchair) 1,995.00

Sideboard, walnut veneer, low crestrail w/broken-scroll center section w/urn finial above the rectangular top w/molded edges above a reeded frieze band over

a pair of large paneled cupboard
doors flanking a long narrow
drawer over a deep drawer w/a
shaped apron, reeded & roundel
trim, baluster-turned reeded
legs 750.00

DUNCAN PHYFE STYLE

Coffee table, walnut, oval rimmed
top on a short urn-form leaf-
carved pedestal on four downswept leaf-carved legs ending in
brass paw caps, branded "Mers-
man Tables" 195.00
Coffee table, mahogany, rectangular
glass-lined tray top, acanthus-
carved pedestal, downswept
legs w/brass paw caps (Not Illus-
trated) 80.00

Dining suite: triple-pedestal drop-
leaf dining table & four side
chairs; mahogany, the chairs
w/plain curved crests above
swag-carved slats, over-upholstered seats, reeded sabre front
legs, 5 pcs. (ILLUS. of part) 498.00
Dining table, mahogany, extension-
type, drop-leaf ends & three
leaves, raised on a triple pedestal
base w/downswept legs ending in
brass paw caps (Not Illustrated) . . 126.50
Drum table, revolving, burled walnut veneer, round top above
six open sections, three w/top
arches, round base raised on
short pedestal w/four downswept
reeded legs ending in brass paw
caps 485.00

Games table, mahogany, rectangular top above an apron w/a single
drawer, lyre-form base w/down-
swept legs ending in brass paw
caps, labeled "Mersman Tables"
(Not Illustrated) 192.50

Side chair, mahogany, plain crestrail
above a lyre-form splat, upholstered slip seat, simple front sabre legs, labeled "Tell City Chair
Co. #566" 45.00

Side chair, mahogany, flat line-
incised crestrail above slender
slat w/oval center panel, red
leather-upholstered seat, reeded
flat seatrail, simple reeded front
sabre legs 99.00

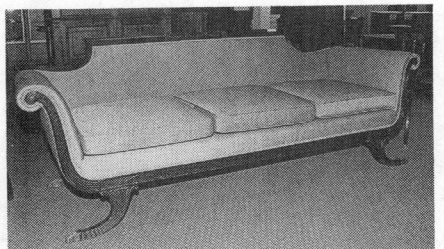

Sofa, mahogany, flat crestrail
w/three carved swags, reeded
downswept rail ends above outswept arms w/reeded arm supports flanking the three-cushion
seat, reeded seatrail w/swag-
carved corner blocks above outswept reeded legs w/brass paw
caps, labeled on platform "Custom
Made by McGilligan's - University
Ave. - Madison" 475.00

Tea table, mahogany, cartouche-
shaped top w/raised rim raised
on a baluster-turned & acanthus-
carved pedestal above four downswept reeded legs w/brass paw
caps, label of Fine Arts Furniture
Co., Grand Rapids, Michigan,
14½ x 25½", 22" h. 125.00

EMPIRE STYLE

Chest of drawers, mahogany,
American Empire-Style, rectangular top above five drawers
flanked by rope-twist pilasters,
bun feet, half-ring drawer pulls
(Not Illustrated) 375.00
Parlor suite: side table, settee &
two armchairs; mahogany w/or-
molu mounts, French Empire-
Style, the chairs w/a flat crestrail
w/ormolu ribbon mount over the
upholstered back, flat arms on
gilt sphinx-carved arm supports,
flat seatrail w/ormolu leaf band
mount, square tapering legs
w/spade feet, 4 pcs. (ILLUS. of
one chair) 1,775.00

Parlor Suite Armchair

LOUIS XVI STYLE

Chest of drawers, gumwood, low
crestrail on the rectangular top
w/molded edges, double row of
fine beading around the four long
drawers above a narrow band-
incised bottom drawer, scrolled
corner blocks on the trumpet-form
short legs 495.00

WINDSOR CHAIRS

Armchair, sackback-type, arched
crestrail above eight turned spin-

dles above a medial rail continuing to arms w/carved handgrips
over turned spindles & canted,
baluster-turned arm supports,
shaped saddle seat, canted
baluster-turned legs joined by
shaped stretchers, 1920's 125.00

Side chair, bow-back type, narrow
arched back above three baluster-
and ring-turned flared spindles,
simple shaped seat, slightly canted baluster- and ring-turned legs
joined by turned stretchers, label
of Heywood-Wakefield, original
finish 95.00

Side chair, bow-back type, walnut,
arched crestrail framing a slender
vase-shaped splat & four slender,
turned spindles, simple rounded,
shaped seat, canted baluster-
turned legs joined by simple
turned stretchers 45.00

WALLACE NUTTING FURNITURE
"Brewster" armchair, spindle back,
rush seat (Not Illustrated) 1,800.00
Highboy, Chippendale-Style, carved
mahogany, two-part construction:
the upper section w/a scrolled

swan's-neck crest surmounted by
three urn-form finials centering a
shell- and leaf-carved tympanum
over a row of three small drawers
over four long, graduated drawers
flanked by colonettes; the lower
section w/a mid-molding over a
long drawer over a pair of deep
drawers flanking a large central
shell- and scroll-carved drawer
above the scalloped & acanthus-
carved apron continuing to
acanthus-carved cabriole legs continuing to ball-and-claw feet, the
interior w/two labels & inscription
"1927 - no.992" & a branded
mark, in the Philadelphia style,
dated 1927, 43 x 46¾", 8' 1" h.
(Not Illustrated) 7,188.00

Lowboy, Chippendale-Style, carved
mahogany, the rectangular top
w/molded edges carved w/a
gadroon & dentil band above a
single long drawer over a pair of
small drawers flanking a deep,
larger center drawer w/ornate
shell & scroll carving, leaf vine-
carved colonettes down the front
corners, the shaped shell- and
scroll-carved apron continuing to
the acanthus-carved cabriole legs
ending in ball-and-claw feet, in
the Philadelphia style, branded
mark, ca. 1920's, 20 x 36½",
31" h. (ILLUS.) 3,163.00
Side chairs, ladder-back style, five
slats between sausage-turned
stiles, rush seat, turned legs, set
of 4 (Not Illustrated) 1,045.00
Tea table, Chippendale-Style, mahogany, the shaped round dished
top tilting above a birdcage support & a baluster-turned & carved
pedestal on a tripod base
w/acanthus-carved cabriole legs
ending in claw-and-ball feet,
branded mark, early 20th c.,
33" d., 28¼" h. (Not Illustrated)........................4,888.00

Windsor armchair, continuous arm style, braced back above shaped seat, turned legs, repaired (Not Illustrated)...................... 900.00

Windsor armchair, sack-back style, the arched crest above nine tapered spindles & a plank seat on turned, canted legs joined by turned stretchers, ca. 1930, branded mark (Not Illustrated) 460.00

Windsor chairs, hoop- & braced-back style, painted green, two armchairs & six side chairs, the set (Not Illustrated) 15,950.00

Windsor settee, double sack-back style (Not Illustrated) 4,400.00

Windsor side chairs, brace-back style, set of six, each (Not Illustrated) 545.00

(End of Special Focus)

FURNITURE

Furniture made in the United States during the 18th and 19th centuries is coveted by collectors. American antique furniture has a European background, primarily English, since the influence of the Continent usually found its way to America by way of England. If the style did not originate in England, it came to America by way of England. For this reason, some American furniture styles carry the name of an English monarch or an English designer. However, we must realize that, until recently, little research has been conducted and even less published on the Spanish and French influences in the areas of the California missions and New Orleans.

After the American Revolution, cabinetmakers in the United States shunned the prevailing styles in England and chose to bring the French styles of Napoleon's Empire to the United States and we have the uniquely named "American Empire" style of furniture in a country that never had an emperor.

During the Victorian period, quality furniture began to be mass-produced in this country with its rapidly growing population. So much walnut furniture was manufactured, the vast supply of walnut was virtually depleted and it was of necessity that oak furniture became fashionable as the 19th century drew to a close.

For our purposes, the general guidelines for dating furniture will be:
Pilgrim Century - 1620-85
William & Mary - 1685-1720
Queen Anne - 1720-50
Chippendale - 1750-85

Federal - 1785-1820
Hepplewhite - 1785-1800
Sheraton - 1800-20
American Empire (Classical) - 1815-40
Victorian - 1840-1900
Early Victorian - 1840-50
Gothic Revival - 1840-90
Rococo (Louis XV) - 1845-70
Renaissance - 1860-85
Louis XVI - 1865-75
Eastlake - 1870-95
Jacobean & Turkish Revival - 1870-90
Aesthetic Movement - 1880-1900
Art Nouveau - 1890-1918
Turn-of-the-Century - 1895-1910
Mission (Arts & Crafts movement) - 1900-15
Art Deco - 1925-40

All furniture included in this listing is American unless otherwise noted. Also see MINIATURES (Replicas), ROYCROFT ITEMS and SHAKER COLLECTIBLES.

BEDS

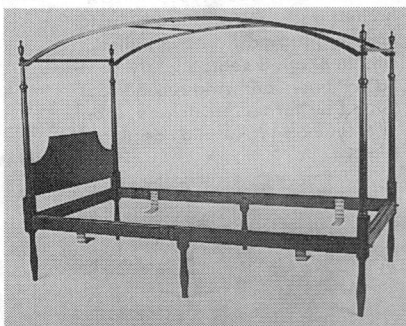

Federal Child's Canopy Bed

Art Nouveau bed, carved & inlaid mahogany, the arched headboard w/whiplash carved & molded corners & footboard w/molded panels, both inlaid w/various woods, mother-of-pearl & copper w/stylized poppy blossoms & undulating leafage, Louis Majorelle, France, ca. 1900, 69 x 85", 5' 11¾" h. $14,300.00

Art Nouveau beds, carved walnut & satinwood, each carved w/birds, irises & cattails, the headboard w/an elaborate floral crest, the footboard w/a squirrel, Ecole de Nancy, France, ca. 1900, 5' h., pr. 3,520.00

Biedermeier twin beds, ebonized birch, rectangular paneled headboard w/circular supports, straight rails & arched footboard fitted w/free-standing columnar supports, the whole outlined w/ebonized borders, Europe, second quarter 19th c., 40" w., 4' 6½" h., pr. 4,125.00

Chippendale tall poster bed, mahogany, the footposts tapering & fluted above a vase-form support, the headposts ring-turned & tapered centering a shaped mahogany headboard, on square legs w/Marlboro feet, Philadelphia, ca. 1760, 56¼" w., 6' 9" h. (top of posts extended) 22,000.00

Classical (American Empire) country-style low poster bed, curly maple, the headboard w/baluster- and ring-turned corner posts topped by ball & disc finials flanking the arched & scroll-cut headboard w/a slender turned blanket roll crest, the footboard w/matching posts flanking a shaped panel below an octagonal blanket bar w/ball- and ring-turned end sections, original rope rails, mellow refinishing, ca. 1830-50, 53 x 69", 5' h...........1,760.00

Empire (American) country-style rope bed, maple w/some curl, the high headboard w/scroll-carved ears flanking a small crest bar w/pointed terminals, the headposts w/turned slightly tapering columns topped by a ring-turned section below the mushroom finial, baluster- and ring-turned legs, the footboard w/a heavy turned blanket rail w/ball- and ring-turned ends, a narrow shaped rail below over the round siderail, turned legs matching the headboard, original siderails, Ohio, 19th c., 52 x 74", 5' ¼" h. (mellow refinishing, pegs replaced on end rails, chip on one post) 400.00

Federal child's tall poster canopy bed, maple & cherry, a wide shaped headboard flanked by turned tapering headposts & matching footposts continuing to turned feet, arched canopy framework, w/siderails, New England, early 19th c., restoration, 38 x 72¼", 5' 2" h. (ILLUS.)......1,650.00

Federal low poster bed, arching headboard between rectangular supports w/flattened ball finials, on turned tapering legs, painted blue, 34½" w., 73" l., 29" h. 770.00

Federal tall poster bed, birch, the double-paneled headboard topped w/a roll bar & flanked by simple turned tapering posts, the footposts spirally-turned & acanthus-carved, on tapered ball feet, New England, ca. 1825, 53 x 78" 3,025.00

Federal tall poster bed, carved mahogany & maple, the footposts reeded & acanthus-carved, w/an urn & sheaf of wheat carving below, the headposts tapering & centering an arched pine headboard, the footposts ending in tapering square legs w/spade feet, Boston-Salem, Massachusetts, ca. 1810, 52¾" x 75"......5,500.00

Mission-style (Arts & Crafts movement) double bed, oak, the headboard & lower footboard w/alternating pairs of narrow slats & one broad slat, arched aprons, complete w/side rails, fine original dark finish, branded mark of The Limbert Furniture Company, Model No. 471, 50 x 54" 2,200.00

Victorian Gothic Revival Bed

Victorian bed, Gothic Revival substyle, carved mahogany, the tall headboard w/three Gothic arch panels below a leaf-carved crestrail, flanked by heavy round ribbed posts topped by ring-turned finials, the lower footposts flanking an arched & paneled footboard, on heavy bun feet, ca. 1850 (ILLUS.) 3,850.00

Victorian bed, Renaissance Revival substyle, ebonized walnut, the paneled & arched headboard centered by a beaded wreath, flanked by stylized anthemia surmounted by a foliate scrolled crest centering a shield, matching footboard, possibly Philadelphia, late 19th c., 5' 5" x 6' 2½", 10' 4" h. 3,300.00

Victorian 'half-tester' bed, Rococo substyle, carved rosewood, the tall arched headboard w/a shell-carved crest w/fruit & nuts, scroll-carved borders & shaped bordered panels flanked by tall tapering

Victorian Rococo Half-Tester Bed
turned headposts supporting the
upholstered half-tester w/a scroll-
carved crest & turned finials, the
paneled sideboards & footboard
w/turned & carved details &
scroll-carved corner braces, attributed to Prudent Mallard, New
Orleans, Louisiana, ca. 1850
(ILLUS.) 13,200.00

BEDROOM SUITES

Late Victorian Mahogany Chest of Drawers

Art Deco: mirrored vanity w/stool,
tall chest of drawers, low chest of
drawers, single bed, side table &
side chair; bird's-eye maple & mahogany, the tall chest w/one long
drawer above two doors opening
to a fitted interior over three long
drawers (missing a pull), the low
chest w/three long drawers, circular bed headboard w/painted details & on fluted feet, tag of the

Widdicomb company, tall chest
19¼ x 33½", 43" h., the set 1,540.00
Late Victorian: double bed, wardrobe, chest of drawers w/mirror &
commode w/mirror; carved mahogany, each piece w/an ornate
stepped & scroll-carved crestrail
above a veneered frieze above
carved side pilasters, the commode & chest of drawers w/ob-
long swiveling beveled mirrors &
red marble tops, mahogany flame
veneering on wardrobe, chest of
drawers & commode fronts, ca.
1890, the set (ILLUS. of chest of
drawers) 6,600.00
Louis XV-Style: double bed & ar-
moire; ormolu-mounted rosewood
& marquetry; arched crest centered by a bold ormolu scroll
finial on the rectangular top
w/molded cornice above a marquetry frieze, the armoire w/a
pair of shaped mirrored doors, ornate scrolled-inlaid sides & a narrow inlaid drawer at base, ormolu
mounts at the front top & bottom
corners & ormolu boss below the
drawer, France, ca. 1890-1900,
bed 63" w., 5' ½" h., armoire
63" w., 8' 2" h., the set 15,400.00

Renaissance Revival Bed & Commode
Victorian Renaissance Revival: double bed, drop-center dresser &
small commode; carved walnut,
the bed w/a high, arched headboard w/an ornately pierce-
carved scrolling crestrail w/a
palmette finial above a carved
bust above a wide arched burl-
veneered panel flanked by turned
columns over carved palmettes &
scrolls & stepped-out sides w/urn-
form finials, the lower footboard
w/narrow burl-veneered panels,

w/matching white marble-topped dresser & commode, bed 9' h. (ILLUS. of bed & commode) 12,650.00

Victorian Rococo: armoire, daybed & commode; bird's-eye maple & rosewood, the single-door armoire w/an arched crestrail w/an ornately carved fruit & flower rosewood crest & turned corner finials, arched mirror in the door & a single long drawer in the base, resting on flattened bun feet, ca. 1850-60, the set 6,425.00

Victorian Rococo: half-tester bed, armoire & three-drawer marble-topped dresser; carved rosewood, the half-tester on the bed w/a scroll-carved crest & bulbous corner finials, the arched headboard w/a scroll & flower-carved crest over a pair of pyramidal panels above a large rectangular panel, the low scroll-carved footboard w/bold turned finials on the posts, attributed to Prudent Mallard, New Orleans, Louisiana, ca. 1850-60, 3 pcs. 18,150.00

BENCHES

Federal Window Bench

Bucket (or water) bench, painted pine, long rectangular top raised on tall canted board ends dovetailed into the top, low arched cut-out on ends & angled braces under the top, old worn green repaint, 11¾ x 32" 269.50

Bucket (or water) bench, pine & poplar, a wide rounded gallery top above a raised shelf flanked by shaped sides above a stepped-out rectangular shelf above a cabinet w/a pair of square paneled doors, on simple bracket feet, old brown finish, Pennsylvania, mid-19th c., 15¼ x 45¼", 45½" h. 2,750.00

Federal window bench, figured mahogany, each end w/a rectangular crotch-figured crest centering a removable slip seat, the crotch-figured seatrail on sabre legs, New York, ca. 1825, 40½" l. (ILLUS.) 2,750.00

Gothic Revival bench, carved mahogany, the angled over-upholstered seat w/carved seatrails centering a quatrefoil, centering a faceted lancet-carved leg, the whole flanked by faceted lancet-carved legs, on molded, faceted feet, 1820-40, 20 x 65", 15½" h. 1,540.00

Hall bench, Arts & Crafts style, oak, the tall flat back w/a large rectangular black leather-upholstered panel, narrow rounded sides continuing down to form low, rounded arms flanking the leather-upholstered seat lifting above a storage compartment, Limbert Furniture Co., Model 95, early 20th c., 20 x 46¼", 4' h. (bottom board on back panel replaced, new leather) 1,320.00

Mission-style Bench by Limbert

Mission-style (Arts & Crafts movement) bench, oak, rectangular seat flanked by slanted panels, four square cut-outs on both sides, new dark finish, branded mark of Limbert Company, Model No. 243, 17¾ x 24¼ x 25" (ILLUS.) 2,750.00

Parlor bench, Louis XV-Style, carved wood, kidney-shaped w/an upholstered top above a frieze carved w/acanthus scrolls, raised on cabriole legs w/carved knees & scroll feet, probably 19th c., 58" l., 20" h. 1,045.00

Primitive pine bench, long rectangular top, bootjack feet mortised through top, old dark finish, 10½ x 96", 18" h. (top weathered) 175.00

BOOKCASES

Small Mission Bookcase

Classical (American Empire) bookcase, mahogany, three-part construction: the upper part w/deeply projecting rectangular cornice over an arched frieze; the middle part a conforming case fitted w/a pair of geometric-glazed cupboard doors enclosing two shelves; the lower part w/rectangular white marble top above a bolection-molded frieze drawer & a pair of paneled cupboard doors enclosing a shelf & centered by engaged colonettes, on foliate-carved & gadrooned bun feet, New York, 1810-30, 24¼ x 47½", 7' 7¼" h. 2,860.00

Directoire-Style bookcase, brass & ormolu-mounted mahogany, burl birch & ebonized wood, the shaped rectangular cornice of breakfront outline w/brass & ebony banded panels w/diamond-decorated inlaid frieze above three glazed doors joined by fluted pilasters w/ormolu *chandelles* decoration raised on a shaped rectangular breakfront plinth w/ormolu leaftip border, France, second half 19th c., 17½ x 72", 7' 1" h. 16,500.00

Federal bookcase, mahogany veneered, four-part construction: a long rectangular top w/a detachable molded cornice; the two bookcase sections each w/pairs of glazed cupboard doors w/twelve rectangular panes below a top row of arched panes opening to adjustable shelves; the lower section centering a butler's fall-front desk drawer over a kneehole area flanked by banks of three cockbead-molded

short drawers & large paneled cupboard doors opening to shelves, on molded bases, Philadelphia, 1790-1810, 17½ x 119", 8' 9¾" h. 24,200.00

Mission-style (Arts & Crafts movement) bookcase, oak, a low galleried top above curve-fronted sides w/inverted spade cut-outs flanking two open shelves above a single glazed cupboard opening to two shelves, slightly arched aprons, original dark finish, paper label of the Limbert Furniture Company, early 20th c., 11¼ x 16½", 46¾" h. (ILLUS.) . . . 2,090.00

Mission-style (Arts & Crafts movement) bookcase-cabinet, oak, three-quarter open gallery above the rectangular top over two pairs of narrow 6-pane glazed cupboard doors w/metal plate & bail pulls opening to shelves above two pairs of small cupboard doors w/large strap hinges & metal plate & bail pulls, painted iron hardware, red decal mark of Gustav Stickley, ca. 1902, 14 x 60", 5' 9" h. 77,000.00

Ellis-Designed Mission Bookcase

Mission-style (Arts & Crafts movement) bookcase-cabinet, oak, low three-quarter open gallery on the rectangular top above a pair of tall 2-pane glazed cupboard doors opening to two shelves above a pair of long cupboard doors, arched front apron & bootjack ends, rectangular metal plate & bail pulls, designed by Harvey Ellis for Gustav Stickley, ca. 1903 (ILLUS.) 20,900.00

Victorian bookcase, Baroque style, ebonized oak, the long top w/rounded ends above two carved bands & an ornate scroll-carved frieze & w/two outset cap-

Victorian Baroque Style Bookcase

itals above free-standing turned,
reeded & acanthus-carved
columns down the front, the
curved ends w/glass-enclosed
shelved cupboards flanking a pair
of central glazed doors opening to
shelves, all above the conforming
base w/the curved end cabinets &
pair of central doors all trimmed
w/boldly carved square raised
panels surrounding ornately
carved fruit clusters or trophies,
the flaring ogee base band carved
w/scrolling leaves & raised on
flattened bun feet, ca. 1870,
95" w., 9' 2" h. (ILLUS.) 6,600.00

Victorian bookcase, Chinese style,
gilt-decorated black lacquer, two-
part construction: the upper
'breakfront' section w/a rectangular top w/a coved molding above
a wide outset center section
flanked by narrower side sections
each w/a single-pane glazed door
opening to three shelves, the
framework decorated w/gilt
scrolls & Oriental detailing & on a
molded mid-molding; the lower
section of conforming design
w/the wide central section w/an
arched & paneled door decorated
w/Chinese figures in a landscape
in gilt & w/gilt edge trim & the
narrower side doors w/similarly
decorated panels, a molded base
w/short bracket feet, England,
19th c., decoration of 20th century
origin, 19½ x 78" w., 7' 3" h. 12,650.00

Victorian bookcase, Eastlake substyle, cherry, a rectangular top
w/a flaring bead-trimmed cornice
above a pair of single-pane
glazed cupboard doors w/carved
oval paterae & scrolls across the

top, interior fitted w/adjustable
shelves, the stepped-out base w/a
pair of line-incised drawers w/bail
pulls, ca. 1880, 15¼ x 47½",
5' 9¼" h. (one shelf replaced) 880.00

Victorian bookcase, Gothic substyle,
walnut, a rectangular top w/a
pierced & arcaded cornice flanked
by spire finials above a pair
of tall glazed cupboard doors
w/Gothic tracery & lower solid
panels, on a plinth base, England,
second quarter 19th c., altera-
tions, 20½ x 38½", 7' 5½" h. ...8,250.00

Renaissance Revival Bookcase

Victorian bookcase, Renaissance Revival substyle, walnut & burl walnut, the rectangular top w/deep
molded cornice centered by a
high arched pediment w/leaf-
carved bands & a female mask
keystone over burl panels over a
pair of tall glazed cupboard doors
opening the shelves, the doors
flanked by raised block & pilaster
burl panels, the stepped-out
base section w/a single drawer
w/raised burl panels flanked by
blocked ends w/raised burl
panels, ca. 1875, 19½ x 41",
9' 1" h. (ILLUS.) 2,420.00

Victorian bookcase, stacking lawyer-
type, oak, four sections w/glass-
fronted doors & a drawer in the
base, made by Globe-Wernicke,
late 19th - early 20th c.......... 340.00

CABINETS

China cabinet, Baroque-Style, carved
mahogany, oblong top w/carved
scrollwork flanked by lions' faces
at the front, three-section glass

Baroque-Style China Cabinet

case w/curved glass at the side
sections, carved half columns
flanking the central door opening to glass shelves & mirrored
back, raised on low carved feet
(ILLUS.) 4,250.00
China cabinet, Mission-style (Arts &
Crafts movement), oak, a low
crestboard w/rounded corners
above the rectangular top
w/rounded corners above tapering sideboards fitted w/a small
open shelf on each side above
tapering corbels, all centering a
cabinet w/a single glazed door
w/three panes above a large lower pane, opening to three adjustable shelves, flat base, small
copper pull, on wheels, burned-in
mark of the Limbert Furniture
Company, Model No. 452, early
20th c., 16 x 45", 4' 10" h. (small
knob missing on pull, replaced
glass panel) 3,630.00

Golden Oak Style "Side-by-Side"

China cabinet-secretary, Golden
Oak style, "side-by-side," rectangular top w/gently rounded
corners above shelf over long
curved-glass cupboard door on
left side opening to shelves, the
right side w/square beveled glass
mirror above two short drawers
w/rounded fronts over a hinged
fall-front lid above three curved
long drawers, each drawer fitted
w/brass bail pulls, on short
cabriole front legs on casters
(ILLUS.) 1,600.00

Art Deco Corner Cabinet

Corner cabinet, Art Deco, mahogany, the rectangular top w/round-
ed corner above a single small
glazed gilt-bronze door opening to
a mirrored compartment, above
three short drawers each set w/a
rectangular shagreen escutcheon,
flanked on the right by a quarter
round door opening to a mirrored
& glass shelved interior, the
whole raised on molded feet ending in gilt-bronze *sabots*, France,
ca. 1925, 16 x 34½", 35½" h.
(ILLUS.) 2,420.00
Liquor cabinet, Mission-style (Arts &
Crafts movement), oak, oblong
top w/slightly rounded ends
above a thin copper pull-out tray
over the large single door
w/hammered copper strap hinges
& a hammered copper keyhole escutcheon w/a small loop pull, low
cut-out arches at sides, paper label of the Lifetime Furniture Company, original dark finish,
17 x 24", 32" h. 1,650.00
Music cabinet, Art Nouveau style,
walnut & marquetry, two doors
above two drawers, all worked in
an overall design of irises, incised
"Emile Galle Nancy," France, ca.
1900, 16 x 23", 51" h. 2,090.00

Side cabinet, Art Deco, ebene' de Macassar, the rectangular top above a pair of wide doors veneered w/a pattern of diagonal squares of matched ebene' de Macassar, opening to a shelved interior in mottled deep red lacquer, the sides & top also w/patterned veneer, raised on a molded base, France, ca. 1930, 21 x 65½", 5' h. 13,200.00

Side cabinets, Oriental, inlaid black lacquer, pair of hinged doors opening to sliding doors, inlaid w/mother-of-pearl depicting watery landscapes, the sides w/brass bail handles, the lower cabinet on a low stand, Korea, 16 x 32 7/8", overall 46¾" h., pr. 3,850.00

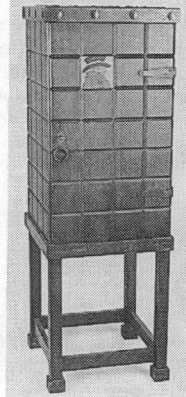

Mission-style Smoker's Cabinet

Smoker's cabinet, Mission-style (Arts & Crafts movement), flat overhanging top w/copper tray, overall paneling w/a deeply incised square design, one decorated w/a character portrait, raised on square legs joined by a box stretcher, square feet, fitted interior (missing turntable), iron hardware, unmarked, 15" w., 44½" h. (ILLUS.) 467.50

Vitrine cabinet, Art Nouveau, ormolu-mounted mahogany & mahogany veneer, of demilune contour, the upper section w/one curved glazed door flanked by two curved glass side panels all within sinuously carved surrounds, the lower section w/a paneled backboard w/diamond design veneering & two slightly arched sinuous carved front supports continuing to a demilune shelf above an arched apron, the whole

w/elaborate ormolu mounts along the supports finely cast as orchid blossoms, buds & leaves, w/the key, Louis Majorelle, France, ca. 1900, 23 x 52¾", 7' 1½" h. 74,250.00

CHAIRS

Thonet Bentwood Armchair

Art Deco armchairs, giltwood, the sloping U-form backrail ending in gently swollen reeded arm supports enclosing a D-shaped seat cushion, one upholstered in pale grey silk velvet & the other in grey & tan striped silk, France, ca. 1925, pr. 15,400.00

Art Deco dining chairs, mahogany, the tall slightly canted back frame w/an arched crestrail above an upholstered panel trimmed w/brass tacks, upholstered seat w/tack trim, square tapering & slightly curved legs, the front legs w/brass *sabots*, France, ca. 1920, eight side chairs & two armchairs, 39¾" h., the set. 2,090.00

Art Deco open armchairs, the upholstered rectangular back raised above the rectangular seat flanked by open shaped rectangular arms, raised on four rectangular slightly curved tapering legs, upholstered in red leatherette, France, ca. 1930, set of 6. . . . . . .2,750.00

Art Deco side chairs, wooden gondola backs & ivory *sabots* on the front legs, upholstered in cream striped fabric, Europe, 35" h., pr. 1,760.00

Art Nouveau armchair, carved mahogany, the horseshoe-shaped back rail above an upholstered back, the front of the arm supports carved w/pine cones & needles & continuing to form the molded front legs similarly carved, dark green leather uphol-

stery, L. Majorelle, France, ca.
1900 . . . . .6,600.00

Art Nouveau desk armchair, mahogany, the curved crestrail continuing to outward flaring arms
enclosing three upholstered
panels above a D-shaped over-
upholstered seat, raised on outward curving molded legs, the
back uprights supporting the set-
back arms continuing downward
as braces for the rear legs, dark
green leatherette upholstery,
Louis Majorelle, France, ca.
1900 . . . . .9,350.00

Bannister-back side chair, painted &
decorated, the wide arched crest
above four splint bannisters
flanked by baluster-turned stiles
w/knob finials over the rushed
seat, on baluster- and block-
turned front legs joined by
baluster-turned front & side rungs,
the back & the front of the legs
decorated w/gold stenciling &
striping on a dark brown ground,
paint added later, New England,
late 18th c., 44" h. 770.00

Bentwood armchair, mahogany,
rounded square back w/vertical
slats between to curved red
leather-upholstered arms over slat
sides flanking the caned seat,
straight square legs, designed by
A. Lorenz, produced by Thonet,
Austria, ca. 1910, 24" w., 34½" h.
(ILLUS.) 1,980.00

Child's armchair, Queen Anne,
painted, yoked crestrail over a
vase-shaped splat flanked by
baluster-turned stiles above
downswept scrolling arms & a
plank seat, on turned legs joined
by stretchers, painted black, New
England, mid to late 18th c.,
21" h. (reduced) 2,860.00

Child's highchair, William & Mary,
oak, the rectangular back w/a
central caned & foliate-carved
panel, the crestrail w/carved
putti holding aloft a crown between spiral-turned stiles w/knob
finials, turned shaped arms on
spiral-turned arm supports above
a caned seat, bobbin- and spiral-
turned front legs joined by a flat
stretcher carved w/putti holding a
crown, spiral-turned back legs &
spiral-turned lower stretchers,
England, late 17th c. (ILLUS. top
next column) 3,300.00

Child's "ladder-back" highchair,
painted maple, the back w/three
rectangular slats flanked by

William & Mary Highchair

turned posts w/button finials continuing to form back legs, rush
seat between slender round arms
on turned arm supports continuing
to form front legs, double stretchers on front & sides, single in
back, partially painted black,
New England, early 18th c. 2,475.00

Child's Ladder-Back Highchair

Child's "ladder-back" highchair,
painted & turned maple & hickory,
two arched slats in the back
flanked by heavy turned stiles
continuing down to form the back
legs, slender turned arms joined
to front stiles forming the front
legs, upholstered seat, three simple turned stretchers on each
side, original red paint, early
19th c. (ILLUS.) 990.00

Chippendale corner chair, carved
walnut, upswept cresting over
continuous flat shaped arms &
vase-shaped splats flanked by
columnar supports above a ser-

pentine slip-seat & cabriole front leg carved w/a scallop shell & pendent bellflower, on a ball-and-claw foot, the remaining turned tapering legs on pad feet joined by block-and-arrow X-stretchers, Rhode Island, 1760-80, 31¾" h. 49,500.00

Chippendale Corner Chair

Chippendale corner chair, walnut, upswept central cresting over continuous flat shaped arms & wide vase-shaped splats flanked by columnar supports above the upholstered seat, deep arched apron above the three cabriole front legs, the center leg ending in a trifid foot, Pennsylvania, ca. 1760, 33½" h. (ILLUS.) 2,200.00

Chippendale Side Chair

Chippendale side chair, carved cherry, oxbow crestrail above a pierced-carved back splat, upholstered seat, square legs w/scroll-carved corner brackets in front, by Eliphalet Chaplin, Connecticut, ca. 1780, 37" h. (ILLUS.) 3,630.00

Chippendale side chair, carved mahogany, the ox-yoke crestrail carved w/leafy scrolls above a pierced vasiform splat, uphol-

Chippendale Side Chair

stered seat w/molded seatrail above square legs joined by box stretchers, old refinish, Philadelphia, 1760-80, 37" h. (ILLUS.).....2,090.00

Chippendale side chair, carved mahogany, bead-molded shaped crestrail centering a carved pendent leaf flanked by carved scrolled ears above a pierced & scroll-carved splat over a trapezoidal slip seat, the front seatrail w/shaped bead molding centering a carved cabochon flanked by scrolls, on cabriole legs w/ball-and-claw feet, Philadelphia, 1765-85, 38" h. 6,050.00

Chippendale side chair, carved mahogany, shaped crest centering a carved shell above a double-heart pierced vase-form splat, upholstered seat above the molded seatrail w/a center carved shell, on cabriole front legs w/claw-and-ball feet, Philadelphia, ca. 1770 (shell on skirt replaced) 5,225.00

Chippendale side chair, walnut, serpentine crestrail centered by a scallop shell flanked by volutes & scrolling ears over a pierced interlacing vase-shaped splat carved w/volutes above a trapezoidal slip seat w/shell-carved seatrail, on cabriole legs headed by shells, on ball-and-claw feet, Pennsylvania, 1760-80, 40" h. 17,600.00

Chippendale wing chair, mahogany, the tall upholstered back w/a serpentine crest flanked by curved wings continuing to out-scrolled arms above the wide upholstered seat, on square tapering molded front legs & square slightly canted rear legs all joined by box stretchers, probably Pennsylvania, 1770-90, refinished, 4' h. (restoration).........................2,530.00

Chippendale-Style, armchair w/open arms, carved mahogany, arched acanthus-carved crestrail above a Gothic carved pierced splat, molded seatrail enclosing an upholstered slip seat, cabriole front legs ending in claw-and-ball feet, Philadelphia, 19th c. 31,900.00

Chippendale-Style Armchair

Chippendale-Style dining chairs, Centennial-type, carved mahogany, the oxbow crestrail carved w/scrolls & continuing into the pierce-carved back splat, the armchair w/curved flat arms ending in curled handgrips over curved arm rests, upholstered seat, front seatrail centered by a carved shell, w/cabriole front legs w/leaf-carved knees & ending in claw-and-ball feet, late 19th c., set of 12 (ILLUS. of armchair) 7,325.00

American Classical Side Chair

Classical (American Empire) side chairs, carved mahogany, wide flat & curved crestrail above a fruit basket & drapery pierce-carved slat flanked by carved stiles continuing down to form the side seatrails, upholstered

seat, curved sabre front legs & canted back legs, New York, ca. 1810, 31¼" h., pr. (ILLUS. of one) 1,760.00

Ladder-Back Armchair

Early American "ladder-back" armchair, turned & painted wood, the tall bobbin- and rod-turned stiles w/ball finials flanking five arched stiles above shaped arms on baluster-turned arm supports continuing to bobbin- and rod-turned front legs, replaced rush seat, double sausage-turned front rungs & plain side & back rungs, old red paint, New England, 18th c., minor imperfections, 44¾" h. (ILLUS.) 2,640.00

Federal dining chairs, carved mahogany, shield-shaped back centering flowerhead- and bell-flower-carved uprights, above leaf- and flowerhead-carved molded arms, the bowed seatrail on molded tapering legs ending in spade feet, New York, ca. 1795, three side chairs & one armchair, the set (one w/repair to crest at juncture w/stile) 25,300.00

Federal "Fancy" Side Chairs

Federal "fancy" side chairs, ring-turned crestrail above a carved & painted palmette over a trapezoidal rushed seat flanked by molded stiles, on baluster-turned legs, entire surface painted & embellished w/gilt highlights, Philadelphia, 19th c., 33" h., set of 4 (ILLUS. of part) 1,320.00

Federal "klismos" chair, mahogany, the carved tablet crest centering intertwined cornucopiae over a lyre splat flanked by scrolled & reeded stiles above a trapezoidal slip-seat w/molded front seatrail, on sabre legs, New York, 1790-1810, 23½" h. 5,280.00

Federal "lolling" armchair, mahogany, the tall upholstered back w/arched crest above open arms w/curved & reeded arm supports, wide upholstered seat on square tapering legs joined by stretchers, Massachusetts, ca. 1795, 45" h. ...5,225.00

Federal "racquet-back" dining chairs, carved mahogany, molded back centering a bellflower- and leaf-carved splat above a serpentine over-upholstered seat, on molded tapering legs, Philadelphia, ca. 1800, three side chairs & one armchair, the set 3,575.00

Federal "shield-back" side chairs, mahogany, the heart-shaped shield back w/a triple-arch crest above a pierce-carved central splat w/a fanned design flanked by slender curved slats carved w/tassels & reeding, the trapezoidal upholstered seat w/tack trim above square tapering front legs ending in spade feet, New York, ca. 1795, 38" h., pr............3,850.00

Federal side chairs, painted & grained maple, concave crestrail & stayrail painted w/stylized shells & scrolls, rush seat, turned front seatrail, turned front legs joined by an ornate flat rung, double side rungs & single back rung, New York or New England, ca. 1815, set of 6 ....4,400.00

Louis XV "fauteuil a la Reine" (open-arm armchair), beechwood, cartouche-shaped upholstered backrest carved w/flowerheads & foliate scrolls, the padded armrests raised on voluted leaf-carved supports, the serpentine-fronted seat carved to match the backrest & raised on cabriole legs carved at the knees w/flowerheads & ending in leaf-carved

Louis XV Fauteuil a la Reine

toes, signed "I. Gourdin," France, mid-18th c. (ILLUS.) 8,800.00

Mission-style (Arts & Crafts movement) armchair, oak, a wide flat crestrail above three low, wide vertical slats flanked by rectangular stiles continuing down to form back legs, flat arms above three wide vertical slats, heavy rectangular arm supports continue down to form front legs, leather-upholstered slip seat, attributed to Harden & Company, 29½" w., 34¾" h. 385.00

Child's Chair by Limbert

Mission-style (Arts & Crafts movement) child's armchair, oak, the back w/two slats w/curved edges flanked by square stiles continuing down to form the back legs, flat shaped arms on set-back arm supports, upholstered seat, square front legs joined by a wide rung arched on the bottom edge, branded mark of Limbert Company, Model No. 873, ca. 1910, 25¾" h. (ILLUS.) 220.00

Mission-style (Arts & Crafts movement) "Morris" armchair, oak, adjustable back w/five horizontal slats, slanted arms over corbels & five vertical side slats, on casters, branded Gustav Stickley mark, Model No. 369, ca. 1912, 36½" w., 41½" h. 4,675.00

Mission-style (Arts & Crafts movement) rocking chair w/arms, oak, slightly curved crestrail over five vertical slats, wide flat arms over four slats, original spring seat w/leather covering, Harden, unmarked, 29 x 33", 36" h. 495.00

Mission-style (Arts & Crafts movement) side chair, inlaid oak, the tall back w/a wide crestrail above a wide center splat flanked by narrow splats, the crestrail & central splat inlaid w/long, slender stylized flowers in colored wood, upholstered seat, heavy straight rectangular legs joined by H-stretchers, Shop of The Crafters paper label, early 20th c., original dark finish, 43½" h. 1,100.00

Mission-style (Arts & Crafts movement) side chairs, oak, a pair of heavy curved slats flanked by heavy square, slightly tapering stiles continuing down to form the back legs, original rush seat, square tapering front legs w/stretchers, remnant of the paper label of The Michigan Chair Company, ca. 1900, 35½" h., pr. 385.00

Mission-style (Arts & Crafts movement) vanity chair, oak, the back w/a wide "H" splat between slats & the stiles, raised above the rush slip-seat, square tapering legs joined by flat stretchers, lacquered black, Gustav Stickley, Model No. 398, 32½" h. 302.50

Modern Chair by Frank Lloyd Wright

Modern style side chair, painted steel & leather, the tall rectangular back w/a black leather-upholstered panel on the brown-painted steel frame, a square black leather seat above the plain angular steel frame, straight legs & rungs, designed by Frank Lloyd Wright for the Larkin Co. Building, Buffalo, New York, 1904 (ILLUS.) 4,675.00

Modern style "Zigzag" side chair, maple, the simple zigzag structure w/indented carrying handle on the reverse, designed by Gerrit Rietveld in 1934, made in 1940 . . .5,500.00

Queen Anne corner chair, cherry, the U-shaped back w/beaded shaped crest ending in outscrolled flat arms above two pierced vase-form splats centered by three ring-turned uprights, upholstered slip-seat above a deep shaped apron, frontal cabriole leg ending in a raised pad foot & turned back legs ending in raised button feet, Connecticut, 1750-80 (one front leg return replaced) 9,900.00

Queen Anne Country-Style Side Chair

Queen Anne country-style side chair, carved & painted, the deeply carved crestrail center terminates in C-scrolls above a spooned splat flanked by molded spooned stiles above an old rush seat, the baluster-turned & blocked legs joined by a bulbous-turned rung & ending in simple Spanish feet, early black paint w/olive accents, New England, ca. 1730-50, very minor imperfections, 41" h. (ILLUS.) 4,675.00

Queen Anne "fiddleback" side chair, yoke-shaped crestrail above ring-turned tapering stiles flanking a circle & heart-pierced vasiform splat over a woven rush seat, on ring-turned cylindrical legs joined by a box stretcher, 19th c., 39¼" h. 825.00

Queen Anne Side Chair

Queen Anne side chair, walnut, yoked crest above a solid vasiform splat above trapezoidal seat, on cabriole legs w/pad feet joined by turned stretchers, Massachusetts, ca. 1760, 39" h. (ILLUS.) 1,320.00

Queen Anne side chair, figured maple, the molded yoked crestrail over an earred vasiform splat flanked by molded serpentine stiles above a balloon-shaped slip-seat, on cabriole legs w/stock-inged pad feet, Pennsylvania, 1740-60, 40¼" h. 9,900.00

Queen Anne wing chair, leather-upholstered turned walnut & maple, the tall back w/serpentine crestrail, upright scrolled arms & seat w/loose cushion covered in black leather, on cabriole legs joined by block- and ring-turned stretchers ending in pad feet, the rear legs chamfered, Boston, Massachusetts, ca. 1760 (minor repair to right rear leg at juncture w/seatrail)....................68,750.00

Regency Armchair

Regency armchairs, painted finish, rectangular back centered by a

tablet painted w/a flower-filled basket, over an X-form splat, the caned seat now w/green & cream patterned cushion, on turned tapering legs, decoration restored, England, early 19th c., pr. (ILLUS. of one) 3,850.00

Victorian Balloon-Back Chair

Victorian country-style "balloon-back" side chairs, painted & decorated, the wide rounded balloon back above a pierced vase-form splat, all in original dark brown painted w/polychrome floral designs w/grey & gold striping, a shaped seat w/gilt trim above ring-turned front legs w/gilt trim, Pennsylvania, ca. 1840, surface wear, 32" h., pr. (ILLUS. of one) .. 220.00

Victorian Gothic Hall Chair

Victorian Gothic Revival hall chairs, oak, w/a pointed, arched & pierced back flanked by block stiles w/pointed finials above a trapezoidal plank seat w/a shaped seatrail, raised on turned & stud-carved legs ending in top-form feet, mid-19th c., England, set of 4 (ILLUS. of one).........2,530.00

Hunzinger Patent Armchair

Victorian "patent" armchair, walnut, a pierce-carved crest above a rectangular upholstered back panel flanked by turned & curved slats & stiles above a low upholstered barrel-back w/the arm frame carved w/classical heads flanking the upholstered seat, pierced & scroll-carved front drop under seat connected to the turned rung joining the carved & turned front legs w/ball feet, front leg stamped "George Hunzinger, NY - patent March 30, 1869," late 19th c. (ILLUS.) 1,870.00

Victorian rocking chair w/arms, copper tubing & sheet copper, the arched crest of copper tubing w/a looped tube band joining it to a tube crossbar between tubing stiles w/knob finials flanking the woven back panel, shaped tube arms continuing to form the front legs, woven seat, double tube rungs at the front & sides, on rockers, 33" h. (one arm needs resoldering) 330.00

Victorian Rococo Office Chair

Victorian Rococo office chair, carved rosewood, an arched flower-carved crestrail joining curved & carved stiles framing the tufted leather-upholstered back, padded closed arms w/curved & scroll-carved arm supports flanking the upholstered seat above a serpentine seatrail w/a boldly scroll-carved drop, raised on a short pedestal base w/four scrolled legs on casters, made in Philadelphia, ca. 1850-60, 33½" w., 4' h. (ILLUS.) 6,600.00

Wicker Child's Rocker

Wicker child's rocker, a large C-scroll wicker crest above the wicker-woven back panel between round stiles w/ball finials, open arms over loops, upholstered seat, simple turned front legs & rung, painted white, late 19th - early 20th c., 27" h. (ILLUS.) 140.00

Wicker rocking chair w/arms, the wide flat woven crest continues down to form wide flat arms above loosely woven panels in the back & under the arms, tightly woven apron above openwork criss-cross bands, natural finish, paper label of Heywood Brothers, Model No. W59D, ca. 1910, 38" h. 220.00

Wicker rocking chair w/arms, alternating ash splints & wicker, the rolled crest above a solidly woven back continuing down to form the seat, the back & seat flanked by S-shaped wicker flat scroll arms, on a rocker base w/arched legs, decal mark of Ordway Mfg. Co., Bristol, Tennessee, ca. 1905, 21" w., 44½" h. (ILLUS. top next page) 715.00

William & Mary armchair, carved walnut, a shaped crest on flat rectangular stiles flanking a vase-

Wicker Rocking Chair

form splat, long shaped arms on
baluster-turned arm supports over
the wide planked seat, on black-
turned front legs joined by a ring-
and baluster-turned front stretcher, double flat stretchers at the
sides & a single stretcher at the
back, Bethlehem, Pennsylvania,
ca. 1720 .39,600.00

William & Mary "bannister-back"
armchair, painted, shaped &
heart-pierced crown crest above
four molded vertical bannisters
flanked by baluster- and ring-
turned stiles & scroll-end arms
over baluster-turned underarm
stretchers above a rush seat, on
turned legs joined by double
turned stretchers, painted black,
attributed to the shop of Thomas
Salmon, Stratford, Connecticut,
1725-35, 43" h. (feet slightly
reduced) .8,800.00

William & Mary "Caned-Back" Chair

William & Mary "caned-back" side
chair, carved & painted, arched
scroll-carved crest above an oxbow crestrail w/carved scrolls
above a shaped back splat centered by a panel of caning
flanked by spooned back stiles,
the caned seat above a shaped
seatrail on baluster-turned &
blocked front legs joined by a
bulbous-turned rung, simple Spanish feet at the front, Boston, Massachusetts, ca. 1720, 45¼" h.
(ILLUS.) 660.00

William & Mary-Style open armchair,
the tall back w/an arched &
pierced scroll crestrail above the
narrow caned panel back flanked
by slender baluster- and ring-
turned stiles above slender
shaped arms ending in scroll
handgrips & raised on baluster-
turned armrests, wide caned
seat, baluster- and ring-turned
front legs ending in Spanish
feet & joined by a double-bulb-
turned front stretcher, a lower
H-stretcher joining the front &
rear legs, original dark finish,
marked "Michigan Chair Co.,"
early 20th c., 4' 3" h. 125.00

Windsor "bamboo-turned" rocking
armchair, painted wood, the
stepped crest raised on very tall
bamboo-turned stiles flanking sev-
en tapered turned spindles above
turned arms on ring- and knob-
turned arm rests over the wide
plank seat, on splayed turned
legs joined by turned stretchers
on rockers, painted red, ca.
1820 . . . . .1,045.00

Windsor "bow-back" & "brace-back"
armchair, painted, molded bowed
crestrail braced w/slender spindles above seven baluster-turned
spindles & serpentine mahogany
arms w/scrolling handgrips above
a shaped saddle seat, on slightly
canted baluster- and ring-turned
legs joined by a swelled H-
stretcher, painted black, Rhode Island, ca. 1800, 39" h. (rear feet
slightly pieced) 1,210.00

Windsor "comb-back" armchair, the
serpentine crestrail w/scrolling
ears over seven spindles & continuous arms w/scrolling knuckled
handrests above baluster- and
ring-turned arm supports, shaped
plank seat on baluster-turned
tapering splayed legs joined by
arrow-turned stretchers, Massachusetts, ca. 1780, 41" h. (me-
dial stretcher restored) 14,300.00

Windsor "continuous arm" armchair,

arched crestrail above seven turned spindles, crest continues to form shaped arms on bamboo-turned arm supports, shaped seat on canted bamboo-turned legs joined by a swelled H-stretcher, overall black paint, New England, ca. 1800, 38" h. (repairs to crest & arms) 357.50

Windsor "Fan-Back" Armchair

Windsor "fan-back" armchair, a slender arched crest w/delicate scrolled ears above seven slender spindles on a medial rail continuing to form curved handgrips & above thicker turned spindles above the wide shaped seat, canted baluster- and ring-turned legs joined by a swelled H-stretcher, traces of old paint under seat & stamped "P.S. Byrn 1708," refinished, one portion of one handgrip replaced, 43½" h. (ILLUS.) . .5,700.00

Windsor "Firehouse" Armchair

Windsor "firehouse" armchairs, painted & decorated wood, heavy molded crestrail tapering to form

thick arms above eight knob- and baluster-turned spindles, D-shaped seat on ring- and rod-turned front legs joined by a turned stretcher, plain side & back stretchers, painted black w/gilt banding, the crestrail centered by a small Masonic symbol, ca. 1860-80, probably Vermont, 30" h., set of 8 (ILLUS. of one) . . .4,180.00

Windsor "sack-back" armchair, bowed crestrail over a seven-spindle back & arm rail ending in shaped knuckled handgrips above baluster-turned arm supports, saddle seat on baluster-turned tapering legs joined by a swelled H-stretcher, Boston, 1780-1800, 41" h. 8,250.00

Windsor "step-down" side chair, the stepped crestrail above curved flattened stiles flanking six bamboo-turned spindles, shaped saddle seat raised on canted bamboo-turned legs joined by box stretchers, old worn green repaint, overall 35" h. (wear, one crest end loose) 325.00

Windsor "step-down rod-back" side chairs, each w/a stepped crest above flattened curved stiles flanking seven turned tapering spindles, above a shaped plank seat on canted bamboo-turned legs joined by bamboo-turned stretchers, refinished, New England, ca. 1815, set of 6 . . . . .3,850.00

Windsor "writing-arm" armchair, painted wood, curved thick crest-rail continuing to a broad oblong writing surface above a drawer & to a scrolling arm now mounted w/a reading stand above the spindled back & baluster- and ring-turned arm supports, shaped plank seat over a drawer, on baluster-turned canted legs joined by H-stretchers, back of crestrail inscribed "L.Beecher," painted green, Connecticut, early 19th c., 30¾" h. 2,860.00

CHESTS & CHESTS OF DRAWERS

Apothecary chest, mahogany, rectangular top above a case w/rows of 12 small square drawers over two larger bottom drawers, each w/a gilt-painted label, raised on bracket feet, old dark stained surface, original turned wood pulls, England, 19th c., minor imperfections, 8½ x 28¼", 36¼" h. (ILLUS.) 1,320.00

English Apothecary Chest

Apothecary chest, painted cherry, a flat gallery above the rectangular top over the case w/43 drawers arranged in eight graduated rows w/the smallest across the top, painted red, New England, 19th c., 15 x 36 1/8", 45¼" h. (no knobs)........................4,400.00

Blanket chest, child's, painted pine, rectangular hinged lid w/molded edge opening to a well, the case w/base molding, on removable ring-turned short legs ending in large ball feet, painted green, probably New England, early 19th c., 12 x 25", 18" h.........1,320.00

Chippendale Blanket Chest

Blanket chest, Chippendale, inlaid walnut, the hinged rectangular lid opening to a well w/till, the front of the case w/the date "1775" centered by an inlaid tulip & a heart w/the initials "IL," two molded drawers below, on bracket feet, minor patches to drawer lips & moldings, Pennsylvania, 1775, 22½ x 49¼", 28¼" h. (ILLUS.).......................13,750.00

Blanket chest, country-style, grain-painted poplar, rectangular top w/molded edge opening to a deep well, dovetailed case w/base molding, raised on short ring- and knob-turned feet, original reddish brown banded flame

graining, mid-19th c., 20 x 45¾", 24" h. (till removed)............ 990.00

Blanket chest, country-style, painted & decorated pine, rectangular top opening to a well w/till, the front painted w/a pair of doves on large tulip blossoms each flanked by balls on curved arms, centered by a round hex sign above an inverted heart, painted in black, orange & white on a very dark blue ground, on simple bracket feet, decorated by Johannes Spitler, Shenandoah County, Virginia, ca. 1800, 21¼ x 47", 22¼" h. (some retouching to paint on top).....26,400.00

Chippendale "block-front" chest of drawers, mahogany, the thumb-molded rectangular top w/blocked-front edge above a conforming case w/four graduated long drawers w/molded surrounds over a molded base, on shaped bracket feet, Boston, Massachusetts, 1760-80, 17½ x 36", 29¾" h. (restorations to feet)....6,050.00

Chippendale chest of drawers, carved walnut, rectangular molded top above a case w/four graduated long drawers, quarter columns flanking, on ogee bracket feet, Pennsylvania, ca. 1780, 20¼ x 35", 33¼" h. (some restoration to lower one inch of feet) 11,000.00

Chippendale Chest of Drawers

Chippendale chest of drawers, cherry, rectangular top w/thumb-molded edge overhanging the case w/four long graduated drawers w/brass bail pulls, a molded base on large ogee bracket feet, New England, probably Vermont, ca. 1790, 20½ x 40¾", 37¾" h. (ILLUS.) 5,500.00

Chippendale chest of drawers, painted birch, overhanging rectangular top above conforming case of four beaded graduated drawers, scroll-carved apron, on bracket feet, original red paint, replaced brasses, Northern New England, ca. 1800, 19½ x 43¾", 41 1/8" h. (minor imperfections) 3,850.00

Chippendale chest-on-chest, curly maple, two-part construction: the upper section w/a molded rectangular cornice above a group of three small drawers, the center one w/a fan carved in the middle above four long drawers; the lower section w/applied waist molding over four long graduated drawers & a molded base w/a shaped center pendant, on tall ogee bracket feet, apparently original butterfly brasses, New Hampshire, 1760-90, 21¼ x 34¼", 6' 6½" h. .17,600.00

Chippendale Chest-on-Chest

Chippendale chest-on-chest, walnut, two-part construction: the upper section w/a rectangular top over a molded cornice edged w/Greek key above three short thumb-molded drawers above a pair of larger short drawers over three long graduated drawers all flanked by divided fluted quarter columns; the lower section w/applied mid-molding over two thumb-molded graduated deep drawers flanked by fluted quarter columns above a molded base, on ogee bracket feet, Pennsylvania, 1760-80, feet restored, 23¾ x 42¾" (ILLUS.) 4,400.00

Chippendale "serpentine front" chest of drawers, mahogany, the rectangular top w/molded edge &

Chippendale Chest of Drawers

serpentine front above a conforming case w/four graduated long drawers w/incised edges, on ogee bracket feet, Massachusetts, ca. 1770, some restoration to feet, 22 x 40½", 32½" h. (ILLUS.) 6,050.00

Chippendale tall chest of drawers, carved curly maple, rectangular top w/molded cornice above a conforming case w/seven thumb-molded graduated long drawers, on bracket feet, 17½ x 40½", 5' 5½" h. .8,250.00

Chippendale Tall Chest of Drawers

Chippendale tall chest of drawers, inlaid walnut, rectangular top w/a molded coved cornice above a book end-inlaid tympanum over three small drawers w/brass bail pulls over a pair of drawers w/two brass bail pulls each over five long graduated drawers w/brass bail pulls, fluted quarter-columns at the sides, a molded base on tall slender ogee bracket feet, Pennsylvania, ca. 1785, some

old cracks to feet, 23½ x 45½",
5' 10" h. (ILLUS.) 9,900.00

Empire (American) chest of drawers,
cherry w/highly figured burl veneer w/burl inlay on facade &
ends, rectangular top over three
short drawers w/rounded fronts
above two double-ogee long
drawers over three graduated
long drawers w/inlaid turned
pulls, flanked by gooseneck
pilasters, on scrolled feet, mellow
refinishing, found in Lowell, Ohio,
23 x 44", 4' 3½" h. (minor age
cracks) 1,100.00

Empire (American) chest of drawers,
curly maple & cherry, a rectangular top above a pair of deep,
square drawers flanking a pair of
short drawers slightly overhanging three long graduated drawers
flanked by half-round baluster-
and ring-turned columns down the
sides, on double-knob turned
legs, all curly maple except
columns & legs in cherry, mid-
19th c., 21½ x 43 3/8", 4' 1" h.
(refinished, minor repairs) 950.00

Federal "bombe' " chest of drawers,
cherry, rectangular top above an
outward-swelling case w/four
long conforming drawers w/oval
stamped brasses & brass keyhole
escutcheons, on tall French feet,
northern Connecticut River Valley,
ca. 1800, 20 x 37", 32½" h. 5,060.00

Federal "bow-front" chest of drawers, flame birch & ivory-inlaid mahogany, the rectangular top
w/bowed front above a conformingly shaped case w/four graduated long drawers each w/cock-
beaded surrounds & three rectangular flame birch panels centering
ivory-inlaid escutcheons, the skirt
w/rectangular inlaid panel continuing to slightly splayed bracket
feet, Portsmouth, New Hampshire, ca. 1805, 21½ x 41¼",
39" h. (minor repairs to ve-
neers) 28,600.00

Federal chest of drawers, inlaid
cherry, rectangular top w/line-
inlaid edge above four long
graduated line-inlaid drawers
flanked by line-inlaid quarter-
round corner columns, molded
base on ogee bracket feet, probably Rhode Island, ca. 1810,
18 x 41½", 35½" h. 1,980.00

Federal chest of drawers, inlaid mahogany, the oblong top w/outset
corners & lunette-inlaid edge

Federal Chest of Drawers

above four cockbeaded drawers
centering oval reserves, reeded
three-quarter-round columns
flanking, the shaped skirt continuing to reeded legs, on brass
casters, probably original lion's
mask pulls, minor repairs to inlay,
Boston area, Massachusetts, ca.
1805, 22 x 41", 39¾" h. (ILLUS.) . .8,800.00

Federal chest of drawers, walnut,
the rectangular top w/molded
edge above a case w/four long
graduated drawers w/butterfly
pulls flanked by chamfered &
reeded front corners, molded
base, on tall tapering French
feet, Pennsylvania, ca. 1790,
21½ x 40", 33" h. 3,520.00

Federal "serpentine-front" chest
of drawers, inlaid walnut, the
rectangular top w/inlaid edge &
serpentine front above a case
w/four beaded & graduated long
drawers outlined w/stringing, the
shaped apron continuing to flaring
bracket feet, Maryland, ca. 1800,
21 x 41½", 37½" h. (patches to
veneer) 9,350.00

Federal tall chest of drawers, inlaid
curly maple, the rectangular top
w/a cove-molded cornice above a
diamond-inlaid frieze over a row
of three small drawers over five
long graduated drawers, intersecting line-inlaid canted front
corners & a diamond-inlaid band
across the base, raised on tall
French feet, probably Lancaster-
Manheim area, Pennsylvania, ca.
1810, 22¼ x 45¼", 5' 5" h. (minor
repairs to feet) 7,820.00

Hepplewhite country-style chest of
drawers, inlaid walnut, rectangular top w/reeded edge above a
case w/four graduated long draw-

ers, each w/an inlaid diamond escutcheon & applied edge beading,
straight bracket feet, refinished,
found in Bullitt County, Kentucky,
17¼ x 40¼", 37" h. (feet have
minor repairs, one back foot replaced, replaced brasses) 1,450.00
Mission-style (Arts & Crafts movement) chest of drawers, oak, rectangular top w/low rounded backsplash over pair of short drawers
above four long drawers, round
wooden pulls, "Handcraft" decal mark of L. & J.G. Stickley,
20¼ x 34", 4' 5" h. 1,870.00
Mission-style (Arts & Crafts movement) tall chest of drawers, oak,
rectangular top above a case
w/five long drawers above curved
apron, on square legs joined by
stretchers at the sides & back,
branded mark of the Limbert
Furniture Co., Model No. 484,
23 x 34", 45" h. (replaced thin
backsplash) 1,760.00

Modern Style Tall Chest of Drawers

Modern style tall chest of drawers,
walnut, rectangular top above a
tall case w/dovetailed corners
above a stack of seven drawers
w/handholds at the top center of
each, raised on shoe feet, designed by George Nakashima,
ca. 1960, 20 x 36", 4' 4¾" h.
(ILLUS.) 2,750.00
Mule chest (box chest w/one or
more drawers below a storage
compartment), Chippendale country style, cherry, the rectangular
lid lifting above a deep well
fronted by two long beaded
sham drawers above two true
long beaded drawers, all w/bat-
wing brasses, molded base on
scrolled bracket feet, late

18th c., 19½ x 44", 42½" h.
(refinished, minor repairs, brasses
replaced) 2,200.00
Mule chest (box chest w/one or
more drawers below storage compartment), grain-painted, rectangular top lifting above a deep
well over two long thumb-molded
drawers, original red & black fanciful graining above black skirt &
feet, original oval brasses, northern New England, early 19th c.,
16½ x 39¾", 31¾" h. 3,025.00

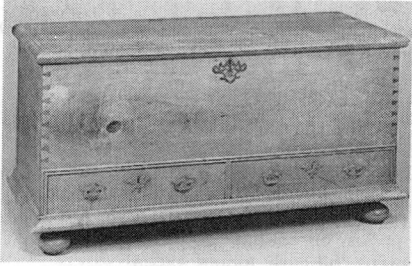

William & Mary Mule Chest

Mule chest, William & Mary, walnut,
the molded hinged lid opening to
an interior w/till w/hinged cover,
the case above two short drawers
& a molded base on ball feet,
probably w/original brasses,
Pennsylvania, early 18th c.,
20¼ x 47½", 25½" h. (feet replaced) 2,420.00
Pilgrim Century chest over drawers,
oak, a rectangular top lifting
above a deep well, the front of
the well w/three recessed panels,
two diamond-shaped flanking a X-
form, each panel separated
w/pairs of rod- and ring-turned
bars above two long bottom
drawers w/their fronts divided
into small panels divided by small
half-round bars & w/longer bars
at the outside edges, scroll corner
blocks at the front bottom, on bun
feet, dated & initialed in the upper center panel "1691" &
"H.C.S.," New England, ca. 1691,
19¾ x 44½", 36½" h. 13,200.00
Queen Anne chest of drawers, walnut, the oblong molded top
w/canted corners above two short
& three long graduated molded
drawers, fluted canted corners
flanking, on bracket feet, lacks
section of central skirt pendant, Philadelphia, ca. 1750,
23½ x 43½", 36¼" h. (ILLUS.
top next column) 9,350.00
Queen Anne country-style chest-on-

Queen Anne Chest of Drawers

Queen Anne Chest-on-Frame

frame, cherry, the rectangular top above a cove-molded cornice over a case w/a pair of small drawers over four long graduated drawers, all w/bail pulls, a base molded over a scalloped apron & bootjack ends, Connecticut, ca. 1770, 20 x 36", 4' 11½" h. (ILLUS.) 3,190.00

Queen Anne tall chest of drawers, maple, two-part construction: the upper section w/molded cornice above a pair of short drawers over four graduated long drawers flanked by fluted pilasters; the lower section w/applied mid-molding above a single long drawer over three short drawers above a scalloped skirt w/drop pendants, on cabriole legs w/peaked slipper feet, New York or Rhode Island, 1725-60, 21 x 38¾", 6' ½" h. 18,700.00

Sheraton country-style "oxbow" chest of drawers, curly birch, rectangular top w/undulating front

above a conforming case w/four long cockbeaded drawers flanked by rounded corners w/single flute, scalloped apron, high turned feet, good old worn & alligatored reddish brown finish, top 20 3/8 x 43", overall 38" h. 3,080.00

Early Stagecoach Chest

Stagecoach chest, painted & decorated, rectangular flat top above a dovetailed case fitted w/three long drawers, original red paint w/yellow lettering on each drawer denoting stage stops including "Worcester & Norwich," "Boston & Dudley," & "Boston & Hartford," New England, 19th c., replaced pulls, minor imperfections, 15¼ x 32¼", 39¼" h. (ILLUS.) . . . 1,650.00

William & Mary blanket chest, grain-painted wood, the rectangular top w/molded edge flanked by shaped cleats lifting above a compartment fitted w/a till, the case w/applied molding w/two sham & two long drawers over a base molding, on ball-turned front feet, Connecticut, 1725-35, 21½ x 41½", 36" h. 3,300.00

William & Mary chest of drawers, painted chestnut & pine, the rectangular top w/molded edge above a conforming case fitted w/a panel-molded long drawer above three geometrically molded & graduated long drawers over a molded base, on turned feet, painted red, eastern Connecticut, 1725-35, 22 x 39½", 35¼" h. . . . 12,100.00

William & Mary chest of drawers, walnut, the molded rectangular top above a case w/two short drawers above three long graduated drawers, all within beaded surrounds, the molded base continuing to compressed ball feet, Pennsylvania, probably Chester County, early 18th c., 22¾ x 41¾", 40¼" h. 8,250.00

CRADLES

Early European Cradle

Country-style low cradle on rockers, painted & chip-carved pine, four splayed & turned corner posts centering arched head- & foot-boards w/single central heart cut-outs, the canted sides w/three shield-shaped cut-outs each, the headboard, footboard & sides decorated w/chip-carved hex symbols & flowers trimmed w/polychrome paint, Scandinavia or Germany, first half 19th c., 27" l. (ILLUS.). 990.00

Country-style low cradle on rockers, painted poplar, turned ball finials & heart cut-outs at head & foot, shaped sides, worn old black & red graining, 42" l. 350.00

Hooded cradle on rockers, galvanized sheet metal, the gently arched hood on flared sides, short rockers, old worn red & blue paint, 26½" l. (some damage) 115.50

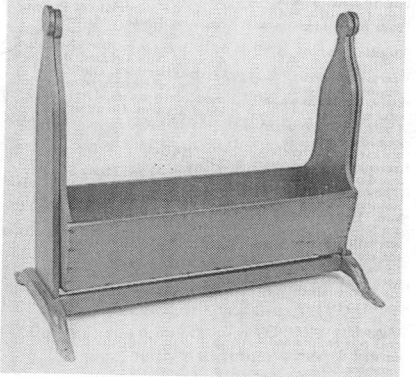

Suspended Swing Cradle

Suspended swing-type cradle, painted wood, flat & tapering end uprights w/flat round finials suspend a rectangular cradle w/deep

slightly canted sides, on a trestle base w/slightly arched feet, overall red paint, probably Pennsylvania, late 18th c., minor surface wear, 39½" l., 37" h. (ILLUS.) 522.50

William & Mary cradle on rockers, painted pine, domed hood w/shaped sides above a rectangular body, on shaped rockers, 40" l. 1,760.00

Windsor country-style cradle on rockers, painted hardwood, bentwood ends, low spindled sides, pinned mortises, old worn green paint, 36" l. (some spindles are old replacements, mortises have added nails) 250.00

CUPBOARDS

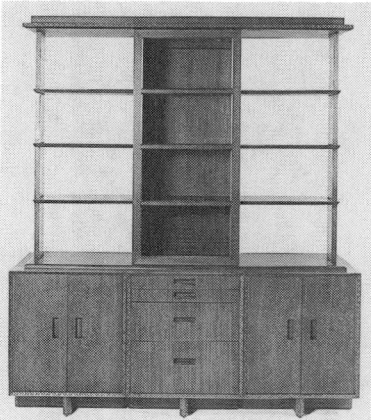

Frank Lloyd Wright Breakfront Cupboard

Breakfront cupboard, Modern style, the flat rectangular top above a pair of open sections w/three shelves flanking a closed three-shelf cupboard all slightly set-back from the base w/a pair of two-door cupboards flanking a stack of four drawers, on a flat base w/three brackets in front, designed by Frank Lloyd Wright, made by Henredon (ILLUS.) 4,675.00

Chimney cupboard, painted poplar, flat rectangular top on very tall narrow cupboard w/a single tall narrow raised panel door opening to shelves, old olive green wash over white, 14 x 19¾", 6' 4" h. (incomplete cast-iron latch, replaced brass thumb latch) 1,000.00

Corner cupboard, Chippendale, carved walnut, two-part construction: the upper section w/a molded & dentil-carved cornice above a single wide arched & geomet-

Chippendale Corner Cupboard

rically-glazed cupboard door
opening to a painted interior
w/three shaped shelves; the lower section w/a mid-molding above
a pair of paneled cupboard doors
opening to a painted shelved interior, on ogee bracket feet,
Pennsylvania, late 18th c., cornice, upper mid-moldings & feet
replaced, 28 x 45", 7' 8½" h.
(ILLUS.) 5,500.00
Corner cupboard, Chippendale, ma-
hogany, two-part construction: the
upper section w/a broken pitched
pediment w/molded dentilled cornice filled w/latticework flanking
a fluted central plinth surmounted
by an asymmetrical peanut-carved
crest over a foliate & geometric
carved blind-fret carved frieze & a
pair of long geometrically-glazed
cupboard doors opening to four
shaped shelves & flanked by fluted canted angles; the lower section w/an applied mid-molding
above a pair of paneled cupboard
doors opening to two shelves &
centered by fluted canted front
corner angles over a molded base
on heavy ogee bracket feet, Philadelphia, 1760-80, 24 x 54½",
8' 10½" h. 33,000.00
Corner cupboard, Classical (Ameri-
can Empire), walnut & walnut-
veneered, two-part construction:
the upper section w/an arched &
scrolled pediment w/three turned
& reeded urn finials above a pair
of arched & geometrically-glazed
cupboard doors opening to three
shelves & flanked by half-round
carved pilasters; the lower section w/three drawers above a

Classical Corner Cupboard

pair of cupboard doors opening to
a single shelf & flanked by half-
round carved & ring-turned pilasters, flat apron, on short knob-
turned feet, Ohio, ca. 1830-40,
refinished, brasses replaced,
24 x 55", 10' 4" h. (ILLUS.) 4,125.00
Corner cupboard, country-style,
painted pine, one-piece construction, perimeter molding w/applied
pierced scalloping across the top
& almost to the base on each
side, double 8-pane doors opening
to butterfly scalloped shelves, interior w/arched baffle w/cut-out
pinwheels, above midsection panel w/reeding & relief carving over
single paneled door flanked by
two similar stationary panels,
cleaned down to traces of old
blue paint, attributed to the
Amish community near Lancaster,
Pennsylvania, 54½" w., 7' 5¼" h.
(minor edge damage, portions of
backboard cut away on one side
at top & bottom corners) 6,500.00

Corner cupboard, Federal 'bow-
front' country-style, painted, two-
part construction: the upper section w/a bowed, molded cornice
hung w/spherules over a frieze
decorated w/applied roundels
over a pair of geometrically-
glazed cupboard doors w/roun-
dels enclosing three shelves &
flanked by feather-carved panels;
the lower section of conforming
form w/a mid-molding above a
pair of molded paneled cupboard
doors enclosing two shelves &
centered by tongue-shaped side
panels above a shaped apron, on
bracket feet, painted red, northern New England, early 19th c.,
28 x 56½", 7' 1" h. (ILLUS.) 11,000.00

Federal "Bow-Front" Corner Cupboard

Early American Court Cupboard

Court cupboard, Pilgrim Century, carved & painted oak, the rectangular top above heavy ring-turned columns flanking a pair of small paneled cupboard doors centered by another panel all slightly stepped-back from the lower section w/a pair of long paneled drawers above a pair of paneled cupboard doors, front stiles form short block feet, probably Massachusetts, 17th c., refinished, restored & pieced feet, 20¾ x 50", 5' 5" h. (ILLUS.) 12,100.00

Hanging corner cupboard, painted pine, the molded cove cornice above a single long raised-panel door opening to a shelf, the tapering backboards forming a rounded point at the bottom flanking a small corner shelf, painted green, Pennsylvania, first quarter 19th c., 16 x 22¾", 37½" h. 2,475.00

Hanging cupboard, Chippendale, painted, the rectangular molded cornice above an arched opening revealing a pair of serpentine shelves over a molded base, red-painted finish, 10 x 18½", 26" h. 2,420.00

Hanging cupboard, grain-painted pine, rectangular top w/projecting cornice above a pair of double-paneled doors, the top panel glazed, opening to a shelf, painted & grained overall in brown & ochre, New England, first half 19th c., 10 x 36¾", 29¾" h. 990.00

Hanging cupboard, painted walnut, the superstructure w/scroll-cut sides centering two open shelves above a single raised-panel door w/wrought-iron rattail hinges, painted black, Pennsylvania, 1750-80, 14¼ x 23½", 44½" h. . . .6,490.00

Hanging cupboards, Edwardian, inlaid satinwood, bone & ebony inlaid arched crest over a single door & arched apron, ca. 1900, 32" h., pr. .1,870.00

Victorian Jelly Cupboard

Jelly cupboard, hardwood, a high rectangular backboard crest above a narrow shelf flanked by shaped end brackets above the rectangular top over a pair of short drawers above a single long drawer above a pair of tall paneled cupboard doors w/rounded corners & line-incised bands, bracket feet, dark stain finish, late 19th c. (ILLUS.) 600.00

Jelly cupboard, painted butternut, rectangular top w/dentil-molded cornice above a paneled door w/porcelain knob, scrolled apron, high cut-out feet, old worn grey paint over earlier red, 18½ x 36½", 59" h. (bottom boards replaced) . . 900.00

Jelly cupboard, painted pine, rectangular top w/flared cornice above a pair of beaded drawers w/turned wood knobs above a pair of long beaded & paneled cupboard doors, tall slender cut-out feet, cleaned to old blue paint w/traces of yellow, 19th c., 19 x 49½", 4' 11" h. (turn-buckle on doors added) 2,550.00

Jelly cupboard, primitive painted yellow pine, rectangular top above a long flat door w/wooden turn latch flanked by wide front boards, side boards form the feet, rough-sawn lumber decorated w/orange stylized pine trees in large diamonds across the front on a green ground, wire nail construction, found in Catawba County, North Carolina, 17 x 36", 6' 1" h. 3,190.00

Chippendale Linen Press

Linen press, Chippendale, mahogany, two-part construction: the upper section w/a rectangular top above a deep flaring cornice w/dentil band above a pair of tall arch-paneled cupboard doors; the lower section w/a medial molding above three long drawers on a molded base w/scroll-cut bracket feet, attributed to Matthew Edgerton, New Brunswick, New Jersey, 18th c., 44" w., 6' 8¼" h. (ILLUS.) 7,150.00

Linen press, Classical, oak, two-part construction: the upper section w/a rectangular top w/outset corners on the stepped, flaring cornice above a pair of cupboard doors each w/two arched panels & flanked by knob- and ring-turned pilasters; the lower section

Canadian Classical Linen Press

w/a row of three drawers over three long graduated drawers, scroll-cut apron & tall bracket feet, Canada, mid-19th c. (ILLUS.) 1,430.00

Linen press, Federal, inlaid mahogany, two-part construction: the upper section w/a rectangular top w/a molded cornice above a pair of hinged paneled doors w/inlaid central flower reserve opening to shelves; the lower section w/four long graduated cockbeaded drawers, on tall slender French feet, New York, ca. 1800, 20½ x 46½", 7' ½" h. (some losses to veneer) 6,600.00

Pewter cupboard, primitive painted hardwood, one-piece construction, rectangular top above an open-fronted case w/two shelves on a stepped-out base w/a pair of long simple cupboard doors w/wooden thumb latch, short square feet, worn layers of old dark paint, 18¾ x 40¼", 6' 1½" h. (one front foot damaged) 1,300.00

Pie safe, hanging-type, pine, rectangular top over case w/pine sides & punched tin circular design panels in back & on door, wrought-iron hooks at top edges, 23½ x 39", 30¼" h. 350.00

Pie safe, butternut, mortised & pinned construction, rectangular top w/low crestrail over two short drawers w/wooden pulls above two hinged doors w/three punched tin figure eight design panels in each, three conforming panels in each end, simple feet, refinished, 17¾ x 37¾", 4' 3" h. plus crest (cornice removed) 825.00

Pie safe, painted pine, rectangular

top slightly overhanging a case
w/two doors each w/two punched
tin panels w/a diamond surrounding a tulip blossom & flanked
by stars, matching double end
panels, a molded apron raised
on tall square legs, old green
repaint over earlier brown, North
Carolina origin, 19th c., 17 x 42",
5' h. 1,540.00
Pie safe, yellow pine, rectangular
top w/a narrow molded cornice
above a tall case w/a pair of cupboard doors, each w/two rectangular tins punched w/stylized
'boteh' designs & framed w/reed-
ed molding, above a central pair
of drawers w/wooden knobs
above another pair of raised-
panel lower cupboard doors,
three matching punched tin panels
& a raised-panel at each side, the
molded base raised on tall square
post legs extending from the cupboard corner posts, found in
Savannah, Georgia, 19th c.,
19½ x 43¾", 5' 10¾" h. (minor repairs, refinished, tins re-
placed) 2,090.00
Step-back wall cupboard, Chippen-
dale country-style, painted pine,
two-part construction: the upper
section w/a rectangular top w/a
narrow molded cornice over a
pair of 6-pane glazed cupboard
doors opening to two shelves
above an open pie shelf; the
stepped-out lower section w/a
pair of drawers flanking a small
central drawer over a pair of
paneled cupboard doors, molded
base band & slightly arched apron
w/cut-out bracket feet, chamfered
corners on both sections, old
worn brown, Pennsylvania, early
19th c., 20 x 47", 6' 6½" h. (wear,
edge damage, feet ended-out,
center drawer front old replace-
ment) 3,025.00
Step-back wall cupboard, country-
style, painted wood, one-piece
construction, a flat rectangular
top on a tall upper open section
w/molding around the edge of
the front framing three open
shelves, the sides w/double
panels, the stepped-out lower section w/a single wide paneled
door, flat base, worn red & pewter green paint, New England,
early 19th c., surface wear &
damage to door, 18 x 34½",
6' 8¼" h. (ILLUS. top next
column) 1,870.00

Country-Style Step-back Cupboard

Step-back wall cupboard, Federal,
painted poplar, two-part construction: the upper section w/molded
cornice above a pair of double-
paneled cupboard doors opening
to a mustard-painted three-
shelved interior over scalloped
supports; the projecting lower
section w/applied mid-molding
above a pair of double-paneled
cupboard doors opening to a single shelf interior flanking four
graduated short drawers, shaped
skirt, bracket feet, door panels &
drawer fronts grain-painted over
natural finish, remainder grain-
painted in brown, Mid-Atlantic
States, 1820-30, 17½ x 55¾",
6' 11¾" h. 13,200.00

Federal Step-back Cupboard

Step-back wall cupboard, Federal
country-style, painted wood, two-
part construction: the upper section w/a rectangular top above

the widely flaring cornice above a pair of 6-pane glazed cupboard doors opening to three shelves above an open pie shelf; the lower section w/three drawers above a pair of paneled cupboard doors, on turnip-turned feet, old red paint, round brass pulls, Pennsylvania, 1835-45, minor imperfections, 19 x 53¼", 7' 3" h. (ILLUS.) 17,600.00

Step-back wall cupboard, grain-painted poplar, two-part construction: the upper section w/a rectangular top w/a flat flaring cornice above a pair of 6-pane glazed doors opening to shelves, above an open pie shelf; the projecting lower section w/a pair of drawers w/wooden knobs above a pair of raised-panel cupboard doors, raised on simple bracket feet, original brown flame graining, 19th c., 19½ x 47", 7' h. (added brass thumb latch on lower door, some paint touch-up, one back foot repaired) 3,080.00

Step-back wall cupboard, walnut w/poplar ends, two-part construction: upper section w/a rectangular top w/a beveled cornice above two paneled cupboard doors set in beaded frames; the projecting lower section w/two paneled cupboard doors set in beaded frames, deeply scalloped apron, high feet, 13¼ x 48¼", 6' 7" h. (small repair to corner of bottom door, base has some reconstruction, refinished) 1,400.00

Painted Wall Cupboard

Wall cupboard, country-style, painted wood, one-piece construction, a rectangular top above a wide

flaring dentil-carved cornice above a single tall four-panel door w/white porcelain door knob, front bracket feet, w/original Spanish brown paint w/the panels in olive green trimmed w/cream designs & black striping, five shelves on the interior, script inscription on the backboards reads "C.W. Robinson - Salisbury, Mass.," Georgia, mid-19th c., 16¾ x 43¼", 6' 4¼" h. (ILLUS.) . .1,320.00

Wall cupboard, country-style, pine, one-piece construction, rectangular top w/molded cornice above two tall cupboard doors w/raised paneling, opening on rattail hinges to an interior w/four shelves, sides continuing to form feet, first half 19th c., 46" w., 4' 10" h. (one shelf missing) 3,080.00

Early New Jersey Cupboard

Wall cupboard, Federal country-style, stained pine, two-part construction: the upper section w/a rectangular top w/a cove-molded cornice over a pair of 6-pane glazed cupboard doors flanked by tall, narrow panels; the lower section w/a medial molding above a long center drawer flanked by small square drawers above a pair of double-paneled cupboard doors w/a narrow panel over a wide panel, the doors flanked by short & tall side panels, Bergen County, New Jersey, first quarter 19th c., 18½ x 51", 6' 9" h. (ILLUS.) 5,500.00

Wall cupboard, Norwegian provincial-style, painted wood, one-piece construction, the rectangular overhanging cornice over a single paneled door decorated w/an ornate carved double-cartouche scroll, the front corners w/rope-turned pilasters, a heavy medial molding below the door & above an open pie shelf w/deeply coved side brackets over a heavy edge molding above a single lower door matching the upper door & also flanked by rope-turned edge pilasters, the whole painted tomato red w/teal blue trim on the cornice, moldings & the door designs & highlighted w/black & yellow scrolled decoration & indistinct initials, dated 1836, 11 x 36¼", 5' 9½" h. 5,500.00

DESKS

Art Deco Lady's Writing Desk

Art Deco lady's writing desk, inlaid rosewood, mahogany & ebonized wood, a narrow rectangular top w/inlaid border band above a slanted writing lid inlaid w/a central cartouche of stylized blossoms in various woods, abalone & ivory, opening to a writing surface, open shelf & two small drawers, above a single long apron drawer w/scalloped edge, raised on tapering legs w/fluted capitals, France, ca. 1925, 15¼ x 26¾", 36½" h. (ILLUS.) 1,870.00

Art Nouveau desk, "Neuphars," gilt-bronze mounted mahogany, the irregular rectangular top inset w/a leather writing surface w/dished outward flaring & curving front corners, supporting an integral superstructure deck at the rear w/three small curved drawers above an open shelf, all above two frieze drawers, the whole supported by curved legs w/flaring buttresses mounted w/gilt-bronze furling lily pads & blossoms, the drawer handles similarly cast, w/the key, Louis

Majorelle, France, ca. 1900, 34 x 55½", 40" h. 57,750.00

Arts & Crafts Partner's Desk

Arts & Crafts style partner's desk, oak, rectangular top over a central long drawer & kneehole flanked by a cabinet door on one side & a bank of three small drawers on the other, chamfered boards at sides & lining the kneehole, wide tapering legs on casters, unmarked, ca. 1910, 34¼ x 54", 30½" h. (ILLUS.) 770.00

Chippendale country-style slant-front desk, curly maple, a narrow rectangular top above the hinged slant-front opening to an interior fitted w/pigeonholes above a row of five small drawers over two longer drawers, the case w/four long, graduated drawers w/batwing brasses, scroll-cut bracket feet, late 18th c., 18 x 35½", 42" h. (minor repairs, age cracks to slant-front) 4,730.00

Chippendale kneehole desk, mahogany, the rectangular molded top over a conforming case w/beaded long drawer opening to a partly fitted interior over tiers of three graduated short drawers flanking a kneehole backed by a paneled cupboard door enclosing two shelves above a molded base, on bracket feet, probably Norfolk, Virginia, 1760-80, 22¼ x 40½", 32" h. 12,650.00

Chippendale slant-front desk, carved walnut, hinged lid opening to an interior fitted w/valanced pigeonholes above eight short drawers centering a prospect door, on a case w/four long graduated drawers, on bracket feet, replaced brasses, refinished, Chester County, Pennsylvania, 1797-1833, 22 x 38", 42¾" h. 13,200.00

Continental provincial-style slant-front desk, painted wood, a deep scroll-cut crest above the rectangular slant-front opening to a well, raised on shaped circular faceted tapering legs, painted blue, Europe, 19th c., 27¾ x 31", 38" h. 990.00

Federal lady's writing desk, mahogany, the rectangular top w/hinged out-folding writing slab, the interior fitted w/three small short drawers & the slab w/two long compartments, over a conforming case w/one long drawer to one side on ring-turned reeded tapering cylindrical legs, on casters, attributed to John or Thomas Seymour, Boston, Massachusetts, 1800-20, 20 x 29", 37" h. 3,300.00

Federal Roll-Top Desk

Federal roll-top desk, inlaid mahogany, the rectangular top over a frieze of two small drawers over a roll-top opening to a fitted interior of pigeonholes above short drawers over the case fitted w/a secretary drawer over three long, graduated drawers, each drawer w/quarter-fan inlay, shaped apron, on French feet, mid-Atlantic States, 1790-1810, some restorations to feet, 20½ x 42", 4' ½" h. (ILLUS.) 4,400.00

Hepplewhite country-style desk-on-frame, butternut, a narrow three-quarter gallery w/scrolled ends above a wide slant-top lifting above a deep dovetailed case fitting into a frame w/a molded edge band above a pair of narrow drawers w/large turned wood pulls, raised on heavy square tapering legs, 19th c., 29½ x 30¼", 36" h. (refinished, repairs, edge band added, lid hinge broken) 385.00

Mission-style (Arts & Crafts movement) drop-front desk, tapered top overhanging paneled drop-front above medial shelf, tapering one-piece end boards w/cut-out

ends, red decal mark of Gustav Stickley, Model No. 706, 11 x 30", 44" h. 2,090.00

Mission-style (Arts & Crafts movement) writing desk, oak, rectangular top above a case w/two pairs of drawers flanking a central kneehole w/a drawer over an indented shelf, early hand-wrought pulls, paneled sides, original dark finish, large red decal mark of Gustav Stickley, Model No. 709, 24 x 42", 29" h. 1,100.00

Modern desk, inlaid palmwood, the elliptical top w/two apron drawers supported by tapering ends, the top & sides set w/mother-of-pearl rectangles over-painted in black w/geometric patterns of concentric circles & triangles, bordered by alternating sections of palmwood & mother-of-pearl & inset w/chrome, 25 x 60", 29¼" h. 1,100.00

Modern style desk, wood & copper, the rectangular top w/rounded corners above three drawers w/copper handles on the right side, the kneehole framed w/two twin rounded copper stretchers, after a design by Gilbert Rohde for the Herman Miller Furniture Co., together w/a dark green leather upholstered side chair w/copper intersected legs, desk 22½ x 44", 29½" h., 2 pcs. 4,400.00

Queen Anne slant-front desk, cherry, rectangular top over the slant front opening to an interior fitted w/five pairs of pigeonholes above a row of five small drawers, the case w/four long graduated drawers w/butterfly brasses, molded base on shaped bracket feet, New England, ca. 1750, 19 x 34¾", 42½" h. 3,080.00

Queen Anne slant-front child's desk, curly maple, the rectangular hinged lid opening to an interior fitted w/small drawers & pigeonholes, a well w/retractable lid below, all above two drawers, on bracket feet, Massachusetts, ca. 1765, 10 x 18", 26½" h. (some restoration) 11,500.00

Rococo-Style fall-front desk, marquetry, a narrow rectangular top above the slanted fall-front inlaid w/leafy scrolls, birds & insects above a shell carving & opening to a compartmentalized interior w/frieze drawers, above a long serpentine drawer over a knee-hole flanked by two short drawers, all inlaid w/flowers & leafy

Dutch Marquetry Rococo Style Desk

vines, raised on simple cabriole
legs w/blossom & line inlay &
ending in brass *sabots*, Holland,
late 19th c., 18 x 27", 38" h.
(ILLUS.) 2,640.00
Victorian "Davenport" desk, ma-
hogany, the square top w/a
slightly canted lid inset w/tooled
leather & opening to a well &
small drawers, the case containing four full drawers on the front
& four sham drawers on the back,
on a molded base w/bracket
feet, England, first half 19th c.,
18½" sq., 32" h. 2,090.00

Wooton Extra Grade Desk

Victorian "patent" desk, Wooton Extra Grade, walnut & bird's-eye
maple & ebonized wood, incised
gilt trim, an ornate carved &
paneled cornice above hinged
doors opening to an interior fitted
throughout with pigeonholes &
small drawers, raised on carved
shoe feet on casters, ca. 1870
(ILLUS.) 18,700.00
Victorian roll-top desk, oak, a nar-
row rectangular top above the S-

Victorian Roll-top Desk

roll top opening to an interior
fitted w/rows of small drawers,
pigeonholes & a central open gallery, the lower case w/a long
narrow drawer over a kneehole
backed by a pair of paneled doors
& flanked by stacks of four drawers each, on a molded base, ca.
1900 (ILLUS.) 5,280.00
William & Mary 'desk-on-frame,'
painted wood, the slant lid opening to an interior w/small compartments above a single drawer,
on a frame w/baluster-, knob-
and ring-turned legs joined by
flat shaped stretchers & ending in
ball feet, dark red & black paint,
New England, early 18th c.,
19½ x 31 1/8", 33" h. (restora-
tion) 4,125.00
William & Mary slant-front desk,
burled walnut veneer, a rectangular top above a slant-front opening to a fitted interior w/end
blocked serpentine small drawers
below open valanced compartments flanking a veneered prospect door & document drawers
w/pilasters, the lower case
w/four long drawers w/burl veneer & batwing brasses, a molded
base on turned turnip feet, Boston area, 1710-30, 20½ x 38¾",
39¾" h. 12,100.00

DINING SUITES

Art Deco: dining table & six armchairs; mahogany, the table
w/round top w/radiating veneers
above a large circular pedestal
decorated w/three bronze rings,
supported by three gently arched
tapering legs ending in bronze
sabots, the chairs w/curved mahogany crestrail above shaped
rectangular upholstered back

flanked by U-shaped mahogany arms centering an oval upholstered seat & raised on tapering cylindrical feet ending in bronze *sabots*, upholstered in textured cream-colored velvet, Jules Leleu, France, ca. 1930, table 47" d., 28½" h., 7 pcs..................7,700.00

Danish Modern: dining table & four side chairs; table w/laminated circular top on three slender, cylindrical legs, the chairs w/narrow concave crestrails over triangular seats, the back stiles forming back legs, stackable, w/the manufacturer's label, designed by Hans Wegner & manufactured by Fritz Hansen, ca. 1950, table 47" d., chairs 28½" h., the set (one chair repaired, some roughness)......................... 550.00

Ornately Carved Dining Table

w/a molded edge over the ornately scroll-carved apron supported on a base composed of four full-figure carved griffins on a cross section centered by a large bulbous reeded center column & on bun feet, late 19th c., 12 pcs. (ILLUS. of table)........16,150.00

Mission-style Sideboard

Mission-style (Arts & Crafts movement): pedestal base dining table Model 409 w/four boxed leaves, sideboard, server & seven dining chairs Model No. 891; oak, all w/branded mark of Limbert Furniture Co., ca. 1910, sideboard 59¼" l., refinished, 10 pcs. (ILLUS. of sideboard).................5,500.00

Modern style: extension dining table & six chairs; walnut, the table w/a rectangular top composed of two broad laminated leaves joined by three butterfly joints, raised on a simple base of canted tapering circular legs & w/two extension leaves for either end, the chairs w/rounded back rail raised on spindle supports & w/woven grass seats raised on four spindle legs conjoined by stretchers, by George Nakashima, ca. 1960, table 36 x 104" (extended), 28½" h., 7 pcs.................9,900.00

Victorian, Baroque style: dining table, sideboard, china cabinet, server & eight chairs; mahogany, the round expandable dining table

Baroque Style Dining Table

Victorian, Baroque style: dining table w/eight leaves, server & 12 upholstered chairs; oak, the round expandable table w/a molded edge above the slightly rounded apron ornately carved w/scrolling leafy vines & cartouches & raised on four heavy cabriole legs w/scroll-carved knees & ending in lion paw feet resting on a wide platform base centered by a heavy column w/a gadrooned base band, late 19th c., table 60" d., 14 pcs. (ILLUS. of table) ..4,250.00

DRY SINKS

Painted pine, long rectangular well on top w/a deep flaring banded edging above the case w/a pair of large cupboard doors composed of narrow wainscoting boards, old worn blue repaint, drain hole through top & interior shelves, well partially refinished, 19th c., 18¾ x 52", 33¼" h............. 350.00

Painted poplar, rectangular well above a pair of paneled cupboard doors, scroll-cut apron continuing to low bracket feet, layers of old worn green paint, 19th c., 16¾ x 39½", 33" h. (cast-iron thumb latch replaced, feet expertly ended-out) 575.00

Painted & Decorated Dry Sink

Painted & decorated oak & pine, superstructure w/three short drawers above scalloped sides above square work surface at one end above a small drawer beside the rectangular well, two paneled doors in base opening to an interior w/two shelves, scroll-cut apron, red & green ground w/polychrome painted decoration, original turned wood pulls, some height loss & paint imperfections, Pennsylvania, last quarter 19th c., 17¼ x 44", 4' 9 5/8" h. (ILLUS.) ... 825.00

Painted & decorated poplar, a low rounded splashback above the rectangular well all lined w/zinc above a wide molded board above a pair of paneled doors & a suspended small drawer under the top at one end, overall oak graining over earlier red, found in Lancaster County, Pennsylvania, 19th c., 20½ x 45¾", 32¾" h. plus crest 715.00

Pine & poplar, rectangular top w/a low rounded splashboard above an inset work section at the right end above a single shelf, a deep well above a pair of paneled cupboard doors, simple bracket feet, 19th c., 18¼ x 46", 37¾" h. (small pieced repair to drawer front) 375.00

Poplar, rectangular well w/molded edge & low rounded splashback above a case w/a pair of paneled cupboard doors, on turnip-shaped

turned feet, 22 x 49", 34¼" h. plus crest (refinished, base & molding damage, feet & bottom board of well replaced) 440.00

GARDEN & LAWN FURNITURE

(Cast iron unless otherwise noted)

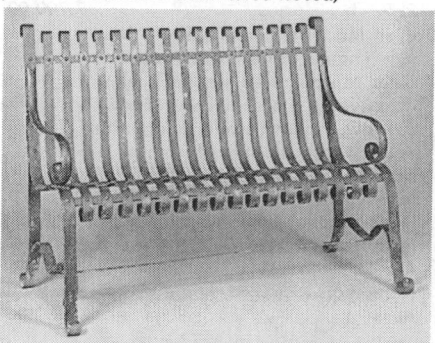

Victorian Strap-Iron Bench

Armchairs, "Curtain" patt., pierced & scrolled rectangular back surmounted w/a crest in the form of a stylized flower, pierced seat, straight legs joined at sides w/a bow-shaped stretcher, stamped "S.S. Bent & Sons N.Y.," late 19th c., pr. 523.00

Armchairs, Fern patt., back composed of a pierced design of fern leaves above a conforming seat, on curved leafy legs, set of 4 ....1,100.00

Bench, semi-circular, the scalloped pierced back composed of berried laurel leaf panels, raised on stylized griffin legs, late 19th c., 38" l. 1,430.00

Bench, three-chairback style, center crestrail cast w/ornate medallion above pierced design, flanked by lower crestrails w/matching medallions, backs composed of scrolling trellis-form casting, back w/nameplate "C. Coughlin, Jr.," green repaint, 44" l. 495.00

Bench, strap-iron, the back & seat composed of long, curved straps of iron w/curled ends between strap scrolled arms, scroll-ended legs joined by strap rungs & a media! bar, painted black, second half 19th c., 45¼" l. (ILLUS.) 1,320.00

Bench, Rustic patt., formed as intertwining branches, 49" l. 2,750.00

Center table, pierced circular top above a standard cast w/dolphins, ending in a scrolling tripod base, stamped w/English registry mark, third quarter 19th c., 22¼" d., 27½" h. 1,100.00

Garden suite: settee & two armchairs; triple chair-back settee w/a stepped crest above each section, center back section cast in a pierced snowflake-type design flanked by sections of a pierced scrolling design, geometric pierced seat & apron, scrolling arms, conforming armchairs, Peter Timmes Son, Brooklyn, New York, last quarter 19th c., settee 44" l., 38" h., 3 pcs. 2,640.00

Plant stands, stylized commodeform, a rectangular top over bombe' sides w/a pierced trellis design & swags w/a large shell at the base of the front, raised on slender, tapering legs ending in bun feet resting on a X-form base, painted white, Europe, 19th c., 30" h., pr. 3,575.00

Victorian Garden Table

Table, oblong pierced top above wide foliate-cast & elaborately scrolled ends joined by a shaped medial bar, painted black, American-made, second half 19th c., 22¼ x 36", 26½" h. (ILLUS.)...... 880.00

HALL RACKS & TREES

Hall rack, Art Nouveau, mahogany, a flaring mahogany panel w/five brass curved coat hooks centered by a mirror, an umbrella stand below, France, early 20th c., 47" w., 7' 1" h. 978.00

Hall rack, Mission-style (Arts & Crafts movement), oak, tall square shaft w/two tiers of four wooden hooks each near the top, half buttresses running up from the cross base on all four sides, on square wafer feet, attributed to Charles Rohlfs, early 20th c., 5' 4" h. 990.00

Hall rack, Mission-style (Arts & Crafts movement), two-sided, two

slender tapering vertical posts ending in shoe feet & joined near the middle by two horizontal slats ending in through-tenons flush w/the sides, each side mounted w/three hooks, fine original medium brown finish, red decal mark of Gustav Stickley, Model No. 53, 13" w., 6' h. 1,600.00

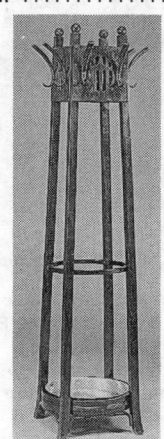

Hall Rack by Joseph Hoffmann

Hall rack, Modern style, stained beechwood, the four square uprights w/ball finials enclosing oval pierced panels w/paired coat hooks at top conjoined by a railing at the middle, the circular base enclosing a shallow umbrella drip pan, drip pan replaced, designed by Joseph Hoffmann, manufactured by Mundus and J. & J. Kohn, ca. 1910, 18" w., 6' 7½" h. (ILLUS.)..............3,575.00

Hall tree, carved walnut, carved as a tall, slender bare-branched tree w/a bear cub at the top & a mother bear climbing from below, looped branches at front to hold umbrellas w/a drip pan in the base, on turned turnip feet, Europe, 19th c., 7' 1" h. 5,175.00

HIGHBOYS & LOWBOYS

Highboys

Chippendale "bonnet-top" highboy, carved walnut, two-part construction: the upper section w/molded swan's neck pediment centering a flame finial above four graduated long drawers; the lower section w/mid-molding above one long & three short drawers, the center fan-carved over a stepped skirt w/two pendant drops, on

Chippendale "Bonnet-Top" Highboy

cabriole legs w/pad-and-disc feet,
Salem, Massachusetts, 1760-80,
22 x 40", 7' h. (ILLUS.) 60,500.00
Chippendale-Style "bonnet-top"
highboy, mahogany, two-part construction: the upper section w/a
broken-arch closed bonnet top
w/three turned urn finials above
a wide frieze carved w/a low,
elongated & arched fan carving
above a pair of drawers above
three long drawers all flanked by
reeded pilasters; the lower section w/a medial molding above a
pair of drawers over two smaller
drawers flanking a deeply arched
center section & a shaped apron
w/drops, cabriole legs w/fan-
carved knees & claw-and-ball
feet, late 19th - early 20th century copy w/some 'old' parts,
17¾ x 40¾", 7' 2" h. (some dam-
age & veneer repairs) 1,870.00
Queen Anne "bonnet-top" highboy,
carved & figured walnut & maple,
two-part construction: the upper
section w/a molded swan's neck
crest surmounted by three
spirally-twisted finials above a
pair of small drawers flanking a
deep center drawer w/large fan-
carving above four long graduated
drawers; the lower section w/a
narrow long drawer above a row
of three deep drawers, the center
one fan-carved, shaped apron
w/two small rounded drops continues to cabriole legs ending
in pad feet, Boston, Massachusetts, ca. 1760, 21 7/8 x 39½",
7' 4¼" h. 60,500.00
Queen Anne "flat-top" highboy, burl
walnut veneer & maple, two-part

construction: the upper section
w/molded cornice above two
short & three long graduated
drawers; the lower section
w/three short drawers, the
shaped skirt below continuing to
cabriole legs ending in pad feet,
probably original bright-cut decorated brasses & escutcheons, Boston, Massachusetts, ca. 1740,
19¼ x 37½", 5' ¾" h. 30,800.00

Queen Anne "Flat-Top" Highboy

Queen Anne "flat-top" highboy, maple, two-part construction: the upper section w/a rectangular top
over a deep molded cornice
above a pair of drawers over
three long graduated drawers; the
lower section w/a mid-molding
above a narrow long drawer over
a pair of deep drawers flanking a
narrow center drawer over a scalloped & shell-carved apron, cabriole legs ending in pad feet,
Goddard-Townsend school, Rhode
Island, 18th c., untouched condi-
tion (ILLUS.) 30,800.00
William & Mary "flat-top" highboy,
painted wood, two-part construction: the upper section w/rectan-
gular molded cornice over two
short drawers above three graduated long drawers; the lower section w/molded waist over a long
drawer, above baluster- and
trumpet-turned legs joined by flat
curved stretchers, on ball feet,
painted black, Pennsylvania,
1720-40, 22 x 39", 4' 2½" h. (feet
restored) .15,400.00

Lowboys

Chippendale lowboy, carved mahogany, molded top above a case

Rare Chippendale Lowboy

w/a frieze drawer above a shell-carved drawer & two small drawers, fluted quarter-columns flanking, the shaped skirt continuing to shell-carved cabriole legs ending in ball-and-claw feet, Philadelphia, ca. 1770, 21½ x 36 7/8", 31½" h. (ILLUS.) 104,500.00

Queen Anne lowboy, carved curly maple, rectangular thumbmolded top above a long narrow drawer over three deep drawers, the center one fan-carved, the scalloped skirt w/two teardrop-turned pendants continuing to angular cabriole legs ending in pad feet, Boston-Salem, Massachusetts, 1760-80, 19½ x 36¾", 31½" h. (patch to top) 55,000.00

Queen Anne lowboy, carved walnut, the rectangular thumbmolded top w/notched corners above one long & two short molded drawers, the skirt centering a carved shell & continuing to shell-carved cabriole legs ending in trifid feet, Philadelphia, ca. 1750, 19 7/8 x 33½", 29" h. 16,500.00

Queen Anne "Japanned" Lowboy

Queen Anne lowboy, japanned & carved walnut & pine, the rectangular molded top above one long

& three short molded drawers, the center drawer fan-carved, the shaped skirt w/turned pendants, continuing to angular cabriole front legs ending in pad feet, painted all over w/chinoiserie motifs including pagodas, weeping willow trees & strapwork designs in red, black & gold, the japanning executed ca. first quarter 19th c., probably original pierced brass hardware, Massachusetts, ca. 1765, old restoration to upper section of right leg, 20¾ x 34", 30¼" h. (ILLUS.) 6,050.00

Queen Anne-Style lowboy, curly maple & cherry, rectangular top overhanging a case w/a single long curly maple drawer above three small curly maple drawers above a scalloped & arched apron, cabriole legs ending in pad feet, hand-made reproduction w/some age, 20th c., 20 x 32", 29½" h. 1,265.00

LOVE SEATS, SOFAS & SETTEES

Louis XVI Canape'

Canape' (small love seat), Louis XVI, beechwood, shaped reeded frame above upholstered back above a loose cushion seat, raised on eight legs, the front legs headed by square medallions, w/stamp of George Jacob, France, late 18th c., 71" l., 37" h. (ILLUS.) 2,310.00

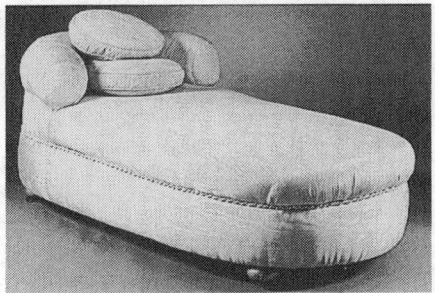

Art Deco Chaise Longue

Chaise longue, Art Deco, the oval

upholstered frame w/semicircular tubular back at one end, raised on bun feet, upholstered in beige taffeta, France, ca. 1925, 6' l. (ILLUS.) 3,300.00

Ornate Classical Couch

Couch, Classical (American Empire), mahogany & mahogany veneer, veneered crestrail terminating in carved parcel gilt water leaf & floral motif, gilt S-scroll dolphin arms over floral & leaf-filled cornucopia & lions' paw feet, New York, ca. 1825, 24¼ x 94", 32¼" h. (ILLUS.) 10,450.00

Daybed, country-style, curly maple w/walnut headboard, curved headboard flanked by ring-turned flat knobs over block- and baluster-turned posts, low conforming posts at foot, old mellow finish, upholstered cushion, 24 x 77" 510.00

Daybed, Mission-style (Arts & Crafts movement), oak, low headboard w/two splats flanking a wider center slat below a heavy crestrail between heavy square uprights continuing to form legs, wide siderails & heavy end legs, original brown finish, reupholstered in green leather, Stickley Brothers, Model No. 3236, early 20th c. 605.00

Rococo Rosewood Daybed

Daybed, Victorian, Rococo substyle, rosewood, the scrolled end & padded seat upholstered in contemporary floral needlework high-

lighted by beadwork, the scrolling foliate seatrail on cabriole legs w/casters, mid-19th c., 62" l. (ILLUS.) 2,420.00

Daybed, William & Mary, carved & painted maple, elaborately carved scrolled & interlaced crest above five vertical molded splats flanked by block- and baluster-turned stiles over a rush seat, on eight baluster- and cylinder-turned legs joined by baluster-turned stretchers, New England, mid-18th c., 22½ x 71", 40" h. (one stile restored) 4,400.00

Diminutive Classical Recamier

Recamier, Classical (American Empire), carved mahogany, the shaped crestrail above an upholstered back & seat, on acanthus-carved legs ending in animal paw feet, minor repairs, probably by Charles White, Philadelphia, ca. 1825, 65½" l. (ILLUS.) 3,575.00

Settee, Art Deco, narrow arched crestrail continuing to curving sloping arms, carved at center w/stylized blossoms & leaves above upholstered back & arms & enclosing a loose cushion, the whole raised on fluted melon-form feet, France, ca. 1925, 54" l. 1,210.00

Child's Settee by Gustav Stickley

Settee, child's, Mission-style (Arts &

Crafts movement), narrow crest-rail above single wide horizontal slat, shaped sides fastened through-tenon & keys continuing to form feet, fine original dark finish, paper label of Gustav Stickley, Model No. 215, together w/long suede pillow, 12¼ x 38", 30" h. (ILLUS.) 935.00

Settee, Federal, inlaid mahogany, the turned crestrail above four rectangular tablets continuing to arms w/turned supports, upholstered back & arms, the bowed seat w/loose cushion, on ring-turned tapering & reeded legs on casters, ca. 1800, 71½" l. (some repairs) 3,850.00

Settee, Federal "Fancy" style, painted & decorated, the long flat & wide crestrail w/rounded corners decorated w/a long band of fruit & foliage in brown w/black striping on the greyish yellow ground, three wide vase-shaped splats in the back & two ring-turned spindles between, scrolled end arms above turned spindles above the long S-scroll plank seat, four ring-turned front legs joined by flat stretchers, the whole decorated w/brown & black striping on the greyish yellow ground, ca. 1830-50, 80½" l. 1,375.00

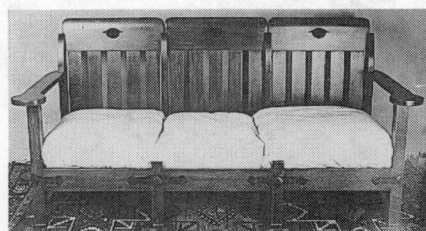

Mission-style Settee

Settee, Mission-style (Arts & Crafts movement), three-section back, each crestrail w/cut-out design, above five-slat back w/divider between each section, paddle arms, front apron applied w/hammered copper straps, branded mark of Gustav Stickley, 32 x 76", 38" h. (ILLUS.) 1,100.00

Settee, Windsor, painted wood, the rod-back crest above twenty-four raked spindles & curved arms on a shaped seat w/chamfered edge, on eight raking legs joined by rod stretchers, original brown-painted surface, 77" l., 32" h. 3,080.00

Settee, Windsor, a continuous arched crestrail above numerous

bamboo-turned spindles, shaped arms over spindles & canted baluster-turned arm supports, the plank saddle seat on eight baluster-turned canted legs joined by turned swelled stretchers, old mellow refinishing, late 18th - early 19th c., 72½" l., 35" h. (old repaired split at end of seat, one repaired spindle) 5,500.00

Country-Style Pine Settle

Settle, country-style, painted pine, the high back w/a flat top above shaped sides above a long hinged seat over a closed base, old Spanish brown paint, New England, early 19th c., imperfections, 13¾ x 54", 4' 7¼" h. (ILLUS.) 3,025.00

Mission-Style Settle

Settle, Mission-style (Arts & Crafts movement), oak, flat molded crestrail over thirteen wide canted vertical slats, molded even arms each over four vertical slats, two-part drop seat w/upholstered cushion, original medium finish, unsigned L. & J.G. Stickley, Onondaga Shops, Model No. 738, ca. 1902, 76¼" l., 38" h. (ILLUS.) 4,510.00

Settle-bed, painted pine, the flat raised back above deeply cut-out sides above a fold-out seat, early brown paint, Canada, ca. 1800, 66½" l., 33" h. (ILLUS. top next page) 880.00

Early Pine Settle-Bed

Settle-bed, pine, paneled back & cut
out sides w/applied moldings,
folds out into a bed, finish
cleaned down to old red paint,
73½" l., 48¾" h. (minor re-
pairs) 700.00

Sofa, Art Deco, polychromed wood,
the scalloped & slightly arched
crestrail centered by a crest
w/stylized overlapping flowerheads polychromed in red & shaded cream, crestrail continues to
upholstered outswept arms
w/fluted & foliate-carved front
supports, three-cushion upholstered seat above a serpentine
seatrail carved w/faceted dentils,
raised on reeded tapering turned
& curved legs, upholstered in
beige satin, in the manner of
Paul Follot, France, ca. 1925,
79½" l. 7,700.00

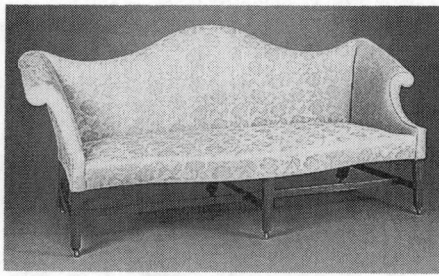

Fine Chippendale Sofa

Sofa, Chippendale 'camelback,'
carved mahogany, arched back
flanked by dramatically outscrolled & sloped arms & serpentine seat on square tapering legs
joined by stretchers, on casters,
Philadelphia, ca. 1770, some restorations to upper section of rear
center leg, 90" l. (ILLUS.) 36,300.00

Sofa, Classical (American Empire),
brass-inlaid mahogany, the narrow brass-, line- and star-inlaid
crestrail w/scrolled ears above a
low upholstered back flanked by
outscrolled arms w/brass-inlaid
arm supports continuing to the
exposed seatrail below the uphol-

stered seat w/two loose bolsters,
on brass-inlaid sabre legs ending
in sleeping lion's head cast brass
caps & on brass casters, attributed to Joseph Barry, Philadelphia,
ca. 1820, 86" l. (slight restoration
to two right legs) 18,400.00

American Classical Sofa

Sofa, Classical (American Empire),
carved mahogany, a rolled &
curved crest ending in florettes
raised above the scroll-cut crestrail above the high rolled arms
w/swan's head-carved arm supports continuing down to form the
molded seatrail below the upholstered seat, on turned tapering &
reeded legs on brass casters, Boston, Massachusetts, ca. 1820,
85" l. (ILLUS.) 2,875.00

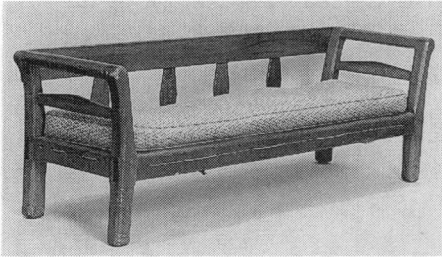

Texas-Made Pine Sofa

Sofa, country-style, pine, a low wide
crestrail above four diamond-
shaped splats, gently outscrolled
even arms above shaped slats
over the rope-strung seat now
fitted w/a cushion, on heavy
square legs w/chamfered corners,
Texas, 19th c. (ILLUS.) 3,430.00

Sofa, Federal, carved mahogany,
the crest carved w/three rectangular reeded panels flanked by
reeded downcurving arms & reeded leaf-carved arm supports, the
bowed seat on reeded tapering
legs ending in vase-form feet, on
brass casters, New York, ca.
1810, 78" l. 4,400.00

Sofa, Federal, carved mahogany,
the paneled crest carved w/drap-
ery swags & tassels centering a

reserve carved w/a bow w/ar-
rows, the reeded arms above a
bowed seat w/loose cushion, on
reeded legs ending in brass ball
feet, New York or Philadelphia,
ca. 1810, 78" l. (minor repairs)...9,350.00

Federal Sofa

Sofa, Federal, inlaid mahogany, the
upholstered back w/a gently
arched crest continuing to form
the upholstered arms w/a flat
wooden arm support fronted by
an arched handrest over a reeded
& baluster-turned spindle, the upholstered seat w/a flat seatrail
raised on four reeded & baluster-
turned front legs, probably Massachusetts, ca. 1810, 71" l., 35" h.
(ILLUS.) 4,125.00

MIRRORS

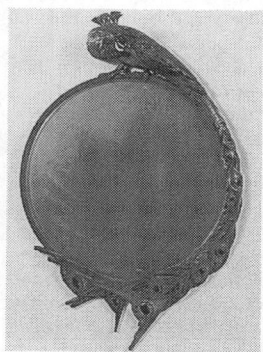

Elegant Art Nouveau Mirror

Art Nouveau wall mirror, lacquered
wood & enameled copper, the circular beveled mirror within a conforming cast metal frame set
w/the figure of a peacock at the
top, its body overlaid in brilliant
blue & turquoise enamels on the
head & tail, the tail continuing
down & around to form the right-
hand side in carved & lacquered
wood w/a rich golden brown &
applied w/golden flecks, the
enameled copper tail 'eyes' in cobalt blue & turquoise, minor
restorations, attributed to A.
Vever, France, ca. 1900, 19" w.,
29" h. (ILLUS.) 13,200.00

Baroque wall mirror, mirrored borders inset w/cobalt blue plaques
fitted w/gilt-metal foliate mounts,
outlined w/twist-turned borders &
surrounded by a mirrored border
& an outer cobalt blue border surrounded by gilt-metal frames &
fitted at each corner w/gilt-metal
flower-filled baskets, surrounding
a rectangular mirror plate, Italy,
late 17th c., 39¼" w., 47" h. ...16,500.00
Chippendale wall mirror, mahogany,
the wide crestrail ornately pierce-
carved w/scrolls & w/scrolled
ears & a central leaf-carved crest,
rectangular mirror plate w/parcel-
gilt liner, frame base crest identical to top crest, England, ca. 1780,
36" h. 1,540.00
Classical (American Empire) convex
wall mirror, giltwood, circular
frame surmounted by a wing-
spread eagle on a rockwork support, the mirror plate flanked by
four projecting candlearms, a
shaped pendant below, first quarter 19th c., 35" w., 44" h. 8,800.00
Empire country-style wall mirror,
carved wood, the rectangular
frame w/square corner blocks
joined by bobbin- and rod-turned
half-round pilasters along the
sides, a reverse-painted panel
section at the top decorated w/a
primitive landscape of a house &
trees above the rectangular mirror plate, mid-19th c., 12¾" w.,
23" h. 450.00

Federal Wall Mirror

Federal wall mirror, giltwood &
eglomise', the flat molded cornice
w/outset corners hung w/spher-
ules over a rectangular eglomise'
panel decorated in white & gilt
w/a central urn issuing florals &
vining foliage above the rectangular mirror plate, twist carving

flanking the mirror, some restoration, New England, 22¼" w.,
36" h. (ILLUS.) 715.00
Federal wall mirror, giltwood, mold-
ed flat crestrail w/outset blocked
corners, a row of spherules above
a lightly carved frieze band over a
rectangular eglomise' panel
featuring an allegorical scene of
"Harmony," above the rectangular
mirror plate flanked by half-round
colonettes up the side, flat base
rail w/corner blocks, New York,
ca. 1800, 21½" w., 46¼" h. 3,850.00
Mission-style (Arts & Crafts movement) wall mirror, oak, rectangular frame, the upper portion
gently curved, the lower portion
w/four iron coat hooks, original
chain for hanging, red decal mark
of Gustav Stickley, Model No. 66,
27¾ x 35¾" 2,860.00
Modern style wall mirror, oak, rectangular w/Greek key-type molding, designed by Frank Lloyd
Wright for Heritage Henredon
Company, stamped "0.2002 MIRR,"
15½ x 19¾" 528.00

Aesthetic Movement Overmantel Mirror

Victorian overmantel mirrors, Aesthetic Movement substyle, giltwood, ornate rectangular frame,
the central rectangular crest decorated w/oak leaves & pendant
acorns, flanked by further repetitive devices & depiction of a bird
& snake on a tree branch, labeled
"L. Uter, 47 Royal Street, New
Orleans," ca. 1880, pr. (ILLUS. of
one). 6,380.00

PARLOR SUITES

Art Deco: settee & a pair of side
chairs; carved & upholstered mahogany, the settee w/an arched
crestrail carved w/reeding ending
in volutes, the sides sweeping out
into a stylized shell form continuing to the lower frame carved
w/an apron resembling stretched
fabric w/fringe, raised on shaped
legs carved w/tassels & ending in
scrolling block feet, upholstered
in tufted teal blue velvet, the
chairs matching, made by Sue et
Mare, France, ca. 1925, settee
48" l., 3 pcs. 44,000.00

Art Deco Armchair

Art Deco: settee, a pair of club
chairs & a marble-topped coffee
table; giltwood & upholstered,
raised flat backs w/giltwood
crestrail above downswept giltwood arm rails above closed
arms, the giltwood arm supports
w/a cluster of carved leaves top-
ping, raised on baluster-turned
giltwood feet, each w/Wedgwood
blue velvet upholstery & over-
stuffed back & seat cushions, the
giltwood table w/an oval white
marble top raised on flat, reeded
legs above a caned lower shelf,
France, ca. 1925, chairs 33" h.,
settee 47" l., table 28 x 40",
25" h., the set (ILLUS. of
chair). 16,100.00
Bentwood: settee & two armchairs;
'Buenos Aires' set, leather-
upholstered bentwood, the settee
w/curved backrail & deep tufted
brown leather back curving to
form rolled arms & enclosing a D-
form upholstered seat, paneled
back & frame decorated w/brass
nailheads, designed by Josef Hoffmann, made by J. & J. Kohn, Austria, w/paper label, ca. 1904,
settee 52¼" l., 3 pcs. 15,400.00
Empire-Style (American): settee, two
armchairs & four side chairs; gilt-
bronze mounted mahogany, each
rectangular back fitted w/gilt-

bronze mounts, continuing to padded arms, raised on square tapering legs, the armchairs & settee headed by winged busts, all ending in gilt-bronze paw *sabots*, late 19th - early 20th c., 7 pcs......18,400.00

Louis XV-Style: settee, two canapes & four armchairs; giltwood, each upholstered back within a foliate & floral carved frame continuing to padded arms & upholstered seat, raised on cabriole legs headed by a shell & ending in scrolled toes, upholstered in figural Aubusson tapestry, third quarter 19th c., 7 pcs..........20,700.00

Louis XVI-Style Canape'

Louis XVI-Style: canape' & two armchairs; giltwood, each w/narrow continuous incurved crestrail continuing down to form hand-holds & curved arm supports & carved w/foliate bands, the oblong upholstered medallion back & side panels upholstered w/figural Aubusson tapestry, upholstered seat above a gently curved seatrail raised on turned tapering reeded legs, France, third quarter 19th c., 3 pcs. (ILLUS. of canape') 4,888.00

Louis XVI-Style: settee & four armchairs; giltwood, the settee w/a three-panel back & the armchairs each w/an oval upholstered back, all within a modeled foliate frame, continuing to scrolled open arms raised on stop-fluted foliate scrolled legs, each upholstered in Aubusson tapestry, the back depicting putti at various pursuits & the seats depicting dogs in pursuit of game, France, third quarter 19th c., 5 pcs...............23,100.00

Napoleon III: sofa, two bergeres, six armchairs, two side chairs & a fire screen; each w/a shaped rectangular leather upholstered back within a conforming frame fitted

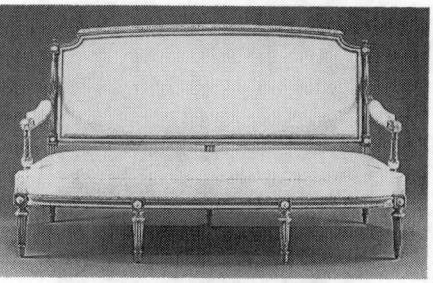

Napoleon III Sofa

w/ormolu beads & leaftip mounts, the sides of fluted columnar form headed by ormolu flowerheads & finials continuing to padded arms supported by spiral urn-form shaped standards, the upholstered seat above a similarly decorated apron raised on circular fluted legs, signed "Lexcellent Paris," France, third quarter 19th c., 12 pcs. (ILLUS. of sofa) 46,000.00

Aesthetic Movement Armchair

Victorian, Aesthetic Movement substyle: settee, two armchairs & two side chairs; ebonized wood, each piece w/an arched fan-shaped crestrail, the settee's flanked by Gothic-style arched side panels, the settee raised on *toupie* legs, the chairs on circular legs, each w/overall Gothic designs, carved leaves & incised decoration, third quarter 19th c., 5 pcs. (ILLUS. of armchair) 4,400.00

Victorian, Rococo substyle: armchair & four side chairs; carved rosewood, each w/a high, swelled balloon back w/the crestrail carved w/an ornate band of flowers, leaves & fruits, the armchair w/curved arms on shaped arm supports carved w/flowers above the demi-cabriole legs, serpentine seatrails w/carved flowers, on

Belter Rococo Armchair

casters, attributed to John Henry
Belter, New York, New York,
ca. 1855, the set (ILLUS. of arm-
chair). 8,625.00

SCREENS

Fire screen, Arts & Crafts style, copper & wood, triptych type w/a
wide central panel flanked by
narrow side panels each topped
by a double-arched crestrail, hammered copper panels decorated
w/stylized fish & naturalistic designs, riveted to a wooden frame,
ca. 1910, 38" w., 36" h. 440.00
Fire screen, brass, ornate rococo
scrollwork around sides centering
sunburst medallion, on bracket
feet, 30¾" h. 750.00
Folding screen, two-fold, painted
paper, continuous landscape
scene w/two samurai outside a
noble's pavilion, gilt clouds &
ground, brocade border, black
lacquer frame, Tosa School, Japan, early 19th c., each panel
23½ x 48" 4,400.00
Folding screen, two-fold, painted
paper, the two panels painted to
form a single landscape scene
w/three ponies & cherry trees in
blossom, brocade silk border, lacquer frame, Japan, late Edo peri-
od, minor tears, 37½ x 68" 5,225.00
Folding screen, three-fold, Art Deco
style, painted wood, the graduated panels painted w/pink & green
blossoms & a white spiderweb on
a silver ground, the reverse in
silk panels of stylized leaping
gazelles in maroon & tan, ca.
1930, 6' 11½" h. 605.00
Folding screen, three-fold, Art Nou-
veau style, mahogany & fruit-

wood, each shaped rectangular
panel carved in the upper section
in low-relief w/lotus leaves &
blossoms amid whiplash devices
above panels inlaid w/tall sailing
galleons & swirling banners,
clouds & waters, raised on relief-
molded scroll & whiplash feet,
signed in marquetry "Cutler &
Girard," Italy, ca. 1902, 5' 2¾" l.,
5' 11¼" h. .4,675.00
Folding screen, four-fold, painted &
giltwood, Louis XVI-Style, each
panel painted w/neoclassical designs including floral & scroll
swags, wreaths w/ribbons & oval
panels at the base, each oval
panel decorated w/an exotic animal, each panel within a molded
giltwood frame topped by a fruit-
and flower-molded wreath, Europe, late 19th - early 20th c.,
each panel 14½" w., 5' 8½" h. . .1,650.00

Rococo Revival Screen

Folding screen, five-fold, giltwood
w/painted panels, rococo revival
style, very ornate pierced scroll-
and lattice-carved frame in giltwood, one end panel headed at
the top corner by a caryatid, each
panel decorated by Georges Antoine Rochegrosse w/a different
landscape scene featuring lovers
in 18th c. costume, France, late
19th c., each panel 27½" w.,
8' 4" h. (ILLUS. of part) 22,000.00
Folding screen, six-fold, mahogany,
Louis Philippe style, each rectangular divided panel w/molded
mahogany borders & now upholstered w/stencil-decorated panels
of baskets of fruit & flowers,
France, early 19th c., each panel
20" w., 5' h. 6,600.00
Folding screen, six-fold, painted

Painted Leather Screen

leather, each panel divided into
three sections depicting a variety
of exotic birds, flora & fauna
in pale tones of red, green &
blue w/calligraphic lines, the
whole w/studded gilt-leather borders, Europe, each panel 22" w.,
7' 6" h. (ILLUS. of part) 2,310.00

Pole screen, Federal style, inlaid
mahogany, an octagonal frame
enclosing a floral-embroidered
needlework panel, the whole sliding on a rod w/removable finial,
the ring-turned standard raised on
three downcurving line-inlaid legs
joined by a shaped plinth, on
ebonized tapered feet, Salem or
Boston area, ca. 1810, 4' 9¼" h.
(some repairs) 1,870.00

Stationary screen, hardwood &
hongmu, an arrangement of five
graduated panels inset w/*famille
rose* porcelain plaques of varying
sizes decorated w/scenes depicting landscapes, people at various
pursuits & flowering plants, on a
gadroon foliate scroll & leaftip-
carved base, the panels surmounted by a conformingly carved
section, China, 19th c., 9' w.,
6' 9" h. 8,800.00

SECRETARIES

Chippendale secretary-bookcase,
cherry, two-part construction: the
upper section w/a rectangular top
w/deep molded cornice above a
pair of paneled cupboard doors
opening to a fitted interior; the
lower section w/applied mid-
molding over a slant lid opening
to a fitted interior w/a prospect
door flanked by valanced pigeonholes over banks of small drawers

all above a case w/four long
graduated drawers, molded base
raised on scroll-carved ogee
bracket feet, probably Connecticut, 1760-80, 20½ x 43½", 6' 9" h.
(restorations to feet, hinge
patches) 6,600.00

Chippendale secretary-bookcase,
cherry, two-part construction: the
upper section w/a broken-arch
bonnet top flanked by flame-
turned corner finials above a pair
of arched paneled doors opening
to a fitted interior; the lower section w/a slant lid opening to a
fitted interior above a case
w/four long graduated drawers
w/butterfly pulls, molded base on
ogee bracket feet, Rhode Island,
ca. 1780, 20½ x 27", 7' 7" h. ...23,100.00

Chippendale secretary-bookcase,
walnut, two-part construction: the
upper section w/a flat rectangular
top w/a molded projecting cornice
above a pair of long paneled
doors opening to adjustable
shelves; the lower section w/a
medial molding above a hinged
slant lid opening to an interior
fitted w/pigeonholes over small
drawers centering a hinged prospect door opening to two pigeonholes & two small drawers, above
a case w/four long graduated
molded drawers, on bracket feet,
probably Pennsylvania, ca. 1775,
16½ x 43", 6' 10½" h. (patches to
case & moldings, some replacement to drawer interiors) 4,125.00

Federal country-style secretary-
bookcase, maple & bird's-eye maple veneer, two-part construction:
the upper section w/a rectangular
top w/a molded cornice above a
pair of paneled doors opening to
shelves over a row of three small
drawers w/bird's-eye maple veneer; the lower section w/a wide
slant lid opening to a fitted interi-
or over a narrow long drawer
stepped-out over three long,
graduated drawers all w/bird's-
eye maple veneer & flanked by
free-standing baluster- and ring-
turned columns, flat apron, raised
on ring- and knob-turned feet,
brass batwing drawer pulls, northern New England, ca. 1825,
20 x 41½", 6' 10" h. 2,200.00

Federal "cylinder-front" secretary-
bookcase, inlaid mahogany, two-
part construction: the upper section w/shaped cornice inlaid
w/rectangular satinwood panels,

above a pair of glazed & mullioned cabinet doors opening to an interior w/two shelves, the lower section w/a retractable cylinder tambour front opening to an interior w/pigeonholes & small drawers w/satinwood fronts, a well w/leather-lined hinged cover below, the case w/five small line-inlaid drawers surrounding a kneehole section & supported on line-inlaid square tapering legs ending in crossbanded cuffs, Philadelphia or Baltimore, ca. 1805, 27 x 36", 6' 8½" h. (tambour lid inoperable) 79,750.00

Federal secretary-bookcase, mahogany & birch veneer, two-part construction: the upper w/shaped pediment centering three finials above a coved cornice over double cupboard doors w/patterned glazing & mullions enclosing six shelves over two line-inlaid cupboard doors, each enclosing two short drawers over three pigeonholes, centering a prospect door enclosing two short drawers; the lower case w/crossbanded & line-inlaid hinged slant writing flap over pair of line-inlaid & cockbeaded cupboard doors flanked by line-inlaid & cockbeaded bottle drawers, above a shaped apron, on ring-turned & tapering reeded legs w/ball-turned feet, New Hampshire, 1800-20, 20¾ x 42", 6' 7" h. (break to writing flap support) 8,800.00

Federal Secretary

Federal secretary-bookcase, tiger maple, two-part construction: the upper section w/a shaped cornice above a pair of glazed cupboard doors opening to an arrangement

of shelves & drawers; the lower section w/a hinged writing flap above two long drawers above a scalloped apron, on baluster- and ring-turned legs, 19 x 39½", 5' 10" h. (ILLUS.) 3,960.00

Federal secretary-bookcase, walnut, two-part construction: the upper section w/a rectangular top over a deep flaring & stepped cornice over a pair of double-paneled long cupboard doors w/the upper panels shorter than the lower ones; the lower section w/a slant lid opening to a fitted interior w/a prospect door flanked by valanced pigeonholes over shelves & short drawers, the lower case w/four long graduated drawers w/crossbanded inlay matching that on the slant lid, on tall French feet, probably Virginia, 1790-1810, 21¼ x 38¾", 7' 6" h. (restorations to feet) 7,150.00

George I Walnut Secretary

George I secretary-bookcase, walnut, two-part construction: the upper section w/an arched molded cornice above a pair of doors w/later beveled glazed plates opening to pigeonholes, small drawers & shelves above a pair of candleslides; the lower section w/a slant front opening to a fitted interior over one long, two short & two long drawers, molded base w/bracket feet, England, ca. 1720, 23 x 40½", 7' 3" (ILLUS.) 27,500.00

Queen Anne secretary-bookcase, walnut, two-part construction: the upper section w/a double arched cornice above a pair of glazed arched cupboard doors; the lower

Queen Anne Walnut Secretary

section w/a slant lid opening to
an interior fitted w/pigeonholes &
small drawers over three graduated long drawers, molded base
w/low bracket feet, England,
18th c. (ILLUS.) 14,500.00
Wallace Nutting-signed Chippendale-
Style secretary-bookcase, mahogany, two-part construction: the
upper section w/a swan's-neck
crest centering three urn-shaped
finials above a tri-paneled door
w/each panel topped by a carved
shell, the door opening to
shelves; the lower section w/a
slanted tri-paneled blocked &
shell-carved lid opening to a
shell-carved interior w/small
drawers & valanced pigeonholes
all above four long, graduated
blocked, shell-carved drawers on
a conforming molded base raised
on ogee bracket feet, in the Newport style, branded & labeled
"no. 933," & inscribed "1930,"
15 x 39¾", 8' 10" h. 14,950.00

SIDEBOARDS

Art Moderne sideboard, bronze-
mounted & lacquered, rectangular
top w/rounded corners above a
pair of long cabinet doors opening
to a fitted interior w/open shelves
& three drawers, raised on short
tapering turned feet, the doors
mounted in the center w/gilt-
bronze shells & the doors, side
panels & feet also mounted
w/thin bronze moldings, lacquered in mottled chocolate
brown & gold, France, ca. 1940,
19½ x 73½", 36½" h. 6,600.00
Biedermeier sideboard, brass-

mounted mahogany, the shaped
rectangular top slightly overhanging one very long drawer w/three
keyholes & a smaller drawer
above a wide central cupboard
door flanked by smaller cupboard
doors, now enclosing sliding
shelves, raised on a plinth base,
brass keyhole escutcheons, Europe, second quarter 19th c.,
24 x 77", 45½" h. 7,150.00

Ornate Edwardian Sideboard

Edwardian sideboard, inlaid satinwood & mahogany, classical style
w/a tubular brass top gallery w/a
high central oval & side posts
mounted w/pairs of candlearms,
rectangular 'breakfront' style top
above a conforming case w/a
band of frieze drawers w/gilt
classical designs above three
short central doors on tall square
tapering legs flanked by a pair of
tall doors above pairs of short
square tapering legs, overall
banded inlay, England, early
20th c. (ILLUS.) 6,325.00
Federal country-style huntboard,
yellow pine, rectangular top
w/under-edge molding on the
apron, three small drawers above
a lower molding, raised on tall
square tapering legs, old dark
reddish black finish, found in
Newberry County, South Carolina,
25½ x 52½", 42" h. (repairs to
drawer fronts) 4,730.00
Federal country-style huntboard,
pine, rectangular top above pairs
of deep end drawers w/oval
brasses flanking a central paneled
door, on turned tapering legs,
Southern U.S., ca. 1820 (ILLUS.
top next page) 2,960.00
Federal huntboard, inlaid mahoga-
ny, the long rectangular top w/a
serpentine front above a conforming apron centered by an oval
figured reserve w/oval inlaid

Federal Country-Style Huntboard

dies at the corners, the sides
fitted w/drawers, on square
tapering line- and bellflower-
inlaid legs ending in crossbanded
cuffs, Baltimore, Maryland, ca.
1795, 26¼ x 66½", 35¾" h.
(drawers replaced, some veneer
patches) 42,550.00

Federal Server

Federal server, mahogany, a low
three-quarter gallery around the
rectangular top slightly overhanging a long beaded drawer w/oval
brass pulls & keyhole escutcheon
raised on turned columnar supports above the galleried medial
shelf on short baluster-turned
legs, probably Philadelphia,
ca. 1810, 17½ x 42½", 37½" h.
(ILLUS.) 3,025.00
Federal server, mahogany & ma-
hogany veneer, the rectangular
top w/ovolu corners & a concave
center section above a conforming
case, the corners above outset
reeded columns continuing to the
short reeded legs, the case w/a
long concave center drawer
flanked by small square drawers
above a pair of concave cupboard
doors flanked by tall bottle drawers above a single long drawer
across the bottom w/a concave

center section flanked by blocked
end panels, arched apron, the facade w/flame-grained veneering
overall, Massachusetts, ca. 1800,
22½ x 40¼", 38½" h. 9,350.00

Federal Serpentine-Front Sideboard

Federal "serpentine-front" sideboard, inlaid mahogany, the rectangular top w/serpentine front
above a conforming case w/a pair
of short end drawers flanking a
long central drawer over a pair of
central cupboard doors flanked
by bottle drawers at each end,
raised on slender square tapering
legs, minor veneer repairs, probably Massachusetts, ca. 1800,
26½ x 69½", 41½" h. (ILLUS.) . . .6,050.00
Federal sideboard, bird's-eye maple
& mahogany inlaid cherry, the oblong top w/outset corners above
a frieze w/inlaid swags & tassels
above a deep drawer flanked by
bottle drawers, above three cockbeaded long drawers, three-
quarter-round columns flanking,
the shaped skirt continuing
to turned front feet, probably
original brasses, New England,
probably Connecticut, ca. 1815,
20¼ x 46", 43 7/8" h. 5,225.00
Federal sideboard, inlaid walnut,
the oblong top w/swelled center
section w/a line-inlaid edge
above a conforming case w/three
frieze drawers, the center long
one paneled to resemble two,
over convex rounded doors
flanked by a pair of hinged cupboard doors, on line-inlaid square
tapering legs ending in crossbanded cuffs, Southern, ca. 1810,
24 x 69", 45 3/8" h. (minor losses
to inlay) 7,700.00
Hepplewhite country-style hunt-
board, painted & decorated pine,
rectangular top above a deep
case w/a long drawer over a narrow pull-out work shelf above another long drawer, turned wood

knobs, slender square tapering
legs, old but not original alligatored brown finish w/black &
gold-painted decoration, top
w/old grey over a yellowed
marbleized paint, early 19th c.,
19½ x 30¾", 38" h. (replaced
pulls on work shelf, replaced
molding on bottom edge)........2,200.00

Jacobean-Style Sideboard

Jacobean-Style sideboard, oak, rectangular top w/outset corners
above a pair of long drawers ornately carved w/leafy scrolls &
separated by three blocks carved
w/lions' masks each above a
boldly carved herm figure
separating two ornately carved
cupboard doors centered by a
grotesque mask, stepped & molded base on short compressed
grotesque mask feet, England,
19th c., 25 x 70¾", 39½" h.
(ILLUS.) 1,100.00

Mission-style (Arts & Crafts movement) server, oak, a plate rack
above the rectangular top over
two short drawers w/square
wooden knobs above an open bay
& shelf over a single long drawer
w/square wooden knobs, red decal mark of Gustav Stickley, Model No. 955, 1902, 23½ x 59",
44¼" h. 4,180.00

Mission-style (Arts & Crafts movement) sideboard, oak, the low
slightly rounded crestrail w/plate
rack above the rectangular top
over a pair of narrow drawers
over a single long drawer over a
pair of paneled cupboard doors,
slightly arched apron, paneled
ends, original suede drawer lining, reddish brown finish, branded mark of the Limbert Furniture Company, Model No. 1320,
19 x 45", 42½" h. (some wood
replaced on plate rack) 1,430.00

Mission-style (Arts & Crafts movement) sideboard, oak, a low upright back section w/two long,
rectangular panels behind a plate

Mission Style Sideboard

rail above the rectangular top
slightly overhanging the case w/a
pair of short drawers over two
longer drawers all flanked by a
pair of end cupboard doors, a
single long drawer all the way
across the bottom, copper strap
hinges & bail pulls, Handcraft
label of L. & J.G. Stickley, Model No. 735, ca. 1910, minor
water mark, 22 x 56", 46½" h.
(ILLUS.) 2,420.00

Modern Style Sideboard

Modern-style sideboard, 'Janus'
type, hardwood, a raised superstructure w/rectangular top over
four double-panel cupboard doors
mounted each w/two unique Japanese carved woodblocks above
four narrow drawers over an
open area above a rectangular
black faux marble drop-in top
over four cupboard doors w/inlaid
panels over a single long drawer
across the bottom, on short
square legs, designed by Edward
Wormley for Dunbar Furniture
Corp., Model Nos. 5723 & 5724,
1957, w/manufacturer's pamphlet,
20 x 66", 6' 5½" h. (ILLUS.) 3,025.00

STANDS

Chippendale 'Tilt-Top' Candlestand

Candlestand, Chippendale, tilt-top, mahogany, the square top w/rounded notched corners tilting above a baluster-turned pedestal on a tripod base w/cabriole legs ending in snake feet, New England, ca. 1780, 20" w., 28" h. (ILLUS.) 1,100.00

Candlestand, Classical (American Empire), tilt-top, curly maple, oblong top w/scalloped sides & rounded corners tilting above a baluster-turned standard carved w/bold acanthus leaves above a tripod base w/tapering S-scroll legs carved at the sides of the knees w/acorn & leaf sprigs, possibly Albany, New York, ca. 1815, 20½" l., 27¼" h. 3,300.00

Candlestand, Classical (American Empire), tilt-top, mahogany, clover-shaped top tilting above a foliate- & rosebud-carved pedestal, on a tripartite base w/sabre legs & acanthus-carved knees, on hairy-paw feet, New York second quarter 19th c., 19½ x 26½", 29½" h. 990.00

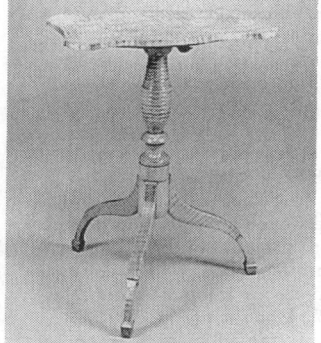

Federal Curly Maple Candlestand

Candlestand, Federal, tilt-top, curly maple, the cartouche-shaped top tilting above a ring-turned standard on a tripod base w/arched & reeded spider legs ending in spade feet, probably New York state, ca. 1820, 13¾ x 21¾", 27½" h. (ILLUS.) 1,870.00

Candlestand, Federal, tilt-top, inlaid mahogany, the octagonal top w/light band inlay around the border tilting above a ring-turned baluster-form pedestal on a tripod base ending in snake feet, Portsmouth, New Hampshire, ca. 1800, 16 x 20½", 28" h. 1,870.00

Candlestand, Federal, tilt-top, mahogany, the octagonal top tilting above a slender urn-turned pedestal on a tripod base w/spider legs ending in spade feet, Massachusetts, ca. 1800, 16" w., 28¼" h. 1,210.00

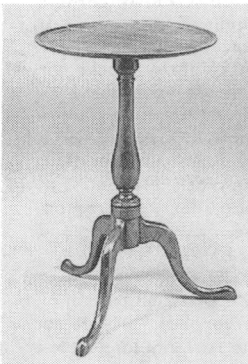

Queen Anne Candlestand

Candlestand, Queen Anne, mahogany & birch, circular dished top above a baluster-form turned standard on a tripod base w/cabriole legs ending in snake feet, New England, ca. 1770, top split & repaired, 18" d., 27½" h. (ILLUS.)....................... 990.00

Candlestand, Queen Anne, maple, octagonal top above a ball- and column-turned pedestal on an X-support w/crimped edges, 13½ x 13¾", 24" h. 1,870.00

Classical country-style two-drawer stand, curly maple, rectangular top overhanging two small drawers w/large wooden mushroom knobs, on slightly tapering square block legs w/ring-turned sections at the top & base, ca. 1850, 19½ x 20", 28¾" h. (refinished) .. 770.00

Drink stand, Mission-style (Arts & Crafts movement), oak, round top overhanging a broad apron &

canted square legs joined by arched cross-stretchers, restored dark finish, decal mark of L. & J.G. Stickley, Model No. 22, early 20th c., 18" d., 28½" h. 1,430.00

Empire (American) country-style two-drawer stand, cherry & curly maple, the rectangular top slightly overhanging a case w/a narrow curly maple drawer w/burl edging & two wooden knobs over a deeper matching drawer, both drawers flanked by boldly baluster- and ring-turned curly maple half-round pilasters, on boldly turned baluster- and ring-turned legs, ca. 1830-40, 19 x 22", 29½" h. (knobs replaced, worn & stained top, repairs to drawer interior) 715.00

Federal country-style one-drawer stand, painted pine & poplar, nearly square top widely overhanging an apron w/a single drawer w/turned wood knob, boldly baluster-turned legs w/ring-turned sections & knob feet, old worn red finish, 18½ x 19", 26¾" h. 495.00

Federal one-drawer stand, bird's-eye maple & mahogany-inlaid birch, the rectangular top overhanging an apron w/a single drawer w/banded inlays, on slender squared tapering legs, New England, ca. 1810, 15 7/8 x 16¼", 28¼" h. 2,070.00

Federal one-drawer stand, cherry, rectangular top above a single drawer frieze, on square tapering splayed legs, probably New England, minor patch to drawer lip, first quarter 19th c., 18½ x 19", 29" h. 1,430.00

Federal one-drawer stand, curly maple, rectangular top w/reeded edge above a single drawer w/turned knob above a reeded band above the baluster-, ring- and knob-turned tapering legs, old mellow refinishing, early 19th c., 19¼ x 19½", 29½" h. (pull replaced) 700.00

Federal one-drawer stand, inlaid mahogany, rectangular top w/line-inlaid edge above a case w/a single drawer w/two small round knobs, on icicle-inlaid square tapering legs ending in crossbanded cuffs, New England, ca. 1800, 16 x 19", 26¼" h. (in need of restoration) 11,550.00

Federal two-drawer stand, carved mahogany, the rectangular top w/outset rounded corners deco-

Federal Carved Mahogany Stand

rated w/molded roundels over a conforming case fitted w/two cockbeaded frieze drawers flanked by engaged colonettes carved w/roses on a star-punched ground, on ring-turned reeded tapering legs, Salem, Massachusetts, 1790-1810, 18¼ x 19½", 28¼" h. (ILLUS.) 4,400.00

Federal two-drawer stand, figured birch & mahogany, the oblong top w/rounded outset corners above two cross-banded drawers, each corner w/three-quarter-round ring-turned colonettes on circular tapering legs ending in tapered feet, Northeastern New England, ca. 1815, 17¾ x 18", 30" h. 3,300.00

Federal two-drawer stand, inlaid walnut, rectangular top widely overhanging the case w/two shallow drawers banded w/cherry & maple inlay & flanked by inlaid corner panels, slender tapering rope-turned legs w/knobbed cuffs above the feet, early 19th c., 20¾ x 21", 30¼" h. (refinished, some edge damage, age cracks, some rebuilding on drawers) 550.00

Federal two-drawer stand, mahogany, the rectangular top above a case w/two drawers, the upper drawer fitted w/a baize-lined hinged adjustable writing surface & a divided well, the lower drawer fitted w/a divided well, fitted at the side w/a sewing bag slide, on ring-turned & reeded tapering legs, Boston, Massachusetts, ca. 1810, 16¼ x 21", 28¾" h. (writing flap replaced, lacks casters) 3,850.00

Hepplewhite country-style one-drawer stand, walnut, rectangular removable two-board top widely overhanging the apron w/a single dovetailed drawer w/turned

wooden knob, square tapering
legs, 19th c., found in Ohio,
21¼ x 25½", 29¼" h. (some edge
damage, drawer front repaired) .. 385.00

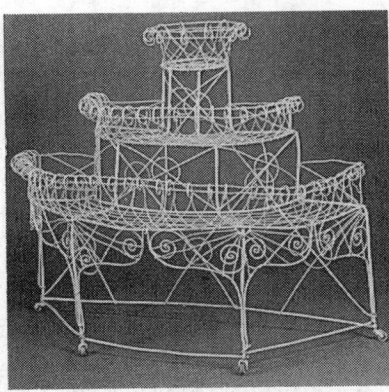

Victorian Wirework Plant Stand

Mission-Style Magazine Stand

Magazine stand, Mission-style (Arts
& Crafts movement), oak, three
wide open shelves between tapering sides, arched aprons, original
reddish brown finish, decal mark
of L. & J.G. Stickley, Model
No. 47, 15 x 19¾", 41½" h.
(ILLUS.) 1,320.00
Music stand, George III-Style, mahogany, reeded & acanthus-carved
support on a tripartite base ending in ball-and-claw feet, late
19th c. 605.00
Nightstands, Art Nouveau, mahogany, marquetry & marble, rectangular red & black marble top inset
within a molded surround above a
single drawer w/burled front, the
molded uprights flanking an open
shelf above a single door opening
to a marble-lined interior, the
door inlaid w/various woods
w/poppy blossoms & leafage, Louis Majorelle, France, ca. 1900,
15 x 17", 36½" h., pr. 8,250.00
Plant stand, Mission-style (Arts &
Crafts movement), oak, four post
legs joined by curved stretchers,
the square top inset w/a square
green-glazed Grueby Pottery tile,
black finish, Gustav Stickley red
decal mark, Model No. 44, ca.
1902, 12½" sq., 29¾" h. 6,600.00
Plant stand, wirework, demilune
form, three-tier, each tier w/an
ornately curled rim, on four slender legs headed by scrolling wire
design & joined by single stretchers w/X-bracing at back, on casters, painted finish, late 19th c.,
45" l., 40" h. (ILLUS.) 523.00

Sheraton country-style two-drawer
stand, grain-painted pine, rectangular top w/outset rounded corners above the apron w/rounded
corners continuing into the
baluster- and ring-turned legs,
two long narrow drawers w/origi-
nal embossed gilt-brass round
pulls, overall red flame graining, early 19th c., 17½ x 21¾",
28½" h. 1,925.00
Washstand, country-style, inlaid
cherry & walnut, a scrolled
splashback w/small central roundel above the rectangular top
flanked by outswept & turned
towel bars above the single long
drawer w/its front composed of
laminated strips of cherry & walnut, on slender turned legs joined
by a medial shelf inlaid w/a design of a running horse, late wire
nail construction, 14¼ x 28½",
35½" h. 385.00

STOOLS

American Folk Art Stool

Country-style stool, painted & decorated poplar, rectangular top

w/shaped apron, painted overall w/red, green & black rose blossoms, berries & leafage on a yellow ground outlined w/red & black pinstriping, the whole raised on bootjack ends, inscribed in pencil on the bottom "E.K. 1840," Landis Valley, Pennsylvania, 9" l., 5" h. (some wear) 4,125.00

Country-style "folk art" stool, painted & decorated, an octagonal seat w/a chamfered edge & trimmed w/a border band of carved hearts, on tall splayed & chamfered legs also trimmed w/carved hearts & joined by slender rungs, overall polychrome paint, probably Fredericksburg, Pennsylvania, late 19th - early 20th c. (ILLUS.) 1,760.00

Footstool, painted & decorated, bowed rectangular top centering a rush seat, on turned cylindrical legs joined by ring- and block-turned stretchers, painted yellow & decorated w/red-painted cherries & leaves, New England, first quarter 19th c., 10¾ x 15¼", 8¾" h. 3,520.00

Louis XV Stool

Louis XV Provincial-style stool, carved wood, rectangular seat w/rounded corners upholstered in a needlepoint tapestry w/tack trim, the scalloped apron carved w/shells & scrolls, the cabriole legs w/scroll-carved knees & acanthus-carved feet, France, 15 x 20" (ILLUS.) 1,072.50

Mission-style (Arts & Crafts movement) footstool, oak, rectangular tacked-on hard leather seat on slender square legs w/double thin rungs at the ends & single wide rungs at the sides, original condition, "Handcraft" label of L. & J.G. Stickley, Model 391, w/retailer's label, 14 x 19", 18" h. (some wear) . . . . 330.00 to 550.00

Modern style stool, chrome & cane, simple tubular framework forming U-shaped legs joined across the top by woven cane to form the seat, designed by Ludwig Mies van der Rohe, 1927, 17¾" h. 4,950.00

Queen Anne stool, painted wood, rectangular rush top on brown-painted baluster-turned legs joined by turned stretchers, the tops of two legs inscribed "H" & "E," probably New England, mid-18th c., 13" h. 990.00

English Queen Anne Stool

Queen Anne stool, walnut, the rounded rectangular seat covered w/ivory silk, on lappet-carved cabriole legs & pad feet, England, early 18th c., 16½ x 23", 16" h. (ILLUS.) 7,150.00

Windsor footstool, thick rectangular top w/chamfered edges, splayed legs, worn & alligatored original painted florals & striping in yellow, red, blue & white on a dark brown ground, 6½ x 11", 6¾" h. 115.50

Windsor stool, oblong plank seat raised on three tall, turned & slightly swelled legs joined by a T-stretcher, traces of old green paint, 19th c., 15" w., 24½" h. . . . 104.50

TABLES

Bentwood Table by Thonet

Art Deco dining table, gilt-metal &
glass, the inset square glass top
over a gilt-metal frieze cast
w/Greek key motifs, raised on
four curved legs similarly
cast, conjoined to a stepped
square base raised on four feet,
48½" sq., 28½" h..............4,950.00

Art Nouveau nesting tables, mahogany marquetry, each rectangular top from the largest to the
smallest inlaid in various woods
w/chestnuts, mulberry leaves,
daffodils & daisies, respectively,
raised on turned legs & shaped
trestle feet, Majorelle, France, ca.
1900, set of 4 ....2,200.00

Bentwood table, the circular top
raised on a pedestal base formed
of four loops centering a pendent drop, further raised on
turned ribbed spheres resting on
discs, Thonet, Austria, ca. 1890,
23¾" d., 30 5/8" h. (ILLUS.) 1,760.00

Billiards table, Jefferson patt.
w/mother-of-pearl inlay, matching
cue and ball racks, in original
condition, ca. 1923, 54 x 108"....6,000.00

Chippendale card table, mahogany,
the hinged thumbmolded serpentine top over a conforming frieze
decorated w/rectangular veneer
panels outlined w/lightwood
stringing centering a similarly outlined short drawer above a
gadrooned molded edge, on
square molded legs headed by
(restored) fretwork brackets,
Rhode Island, 1770-90, 15 x 32¾",
29½" h. 7,150.00

Chippendale Pembroke Table

Chippendale Pembroke table, mahogany, the rectangular top
flanked by rectangular leaves
above a single drawer, fretwork
brackets on end aprons, square
legs w/inside chamfer joined by

cut-out cross stretcher, old finish
(ILLUS.) 12,000.00

Chippendale tea table, mahogany,
rectangular top w/molded edge &
rounded corners above a rounded
projecting apron w/shaped centered pendants on cabriole legs
ending in claw-and-ball feet, New
York or Philadelphia, 1740-60,
16½ x 30", 26½" h. (lacks tray
molding on top, repairs to legs,
underside now painted brown)..26,400.00

Classical (American Empire) dining
table, carved mahogany, two-
part, each section w/a rectangular top w/a single hinged leaf
w/rounded corners above a
rounded apron w/leaf & flower-
carved corner panel & raised on a
heavy turned & acanthus-carved
pedestal on a curve-sided plinth
base on scrolling acanthus-carved
animal paw feet w/casters, Philadelphia, ca. 1830, 46 x 89½" extended, 27" h. (minor repairs to
veneer)......................4,950.00

Classical Dressing Table

Classical (American Empire) dressing table w/mirror, mahogany,
surmounted by a rectangular mirror pivoting between two obelisks
above two short drawers, the
projecting lower section w/one
long drawer above a pair of
scrolled uprights, a molded base
below, attributed to the workshop
of Duncan Phyfe & Sons, New
York, ca. 1845, 21 x 47 7/8",
6' 4¾" h. (ILLUS.)..............7,700.00

Classical (American Empire) swivel-
top card tables, carved mahogany, oblong top w/hinged leaf
swiveling above a well, the plain
frieze on acanthus- and volute-
carved lyre-form standard & plinth

base on molded down-curving legs ending in brass animal paw feet, Boston, Massachusetts, ca. 1825, 17 7/8 x 36½", 29" h., pr. (minor veneer repairs) 3,300.00

Country-style "harvest" table, painted birch & pine, long rectangular top flanked by a pair of 11½" w. drop leaves, on slender turned tapering legs ending in brass casters, original overall red paint, 22¼ x 95½" plus leaves, 30" h. (minor paint wear). 8,800.00

Federal Card Table

Federal card table, mahogany & flame birch-veneered, the hinged rectangular top w/outset rounded corners edged w/foliate banding above a conforming apron centering a crossbanded panel, on turned tapering reeded legs headed by ring turnings, North Shore, Massachusetts, 1790-1810, 17¾ x 35¾", 29¾" h. (ILLUS.) . . .2,420.00

Federal country-style drop-leaf breakfast table, cherry, the rectangular top flanked by a pair of serpentine drop leaves w/round corners, above the serpentine skirt, raised on four square tapering molded legs, old refinish, New England, ca. 1790, 34 x 34" open, 27¾" h. (minor restoration). 2,200.00

Federal country-style drop-leaf side table, cherry & bird's-eye maple, rectangular top flanked by two 9" w. drop leaves w/cut-out notched corners above a deep apron w/two bird's-eye maple veneer drawers w/wooden knobs, delicate ring- and baluster-turned tapering legs, 15¼ x 23¾" plus leaves, 27¼" h. (refinished, slight damage) 715.00

Federal country-style tea table, cherry & pine, rectangular top w/deeply scalloped sides, outset rounded corners & chamfered cyma-curve edge above a plain skirt on square tapering legs, New England, early 19th c., 21½ x 35", 28" h. 2,420.00

Federal dressing table, painted & decorated pine, a high crestrail w/scrolled ends decorated w/graining, pinstriping & a stenciled fruit cluster above a rectangular top w/serpentine sides above a deep apron w/wood graining & a fruit cluster, slender square tapering legs, possibly Maine, ca. 1820 . . . . 990.00

Federal Pembroke table, tiger stripe maple, rectangular flanked by a pair of scalloped drop-leaves w/rounded corners, raised on slender square tapering legs, New England, ca. 1800, closed 17½ x 35", 28¼" h. 5,500.00

Federal work table, mahogany, the rectangular top w/outset ovolu corners above ring-turned corner posts flanking a pair of narrow drawers w/round stamped brass pulls, on tapering ring- and rope-turned legs w/knobbed cuffs, early 19th c., 18½ x 19¼", 29¼" h. 935.00

![Ornate George II Side Table]

Ornate George II Side Table

George II side table, marble & giltwood, the rectangular *verde antico* marble top w/shaped corners above a frieze elaborately carved w/shells & scrolling foliage, on hipped cabriole legs headed by shells & w/flowerhead brackets issuing foliage, on scrolled toes carved w/long leaves, England, mid-18th c., regilt, 27 x 41½", 31½" h. (ILLUS.). 17,600.00

Hepplewhite country-style drop-leaf table, walnut, rectangular top flanked by two rectangular drop leaves over a mortised & pinned apron w/bottom edge molding & single drawer, square tapered legs, old refinishing, 20½ x 39" plus 12" w. leaves, 28" h. (replaced oval brass, added center brace, one leg ended out about 1") 650.00

Hepplewhite-Style card table, inlaid mahogany, hinged fold-over D-shaped top above a conforming apron w/inlaid veneer rectangular panels & oval reserves, on slender square tapering legs w/line inlay, 20th c. reproduction, 19 x 38" closed, 31" h. (minor wear) 625.00

Hutch (or chair) table, cherry, round top tilting above a rectangular deep apron above flat, shaped ends raised on shoe feet joined by a side stretcher, probably New York, 18th c., 47½" d., 29" h. ...2,970.00

Hutch table, stained pine & birch, rectangular removable top tilting above a medial section w/a hinged lid opening to a well, the side panel now hinged, the sides forming bootjack feet, first half 19th c., 29 x 60", 30½" h. (lower side panel once stationary) 3,025.00

Louis XV writing table, tulipwood parquetry, the shaped rectangular top veneered w/trellis parquetry, the front w/a frieze drawer fitted w/a hinged writing tablet & veneered all around w/herringbone parquetry, raised on cabriole legs, France, mid-18th c., 12¾ x 16¾", 28¼" h. 5,750.00

Mission-style (Arts & Crafts movement) dining table, oak, round top over a plain apron, five square legs w/wide corbels, branded mark, Limbert Company, Model No. 418, ca. 1910, 48" d., 29" h. 1,980.00

Mission Style Dining Table
Mission-style (Arts & Crafts movement) dining table, oak, the

round top overhanging a conforming apron raised on heavy square legs joined by arched cross-stretchers, paper label of Gustav Stickley, Model No. 629, ca. 1907, edge roughness, 47½" d., 30" h. (ILLUS.) 3,410.00

Gustav Stickley Directors' Table
Mission-style (Arts & Crafts movement) directors' table, oak, rectangular top widely overhanging a deep skirt joined to square canted legs by three large round-top pegs, trestle feet, branded mark of Gustav Stickley, Model No. 631½, ca. 1907, 36 x 72", 29½" h. (ILLUS.) 16,500.00

Mission-style (Arts & Crafts movement) hall table, oak, rectangular top overhanging ends composed of three narrow square spindles joined to stretchers fitted into square tapering legs & joined by a cross-stretcher, original color, recent dark finish, brass tag mark of Stickley Brothers, 18 x 30", 30" h. 1,100.00

Mission-style (Arts & Crafts movement) tea table, octagonal "framed" top raised on four flat legs w/shoe feet joined by a lower medial shelf, fine original dark finish, unmarked L. & J.G. Stickley, Model No. 515, 20" w., 24" h. 2,970.00

Modern style center table, cypress, hexagonal top on three triangular supports joined by flat stretchers & on short angled block legs, designed by Frank Lloyd Wright for Auldbrass Plantation, Yemasse, South Carolina, ca. 1940, 59¼" w., 29½" h. 17,600.00

Modern style console table, Formica, aluminum & chromium-plated metal, the rectangular black Formica top w/triple-band aluminum edge on three curved chromium-plated legs on a runner base formed by two tubular supports, designed by Gilbert Rohde for the Troy Sunshade Metal Co., Model No. 56-B, ca. 1930's, 12 x 42", 26" h. 1,430.00

Modern Style End Tables

Modern style end tables, hardwood, G-shaped w/a small tier raised above a long rectangular tier raised above a platform base, blond finish, unsigned, ca. 1950, 12¼ x 26¾", 26" h., pr. (ILLUS.).. 247.50

Queen Anne "butterfly" tavern table, maple, the oblong top w/two hinged D-shaped leaves above a molded skirt w/single drawer, on splayed turned legs joined by a box stretcher, each long end w/swinging leaf supports, on ball feet, 36" l., extended 37¼" w., 27¾" h. 9,350.00

Queen Anne dining table, cherry, the rectangular top w/rounded ends flanked by a pair of wide rounded drop leaves, a scalloped apron & cabriole legs ending in pad feet, New England, ca. 1760, open 53 x 54", 28" h. 7,150.00

Queen Anne Dressing Table

Queen Anne dressing table, cherry, the rectangular top w/molded rim & rounded corners overhanging a case w/a single long drawer above three small drawers, the center one fan-carved, shaped apron w/two acorn drops, cabriole legs ending in pad feet, Connecticut, ca. 1760, 30" w., 28½" h. (ILLUS.) 10,450.00

Queen Anne "handkerchief" table, mahogany, the triangular top w/molded edge above a triangular drop leaf opening to a compartment over a plain apron, on

four cylindrical tapering legs w/pad & disc feet, probably Charleston, South Carolina, 1740-60, open 35½ x 35¾", 28" h. (one pad foot slightly pieced) 33,000.00

Queen Anne tavern table, painted, the rectangular top w/batten ends over a molded frieze, ring-turned & tapering splayed legs joined by molded stretchers, on turned feet, painted red, 18th c., 20½ x 31½", 25" h. 2,640.00

"Sawbuck" table, country-style, painted poplar, rectangular one-board top w/breadboard ends slightly overhanging a narrow apron & raised on heavy X-legs joined by a high stretcher, original dark mustard paint on base & old natural finish on the top, found in Vermont, 19th c., 21¼ x 43", 33¾" h. (minor age cracks in top) 770.00

Sheraton country-style side table, cherry, rectangular two-board top w/rounded corners above deep slightly canted apron w/reeded edges, on slender turned & tapering legs w/ball-turned cuffs & flattened knob feet, early 19th c., 19¼ x 24¼", 30¼" h. (wear, stains on top) 935.00

Swedish provincial-style trestle table, pine, the rectangular top w/canted corners raised on H-form trestle supports, joined by a wide rectangular stretcher dated "1776" & w/indistinct initials, traces of red paint, 33 x 64", 31½" h. 2,200.00

Tavern table, country-style, painted maple, scrubbed rectangular top w/shaped corners widely overhanging a brown-stained base w/straight skirt & raised on tapering turned legs w/small ankled feet, New England, 18th c., 25¼ x 35½", 28" h. (imperfections).......................2,475.00

Victorian dressing table, Rococo substyle, carved rosewood, a high ornately pierce-carved superstructure w/a large cartouche-form center mirror w/carved crest & urn finial flanked by scroll-carved side wings fitted w/graduated open shelves joined by bobbin-turned supports all above the serpentine-fronted white marble top above a deep conforming apron w/floral & scroll-carved edging, raised on four offset S-scroll legs joined by a scrolled

Victorian Rococo Dressing Table

cross stretcher w/small center
round shelf above conjoined
C-scrolls, attributed to Prudent
Mallard, New Orleans, Louisiana,
ca. 1850 (ILLUS.) 8,250.00
Victorian library table, Aesthetic
Movement substyle, inlaid rosewood, inlaid rectangular top
w/rounded corners above an
apron w/two drawers each inlaid
w/stylized flower clusters & scattered blossoms w/similar inlay
around the sides, raised on
square incised legs joined by an
H-stretcher, on casters, stamped
"Herter Bros.," New York, late
19th c., 32" w., 30" h. 19,800.00

Victorian Baroque-Style Library Table

Victorian library table, Baroque-
Style, carved mahogany, a rectangular top w/molded edge above a
curved apron w/two drawers
w/brass bail pulls over a carved
frieze band raised on four large
full-figure carved seated griffin
legs joined by a shaped shelf
stretcher raised on squatty bun
feet, late 19th c., 49" l. (ILLUS.) . .2,750.00
Victorian library table, Egyptian Revival substyle, parcel-gilt & patinated gilt-bronze walnut, the
rectangular top w/wide canted

corners & inset w/a baize writing
surface surrounded by a geometric decorated border, the front &
back fitted w/a gilt-metal plaque
depicting a lizard climbing a lattice applied w/a stylized flowerhead, the corners fitted w/a
drawer adorned w/a lion ring
handle, raised on stylized animal
legs w/hoof feet joined by an angular pierced stretcher centered
by an urn, handles stamped "P.S.,"
attributed to Pottier & Stymus,
New York, third quarter 19th c.,
39 x 62", 28¼" h. 41,400.00
Victorian parlor center table, East-
lake substyle, *pietra dura* marble
& ebonized wood, the circular top
inset w/a floral wreath, the conforming ebonized border & apron
supported by turned legs & spindles, ending in an X-shaped base,
third quarter 19th c., 27" d.,
29½" h. .2,875.00

Renaissance Revival Parlor Table

Victorian parlor center table,
Renaissance Revival substyle,
carved rosewood, the cartouche-
shaped top inset w/white marble
above a conforming apron
w/carved roundels w/a carved
bust centered on each side, raised
on long S-scrolls joined at a central column & raised on four
square posts above a cross
stretcher raised on heavy scroll-
carved feet, each foot topped by
a full-figure classical lady's bust,
on casters, attributed to John Jel-
liff, ca. 1865 (ILLUS.) 7,150.00
Victorian parlor center table, Rococo
substyle, carved rosewood, the
white marble 'turtle' top above a
conforming apron ornately pierce-
carved w/leafy scrolls & central
fruit clusters, on floral-carved
S-scroll legs joined by serpentine
scroll-carved stretchers centered

Victorian Rococo Parlor Table

by a gadroon-carved urn finial &
drop, attributed to J. & J.W.
Meeks, ca. 1855 (ILLUS.).......14,300.00
William & Mary dressing table,
figured maple, rectangular top
w/molded edge & cusped corners
over a case fitted w/a pair of
thumb-molded short drawers over
a further pair of drawers &
shaped apron, on square cabriole legs w/Spanish feet, Delaware River Valley, 1730-50,
21½ x 35½", 30¾" h. 8,250.00
William & Mary drop-leaf "gate-leg"
table, maple, rectangular drop-
leaf top w/butterfly wing supports
over a plain apron, on double
baluster-turned legs joined by
a box stretcher, New England,
1730-50, 44 x 46", 26¾" h. 19,800.00

William & Mary Side Table

William & Mary side table, painted
& turned cherry, the oval top
above a plain skirt on ring- and
block-turned legs joined by flat
stretchers, on flared feet, painted
grey over red, New York or Connecticut, 1710-50, 18½ x 21¾",
22" h. (ILLUS.) 13,800.00
William & Mary "trestle-base" table,
painted, oval top above double

baluster-turned legs joined by
a similarly turned stretcher, on
trestle feet, painted black, New
England, 1730-50, 22 x 28¼",
26½" h. 20,900.00

WARDROBES & ARMOIRES

Art Nouveau Armoire

Armoire, Art Nouveau, carved walnut, the arched crest carved w/a
cluster of pendent fruits & leaves
above a mirrored door opening
to a shelved interior above a
shaped oval drawer, raised on
molded feet, France, ca. 1900,
20¼ x 43½", 7' 5½" h. (ILLUS.) ..4,400.00
Armoire, Art Nouveau, inlaid mahogany, the boldly serpentine
molded top above a large central
door w/beveled mirror plate
flanked by side cabinets beneath
open shelves backed by diapered
floral marquetry, all above a central drawer flanked by one drawer on either side, each mounted
w/a foliate bronze handle, the
side doors inlaid w/various woods
w/stylized undulating poppy blossoms & leafage, Louis Majorelle,
France, ca. 1900, 22" deep,
81" w., 8' 9½" h. 7,700.00
Armoire, Scandinavian provincial-
style, painted wood, the serpentine stepped cornice centered by
a keystone w/dentils above the
conforming hinged cupboard door
enclosing partitions, flanked by
canted corners, raised on square
heavy tapering legs, painted
w/floral reserves on the corners &
sides, the central door panel
painted w/a religious scene surrounded by flower-filled urns in
tones of iron-red, blue, green,
burgundy, yellow, cream & brown,

bearing two embossed leather labels stamped "H. Chatarina," dated 1835, 22½ x 43", 6' 1" h. . .4,400.00

Kas (American version of the Netherlands *Kast* or wardrobe), William & Mary, carved cherry, deeply molded projecting cornice above a pair of panel covered doors opening to a shelved interior, two drawers below, on compressed ball feet, Hudson River Valley, early 18th c., 26½ x 73", 6' 5" h. (feet replaced & other repairs) 6,600.00

William & Mary Gumwood Kas

Kas, William & Mary, gumwood, two-part construction: the upper section w/an elaborately molded bold cornice above two fielded panel double cupboard doors enclosing two shelves, one fitted w/a short drawer centering three pilasters w/double vertical molded panels & three horizontal applied short moldings over a single long drawer panel molded to appear as two drawers, on removable large compressed ball feet, segment of one shelf removed, New York, 1725-55, 22¼ x 65½", 6' 1½" h. (ILLUS.) 4,950.00

Wardrobe, Classical (American Empire), mahogany, in several parts, removable molded cornice & recessed center flanked by dies w/gilt-stenciled foliate decoration above a pair of double paneled doors, each w/a border of gilt-stenciled decoration in the form of stylized leafage, within ebonized borders & opening to an interior w/three small drawers, two w/brass handles in the form of fruit & flower-filled baskets, the drawers centered by pull-out

Classical Mahogany Wardrobe

slides, each end fitted w/a cupboard door now w/flush brass handle, the whole flanked by turned columns w/leaf-carved capitals supported on a gilt-stenciled removable base, frontal stylized carved paw feet, the rear legs ring-turned & tapered, New York, possibly by Joseph Meeks & Sons, ca. 1820, 26¼ x 54½", 7' 4" h. (ILLUS.) 10,450.00

Wardrobe, Classical (American Empire), gilded & ebonized mahogany, in several parts, a rectangular top w/projecting removable cove-molded cornice above a projecting central section w/a pair of paneled cupboard doors opening to an interior fitted w/sliding linen trays, above a pair of drawers over two long drawers, the side sections w/tall three-paneled cupboard doors, the plinth base raised on short ebonized & gilded acanthus-carved animal paw feet, probably Philadelphia, ca. 1815, 24 x 107½", 6' 5½" h. (gilding & ebonizing on feet later) 6,325.00

Wardrobe, Modern style, walnut, plain rectangular top above a pair of plain, tall doors w/demi-lune metal handles, plain interior, designed by Lily Reich, ca. 1930's, 24 x 49¼", 6' 5" h. 5,500.00

WHATNOTS & ETAGERES

Etagere, Art Nouveau, mahogany, a small round shelf w/molded edge raised on two slender sinuous supports centering two lower circular shelves similarly molded, raised on four flaring legs conjoined by an X-stretcher continuing to angular feet, Serrurier-Bovy, France, ca. 1900, 20½" w., 4' 9¾" h. 4,400.00

Federal Three-Tier Etagere

Etagere, Federal, mahogany, three-tiered, each tier centered by ring-turned supports over a single drawer w/two turned wood pulls, on turned feet, probably Boston, ca. 1820, 13¾ x 18", 45½" h. (ILLUS.) 2,310.00

Etagere, Regency, rosewood, the three square shelves on double baluster supports w/gadrooned finials & legs, brass feet & casters, England, first quarter 19th c., 13 x 15", 29½" h. 1,540.00

Ornate Victorian Etagere

Etagere, Victorian, Oriental-style, parcel-gilt black & scarlet japanned & bamboo carved, the canted fretted cornice above various asymmetrical shelves, decorated w/birds & flowers, the base w/four frieze drawers above a pair of doors, late 19th c., 19 x 56", 6' 4½" h. (ILLUS.) 2,860.00

(End of Furniture Section)

GAMES & GAME BOARDS

For related items see the CHARACTER COLLECTIBLES and DISNEY COLLECTIBLES categories.

Six Day Bike Race Game

Across the Border board game, game board depicts soldiers charging the Mexican border, Milton Bradley $225.00

Across the Continent - The United States Game, board game about railroad travel, Parker Brothers, 1952, excellent condition, w/box . . . . .20.00 to 40.00

Alee Oop game, skill-type, Roy-Toy Company, ca. 1939, mint in tin . . .   30.00

Annette's Secret Passage board game, Disney & Parker Bros., 1958 . . . .   40.00

Astron board game, Parker Bros., 1955 . . . . 200.00

Barnabas Collins board game, based on TV's 'Dark Shadows,' 1969 . . . . .   28.00

Baseball Card Game, Olson Game Co., ca. 1922, complete in box . . .   35.00

Ben Casey board game, based on the TV series, early 1960's 15.00

Black Sambo target game, self-framed tin, Wyandotte Toys, 11 x 23½" 325.00

Bugville, w/four lithographed tin friction-type bugs, unused condition, 1915 . . . . .125.00 to 135.00

Camelot board game, Parker Brothers, ca. 1930 . . . .   32.50

Campaign, Civil War theme board game, 1961, unopened worn box 18.00

Carrom board w/stand, instruction book dated 1901, two cloth bags w/game pieces, marked "The Carrom Co. 1889" 125.00

Checkerboard, painted & decorated pine, rectangular, red & blue painted playing surface, America, 19th c., 14 1/8 x 17½" (some wear) 495.00

Checkerboard, painted pine, crudely repainted w/black & orange squares & green edging, 15" sq. . . 150.00

Checkerboard, painted pine, rectangular, black-painted applied lip w/a playing surface painted in red & black squares, the borders w/large alternating red & black scallops on a yellow ground, America, late 19th c., 18½ x 21½" 7,425.00

Checkerboard, pine, simple narrow frame & border painted red, playing surface in natural & black, 14¼ x 15" (paint worn) 195.00

Checkerboard, reverse-painted glass, abalone shell star in each corner on black paper, center of each side w/photograph of "Wm. Savill," black frame, 22½" sq. 100.00

Chenkek Check game board, w/instructions & marbles in original bag, 1937 . . . . 17.00

Chess set, carved salmon & white coral, the kings & queens as deities, the bishops as priests, the knights on horseback, the rooks as elephants w/turrets & the pawns as tunic-clad figures, China, 19th c., 1 3/8" to 2¾" h., 32 pcs. in fitted box 5,225.00

Climbing Monkeys (The) board game, consisting of a lithographed board together w/seven flat h.p. metal monkeys, Spears, Germany, ca. 1915, in original lithographed box 198.00

Croquet set, child's, pictures children, reads "Kro-Kay" - "For Gay Play Every Day," ca. 1920's, mint in box 35.00

Donkey Party, lithographed fabric, w/22 die-cut tails, package shows black man holding tail, 24 x 36" (package rough) 66.00

Elsie the Cow game, Selchow & Righter, 1941 . . . . 65.00

Flinch card game, Parker Bros., 1938 . . . . 12.00

Flying G-Men board game, 1939, unused mint condition 250.00

Frankenstein Mystery board game, Hasbro, Universal Pictures, 1963 . . 95.00

Game of Famous Authors, Parker Bros., 1943 . . . . 15.00

Game of States board game, graphic game board, four plastic truck playing pieces, ca. 1930's, in large worn box 35.00

Gee-Wiz Race, mechanical-type,

tin, Wolverine, 1923, in original box . . . . 100.00 to 125.00

Going To Market card game, advertising-type, featuring ads for Grape-Nuts, Welch's, Beech-Nut, Western Electric, Libby, etc., Beech-Nut Packing Co., ca. 1910 . . 95.00

Hickory Dickory Dock mechanical marble game, wooden, ca. 1930's, mint in box 110.00

Hokum card game, Parker Bros., 1927 . . . . 20.00

India board game, Parker Bros., 1940 . . . . 25.00

Kentucky Derby Racing Game, board-type, Whitman, 1938 . . . . 25.00

Lindy card game, Parker Bros., 1929 . . . . 25.00

Lotto card game, cardboard cards & wooden playing pieces, in wooden box w/original green paint, orange trim & worn gilt label "Lotto," 7¾" l. 45.00

Mr. Potato Head game, double set, Hasbro, 1950, mint in box 65.00

Nancy & Sluggo game, Whitman, 1944 . . . . 40.00

Ouija Board, Baltimore Talking Board Co., sample size, ca. 1920, in original premium mailer, 6 x 9" 20.00

Parcheesi game board, painted wood, square, painted in brilliant tones of red, green, yellow & orange, the corners decorated w/neoclassical leaf designs, America, late 19th - early 20th c., 14" sq. (minor chipping) 1,100.00

Pigskin - Tom Hamilton's football game, Parker Bros., 1935 . . . . 40.00

Pirate and Traveller board game, Milton Bradley, 1936 . . . . 32.00

Pit card game, Parker Bros., 1903, in box 85.00

Politics Game (The), board-type, Oswald B. Lord, New York, New York, ca. 1935 . . . . 25.00

Polly Put The Kettle On, skill-type, ten wooden pieces, Parker Bros., 1923, boxed, 6 5/8 x 7 5/8" 35.00

Quien Sabe card game, Parker Bros., 1906 . . . . 30.00

Radio Game, board-type, Milton Bradley, 1926 . . . . 75.00

Range Commandos, Parker Brothers, 1942, mint in box 45.00

Six Day Bike Race board game, lithographed tin board, Linstrom Tool & Toy Co., Bridgeport, Connecticut, ca. 1930's, unplayed-with condition, 9½ x 15¼" (ILLUS.) 44.00

Snake Eyes boxed card game, Selchow & Righter, 1930's, complete 90.00

Spoof card game, Milton Bradley,
1918 . . . . 28.00
Sweep the Country board game, po-
litical election game, book-form,
w/cartoon images of Democrats &
Republicans, 1936 . . . . 35.00
Tiddly Winks, Milton Bradley, 1932 . . 15.00
Wahoo Pick 'Em Up Sticks game,
skill-type, "The gayest game of
all," Indian head graphics in col-
or, Peters Weather Bird Shoes
advertisement on back, mint con-
tents in mint box 45.00
White Squadron card game, Fireside
Game Co., box illustrates U.S.
Navy ships, 1896 . . . . 175.00
World Cruise Travel Game, Lowell
Thomas, Parker Bros., 1937 . . . . . . 150.00
World Educator and Game (The),
board-type, Reed Toy Co., ca.
1887 . . . . 125.00

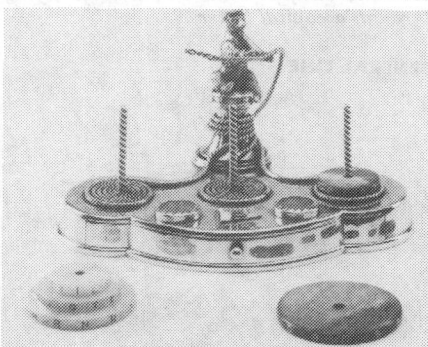

Hand-Crafted Yachting Game

Yachting game, skill-type, silver, enamel & mother-of-pearl, shaped
oval base set w/two compasses, a
blue & white enamel burgee &
three pegs formed as coiled lines,
the lines joining behind at a
winch surmounted by a bear in
nautical uniform, w/a drawer for
seven white & purple-stained
mother-of-pearl playing chips, the
base inscribed "ON BOARD THE
DREAMER" & a description of the
specially-made hand-crafted set,
w/original fitted blue leather
case, made by Tiffany & Co., New
York, 1900-02, case 6 5/8" l.
(ILLUS. of part) 4,180.00
Young America Target, skill-type,
Parker Bros., ca. 1895, in box 68.00

GARDEN
FOUNTAINS & ORNAMENTS

*Ornamental garden or yard fountains, urns
and figures often enhanced the formal plant-*
*ings on spacious lawns of mansion-sized
dwellings during the late 19th and early 20th
century. While fountains were usually reserved for the lawns of estates, even modest
homes often had a latticework arbor or cast
iron urn in the yard. Today garden enthusiasts look for these ornamental pieces to
lend an aura of elegance to their landscaping.*

Figure of a Classical Woman

Armillary, bronze, on a cast stone
cylindrical standard carved
w/scrolling acanthus leaves, ending in a stepped circular base further raised on a low square base,
4' 8" h. $2,530.00
Bench, marble, shaped rectangular
back w/scrolled cresting, centering a musical trophy flanked by
grotesques, foliate-carved scrolled
sides, rectangular seat raised on
scrolled supports, carved w/gro-
tesque fish, late 19th - early
20th c., 81" l. 9,350.00
Figure of a woman, zinc, classical
figure in flowing garments holding
a ewer & chalice, raised on a
rockwork base, marked "A B and
W T. Westervelt, New York,"
late 19th c., overall 6' 8" h.
(ILLUS.) 6,600.00
Fountain, bronze, depicting a young
boy playing the panpipes, w/three
frogs at his feet issuing spouts
for water, green patina, signed
"Berge and Roman Bronze Works,
N.Y.," 42" h. 7,700.00
Fountain, cast iron, the welled base
w/a lily pad & frog cast rim, supporting a central standard formed
as three egrets, supporting three
graduated foliate tiers, stamped
"J.W. Fiske, N.Y.," late 19th c.,
5' 10" d., overall 9' 2" h. 10,450.00
Fountain, marble, depicting a young
boy riding the back of a snail, the

snail incorporating a nozzle,
raised on a rocky ground,
4' h. 13,200.00

Fountain, wall-type, marble, shield-
form w/ornately scrolled edges,
center carved w/a dancing bear,
late 19th - early 20th c., 38" h. . .2,530.00

Hose caddy, figural, painted wood &
metal, a flat cut-out of a standing
black man wearing a hat, striped
shirt & bib overall, holding in one
hand a curved bar to support the
hose, original polychrome paint,
marked "Sprinkling Sambo, The
Firestone Tire & Rubber Co.,"
20th c., 33½" h. 165.00

Jardiniere, marble, octagonal,
carved on sides w/a continuous
line of young girls & boys holding
foliate swags, 19" h. 6,050.00

Model of a rabbit, cast iron, in seated position w/ears up, layers of
worn & weathered white paint,
12" h. 175.00

Models of cranes, bronze, one
modeled w/his neck held erect,
the other looking back over his
shoulder, patinated finish, tallest
6' 9" h., pr. 1,980.00

Models of lions, cast stone, seated
animal w/partially open mouth
holding a shield in one raised
paw, raised on a rectangular
plinth, 30" h., pr. 3,080.00

Models of sphinxes, marble, recumbent figure w/floral-draped
nemes, late 19th - early 20th c.,
37" l., 24½" h., pr. 14,850.00

Urn, cast iron, gadrooned body,
raised on a paneled standard
above a floral band, on a low
square base, stamped "J. W.
Fiske, N.Y.," late 19th c.,
24" h. 1,320.00

Urn, cast iron, campana-shaped
bowl w/rolled leaf-molded rim &
base flanked by large slender
griffin-form handles, each animal
w/a looped & pointed tail, raised
on a cattail-molded pedestal surrounded by three standing cranes,
on a molded round base, painted
white, J.W. Fiske & Co., New
York, New York, ca. 1893, 48" d.,
4' 10" h. 3,025.00

Urns, cast iron, the wide rounded
bowl w/rolled & scalloped rim
cast on the exterior w/scrolling
leaves, raised on a shaped pedestal surrounded by three figures of
egrets, on a circular base, painted
white, attributed to J.W. Fiske &
Co., New York, ca. 1893, 33½" d.,
36¼" h., pr. 4,400.00

Wall ornament, wrought iron,
modeled as a woven basket issuing a swirling spray of ivy-type
vines & leaves, 6' h. 4,400.00

GLASS

AKRO AGATE

This glass was made by the Akro Agate Company in Clarksburg, West Virginia between 1932 and 1951. The company was famous for their marble production but also produced many novelty items in various colors of marbleized glass and offered a popular line of glass children's dishes in plain colors and marbleized glass. Most articles bear the company mark of a crow flying through a capital letter A.

GENERAL LINE

Colonial Lady Powder Box

Ashtray, ellipsoid, marbleized blue
& white $12.00

Ashtray, leaf-shaped, marbleized
green swirls 8.00

Ashtray, square, marbleized orange
& white 4.00

Ashtrays, bridge set, green, set
of 4 . . . . 35.00

Bowl, 7¼" d., tab-handled, marbleized orange & white 35.00

Cornucopia-vase, marbleized blue &
white 9.00

Flowerpot, miniature, marbleized
deep blue & white, 2½" h. 5.00

Flowerpot, miniature, marbleized
orange & white w/graduated
darts design, 2" h. 8.00

Night light w/eagle on ball finial,
marbleized blue & white 110.00

Planter, oval, marbleized red &
creamy white 20.00

Powder box, Colonial Lady cover,
cobalt blue, 6¼" h. 80.00

Powder box, Colonial Lady cover,
  green, 6¼" h. 170.00
Powder box, Colonial Lady cover,
  milk white, 6¼" h. 45.00
Powder box, Colonial Lady cover,
  powder blue opaque, 6¼" h.
  (ILLUS.) 75.00

Scottie Dog Powder Jar

Powder jar, Scottie dog cover, blue
  opaque (ILLUS.) 85.00

CHILDREN'S DISHES
Bowl, cereal, Concentric Rib patt.,
  blue opaque, 3 3/8" d. 20.00
Bowl, cereal, Concentric Rib patt.,
  lime green opaque, 3 3/8" d. 6.00
Bowl, cereal, Interior Panel
  patt., marbleized green & white,
  3 3/8" d. 20.00
Bowl, cereal, Octagonal patt., green
  opaque, 3 3/8" d. 5.00
Creamer, Concentric Rib patt.,
  blue 25.00
Creamer, Octagonal patt., blue 4.00
Cup, Raised Daisy patt., blue,
  1¾" h. 25.00
Cup & saucer, Concentric Rib patt.,
  green opaque 12.00
Cup & saucer, Stippled Band patt.,
  light amber 13.00
Cups & saucers, Octagonal patt.,
  pumpkin, w/original box,
  16 pcs. 130.00
Pitcher, Interior Panel patt., tur-
  quoise 10.00
Pitcher, Stippled Band patt., trans-
  parent green, 2 7/8" h. 9.00
Plate, dinner, 3 3/8" d., Chiquita
  patt., green opaque 2.50
Plate, dinner, 3 3/8" d., Concentric
  Rib patt., green opaque 6.50
Plate, dinner, 3 3/8" d., Octagonal-
  O patt., green opaque 4.50
Plate, dinner, 4¼" d., Interior Panel
  patt., green opaque 7.50
Plate, dinner, 4¼" d., Interior Panel
  patt., marbleized green & white . . 10.00

Plates, dinner, 4¼" d., Stippled
  Band patt., transparent green, set
  of 4 . . . . 16.00
Plates, dinner, 4¼" d., Octagonal
  patt., green opaque, set of 10 . . . . 25.00
Teapot, cov., Concentric Rib patt.,
  blue opaque 18.00
Teapot, cov., Interior Panel patt.,
  transparent green 17.50
Teapot, cov., Stacked Disc patt.,
  dark blue 10.00
Teapot, cov., Stacked Disc & Panel
  patt., cobalt blue teapot & custard
  cover 35.00
Teapot, cov., Stippled Band patt.,
  marbleized lemonade & white 20.00
Tumbler, Stacked Disc patt., pink . . . 4.50
Tumblers, Stippled Band patt., transparent green, set of 6 . . . . 40.00

AMBERINA

Pressed Amberina Berry Bowl

*Amberina was developed in the late 1880's
by the New England Glass Company and a
pressed version was made by Hobbs, Brockunier & Company (under license from the
former). A similar ware, called Rose Amber,
was made by the Mt. Washington Glass
Works. Amberina-Rose Amber shades from
amber to deep red or fuchsia and cut and plated (lined with creamy white) examples were
also made. The Libbey Glass Company briefly revived blown Amberina, using modern
shapes, in 1917.*

Basket, footed, squatty bulbous
  shape w/crimped rim, applied
  squared amber handle w/berry
  prunts on each side, raised
  squared hob pattern, three applied amber feet, 6½" d., 7" h. . . $395.00
Basket, 'poke bonnet' form w/an
  applied pointed amber handle at
  the flared rim, applied amber
  wishbone feet & rim edging, gold
  enameled flowers & fence on one
  side & gold flowers on the rim,
  6½ x 8¾", 14½" h. 695.00
Bowl, individual berry, 5" w.,

square, pressed Daisy & Button
patt. (ILLUS.)................... 70.00
Bowl, 7½" d., 3½" h., squared ruffled rim, Hobnail patt........... 395.00
Bowl, 10" l., 6¼" h., oval, applied
amber wishbone-form rim band,
end handles & feet 275.00
Butter dish, cover w/applied ball
finial, Inverted Thumbprint patt. .. 235.00
Celery vase, cylindrical w/squared
scalloped rim, Inverted Thumbprint patt., 6½" h. 515.00
Celery vase, tall cylindrical form
w/a flaring scalloped rim,
10 7/8" h. 130.00
Compote, cov., 7" d., 9¾" h.,
domed cover w/applied amber
finial & pedestal base, Swirl
patt. 265.00
Creamer, bulbous base tapering to
a cylindrical rim w/pinched lip,
applied amber handle, 3½" d.,
4¾" h. 135.00
Cruet w/original amber facet-cut
stopper, cylindrical body w/round
shoulder tapering to a short narrow cylindrical neck w/slightly
flared rim, applied amber handle,
2½" d., 5¾" h. 145.00
Cruet w/original stopper, Reverse
Amberina, Inverted Thumbprint
patt. 365.00
Dish, cov., low cylindrical Swirl patt.
base w/applied amber stick handle on side, matching slightly
domed cover w/applied amber
button finial, 5¾" d., 4¼" h...... 245.00
Finger bowl, tricorner folded rim,
Diamond Quilted patt. 340.00
Finger bowl, Swirl patt., 4½" d.,
2½" h. 165.00
Lemonade set: 10" h., 4¼" d. footed
pitcher w/ovoid body & wide flaring neck & applied amber handle
& four 4½" h. cylindrical tumblers; fine molded interior ribbing, 5 pcs.................... 425.00
Mug, lemonade, applied snake handle w/curl at base, Swirl patt.,
5" h. 225.00
Pickle castor, mold-blown Inverted
Thumbprint patt. bulbous insert in
a footed, braided silver plate
frame 325.00
Pitcher, 4½" h., 3½" d., bulbous
body w/a wide cylindrical neck
w/pinched spout, applied angled
amber handle.................. 145.00
Pitcher, 5¼" h., applied reeded amber handle, Wide Optic patt. 210.00
Pitcher, 6" h., mold-blown bulbous
ovoid body w/squared flaring
neck, applied reeded amber handle, Inverted Thumbprint patt..... 302.50

Pitcher, 10" h., 5 1/8" d., bulbous
body tapering to a slender cylindrical neck w/pinched lip, applied
amber handle, Inverted Thumbprint patt. 225.00
Plate, 7" d., Inverted Thumbprint
patt., New England Glass Co. 145.00
Punch cup w/applied amber handle, Diamond Thumbprint patt.,
2¾" d., 2¾" h. 135.00
Spooner, Inverted Thumbprint
patt.......................... 180.00
Spooner, corset-shaped, Swirled Rib
patt.......................... 245.00
Toothpick holder, cylindrical body
w/tricornered rim, Diamond Quilted patt., Mt. Washington Glass
Co. 250.00

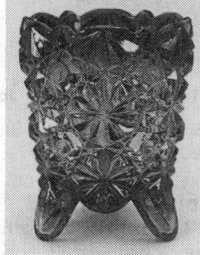

Amberina Daisy & Button Toothpick Holder

Toothpick holder, pressed Daisy &
Button patt. (ILLUS.) 335.00
Tumbler, Swirled Rib patt., decorated w/multicolored florals & white
dotting, 4" h. 125.00
Tumbler, whiskey, cylindrical, Diamond Quilted patt., New England
Glass Co., 2" d., 2 5/8" h. 195.00
Vase, 5" h., 4½" d., squatty bulbous
body tapering to a flaring squared
neck, Swirled Rib patt., enameled
w/gold roses, leaves & trim 245.00

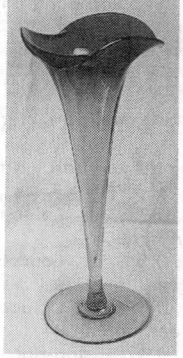

Amberina Lily-Form Vase

Vase, 7" h., lily-form, New England
Glass Co. (ILLUS.) 295.00

Vases, 8¼" h., 2 7/8" d., footed, cone shaped w/scalloped rim, applied amber shell-shaped feet, Optic Rib patt., pr. 195.00

Vase, bud, 9" h., bottle-shaped, Swirled Rib patt., signed "Libbey" 450.00

Vase, bud, 11¾" h., tall very slender body slightly swelled at the upper half, on an amber disc foot, Libbey Glass Co. 330.00

Water set: 7" h., 5" d. bulbous tapering cylindrical pitcher & six 2½" d., 3¾" h. footed tumblers; Swirled Rib patt., 7 pcs. 375.00

Whimsey, model of a canoe, pressed Daisy & Button patt. 195.00

Wine cruet w/original amber bubble stopper, bulbous body w/a slender cylindrical neck, applied angled amber handle, Swirled Rib patt., 4 3/8" d., 8¾" h. 245.00

ANIMALS

Fish Vase by Heisey

Americans evidently like to collect glass animals and, for the past fifty years, American glass manufacturers have turned out a wide variety of animals to please the buying public. Some were produced for long periods and some were later reproduced by other companies, while others were made for only a short period of time and are rare. We have not included late productions in our listings and have attempted to date the productions where possible. Evelyn Zemel's book, American Glass Animals A to Z *will be helpful to the novice collector.*

Angelfish book ends, clear, A.H. Heisey & Co., 1942-52, 2¼ x 3½" wave base, 7" h., pr. $186.00

Asiatic Pheasant, clear, A.H. Heisey & Co., 1944-45, 7¼" l., 10¼" h. . . 300.00

Chicks, clear, heads up or heads down, A.H. Heisey & Co., 1948-49, 1" h., each 82.00

Chinese Pheasant, blue, Paden City Glass Mfg. Co., ca. 1940, 13¾" l., 5¾" h. . . . . .95.00 to 125.00

Cygnet (Baby Swan), clear, A.H. Heisey & Co., 1947-49, 2¼" h. 200.00

Cygnet (Baby Swan), caramel slag, Imperial Glass Co. (Heisey mold), 1982-83, 2 1/8" h. 45.00

Deer sitting, milk white, Fostoria Glass Co., 1954-58, 1 x 2" base, 2¼" h. 30.00

Deer standing, blue, Fostoria Glass Co., 1977, 1 x 2" base, 4¼" h. . . . 40.00

Deer standing, frosted, Fostoria Glass Co., 1940-43, 1 x 2" base, 4¼" h. 40.00

Deer standing, milk white, Fostoria Glass Co., 1954-58, 1 x 2" base, 4¼" h. 37.50

Duck (Mallard) w/wings up, clear, A.H. Heisey & Co., 1942-53, 6½" h. 150.00

Duck floral block, Hawthorne (light amethyst), A.H. Heisey & Co., late 1920's-early 1930's, 5¼" d., 5" h. 295.00

Elephant w/long trunk extended, clear, A.H. Heisey & Co., 1944-53, medium (6¾" l.) 230.00

Elephant book ends, clear, New Martinsville Glass Mfg. Co., prior to 1945, 3¼ x 5¼" base, 6¼" l., 5¼" h., pr. . . . . .160.00 to 190.00

Fish candleholder, clear, A.H. Heisey & Co., 1941-48, 5" h. 165.00

Fish vase on wave base, clear, A.H. Heisey & Co., 1941-46, 9" h. (ILLUS.) . . . . .325.00 to 400.00

Gazelles, Ultra blue, Imperial Glass Co. (Heisey mold), 1982, 11" h., pr. 220.00

Giraffe w/head straight, clear, A.H. Heisey & Co., 1942-52, 11¼" h. 200.00

Goose (The Fat Goose), clear, Duncan & Miller Glass Co., 6" l., 6½" h. 235.00

Goose, wings down, clear, A.H. Heisey & Co., 1942-53, 10½" l., 2" h. . . . . .385.00 to 425.00

Horse, Clydesdale, clear, A.H. Heisey & Co., 1942-48, 8" l., 8" h. 350.00

Horse, Plug (Sparky), cobalt blue, A.H. Heisey & Co., 1941-46, 4" l., 4" h. 1,500.00

Horse, Plug (Sparky), Horizon blue, Imperial Glass Co. (Heisey mold), marked HCA-IG-81, 1981, 4" h. 35.00

Horse, Pony kicking, clear, A.H. Heisey & Co., 1941-45, 1½ x 2¼" base, 3" l., 4" h. . . . . .160.00 to 195.00

Horse rearing book end, dark

green, L.E. Smith, 1940's, 3 x 5½"
base, 5¾" l., 8" h. 50.00

Horse Head book end, clear, A.H.
Heisey & Co., 1937-55, 2¾ x 4¼"
base, 7" h. ....125.00 to 155.00

Horse Head book ends, clear, hollow, Federal Glass Co., 1940's,
3½ x 4¾" base, 5¾" h., pr. 44.00

Pig, Mama, clear, A.H. Heisey &
Co., 1948-49, 3 1/8" h. 1,050.00

Piglet standing, clear, A.H. Heisey &
Co., 1948-49, 1" h. 125.00

Piranha Fish, clear, bubbly texture,
unmarked, 4½" h. 65.00

Police Dog (German Shepherd) book
end, amethyst w/frosted base,
New Martinsville Glass Mfg. Co.,
1937-50, 5 1/8" h. 82.00

Porpoise book ends, clear, New
Martinsville Glass Mfg. Co., ca.
1940's, 6" w., 6½" h., pr. 525.00

Rabbit, caramel slag, Imperial
Glass Co. (Heisey mold), 1982,
4 5/8" h. 45.00

Rabbit, clear, New Martinsville
Glass Mfg. Co., 1½ x 3¼" base,
5" l., 3" h. 200.00

Ringneck Pheasant, clear, A.H.
Heisey & Co., 1942-53, 11" l.,
4¾" h. ....140.00 to 170.00

Rooster, clear, A.H. Heisey & Co.,
1948-49, 5 3/8" h. 475.00

Rooster fighting (Chanticleer), clear,
A.H. Heisey & Co., 1940-46,
8½" h. ....145.00 to 165.00

Rooster w/head down, clear, Paden
City Glass Mfg. Co., 3¾ x 5¼"
oval base, 8¾" h. 65.00

Scottie Dog book ends, clear, A.H.
Heisey & Co., 1941-46, 3¾" l.
base, 5" h., pr. ....155.00 to 175.00

Seal w/ball, clear, New Martinsville
Glass Mfg. Co., 7¼" h. 60.00

Sparrow, clear, A.H. Heisey & Co.,
1942-45, 4" l., 2¼" h. at raised
tail 110.00

Swan dish, Crown Tuscan, Cambridge Glass Co., 8½" l. 150.00

Swan dish, red, Sylvan patt., Duncan & Miller Glass Co., 10½" l.... 80.00

Swan dish, red w/clear neck, Duncan & Miller Glass Co., 7" l....... 35.00

Swan dish, green w/clear neck,
Duncan & Miller Glass Co.,
12" l. 67.00

Swan dish, ruby, Duncan & Miller
Glass Co., 12" l. 65.00

Swan figure, Pall Mall patt.,
clear, Duncan & Miller Glass
Co., 3¼" l., 3¼" h. 20.00

Swan figure, Pall Mall patt., clear,
Duncan & Miller Glass Co., 5" l.,
4½" h. 25.00

Swan figure, clear, Vallerysthal,
5¾" l., 5½" h................... 135.00

Tiger paperweight, caramel slag,
Imperial Glass Co. (Heisey mold),
1982-83, 8" l., 2¾" h............. 145.00

Viking Duck ashtray, clear, A.H.
Heisey & Co., 4¾" l. 75.00

ART GLASS BASKETS

*Popular in the late Victorian era, these or-
nate hand-crafted glass baskets were often
given as gifts. Sometimes made with unusually tall handles and applied feet, these fragile
ornaments usually command a good price
when they survive intact.*

Cased, creamy white exterior, deep
rose interior, ruffled rim, applied
amber edging & applied amber
spiral twist handle, 5 x 6 1/8",
7¼" h. $165.00

Cased, maroon, green, pink & yellow spatter exterior, embossed
Swirl patt., white interior, square
ruffled rim, applied clear angular
thorn handle, 5½" d., 7½" h. 165.00

Cased, pink & white spatter exteri-
or, white interior, star-shaped
rim, applied clear twisted thorn
handle, 5 1/8" d., 7¼" h. 135.00

Cased, raspberry pink exterior,
white interior, a flattened oblong
shape w/a lightly crimped rim,
decorated overall w/tiny polychrome blossoms, leaves & gilt
tracery & applied w/an amber
leaf sprig & pears or cherries &
raised on four applied amber
feet, an applied amber twist handle across the top, attributed
to Stevens & Williams, England,
11" l., 11" h. (one cherry stem
missing) 660.00

Cased, shaded heavenly blue satin
mother-of-pearl Diamond Quilted
patt., white interior, applied clear
frosted angular handle, 4½" d.,
6¾" h. 375.00

Cased, white exterior, shaded blue
interior, applied clear rigaree
around ruffled rim, applied clear
thorn handle, 8½" d., 9" h. 245.00

Cranberry, bulbous body, ruffled rim
w/applied clear edging, six tiny
applied clear feet, applied clear
reeded handle, 5½" d., 8" h. 265.00

Green opalescent, scalloped rim,
applied pink spatter flowers,
vaseline leaves & branches,
applied vaseline twist handle,
6 3/8" d., 8¾" h. 195.00

Pink opalescent, lightly ruffled rim,
applied clear twist handle & pink

flower w/clear branch, 5¼" d.,
6¾" h. 145.00
Pink shaded to amber w/opalescent
swirls, melon-ribbed body
w/turned down rim on each
side, applied pink twist handle,
4 1/8" d., 7¼" h. 145.00
Spangled, heavenly blue exterior
w/stripes of silver mica flecks,
white interior, bulbous body
w/ruffled rim, applied clear twist
handle, 5½" d., 8¾" h. 195.00
Spangled, salmon pink w/gold mica
flecks, molded rib design, bulbous
body w/ruffled rim, applied amber twist handle & edge trim,
4¼" d., 7¾" h. 125.00
Spatter, blue & white spatter exteri-
or, bulbous w/crimped rim, applied sapphire blue handle,
5½" d., 6½" h. 165.00
Spatter, green embossed Basket-
weave patt. w/white spatter exterior, white interior, rectangular body w/ruffled rim, applied
clear twisted thorn handle,
3¾ x 4 7/8", 6¼" h. 118.00
Spatter, pink & gold spatter exteri-
or, white interior, bulbous base
w/crimped rim, applied clear
angular thorn handle, 4¼" d.,
6¼" h. 155.00
White w/applied cranberry ruffled
rim, applied clear twisted thorn
handle, 4½" d., 7½" h. 145.00
Yellow opaque Diamond Quilted
patt., tightly ruffled rim w/applied
clear edging, applied clear thorn
handle, 5¼" d., 8¼" h. 195.00

BACCARAT

Baccarat Candlesticks

*Baccarat glass has been made by Cristaller-
ies de Baccarat, France, since 1765. The firm
has produced various glasswares of excellent
quality and paperweights. Baccarat's Rose
Tiente is often referred to as Baccarat's
Amberina.*

Box, cov., rectangular, Rose Tiente
Swirl patt., marked, 8" l., 5" h. . . . $345.00
Candlestick, Rose Tiente Swirl patt.,
marked, 4¼" d., 7¼" h. 145.00
Candlesticks, clear w/tulip-shaped
candle socket above a baluster-
form shaft on a flaring foot, all
w/a bold swirled pattern, w/a
matching swirled bobeche,
signed, 9" h., pr. (ILLUS.) 357.50
Jar, cov., cylindrical, Rose Tiente
Swirl patt., 6" d., 3¼" h. 85.00
Salt dip, Rose Tiente Swirl patt. 32.00
Toothpick holder w/scalloped rim,
Diamond Point patt., clear 45.00
Tumblers, Rose Tiente Swirl patt.,
8 oz., set of 6. . . . . 285.00
Vases, 13 7/8" h., thick clear body
of square section w/round base &
rim, finely wheel-carved w/scenes
of birds & flowers w/Oriental-
inspired borders, mounted on silver plated base of conforming design, base stamped "BACCARAT,"
ca. 1878, pr. 4,675.00

BLOWN THREE MOLD

*This type of glass was entirely or partially
blown in a mold from about 1820 in the United States. The object was formed and the
decoration impressed upon it by blowing the
glass into a metal mold, usually of three but
sometimes more sections, hinged together.
Mold-blown glass actually dates back to ancient times. Recent research reveals that certain geometric patterns were reproduced in
the 1920's and collectors are urged to read all
recent information available. Reference numbers are from George L. and Helen Mc-
Kearin's book,* American Glass.

Creamer, geometric, ovoid body
tapering up to a wide flaring rim,
applied handle, diamond point
band w/sunburst panels, clear
(GIII-12) $935.00
Decanter w/blown bulbous stopper,
geometric, ribbed w/panel molded in relief w/"Brandy," possibly
Mt. Vernon Glass Works, Vernon,
New York, clear, qt. (GIII-2) 550.00
Decanter w/original tam-o-shanter
stopper, geometric, molded ribbing, Boston & Sandwich Glass
Works, Sandwich, Massachusetts,
cobalt blue, ½ pt., GI-29 (¼" flat
chip on underside of mouth) 467.50
Decanter w/blown bulbous stopper,
Heart & Chain patt., clear, 8¾" h.
plus stopper, GV-16 (minor
stain) 412.50

Decanter, no stopper, geometric, diamond point band w/sunburst panels, Keene Marlboro Street Glassworks, Keene, New Hampshire, deep forest green, pt. (GIII-16) 2,310.00

Decanter, no stopper, geometric, diamond point band around the middle, Keene Marlboro Street Glassworks, Keene, New Hampshire, olive amber, qt. (GIII-19) ... 935.00

Decanter, no stopper, geometric, molded interior swirled ribbing w/diamond point band around the center, flared mouth, pontil scar, Mt. Vernon Glass Works, Vernon, New York, light yellowish green, 6¾" h., pt. (GII-2) 6,600.00

Flask, geometric, rolled mouth, pontil scar, clear, pt., GI-22 (small ground spot at bubble burst inside mouth) 1,210.00

Flip glass, geometric, flaring cylindrical shape, diamond point band design, clear, 4 3/8" h. (GIII-23) .. 176.00

Inkwell, geometric, low cylindrical form w/rounded edges, olive amber (GII-16) 110.00

Lamp, spherical footed body, molded interior ribbing, clear, 1¾" d., 2 3/8" h., mold similar to GI-6 (exterior stain, brass collar missing) 357.50

Tumbler, clear, 6" h. (GII-22) 137.50

Whimsey, model of a top hat, geometric, clear, 2½" d. (GII-7)...... 110.00

Whimsey, model of a top hat, geometric, clear (GII-16) 77.00

Whimsey, model of a top hat, geometric, folded rim, clear, 2¼" h. (GIII-3) 121.00

BOHEMIAN

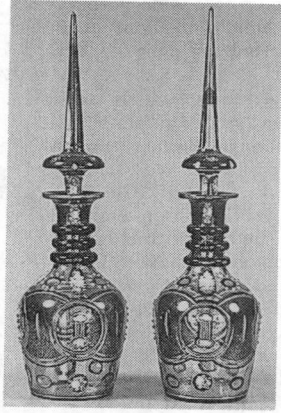

Ornate Cut Overlay Decanters

Numerous types of glass were made in the once-independent country of Bohemia and fine colored, cut and engraved glass was turned out. Flashed and other inexpensive wares also were made and many of these, including amber- and ruby-shaded glass, were exported to the United States last century and in the present one. One favorite pattern in the late 19th and early 20th centuries was Deer & Castle. Another was Deer and Pine Tree.

Basket, etched Deer & Castle patt., amethyst & clear, 8" h. $85.00

Box, cov., "Lithyalin," rectangular casket-form in marbleized sealing-wax red, the sides & cover w/formal gilt scrolls & floral sprays & garlands in opaque white enamel, between gilt line & enamel dot borders, late 19th c., 4¾ x 9 1/8" 1,148.00

Candy dish, cov., three-footed, etched Vintage Grape patt., ruby & clear 125.00

Compote, open, 7 5/8" h., amber-stained, deep flaring paneled bowl w/ten-lobed rim, a roundel in each lobe, each roundel engraved w/a German landscape view including Coblenz & one w/the initial "K," thick facet-cut stem & scalloped foot w/a star-cut base, ca. 1850 ....1,340.00

Decanters w/tall slender spire stoppers, cut overlay, clear overlaid w/ruby & cut w/round panels & arches, three applied rings at the neck, decorated overall w/ornate gold trim & delicate colored florals, 23½" h., pr. (ILLUS.) 1,540.00

Decanter set: ball-shaped decanter & six ball-shaped shot glasses; etched Deer & Castle patt., ruby & clear, 8" h. decanter, 7 pcs....... 185.00

Goblets, cut overlay, tulip-shaped bowl on a notched tapering stem, clear crystal overlaid in cranberry & cut back to clear w/grapes & stars, 8¼" h., set of 6 .... 130.50

Scent bottle w/original stopper, "Lithyalin," upright square footed bottle in sealing-wax red, the sides & stopper faceted & painted in opaque white enamel & gilt w/flower & leaf sprays between gilt line & enamel dot borders, gilt rim, late 19th c., 7½" h. (gilding worn)..................... 957.00

Tumbler, "Lithyalin," Biedermeier-style, decorated in gilt w/a scene of Aesop before King Croesus, signed, ca. 1830, 4½" h. 4,400.00

Tumbler, footed, clear, decorated

w/four varicolor-applied & engraved oval vignettes w/the inscriptions "Bringe Ihuen die Ziet," "Gezundheit," "Gluet," & "Und Freude," mid- to late 19th c. 60.00

Vase, 8½" h., 8" w., fan-shaped, etched Deer & Castle patt., blue & clear 120.00

Ornate Cut & Stained Vases

Vases, cov., 22" h., amber-stained, flaring cylindrical body raised on a facet-cut & knopped pedestal on a domed foot, the cover tapering to a tall, knopped & facet-cut finial, the body w/a wide upper band etched w/leaf swags framing pairs of birds above a wide diamond-cut band, further etched leaf swags around base of bowl & on the foot, 19th c., pr. (ILLUS.) . . 1,650.00

Vase, 23½" h., trumpet-form, faceted sides, amber, late 19th c. 1,210.00

Wine, etched Deer & Castle patt., ruby & clear 40.00

Wines, cut-overlay, globular bowl above clear stem & base, each bowl flashed in either blue, red, green, yellow or amethyst & cut w/a design of grapes & hobstars, 7¾" h., set of 12 . . . . 192.50

BRIDE'S BASKETS & BOWLS

These are berry or fruit bowls, once popular as wedding gifts, hence the name.

Amethyst bowl, enameled w/white leaves & butterflies, in original ornate silver plate frame, 9½" d. bowl, 14" h. frame $195.00

Cased bowl, butterscotch w/gold mica flecks interior, white exterior, crimped rim, silver plate frame marked "Tufts" 245.00

Fine Satin Glass Bride's Bowl

Cased bowl, gold satin mother-of-pearl Diamond Quilted patt. exterior decorated w/white blossoms on branches & small bluebirds, pink interior, deeply crimped & ruffled rim, raised on an ornate silver plate stand w/three figural putti on a trilobed footed base, attributed to Thomas Webb & Sons, late 19th c. (ILLUS.) 1,950.00

Cased bowl, heavenly blue satin interior w/enameled white daisies & gold branches, white exterior, undulating rim w/one side turned-up, 13½" d., 6½" h. 325.00

Cased bowl, light cranberry shaded to pink interior, white exterior, applied clear rigaree on ruffled rim, 11" d., 3 7/8" h. 115.00

Cased bowl, pink interior w/white Coralene herringbone pattern decoration, white exterior, in an ornate peacock pattern silver plate frame, bowl 9" d. 400.00

Cased bowl, pink shaded satin mother-of-pearl Diamond Quilted patt. exterior, white interior, rectangular w/crimped rim, ornate silver plate frame marked "Manhattan Silver Plating Co.," bowl 7 x 12", overall 11" h. 795.00

Cased bowl, purple shaded to soft green interior, white exterior, ruffled rim, footed brass frame w/scrolling trim in handle, 10 3/8" d., overall 7¾" h. 225.00

Cased bowl, purple shaded mother-of-pearl satin glass interior decorated w/dainty lavender & white flowers & green leaves, white exterior, tightly ruffled rim, in ornate silver plate frame, 12¼" d., 8½" h. 295.00

Cased bowl, rich green shaded to pale green interior decorated w/embossed lattice design around the edge, white exterior, ruffled rim, no frame, 11½" d., 3¾" h. . . . 225.00

Cased bowl, turquoise blue interior decorated w/white flowers w/green & yellow centers, creamy white exterior, deep three-lobed shape w/tightly crimped edge, in an ornate, footed ormolu frame w/bow at top of handle, 6½ x 9", 8½" h. 245.00

Cased bowl, white interior w/enameled flower sprays, shaded pink satin exterior decorated w/enameled flowers, four-lobe crimped edge, in an ornate footed resilvered frame marked "Meriden," 9¼" d., overall 8½" h. 395.00

Cased bowl, white interior, shaded pink satin mother-of-pearl Diamond Quilted patt. exterior, tightly ruffled rim, ornate footed silver plate frame w/high overhead handle, marked "Manhattan," 11½" d., overall 10½" h. 795.00

Cased bowl, yellow interior, white exterior decorated overall w/blue & pink daisy-like flowers, leaves & branches all outlined finely in gold, widely rolled sides, ruffled rim, ormolu footed frame w/ornate handle, 7" d., overall 9¾" h. 236.00

Cranberry bowl, applied clear rigaree rim band pulled to scalloped points, applied clear wafer foot, no frame, 9½" d., 4" h. 225.00

Rubina opalescent bowl, exterior decorated w/opalescent thistle blossoms & leaves, scalloped & crimped rim, no frame, 11 5/8" d., 3 3/8" h. 245.00

Spangled bowl, elongated oblong shape, white interior decorated w/multicolored enameled flowers & leaves, red exterior w/silver mica flecks, ornate silver plate stand w/long swirled loop end handles & domed foot, 16" l., 7" h. 450.00

BRISTOL

While glass was made in several glasshouses in Bristol, England, the generic name Bristol glass is applied today by collectors to a variety of semi-opaque glasses, frequently decorated by enameling, and made both abroad and in United States glasshouses in the 19th and 20th centuries.

Candlestick, decorated w/small orange & white flowers in gold trimmed garlands around top, middle & base, turquoise blue ground, 3½" d., 6¾" h. $95.00

Cologne bottle w/original tulip-shaped stopper, footed bulbous body tapering to a slender neck w/flared rim, decorated w/white & grey enameled decoration on a blue satin ground, 3" d., 8¼" h. . . . 110.00

Cracker jar, cov., cylindrical body decorated w/herons & trees on a tan ground, silver plate rim, flat cover w/strawberry finial & bail handle, 4¾" d., 7½" h. 195.00

Cracker jar, cov., slightly rounded sides, grey & white enameled herons front & green palm trees, pink flowers & marsh reverse against a turquoise blue ground, silver plate rim, flat cover & bail handle, 5" d., 12¼" h. 650.00

Jam jar, cov., white satin ground w/h.p. floral decoration, silver plate frame, cover & bail handle 65.00

Mustard pot, cov., decorated w/yellow, pink & blue daisies & green leaves on a green opaque body, silver plate hinged lid, w/silver plate spoon, 1¾" d., 3 1/8" h., 2 pcs. 40.00

Perfume bottle w/original blue bubble-shaped stopper trimmed in gold, enameled cream & gold flowers & white enameled scroll decoration on a turquoise blue ground, 1 7/8" d., 5¼" h. 75.00

Perfume bottle w/original blue stopper, bulbous base tapering to a cylindrical neck w/slightly flared rim, decorated w/pink & white flowers & white & green leaves on a turquoise blue ground, 2¼" d., 5 3/8" h. 110.00

Salt dip, bucket-shaped w/silver plate rim & bail handle, enameled bird, butterfly & trees in white, green & brown on a turquoise blue body, 2½" d., 1 5/8" h. 75.00

Vase, 7" h., 3½" d., cylindrical body tapering in slightly & flaring to a short rim, applied turquoise ring handles, decorated w/enameled pink, yellow & white flowers, green leaves & brown & gold birds on a turquoise ground 95.00

Vase, 12" h., 4" d., footed, baluster-form w/slightly flared rim, enameled pink flowers w/green leaves, bird sitting on a branch & white dot trim decoration on a turquoise blue ground 125.00

Vases, 14½" h., footed baluster-form w/slightly flared rim, deco-

rated w/enameled lily-type flowers in lavender, blue, yellow &
brown on a bright yellowish green
ground, pr. 350.00

BURMESE

Footed Burmese Vase

*Burmese is a single-layer glass that shades
from pink to pale yellow. It was patented by
Frederick S. Shirley and made by the Mt.
Washington Glass Co. A license to produce
the glass in England was granted to Thomas
Webb & Sons, which called its articles
Queen's Burmese. Gundersen Burmese was
made briefly about the middle of this century, and the Pairpoint Crystal Company is
making limited quantities at the present time.*

Bowl, 3 7/8" d., 2¼" h., bulbous
base w/folded over star-shaped
rim, satin finish, unsigned Webb. . $210.00
Bowl, 3 7/8" d., 2 7/8" h., bulbous
body w/six-sided rim, enameled
lavender flowers & green & brown
foliage decoration, satin finish . . . 310.00
Bowl, 4¾" d., 2¼" h., footed, ruffled rim, marked "Queen's Bur-
mese Thomas Webb" 120.00
Compote, open, 6" d., 4½" h.,
glossy finish, Gundersen 70.00
Finger bowl, scalloped rim, satin
finish 325.00
Ice cream dish, ruffled rim, Mt.
Washington Glass Co., 4¾" d. . . . 295.00
Marmalade jar, cov., glossy finish,
Thomas Webb & Sons 200.00
Pitcher, 4¾" h., 3½" d., ovoid body
w/square flaring neck, applied
yellow reeded handle, decorated
w/yellow mums on one side &
white mums on other, satin finish,
Mt. Washington Glass Co. 595.00
Plate, 4¾" d., footed, satin finish,
Pairpoint Corporation, original pa-
per label 150.00

Rose bowl, miniature, eight-crimp
rim, lavender five-petal flowers &
green leaves decoration, satin fin-
ish, 2½" d., 2¼" h. 295.00
Rose bowl, eight-crimp rim, decorat-
ed w/lavender five-petal flowers
& green & brown leaves, satin
finish, unsigned Webb, 3¼" d.,
3¼" h. 395.00
Salt & pepper shakers w/original
tops, cylindrical ribbed body, satin
finish, pr. 250.00
Salt & pepper shakers w/original
tops & original silver plate frame,
cylindrical ribbed shakers w/satin
finish, shakers by Mt. Washington Glass Co., frame marked
"Rockford Silver Plate," holder
2½ x 5½", 4½" h., 3 pcs. 350.00
Sweetmeat jar, cov., melon-ribbed
body, decorated w/enameled pansies, original marked silver plate
base, rim & cover, attributed to
Mt. Washington Glass Co. 250.00
Toothpick holder, bulbous base
w/square top, satin finish, Mt.
Washington Glass Co., 2 7/8" h. . . 485.00
Toothpick holder, crimped top, Diamond Quilted patt., satin finish . . . 675.00
Tumbler, cylindrical, h.p. enameled
violets, Mt. Washington Glass
Co. 750.00
Tumbler, decorated w/h.p. roses &
blue forget-me-nots & the verse
"But I will woo the dainty Rose..."
by Thos. Hood, Mt. Washington
Glass Co. 1,300.00
Vase, 3" h., 2 5/8" d., bulbous body
tapering to a short star-shaped
neck, decorated w/blue & white
enameled flowers & brown
leaves, satin finish 300.00
Vase, 3 3/8" h., 2 5/8" d., squatty
bulbous base tapering to a short
cylindrical neck w/flaring & folded
over star-shaped rim, satin finish,
unsigned Webb 200.00
Vase, 3¾" h., 2¾" d., cylindrical
body w/slightly flaring ruffled rim
& ruffled foot, enameled w/lav-
ender blue flowers & green &
brown leaves, satin finish, Thom-
as Webb 300.00
Vase, 4" h., 2¾" d., rounded cylin-
drical body flaring to a ruffled rim
& raised on a round ruffled pedes-
tal foot, satin finish 225.00
Vase, 4¼" h., bell-shaped body
w/flared & crimped rim, decorated w/lavender flowers & green &
brown foliage, satin finish 325.00
Vase, 6½" h., bulbous body w/tall,
flaring neck w/fluted rim, satin

finish, Mt. Washington Glass
Co. 375.00
Vase, 8" h., footed, lily-form
w/tricorner rim, decorated overall
w/delicate clusters of forget-me-
nots, Mt. Washington Glass Co. .. 975.00
Vase, 8¼" h., 3 7/8" d., bulbous
body tapering to a tall cylindrical
stick neck, enameled w/green ivy
leaves, satin finish, signed "Thos.
Webb - Queen's Burmese Ware".. 695.00
Vase, 8¼" h., footed, very slender
cylindrical base swelling gradually
at the upper half, decorated
w/dainty white enameled daisies
on thin stems & surrounded by
pastel leaves, three gold stripes
on foot & rim 685.00
Vase, 8½" h., 3 7/8" d., bulbous
base tapering to a cylindrical
neck, enameled red rose buds &
green & brown leaves, satin finish, unsigned 695.00
Vase, 10" h., 4¼" widest d., footed
trumpet-shaped body w/lightly
ruffled flaring rim, satin finish,
Mt. Washington Glass Co. 375.00
Vase, 11" h., bulbous base w/long
stick neck, Mt. Washington Glass
Co. 375.00
Vase, 11½" h., squatty bulbous
base w/tall stick neck & small applied loop handles at the base of
the neck, gold enameled blossoms
& threading overall 4,750.00
Vases, 9" h., tapering ovoid body
w/closed rim, finely decorated
w/four swallows in flight, white
enamel beaded border, labeled
"Mt. W.G. Co. Burmese pat'd Dec.
15, 1885," pr. 3,300.00
Vases, 10½" h., gently flaring cylindrical bowl w/widely flaring ruffled rim, on a knopped pedestal &
round foot, glossy interior, satin
exterior, pr. (ILLUS. of one) 550.00
Vases, 12" h., 5¼" d., footed tapering cylinder, decorated w/flow-
ering vines & two small birds,
signed "Webb," pr. 4,230.00
Water set, pitcher & five tumblers,
6 pcs. 725.00

CAMBRIDGE

*The Cambridge Glass Company was found-
ed in Ohio in 1901. Numerous pieces are now
sought, especially those designed by Arthur
J. Bennett, including Crown Tuscan. Other
productions included crystal animals, "Black
Amethyst," "blanc opaque," and other types
of colored glass. The firm was finally closed*
*in 1954. It should not be confused with the
New England Glass Co., Cambridge, Massachusetts.*

Feather Pattern Cracker Jar

Ashtray, shell-shaped, Mandarin
Gold (medium yellow), 4" w...... $17.50
Ashtray, Statuesque line, Amethyst
bowl, clear Nude Lady stem...... 295.00
Ashtray, Statuesque line, Carmen
(ruby red) bowl, clear Nude Lady
stem 200.00
Bouillon cup & saucer, etched Cleo
patt., blue, 2 pcs. 40.00
Bowl, 10" d., 4¼" h., fluted rim,
etched Diane patt., Crystal 65.00
Bowl, 10" d., etched Rose Point
patt., No. 3400/1185, Crystal 52.00
Bowl, 10½" d., Tally-Ho line,
Carmen 65.00
Bowl, 11½" d., etched Portia patt.,
Crystal 65.00
Bowl, 12" oval, handled, four-
footed, etched Chantilly patt.,
Crystal 49.00
Bowl, 12" oblong, footed, etched Di-
ane patt., No. 3400/160, Crystal .. 50.00
Bowl, 13½" d., crimped rim, footed,
pressed Caprice patt., Moonlight
(pale blue) 60.00
Brandy, Statuesque line, Amethyst
bowl, clear Nude Lady stem..... 115.00
Brandy, Statuesque Line, Carmen
bowl, frosted Nude Lady stem 125.00
Brandy, Statuesque line, Moonlight
bowl, clear Nude Lady stem...... 250.00
Butter dish, cov., etched Elaine
patt., Crystal 65.00
Cake plate, handled, etched Wild-
flower patt., Crystal, 13½" d. 48.00
Candlesticks, one-light, footed C-
shape suspending a single prism,
pressed Caprice patt., No. 70,
Moonlight, 7" h., pr. ....100.00 to 125.00
Candlesticks, three-light, etched
Chantilly patt., Crystal, pr. 70.00
Candlesticks, two-light, No. 647,
Carmen, w/original paper labels,
pr. 150.00

Candlesticks, two-light, gold-encrusted etched Rose Point patt., pr. 185.00

Candlesticks, one-light, Sea Shell line, Windsor Blue (pale blue opaque), 2" h., pr. 225.00

Candlestick, two-light, etched Wildflower patt., No. 647, Crystal 65.00

Candy box, cov., Cascade line, Forest Green (dark green) 80.00

Candy box, cov., etched Chantilly patt., Crystal, 6" l. 50.00

Candy box, cov., Pristine line, Crystal, 6" d. 58.00

Celery dish, etched Rose Point patt., Crystal, 11" l. 45.00

Champagne, engraved Candlelight patt., Crystal 27.00

Champagne, Statuesque line, Crystal bowl, clear Nude Lady stem 99.00

Claret, Pristine line, Crystal, 4½ oz. 14.00

Claret, Statuesque line, Emerald Green (light green) bowl, clear Nude Lady stem . . . . 100.00 to 125.00

Cocktail, Martha Washington line, blue, 3 oz. 12.00

Cocktail, Statuesque line, Amber bowl, clear Nude Lady stem 90.00

Cocktail, Statuesque line, Carmen bowl, clear Nude Lady stem 95.00

Cocktail, Statuesque line, Pistachio (delicate pastel green) bowl, clear Nude Lady stem 105.00

Compote, open, 6" d., w/pie crust rim, etched Rose Point patt., Crystal 50.00

Compote, open, 7" d., Statuesque line, Carmen bowl, clear Nude Lady stem 150.00

Compote, open, 7½" d., Mt. Vernon line, No. 11, Crystal 20.00

Console set: 9" d. Gadroon (No. 3500) line ram's head-handled bowl & a pair of 9½" h. Doric Column candlesticks; Ivory, 3 pcs. 350.00

Cordial, Statuesque line, Carmen bowl, clear Nude Lady stem 595.00

Cracker jar, cov., Feather patt., Near Cut line, ca. 1910, clear (ILLUS.) 86.00

Creamer, etched Chantilly patt., Crystal 14.50

Creamer & open sugar bowl, Gadroon (No. 3500) line, Crystal, pr. 35.00

Creamer & open sugar bowl, individual size, etched Rose Point patt., No. 3500/15, Crystal, pr. . . . 42.50

Crown Tuscan bowl, 11" l., Sea Shell line, three-footed 75.00

Crown Tuscan candlesticks, Dolphin patt., 3½" h., pr. 250.00

Crown Tuscan candlesticks, Statuesque line, Nude Lady stem, 8" h., pr. 525.00

Crown Tuscan candy dish, cov., footed, Sea Shell line, W107, 6" l. 55.00

Crown Tuscan compote, open, 4½" h., Sea Shell line, decorated w/h.p. flowers 85.00

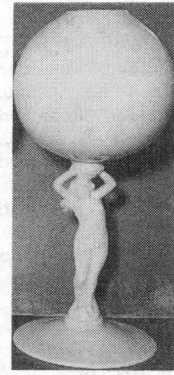

Crown Tuscan Ivy Ball

Crown Tuscan ivy ball, Nude Lady stem, 9½" h. (ILLUS.) 225.00

Crown Tuscan lamp, table model, urn-shaped, gold-encrusted etched Rose Point patt. 550.00

Crown Tuscan model of a swan, 9" l. 85.00

Crown Tuscan nut dish, Sea Shell line, three shell-shaped feet, 3" l. 7.00

Crown Tuscan vase, 10½" h., cornucopia-shaped w/sea shell base 52.00

Cruet w/original stopper, footed, etched Rose Point patt., No. 3400/161, Crystal, 6 oz. 200.00 to 225.00

Cup & saucer, etched Apple Blossom patt., green 38.50

Cup & saucer, Decagon line, green 12.00

Figure flower holder, "Bashful Charlotte," Crystal, 6½" h. 75.00

Figure flower holder, "Bashful Charlotte," green, 6½" h. 145.00

Figure flower holder, "Bashful Charlotte," pink, 6½" h. 135.00

Figure flower holder, "Bashful Charlotte," Crystal, 11" h. 155.00

Figure flower holder, "Bashful Charlotte," Forest Green, 11" h. 225.00

Figure flower holder, "Bashful Charlotte," frosted blue, 11" h. 495.00

Figure flower holder, "Bashful Charlotte," frosted Peach-Blo (light pink), 11" h. 200.00

Figure flower holder, "Draped Lady," Amber, 8½" h. . . . 135.00 to 155.00

Figure flower holder, "Draped
Lady," Crystal, 8½" h. 75.00
Figure flower holder, "Draped
Lady," Mandarin Gold, 8½" h. . . .   225.00
Figure flower holder, "Draped
Lady," Moonlight,
8½" h. . . . . .325.00 to 375.00
Figure flower holder, "Draped
Lady," Amber, 13" h. 275.00
Figure flower holder, "Draped
Lady," frosted blue, 13" h. 350.00
Figure flower holder, "Mandolin
Lady," Crystal, 9" h. . . . . .200.00 to 225.00
Figure flower holder, "Rose Lady,"
Amber, 8½" h. . . . . .250.00 to 275.00
Figure flower holder, "Rose Lady,"
Crystal, 8½" h. 225.00
Figure flower holder, "Rose Lady,"
green, 8½" h. . . . . .200.00 to 245.00
Figure flower holder, "Rose Lady,"
pink, 8½" h. 140.00
Figure flower holder, "Two-Kid,"
Amber, 8¾" h. 245.00
Figure flower holder, "Two-Kid,"
Forest Green, 8¾" h. 190.00
Figure flower holder, "Two-Kid,"
Peach-Blo, 8¾" h. 275.00

Heron Flower Holder

Flower holder, Heron, Crystal, 9" h.
(ILLUS.) . . . . .75.00 to 100.00
Flower holder, Sea Gull, Crystal,
8" h. . . . . .50.00 to 75.00
Goblet, water, Decagon line, Moon-
light (pale blue), 7¼" h., 9 oz. . . .   30.00
Goblet, Gadroon (No. 3500) line,
Crystal, 8½" h. 35.00
Goblet, table, Statuesque line, Car-
men (deep red) "crackle" bowl,
clear Nude Lady stem 795.00
Goblet, Statuesque line, Emerald
Green (light green) bowl, clear
Nude Lady stem. 115.00
Goblet, water, Tally-Ho line,
Carmen 35.00
Hurricane lamp shade, etched Rose
Point patt., Crystal 100.00
Ice bucket, pressed Caprice patt.,
Moonlight 130.00

Ice bucket w/chrome handle, etched
Chantilly patt., Crystal 70.00
Ice bucket, etched Rose Point patt.,
No. 851, Crystal 145.00
Ivy ball, Statuesque line, Amethyst
bowl, frosted Nude Lady stem 290.00
Luncheon set: twelve 8½" d. plates,
twelve bread & butter plates &
twelve cups & saucers; No. 3400
line, Carmen, 48 pcs. 400.00
Martini pitcher, etched Rose Point
patt., Crystal 475.00
Model of a swan, Forest Green
(dark green), 3" l. 55.00
Oyster cocktail, etched Chantilly
patt., Crystal 25.00
Perfume bottle w/atomizer, Colonial
(No. 2630) line, green 79.00
Pitcher, 10" h., etched Apple Blos-
som patt., No. 1205, Crystal 250.00
Pitcher, ball-shaped, pressed
Caprice patt., No. 179, Moonlight,
32 oz. 175.00
Pitcher, tall, Doulton-style, pressed
Caprice patt., No. 178, Crystal,
90 oz. 975.00
Pitcher, ball-shaped, Mt. Vernon
line, Crystal, 80 oz. 65.00
Pitcher, ball-shaped, etched Rose
Point patt., Carmen, 80 oz. 165.00
Plate, 7½" d., Laurel Wreath patt.,
Crystal 81.00
Plate, tea, 7½" d., etched Apple
Blossom patt., blue 22.00
Plate, salad, 8" d., etched Chantilly
patt., Crystal 15.00
Plate, salad, 8" d., Decagon line,
Moonlight 10.00
Plate, 8" d., etched Rose Point patt.,
Crystal 20.00
Plate, 8½" d., etched Apple Blos-
som patt., green 22.00
Plate, luncheon, 8½" d., etched
Rose Point patt., Crystal 25.00
Plate, dinner, 10½" d., etched Ap-
ple Blossom patt., green 110.00
Plate, dinner, 10½" d., etched Ap-
ple Blossom patt., yellow 95.00
Plate, 10½" d., etched Chantilly
patt., Crystal 52.50
Plate, 14" d., footed, etched Wild-
flower patt., clear 50.00
Plate, 14¼", rolled rim, etched Daf-
fodil patt., Crystal 35.00
Relish dish, etched Apple Blossom
patt., Amber, 8" l. 27.50
Relish, two-part, etched Rose Point
patt., Crystal, 6" l. 30.00
Relish, three-part, etched Rose Point
patt., Crystal, 7½" l. 40.00

(Cambridge Glass - Continued on page 504)

CARNIVAL GLASS

Earlier called Taffeta glass, the Carnival glass now being collected was introduced early in this century. Its producers gave it an iridescence that attempted to imitate that of some Tiffany glass. Collectors will find available books by leading authorities Donald E. Moore, Sherman Hand, Marion T. Hartung and Rose M. Presznick.

ACANTHUS (Imperial)

Bowl, 7" d., green	$20.00
Bowl, 7" d., marigold	46.50
Bowl, 7½" d., purple	80.00
Bowl, 7¾" d., smoky	45.00
Bowl, 8" to 9" d., green	65.00
Bowl, 8" to 9" d., marigold	62.00
Bowl, 8" to 9" d., purple	95.00
Bowl, 8" to 9" d., smoky	76.00
Plate, 9" to 10" d., marigold	193.00
Plate, 9" to 10" d., smoky	250.00

ACORN (Fenton)

Bowl, 3½" d., marigold	50.00
Bowl, 5" d., milk white w/marigold overlay	322.00
Bowl, 6" d., blue	45.00
Bowl, 6" d., vaseline	40.00
Bowl, 7" d., ruffled, amber	100.00
Bowl, 7" d., aqua	85.00
Bowl, 7" d., blue	44.00
Bowl, 7" d., green	68.00
Bowl, 7" d., lime green	55.00
Bowl, 7" d., marigold	30.00
Bowl, 7" d., peach opalescent	185.00
Bowl, 7" d., ruffled, peach opalescent	300.00
Bowl, 7" d., purple	45.00
Bowl, 7" d., red	550.00 to 600.00
Bowl, 7" d., ruffled, vaseline	100.00 to 125.00
Bowl, 8" to 9" d., blue	55.00
Bowl, 8" to 9" d., marigold w/opalescent rim	300.00
Bowl, 8" to 9" d., ribbon candy rim, purple	50.00
Bowl, 8" to 9" d., ruffled, red	700.00 to 750.00
Bowl, ice cream shape, aqua	125.00
Bowl, ice cream shape, blue	35.00
Bowl, ice cream shape, green	65.00
Bowl, ice cream shape, ice blue w/marigold overlay	75.00
Bowl, ice cream shape, moonstone	185.00
Bowl, ice cream shape, red slag	650.00
Bowl, ice cream shape, teal blue	75.00
Bowl, ruffled, aqua opalescent	125.00
Bowl, ruffled, green	70.00
Bowl, ruffled, marigold	30.00
Bowl, ruffled, moonstone	450.00
Bowl, ruffled, peach opalescent	362.00
Bowl, white	180.00

ACORN BURRS (Northwood)

Acorn Burrs Butter Dish

Berry set: master bowl & 6 sauce dishes; green, 7 pcs.	350.00
Berry set: master bowl & 6 sauce dishes; marigold, 7 pcs.	208.00
Bowl, master berry, 10" d., green	80.00
Bowl, master berry, 10" d., marigold	78.00
Bowl, master berry, 10" d., purple	175.00
Butter dish, cov., green	300.00 to 375.00
Butter dish, cov., marigold	178.00
Butter dish, cov., purple (ILLUS.)	175.00 to 200.00
Creamer, green	90.00
Creamer, marigold	100.00
Creamer, purple	100.00
Pitcher, water, marigold	325.00
Pitcher, water, purple	350.00 to 400.00
Punch cup, aqua opalescent	1,800.00
Punch cup, blue	90.00
Punch cup, green	45.00
Punch cup, ice blue	100.00
Punch cup, ice green	90.00
Punch cup, marigold	21.00
Punch cup, purple	30.00
Punch cup, white	55.00
Punch cups, blue, set of 6, set	450.00
Punch set: bowl, base & 5 cups; green, 7 pcs.	1,200.00 to 1,600.00
Punch set: bowl, base & 6 cups; ice blue, 8 pcs.	7,000.00
Punch set: bowl, base & 6 cups; marigold, 8 pcs.	1,000.00
Punch set: bowl, base & 6 cups; purple, 8 pcs.	1,500.00
Punch set: bowl, base & 6 cups; white, 8 pcs.	4,000.00
Sauce dish, green	37.50
Sauce dish, marigold	30.00
Sauce dish, purple	45.00
Spooner, green	78.00
Spooner, marigold	88.00
Spooner, purple	100.00 to 125.00
Table set: cov. sugar bowl, creamer, spooner & cov. butter dish; marigold, 4 pcs.	900.00
Table set, purple, 4 pcs.	1,000.00

Tumbler, green 85.00
Tumbler, marigold................. 50.00
Tumbler, purple.................. 55.00
Water set: pitcher & 4 tumblers;
   marigold, 5 pcs................. 650.00
Water set: pitcher & 6 tumblers;
   green, 7 pcs..................1,200.00
Water set: pitcher & 6 tumblers;
   purple, 7 pcs...........750.00 to 800.00

ADVERTISING & SOUVENIR ITEMS

Bernheimer Brothers Bowl

Basket, "Feldman Bros. Furniture,
  Salisbury, Md.," open edge,
  marigold 75.00
Basket, "John H. Brand Furniture
  Co., Wilmington, Del.," mari-
  gold 60.00
Bell, souvenir, BPOE Elks, "Atlantic
  City, 1911," blue...............1,400.00
Bell, souvenir, BPOE Elks, "Parkers-
  burg, 1914," blue 1,250.00
Bowl, "Isaac Benesch," 6¼" d., pur-
  ple (Millersburg) ....250.00 to 300.00
Bowl, "Bernheimer Brothers," blue
  (ILLUS.) 1,000.00
Bowl, "Dreibus Parfait Sweet," ruf-
  fled, smoky lavender 400.00
Bowl, "Horlacher," Peacock Tail
  patt., green 100.00
Bowl, "Horlacher," Thistle patt.,
  green 100.00
Bowl, "Ogden Furniture Co.,"
  purple 225.00
Bowl, "Sterling Furniture," purple ... 600.00
Bowl, souvenir, BPOE Elks, "Atlantic
  City, 1911," blue, one-eyed Elk ... 488.00
Bowl, souvenir, BPOE Elks, "Detroit,
  1910," blue, one-eyed Elk 550.00
Bowl, souvenir, BPOE Elks, "Detroit,
  1910," green, one-eyed Elk 1,000.00
Bowl, souvenir, BPOE Elks, "Detroit,
  1910," ruffled, green 250.00
Bowl, souvenir, BPOE Elks, "Detroit,
  1910," purple, one-eyed Elk 385.00
Bowl, souvenir, BPOE Elks, "Detroit,

1910," purple, two-eyed Elk
  (Millersburg).................... 932.00
Bowl, souvenir, "Brooklyn Bridge,"
  marigold 325.00
Bowl, souvenir, Brooklyn Bridge, un-
  lettered, marigold.............. 550.00
Bowl, souvenir, "Millersburg Court-
  house," purple 550.00
Bowl, souvenir, Millersburg Court-
  house, unlettered, purple 965.00
Card tray, "Fern Brand Chocolates,"
  turned-up sides, 6¼" d., purple .. 175.00
Card tray, "Isaac Benesch," Holly
  Whirl patt., marigold 70.00
Dish, "Compliments of Pacific Coast
  Mail Order House, Los Angeles,
  California".................... 700.00
Hat, "Arthur O'Dell," green 75.00
Hat, "General Furniture Co." 1910,
  Peacock Tail patt., green 75.00
Hat, "Horlacher," Peacock Tail patt.,
  green 70.00
Hat, "John Brand Furniture,"
  green 42.00
Hat, "John Brand Furniture," open
  edge, marigold 45.00
Hat, "Miller's Furniture - Harris-
  burg," basketweave, marigold.... 75.00
Paperweight, souvenir, BPOE Elks,
  green 625.00
Paperweight, souvenir, BPOE Elks,
  purple (Millersburg) .....600.00 to 700.00
Plate, "Ballard, California," purple
  (Northwood) 900.00
Plate, "Bird of Paradise," purple 220.00
Plate, "Brazier Candies," w/hand-
  grip, 6" d., purple 250.00
Plate, "Davidson Chocolate Society,"
  6¼" d., purple................ 230.00
Plate, "Eagle Furniture Co.,"
  purple 750.00
Plate, "Fern Brand Chocolates,"
  6" d., purple.................. 700.00
Plate, "Gervitz Bros., Furniture &
  Clothing," w/handgrip, 6" d.,
  purple 350.00
Plate, "Greengard Furniture Co.,"
  purple 625.00
Plate, "E.A. Hudson Furniture Co.,"
  7" d., purple (Northwood)........ 225.00
Plate, "Jockey Club," w/handgrip,
  6" d., purple.................. 425.00
Plate, "Old Rose Distillery," Grape
  & Cable patt., stippled, 9" d.,
  green 370.00
Plate, "Roods Chocolate, Pueblo,"
  purple 750.00
Plate, "Season's Greetings - Eat
  Paradise Soda Candies," 6" d.,
  purple 178.00
Plate, "Spector's Department Store,"
  Heart & Vine patt., 9" d., mari-
  gold 450.00

Plate, "Utah Liquor Co.," w/hand-
grip, 6" d., purple 950.00
Plate, "We Use Brocker's," 7" d.,
purple 495.00
Plate, souvenir, BPOE Elks, "Atlantic
City, 1911," blue . . . . 800.00 to 900.00
Plate, souvenir, BPOE Elks, "Par-
kersburg, 1914," 7½" d., blue 865.00
Vase, "Howard Furniture," Four Pil-
lars patt., green 80.00

APPLE BLOSSOMS

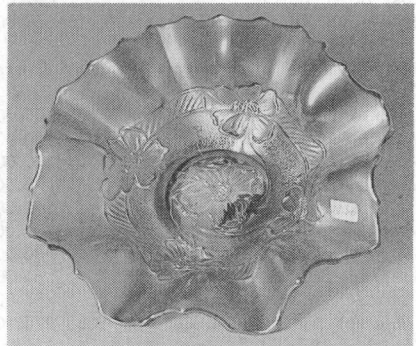

Apple Blossoms Bowl

Bowl, 5½" d., purple 42.50
Bowl, 6" d., marigold 20.00
Bowl, 6" d., deep, purple 30.00
Bowl, 7" d., collared base, marigold
(ILLUS.) 32.00
Bowl, 7" d., collared base, purple . .   70.00
Bowl, 7" d., ribbon candy rim,
marigold 25.00
Bowl, 7" d., ribbon candy rim,
white 135.00
Rose bowl, marigold 35.00
Tumbler, enameled, blue 120.00

AUSTRALIAN

Australian Swan Bowl

Berry set: master bowl & 6 sauce
dishes; Magpie, marigold,
7 pcs. 325.00
Bowl, 5½" d., Swan, marigold 45.00

Bowl, 9" to 10" d., Emu, aqua 550.00
Bowl, 9" to 10" d., Emu, marigold . . 145.00
Bowl, 9" to 10" d., Kangaroo,
marigold 100.00
Bowl, 9" to 10" d., Kangaroo,
purple 170.00
Bowl, 9" to 10" d., Kingfisher,
purple 150.00
Bowl, 9" to 10" d., Kiwi, ruffled,
marigold 250.00
Bowl, 9" to 10" d., Kiwi, purple 250.00
Bowl, 9" to 10" d., Kookaburra,
marigold 98.00
Bowl, 9" to 10" d., Magpie, mari-
gold 115.00
Bowl, 9" to 10" d., Magpie, purple . . 110.00
Bowl, 9" to 10" d., Swan, purple
(ILLUS.) 165.00
Bowl, 9" to 10" d., Thunderbird,
marigold 200.00
Bowl, 9" to 10" d., Thunderbird,
purple 165.00
Bowl, 11" d., ice cream shape,
Kookaburra, marigold 135.00
Bowl, 11" d., ice cream shape,
Kookaburra variant, marigold 135.00
Bowl, 11" d., ice cream shape,
Kookaburra variant, purple 300.00
Bowl, pin-up, purple 65.00
Cake plate, Butterfly & Bells,
marigold 78.00
Compote, Butterflies & Waratah,
aqua 135.00
Compote, Butterflies & Waratah,
marigold 125.00
Compote, Butterflies & Waratah,
purple 210.00
Compote, Butterfly & Bush, mari-
gold 86.00
Sauce dish, Kangaroo, marigold 70.00
Sauce dish, Kangaroo, purple 64.00
Sauce dish, Kingfisher, marigold 60.00
Sauce dish, Kookaburra, marigold . .   65.00
Sauce dish, Kookaburra, purple 45.00
Sauce dish, Swan, marigold 65.00
Sauce dish, Thunderbird, marigold . .   65.00
Sauce dish, Thunderbird, purple 85.00

BASKET (FENTON'S OPEN EDGE)
Amber 250.00
Amberina, w/two rows, two sides
turned up 125.00
Aqua 74.00
Aqua, w/two rows, jack-in-the-
pulpit shape 125.00
Aqua, w/two rows, two sides
turned up 110.00
Aqua opalescent 145.00
Black amethyst 365.00
Blue 56.00
Celeste blue 92.00
Green 53.00
Green, hat shape 85.00

Green, low sides 175.00
Ice blue 195.00
Ice blue, w/two rows, open edge,
  six ruffled . . . . .225.00 to 295.00
Ice blue, w/three rows 525.00
Ice green 225.00
Ice green, w/three rows 394.00
Marigold 40.00
Purple 110.00
Red 340.00
Red, hat shape 400.00
Red, jack-in-the-pulpit
  shape . . . . .325.00 to 425.00
Red, w/two rows, small . . .300.00 to 325.00
Reverse Amberina 650.00
Vaseline 115.00
Vaseline, plain interior 275.00
Vaseline, w/two rows, large 85.00
White, w/two rows 150.00

BASKET or BUSHEL BASKET (Northwood)

Northwood Basket

Aqua, 4½" d., 4¾" h. 425.00
Aqua opalescent, 4½" d., 4¾" h. . . 405.00
Blue (ILLUS.) 118.00
Celeste blue 1,900.00
Clambroth 400.00
Cobalt blue 115.00
Electric blue 165.00
Green . . . . .500.00 to 525.00
Honey amber . . . . .400.00 to 500.00
Horehound, variant 1,250.00
Ice blue . . . . .600.00 to 800.00
Ice green 335.00
Lavender 190.00
Lime green 350.00
Lime green opalescent 1,500.00
Marigold 115.00
Olive green 550.00
Purple 135.00
Sapphire blue 1,750.00
Smoky 750.00
Vaseline 2,600.00
White 157.00

BEADED CABLE (Northwood)

Bowl, 7" d., three-footed, green 50.00
Bowl, 7" d., three-footed, ruffled,
  marigold 35.00

Candy dish, green 50.00
Candy dish, marigold 30.00
Candy dish, purple 55.00
Rose bowl, aqua 350.00
Rose bowl, aqua opalescent 307.00
Rose bowl, blue 137.00
Rose bowl, electric blue 300.00
Rose bowl, green 108.00
Rose bowl, ice blue . . . . .850.00 to 1,000.00
Rose bowl, ice green . . . .950.00 to 1,300.00
Rose bowl, lime green opalescent . .1,200.00
Rose bowl, marigold 70.00
Rose bowl, purple 92.00
Rose bowl, white . . . . .550.00 to 660.00

BEADED SHELL (Dugan or Diamond Glass Co.)

Creamer, marigold 65.00
Mug, blue 150.00
Mug, marigold 120.00
Mug, purple 70.00
Mug, purple, souvenir 150.00
Mug, white 1,000.00
Sauce dish, marigold 30.00
Spooner, footed, marigold 65.00
Sugar bowl, cov., marigold 55.00
Table set, marigold, 4 pcs. 275.00
Tumbler, blue 118.00
Tumbler, lavender 80.00
Tumbler, marigold 55.00
Tumbler, purple 59.00

BEADS & BELLS

Beads & Bells Bowl

Bowl, 7" d., peach opalescent
  (ILLUS.) 75.00
Bowl, 7" d., purple 53.00

BIG FISH BOWL (Millersburg)

Green 595.00
Green, square 1,000.00
Marigold 495.00
Marigold, ice cream shape 550.00
Marigold, square 850.00
Purple, ice cream shape 660.00
Purple, ruffled 704.00
Purple, square 700.00

BLACKBERRY (Fenton)

Basket, aqua	150.00
Basket, blue	38.00
Basket, green	95.00
Basket, marigold	65.00
Basket, purple	72.00
Basket, red	250.00
Basket, smoky w/marigold over-lay	75.00
Bowl, 5" d., purple	30.00
Bowl, 7" d., purple	75.00
Bowl, 8" to 9" d., ruffled, green	90.00
Bowl, 8" to 9" d., ruffled, marigold	50.00
Bowl, 8" to 9" d., ruffled, purple	58.00
Bowl, 10" d., ruffled, blue	650.00
Bowl, nut, open edge, Basketweave exterior, purple	60.00
Plate, openwork rim, marigold	450.00
Vase, whimsey, open edge, blue opalescent	900.00
Vase, whimsey, open edge, marigold	650.00

BLACKBERRY BLOCK (Fenton)

Blackberry Block Pitcher

Pitcher, water, marigold	465.00
Pitcher, water, purple (ILLUS.)	1,000.00
Tumbler, blue	60.00
Tumbler, green	195.00
Tumbler, marigold	35.00
Tumbler, pastel marigold	85.00
Tumbler, purple	72.00
Tumbler, white	500.00
Water set: pitcher & 6 tumblers; marigold, 7 pcs.	775.00

BLACKBERRY SPRAY

Bonbon, marigold	30.00
Bowl, 7" d., marigold	25.00
Hat shape, amber	165.00
Hat shape, Amberina	300.00
Hat shape, aqua	75.00
Hat shape, jack-in-the-pulpit shape, crimped rim, aqua	85.00

Hat shape, aqua opalescent	350.00
Hat shape, jack-in-the-pulpit, aqua opalescent	300.00
Hat shape, blue	42.50
Hat shape, blue opalescent	585.00
Hat shape, jack-in-the-pulpit, crimped rim, clambroth	27.00
Hat shape, green	75.00
Hat shape, ice green opalescent	350.00
Hat shape, jack-in-the-pulpit, lime green w/marigold overlay	35.00
Hat shape, lime green opalescent	325.00
Hat shape, marigold	35.00
Hat shape, purple	50.00
Hat shape, red	350.00 to 375.00
Hat shape, red slag	475.00
Hat shape, Reverse Amberina	300.00
Hat shape, vaseline	72.00
Hat shape, vaseline w/marigold overlay	54.00

BLACKBERRY WREATH (Millersburg)

Bowl, 5" d., green	48.00
Bowl, 5" d., marigold	25.00
Bowl, 5" d., ruffled, marigold	35.00
Bowl, 5" d., purple	55.00
Bowl, 7" d., green	65.00
Bowl, 7" d., marigold	35.00
Bowl, 7" d., purple	70.00
Bowl, 8" to 9" d., green	85.00
Bowl, 8" to 9" d., marigold	45.00
Bowl, 8" to 9" d., purple	75.00
Bowl, 10" d., blue	750.00
Bowl, 10" d., green	82.00
Bowl, 10" d., marigold	90.00
Bowl, 10" d., purple	155.00
Bowl, ice cream, large, marigold	70.00
Bowl, ice cream, large, purple	225.00

BUSHEL BASKET - See Basket (Northwood) Pattern

BUTTERFLIES (Fenton)

Butterflies Bonbon

Bonbon, blue	50.00
Bonbon, green	49.00
Bonbon, marigold	40.00
Bonbon, purple (ILLUS.)	50.00

BUTTERFLY (Northwood)

Bonbon, threaded exterior, blue	235.00
Bonbon, handled, threaded exterior, electric blue	450.00
Bonbon, threaded exterior, ice blue	1,600.00
Bonbon, green	85.00
Bonbon, marigold	45.00
Bonbon, purple	78.00
Bonbon, threaded exterior, purple ..	239.00
Bonbon, smoky	350.00

BUTTERFLY & BERRY (Fenton)

Berry set: master bowl & 6 sauce dishes; marigold, 7 pcs.	288.00
Bowl, 7" d., three-footed, marigold	65.00
Bowl, 8" to 9" d., footed, blue	68.00
Bowl, 8" to 9" d., footed, marigold	65.00
Bowl, 8" to 9" d., footed, purple	175.00
Bowl, master berry or fruit, four-footed, blue	90.00
Bowl, master berry or fruit, four-footed, green	150.00
Bowl, master berry or fruit, four-footed, marigold	82.00
Bowl, master berry or fruit, four-footed, purple	120.00
Bowl, master berry or fruit, four-footed, white ....250.00 to	275.00
Butter dish, cov., blue	250.00
Butter dish, cov., green	280.00
Butter dish, cov., marigold	114.00
Centerpiece bowl, purple	500.00
Creamer, blue	85.00
Creamer, marigold	65.00
Creamer, purple	145.00
Hatpin holder, blue	1,900.00
Hatpin holder, marigold	1,700.00
Nut bowl, purple	437.00
Pitcher, water, blue	425.00
Pitcher, water, marigold	195.00
Sauce dish, blue	42.00
Sauce dish, green	45.00
Sauce dish, marigold	25.00
Sauce dish, purple	95.00
Spooner, blue	120.00
Spooner, marigold..............	62.00
Sugar bowl, cov., blue	120.00
Sugar bowl, cov., marigold........	82.00
Table set, marigold, 4 pcs.	325.00
Tumbler, blue..................	50.00
Tumbler, green	100.00
Tumbler, marigold	30.50
Tumbler, purple................	325.00
Vase, 6" h., marigold	35.00
Vase, 7" h., blue	65.00
Vase, 7" h., green	145.00
Vase, 8" h., blue	65.00
Vase, 8" h., marigold	35.00
Vase, 9" h., blue	76.00
Vase, 9" h., marigold...........	45.00
Vase, 9" h., purple	50.00
Vase, 10" h., blue..............	50.00
Vase, amber...................	130.00
Vase, green	170.00
Water set: pitcher & 6 tumblers; marigold, 7 pcs.................	315.00

BUTTERFLY & FERN (Fenton)

Pitcher, water, blue	425.00
Pitcher, water, green	425.00
Pitcher, water, marigold	275.00
Tumbler, blue..................	45.00
Tumbler, green	59.00
Tumbler, marigold	32.00
Tumbler, pastel marigold	35.00
Tumbler, purple................	46.00
Water set: pitcher & 6 tumblers; green, 7 pcs.	850.00
Water set: pitcher & 6 tumblers; marigold, 7 pcs.................	515.00

BUTTERFLY & TULIP

Bowl, 9" w., 5½" h., footed, marigold ....350.00 to	375.00
Bowl, 9" w., footed, purple	700.00
Bowl, 10½" square flat shape, footed, marigold..................	500.00
Bowl, 10½" square flat shape, footed, purple..................	1,875.00
Bowl, 12" d., upturned sides, footed, marigold....................	332.00

CARNIVAL HOLLY - See Holly Pattern

CAROLINA DOGWOOD

Bowl, 8½" d., blue opalescent ....350.00 to	375.00
Bowl, 8½" d., marigold	65.00
Bowl, 8½" d., milk white w/marigold overlay ....250.00 to	275.00
Bowl, 8½" d., peach opalescent	155.00
Bride's bowl, peach opalescent	325.00
Plate, 8½" d., peach opalescent	475.00

CATHEDRAL

Celery vase, chalice shape, footed, marigold	145.00

CATTAILS & WATER LILY - See Water Lily & Cattails Pattern

CHERRY (Dugan)

Bowl, 6" d., clambroth opalescent ..	30.00
Bowl, 6" d., Jeweled Heart exterior, purple	45.00
Bowl, 6" d., purple	60.00
Bowl, 7" d., three-footed, crimped rim, peach opalescent	95.00
Bowl, 8" d., ruffled, purple........	125.00
Bowl, 8" to 9" d., three-footed, marigold	113.00
Bowl, 8" to 9" d., three-footed, peach opalescent...............	300.00

Bowl, 8" to 9" d., three-footed,
purple 100.00
Bowl, 10" d., Jeweled Heart exteri-
or, purple 260.00
Bowl, large, peach opalescent 240.00
Bowl, large, Jeweled Heart exterior,
purple 275.00
Dish, ruffled, marigold, 6" d. 80.00
Dish, ruffled, purple, 6" d. 38.00
Plate, 6" d., ruffled, purple 150.00
Plate, 6½" d., ruffled, Jeweled
Heart exterior, purple 95.00
Sauce dish, peach opalescent 65.00
Sauce dish, Jeweled Heart exterior,
ruffled, peach opalescent 75.00
Sauce dish, purple 50.00

CHERRY or HANGING CHERRIES (Millersburg)

Banana compote (whimsey), blue ... 625.00
Banana compote (whimsey),
green 1,500.00
Banana compote (whimsey), mari-
gold 735.00
Bowl, 4" d., green 75.00
Bowl, 5" d., blue ....825.00 to 875.00
Bowl, 5" d., green 62.00
Bowl, 5" d., ruffled, marigold 50.00
Bowl, 5" d., piecrust rim, purple 49.00
Bowl, 6" d., ruffled, green 95.00
Bowl, 7" d., marigold 75.00
Bowl, 7" d., purple 90.00
Bowl, 8" to 9" d., ruffled, green 264.00
Bowl, 8" to 9" d., ice cream shape,
green 175.00
Bowl, 8" to 9" d., dome-footed,
marigold 70.00
Bowl, 8" to 9" d., purple 60.00
Bowl, 9" d., Hobnail exterior,
marigold 795.00
Bowl, 10" d., ice cream shape,
green 154.00
Bowl, 10" d., ice cream shape,
marigold 125.00
Bowl, 10" d., ice cream shape,
purple 169.00
Bowl, 10" d., ice cream shape, teal
blue 850.00
Bowl, 10" d., three-in-one rim,
marigold 245.00
Bowl, 10" d., purple 310.00
Bowl, ruffled, Hobnail exterior, mar-
igold, large 468.00
Butter dish, cov., green 227.00
Butter dish, cov., marigold 190.00
Compote, green 1,400.00
Creamer, green 77.00
Creamer, marigold 55.00
Creamer, purple 75.00
Pitcher, milk, marigold 600.00
Pitcher, milk, purple.............. 418.00
Pitcher, water, marigold 200.00

Pitcher, water, purple 600.00
Plate, 7" d., purple............... 225.00
Spooner, green 68.00
Spooner, marigold................. 60.00
Sugar bowl, cov., marigold 85.00
Tumbler, green 290.00
Tumbler, marigold................. 200.00

CHRYSANTHEMUM or WINDMILL & MUMS

Bowl, 8" to 9" d., three-footed,
green 78.00
Bowl, 8" to 9" d., three-footed,
marigold 46.00
Bowl, 9" d., ruffled, blue 128.00
Bowl, 9" d., ruffled, green 275.00
Bowl, 9" d., marigold 52.00
Bowl, 9" d., ruffled, marigold 130.00
Bowl, 9" d., ruffled, purple........ 150.00
Bowl, 9" d., red w/amber center ...4,100.00
Bowl, 10" d., three-footed, blue 160.00
Bowl, 10" d., three-footed, mari-
gold 89.00
Bowl, 10" d., three-footed, purple .. 75.00
Bowl, 10" d., collared base, red....5,000.00
Bowl, 11" d., three-footed, blue ... 150.00
Bowl, 11" d., three-footed, green .. 250.00
Bowl, 11" d., three-footed, mari-
gold 52.00
Bowl, 12" d., three-footed, ruffled,
black amethyst................... 575.00
Bowl, 12" d., three-footed, vase-
line 275.00
Bowl, collared base, green 238.00
Bowl, collared base, marigold 52.50
Bowl, collared base,
purple ....300.00 to 350.00
Bowl, orange, footed, vaseline 350.00

COIN SPOT (Dugan)

Compote, 7" d., marigold 35.00
Compote, 7" d., peach opalescent .. 50.00
Compote, 7" d., fluted, peach opal-
escent 100.00
Compote, 7" d., fluted, purple...... 65.00
Vase, 10" h., purple 25.00
Water set: lemonade pitcher & 4
tumblers; marigold, 5 pcs. 365.00

CONCORD (Fenton)

Bowl, 8½" d., piecrust rim,
marigold 75.00
Bowl, blue....................... 118.00
Bowl, ribbon candy rim, blue 225.00
Bowl, green 225.00
Bowl, marigold................... 110.00
Bowl, purple 175.00
Bowl, three-in-one edge, green..... 120.00
Bowl, three-in-one edge, marigold .. 65.00
Bowl, three-in-one edge, purple 250.00
Plate, green 750.00
Plate, marigold..................1,250.00

CORN BOTTLE

Corn Bottle

Green............................ 232.00
Ice green.................250.00 to 275.00
Marigold ....250.00 to 300.00
Smoky (ILLUS.) 210.00

CORN VASE (Northwood)

Aqua opalescent 1,500.00
Aqua w/light marigold overlay 1,975.00
Green............................ 800.00
Ice blue 1,400.00
Ice green.................375.00 to 400.00
Marigold 900.00
Pastel marigold 475.00
Purple 625.00
White 274.00

COSMOS & CANE (U.S. Glass Co.)

Bowl, 6" d., ice cream shape, honey
    amber 50.00
Bowl, 7" d., Headdress interior,
    purple 175.00
Bowl, 8" to 9" sq., white.......... 155.00
Bowl, 10" d., marigold............ 115.00
Bowl, 10" d., white............... 120.00
Butter dish, cov., amber.......... 235.00
Butter dish, cov., marigold 215.00
Butter dish, cov., purple 100.00
Butter dish, cov., white 275.00
Compote, amber 500.00
Compote, marigold 160.00
Compote, purple 350.00
Compote, white 850.00
Creamer, honey amber 180.00
Creamer, marigold 110.00
Cuspidor, honey amber 7,000.00
Pitcher, honey amber 1,500.00
Pitcher, white 1,000.00
Rose bowl, pedestal footed, honey
    amber 1,300.00
Rose bowl, Headdress interior,
    marigold 400.00
Sauce dish, green 40.00
Sauce dish, honey amber 55.00
Sauce dish, honey amber, squat 225.00

Sauce dish, marigold 35.00
Sauce dish, white 50.00
Sugar bowl, cov., honey amber..... 85.00
Table set, amber, 4 pcs. 595.00
Tumbler, amber 110.00
Tumbler, honey amber............ 75.00
Tumbler, marigold................. 70.00
Tumbler, marigold, w/advertising... 175.00
Tumbler, white ....150.00 to 200.00

CRUCIFIX

Candlesticks, marigold, pr. 1,000.00

CUT COSMOS

Tumbler, marigold................. 258.00

DAHLIA (Dugan or Diamond Glass Co.)

Dahlia Tumbler

Berry set: master bowl & 4 sauce
    dishes; marigold, 5 pcs. 295.00
Berry set: master bowl & 4 sauce
    dishes; white, 5 pcs. 600.00
Bowl, master berry, 10" d., footed,
    white 190.00
Butter dish, cov., white 300.00
Creamer, marigold 60.00
Creamer, purple 125.00
Creamer, white 180.00
Pitcher, water, marigold 650.00
Pitcher, water, purple .....675.00 to 700.00
Pitcher, water, white 718.00
Sauce dish, marigold 40.00
Sauce dish, purple 50.00
Sauce dish, white 60.00
Sugar bowl, open, purple 85.00
Table set: cov. sugar bowl, creamer,
    spooner & cov. butter dish; mari-
    gold, 4 pcs. 425.00
Table set, white, 4 pcs. 1,150.00
Tumbler, amber.................. 95.00
Tumbler, marigold (ILLUS.) 115.00
Tumbler, pastel marigold 135.00
Tumbler, purple.................. 195.00
Tumbler, white ....125.00 to 150.00
Tumbler, white w/blue flower 275.00
Tumbler, white w/gold flower 195.00
Tumbler, white w/red flower 275.00
Tumbler, white w/silver band 300.00
Water set: pitcher & 6 tumblers;
    white w/blue flowers, 7 pcs. 2,000.00

DAISIES & DRAPE VASE (Northwood)

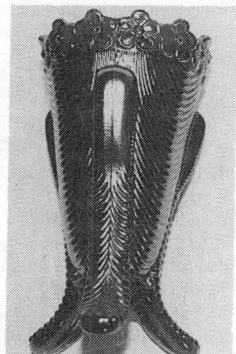

Daisies & Drape Vase

Aqua opalescent	600.00
Cobalt blue (ILLUS.)	1,100.00
Green	4,500.00
Marigold	800.00
Purple	800.00
White	155.00

DAISY SQUARES

Bowl, 6" d., clear w/marigold	425.00
Compote, amber	265.00
Compote, green	575.00 to 675.00
Compote, marigold	400.00 to 425.00
Goblet, green	275.00
Goblet, purple	800.00
Rose bowl, stemmed, green	550.00 to 650.00
Rose bowl, jack-in-the-pulpit type, light green w/marigold overlay	725.00
Rose bowl, marigold	550.00

DANDELION (Northwood)

Mug, aqua opalescent	500.00 to 550.00
Mug, blue	440.00 to 480.00
Mug, green	500.00 to 600.00
Mug, ice blue opalescent	895.00
Mug, marigold	400.00 to 450.00
Mug, pastel marigold	300.00 to 325.00
Mug, purple	275.00
Mug, Knights Templar, ice blue	1,000.00
Mug, Knights Templar, ice green	1,100.00
Mug, Knights Templar, marigold	500.00
Mug, Knights Templar, purple	295.00
Pitcher, water, tankard, green	985.00
Pitcher, water, tankard, marigold	400.00 to 450.00
Pitcher, water, tankard, purple	650.00 to 750.00
Tumbler, blue	50.00
Tumbler, green	100.00
Tumbler, ice blue	200.00
Tumbler, ice green	900.00
Tumbler, lavender	225.00
Tumbler, marigold	45.00
Tumbler, purple	60.00
Tumbler, smoky	250.00
Tumbler, white	180.00

Water set: pitcher & 1 tumbler; white, 2 pcs.	2,500.00
Water set: pitcher & 2 tumblers; pastel marigold, 3 pcs.	875.00
Water set: pitcher & 5 tumblers; green, 6 pcs.	1,400.00
Water set: pitcher & 6 tumblers; purple, 7 pcs.	950.00 to 1,000.00

DANDELION, PANELED (Fenton)

Paneled Dandelion Pitcher

Pitcher, water, blue (ILLUS.)	450.00
Pitcher, water, green	475.00
Pitcher, water, marigold	350.00
Pitcher, water, purple	400.00 to 500.00
Tumbler, blue	65.00
Tumbler, green	40.00
Tumbler, marigold	40.00
Tumbler, purple	50.00
Water set: pitcher & 1 tumbler; blue, 2 pcs.	130.00
Water set: pitcher & 6 tumblers; blue, 7 pcs.	875.00

DIAMOND & RIB VASE (Fenton)

Vase, 6" h., green	45.00
Vase, 7" h., purple	34.00
Vase, 9" h., white	75.00
Vase, 10" h., blue	40.00
Vase, 10" h., green	40.00
Vase, 10" h., marigold	35.00
Vase, 10" h., purple	35.00
Vase, 10" h., white	85.00
Vase, 11" h., aqua	35.00
Vase, 11" h., green	38.00
Vase, 11" h., ice green	60.00
Vase, 11" h., marigold	70.00
Vases, 11" h., purple, pr.	80.00
Vase, 12" h., purple	32.50
Vase, 13" h., blue	35.00
Vase, 15" h., marigold	55.00
Vase, 16" h., purple	50.00 to 75.00
Vase, 19" h., purple	95.00
Vase, 19" h., funeral, purple	1,150.00

DIAMOND LACE (Imperial)

Bowl, 8" to 9" d., clambroth	65.00
Bowl, 8" to 9" d., marigold	48.00
Bowl, 8" to 9" d., purple	65.00

Diamond Lace Pitcher

Pitcher, water, purple
(ILLUS.) ....175.00 to 200.00
Sauce dish, marigold, 5" d. 25.00
Sauce dish, purple, 5" d........... 35.00
Tumbler, marigold................. 425.00
Tumbler, purple...........45.00 to 50.00
Water set: pitcher & 6 tumblers;
purple, 7 pcs...........550.00 to 600.00

DIAMOND RING (Imperial)

Bowl, 8" to 9" d., marigold........ 60.00
Bowl, 8" to 9" d., purple........... 75.00
Bowl, 8" to 9" d., smoky.......... 45.00
Rose bowl, marigold.............. 300.00
Sauce dish, marigold.............. 22.50
Sauce dish, smoky 28.00

DIAMONDS (Millersburg)

Pitcher, water, aqua.............. 225.00
Pitcher, water, green............. 225.00
Pitcher, water, marigold 150.00
Pitcher, water, purple 160.00
Punch bowl & base, green, 2 pcs. ..2,000.00
Tumbler, aqua 85.00
Tumbler, green 55.00
Tumbler, lavender................ 70.00
Tumbler, marigold................ 40.00
Tumbler, purple.................. 52.00
Water set: pitcher & 1 tumbler; mar-
igold, 2 pcs. 250.00
Water set: pitcher & 4 tumblers;
purple, 5 pcs.................. 475.00
Water set: pitcher & 6 tumblers;
green, 7 pcs. 600.00

DOGWOOD SPRAYS

Bowl, 7" d., collared base, peach
opalescent..................... 60.00
Bowl, 8" to 9" d., dome-footed,
marigold 36.00
Bowl, 8" to 9" d., dome-footed,
peach opalescent.............. 85.00
Bowl, 8" to 9" d., dome-footed,
purple 65.00

**DRAGON & BERRY - See Dragon & Straw-
berry Bowl Pattern**

DRAGON & LOTUS (Fenton)

Bowl, 7" to 9" d., three-footed,
blue 72.00
Bowl, 7" to 9" d., three-footed,
green 55.00
Bowl, 7" to 9" d., three-footed,
lavender 125.00
Bowl, 7" to 9" d., three-footed, lime
green opalescent............... 300.00
Bowl, 7" to 9" d., three-footed,
marigold 45.00
Bowl, 7" to 9" d., three-footed,
peach opalescent............... 500.00
Bowl, 7" to 9" d., three-footed,
purple 75.00
Bowl, 8" to 9" d., collared base,
amber ....200.00 to 225.00
Bowl, 8" to 9" d., collared base,
blue 116.00
Bowl, 8" to 9" d., collared base,
green 108.00
Bowl, 8" to 9" d., collared base,
lime green 325.00
Bowl, 8" to 9" d., collared base,
lime green opalescent ...550.00 to 650.00
Bowl, 8" to 9" d., collared base,
marigold 50.00
Bowl, 8" to 9" d., collared base,
moonstone 1,100.00
Bowl, 8" to 9" d., collared base,
peach opalescent............... 550.00
Bowl, 8" to 9" d., collared base,
purple 100.00
Bowl, 8" to 9" d., red 1,750.00
Bowl, 9" d., ice cream shape, col-
lared base, amber ......150.00 to 200.00
Bowl, 9" d., ice cream shape, col-
lared base, aqua opalescent.....3,400.00
Bowl, 9" d., ice cream shape, col-
lared base, blue 78.00
Bowl, 9" d., ice cream shape, col-
lared base, marigold 55.00
Bowl, 9" d., ice cream shape, col-
lared base, moonstone 1,250.00
Bowl, 9" d., ice cream shape, col-
lared base, red................1,400.00
Bowl, 9" d., ice cream shape, col-
lared base, Reverse Amberina ... 765.00
Bowl, 9" d., marigold............ 85.00
Bowl, ruffled, lavender 195.00
Bowl, ruffled, marigold opalescent.. 675.00
Plate, 9" d., marigold 2,600.00
Plate, collared base,
blue ....1,500.00 to 2,000.00
Plate, collared base, ruffled, mari-
gold.........................2,200.00
Plate, edge turned up, blue 250.00
Plate, spatula-footed, marigold 638.00

DRAGON & STRAWBERRY BOWL or DRAG-
ON & BERRY (Fenton)

Bowl, 9" d., blue................. 550.00
Bowl, 9" d., green 682.00

Bowl, 9" d., marigold 375.00
Bowl, 9" d., purple 625.00

DRAPERY (Northwood)

Candy dish, tricornered, ice
    blue . . . . 150.00 to 175.00
Candy dish, tricornered, ice
    green . . . . 150.00 to 200.00
Candy dish, tricornered, marigold . . 62.50
Candy dish, tricornered, purple 400.00
Candy dish, tricornered, white 130.00
Rose bowl, aqua opalescent 325.00
Rose bowl, blue 325.00
Rose bowl, electric blue 600.00
Rose bowl, ice blue . . . . . . 800.00 to 1,000.00
Rose bowl, lavender 110.00
Rose bowl, marigold . . . . . 325.00 to 425.00
Rose bowl, pastel marigold 385.00
Rose bowl, purple . . . . 200.00 to 250.00
Rose bowl, white 435.00
Vase, 4" h., ice blue 170.00
Vase, 7" h., blue 67.50
Vase, 7" h., ice green 80.00
Vase, 7" h., marigold 50.00
Vase, 8" h., blue 50.00
Vase, 8" h., ice blue 60.00
Vase, 8" h., ice green 150.00
Vase, 8" h., marigold 42.00
Vase, 8" h., white 100.00
Vase, 9" h., blue 95.00
Vase, 9" h., purple 150.00
Vase, 10" h., ice blue . . . . . 200.00 to 250.00
Vase, 10" h., ice green 185.00
Vase, 10" h., marigold . . . . . 75.00 to 100.00

EMBROIDERED MUMS (Northwood)

Embroidered Mums Bowl

Bonbon, stemmed, white 1,150.00
Bowl, 8" to 9" d., amber 1,000.00
Bowl, 8" to 9" d., ruffled, aqua
    opalescent 3,400.00
Bowl, 8" to 9" d., blue . . . . . 425.00 to 450.00
Bowl, 8" to 9" d., ruffled, blue 1,350.00
Bowl, 8" to 9" d., electric blue 500.00
Bowl, 8" to 9" d., ice blue 900.00
Bowl, 8" to 9" d., ice
    green . . . . 900.00 to 1,000.00

Bowl, 8" to 9" d., marigold 525.00
Bowl, 8" to 9" d., ruffled, mari-
    gold 230.00
Bowl, 8" to 9" d., pastel marigold . . 500.00
Bowl, 8" to 9" d., purple
    (ILLUS.) . . . . 400.00 to 450.00
Bowl, aqua 1,400.00
Bowl, lavender 1,600.00
Bowl, lime green opalescent 1,800.00
Bowl, piecrust rim, sapphire blue . . 2,700.00
Plate, ice green . . . . 2,000.00 to 2,500.00

FAN (Dugan)

Sauceboat, peach opalescent 110.00
Sauceboat, purple 60.00

FANCIFUL (Dugan)

Fanciful Bowl

Bowl, 8" to 9" d., blue 85.00
Bowl, 8" to 9" d., piecrust rim,
    marigold . . . . 100.00 to 125.00
Bowl, 8" to 9" d., peach opales-
    cent 150.00
Bowl, 8" to 9" d., ruffled, purple
    (ILLUS.) 135.00
Bowl, 8" to 9" d., ruffled, white 200.00
Bowl, 10" d., ruffled,
    white . . . . 150.00 to 175.00
Bowl, ice cream shape, marigold . . . 60.00
Bowl, ice cream shape, peach
    opalescent 95.00
Bowl, ice cream shape, purple 135.00
Bowl, ice cream shape, white 95.00
Plate, 9" d., blue . . . . 275.00 to 300.00
Plate, 9" d., marigold . . . . . 100.00 to 150.00
Plate, 9" d., peach opales-
    cent . . . . 275.00 to 325.00
Plate, 9" d., purple 275.00
Plate, 9" d., white 225.00
Plate, 9½" d., ruffled, white 190.00

FARMYARD (Dugan)

Bowl, purple 2,600.00
Bowl, fluted, purple 3,900.00
Bowl, ribbon candy rim, purple 3,500.00
Bowl, square, purple 2,900.00
Plate, 10" d., purple 6,000.00

FASHION (Imperial)

Fashion Punch Set

Bowl, 9" d., clambroth	30.00
Bowl, 9" d., marigold	25.00
Bowl, 9" d., ruffled, smoky	40.00
Creamer, marigold	25.00
Creamer, smoky	130.00
Creamer & sugar bowl, marigold, pr.	60.00
Creamer & sugar bowl, purple, pr.	325.00
Pitcher, water, marigold ...100.00 to	125.00
Pitcher, water, purple	950.00
Punch bowl & base, marigold, 12" d., 2 pcs.	104.00
Punch cup, marigold	15.00
Punch cup, red	325.00
Punch cups, marigold, set of 6	105.00
Punch set: bowl, base & 8 cups; marigold, 10 pcs. (ILLUS. of part)	325.00
Rose bowl, green	425.00
Rose bowl, marigold, 7" d.	98.00
Tumbler, marigold	22.00
Tumbler, purple	175.00
Tumbler, smoky	90.00
Water set: pitcher & 3 tumblers; smoky, 4 pcs.	700.00
Water set: pitcher & 6 tumblers; marigold, 7 pcs.	350.00

FEATHER & HEART

Feather & Heart Tumbler

Pitcher, water, green	450.00
Pitcher, water, marigold ...300.00 to	350.00
Tumbler, green	200.00
Tumbler, marigold	70.00
Tumbler, purple (ILLUS.)	92.50

FENTONIA

Berry set: master bowl & 4 sauce dishes; marigold, 5 pcs.	175.00
Bowl, master berry, blue	95.00
Bowl, master berry, marigold	50.00
Butter dish, cov., footed, marigold	137.50
Creamer, blue	110.00
Pitcher, water, blue	700.00
Pitcher, water, marigold	225.00
Spooner, marigold	60.00
Sugar bowl, cov., blue	115.00
Table set: creamer, cov. sugar bowl & spooner; blue, 3 pcs.	350.00
Tumbler, blue	60.00
Tumbler, marigold	44.00

FENTON'S FLOWERS ROSE BOWL - See Orange Tree Pattern

FILE (Imperial)

Pitcher, water, marigold	650.00
Spooner, marigold	70.00
Tumbler, marigold ....175.00 to	200.00
Vase, marigold	250.00

FINECUT & ROSES (Northwood)

Candy dish, three-footed, aqua opalescent ....400.00 to	450.00
Candy dish, three-footed, electric blue	67.50
Candy dish, three-footed, green	62.00
Candy dish, three-footed, ice blue	350.00
Candy dish, three-footed, ice green	175.00
Candy dish, three-footed, marigold	40.00
Candy dish, three-footed, purple	50.00
Candy dish, three-footed, white	125.00
Rose bowl, amber	550.00
Rose bowl, aqua opalescent ....1,000.00 to	1,300.00
Rose bowl, green	250.00
Rose bowl, ice blue	325.00
Rose bowl, marigold	102.00
Rose bowl, purple	85.00
Rose bowl, white ....425.00 to	450.00
Rose bowl/whimsey, straight top, lavender	650.00
Rose bowl/whimsey, purple	195.00

FINE RIB (Northwood & Fenton)

Bowl, master berry, 9" d., marigold	35.00
Bowl, 10½" d., green	50.00
Bowl, purple	35.00
Compote, ruffled, green	45.00
Plate, 9" d., eight-sided, marigold	85.00
Sauce dish, vaseline	25.00
Vase, 6½" h., 5" d., blue	25.00
Vase, 6½" h., 5" d., green	30.00
Vase, 6½" h., 5" d., marigold	25.00
Vase, 7" h., green	42.50
Vase, 7" h., marigold	35.00
Vase, 7½" h., white	80.00

Vase, 8" h., aqua 62.50
Vase, 8½" h., blue............... 38.00
Vase, 8½" h., red................ 195.00
Vase, 9" h., green 34.00
Vase, 9" h., purple 25.00
Vase, 9" h., red (Fenton) 275.00
Vase, 9½" h., blue................ 45.00
Vase, 9½" h., vaseline (Fenton) 45.00
Vase, 10" h., amber (Fenton)....... 45.00
Vase, 10" h., aqua (Northwood) 70.00
Vase, 10" h., purple 45.00
Vase, 10" h., red (Fen-
  ton)..................400.00 to 475.00
Vase, 12" h., blue................ 45.00
Vase, 12" h., green 35.00
Vase, 12" h., red (Fenton) 650.00
Vase, 12" h., vaseline (Fenton) 75.00
Vase, 15" h., blue................ 60.00
Vase, 16" h., marigold........... 45.00
Vase, 17" h., marigold........... 85.00

FISHERMAN'S MUG

Fisherman's Mug

Marigold ....190.00 to 210.00
Marigold opalescent 1,200.00
Pastel marigold 250.00
Peach opalescent ......1,100.00 to 1,250.00
Purple (ILLUS.) 115.00

FISHSCALE & BEADS

Banana boat, peach opalescent,
  7" l. 73.00
Bonbon, marigold, 6" 35.00
Bonbon, peach opalescent, 6" 55.00
Bowl, 7" d., marigold............. 21.00
Card tray, peach opalescent,
  4 x 7"........................ 68.00
Plate, 7" d., marigold 75.00
Plate, 7" d., pastel marigold 75.00
Plate, 7" d., ruffled rim, peach
  opalescent ....125.00 to 150.00
Plate, 7" d., purple............... 375.00
Plate, 7" d., white 95.00
Plate, 7½" d., marigold 110.00
Plate, 7½" d., purple 150.00
Plate, 8" d., purple.............. 500.00

FLEUR DE LIS (Millersburg)

Bowl, 8" to 9" d., dome-footed, purple (ILLUS.) 267.00

Fleur-de-Lis Bowl

Bowl, 10" d., green ....250.00 to 275.00
Bowl, 10" d., marigold............. 180.00
Bowl, 10" d., purple.......300.00 to 400.00
Bowl, dome-footed, ruffled, mari-
  gold 175.00
Bowl, dome-footed, purple 350.00
Bowl, tricornered, footed, mari-
  gold 250.00
Bowl, tricornered, footed, purple ... 245.00
Rose bowl, dome-footed, purple ...3,300.00

FLOWERS & FRAMES

Flowers & Frames Bowl

Bowl, 7" d., single handle, peach
  opalescent...................... 33.00
Bowl, 7" d., dome-footed, purple ... 100.00
Bowl, 9" d., dome-footed, green 275.00
Bowl, 9" d., dome-footed, peach
  opalescent...................... 145.00
Bowl, 9" d., dome-footed, fluted,
  purple (ILLUS.) ....150.00 to 200.00
Bowl, tricornered, peach opales-
  cent 130.00
Bowl, tricornered, dome-footed,
  purple 125.00

**FLUFFY PEACOCK - See Peacock, Fluffy Pat-
tern**

FLUTE (Imperial)

Bowl, 8" to 9" d., marigold	28.00
Bowl, 8" to 9" d., purple	65.00
Butter dish, cov., marigold	60.00
Compote, green	25.00
Creamer, breakfast size, marigold . .	50.00
Creamer, breakfast size, purple	60.00
Creamer & open sugar bowl, break-	
fast size, purple, pr.	130.00
Match holder, purple	900.00
Pitcher, water, clambroth	175.00
Pitcher, water, marigold	275.00
Pitcher, water, purple	293.00
Punch cup, green	25.00
Punch cup, marigold	35.00
Punch cup, purple	25.00
Punch set: bowl, base & 6 cups; pur-	
ple, 8 pcs. . . . . 750.00 to	850.00
Rose bowl, marigold	24.00
Sauce dish, green	34.00
Sauce dish, marigold	15.00
Sauce dish, purple	50.00
Sugar bowl, open, breakfast size,	
amber	65.00
Sugar bowl, open, breakfast size,	
green	60.00
Sugar bowl, open, breakfast size,	
purple	60.00
Toothpick holder, green	48.00
Toothpick holder, lavender	110.00
Toothpick holder, marigold	50.00
Toothpick holder, purple	60.00
Tumbler, aqua	175.00
Tumbler, cobalt blue	400.00
Tumbler, marigold	50.00
Tumbler, purple	82.00
Tumbler, red	275.00
Tumbler, smoky	425.00
Vase, 9" h., aqua	70.00
Vase, 9" h., purple	82.00
Vase, 12" h., funeral, green	32.00
Vase, 17" h., green	65.00

FLUTE (Northwood)

Pitcher, water, clambroth	175.00
Salt dip, master size, blue	45.00
Tumbler, marigold	55.00
Tumbler, marigold, variant	85.00
Tumbler, dark marigold	95.00
Vase, 13" h., funeral, marigold	35.00
Vase, funeral, green	175.00

FOUR FLOWERS - See Pods & Posies Pattern

FOUR SEVENTY FOUR (Imperial)

Compote, green	95.00
Goblet, water, marigold	75.00
Pitcher, milk, green . . . . 275.00 to	375.00
Pitcher, milk, marigold	162.00
Pitcher, water, marigold	150.00
Pitcher, water, purple (ILLUS. top	
next column)	575.00
Punch cup, green	60.00

Four Seventy Four Pitcher

Punch cup, marigold	22.00
Punch cup, purple	50.00
Tumbler, blue	200.00
Tumbler, marigold	35.00
Tumbler, purple	75.00
Water set: pitcher & 6 tumblers;	
marigold, 7 pcs.	385.00
Water set: pitcher & 6 tumblers;	
purple, 7 pcs. 1,800.00	

FROLICKING BEARS (U.S. Glass)

Frolicking Bears Pitcher

Pitcher, green (ILLUS.) . .5,000.00 to 7,000.00	
Tumbler, green 9,500.00	

FROSTED BLOCK

Bowl, 6" d., marigold	19.00
Bowl, 8" to 9" d., scalloped & fluted,	
clambroth	35.00
Bowl, square, clambroth	30.00
Bowl, square, marigold	40.00
Bowl, square, "USA," white	45.00
Compote, clambroth	100.00
Compote, white	150.00
Nut dish, clambroth	55.00
Nut dish, marigold	45.00
Pitcher, milk, marigold	50.00
Plate, 7¾" sq., marigold	30.00
Plate, 7¾" sq., smoky	100.00
Plate, 9" d., clambroth	70.00
Plate, 9" d., marigold	50.00

Plate, 9" d., smoky	50.00
Relish, marigold	35.00
Rose bowl, clambroth	280.00
Rose bowl, marigold	35.00
Rose bowl, white	58.00
Vase, smoky	35.00

FRUITS & FLOWERS (Northwood)

Berry set: master bowl & 4 sauce dishes; purple, 5 pcs.	395.00
Bonbon, stemmed, two-handled, amber	375.00
Bonbon, stemmed, two-handled, aqua opalescent	475.00 to 500.00
Bonbon, stemmed, two-handled, blue	100.00
Bonbon, stemmed, two-handled, electric blue	195.00
Bonbon, stemmed, two-handled, green	105.00
Bonbon, stemmed, two-handled, ice blue	700.00 to 750.00
Bonbon, stemmed, two-handled, ice green	450.00
Bonbon, stemmed, two-handled, lavender	650.00
Bonbon, stemmed, two-handled, marigold	90.00
Bonbon, stemmed, two-handled, olive green	135.00
Bonbon, stemmed, two-handled, pastel marigold	115.00
Bonbon, stemmed, two-handled, purple	95.00
Bonbon, stemmed, two-handled, white	375.00 to 400.00
Bowl, 6" d., ruffled, green	48.00
Bowl, 6" d., ruffled, marigold	60.00
Bowl, 6" d., ruffled, purple	48.00
Bowl, 7" d., blue	85.00
Bowl, 7" d., electric blue	300.00 to 350.00
Bowl, 7" d., green	53.00
Bowl, 7" d., purple	60.00
Bowl, 7" d., ruffled, blue	275.00
Bowl, 7" d., ruffled, marigold	15.00
Bowl, 9½" d., ruffled, Basketweave exterior, purple	61.00
Bowl, master berry, 10" d., green	82.00
Bowl, master berry, 10" d., marigold	45.00
Bowl, master berry, 10" d., purple	66.00
Bowl, 10" d., ruffled, ice green	475.00
Bowl, 10" d., ruffled, purple	150.00
Bowl, piecrust rim, purple	225.00
Card tray, green	125.00
Plate, 7" d., green	170.00
Plate, 7" d., marigold	125.00
Plate, 7" d., purple	175.00
Plate, 7½" d., hand-grip, green	165.00
Plate, 7½" d., hand-grip, purple	125.00 to 150.00
Sauce dish, marigold	31.00
Sauce dish, purple	45.00

GOD & HOME

God & Home Water Set

Pitcher, blue	1,130.00
Tumbler, blue	225.00
Water set: pitcher & 6 tumblers; blue, 7 pcs. (ILLUS.)	2,500.00

GOOD LUCK (Northwood)

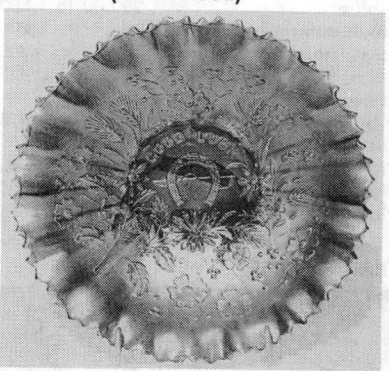

Good Luck Bowl

Bowl, 8" d., ruffled, blue	200.00 to 225.00
Bowl, 8" d., ruffled, stippled, blue	374.00
Bowl, 8" d., ruffled, electric blue	285.00
Bowl, 8" d., ruffled, stippled, electric blue	325.00
Bowl, 8" d., ruffled, green	263.00
Bowl, 8" d., ruffled, Basketweave exterior, green	250.00 to 300.00
Bowl, 8" d., ruffled, marigold	125.00
Bowl, 8" d., ruffled, Basketweave exterior, marigold	150.00 to 200.00
Bowl, 8" d., ruffled, stippled, marigold	130.00
Bowl, 8" d., ruffled, purple	200.00
Bowl, 8" d., ruffled, Basketweave exterior, purple	186.00
Bowl, 8" to 9" d., piecrust rim, aqua opalescent	1,800.00
Bowl, 8" to 9" d., piecrust rim, blue (ILLUS.)	302.00
Bowl, 8" to 9" d., piecrust rim, stippled, blue	321.00
Bowl, 8" to 9" d., piecrust rim, clambroth	450.00
Bowl, 8" to 9" d., piecrust rim, green	375.00 to 425.00
Bowl, 8" to 9" d., piecrust rim, lavender	700.00

Bowl, 8" to 9" d., piecrust rim, marigold 162.00

Bowl, 8" to 9" d., piecrust rim, stippled, marigold 190.00

Bowl, 8" to 9" d., piecrust rim, purple 280.00

Bowl, 8" to 9" d., piecrust rim, teal blue ....2,500.00 to 3,000.00

Bowl, 8" to 9" d., ruffled, aqua opalescent 1,300.00

Bowl, 8" to 9" d., ruffled, green 800.00

Bowl, 8" to 9" d., ruffled, lavender ....200.00 to 250.00

Bowl, 8" to 9" d., ruffled, marigold 115.00

Bowl, 8" to 9" d., ruffled, purple ... 255.00

Bowl, 8" to 9" d., ruffled, red 850.00

Bowl, 8" to 9" d., ruffled, teal blue ....1,200.00 to 1,500.00

Bowl, aqua 1,200.00

Bowl, ruffled, sapphire blue 1,300.00

Plate, 9" d., blue................... 425.00

Plate, 9" d., electric blue ....1,250.00 to 1,275.00

Plate, 9" d., green 700.00

Plate, 9" d., marigold 500.00

Plate, 9" d., purple................. 475.00

Plate, 9" d., stippled, purple 600.00

GRAPE & CABLE

Grape & Cable Punch Set

Banana boat, blue.................. 330.00

Banana boat, banded rim, stippled, blue........................1,200.00

Banana boat, green 303.00

Banana boat, stippled, green 400.00

Banana boat, ice blue .....550.00 to 600.00

Banana boat, ice green 750.00

Banana boat, marigold 140.00

Banana boat, stippled, marigold 225.00

Banana boat, purple.............. 225.00

Banana boat, white ....650.00 to 685.00

Berry set: master bowl & 6 sauce dishes; marigold, 7 pcs. 275.00

Berry set: master bowl & 6 sauce dishes; purple, 7 pcs.....375.00 to 400.00

Bonbon, two-handled, blue......... 85.00

Bowl, 5" d., blue (Fenton).......... 50.00

Bowl, 5" d., green 37.50

Bowl, 5" d., marigold 40.00

Bowl, 5" d., purple 38.00

Bowl, 6" d., red (Fenton).......... 360.00

Bowl, 6½" d., marigold 38.00

Bowl, 7" d., ice cream shape, aqua (Fenton)...................... 300.00

Bowl, 7" d., ice cream shape, marigold (Fenton) 125.00

Bowl, 7" d., ice cream shape, milk white w/marigold overlay (Fenton)....................150.00 to 250.00

Bowl, 7" d., ice cream shape, red (Fenton) 750.00

Bowl, 7½" d., ball-footed, aqua (Fenton) 96.00

Bowl, 7½" d., ball-footed, blue (Fenton) 65.00

Bowl, 7½" d., ball-footed, green (Fenton) 42.00

Bowl, 7½" d., ball-footed, marigold (Fenton) 40.00

Bowl, 7½" d., ball-footed, purple (Fenton) 92.50

Bowl, 7½" d., ball-footed, red (Fenton) 550.00

Bowl, 7½" d., ball-footed, vaseline (Fenton) 82.50

Bowl, 8" d., ice cream shape, footed, blue (Fenton)................ 65.00

Bowl, 8" d., ice cream shape, stippled, blue 130.00

Bowl, 8" d., ice cream shape, footed, celeste blue (Fenton) 600.00

Bowl, 8" d., ice cream shape, footed, green (Fenton) 58.00

Bowl, 8" d., red (Fenton).......... 475.00

Bowl, 8¾" d., ruffled rim, purple ... 94.00

Bowl, 8" to 9" d., piecrust rim, aqua opalescent (Northwood) 3,200.00

Bowl, 8" to 9" d., piecrust rim, electric blue 350.00

Bowl, 8" to 9" d., piecrust rim, stippled, blue 340.00

Bowl, 8" to 9" d., piecrust rim, green 147.00

Bowl, 8" to 9" d., piecrust rim, ice blue 1,000.00

Bowl, 8" to 9" d., piecrust rim, marigold 100.00

Bowl, 8" to 9" d., piecrust rim, purple ....250.00 to 275.00

Bowl, 8" to 9" d., ball-footed, blue (Fenton) 85.00

Bowl, 8" to 9" d., ball-footed, celeste blue (Fenton) 550.00

Bowl, 8" to 9" d., ball-footed, green (Fenton) 76.00

Bowl, 8" to 9" d., ball-footed, pastel marigold (Fenton) 45.00

Bowl, 8" to 9" d., ball-footed, purple (Fenton)...................... 50.00

Bowl, 8" to 9" d., ball-footed, smoky (Fenton) 275.00

Bowl, 8" to 9" d., ball-footed, teal blue 275.00

Bowl, 8" to 9" d., spatula-footed, blue (Northwood) 65.00

Bowl, 8" to 9" d., spatula-footed, clambroth (Northwood) 90.00

Bowl, 8" to 9" d., spatula-footed, green (Northwood) 70.00

Bowl, 8" to 9" d., spatula-footed, marigold (Northwood) 55.00

Bowl, 8" to 9" d., spatula-footed, ruffled, purple (Northwood)................75.00 to 100.00

Bowl, 8" to 9" d., stippled, blue 400.00

Bowl, 8" to 9" d., stippled, green ... 325.00

Bowl, 8" to 9" d., stippled, ice blue............1,000.00

Bowl, 8" to 9" d., stippled, purple .. 225.00

Bowl, berry, 9" d., clambroth....... 100.00

Bowl, berry, 9" d., green 110.00

Bowl, berry, 9" d., ice green 1,100.00

Bowl, berry, 9" d., marigold....... 101.00

Bowl, berry, 9" d., purple 82.00

Bowl, orange, 10½" d., footed, Persian Medallion interior, blue (Fenton)...............225.00 to 250.00

Bowl, orange, 10½" d., footed, Persian Medallion interior, green (Fenton)...............225.00 to 250.00

Bowl, orange, 10½" d., footed, Persian Medallion interior, marigold (Fenton) 143.00

Bowl, orange, 10½" d., footed, Persian Medallion interior, purple (Fenton)..............200.00 to 225.00

Bowl, orange, 10½" d., footed, blue 350.00

Bowl, orange, 10½" d., footed, clambroth 350.00

Bowl, orange, 10½" d., footed, stippled, electric blue (Northwood)... 680.00

Bowl, orange, 10½" d., footed, green ....250.00 to 300.00

Bowl, orange, 10½" d., footed, ice blue 875.00

Bowl, orange, 10½" d., footed, ice green.................950.00 to 1,150.00

Bowl, orange, 10½" d., footed, marigold.................150.00 to 175.00

Bowl, ice cream, 11" d., blue....... 700.00

Bowl, ice cream, 11" d., green 300.00

Bowl, ice cream, 11" d., Basketweave exterior, green 1,250.00

Bowl, ice cream, 11" d., ice blue ....2,100.00 to 2,750.00

Bowl, ice cream, 11" d., ice green ....1,200.00 to 1,500.00

Bowl, ice cream, 11" d., marigold................400.00 to 500.00

Bowl, ice cream, 11" d., Basketweave exterior, marigold 150.00

Bowl, ice cream, 11" d., purple..... 300.00

Bowl, ice cream, 11" d., Basketweave exterior, purple 450.00

Bowl, ice cream, 11" d., white ....300.00 to 325.00

Butter dish, cov., amber 155.00

Butter dish, cov., green............ 176.00

Butter dish, cov., ice green 250.00

Butter dish, cov., marigold 145.00

Butter dish, cov., purple 198.00

Candle lamp, green ....650.00 to 700.00

Candle lamp, marigold ....500.00 to 550.00

Candle lamp, purple .....500.00 to 600.00

Candlestick, green 135.00

Candlestick, marigold.............. 90.00

Candlestick, purple.........100.00 to 125.00

Candlesticks, blue, pr............. 275.00

Card tray, green 350.00

Card tray, horehound............. 80.00

Card tray, marigold 50.00

Card tray, purple 80.00

Centerpiece bowl, green 900.00

Centerpiece bowl, ice blue 825.00

Centerpiece bowl, ice green ....800.00 to 850.00

Centerpiece bowl, marigold 250.00

Centerpiece bowl, purple 425.00

Centerpiece bowl, white 632.00

Cologne bottle w/stopper, green ....175.00 to 200.00

Cologne bottle w/stopper, ice blue 950.00

Cologne bottle w/stopper, marigold 165.00

Cologne bottle w/stopper, purple ....225.00 to 250.00

Cologne bottle w/stopper, sapphire blue 795.00

Cologne bottle w/stopper, white ... 650.00

Compote, cov., large, green 425.00

Compote, cov., large, marigold 1,450.00

Compote, cov., small, purple ....325.00 to 350.00

Compote, cov., large, purple 450.00

Compote, open, large, green....... 425.00

Compote, open, large, marigold ....300.00 to 350.00

Compote, open, large, purple ....425.00 to 525.00

Cracker jar, cov., blue............. 500.00

Cracker jar, cov., ice green 800.00

Cracker jar, cov., marigold......... 300.00

Cracker jar, cov., purple 400.00

Cracker jar, cov., white 875.00

Creamer, green 125.00

Creamer, marigold 90.00

Creamer, purple 88.00

Creamer, individual size, green 65.00

Creamer, individual size, marigold .. 70.00

Creamer, individual size, purple 75.00

Creamer & cov. sugar bowl, purple, pr........................... 278.00

Fernery, ice blue 1,300.00

Fernery, marigold 980.00

Fernery, purple 700.00

Fernery, white ....700.00 to 1,000.00

Hatpin holder, aqua opalescent (rare).........................12,000.00

Hatpin holder, blue ....1,000.00 to 1,200.00

Hatpin holder, green 267.00

Hatpin holder, ice blue...........1,900.00

Hatpin holder, ice green 1,700.00
Hatpin holder, lavender ...400.00 to 450.00
Hatpin holder, marigold ...200.00 to 225.00
Hatpin holder, purple .....250.00 to 275.00
Hatpin holder, white 1,800.00
Hat shape, green ....225.00 to 250.00
Hat shape, marigold 50.00
Hat shape, purple 50.00
Humidor (or tobacco jar), cov.,
  blue 1,000.00
Humidor, cov., stippled, blue 1,500.00
Humidor, cov., marigold ...275.00 to 300.00
Humidor, cov., stippled, marigold ... 160.00
Humidor, cov., purple ....700.00 to 900.00
Ice cream set: master bowl & 1 in-
  dividual dish; marigold, 2 pcs..... 425.00
Ice cream set: master bowl & 6 in-
  dividual dishes; white, 7 pcs. 1,500.00
Nappy, single handle, green 75.00
Nappy, single handle, ice blue 600.00
Nappy, single handle, marigold 47.00
Nappy, single handle, purple 130.00
Nappy, cup whimsey, hairpin,
  purple 50.00
Perfume bottle w/stopper, mari-
  gold 425.00
Perfume bottle w/stopper, purple .. 670.00
Pin tray, green.................... 225.00
Pin tray, ice blue................ 900.00
Pin tray, marigold........140.00 to 150.00
Pin tray, purple ....250.00 to 275.00
Pitcher, water, 8¼" h., green 500.00
Pitcher, water, 8¼" h., marigold ... 205.00
Pitcher, water, 8¼" h., pur-
  ple ....250.00 to 300.00
Pitcher, tankard, 9¾" h., green 1,500.00
Pitcher, tankard, 9¾" h., mari-
  gold 425.00
Pitcher, tankard, 9¾" h., purple 600.00
Pitcher, smoky 600.00
Plate, 5" to 6" d., purple (North-
  wood) 130.00
Plate, 7½" d., turned-up handgrip,
  green 95.00
Plate, 7½" d., turned-up handgrip,
  marigold ....100.00 to 125.00
Plate, 7½" d., turned-up handgrip,
  purple ....75.00 to 100.00
Plate, 8" d., clambroth 850.00
Plate, 8" d., footed, green (Fen-
  ton).................... 110.00
Plate, 8" d., green (Northwood) 140.00
Plate, 8" d., footed, mari-
  gold ....50.00 to 75.00
Plate, 8" d., footed, purple........ 84.00
Plate, 8" d., purple............... 225.00
Plate, 9" d., blue................ 250.00
Plate, 9" d., spatula-footed, blue ... 150.00
Plate, 9" d., stippled, blue 600.00
Plate, 9" d., green ....300.00 to 400.00
Plate, 9" d., spatula-footed, green .. 137.00
Plate, 9" d., spatula-footed, ice
  green ....850.00 to 875.00
Plate, 9" d., marigold 90.00

Plate, 9" d., spatula-footed,
  marigold 85.00
Plate, 9" d., purple........100.00 to 125.00
Plate, 9" d., spatula-footed, pur-
  ple 125.00
Plate, 9" d., Basketweave exterior,
  green 150.00
Plate, 9" d., Basketweave exterior,
  marigold 90.00
Plate, 9" d., Basketweave exterior,
  purple 147.00
Plate, 9" d., stippled, blue 485.00
Plate, 9" d., stippled, green 302.00
Plate, 9" d., stippled, green, var-
  iant 900.00
Plate, 9" d., stippled, marigold 150.00
Powder jar, cov., blue 600.00
Powder jar, cov., green............ 110.00
Powder jar, cov., marigold 85.00
Powder jar, cov., purple ....75.00 to 100.00
Punch bowl & base, green, 11" d.,
  2 pcs..................... 600.00
Punch bowl & base, marigold,
  11" d., 2 pcs. 250.00
Punch bowl & base, purple, 11" d.,
  2 pcs..................... 425.00
Punch bowl & base, purple, 14" d.,
  2 pcs.................500.00 to 525.00
Punch cup, aqua opalescent 895.00
Punch cup, blue 40.00
Punch cup, stippled, blue ...50.00 to 75.00
Punch cup, green 38.00
Punch cup, stippled, green 45.00
•Punch cup, ice blue 90.00
Punch cup, ice green 80.00
Punch cup, lavender 25.00
Punch cup, marigold............. 20.00
Punch cup, purple 25.00
Punch cup, white................ 60.00
Punch set: 11" bowl & 6 cups; blue,
  7 pcs. 1,100.00
Punch set: 11" bowl & 6 cups; mari-
  gold, 7 pcs................. 425.00
Punch set: 11" bowl & 6 cups; white,
  7 pcs.................... 1,750.00
Punch set: 11" bowl, base & 6 cups;
  green, 8 pcs. 825.00
Punch set: 14" bowl & 10 cups; ice
  green, 11 pcs................ 2,300.00
Punch set: 14" bowl, base & 5 cups;
  purple, 7 pcs................ 895.00
Punch set: 14" bowl, base & 6 cups;
  marigold, 8 pcs.............. 585.00
Punch set: 14" bowl, base & 6 cups;
  white, 8 pcs. (ILLUS.)........... 3,500.00
Punch set: 14" bowl, base & 8 cups;
  blue, 10 pcs................ 2,300.00
Punch set: 17" bowl, base & 6 cups;
  purple, 8 pcs................ 2,000.00
Punch set: 17" bowl, base &
  10 cups; blue, 12 pcs. 4,200.00
Punch set: 17" bowl, base &
  10 cups; white, 12 pcs.......... 6,000.00

Sherbet or individual ice cream dish, green 35.00

Sherbet or individual ice cream dish, ice green..................... 175.00

Sherbet or individual ice cream dish, marigold 35.00

Sherbet or individual ice cream dish, purple 35.00

Sherbet or individual ice cream dish, white ....175.00 to 200.00

Spooner, green 125.00

Spooner, marigold................. 42.00

Spooner, purple 100.00

Sugar bowl, cov., green 85.00

Sugar bowl, cov., marigold......... 85.00

Sugar bowl, cov., purple 104.00

Sugar bowl, individual size, green .. 60.00

Sugar bowl, individual size, marigold 35.00

Sugar bowl, individual size, purple.. 60.00

Sweetmeat jar, cov., marigold 1,800.00

Sweetmeat jar, cov., purple ....225.00 to 275.00

Tumbler, green ....45.00 to 65.00

Tumbler, ice green ....700.00 to 800.00

Tumbler, marigold................. 32.00

Tumbler, stippled, marigold 60.00

Tumbler, purple.................... 40.00

Tumbler, stippled, purple 50.00

Tumbler, tankard, blue 72.00

Tumbler, tankard, green 225.00

Tumbler, tankard, marigold 58.00

Tumbler, tankard, stippled, marigold 65.00

Tumbler, tankard, purple 45.00

Tumbler, tankard, stippled, purple .. 89.00

Water set: pitcher & 4 tumblers; purple, 5 pcs..................... 625.00

Water set: pitcher & 6 tumblers; green, 7 pcs. 575.00

Water set: pitcher & 6 tumblers; marigold, 7 pcs.......500.00 to 550.00

Water set: tankard pitcher & 6 tumblers; marigold, 7 pcs....700.00 to 800.00

Water set: tankard pitcher & 6 tumblers; purple, 7 pcs............. 850.00

GRAPE ARBOR (Northwood)

Bowl, 10" d., footed, blue (Dugan).. 210.00

Bowl, 10" d., footed, marigold (Dugan) 90.00

Bowl, 10" d., footed, purple (Dugan) ....350.00 to 375.00

Hat shape, blue.................... 75.00

Hat shape, marigold ....75.00 to 100.00

Hat shape, white.................. 110.00

Pitcher, tankard, marigold ....225.00 to 250.00

Pitcher, tankard, purple 600.00

Pitcher, tankard, white ....550.00 to 650.00

Tumbler, blue ....200.00 to 250.00

Tumbler, ice blue ....125.00 to 175.00

Tumbler, ice green ....400.00 to 500.00

Tumbler, lavender................. 175.00

Tumbler, marigold................. 30.00

Tumbler, pastel marigold 40.00

Tumbler, purple................. 60.00

Tumbler, teal blue 175.00

Tumbler, white ....100.00 to 125.00

Water set: tankard pitcher & 4 tumblers; purple, 5 pcs.............. 800.00

Water set: tankard pitcher & 4 tumblers; white, 5 pcs. 1,250.00

Water set: tankard pitcher & 6 tumblers; marigold, 7 pcs....500.00 to 575.00

GRAPEVINE LATTICE

Bowl, 7" d., ruffled, ice white 185.00

Bowl, 7" d., ruffled, white ...50.00 to 60.00

Bowl, fluted, white 85.00

Hat shape, white.................. 150.00

Pitcher, water, blue 287.00

Pitcher, water, purple .....450.00 to 475.00

Pitcher, water, white ......600.00 to 800.00

Plate, 6" to 7" d., marigold 50.00

Plate, 6" to 7" d., purple ..150.00 to 175.00

Plate, 6" to 7" d., white ....75.00 to 100.00

Plate, 8" d., ruffled, marigold 110.00

Tumbler, marigold................. 40.00

Tumbler, purple 50.00

Tumbler, smoky 40.00

Tumbler, white................... 165.00

Water set: pitcher & 6 tumblers; marigold, 7 pcs. ....475.00 to 525.00

GREEK KEY (Northwood)

Bowl, 8" to 9" d., blue............ 500.00

Bowl, 8" to 9" d., fluted, green 185.00

Bowl, 8" to 9" d., ruffled, marigold 85.00

Bowl, 8" to 9" d., purple...100.00 to 150.00

Bowl, 8" to 9" d., ruffled, purple ... 245.00

Bowl, eight-sided, 6½" w., 4" h., purple 85.00

Bowl, dome-footed, green 55.00

Bowl, piecrust rim, electric blue....1,950.00

Bowl, piecrust rim, green 400.00

Pitcher, water, green 1,450.00

Pitcher, water, purple .....500.00 to 700.00

Plate, 9" d., blue 2,800.00

Plate, 9" d., green 600.00

Plate, 9" d., marigold 800.00

Plate, 9" d., purple........300.00 to 400.00

Tumbler, green 110.00

Tumbler, marigold................. 60.00

Tumbler, purple............75.00 to 100.00

Water set: pitcher & 4 tumblers; purple, 5 pcs. 1,250.00

HANGING CHERRIES - See Cherry (Millersburg) Pattern

HARVEST FLOWER (Dugan or Diamond Glass)

Pitcher, tankard, marigold (ILLUS. top next page)......1,200.00 to 1,500.00

Tumbler, amber................. 125.00

Harvest Flower Pitcher

Tumbler, marigold................ 85.00
Tumbler, purple.................. 900.00

HEARTS & FLOWERS (Northwood)

Hearts & Flowers Plate

Bowl, 8" to 9" d., aqua opales-
  cent ....1,000.00 to 1,500.00
Bowl, 8" to 9" d., blue............ 650.00
Bowl, 8" to 9" d., piecrust rim,
  blue 465.00
Bowl, 8" to 9" d., piecrust rim, elec-
  tric blue 1,175.00
Bowl, 8" to 9" d., piecrust rim, ice
  blue ....550.00 to 650.00
Bowl, 8" to 9" d., piecrust rim, ice
  green ....1,400.00 to 1,700.00
Bowl, 8" to 9" d., piecrust rim,
  marigold 600.00
Bowl, 8" to 9" d., piecrust rim, pur-
  ple ....350.00 to 375.00
Bowl, 8" to 9" d., ruffled, blue 450.00
Bowl, 8" to 9" d., ruffled, green 700.00
Bowl, 8" to 9" d., ruffled, ice
  blue ....450.00 to 475.00
Bowl, 8" to 9" d., ruffled, ice
  green...............800.00 to 1,000.00

Bowl, 8" to 9" d., ruffled, mari-
  gold 350.00
Bowl, 8" to 9" d., ruffled, pur-
  ple ....400.00 to 425.00
Bowl, 8" to 9" d., ruffled, white 275.00
Compote, 6¾" h., aqua opales-
  cent ....500.00 to 600.00
Compote, 6¾" h., blue ....475.00 to 500.00
Compote, 6¾" h., blue opales-
  cent 1,500.00
Compote, 6¾" h., electric blue 270.00
Compote, 6¾" h.,
  green ....2,250.00 to 2,700.00
Compote, 6¾" h., ice blue 950.00
Compote, 6¾" h., ice
  green................750.00 to 1,000.00
Compote, 6¾" h., mari-
  gold ....150.00 to 200.00
Compote, 6¾" h., moonstone......3,000.00
Compote, 6¾" h., purple ..450.00 to 500.00
Compote, 6¾" h., sapphire blue.... 895.00
Compote, 6¾" h., white ...150.00 to 175.00
Plate, green 1,700.00
Plate, ice blue..................1,750.00
Plate, ice green 3,900.00
Plate, marigold ....700.00 to 1,000.00
Plate, purple (ILLUS.).....900.00 to 1,000.00
Plate, white.....................2,500.00

HEAVY GRAPE (Dugan, Diamond Glass or Millersburg)

Bowl, 7" d., ruffled, vaseline 40.00
Bowl, 8" sq., ruffled, electric blue .. 325.00
Bowl, 8" d., marigold 85.00
Bowl, 10" d., marigold............ 45.00
Bowl, master berry, 10" d., peach
  opalescent..................... 650.00
Bowl, master berry, 10" d., purple.. 350.00
Compote, purple (Millersburg) 850.00
Nappy, marigold 28.00
Nappy, purple 50.00
Sauce dish, electric blue, 5" sq. 95.00

HEAVY GRAPE (Imperial)

Bowl, 4" d., lavender 25.00
Bowl, 5" d., 2" h., marigold 30.00
Bowl, 5" d., purple............... 150.00
Bowl, 6" d., marigold............. 45.00
Bowl, 6" d., purple............... 38.00
Bowl, 7" d., fluted, green 30.00
Bowl, 7" d., marigold 20.00
Bowl, 7" d., purple 42.50
Bowl, 8" to 9" d., green 58.00
Bowl, 8" to 9" d., marigold........ 55.00
Bowl, 8" to 9" d., purple 65.00
Bowl, 8" to 9" d., smoky 75.00
Bowl, 10" d., marigold............ 80.00
Bowl, 10" d., purple 335.00
Bowl, square, purple 550.00
Compote, green.................. 850.00
Nappy, handled, green 38.00
Nappy, handled, margiold 28.00

Nappy, handled, purple............ 35.00
Plate, 7" to 8" d., amber ..150.00 to 200.00
Plate, 7" to 8" d., blue-green....... 195.00
Plate, 7" to 8" d., green 55.00
Plate, 7" to 8" d., lavender 140.00
Plate, 7" to 8" d., marigold 56.00
Plate, 7" to 8" d., purple 112.00
Plate, 7" to 8" d., smoky........... 125.00
Plate, chop, 11" d., am-
ber ....450.00 to 650.00
Plate, chop, 11" d., blue 400.00
Plate, chop, 11" d., green......... 225.00
Plate, chop, 11" d., mari-
gold ....150.00 to 175.00
Plate, chop, 11" d., pur-
ple ....300.00 to 325.00
Plate, chop, 11" d., smoky 950.00
Punch cup, amber 25.00
Punch cup, green 45.00
Punch cup, marigold.............. 20.00
Punch cup, purple 38.00
Punch set: bowl, base & 4 cups; pur-
ple, 6 pcs...................... 800.00

HOBNAIL, SWIRL - See Swirl Hobnail Pattern

HOBSTAR & FEATHER (Millersburg)

Hobstar & Feather Punch Bowl

Punch bowl & base, purple
(ILLUS.) 3,300.00
Punch cup, blue 65.00
Punch cup, marigold............... 25.00
Punch cup, purple 100.00
Punch set: bowl, base & 6 cups;
marigold, 8 pcs. 1,250.00
Rose bowl, green, 7½" top d.,
13" h. 1,235.00
Whimsey, cuspidor-shaped, pur-
ple 5,000.00

HOBSTAR BAND
Pitcher, marigold ....150.00 to 200.00
Tumbler, marigold................. 40.00

HOLLY, HOLLY BERRIES & CARNIVAL HOLLY

Bonbon, two-handled, green 60.00
Bonbon, two-handled, marigold..... 65.00

Bonbon, two-handled, purple 50.00
Bowl, 5" d., marigold.............. 25.00
Bowl, 5" d., scalloped, red (Fen-
ton).......................... 450.00
Bowl, 8" to 9" d., amber 125.00
Bowl, 8" to 9" d., aqua ....300.00 to 350.00
Bowl, 8" to 9" d., blue............ 55.00
Bowl, 8" to 9" d., green 65.00
Bowl, 8" to 9" d., lav-
ender ....175.00 to 200.00
Bowl, 8" to 9" d., light blue w/mari-
gold overlay 200.00
Bowl, 8" to 9" d., marigold...40.00 to 50.00
Bowl, 8" to 9" d., milk white
w/marigold overlay 1,050.00
Bowl, 8" to 9" d., purple 62.50
Bowl, 8" to 9" d., red (Fen-
ton)................1,000.00 to 1,125.00
Bowl, 8" to 9" d., teal blue........ 500.00
Bowl, 8" to 9" d., vaseline 85.00
Bowl, 8" to 9" d., white ...100.00 to 125.00
Bowl, 8" to 9" d., ice cream shape,
celeste blue 4,000.00
Bowl, 8" to 9" d., ice cream shape,
clambroth 85.00
Bowl, 8" to 9" d., ice cream shape,
cobalt blue 275.00
Bowl, 8" to 9" d., ice cream shape,
green 95.00
Bowl, 8" to 9" d., ice cream shape,
ice green 3,200.00
Bowl, 8" to 9" d., ice cream shape,
marigold 80.00
Bowl, 8" to 9" d., ice cream shape,
moonstone ....800.00 to 850.00
Bowl, 8" to 9" d., ice cream shape,
purple 52.50
Bowl, 8" to 9" d., ice cream shape,
red...........................1,300.00
Bowl, 8" to 9" d., ice cream shape,
white 135.00
Bowl, 8" to 9" d., ribbon candy rim,
amethyst ....100.00 to 125.00
Bowl, 8" to 9" d., ribbon candy rim,
blue 55.00
Bowl, 8" to 9" d., ribbon candy rim,
green 135.00
Bowl, 8" to 9" d., ribbon candy rim,
marigold 50.00
Bowl, 8" to 9" d., ribbon candy rim,
pastel green 65.00
Bowl, 8" to 9" d., ribbon candy rim,
purple 85.00
Bowl, 8" to 9" d., ruffled, blue
opalescent 1,400.00
Bowl, 8" to 9" d., ruffled,
green ....100.00 to 125.00
Bowl, 8" to 9" d., ruffled, mari-
gold 32.50
Bowl, 8" to 9" d., ruffled, pastel
blue ....50.00 to 75.00
Bowl, 8" to 9" d., ruffled, purple
(ILLUS. top next page) ....75.00 to 100.00

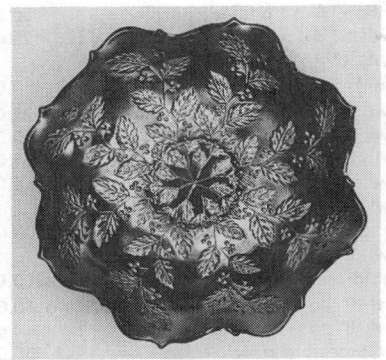

Holly Bowl

Bowl, 8" to 9" d., ruffled,
red .... 900.00 to 1,000.00
Bowl, 8" to 9" d., ruffled, vaseline . . 225.00
Bowl, 8" to 9" d., ruffled, white 100.00
Card tray, green, 6¾" 80.00
Card tray, marigold, 6¾" 40.00
Compote, small, aqua w/marigold
overlay 100.00
Compote, small, blue 40.00
Compote, small, green 45.00
Compote, small, lavender .... 50.00 to 75.00
Compote, small, lime green opales-
cent 735.00
Compote, small, marigold 28.00
Compote, small, marigold w/vase-
line stem 65.00
Compote, small, purple .... 100.00 to 125.00
Compote, small, red (Fenton) 450.00
Compote, small, vaseline 75.00
Compote, ice blue 50.00
Compote, ice green 75.00
Compote, ice green opalescent 625.00
Compote, lime green 90.00
Compote, red 1,000.00
Dish, hat-shaped, amber, 5¾" 40.00
Dish, hat-shaped, Amberina 450.00
Dish, hat-shaped, amethyst opales-
cent 425.00
Dish, hat-shaped, aqua, 5¾" 72.50
Dish, hat-shaped, aqua opalescent .. 275.00
Dish, hat-shaped, blue, 5¾" 40.00
Dish, hat-shaped, green, 5¾" 36.00
Dish, hat-shaped, green w/marigold
overlay.......................... 29.00
Dish, hat-shaped, ice blue w/mari-
gold overlay, 5¾"............... 75.00
Dish, hat-shaped, lime green,
5¾" ....50.00 to 75.00
Dish, hat-shaped, marigold, 5¾" ... 30.00
Dish, hat-shaped, milk white
w/marigold overlay 118.00
Dish, hat-shaped, moonstone 200.00
Dish, hat-shaped, purple, 5¾" 35.00
Dish, hat-shaped, purple opalescent,
5¾" 300.00
Dish, hat-shaped, red, 5¾" 470.00
Dish, hat-shaped, vaseline, 5¾".... 72.00

Goblet, blue 35.00
Goblet, green.................... 70.00
Goblet, marigold 27.00
Goblet, red (Fenton).............. 429.00
Plate, 9" to 10" d., amethyst.......1,050.00
Plate, 9" to 10" d., blue .. 350.00 to 450.00
Plate, 9" to 10" d., celeste blue
(Fenton) 9,500.00
Plate, 9" to 10" d., clambroth 125.00
Plate, 9" to 10" d., green ..650.00 to 850.00
Plate, 9" to 10" d., lavender 210.00
Plate, 9" to 10" d., mari-
gold ....125.00 to 175.00
Plate, 9" to 10" d., pastel mari-
gold 90.00
Plate, 9" to 10" d., pur-
ple ....400.00 to 600.00
Plate, 9" to 10" d., white ..200.00 to 225.00
Plate, lavender 200.00
Sauceboat, handled, peach opales-
cent (Dugan).................... 102.00
Sauceboat, handled, purple 110.00
Sherbet, blue 42.50
Sherbet, green 25.00
Sherbet, lime green 75.00
Sherbet, lime green opalescent 675.00
Sherbet, marigold 35.00
Sherbet, red (Fenton) 425.00

HOLLY SPRIG - See Holly Whirl Pattern

**HOLLY WHIRL or HOLLY SPRIG (Millersburg,
Fenton & Dugan)**
Bowl, 6" w., tricornered, amethyst.. 125.00
Bowl, 6" w., tricornered, green..... 85.00
Bowl, 6" d., ruffled, marigold 62.50
Bowl, 6" d., ruffled, purple........ 92.50
Bowl, 7" d., green 55.00
Bowl, 7" d., marigold 55.00
Bowl, 7" d., ruffled, purple........ 60.00
Bowl, 8" d., ice cream shape, mari-
gold, variant.................... 68.00
Bowl, 8" d., ice cream shape,
white 110.00
Bowl, 8" to 9" d., ruffled, blue 50.00
Bowl, 8" to 9" d., green 75.00
Bowl, 8" to 9" d., marigold........ 60.00
Bowl, 8" to 9" d., peach opales-
cent 75.00
Bowl, 8" to 9" d., purple....75.00 to 100.00
Bowl, 10" d., ruffled, marigold 50.00
Bowl, 10" d., ruffled, purple........ 110.00
Hat shape, green, 6" 38.00
Nappy, single handle, marigold 45.00
Nappy, single handle, peach opales-
cent (Dugan)................... 62.00
Nappy, single handle, purple
(Dugan) ....75.00 to 100.00
Nappy, tricornered, green (Dugan).. 110.00
Nappy, tricornered, marigold (Mil-
lersburg) 110.00
Nappy, tricornered, purple
(Dugan) 100.00
Nappy, tricornered, purple (Millers-
burg) ....175.00 to 200.00

Nappy, two-handled, amethyst (Millersburg)	68.00
Nappy, two-handled, green (Dugan)	75.00 to 100.00
Nappy, two-handled, green (Millersburg)	80.00
Nut dish, two-handled, green	75.00
Nut dish, two-handled, marigold	60.00
Nut dish, two-handled, purple	72.50
Rose bowl, blue	290.00
Rose bowl, small, marigold	325.00
Sauceboat, peach opalescent (Dugan)	135.00
Sauce dish, purple, 5½" d. (Millersburg)	145.00
Sauce dish, marigold, 5¾" d.	125.00
Sauce dish, green, 6½" d. (Millersburg)	100.00 to 125.00
Sauce dish, deep, purple	350.00

HORSE HEADS or HORSE MEDALLION (Fenton)

Bowl, 5" d., footed, marigold	57.00
Bowl, 6" d., blue	60.00
Bowl, 6" d., collared base, marigold	85.00
Bowl, 7" to 8" d., amber	395.00
Bowl, 7" to 8" d., blue	115.00
Bowl, 7" to 8" d., green	135.00
Bowl, 7" to 8" d., marigold	75.00 to 100.00
Bowl, 7" to 8" d., purple	118.00
Bowl, 7" to 8" d., red	1,800.00
Bowl, ice cream shape, amber	280.00
Bowl, ice cream shape, blue	235.00
Bowl, 7" d., ice cream shape, purple	425.00
Bowl, ruffled, collared base, Amberina	450.00
Bowl, jack-in-the-pulpit shaped, amber	495.00
Bowl, jack-in-the-pulpit shaped, blue	150.00 to 175.00
Bowl, jack-in-the-pulpit shaped, green	250.00 to 300.00
Bowl, jack-in-the-pulpit shaped, marigold	130.00
Bowl, jack-in-the-pulpit shaped, purple	265.00
Bowl, jack-in-the-pulpit shaped, teal green	675.00
Bowl, jack-in-the-pulpit shaped, vaseline	400.00 to 425.00
Nut bowl, three-footed, amethyst	225.00
Nut bowl, three-footed, blue	135.00
Nut bowl, three-footed, marigold	85.00
Nut bowl, three-footed, red	1,800.00
Nut bowl, three-footed, vaseline	250.00 to 300.00
Plate, 7" to 8" d., blue	750.00
Plate, 7" to 8" d., marigold	200.00 to 225.00
Rose bowl, blue	225.00
Rose bowl, marigold	130.00

Rose bowl, smoky blue	400.00
Rose bowl, vaseline	750.00

IMPERIAL GRAPE (Imperial)

Imperial Grape Water Bottle

Basket, marigold	80.00
Basket, smoky	118.00
Berry set: master bowl & 2 sauce dishes; purple, 3 pcs.	225.00
Berry set: master bowl & 4 sauce dishes; green, 5 pcs.	125.00 to 150.00
Bowl, 7" d., 2½" h., green	42.00
Bowl, 7" d., 2½" h., marigold	20.00
Bowl, 7" d., 2½" h., ruffled, purple	70.00
Bowl, 8" to 9" d., green	48.00
Bowl, 8" to 9" d., marigold	28.00
Bowl, 8" to 9" d., purple	50.00
Bowl, 10" d., green	40.00
Bowl, 10" d., marigold	45.00
Bowl, 10" d., purple	117.00
Bowl, 10" d., smoky	33.00
Bowl, 10" d., white	45.00
Bowl, 11" d., ruffled, purple	100.00
Compote, amber	60.00
Compote, clambroth	35.00
Compote, green	48.00
Compote, lavender swirled w/amber	140.00
Compote, purple	500.00
Compote, smoky	35.00
Cup, purple	20.00
Cup & saucer, amber	65.00
Cup & saucer, green	85.00
Cup & saucer, marigold	80.00
Decanter w/stopper, green	125.00 to 150.00
Decanter w/stopper, marigold	88.00
Decanter w/stopper, purple	225.00 to 250.00
Goblet, aqua teal	90.00
Goblet, clambroth	75.00
Goblet, green	35.00
Goblet, marigold	35.00
Goblet, purple	55.00
Goblet, smoky	75.00 to 100.00
Pitcher, water, amber	650.00

Pitcher, water, green 250.00
Pitcher, water, marigold . . . .75.00 to 100.00
Pitcher, water, purple 300.00
Pitcher, water, smoky . . . . .300.00 to 400.00
Plate, 6" d., amber . . . . .125.00 to 150.00
Plate, 6" d., green 60.00
Plate, 6" d., marigold 50.00
Plate, 6" d., purple . . . . .100.00 to 150.00
Plate, 7" d., green 85.00
Plate, 7" d., marigold 30.00
Plate, 8" d., green 75.00
Plate, 8" d., marigold 50.00
Plate, 8" d., purple . . . . .75.00 to 100.00
Plate, 9" d., ruffled, clambroth 75.00
Plate, 9" d., flat, green 65.00
Plate, 9" d., ruffled, green 137.00
Plate, 9" d., flat, marigold 100.00
Plate, 9" d., ruffled, mari-
    gold .50.00 to 100.00
Plate, 9" d., purple 310.00
Plate, 9" d., ruffled, purple 100.00
Plate, 9" d., ruffled, white 50.00
Rose bowl, amber 675.00
Rose bowl, green 65.00
Rose bowl, white 70.00
Sauce dish, amber 17.00
Sauce dish, green 25.00
Sauce dish, ruffled, marigold 17.00
Tray, center handle, clambroth 45.00
Tray, center handle, marigold 75.00
Tray, center handle, smoky 32.00
Tumbler, amber 98.00
Tumbler, aqua 130.00
Tumbler, green 28.00
Tumbler, lilac 59.00
Tumbler, marigold 20.00
Tumbler, purple 50.00
Tumbler, smoky 75.00
Water bottle, green . . . . . . .100.00 to 125.00
Water bottle, marigold 115.00
Water bottle, purple
    (ILLUS.) . . . . .150.00 to 175.00
Water bottle, smoky 450.00
Water set: pitcher & 1 tumbler; am-
    ber, 2 pcs. 850.00
Water set: pitcher & 6 tumblers;
    marigold, 7 pcs. 225.00
Water set: pitcher & 6 tumblers;
    purple, 7 pcs. 700.00
Wine, clambroth 18.00
Wine, green 30.00
Wine, marigold 28.00
Wine, purple 35.00
Wine, smoky 75.00
Wine, vaseline 40.00
Wine set: decanter w/stopper &
    6 wines; marigold, 7 pcs. 260.00
Wine set: decanter w/stopper &
    6 wines; purple, 7 pcs. . .475.00 to 500.00

INVERTED FEATHER (Cambridge)
Compote, jelly, marigold 75.00
Cracker jar, cov., green
    (ILLUS.) . . . . .200.00 to 250.00

Inverted Feather Cracker Jar

Cracker jar, cov., purple 750.00
Parfait, marigold 90.00
Pitcher, milk, marigold 750.00
Pitcher, milk, pastel marigold 475.00
Tumbler, green 750.00
Vase, 6" h., marigold (Cambridge) . . 75.00
Vase, 6" h., marigold (Northwood) . . 45.00

INVERTED STRAWBERRY (Cambridge)
Bowl, 6½" d., green, marked Near-
    Cut 52.00
Bowl, 7" d., green 125.00
Candlestick, marigold 128.00
Candlesticks, green, 7" h., pr. 225.00
Celery, blue .1,200.00
Compote, open, 5" d., 6" h.,
    marigold 230.00
Compote, open, giant, mari-
    gold . . . . .225.00 to 250.00
Cuspidor, green 1,000.00
Cuspidor, marigold . . . . .800.00 to 850.00
Pitcher, tankard, marigold 950.00
Powder jar, cov., green . . .150.00 to 200.00
Powder jar, cov., marigold 90.00
Sherbet w/flared sides, blue 625.00
Spooner, green 225.00
Table set, marigold, 4 pcs. 1,000.00
Table set, purple, 4 pcs. 1,500.00
Tumbler, green 275.00
Tumbler, marigold . . . . .125.00 to 150.00
Tumbler, purple . . . . .175.00 to 200.00
Water set: pitcher & 1 tumbler;
    green, 2 pcs. 1,500.00
Water set: pitcher & 6 tumblers;
    marigold, 7 pcs. . . . . .1,500.00 to 1,700.00

JEWELLED HEART (Dugan or Diamond Glass)
Basket, peach opalescent,
    6" h. . . . . .525.00 to 625.00
Bowl, master berry, 10½" d., fluted,
    peach opalescent 135.00
Bowl, 10" d., purple 100.00
Bowl, white 165.00
Sauce dish, peach opalescent 38.00
Sauce dish, peach opalescent
    w/rayed interior 32.00

Sauce dish, purple 41.00
Tumbler, amber.................. 115.00
Tumbler, green 35.00
Tumbler, marigold............... 65.00

KITTENS (Fenton)

Kittens Cup & Saucer

Bowl, cereal, blue ....450.00 to 500.00
Bowl, cereal, marigold ....150.00 to 175.00
Bowl, ruffled, blue 775.00
Bowl, ruffled, marigold ...100.00 to 125.00
Bowl, four-sided, ruffled, aqua 225.00
Bowl, four-sided, blue 350.00
Bowl, four-sided, ruffled, mari-
    gold ....100.00 to 150.00
Bowl, six-sided, ruffled, marigold ... 200.00
Cup, blue...................... 675.00
Cup, marigold ....100.00 to 125.00
Cup & saucer, blue 2,600.00
Cup & saucer, marigold
    (ILLUS.) ....200.00 to 275.00
Dish, turned-up sides, blue......... 550.00
Dish, turned-up sides, mari-
    gold ....125.00 to 150.00
Dish, turned-up sides, purple 525.00
Plate, 4½" d., marigold ...125.00 to 150.00
Spooner, blue..................... 280.00
Spooner, marigold................ 150.00
Toothpick holder, blue.....400.00 to 475.00
Toothpick holder, marigold......... 185.00
Vase, blue........................ 215.00
Vase, marigold 250.00
Vase, child's, ruffled, marigold 145.00

LEAF & BEADS (Northwood)

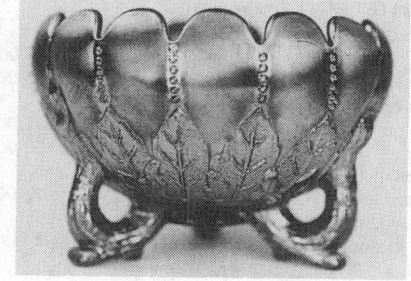

Leaf & Beads Rose Bowl

Candy bowl, footed, aqua
    opalescent..................... 500.00
Candy bowl, footed, green 50.00

Candy bowl, footed, marigold 40.00
Candy bowl, footed, purple 57.50
Nut bowl, aqua opalescent........ 575.00
Nut bowl, handled, green 60.00
Nut bowl, handled, mari-
    gold ....75.00 to 100.00
Nut bowl, handled, purple 95.00
Rose bowl, aqua 300.00
Rose bowl, aqua opales-
    cent ....325.00 to 350.00
Rose bowl, blue ....200.00 to 250.00
Rose bowl, electric blue 200.00
Rose bowl, green 85.00
Rose bowl, interior pattern,
    green ....75.00 to 85.00
Rose bowl, ice blue.............1,400.00
Rose bowl, lime green............ 450.00
Rose bowl, marigold ....75.00 to 100.00
Rose bowl, interior pattern, mari-
    gold ....75.00 to 100.00
Rose bowl, olive green ....225.00 to 275.00
Rose bowl, pastel marigold 50.00
Rose bowl, purple (ILLUS.) 75.00
Rose bowl, purple w/smooth
    rim ....350.00 to 375.00
Rose bowl, interior pattern, pur-
    ple 150.00
Rose bowl, interior pattern, teal
    blue........................1,000.00
Rose bowl, white................. 900.00

LEAF CHAIN (Fenton)

Bowl, 5" d., ruffled, marigold 45.00
Bowl, 6" d., ruffled, red 600.00
Bowl, 7" d., ruffled, Amberina 450.00
Bowl, 7" d., aqua ....100.00 to 150.00
Bowl, 7" d., blue 52.00
Bowl, 7" d., lavender 150.00
Bowl, 7" d., marigold............. 48.00
Bowl, 7" d., red.......1,000.00 to 1,200.00
Bowl, 7" d., vaseline 100.00
Bowl, 7" d., white 62.00
Bowl, 8" to 9" d., blue 62.00
Bowl, 8" to 9" d., clambroth 48.00
Bowl, 8" to 9" d., green 65.00
Bowl, 8" to 9" d., marigold........ 25.00
Bowl, 8" to 9" d., purple 68.00
Bowl, 8" to 9" d., vaseline 110.00
Bowl, 8" to 9" d., white 85.00
Plate, 7" to 8" d., blue 80.00
Plate, 7" to 8" d., marigold 74.00
Plate, 9" d., clambroth ....115.00 to 130.00
Plate, 9" d., green 128.00
Plate, 9" d., marigold .....125.00 to 175.00
Plate, 9" d., white ....200.00 to 225.00

LEAF RAYS NAPPY

Marigold 25.00
Peach opalescent................. 45.00
Purple (ILLUS. top next page)...... 40.00
Purple, "Souvenir of Cedar City,
    Michigan" 60.00
White 50.00

Leaf Rays Nappy

LION (Fenton)

Bowl, 5" d., marigold	105.00
Bowl, 6" d., marigold	148.00
Bowl, 7" d., blue	225.00 to 250.00
Bowl, 7" d., marigold	132.00
Bowl, 7" d., ice cream shape, blue	315.00
Bowl, 7" d., ice cream shape, marigold	104.00
Bowl, ruffled, red	675.00
Plate, 7" d., marigold	500.00

LITTLE BARREL PERFUME

Green	85.00
Marigold	77.50
Smoky	97.00

LITTLE FISHES (Fenton)

Little Fishes Bowl

Bowl, 6" d., three-footed, marigold	62.50
Bowl, 6" d., three-footed, purple	144.00
Bowl, 8" to 9" d., three-footed, blue	185.00
Bowl, 8" to 9" d., three-footed, marigold	135.00
Bowl, 10" d., three-footed, blue (ILLUS.)	250.00
Bowl, 10" d., three-footed, marigold	110.00
Bowl, 10" d., three-footed, white	1,000.00
Sauce dish, three-footed, aqua, 5" d.	210.00
Sauce dish, three-footed, blue, 5" d.	90.00
Sauce dish, three-footed, marigold, 5" d.	52.00
Sauce dish, three-footed, vaseline, 5" d.	95.00

LOTUS & GRAPE (Fenton)

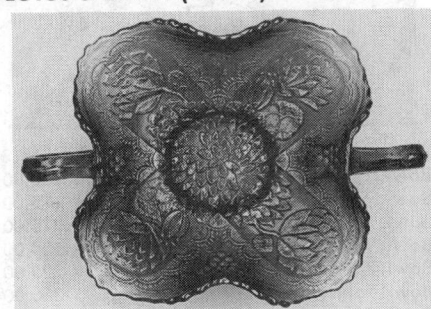

Lotus & Grape Bonbon

Bonbon, two-handled, green (ILLUS.)	90.00
Bonbon, two-handled, marigold	45.00
Bonbon, two-handled, red	1,800.00
Bonbon, two-handled, vaseline	90.00
Bowl, 5" d., footed, blue	40.00
Bowl, 5" d., footed, green	67.00
Bowl, 5" d., footed, marigold	45.00
Bowl, 7" d., footed, marigold	45.00
Bowl, 7½" d., ice cream shape, blue	65.00
Bowl, 8" d., collared base, ruffled, marigold on vaseline	75.00
Bowl, 8" to 9" d., blue	80.00
Bowl, 8" to 9" d., green	90.00
Bowl, 8" to 9" d., marigold	125.00
Bowl, 8½" d., ice cream shape, Persian blue	400.00
Plate, 9" d., blue	900.00
Plate, 9" d., green	1,200.00

LUSTRE ROSE (Imperial)

Bowl, 7" d., three-footed, clambroth	75.00
Bowl, 7" d., three-footed, green	35.00
Bowl, 7" d., three-footed, marigold	42.00
Bowl, 7" d., three-footed, vaseline	100.00
Bowl, 8" to 9" d., three-footed, amber	72.00
Bowl, 8" to 9" d., three-footed, clambroth	45.00
Bowl, 8" to 9" d., three-footed, green	45.00
Bowl, 8" to 9" d., three-footed, marigold	40.00
Bowl, 8" to 9" d., three-footed, purple	117.00

Bowl, 8" to 9" d., ruffled, smoky ... 35.00
Bowl, 8" to 9" d., three-footed,
  vaseline 125.00
Bowl, 10½" d., three-footed,
  clambroth 50.00
Bowl, 10½" d., three-footed,
  marigold 56.00
Bowl, 10½" d., three-footed, pur-
  ple 400.00
Bowl, 10½" d., three-footed,
  smoky 74.00
Bowl, 11" d., ruffled, collared base,
  green 85.00
Bowl, 11" d., ruffled, footed,
  marigold 50.00
Bowl, 11" d., ruffled, footed, pur-
  ple 650.00
Bowl, fruit, red 2,400.00
Bowl, whimsey, centerpiece, am-
  ber 250.00
Bowl, whimsey, centerpiece, pur-
  ple 550.00
Butter dish, cov., marigold 65.00
Butter dish, cov., purple 110.00
Fernery, amber 80.00
Fernery, green w/marigold over-
  lay............................... 125.00
Fernery, marigold 40.00
Fernery, olive..................... 70.00

Lustre Rose Fernery

Fernery, purple (ILLUS.) 95.00
Fernery, red 1,000.00
Pitcher, water, clambroth 65.00
Pitcher, water, green 90.00
Pitcher, water, marigold 85.00
Plate, 9" d., green 75.00
Plate, 9" d., marigold 65.00
Plate, 9" d., purple 600.00
Plate, 10½" d., marigold 85.00
Rose bowl, amber 70.00
Rose bowl, green 40.00
Rose bowl, marigold.............. 45.00
Rose bowl, purple 30.00
Sauce dish, clambroth 30.00
Sauce dish, green 24.00
Sauce dish, marigold 12.00
Sugar bowl, cov., green 50.00

Table set: cov. sugar bowl, creamer,
  spooner & cov. butter dish; mari-
  gold, 4 pcs...................... 160.00
Table set, purple, 4 pcs. 400.00
Table set, vaseline, 4 pcs. 375.00
Tumbler, amber 17.00
Tumbler, aqua 395.00
Tumbler, green 38.00
Tumbler, honey amber........... 45.00
Tumbler, marigold............... 25.00
Tumbler, purple 45.00
Tumbler, white.................. 39.00
Water set: pitcher & 4 tumblers;
  purple, 5 pcs. 700.00
Water set: pitcher & 6 tumblers;
  marigold, 7 pcs................. 200.00
Whimsey, flattened fernery, green .. 110.00

MANY FRUITS (Dugan)

Many Fruits Punch Bowl

Punch bowl & base, marigold,
  2 pcs. 400.00
Punch bowl & base, purple, 2 pcs.
  (ILLUS.)........................ 715.00
Punch cup, blue 50.00
Punch cup, green 35.00
Punch cup, marigold............. 21.00
Punch cup, purple 28.00
Punch set: bowl, base & 6 cups;
  white, 8 pcs. 1,600.00

MAPLE LEAF (Dugan)

Berry set: master bowl & 6 small
  berry bowls; pedestaled, purple,
  7 pcs. 300.00
Bowl, 6" d., small berry, marigold .. 25.00
Bowl, 6" d., small berry, purple 30.00
Bowl, master berry or fruit, pur-
  ple 100.00
Bowl, ice cream, footed, marigold .. 35.00
Butter dish, cov., blue 82.50
Butter dish, cov., marigold 175.00
Butter dish, cov., purple 195.00
Creamer, blue 60.00
Creamer, marigold 42.00
Creamer, purple 60.00
Pitcher, water, blue 275.00

Spooner, blue.................... 70.00
Spooner, marigold............... 43.00
Spooner, purple................. 60.00
Sugar bowl, cov., marigold......... 40.00
Sugar bowl, cov., purple........... 95.00
Tumbler, amber................. 75.00
Tumbler, blue.................. 65.00
Tumbler, lavender.............. 150.00
Tumbler, marigold............... 24.00
Tumbler, pastel marigold 75.00
Tumbler, purple................. 38.00
Water set: pitcher & 6 tumblers;
  purple, 7 pcs................... 725.00

MILADY (Fenton)

Milady Water Set

Pitcher, water, blue.............1,000.00
Pitcher, water, marigold 675.00
Tumbler, blue.................... 89.00
Tumbler, green 675.00
Tumbler, marigold............... 84.00
Tumbler, purple................. 116.00
Water set: pitcher & 6 tumblers;
  blue, 7 pcs. (ILLUS.) 800.00

**MILLERSBURG PIPE HUMIDOR - SEE PIPE HU-
MIDOR Pattern**

**MILLERSBURG TROUT & FLY - See Trout &
Fly**

MULTIFRUITS & FLOWERS (Millersburg)

Pitcher, water, marigold 3,300.00
Pitcher, water, purple.............4,500.00
Punch bowl & base, marigold,
  2 pcs. 600.00
Punch bowl & base, purple, 2 pcs. ... 850.00
Punch cup, green 60.00
Punch cup, marigold.............. 70.00
Punch cup, purple............... 40.00
Punch set: bowl, base & 5 cups;
  green, 7 pcs................... 1,675.00
Tumbler, green 1,000.00
Tumbler, marigold 1,000.00

NAUTILUS (Dugan)

Bowl, peach opalescent....200.00 to 250.00
Bowl, footed, purple............... 175.00
Creamer, peach opalescent 150.00
Creamer, purple ....225.00 to 250.00
Dish, flattened boat shape, peach
  opalescent, 6 x 7½", 3" h....... 295.00
Sugar bowl, open, peach opales-
  cent 250.00
Sugar bowl, open, purple 225.00

NESTING SWAN (Millersburg)

Bowl, 10" d., amber 325.00
Bowl, 10" d., green ......300.00 to 325.00
Bowl, 10" d., marigold.....150.00 to 175.00
Bowl, 10" d., purple......275.00 to 300.00

NU-ART CHRYSANTHEMUM PLATE (Imperial)

Nu-Art Chrysanthemum Plate

Amber 600.00
Marigold 495.00
Purple (ILLUS.) 1,200.00
Smoky 530.00
White 700.00

NU-ART HOMESTEAD PLATE (Imperial)

Nu-Art Homestead plate

Amber........................1,600.00
Blue (ILLUS.) 5,250.00

Emerald green	3,000.00
Green .... 750.00 to	850.00
Helios	395.00
Lavender	900.00
Marigold	400.00
Purple .... 875.00 to	975.00
White	758.00

OCTAGON (Imperial)

Bowl, 8" to 9" d., marigold	38.00
Butter dish, cov., marigold	100.00
Creamer, marigold	60.00
Creamer, purple	165.00
Decanter w/stopper, green	700.00
Decanter w/stopper, marigold	60.00
Decanter w/stopper, purple	230.00
Goblet, water, light blue w/marigold overlay	70.00
Goblet, water, marigold	45.00
Pitcher, milk, marigold	88.00
Pitcher, milk, purple ...... 250.00 to	275.00
Pitcher, water, 8" h., marigold	89.00
Pitcher, water, 8" h., purple	525.00
Pitcher, water, tankard, 9¾" h., marigold	100.00
Pitcher, water, tankard, 9¾" h., purple	400.00
Punch set: bowl, ladle & 12 cups; marigold, 14 pcs.	2,400.00
Salt shaker, purple	95.00
Spooner, marigold	45.00
Spooner, purple	165.00
Sugar bowl, cov., marigold	50.00
Toothpick holder, marigold	135.00
Tumbler, green	150.00
Tumbler, marigold	25.00
Tumbler, purple .... 125.00 to	175.00
Vase, 8" h., marigold	100.00
Water set: pitcher & 1 tumbler; marigold, 2 pcs.	185.00
Water set: pitcher & 6 tumblers; purple, 7 pcs.	950.00
Wine, marigold	22.00
Wine, purple	50.00
Wine set: decanter & 1 wine; purple, 2 pcs.	450.00
Wine set: decanter & 6 wines; marigold, 7 pcs.	275.00

ORANGE TREE (Fenton)

Bowl, 7" d., white	64.00
Bowl, 8" to 9" d., blue	68.00
Bowl, 8" to 9" d., clambroth	83.00
Bowl, 8" to 9" d., green	155.00
Bowl, 8" to 9" d., marigold	57.00
Bowl, 8" to 9" d., pastel marigold ..	60.00
Bowl, 8" to 9" d., purple .... 75.00 to	100.00
Bowl, 8" to 9" d., red	2,100.00
Bowl, 8" to 9" d., white	165.00
Bowl, 10" d., three-footed, blue	210.00
Bowl, 10" d., three-footed, green ...	235.00
Bowl, 10" d., three-footed, marigold	85.00
Bowl, 10" d., three-footed, purple ..	325.00
Bowl, 10" d., three-footed, white ...	150.00
Bowl, 10" d., Rose Tree interior, blue	1,100.00
Bowl, ice cream shape, green	185.00
Bowl, ice cream shape, marigold ...	55.00
Bowl, ice cream shape, red	1,400.00
Bowl, ice cream shape, white	125.00
Bowl, milk white w/marigold overlay	1,400.00
Bowl, moonstone	2,000.00
Bowl, peach opalescent	1,900.00
Breakfast set: individual size creamer & cov. sugar bowl; blue, pr. ...	130.00
Breakfast set: individual size creamer & cov. sugar bowl; marigold, pr.	195.00
Breakfast set: individual size creamer & cov. sugar bowl; purple, pr.	130.00
Breakfast set: individual size creamer & cov. sugar bowl; white, pr. ...	150.00
Butter dish, cov., blue	400.00
Butter dish, cov., electric blue	350.00
Butter dish, cov., marigold	250.00
Centerpiece bowl, footed, marigold, 12" d., 4" h.	80.00
Compote, 5" d., blue	62.50
Compote, 5" d., marigold	35.00
Creamer, footed, blue	80.00
Creamer, footed, purple	50.00
Creamer, individual size, blue	45.00
Creamer, individual size, marigold ..	37.50
Creamer, individual size, purple	75.00
Creamer, individual size, white	85.00
Creamer & sugar bowl, footed, blue, pr.	100.00
Dish, ice cream, footed, blue	38.00
Dish, ice cream, footed, marigold ...	50.00
Goblet, amber	62.50
Goblet, aqua	110.00
Goblet, blue	75.00
Goblet, green	190.00
Goblet, marigold	48.00
Hatpin holder, blue .... 275.00 to	300.00
Hatpin holder, green	800.00
Hatpin holder, marigold	239.00
Hatpin holder, purple	250.00
Loving cup, blue	225.00
Loving cup, green	350.00
Loving cup, marigold ...... 175.00 to	200.00
Loving cup, purple	400.00
Mug, amber	114.00
Mug, Amberina	395.00
Mug, aqua	163.00
Mug, blue	45.00
Mug, green	850.00
Mug, lavender	135.00
Mug, lime green	500.00
Mug, lime green w/vaseline base ..	150.00
Mug, marigold	30.00
Mug, marigold, souvenir	75.00
Mug, marigold w/aqua base	75.00
Mug, marigold w/blue base	157.00

Mug, marigold w/vaseline base 150.00
Mug, purple 80.00
Mug, red 330.00
Mug, sapphire blue............... 350.00
Mug, smoky blue.................. 155.00
Mug, vaseline.................... 100.00
Mug, white 1,000.00
Plate, 9" d., flat, blue .....350.00 to 400.00
Plate, 9" d., flat, clambroth 175.00
Plate, 9" d., flat, green 2,000.00
Plate, 9" d., flat, marigold 175.00
Plate, 9" d., flat, pastel marigold ... 140.00
Plate, 9" d., flat, teal blue 375.00
Plate, 9" d., flat, white 210.00
Plate, 9" d., flat, Beaded Berry ex-
    terior, blue 550.00
Plate, 9" d., trunk center, flat,
    Beaded Berry exterior, marigold .. 185.00
Plate, 9" d., trunk center,
    white ....250.00 to 275.00
Plate, 9" d., Blackberry exterior,
    "Souvenir of Hershey," blue 245.00
Powder jar, cov., blue 104.00
Powder jar, cov., green............ 412.00
Powder jar, cov., marigold 65.00
Powder jar, cov., purple 160.00
Punch bowl & base, blue, 2 pcs. 255.00
Punch bowl & base, marigold,
    2 pcs. 153.00
Punch bowl & base, white,
    2 pcs.................700.00 to 800.00
Punch cup, blue 25.00
Punch cup, green 90.00
Punch cup, marigold............... 12.00
Punch cup, white.................. 35.00
Punch set: bowl, base & 4 cups;
    marigold, 6 pcs.................. 365.00
Punch set: bowl, base & 6 cups;
    blue, 8 pcs. ....500.00 to 600.00
Rose bowl, blue 84.00
Rose bowl, green 80.00
Rose bowl, marigold............... 58.00
Rose bowl, purple 95.00
Rose bowl, red ....900.00 to 1,200.00
Sauce dish, footed, blue 30.00
Sauce dish, footed, marigold 21.00
Sauce dish, footed, white 65.00
Shaving mug, amber 125.00
Shaving mug, Amberina 450.00
Shaving mug, blue 50.00
Shaving mug, clambroth 35.00
Shaving mug, green 850.00
Shaving mug, marigold............. 28.00
Shaving mug, marigold, large 125.00
Shaving mug, purple 265.00
Shaving mug, red 650.00
Shaving mug, vaseline............. 110.00
Spooner, marigold................. 50.00
Sugar bowl, cov., blue 60.00
Sugar bowl, cov., marigold......... 110.00
Sugar bowl, cov., white........... 100.00
Sugar bowl, open, individual size,
    marigold 40.00

Sugar bowl, open, individual size,
    purple 52.00
Sugar bowl, open, individual size,
    white 75.00
Tumbler, blue..................... 44.00
Tumbler, clambroth................ 55.00
Tumbler, marigold................. 45.00
Tumbler, pastel marigold 49.00
Tumbler, purple................... 30.00
Tumbler, white.................... 100.00
Wine, aqua 300.00
Wine, blue 52.00
Wine, clambroth 65.00
Wine, marigold 25.00

ORIENTAL POPPY (Northwood)
Pitcher, water, green 1,250.00
Pitcher, water, marigold 325.00
Pitcher, water, purple 634.00
Pitcher, water, white.....895.00 to 1,200.00
Tumbler, blue..................... 200.00
Tumbler, green 60.00
Tumbler, ice blue 155.00
Tumbler, ice green 475.00
Tumbler, lilac 39.00
Tumbler, marigold................. 40.00
Tumbler, pastel marigold 45.00
Tumbler, purple................... 45.00
Tumbler, white.................... 135.00
Water set: pitcher & 1 tumbler;
    white, 2 pcs. 1,900.00
Water set: pitcher & 4 tumblers;
    green, 5 pcs...................1,470.00
Water set: pitcher & 6 tumblers; ice
    blue, 7 pcs. 5,000.00
Water set: pitcher & 6 tumblers; ice
    green, 7 pcs...................4,000.00
Water set: pitcher & 6 tumblers;
    purple, 7 pcs. 1,600.00

PALM BEACH (U.S. Glass Co.)
Bowl, 8½" d., marigold........... 50.00
Butter dish, cov., white 250.00
Creamer, marigold 68.00
Pitcher, water, marigold 450.00
Pitcher, water, white............. 700.00
Rose bowl, amber................. 125.00
Rose bowl, white.................. 75.00
Rose bowl, w/Gooseberry interior,
    white 225.00
Sauce dish, marigold 30.00
Sauce dish, white................. 48.00
Spooner, marigold................. 80.00
Spooner, white.................... 125.00
Sugar bowl, cov., marigold........ 75.00
Table set, white, 4 pcs. 975.00
Tumbler, amber................... 175.00
Tumbler, white................... 125.00
Whimsey banana boat, marigold,
    6" ....75.00 to 90.00
Whimsey banana boat, purple, 6"... 120.00
Whimsey vase, white 190.00

**PANELED DANDELION - See Dandelion,
Paneled Pattern**

PANSY and PANSY SPRAY

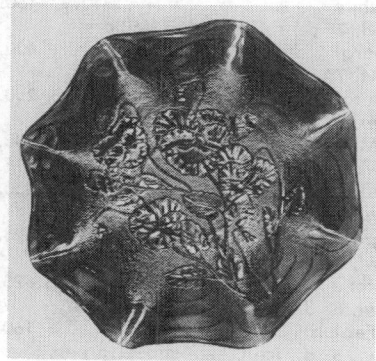

Pansy Bowl

Bowl, 8" to 9" d., amber 50.00
Bowl, 8" to 9" d., green 42.00
Bowl, 8" to 9" d., marigold 38.00
Bowl, 8" to 9" d., purple 90.00
Bowl, 9" d., fluted, marigold 65.00
Bowl, 9" d., fluted, purple (ILLUS.) . . 75.00
Bowl, 9" d., stippled, purple 45.00
Bowl, 9" d., ruffled, smoky 95.00
Breakfast set: individual size cream-
   er & sugar bowl; purple, pr. 35.00
Compote, white 160.00
Creamer, amber 85.00
Creamer, green 55.00
Creamer, marigold 25.00
Creamer, purple 38.00
Creamer & sugar bowl, marigold,
   pr. 60.00
Creamer & sugar bowl, purple,
   pr. . . . . .100.00 to 125.00
Dresser tray, green 55.00
Dresser tray, marigold 40.00
Nappy, green 45.00
Nappy, marigold 25.00
Nappy, purple 60.00
Pickle (or relish) dish, amber,
   6 x 9" 48.00
Pickle (or relish) dish, aqua opales-
   cent, 6 x 9" 425.00
Pickle (or relish) dish, blue, 6 x 9" . . 60.00
Pickle (or relish) dish, clambroth,
   6 x 9" 30.00
Pickle (or relish) dish, green,
   6 x 9" 42.00
Pickle (or relish) dish, marigold,
   6 x 9" 30.00
Pickle (or relish) dish, purple,
   6 x 9" 55.00
Pickle (or relish) dish, smoky,
   6 x 9" 55.00
Plate, 9" d., ruffled, marigold 75.00
Plate, 9" d., ruffled, purple 85.00
Plate, 9" d., ruffled, smoky 65.00
Spooner, green 35.00
Sugar bowl, amber 35.00
Sugar bowl, aqua 110.00

Sugar bowl, green 55.00
Sugar bowl, marigold 18.00
Sugar bowl, breakfast size, purple . . 54.00

PANTHER (Fenton)
Berry set: master bowl & 4 sauce
   dishes; marigold, 5 pcs. 325.00
Bowl, 5" d., footed, aqua 425.00
Bowl, 5" d., footed, blue 85.00
Bowl, 5" d., footed, clambroth 35.00
Bowl, 5" d., footed, green 90.00
Bowl, 5" d., footed, marigold 52.00
Bowl, 5" d., footed, red . . 900.00 to 1,000.00
Bowl, 9" d., claw-footed, blue 350.00
Bowl, 9" d., claw-footed,
   green . . . . .525.00 to 625.00
Bowl, 9" d., claw-footed, marigold . . 150.00
Bowl, 9" d., claw-footed, white 750.00
Bowl, berry, Butterfly & Berry ex-
   terior, marigold 35.00
Bowl, low, marigold 300.00
Centerpiece bowl, mari-
   gold . . . . .575.00 to 600.00

PEACOCK & GRAPE (Fenton)
Bowl, 8" d., collared base, amber . . 120.00
Bowl, 8" d., collared base, blue 53.00
Bowl, 8" d., collared base, ruffled,
   green 75.00
Bowl, 8" d., collared base, ruffled,
   ice green 225.00
Bowl, 8" d., collared base, mari-
   gold 40.00
Bowl, 8" d., collared base, peach
   opalescent 580.00
Bowl, 8" d., collared base, purple . . 72.00
Bowl, 8" d., collared base, ruffled,
   red 1,200.00
Bowl, 8" d., collared base, smoky . . 585.00
Bowl, 8" d., collared base, vase-
   line 275.00
Bowl, 8" d., collared base, ribbon
   candy rim, blue 80.00
Bowl, 8" d., collared base, ribbon
   candy rim, lavender 75.00
Bowl, 8" d., spatula-footed, blue . . . 50.00
Bowl, 8" d., spatula-footed, green . . 72.00
Bowl, 8" d., spatula-footed, ice
   green opalescent 418.00
Bowl, 8" d., spatula-footed,
   lavender 200.00
Bowl, 8" d., spatula-footed,
   marigold 60.00
Bowl, 8" d., spatula-footed, milk
   white w/marigold overlay 360.00
Bowl, 8" d., spatula-footed, peach
   opalescent . . . . .325.00 to 350.00
Bowl, 8" d., spatula-footed, purple . . 68.00
Bowl, 8" d., spatula-footed, red 934.00
Bowl, 8" d., spatula-footed, smoky . . 90.00
Bowl, 8" d., spatula-footed, vase-
   line 125.00
Bowl, 8" d., spatula-footed, vaseline
   opalescent 450.00

Bowl, ice cream shape, Amberina .. 650.00
Bowl, 8" d., ice cream shape,
  green 85.00
Bowl, 8" d., ice cream shape,
  marigold 90.00
Bowl, 8" d., ice cream shape, red ..1,650.00
Bowl, ice cream shape, collared
  base, vaseline 185.00
Bowl, 9" d., ruffled, collared base,
  blue 70.00
Bowl, 9" d., ruffled, purple......... 75.00
Bowl, 9" d., ruffled, red 300.00
Bowl, ruffled, iridized moonstone ... 325.00
Plate, 9" d., collared base, blue 325.00
Plate, 9" d., collared base, mari-
  gold 275.00
Plate, 9" d., collared base, berry ex-
  terior, smoky ice blue 800.00
Plate, 9" d., spatula-footed,
  green ....150.00 to 175.00
Plate, 9" d., spatula-footed,
  marigold 350.00
Plate, 9" d., spatula-footed, pur-
  ple 260.00

PEACOCK & URN (Millersburg Peacock)

Peacock & Urn Bowl

Berry set: master bowl & 5 sauce
  dishes; purple, 6 pcs.....750.00 to 850.00
Bowl, 5½" d., ruffled, blue (Millers-
  burg)........................1,240.00
Bowl, 6" d., ice cream shape, blue,
  stippled 175.00
Bowl, 6" d., ice cream shape, green
  (Millersburg)................... 175.00
Bowl, 6" d., ice cream shape, mari-
  gold (Millersburg) 75.00
Bowl, 6" d., ice cream shape, mari-
  gold (Northwood) 50.00
Bowl, 6" d., ice cream shape, pur-
  ple 75.00
Bowl, 6" d., ice cream shape, purple
  (Millersburg)................... 162.00
Bowl, 6" d., ice cream shape, purple
  satin 195.00

Bowl, 6" d., ice cream shape,
  white 150.00
Bowl, 7" d., ruffled, blue (Millers-
  burg) 400.00
Bowl, 7" d., ruffled, green (Millers-
  burg) 250.00
Bowl, 7" d., ruffled, marigold
  (Millersburg) 288.00
Bowl, 7" d., ruffled, purple (Millers-
  burg) 350.00
Bowl, 7½" d., "shotgun," ruffled,
  green 425.00
Bowl, 8" d., collared base, moon-
  stone 1,825.00
Bowl, 8" d., ice cream shape, blue
  (Fenton) 160.00
Bowl, 8" d., ice cream shape, green
  (Fenton) 200.00
Bowl, 8" d., ice cream shape, ice
  blue 350.00
Bowl, 8" d., ice cream shape, mari-
  gold (Fenton) 108.00
Bowl, 8" d., ice cream shape,
  white 350.00
Bowl, 8" to 9" d., blue (Fenton)..... 214.00
Bowl, 8" to 9" d., green (Fenton) ... 300.00
Bowl, 8" to 9" d., green (Millers-
  burg) ....400.00 to 425.00
Bowl, 8" to 9" d., marigold (Fen-
  ton).......................... 94.00
Bowl, 8" to 9" d., ruffled, marigold
  (Millersburg)..........200.00 to 250.00
Bowl, 8" to 9" d., purple (Fenton)... 180.00
Bowl, 8" to 9" d., purple (Millers-
  burg) 275.00
Bowl, 8" to 9" d., white (Fenton) ... 165.00
Bowl, 9" d., ruffled, blue ..175.00 to 200.00
Bowl, 9" d., ruffled, purple (Fen-
  ton).......................... 400.00
Bowl, 9" d., ruffled, vaseline 675.00
Bowl, 9½" d., berry, purple (Millers-
  burg) 525.00
Bowl, 10" d., fluted, green (Millers-
  burg) 400.00
Bowl, 10" d., fluted, lavender
  (Millersburg).................. 600.00
Bowl, 10" d., fluted, marigold
  (Millersburg).................. 275.00
Bowl, 10" d., ruffled, marigold 150.00
Bowl, 10" d., ruffled, purple........ 492.00
Bowl, ice cream, 10" d., aqua
  opalescent.................... 950.00
Bowl, ice cream, 10" d., blue
  (Northwood) 625.00
Bowl, ice cream, 10" d., blue, stip-
  pled 1,250.00
Bowl, ice cream, 10" d., electric
  blue (Northwood)..............1,450.00
Bowl, ice cream, 10" d., green
  (Northwood)..................2,500.00
Bowl, ice cream, 10" d., green,
  w/bee (Millersburg) 795.00
Bowl, ice cream, 10" d., ice blue
  (Northwood) 900.00

Bowl, ice cream, 10" d., ice green
(Northwood) ....1,200.00 to 1,300.00
Bowl, ice cream, 10" d., marigold
(Millersburg) 375.00
Bowl, ice cream, 10" d., marigold
(Northwood) 443.00
Bowl, ice cream, 10" d., pastel mari-
gold (Northwood) ......650.00 to 700.00
Bowl, ice cream, 10" d., purple
(Millersburg) 465.00
Bowl, ice cream, 10" d., purple,
Northwood (ILLUS.) ......550.00 to 575.00
Bowl, ice cream, 10" d., smoky
(Northwood) 900.00
Bowl, ice cream, 10" d., white
(Northwood) ....575.00 to 600.00
Bowl, 10½" d., ruffled, green
(Millersburg)...........375.00 to 400.00
Bowl, 10½" d., ruffled, marigold
(Millersburg) 250.00
Bowl, 10½" d., ruffled, pur-
ple ....225.00 to 250.00
Bowl, 10½" d., ruffled, purple
(Millersburg)...........400.00 to 450.00
Compote, 5½" d., 5" h., aqua (Fen-
ton)............................ 325.00
Compote, 5½" d., 5" h., blue (Fen-
ton)............................ 100.00
Compote, 5½" d., 5" h., green (Fen-
ton)............................ 230.00
Compote, 5½" d., 5" h., ice green
(Fenton) 135.00
Compote, 5½" d., 5" h., marigold
(Fenton) 50.00
Compote, 5½" d., 5" h., marigold
over ice blue (Fenton) 85.00
Compote, 5½" d., 5" h., red (Fen-
ton)............................ 800.00
Compote, 5½" d., 5" h., vaseline
(Fenton) 150.00
Compote, 5½" d., 5" h., white (Fen-
ton)..................250.00 to 300.00
Compote, green (Millersburg
Giant) 1,350.00
Compote, marigold (Millersburg
Giant) 1,900.00
Compote, purple (Millersburg
Giant) 3,000.00
Goblet, marigold (Fenton).......... 50.00
Ice cream dish, purple, 5¾" d.
(Millersburg)...........350.00 to 400.00
Ice cream dish, aqua opalescent,
small (Northwood) 1,500.00
Ice cream dish, blue, stippled, small
(Northwood) 145.00
Ice cream dish, blue, small (North-
wood) 82.50
Ice cream dish, electric blue,
small 175.00
Ice cream dish, green, small 145.00
Ice cream dish, ice blue, small 600.00
Ice cream dish, ice green, small 425.00
Ice cream dish, lavender, small
(Northwood) 225.00

Ice cream dish, marigold, small 85.00
Ice cream dish, purple, small....... 86.00
Ice cream dish, white, small 150.00
Ice cream set: large bowl &
6 small dishes; marigold,
7 pcs..................650.00 to 700.00
Ice cream set: large bowl & 6 small
dishes; purple, 7 pcs. (Millers-
burg) ....800.00 to 1,000.00
Plate, 6½" d., green 3,600.00
Plate, 6½" d., marigold 155.00
Plate, 6½" d., purple........... 500.00
Plate, 6½" d., white 350.00
Plate, 9" d., blue............. 550.00
Plate, 9" d., green.............1,000.00
Plate, 9" d., marigold 408.00
Plate, 9" d., white ......450.00 to 500.00
Plate, chop, 11" d., marigold
(Millersburg) 2,200.00
Plate, chop, 11" d., marigold (North-
wood)........................ 995.00
Plate, chop, 11" d., purple (Millers-
burg) 2,700.00
Plate, chop, 11" d., purple (North-
wood)...............1,200.00 to 1,400.00
Sauce dish, blue (Millersburg) 250.00
Sauce dish, blue (Northwood) 120.00
Sauce dish, green (Millersburg) 75.00
Sauce dish, ice blue, 6" d. 70.00
Sauce dish, ice green, 6" d. (North-
wood)........................ 415.00
Sauce dish, lavender (Millersburg) .. 45.00
Sauce dish, marigold (Northwood) .. 50.00
Sauce dish, purple (Millersburg) .. 116.00
Sauce dish, purple (Northwood) 65.00
Sauce dish, white (Northwood) 185.00
Whimsey sauce dish, marigold,
5¼" d. (Millersburg)............. 175.00
Whimsey sauce dish, purple,
5¼" d.................275.00 to 300.00

PEACOCK AT FOUNTAIN (Northwood)

Peacock at Fountain Punch Set

Berry set: master bowl & 4 sauce
dishes; purple, 5 pcs............. 450.00
Berry set: master bowl & 6 sauce
dishes; blue, 7 pcs............... 600.00
Bowl, master berry, blue 325.00
Bowl, master berry, green 600.00

Bowl, master berry, ice blue 380.00
Bowl, master berry, marigold 150.00
Bowl, master berry, purple 200.00
Bowl, master berry, white 250.00
Bowl, orange, three-footed, aqua
   opalescent 1,100.00
Bowl, orange, three-footed, blue ... 1,000.00
Bowl, orange, three-footed,
   lavender 525.00
Bowl, orange, three-footed,
   marigold 200.00
Bowl, orange, three-footed, pur-
   ple ....300.00 to 350.00
Butter dish, cov., green 500.00
Butter dish, cov., marigold 210.00
Butter dish, cov., purple 288.00
Compote, aqua opalescent 3,100.00
Compote, blue 537.00
Compote, ice blue 1,200.00
Compote, ice green 1,400.00
Compote, marigold 400.00
Compote, purple 800.00
Compote, white ....550.00 to 650.00
Creamer, marigold 65.00
Creamer, purple 125.00
Pitcher, water, blue 450.00
Pitcher, water, ice blue 1,600.00
Pitcher, water, marigold 250.00
Pitcher, water, purple 305.00
Pitcher, water, white 775.00
Punch bowl & base, blue,
   2 pcs. .... 1,000.00 to 1,200.00
Punch bowl & base, ice blue,
   2 pcs. 6,700.00
Punch bowl & base, ice green,
   2 pcs. 9,500.00
Punch bowl & base, marigold,
   2 pcs. 900.00
Punch bowl & base, purple, 2 pcs. .. 725.00
Punch cup, aqua opalescent 1,400.00
Punch cup, blue 50.00
Punch cup, electric blue 95.00
Punch cup, ice blue 125.00
Punch cup, ice green 525.00
Punch cup, lavender 88.00
Punch cup, marigold 32.00
Punch cup, purple 38.00
Punch cup, white 75.00
Punch set: bowl, base & 2 cups;
   marigold, 4 pcs. 625.00
Punch set: bowl, base & 5 cups; ice
   green, 7 pcs. 10,750.00
Punch set: bowl, base & 6 cups; ice
   blue, 8 pcs. 7,000.00
Punch set: bowl, base & 6 cups;
   white, 8 pcs. (ILLUS.) 6,000.00
Sauce dish, blue 40.00
Sauce dish, ice blue 100.00
Sauce dish, marigold 21.00
Sauce dish, purple 31.00
Sauce dish, white 50.00
Spooner, blue 150.00
Spooner, ice blue 260.00
Spooner, marigold 76.00

Spooner, purple 90.00
Spooner, white 175.00
Sugar bowl, cov., ice blue 265.00
Sugar bowl, cov., marigold 85.00
Table set, marigold, 4 pcs. 475.00
Table set, purple, 4 pcs. ...450.00 to 500.00
Tumbler, amber 89.00
Tumbler, blue 50.00
Tumbler, green ....300.00 to 350.00
Tumbler, ice blue ....400.00 to 425.00
Tumbler, lavender 125.00
Tumbler, marigold 45.00
Tumbler, purple 55.00
Tumbler, teal blue 139.00
Tumbler, white 232.00
Water set: pitcher & 5 tumblers;
   marigold, 6 pcs. 500.00
Water set: pitcher & 6 tumblers;
   blue, 7 pcs. 775.00
Water set: pitcher & 6 tumblers;
   purple, 7 pcs. 900.00

PEACOCK, FLUFFY (Fenton)
Pitcher, water, green 750.00
Pitcher, water, purple .....575.00 to 600.00
Tumbler, blue 85.00
Tumbler, green 75.00
Tumbler, marigold 63.00
Tumbler, purple 75.00
Tumbler, violet 75.00

PEACOCKS ON FENCE (Northwood Peacocks)
Bowl, 8" to 9" d., aqua opales-
   cent ....1,000.00 to 1,100.00
Bowl, 8" to 9" d., electric blue 995.00
Bowl, 8" to 9" d., piecrust rim, aqua
   opalescent 3,000.00
Bowl, 8" to 9" d., piecrust rim,
   blue 485.00
Bowl, 8" to 9" d., piecrust rim, blue,
   stippled w/ribbed back 795.00
Bowl, 8" to 9" d., piecrust rim,
   green ....1,600.00 to 1,800.00
Bowl, 8" to 9" d., piecrust rim, elec-
   tric blue 695.00
Bowl, 8" to 9" d., piecrust rim, ice
   blue 1,675.00
Bowl, 8" to 9" d., piecrust rim, ice
   green 1,850.00
Bowl, 8" to 9" d., piecrust rim,
   lavender 550.00
Bowl, 8" to 9" d., piecrust rim,
   marigold 275.00
Bowl, 8" to 9" d., piecrust rim, stippled, marigold 425.00
Bowl, 8" to 9" d., piecrust rim, pastel marigold ....300.00 to 325.00
Bowl, 8" to 9" d., piecrust rim,
   purple 500.00
Bowl, 8" to 9" d., piecrust rim,
   white 850.00
Bowl, 8" to 9" d., ruffled rim, aqua
   opalescent 650.00

Bowl, 8" to 9" d., ruffled rim, blue . . 525.00
Bowl, 8" to 9" d., ruffled rim,
green . . . . .1,000.00 to 1,100.00
Bowl, 8" to 9" d., ruffled rim, ice
blue 1,750.00
Bowl, 8" to 9" d., ruffled rim, ice
green 1,400.00
Bowl, 8" to 9" d., ruffled rim,
marigold 200.00
Bowl, 8" to 9" d., ruffled rim, pur-
ple 360.00
Bowl, 8" to 9" d., ruffled rim,
smoky 2,500.00
Bowl, 8" to 9" d., ruffled rim,
white 650.00
Bowl, 9" d., stippled, green 1,100.00
Bowl, ruffled, lime green opales-
cent 4,000.00
Bowl, ruffled, ribbed back, white . . . 875.00
Plate, 8" d., blue . . . . .700.00 to 750.00
Plate, 9" d., stippled, cobalt
blue . . . . .650.00 to 700.00
Plate, 9" d., electric blue 1,050.00
Plate, 9" d., green . . . . .1,550.00 to 1,650.00
Plate, 9" d., ice blue . . .1,650.00 to 1,750.00
Plate, 9" d., ice green 450.00
Plate, 9" d., lavender . .1,100.00 to 1,200.00
Plate, 9" d., marigold 456.00
Plate, 9" d., stippled, mari-
gold . . . . .450.00 to 500.00
Plate, 9" d., purple . . . . . . .625.00 to 650.00
Plate, 9" d., white 470.00
Plate, 9" d., white, decorated 1,100.00

PERSIAN GARDEN (Dugan)

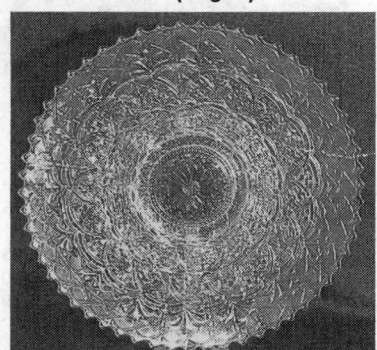

Persian Garden Chop Plate

Berry set: 11½" d. fruit bowl &
4 sauce dishes; peach opalescent,
5 pcs. 650.00
Bowl, 5" d., peach opalescent 45.00
Bowl, 5" d., white 83.00
Bowl, 9" d., ruffled, marigold 150.00
Bowl, ice cream, 11" d., lavender
tint 345.00
Bowl, ice cream, 11" d., peach
opalescent . . . . .850.00 to 900.00
Bowl, ice cream, 11" d., purple 800.00
Bowl, ice cream, 11" d., white 250.00

Fruit bowl (no base), peach opales-
cent, 11½" d. 350.00
Fruit bowl (no base), white,
11½" d. 250.00
Fruit bowl & base, marigold,
2 pcs. 275.00
Fruit bowl & base, peach opales-
cent, 2 pcs. 650.00
Fruit bowl & base, purple, 2 pcs. . . 800.00
Fruit bowl & base, white, 2 pcs. 500.00
Hair receiver, blue 115.00
Hair receiver, marigold 75.00
Plate, 6" to 7" d., marigold 92.00
Plate, 6" to 7" d., pastel marigold . . 50.00
Plate, 6" to 7" d., peach opales-
cent 260.00
Plate, 6" to 7" d., white 130.00
Plate, 9" d., marigold 125.00
Plate, chop, 11" d., purple 5,500.00
Plate, chop, 11" d., white (ILLUS.) . . 900.00

PETER RABBIT (Fenton)

Peter Rabbit Bowl

Bowl, 8" d., blue 1,100.00
Bowl, 8" d., green . . . . . . .850.00 to 900.00
Bowl, 8" d., marigold (ILLUS.) 1,550.00

PINE CONE (Fenton)

Bowl, 5" d., aqua 75.00
Bowl, 5" d., blue 45.00
Bowl, 5" d., marigold 40.00
Bowl, 5" d., purple 35.00
Bowl, 6" d., ruffled, blue 45.00
Bowl, 6" d., marigold 27.00
Bowl, 7" d., ruffled, blue 50.00
Bowl, 7" d., ruffled, green 35.00
Bowl, 7" d., marigold 30.00
Bowl, 7" d., ruffled, purple 40.00
Plate, 5" d., aqua 95.00
Plate, 6½" d., amber 400.00
Plate, 6½" d., blue 87.00
Plate, 6½" d., green 225.00
Plate, 6½" d., marigold 50.00
Plate, 6½" d., purple 110.00
Plate, 7½" d., amber 425.00
Plate, 7½" d., blue 150.00
Plate, 7½" d., marigold 100.00

Plate, 7½" d., purple 65.00
Plate, 7¾" d., blue 225.00

PIPE HUMIDOR (Millersburg)

Pipe Humidor

Green (ILLUS.) 6,500.00
Marigold 5,000.00

PODS & POSIES or FOUR FLOWERS (Dugan)

Pods & Posies Plate

Bowl, 6" d., peach opalescent 68.00
Bowl, 6" d., purple 55.00
Bowl, 8" to 9" d., green 160.00
Bowl, 8" to 9" d., marigold 45.00
Bowl, 8" to 9" d., purple 50.00
Bowl, 10" d., peach opales-
   cent . . . . 150.00 to 175.00
Bowl, 10" d., purple 145.00
Plate, 6" d., green 350.00
Plate, 6" d., peach opalescent 175.00
Plate, 6" d., purple 295.00
Plate, 6" to 7" d., w/exterior pat-
   tern, peach opalescent 102.00
Plate, 9" d., green 575.00
Plate, 9" d., purple (ILLUS.) 500.00
Plate, chop, 11" d., peach opales-
   cent . . . . 450.00 to 500.00
Plate, chop, 11" d., purple 750.00

POINSETTIA (Imperial)

Poinsettia Pitcher

Pitcher, milk, green 245.00
Pitcher, milk, marigold (ILLUS.) 108.00
Pitcher, milk, smoky 135.00

POLO
Ashtray, marigold 35.00

PONY

Pony Bowl

Bowl, 8" to 9" d., aqua . . . . 450.00 to 500.00
Bowl, 8" to 9" d., ice green 896.00
Bowl, 8" to 9" d., marigold
   (ILLUS.) 65.00
Bowl, 8" to 9" d., purple . . . 200.00 to 250.00
Plate, marigold 275.00

POPPY (Millersburg)
Compote, green 500.00
Compote, marigold 375.00
Compote, purple . . . . 800.00 to 850.00

POPPY (Northwood)
Pickle dish, amber 225.00
Pickle dish, aqua opalescent 1,200.00
Pickle dish, blue 146.00
Pickle dish, green 325.00
Pickle dish, ice blue 700.00
Pickle dish, marigold 110.00
Pickle dish, pastel marigold 50.00
Pickle dish, purple . . . . 200.00 to 250.00
Pickle dish, white . . . . 450.00 to 500.00

POPPY SHOW (Northwood)
Bowl, 8" to 9" d., aqua opales-
cent 18,500.00
Bowl, 8" to 9" d., blue . . . . .550.00 to 600.00
Bowl, 8" to 9" d., electric
blue . . . . .500.00 to 1,000.00
Bowl, 8" to 9" d., green 1,300.00
Bowl, 8" to 9" d., ice blue 1,800.00
Bowl, 8" to 9" d., ice green 1,950.00
Bowl, 8" to 9" d., mari-
gold . . . . .525.00 to 600.00
Bowl, 8" to 9" d., purple 650.00
Bowl, 8" to 9" d., white 375.00
Plate, blue 3,000.00
Plate, electric blue 1,750.00
Plate, green 5,800.00
Plate, ice blue . . . . .1,600.00 to 2,000.00
Plate, ice green . . . . .3,800.00 to 4,200.00
Plate, marigold 725.00
Plate, pastel marigold 1,000.00
Plate, purple . . . . .1,200.00 to 1,400.00
Plate, white 600.00

PRIMROSE BOWL (Millersburg)
Blue 2,400.00
Green 116.00
Marigold 72.00
Purple 113.00

PUZZLE
Bonbon, marigold 36.00
Bonbon, stemmed, peach opales-
cent 55.00
Bonbon, white 65.00
Compote, marigold 25.00
Compote, peach opalescent 65.00
Compote, purple 58.00

QUESTION MARKS
Bonbon, footed, marigold, 6" d.,
3¾" h. 38.00
Bonbon, footed, peach opalescent,
6" d., 3¾" h. 80.00
Bonbon, footed, purple, 6" d.,
3¾" h. 45.00
Bonbon, footed, white, 6" d.,
3¾" h. 130.00
Bonbon, stemmed, marigold 20.00
Bonbon, stemmed, peach opales-
cent 45.00
Bonbon, stemmed, purple 60.00
Bonbon, stemmed, white 48.00
Compote, crimped edge, marigold . .   45.00
Compote, crimped edge, peach
opalescent 83.00
Plate, dome-footed, Georgia Peach
exterior, purple 250.00
Plate, stemmed, marigold 80.00
Plate, stemmed, white 325.00

QUILL (Dugan or Diamond Glass Co.)
Pitcher, water, marigold 2,500.00
Pitcher, water, purple (ILLUS.) 950.00

Quill Pitcher

Tumbler, blue 40.00
Tumbler, marigold 250.00
Tumbler, pastel marigold 195.00
Tumbler, purple 300.00
Water set: pitcher & 6 tumblers;
purple, 7 pcs. 4,000.00

RASPBERRY (Northwood)
Pitcher, milk, green 260.00
Pitcher, milk, ice blue 1,900.00
Pitcher, milk, marigold 125.00
Pitcher, milk, purple 290.00
Pitcher, milk, white . . . .1,000.00 to 1,200.00
Pitcher, water, green . . . . . .275.00 to 295.00
Pitcher, water, ice blue 2,100.00
Pitcher, water, marigold 125.00
Pitcher, water, purple . . . . .225.00 to 250.00
Sauceboat, green 225.00
Sauceboat, marigold 70.00
Sauceboat, purple 80.00
Tumbler, green 60.00
Tumbler, ice blue . . . . .275.00 to 300.00
Tumbler, ice green . . . . . . .550.00 to 650.00
Tumbler, marigold 35.00
Tumbler, purple 42.00
Tumbler, white 675.00
Water set: pitcher & 4 tumblers;
purple, 5 pcs. 450.00
Water set: pitcher & 6 tumblers;
marigold, 7 pcs. 335.00

RIPPLE VASE
Amber, 7½" h. 58.00
Amber, 10" h.   60.00
Amber, 11½" h. 75.00
Amber, 15¼" h. 81.00
Aqua, 12" h. 78.00
Green, 6" h. 95.00
Green, 13" h.   45.00
Green, 14½" h. 75.00
Green, 18¾" h. 163.00
Marigold, 5" h. 70.00
Marigold, 6" h. . . . . .100.00 to 150.00
Marigold, 6½" h. 55.00
Marigold, 8" h. 35.00
Marigold, 9½" h. 30.00

Marigold, 10½" h. 40.00
Marigold, 12" h. 50.00
Marigold, 15" h. 45.00
Marigold, 16½" h., funeral........ 50.00
Marigold, 17" h. 65.00
Marigold, 20" h. ....150.00 to 200.00
Purple, 10" h. 45.00
Purple, 11" h. 55.00
Smoky, 12" h. 95.00
Teal blue, 10½" h. 100.00
White, 8" h. 155.00

ROBIN (Imperial)

Robin Mug

Mug, green w/marigold overlay,
    green base 50.00
Mug, marigold (ILLUS.)............. 42.00
Mug, smoky 275.00
Mug, smoky w/marigold overlay ... 158.00
Pitcher, water, marigold 300.00
Tumbler, marigold................ 40.00

ROCOCO

Bowl, 6" d., dome-footed, mari-
    gold 20.00
Bowl, 8¼" d., dome-footed, ice
    cream shape, marigold 160.00
Candy dish, smoky 45.00
Vase, marigold 108.00
Vase, smoky.................... 145.00

ROSE SHOW

Rose Show Plate

Bowl, 9" d., amber 750.00

Bowl, 9" d., aqua ....650.00 to 750.00
Bowl, 9" d., aqua opalescent 1,400.00
Bowl, 9" d., blue 566.00
Bowl, 9" d., blue opales-
    cent ....1,500.00 to 1,950.00
Bowl, 9" d., electric blue 1,250.00
Bowl, 9" d., green ....3,000.00 to 4,000.00
Bowl, 9" d., ice blue 1,600.00
Bowl, 9" d., ice green ..1,500.00 to 2,000.00
Bowl, 9" d., ice green opalescent ..2,150.00
Bowl, 9" d., lavender 3,500.00
Bowl, 9" d., marigold 552.00
Bowl, 9" d., purple 1,275.00
Bowl, 9" d., sapphire blue 3,200.00
Bowl, 9" d., smoky 1,100.00
Bowl, 9" d., white........350.00 to 400.00
Plate, 9" d., aqua opalescent 8,000.00
Plate, 9" d., blue (ILLUS.)..........1,200.00
Plate, 9" d., clambroth 1,350.00
Plate, 9" d., custard 4,500.00
Plate, 9" d., electric green 7,500.00
Plate, 9" d., green...............3,600.00
Plate, 9" d., ice blue ...1,800.00 to 2,000.00
Plate, 9" d., marigold .....650.00 to 750.00
Plate, 9" d., moonstone 7,000.00
Plate, 9" d., pastel mari-
    gold ....1,000.00 to 1,500.00
Plate, 9" d., purple 1,500.00
Plate, 9" d., vaseline 3,400.00
Plate, 9" d., white 500.00

ROSETTE

Bowl, 7" d., purple 35.00
Bowl, footed, green 110.00
Bowl, footed, purple (Northwood) .. 85.00

RUSTIC VASE

Blue, 9" h.................... 60.00
Blue, 10½" h................. 35.00
Blue, 11" h................. 45.00
Blue, 16" h. ....100.00 to 150.00
Blue, funeral, 18" h. 500.00
Blue, funeral, 19½" h. 795.00
Blue, elephant base 425.00
Green, 14" h.................. 45.00
Green, 16" h.................. 90.00
Lime green opalescent, 11" h. 600.00
Marigold, 9½" h. 75.00
Marigold, 11" h. 30.00
Marigold, 15" h. 80.00
Marigold, 16" to 20" h. 250.00
Marigold, funeral, 21½" h........... 300.00
Purple, 11" h.................. 50.00
Purple, 14" h.................. 90.00
Purple, 16" h.................. 195.00
Purple, 18½" h.................. 325.00
Purple, elephant base 400.00
Purple, funeral 1,050.00
Red, 10" h., crimped top 3,700.00
White, 6" h. 46.00
White, 8" h. 80.00
White, 12½" h. 60.00
White, 14" h. 160.00
White, 20" h. 410.00

SAILBOATS (Fenton)
Bowl, 5" d., amber 250.00
Bowl, 5" d., ruffled, Amberina 400.00
Bowl, 5" d., aqua 110.00
Bowl, 5" d., ruffled, blue 55.00
Bowl, 5" d., green 125.00
Bowl, 5" d., marigold 28.00
Bowl, 5" d., ice cream shape,
   marigold 50.00
Bowl, 5" d., purple 120.00
Bowl, 5" d., ruffled, red . . . 500.00 to 550.00
Bowl, 5" d., vaseline 175.00
Bowl, 6" d., ruffled, green 105.00
Bowl, 6" d., ruffled, marigold 32.00
Bowl, 6" d., Orange Tree exterior,
   marigold 60.00
Bowl, 6" d., ruffled, purple 150.00
Bowl, ruffled, vaseline 250.00
Compote, blue 220.00
Compote, marigold 65.00
Dish, square, marigold 115.00
Goblet, water, green . . . . . . 250.00 to 350.00
Goblet, water, marigold 128.00
Goblet, water, purple 300.00
Plate, 6" d., blue 195.00
Plate, 6" d., marigold . . . . . 400.00 to 425.00
Wine, blue 120.00
Wine, marigold 35.00

SCOTCH THISTLE COMPOTE
Blue 55.00
Green 70.00
Marigold 38.00
Purple 55.00

SCROLL EMBOSSED
Bowl, 5½" d., File exterior, pur-
   ple 25.00
Bowl, 7" d., aqua 85.00
Bowl, 7" d., purple 45.00
Bowl, 8" d., clambroth 35.00
Bowl, 8" to 9" d., aqua 60.00
Bowl, 8" to 9" d., green 39.00
Bowl, 8" to 9" d., marigold 40.00
Bowl, 8" to 9" d., pastel marigold . . 43.00
Bowl, 8" to 9" d., purple 45.00
Bowl, 8" to 9" d., ruffled, File ex-
   terior, purple 68.00
Compote, green 75.00
Compote, marigold 49.00
Compote, File exterior, marigold . . . 50.00
Compote, purple 76.00
Plate, 9" d., green . . . . 90.00 to 100.00
Plate, 9" d., marigold 125.00
Plate, 9" d., pastel marigold 125.00
Plate, 9" d., purple 265.00
Sauce dish, purple, 5½" d. 35.00
Sauce dish, ruffled, purple,
   5¾" d. 85.00

SEAWEED (Millersburg)
Bowl, 8½" d., ice cream shape,
   marigold 350.00

Bowl, 8¾" d., low, mari-
   gold . . . . .450.00 to 525.00
Bowl, 10" d., ruffled, green 275.00
Bowl, 10" d., ruffled, mari-
   gold . . . . .175.00 to 200.00
Bowl, 10" d., ruffled, pur-
   ple .300.00 to 350.00
Bowl, ice cream shape, green 1,650.00
Lamp, marigold 300.00

SHELL & JEWEL
Creamer, cov., green 40.00
Creamer, cov., marigold 25.00
Creamer & cov. sugar bowl, green,
   pr. 90.00
Sugar bowl, cov., marigold 35.00
Sugar bowl, open, green 11.00

SHELL & SAND

Shell & Sand Plate
Bowl, 7" d., purple 55.00
Bowl, 8" to 9" d., marigold 50.00
Bowl, 8" to 9" d., ruffled, purple . . . 69.00
Plate, purple .1,025.00
Plate, smoky (ILLUS.) 450.00
Tumbler, purple 50.00

SHIP & STARS PLATE
Marigold 31.00

SINGING BIRDS (Northwood)
Berry set: master bowl & 3 sauce
   dishes; green, 4 pcs. 132.00
Berry set: master bowl & 6 sauce
   dishes; purple, 7 pcs. 325.00
Bowl, ice cream shape, green 48.00
Bowl, ice cream shape, marigold . . . 48.00
Bowl, master berry, blue 225.00
Bowl, master berry, marigold 75.00
Butter dish, cov., green 230.00
Butter dish, cov., marigold 138.00
Butter dish, cov., purple 350.00
Creamer, green 150.00
Creamer, marigold 52.00
Creamer, purple . . . . 125.00 to 150.00
Mug, aqua opalescent 950.00
Mug, blue 175.00

Mug, stippled, blue 575.00
Mug, electric blue . . . . .150.00 to 200.00
Mug, green 250.00
Mug, stippled, green 424.00
Mug, ice blue . . . . .750.00 to 800.00
Mug, lavender 400.00
Mug, marigold 104.00
Mug, stippled, marigold . . .100.00 to 125.00
Mug, purple 96.00
Mug, purple, w/advertising, "Ama-
    zon Hotel" 125.00
Mug, purple, w/advertising, "Hotel
    Verdome" 133.00
Mug, white 585.00
Pitcher, green . . . . .275.00 to 325.00
Pitcher, marigold . . . . .250.00 to 275.00
Pitcher, purple . . . . .350.00 to 400.00
Sauce dish, blue 65.00
Sauce dish, electric blue 90.00
Sauce dish, green 28.00
Sauce dish, marigold 32.00
Sauce dish, purple 30.00
Spooner, green 150.00
Spooner, marigold 62.00
Sugar bowl, cov., green 185.00
Sugar bowl, cov., marigold 90.00
Table set: cov. butter dish, cov. sug-
    ar bowl, creamer & spooner; mar-
    igold, 4 pcs. 375.00
Table set, purple, 4 pcs. 750.00
Tumbler, amber 60.00
Tumbler, green 45.00
Tumbler, marigold 40.00
Tumbler, purple 55.00
Water set: pitcher & 6 tumblers;
    green, 7 pcs. 790.00
Water set: pitcher & 6 tumblers;
    marigold, 7 pcs. 510.00
Water set: pitcher & 6 tumblers;
    purple, 7 pcs. 795.00

SIX PETALS (Dugan)

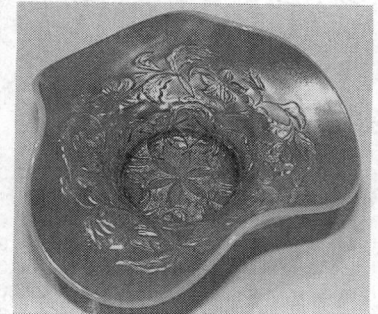

Six Petals Tricornered Bowl

Bowl, 7" d., crimped, peach
    opalescent 35.00
Bowl, 7" w., tricornered, peach
    opalescent (ILLUS.) 85.00
Bowl, 7" w., tricornered, purple 51.00
Bowl, 7" d., purple 190.00

Bowl, 7" d., white 50.00
Bowl, 8" d., peach opalescent 80.00
Bowl, 8" d., purple 75.00
Bowl, 8" d., white 85.00
Bowl, 9" d., dome-footed, peach
    opalescent 70.00

SKI STAR (Dugan)

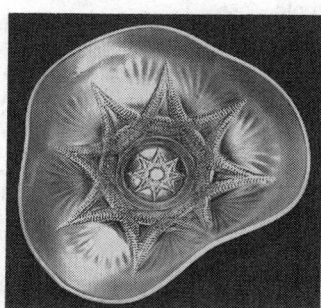

Ski Star Tricornered Bowl

Banana bowl, peach opalescent 175.00
Banana bowl, purple 92.00
Basket, peach opalescent 520.00
Berry set: master bowl & 6 sauce
    dishes; peach opalescent, 7 pcs. . . . 600.00
Bowl, 5" d., peach opalescent 40.00
Bowl, 5" d., fluted, peach opales-
    cent 35.00
Bowl, 5" d., ruffled, peach opales-
    cent 45.00
Bowl, 5" d., ruffled, purple 55.00
Bowl, 6" d., ruffled, peach opales-
    cent 50.00
Bowl, 8" d., ruffled, pur-
    ple . . . . .425.00 to 450.00
Bowl, 8" to 9" d., dome-footed,
    peach opalescent 110.00
Bowl, 10" d., marigold 62.00
Bowl, 10" d., peach opalescent 80.00
Bowl, 10" d., purple 178.00
Bowl, 11" d., peach opales-
    cent . . . . .125.00 to 175.00
Bowl, 11" d., purple 185.00
Bowl, tricornered, dome-footed,
    peach opalescent (ILLUS.) 120.00
Plate, 6" d., crimped rim, peach
    opalescent . . . . .150.00 to 200.00
Plate, 8½" d., dome-footed,
    w/handgrip, peach opales-
    cent . . . . .165.00 to 185.00
Plate, 8½" d., dome-footed,
    w/handgrip, purple 295.00

SOUTACHE (Dugan)

Bowl, 8" d., dome-footed, ruffled,
    peach opalescent 85.00
Bowl, 8" to 9" d., dome-footed,
    piecrust rim, peach opalescent . . . 145.00
Plate, 9½" d., dome-footed, peach
    opalescent . . . . .250.00 to 300.00

"S" REPEAT (Dugan)

Punch cup, purple 98.00
Punch set: bowl, base & 8 cups; pur-
   ple, 10 pcs. 2,850.00
Toothpick holder, blue 100.00
Toothpick holder, marigold 28.00
Tumbler, marigold ....450.00 to 500.00
Tumbler, w/advertising, dated 1910,
   marigold 350.00

STAG & HOLLY (Fenton)

Stag & Holly Bowl

Bowl, 7" d., spatula-footed,
   blue .... 125.00 to 175.00
Bowl, 7" d., spatula-footed, mari-
   gold 55.00
Bowl, 7" d., spatula-footed, purple.. 78.00
Bowl, 7" d., spatula-footed, red 2,500.00
Bowl, 8" d., footed, ice cream
   shape, blue................... 185.00
Bowl, 8" d., footed, ice cream
   shape, green 195.00
Bowl, 8" to 9" d., spatula-footed,
   blue ....225.00 to 250.00
Bowl, 8" to 9" d., spatula-footed,
   green 228.00
Bowl, 8" to 9" d., spatula-footed,
   lavender ....175.00 to 200.00
Bowl, 8" to 9" d., spatula-footed,
   marigold 90.00
Bowl, 8" to 9" d., spatula-footed,
   peach opalescent 1,900.00
Bowl, 8" to 9" d., spatula-footed,
   purple 140.00
Bowl, 10" to 11" d., three-footed,
   amber ....450.00 to 500.00
Bowl, 10" to 11" d., three-footed,
   Amberina 838.00
Bowl, 10" to 11" d., three-footed,
   aqua......................... 800.00
Bowl, 10" to 11" d., three-footed,
   blue (ILLUS.) 325.00
Bowl, 10" to 11" d., three-footed,
   cobalt blue 125.00
Bowl, 10" to 11" d., three-footed,
   green 425.00
Bowl, 10" to 11" d., three-footed,
   marigold 125.00

Bowl, 10" to 11" d., three-footed,
   purple 435.00
Bowl, 10" to 11" d., three-footed,
   vaseline.................175.00 to 275.00
Bowl, 11" d., flat, amber ..500.00 to 600.00
Bowl, 11" d., flat, electric blue 325.00
Bowl, 11" d., flat, green...........1,250.00
Bowl, 11" d., flat, mari-
   gold ....100.00 to 125.00
Bowl, 11" d., ruffled,
   blue ....150.00 to 200.00
Bowl, 11" d., ruffled, green w/mari-
   gold overlay 250.00
Bowl, 12" d., ice cream shape,
   blue 325.00
Bowl, 12" d., ice cream shape,
   green 170.00
Bowl, 12" d., ice cream shape,
   marigold 125.00
Bowl, spatula-footed,
   red ....1,325.00 to 1,375.00
Plate, 9" d., marigold .....300.00 to 350.00
Plate, chop, 12" d., three-footed,
   marigold ....750.00 to 850.00
Rose bowl, blue, large............. 995.00
Rose bowl, marigold, large 275.00

STAR & FILE (Imperial)

Bowl, 5" d., marigold 22.00
Bowl, 7" d., marigold 22.00
Bowl, 8" d., ice cream shape,
   marigold 15.00
Bowl, two-handled, marigold 35.00
Card tray, two turned-up sides, mar-
   igold, 6¼" d. 32.00
Celery vase, two-handled,
   clambroth 35.00
Celery vase, two-handled, mari-
   gold 65.00
Compote, jelly, marigold 55.00
Compote, large, marigold 30.00
Creamer, marigold 30.00
Pitcher, milk, marigold 70.00
Pitcher, water, marigold ...100.00 to 120.00
Plate, 6" d., marigold 110.00
Relish tray, two-handled, marigold.. 34.00
Rose bowl, marigold............... 50.00
Sherbet, marigold 25.00
Sugar bowl, marigold............. 12.00
Tumbler, marigold................. 106.00
Water set: pitcher & 6 tumblers;
   marigold, 7 pcs. 750.00
Wine, marigold 70.00
Wine decanter w/stopper, mari-
   gold 275.00

STARFISH

Bonbon, peach opalescent 120.00
Bonbon, purple 58.00
Compote, peach opalescent 65.00
Compote, purple 45.00

STAR OF DAVID (Imperial)

Bowl, 7" d., ruffled, purple......... 140.00

Bowl, 8" to 9" d., collared base,
blue 75.00
Bowl, 8" to 9" d., collared base,
green 85.00
Bowl, 8" to 9" d., collared base,
marigold 48.00
Bowl, 8" to 9" d., collared base,
purple 82.00
Bowl, 9" d., flat, ruffled, purple 80.00

STIPPLED RAYS

Stippled Rays Bonbon

Bonbon, two-handled, green
(ILLUS.) 48.00
Bonbon, two-handled, lime green ... 200.00
Bonbon, two-handled, marigold..... 30.00
Bonbon, two-handled, purple 28.00
Bonbon, two-handled, red........ 350.00
Bowl, 5" d., amber 25.00
Bowl, 5" d., Amberina 175.00
Bowl, 5" d., blue 50.00
Bowl, 5" d., green 33.00
Bowl, 5" d., marigold............. 20.00
Bowl, 5" d., purple 30.00
Bowl, 5" d., red...........350.00 to 400.00
Bowl, 6" d., Amberina 225.00
Bowl, 6½" d., ruffled,
red ....300.00 to 350.00
Bowl, 7" d., dome-footed, green.... 32.00
Bowl, 7" d., red 250.00
Bowl, 7" d., ruffled rim, red........ 450.00
Bowl, 8" to 9" d., green 55.00
Bowl, 8" to 9" d., ribbon candy rim,
green 75.00
Bowl, 8" to 9" d., marigold......... 32.00
Bowl, 8" to 9" d., ribbon candy rim,
marigold 33.00
Bowl, 8" to 9" d., purple 46.00
Bowl, 8" to 9" d., ribbon candy rim,
purple 70.00
Bowl, 8" to 9" d., red............. 605.00
Bowl, 10" d., green 65.00
Bowl, 10" d., ruffled, green 110.00
Bowl, 10" d., ruffled, lavender 75.00
Bowl, 10" d., ruffled, marigold 44.00
Bowl, 10" d., purple 55.00
Bowl, 10" d., white........150.00 to 200.00
Bowl, 10" w., tricornered, crimped
rim, green 85.00
Bowl, 11" d., Basketweave exterior,
ruffled, marigold 60.00

Bowl, 11" sq., dome-footed, ribbon
candy rim, green................ 115.00
Bowl, ruffled, red 330.00
Creamer, blue 25.00
Creamer, green 40.00
Creamer, footed, marigold 12.00
Creamer & sugar bowl, marigold,
pr............................. 45.00
Plate, 6" to 7" d., marigold 32.00
Plate, 6" to 7" d., red.............1,250.00
Rose bowl, green 80.00
Rose bowl, purple 65.00
Sherbet, Amberina 275.00
Sugar bowl, individual size, mari-
gold 10.00
Sugar bowl, open, blue 25.00
Sugar bowl, open, marigold 18.00

STORK (Imperial)
Vase, marigold 50.00

STORK & RUSHES (Dugan or Diamond Glass Works)
Basket, handled, marigold 175.00
Berry set: master bowl & 6 sauce
dishes; marigold, 7 pcs. 245.00
Bowl, master berry or fruit, mari-
gold 55.00
Butter dish, cov., marigold 135.00
Creamer, marigold 72.00
Hat shape, blue 40.00
Mug, amethyst................... 40.00
Mug, lavender 175.00
Mug, marigold 25.00
Mug, purple 125.00
Pitcher, water, blue 375.00
Pitcher, water, marigold 375.00
Pitcher, water, purple 400.00
Punch bowl & base, marigold,
2 pcs. 225.00
Punch bowl & base, purple, 2 pcs. ... 185.00
Punch cup, marigold.............. 17.50
Punch cup, purple 24.00
Punch set: bowl, base & 6 cups;
marigold, 8 pcs................. 325.00
Sauce dish, marigold 50.00
Sauce dish, purple 75.00
Spooner, marigold................ 80.00
Tumbler, aqua 210.00
Tumbler, blue................... 53.00
Tumbler w/lattice band, blue....... 55.00
Tumbler, marigold................ 26.00
Tumbler w/lattice band, marigold .. 30.00
Tumbler, marigold w/pale blue
base 128.00
Tumbler, purple................. 35.00
Tumbler w/lattice band, purple..... 69.00
Vase, marigold 22.00
Water set: pitcher & 1 tumbler;
blue, 2 pcs. ....450.00 to 500.00

STRAWBERRY (Fenton)
Bonbon, Amberina 200.00
Bonbon, reverse Amber-
ina ....325.00 to 400.00

Bonbon, one-handled, marigold..... 135.00
Bonbon, two-handled, amber 75.00
Bonbon, two-handled, blue......... 65.00
Bonbon, two-handled, green 59.00
Bonbon, two-handled, ice green
    opalescent..................... 450.00
Bonbon, two-handled, marigold..... 32.00
Bonbon, two-handled, purple 29.00
Bonbon, two-handled, vaseline
    w/marigold iridescence.......... 155.00
Bonbon, two-handled, vaseline
    opalescent ....600.00 to 650.00

STRAWBERRY (Millersburg)

Bowl, 7" d., green 95.00
Bowl, 7" d., purple 115.00
Bowl, 8" to 9" d., marigold........ 260.00
Bowl, 8" to 9" d., purple...225.00 to 250.00
Bowl, 8" to 9" d., vaseline........1,200.00
Bowl, 9" w., tricornered, marigold .. 200.00
Bowl, 9½" w., square, green....... 600.00
Bowl, 9½" w., square, ribbon candy
    rim, purple 400.00
Bowl, 9½" d., Basketweave exteri-
    or, marigold 55.00
Bowl, 9½" d., Basketweave exteri-
    or, purple 70.00
Bowl, 10" w., tricornered, ribbon
    candy rim, purple 450.00
Compote, green................... 250.00
Compote, marigold................ 275.00
Compote, purple 225.00

STRAWBERRY (Northwood)

Northwood Strawberry Bowl

Bonbon, amber 50.00
Bonbon, blue 60.00
Bonbon, marigold 135.00
Bonbon, purple 150.00
Bonbon, vaseline................ 145.00
Bonbon, vaseline opalescent 700.00
Bowl, 5" d., fluted, purple 40.00
Bowl, 7" d., purple 33.00
Bowl, 8" to 9" d., stippled, blue 350.00
Bowl, 8" to 9" d., stippled, ribbon
    candy rim, green ....100.00 to 150.00
Bowl, 8" to 9" d., stippled, ice
    green 1,100.00

Bowl, 8" to 9" d., stippled,
    purple ....200.00 to 250.00
Bowl, 8" to 9" d., ruffled, Basket-
    weave exterior, green........... 90.00
Bowl, 8" to 9" d., ruffled, Basket-
    weave exterior, marigold 65.00
Bowl, 8" to 9" d., ruffled, Basket-
    weave exterior, purple 85.00
Bowl, 8" to 9" d., ruffled, white....1,350.00
Bowl, 8" to 9" d., blue........... 80.00
Bowl, 8" to 9" d., marigold........ 40.00
Bowl, 8" to 9" d., piecrust rim,
    purple (ILLUS.) 75.00
Plate, 6" to 7" d., w/handgrip,
    green 210.00
Plate, 6" to 7" d., w/handgrip,
    purple 105.00
Plate, 9" d., green 135.00
Plate, 9" d., marigold 115.00
Plate, 9" d., pastel marigold 125.00
Plate, 9" d., purple............. 210.00
Plate, 9" d., Basketweave exterior,
    green ....200.00 to 275.00
Plate, 9" d., Basketweave exterior,
    marigold ....125.00 to 150.00
Plate, 9" d., Basketweave exterior,
    purple 165.00
Plate, 9" d., stippled, Basketweave
    exterior, green 400.00
Plate, 9" d., stippled, green........ 750.00
Plate, 9" d., stippled, mari-
    gold ....800.00 to 1,000.00
Plate, 9" d., stippled, purple 650.00
Plate, 9" d., stippled, ribbed, pur-
    ple 475.00

SUNFLOWER PIN TRAY (Millersburg)

Green ....175.00 to 200.00
Marigold 450.00
Purple ....450.00 to 475.00

SWAN PASTEL NOVELTIES (Dugan)

Salt dip, celeste blue 38.00
Salt dip, ice blue................. 36.00
Salt dip, ice green 40.00
Salt dip, marigold 75.00
Salt dip, peach opalescent 300.00
Salt dip, pink 35.00
Salt dip, purple 175.00
Salt dip, vaseline................. 58.00

SWIRL HOBNAIL (Millersburg)

Swirl Hobnail Cuspidor

Cuspidor, marigold 600.00
Cuspidor, purple (ILLUS.) 475.00
Rose bowl, marigold 300.00
Rose bowl, purple . . . . 275.00 to 325.00
Vase, green . . . . 275.00 to 300.00
Vase, marigold 200.00
Vase, purple 225.00

TEN MUMS (Fenton)
Bowl, 8" to 9" d., ribbon candy rim,
  blue 140.00
Bowl, 8" to 9" d., ribbon candy rim,
  green 125.00
Bowl, 8" to 9" d., ribbon candy rim,
  purple 135.00
Bowl, 10" d., ruffled, blue 130.00
Bowl, 10" d., footed, green 80.00
Bowl, 10" d., ribbon candy rim,
  green 175.00
Bowl, 10" d., footed, marigold 225.00
Bowl, 10" d., ribbon candy rim,
  marigold 300.00
Bowl, 10" d., ruffled, marigold 105.00
Bowl, 10" d., ribbon candy rim,
  purple 110.00
Bowl, 10" d., ruffled, purple 155.00
Pitcher, water, blue 1,650.00
Pitcher, water, marigold 475.00
Tumbler, amber 65.00
Tumbler, blue 75.00
Tumbler, marigold 50.00
Tumbler, purple 65.00
Tumbler, white 153.00
Water set: pitcher & 1 tumbler; mar-
  igold, 2 pcs. 575.00

THIN RIB VASE
8" h., aqua 60.00
8" h., green 30.00
9" h., aqua opalescent 85.00
9" h., blue 35.00
9" h., green 40.00
9" h., teal blue 105.00
9½" h., green (Northwood) 45.00
10" h., blue 35.00
10" h., green (Northwood) 40.00
10" h., marigold 48.00
10" h., purple (Northwood) 32.50
10" h., vaseline 45.00
10" h., white 70.00
11" h., aqua opalescent 125.00
11" h., green 75.00
11¼" h., marigold 40.00
12" h., aqua 75.00
12" h., green 85.00
12" h., purple 45.00
13" h., aqua opalescent (North-
  wood) 1,100.00
13" h., green . . . . 100.00 to 125.00
13" h., purple 100.00
13" h., funeral, white 200.00
14" h., funeral, green (North-
  wood) 100.00

14" h., funeral, purple 135.00
16½" h., green 135.00

THREE FRUITS (Northwood)

Three Fruits Plate

Bowl, 5" d., marigold 30.00
Bowl, 5" d., purple 30.00
Bowl, 6" d., green 40.00
Bowl, 6" d., marigold 30.00
Bowl, 8" d., ruffled, green 70.00
Bowl, 8" d., ruffled, mari-
  gold . . . . 75.00 to 100.00
Bowl, 8" d., ruffled, purple 90.00
Bowl, 8" d., dome-footed, Basket-
  weave & Grapevine exterior,
  white 350.00
Bowl, 8½" d., collared base,
  Basketweave & Grapevine exteri-
  or, green 65.00
Bowl, 8½" d., dome-footed,
  green . . . . 150.00 to 175.00
Bowl, 8½" d., piecrust rim, green . . 98.00
Bowl, 8½" d., piecrust rim,
  marigold 60.00
Bowl, 8½" d., purple 100.00
Bowl, 8½" d., piecrust rim, purple . . 70.00
Bowl, 9" d., footed, Meander re-
  verse, black amethyst 750.00
Bowl, 9" d., ruffled, stippled, aqua
  opalescent 875.00
Bowl, 9" d., ruffled, blue 210.00
Bowl, 9" d., green 66.00
Bowl, 9" d., ruffled, green 110.00
Bowl, 9" d., stippled, marigold 125.00
Bowl, 9" d., ruffled, pastel mari-
  gold 90.00
Bowl, 9" d., ruffled, collared base,
  marigold 60.00
Bowl, 9" d., purple 88.00
Bowl, 9" d., stippled, purple 200.00
Bowl, 9" d., ruffled, violet 55.00
Bowl, 9" d., stippled, white 762.50
Bowl, 9" d., dome-footed, Basket-
  weave & Grapevine exterior,
  green 70.00
Bowl, 9" d., dome-footed, Basket-
  weave & Grapevine exterior, ice
  green 675.00

Bowl, 9" d., dome-footed, Basketweave & Grapevine exterior, marigold 85.00

Bowl, 9" d., dome-footed, Basketweave & Grapevine exterior, purple 60.00

Bowl, 9" d., dome-footed, Basketweave & Grapevine exterior, white ....350.00 to 380.00

Bowl, 9" d., piecrust rim, stippled, Ribbed exterior, green 795.00

Bowl, 9" d., spatula-footed, aqua opalescent...................... 580.00

Bowl, 9" d., spatula-footed, blue ... 100.00

Bowl, 9" d., spatula-footed, ruffled, green 60.00

Bowl, 9" d., spatula-footed, ice green 1,100.00

Bowl, 9" d., spatula-footed, marigold 95.00

Bowl, 9" d., spatula-footed, pastel honey amber (smoke tint)........ 350.00

Bowl, 9" d., spatula-footed, purple.. 157.00

Bowl, 9" d., spatula-footed, white .. 360.00

Bowl, 10" d., purple 67.00

Bowl, 10" d., ruffled, Basketweave & Grapevine exterior, ice green 375.00

Bowl, collared base, aqua opalescent ....800.00 to 1,200.00

Bowl, piecrust rim, stippled, green 1,425.00

Bowl, spatula-footed, stippled, purple 175.00

Bowl, stippled, ruffled, blue 700.00

Bowl, collared base, stippled, marigold 78.00

Bowl, collared base, stippled, white ....750.00 to 775.00

Bowl, piecrust rim, stippled, green ....1,000.00 to 1,200.00

Bowl, ruffled, stippled, footed, ice blue ....800.00 to 1,000.00

Plate, 7½" d., Basketweave & Grapevine exterior, green 175.00

Plate, 8" d., w/handgrip, ribbed exterior, purple 150.00

Plate, 9" d., stippled, aqua opalescent ....1,850.00 to 2,000.00

Plate, 9" d., clambroth 100.00

Plate, 9" d., stippled, electric blue (ILLUS.)....................... 950.00

Plate, 9" d., green 168.00

Plate, 9" d., horehound 295.00

Plate, 9" d., lavender............. 325.00

Plate, 9" d., stippled, lavender ....1,250.00 to 1,400.00

Plate, 9" d., marigold 107.00

Plate, 9" d., stippled, marigold 221.00

Plate, 9" d., purple............. 142.00

Plate, 9" d., stippled, purple 340.00

Plate, 9" d., stippled, ribbed exterior, purple 950.00

Plate, 9" d., stippled, teal blue ...3,500.00

Plate, 9½" w., 12-sided, blue (Fenton)............................ 100.00

Plate, 9½" w., 12-sided, green (Fenton)............................ 150.00

Plate, 9½" w., 12-sided, marigold (Fenton) 130.00

Plate, 9½" w., 12-sided, purple (Fenton)............................ 110.00

Plate, plain back, stretch "electric" finish, purple 275.00

Plate, two sides up, green 150.00

Plate, Basketweave exterior, marigold 125.00

Plate, Basketweave exterior, purple 110.00

TIGER LILY (Imperial)

Tiger Lily Pitcher

Pitcher, water, green (ILLUS.) 204.00

Pitcher, water, marigold 100.00

Pitcher, water, purple 365.00

Tumbler, aqua 204.00

Tumbler, blue..................... 89.00

Tumbler, clambroth................ 65.00

Tumbler, green 34.00

Tumbler, marigold................. 30.00

Tumbler, olive green 115.00

Tumbler, purple................... 80.00

Water set: pitcher & 4 tumblers; marigold, 5 pcs. 310.00

Water set: pitcher & 6 tumblers; aqua, 7 pcs....................2,205.00

Water set: pitcher & 6 tumblers; purple, 7 pcs.................. 900.00

TOWN PUMP NOVELTY (Northwood)

Green 2,600.00

Marigold ....1,275.00 to 1,300.00

Purple 750.00

TREE TRUNK VASE (Northwood)

6" h., purple, squatty............. 150.00

6¼" h., purple.................... 40.00

7" h., green 45.00

7" h., ice blue 400.00

7½" h., green, squatty 150.00

7" to 11" h., ice green.....134.00 to 220.00

8" to 10" h., blue 92.00

8" to 10" h., ice blue	250.00
8" to 11" h., green	35.00
9" h., aqua	95.00
9" h., white	100.00
9" to 12" h., aqua opalescent	475.00
9" to 10" h., marigold	35.00
9" to 10" h., purple	52.50
10½" h., electric blue	70.00
11" h., ice blue	350.00
11" h., purple	85.00
11" h., white	70.00
12" h., blue	150.00 to 175.00
12" h., ice blue	275.00
12" h., ice green	440.00
12" h., marigold	130.00
12" h., purple	185.00
12" h., white	175.00
13" h., green	175.00 to 200.00
13" h., purple	300.00
13½" h., blue	425.00
14" h., purple	125.00
15" h., purple, w/elephant foot	1,300.00
17" h., white, funeral	1,000.00
18" h., green	550.00
18" h., purple	975.00
19" h., purple, funeral	1,800.00
20" h., cobalt blue, funeral	1,300.00

TROUT & FLY (Millersburg)

Bowl, ice cream shape, green	850.00
Bowl, ice cream shape, lavender	1,350.00
Bowl, ice cream shape, marigold	425.00 to 475.00
Bowl, ice cream shape, purple	595.00
Bowl, ribbon candy rim, green	712.00
Bowl, ribbon candy rim, lavender	1,400.00
Bowl, ribbon candy rim, marigold	350.00
Bowl, ribbon candy rim, purple	575.00
Bowl, ruffled, green	450.00 to 500.00
Bowl, ruffled, lavender	1,800.00
Bowl, ruffled, marigold	475.00
Bowl, ruffled, marigold, satin finish	385.00
Bowl, ruffled, pastel marigold, satin finish	500.00
Bowl, ruffled, purple	550.00
Bowl, ruffled, purple, satin finish	675.00
Bowl, square, green	1,400.00 to 1,500.00
Bowl, square, marigold	700.00
Bowl, square, purple	825.00

TULIP & CANE

Bowl, small, berry, marigold	25.00
Compote, marigold	50.00
Goblet, marigold, 4 oz.	60.00
Goblet, marigold	55.00

TWO FLOWERS (Fenton)

Bonbon, stemmed, blue	85.00
Bowl, 6" d., footed, aqua	155.00
Bowl, 6" d., footed, blue	75.00
Bowl, 6" d., footed, lime green	45.00
Bowl, 6" d., footed, marigold	26.00
Bowl, 6" d., footed, purple	75.00
Bowl, 6" d., footed, vaseline	100.00 to 125.00
Bowl, 7" to 8" d., footed, blue	60.00
Bowl, 7" to 8" d., footed, clambroth	90.00
Bowl, 7" to 8" d., footed, green	80.00 to 100.00
Bowl, 7" to 8" d., footed, marigold	45.00
Bowl, 7" to 8" d., footed, fluted, purple	47.00
Bowl, 7" to 8" d., footed, red	2,247.00
Bowl, 8" d., footed, Amberina	1,500.00 to 1,900.00
Bowl, 8" d., collared base, marigold	100.00 to 125.00
Bowl, 8" d., collared base, ice cream shape, marigold	175.00
Bowl, 8½" d., footed, blue	99.00
Bowl, 9" d., footed, marigold	75.00
Bowl, 9" d., footed, ice cream shape, marigold	125.00
Bowl, 9½" d., ruffled, purple	150.00
Bowl, 10" d., footed, scalloped rim, blue	85.00
Bowl, 10" d., footed, scalloped rim, green	75.00
Bowl, 10" d., footed, scalloped rim, marigold	65.00
Bowl, 10" d., footed, aqua	237.00
Bowl, 10" d., footed, blue	100.00 to 125.00
Bowl, 10" d., footed, marigold	80.00 to 100.00

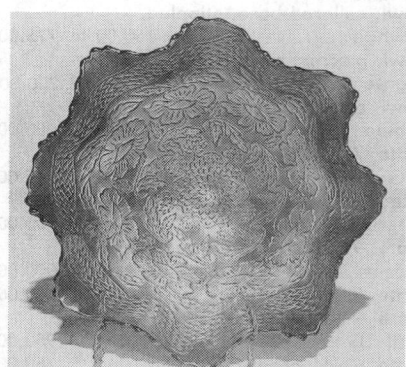

Two Flowers Bowl

Bowl, 10" d., ruffled, footed, red (ILLUS.)	2,000.00
Bowl, 10" d., footed, vaseline	350.00
Bowl, 10" d., footed, white	750.00
Bowl, 10½" d., ruffled, blue	180.00
Bowl, 11" d., aqua	650.00
Bowl, 11" d., green	1,050.00
Bowl, 11" d., footed, ruffled, purple	750.00

Bowl, 11" d., ice cream shape,
  blue 125.00
Bowl, 11½" d., footed, blue 125.00
Bowl, 11½" d., ball footed,
  marigold 55.00
Plate, 6½" d., marigold 125.00
Plate, 9" d., footed, marigold 425.00
Plate, chop, 11½" d., three-footed,
  marigold 350.00
Plate, chop, 13" d., three-footed,
  marigold 575.00
Rose bowl, three-footed, blue 153.00
Rose bowl, three-footed, mari-
  gold ....50.00 to 75.00
Rose bowl, three-footed, purple 257.00

VENETIAN GIANT ROSE BOWL (Cambridge)

Venetian Giant Rose Bowl

Green (ILLUS.).....................1,200.00
Marigold.........................1,700.00

VINEYARD

Pitcher, water, marigold 100.00
Pitcher, water, peach opalescent ...1,200.00
Pitcher, water, purple 315.00
Tumbler, amber 29.00
Tumbler, green 39.00
Tumbler, lavender................. 79.00
Tumbler, marigold................. 26.00
Tumbler, purple 55.00

VINTAGE or VINTAGE GRAPE

Bonbon, two-handled, blue (Fen-
  ton)........................... 50.00
Bonbon, two-handled, green (Fen-
  ton)........................... 57.00
Bonbon, two-handled, marigold
  (Fenton) 30.00
Bonbon, two-handled, purple (Fen-
  ton)........................... 35.00
Bowl, 6" d., blue (Fenton).......... 29.00
Bowl, 6" d., green (Fenton) 45.00
Bowl, 6" d., purple (Fenton) 32.50
Bowl, 6½" d., ice cream shape,
  green 30.00
Bowl, 7" d., fluted, aqua opalescent
  (Fenton) 925.00
Bowl, 7" d., fluted, green (Fenton) .. 32.50

Bowl, 7" d., fluted, purple (Fen-
  ton)........................... 28.00
Bowl, 7" d., purple (Millers-
  burg) ....50.00 to 75.00
Bowl, 7" d., ruffled, vaseline ... 110.00
Bowl, 7½" d., ice cream shape,
  blue 36.00
Bowl, 7½" d., ice cream shape,
  green 32.00
Bowl, 7½" d., ice cream shape,
  purple 35.00
Bowl, 8" d., ribbon candy rim, aqua
  opalescent ....1,600.00 to 1,900.00
Bowl, 8" d., ribbon candy rim, Wide
  Panel exterior, blue 55.00
Bowl, 8" to 9" d., aqua opales-
  cent ....1,000.00 to 1,200.00
Bowl, 8" to 9" d., ruffled, aqua
  opalescent ....850.00 to 1,000.00
Bowl, 8" to 9" d., footed, blue (Fen-
  ton)........................... 42.50
Bowl, 8" to 9" d., ruffled, blue 50.00
Bowl, 8" to 9" d., green (Fenton) ... 50.00
Bowl, 8" to 9" d., green (Millers-
  burg) 30.00
Bowl, 8" to 9" d., marigold (Fen-
  ton)........................... 35.00
Bowl, 8" to 9" d., fluted, Persian
  blue 630.00
Bowl, 8" to 9" d., footed, purple
  (Fenton) 38.00
Bowl, 8" to 9" d., ruffled,
  red ....1,700.00 to 1,800.00
Bowl, 8" to 9" d., fluted, teal blue .. 75.00
Bowl, 8" to 9" d., vaseline 225.00
Bowl, 9½" d., ruffled, dome-footed,
  marigold 68.00
Bowl, 10" d., blue ....75.00 to 100.00
Bowl, 10" d., green, Hobnail exteri-
  or (Millersburg) 950.00
Bowl, 10" d., marigold, Hobnail ex-
  terior (Millersburg) 575.00
Bowl, 10" d., ruffled, green 85.00
Bowl, 10" d., ruffled, purple........ 55.00
Bowl, 10" d., ruffled, red 3,250.00
Bowl, 10" d., ice cream shape,
  blue 200.00
Bowl, 10" d., ice cream shape, red
  (Fenton).............1,300.00 to 1,900.00
Bowl, 10" d., ice cream shape, vase-
  line (Fenton) 225.00
Bowl, 11" d., ice cream shape, blue
  (Fenton) 190.00
Bowl, 11" d., ice cream shape,
  marigold 600.00
Bowl, ruffled, domed base, celeste
  blue 825.00
Compote, 7" d., blue (Fenton) 75.00
Compote, 7" d., fluted, green (Fen-
  ton)........................... 46.00
Compote, 7" d., marigold (Fenton) .. 40.00
Compote, 7" d., purple (Fenton) 50.00
Cuspidor, marigold 2,300.00
Epergne, blue (Fenton) 150.00

Epergne, green (Fenton) 150.00
Epergne, large, green 235.00
Epergne, marigold (Fenton) 150.00
Epergne, purple, small 110.00
Epergne, purple, large 365.00
Epergne, purple (Fenton) 130.00
Fernery, footed, blue (Fenton) 58.00
Fernery, footed, green (Fenton) 75.00
Fernery, footed, marigold (Fenton) . . 45.00
Fernery, footed, purple (Fenton) 55.00
Fernery, footed, red (Fenton) 1,400.00
Ice cream set: master ice cream
  bowl & four 6" d. bowls; cobalt
  blue, 5 pcs. 450.00
Nut dish, footed, blue, 6" d. (Fen-
  ton). 55.00
Nut dish, footed, green, 6" d. (Fen-
  ton). 75.00
Nut dish, footed, marigold, 6" d.
  (Fenton) 48.00
Nut dish, footed, purple, 6" d. (Fen-
  ton). 62.00
Nut dish, footed, red 430.00
Plate, 5" d., blue 75.00
Plate, 6" d., blue 140.00
Plate, 6" d., green 90.00
Plate, 6" d., purple 65.00
Plate, 6½" d., stippled, marigold . . . 50.00
Plate, 7" d., blue (Fenton) . . . 65.00 to 75.00
Plate, 7" d., blue (Millersburg) 155.00
Plate, 7" d., green (Fenton) 175.00
Plate, 7" d., marigold (Fenton) 125.00
Plate, 7" d., purple (Fen-
  ton). . . . . 125.00 to 150.00
Plate, 7" d., purple 70.00
Plate, 8" d., blue 125.00
Plate, 8" d., green 165.00
Powder jar, cov., marigold (Fen-
  ton). 80.00
Powder jar, cov., marigold 75.00
Powder jar, cov., purple (Fenton) . . . 100.00
Sandwich tray, handled, marigold . . 23.00
Sandwich tray, handled, purple 30.00
Sauce dish, blue 30.00
Sauce dish, blue, Hobnail exterior
  (Millersburg) 450.00
Sauce dish, green 25.00
Sauce dish, marigold (Fenton) 20.00
Sauce dish, ice cream shape, Hob-
  nail exterior, marigold (Millers-
  burg) 700.00
Tumbler, marigold (Fenton) 25.00
Wine, marigold (Fenton) 25.00
Wine, purple (Fenton) 32.00

VINTAGE GRAPE - See Vintage Pattern

WATER LILY & CATTAILS
Banana boat, blue . . . . 150.00 to 185.00
Bonbon, two-handled, marigold,
  large. 50.00
Bowl, 5" d., marigold 32.00
Bowl, 9" d., purple 60.00
Butter dish, cov., marigold 156.00

Dish, three turned up sides, mari-
  gold, 6" d. 29.00

Water Lily & Cattails Pitcher

Pitcher, water, marigold (ILLUS.) 548.00
Plate, 6" d., marigold 55.00
Rose bowl, marigold 20.00
Sauce dish, marigold 12.00
Sauce dish, footed, vaseline w/mari-
  gold overlay 75.00
Spooner, marigold 50.00
Sugar bowl, cov., marigold 75.00
Table set: cov. sugar bowl, creamer,
  spooner & cov. butter dish; mari-
  gold, 4 pcs. 675.00
Toothpick holder, marigold 65.00
Tumbler, blue 2,700.00
Tumbler, marigold. 51.00
Tumbler, purple 22.50
Water set: pitcher & 6 tumblers;
  marigold, 7 pcs. 725.00
Whimsey, marigold 32.50
Whimsey, purple 55.00

WHITE OAK TUMBLER
Tumbler, marigold. 242.00

WIDE PANEL

Wide Panel Epergne

Banana bowl, amber 40.00
Basket, green. 80.00
Bowl, 8" to 9" d., marigold. 19.00

Bowl, 8" to 9" d., purple 28.00
Bowl, 8½" d., Ragged Robin, 3 in 1
   rim, blue 135.00
Bowl, 10" d., console, blue 40.00
Bowl, 10" d., console, vaseline 40.00
Bowl, 12" d., marigold 45.00
Candy dish, cov., marigold 30.00
Candy dish, cov., red 350.00
Candy dish, cov., white 55.00
Compote, vaseline 65.00
Epergne, four-lily, green (ILLUS.) . . .1,250.00
Epergne, four-lily, ice blue 225.00
Epergne, four-lily, marigold 525.00
Epergne, four-lily, purple 950.00
Epergne, four-lily, white 2,600.00
Goblet, marigold 18.00
Goblet, red 175.00
Plate, 8" d., marigold 35.00
Plate, 8" d., red 57.00
Plate, chop, 12" d., vaseline 50.00
Plate, chop, 14" d., marigold 40.00
Plate, chop, 14" d., red 195.00
Plate, chop, 14" d., smoky 53.00
Plate, chop, 14" d., white 28.00
Rose bowl, clambroth 20.00
Rose bowl, marigold 25.00
Rose bowl, purple 29.00
Salt set: master pedestal salt dip &
   6 individual size salt dips; mari-
   gold (Northwood), 7 pcs 150.00
Vase, 6" h., marigold 55.00
Vase, 8½" h., 7½" d., smoke over
   milk white glass 185.00
Vase, 13" h., ice blue 45.00
Vase, 15" h., marigold 110.00

WILD ROSE

Wild Rose Syrup Pitcher

Bowl, 5½" d., three-footed, open
   heart rim, green 47.00
Bowl, 7" d., three-footed, open
   heart rim, green (Northwood) 48.00
Bowl, 7" d., three-footed, open
   heart rim, marigold (North-
   wood) 52.00
Bowl, 7" d., three-footed, open
   heart rim, purple (Northwood) . . .   72.00

Bowl, 8" to 9" d., marigold (North-
   wood) 32.50
Bowl, 8" to 9" d., green (North-
   wood) 38.00
Candy dish, open edge, blue,
   5¾" d. 150.00
Candy dish, open edge, green 75.00
Candy dish, open edge, purple 90.00
Lamp, three portrait medallions,
   w/original burner & etched chim-
   ney shade, green, small (Millers-
   burg) 850.00
Lamp, w/original burner & etched
   chimney shade, green, medium
   (Millersburg) 1,450.00
Lamp, w/original burner & etched
   chimney shade, marigold, medium
   (Millersburg) . . . . .1,100.00 to 1,300.00
Lamp, w/original burner & etched
   chimney shade, purple (Millers-
   burg) 1,400.00
Syrup pitcher, marigold
   (ILLUS.) . . . . .575.00 to 625.00

WILD STRAWBERRY (Northwood)

Bowl, 6" d., green 55.00
Bowl, 6" d., purple 48.00
Bowl, 6" d., ruffled, purple 100.00
Bowl, 7" d., marigold 85.00
Bowl, 10" d., green 285.00
Bowl, 10" d., ice green 1,750.00
Bowl, 10" d., marigold 85.00
Bowl, 10" d., purple 185.00
Plate, 6" to 7" d., w/handgrip,
   green . . . . .200.00 to 225.00
Plate, 6" to 7" d., w/handgrip,
   marigold 160.00
Plate, 6" to 7" d., w/handgrip,
   purple 125.00
Plate, 8" d., w/handgrip, green 100.00
Plate, 8" d., w/handgrip, purple 150.00

WINDFLOWER

Bowl, 8" to 9" d., blue 60.00
Bowl, 8" to 9" d., marigold 32.00
Bowl, 8" to 9" d., pastel marigold . .   75.00
Bowl, 8" to 9" d., purple 60.00
Bowl, 8" to 9" d., smoky 125.00
Plate, 8" d., marigold 130.00
Plate, 9" d., blue 175.00
Plate, 9" d., marigold 65.00
Plate, 9" d., pastel marigold 125.00
Sauceboat, ice green 425.00
Sauceboat, marigold 40.00
Sauceboat, purple 35.00
Tumbler, marigold 200.00
Tumbler, purple 50.00

WINDMILL or WINDMILL MEDALLION (Imperial)

Bowl, 7" d., green 45.00
Bowl, 7" d., marigold 40.00
Bowl, 7" d., purple 56.00
Bowl, 8" to 9" d., green 35.00

Bowl, 8" to 9" d., ruffled, mari-
gold 75.00
Bowl, 8" to 9" d., ruffled, purple ... 145.00
Bowl, 8" to 9" d., ruffled, vaseline .. 65.00
Bowl, 8" to 9" d., ruffled, smoky ... 52.00
Bowl, 9" d., footed, marigold 30.00
Bowl, 9" d., ribbon candy rim, milk
white w/marigold overlay 145.00
Bowl, 9" d., footed, purple 115.00
Dresser tray, oval, marigold 48.00
Pickle dish, aqua teal 275.00
Pickle dish, green 50.00
Pickle dish, lavender 70.00
Pickle dish, marigold 28.00
Pickle dish, purple 50.00
Pitcher, milk, clambroth 45.00
Pitcher, milk, ice green 110.00
Pitcher, milk, marigold 60.00
Pitcher, milk, purple 500.00
Pitcher, milk, smoky 225.00
Pitcher, water, marigold 78.00
Pitcher, water, purple 550.00
Plate, 8" d., marigold 18.00
Sauce dish, clambroth 35.00
Sauce dish, green 32.00
Sauce dish, marigold 20.00
Sauce dish, purple 35.00
Tumbler, green 39.00
Tumbler, marigold 35.00
Tumbler, purple 100.00
Water set: pitcher & 1 tumbler; mar-
igold, 2 pcs. 130.00
Water set: pitcher & 2 tumblers;
purple, 3 pcs. 1,200.00

WINDMILL & MUMS - See Chrysanthemum Pattern

WINDMILL MEDALLION - See Windmill Pattern

WINE & ROSES
Goblet, blue 75.00
Goblet, vaseline 75.00
Water set: pitcher & 6 goblets; mari-
gold, 7 pcs. 362.00
Wine, marigold 32.00

WISHBONE (Northwood)
Bowl, 7" d., three-footed, ruffled
rim, marigold 50.00
Bowl, 8" to 9" d., footed, blue 300.00
Bowl, 8" to 9" d., footed, clam-
broth 90.00
Bowl, 8" to 9" d., footed, green 103.00
Bowl, 8" to 9" d., footed, ice blue ..2,200.00
Bowl, 8" to 9" d., footed, ice
green 1,850.00
Bowl, 8" to 9" d., footed, lavender .. 200.00
Bowl, 8" to 9" d., footed, lime
green 80.00
Bowl, 8" to 9" d., footed, mari-
gold 75.00
Bowl, 8" to 9" d., footed, purple 89.00

Bowl, 8" to 9" d., footed, white 550.00
Bowl, 10" d., footed,
blue ....500.00 to 600.00
Bowl, 10" d., piecrust rim, electric
blue 2,300.00
Bowl, 10" d., piecrust rim,
green ....200.00 to 225.00
Bowl, 10" d., piecrust rim, Basket-
weave exterior, green 1,175.00
Bowl, 10" d., piecrust rim, mari-
gold 92.00
Bowl, 10" d., piecrust rim, Basket-
weave exterior, marigold 140.00
Bowl, 10" d., ruffled, green 145.00
Bowl, 10" d., ruffled, marigold 150.00
Bowl, 10" d., piecrust rim,
purple ....125.00 to 150.00
Bowl, 10" d., footed, ruffled,
purple 135.00
Bowl, 10" d., footed, piecrust rim,
smoky 1,300.00
Bowl, 10" d., footed, piecrust rim,
white 750.00
Bowl, footed, clambroth 115.00
Epergne, ice blue 2,500.00
Epergne, green 675.00
Epergne, marigold ....400.00 to 450.00
Epergne, purple ....400.00 to 450.00
Epergne, white 1,950.00
Pitcher, water, green 1,800.00
Pitcher, water, marigold 1,500.00
Pitcher, water, purple ..1,150.00 to 1,250.00
Plate, 8½" d., footed, marigold 475.00
Plate, 8½" d., footed, purple 300.00
Plate, 8½" w., footed, tricornered,
green 675.00
Plate, 8½" w., footed, tricornered,
purple 400.00
Plate, chop, 11" d., marigold 500.00
Plate, chop, 11" d., purple 645.00
Tumbler, green 180.00
Tumbler, marigold 130.00
Tumbler, purple 135.00

WREATHED CHERRY (Dugan)
Berry set: master bowl & 4 sauce
dishes; marigold, 5 pcs. 140.00
Berry set: master bowl & 4 sauce
dishes; white, 5 pcs. 675.00
Bonbon, two-handled, green, 8" 45.00
Bonbon, two-handled, marigold,
8" 40.00
Bowl, berry, 9 x 12" oval, laven-
der 65.00
Bowl, berry, 9 x 12" oval, mari-
gold 90.00
Bowl, berry, 9 x 12" oval, peach
opalescent....................... 250.00
Bowl, berry, 9 x 12" oval, purple ... 132.00
Bowl, berry, 9 x 12" oval, white 245.00
Butter dish, cov., marigold 70.00
Butter dish, cov., purple ...175.00 to 225.00
Compote, three-footed, peach
opalescent....................... 75.00

Creamer, blue 55.00
Creamer, marigold 55.00
Pitcher, water, marigold 225.00
Pitcher, water, white w/gold cher-
ries .... 700.00 to 750.00
Sauce dish, 5" to 6", oval, mari-
gold 30.00
Sauce dish, 5" to 6", oval, peach
opalescent.................... 140.00
Sauce dish, 5" to 6", oval, purple ... 40.00
Sauce dish, 5" to 6", oval, white 42.50
Spooner, marigold................. 65.00
Spooner, purple.................. 60.00
Spooner, white.................. 95.00
Tumbler, marigold............... 32.50
Tumbler, purple 65.00
Tumbler, white.................. 100.00
Tumbler, white w/red-stained
cherries 115.00
Water set: pitcher & 4 tumblers;
marigold, 5 pcs................ 400.00

WREATH OF ROSES
Bonbon, two-handled, blue, 8" d. ... 46.00
Bonbon, two-handled, green, 8" d... 55.00
Bonbon, two-handled, marigold,
8" d. 50.00
Bonbon, two-handled, purple,
8" d.................... 100.00 to 125.00
Bonbon, two-handled, white, 8" d. ... 150.00
Compote, 6" d., blue 65.00
Compote, 6" d., fluted, green 50.00
Compote, 6" d., honey amber (vari-
ant)......................... 35.00
Compote, 6" d., marigold 46.00
Compote, 6" d., fluted, purple 45.00
Punch bowl, Persian Medallion in-
terior, blue 300.00
Punch bowl, Vintage interior,
purple 145.00
Punch bowl & base, Persian Medal-
lion interior, marigold, 2 pcs. 225.00
Punch cup, blue 22.00
Punch cup, Persian Medallion interi-
or, blue 32.00
Punch cup, Vintage interior, blue ... 25.00
Punch cup, green 25.00
Punch cup, Persian Medallion interi-
or, green 38.00
Punch cup, Vintage interior, green .. 25.00
Punch cup, marigold 14.00
Punch cup, Persian Medallion interi-
or, marigold 25.00
Punch cup, Vintage interior,
marigold 30.00
Punch cup, purple 25.00
Punch cup, Persian Medallion interi-
or, purple 27.00
Punch cup, Vintage interior, pur-
ple 25.00
Punch set: bowl, base & 2 cups;
green, 4 pcs. 425.00
Punch set: bowl, base & 4 cups; Per-

sian Medallion interior, marigold,
6 pcs........................ 395.00
Punch set: bowl, base & 5 cups; Vin-
tage interior, purple, 7 pcs. 800.00
Punch set: bowl, base & 6 cups;
blue, 8 pcs.................... 695.00
Rose bowl, marigold (Dugan) 50.00
Rose bowl, purple (Dugan) 55.00
Whimsey, tricornered, marigold
(Dugan) 45.00

ZIG ZAG (Millersburg)
Bowl, 9½" d., marigold........... 195.00
Bowl, 9½" d., green 420.00
Bowl, 10" d., green 275.00
Bowl, 10" d., marigold........... 185.00
Bowl, 10" d., purple 240.00
Bowl, 10" w., tricornered, piecrust
rim, green.................... 200.00
Bowl, 10" w., tricornered, mari-
gold 275.00
Bowl, 10" w., tricornered, purple ... 430.00
Bowl, 10", ribbon candy rim,
green 95.00
Bowl, ribbon candy rim, marigold ... 225.00
Bowl, ribbon candy rim, pur-
ple .... 250.00 to 300.00

ZIPPERED HEART

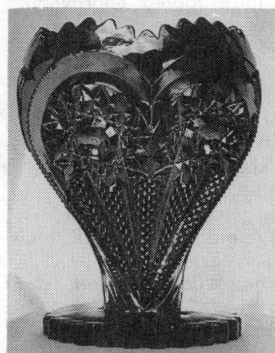

Zippered Heart Rose Bowl

Bowl, berry, 10" d., purple 130.00
Rose bowl, green (ILLUS.) 3,600.00
Sauce dish, purple, 5" d........... 22.50
Vase, 9" h., green 2,100.00
Vase, marigold 550.00

ZIPPERED LOOP LAMP (Imperial)
Hand, marigold, 4½" h............ 1,200.00
Hand, marigold, medium........... 675.00
Sewing, marigold, small 325.00
Sewing, marigold,
medium .... 600.00 to 675.00
Sewing, smoky,
medium............... 950.00 to 1,000.00
Sewing, marigold, large ... 550.00 to 575.00

(End of Carnival Glass Section)

(Cambridge Glass - Continued from page 452)

Salt & pepper shakers w/original
   tops, etched Chantilly patt., Crys-
   tal, pr. 37.50
Salt & pepper shakers w/original
   tops, etched Gloria patt., yellow,
   pr. 150.00
Sandwich tray w/center handle,
   etched Rose Point patt., Crystal,
   11" d. 140.00
Sherbet, etched Chantilly patt.,
   Crystal, 6 oz. 17.50
Sherbet, tall, etched Elaine patt.,
   Crystal, 6 oz. 18.50
Sherbet, low, engraved Lynbrook
   patt., clear 8.50
Sherry decanter w/original stopper,
   Amber, 32 oz., in original Farber
   chrome holder, 14¾" h. 60.00
Sugar bowl, open, etched Chantilly
   patt., Crystal 13.50
Tumbler, Cascade (No. 4000) line,
   Crystal, 5½" h., 8 oz. 10.00
Tumbler, etched Hunt Scene patt.,
   pink, 2 3/8" h., 1½ oz. 110.00
Tumbler, iced tea, engraved King
   Edward patt., clear 16.00
Tumbler, juice, footed, engraved
   Lynbrook patt., clear, 5" h. 13.50
Vase, bud, 6" h., No. 6004 line,
   Carmen 19.50
Vase, 10" h., etched Gloria patt.,
   Gold Krystol (golden tint) 225.00
Vase, 10½" h., cornucopia-shaped
   w/sea shell base, Windsor Blue
   (pale blue opaque) 190.00
Water set: pitcher & four tumblers;
   etched Apple Blossom patt., blue,
   5 pcs. 200.00
Wine, etched Wildflower patt., clear
   w/gold trim 35.00
Wine set: decanter & six wines;
   Nautilus (No. 3450) line, Cobalt
   Blue, 7 pcs. 200.00

CHOCOLATE

*This glass is often called Caramel Slag. It
was made by the Indiana Tumbler and Goblet Company of Greentown, Indiana, and other glasshouses, beginning at the turn of this
century. Various patterns were produced,
highly popular among them being Cactus and
Leaf Bracket.*

Animal covered dish, Cat on Low
   Hamper, Greentown $575.00
Animal covered dish, Dolphin, saw-
   tooth rim, Greentown . . .250.00 to 275.00
Animal covered dish, Rabbit on Bas-
   ket, Greentown 385.00

Berry set: master bowl & five sauce
   dishes; Dewey patt., Greentown,
   6 pcs. 285.00
Butter dish, cov., flat base, Cactus
   patt., Greentown 180.00
Butter dish, cov., small, Leaf Brack-
   et patt., Greentown 98.00
Compote, open, 5¼" d., Cactus
   patt., Greentown . . . . . .175.00 to 200.00
Compote, open, 5¼" d., Leaf Brack-
   et patt., Greentown 225.00
Compote, jelly, Geneva patt.,
   McKee 125.00
Cracker jar, cov., Cactus patt.,
   Greentown 295.00
Creamer, large, Austrian patt.,
   Greentown 125.00
Cruet w/original stopper, Cactus
   patt., Greentown . . . . . . .175.00 to 200.00

Leaf Bracket Cruet

Cruet w/original stopper, Leaf
   Bracket patt., Greentown
   (ILLUS.) . . . . .200.00 to 225.00
Dresser box, cov., rectangular,
   Aurora patt., National Glass Co.,
   5½ x 9" 995.00
Mug, Cactus patt., Greentown 78.00
Mug, Indoor Drinking Scene, Green-
   town, 5" h. . . . . .125.00 to 150.00
Mug, Outdoor Drinking Scene,
   Greentown . . . . .100.00 to 125.00
Nappy, triangular, handled, Leaf
   Bracket patt., Greentown 66.00
Nappy, triangular, Masonic patt.,
   McKee 135.00
Pickle dish, Aurora patt., National
   Glass Co., 8½" l. 195.00
Pitcher, water, Squirrel patt.,
   Greentown 630.00
Plate, 6¼" d., Serenade (or Trouba-
   dour) patt., McKee 175.00
Relish, oval, Leaf Bracket patt.,
   Greentown, 4½ x 7¼" 120.00
Salt shaker w/original top, Cactus
   patt., Greentown 70.00
Syrup jug w/original metal top, Cac-
   tus patt., Greentown (ILLUS.) 295.00

Cactus Syrup Jug

Toothpick holder, Cactus patt.,
  Greentown 75.00
Toothpick holder, figural Indian
  head, Greentown 195.00
Tumbler, Cactus patt., Greentown,
  4" h. 55.00
Tumbler, File patt., National Glass
  Co. 100.00
Tumbler, Leaf Bracket patt.,
  Greentown 65.00
Vase, 6" h., Masonic patt., McKee . . 250.00

CONSOLIDATED

The Consolidated Lamp and Glass Company of Coraopolis, Pennsylvania was founded in 1894 and for a number of years was noted for its lighting wares but also produced popular lines of pressed and blown tablewares. Highly collectible glass patterns of this early era include the Cone, Florette and Guttate lines.

Lamps and shades continued to be good sellers but in 1926 a new "art" line of molded decorative wares was introduced. This "Martele' " line was developed as a direct imitation of the fine glasswares being produced by Rene' Lalique of France and many Consolidated patterns resembled their French counterparts. Other popular lines produced during the 1920's and 1930's were "Dancing Nymph," the delightfully Art Deco "Ruba Rombic," introduced in 1928, and the "Catalonian" line, imitating 17th century Spanish glass, which debuted in 1927.

Although the factory closed in 1933, it was reopened under new management in 1936 and prospered through the 1940's. It finally closed in 1967. Collectors should note that many later Consolidated patterns closely resemble wares of other competing firms, especially the Phoenix Glass Company. Careful study is needed to determine the maker of pieces from the 1920-40 era.

A recent book which will be of help to collectors is Phoenix & Consolidated Art Glass, 1926-1980, *by Jack D. Wilson (Antique Publications, 1989).*

Bulging Loops
Mustard jar, cov., cased pink $135.00
Pitcher, milk, cased pink 120.00
Toothpick holder, blue opaque 95.00

Cone
Cruet w/original stopper, cased
  pink 175.00
Mustard jar, cov., pink 115.00
Pickle castor, cranberry, extremely
  ornate silver plate frame on ped-
  estal base 395.00
Pickle castor, yellow, silver plate
  frame 350.00
Sugar bowl, cov., yellow 95.00

Florette

Florette Cracker Jar

Cracker jar, cov., cased apricot, silver plate rim, lid & bail handle . . . 350.00
Cracker jar w/original glass cover,
  cased pink, Regent line, ca. 1940's
  (ILLUS.) 215.00
Cracker jar w/original silver plate
  rim, lid & bail handle, cased pink
  satin . . . . .250.00 to 300.00
Cracker jar w/original silver plate
  rim, lid & bail handle, cased red
  satin 290.00
Creamer & cov. sugar bowl, cased
  pink, silver plate cover, rims &
  handles, creamer 4" d., 3¾" h.,
  sugar bowl 5¾" d., 5½" h., pr.
  (resilvered) 235.00
Salt shaker w/original top, cased
  yellow 45.00

Later Lines
Bowl, 7" d., footed, flared rim,
  Line 700, light green wash 75.00
Bowl, 9" d., Ruba Rombic line,
  lilac. 325.00
Bowl, 15" d., Fish patt., Martele'
  line, yellow wash 410.00

Box, cov., shaped oval, pound-type, Five Fruits & Olive patt., Martele' line, green wash 50.00

Candlesticks, slightly domed oval base, flared oval candlecup, flat horizontal oval connector, Hummingbird & Orchids patt., Martele' line, purple, 8" h., pr. 125.00

Charger, Bird of Paradise patt., Martele' line, green wash, 12" d. 175.00

Compote, 9", Fish patt., Martele' line, green wash 150.00

Goblet, Five Fruits patt., Martele' line, yellow, 9 oz. 26.00

Lamp, table model, brass base & shade cap, Foxglove patt., Martele' line, satin custard ground ... 150.00

Lamp, table model, brass fittings, ovoid, Love Bird patt., Martele' line, ruby-stained 185.00

Pitcher, water, footed, Five Fruits patt., Martele' line, green wash, ½ gal. 325.00

Plate, 8" d., Five Fruits patt., Martele' line, green wash 40.00

Plate, 12" d., Bird of Paradise patt., Martele' line, pink wash 95.00

Puff box, cov., Love Bird patt., Martele' line, pink wash 140.00

Relish dish, six-part, Catalonian line, amethyst wash 45.00

Sherbet, footed, Dancing Nymph line, clear frosted 65.00

Sherbet, footed, Five Fruits patt., Martele' line, russet wash 15.00

Sherbet, footed, Five Fruits patt., Martele' line, yellow wash 25.00

Sherbet, footed, Line 700, yellow wash 40.00

Tumbler, Catalonian line, jade green wash, 5" h. 10.00

Tumbler, Catalonian line, honey (amber) wash, 6½" h. 40.00

Tumbler, footed, Five Fruits patt., Martele' line, green wash, 5¾" h. 40.00

Vase, 6" h., Ruba Rombic line, lavender 850.00

Vase, 6" h., Screech Owls patt., Martele' line, gold decoration on a milk white ground 125.00

Vases, 6" h., 4" d., ovoid, Dragonfly & Cattails patt., Martele' line, light blue, fitted in an ornate ormolu footed stand w/decorative ormolu handles at the rim, pr. ... 250.00

Vase, 8" h., ovoid, Katydid patt., Martele' line, green decoration on a milk white ground 135.00

Vase, 9¼" h., flattened baluster-form, Bird of Paradise patt., Martele' line, blue wash on crystal ... 265.00

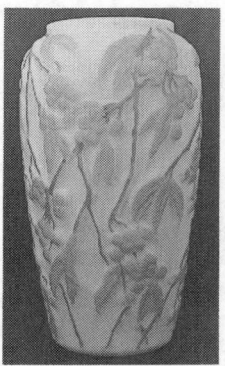

Bittersweet Pattern Vase

Vase, 9½" h., baluster-form, Bittersweet patt., Martele' line, blue berries, green leaves & brown branches on a satin milk white ground (ILLUS.).................. 135.00

Vase, 10" h., triangular, Catalonian line, amethyst wash 225.00

Vase, 10½" h., Dogwood patt., Martele' line, three-color decoration on a white ground 135.00

Vase, sweet pea-type, Catalonian line, No. 1154, amethyst wash.... 40.00

Whiskey decanter w/original stopper, Catalonian line, emerald green 95.00

CORALENE

Coralene is a method of decorating glass, usually satin glass, with the use of a beaded-type decoration customarily applied to the glass with the use of enamels, which were melted. Coralene decoration has been faked with the use of glue.

Creamer, bulbous base tapering to a cylindrical slightly flaring rim, applied clear handle, cranberry exterior w/pink & yellow "seaweed" coralene beading, 2" d., 2¾" h. $225.00

Punch cup, shaded rose mother-of-pearl satin Diamond Quilted patt. exterior w/yellow "seaweed" coralene beading, white lining, 3" d., 2 3/8" h. 495.00

Rose bowl, cranberry background covered w/coralene beading, marked "Patent," 7¼" d., 6¼" h. 1,050.00

Toothpick holder, bulbous base tapering to a cylindrical rim, glossy ground decorated w/yellow "seaweed" coralene beading 295.00

Vase, 5" h., 4¼" d., squatty bulbous

base w/short flaring rim, shaded
heavenly blue satin body decorated w/overall coralene beading ... 395.00

Vase, 7¾" h., 4¾" d., ovoid body
tapering to a short flaring neck,
pink & green striped satin ground
decorated w/overall yellow "seaweed" coralene beading, white
lining 475.00

Vase, 10½" h., 4½" d., yellow
mother-of-pearl satin Diamond
Quilted patt. decorated w/pink &
white "seaweed" coralene beading 905.00

Vase, 11¼" h., bulbous base tapering to a tall stick neck, painted
dusty rose shading to white then
blue satin ground decorated overall w/coralene beading in a "crazy quilt" patch design, each patch
filled w/small "snowflake" coralene beading 665.00

COSMOS

Cosmos Water Pitcher

*One of the most popular and widely collect-
ed of the glass patterns produced by The Consolidated Lamp and Glass Company of
Coraopolis, Pennsylvania, the pieces were
produced in milk white glass with molded
groupings of Cosmos blossoms. The blossoms
and edge bands were then stained with various pastel colors including pink, blue and yellow. For information on other Consolidated
patterns see that listing.*

Butter dish, cov., pink band
decoration..................... $230.00
Lamp, miniature, yellow band
decoration.................... 190.00
Pickle castor, pink band decoration,
w/original silver plate footed
frame & cover 375.00
Pitcher, water, 8½" h., 7" d., pink
band decoration (ILLUS.) 245.00

Sugar bowl, cov., pink band decoration....................165.00 to 195.00
Tumbler, pink band decoration 80.00

CRACKLE

Crackle Glass Pitcher

*This type of glassware has been made for
centuries by submersing hot glass in cold water, reheating it and then blowing it to produce a crackled or fine spider web effect
throughout the body of the piece. Another
glass sometimes called "Craquelle" is
produced by a different technique and is listed in this guide under "Overshot" glass
(which see).*

Cruet w/original clear bubble stopper, bulbous cranberry body w/a
cylindrical neck w/pinched spout,
applied clear handle & ring foot,
4¼" d., 8" h. $145.00
Lemonade set, clear pitcher w/ap-
plied sea green handle & base &
six clear tumblers w/applied
green bases, 7 pcs. 175.00
Pitcher, 6½" h., ovoid body tapering
to a wide mouth w/pinched spout,
green w/applied green handle &
foot (ILLUS.) 25.00
Pitcher, lemonade, w/ice lip, clear
w/applied amber handle......... 150.00
Tumbler, Amberina, 2 7/8" d.,
4¼" h. 50.00
Tumbler, clear 15.00
Tumbler, lemonade, footed, clear
w/applied amber handle......... 20.00

CRANBERRY

*Gold was added to glass batches to give
this glass its color on reheating. It has been
made by numerous glasshouses for years and
is currently being reproduced. Both blown
and molded articles were produced. A less ex-*

pensive type of cranberry was made with the substitution of copper for gold.

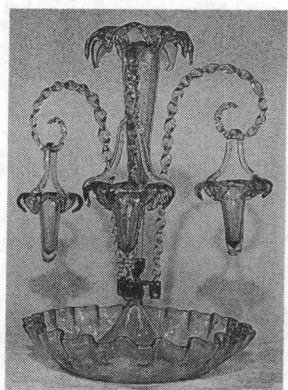

Victorian Cranberry Epergne

Bowl, 3 7/8" d., 3¾" h., spherical wide-mouthed body on three applied clear scroll feet w/small lions' heads, body decoration w/three applied clear stars w/berry centers & applied clear rigaree around the rim, the exterior w/silver mica flecks creating a faint craquelled effect, berry pontil $165.00

Box w/hinged lid, decorated overall w/h.p. gold-enameled florals and butterflies, silver plate fittings, 2¼" d., 1¼" h. 225.00

Candle lamp, cylindrical body decorated w/blue & white flowers, green leaves & a gold butterfly & set within a delicate brass wire footed framework w/a loop side handle, 3¼" d., 6½" h. 295.00

Candlesticks w/bobeches, Diamond Quilted patt., 3¾" d., pr. 110.00

Celery vase, Inverted Thumbprint patt., w/silver plated frame w/twisted rope handle & two medallion head decorations 350.00

Cheese dish, cov., the high domed cover w/tall, pointed finial & the underplate both ornately enameled w/white scrolls & tiny blossoms, underplate 10" d., overall 9" h. 515.00

Cracker jar, cov., Inverted Thumbprint patt., decorated w/enameled florals & gold leaves, ornate silver plate cover, 6½" h. 375.00

Creamer, footed ovoid body tapering to a wide, arched spout, applied clear handle trimmed in gold, the body decorated w/lacy gold flowers & foliage accented w/tiny blue flowers, 2¾" d., 4½" h. 135.00

Cruet w/original clear cut bubble stopper, footed spherical body w/a tall, slender neck w/a tri-lobed rim, applied clear reeded handle, decorated w/green leaves & blue & yellow berries, 3¼" d., 7½" h. 195.00

Decanter w/original clear bubble stopper, baluster-form body tapering to a cylindrical neck & petal-shaped lip, clear applied handle, white enameled flowers w/blue centers & overall white dotting decoration, 4" d., 10¼" h. 195.00

Epergne, four-lily, a flaring & deeply ruffled base bowl tapering up to metal fittings supporting a tall central lily w/a rolled petal rim, central lily flanked by three tall slender clear twisted hook branches suspending three small lilies w/rolled petal rims (ILLUS.) 875.00

Liqueur set: a 6¼" h. & a 10" h. bulbous, bottle-shaped decanter each w/a clear stopper, two 4½" h. footed tumblers & a round tray; all decorated w/heavy gold fuchsia-like flowers & leaves, tumblers w/clear applied feet, 5 pcs. 525.00

Mug, cylindrical w/clear applied handle, decorated w/sanded gold flowers & blue & white outlining, 2 1/8" d., 3" h. 75.00

Pitcher, 5" h., 2¾" d., footed ovoid body tapering to a widely flaring ruffled rim w/pinched spout, clear applied handle 65.00

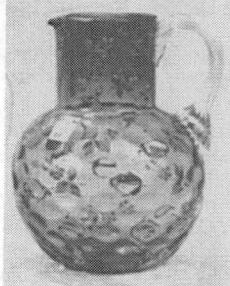

Decorated Cranberry Pitcher

Pitcher, 8½" h., Inverted Thumbprint patt., bulbous spherical body below a wide cylindrical neck w/pinched spout, applied clear reeded handle, decorated overall w/scattered small sprigs of blue flowers & green leaves (ILLUS.) . . . 260.00

Pitcher, tankard, 11½" h., 5" d., Optic patt., clear applied handle 198.00

Rose bowl, footed egg shape, eight-crimp rim, decorated w/gold & silver enameled flowers & leaves on the front & gold & silver birds on the back, clear applied feet, signed "E" & spider web on base for Sir Edward Webb, superintendent of Whitehouse Glass Works, Stourbridge, 3" d., 4¼" h. 210.00

Salt dip, master size, rectangular, gold & creamy white decoration all around, 1½ x 2¾", 1¼" h. . . . 95.00

Salt dip, squatty bulbous shape w/applied clear ruffled rigaree rim, Ribbed patt., silver plate claw-footed holder, 1 7/8" d., 1¾" h. 145.00

Toothpick holder, barrel-shaped, Inverted Thumbprint patt., applied vaseline feet. 195.00

Tumble-up (water carafe w/tumbler lid), Optic patt., corseted body w/matching tumbler, bottle 3 7/8" d., overall 8 3/8" h. 175.00

Vase, 3½" h., 3¼ x 6¼", trough-shaped, w/applied clear flower prunts on each end & decorated overall w/lacy gold scrolls & dainty gold flowers. 165.00

Vase, 5¾" h., 2 3/8" d., bulbous squatty base tapering to a tall slender cylindrical neck, decorated w/small blue & peach enameled flowers, gold leaves, gold neck w/six small amber jewels 95.00

Vase, 10¼" h., 3 7/8" d., Rosette patt., the tall slender footed pedestal base supports a bulbous body w/a short flaring rim, applied clear leaf feet, applied clear leaves around lower rim of the body 145.00

Vase, 10¾" h., 3½" d., swelled cylindrical body on a cushion foot, the rim applied w/a clear band pulled into points, the body decorated w/a white enameled scene of a heron among foliage & flowers. 325.00

Vases, 8½" h., 4" d., bulbous base tapering to a tall slender flaring neck, decorated w/gold swirled bands & leaves & gold & yellow flowers, pr. 325.00

Water set: pitcher & four tumblers; Florentine Cameo ware, enameled w/tropical foliage & birds decoration, 5 pcs. 525.00

Water set: 10" h., 4¼" d. ovoid tankard pitcher w/ruffled rim & applied clear handle & six 4" h. matching tumblers; each decorated w/enameled dots, blue grapes,

white leaves & white bands of triangles, 7 pcs. 450.00

Whimsey, model of a top hat, Honeycomb patt., 1½ x 3¾" 95.00

CROWN MILANO

Enameled Crown Milano Vase

This glass, produced by Mt. Washington Glass Company late last century, is opal glass decorated by painting and enameling. It appears identical to a ware termed Albertine, also made by Mt. Washington.

Cracker jar, cov., cylindrical, decorated w/six pastel pansies highlighted w/gold trim, silver plate rim, floral embossed cover w/an applied butterfly & bail handle, signed & numbered, 4¼" d., 5" h. $785.00

Cracker jar, cov., squatty bulbous body molded overall w/small stars, decorated w/apricot chrysanthemums & a jeweled starfish design, ornate silver plate rim, flower-engraved cover & bail handle, cover marked "MW 4417," 4" h. 660.00

Cracker jar, cov., squatty bulbous body decorated w/starfish & coral branches, heavy gilt trim 1,045.00

Jar w/hinged lid, bulbous sides molded w/twelve swirled panels, four decorated w/tan reserve outlined in gold & the others w/two trailing chrysanthemum branches w/purple flowers & green foliage, flat cover inset w/mirror on both sides, gold-plated rim & collar, metal clasp a replica of the Mt. Washington wreath, marked "456-0/928," 8" d., 4" h. 585.00

Mustard jar, cov., white ground decorated w/h.p. roses, pansies & raised gold decoration, silver plate lid & rim 595.00

Pitcher, molded quilted body decorated w/h.p. enameled holly berry & leaf decoration 3,300.00

Rose bowl, six-crimp rim, decorated overall w/h.p. pansies against a painted white shading to yellow background, 4" d., 3" h. 225.00

Salt & pepper shakers w/original tops, embossed ribbing, decorated w/delicate pink florals on a white satin ground, pr................ 195.00

Sweetmeat jar, cov., decorated w/enameled gold & bronze-tone roses w/applied jeweled centers & foliage, silver plate rim, cover w/turtle finial & bail handle, signed & numbered............. 875.00

Syrup pitcher w/original top, melon-ribbed body decorated w/sprays of roses, pansies, daisies & forget-me-nots, gold scrollwork around the rim, domed pewter top w/ornate finial, rim & handle 685.00

Tray, rolled rim, center decorated w/two large iris blossoms & green foliage, gold trim on the rim, 6¾ x 9½".................... 370.00

Tumbler, gold floral decoration, glossy finish, signed 285.00

Vase, 3" h., 2¼" d., bulbous body tapering to a tiny neck w/flared rim, decorated w/white enameled scrolls & dots & gold trim 40.00

Vase, 8" h., spherical body on a tiny footring, w/a short cylindrical neck w/flared rim flanked by slender pointed applied handles, decorated w/round medallions of griffin's heads scattered around the sides & joined by overall branches of prunus blossoms in gold & brown 1,540.00

Vase, 9¼" h., spherical body raised on a thick, round foot, tapering at the top to a small mouth w/out-wardly looped rim forming small rim handles, creamy ground decorated in gilt w/frolicking putti within gilt cartouches reserved against a ground further decorated overall w/delicate gilt scrolls, flowers & leafage, "CM" & crown mark & "593" (ILLUS.) 1,320.00

Vase, 9¾" h., spherical body tapering to a tiny neck below a flaring cupped rim, creamy ground decorated on the obverse w/three flamingoes wading in shallow waters within a leafy surround, the reverse w/two flamingoes in flight, in shades of rose, pink, white, salmon, olive green & rust trimmed w/gold, two C-scroll handles at the shoulder, unsigned ...2,750.00

CRUETS

Log & Star Pattern Cruet

Amber, blown, footed ovoid body w/short neck & tricorner rim, decorated w/blue daisies & gold leaves, applied amber handle, amber ball stopper, 3 1/8" d., 8" h................................$110.00

Amber, mold-blown, French Hobnail patt., applied blue handle, original stopper 150.00

Amber, pressed, Log & Star patt., original stopper (ILLUS.) 60.00

Blue, pressed, Challinor's Tree of Life patt., original stopper 95.00

Cased, blown, yellow exterior, pink interior, bulbous body w/trefoil rim, applied clear handle, original bulbous stopper................ 150.00

Clear, pressed, Paneled Sunflower patt., original stopper 35.00

Cobalt blue, pressed, Medallion Sprig patt., original cobalt to clear stopper 150.00

Cranberry, blown, teepee-shaped, engraved initials w/ferns, ground pontil, original cut stopper 195.00

Green, pressed, Beaded Ovals in Sand patt., original stopper 175.00

Green, pressed, Beaded Scroll patt., original stopper 205.00

Green, pressed, Beaumont's Flora patt., gold trim, original stopper.. 225.00

Green, pressed, Double Circle patt., original stopper 110.00

Lavender, blown, footed spherical body w/slender cylindrical neck, decorated w/gold flowers & bows, applied clear handle & foot, clear facet-cut stopper, 7¼" h. 210.00

Milk white, pressed, Beaded Swag patt., gold trim, original stopper.. 185.00

Sapphire blue, blown, bulbous body w/a slender cylindrical neck, enameled w/white wreaths, scrolls & dots, applied sapphire blue handle, original enameled ball stopper, 3¼" d., 7¼" h...... 125.00

Sapphire blue, blown, footed ovoid
body w/slender cylindrical neck,
decorated w/a gold bird, applied
clear twisted handle & disc foot,
clear facet-cut stopper, 8" h. 235.00
Sapphire blue, blown, ovoid body
w/tall slender neck, applied amber handle, amber ball stopper,
3 5/8" d., 8 3/8" h. 70.00
Sapphire blue, mold-blown, Swirl
patt., ovoid body w/a tall slender
neck w/four-crimp rim, applied
clear handle, clear bubble stop-
per, 3" d., 8¾" h. 88.00

CUSTARD GLASS

This ware takes its name from its color and is a variant of milk white glass. It was produced largely between 1890 and 1915 by the Northwood Glass Co., Heisey Glass Company, Fenton Art Glass Co., Jefferson Glass Co., and a few others. There are 21 major patterns and a number of minor ones. The prime patterns are considered Argonaut Shell, Chrysanthemum Sprig, Inverted Fan and Feather, Louis XV and Winged Scroll. Most custard glass patterns are enhanced with gold and some have additional enameled decoration or stained highlights. Unless otherwise noted, items in this listing are fully decorated.

ARGONAUT SHELL (Northwood)

Argonaut Shell Sugar & Spooner

Berry set, master bowl & 6 sauce
dishes, 7 pcs. $575.00
Bowl, master berry or fruit, 10½" l.,
5" h. . . . . .185.00 to 225.00
Butter dish, cov. 250.00
Compote, jelly, 5" d., 5" h. 126.00
Creamer 131.00
Cruet w/original stopper . .450.00 to 500.00
Pitcher, water 375.00
Salt & pepper shakers w/original
tops, pr. . . . . .325.00 to 350.00
Sauce dish. 57.00
Spooner (ILLUS. right). 150.00
Sugar bowl, cov. (ILLUS. left) 205.00
Toothpick holder 345.00
Tumbler 85.00

BEADED CIRCLE (Northwood)

Beaded Circle Creamer

Butter dish, cov. 272.00
Creamer (ILLUS.) 130.00
Pitcher, water . . . . .600.00 to 650.00
Spooner 124.00
Sugar bowl, cov. 175.00
Tumbler 130.00

BEADED SWAG (Heisey)

Goblet . . . . .55.00 to 65.00
Goblet, souvenir 62.50
Sauce dish. 25.00
Sauce dish, souvenir. 35.00
Wine. 48.50
Wine, souvenir. 58.00

CARNELIAN - See Everglades Pattern

CHRYSANTHEMUM SPRIG (Northwood)

Chrysanthemum Sprig Cruet

Berry set, master bowl & 6 sauce
dishes, 7 pcs. 590.00
Bowl, master berry or fruit, 10½"
oval, decorated 165.00
Bowl, master berry or fruit, 10½"
oval, undecorated. . . . . . .125.00 to 140.00
Butter dish, cov. 270.00
Celery vase. 715.00
Compote, jelly, decorated. 125.00
Compote, jelly, undecorated 75.00
Condiment tray 615.00
Creamer 120.00
Cruet w/original stopper
(ILLUS.) . . . . .275.00 to 300.00
Pitcher, water, decorated 345.00
Pitcher, water, undeco-
rated . . . . .200.00 to 250.00
Salt & pepper shakers w/original
tops, pr. 210.00

Sauce dish........................ 62.00
Sauce dish, blue trim 135.00
Spooner 86.00
Sugar bowl, cov., decorated....... 210.00
Sugar bowl, cov., undecorated 145.00
Toothpick holder w/gold trim &
   paint, signed 270.00
Toothpick holder, undecorated 175.00
Tumbler 57.50
Water set, pitcher & 6 tumblers,
   7 pcs. 745.00

DIAMOND WITH PEG (Jefferson)
Butter dish, cov. 285.00
Creamer, individual size 30.00
Creamer, individual size, souvenir .. 85.00
Creamer 75.00
Mug, souvenir ....35.00 to 45.00
Napkin ring....................... 145.00
Pitcher, 5½" h. 140.00
Pitcher, tankard, 7½" h............ 250.00
Pitcher, tankard, 7½" h., souvenir .. 230.00
Spooner 95.00
Sugar bowl, cov..........125.00 to 150.00
Toothpick holder 75.00
Tumbler 50.00
Tumbler, souvenir 39.00
Whiskey shot glass 45.00
Wine............................. 37.50
Wine, souvenir.................... 55.00

EVERGLADES or CARNELIAN (Northwood)
Bowl, master berry or fruit, footed
   compote ....165.00 to 185.00
Compote, jelly 250.00
Salt shaker w/original top 150.00
Sauce dish........................ 60.00
Spooner 130.00
Table set, cov. butter dish, cov.
   sugar bowl, creamer & spooner,
   4 pcs. 850.00
Tumbler 105.00

FAN (Dugan)
Bowl, master berry or
   fruit ....175.00 to 200.00
Creamer 90.00
Ice cream dish 42.00
Pitcher, water 290.00
Sauce dish........................ 60.00
Spooner 60.00
Tumbler 72.50
Water set, pitcher & 4 tumblers,
   5 pcs. 545.00

**FLUTED SCROLLS WITH FLOWER BAND - See
Jackson Pattern**

GENEVA (Northwood)
Banana boat, four-footed,
   11" oval.................95.00 to 125.00
Banana boat, four-footed, green
   stain, 11" oval 145.00

Berry set, oval master bowl &
   6 sauce dishes, 7 pcs. 318.00
Bowl, master berry or fruit, 8½"
   oval, four-footed 95.00
Bowl, master berry or fruit, 8½"
   oval, four-footed, green stain 85.00
Bowl, master berry or fruit, 8½" d.,
   three-footed 102.00
Butter dish, cov. 145.00
Compote, jelly 80.00
Creamer ....80.00 to 90.00
Cruet w/original stopper ..350.00 to 450.00
Salt & pepper shakers w/original
   tops, pr......................... 195.00
Sauce dish, round 37.50
Spooner ....75.00 to 100.00
Sugar bowl, cov..........125.00 to 150.00

Geneva Syrup Pitcher

Syrup pitcher w/original top
   (ILLUS.)........................ 275.00
Table set, 4 pcs. ....450.00 to 500.00
Toothpick holder, decorated........ 125.00
Toothpick holder, undecorated 60.00
Tumbler 55.00

GEORGIA GEM or LITTLE GEM (Tarentum)
Bowl, master berry or fruit,
   decorated 72.00
Butter dish, cov., deco-
   rated ....175.00 to 200.00
Butter dish, cov., undecorated...... 98.00
Celery vase....................... 132.00
Creamer, decorated 35.00
Creamer, breakfast size 30.00
Creamer & cov. sugar bowl, sou-
   venir, pr.................75.00 to 125.00
Creamer & open sugar bowl, break-
   fast size, souvenir, pr........... 90.00
Cruet w/original stopper ..150.00 to 200.00
Hair receiver, souvenir 45.00
Powder jar, cov., souvenir 52.00
Salt shaker w/original top 50.00
Sauce dish, decorated 27.00
Spooner 65.00
Sugar bowl, cov., decorated........ 105.00
Sugar bowl, cov., undecorated 45.00
Toothpick holder 105.00
Toothpick holder, souvenir 32.00
Tumbler 50.00
Tumbler, souvenir 35.00

GRAPE & CABLE - See Northwood Grape Pattern

GRAPE & GOTHIC ARCHES (Northwood)

Grape & Gothic Arches Goblet

Berry set, master bowl & 3 sauce
   dishes, 4 pcs. 215.00
Bowl, master berry or fruit........ 125.00
Goblet (ILLUS.) 55.00
Spooner ....50.00 to 75.00
Sugar bowl, cov. 195.00
Sugar bowl, cov., blue stain........ 195.00
Tumbler 55.00
Vase, 10" h. ("favor" vase made
   from goblet mold) 75.00
Water set, pitcher & 6 tumblers,
   7 pcs. ....550.00 to 650.00

GRAPE & THUMBPRINT - See Northwood Grape Pattern

INTAGLIO (Northwood)

Bowl, fruit, 7½" d. footed com-
   pote 142.00
Bowl, fruit, 9" d. footed com-
   pote ....300.00 to 350.00
Butter dish, cov. 245.00
Compote, jelly 95.00
Creamer 100.00
Cruet w/original stopper........... 315.00
Pitcher, water 335.00
Salt shaker w/original top 85.00
Sauce dish........................ 47.00
Spooner 100.00
Sugar bowl, cov. 150.00
Table set, green stain, 4 pcs........ 540.00
Tumbler 60.00
Water set, pitcher & 6 tumblers,
   7 pcs. 750.00

INVERTED FAN & FEATHER (Northwood)

Berry set, master bowl & 6 sauce
   dishes, 7 pcs...........575.00 to 600.00
Bowl, master berry or fruit, 10" d.,
   5½" h., four-footed 250.00
Butter dish, cov. ....250.00 to 275.00
Compote, jelly ....350.00 to 425.00
Creamer 125.00
Punch cup 265.00

Salt & pepper shakers w/original
   tops, pr.......................... 495.00
Sauce dish........................ 54.00
Spooner 105.00
Sugar bowl, cov. 215.00
Table set, 4 pcs. 800.00
Toothpick holder 650.00
Tumbler 75.00
Water set, pitcher & 6 tumblers,
   7 pcs. 895.00

IVORINA VERDE - See Winged Scroll Pattern

JACKSON or FLUTED SCROLLS WITH FLOWER BAND (Northwood)

Jackson Creamer

Bowl, master berry or fruit......... 85.00
Creamer (ILLUS.) 90.00
Cruet, no stopper ....100.00 to 125.00
Salt shaker w/original top, un-
   decorated 58.00
Salt & pepper shakers w/original
   tops, pr.......................... 135.00
Tumbler 37.00
Water set, pitcher & 4 tumblers,
   5 pcs. ....365.00 to 385.00

LITTLE GEM - See Georgia Gem Pattern

LOUIS XV (Northwood)

Berry set, master bowl & 5 sauce
   dishes, 6 pcs. 425.00
Bowl, berry or fruit, 7¾ x 10"
   oval ....135.00 to 150.00
Butter dish, cov. ....150.00 to 175.00
Creamer ....60.00 to 75.00
Cruet w/original stopper........... 235.00
Pitcher, water 210.00
Salt & pepper shakers w/original
   tops, pr.......................... 215.00
Sauce dish, footed, 5" oval........ 39.00
Spooner ....60.00 to 75.00
Sugar bowl, cov. 112.00
Table set, 4 pcs. ....500.00 to 550.00
Tumbler 55.00

MAPLE LEAF (Northwood)

Banana bowl....................... 175.00
Butter dish, cov. 270.00

Compote, jelly ....450.00 to 500.00
Creamer 145.00
Pitcher, water ....300.00 to 350.00
Sauce dish...................... 80.00
Spooner 128.00
Sugar bowl, cov. 185.00
Toothpick holder 650.00
Tumbler 90.00

NORTHWOOD GRAPE, GRAPE & CABLE or GRAPE & THUMBPRINT

Northwood Grape Creamer & Sugar

Bowl, 7½" d., ruffled rim 45.00
Bowl, master berry or fruit, 11" d.,
   ruffled, footed 445.00
Butter dish, cov. 250.00
Cologne bottle w/original stop-
   per ....400.00 to 500.00
Cracker jar, cov., two-
   handled ....575.00 to 600.00
Creamer ....125.00 to 150.00
Creamer & open sugar bowl, break-
   fast size, pr. (ILLUS.) 125.00
Dresser tray ....275.00 to 325.00
Humidor, cov.................... 650.00
Pin dish 165.00
Plate, 7" d. 55.00
Plate, 8" w., six-sided 60.00
Plate, 8" d.................20.00 to 35.00
Punch cup 75.00
Sauce dish, flat 30.00
Sauce dish, footed 42.00
Spooner 135.00
Sugar bowl, cov. 150.00
Sugar bowl, open, breakfast size ... 62.00
Tumbler 55.00
Water set, pitcher & 6 tumblers,
   7 pcs. 1,250.00

PUNTY BAND (Heisey)

Creamer, individual size, souvenir .. 35.00
Cuspidor, lady's 75.00
Mug, souvenir 55.00
Mug, 4½" h...................... 29.00
Toothpick holder, souvenir 45.00
Tumbler, floral decoration, sou-
   venir.......................... 45.00

RIBBED DRAPE (Jefferson)

Compote, jelly 145.00
Creamer 125.00
Pitcher, water 255.00
Sauce dish..................... 35.00
Spooner (ILLUS.).............. 115.00
Sugar bowl, cov................ 185.00

Ribbed Drape Spooner

Table set, 4 pcs. (open sugar) 575.00
Toothpick holder w/rose decora-
   tion 195.00
Tumbler 82.00

RING BAND (Heisey)

Berry set, master bowl & 6 sauce
   dishes, 7 pcs...........450.00 to 500.00
Bowl, master berry or fruit,
   decorated 295.00
Butter dish, cov. ....235.00 to 250.00
Compote, jelly ....145.00 to 175.00
Creamer 80.00
Cruet w/original stopper 300.00
Pitcher, water 250.00
Salt shaker w/original top, un-
   decorated 55.00
Sauce dish..................... 37.50
Spooner 120.00
Sugar bowl, cov. ....150.00 to 175.00
Syrup pitcher w/original top 295.00
Toothpick holder, decorated........ 120.00
Toothpick holder, undecorated 93.00
Toothpick holder, souvenir 75.00
Tumbler, decorated............... 75.00
Tumbler, undecorated 45.00
Tumbler, souvenir 40.00
Water set, pitcher & 6 tumblers,
   7 pcs. 550.00

VICTORIA (Tarentum)

Butter dish, cov. ....275.00 to 325.00
Celery vase ....150.00 to 200.00
Spooner, decorated................ 145.00
Spooner, undecorated 72.00
Vase, bud 60.00

WINGED SCROLL or IVORINA VERDE (Heisey)

Berry set, master bowl & 6 sauce
   dishes, decorated, 7 pcs. 320.00
Bowl, fruit, 8½" d. 157.00
Butter dish, cov. ....165.00 to 200.00
Celery vase ....275.00 to 300.00
Cigarette jar..............145.00 to 175.00
Compote, 10¾" d., 6¾" h.......... 495.00
Creamer, decorated 93.00
Creamer, undecorated 55.00
Cruet w/original stopper, deco-
   rated ....175.00 to 200.00

Cruet w/original stopper, undeco-
rated 100.00
Match holder ....190.00 to 225.00
Nappy, folded side handle, 6" 50.00
Pin tray, small 195.00
Pitcher, water, 9" h., bulbous 230.00
Pitcher, water, tankard, deco-
rated ....250.00 to 275.00
Pitcher, water, tankard, undeco-
rated 235.00
Powder jar, cov. 99.00
Powder jar, cov., souvenir 55.00
Salt & pepper shakers w/original
tops, pr.......................... 135.00
Sauce dish, 4½" d. 39.00

Winged Scroll Toothpick & Spooner

Spooner (ILLUS. right).............. 72.00
Sugar bowl, cov., deco-
rated ....100.00 to 150.00
Sugar bowl, cov., undecorated 95.00
Syrup pitcher w/original top 365.00
Toothpick holder (ILLUS. left) 95.00
Tumbler 77.50
Vase, 9" h. 190.00
Water set, bulbous pitcher & 4 tum-
blers, 5 pcs. 550.00

MISCELLANEOUS PATTERNS

Delaware
Berry set, master bowl & 5 sauce
dishes, 6 pcs. 190.00
Bowl, 5½" (hat-shaped)............ 45.00
Creamer, individual size 36.00
Creamer w/rose decoration 67.00
Pin tray w/blue decoration 62.00
Pin tray w/green decoration, 7" 70.00
Pin tray w/rose stain, 4½" 60.00
Punch cup 40.00
Ring tree, 4" h. 80.00
Sauce dish w/blue decoration 45.00
Sauce dish w/rose stain 65.00
Spooner 65.00
Sugar bowl, breakfast size 45.00
Tumbler w/blue decoration 55.00
Tumbler w/green decoration 45.00

Heart with Thumbprint
Creamer 40.00
Creamer & sugar bowl, individual
size, pr......................... 125.00
Finger lamp, w/green decoration ... 250.00
Sugar bowl, individual size, w/green
decoration..................... 55.00

Peacock and Urn
Bowl, master berry 130.00
Ice cream bowl, master, w/nutmeg
stain, 9¾" d. ....300.00 to 375.00
Ice cream dish, individual, w/nut-
meg stain 65.00
Sauce dish........................ 38.00

Vermont
Bowl, master berry........100.00 to 125.00
Butter dish, cov. 104.00
Candlestick, finger 73.00
Card basket, 7½" d. 95.00
Celery vase...................... 225.00
Creamer w/blue decoration 97.00
Creamer w/green & pink florals 94.00
Pickle tray....................... 30.00
Pitcher w/blue trim & enameled
decoration..................... 250.00
Salt shaker w/original top,
enameled decoration 77.50
Salt & pepper shakers w/original
tops, blue decoration, pr. 135.00
Spooner 75.00
Spooner w/green decoration 75.00
Toothpick holder w/blue trim &
enameled decoration 90.00
Toothpick holder w/green deco-
ration 135.00
Tumbler 70.00
Tumbler w/blue decoration 60.00
Vase............................ 25.00
Vase w/enameled decoration 70.00

Wild Bouquet
Butter dish, cov. 565.00
Creamer 140.00
Cruet w/original stopper, w/enam-
eling & gold trim 570.00
Cruet w/original stopper, undeco-
rated 300.00
Sauce dish....................... 50.00
Spooner w/gold trim & colored
decoration..................... 138.00
Spooner, undecorated 65.00
Toothpick holder, decorated........ 475.00
Tumbler, undecorated 86.00

(End of Custard Glass Section)

CUT GLASS

Cut glass most eagerly sought by collectors is American glass produced during the so-called "Brilliant Period" from 1880 to about 1915. Pieces listed below are by type of article in alphabetical order.

BOWLS
Egginton signed, Trellis patt.,
9¼" d., 3" h. $1,600.00
Expanding Star patt., fan, hobstar,

star & strawberry diamond,
8" d. 275.00
Hawkes signed, Gravic Iris patt.,
8" d. 200.00
Hawkes' Chrysanthemum patt., split
vesicas, hobstars, cane & other
cutting, 11" d., 6" h. 750.00

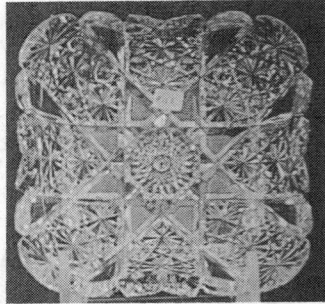

Hawkes' Grecian Pattern Bowl

Hawkes' Grecian patt., vesica, fan,
Russian motif & other cutting,
turned in rim, 8" sq. (ILLUS.) 500.00
Hoare signed, Comet patt., 9¼" d.,
4" h. 825.00
Hoare's Carolyn patt. variant, small
cane, hobstars & plain vesicas
surrounded by fine silver diamonds & hobstars around scalloped top, 9" d. 525.00
Hobstar & cane, heart-shaped,
4 x 8 x 9" 550.00
Hunt's Royal patt., Russian motif
w/hobstar button, five-sided
strawberry diamond lozenge &
large hobstars, shallow, 8" d. 425.00
Libbey's Colonna patt., chain of hobstars, crosshatched triangle, fan,
star & strawberry diamond, shallow, 10" d. 175.00
Libbey's Puritania patt., cane, cross-
cut diamond, fan & hobstar,
7" sq. 400.00
Libbey's Stratford patt., cluster of
hobstars around hexagon center,
turned in rim, 9" sq. 550.00
Mayonnaise, Meriden's Alhambra
(Greek Key) patt. 1,000.00
Sinclaire's Adam patt., intaglio-
cut floral baskets, octagonal,
9½" w. 350.00
Tuthill's Phlox patt., intaglio-cut
flowers & other cutting, heart-
shaped, 7" w. 225.00
Tuthill's Wild Rose patt., intaglio-cut
rose blossoms & foliage & other
cutting, 7" d. 400.00

BOXES

Dresser, Russian patt. on hinged lid
& around sides, hobstar in base,
7" d. 600.00

Glove, Hawkes' Gravic Iris patt. 400.00

Tuthill Handkerchief Box

Handkerchief, Tuthill, hinged square
lid cut w/a chain of hobstars interrupted at the corners w/fan
cutting & surrounding central deep
intaglio-cut flowers, the sides cut
in double thumbprints w/cross-cut
diamond, star-cut base (ILLUS.) ..1,875.00
Trinket, Sinclaire signed, oval, lid
cut w/ferns in an oval & notching,
sides cut w/hobstars, crosshatching & notching 245.00

BUTTER DISHES & TUBS

Covered dish, pinwheel & hobstar,
dome lid & matching underplate .. 200.00
Covered dish, Straus' Americus
patt., fan, hobstar, star & strawberry diamond, dome lid & matching underplate 800.00
Tub, hobstars & other cutting, two-
handled, 3½ x 7" 380.00

CANDLESTICKS & CANDLEHOLDERS

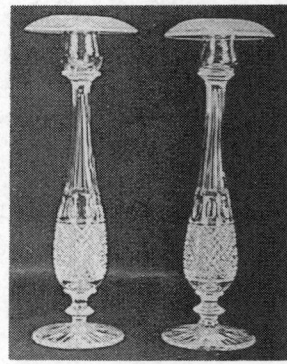

Brilliant Period Candlesticks

Baluster-form hollow stem, engraved w/flowers & cut w/ovals &
honeycomb, 13" h., pr. 302.50
Cross-cut diamond on lower portion
of stem beneath a band of bull's-
eyes, everted conformingly cut

rim, rayed base, 15" h., pr.
(ILLUS.) 1,250.00
Hawkes signed, Sheraton patt.,
bands of triple mitre cutting &
medallions engraved w/fruit
baskets & cornucopias, honeycomb stem w/teardrop, 9" h...... 350.00
Prism & beading on stem w/two
lapidary-cut knobs & teardrop,
24-point hobstar base, 10" h...... 400.00
Rock Crystal-style design of flowers
& leaves on ovoid stem, Sinclaire-
type elliptical ovals on base,
10½" h., pr. 500.00
Teardrop-shaped panels (6) w/prism
cutting on each edge, bulbous
form, 10" h., pr. 600.00

Other
Candelabrum, five-light, Bergen's
Pyramid patt., fan, hobstar, ovals
& strawberry diamond, w/silver
plate fittings, 15" h. 700.00
Chamberstick, flute & strawberry
diamond, triple-notched handle,
4" d. 275.00

CARAFES
Hawkes signed, hobstars, deep
mitres & other cutting, ring-cut
neck, 24-point star base, 8" h. ... 125.00
Hawkes' Kensington patt. 395.00
Hobstars, cane & cross-cut diamond,
8¼" h.......................... 85.00

CELERY TRAYS
Cane patt. & intaglio cutting, boat-
shaped, 11½" l................. 190.00
Hobstars & diamonds overall,
11" l.......................... 125.00
Russian patt., large 500.00

CHAMPAGNES, CORDIALS & WINES
Champagne, Libbey's Kimberly patt.,
fan, hobstar & strawberry diamond (single) 275.00
Champagnes, Hawkes' Gravic Iris
patt., set of 4 .... 280.00
Cordial, Libbey's Imperial patt.,
cane, fan, hobstar & star 160.00
Wine, cranberry cut to clear,
Hawkes' Venetian patt., chain of
hobstars, fan, star & strawberry
diamond split vesica 375.00
Wine, cranberry cut to clear, Russian patt....................... 325.00
Wines, cranberry cut to clear,
Hoare's Monarch patt., cross-cut
vesicas w/split, pr.............. 600.00
Wines, green cut to clear, Honey-
comb patt., set of 6 .... 660.00
Wines, Sinclaire's Adam patt.,
intaglio-cut floral baskets, pr. 160.00

COMPOTES

Averbeck's Marietta Pattern Compote

Averbeck's Marietta patt., hobstars,
double cross-cut vesicas & other
cutting, notch-cut stem w/tear-
drop, hobstar base, pr. (ILLUS. of
one) 500.00
Hoare's Comet patt., teardrop stem
cut in St. Louis diamond, hobstar
base, 6" d., 11½" h. 700.00
Hobstar & cane, 7" 150.00
Hobstar & fan, teardrop stem,
9¼" 90.00
Hobstar & fan, teardrop stem,
9½" 225.00

CREAMERS & SUGAR BOWLS
Alhambra (Greek Key) patt., pr..... 350.00
Buzz star & deep mitre cutting, low
footed w/star-cut base, cut handles, pr........................ 225.00
Expanding Star patt., fan, hobstar,
star & strawberry diamond, triple-
notched handles, pedestal base,
pr............................. 350.00
Hawkes signed, chain of hobstars,
pedestal base, pr................ 275.00
Hoare signed, Monarch patt., cross-
cut vesica w/split, pr. 270.00
Hobstar & fan, pedestal base,
pr....................100.00 to 125.00
Libbey signed, Wheat patt., pr...... 210.00
Libbey's Neola patt., feather-type
motif w/hobstars & other cutting,
pr............................. 300.00
Russian patt., starred conical foot,
covered sugar bowl has knurled
tab handle on either side, pr. 450.00

CRUETS
Diamond & fan, rayed base, bulbous
body, faceted stopper 60.00
Hawkes signed, Russian patt., rayed
base, bulbous body, tri-pour lip .. 300.00
Hoare's Hindoo patt., chain of hobstars, beading & fan............ 130.00

Hobstar & cane, original cut
   stopper 85.00
Hobstar & fan, tri-pour lip.......... 140.00
Hobstar, zipper, file & other cutting,
   step-cut neck, notch-cut handle,
   matching stopper............... 98.00

DECANTERS

Egginton's Trellis Pattern Decanter

Chain of hobstars & fan, conformingly cut mushroom-shaped stopper, 10" h. 90.00
Cross-cut diamond, fan & stars,
   matching stopper, 14¾" h........ 195.00
Egginton's Trellis patt., checker-
   board-type design, beading & horizontal step-cutting at neck, faceted stopper, 12½" h. (ILLUS.).....2,600.00
Hobstar & fan, triple ring-cut neck,
   11" h......................... 250.00
Hobstars, herringbone, prism &
   cane, double-notched handle,
   teardrop lapidary-cut stopper,
   pyramid-shaped, 14½" h. 950.00
Hobstars, miters & fan, sterling silver neck & rim, matching stopper,
   3" sq., 11" h. 185.00
Pinwheel & cane, corset-shaped,
   notched neck, 14" h. 180.00
Russian patt. w/starred buttons,
   globular w/faceted rings at neck,
   original conformingly cut stopper,
   11½" h........................ 325.00

DISHES, MISCELLANEOUS

Bonbon, Russian patt., leaf-shaped,
   5½ x 7½"..................... 140.00
Mint dish, Sinclaire's Snowflake &
   Holly patt...................... 700.00
Relish, Libbey's Columbia patt.,
   clear tusks, hobstars & other cutting, turned-in sides, serrated rim,
   6 x 12" (ILLUS.) 1,400.00

Libbey's Columbia Pattern Relish

Relish, Libbey's Marcella patt., cluster of hobstars around hexagon
   center, 6 x 12", 3" h............ 600.00
Relish, Meriden's Old Irish patt.,
   fan, prism & relief diamond 210.00

JARS

Tobacco Jar by Dorflinger

Cigar, Harvard patt., matching cover, 9" h........................ 550.00
Horseradish, overall pinwheel cutting, original stopper 75.00
Mustard, buttons, cane & floral, cover w/cut finial 110.00
Powder, fans & crosshatching,
   16-point star at center of cover
   & on bottom 85.00
Powder, Hawkes' Venetian patt.,
   chain of hobstars, fan, star &
   strawberry diamond split vesica,
   silver plate lid 140.00
Tobacco, cranberry cut to clear, Dorflinger, chain of hobstars & fan
   above plain paneled sides headed
   w/cross-hatching, row of bull's-
   eye on shoulder, silver collar,
   compressed ball stopper cut in
   pattern, 8" d., 9" h. (ILLUS.) 6,500.00

LAMPS

Boudoir, domed shade w/hobstars
   & other cutting, conforming
   baluster-form base, silver plate
   fittings, 6" d. shade, 15" h. 495.00
Table, domed shade w/floral & Harvard patt., conformingly cut stem
   & flaring base w/serrated edge,

silver rim w/prisms, 8" d. shade,
23" h. 850.00
Table, domed shade, floral cutting
alternating w/squares of cane cutting, matching serrated & scalloped petticoat base, metal rim
w/prisms, 12" d. shade, 23" h. . . . 880.00
Table, domed shade, double star,
hobstar & fan, slightly flaring
cylindrical standard w/horizontal
step-cutting above conforming
pattern, silver rim w/notch-cut
prisms, 30" h. 1,210.00

"Street Lamp" Style Table Lamp

Table, "Street Lamp" style, mushroom shaped central shade cut in
pinwheel w/hobstar & fan,
flanked by four teardrop ball
shades conformingly cut, horizontally stepped flared base w/scal-
loped & serrated rim, silver
fittings hung w/spear-point
prisms, 31" h. (ILLUS.). 26,400.00

MISCELLANEOUS

Banana Boat by Libbey

Banana boat, Libbey's Pattern
No. 202, hobstars, fan & other
cutting, pedestal base w/star-cut
foot, scalloped & serrated rim
(ILLUS.) 1,700.00

Cuspidor, lady's, hobstars & fans . . . 75.00
Finger bowl, Bergen's Glenwood
patt., hobstars, five-sided strawberry diamond lozenge & other
cutting 60.00
Finger bowl, cross-cut diamond &
fan 50.00
Finger bowl, Egginton signed, chain
of hobstars separated by half diamonds of cross-cut diamonds . . 175.00
Finger bowl, Hawkes' Millicent patt.,
bands of triple miter cutting alternating w/medallions of engraved
fruit baskets 150.00
Finger bowl, Libbey's Imperial patt.,
cane, fan, hobstar & star 220.00
Flower center, hobstars, fan, fine
cut & cane, horizontal stepped
neck, scalloped rim, 14½" d.,
8¾" h. (minor roughness) 1,540.00
Ice cream knife, handle cut in
honeycomb & Russian patt.
w/clear button, floral engraved
silver blade marked "1834 J. Rus-
sel & Co." 350.00
Lemonade set: 7¾" h. pitcher & four
4" h. handled mugs w/pedestal
base; Tuthill signed, Vintage
patt., 5 pcs. 495.00
Napkin ring, bull's-eye & hobstar . . . 70.00
Napkin ring, Cane patt. 75.00
Pickle castor, St. Louis Diamond cut-
ting on lower half, the top half
w/etched florals & foliage, in
an ornate silver plate frame
w/cover 250.00
Salad serving fork & spoon, Cane
patt. handles w/teardrop, silver
plate tines & bowl, pr. 525.00
Sugar shaker, Russian patt. alternat-
ing w/clear panels, original silver
top 375.00
Whipped cream bowl & underplate,
Libbey's Wedgemere patt., beading, flute, hobstar & strawberry
diamond, 2 pcs. 1,100.00
Whiskey tumbler, Hawkes' Gladys
patt., chain of hobstars, fan &
strawberry diamond 40.00
Whiskey tumbler, Hoare's Monarch
patt., cross-cut vesicas w/split . . . 50.00
Whiskey tumbler, Hoare's Pluto
patt., chain of hobstars, beading,
fan & strawberry diamond 60.00
Whiskey tumbler, Libbey's Florence
patt., chain of hobstars, fan, star
& strawberry diamond 40.00

NAPPIES

Hobstar & cane, two-handled 80.00
Hobstars & other cutting, clover-
shaped, stem forms handle,
4 x 5" 95.00

Hobstars, flowers & foliage, serrated rim, loop handle, 6" d. 75.00

Libbey's Somerset patt., crossed ovals, hobstars, hobnail & beading, heart-shaped, 5 x 5½" 95.00

Meriden's Florence patt., Florence hobstars w/notched prism & fans, tri-shell shaped handle folds in to center......................... 150.00

Stars & vesicas, single handle, 6" d........................... 45.00

PERFUME & COLOGNE BOTTLES

Cologne, Dorflinger's Parisian patt., strawberry diamond, star, fan & beading, large 400.00

Cologne, Harvard patt., square w/step-cut shoulders & rayed neck, 6" h. 100.00

Cologne, Hawkes' Gravic Iris patt. ... 300.00

Cologne, hobstars & fields of Kohinoor, hobstar bottom, signed Wilcox sterling silver repousse' stopper, 6" h., pr. 800.00

Cologne, red cut to clear, Harvard patt., conformingly cut stopper, 7½" h........................ 850.00

Cologne, Tuthill signed, Wild Rose patt., Gorham sterling silver repousse' stopper, 6" h. 750.00

Perfume, Cane patt., w/glass stopper & sterling silver top......... 175.00

Perfume, cylindrical, the sides cut w/rows of ovals, hinged sterling silver cover centering a polychrome portrait of a lady under glass, 7" h. 220.00

Perfume, Tuthill's Phlox patt........ 225.00

PITCHERS

Cut Glass Tankard Pitcher

Champagne, hobstars, notched prism, crosshatching & other cutting, Gorham signed sterling silver collar, 4½" base d., 10" h. 275.00

Cider, hobstars & fan, 6½" h. 175.00

Creamer, Hawkes' Gravic Iris patt.......................... 50.00

Lemonade, Hawkes' Middlesex patt., chain of hobstars & fan 550.00

Tankard, cranberry cut to clear, vertical panels of hobstars alternating w/clusters of cane, strawberry diamond & other cutting, scalloped & serrated rim (ILLUS.) 6,500.00

Tankard, expanding star, hobstar & cane, 12" h. 200.00

Water, hobstars & fan, notch-cut handle, 8" h. 250.00

Water, diamond point & prism, sterling silver rim, 10" h............. 750.00

Water, Libbey signed, hobstars, cross-cut diamond & fan, scalloped & serrated rim, 5¼" d., 8" h. 295.00

Water, Sinclaire's Adam patt., intaglio-cut floral baskets, silver top, 11" h.................... 240.00

Water, Mt. Washington's Wheeler patt., cross-cut diamond, fan, star & strawberry diamond, 11½" h. .. 375.00

Water, Hawkes' Classic patt., spray of flowers against a fish-scale ground 275.00

Water, sunburst motif w/hobstar & cane 150.00

PLATES

5" d., Dorflinger's Hob & Lace patt., double miter cane 85.00

5¾" d., Sinclair signed, Adam patt., intaglio-cut baskets & other cutting 150.00

7" d., Bergen's Prism patt., 24-point hobstar center w/radiating beading 225.00

7" d., comet motif comprised of swirls of notched prism & hobstars 125.00

7" d., Egginton's Tokio patt., sunburst motif w/hobstars & other cutting 220.00

7" d., Hawkes signed, hobstars, fan & cane 145.00

7 x 9" oval, Tuthill's Vintage patt., intaglio-cut grape clusters & foliage 750.00

8" d., cranberry cut to clear, Dorflinger's Vintage patt. 495.00

8" d., Hawkes signed, strawberry diamond & fan 75.00

8" d., Hawkes signed, wide line-cut band, center w/floral design 95.00

8" d., Pairpoint's Vintage patt., intaglio-cut, cobalt blue.......... 170.00

10" d., Hawkes signed, hobstar center surrounded by intaglio-cut ferns & flowers, chain of hobstars border 325.00

10" d., Three Fruits patt., attributed to Tuthill, intaglio-cut cherries, pears & grapes & foliage, scalloped & serrated rim 375.00

Rosaceae Pattern Plate

10" d., Tuthill's Rosaceae patt., chain of hobstars border surrounding a band of rose blossoms & foliage, large hobstar center (ILLUS.) 600.00

PUNCH BOWLS

Alford signed, Triest patt., notched prism w/large triangle from side to base to side, further cut w/hobstars alternating w/crosshatching, 12" d., 5½" h. 750.00

Hobstars, single stars, miter cutting & a foliate design, matching flared base w/an undulating thumbprint foot, 10" d., overall 10¼" h., 2 pcs. 660.00

Hunt's Royal patt., Russian motif w/hobstar button, five-sided strawberry diamond lozenge & large hobstars, matching base, 12" d., 2 pcs. 1,500.00

Libbey signed, Colonna patt., chain of hobstars, crosshatched triangle, fan, star & strawberry diamond, 14" d., together w/matching ladle, the set 2,100.00

Libbey's Kimberly patt., cross-cut diamond, fan & hobstar, 12" d., 6" h. 850.00

PUNCH CUPS

Hawkes' Nautilus patt., beading, cane, hobstar & star 425.00

Hoare's Monarch patt., cross-cut vesica w/split, hobstars & other cutting, footed 60.00

Hunt's Royal patt., Russian motif w/hobstar button, five-sided strawberry diamond lozenge & large hobstars 30.00

Libbey's Harvard patt. 25.00

Libbey's Marcella patt., cluster of hobstars around hexagon center .. 55.00

Pinwheel & fan 28.50

ROSE BOWLS

Cranberry cut to clear, strawberry diamond & fan w/deep miter cutting, 5" d., 4" h. 350.00

Cranberry cut to clear, Zipper patt., star-cut bottom, 2" d. opening, 3" h. 350.00

Hobstars, crosshatching & fan, 9" h. 935.00

Hope signed, Carnation patt., intaglio-cut blossoms & foliage ... 425.00

Strawberry diamond overall, 6" d. .. 275.00

SALT & PEPPER SHAKERS

Hobstar & drape cutting, brass tops, pr. 95.00

Libbey signed, intaglio-cut flowers & swags, baroque Wilson sterling silver tops, pr. 250.00

Notched prism, sterling silver tops, 1¾" h., pr. 50.00

SALT DIPS

Comet motif 50.00

Cranberry cut to clear, overall strawberry diamond, serrated rim 95.00

Green cut to clear, finecut & button around sides, 1¾" d., 7/8" h. 65.00

Hobstars & fan, paperweight-type w/hobstar in bottom, master size, 3" d. 70.00

Hobstars & fan, pedestal base, rayed foot, master size 125.00

Notched prism, set of 6 .... 82.50

SPOONERS

Hobstars, buttons & crosshatching, large hobstar in base, scalloped & serrated rim, child's size, 2¾" d., 3½" h. 195.00

Maple City signed, large hobstars, fields of cane, double miters separated by double lozenges of crosshatching, vertical notching on each side, triple-cut handles, 5½" h. 225.00

Strawberry diamond & fan 175.00

SYRUP PITCHERS & JUGS

Hobstars overall, rayed base, sterling silver hinged lid 250.00

Hobstar (large) on front & back, surrounded by fans, crosshatching & other cutting, sterling silver handle & hinged lid 245.00

Zipper cutting overall, silver plate handle & hinged lid 110.00

TOOTHPICK HOLDERS

Crosscut diamond & fan, 2" h. 20.00
Crosshatching & fan, 2½" h. 55.00
Hobstars & other cutting 75.00
Zipper cutting overall, 2" h. 35.00

TRAYS

Hawkes' Holland Pattern Tray

Allen Cut Glass Company's Lotus
   patt., intaglio-cut, 12" d. 695.00
Bread, Colonna patt., chain of
   hobstars, crosshatched triangle,
   fan, star & strawberry diamond,
   8 x 11" 450.00
Bread, hobstars & button, rectan-
   gular w/sloped ends, 4¼ x 11",
   3" h. 135.00
Bread, Sinclaire signed, intaglio-cut
   dahlias w/dot border, 6 x 13½"
   oval 350.00
Card, Oxford patt., fan, hobstar &
   zipper, 5" 100.00
Celery, Harvard patt. border, floral
   center, 9" l. 45.00
Celery, strawberry diamond & fan,
   scalloped & serrated rim, 13" l. 121.00
Dresser, Tuthill's Vintage patt.,
   intaglio-cut grapes & foliage,
   5½ x 7½" 425.00
Egginton's Calve' patt., checker-
   board-type motif, 8 x 10" 2,100.00
Harvard patt., tab handles, 8" w.,
   overall 13" l. 350.00
Hawkes' Holland patt., hobstars,
   strawberry diamond, fan & other
   cutting, large hobstar center, scalloped & serrated rim, 13" d.
   (ILLUS.) 1,300.00
Ice cream, four large sunbursts cen-
   ter in triangle of cane, hobstars
   & crosshatching w/cross-cut dia-
   monds, 18" 685.00
Ice cream, overall strawberry dia-
   mond, 9 x 16" 250.00
Ice cream, single stars, fan, cross-
   hatching, notched vesicas & other
   cutting within a border of hob-
   stars, serrated rim, 15" l. 550.00

Pin, chain of hobstars around edge,
   center w/three hobstars & four
   diamonds of crosshatching,
   2¾ x 4½" oval 125.00
Sinclaire signed, chain of hobstars
   separated by diamonds of crosshatching, 11½" l., 2½" h. 110.00
Sterling's Arcadia patt., strawberry
   diamond pentagon, hobstar &
   star, 7 x 11" 375.00
Strauss' Imperial patt., chain of
   hobstars & strawberry diamond,
   8¾ x 14" 500.00
Tuthill's Rosemere patt., intaglio-cut
   florals & foliage w/geometric cut-
   ting, 3 x 7½" oval 225.00

TUMBLERS

Butterfly & deeply cut floral
   decoration 75.00
Hawkes signed, hobstar w/clear hob
   & fan 25.00
Hobstars, cross-cut diamond &
   fan, 12-point hobstar in base,
   3½" h. 110.00
Libbey signed, hobstars & finecut . . . 45.00
Libbey's Harvard patt. 55.00

VASES

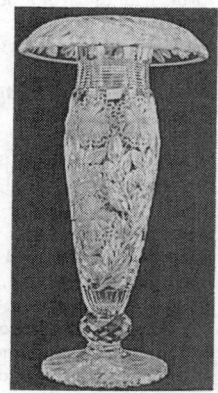

Intaglio-cut Vase

Butterfly & daisy pattern w/mitered
   foliage, hobstar base, compressed
   bulbous body w/narrow fluted &
   notch-cut neck, 7½" h. 121.00
Cane panels alternating w/hobstar
   panels, cylindrical w/slightly flaring base, scalloped & serrated
   rim, 26" h. .5,775.00
Flower & Harvard patt., cosmos
   blossoms w/strawberry diamond
   centers & long vining stems, further cut in Harvard patt., 24-point
   star base, 6¾" d., 16¼" h. 480.00
Hawkes signed "Gravic Glass," Iris
   patt., sterling silver base,
   14" h. 525.00

Hawkes signed, Queens patt.,
chain of hobstars & bull's-eye,
15½" h. 1,850.00
Hawkes' Brunswick patt., chain of
hobstars, zipper-type beading &
flute, 14" h. 525.00
Hobstars, button, crosshatching &
other cutting, large hobstar in
base, scalloped & serrated rim,
2¾" d., 3½" h. 110.00
Hobstars, pinwheel & other cutting,
corset-shaped, 8½" h. 115.00
Hobstars & stars, cylindrical
w/flared mouth & scalloped & serrated rim, 15" h. 330.00
Hobstars, cross-cut diamond, crosshatching & notch-cutting interspersed w/daisies, fans & miters,
scalloped & serrated rim, hobstar
base, 25½" h. 2,530.00
Hobstar diamonds, cross-cut diamond & fan, circular hobstar
base, scalloped & serrated rim,
hourglass-form, 13½" h. 660.00
Intaglio-cut florals overall, horizontal step-cutting at neck, conformingly cut everted rim, facet-cut
knob above serrated pattern-cut
foot, 18" h. (ILLUS.) 1,900.00
Pairpoint's Savoy patt., bull's-eye &
cross-cut diamond, 10" h. 395.00
Walsh signed, cobalt blue cut to
clear forming six scalloped
panels, each w/an intaglio-cut
vintage design, cobalt blue ring &
band around cobalt blue bottom,
scalloped rim, 8" h. 395.00

WATER SETS

Blackberry Pattern Water Set

Pitcher & four tumblers, Tuthill's
Blackberry patt., panels of
intaglio-cut blackberries & foliage
alternating w/panels of flashed
hobstars & other cutting, 5 pcs.
(ILLUS.)........................ 850.00
Pitcher & six tumblers, chain of cosmos & fan, rayed base, pitcher
10" h., 7 pcs. 275.00

Pitcher & six tumblers, Heart patt.,
7 pcs. 1,450.00

(End of Cut Glass Section)

CZECHOSLOVAKIAN

Czechoslovakian Liqueur Set

*At the close of World War I, Czechoslova-
kia was declared an independent republic and
immediately developed a large export industry. Czechoslovakian glass factories produced
a wide variety of colored and hand-painted
glasswares from about 1918 until 1939, when
the country was occupied by Germany at the
outset of World War II. Between the wars,
fine quality blown glasswares were produced
along with a deluge of cheaper, vividly colored spatterwares for the American market.
Subsequent production was primarily limited to cut crystal or Bohemian-type etched
wares for the American market. Although it
was marked, much Czechoslovakian glass is
mistaken for the work of Tiffany, Loetz, or
other glass artisans it imitates. It is often
misrepresented and overpriced.*

*With the recent break-up of Czechoslova-
kia into two republics, such wares should gain
added collector appeal.*

Basket w/ruffled rim, applied twisted cobalt blue handle, lavender,
pink & white spatter w/embossed
raindrop design exterior, white
lining, 3 3/8" d., 6½" h. $75.00
Bowl, 9" d., 4½" h., footed, orange
iridescent ground, applied cobalt
blue rim & ball feet 220.00
Console set: bowl & candlesticks;
black exterior & red interior,
polished pontils, 3 pcs. 275.00
Decanter w/original stopper, Hobnail patt., lavender opalescent,
10" h. 150.00
Figure of a gentleman talking
w/one hand extended out & one
hand behind his back holding a
book, 8" h. 165.00

Figure of a teacher reading from a book, dressed in a grey & brown suit, 7½" h. 165.00

Jar, cov., footed, melon-shaped, domed cover w/bulbous finial, pink spatter w/deeper pink stripes, on applied black feet, 3½" d., 7¼" h. 45.00

Liqueur set: 9" h. decanter w/pointed stopper & six short tumblers; the domical hexagonal decanter decorated w/cut & black-enameled geometric designs, the faceted tumblers similarly decorated, original paper labels, ca. 1925, 7 pcs. (ILLUS.) 1,100.00

Model of an owl, yellow ground, signed "Prof. Cerny" 225.00

Powder jar, cov., yellow & orange mottled exterior w/black rim, applied flowers on the cover, 4½" h. 225.00

Punch set: covered bowl, six footed, handleless punch cups & a ladle; orange w/garland & peacock silver overlay, cups 4½" h., bowl 10½" h., 8 pcs. 375.00

Tumbler, cylindrical w/a faceted base, enameled w/a large jumping fish in heavy relief on a clear ground, 6" h. 75.00

Tumblers, cylindrical, clear w/etched birds & swirl decoration, set of 12 .... 275.00

Vase, 5¾" h., footed octagonal body w/a flared eight-petal shaped rim, golden amber, signed 34.00

Vase, 10" h., iridescent gold textured body w/orange pulled-feather decoration 150.00

Vase, 10" h., urn-form on a pedestal base, the upper body in lemon yellow, the lower body & base in silvery iridescent blue, design attributed to Dagobert Peche, stamped "CZECHOSLOVAKIA" 1,320.00

D'ARGENTAL

Glass known by this name is so-called after its producer, who fashioned fine cameo pieces in St. Louis, France late last century and up to 1918.

Cameo jar, cov., egg-shaped, the grey walls infused w/egg yolk yellow, overlaid w/deep umber & cut w/a pattern of crocus blossoms about the base & fluttering fritillaries on the lid, signed in cameo "D'Argental" & w/the cross of Lorraine, ca. 1920, 6" h. (minor chip to inner rim of base) $1,760.00

Cameo lamp, table-type, the domical shade & baluster base in opalescent lemon yellow splashed w/rose red, overlaid in deepest rose red & strawberry red & cut w/trailing vines of morning glories & columbine blossoms & leafage, foliate wrought-iron mounts, signed in cameo "d'Argental" w/cross of Lorraine, ca. 1920, shade 13" d., 24¾" h. 5,500.00

Cameo vase, 5½" h., ovoid body tapering to a small flat mouth, frosted amber overlaid in burgundy & etched & wheel-cut w/a scene of city roof tops w/storks in a chimney nest, cameo signature "D'Argental" 1,210.00

Cameo vase, 7" h., tall ovoid body tapering to a short neck w/flaring rim, pale yellow splashed & overlaid in cherry red & cut w/pendent passion flowers & leaves, signed in cameo "D'Argental" & the cross of Lorraine, ca. 1920.... 660.00

Cameo vase, 9¾" h., baluster-form, grey mottled w/lemon yellow, overlaid in cherry red & deep amber & cut w/a scenic landscape, signed in cameo "D'Argental" w/the cross of Lorraine, ca. 1915 .... 1,320.00

Tall D'Argental Cameo Vase

Cameo vase, 10" h., baluster-shaped, lemon yellow overlaid in deep amber & chocolate brown & cut w/orchid blossoms & leafage, signed in cameo "D'Argental" w/the cross of Lorraine, ca. 1910 (ILLUS.) 770.00

Cameo vase, 13 7/8" h., slightly shouldered ovoid body in grey invested w/lemon yellow opalescence, overlaid in salmon & chocolate brown & cut w/a landscape of a lake surrounded by tall leafy trees, signed in cameo "D'Argental," ca. 1920 .... 2,090.00

DAUM NANCY

Daum Nancy Ewer

This fine glass, much of it cameo, was made by Auguste and Antonin Daum, who founded a factory in 1875 in Nancy, France. Most of their cameo and enameled glass was made from the 1890's into the early 20th century.

Bottle w/original stopper, cylindrical w/short wide neck, mottled blue & orange ground etched & enameled w/a Dutch winter landscape w/windmills, houses & trees under snow, frosted glass stopper, etched signature "Daum Nancy," 3" h. $1,430.00

Bowl, 6" h., deep flaring conical form w/molded banding, tapering to a small circular foot, yellow, engraved "DAUM NANCY FRANCE" w/cross of Lorraine. 880.00

Cameo box, cov., flattened spherical base & cover w/squared edges, grey splashed w/cream, ochre, turquoise & purple, overlaid & finely wheel carved w/berried leafy branches in shades of rust, lemon yellow, emerald green, amber, olive green & cinnamon, signed in intaglio "DAUM - NANCY" w/cross of Lorraine, ca. 1900, 5½" d. 4,950.00

Cameo creamer, squared bulbous shape w/round rim & applied handle, mottled gold down to mottled brown frosted ground & cut to green leaves & brown berries, cameo signature "Daum Nancy," 3" d., 3 1/8" h. 1,650.00

Cameo scent bottle, cylindrical, clear overlaid in pale orange, cut w/daisies & leafage & heightened in gilt, clear glass stopper & hinged silver mount, inscribed "Daum - Nancy" w/cross of Lorraine, ca. 1910, 3¾" h. 495.00

Cameo vase, 6½" h., in the form of an emerging flower w/an asymmetrical rim, acid-etched clear walls mottled w/lemon yellow shading to ochre, cherry red & deep rose, overlaid & enameled w/sprays of bleeding heart blossoms, buds & leafage in shades of rose, Chinese red, lemon yellow, emerald green, lime green & avocado, signed in cameo "DAUM - NANCY" w/the cross of Lorraine, ca. 1910 . . . . .7,150.00

Ewer, cov., the shouldered bulbous creamy opalescent glass body cut w/lilies of the valley & leafage trimmed in gilt, fitted w/a silver neck band, hinged cover, angled handle & a pierced footring all cast w/stylized flowerheads, signed in gilt "Daum Nancy" w/the cross of Lorraine, stamped marks on the silver, ca. 1900, 4½" h. (ILLUS.) 2,475.00

Lamp, table model, 15½" d. domed glass shade on a high-domed matching base w/molded foot, each in pale salmon deeply etched w/stylized geometric designs, acid-etched "DAUM NANCY FRANCE," overall 19" h. 20,900.00

Perfume flask, cov., cylindrical, green etched w/mistletoe w/white enameled berries & gilt trim, fitted w/a silver rim & hinged silver cover decorated w/repousse' mistletoe, cover opens to an etched glass stopper, gilt signature "Daum Nancy," 3 1/8" h. 1,430.00

Vase, 6" h., flared cylindrical body on a raised foot, mottled yellow & apricot ground w/*martele'* finish, etched to depict various wild mushrooms, enameled in shades of red, green & brown, the undersides of the mushrooms & the grass delicately carved, long applied angled handles from the shoulder to the foot, enameled "DAUM NANCY" 7,700.00

Vase, 11¾" h., conical sides on a bulbous swollen base, three thick applied loop handles, the background shading from emerald green to aqua below, finely etched & enameled *en grisaille* to depict cranes in flight above a pond w/water lilies, gilt & rose floral sprays cascading from a stylized floral gilt band at the rim, enameled signature "Daum Nancy" 47,300.00

DEPRESSION GLASS

The phrase "Depression Glass" is used by collectors to denote a specific kind of transparent glass produced primarily as tablewares, in crystal, amber, blue, green, pink, milky-white, etc., during the late 1920's and 1930's when this country was in the midst of a financial depression. Made to sell inexpensively, it was turned out by such producers as Jeannette, Hocking, Westmoreland, Indiana and other glass companies. We compile prices on all the major Depression Glass patterns. Collectors should consult Depression Glass references for information on those patterns and pieces which have been reproduced.

ADAM (Process-etched)

Adam Pitcher

Ashtray, clear, 4½" sq.	$8.50
Ashtray, green, 4½" sq.	17.50
Bowl, cereal, 5¾" sq., green or pink	34.00
Bowl, nappy, 7¾" sq., green	19.00
Bowl, nappy, 7¾" sq., pink	15.00
Bowl, cov., 9" sq., green	75.00
Bowl, cov., 9" sq., pink	45.50
Bowl, 9" sq., pink	18.00
Bowl, 10" oval vegetable, green or pink	22.00
Butter dish, cov., green	292.00
Butter dish, cov., pink	68.50
Cake plate, footed, green or pink, 10" sq.	18.50
Candlestick, green, 4" h.	45.00
Candlesticks, pink, 4" h., pr.	74.00
Candy jar, cov., green	96.50
Candy jar, cov., pink	78.50
Coaster, green, 3¼" sq.	14.00
Coaster, pink, 3¼" sq.	18.50
Creamer, green	16.50
Creamer, pink	15.00
Cup & saucer, green	23.50
Cup & saucer, pink	25.50
Pitcher, 8" h., 32 oz., cone-shaped, green (ILLUS.)	35.50
Pitcher, 8" h., 32 oz., cone-shaped, pink	28.00
Plate, sherbet, 6" sq., green	4.50
Plate, sherbet, 6" sq., pink	6.00
Plate, salad, 7¾" sq., green or pink	9.00
Plate, salad, round, pink	60.00
Plate, salad, round, yellow	110.00
Plate, dinner, 9" sq., green	18.50
Plate, dinner, 9" sq., pink	22.50
Plate, grill, 9" sq., green	13.00
Plate, grill, 9" sq., pink	15.50
Platter, 11¾" l., green or pink	19.00
Salt & pepper shakers, footed, green, 4" h., pr.	76.00
Salt & pepper shakers, footed, pink, 4" h., pr.	59.50
Sherbet, green, 3" h.	31.50
Sherbet, pink, 3" h.	22.50
Sugar bowl, cov., green	41.00
Sugar bowl, cov., pink	25.00
Tumbler, cone-shaped, green, 4½" h., 7 oz.	21.00
Tumbler, cone-shaped, pink, 4½" h., 7 oz.	22.00
Tumbler, iced tea, green, 5½" h., 9 oz.	39.50
Vase, 7½" h., green	41.50
Vase, 7½" h., pink	189.00

AMERICAN SWEETHEART (Process-etched)

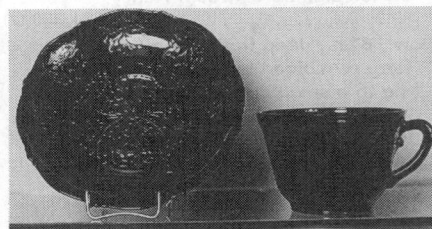

American Sweetheart Cup & Saucer

Bowl, berry, 3¾" d., pink	36.50
Bowl, cream soup, 4½" d., Monax	67.50
Bowl, cereal, 6" d., Monax or pink	12.00
Bowl, berry, 9" d., Cremax	28.50
Bowl, berry, 9" d., Monax	56.50
Bowl, soup w/flange rim, 9½" d., pink	39.00
Bowl, 11" oval vegetable, Monax	59.50
Bowl, 11" oval vegetable, pink	40.50
Console bowl, Monax, 18" d.	375.00
Creamer, footed, blue	95.00
Creamer, footed, Monax	8.00
Creamer, footed, pink	13.50
Creamer, footed, ruby red	120.00
Cup, ruby red (ILLUS. right)	86.00
Cup & saucer, Monax	11.50
Cup & saucer, pink	16.00
Lamp shade, Monax	446.00

Pitcher, 7½" h., 60 oz., jug-type,
 pink 308.00
Pitcher, 8" h., 80 oz., pink 442.00
Plate, bread & butter, 6" d., Monax
 or pink 4.00
Plate, salad, 8" d., blue 72.50
Plate, salad, 8" d., ruby red 65.50
Plate, luncheon, 9" d., Monax 9.00
Plate, dinner, 9¾" d., Monax 18.50
Plate, dinner, 9¾" d., pink 24.50
Plate, dinner, 10¼" d., Monax 19.50
Plate, chop, 11" d., Monax 12.50
Plate, salver, 12" d., Monax 12.50
Plate, salver, 12" d., pink 14.00
Plate, salver, 12" d., ruby red 169.00
Plate, 15½" d., w/center handle,
 Monax 194.00
Platter, 13" oval, Monax 48.00
Platter, 13" oval, pink 33.00
Salt & pepper shakers, footed,
 Monax, pr. 239.00
Salt & pepper shakers, footed, pink,
 pr. 283.00
Saucer, ruby red (ILLUS. left) 35.00
Sherbet, footed, pink, 3¾" h. 15.50
Sherbet, footed, Monax, 4¼" h. 16.00
Sherbet, footed, pink, 4¼" h. 12.00
Sherbet, metal holder, clear 7.50
Sugar bowl, cov., Monax (only) 169.00
Sugar bowl, open, Monax 6.00
Sugar bowl, open, pink 11.50
Tidbit server, two-tier, Monax 73.50
Tidbit server, two-tier, pink 58.00
Tidbit server, two-tier, ruby red 225.00
Tidbit server, three-tier, Monax 158.00
Tumbler, pink, 3½" h., 5 oz. 66.00
Tumbler, pink, 4¼" h., 9 oz. 65.00
Tumbler, pink, 4¾" h., 10 oz. 73.50
Water set: 7½" h. pitcher & four
 9 oz. tumblers; pink, 5 pcs. 525.00

BLOCK or Block Optic (Press-mold)

Block Creamer & Sugar Bowl

Bowl, 4½" d., green 24.50
Bowl, cereal, 5¼" d., green 10.00
Bowl, salad, 7" d., green 27.50
Bowl, large berry, 8½" d., green . . . 21.50
Butter dish, cov., rectangular,
 green, 3 x 5" 39.00
Butter dish, cov., rectangular,
 green clambroth, 3 x 5" 350.00

Candlesticks, amber, 1¾" h., pr. . . . 100.00
Candlesticks, green, 1¾" h., pr. 97.00
Candlesticks, pink, 1¾" h., pr. 67.50
Candy jar, cov., green, 2¼" h. 39.50
Candy jar, cov., pink, 2¼" h. 36.50
Candy jar, cov., yellow, 2¼" h. 47.50
Candy jar, cov., clear, 6¼" h. 24.50
Candy jar, cov., green, 6¼" h. 44.50
Candy jar, cov., pink, 6¼" h. 81.00
Compote, 4" d., cone-shaped,
 green 19.50
Creamer, various styles, green
 (ILLUS. right) 10.50
Creamer, various styles, pink 11.00
Creamer, various styles, yellow 10.00
Cup & saucer, green 12.50
Cup & saucer, pink 11.00
Cup & saucer, yellow 10.00
Goblet, cocktail, pink, 4" h. 20.50
Goblet, wine, clear, 4½" h. 12.50
Goblet, wine, green, 4½" h. 31.50
Goblet, wine, pink, 4½" h. 29.50
Goblet, clear, 5¾" h., 9 oz. 9.00
Goblet, green, 5¾" h., 9 oz. 17.00
Goblet, pink, 5¾" h., 9 oz. 25.00
Goblet, clear, 7¼" h., 9 oz. 8.00
Goblet, green, 7¼" h., 9 oz. 19.50
Goblet, pink, 7¼" h., 9 oz. 18.50
Goblet, yellow, 7¼" h., 9 oz. 26.00
Ice bucket, w/metal bail handle,
 clear 17.50
Ice bucket, w/metal bail handle,
 green 36.00
Ice tub, tab handles, green 36.50
Ice tub, tab handles, pink 77.00
Mug, green 35.00
Pitcher, 8" h., 80 oz., clear 25.00
Pitcher, 8" h., 80 oz., green 53.00
Pitcher, 8" h., 80 oz., pink 35.50
Pitcher, 8½" h., 54 oz., clear 17.00
Pitcher, 8½" h., 54 oz., green 35.50
Pitcher, 8½" h., 54 oz., pink 34.00
Plate, sherbet, 6" d., clear 1.50
Plate, sherbet, 6" d., green, pink or
 yellow 2.00
Plate, luncheon, 8" d., clear 2.00
Plate, luncheon, 8" d., green 3.00
Plate, luncheon, 8" d., pink or
 yellow 4.00
Plate, dinner, 9" d., green 13.50
Plate, dinner, 9" d., yellow 29.00
Plate, grill, 9" d., green 12.50
Plate, sandwich, 10¼" d., clear 12.00
Plate, sandwich, 10¼" d., green 19.50
Salt & pepper shakers, squat, green,
 pr. 59.00
Salt & pepper shakers, footed,
 clear, pr. 22.00
Salt & pepper shakers, footed,
 green, pr. 31.00
Salt & pepper shakers, footed, pink,
 pr. 59.50
Salt & pepper shakers, footed, yel-
 low, pr. 65.00

Sandwich server w/center handle,
   green 42.00
Sandwich server w/center handle,
   pink 48.00
Sherbet, cone-shaped, footed,
   green 3.50
Sherbet, stemmed, clear, 3¼" h.,
   5½" oz. 3.00
Sherbet, stemmed, green, 3¼" h.,
   5½" oz. 4.00
Sherbet, stemmed, pink, 3¼" h.,
   5½ oz. 7.50
Sherbet, stemmed, yellow, 3¼" h.,
   5½ oz. 6.50
Sherbet, stemmed, clear, 4¾" h.,
   6 oz. 5.00
Sherbet, stemmed, green or yellow,
   4¾" h., 6 oz. 12.50
Sherbet, stemmed, pink, 4¾" h.,
   6 oz. 11.50
Sugar bowl, open, various styles,
   clear 7.00
Sugar bowl, open, various styles,
   green (ILLUS. left) 9.00
Sugar bowl, open, various styles,
   pink 8.50
Sugar bowl, open, various styles,
   yellow 9.00
Tumbler, footed, pink, 2 5/8" h.,
   3 oz. 23.50
Tumbler, juice, green, 3½" h.,
   5 oz. 15.50
Tumbler, juice, pink, 3½" h.,
   5 oz. 19.00
Tumbler, green, 3 7/8" h., 9½ oz. ... 14.50
Tumbler, pink, 3 7/8" h., 9½ oz. .. 10.50
Tumbler, iced tea, footed, green or
   pink, 6" h., 10 oz. 21.50
Tumbler, green or pink, 4 7/8" h.,
   12 oz. 19.50
Tumbler, green, 5¼" h., 15 oz. 33.00
Tumbler, pink, 5¼" h., 15 oz. 34.00
Tumble-up set: bottle & 3" h. tum-
   bler; green, 2 pcs. 51.50

BUBBLE, Bullseye or Provincial (Press-mold)

Bubble Bowl

Bowl, berry, 4" d., blue 13.00

Bowl, fruit, 4½" d., blue 9.00
Bowl, fruit, 4½" d., clear or milk
   white 3.50
Bowl, fruit, 4½" d., green or ruby
   red 6.00
Bowl, soup, 7¾" d., blue 11.00
Bowl, soup, 7¾" d., clear 7.00
Bowl, soup, 7¾" d., pink 10.00
Bowl, 8 3/8" d., blue or green 12.50
Bowl, 8 3/8" d., clear 6.50
Bowl, 8 3/8" d., milk white 5.50
Bowl, 8 3/8" d., ruby red (ILLUS.) .. 19.00
Candlesticks, clear, pr. 13.50
Creamer, blue 27.50
Creamer, clear 5.50
Creamer, green 10.00
Cup & saucer, green 9.00
Cup & saucer, ruby red 8.00
Lamp, clear 34.00
Pitcher w/ice lip, 64 oz., clear 65.00
Pitcher w/ice lip, 64 oz., ruby red .. 45.50
Plate, bread & butter, 6¾" d.,
   blue 3.00
Plate, bread & butter, 6¾" d.,
   green 5.50
Plate, dinner, 9 3/8" d., green 13.00
Plate, dinner, 9 3/8" d., ruby red ... 8.00
Plate, grill, 9 3/8" d., blue 17.00
Plate, grill, 9 3/8" d., clear 7.50
Platter, 12" oval, green 13.00
Platter, 12" oval, clear 8.00
Sugar bowl, open, blue 14.50
Sugar bowl, open, clear 5.50
Sugar bowl, open, green 9.00
Sugar bowl, open, milk white 4.50
Tidbit server, two-tier, blue 44.00
Tumbler, juice, ruby red, 6 oz. 7.00
Tumbler, old fashioned, clear,
   3¼" h., 8 oz. 4.00
Tumbler, old fashioned, ruby red,
   3¼" h., 8 oz. 13.50
Tumbler, water, ruby red, 9 oz. 9.00
Tumbler, iced tea, ruby red, 4½" h.,
   12 oz. 9.00
Tumbler, lemonade, ruby red,
   5 7/8" h., 16 oz. 16.50

CAMEO or Ballerina or Dancing Girl (Process-etched)

Bowl, sauce, 4¼" d., clear 7.50
Bowl, cereal, 5½" d., clear 6.50
Bowl, cereal, 5½" d., green 27.00
Bowl, cereal, 5½" d., yellow 28.00
Bowl, salad, 7¼" d., green 50.50
Bowl, large berry, 8¼" d., green ... 33.50
Bowl, soup w/flange rim, 9" d.,
   green 44.00
Bowl, 10" oval vegetable, green 21.50
Bowl, 10" oval vegetable, yellow ... 36.50
Butter dish, cov., green 160.00
Cake plate, three-footed, green,
   10" d. 18.00
Candlesticks, green, 4" h., pr. 103.00

Cameo Candy Jar

Candy jar, cov., green, 4" h.
(ILLUS.) 58.50
Candy jar, cov., yellow, 4" h. 64.00
Candy jar, cov., green, 6½" h. 134.00
Compote, mayonnaise, 5" d., 4" h.,
cone-shaped, green 28.50
Console bowl, three-footed, yellow,
11" d. 74.00
Cookie jar, cov., green 42.50
Creamer, green, 4¼" h. 19.00
Creamer, pink, 4¼" h. 65.00
Cup & saucer, yellow 9.50
Decanter w/stopper, green, 10" h. . .   120.00
Domino tray, clear, 7" d. 85.00
Domino tray, green, 7" d. 118.00
Goblet, wine, green, 4" h. 62.00
Goblet, water, green, 6" h. 49.00
Goblet, water, pink, 6" h. 140.00
Ice bowl, tab handles, green,
5½" d., 3½" h. 155.00
Jam jar, cov., closed handles,
green, 2" 133.00
Pitcher, syrup or milk, 5¾" h.,
20 oz., green 196.00
Pitcher, juice, 6" h., 36 oz., green . .   48.00
Pitcher, water, 8½" h., 56 oz., jug-
type, green 49.50
Plate, sherbet (or ringless saucer),
6" d., green or yellow 3.00
Plate, salad, 7" d., clear 3.00
Plate, luncheon, 8" d., green or
yellow 9.50
Plate, 8½" sq., green 32.00
Plate, sandwich, 10" d., green 14.50
Plate, sandwich, 10" d., pink 38.50
Plate, dinner, 10¼" d., rimmed,
green 10.00
Plate, 10½" d., closed handles,
green 13.00
Plate, grill, 10½" d., closed han-
dles, green 54.50
Plate, grill, 10½" d., closed han-
dles, yellow 7.50
Platter, 12", closed handles, green . .   20.50
Platter, 12", closed handles,
yellow 37.00
Relish, footed, three-part, green,
7½" 25.00

Salt & pepper shakers, green, pr. . . .   69.50
Salt & pepper shakers, pink, pr. 950.00
Sherbet, pink, 3 1/8" h. 69.00
Sherbet, yellow, 3 1/8" h. 35.00
Sherbet, thin, high stem, green,
4 7/8" h. 27.00
Sherbet, thin, high stem, yellow,
4 7/8" h. 34.50
Sugar bowl, open, green, 4¼" h. 19.00
Sugar bowl, open, pink, 4¼" h. 67.50
Tumbler, juice, footed, green,
3 oz. 57.50
Tumbler, juice, green, 3¾" h.,
5 oz. 24.50
Tumbler, water, clear, 4" h., 9 oz. . .   9.00
Tumbler, water, green, 4" h.,
9 oz. 24.00
Tumbler, footed, green, 5" h.,
9 oz. 25.50
Tumbler, green, 5" h., 11 oz. 25.50
Tumbler, yellow, 5" h., 11 oz. 58.00
Tumbler, footed, green, 5¾" h.,
11 oz. 55.00
Tumbler, green, 5¼" h., 15 oz. 58.50
Vase, 5¾" h., green 160.00
Vase, 8" h., green 24.00
Water bottle, dark green "White
House Vinegar" base, 8½" h. 23.00

CHERRY BLOSSOM (Process-etched)

Cherry Blossom Pitcher

Bowl, berry, 4¾" d., Delphite or
pink 12.00
Bowl, berry, 4¾" d., green 13.50
Bowl, cereal, 5¾" d., green or
pink 29.50
Bowl, soup, 7¾" d., green 48.50
Bowl, soup, 7¾" d., pink 56.00
Bowl, berry, 8½" d., Delphite 35.50
Bowl, berry, 8½" d., green 37.00
Bowl, berry, 8½" d., pink 38.50
Bowl, 9" d., two-handled, Delphite . .   25.50
Bowl, 9" d., two-handled, green 27.50
Bowl, 9" d., two-handled, pink 29.00
Bowl, 9" oval vegetable, Delphite . . .   36.00
Bowl, 9" oval vegetable, green 31.00
Bowl, 9" oval vegetable, pink 34.00
Bowl, fruit, 10½" d., three-footed,
green 71.50

Butter dish, cov., green	75.00
Butter dish, cov., pink	61.00
Cake plate, three-footed, pink, 10¼" d.	23.50
Coaster, green	11.00
Coaster, pink	14.00
Creamer, Delphite	20.00
Creamer, green	16.50
Creamer, pink	15.50
Cup & saucer, Delphite	24.50
Cup & saucer, green	21.50
Cup & saucer, pink	18.00
Mug, green, 7 oz.	155.00
Mug, pink, 7 oz.	180.00
Pitcher, 6¾" h., 36 oz., overall patt., Delphite (ILLUS.)	77.00
Pitcher, 6¾" h., 36 oz., overall patt., green	51.00
Pitcher, 6¾" h., 36 oz., overall patt., pink	43.00
Pitcher, 8" h., 36 oz., footed, cone-shaped, patt. top, Delphite	66.00
Pitcher, 8" h., 36 oz., footed, cone-shaped, patt. top, green	49.50
Pitcher, 8" h., 42 oz., patt. top, pink	41.50
Plate, sherbet, 6" d., Delphite	8.50
Plate, sherbet, 6" d., green	6.00
Plate, sherbet, 6" d., pink	7.00
Plate, salad, 7" d., green or pink	17.00
Plate, dinner, 9" d., Delphite	19.00
Plate, dinner, 9" d., green or pink	18.50
Plate, grill, 9" d., green	22.00
Plate, grill, 9" d., pink	18.50
Platter, 11" oval, green	30.50
Platter, 11" oval, pink	32.50
Platter, 13" oval, green	42.50
Platter, 13" oval, divided, pink	46.50
Salt & pepper shakers, green, pr.	1,085.00
Sandwich tray, handled, Delphite, 10½" d.	19.50
Sandwich tray, handled, pink, 10½" d.	18.50
Sherbet, Delphite	11.50
Sherbet, green	15.00
Sherbet, pink	13.50
Sugar bowl, cov., clear	15.00
Sugar bowl, cov., Delphite	35.00
Sugar bowl, cov., green	29.00
Sugar bowl, cov., pink	26.50
Sugar bowl, open, Delphite	17.00
Sugar bowl, open, green	12.00
Sugar bowl, open, pink	11.00
Tumbler, patt. top, green, 3½" h., 4 oz.	21.50
Tumbler, patt. top, pink, 3½" h., 4 oz.	15.50
Tumbler, juice, footed, overall patt., Delphite, 3¾" h., 4 oz.	18.00
Tumbler, footed, overall patt., green, 4½" h., 8 oz.	29.00
Tumbler, footed, overall patt., pink, 4½" h., 8 oz.	26.50

Tumbler, patt. top, green, 4¼" h., 9 oz.	18.00
Tumbler, footed, overall patt., Delphite, 4½" h., 9 oz.	18.50
Tumbler, footed, overall patt., green, 4½" h., 9 oz.	28.00
Tumbler, footed, overall patt., pink, 4½" h., 9 oz.	29.00
Tumbler, patt. top, green, 5" h., 12 oz.	65.00
Tumbler, patt. top, pink, 5" h., 12 oz.	48.00

JUNIOR SET:

Creamer, Delphite	39.00
Creamer, pink	36.00
Cup & saucer, Delphite	36.00
Cup & saucer, pink	32.00
Plate, 6" d., Delphite	10.50
Plate, 6" d., pink	7.50
Sugar bowl, Delphite	36.50
Sugar bowl, pink	35.00
14 pc. set, Delphite	230.00
14 pc. set, pink	245.00

COLONIAL or Knife & Fork (Press-mold)

Colonial Creamer & Sugar Bowl

Bowl, berry, 3¾" d., pink	40.00
Bowl, berry, 4½" d., clear	5.00
Bowl, berry, 4½" d., green or pink	11.50
Bowl, cream soup, 4½" d., clear	35.00
Bowl, cream soup, 4½" d., green	50.00
Bowl, cereal, 5½" d., green	56.50
Bowl, soup, 7" d., green	46.50
Bowl, soup, 7" d., pink	50.00
Bowl, 9" d., clear	12.50
Bowl, 9" d., green	23.00
Bowl, 10" oval vegetable, pink	25.50
Butter dish, cov., clear	29.50
Butter dish, cov., green	47.00
Celery or spooner, clear	57.50
Celery or spooner, green	109.00
Creamer or milk pitcher, green, 5" h., 16 oz. (ILLUS. right)	19.50
Creamer or milk pitcher, pink, 5" h., 16 oz.	25.00
Cup & saucer, milk white	8.50
Cup & saucer, pink	13.50
Goblet, cordial, clear, 3¾" h., 1 oz.	15.50

Goblet, cordial, green, 3¾" h., 1 oz.	25.50
Goblet, cocktail, clear, 4" h., 3 oz.	10.50
Goblet, cocktail, green, 4" h., 3 oz.	22.50
Goblet, claret, clear, 5¼" h., 4 oz.	13.50
Goblet, claret, green, 5¼" h., 4 oz.	22.00
Goblet, clear, 5¾" h., 8½ oz.	13.00
Goblet, green, 5¾" h., 8½ oz.	26.50
Pitcher, ice lip or plain, 7" h., 54 oz., clear	23.50
Pitcher, ice lip or plain, 7" h., 54 oz., green	42.50
Pitcher, ice lip or plain, 7¾" h., 68 oz., pink	49.00
Plate, sherbet, 6" d., clear	2.50
Plate, sherbet, 6" d., green or pink	4.00
Plate, luncheon, 8½" d., clear	3.50
Plate, luncheon, 8½" d., green or pink	7.50
Plate, dinner, 10" d., clear	22.00
Plate, dinner, 10" d., green	46.50
Plate, grill, 10" d., green or pink	21.50
Platter, 12" oval, pink	26.00
Salt & pepper shakers, clear, pr.	46.00
Salt & pepper shakers, green, pr.	117.50
Salt & pepper shakers, pink, pr.	112.00
Sherbet, pink, 3" h.	15.50
Sherbet, pink, 3 3/8" h.	8.00
Sugar bowl, cov., clear	21.00
Sugar bowl, cov., green (ILLUS. left)	25.50
Tumbler, whiskey, green, 2½" h., 1½ oz.	12.00
Tumbler, whiskey, pink, 2½" h., 1½ oz.	10.00
Tumbler, cordial, footed, clear, 3¼" h., 3 oz.	11.00
Tumbler, cordial, footed, green, 3¼" h., 3 oz.	22.00
Tumbler, juice, pink, 3" h., 5 oz.	14.00
Tumbler, footed, clear, 4" h., 5 oz.	10.50
Tumbler, footed, green, 4" h., 5 oz.	24.00
Tumbler, footed, pink, 4" h., 5 oz.	21.00
Tumbler, water, clear, 4" h., 9 oz.	10.00
Tumbler, water, green, 4" h., 9 oz.	22.00
Tumbler, footed, green or pink, 5¼" h., 10 oz.	41.50
Tumbler, pink, 5 1/8" h., 11 oz.	32.00
Tumbler, iced tea, green, 12 oz.	32.00
Tumbler, iced tea, pink, 12 oz.	40.00
Tumbler, lemonade, green, 15 oz.	73.00

CUBE or CUBIST (Press-mold)

Bowl, dessert, 4½" d., green	6.00
Bowl, dessert, 4½" d., pink	5.00
Bowl, 4½" d., deep, pink	6.00
Bowl, salad, 6½" d., clear	5.00
Bowl, salad, 6½" d., ultramarine	55.00
Butter dish, cov., green	46.00
Butter dish, cov., pink	42.50
Candy jar, cov., green, 6½" h.	26.00
Candy jar, cov., pink, 6½" h.	22.50
Coaster, green or pink, 3¼" d.	6.50

Cube Creamer & Sugar Bowl

Creamer, clear, 2 5/8" h. (ILLUS. right)	1.00
Creamer, pink, 3½" h.	5.50
Cup & saucer, green	11.50
Cup & saucer, pink	9.00
Pitcher, 8¾" h., 45 oz., green	190.00
Pitcher, 8¾" h., 45 oz., pink	139.00
Plate, sherbet, 6" d., clear	1.00
Plate, sherbet, 6" d., green or pink	2.50
Plate, luncheon, 8" d., green	5.50
Plate, luncheon, 8" d., pink	4.50
Powder jar, cov., three-footed, green or pink	19.00
Salt & pepper shakers, green or pink, pr.	30.50
Sherbet, footed, green or pink	5.50
Sugar bowl, cov., green, 3" h.	18.50
Sugar bowl, cov., pink, 3" h.	10.00
Sugar bowl, open, clear, 2 3/8" h. (ILLUS. left)	1.00
Tumbler, green or pink, 4" h., 9 oz.	45.00

DAISY or Number 620 (Press-mold)

Daisy Cereal Bowl

Bowl, berry, 4½" d., amber	7.00
Bowl, cream soup, 4½" d., clear	6.50
Bowl, cereal, 6" d., amber (ILLUS.)	24.50
Bowl, cereal, 6" d., clear	9.00

Bowl, berry, 7 3/8" d., amber	14.50
Bowl, berry, 7 3/8" d., clear	6.00
Bowl, berry, 9 3/8" d., amber	25.00
Bowl, 10" oval vegetable, amber	13.50
Creamer, footed, amber	7.00
Cup & saucer, clear	3.50
Plate, sherbet, 6" d., amber	2.00
Plate, salad, 7 3/8" d., amber	6.00
Plate, luncheon, 8 3/8" d., amber	5.50
Plate, dinner, 9 3/8" d., clear	4.50
Plate, grill, 10 3/8" d., amber	13.00
Plate, grill, 10 3/8" d., clear	4.50
Plate, 11½" d., amber	11.00
Plate, 11½" d., clear	7.50
Platter, 10¾" l., amber	11.50
Relish dish, three-part, amber, 8 3/8"	27.00
Sherbet, footed, amber	7.00
Sherbet, footed, clear	3.00
Sugar bowl, open, footed, amber	6.00
Tumbler, footed, clear, 9 oz.	8.00
Tumbler, footed, amber, 12 oz.	29.50
Tumbler, footed, clear, 12 oz.	19.00

DIANA (Press-mold)

Diana Salad Bowl

Ashtray, green, 3½" d.	3.00
Bowl, cereal, 5" d., amber	10.00
Bowl, cream soup, 5½" d., clear or pink	4.00
Bowl, salad, 9" d., pink (ILLUS.)	14.50
Bowl, 12" d., scalloped rim, amber or clear	7.50
Candy jar, cov., round, clear	13.00
Candy jar, cov., round, pink	20.00
Coaster, clear, 3½" d.	2.50
Coaster, pink, 3½" d.	5.50
Console bowl, amber, 11" d.	9.00
Creamer, oval, pink	6.00
Cup & saucer, demitasse, clear	9.50
Cup & saucer, demitasse, pink	37.50
Cup & saucer, pink	14.50
Plate, dinner, 9½" d., amber	7.50
Plate, dinner, 9½" d., clear	4.50
Plate, sandwich, 11¾" d., clear	4.50
Platter, 12" oval, amber	10.00
Salt & pepper shakers, amber, pr.	81.00
Salt & pepper shakers, clear, pr.	20.00

Salt & pepper shakers, pink, pr.	45.00
Sherbet, amber or pink	9.50
Sugar bowl, open, oval, amber	6.50
Tumbler, amber, 4 1/8" h., 9 oz.	22.00
Junior set: 6 cups, saucers & plates w/round rack; clear, set	68.00

DOGWOOD or Apple Blossom or Wild Rose (Process-etched)

Dogwood Cup & Saucer

Bowl, cereal, 5½" d., green	20.50
Bowl, cereal, 5½" d., pink	21.50
Bowl, berry, 8½" d., Cremax	31.00
Bowl, berry, 8½" d., green	75.00
Bowl, fruit, 10¼" d., green	106.00
Bowl, fruit, 10¼" d., pink	241.00
Cake plate, heavy solid foot, green, 13" d.	80.00
Creamer, thin, green, 2½" h.	37.00
Creamer, thin, pink, 2½" h.	16.50
Cup & saucer, Cremax	34.50
Cup & saucer, green (ILLUS.)	23.00
Pitcher, 8" h., 80 oz., American Sweetheart style, pink	563.00
Pitcher, 8" h., 80 oz., decorated, green	413.00
Pitcher, 8" h., 80 oz., decorated, pink	140.00
Plate, bread & butter, 6" d., green	5.00
Plate, luncheon, 8" d., green or pink	6.50
Plate, dinner, 9¼" d., pink	24.00
Plate, grill, 10½" d., overall patt. or border design only, green or pink	15.00
Plate, salver, 12" d., Monax	17.00
Plate, salver, 12" d., pink	29.50
Platter, 12" oval, pink	235.00
Sherbet, low foot, green	40.00
Sherbet, low foot, pink	25.50
Sugar bowl, open, thin, green, 2½" h.	35.00
Sugar bowl, open, thick, footed, pink, 3¼" h.	13.00
Tumbler, decorated, pink, 3½" h., 5 oz.	230.00
Tumbler, decorated, green, 4" h., 10 oz.	65.00

Tumbler, decorated, pink, 4¾" h.,
11 oz. 34.00
Tumbler, decorated, pink, 5" h.,
12 oz. 45.00

DORIC (Press-mold)

Doric Relish Tray

Bowl, berry, 4½" d., green or
pink 7.00
Bowl, cereal, 5½" d., green 55.00
Bowl, cereal, 5½" d., pink 46.00
Bowl, large berry, 8¼" d., green ... 16.50
Bowl, 9" d., two-handled, pink 11.50
Bowl, 9" oval vegetable, green 27.00
Bowl, 9" oval vegetable, pink 22.50
Butter dish, cov., green 75.00
Butter dish, cov., pink 58.00
Cake plate, three-footed, green,
10" d. 24.50
Candy dish, three-section, green,
6" 10.00
Candy jar, cov., pink, 8" h. 32.00
Coaster, green, 3" d. 19.00
Coaster, pink, 3" d. 20.00
Creamer, green or pink, 4" h. 11.50
Cup & saucer, green 11.50
Pitcher, 6" h., 36 oz., pink 32.00
Pitcher, 7½" h., 48 oz., footed,
pink 425.00
Plate, sherbet, 6" d., green or
pink 3.50
Plate, salad, 7" d., green 16.50
Plate, dinner, 9" d., pink 10.50
Plate, grill, 9" d., green 15.00
Plate, grill, 9" d., pink 16.50
Platter, 12" oval, green or pink 20.00
Relish tray, pink, 4 x 8" (ILLUS.) 7.50
Relish or serving tray, green or
pink, 8 x 8" 14.50
Relish set: two 4 x 4" dishes & one
4 x 8" dish on 8 x 8" undertray;
pink, 4 pcs. 46.50
Salt & pepper shakers, green, pr.... 33.50
Salt & pepper shakers, pink, pr. 30.50
Sandwich tray, handled, pink,
10" d. 13.50
Sherbet, footed, Delphite 5.00
Sherbet, footed, green or pink 12.00
Sugar bowl, cov., green 27.00
Sugar bowl, cov., pink 23.50
Tumbler, green, 4½" h., 9 oz. 81.00
Tumbler, pink, 4½" h., 9 oz. 57.00
Tumbler, footed, pink, 4" h.,
10 oz. 42.00

Tumbler, footed, green, 5" h.,
12 oz. 87.50

DORIC & PANSY (Press-mold)

Bowl, berry, 4½" d., ultramarine ... 14.50
Bowl, large berry, 8" d., pink 18.00
Bowl, large berry, 8" d., ultra-
marine 61.00
Bowl, 9" d., handled, ultramarine... 25.00
Butter dish, cov., ultramarine 480.00
Creamer, ultramarine 175.00
Cup & saucer, clear 14.50
Cup & saucer, ultramarine 25.00
Plate, sherbet, 6" d., clear 8.00
Plate, salad, 7" d., ultramarine 28.00
Plate, dinner, 9" d., ultramarine 27.50
Salt & pepper shakers, ultramarine,
pr. 393.00
Sugar bowl, open, ultramarine 152.00
Tray, handled, ultramarine, 10" 21.00
Tumbler, ultramarine, 4½" h.,
9 oz. 70.00

PRETTY POLLY PARTY DISHES

Creamer, pink 28.50
Cup, ultramarine 29.50
Cup & saucer, pink 28.50
Cup & saucer, ultramarine 44.00
Plate, pink 6.50
Saucer, ultramarine 7.50
Sugar bowl, pink 25.00
Sugar bowl, ultramarine 37.50
14 piece set, pink 200.00
14 piece set, ultramarine 210.00

ENGLISH HOBNAIL (Handmade - not true Depression)

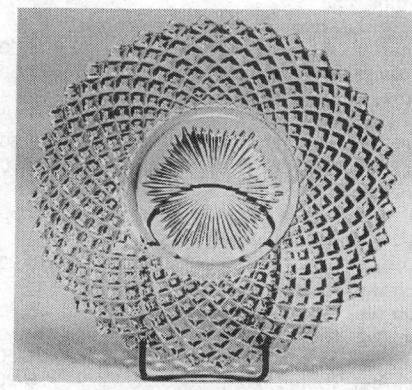

English Hobnail Dinner Plate

Bowl, nappy, 4½" d., green 9.50
Bowl, nappy, 4½" sq., clear 5.50
Bowl, cream soup, 4¾" d., clear ... 6.50
Bowl, fruit, 8" d., two-handled, foot-
ed, green 41.00
Bowl, nappy, 8" d., amber 17.00
Bowl, 12" d., flared, green 40.00

Candlesticks, amber, 3½" h., pr. ...	22.50
Candlesticks, blue, 3½" h., pr.	33.50
Candlesticks, clear, 8½" h., pr.	58.00
Candlesticks, green, 8½" h., pr.	67.50
Candlesticks, turquoise, 8½" h., pr.	61.00
Candy dish, cov., cone-shaped, amber, ½ lb.	39.50
Candy dish, cov., cone-shaped, green, ½ lb.	61.00
Candy dish, cov., urn-shaped, green, 15" h.	300.00
Celery tray, clear, 12" l.	17.00
Cigarette box, cov., clear	32.00
Cologne bottles w/stoppers, cobalt blue, pr.	91.50
Creamer, flat or footed, blue	37.50
Cup & saucer, demitasse, pink	39.00
Cup & saucer, clear	8.00
Cup & saucer, pink	20.00
Dish, cov., three-footed, clear	21.50
Dish, cov., three-footed, green	57.00
Egg cup, clear	17.00
Goblet, cordial, clear, 1 oz.	16.50
Goblet, wine, clear, 2 oz.	8.50
Goblet, cocktail, clear, 3 oz.	11.00
Goblet, cobalt blue, 6¼ oz.	35.00
Goblet, green, 6¼ oz.	21.50
Goblet, pink, 6¼ oz.	18.00
Goblet, turquoise, 6¼ oz.	44.00
Lamp, electric, clear, 6¼" h.	30.50
Lamp, electric, pink, 6¼" h.	43.00
Lamp, electric, amber, 9¼" h.	71.00
Lamp, electric, blue, 9¼" h.	85.00
Marmalade jar, cov., green	35.00
Marmalade jar, cov., pink	31.50
Pitcher, 23 oz., clear	75.00
Plate, luncheon, 8" round or square, pink	7.50
Plate, luncheon, 8" round or square, turquoise	15.00
Plate, dinner, 10" d., amber	17.50
Plate, dinner, 10" d., clear (ILLUS.)	7.50
Puff box, cov., clear	27.50
Puff box, cov., green	34.50
Rose bowl, clear, 6"	24.50
Salt & pepper shakers, amber, pr. ...	72.50
Salt & pepper shakers, turquoise, pr.	110.00
Salt dip, footed, cobalt blue, 2"	31.00
Salt dip, footed, green, 2"	16.50
Salt dip, footed, pink, 2"	14.50
Salt dip, footed, turquoise, 2"	21.50
Sherbet, footed, clear	9.00
Sherbet, footed, green	14.00
Sugar bowl, open, footed or flat, pink	17.00
Tumbler, whiskey, clear, 1½ oz.	8.00
Tumbler, whiskey, clear, 3 oz.	15.50
Tumbler, clear, 3¾" h., 5 oz.	8.50
Tumbler, footed, clear, 7 oz.	11.50
Tumbler, footed, clear, 9 oz.	12.00

Tumbler, iced tea, clear, 4" h., 10 oz.	8.50
Tumbler, footed, clear, 12½ oz.	12.50
Vase, 7¼" h., clear	42.50
Vase, 7¼" h., pink	101.00

FLORAL or Poinsettia (Process-etched)

Floral Candy Jar

Bowl, berry, 4" d., green or pink ...	15.50
Bowl, salad, 7½" d., green	17.00
Bowl, cov. vegetable, 8" d., pink ...	39.00
Bowl, 9" oval vegetable, green	15.00
Butter dish, cov., pink	82.00
Candlesticks, green, 4" h., pr.	78.50
Candlesticks, pink, 4" h., pr.	63.00
Candy jar, cov., green (ILLUS.)	34.00
Candy jar, cov., pink	32.50
Canister, cov., Jadite	28.00
Coaster, green, 3¼" d.	8.50
Creamer, pink	12.50
Cup & saucer, green	20.00
Cup & saucer, pink	18.00
Ice tub, oval, pink, 3½" h.	500.00
Lamp, green	275.00
Lamp, pink	225.00
Pitcher, 5½" h., 24 oz., green	715.00
Pitcher, 8" h., 32 oz., cone-shaped, green	31.50
Pitcher, lemonade, 10¼" h., 48 oz., pink	184.00
Plate, sherbet, 6" d., green	6.00
Plate, sherbet, 6" d., pink	5.00
Plate, salad, 8" d., green or pink ...	8.50
Plate, dinner, 9" d., green or pink ..	14.50
Platter, 10¾" oval, green or pink ...	14.50
Refrigerator dish, cov., green, 5" sq.	54.00
Relish, two-part, oval, green	14.50
Relish, two-part, oval, pink	13.50
Salt & pepper shakers, footed, green, 4" h., pr.	45.00
Salt & pepper shakers, flat, pink, 6" h., pr.	47.50
Sherbet, green	15.50
Sherbet, pink	13.50
Sugar bowl, cov., green	22.50
Tray, closed handles, green, 6" sq.	21.00

Tray, closed handles, pink, 6" sq.... 13.00
Tray, dresser, green, 9¼" oval 450.00
Tumbler, juice, footed, green, 4" h.,
   5 oz............................ 18.00
Tumbler, water, footed, pink,
   4¾" h., 7 oz. 16.00
Tumbler, green, 4½" h., 9 oz....... 190.00
Tumbler, lemonade, footed, green,
   5¼" h., 9 oz. 42.00
Vase, 6 7/8" h., octagonal, clear ... 300.00
Vase, 6 7/8" h., octagonal, green .. 490.00

(OLD) FLORENTINE or Poppy No. 1 (Process-etched)

Old Florentine Pitcher & Tumblers

Ashtray, clear, 5½" 18.00
Ashtray, green, 5½" 20.00
Bowl, berry, 5" d., cobalt blue 16.00
Bowl, berry, 5" d., green 11.00
Bowl, 8½" d., pink 30.00
Bowl, 8½" d., yellow 33.50
Bowl, cov. vegetable, 9½" oval,
   green 35.00
Bowl, cov. vegetable, 9½" oval,
   pink 50.00
Butter dish, cov., pink 154.00
Butter dish, cov., yellow 128.00
Creamer, plain rim, green, pink or
   yellow 11.00
Creamer, ruffled rim, clear 21.50
Creamer, ruffled rim, cobalt blue ... 50.00
Cup & saucer, green 11.00
Cup & saucer, pink or yellow 12.50
Nut dish, handled, ruffled rim, clear
   or pink 13.00
Nut dish, handled, ruffled rim, co-
   balt blue 41.00
Pitcher, 6½" h., 36 oz., footed,
   yellow 44.50
Pitcher, 7½" h., 48 oz., clear
   (ILLUS.)..................... 59.00
Pitcher, 7½" h., 48 oz., pink 97.00
Plate, sherbet, 6" d., green 7.50
Plate, sherbet, 6" d., pink 5.00
Plate, salad, 8½" d., clear 5.00
Plate, salad, 8½" d., green 7.00
Plate, dinner, 10" d., green 13.50

Plate, dinner, 10" d., pink 21.00
Plate, dinner, 10" d., yellow 14.00
Plate, grill, 10" d., green 11.00
Plate, grill, 10" d., pink or yellow .. 12.00
Platter, 11½" oval, clear 9.00
Platter, 11½" oval, green or pink ... 17.50
Salt & pepper shakers, footed, pink,
   pr........................... 48.50
Salt & pepper shakers, footed, yel-
   low, pr. 52.00
Sherbet, footed, clear, 3 oz. 7.00
Sherbet, footed, green, pink or yel-
   low, 3 oz. 9.00
Sugar bowl, cov., pink 25.00
Sugar bowl, cov., yellow 28.00
Sugar bowl, open, pink or yellow ... 11.00
Sugar bowl, open, ruffled rim, co-
   balt blue 45.00
Sugar bowl, open, ruffled rim,
   pink 28.00
Tumbler, footed, green, 3¼" h.,
   4 oz. 11.50
Tumbler, juice, footed, clear,
   3¾" h., 5 oz. (ILLUS.)........ 9.00
Tumbler, juice, footed, yellow,
   3¾" h., 5 oz. 17.00
Tumbler, ribbed, clear or pink,
   4" h., 9 oz. 12.00
Tumbler, water, footed, green or
   yellow, 4¾" h., 10 oz. 19.00
Tumbler, iced tea, footed, pink,
   5¼" h., 12 oz. 17.50
Tumbler, iced tea, footed, yellow,
   5¼" h., 12 oz. 21.50

FLORENTINE or Poppy No. 2 (Process-etched)

Florentine Covered Vegetable Bowl

Bowl, berry, 4½" d., pink.......... 14.00
Bowl, berry, 4½" d., yellow........ 15.50
Bowl, cream soup, plain rim,
   4¾" d., green 10.50
Bowl, 5½" d., green 45.00
Bowl, 5½" d., yellow............. 32.00
Bowl, cereal, 6" d., clear 19.50
Bowl, cereal, 6" d., green......... 27.00
Bowl, 8" d., yellow 26.50
Bowl, cov. vegetable, 9" oval,
   clear....................... 45.00
Bowl, cov. vegetable, 9" oval, yel-
   low (ILLUS.)................. 56.00
Bowl, 9" oval vegetable, green 20.00

Bowl, 9" oval vegetable, yellow	26.00
Butter dish, cov., green...........	92.50
Butter dish, cov., yellow	128.00
Candlesticks, yellow, 2¾" h., pr. ...	54.00
Candy dish, cov., pink	118.00
Candy dish, cov., yellow	147.00
Coaster, clear, 3¼" d.............	8.50
Coaster, green, 3¼" d.............	12.50
Coaster-ashtray, clear or green, 3¾" d......................	15.00
Compote, 3½", ruffled, clear or green	21.50
Compote, 3½", ruffled, cobalt blue	50.00
Creamer, clear..................	4.50
Creamer, green or yellow..........	7.50
Cup & saucer, clear	8.00
Cup & saucer, yellow	12.00
Custard cup, clear	25.50
Custard cup, green or yellow.......	70.00
Gravy boat, yellow	48.50
Pitcher, 6¼" h., 24 oz., cone-shaped, yellow.................	116.50
Pitcher, 7½" h., 28 oz., cone-shaped, green	33.50
Pitcher, 7½" h., 48 oz., straight sides, pink	107.50
Pitcher, 7½" h., 48 oz., straight sides, yellow	144.00
Pitcher, 8" h., 76 oz., pink	219.00
Plate, sherbet, 6" d., clear or green	3.50
Plate, sherbet, 6" d., yellow	4.50
Plate, 6¼" d., w/indentation, yellow	27.50
Plate, salad, 8½" d., clear or pink ..	5.50
Plate, salad, 8½" d., green or yellow	8.00
Plate, dinner, 10" d., clear	9.50
Plate, grill, 10¼" d., green	13.50
Platter, 11" oval, clear...........	10.50
Platter, 11½", for gravy boat, yellow	41.00
Relish dish, three-part or plain, clear, 10".....................	13.00
Relish dish, three-part or plain, pink or yellow, 10"	24.50
Salt & pepper shakers, clear, pr. ...	35.00
Salt & pepper shakers, green, pr....	38.50
Salt & pepper shakers, yellow, pr...	44.00
Sherbet, clear or green	8.50
Sherbet, yellow	9.50
Sugar bowl, cov., green	16.00
Sugar bowl, cov., yellow..........	29.50
Sugar bowl, open, clear	6.00
Sugar bowl, open, green or yellow	7.50
Tumbler, footed, green or yellow, 3¼" h., 5 oz.	12.50
Tumbler, juice, green, 3½" h., 5 oz..........................	11.00
Tumbler, footed, yellow, 4" h., 5 oz..........................	14.00

Tumbler, blown, green, 3½" h., 6 oz...........................	12.50
Tumbler, water, clear, 4" h., 9 oz. ...	9.50
Tumbler, water, yellow, 4" h., 9 oz...........................	17.50
Tumbler, footed, green, 4½" h., 9 oz...........................	19.00
Tumbler, footed, yellow, 4½" h., 9 oz...........................	27.50
Tumbler, blown, green, 5" h., 12 oz..........................	16.00
Tumbler, iced tea, clear, 5" h., 12 oz..........................	20.00
Tumbler, iced tea, pink, 5" h., 12 oz..........................	55.00
Vase (or parfait), 6" h., green	42.50
Vase (or parfait), 6" h., yellow	59.00

GEORGIAN or Lovebirds (Process-etched)

(All items in green only)

Bowl, berry, 4½" d.	7.00
Bowl, cereal, 5¾" d.	18.50
Bowl, 9" oval vegetable	62.50
Butter dish, cov.	70.00
Creamer, footed, 3" h.	11.00
Cup & saucer	11.50
Hot plate, center design, 5" d.	43.50
Plate, luncheon, 8" d.	7.50
Plate, dinner, 9¼" d..............	25.00
Platter, 11½" oval, closed handles..	58.00
Sherbet	10.00
Sugar bowl, cov., footed, 4" h.	76.00
Tumbler, 4" h., 9 oz.	45.50
Tumbler, 5¼" h., 12 oz.	108.00

IRIS or Iris & Herringbone (Press-mold)

Iris Tumbler

Bowl, berry, 4½" d., beaded rim, clear	35.50
Bowl, cereal, 5" d., clear	73.00
Bowl, sauce, 5" d., ruffled rim, amber iridescent	21.00
Bowl, soup, 7½" d., clear.........	127.00
Bowl, berry, 8" d., beaded rim, amber iridescent	19.50

Bowl, salad, 9½" d., amber irides-
cent or clear 11.00
Bowl, fruit, 11" d., straight rim,
clear 56.00
Bowl, fruit, 11½" d., ruffled rim,
clear 10.00
Butter dish, cov., amber iridescent . . 39.00
Candlesticks, two-branch, clear,
pr. 34.00
Candy jar, cov., clear 132.00
Coaster, clear 76.50
Creamer, footed, amber iridescent . . 11.50
Creamer, footed, clear 9.00
Cup & saucer, demitasse, clear 142.00
Cup & saucer, demitasse, ruby 92.50
Cup & saucer, amber iridescent 18.50
Goblet, cocktail, clear, 4¼" h.,
4 oz. 19.50
Goblet, clear, 5¾" h., 8 oz. 18.50
Lamp shade, blue 42.00
Lamp shade, clear 37.00
Lamp shade, clear frosted 72.00
Lamp shade, pink 62.00
Pitcher, 9½" h., footed, clear 32.00
Plate, sherbet, 5½" d., amber
iridescent 9.50
Plate, sherbet, 5½" d., clear 13.00
Plate, luncheon, 8" d., clear 75.00
Plate, dinner, 9" d., clear 47.50
Plate, sandwich, 11¾" d., amber
iridescent 24.50
Sherbet, footed, clear, 2½" h. 19.50
Sherbet, footed, amber iridescent,
4" h. 12.00
Sugar bowl, cov., footed, amber
iridescent or clear 20.00
Tumbler, clear, 4" h. 83.00
Tumbler, footed, amber iridescent,
6" h. 15.00
Tumbler, footed, clear, 6½" h.
(ILLUS.) 26.50
Vase, 9" h., pink 66.00

LACE EDGE or Open Lace (Press-mold)

Lace Edge Butter Dish

Bowl, cereal, 6½" d., pink 15.50
Bowl, 7¾" d., ribbed, pink 38.00
Bowl, 9½" d., plain or ribbed,
pink 19.50
Butter dish or bonbon, cov., pink
(ILLUS.) 59.00
Candlesticks, pink, pr. 235.00
Candlesticks, pink frosted, pr. 50.00

Candy jar, cov., ribbed, pink,
4" h. 45.00
Compote, cov., 7" d., footed, pink . . 47.50
Compote, open, 7" d., footed,
pink 18.00
Console bowl, three-footed, pink,
10½" d. 168.00
Cookie jar, cov., pink, 5" h. 51.00
Creamer, pink 20.50
Cup & saucer, pink 29.00
Flower bowl w/crystal block, pink . . 23.50
Plate, salad, 7¼" d., pink 19.00
Plate, luncheon, 8¾" d., pink 18.00
Plate, dinner, 10½" d., pink 22.50
Plate, grill, 10½" d., pink 16.00
Plate, 13" d., solid lace, pink 28.00
Platter, 12¾" oval, pink 23.50
Relish dish, three-part, deep, pink,
7½" d. 58.00
Relish plate, four-part, solid lace,
pink, 13" d. 25.50
Sherbet, footed, pink 75.00
Sugar bowl, open, pink 17.00
Tumbler, pink, 3½" h., 5 oz. 26.00
Tumbler, pink, 4½" h., 9 oz. 15.50
Vase, 7" h., pink frosted 47.50

LORAIN or Basket or Number 615 (Process-etched)

Lorain Cup & Saucer

Bowl, cereal, 6", yellow 49.50
Bowl, salad, 7¼", green 33.00
Bowl, berry, 8", yellow 137.00
Bowl, 9¾" oval vegetable, green . . . 35.00
Creamer, footed, yellow 17.50
Cup, green 10.50
Cup & saucer, clear 14.00
Cup & saucer, yellow (ILLUS.) 17.50
Plate, sherbet, 5½", green 6.00
Plate, salad, 7¾", green or yel-
low 12.50
Plate, luncheon, 8 3/8", green 10.50
Plate, dinner, 10¼", yellow 47.00
Platter, 11½", green 23.00
Relish, four-part, green, 8" 16.00
Relish, four-part, yellow, 8" 28.50
Sherbet, footed, green 17.50
Sherbet, footed, yellow 26.50
Sugar bowl, open, footed, yellow . . . 18.00
Tumbler, footed, yellow, 4¾" h.,
9 oz. 22.50

MADRID (Process-etched)

Madrid Salt & Pepper Shakers

Ashtray, amber, 6" sq. 221.00
Bowl, sauce, 5" d., amber or pink . . 5.50
Bowl, sauce, 5" d., blue 35.00
Bowl, soup, 7" d., blue 20.00
Bowl, soup, 7" d., green 16.50
Bowl, salad, 8" d., blue. 46.50
Bowl, large berry, 9 3/8" d., pink. . . 12.50
Bowl, salad, 9½" d., deep, amber . . 28.50
Bowl, 10" oval vegetable, amber . . . 14.00
Bowl, 10" oval vegetable, blue 29.00
Butter dish, cov., amber 64.00
Butter dish, cov., clear 49.00
Butter dish, cov., green 78.00
Cake plate, amber, 11¼" d. 14.00
Candlesticks, iridescent, 2¼" h.,
   pr. 17.50
Candlesticks, pink, 2¼" h., pr. 13.50
Console bowl, flared, amber,
   11" d. 12.50
Console set: bowl & pair of candle-
   sticks; pink, 3 pcs. 33.50
Cookie jar, cov., amber. 38.00
Cookie jar, cov., clear 32.50
Creamer, blue 14.00
Creamer, clear. 5.00
Cup & saucer, blue 22.50
Cup & saucer, clear 7.00
Cup & saucer, green 13.50
Gelatin mold, amber, 2 1/8" h. 11.50
Gravy boat & platter, amber. 1,575.00
Gravy boat platter, amber 500.00
Hot dish coaster, amber, 5" d. 38.50
Hot dish coaster, w/indentation,
   amber 35.00
Hot dish coaster w/indentation,
   green 29.00
Jam dish, amber, 7" d. 16.50
Jam dish, blue, 7" d. 27.50
Pitcher, juice, 5½" h., 36 oz.,
   amber 33.00
Pitcher, 8" h., 60 oz., square, blue. . 127.00
Pitcher, 8" h., 60 oz., square,
   green 140.00
Pitcher, 8½" h., 80 oz., jug-type,
   amber 59.50

Pitcher, 8½" h., 80 oz., jug-type,
   green 188.50
Pitcher w/ice lip, 8½" h., 80 oz.,
   amber 52.00
Plate, sherbet, 6" d., blue 10.50
Plate, salad, 7½" d., blue 17.00
Plate, luncheon, 8 7/8" d., amber . . 6.50
Plate, luncheon, 8 7/8" d., green . . . 9.50
Plate, dinner, 10½" d., amber. 34.00
Plate, dinner, 10½" d., blue 58.00
Plate, grill, 10½" d., green 15.00
Platter, 11½" oval, amber 13.50
Platter, 11½" oval, blue 29.00
Relish plate, pink, 10½" d 9.00
Salt & pepper shakers, green,
   3½" h., pr. 42.50
Salt & pepper shakers, footed, am-
   ber, 3½" h., pr. (ILLUS.) 53.00
Salt & pepper shakers, footed, blue,
   3½" h., pr. 126.00
Sherbet, blue 10.00
Sherbet, green 8.50
Sugar bowl, cov., amber 38.00
Sugar bowl, cov., clear 29.50
Sugar bowl, cov., green 47.50
Tumbler, juice, blue, 3 7/8" h.,
   5 oz. 29.00
Tumbler, juice, green, 3 7/8" h.,
   5 oz. 48.00
Tumbler, footed, amber, 4" h.,
   5 oz. 18.50
Tumbler, green, 4½" h., 9 oz. 19.00
Tumbler, pink, 4½" h., 9 oz. 13.00
Tumbler, footed, amber, 5¼" h.,
   10 oz. 22.50
Tumbler, blue, 5½" h., 12 oz. 39.00
Tumbler, green, 5½" h., 12 oz. 32.00

MANHATTAN or Horizontal Ribbed (Press-mold)

Ashtray, clear w/gold trim,
   4½" sq. 16.00
Bowl, sauce, 4½" d., two-handled,
   clear 8.00
Bowl, cereal, 5½" d., clear 25.00
Bowl, large berry, 7½" d., clear 13.00
Bowl, salad, 9" d., pink. 16.00
Bowl, fruit, 9½" d., clear 26.00
Candlesticks, double, clear, 4¼" h.,
   pr. 32.00
Candy dish, cov., clear 33.00
Candy dish, open, three-footed,
   pink 9.50
Coaster, clear, 3½" d. 11.50
Compote, 5¾" h., pink 29.00
Creamer, oval, clear 8.50
Creamer, oval, pink 10.50
Cup & saucer, clear or pink 20.00
Pitcher, juice, 42 oz., ball tilt-type,
   clear or pink 24.50
Pitcher w/ice lip, 80 oz., ball tilt-
   type, pink 45.50

Plate, sherbet or saucer, 6" d., pink	6.00
Plate, salad, 8½" d., clear	11.50
Plate, dinner, 10¼" d., clear	16.00
Plate, dinner, 10¼" d., pink	12.50
Relish tray, five-part, clear w/ruby inserts, 14" d.	41.50
Relish tray, five-part, pink w/pink inserts, 14" d.	36.50
Salt & pepper shakers, square, pink, 2" h., pr.	34.00
Sherbet, clear	7.00
Sherbet, pink	11.50
Sugar bowl, open, oval, clear	9.00
Tumbler, footed, green or pink, 10 oz.	16.00
Vase, 8" h., clear	15.00
Water bottle, cov., clear	22.00
Wine, clear, 3½" h.	5.00

MAYFAIR or Open Rose (Process-etched)

Mayfair Pitcher

Bowl, cream soup, 5", pink	33.50
Bowl, cereal, 5½", blue	50.50
Bowl, vegetable, 7", pink	21.00
Bowl, 9½" oval vegetable, blue	55.00
Bowl, 9½" oval vegetable, yellow	175.00
Bowl, 10", cov. vegetable, blue	135.00
Bowl, 10", open vegetable, pink	21.50
Bowl, 11¾" d., low, blue	62.00
Bowl, 11¾" d., low, green	31.00
Bowl, fruit, 12" d., deep, scalloped, green	31.00
Bowl, fruit, 12" d., deep, scalloped, yellow	250.00
Butter dish, cov., blue	265.00
Butter dish, cov., pink	53.00
Cake plate, footed, blue, 10"	56.50
Cake plate, handled, pink, 12"	31.00
Candy jar, cov., blue	240.00
Candy jar, cov., pink	51.00
Celery dish, pink, 10" l.	31.50
Celery dish, two-part, blue, 10" l.	46.50
Celery dish, two-part, pink, 10" l.	127.00
Cookie jar, cov., blue	246.00
Cookie jar, cov., pink	41.00

Cookie jar, cov., pink frosted	28.50
Creamer, footed, blue	65.00
Creamer, footed, pink	21.00
Creamer, footed, pink frosted	10.00
Cup & 5¾" underplate, blue	60.00
Cup & 5¾" underplate, pink	25.50
Cup & saucer w/cup ring, pink	41.50
Decanter w/stopper, pink, 10" h., 32 oz.	127.50
Goblet, cocktail, pink, 4" h., 3½ oz.	65.50
Goblet, water, pink, 5¾" h., 9 oz.	58.00
Goblet, water, thin, blue, 7¼" h., 9 oz.	165.00
Pitcher, juice, 6" h., 37 oz., clear	14.50
Pitcher, juice, 6" h., 37 oz., pink	44.50
Pitcher, 8" h., 60 oz., jug-type, pink (ILLUS.)	46.50
Pitcher, 8½" h., 80 oz., jug-type, blue	154.00
Plate (or saucer), 5¾", pink	11.50
Plate, sherbet, 6½" d., pink	11.00
Plate, sherbet, 6½" d., off-center indentation, blue	20.50
Plate, luncheon, 8½", blue	35.50
Plate, dinner, 9½", pink	45.50
Plate, dinner, 9½", yellow	117.50
Plate, grill, 9½", blue	36.00
Platter, 12" oval, open handles, clear	13.00
Platter, 12" oval, open handles, yellow	215.00
Platter, 12½" oval, closed handles, yellow	200.00
Relish, four-part, blue, 8 3/8"	48.50
Relish, four-part, pink, 8 3/8"	26.00
Salt & pepper shakers, flat, blue, pr.	243.00
Salt & pepper shakers, flat, pink frosted, pr.	39.00
Sandwich server w/center handle, blue, 12"	64.00
Sandwich server w/center handle, green, 12"	26.50
Saucer w/cup ring, pink	27.50
Sherbet, flat, blue, 2¼" h.	112.00
Sherbet, flat, pink, 2¼" h.	153.00
Sherbet, footed, pink, 4¾" h.	72.50
Sugar bowl, open, footed, blue	69.00
Sugar bowl, open, footed, pink	21.00
Tumbler, cocktail, pink, 2 oz.	65.00
Tumbler, juice, footed, pink, 3¼" h., 3 oz.	66.50
Tumbler, juice, blue, 3½" h., 5 oz.	100.00
Tumbler, water, pink, 4¼" h., 9 oz.	26.00
Tumbler, footed, blue, 5¼" h., 10 oz.	113.00
Tumbler, water, pink, 4¾" h., 11 oz.	92.00
Tumbler, iced tea, pink, 5¼" h., 13½ oz.	41.00

Tumbler, iced tea, footed, blue,
6½" h., 15 oz. 140.00
Vase, 5½ x 8½", sweetpea, hat-
shaped, pink. 142.00

MISS AMERICA (Press-mold)

Miss America Relish

Bowl, berry, 4½" d., green 10.00
Bowl, berry, 6¼" d., clear 8.00
Bowl, fruit, 8" d., curved in at top,
pink 67.00
Bowl, fruit, 8¾" d., deep, clear 33.00
Bowl, 10" oval vegetable, pink 28.00
Butter dish, cov., clear 186.50
Butter dish, cov., pink 388.00
Cake plate, footed, clear, 12" d. 23.50
Candy jar, cov., pink, 11½" h. 116.00
Celery tray, clear, 10½" oblong 10.00
Coaster, pink, 5¾" d. 21.00
Compote, 5" d., clear. 11.50
Compote, 5" d., pink 22.00
Creamer, footed, clear 8.00
Creamer, footed, pink 16.00
Cup & saucer, pink 25.00
Goblet, wine, clear, 3¾" h., 3 oz. . . 17.50
Goblet, juice, pink, 4¾" h., 5 oz. . . . 75.00
Goblet, water, clear, 5½" h.,
10 oz. 20.00
Goblet, water, green, 5½" h.,
10 oz. 16.00
Pitcher, 8" h., 65 oz., pink 110.00
Pitcher w/ice lip, 8½" h., 65 oz.,
clear 48.50
Plate, sherbet, 5¾" d., clear 4.50
Plate, sherbet, 5¾" d., pink 7.50
Plate, 6¾" d., green 7.50
Plate, salad, 8½" d., clear 7.00
Plate, dinner, 10¼" d., pink 28.50
Plate, grill, 10¼" d., clear 9.00
Plate, grill, 10¼" d., pink. 20.50
Platter, 12¼" oval, clear. 13.50
Relish, four-part, pink, 8¾" d.
(ILLUS.). 19.00
Relish, divided, clear, 11¾" d. 18.50
Salt & pepper shakers, green, pr. . . . 180.00
Salt & pepper shakers, pink, pr. 60.00
Sherbet, clear. 7.50

Sherbet, pink 12.50
Sugar bowl, open, footed, clear 7.00
Tumbler, juice, pink, 4" h., 5 oz. . . . 40.00
Tumbler, water, clear, 4½" h.,
10 oz. 13.50
Tumbler, water, green, 4½" h.,
10 oz. 15.00
Tumbler, iced tea, clear, 6¾" h.,
14 oz. 26.00
Tumbler, iced tea, pink, 6¾" h.,
14 oz. 73.00

MODERNTONE (Press-mold)

Moderntone Cup & Saucer

Ashtray w/match holder, cobalt
blue, 7¾" d. 200.00
Bowl, cream soup, 4¾" d., ame-
thyst 15.50
Bowl, cream soup, 4¾" d., cobalt
blue 18.00
Bowl, berry, 5" d., platonite 6.50
Bowl, cream soup w/ruffled rim,
5" d., cobalt blue 52.50
Bowl, cereal, 6½" d., cobalt blue . . . 65.00
Bowl, cereal, 6½" d., platonite 6.00
Bowl, soup, 7½" d., cobalt blue 119.00
Bowl, large berry, 8¾" d., cobalt
blue 50.00
Bowl, large berry, 8¾" d., pla-
tonite 7.00
Butter dish w/metal lid, cobalt
blue 82.50
Cheese dish w/metal lid, cobalt
blue, 7" d. 232.50
Creamer, amethyst 8.50
Creamer, cobalt blue 10.50
Cup & saucer, amethyst. 11.50
Cup & saucer, cobalt blue (ILLUS.) . . 13.50
Custard cup, amethyst 10.50
Plate, sherbet, 5 7/8" d., cobalt
blue 6.00
Plate, salad, 6¾" d., cobalt blue . . . 9.00
Plate, luncheon, 7¾" d., platonite . . 4.50
Plate, dinner, 8 7/8" d., amethyst . . 10.50
Plate, dinner, 8 7/8" d., cobalt
blue 15.50
Plate, sandwich, 10½" d., pla-
tonite 13.50

Platter, 11" oval, amethyst	17.50
Platter, 11" oval, cobalt blue	41.50
Platter, 12" oval, cobalt blue	48.00
Platter, 12" oval, platonite	12.50
Salt & pepper shakers, amethyst, pr.	43.00
Salt & pepper shakers, cobalt blue, pr.	37.50
Sherbet, amethyst	9.00
Sherbet, cobalt blue	11.50
Sugar bowl, open, cobalt blue	9.50
Sugar bowl, open, platonite	6.50
Sugar bowl w/metal lid, cobalt blue	35.00
Tumbler, whiskey, clear, 1½ oz.	5.50
Tumbler, juice, cobalt blue, 5 oz.	30.00
Tumbler, juice, platonite, 5 oz.	6.00
Tumbler, water, cobalt blue, 4" h., 9 oz.	29.50
Tumbler, iced tea, amethyst, 12 oz.	67.00

LITTLE HOSTESS PARTY SET

Creamer, 1¾" h., dark or pastel	9.50
Cup, 1¾" h., dark	10.00
Cup, 1¾" h., pastel	7.00
Plate, 5¼" d., dark or pastel	8.00
Saucer, 3 7/8" d., dark	5.50
Saucer, 3 7/8" d., pastel	6.50
Sugar bowl, 1¾" h., dark or pastel	9.50
Teapot, cov., 3½" h., dark	67.50
Teapot, cov., 3½" h., pastel	60.00
Tea set, pastel, 16 pcs.	265.00
Tea set, dark, 16 pcs.	195.00

NORMANDIE or Bouquet and Lattice (Process-etched)

Normandie Cup & Saucer

Bowl, berry, 5" d., amber or pink	5.50
Bowl, cereal, 6½" d., Sunburst iridescent	7.50
Bowl, large berry, 8½" d., Sunburst iridescent	13.00
Bowl, 10" oval vegetable, pink	21.00
Creamer, footed, pink	7.00
Cup & saucer, amber	8.50
Cup & saucer, pink	10.00
Cup & saucer, Sunburst iridescent (ILLUS.)	7.00
Pitcher, 8" h., 80 oz., amber	63.00

Pitcher, 8" h., 80 oz., pink	100.00
Plate, sherbet, 6" d., pink	3.50
Plate, salad, 8" d., amber	7.50
Plate, luncheon, 9¼" d., pink	12.00
Plate, dinner, 11" d., amber	19.50
Plate, dinner, 11" d., pink	116.00
Plate, grill, 11" d., amber	7.00
Platter, 11¾" oval, amber	15.00
Platter, 11¾" oval, pink	29.00
Salt & pepper shakers, amber, pr.	35.00
Salt & pepper shakers, pink, pr.	53.50
Sherbet, amber, clear or Sunburst iridescent	5.50
Sherbet, pink	8.00
Sugar bowl, cov., amber	67.00
Tumbler, juice, pink, 4" h., 5 oz.	35.00
Tumbler, water, amber, 4½" h., 9 oz.	13.00
Tumbler, iced tea, amber, 5" h., 12 oz.	18.00
Tumbler, iced tea, pink, 5" h., 12 oz.	82.50

NUMBER 612 or Horseshoe (Process-etched)

Number 612 Tumbler

Bowl, berry, 4½" d., yellow	18.00
Bowl, cereal, 6½" d., green	22.50
Bowl, salad, 7½" d., yellow	18.50
Bowl, vegetable, 8½" d., green	19.00
Bowl, large berry, 9½" d., yellow	28.00
Bowl, 10½" oval vegetable, green	17.00
Butter dish, cov., green	550.00
Candy in metal holder, motif on lid, green	165.00
Creamer, footed, yellow	14.00
Cup & saucer, green	11.50
Cup & saucer, yellow	14.00
Pitcher, 8½" h., 64 oz., green	200.00
Plate, sherbet, 6" d., yellow	5.00
Plate, salad, 8 3/8" d., green or yellow	7.50
Plate, luncheon, 9 3/8" d., green	9.50
Plate, dinner, 10 3/8" d., green	16.50
Plate, grill, 10 3/8" d., green	65.00
Plate, sandwich, 11" d., green	13.00
Plate, sandwich, 11" d., yellow	15.50

Platter, 10¾" oval, green or yellow	18.00
Relish, three-part, footed, green	15.00
Sherbet, yellow	14.00
Sugar bowl, open, footed, green	10.50
Tumbler, footed, yellow, 9 oz.	18.00
Tumbler, footed, green, 12 oz. (ILLUS.)	79.00
Tumbler, footed, yellow, 12 oz.	102.50

OLD CAFE (Press-mold)

Old Cafe Cup & Saucer

Bowl, berry, 3¾" d., clear	4.00
Bowl, berry, 3¾" d., pink	8.00
Bowl, 9" d., handled, pink	7.50
Bowl, 9" d., handled, ruby	10.50
Candy dish, ruby, 8" d.	10.00
Cup & saucer, pink	9.50
Cup & saucer, ruby cup, clear saucer (ILLUS.)	7.50
Lamp, pink	12.50
Pitcher, 6" h., 36 oz., clear	25.00
Pitcher, 6" h., 36 oz., pink	72.50
Pitcher, 8" h., 80 oz., pink	83.00
Plate, sherbet, 6" d., clear	4.00
Plate, sherbet, 6" d., pink	10.50
Plate, dinner, 10" d., clear	20.00
Plate, dinner, 10" d., pink	28.50
Sherbet, low foot, clear	3.50
Sherbet, low foot, pink	8.00
Tumbler, juice, pink, 3" h.	11.50
Tumbler, water, pink or ruby, 4" h.	12.00
Vase, 7¼" h., clear	9.00

OYSTER & PEARL (Press-mold)

Bowl, 5¼" heart-shaped, w/handle, clear, pink or white w/green	7.00
Bowl, 5½" d., w/handle, clear	8.50
Bowl, 5½" d., w/handle, ruby	13.00
Bowl, 6½" d., handled, pink	9.00
Bowl, 6½" d., handled, ruby	17.00
Bowl, fruit, 10½" d., clear	16.00
Bowl, fruit, 10½" d., pink	21.50
Bowl, fruit, 10½" d., ruby	37.50
Bowl, fruit, 10½" d., white w/pink	13.00

Candleholders, clear, 3½" h., pr.	20.50
Candleholders, pink, 3½" h., pr.	17.00
Candleholders, ruby, 3½" h., pr.	35.50
Plate, sandwich, 13½" d., pink	18.00
Plate, sandwich, 13½" d., ruby	32.00
Relish, divided, clear, 10¼" oval	8.00
Relish, divided, pink, 10¼" oval	10.00

PARROT or Sylvan (Process-etched)

Parrot Butter Dish

Bowl, berry, 5" sq., amber or green	15.00
Bowl, soup, 7" sq., amber	26.50
Bowl, soup, 7" sq., green	36.50
Bowl, 10" oval vegetable, green	40.00
Butter dish, cov., green (ILLUS.)	325.00
Creamer, footed, green	33.50
Cup & saucer, amber	33.00
Cup & saucer, green	43.50
Hot plate, green, scalloped edge	775.00
Plate, sherbet, 5¾" sq., green	18.00
Plate, salad, 7½" sq., green	25.00
Plate, dinner, 9" sq., amber	25.00
Plate, dinner, 9" sq., green	37.00
Plate, grill, 10½" sq., amber	18.00
Plate, grill, 10½" d., green	27.00
Platter, 11¼" oblong, amber	44.50
Platter, 11¼" oblong, green	39.50
Salt & pepper shakers, green, pr.	205.00
Sherbet, green, 4¼" h.	16.50
Sugar bowl, cov., green	150.00
Sugar bowl, open, amber	18.50
Sugar bowl, open, green	21.00
Tumbler, green, 4¼" h., 10 oz.	97.50
Tumbler, footed, amber, 5½" h., 10 oz.	118.00
Tumbler, footed, cone-shaped, amber, 5¾" h.	112.00

PATRICIAN or Spoke (Process-etched)

Bowl, cream soup, 4¾" d., amber	13.50
Bowl, cream soup, 4¾" d., clear, green or pink	15.00
Bowl, berry, 5" d., pink	11.00
Bowl, cereal, 6" d., amber	21.00
Bowl, cereal, 6" d., clear or green	18.00
Bowl, cereal, 6" d., pink	20.00
Bowl, large berry, 8½" d., amber	41.00
Bowl, large berry, 8½" d., clear	33.50

Bowl, 10" oval vegetable, green 29.00
Bowl, 10" oval vegetable, pink 18.00
Butter dish, cov., amber or clear . . .   78.00
Butter dish, cov., green 95.00
Butter dish, cov., pink 227.00
Cookie jar, cov., amber or clear 76.00
Cookie jar, cov., green 390.00
Creamer, footed, amber, clear or
    pink 9.00

Patrician Cup & Saucer

Cup & saucer, green (ILLUS.) 15.00
Cup & saucer, pink 17.00
Jam dish, amber, 6" 25.00
Jam dish, green, 6" 29.00
Pitcher, 8" h., 75 oz., molded han-
    dle, clear 90.00
Pitcher, 8" h., 75 oz., molded han-
    dle, green 107.00
Pitcher, 8" h., 75 oz., molded han-
    dle, pink 99.00
Pitcher, 8¼" h., 75 oz., applied han-
    dle, amber 95.00
Pitcher, 8¼" h., 75 oz., applied han-
    dle, clear 116.00
Pitcher, 8¼" h., 75 oz., applied han-
    dle, green 110.00
Plate, sherbet, 6" d., clear or
    green 5.50
Plate, sherbet, 6" d., pink 7.50
Plate, salad, 7½" d., amber or
    clear 12.00
Plate, luncheon, 9" d., clear or
    green 8.50
Plate, dinner, 10½" d., green 35.00
Plate, dinner, 10½" d., pink 43.00
Plate, grill, 10½" d., amber 12.00
Plate, grill, 10½" d., clear or pink . .   10.00
Plate, grill, 10½" d., green 8.00
Platter, 11½" oval, amber 28.00
Platter, 11½" oval, clear 25.00
Salt & pepper shakers, pink, pr. 75.00
Sherbet, amber or clear 10.00
Sherbet, green 11.00
Sherbet, pink 12.50
Sugar bowl, cov., amber 57.50
Sugar bowl, open, pink 10.50
Tumbler, amber, 4" h., 5 oz. 25.50
Sugar bowl, cov., clear 54.00
Sugar bowl, cov., green 43.50

Sugar bowl, cov., pink 52.00
Tumbler, pink, 4" h., 5 oz. 21.00
Tumbler, footed, amber, 5¼" h.,
    8 oz. 41.00
Tumbler, footed, green, 5¼" h.,
    8 oz. 39.00
Tumbler, amber, 4½" h., 9 oz. 24.00
Tumbler, clear, green or pink,
    4½" h., 9 oz. 22.00
Tumbler, iced tea, amber, 5½" h.,
    14 oz. 37.50
Tumbler, iced tea, clear, 5½" h.,
    14 oz. 31.50
Tumbler, iced tea, green, 5½" h.,
    14 oz. 35.00
Tumbler, iced tea, pink, 5½" h.,
    14 oz. 40.00

PETALWARE (Press-mold)

Bowl, cream soup, 4½" d., clear . . .   5.50
Bowl, cream soup, 4½" d., plain
    Cremax or Monax 9.00
Bowl, cream soup, 4½" d., decorat-
    ed Cremax or Monax 10.00
Bowl, cereal, 5¾" d., decorated
    Cremax or Monax 7.50
Bowl, cereal, 5¾" d., Florette 9.50
Bowl, cereal, 5¾" d., pink 8.50
Bowl, large berry, 9" d., clear 11.00
Bowl, large berry, 9" d., decorated
    Cremax or Monax 22.00
Bowl, large berry, 9" d., Florette . . .   20.00
Bowl, large berry, 9" d., pink 16.00
Creamer, footed, decorated Cremax
    or Monax 9.50
Creamer, footed, Florette 9.50
Cup & saucer, clear w/platinum
    trim 5.00
Cup & saucer, plain Cremax or
    Monax 7.50
Cup & saucer, Florette or Red Trim
    Floral 10.00
Cup & saucer, pink 9.00
Lamp shade, Monax, 6" h. 8.00
Lamp shade, Monax, 11" h. 15.00
Lamp shade, pink, 12" h. 21.00
Mustard jar w/metal cover, cobalt
    blue 15.00
Plate, sherbet, 6" d., clear 1.50
Plate, sherbet, 6" d., plain Cremax
    or Monax 3.00
Plate, sherbet, 6" d., decorated Cre-
    max or Monax 4.00
Plate, salad, 8" d., decorated Cre-
    max or Monax 7.50
Plate, salad, 8" d., Florette 8.00
Plate, salad, 8" d., Red Trim
    Floral 7.00
Plate, salad, 8" d., pink 4.50
Plate, dinner, 9" d., clear 6.00
Plate, dinner, 9" d., plain Cremax or
    Monax 7.00

Plate, dinner, 9" d., decorated Cremax or Monax 11.00

Plate, salver, 11" d., clear w/platinum trim 5.00

Plate, salver, 11" d., plain Cremax or Monax. 8.00

Plate, salver, 11" d., Florette 15.00

Plate, salver, 11" d., pink 12.50

Plate, salver, 12" d., Florette 14.50

Platter, 13" oval, plain Cremax or Monax 16.00

Platter, 13" oval, decorated Cremax or Monax. 13.50

Sherbet, low foot, cobalt blue, 4½" h. 12.00

Sherbet, low foot, plain Cremax or Monax, 4½" h. 7.50

Sherbet, low foot, Red Trim Floral, 4½" h. 30.00

Sherbet, low foot, pink, 4½" h. 7.50

Sugar bowl, open, footed, decorated Cremax or Monax 8.00

Sugar bowl, open, footed, Florette . . 9.50

Sugar bowl, open, pink 6.50

Tidbit server, plain Cremax or Monax 23.00

Tumbler, juice, pink 5.00

Tumbler, pink, 4¼" h. 29.00

Tumbler, pink, 4¾" h. 29.00

PINEAPPLE & FLORAL or Number 618 or Wildflower (Press-mold)

Ashtray, clear, 4½" l. 13.00

Bowl, berry, 4¾" d., amber 15.00

Bowl, berry, 4¾" d., clear 24.50

Bowl, cream soup, 4 5/8" d., amber 16.00

Bowl, cream soup, 4 5/8" d., clear . . 18.00

Bowl, cereal, 6" d., amber or clear 21.00

Bowl, salad, 7" d., clear 5.00

Bowl, 10" oval vegetable, amber . . . 18.00

Bowl, 10" oval vegetable, clear 23.00

Compote, diamond-shaped, amber . . 5.00

Compote, diamond-shaped, clear . . . 3.50

Creamer, diamond-shaped, amber . . 8.50

Creamer, diamond-shaped, clear . . . 6.00

Cup & saucer, amber or clear 12.00

Plate, sherbet, 6" d., amber or clear 3.50

Plate, salad, 8 3/8" d., amber or clear 7.00

Plate, dinner, 9 3/8" d., amber or clear 12.50

Plate, sandwich, 11½" d., amber . . . 14.50

Plate, sandwich, 11½" d., clear 12.50

Plate, 11½" d., w/indentation, clear 14.00

Platter, 11", closed handles, amber 15.50

Platter, 11", closed handles, clear . . 12.50

Relish, divided, clear, 11½" 14.50

Sherbet, footed, amber or clear 16.00

Sugar bowl, open, diamond-shaped, amber 9.00

Sugar bowl, open, diamond-shaped, clear 6.50

Tumbler, clear, 4¼" h., 8 oz. 31.00

Tumbler, iced tea, clear, 5" h., 12 oz. 36.50

Vase, 12½" h., cone-shaped, clear 42.00

Vase, 12½" h., cone-shaped, clear w/holder 60.00

PRINCESS (Process-etched)

Princess Sugar Bowl

Ashtray, green, 4½" 68.50

Bowl, berry, 4½", green 20.00

Bowl, berry, 4½", pink 17.50

Bowl, berry, 4½", yellow 42.00

Bowl, salad, 9" octagon, pink 27.00

Bowl, salad, 9" octagon, yellow 93.00

Bowl, 9½" hat shape, green 34.00

Bowl, 9½" hat shape, pink 28.50

Bowl, 10" oval vegetable, green or pink 23.50

Butter dish, cov., pink 87.50

Butter dish, cov., yellow 560.00

Cake stand, green or pink, 10" 18.00

Candy jar, cov., green 50.00

Candy jar, cov., pink 44.00

Cookie jar, cov., green 48.00

Cookie jar, cov., pink 46.50

Creamer, oval, green 13.00

Creamer, oval, pink 10.00

Creamer, oval, yellow 11.50

Cup & saucer, amber 9.00

Cup & saucer, green or pink 16.00

Cup & saucer, yellow 10.00

Pitcher, 6" h., 37 oz., jug-type, green 41.00

Pitcher, 6" h., 37 oz., jug-type, pink 47.00

Pitcher, 7 3/8" h., 24 oz., footed, pink 800.00

Pitcher, 8" h., 60 oz., jug-type, green or pink 47.50

Plate, sherbet, 5½", green or pink 8.00

Plate, sherbet, 5½", yellow 3.50

Plate, salad, 8", amber or yellow . . . 8.00

Plate, salad, 8", green 13.00

Plate, salad, 8", pink 11.00

Plate, dinner, 9", pink 19.00

Plate, dinner, 9", yellow 11.50

Plate, grill, 9", amber or yellow 7.00
Plate, grill, 9", green 11.50
Plate, grill, 9", pink 9.00
Plate, grill, 10½", closed handles,
  amber or yellow 5.00
Plate, grill, 10½", closed handles,
  pink 7.00
Plate, sandwich, 11¼", handled,
  green 18.00
Platter, 12" oval, closed handles,
  green or pink 19.00
Relish, green, 7½" 103.00
Relish, pink, 7½" 300.00
Relish, divided, green, 7½" 21.50
Relish, divided, pink, 7½" 17.00
Salt & pepper shakers, green,
  4½" h., pr. 44.50
Salt & pepper shakers, yellow,
  4½" h., pr. 65.00
Salt & pepper (or spice) shakers,
  green, 5½" h., pr. 38.00
Sherbet, footed, green or pink 17.00
Sherbet, footed, yellow 29.00
Sugar bowl, cov., green (ILLUS.) 27.50
Sugar bowl, cov., pink 33.00
Sugar bowl, cov., yellow 23.50
Sugar bowl, open, pink frosted 5.50
Tumbler, juice, green, 3" h., 5 oz. .. 27.00
Tumbler, juice, pink, 3" h., 5 oz. ... 21.00
Tumbler, water, pink, 4" h., 9 oz. .. 21.00
Tumbler, water, yellow, 4" h.,
  9 oz. 19.50
Tumbler, footed, green, 5¼" h.,
  10 oz. 27.00
Tumbler, footed, yellow, 5¼" h.,
  10 oz. 18.50
Tumbler, footed, green, 6½" h.,
  12½ oz. 84.00
Tumbler, footed, pink, 6½" h.,
  12½ oz. 67.50
Tumbler, iced tea, green, 5¼" h.,
  13 oz. 35.00
Tumbler, iced tea, pink, 5¼" h.,
  13 oz. 25.00
Tumbler, iced tea, yellow, 5¼" h.,
  13 oz. 22.50
Vase, 8" h., green or pink 29.50
Vase, 8" h., green frosted 14.00
Vase, 8" h., pink frosted 20.00

QUEEN MARY or Vertical Ribbed (Press-mold)

Ashtray, clear, 3½" d. 5.50
Ashtray, ruby, 3½" d. 8.00
Bowl, nappy, 4" d., clear or pink ... 4.50
Bowl, nappy, 4" d., single handle,
  pink 5.00
Bowl, berry, 5" d., clear or pink 5.50
Bowl, cereal, 6" d., pink 18.50
Bowl, nappy, 7" d., clear 9.50
Bowl, nappy, 7" d., pink 23.00
Bowl, large berry, 8¾" d., clear 10.50
Bowl, large berry, 8¾" d., pink 14.00

Butter (or jam) dish, cov., clear 28.00
Butter (or jam) dish, cov., pink 80.00
Candlesticks, two-light, clear,
  4½" h., pr. 16.00
Candy dish, cov., clear 21.00
Candy dish, cov., pink 33.00
Celery (or pickle) dish, pink, 5 x 10"
  oval 17.00
Cigarette jar, clear, 2 x 3" oval..... 4.50
Coaster, clear, 3½" d. 2.50
Coaster, pink, 3½" d. 4.00
Compote, 5¾" d., clear 7.00
Creamer, oval, clear 4.50
Creamer, oval, pink 11.00
Cup & saucer, clear 8.50

Queen Mary Cup & Saucer

Cup & saucer, pink (ILLUS.) 8.00
Plate, sherbet, 6" d., clear 2.50
Plate, sherbet, 6" d., pink 4.00
Plate, 6 5/8" d., clear 4.50
Plate, 6 5/8" d., pink 10.50
Plate, salad, 8½" d., clear 5.00
Plate, dinner, 9¾" d., clear 14.50
Plate, dinner, 9¾" d., pink 36.00
Plate, sandwich, 12" d., clear 8.50
Plate, sandwich, 12" d., pink 15.00
Relish, four-part, clear, 14" d. 10.00
Salt & pepper shakers, clear, pr. ... 16.50
Sherbet, footed, clear 4.50
Sherbet, footed, pink 6.50
Sugar bowl, open, oval, clear 4.50
Sugar bowl, open, oval, pink 7.50
Tumbler, juice, pink, 3½" h.,
  5 oz. 9.50
Tumbler, water, clear, 4" h., 9 oz. .. 6.50
Tumbler, water, pink, 4" h., 9 oz. .. 10.50
Tumbler, footed, clear, 5" h.,
  10 oz. 17.50

RING or Banded Rings (Press-mold)

Bowl, berry, 5" d., clear 3.50
Bowl, berry, 5" d., clear w/mul-
  ticolored bands or green 5.50
Bowl, soup, 7" d., clear 11.50
Bowl, soup, 7" d., green 8.50
Bowl, large berry, 8" d., green 9.00
Butter tub, clear w/multicolored
  bands 23.50

Cocktail shaker, clear 12.50
Cocktail shaker, clear w/mul-
  ticolored bands 26.50
Creamer, footed, green 8.50
Cup & saucer, clear 5.50
Cup & saucer, clear w/multicolored
  bands, clear w/platinum trim or
  green 5.00
Cup & saucer, green w/platinum
  trim 6.50
Decanter w/stopper, clear 19.00
Decanter w/stopper, clear w/mul-
  ticolored bands 26.00
Goblet, clear w/multicolored bands
  or green, 7¼" h., 9 oz. 10.50
Goblet, clear w/platinum trim,
  7¼" h., 9 oz. 11.50
Ice bucket w/tab handles, clear 10.50
Ice bucket w/tab handles, clear
  w/multicolored bands or green ... 17.50
Pitcher, 8" h., 60 oz., clear 13.00
Pitcher, 8" h., 60 oz., clear w/mul-
  ticolored bands 16.00
Pitcher, 8½" h., 80 oz., clear
  w/multicolored bands 33.00
Pitcher, 8½" h., 80 oz., green 22.50
Plate, sherbet, 6¼" d., green 2.50
Plate, 6½" d., off-center ring, clear
  or clear w/platinum trim 1.50
Plate, 6½" d., off-center ring, clear
  w/multicolored bands 4.50
Plate, luncheon, 8" d., clear w/mul-
  ticolored bands 2.50
Plate, luncheon, 8" d., green 5.00
Salt & pepper shakers, clear, 3" h.,
  pr. 18.00
Salt & pepper shakers, clear w/mul-
  ticolored bands, 3" h., pr. 24.00
Sandwich server w/center handle,
  clear or clear w/platinum trim ... 14.00
Sandwich server w/center handle,
  green 19.50
Sherbet, low, clear 6.00
Sherbet, low, clear w/multicolored
  bands 16.00
Sherbet, footed, clear w/mul-
  ticolored bands, 4¾" h. 6.50
Sherbet, footed, green, 4¾" h. 8.00
Sugar bowl, open, footed, clear or
  clear w/multicolored bands 4.50
Tumbler, whiskey, clear w/mul-
  ticolored bands, 2" h., 1½ oz. 7.00
Tumbler, clear, 3½" h., 5 oz. 3.00
Tumbler, clear w/multicolored
  bands, 3½" h., 5 oz. 8.50
Tumbler, clear, 4¼" h., 9 oz. 6.00
Tumbler, clear w/multicolored
  bands, 4¼" h., 9 oz. 8.00
Tumbler, green, 4¼" h., 9 oz. 11.00
Tumbler, green, 4¾" h., 10 oz. 15.00
Tumbler, clear, 5 1/8" h., 12 oz. 5.50
Tumbler, green, 5 1/8" h., 12 oz. ... 13.50
Tumbler, pink, 5 1/8" h., 12 oz. 7.00

Tumbler, cocktail, footed, clear
  w/multicolored bands, 3½" h. 6.50
Tumbler, cocktail, footed, green,
  3½" h. 12.00
Tumbler, water, footed, clear,
  5½" h. 4.50
Tumbler, water, footed, clear
  w/multicolored bands, 5½" h. 6.00
Tumbler, iced tea, footed, clear
  w/platinum trim, 6½" h. 9.00
Tumbler, iced tea, footed, clear
  w/multicolored bands, 6½" h. 8.50
Vase, 8" h., clear 12.50
Vase, 8" h., clear w/multicolored
  bands 25.00

ROULETTE or Many Windows (Press-mold)
Bowl, fruit, 9" d., green 14.00
Cup & saucer, green 8.00
Pitcher, 8" h., 64 oz., green 30.00
Pitcher, 8" h., 64 oz., pink 26.50
Plate, sherbet, 6" d., green 3.50
Plate, luncheon, 8½" d., clear 4.00
Plate, luncheon, 8½" d., green 5.50
Plate, sandwich, 12" d., green 15.00
Sherbet, green 5.00
Tumbler, whiskey, pink, 2½" h.,
  1½ oz. 11.00
Tumbler, juice, green, 3¼" h.,
  5 oz. 18.50
Tumbler, old fashioned, pink,
  3¼" h., 7½ oz. 19.00
Tumbler, water, green or pink,
  4 1/8" h., 9 oz. 15.50
Tumbler, footed, clear, 5½" h.,
  10 oz. 17.50
Tumbler, footed, green, 5½" h.,
  10 oz. 21.00
Tumbler, iced tea, green, 5 1/8" h.,
  12 oz. 21.50

ROYAL LACE (Process-etched)

Royal Lace Dinner Plate

Bowl, cream soup, 4¾" d., green or
  pink 25.50
Bowl, berry, 5" d., blue 35.00
Bowl, berry, 5" d., green 28.00
Bowl, berry, 5" d., pink 22.50
Bowl, berry, 10" d., blue 42.50

Bowl, berry, 10" d., pink 30.00
Bowl, 10" d., three-footed, rolled edge, blue 250.00
Bowl, 10" d., three-footed, ruffled edge, blue 280.00
Bowl, 10" d., three-footed, ruffled edge, green 55.00
Bowl, 10" d., three-footed, ruffled edge, pink 43.00
Bowl, 10" d., three-footed, straight edge, blue 69.00
Bowl, 10" d., three-footed, straight edge, green 25.00
Bowl, 11" oval vegetable, blue 43.50
Bowl, 11" oval vegetable, pink 29.50
Butter dish, cov., blue 465.00
Butter dish, cov., clear 62.00
Butter dish, cov., green 250.00
Butter dish, cov., pink 139.00
Candlesticks, rolled edge, blue, pr. 167.50
Candlesticks, rolled edge, pink, pr. 42.50
Candlesticks, ruffled edge, blue, pr. 119.00
Candlesticks, ruffled edge, clear, pr. 21.00
Candlesticks, ruffled edge, pink, pr. 39.00
Candlesticks, straight edge, clear, pr. 32.00
Candlesticks, straight edge, green, pr. 62.50
Cookie jar, cov., blue 348.00
Cookie jar, cov., clear 32.50
Cookie jar, cov., green 78.50
Creamer, footed, clear 10.00
Creamer, footed, green 20.00
Creamer, footed, pink 17.00
Cup & saucer, blue 36.50
Cup & saucer, pink 18.50
Nut bowl, green 185.00
Pitcher, 48 oz., straight sides, blue 117.00
Pitcher, 48 oz., straight sides, green 95.50
Pitcher, 8" h., 64 oz., without ice lip, blue 156.00
Pitcher, 8" h., 64 oz., without ice lip, green 80.00
Pitcher, 8" h., 68 oz., w/ice lip, clear 40.00
Pitcher, 8" h., 68 oz., w/ice lip, pink 53.50
Pitcher, 8" h., 86 oz., without ice lip, green 85.50
Pitcher, 8" h., 86 oz., without ice lip, pink 70.00
Pitcher, 8½" h., 96 oz., w/ice lip, blue 257.00
Pitcher, 8½" h., 96 oz., w/ice lip, green 150.00
Plate, sherbet, 6" d., blue 14.00
Plate, sherbet, 6" d., clear 3.00
Plate, dinner, 9 7/8" d., clear 18.00
Plate, dinner, 9 7/8" d., green 20.00
Plate, dinner, 9 7/8" d., pink (ILLUS.) 20.00
Plate, luncheon, 8½" d., blue 31.50
Plate, luncheon, 8½" d., clear 5.00
Plate, dinner, 9 7/8" d., blue 36.00
Plate, grill, 9 7/8" d., green 14.00
Plate, grill, 9 7/8" d., pink 10.50
Platter, 13" oval, blue 46.50
Platter, 13" oval, clear 14.00
Salt & pepper shakers, blue, pr. 225.00
Salt & pepper shakers, clear, pr. 37.00
Salt & pepper shakers, green, pr. 121.00
Salt & pepper shakers, pink, pr. 58.50
Sherbet, footed, blue 34.50
Sherbet, footed, pink 13.00
Sherbet in metal holder, amethyst 34.00
Sherbet in metal holder, blue 23.50
Sugar bowl, cov., blue 198.00
Sugar bowl, cov., clear 21.00
Sugar bowl, cov., green 57.00
Sugar bowl, cov., pink 38.00
Sugar bowl, open, blue 39.50
Toddy or cider set: cookie jar w/metal lid, 7 roly-poly tumblers & metal tray; amethyst, 9 pcs. 145.00
Toddy or cider set: cookie jar w/metal lid, 8 roly-poly tumblers, metal tray & ladle; blue, 11 pcs. 170.00
Tumbler, blue, 3½" h., 5 oz. 40.00
Tumbler, clear, 3½" h., 5 oz. 13.00
Tumbler, green, 3½" h., 5 oz. 21.50
Tumbler, clear, 4 1/8" h., 9 oz. 9.00
Tumbler, green, 4 1/8" h., 9 oz. 26.00
Tumbler, green, 4 7/8" h., 10 oz. 45.00
Tumbler, pink, 4 7/8" h., 10 oz. 35.00
Tumbler, blue, 5 3/8" h., 12 oz. 66.00
Tumbler, pink, 5 3/8" h., 12 oz. 37.50

ROYAL RUBY (Press-mold)

(All items in ruby red)

Ashtray, 4½" sq. 4.50
Bowl, berry, 4¼" d. 5.50
Bowl, 5¼" d. 9.50
Bowl, soup, 7½" d. 11.00
Bowl, 8" oval vegetable 35.00
Bowl, salad, 11½" d. 30.00
Creamer, flat 7.00
Creamer, footed 9.00
Cup & saucer 6.00
Goblet, ball stem 10.00
Juice set, 22 oz. tilted pitcher & six 5 oz. tumblers, 7 pcs. 67.50
Pitcher, 22 oz., tilted or upright 26.50
Pitcher, 3 qt., tilted or upright 38.50
Plate, salad, 7" d. 4.50
Plate, luncheon, 7¾" d. 5.50
Plate, dinner, 9" d. 11.00
Plate, 13¾" d. 23.00
Playing card or cigarette box, divided, clear base 78.00

Popcorn set, 10" d. serving bowl & eight 5¼" d. bowls, 9 pcs.	125.00
Punch bowl & base	59.00
Punch cup	2.50
Sherbet, footed	7.50
Sugar bowl, flat	6.50
Sugar bowl, footed	9.00
Sugar bowl w/slotted lid, footed. . . .	16.00
Tumbler, cocktail, 3½ oz.	10.00
Tumbler, juice, 5 oz.	4.50
Tumbler, water, 9 oz.	5.00
Tumbler, water, 10 oz.	7.00
Tumbler, iced tea, footed, 6" h., 12 oz.	12.50
Vase, 5" h., ball-shaped	10.00
Vase, bud, 5½" h., ruffled top	6.00
Vase, 6½" h., bulbous	5.00
Wine, footed, 2½ oz.	10.00

SAILBOAT or Ships or Sportsman Series

(All items in cobalt blue with white decoration)

Ashtray	27.50
Cocktail mixer w/stirrer	22.00
Cocktail shaker w/metal lid	48.00
Ice bowl	30.00
Pitcher without ice lip, 82 oz.	62.50
Pitcher w/ice lip, 86 oz.	72.50
Plate, bread & butter, 5 7/8" d.	18.00
Plate, salad, 8" d.	23.50
Plate, dinner, 9" d.	33.50
Saucer	14.00
Tray, wooden handles (blue boat on white)	105.00
Tumbler, juice, 3¾" h., 5 oz.	10.50
Tumbler, roly poly, 6 oz.	9.00
Tumbler, old fashioned, 3 3/8" h., 8 oz.	13.50
Tumbler, water, 4 5/8" h., 9 oz.	11.00
Tumbler, iced tea, 4 7/8" h., 10½ oz.	12.50
Tumbler, iced tea, 12 oz.	21.00

SANDWICH (Press-mold)

Sandwich Punch Set

Bowl, 4 5/16" d., clear	4.50
Bowl, 4 5/16" d., green	3.50
Bowl, berry, 4 7/8" d., amber	3.00

Bowl, berry, 4 7/8" d., clear	5.50
Bowl, 5¼" d., scalloped, clear	8.00
Bowl, 5¼" d., ruby	17.00
Bowl, cereal, 6½" d., amber	12.00
Bowl, cereal, 6½" d., clear	25.50
Bowl, 6½" d., smooth or scalloped, amber	6.50
Bowl, 6½" d., smooth or scalloped, green	47.50
Bowl, salad, 7" d., clear	6.00
Bowl, salad, 7" d., green	52.00
Bowl, 8" d., scalloped, green	66.00
Bowl, 8" d., scalloped, pink	12.00
Bowl, 8" d., scalloped, ruby	34.50
Bowl, 8½" oval vegetable, clear	7.00
Bowl, salad, 9" d., amber	23.50
Bowl, salad, 9" d., clear	22.00
Butter dish, cov., clear	37.50
Cookie jar, cov., amber	34.50
Cookie jar, cov., clear	35.50
Creamer, green	24.50
Cup & saucer, amber	6.00
Cup & saucer, clear	4.00
Cup & saucer, green	29.50
Custard cup, clear or green	4.00
Custard cup liner, green	2.00
Pitcher, juice, 6" h., clear	64.50
Pitcher, juice, 6" h., green	143.00
Pitcher w/ice lip, 2 qt., clear	65.00
Pitcher w/ice lip, 2 qt., green	235.00
Plate, dessert, 7" d., amber	8.00
Plate, dessert, 7" d., clear	9.50
Plate, 8" d., clear	6.00
Plate, dinner, 9" d., amber	7.50
Plate, dinner, 9" d., clear	15.50
Plate, dinner, 9" d., green	74.00
Punch bowl & base, clear	41.00
Punch bowl & base, opaque white . .	22.50
Punch cup, clear	2.50
Punch cup, opaque white	2.00
Punch set: punch bowl, base & 10 cups; clear, 12 pcs. (ILLUS. of part)	70.00
Sugar bowl, cov., green	24.00
Sugar bowl, open, clear	5.00
Sugar bowl, open, green	20.00
Tumbler, clear, 5 oz.	6.00
Tumbler, green, 5 oz.	4.00
Tumbler, water, clear, 9 oz.	8.00
Tumbler, water, green, 9 oz.	4.50
Tumbler, footed, amber, 9 oz.	22.00
Tumbler, footed, clear, 9 oz.	20.50

SHARON or Cabbage Rose (Chip-mold)

Bowl, berry, 5" d., amber	6.50
Bowl, berry, 5" d., green or pink . . .	10.50
Bowl, cream soup, 5" d., amber	22.50
Bowl, cream soup, 5" d., green.	41.00
Bowl, cereal, 6" d., green	23.00
Bowl, cereal, 6" d., pink	20.00
Bowl, soup, 7½" d., amber or pink	36.00
Bowl, berry, 8½" d., amber	5.50

Bowl, berry, 8½" d., green or pink	24.00
Bowl, 9½" oval vegetable, amber	15.00
Bowl, fruit, 10½" d., green	26.50
Bowl, fruit, 10½" d., pink	34.00
Butter dish, cov., amber	41.00
Butter dish, cov., green	76.00
Butter dish, cov., pink	47.00
Cake plate, footed, clear, 11½" d.	11.50
Cake plate, footed, green, 11½" d.	48.50
Candy jar, cov., green	160.00
Candy jar, cov., pink	45.00
Cheese dish, cov., amber	177.00
Cheese dish, cov., pink	805.00
Creamer, amber	11.50
Creamer, green	18.00
Cup & saucer, green	21.50
Cup & saucer, pink	19.50
Jam dish, amber, 7½" d., 1½" h.	27.50
Jam dish, green, 7½" d., 1½" h.	34.50
Jam dish, pink, 7½" d., 1½" h.	150.00
Pitcher, 9" h., 80 oz., amber	110.00
Pitcher, 9" h., 80 oz., green	448.00
Pitcher w/ice lip, 9" h., 80 oz., green	322.00
Pitcher w/ice lip, 9" h., 80 oz., pink	138.50
Plate, bread & butter, 6" d., green or pink	6.00
Plate, salad, 7½" d., amber	14.00
Plate, salad, 7½" d., green	18.50
Plate, dinner, 9¼" d., green	13.50
Plate, dinner, 9¼" d., pink	16.50
Platter, 12¼" oval, amber	12.50
Platter, 12¼" oval, green	22.50
Platter, 12¼" oval, pink	20.50
Salt & pepper shakers, amber, pr.	36.00
Salt & pepper shakers, green, pr.	61.00
Salt & pepper shakers, pink, pr.	43.50
Sherbet, footed, amber	9.50
Sherbet, footed, green	29.00
Sherbet, footed, pink	12.50
Sugar bowl, cov., amber	30.00
Sugar bowl, cov., green	40.50
Sugar bowl, cov., pink	37.00

Sharon Pattern

Tumbler, amber, 4" h., 9 oz.	22.00
Tumbler, green, 4" h., 9 oz.	63.50
Tumbler, pink, 4" h., 9 oz.	33.50
Tumbler, amber, 5¼" h., 12 oz. (ILLUS. left previous column)	49.00
Tumbler, green, 5¼" h., 12 oz.	83.50
Tumbler, pink, 5¼" h., 12 oz.	37.00
Tumbler, footed, amber, 6½" h., 15 oz. (ILLUS. right previous column)	80.00
Tumbler, footed, pink, 6½" h., 15 oz.	43.50

SIERRA or Pinwheel (Press-mold)

Bowl, berry, 8½" d., green	23.50
Bowl, berry, 8½" d., pink	27.50
Bowl, 9½" oval vegetable, green	70.00
Bowl, 9½" oval vegetable, pink	49.00
Butter dish, cov., green	64.00
Butter dish, cov., pink	56.50
Creamer, green	19.50
Creamer, pink	11.50
Cup & saucer, green	17.50
Cup & saucer, pink	15.00
Pitcher, 6½" h., 32 oz., green	115.00
Plate, dinner, 9" d., pink	15.00
Platter, 11" oval, green	41.00
Platter, 11" oval, pink	35.00
Salt & pepper shakers, green, pr.	35.50
Salt & pepper shakers, pink, pr.	39.00
Sugar bowl, cov., green	30.00
Sugar bowl, cov., pink	16.50
Tumbler, footed, green, 4½" h., 9 oz.	69.50
Tumbler, footed, pink, 4½" h., 9 oz.	46.50

SPIRAL (Press-mold)

Spiral Pitcher

Bowl, berry, 8" d., green	7.50
Creamer, flat or footed, green	7.50
Cup & saucer, green	6.00
Ice or butter tub, green	25.00
Pitcher, 7 5/8" h., 58 oz., green (ILLUS.)	28.50
Plate, sherbet, 6" d., green	1.50
Plate, luncheon, 8" d., green	4.00
Platter, 12" oval, green	16.50

Sandwich server, w/center handle,
green 30.00
Sugar bowl, flat or footed, green ... 7.00
Tumbler, water, green, 5" h.,
9 oz. 11.50

SWANKY SWIGS (Kraft cheese glasses)

Antique No. 1, black, blue, brown,
green, orange or red 3.50
Band No. 1 .... 3.50
Band No. 2 .... 3.00
Bustlin' Betsy, blue, brown, green,
orange, red or yellow 3.50
Carnival, cobalt blue or red 3.50
Checkerboard, green & white 25.00
Checkerboard, red & white 20.00
Circles & Dot, blue or green 5.50
Forget-Me-Not, dark blue, light
blue, red or yellow 3.00
Kiddy Kup, black, blue, brown,
green, orange or red 5.00
Posy - Cornflower No. 1, 3½" h..... 3.50
Posy - Cornflower No. 1, 4½" h..... 15.00
Posy - Jonquil 4.00
Posy - Tulip 3.50
Posy - Violet 4.00
Sailboat No. 1 (3 boats), blue 13.50
Sailboat No. 2 (4 boats), blue 12.50
Texas Centennial, black 7.50
Texas Centennial, red 24.00
Tulip No. 1, red or green, 4½" h. .. 6.50
Tulip No. 2, black, blue, green or
red 10.00
Tulip No. 3, dark blue, light blue or
yellow 3.00

SWIRL or Petal Swirl (Press-mold)

Swirl Creamer & Sugar Bowl

Bowl, cereal, 5¼" d., Delphite 11.00
Bowl, cereal, 5¼" d., pink 7.00
Bowl, salad, 9" d., pink 15.00
Bowl, salad, 9" d., ultramarine 23.00
Bowl, 9" d., rimmed, ultramarine ... 19.50
Bowl, fruit, 10" d., closed handles,
footed, ultramarine 27.00
Butter dish, cov., pink 165.00
Butter dish, cov., ultramarine 211.00
Candleholders, double, ultramarine,
pr. 35.50
Candy dish, cov., pink 92.00
Candy dish, cov., ultramarine 139.00
Candy dish, open, three-footed,
ultramarine, 5½" d. 14.50
Coaster, pink, 3¼" d., 1" h. 8.50

Console bowl, footed, pink,
10½" d. 16.00
Console bowl, footed, ultramarine,
10½" d. 23.50
Creamer, Delphite (ILLUS. right) 9.00
Creamer, pink 9.50
Cup & saucer, pink 7.50
Cup & saucer, ultramarine 17.50
Plate, sherbet, 6½" d., Delphite 4.50
Plate, sherbet, 6½" d., pink 3.50
Plate, sherbet, 6½" d., ultra-
marine 5.50
Plate, 7¼" d., ultramarine 12.00
Plate, salad, 8" d., Delphite 5.00
Plate, salad, 8" d., pink 4.00
Plate, dinner, 9½" d., Delphite 12.00
Plate, dinner, 9½" d., pink 10.50
Plate, dinner, 9½" d., ultramarine .. 15.00
Plate, sandwich, 12½" d., pink 18.00
Plate, sandwich, 12½" d., ultra-
marine 21.50
Platter, 12" oval, Delphite 29.00
Salt & pepper shakers, Delphite,
pr. 95.00
Salt & pepper shakers, ultramarine,
pr. 37.50
Sherbet, pink 10.00
Soup bowl w/lug handles, ultra-
marine 25.00
Sugar bowl, open, Delphite (ILLUS.
left) 8.00
Sugar bowl, open, pink 9.00
Sugar bowl, open, ultramarine 11.50
Tumbler, pink, 4" h., 9 oz. 9.00
Tumbler, ultramarine, 4" h., 9 oz. .. 16.50
Tumbler, pink, 5 1/8" h., 13 oz. 25.50
Tumbler, ultramarine, 5 1/8" h.,
13 oz. 80.00
Vase, 6½" h., pink 11.00
Vase, 6½" h., ultramarine 17.00
Vase, 8½" h., ultramarine 23.00

TEA ROOM (Press-mold)

Tea Room Tumbler

Banana split dish, flat, green,
7½" 98.00
Banana split dish, footed, green,
7½" 81.00
Bowl, salad, 8¾" d., green 81.00

Bowl, salad, 8¾" d., pink	52.00
Bowl, 9½" oval vegetable, green	68.50
Bowl, 9½" oval vegetable, pink	62.00
Candlesticks, green, pr.	76.50
Candlesticks, pink, pr.	50.50
Celery or pickle dish, green, 8½"	26.00
Celery or pickle dish, pink, 8½"	60.00
Creamer, green, 3¼" h.	14.50
Creamer, clear or pink, 4" h.	11.50
Creamer, footed, pink, 4½" h.	14.50
Creamer, rectangular, green or pink	15.50
Creamer & open sugar bowl on center-handled tray, green	55.00
Creamer & open sugar bowl on center-handled tray, pink	86.00
Creamer & open sugar bowl on rec- tangular tray, green	108.00
Cup & saucer, green	44.00
Cup & saucer, pink	63.50
Finger bowl, green	85.00
Goblet, pink, 9 oz.	74.00
Ice bucket, green	70.00
Ice bucket, pink	85.00
Lamp, electric, clear, 9"	95.00
Lamp, electric, green, 9"	61.50
Mustard, cov., clear	72.00
Parfait, clear	65.00
Pitcher, 64 oz., pink	150.00
Plate, sherbet, 6½" d., pink	17.00
Plate, luncheon, 8¼" d., green	32.00
Plate, 10½" d., two-handled, green	50.00
Plate, sandwich, w/center handle, green	151.00
Relish, divided, green	22.50
Relish, divided, pink	13.00
Salt & pepper shakers, green, pr.	64.00
Salt & pepper shakers, pink, pr.	53.00
Sherbet, low footed, green	30.00
Sherbet, low, flared edge, green	27.50
Sherbet, tall footed, clear	27.50
Sherbet, tall footed, green	37.00
Sherbet, tall footed, pink	31.00
Sugar bowl, cov., pink, 3" h.	130.00
Sugar bowl, cov., green, 3" h.	100.00
Sugar bowl, cov., footed, green, 4½" h.	17.50
Sugar bowl, open, rectangular, green	17.50
Sundae, footed, ruffled, clear	56.00
Sundae, footed, ruffled, green	135.00
Tray, rectangular, for creamer & sugar bowl, pink	38.00
Tray w/center handle, for creamer & sugar bowl, green	209.00
Tumbler, footed, green, 6 oz.	43.50
Tumbler, footed, pink, 6 oz.	30.00
Tumbler, green, 4 3/16" h., 8 oz.	105.00
Tumbler, pink, 4 3/16" h., 8 oz.	32.50
Tumbler, footed, green, 11 oz. (ILLUS.)	62.50
Tumbler, footed, clear, 12 oz.	45.00

Tumbler, footed, green, 12 oz.	82.00
Vase, 9½" h., ruffled rim, amber	150.00
Vase, 9½" h., ruffled rim, clear	18.50
Vase, 9½" h., ruffled rim, green	146.00
Vase, 11" h., ruffled rim, clear	110.00
Vase, 11" h., straight, green	153.00
Vase, 11" h., straight, pink	115.00

TWISTED OPTIC (Press-mold)

Bowl, cream soup, 4¾" d., pink	8.50
Bowl, cereal, 5" d., amber	6.50
Candlesticks, yellow, 3", pr.	19.00
Candy jar, cov., green	23.50
Candy jar, cov., yellow	25.00
Creamer, green	7.00
Plate, sherbet, 6" d., amber	1.50
Plate, luncheon, 8" d., amber	3.00
Plate, luncheon, 8" d., green or pink	3.50
Preserve jar w/slotted lid, green	22.00
Sandwich server w/center handle, green	16.00
Sandwich server w/center handle, yellow	29.00
Sherbet, green	4.50
Sherbet, pink	6.00
Sugar bowl, open, green	8.00
Sugar bowl, open, pink	6.00

WATERFORD or Waffle (Press-mold)

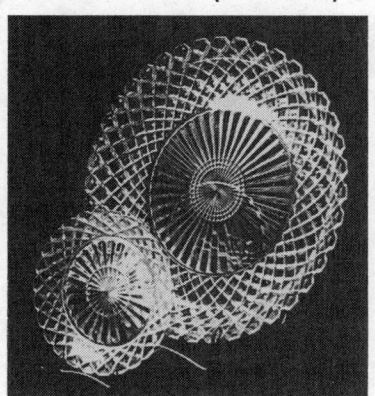

Waterford Plates

Ashtray, clear, 4"	5.50
Bowl, berry, 4¾" d., clear	5.00
Bowl, cereal, 5¼" d., pink	19.00
Bowl, berry, 8¼" d., clear	10.00
Bowl, berry, 8¼" d., pink	8.50
Butter dish, cov., clear	23.00
Butter dish, cov., pink	190.00
Cake plate, handled, pink, 10¼" d.	10.00
Coaster, clear, 4" d.	3.00
Creamer, oval, clear	4.00
Goblet, amber, 5¼" h.	125.00
Goblet, clear, 5¼" h.	14.00
Goblet, clear, 5½" h. (Miss America style)	28.50

Pitcher, juice, 42 oz., tilt-type,
clear 19.00
Pitcher w/ice lip, 80 oz., clear 29.00
Pitcher w/ice lip, 80 oz., pink 147.50
Plate, salad, 7½" d., clear (ILLUS.
left) 4.00
Plate, salad, 7½" d., pink 6.00
Plate, dinner, 9 5/8" d., clear 7.50
Plate, dinner, 9 5/8" d., pink 13.50
Plate, sandwich, 13¾" d., clear
(ILLUS. right) 7.50
Plate, sandwich, 13¾" d., pink 24.00
Relish, five-section, clear, 13¾" d. . . . 13.50
Salt & pepper shakers, clear, short
or tall, pr. 7.00
Saucer, clear 2.00
Saucer, pink 4.00
Sherbet, footed, clear 3.50
Sherbet, footed, pink 7.50
Sugar bowl, cov., oval, clear 7.00
Sugar bowl, cov., oval, pink 27.50
Sugar bowl, open, footed, clear
(Miss America style) 2.00
Tumbler, footed, clear, 5" h.,
10 oz. 9.50
Tumbler, footed, pink, 5" h.,
10 oz. 13.00

WINDSOR DIAMOND or Windsor (Press-mold)

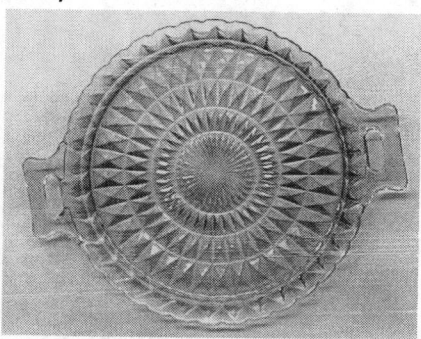

Windsor Sandwich Plate

Ashtray, pink, 5¾" d. 33.00
Ashtray w/patterned rim, pink 475.00
Bowl, berry, 4¾" d., clear 4.00
Bowl, berry, 4¾" d., green or
pink 7.00
Bowl, 5" d., pointed edge, clear 5.50
Bowl, 5" d., pointed edge, pink 19.00
Bowl, cream soup, 5" d., green 18.00
Bowl, cream soup, 5" d., pink 23.00
Bowl, cereal, 5 1/8" or 5 3/8" d.,
clear 7.00
Bowl, cereal, 5 1/8" or 5 3/8" d.,
green or pink 18.50
Bowl, 7" d., three-footed, clear 7.00
Bowl, 7" d., three-footed, pink 23.50
Bowl, 8" d., pointed edge, clear 11.00

Bowl, 8" d., pointed edge, pink 34.00
Bowl, 8" d., two-handled, clear 5.50
Bowl, 8" d., two-handled, green 21.50
Bowl, 8" d., two-handled, pink 14.50
Bowl, berry, 8½" d., clear 8.00
Bowl, berry, 8½" d., green 15.00
Bowl, berry, 8½" d., pink 16.00
Bowl, 9½" oval vegetable, clear 8.50
Bowl, 9½" oval vegetable, pink 17.50
Bowl, 10½" d., pointed edge,
clear 25.00
Bowl, 10½" d., pointed edge,
pink 107.50
Bowl, 7 x 11¾" boat shape, clear . . 17.50
Bowl, 7 x 11¾" boat shape, green . . 29.00
Bowl, 7 x 11¾" boat shape, pink . . . 32.00
Bowl, fruit, 12½" d., clear 26.00
Bowl, fruit, 12½" d., pink 104.00
Butter dish, cov., clear 22.50
Butter dish, cov., green 65.00
Butter dish, cov., pink 47.00
Cake plate, footed, clear, 10¾" d. . . . 7.00
Cake plate, footed, green or pink,
10¾" d. 18.50
Candlesticks, clear, 3" h., pr. 14.50
Candlesticks, pink, 3" h., pr. 81.00
Candy jar, cov., clear 11.00
Coaster, clear, 3¼" d. 7.00
Coaster, green, 3¼" d. 15.50
Coaster, pink, 3¼" d. 13.50
Creamer, flat, clear 3.50
Creamer, flat, green or pink 10.50
Creamer, footed, clear 4.50
Cup & saucer, clear 5.00
Cup & saucer, green 13.00
Cup & saucer, pink 11.00
Pitcher, 4½" h., 16 oz., Amberina
red 600.00
Pitcher, 4½" h., 16 oz., clear 16.50
Pitcher, 4½" h., 16 oz., pink 128.00
Pitcher, 6¾" h., 52 oz., clear 13.00
Pitcher, 6¾" h., 52 oz., green 46.00
Pitcher, 6¾" h., 52 oz., pink 25.50
Plate, sherbet, 6" d., clear 2.00
Plate, sherbet, 6" d., green 5.50
Plate, sherbet, 6" d., pink 3.50
Plate, salad, 7" d., green 17.00
Plate, salad, 7" d., pink 15.00
Plate, dinner, 9" d., clear 5.00
Plate, dinner, 9" d., green 16.50
Plate, dinner, 9" d., pink 14.00
Plate, sandwich, 10¼", handled,
clear 7.50
Plate, sandwich, 10¼", handled,
green 11.50
Plate, sandwich, 10¼", handled,
pink (ILLUS.) 14.00
Plate, chop, 13 5/8" d., clear 8.50
Plate, chop, 13 5/8" d., green 38.00
Plate, chop, 13 5/8" d., pink 34.00
Platter, 11½" oval, clear 6.00
Platter, 11½" oval, green 18.50
Platter, 11½" oval, pink 16.50
Powder jar, cov., clear 10.50

Powder jar, cov., pink	225.00
Relish, divided, clear, 11½"	9.00
Relish, divided, pink, 11½"	187.50
Salt & pepper shakers, green, pr.	40.00
Salt & pepper shakers, pink, pr.	32.00
Sherbet, footed, clear	4.50
Sherbet, footed, green	12.00
Sherbet, footed, pink	9.50
Sugar bowl, cov., flat, clear	6.00
Sugar bowl, cov., flat, green	25.00
Sugar bowl, cov., flat, pink	22.50
Sugar bowl, cov., footed, clear	6.00
Sugar bowl, open, clear	3.00
Sugar bowl, open, green	12.00
Sugar bowl, open, pink	8.50
Tray, clear, 4" sq., without handles	5.00
Tray, pink, 4" sq., without handles	37.00
Tray, green, 4 1/8 x 9", w/handles	12.50
Tray, pink, 4 1/8 x 9", w/handles	10.50
Tray, clear, 4 1/8 x 9", without handles	10.00
Tray, pink, 4 1/8 x 9", without handles	43.50
Tray, clear, 8½ x 9¾", w/handles	4.00
Tray, green, 8½ x 9¾", w/handles	29.00
Tray, pink, 8½ x 9¾", w/handles	22.00
Tray, clear, 8½ x 9¾", without handles	12.00
Tray, pink, 8½ x 9¾", without handles	75.00
Tumbler, clear, 3¼" h., 5 oz.	7.00
Tumbler, green, 3¼" h., 5 oz.	25.00
Tumbler, pink, 3¼" h., 5 oz.	19.50
Tumbler, clear, 4" h., 9 oz.	6.50
Tumbler, footed, clear, 4" h., 9 oz.	6.00
Tumbler, green, 4" h., 9 oz.	24.00
Tumbler, pink, 4" h., 9 oz.	15.00
Tumbler, footed, clear, 5" h., 11 oz.	8.50
Tumbler, clear, 5" h., 12 oz.	9.00
Tumbler, green, 5" h., 12 oz.	35.50
Tumbler, pink, 5" h., 12 oz.	24.00
Tumbler, footed, clear, 7¼" h.	11.50
Water set: pitcher & 4 tumblers; pink, 5 pcs.	60.00

(End of Depression Glass Section)

DE VEZ & DEGUE

Cameo glass with the name DeVez was made in Pantin, France, by Saint-Hilaire, Touvier De Varreaux and Company. Some pieces made by this firm were signed "Degue" after one of the firm's glassmakers.

The official company name was "Cristallerie de Pantin."

Cameo vase, 3 7/8" h., wide flattened heart-shaped body w/a short cylindrical neck & raised on a short pedestal w/cushion foot, frosted white overlaid in amethyst & cut w/a harbor scene on front & back, signed "Devez" $605.00

Cameo vase, 7" h., 7½" d., squatty bulbous base tapering to tall, flaring sides, mottled white & pale yellow acid-etched & brightly enameled in stylized orange & blue repeating poppy blossoms & leaves, engraved mark "Degue France" 605.00

DeVez Cameo Vase

Cameo vase, 10 3/8" h., swollen cylindrical body, grey mottled w/lemon yellow & red-orange, overlaid in red-orange & purple & cut w/a mountain landscape w/leafy blossoming trees in the foreground, signed in cameo "De Vez," ca. 1920 (ILLUS.) 1,210.00

Cameo vase, 16¼" h., balusterform, grey streaked w/sea green, overlaid in striated caramel & cut w/tiers of triangles, signed in intaglio "Degue," underside acidstamped "Made in France No. 18," ca. 1925 ....3,300.00

Vase, 3¾" h., bucket-shaped w/slightly tapering cylindrical sides & small tab rim handles, blue cased in blue & green & cut w/an expansive landscape centering a fisherman & his boat, cameo-signed "Devez" 880.00

Vase, 11 7/8" h., shouldered ovoid body w/flaring rim & base, grey overlaid in mottled blue shading to deep cobalt blue & cut w/a geometric pattern, inscribed "Degue," acid-stamped "MADE IN FRANCE," ca. 1925 ....1,100.00

Special Focus:

The Colorful Story of
Dugan - Diamond Glass

by Dr. James S. Measell

Over a decade ago, through columns in *The Antique Trader Weekly*, William Heacock opened glass collectors' eyes to a facet of American glassmaking that was virtually unknown — the Dugan and Diamond glass interests in Indiana, Pennsylvania. Harry Northwood had had an impact upon Indiana, too, but Northwood was actually there less than four years between early 1896 and late 1899 (see *The Antique Trader Price Guide to Antiques* for February, 1992). Many patterns and items credited to Northwood by earlier glass researchers were actually made by the Dugan or Diamond concerns.

A photograph of Alfred Dugan, ca. 1901.

Between 1904 and 1931, these two important firms operated in Indiana: from 1904 until early 1913, the old Northwood factory was run as the Dugan Glass Company, and both Thomas E.A. Dugan (1865-1944) and Alfred Dugan (1867-1928) held key posts; from 1913 until its destruction by fire in 1931, the concern was known as the Diamond Glass (or

Glass-Ware) Company. Thomas E.A. Dugan was not connected with this latter enterprise, but Alfred Dugan was factory manager for about 13 years until his death in 1928.

The Dugans were Harry Northwood's cousins on his mother's side (her maiden name was Elizabeth Duggan). Another important character was another Thomas Dugan (1834-1926), who emigrated to the U.S. during the Civil War, changing his surname from Duggan to Dugan. He established himself at Pittsburgh, achieved some wealth as proprietor of various hotels, and became involved in the economic development of Ellwood City, Pa.

The Dugans came to the United States in April, 1881, about six months before Harry Northwood. The cousins were employed at the Hobbs-Brockunier plant in Wheeling, and when Harry Northwood established his first plant in nearby Martins Ferry, Ohio, the Dugan men continued to learn the glass trade from him. Northwood and the Dugans went to Ellwood City, Pa., when the company moved there in 1892. "Uncle Tommie" Dugan had parlayed his success in Pittsburgh into even more lucrative investments in Ellwood City, which was being developed by real estate interests in 1891-92.

The plant at Ellwood City was not successful, despite Northwood's creativity and skilled workers such as the Dugans. Batch books kept by Thomas E.A. Dugan preserve many of the formulas for the colors produced in blown glass at Ellwood City between 1893 and early 1896. These include a wide variety of pale opaque colors in pink, green and blue.

In March, 1896, Northwood and the Dugans left Ellwood City for Indiana, Pa. In-

Upper right: two *Grape Delight* Carnival glass bowls as shown in a 1915 Butler Brothers catalog.

vestors sought to re-open a glass plant which had been closed since 1894. Northwood agreed to run the factory, and Uncle Tommie Dugan later provided about $8,000. The National Glass Company purchased the plant in 1899, and Northwood became sales manager for the London office. In November, 1899, the Northwoods returned to England, but the Dugans remained in Indiana. Both Thomas E.A. Dugan and Alfred Dugan had substantial roles in the glass factory. Thomas E.A. Dugan was factory superintendent from mid-1900 through early 1904, when new investors purchased the plant and formed the Dugan Glass Co. This firm lasted from January, 1904, until 1913, when both Thomas E.A. Dugan and Alfred Dugan left for a glassmaking venture in Lonaconing, Maryland. This enterprise, also known as the Dugan Glass Co., was beset by friction among the investors in March, 1915. Alfred Dugan returned to Indiana, becoming factory manager of the Diamond firm. Thomas E.A. Dugan settled at the Hocking Glass Company in Lancaster, Ohio, where he worked until his death in 1944.

Between 1904 and 1907, the Dugan Glass Co. produced colored pattern glass, and many of the designs made — such as those now known as *S-Repeat, Beaded Shell, Beaded Ovals in Sand, Jewelled Heart,* and *Fan* — have been credited to Harry Northwood. Some collectors have, no doubt, purchased items because of this association. These patterns occur in a variety of transparent and opalescent colors — amethyst, crystal, blue, and several shades of green.

The *S-Repeat* and *Beaded Shell* patterns debuted in 1904, but their original names were *National* and *New York*, respectively. The *National (S-Repeat)* line is extensive, consisting of a table set, water set, berry set and syrup jug as well as a condiment set (cruet, salt & pepper shakers and toothpick holder on a tray), punch set, and wine sets with two sizes of decanters and both wines and goblets. The flat-bottomed berry bowl is also the base for the punch bowl. The *New York (Beaded Shell)* line is not as large, but the table set, water set and berry set are known, as is the condiment set (cruet, salt & pepper shakers and toothpick holder), which employs the *National* tray.

The pattern now called *Jewelled Heart* was introduced in 1905, and it was originally called *Victor. Beaded Ovals in Sand*, originally called *Erie*, was probably made about the same time. *Victor (Jewelled Heart)* occurs in table sets and water sets as well as syrup jugs, sugar shakers and a condiment set consisting of cruet, salt & pepper shakers and toothpick holder on a round, flat plate which functions as a tray. Some *Victor* pieces are shown in Butler Brothers and G. Sommers

and Co. catalogs from 1905-06. At least one piece of *Victor*, a green opalescent spooner with crimped rim, has Dugan's "Diamond-D" mark, which was introduced in late 1906.

Dugan's "Diamond-D" trademark, introduced in late 1906.

The *Erie (Beaded Ovals in Sand)* table set, berry set and water set are shown by Butler Brothers in mid-1906 and the condiment set is in a 1907 Dugan factory catalog. The *Erie* cruet uses the same stopper as that which is used in the *National* and *Victor* lines. *Erie* articles are usually found in a light green which is called "apple green" by some collectors.

Several other Dugan patterns deserve brief mention here. *Circled Scroll* was an extensive line, consisting of water set, table set and berry set as well as condiment items — cruet, salt & pepper shakers and tray — and a jelly compote. In late 1906, the *Fan* line was introduced. Called "Northwood's Fan" for many years, *Fan* table sets, water sets and berry sets occur in green, blue and Ivory (custard) glass; articles are typically decorated with very bright gold, and most bear the Diamond-D mark. The creamer is sometimes altered to produce a "gravy boat."

The colors used for *Fan* — green, blue and Ivory — are identical to those used for a line originally called *Filigree* which is now known as *Dugan's Maple Leaf*. Pieces are usually decorated with silver or gold. A few items are known in light blue opalescent glass which has no decoration, and the pattern is quite difficult to recognize without the filigree decor. Closely related to *Fan* and *Maple Leaf* are motifs known as *Cornflower, Quill*, and *Waving Quill*. Still another pattern, known today as *Diamonds and Clubs* (or *Clubs and Spades*) was part of Dugan's Filigree line.

About 1908 or 1909, the Dugan firm revived a pattern called *Inverted Fan and Feather* (originally designed by Harry Northwood about 1898 or 1899 for Ivory glass). The Dugan firm produced *Inverted Fan and Feather* in two new colors — emerald green and a vivid opalescent blue — both decorated with heavy gold. The table set, berry set and water set are in Butler Brothers catalogs in 1909.

During the 1904-09 period, night lamps became an important part of the Dugan Glass Company's production. These are popular today, and collectors call them "miniature lamps." The *Crocodile Tears* lamp is known in Ivory (custard) glass as well as amethyst, light green, blue and opaque white.

In 1905-06, the Dugan firm made vases and rose bowls called *Japanese, Venetian* and *Pompeian.* Produced in ruby and various shades of blue and green, these represent the Dugan firm's desire to imitate art glass imported from Webb and Loetz as well as the wares being made in the United States by Tiffany and Carder.

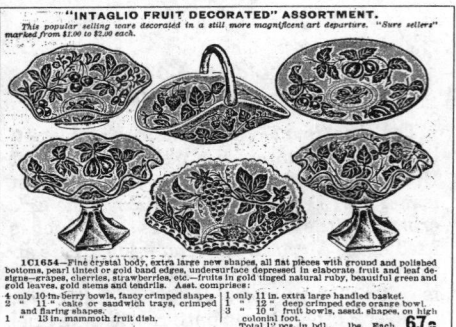

An early advertisement showing a selection of Dugan's "Intaglio" line, now called *goofus* glass. From a Butler Brothers catalog of 1908.

Also in 1905, the Dugan concern introduced its "Intaglio Ware," which is known as *"goofus"* glass today. Although other firms, such as Northwood, imitated the ware, Dugan was the originator. Dugan's *Intaglio* is pressed crystal glass which has a pattern (often a fruit motif) on the outside surface of such articles as bowls, plates and stemmed comports. The pattern is not raised from the surface of the glass as is typical in pattern glass; it is below the surface of the glass, i.e., in hollow relief. Hence, the "intaglio" appellation. The 1907 Dugan catalog offered a variety of Intaglio motifs - Fruit; Cherry; Strawberry; Tulip; Poppy; Holly; Pear and Plum; and Rose and Butterfly. A "Grape Intaglio" was also made. The gold paint on intaglio pieces is subject to chipping and flaking, and these wares were certainly intended for the mass market.

From 1909 through 1912, the Dugan Glass Company was heavily engaged in making the iridescent ware now called Carnival glass. Although the Dugan firm entered this market well after Fenton and Northwood, the Indiana-based concern produced several interesting colors. The most noteworthy is "Peach Opal," which consists of a vivid marigold color applied by spraying opalescent crystal glass. A fire in mid-1912 may have curtailed production of some Carnival patterns whose moulds were damaged or destroyed.

Some items in Dugan's Carnival glass were made from moulds used for pattern glass lines — *National (S-Repeat), New York (Beaded Shell), Victor, Fan, Quill,* and *Inverted Fan*

and Feather. A few others *(Cherry, Fanciful,* and *Peach and Pear)* resemble pieces from the Intaglio line. Still others were probably created especially for iridescent ware, and they are among the most popular Carnival motifs today: *Apple Blossom Twigs; Butterfly and Tulip; Farmyard; Floral and Grape; God and Home; Lattice and Daisy; Persian Garden; Stork and Rushes;* and *Windflower.* For these and other Dugan Carnival articles, readers should consult the Carnival glass section of this and other issues of *The Antique Trader Price Guide to Antiques.*

In 1913, the Dugan men left the firm, and the new management changed the name to the Diamond Glass Company. By 1915, the name had become Diamond Glass-Ware Company, and Alfred Dugan had returned and resumed his post as factory manager. The company produced several candy containers (cash register, fire engine, locomotive and automobile) under interim manager Edward J. Rowland in 1913-14. Readers interested in these should consult the 1986 edition of Eikelberner and Agadjanian's fine book, *The Compleat American Glass Candy Containers Handbook.* Several containers made by the Diamond firm are illustrated there.

OPTIC EFFECT 7 PC. WINE OR LIQUEUR SET.

C1847 — 2 styles, 1 qt., decanter 12 in., SIX 2 oz. wine glasses, Bohemian shapes and designs, optic effect, fire gold decorated handled decanters, enameled daisies and lilies-of-the-valley, green leaves and gold flashes. 2 sets in shipping carton, 20 lbs.
(Total, $1.50)   Set. **75c**

A 1918 Butler Brothers ad for a wine set produced by the Diamond Glass-Ware Company.

In 1915, the Diamond firm added a cutting shop to its premises, but the products of this enterprise have been difficult to document. The cutting seems to be simple stars and floral motifs, but both crystal and colored glass items can be found.

Between 1916-18, innovative designs in decorated crystal glass involving bluebirds or butterflies were on the market. For the

1916 season, the Diamond firm offered a "Blue Bird" line. The glass is thin blown crystal ware, light in weight, and highlighted by the gold edges and blue hand-painting (probably done with the aid of a stencil). The same shapes — tankard pitcher, table set, puff box, vases, etc. — were used for the Butterfly line in 1917-18.

Iridescent colors continued in production throughout the early 1920's, as the Diamond firm made what is called "stretch glass" today. A number of different utilitarian items were made, but one usually sees console bowls on black bases with a pair of candlesticks. Three "Lustre" colors were introduced in 1922: *Egyptian Lustre* is black stretch glass, and *Rainbow Lustre* and *Royal Lustre* are marigold and cobalt blue, respectively. Pale pink and pale green are also known, but there were some mysterious colors introduced between 1917-20: twilight wisteria; ambrosia; and cerulean blue.

Black glass (not iridized) items were made in considerable quantity, and many were decorated with plain gold bands or gold bands designed to simulate a hammered or chipped effect. One noteworthy line, called *Jack and the Bean Stalk*, features a beanstalk decoration on the left half of the bases of candleholders and bowls (Jack is nowhere to be seen!).

In 1925-26 the *No. 900* (now called *Adam's Rib)* line was made. References to this pattern (which comes in amber, blue, green and pink) can be found in discussions of Depression-era glass. Iridescent and decorated pieces are much sought by collectors.

From 1927-31, the Diamond plant produced an array of unrelated lines and articles. A Spanish-style line, "Barcelona," which debuted in 1928, was short-lived, but the *Victory* assortments were made for several years (like *Adam's Rib*, these appear in amber, blue, green as well as a pink color originally called "rose"). Console sets (candleholders and bowls on black bases) and vanity sets also seem to have been popular.

On June 27, 1931, fire destroyed much of the plant and the inventory of glassware on hand. Because of conflicts among the investors and the economic effects of the Depression, the plant was not rebuilt. Glassmaking in Indiana, Pennsylvania, came to an end.

ABOUT THE AUTHOR: *Dr. James S. Measell, who teaches at Wayne State University in Detroit, is also Director of Glass History Research for Antique Publications. He is co-author of* Dugan/Diamond: The Story of Indiana, Pennsylvania, Glass *as well as books on Northwood glass, Findlay glass and Greentown glass. For information about these and other books on glass, contact An-*tique Publications, Box 553, Marietta, OH 45750-0553 (toll free, 1-800-533-3433).*

PRICE LISTINGS:

All items are illustrated unless otherwise indicated.

DUGAN PATTERNS:

Early Colored and Opalescent Lines

Beaded Ovals in Sand (Erie) pitcher, water, green (Not Illus.) $175.00
Beaded Ovals in Sand spooner, light green (Not Illus.) 100.00
Beaded Ovals in Sand toothpick holder, light green (Not Illus.) 250.00
Beaded Shell (New York) bowl, master berry, blue opalescent (Not Illus.) 160.00
Beaded Shell butter dish, cov., light green (Not Illus.) 400.00
Beaded Shell creamer, light green (Not Illus.) 125.00
Beaded Shell pitcher, water, light green (Not Illus.) 450.00
Beaded Shell sugar bowl, cov., light green (Not Illus.) 250.00
Beaded Shell tumbler, light green (Not Illus.) 65.00

Figure 1

Cornflower pitcher, emerald green & gold (ILLUS. left, Fig. 1) 125.00
Cornflower tumbler, emerald green & gold (ILLUS. right) 45.00
Fan bowl, master berry, Custard (Not Illus.) 125.00
Fan butter dish, cov., green (Not Illus.) 185.00
Fan creamer, dark blue w/gold, "Diamond-D" mark, ca. 1907 (Fig. 2 top next page) 145.00

Figure 2

Fan creamer, green (Not Illus.) 100.00

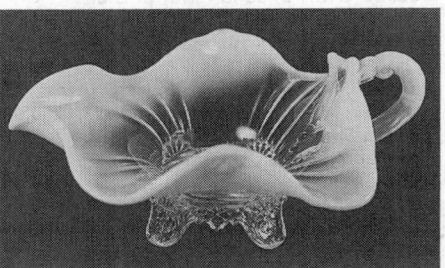

Figure 3

Fan gravy boat, clear opalescent,
  "Diamond-D" mark (Fig. 3) 90.00
Fan pitcher, water, Custard (Not
  Illus.) 250.00
Fan sugar bowl, cov., blue w/gold
  (Not Illus.). 175.00
Fan sugar bowl, cov., green (Not
  Illus.) 135.00
Inverted Fan & Feather butter dish,
  cov., blue opalescent (Not Illus.). . 450.00
Inverted Fan & Feather creamer,
  blue opalescent (Not Illus.). 200.00

Figure 4

Inverted Fan & Feather creamer,
  green w/gold (Fig. 4). . . .100.00 to 125.00
Inverted Fan & Feather pitcher, water, green w/gold (Not Illus.). 175.00
Inverted Fan & Feather sauce dish,
  green w/gold (Not Illus.) 50.00

Figure 5

Inverted Fan & Feather spooner,
  blue opalescent w/gold (Fig. 5). . . 200.00
Inverted Fan & Feather spooner,
  green w/gold (Not Illus.) 100.00
Jewelled Heart (Victor) pitcher, wa-
  ter, light green (Not Illus.) 150.00
Jewelled Heart spooner, clear
  opalescent (Not Illus.) 60.00
Jewelled Heart sugar shaker
  w/original metal lid, blue (Not
  Illus.) 250.00

Figure 6

Jewelled Heart syrup jug w/original
  metal lid, blue, ca. 1905 (Fig. 6) . . 450.00
Jewelled Heart tumbler, green
  opalescent (Not Illus.) 45.00
Jewelled Heart tumbler, light green
  (Not Illus.). 30.00
Maple Leaf butter dish, cov., Cus-
  tard (Not Illus.) 350.00
Maple Leaf creamer, blue w/gold
  (Not Illus.). 150.00
Maple Leaf sugar bowl, cov., blue
  w/gold (Not Illus.) 175.00
Nestor compote, open, jelly, blue
  (Not Illus.). 65.00
Nestor cruet w/original stopper,
  amethyst (Not Illus.). 250.00
Nestor pitcher, water, amethyst
  (Not Illus.). 175.00

Figure 7

Nestor salt shaker w/original lid,
   amethyst w/gold & white trim, ca.
   1905 (Fig. 7) 80.00
S-Repeat (National) cruet w/original
   stopper, blue (Not Illus.) 250.00

Figure 8

S-Repeat decanter, wine, w/orig-
   inal stopper, purple w/gold trim
   (ILLUS. right, Fig. 8, top of photo
   cropped) 175.00
S-Repeat goblet, blue (Not Illus.) ... 75.00
S-Repeat pitcher, water, purple (Not
   Illus.) 175.00
S-Repeat punch cup, purple (Not
   Illus.) 45.00
S-Repeat syrup jug w/original metal
   lid, light green (Not Illus.) 450.00
S-Repeat tumbler, blue (Not Illus.) .. 50.00
S-Repeat wine, purple w/gold
   (ILLUS. left, Fig. 8) 75.00

"Goofus" Lines

Cherry open compote, ruffled sides,
   hexagonal base (Fig. 9 Illus. top
   next column) 55.00
Holly bowl, smooth rim (Fig. 10
   Illus. next column) 50.00

Figure 9

Figure 10

Carnival Glass Lines

Figure 11

Brooklyn Bridge bowl, marigold
   (Fig. 11) 60.00
Butterfly & Tulip interior bowl,
   Feather Scroll exterior, mari-
   gold (Fig. 12 Illus. top next
   page) 150.00
Grape Delight bowl, purple (Fig. 13
   Illus. next page) 65.00

Figure 12

Figure 13

Figure 14

Figure 15

Grape & Cable perfume bottle
w/stopper, purple (Fig. 14) 650.00
Lattice & Daisy pitcher, tankard-
type, marigold (Fig. 15) 175.00

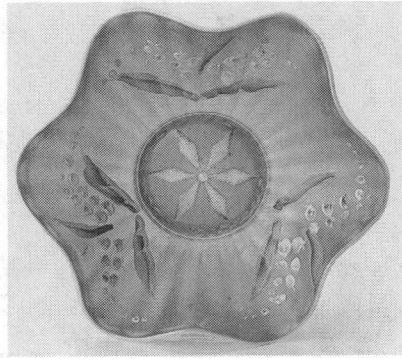

Figure 16

Stippled Petals bowl, peach opal
w/h.p. lily of the valley decora-
tion inside (Fig. 16) 145.00

DIAMOND GLASS-WARE COMPANY PATTERNS:

Black Glass

Figure 17

Candleholder, hexagonal socket &
round foot, "Jack and the Bean
Stalk" decoration, ca. 1928
(Fig. 17) 25.00

Figure 18

Console bowl & base, gold band
decoration, ca. 1924-28 (Fig. 18) . . 45.00

Figure 19

Vase, tall ovoid body w/short cylindrical neck, "hammered gold"
band decoration (Fig. 19) 100.00

Clear Decorated Items

Figure 20

Pitcher, tall footed tankard style
w/ruffled rim, applied angled
handle, h.p. decorated bands
around the middle, ca. 1920
(Fig. 20) 75.00

Figure 21

Tumblers, Blue Bird decoration, ca.
1916, each (Fig. 21) 25.00

Figure 22

Wine decanter w/bulbous stopper,
h.p. w/large daisy-like blossoms,
leaves & bands (Fig. 22) 65.00

Cut Pieces

Figure 23

Basket, shallow upturned sides, applied center handle, cut flowers
around the sides (Fig. 23) 50.00

Figure 24

Vase, wide slightly flaring cylindrical iridescent blue body
w/swelled, closed mouth, cut

w/stylized swags & berries
(Fig. 24)....................... 100.00

Stretch Glass

Figure 25

Console bowl, shallow widely flaring
sides, blue stretch, on a separate
black glass base, ca. 1924
(Fig. 25)....................... 50.00

Figure 26

Pitcher, tankard-type, "Adam's Rib"
patt., blue stretch (Fig. 26)....... 600.00

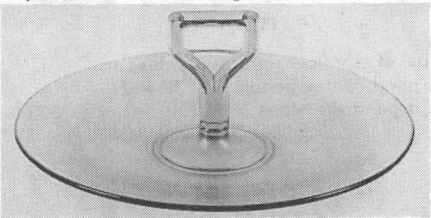

Figure 27

Sandwich server w/central handle,
green stretch, ca. 1927 (Fig. 27).. 55.00

Figure 28

Sherbet, footed, blue stretch
(Fig. 28)....................... 20.00

Other Lines

Figure 29

Figure 30

Figure 31

Figure 32

Candleholder, green w/fluted base,
ca. 1928 (Fig. 29) 20.00
Candleholder, amber w/gold leafy
decorative base band, ca. 1927
(Fig. 30) 20.00
Vanity set: a pair of tall bottles,
cov. powder dish & oblong tray;
rose-pink, gold band trim, the
set (Fig. 31) 125.00
Vase, "Barcelona" line, black glass
w/twisted body & flared rim
(Fig. 32) 125.00

(End of Special Focus)

DUNCAN & MILLER

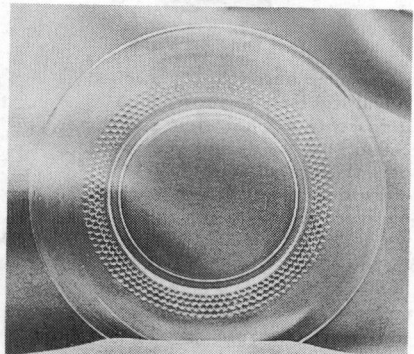

Duncan & Miller Teardrop Pattern Plate

Duncan & Miller Glass Company, a successor firm to George A. Duncan & Sons Company, produced a wide range of pressed wares and novelty pieces during the late 19th century and into the early 20th century. During the Depression era and after, they continued making a wide variety of more modern patterns, including mold-blown types and also introduced a number of etched and engraved patterns. Many colors, including opalescent hues, were produced during this era and especially popular today are the graceful swan dishes they produced in the Pall Mall and Sylvan patterns. The numbers after the pattern name indicate the original factory pattern number. The Duncan factory was closed in 1955. Also see ANIMALS and PATTERN GLASS in Glass section.

Ashtrays, individual size, Teardrop
patt. (No. 301), clear, set of 3 .... $12.00
Basket, handled, Canterbury patt.
(No. 115), clear, 11½" h. 65.00
Bonbon, four closed handles, Teardrop patt., clear, 6" 12.00
Bowl, 6 x 10" oval, Canterbury patt.,
clear 20.00

Bowl, grapefruit, Spiral Flutes patt.
(No. 40), green 7.00
Butter (or cheese) dish, cov., Early
American Sandwich patt. (No. 41),
clear, 8" d. 100.00
Cake plate, footed, Early American
Sandwich patt., clear, 12" d. 87.00
Candleholders w/prisms, Caribbean
patt. (No. 112), clear, 7½" h.,
pr. 110.00
Candy dish, open, heart-shaped,
divided, Teardrop patt., clear 15.00
Cocktail, Canterbury patt., clear 8.00
Cocktail, Hobnail patt. (No. 118),
clear 7.00
Compote, cheese, etched Language
of Flowers patt., clear 18.50
Creamer & sugar bowl, Caribbean
patt., clear, pr. 28.00
Cruet w/original stopper, Spiral
Flutes patt., clear 85.00
Cruet set: oil & vinegar cruets
w/original stoppers & undertray;
Teardrop patt., clear, 3 pcs. 55.00
Goblet, ball stem, Caribbean patt.,
blue, 5¾" h., 8 oz. 40.00
Goblet, water, Mardi Gras patt.
(No. 42), clear 26.00
Marmalade jar, cov., etched First
Love patt., clear 24.00
Mayonnaise bowl & underplate,
Teardrop patt., clear, 2 pcs. 20.00
Model of a swan, Sylvan patt.
(No. 122), clear, 7" l. 23.00
Model of a swan, nesting-type,
avocado, 10½" l. 60.00
Model of a swan, nesting-type, Biscayne green, 12" l. 195.00
Mustard jar, cov., Caribbean patt.,
blue 75.00
Mustard pot, cov., Teardrop patt.,
clear 32.00
Nappy w/handle, Caribbean patt.,
blue, 5" 35.00
Oyster cocktail, etched Language of
Flowers patt., clear, 4½ oz. 22.00
Pitcher, martini, Canterbury patt.,
clear 125.00
Pitcher, milk, Caribbean patt.,
blue 350.00
Plate, fruit, 5½" d., w/applied handle, etched First Love patt.,
clear 21.00
Plate, 6" d., Early American Sandwich patt., clear 6.00
Plate, 8" d., Teardrop patt., clear
(ILLUS.) 5.00
Plate, 9" d., Canterbury patt.,
clear 12.00
Plate, dinner, 10½" d., Teardrop
patt., clear 52.00
Plate, dinner, 11" d., Canterbury
patt., clear 40.00

Plate, sandwich, 12¼" d., etched
First Love patt., clear 60.00

Plate, 13½" d., Caribbean patt.,
blue 55.00

Plate, torte, 14" d., Early American
Sandwich patt., amber 40.00

Plate, 15" d., star-shaped, American
Way patt. (No. 71), ruby red 65.00

Platter, Sanibel patt. (No. 130), blue
opalescent 65.00

Punch cups, Caribbean patt., clear
w/ruby handles, set of 12 . . . .   125.00

Punch set: punch bowl & ten cups;
Caribbean patt., clear bowl &
clear cups w/amber handles,
11 pcs. 148.00

Relish dish, two-part, Sanibel patt.,
yellow opalescent, 8½" l. 32.00

Relish dish, two-part, Teardrop
patt., clear, 6" l. 14.00

Rose bowl, Canterbury patt., clear,
4½" h. 15.00

Sandwich server w/center handle,
Georgian patt. (No. 103), green . .   35.00

Sherbet, footed, Canterbury patt.,
clear, 4¼" h. 12.00

Sherbet, crimped rim, etched First
Love patt., clear, 5½" h. 20.00

Sugar shaker w/original top, Early
American Sandwich patt., clear . . .   95.00

Toothpick holder, Mardi Gras patt.,
clear 25.00

Tray, Sanibel patt., yellow opales-
cent, 13" l.   45.00

Tumbler, iced tea, footed, Early
American Sandwich patt., clear . . .   15.00

Tumbler, bar, Mardi Gras patt.,
clear 20.00

Tumbler, iced tea, flat, Spiral Flutes
patt., pink, 5½" h. 40.00

Tumbler, water, Spiral Flutes patt.,
green, 7 oz.   12.00

Vase, 8" h., cornucopia-shaped,
etched First Love patt., clear 75.00

Vase, 8" h., trumpet-form, Mardi
Gras patt., light amber 125.00

Vase, 8" h., Sanibel patt., yellow
opalescent 145.00

Vase, 9½" h., footed, Caribbean
patt., blue 125.00

Vase, 10½" h., Spiral Flutes patt.,
clear 30.00

Wine, Terrace patt. (No. 111),
clear 20.00

Wines, Mardi Gras patt., clear
w/gold trim, pr. 50.00

DURAND

Fine decorative glass similar to that made by Tiffany and other outstanding glasshouses of its day was made by the Vineland Flint

Glass Works Co. in Vineland, New Jersey, first headed by Victor Durand, Sr., and subsequently by his son Victor Durand, Jr., in the 1920's.

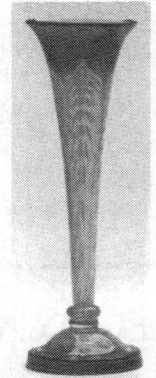

Tall Durand Vase

Boudoir lamp base, slightly swelled
cylindrical body in silvery blue
iridescence w/opal white swirling
coiled King Tut design, mounted
on a domed gilt-metal base & an
electric socket at the top supporting a conical white silk shade,
overall 11½" h. $275.00

Box, cov., squatty bulbous footed
body fitted w/a low domed cover,
coiled green King Tut design on
iridescent ambergris cased in
white opal w/gold iridescence,
star-cut pontil, unsigned, 5" d.,
4" h. 770.00

Center bowl, broad flaring bowl
tapering sharply to a double knop
& domed platform foot, brilliant
ruby w/pink & white pulled-
feather designs in the bowl &
foot, wide border of Bridgeton
Rose pattern designed & cut by
Charles Link, 14" d., 7¾" h. 880.00

Champagne, decorated w/a white
pulled feather on a pink ground,
4½" h. 150.00

Lamp, table-type, the deeply waisted cylindrical glass base w/a bulbous base & top & decorated
overall w/a coiled King Tut design
in green & gold iridescence,
w/metal neck fittings & raised
on a low flaring gold & green-
enameled metal platform base
w/four wide scroll feet, base
12½" h., overall 28" h. 605.00

Powder box, cov., mirror bright ambergris w/wheel-engraved cover,
base inscribed "Durand," 4¾" d.,
3½" h. 330.00

Torcheres, floor-type, conical shade

w/slightly flaring rim, reddish amber 'crackle' finish, on a slender knopped standard w/a pierced gilt-metal hexagonal base, shade 12" h., overall 5' 1" h., pr. 880.00

Vase, 6¼" h., bulbous ovoid footed base tapering to a widely flaring neck, King Tut decoration in golden opalescent decorated w/damascene trailing in pale mint green against an amber iridescent ground, interior w/amber iridescence, signed "Durand - 1700 - 6" 660.00

Vase, 8" h., wide ovoid shouldered body w/a short wide flaring neck, molded vertical ribbing, emerald green exterior cased in white opal w/gold iridescence, signed "Durand 1710-8" 1,045.00

Vase, 8½" h., wide ovoid shouldered body w/a short widely flaring neck, molded w/ten slender ribs, ruby red cased w/white opal & amber w/gold iridescence, unsigned 1,540.00

Vase, 9½" h., wide shouldered ovoid body w/a short cylindrical neck, peach iridescent ground decorated overall w/green scrolling lines in the King Tut design, enameled mark "DURAND 1964-10" 1,760.00

Vase, 10¼" h., wide expanding cylindrical body w/a wide flat mouth, deep cobalt blue decorated on the exterior w/fine random threading, the whole in silvery blue iridescence, signed "Durand - 1970 - 10" 1,100.00

Vase, 14" h., corset-shaped, overall gold iridescence, inscribed "V Durand 1982-14" 660.00

Vases, 14" h., tall slender trumpet-form bowl above a compressed knop & domed platform foot, transparent ruby w/opaque white & pink pulled-feather design & cut Bridgeton Rose border pattern by master cutter Charles Link, feather design repeated on foot, pr. (ILLUS. of one) 990.00

FENTON

Fenton Art Glass Company began producing glass at Williamstown, West Virginia, in January 1907. Organized by Frank L. and John W. Fenton, the company began operations in a newly built glass factory with an experienced master glass craftsman, Jacob Rosenthal, as their factory manager. Fenton

has produced a wide variety of collectible glassware through the years, including Carnival (which see). Still in production today, their current productions may be found at finer gift shops across the country.

Fenton Hobnail Basket

Basket, Hobnail patt., milk white w/clear applied crimped handle, 5½" l., 7" h. (ILLUS.) $40.00
Basket, Coin Dot patt., cranberry opalescent, 6½" h. 115.00
Basket, Gold Crest, 7" h. 42.00
Basket, Vasa Murrhina, 7" h. 80.00
Basket, French Opalescent, 9½" h. 95.00
Bonbon, Hobnail patt., French Opalescent, 5" d. 10.00
Bonbon w/handle, Water Lily & Cattails patt., lavender opalescent, ca. 1910 . . . . 45.00
Bowl, 6" d., 3" h., footed, Mandarin Red 45.00
Bowl, 7" d., double crimped rim, Silver Crest 30.00
Bowl, 7½" d., Celeste Blue Stretch glass 35.00
Bowl, 8" d., crimped rim, footed, Hobnail patt., milk white 14.00
Bowl, fruit, 9" d., footed, deep crimped sides, Mandarin Red 69.00
Bowl, 10" d., Hobnail patt., cranberry opalescent 110.00
Bowl, 10" d., pedestal base, Hobnail patt., No. 3731, Plum Opalescent, ca. 1960 . . . . 110.00
Bowl, 11½" d., Gold Crest 33.00
Butter dish, cov., Hobnail patt., Topaz Opalescent, 1 lb., 1959-60 . . . . 110.00
Cake stand, Hobnail patt., milk white, 12½" d. 35.00
Cake stand, Emerald Crest, 13" d. . . 92.50
Candlesticks, saucer base, No. 315, Chinese Yellow, ca. 1925, 3½" h., pr. 65.00
Candlesticks, cornucopia-form, Mandarin Red, 5" h., pr. 135.00
Candlesticks, Hobnail patt., milk white, 6" h., pr. 18.00

Candlesticks, tall paneled form,
No. 449, Ebony, 8½" h., pr. 120.00

Candy box, cov., Hobnail patt.,
No. 3883, milk white 18.00

Champagne, Plymouth patt., ruby . . 15.00

Cocktail, Lincoln Inn patt., clear 15.00

Compote, open, 7" d., Silver Crest
w/Violets in the Snow, No. 7429,
1968-83 . . . . 24.00

Compote, cov., 1976 American Bi-
centennial - Jefferson Commemorative, No. 8476, Chocolate 160.00

Console bowl, Silver Crest, 13" d. . . 35.00

Cookie jar, cov., Big Cookies
(No. 1681) patt., Ebony 125.00

Creamer, Hobnail patt., cranberry
opalescent 40.00

Cruet w/original stopper, free-
blown, Hanging Heart patt., Cus-
tard, 1976 . . . . 165.00

Cruet w/original stopper, oil, tapering cylindrical body, Hobnail patt.,
No. 3869, milk white 13.00

Epergne, three-lily, Diamond Lace
patt., No. 4808, white opales-
cent 195.00

Goblet, water, Plymouth patt.,
ruby 20.00

Lamp, banquet-type, Coin Dot patt.,
cranberry opalescent, 26" h. 550.00

Nappy, Lotus & Grape patt., Cus-
tard, ca. 1915 . . . . 65.00

Novelty, top hat, Coin Dot patt.,
No. 1924, French Opalescent,
3¼" h. 30.00

Novelty, top hat, Rib Optic patt.,
10" d., 6½" h. 145.00

Pitcher, 6½" h., Hobnail patt.,
green opalescent 42.00

Pitcher, 7" h., w/applied white
opalescent reeded handle, Spanish Lace patt., cranberry opales-
cent 85.00

Pitcher, 10½" h., applied cranberry
reeded handle, Daisy & Fern
patt., cranberry opalescent 145.00

Pitcher, water, Drapery patt., blue
opalescent, early 20th c. 175.00

Plate, 12" d., Silver Crest 22.00

Salad bowl & underplate, New
World patt., lime opalescent,
2 pcs. 225.00

Salt & pepper shakers w/original
tops, Hobnail patt., cranberry
opalescent, pr. 58.00

Salt & pepper shakers w/original
tops, Rib Optic patt., cranberry,
pr. 95.00

Sugar bowl, cov., Cactus patt., Topaz Opalescent, 1959-60 . . . . 65.00

Tidbit tray, two-tiered, Emerald
Crest, 8" & 12" d. plates 45.00

Tumblers, Buttons & Braids patt.,

green opalescent, ca. 1910, set
of 6 . . . . 95.00

Tumbler, Hobnail patt., blue opales-
cent, 3½" h., 5 oz. 8.00

Tumbler, Georgian patt., Jade
Green, 2½ oz. 18.00

Tumbler, footed, No. 1639 Line,
Jade Green w/Ebony foot 18.00

Vase, 4" h., Vasa Murrhina, cushion
foot w/squatty bulbous body
w/flaring & ruffled rim,
No. 6454GB, Aventurine Green
w/blue, white lining 38.00

Vase, 4½" h., fan-shaped, Emerald
Crest 20.00

Vase, 5½" h., Hobnail patt., cran-
berry opalescent 58.00

Vase, 6" h., Cactus patt., Topaz
Opalescent, 1956-60 . . . . 45.00

Vase, 6" h., wafer foot, wide ovoid
body tapering to a wide ruffled
rim, Jacqueline patt., cased Wild
Rose, 1961-62 . . . . 75.00

Vase, 6½" h., melon-ribbed, Crystal
Crest 45.00

Vase, 12" h., footed, Hobnail patt.,
Topaz Opalescent, 1956-60 . . . . 60.00

Water set: 9" h. pitcher & five tumblers; etched San Toy patt., clear
satin, ca. 1936, 6 pcs. 165.00

Water set: 9" h. pitcher & six tumblers; Coin Dot patt., French
Opalescent, 7 pcs. 275.00

Water set: 9" h. pitcher & six tumblers; Dot Optic patt., cranberry
opalescent, 7 pcs. 355.00

Wine, Historic America patt., Fort
Dearborn scene, 1937 . . . . 23.50

Wine, Lincoln Inn patt., clear 14.00

FOSTORIA

American Pattern Console Set

*Fostoria Glass Company, founded in 1887,
produced numerous types of fine glassware
over the years. Their factory in Moundsville,
West Virginia closed in 1986. Also see
ANIMALS under Glass.*

Ashtray, Coin patt., frosted amber . . $25.00

Ashtray, Coin patt., frosted light
blue 22.50

Bonbon, three-toed, American patt.,
canary yellow 165.00

Bonbon, Versailles etching, green .. 27.00

Book ends, Lyre carving, clear, pr... 70.00

Bowl, 4 3/8" d., three-footed, Baroque patt., blue 25.00

Bowl, cereal, 5" d., Coronet patt., clear 8.00

Bowl, 5" d., Vernon etching, blue... 20.00

Bowl, cereal, 6" d., Fairfax patt., Orchid etching, clear 20.00

Bowl, 6¾" d., three-footed, Kashmir etching, yellow 30.00

Bowl, 8" d., Coin patt., frosted red 40.00

Bowl, 8½" d., two-handled, Chintz etching, clear 50.00

Bowl, 9" d., handled, Corsage etching, clear 70.00

Bowl, 9" oval, Coin patt., emerald green 145.00

Bowl, 9¾" oval, divided, American patt., clear 30.00

Bowl, 10" d., handled, Buttercup etching, clear 46.50

Bowl, 10" d., handled, Oak Leaf etching, pink 75.00

Bowl, 11" d., rolled edge, Baroque patt., yellow 40.00

Bowl, cream soup, Chateau etching, clear 8.00

Box, cov., American patt., amber, 3" sq. 150.00

Butter dish, cov., Colony patt., clear, ¼ lb. 38.00

Butter dish, cov., Fairfax patt., amber 60.00

Butter dish, cov., Pioneer patt., green 60.00

Cake plate, handled, Chintz etching, clear, 10" d. 42.50

Cake plate, handled, Navarre etching, clear, 10" d. 42.00

Cake stand, footed, Coin patt., frosted clear 75.00

Candelabrum, three-light, Navarre etching, clear, pr. 65.00

Candlesticks, Arvida cutting, clear, 4" h., pr. 40.00

Candlesticks, two-light, Chintz etching, clear, 3½" h., pr. 55.00

Candlesticks, Coin patt., olive green, 8" h., pr. 65.00

Candlesticks, June etching, topaz, 2" h., pr. 40.00

Candlesticks, Versailles etching, topaz, 5" h., pr. 80.00

Candy dish, cov., Coin patt., frosted red 50.00

Candy dish, cov., Trojan etching, yellow, ½ lb. size 145.00

Catsup bottle w/original top, American patt., clear, 6¾" h. 100.00

Champagne, saucer-shaped, Arcady etching, clear 15.00

Champagne, Corsage etching, clear 12.00

Champagne, Cynthia cutting, clear .. 17.50

Champagne, Meadow Rose etching, clear, 6 oz. 25.00

Champagne, Seville etching, amber 18.00

Cigarette box, cov., Coin patt., frosted amber 70.00

Cigarette box, cov., Morning Glory carving, clear 36.00

Claret, Brunswick etching, amber ... 25.00

Claret, Romance etching, clear 30.00

Claret, Willow etching, clear 18.00

Cocktail, Bouquet cutting, clear, 4 oz. 13.00

Compote, open, 4¾" h., Lido etching, clear 22.50

Compote, open, 6", June etching, blue 125.00

Compote, jelly, 8" h., Midnight Rose etching, clear 110.00

Console bowl, Grape etching, green, 12¾" d. 38.50

Console set: 10" d., 5" h. bowl & pair of 6" h. candlesticks; American patt., clear, the set (ILLUS.) .. 65.00

Cordial, Christiana cutting, clear, 1 oz. 15.00

Cordial, Holly cutting, clear 22.00

Creamer, footed, Baroque patt., clear, 3¾" h. 10.00

Creamer, Trojan etching, pink 27.50

Creamer & cov. sugar bowl, Fairfax patt., topaz, pr. 24.00

Creamer & open sugar bowl, Chintz etching, clear, pr. 35.00

Creamer & open sugar bowl, Kashmir etching, yellow, pr. 60.00

Cruet w/original stopper, American patt., clear 35.00

Cruet w/original stopper, Fairfax patt., blue 120.00

Cruet w/original stopper, Mayfair patt., green 95.00

Cup & saucer, American patt., clear 8.50

Cup & saucer, Colony patt., clear ... 10.00

Cup & saucer, Mayfair patt., amber 7.50

Cup & saucer, Navarre etching, clear 27.50

Cup & saucer, Pioneer patt., green 6.00

Cup & saucer, Trojan etching, yellow 20.00

Dresser set: two cologne bottles w/original stoppers, a 2 x 2" sq. box & a filigree metal & glass undertray; American patt., clear, 4 pcs. 450.00

Epergne, single-lily, Heirloom cutting, pink opalescent, oblong bowl 14½" l., lily 9" h. 95.00

Finger bowl, Seville etching,
amber 18.00
Goblet, Baroque patt., blue, 6¾" h.,
9 oz. 32.00
Goblet, Chintz etching, clear,
9 oz. 25.00
Goblet, Coin patt., olive green 45.00
Goblet, Cynthia cutting, clear 27.50
Goblet, Holly cutting, clear, 8" h. 22.00
Goblet, Jamestown patt., pink,
10 oz. 16.00
Goblet, Mayflower etching, clear,
7 3/8" h., 9 oz. 15.00
Goblet, Sunray patt., clear,
5¾" h. 14.00
Goblet, Versailles etching, green,
6" h. 23.00
Goblet, Willowmere etching, clear .. 25.00
Ice bucket, Seville etching, amber .. 43.00
Ice bucket, Trojan etching, topaz ... 95.00
Mayonnaise bowl & underplate,
Navarre etching, clear, 2 pcs. 35.00
Muffin tray, Colony patt., clear 40.00
Mustard jar, cov., Hermitage patt.,
topaz 32.50
Mustard jar, cover & original spoon,
American patt., clear, 3 pcs. 30.00
Novelty, model of a hat, American
patt., clear, 2 1/8" h. 12.00
Oyster cocktail, Buttercup etching,
clear 18.00
Oyster cocktail, Navarre etching,
clear, 3½ oz. 21.00
Parfait, June etching, topaz,
5¼" h. 60.00
Pickle dish, Chintz etching, clear,
8" l. 30.00
Pitcher, 5¾" h., Jamestown patt.,
amethyst, 3 pt. 100.00
Pitcher, 7¼" h., Hermitage patt.,
yellow 125.00
Pitcher, Coin patt., emerald green
frosted, 1 qt. 225.00
Plates, 6" d., Fairfax patt., rose, set
of 4 .... 25.00
Plate, 7" d., Chintz etching, clear ... 12.00
Plate, 7" d., Colony patt., clear 8.50
Plate, 7" d., June etching, blue 12.50
Plate, 7½" d., Holly cutting, clear .. 8.00
Plate, 7½" d., Midnight Rose etch-
ing, clear 18.50
Plate, 8½" d., Oak Leaf etching,
clear 8.00
Plate, 8½" d., Versailles etching,
blue 22.50
Plate, 8¾" d., Trojan etching,
yellow 9.50
Plate, 9" d., Baroque patt., yellow .. 45.00
Plate, 9½" d., Beverly etching,
green 25.00
Plate, 9½" d., Century patt., clear .. 16.00
Plate, 10¼" d., Kashmir etching,
yellow 35.00

Plate, chop, 13½" d., ruffled rim,
Chintz etching, clear 40.00
Plate, torte, 14" d., Holly cutting,
clear 45.00
Platter, 13" oval, American patt.,
clear 55.00
Platter, 15" oval, Seville etching,
amber 75.00
Punch set: punch bowl & ten cups;
Baroque patt., clear, 11 pcs. 265.00
Relish dish, three-part, Hermitage
patt., clear, 7½" l. 16.00
Relish dish, divided, June etching,
blue, 8½" l. 54.00
Relish dish, three-part, Holly cutting,
clear, 10" d. 27.00
Salt shaker w/original top, Coin
patt., emerald green 20.00
Sandwich server w/center handle,
American patt., clear, 10½" d. 35.00
Sandwich server w/center handle,
Chintz etching, clear, 12" d. 28.00
Sandwich server w/center handle,
Coronet patt., clear 22.00
Sherbet, low, American patt., clear,
5 oz. 9.00
Sherbet, Chintz etching, clear,
4 3/8" h., 6 oz. 19.00
Sherbet, Jamestown patt., red,
4 1/8" h. 10.00
Sherbet, Sunray patt., clear,
3 5/8" h. 11.00
Sherbet, Trojan etching, topaz,
6" h. 19.00
Sugar bowl, individual size, Baroque
patt., blue 23.00
Sugar bowl, cov., Coin patt., olive
green 35.00
Sugar bowl, cov., footed, Fairfax
patt., amber 6.00
Sugar pail, Trojan etching, topaz ... 125.00
Toothpick holder, Victoria patt.,
clear & frosted, ca. 1890 .... 110.00
Tumbler, footed, American patt.,
clear, 5½" h., 6 oz. 10.00
Tumbler, footed, Cordelia etching,
clear, 9 oz. 20.00
Tumbler, footed, Jamestown patt.,
blue, 6" h. 15.00
Tumbler, footed, Lafayette patt.,
wisteria 35.00
Tumbler, water, footed, Lido etch-
ing, clear 8.00
Tumbler, iced tea, Willowmere etch-
ing, clear 29.00
Vase, 5½" h., flared rim, American
patt., clear 25.00
Vase, 7¼" h., handled, Century
patt., clear 58.00
Vase, 8" h., June etching, blue ... 135.00
Vase, 24" h., swung-type, Heirloom
cutting, pink 95.00
Water set: pitcher & four tumblers;
Vernon etching, green, 5 pcs. 375.00

Wine, Chintz etching, clear......... 40.00
Wine, Colony patt., clear 14.00
Wine, Willowmere etching, clear,
   3½ oz......................... 26.00

FRANCES WARE

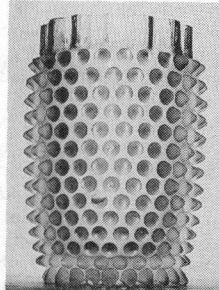

Frances Ware Celery Vase

This glass was made by Hobbs, Brockunier & Co., Wheeling, West Virginia, in the 1880's. It is frosted or clear glass with stained amber tops or rims and was both mold-blown and pressed. It has either a pattern of hobnails or swirled ribs.

Berry set: master bowl & five sauce
   dishes; frosted hobnail w/amber
   rim, 6 pcs...................$175.00
Bowl, 7½" d., frosted hobnail
   w/amber rim 70.00
Butter dish, cov., frosted hobnail
   w/amber rim 75.00
Cake plate, frosted hobnail w/am-
   ber rim....................... 35.00
Celery vase, frosted hobnail w/am-
   ber rim, 8" h. (ILLUS.) 75.00
Lemonade set: pitcher & six tumblers; frosted hobnail w/amber
   rim, 7 pcs.................... 350.00
Pitcher, 8½" h., frosted hobnail
   w/amber rim 180.00
Plate, 5½" d., frosted hobnail
   w/amber rim 30.00
Salt shaker w/original top, frosted
   hobnail w/amber rim 135.00
Sugar bowl, cov., frosted hobnail
   w/amber rim 75.00
Table set: cov. butter dish, cov. sugar bowl, creamer & spooner;
   frosted hobnail w/amber rim,
   4 pcs........................ 325.00
Toothpick holder, frosted swirl
   w/amber rim 37.50

FRY

Numerous types of glass were made by the H.C. Fry Company, Rochester, Pennsylvania. One of its art lines was called Foval and was blown in 1926-27. Cheaper was its milky-

opalescent ovenware (Pearl Oven Ware) made for utilitarian purposes but also now being collected. The company also made fine cut glass.

Collectors of Fry Glass will be interested in the recent publication of a good reference book, The Collector's Encyclopedia of Fry Glassware, *by The H.C. Fry Glass Society (Collector Books, 1990).*

Bake set, child's, "Little Mother's
   Kidi-bake Set," in original box....$250.00
Candlestick, Foval, applied green
   trim, 12" h..................... 30.00
Casserole dish, cov., Pearl Oven
   Ware, 9" oval 25.00
Coffeepot, cov., Foval, applied blue
   handle 250.00
Compote, 4" d., 6" h., clear w/gold
   threaded controlled bubble de-
   sign, teardrop-shaped stem 135.00
Console set: 14" d. ruffled bowl &
   two 5¼" h. candlesticks w/ruffled
   tops; random reeding & controlled
   bubbles, blue, unsigned, 3 pcs.... 295.00
Cookie jar, cov., Sunnybrook patt.,
   green 225.00
Cordial, etched Sheraton patt....... 35.00
Creamer & cov. sugar bowl, Foval,
   applied blue handles, pr. 150.00
Cruet w/original stopper, Star & Fan
   patt., clear 135.00
Cup & saucer, Foval, applied cobalt
   blue handle................... 60.00
Cups & saucers, Foval, applied
   green handles, 4 sets........... 280.00
Parfait, Narrow Optic patt., green,
   6¼" h. 47.00
Pitcher, "crackle" glass, Foval, applied green handle & foot 79.00
Reamer, embossed "Sunkist," green
   opalescent.................... 395.00
Sherry, etched Sheraton patt., clear,
   1½ oz....................... 15.00
Smoke bell (for hanging lamp),
   etched decoration, clear w/blue
   trim......................... 65.00
Tea set: cov. teapot w/applied blue
   handle, six cups w/applied blue
   handles & six sauces w/blue trim;
   Foval, 13 pcs................. 425.00
Tumbler, etched Sheraton patt.,
   clear, 5 oz. 12.00
Vase, 6¼" h., footed, pale robin's
   egg blue body w/opaque threading & applied opaque prunts at
   the collar, on an opaque foot 110.00
Vase, 8" h., Foval, campana urn-
   form w/an applied glass handle,
   the body in opalescent white
   raised on a circular foot, the handle in sky blue................. 264.00
Wine, etched Rose patt., clear...... 18.00
Wine, Wide Optic patt., No. 3101
   line, amber 25.00

GALLE'

Galle' Etched & Enameled Bowl

Galle' glass was made in Nancy, France, by Emile Galle', a founder of the Nancy School and a leader in the Art Nouveau movement in France. Much of his glass, both enameled and cameo, is decorated with naturalistic motifs. The finest pieces were made in the last two decades of the 19th century and the opening years of the present one. Pieces marked with a star preceding the name were made between 1904, the year of Galle's death, and 1914.

Bottle w/stopper, squatty bulbous body w/stepped shoulder & short cylindrical neck fitted w/an acorn stopper, swirled celadon green body enameled *en grisaille* to depict a desolate lake scene w/architectural ruins, framed by a curving branch in sienna & umber interspersed w/finely enameled shells in high-relief, the stopper decorated w/a similar shell, enameled "Cristallerie d'Emile Galle Nancy - Modele et decor deposes - 4," 7½" h. $20,900.00

Bowl, 5¼" l., 2¼" h., compressed quatrefoil form, the topaz ground finely etched to depict branches, leaves & Oriental-inspired lily pads, thickly enameled in burnt orange, burgundy, green & brown, signed "Galle' " (ILLUS.) . .6,600.00

Cameo bowl, 11" l., boat-shaped curved sides tapering to pointed ends, grey overlaid w/opaque white, lavender & soft green, the interior overlaid w/pink, the exterior cameo carved w/delicate blossoms, the interior carved w/blossoms in pink, signed in cameo 2,200.00

Cameo box, cov., circular w/fitted cover, cream overlaid in burnt orange, etched w/trailing poppies & pods, signed in cameo, 4 1/8" d. 1,210.00

Cameo box, cov., compressed circular base, conforming lid, grey mottled in brilliant yellow, over-

laid in deep purple & cut w/leafy branches & berries, signed in cameo "Galle'," ca. 1900, 5¼" d. 1,430.00

Cameo compote, open, 7¾" d., 4" h., golden amber flared bowl layered within in pink & deep red & acid-etched, wheel-cut & polished w/cyclamen blossoms, buds & leafy stems, incised signature in center 1,430.00

Cameo creamer w/applied frosted handle, frosted peach overlaid w/red, cameo-cut w/leaves & berries, 2¼" d., 3¼" h. 1,500.00

Cameo jar, cov., squared cylindrical form, the frosted yellow ground overlaid in ruby red, each side etched w/an oval panel depicting flowering branches & foliage, the circular cover etched w/a fierce fire-breathing dragon, jar & cover signed, 7" h. 5,500.00

Cameo liqueur set: decanter & two liqueur glasses; the decanter of flattened teardrop form, the grey sides streaked w/lime green, overlaid in lime green & deep olive green & cut w/ferns & grasses, the domed stopper & cylindrical glasses w/conforming decoration, decanter & glasses signed in cameo "Galle'," ca. 1900, decanter 11 5/8" h., 3 pcs. 2,750.00

Cameo perfume atomizer, pyriform, grey splashed w/amber & olive green, overlaid in olive green & chocolate brown & cut w/a tranquil river w/leafy trees in the foreground, simple metal mounts, signed in intaglio "Galle'," ca. 1900, overall 8¼" h. 770.00

Cameo perfume burner, flattened spherical vessel, grey infused w/lemon yellow opalescence, overlaid w/deepest cherry red & cut w/cyclamen blossoms, buds & leafage, metal mount, signed in cameo "Galle'," ca. 1900, 6 7/8" h. 1,045.00

Cameo vase, 3¾" h., footed ovoid body w/the rim folded over into serrated points, clear overlaid in palest lavender & etched to depict aquatic plants & a broken honeycomb pattern, w/silver foil inclusions & w/a martele' finish in areas, engraved "Galle' " 7,700.00

Cameo vase, 5¾" h., ovoid w/everted rim, opalescent lemon yellow walls overlaid in amber & cut w/rose blossoms, buds & leafage, signed in cameo "Galle'," ca. 1900 . . . . .2,970.00

Cameo vase, 7½" h., ovoid body tapering to a short cylindrical neck w/flat rim, frosted white ground mottled w/palest yellow, overlaid in crimson & etched to depict flowering bleeding heart stems & foliage, cameo signature 2,530.00

Cameo vase, 8¼" h., flattened flask-form w/everted rim, rich yellow frosted ground overlaid in crimson & etched to depict pendant fuchsia blossoms 3,960.00

Cameo vase, 9 1/8" h., 'marquetrie-sur-verre,' cylindrical w/trilobate rim, deep butterscotch opalescent shaded at the bottom w/deep amber & overlaid in opaque mossy green, inlaid w/white overlaid by lavender, deep amber, pale blue overlaid by olive green & mossy green, finely wheel-carved w/an iris blossom & a bud above leafage, inscribed "Galle'," ca. 1900 .... 58,300.00

Cameo vase, 22" h., trumpet-form footed body w/a bulging knop at the top below the short, flared neck, cream ground overlaid in lime green & caramel, cameo-cut to depict flowering plants & foliage, cameo signature 2,530.00

Cameo *veilleuse* (night light), spherical body w/opalescent lemon yellow sides overlaid in emerald green & periwinkle blue & cut w/sprays of wildflowers & leafage, pierced gilt-metal domed cover w/button & disc finial, signed in cameo, ca. 1900, 7" h. 3,575.00

Cameo wall sconce, half-round demi-lune form, deep rich yellow ground overlaid in blue & umber, cameo-cut w/thorny berried branches, cameo signature, mounted in foliate gilt-metal fixture, 21½" l. 6,325.00

Galle' Cordial Set

Cordial set: footed decanter w/bulbous stepped stopper & two goblets; the bulbous decanter tapering to a slender stick neck & w/an applied ropetwist handle, goblets w/flaring bowl raised on a domed foot, all in clear rib-molded bodies decorated w/enameled stylized flowers & gilt trim, enameled "Emile Galle' a Nancy," decanter 12" h. (ILLUS. of part) 1,650.00

Ewer, the waisted cylindrical body w/applied loop handle, the rim rising diagonally from the handle to the shaped spout, the body further applied w/thick trailings in amber, the sides broadly wheel-carved w/diagonal fluting & carved on one side w/lily blossoms & leafage, enameled in pale pink & brown, heightened in gilt, inscribed "Cristallerie - d'Emile Galle' - Nancy - Modele et decor Deposes," ca. 1890, 13 1/8" h. 5,500.00

Tumbler, 'teaching' style, ribbed cylindrical body in clear decorated w/a colorful enameled rooster teacher & chick students & inscribed "L'Instruction Histoire," signed on the base "E. Galle' - depose," 4 5/8" h. 550.00

Vase, 3 7/8" h., paneled expanding quatrefoil form w/a flat molded rim, raised on four short shaped feet, deep topaz, the surface selectively *martele'* & finely enameled w/insects in flight in shades of pink, blue, green, red & black, the whole trimmed in gilt, signed in enamel "Emile Galle'," ca. 1890 .... 5,775.00

Enameled Galle' Vases

Vases, 4 7/8" h., wide cylindrical body w/slightly flaring ruffled rim, clear topaz, one enameled in naturalistic tones to depict field flowers, the other enameled to depict a Cross of Lorraine among thistles, both etched "E. Galle' Nancy," pr. (ILLUS.) 2,200.00

Vase, 7 1/6" h., raised on a circular foot w/crimped edges in spiralling

tones of clay & red, onion-form
w/tapering neck & bulbous clear
body internally streaked w/au-
tumn red shaded w/lemon yellow
in the lower body, the body w/sil-
ver foil inclusions, the surface
finely wheel-carved to suggest
various layers, the whole against
a *martele'* ground, signed in intaglio "Galle'," ca. 1900 . . . . . . .15,400.00

Vase, 10" h. swelling cylindrical
body, topaz etched & enameled to
depict flower blossoms & foliage,
in green, turquoise, violet & yellow, the ground etched to create
an atmospheric effect, signed 3,080.00

Vase, 18¾" h., tall slender oviform
body w/a peaked trefoil rim, pale
aqua ground etched & enameled
to depict flower blossoms & foliage in violet, green & yellow,
trimmed w/gilt, the ground
etched to create an atmospheric
effect, engraved "Galle' depose'
g.g." 7,700.00

GOOFUS

Goofus Glass Plate

*This is a name collectors have given a
pressed glass whose colors were sprayed on
and then fired. Most pieces have intaglio or
convex designs and were produced by the
Northwood Glass Co.*

Berry set: master bowl & four sauce
dishes; relief-molded Bird &
Strawberry patt. on gold, 5 pcs. . .$145.00

Bowl, 9" d., relief-molded red
florals on gold 17.50

Bowl, 10" d., relief-molded blue &
red Bird & Strawberry patt. on
gold 135.00

Plate, 8" d., relief-molded red roses
on gold (ILLUS.) 40.00

Tray, handled, relief molded red
poppies, 12" oval 35.00

Vase, 9" h., octagonal, relief-
molded red poppies on silver 17.00

GREENTOWN

Greentown Hen on Basket Dish

*Greentown glass was made in Greentown,
Indiana, by the Indiana Tumbler & Goblet
Co. from 1894 until 1903. In addition to its
famed Chocolate and Holly Amber glass,
which see, it produced other types of clear and
colored glass. Miscellaneous pieces are listed here. Also see PATTERN GLASS - Cord
Drapery, Dewey and Teardrop & Tassel.*

Animal covered dish, Cat on Ham-
per, Nile green $1,225.00

Animal covered dish, Fighting
Cocks, emerald green 1,400.00

Animal covered dish, Hen on Bas-
ket, amber, 5½" l. (ILLUS.) 135.00

Animal covered dish, Hen on Bas-
ket, blue, 5½" l. 150.00

Animal covered dish, Hen on Bas-
ket, emerald green, 5½" l. 160.00

Animal covered dish, Hen on Basket, Nile green, 5½" l. (rim
chips) 1,400.00

Animal covered dish, Rabbit on Bas-
ket, amber 135.00

Animal covered dish, Rabbit on Bas-
ket, emerald green 135.00

Compote, 8½" d., high stand, Aus-
trian patt., clear 65.00

Cordial, Austrian patt., vaseline 130.00

Cordial, Herringbone Buttress patt.,
emerald green 235.00

Creamer, large, Austrian patt.,
clear 25.00

Creamer & cov. sugar bowl, Cactus
patt., canary, pr. 190.00

Goblet, Austrian patt., clear 55.00

Greentown Dog's Head Toothpick Holder

Mug, Dewey patt., Nile green 170.00

Syrup pitcher w/original top, Herringbone Buttress patt., clear 145.00

Toothpick holder, model of a dog's head, Nile green (ILLUS. previous page) 150.00

Vase, 10" h., Austrian patt., clear .. 70.00

Wine, Austrian patt., clear 32.50

HEISEY

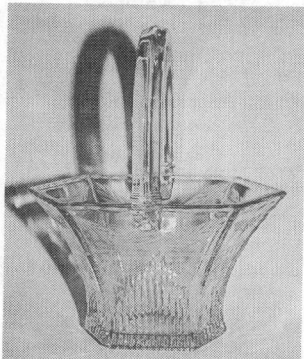

Heisey Basket with Cut Decoration

Numerous types of fine glass were made by A.H. Heisey & Co., Newark, Ohio, from 1895. The company's trade-mark — an H enclosed within a diamond — has become known to most glass collectors. The company's name and molds were acquired by Imperial Glass Co., Bellaire, Ohio, in 1958, and some pieces have been reissued. The glass listed below consists of miscellaneous pieces and types. Also see ANIMALS under Glass and PATTERN GLASS.

Ashtray, Crystolite patt., clear $7.50

Ashtray, Old Sandwich patt., clear .. 30.00

Basket, Colonial patt. w/floral etching, clear, 7" h. 225.00

Basket, Lariat patt., clear, 8" h. 180.00

Basket, Picket patt., decorated w/cut leafy swags & dots, clear, 8" w., 11" h. (ILLUS.) 165.00

Berry set: master berry bowl & six sauce dishes; Empress patt., Flamingo (pink), 7 pcs. 75.00

Bowl, 4" d., Crystolite patt., clear .. 15.00

Bowl, 7½" d., three-footed, Queen Ann patt., Orchid etching, clear .. 42.00

Bowl, fruit, 9" d., Plantation Ivy etching (No. 516), clear 135.00

Bowl, 10" d., Lariat patt., Moongleam (green) 35.00

Bowl, floral, 12" d., footed, scalloped rim, Old Sandwich patt., Sahara (yellow) 100.00

Bowl, 13½" d., Lodestar patt., Dawn (light grey) 180.00

Butter dish, cov., Orchid etching, clear 155.00

Butter dish, cov., Rose etching, clear 155.00

Cake stand, Orchid etching, clear, 13½" d. 275.00

Candleholders, two-light, Fern patt., clear, pr. 100.00

Candleholders, two-light, Lariat patt., clear, pr. 69.00

Candlesticks, Empress patt., Sahara, 6" h., pr. 135.00

Candlesticks, Miss Muffet patt., Flamingo, pr. 50.00

Candlesticks, two-light, Trident patt., clear 100.00

Candy box, cov., w/bow knot finial, Waverly patt., Rose etching, clear 175.00

Candy dish, cov., Ipswich patt., clear 55.00

Candy dish, cov., footed, Plantation patt., clear 162.00

Celery dish, Flat Panel patt., clear .. 22.00

Celery dish, Greek Key patt., clear 34.00

Champagne, Carcassone patt. w/Lafayette etching, clear, 6 oz. 10.00

Champagne, Lariat patt., clear, 6 oz. 8.00

Clarets, Rose etching, clear, 4 oz., set of 4 .... 304.00

Cocktail, figural goose stem, clear .. 200.00

Cocktail, Minuet etching, clear 38.00

Cocktail shaker, Orchid etching, clear, 12" h. 85.00

Compote, jelly, 4" d., Peerless patt., clear 40.00

Console bowl, Ridgeleigh patt., Zircon (blue-green), 11½" d. 325.00

Creamer, Beaded Swag patt., clear 32.00

Creamer, Lariat patt., clear 11.50

Creamer, Winged Scroll patt., emerald green w/gold trim 70.00

Creamer & sugar bowl, Mahabar patt., clear, pr. 22.00

Creamer & sugar bowl, Minuet etching, clear, pr. 90.00

Creamer & sugar bowl, Yeoman patt., Moongleam, pr. 30.00

Cruet w/original stopper, Crystolite patt., clear 47.00

Cruet w/original stopper, Greek Key patt., clear, 3 oz. 50.00

Cruet w/original stopper, Twist patt., Flamingo 95.00

Cup & saucer, Cabochon patt., clear 22.50

Goblet, water, Ipswich patt., clear 24.00

Goblet, Old Williamsburg patt., clear 12.00

Goblet, Victorian patt., clear, 5¼" h. 15.00

Hair receiver, cov., Squared Fan patt., clear, silver plate cover 68.00

Humidor, cov., Fancy Loop patt., clear, silver plate cover 145.00

Ice bucket, Empress patt., Sahara (yellow) 95.00

Ice bucket, Octagon patt., Moongleam (green) 75.00

Ice bucket, Queen Anne patt., clear 100.00

Lemon dish, cov., oval, dolphin finial, Empress patt., clear, in Farberware metal holder, 6½" l. 55.00

Marmalade jar, cover & ladle, Yeoman patt., Moongleam, 3 pcs. 55.00

Mayonnaise bowl w/ladle, Waverly patt., Orchid etching, clear, 2 pcs. 50.00

Mayonnaise bowl & underplate, Fern patt., Belvedere etching, clear, 2 pcs. 75.00

Mayonnaise bowl, underplate & ladle, Ridgeleigh patt., clear, 3 pcs. 45.00

Mug, Punty Band patt., personalized w/name in gold enameling, clear 45.00

Mustard jar, cov., Colonial patt., clear 35.00

Mustard jar, cov., Saturn patt., clear 28.00

Mustard jar, cover & spoon, Puritan patt., clear, 3 pcs. 35.00

Nut cup, Octagon patt., Moongleam 18.00

Nut cups, Twist patt., green, set of six 102.00

Oyster cocktail, Crystolite patt., clear, 3½ oz. 14.00

Oyster cocktail, Ipswich patt., Flamingo (pink) 30.00

Oyster cocktail, New Era patt., clear w/gold trim & wide burgundy bands 20.00

Pitcher, Chantilly cutting, clear, 80 oz. 200.00

Pitcher, tankard, Colonial patt., w/floral cutting, clear, ½ gal. 135.00

Pitcher, Crystolite patt., clear, ½ gal. 95.00

Pitcher, Greek Key patt., clear, 3 pt. . . . . 250.00 to 275.00

Pitcher, water, 6¾" h., Narrow Flute patt., Sahara w/gold band border 335.00

Pitcher, tankard, Orchid etching, clear, 64 oz. 500.00

Pitcher w/ice lip, Plantation patt., clear, ½ gal. 145.00

Pitcher, jug-type, Rose etching, No. 4164, clear, 73 oz. 425.00

Plate, 7" d., Orchid etching, clear . . 18.00

Plate, 7" d., Waverly patt., Rose etching, clear 17.00

Plate, 7½" d., Lariat patt., clear. . . . 12.00

Plate, 7½" d., Twist patt., Flamingo 9.00

Plate, 8" d., Empress patt., Alexandrite (lavender) 65.00

Plate, 8½" d., Colonial Star patt., clear 22.50

Plate, dinner, 10" d., Crystolite patt., clear 65.00

Plate, torte, 13" d., Whirlpool (Provincial) patt., clear 150.00

Plates, 5" d., Yeoman patt., pink, set of 9 . . . . 60.00

Plates, 6" d., Empress patt., Tangerine (deep orangish red), set of 3 . . . . 85.00

Plates, 7" d., Ipswich patt., clear, set of 12 . . . . 148.00

Plates, 8" d., Octagon patt., Flamingo, set of 6 . . . . 60.00

Plates, salad, 8" d., Plantation patt., clear, set of 4 . . . . 68.00

Plates, 8¼" d., Crystolite patt., clear, set of 7 . . . . 105.00

Plates, 9" d., Pleat & Panel patt., Moongleam, set of 4 . . . . 88.00

Punch bowl, Punty Band patt., clear 275.00

Punch bowl & stand, Pinwheel & Fan patt., clear, 2 pcs. 450.00

Punch cup, Crystolite patt., clear . . 10.00

Punch cup, Greek Key patt., clear . . 16.00

Punch cups, Fancy Loop patt., clear, set of 8 . . . . 100.00

Punch set: bowl, underplate, ten cups & ladle; Lariat patt., clear, 13 pcs. 275.00

Punch set: punch bowl, underplate & twelve cups; Crystolite patt., clear, 14 pcs. 325.00

Punch set: bowl, 14 cups & ladle; Puritan patt., clear, bowl 14" d., 16 pcs. 495.00

Relish dish, four-part, Crystolite patt., clear, 9" d. 22.50

Relish dish, Empress patt., Sahara, 10" l. 33.00

Relish dish, three-part, Ridgeleigh patt., clear, 11" l. 62.50

Salt & pepper shakers w/original tops, Empress patt., clear, pr. 40.00

Salt & pepper shakers w/original tops, Fandango patt., clear, pr. 95.00

Sherbet, Carcassone patt., Alexandrite, 6 oz. 135.00

Sherbet, Ipswich patt., clear, 4 oz. . . 24.00

Sherbet, Monte Cristo patt., clear, 6 oz. 30.00

Sherbet, Orchid etching, clear 30.00

Sherbet, Symphone patt., Minuet etching, No. 5010, clear, 6 oz. 20.00

Sugar bowl, open, Quator patt.,
Moongleam 35.00
Sugar bowl, open, Saturn patt.,
clear 25.00
Syrup pitcher w/original top, Planta-
tion patt., clear 65.00
Table set: cov. butter dish, cov. sug-
ar bowl, creamer & spooner;
Beaded Swag patt., milk white
w/pink flowers decoration,
4 pcs. 365.00
Table set: cov. butter dish, cov. sug-
ar bowl, creamer & spooner;
Winged Scroll patt., green w/gold
trim, 4 pcs. 325.00
Toothpick holder, Beaded Swag
patt., ruby-stained 35.00

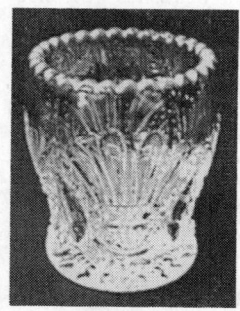

Prince of Wales Plumes Toothpick Holder

Toothpick holder, Prince of Wales
Plumes patt., clear (ILLUS.) 110.00
Toothpick holder, Punty Band patt.,
ruby-stained w/etched florals &
souvenir inscription 45.00
Toothpick holder, Winged Scroll
patt., green w/gold trim 450.00
Tumbler, Arch patt., No. 1417,
clear, 1933-39 . . . .   75.00
Tumbler, iced tea, footed, Carcas-
sonne patt., cobalt blue, 12 oz. . . .   85.00
Tumbler, Chantilly cutting, clear,
13 oz. 25.00
Tumbler, iced tea, Enchantress cut-
ting, clear 50.00
Tumbler, Fancy Loop patt., clear 32.00
Tumbler, iced tea, footed, Orchid
etching, clear, 12 oz. 50.00
Tumbler, Pleat & Panel patt., Moon-
gleam, 8 oz.   75.00
Tumbler, Twist patt., Flamingo,
5 oz. 15.00
Vase, 4" h., Orchid etching, clear . .   95.00
Vase, 7" h., fan-shaped, Lariat
patt., Orchid etching, clear 75.00
Vase, 8" h., crimped rim, Lodestar
patt., Dawn (light grey) 125.00
Vase, 9" h., footed tulip shape,
No. 1420, cobalt blue 500.00
Vase, 12" h., Fairacre patt.,
Moongleam 135.00

Water set: pitcher & six tumblers;
Beaded Swag patt., milk white
w/pink trim, 7 pcs. 175.00
Water set: tankard pitcher & four
tumblers; Orchid etching, clear,
5 pcs. 275.00
Wine, Chateau cutting, clear 60.00
Wine, Gascony patt., Tangerine,
3" h. 160.00
Wine, Locket on Chain patt., clear . .   65.00
Wine, Old Williamsburg patt.,
clear 18.00
Wine, Wildflower etching, clear
w/gold trim 40.00
Wine, Triple Triangle patt., clear . . .   30.00

HISTORICAL & COMMEMORATIVE

Jenny Lind Compote

*Reference numbers are to Bessie M. Lind-
sey's book,* American Historical Glass. *Also
see MILK WHITE GLASS.*

Battleship Olympia dish, cov., milk
white, 6 3/8" l., 3 5/8" w., 4" h.,
No. 468 . . . . $60.00
Battleship Oregon dish, cov., milk
white, 6 3/8" l., 3 5/8" w., 4" h.,
No. 469 . . . . .50.00 to 60.00
Battleship Wheeling dish, cov., milk
white, 6 3/8" l., 3 5/8" w., 4" h.,
No. 470 . . . . .50.00 to 60.00
British Lion paperweight, head of
lion & front paws on round base,
Gillinder & Sons, unsigned, frost-
ed, 2½" d., 2½" h. 95.00
British Lion paperweight, frosted,
2¾ x 5 5/8", 2¾" h., No. 516 . . . .   170.00
Cleveland bottle, bust of Cleve-
land, clear & frosted finish,
10" h., No. 318 . . . .   225.00
Columbia bread tray, shield-
shaped, Columbia superimposed
against 13 vertical bars, blue,
9½ x 11½", No. 54 . . . . .200.00 to 225.00

Dewey (Admiral) pitcher, bust portrait of Dewey & flagship Olympia reverse, w/mounted cannons, crossed rifles, U.S. & Cuban flags & stacks of cannon balls toward base, clear, 9½" h., No. 400 ..... 82.00

Dewey (Admiral) pitcher, portrait of Dewey within laurel leaves, "Gridley You May Fire When Ready," eagle, w/shield, etc., clear, 9¼" h., No. 401 .... 115.00

Dewey (Admiral) statuette, bust of Dewey, frosted, 5" h., No. 383 ... 55.00

Dewey (Admiral) tumbler, transfer commemorating Manila Bay Battle, clear, 3 5/8" h., No. 397 ..... 48.00

Emblem lamp, applied handle, six shields around bowl, inscribed on metal collar "Pat'd. Apr. 19, 1875. M'ch 21, 1876.," clear, 4" d., 3½" h., No. 63 .... 195.00

Emblem mug, "E Pluribus Unum," shield w/arrows & 13 stars, clear, 2½" d., 5" h., No. 56 .... 60.00

Emblem pickle dish, eagle, shield, arrows & olive branches, clear, 5¾ x 10", No. 58 .... 45.00 to 55.00

Flaming Sword relish dish, sapphire blue, 4¼ x 10", No. 209 ...40.00 to 50.00

Garfield Memorial mug, handled, embossed bust of Garfield, date of birth & death, clear, 2 5/8" h., No. 294 .... 70.00

Garfield plate, frosted bust of Garfield center, 1-0-1 border, clear, 9" d., No. 300 .... 45.00

Garfield Star plate, frosted bust of Garfield center, star border, clear, 6" d., No. 299 .... 35.00

Grant Memorial plate, portrait of Grant center, laurel wreath on stippled border, clear, 10" d., No. 288 .... 55.00

Jones (John Paul) flask, amber, No. 48 .... 20.00

Kitchen stove dish, cov., clear, 4½ x 6¾", 4½" h., No. 149 ...... 150.00

Knights of Labor mug, laborer clasping hands w/bearded man wearing high hat & frock coat, handle w/thumbrest, inscribed "Arbitration," clear, 3" d., 7" h., No. 514 .... 45.00

Lee (Major General Fitzhugh) plate, portrait transfer against a flag background, club border, milk white, 7¼" d., No. 379 .... 44.00

Lind (Jenny) compote, clear bowl w/frosted bust pedestal base, scalloped rim, No. 424 (ILLUS.) ... 145.00

Lind (Jenny) compote, milk white, 8¼" d., 8" h., No. 424 .... 170.00

McKinley tumbler, "Our President

1897-1901," clear, 3¾" h., No. 351 .... 24.00

Moses in the Bulrushes Tray

Moses in the Bulrushes tray, blue opaque, 6 5/8 x 8¾", No. 213 (ILLUS.)..................... 125.00

Moses in the Bulrushes tray, milk white, 6 5/8 x 8¾", No. 213 ....85.00 to 125.00

Old Abe (eagle) butter dish, cov., clear, No. 478 .... 115.00

Old Statehouse tray, shows Independence Hall above "Old Statehouse, Philadelphia, Erected 1735," clear, round, No. 32 ....75.00 to 100.00

Plymouth Rock paperweight, "Mary Chilton was, etc." & "Inkstand Co., Prov., R.I.," clear, No. 19 ....80.00 to 100.00

Preparedness plate, crossed flags center above "Preparedness," wide border w/the figure of a soldier or sailor, two of each, alternating w/a large spreadwinged eagle, clear, 10¾" d. 550.00

Queen Victoria plate, bust of mature Queen superimposed on bust of youthful Queen framed by sunburst, clear, 10" d., No. 435 ...... 60.00

Railroad Train Platter

Railroad train platter, Union Pacific Engine No. 350, clear, 9 x 12", No. 134 (ILLUS.).........95.00 to 115.00

Rock of Ages bread tray, milk white, No. 236 .... 165.00

Roosevelt (Theodore) platter,
portrait center, Teddy bears,
etc., border, clear, 7¾ x 10",
No. 357 .... 155.00
Symbolical platter, Plymouth Rock
"1620," sinking "1776" ship & sun
rising above water & full-rigged
"1876" ship, clear, 9 x 12½",
No. 20 .... 195.00
Three Graces plate, "Faith, Hope &
Charity," clear, 10" d., No. 230 ... 57.00
Three Presidents goblet, frosted
bust portraits of Washington, Lincoln & Garfield framed in medallion settings, clear, 3" d., 6¼" h.,
No. 250 .... 325.00

Three Shields Covered Dish

Three Shields covered dish, shield-
shaped, clear, 5½" w., 8½" l.,
No. 60 (ILLUS.) 170.00
Uncle Sam dish, cov., figure of Uncle Sam sitting on lid, milk white,
3 x 6", 4½" h., No. 112 .... 68.00
Unidentified Lady platter, portrait of
a lady framed in a diamond shape
formed by converging diagonal
lines, further decorated by floral
border in high-relief, milk white,
7½ x 11", No. 453 .... 92.50

HOLLY AMBER

Holly Amber Butter Dish

*Holly Amber, originally marketed under
the name "Golden Agate," was produced for
only a few months in 1903 by the Indiana
Tumbler and Goblet Company of Greentown,
Indiana. When this factory burned in June
1903 all production of this ware ceased, mak-*

*ing it very rare today. The same "Holly"
pressed pattern was also produced in clear
glass by the Greentown factory. Collectors
should note that the St. Clair Glass Company
has reproduced some Holly Amber pieces.*

Bowl, 8½" d. ....$475.00 to 550.00
Butter dish, cov. (ILLUS.) 1,025.00
Compote, cov., 7 3/8" d.,
6½" h.................900.00 to 950.00
Creamer & cov. sugar bowl, pr....1,550.00
Cruet w/original stopper 1,500.00
Relish, oval, footed, 4½ x 7 3/8" ..1,025.00
Sauce dish, 4½" d........225.00 to 250.00
Spooner, w/beaded rim, 3½" d.,
4" h............................. 550.00
Sugar bowl, cov. 1,800.00
Toothpick holder ....350.00 to 375.00
Tumbler, 3 7/8" h. ....225.00 to 250.00

IMPERIAL

*Imperial Glass Company, Bellaire, Ohio,
was organized in 1901 and was in continuous
production, except for very brief periods, until its closing in June 1984. It had been a major producer of Carnival Glass (which see)
earlier in this century and also produced other
types of glass, including an Art Glass line
called "Free Hand Ware" during the 1920's
and its "Jewels" about 1916. The company
acquired a number of molds of other earlier
factories, including the Cambridge and A.H.
Heisey companies, and reissued numerous
items through the years. Also see ANIMALS
under Glass.*

CANDLEWICK PATTERN

Ashtray, w/embossed eagle cen-
ter, No. 400/150, milk white,
5¾" d. $50.00
Bell, No. 400/108, clear, 5" h. 30.00
Bowl, 7" square, No. 400/233,
clear 120.00
Butter dish, cov., California,
No. 400/276, clear 65.00
Candleholders, No. 400/40F, clear,
6" d., pr. 48.00
Candy box, cov., partitioned,
No. 400/110, clear, 7" d......... 140.00
Condiment set: salt & pepper shak-
ers w/chrome tops, vinegar
cruet w/stopper & 8" tray;
No. 400/2769, clear, the set 120.00
Deviled egg server, No. 400/154,
clear, 11½" d. 115.00
Goblet, iced tea or hiball, No. 4000,
clear, 12 oz. 25.00
Ice tub, No. 400/63, clear, 8" d.,
5½" h........................... 155.00
Muddler (drink stirrer), No. 400/19,
clear, 4½" h. 25.00

Nappy, fruit, No. 400/1F, clear,
5" d. 8.00
Parfait, No. 3400, clear, 6 oz. 45.00
Pitcher, juice or cocktail,
No. 400/19, clear, 40 oz. 125.00
Plate, 5½" d., open handles,
No. 400/42D, clear 6.50
Plate, torte, 12½" d., cupped edge,
No. 400/75V, clear 27.50
Plate, 14" d., No. 400/92D, clear
w/gold & silver overlay 80.00
Punch set: 6 qt. bowl, 17" d. under-
plate, twelve cups & ladle; clear,
15 pcs. 225.00
Relish, two-part, No. 400/256, clear,
11" oval 18.00
Seafood icer or fruit cocktail, foot-
ed, No. 3800, clear, 2 pcs. 65.00
Tidbit set, two-tier, No. 400/2701,
green 375.00
Tumbler, juice, low foot, one bead,
No. 3400, clear, 5 oz. 20.00
Vase, bud, 8½" h., footed,
No. 400/28C, clear 45.00

CAPE COD PATTERN

Basket, handled, No. 160/40, clear,
11" h. 100.00
Bowl, finger, 4" d., No. 1604½A,
clear 12.50
Bowl, 10" oval, No. 160/221, clear . . 85.00
Claret, stemmed, No. 1602, clear,
5 oz. 9.50
Cruet w/original stopper,
No. 160/70, clear, 5 oz. 38.00
Horseradish bottle w/original stop-
per, No. 160/226, clear, 5 oz. 57.50
Pepper mill, No. 160/236, clear 35.00
Pitcher w/ice lip, No. 160/19, clear,
40 oz. 57.50
Plate, 13" d., birthday w/72 candle
holes, No. 160/72, clear 195.00
Relish, three-part, No. 160/55, clear,
9½" oval 27.00
Salt & pepper shakers w/original
tops, footed, No. 160/116, clear,
pr. 16.00
Tray, pastry, center handle,
No. 400/68D, amber, 11" d. 85.00
Tumbler, juice, footed, No. 1602,
amber, 6 oz. 12.00
Tumbler, water, footed, No. 1602,
clear, 10 oz. 7.00

FREE HAND WARE

Vase, 6" h., spherical, iridized
green leaf & vine design, orange
interior, "Free Hand Made in USA
Im-Pe-Ri-Al" label 412.50
Vase, 6¼" h., decorated in irides-
cent peacock bluish green & aubergine, signed "Imperial" 60.00
Vase, 6 5/8" h., 4 1/8" d., ovoid
body tapering to a short neck

w/flattened flaring rim, oyster
white iridescent body decorated
w/green hearts & vines, deep
bronze interior 325.00
Vase, 8½" h., cylindrical, white
opal body decorated w/yellow
drag loops, orange iridescent
interior 175.00
Vase, 9" h., orange iridescent
ground w/gold drag loops 179.00
Vase, 11¼" h., tall slender ovoid
body tapering slightly to a flared
rim, glossy cobalt blue exterior
w/white hearts & random vine
decoration, orange iridescent
interior 550.00

MISCELLANEOUS PATTERNS & LINES

Animal covered dish, duck, brown
slag, 4½" 45.00
Animal covered dish, lion on lacy
base, purple slag 175.00
Animal covered dish, owl on basket
base, caramel slag 125.00

IOWA CITY GLASS

This ware, made by the Iowa City Glass Manufacturing Co., Iowa City, Iowa, from 1880 to about 1883, was produced in many shapes and patterns. The Frosted Stork pattern and pieces decorated with mottos and various animals are probably best known among collectors.

ABC plate, Frosted Stork center, al-
phabet border $60.00
Bread plate, round, "Elaine," 1-0-1
border, frosted center 95.00
Goblet, Paneled Sage patt., clear . . . 125.00
Platter, oval, "Be Industrious," clear
beehive center, plain border 75.00

JACK-IN-THE-PULPIT VASES

Glass vases in varying sizes and resembling in appearance the flower of this name have been popular with collectors since the 19th century. They were produced in various solid colors and in shaded wares.

Cased, Bristol white exterior decorated w/dainty blue, pink & yellow flowers & green leaves,
shaded pink rim, squatty bulbous
base, 4 5/8" d., 5 5/8" h. $85.00
Cased, creamy exterior, tomato red
interior, ruffled top w/tri-lobed
base, embossed swirl design,
3¾" d., 4¼" h. 125.00

Cased, white exterior, green interi-
or, bulbous base w/petal-form
top, applied clear petal feet,
5¾" d., 7" h. 95.00
Cased, white exterior, shaded green
interior, 5" d., 8" h. 85.00
Cranberry w/applied clear ruffled
edging around the rim & squatty
bulbous base, 5¾" d., 5½" h. 185.00
Cranberry w/white opaque wavy
embedded threading, slender
trumpet-form w/crimped rim,
4½" d., 7¾" h. 135.00
Emerald green w/cream & brown
swirls, tapering cylindrical base
w/slightly ruffled rim, 2½"
base d., 6½" h., pr. 200.00
Orange w/spiral twist at base of
slender trumpet-form body, applied vaseline petal-shaped rim &
applied vaseline feet, 2¾" d.,
7 1/8" h. 85.00
Spangled, white, green & purple
spatter w/silver mica flecks,
tapering cylindrical base w/flaring
rim, 4¼" d., 7" h. 85.00
Spatter, slender trumpet-form body
on a squatty foot, maroon & white
spatter w/applied vaseline
opalescent curled five-petal top,
5¾" d., 11" h. 95.00

KELVA

Kelva was made early in this century by the C.F. Monroe Co., Meriden, Connecticut, and was a type of decorated opal glass very like the same company's Wave Crest and Nakara wares. This type of glass was produced until about the time of the first World War. Also see NAKARA and WAVE CREST.

Box w/hinged lid, pink flowers on
blue-grey ground, mirror in lid,
4½" d. $515.00
Box w/hinged lid, h.p. rose & white
orchids, 5" d., 2½" h. 425.00
Box w/hinged lid, pink ground
w/enameled blue & white daisies
decoration, set on ormolu footed
frame, 5½" d., 4" h. 650.00
Box w/hinged lid, pink hibiscus
flowers & green leaves on a deep
green mottled background,
7¾" d., 3½" h. 650.00
Toothpick holder, robin's egg blue
ground decorated w/h.p. pink &
white daisies & white dotted
rim 225.00
Vase, 14½" h., mottled green

ground w/h.p. bright pink & white
flowers, on ormolu footed base &
ornate ormolu handles, signed ... 850.00

LACY

Lacy Glass is a general term developed by collectors many years ago to cover the earliest type of pressed glass produced in this country. "Lacy" refers to the fact that most of these early patterns consisted of scrolls and geometric designs against a finely stippled background which gives the glass the look of fine lace. Formerly this glass was often referred to as "Sandwich" for the Boston & Sandwich Glass Company of Sandwich, Massachusetts which produced a great deal of this ware. Today, however, collectors realize that many other factories on the East Coast and in the Pittsburgh, Pennsylvania and Wheeling, West Virginia areas also made lacy glass from the 1820's into the 1840's. All pieces listed are clear unless otherwise noted. Numbers after salt dips refer to listings in Pressed Glass Salt Dishes of the Lacy Period, 1825-1850, *by Logan W. and Dorothy B. Neal. Also see SANDWICH GLASS.*

Bowl, 7½" d., low, scalloped rim,
Rayed Peacock Eye patt. $210.00
Compote, open, 7 3/8" d., 3 5/8" h.,
flaring rim on a shallow rounded
bowl, applied wafer & knob stem
on lacy foot, Peacock Eye patt. 495.00
Dish, round w/scalloped hairpin pattern rim & an octagonal center
w/small diamonds around a four-
petal blossom in the middle,
5¾" d. (minor chips) 49.50
Plate, 6" d., Hairpin patt., clear 80.00
Plate, 6" d., Shell patt., clear 160.00
Plate, 7" d., Rayed Peacock Eye
patt., clear 95.00
Plate, 8" d., band of diamonds
around the rim & another band
around the center, six-point star &
leaves in the middle, clear, Pittsburgh, ca. 1840 (some usual rim
flaking) 93.50
Plate, 9¼" d., early Roman Rosette
patt., fiery opalescent, ca. 1840 .. 715.00
Salt dip, boat-shaped, model of an
early sidewheeler w/"Lafayette" on
each side & "Sandwich" inside &
"B.&S. Glass Co." on stern, Boston
& Sandwich Glass Co., deep cobalt blue, ca. 1840 (minor flaking,
two shallow chips on stern) 485.00
Salt dip, boat-shaped, model of an
early sidewheeler w/"Lafayet" on
each side & "Sandwich" on inside
& the base & "B.&S. Glass Co." on
stern, Boston & Sandwich Glass

Co., opaque lavender blue, ca.
1840 (usual base & rim flaking) ... 797.50

Salt dip, boat-shaped, model of an
early sidewheeler w/"Pittsburgh"
on the stern, cobalt blue, ca. 1840
(stress crack on side) 385.00

Salt dip, deep rounded oblong sides
w/scalloped rim, large scrolls
flanking six-point stars on the
sides, on a short flared foot,
medium amethyst, ca. 1840 (some
minor rim flaking) 632.50

Salt dip, rectangular casket-shape
w/flared sides, on small knob
feet, Grecian horses & chariot
w/cornucopia design on sides,
opaque powder blue, ca. 1840
(several small edge flakes) 522.50

Salt dip, sleigh-shaped, raised
standing American eagle at each
corner looking over its shoulder,
American shield at the center of
the sides, on scrolled feet, medium fiery opalescent, ca. 1840 .... 357.50

Salt dip, wagon-shaped, deep rectangular sides on small molded
wheels, a diamond in a panel
flanked by stars on the sides,
clear, WN-1 (chips) 30.00

Sauce dish, early Roman Rosette
patt., light opalescent clear, ca.
1850, 3½" d. 77.00

Sugar bowl, cov., Gothic Arch patt.,
attributed to Boston & Sandwich
Glass Co., clear 140.00

Sugar bowl, cov., octagonal, footed,
Gothic Arch patt., turquoise blue,
ca. 1840 (small flaking on lid).... 1,210.00

Toddy plate, American eagle &
shield in center, scrolls & leaves
border, deep brilliant cobalt blue,
ca. 1840, 4 3/8" d. 522.50

Toddy plate, Harp patt., brilliant
sapphire blue, ca. 1840, 4½" d. .. 275.00

Tray, rectangular w/cut corners,
Pineapple Gothic patt., 9" l. (minor chips) 170.50

Whiskey taster, cylindrical body on
a low foot, a band of shields centering oval buttons, canary yellow, attributed to the Boston &
Sandwich Glass Co., ca. 1840
(small chips & roughage around
foot) 82.50

LALIQUE

*Fine glass, which includes numerous ex-
traordinary molded articles, has been made
by the glasshouse established by Rene' Lalique early in this century in France. The firm
was carried on by his son, Marc, until his
death in 1977 and is now headed by Marc's
daughter, Marie-Claude. All Lalique glass is
marked, usually on, or near, the bottom with
either an engraved or molded signature. Unless otherwise noted, we list only those pieces
marked "R. Lalique" produced before the
death of Rene' Lalique in 1945.*

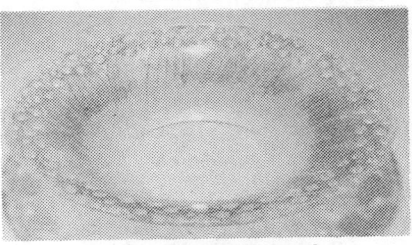

Lalique Console Bowl

Atomizer, "Le Parisien," cylindrical
body, molded w/a procession of
women in diaphanous gowns,
trimmed in amber patina, molded
"R. LALIQUE MADE IN FRANCE,"
6" h. $715.00

Beverage set: six tumblers & an
18" d. tray; "Setubal," each tumbler w/flaring clear sides above a
frosted bulbous base molded w/a
leaf & berry design, the clear tray
w/frosted leaf & berry-molded tab
handles, each piece marked "R.
Lalique," the set 770.00

Book ends, "Tete d'Aigle," molded
as the head of an eagle fitting
into a circular domed-metal mount
attached to a rectangular black
glass base, grey, each molded "R.
LALIQUE," bases acid-stamped "R.
LALIQUE - FRANCE," ca. 1928,
5¼" h., pr. (beak & eyebrow on
one chipped, chips to bases) 3,300.00

Bowl, 8½" d., "Volubilis," the shallow opalescent bowl molded on
the underside w/three large
round feathered & ribbed discs
forming the short feet, raised
mark "R. Lalique" 330.00

Bowl, 12 3/8" d., "Rosace," shallow
body in deep cobalt blue molded
w/graduated rows of raised triangles, raised on four triangular
feet, acid-stamped "R. LALIQUE
FRANCE," introduced in 1930 .... 4,400.00

Box, cov., "Cleones," round w/low
domical cover molded on the interior w/scarabs randomly placed
among foliage, amber, molded "R.
LALIQUE," ca. 1921, 6 5/8" d.... 1,650.00

Box, cov., "Saint-Nectaire," hexagonal, the cover molded w/a design of swirled fern-like leaves
w/grey-green patination, en-

graved "R. LALIQUE FRANCE,"
3 3/8" w. 880.00
Bracelet, "Poussins," comprised of
11 half-cylindrical pieces, each
molded w/chicks' heads, trimmed
w/grey patina, elasticized, engraved "R. Lalique France,"
1" w. 605.00
Candlesticks, the standard molded
w/a blossoming wreath w/a pair
of birds inside, on a six-sided
foot, clear, engraved "Lalique
France," 6½" h., pr. 605.00
Charger, "Sirenes," footed, frosted
clear circular form molded w/a
sinuous nude maiden amid the
surf, blue patina, molded "R.LA-
LIQUE," 14½" d. 3,080.00
Clock, "Dahlia," the pentagonal case
molded on the obverse w/stylized
flower blossom, the petals edged
in black enamel, frosted, inscribed "R. LALIQUE FRANCE,"
clock face signed "ATO - PRIEUR -
BREST," introduced in 1926,
6¾" h. (chip to top back edge) . . 2,200.00
Console bowl, low widely flaring
sides molded w/lily-of-the-valley
blossoms & leaves radiating from
the center, opalescent w/blue
patination, stamped "R. LALIQUE
FRANCE," base slightly polished,
12½" d. (ILLUS.) 1,760.00
Cordials, frosted clear, the stems
molded w/berries on curling vine,
each engraved "R. Lalique
France," 3½" h., set of 12 . . . . 935.00
Decanters w/tall pointed stoppers,
"Vigne Strie'," clear frosted slightly rounded conical form w/a narrow neck & high flared rim,
molded w/vertical delicate stringing, the neck w/a band molded
w/berried vines, matching stopper, inscribed "R. Lalique," stopper molded "LALIQUE," ca. 1920,
12" h., pr. (chips) 2,200.00
Figure, "Cote D'Azur," modeled as a
nude maiden w/arched back &
flowing tresses on a raised base,
pale champagne tint, molded
"COTE D'AZUR PULLMAN EXPRESS
- 9 DECEMBRE 1929" & w/mono-
grams "WL" & "PML," inscribed
"R. Lalique," introduced 1929,
6½" h. 5,720.00
Hood ornament, figural, "Chrysis,"
frosted nude woman on her knees
& arched backward w/her arms &
flowing hair trailing back, on a
round pedestal base, signed in
block letters "R. Lalique France,"
ca. 1928, 5¼" h. 2,200.00

Hood ornament, "Victoire," frosted
& clear model of a woman's head
w/streaming stylized hair, mounted in original metal radiator
cap & on a black stepped plinth,
molded "R.LALIQUE FRANCE,"
9¼" h. 9,900.00
Inkwell, "Quatre Sirenes," the flat-
tened domical body molded on
the interior w/four mermaids in
various poses, w/small domical
lid, frosted grey, molded "LA-
LIQUE," introduced 1920, 6¼" d.,
1¾" h. 1,725.00
Lamp, table-type, "Bague Person-
nages," the inverted conical shade
& trumpet-form base w/slightly
ribbed sides centering a band
molded in high-relief w/nude female figures cavorting in a bower, grey patina, introduced in
1913, inscribed "R. Lalique France"
at a later date, 18½" h. 19,800.00
Lemonade set: spherical pitcher,
eight glasses & a circular handled
tray; "Setubal," each piece in pale
amber molded overall w/knobby
fruits among leafy branches, each
piece marked, tray 18 1/8" l., the
set 4,830.00

Lalique Wall Mirror

Mirror, wall-type, circular, "Eglantine," the mirror plate framed by
six curved sections molded w/a
profusion of poppy blossoms &
stems interrupted by narrow metal sections cast w/overlapping
rays, frosted clear, inscribed "R.
Lalique," 17 1/8" (ILLUS.) 5,175.00
Model of lovebirds, "Deux Tour-
telles," cast in full-relief in yellow
& blue tinged opalescence, the
entwined birds perched on a
flower-strewn circular base, inscribed "R. Lalique," introduced in
1925, 4 5/8" h. 1,320.00
Panel, "Figurine et Raisins Tete Lev-
ee," the rectangular panel molded

Lalique Frosted Glass Panel

in low-relief w/a nude maiden
w/clusters of grapes & coiling
vines, frosted clear, introduced
in 1928, unsigned, framed,
6¼ x 18¼" (ILLUS.) 5,463.00
Paperweight, "St. Christophe," a
thin upright disc intaglio-molded &
frosted w/a design of a stooped
St. Christopher carrying the Christ
Child, on a small round foot,
4½" h. 715.00
Perfume bottle w/stopper, "Cigalia,"
tapering rectangular bottle molded w/a frosted clear winged cica-
da at each corner, the lozenge-
shaped stopper molded w/stylized
branches, clear ground, in original
decorated wooden box, 5¼" h. . . 7,700.00
Perfume bottle, "Telline," molded
in relief as a clam shell, 4" h. . . .1,045.00
Plaque, commemorative, circular,
molded w/the profile of Louis
Pasteur enhanced by grey patina,
molded signature "R. LALIQUE" &
"LOUIS PASTEUR," in original
fitted box, ca. 1922, 4" d. 920.00
Plates, ice cream, 7½" d., "Ricque-
wihr," clear decorated w/a molded garland of grapes, etched
signature "R. LALIQUE," set
of 17 . . . . 440.00
Plate, 10¾" d., "Ondines," round,
molded around the middle w/a
band of languorous nude females
in waves, clear opalescent, engraved "R. LALIQUE FRANCE" 1,210.00
Powder box, cov., "Chantilly," circular w/a central clear cabochon on
the cover, surrounded by a design
of deer amid foliage, frosted
clear, molded "R. LALIQUE,"
3 5/8" d. 575.00
Vase, 5½" h., "Canard," ovoid body
tapering to a widely flared rim,

molded w/spiraling bands each
w/graduated rows of ducks, frosted amber, stenciled "R. LALIQUE
FRANCE". .1,650.00
Vase, 9½" h., "Borromee," wide
ovoid body tapering to a flared
rim, frosted blue molded on the
upper half w/an array of peacock
heads w/white patination in the
recessed areas, stamped "R. LA-
LIQUE FRANCE" 16,500.00
Vase, 11 3/8" h., "Gros Scarabees,"
large ovoid body molded in low-
relief w/large scarab beetles,
frosted deep amber w/pale
opaque patina, molded "R. LA-
LIQUE," inscribed "France," in-
troduced 1923 . . . . .9,320.00
Wax letter seal, "Aigles," molded as
a seated eagle on a square base,
frosted clear, engraved signature
"R. Lalique France No. 175,"
3½" h. 1,650.00

LEGRAS

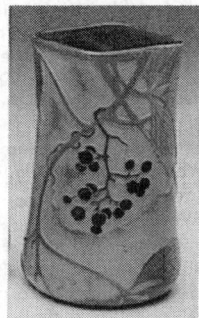

Legras Cameo Vase

*Cameo and enameled glass somewhat simi-
lar to that made by Galle', Daum Nancy and
other factories of the period was made at the
Legras works in Saint Denis, France, late last
century and until the outbreak of World
War I.*

Box, cov., round w/gently tapering sides & a low domed cover,
enameled around the sides w/a
winter landscape w/barren trees,
birds & snow-covered ground,
signed, 5" d. $385.00
Cameo bowl, 7" d., 4¾" h., a wide
& deep base tapering up to a
widely flaring shallow & incurved
rim, opaque white overlaid w/am-
ber & cameo-cut w/clusters of
broad leaves further enameled &
polished in green & reddish am-
ber, cameo mark "Legras SD" 715.00

Cameo vase, 6 5/8" h., cylindrical body w/squared rim, fiery amber layered in opaque opal, cameo-carved & enameled w/leafy stems & berry clusters, signed "Legras SD" (ILLUS.).................... 770.00

Cameo vase, 7" h., tall slender cylindrical body tapering to a small, flat rim, opaque white overlaid in amber & acid-etched overall w/mistletoe leaves & berries, decorated w/naturalistic enameled trim, cameo signature "Legras S+D".................. 495.00

Cameo vase, 21¼" h., ovoid, opalescent splashed w/deep umber & cased within clear, acid-etched about the upper section w/seagulls in flight, the design rubbed w/dark brown stain, signed in cameo "Legras," ca. 1930.......................1,035.00

Vase, 6" h., a cylindrical body flaring at the foot, clear painted w/a continuous landscape of tall black trees against an orange sky above snow-covered ground, signed 357.50

Vase, 15¾" h., tall ovoid body tapering to a short flared neck, enameled overall w/a continuous winter landscape of tall trees against a sunset-colored ground, signed on the side 990.00

Vase, 25½" h., gourd-form, grey cut w/a spray of berry-laden leafy branches enameled in burgundy, signed in enamel cameo "Legras," ca. 1925 ....1,320.00

LE VERRE FRANCAIS

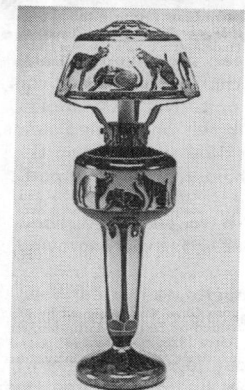

Le Verre Francais Cameo Lamp

This glass was made in France by Charles Schneider and fairly large quantities of the

cameo ware were exported to the United States in the early part of this century. Much of it was sold by Ovingtons, New York City. See SCHNEIDER for further details on this company.

Cameo bowl, 6½" h., squat bulbous body in frosted mottled yellow & orange overlaid in orange & etched to depict stylized oleander branches, cameo signature "Charder" & etched "Le Verre Francais" $1,380.00

Cameo bowl, 14" d., 10" h., footed conical form on a circular foot, orange overlaid in burgundy to orange, etched w/long stems & stylized blossoms, signed "Le Verre Francais - France" 825.00

Cameo box, cov., compressed circular base & domed cover surmounted w/a purple ball handle, grey walls mottled in sunshine yellow & pumpkin, overlaid in tomato red shading to burgundy & decorated w/thistle blossoms & leafage, signed in cameo "Charder," acid-stamped "Le Verre Francais" & "FRANCE," ca. 1925, 7" d. 1,210.00

Cameo lamp, table model, the 7" d. helmet-form shade in mottled lemon yellow & Chinese red overlaid in aubergine & cut w/a frieze of cats in various stances, the top w/cut brickwork, the baluster-form footed base w/bulging shoulder cut w/a similar frieze band, wrought-iron mounts, overall 17½" h. (ILLUS.) 3,738.00

Cameo vase, 10¼" h., flared cylindrical form on a knopped circular foot, mottled white overlaid in red & green, etched w/stylized palmettes, engraved "Le Verre Francais" & signed in cameo "Charder" & etched "FRANCE" 825.00

Cameo vase, 12¼" h., thick cushion foot narrowing to a short stem supporting the tall ovoid body w/a short, narrow flared rim, mottled & shaded white to aqua blue overlaid in orange shading to royal blue at the base & cut w/a continuous band of variously sized flying butterflies around the top half, inscribed "Le Verre Francais" on the foot & "France - Ovington" on the base 1,430.00

Cameo vase, 14½" h., conical body on knopped circular foot, mottled amber ground overlaid w/mottled cinnabar, etched w/pendant pods & branches, engraved "Le Verre Francais" & etched "FRANCE" 880.00

Cameo vase, 16½" h., Art Deco
style, a thick cushion foot & short
pedestal supporting the tall ovoid
body tapering to a flaring neck,
yellow & orange overlaid in bright
blue shading to orange & cut w/a
continuous design of suspended
stylized large blossoms, leaves &
vines, signed 935.00

Cameo *veilleuse* (night light),
peaked-form, pale blue overlaid
in darker blue, etched w/balloon-
like blossoms, engraved signature
"Le Verre Francais - France," on a
wrought-iron base, 7" h. 990.00

Vase, 10" h., topaz w/etched pine
cones decoration, signed "Char-
der," ca. 1930. . . . . 330.00

LIBBEY

Maize Pattern Celery Vase

In 1878, William L. Libbey obtained a lease
on the New England Glass Company of Cambridge, Massachusetts, changing the name to
the New England Glass Works, W.L. Libbey
and Son, Proprietors. After his death in 1883,
his son, Edward D. Libbey, continued to operate the company at Cambridge until 1888
when the factory was closed. Edward Libbey
moved to Toledo, Ohio, and set up the company subsequently known as Libbey Glass
Co. During the 1880's, the firm's master tech-
nician, Joseph Locke, developed the now
much desired colored art glass lines of Aga-
ta, Amberina, Peach Blow and Pomona. Renowned for its Cut Glass of the Brilliant
Period (see CUT GLASS), the company continues in operation today as Libbey Glassware, a division of Owens-Illinois, Inc.

Candlesticks, Silhouette patt., clear
cup, opalescent figural camel
stem, pr. $300.00

Champagne, fluted rim, Amberina . . 280.00

Champagne, Silhouette patt., clear
bowl, opalescent figural rabbit
stem 95.00

Champagne, Silhouette patt., clear
bowl, opalescent figural squirrel
stem 85.00

Cordials, clear deep ovoid bowl on
a tall slender stem w/a jade
green knop just above the clear
foot, Libbey-Nash series, engraved Empire patt., each marked
w/"Libbey" in a circle, 5" h., set
of 8 . . . . 385.00

Maize bowl, 9" d., 3½" h., creamy
opaque w/green leaves 210.00

Maize celery vase, clear w/amber
iridescent kernels & blue husks
(ILLUS.). 170.00

Maize celery vase, creamy opaque
w/green husks . . . . .150.00 to 175.00

Maize finger bowl, creamy opaque
w/yellow husks outlined in gold . . 165.00

Maize salt shaker w/original top,
creamy opaque w/green husks . . . 125.00

Plates, 8½" d., cut leaf design,
signed, set of 8 . . . . 295.00

Sherbet, Silhouette patt., clear
bowl, black figural rabbit
stem. .75.00 to 100.00

Sherbet, Silhouette patt., clear
bowl, opalescent figural squirrel
stem, 4" h. 95.00

American Prestige Stemware

Stemware set: seventeen goblets,
wines & champagnes; American
Prestige patt. (No. 7000 Line),
rounded bowls on paneled stems,
clear, ca. 1942 (ILLUS. of part). . . . 330.00

Toothpick holder, Little Lobe patt.,
clear 100.00

Vase, 9¼" h., applied clear handles, clear w/fuchsia engraving,
signed 150.00

Wine, Silhouette patt., clear bowl,
opalescent figural cat stem,
6" h. 95.00

Wine, Silhouette patt., clear bowl,
opalescent figural kangaroo stem,
6" h. 95.00

Wine, Silhouette patt., clear bowl,
opalescent figural polar bear
stem, 6" h. 125.00

LOETZ

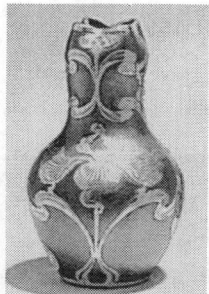

Loetz Vase with Silver Overlay

Iridescent glass, some of it somewhat resembling that of Tiffany and other contemporary glasshouses, was produced by the Bohemian firm of J. Loetz Witwe of Klostermule and is referred to as Loetz. Some cameo pieces were also made. Not all pieces are marked.

Bowl, 9½" d., deep ovoid body w/a wide ruffled rim, pink iridescence w/raised, pulled & trailed decoration in iridescent blue, gold & purple $880.00

Bowl-vase, paperweight-type, compressed bulbous form w/short neck & everted rim, clear walls decorated on the interior w/rich tangerine & on the exterior w/trailings in silvery mint green shading to a deep lime green, unsigned, ca. 1900, 3 1/8" h. 3,520.00

Cameo vase, 7¼" h., cylindrical base flaring to a wider cylindrical top section, clear overlaid in amethyst & etched w/a linear design w/stylized floral designs, the ground w/a 'rough' finish, designed by Josef Hoffmann, cameo signature "Loetz" (small chip on base) 7,150.00

Cameo vase, 17" h., tall cylindrical shape slightly tapering at the rim, bronze ground overlaid in pale green iridescence, etched pine cone & branch decoration 750.00

Decanter w/bulbous pointed stopper, the trumpet-form tall neck flaring down to a squatty bulbous body, ruby red decorated w/silvery blue oil spottings & set within an intricate foliate silver framework cast w/irises amid tall grasses & w/a "BG" monogram, the stopper completely overlaid in silver, inscribed "1/10," ca. 1900, 10¾" h. 3,080.00

Model of a stork, the body in yellow iridescence, the beak & wings in purple iridescence, on a circular textured base, signed "Loetz Austria," ca. 1904, 19¼" h. (base restored) 825.00

Perfume bottle w/stopper, ovoid body tapering to a short flared neck, cobalt blue w/gold iridized spotted surface, the rim overlaid w/a silver band & the bulbous stopper overlaid w/silver in an embossed floral design, silver marked "Sterling," 6½" h. 550.00

Vase, miniature, 2¾" h., wide ovoid body tapering to a flared wide rim, gold w/an iridescent spotted surface, decorated w/a silver overlay engraved scrolling foliate Art Nouveau design 467.50

Vase, 4" h., 6" d., wide flat-bottomed domed form w/a pinched & folded tricorner rim & deeply indented sides, cobalt blue w/pulled metallic silvery gold iridized ribbons, inscribed on the pontil "Loetz Austria" 1,430.00

Vase, 4¾" h., a conical body tapering to a short flared neck, cased blue decorated w/silver & green iridescent waves & overlaid w/openwork silver in a lily-of-the-valley design 3,220.00

Vase, 4¾" h., squatty lozenge-shaped body tapering to a small conforming flaring neck, iridescent peach decorated w/iridescent blue waves & serrated lines, marked 3,300.00

Vase, 5" h., ovoid w/pulled scrolling lip, olive green decorated w/silvery blue iridescent damascene trailings, inscribed "Loetz - Austria," ca. 1900 ....2,475.00

Vase, 5½" h., pyriform w/indented sides, rich lemon yellow iridescence decorated w/silvery blue, purple & lavender drippings, trailings & bosses, inscribed "Loetz - Austria," ca. 1900 ....3,850.00

Vase, 5¾" h., double conical form w/bulbous neck, pale amber decorated w/trailings in watermelon pink, silvery blue, ochre & black iridescence, overlaid w/silver whiplash devices, inscribed "Phen - 733 - 358 - A," ca. 1900 ..2,200.00

Vase, 6¼" h., bulbous body tapering to a cylindrical neck w/quatrefoil mouth, blue iridescent overlaid w/an overall sinuous floral design in silver (ILLUS.) 880.00

Vase, 6¼" h., footed bulbous body w/elongated neck, dark red w/iridescent blue decoration & overlaid w/silver flowering designs 825.00

Vase, 9" h., beaker-shaped conical body, silver iridescent waves on a salmon ground & applied w/five spiraling striped iridescent trailing drips, engraved "Loetz Austria" . . 8,800.00

Vase, 9 3/8" h., footed trumpet-form body w/rounded sides flaring to a flat everted rim, deep cobalt blue streaked overall w/silvery blue iridescence 1,760.00

Vase, 9 7/8" h., tall cylindrical form flaring outward at foot & mouth, deep blue decorated w/iridescent green in a pulled & trailed design 770.00

Vase, 10¼" h., swelled tapering double gourd-form body w/a cushion foot, violet ground decorated w/striated rainbow iridescent spots 1,870.00

Vase, 11" h., conical base & long slender cylindrical neck, lime green decorated w/silvery blue, amber & purple iridescent loopings & trailings, engraved crossed arrows factory mark & signed, ca. 1899 . . . . 4,840.00

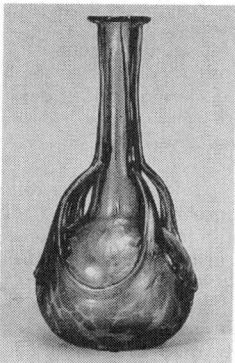

Unusual Loetz Vase

Vase, 12" h., bottle-form, bulbous base tapering to a tall slender cylindrical neck w/flared rim, the bottom overlaid w/another layer pulled up into four loop handles which attach to the base of the neck & trail up its sides, iridescent deep amber ground decorated w/blue-green iridescent oil spot design, signed (ILLUS.) 12,750.00

Vase, 12½" h., tall slender tapering double-gourd form w/everted rim, iridescent rose decorated w/striated silver rainbow iridescent spots, ca. 1902 . . . . 2,420.00

Vase, 14½" h., spherical base w/indented sides below a tall swelling & waisted neck w/a peaked tre-

foil rim, deep cobalt blue ground streaked overall w/silvery blue iridescence 2,420.00

LUSTRES

Bohemian Glass Lustres

Lustres are glass vase-like decorative vessels with prisms, designed to hold candles and intended as mantel and tabletop decorative adjuncts.

Blue opaque, cylindrical bowl w/scalloped rim, decorated w/gold enameled florals, hung w/faceted prisms, 9" h., pr. $225.00

Clear, cut overall in strawberry diamond & fan, hung w/6" l. notch-cut prisms, 6" d., 10½" h., pr. . . . 1,800.00

Cranberry, tulip-shaped bowl, decorated w/enameled daisies, blue bells & dotting, gold trim, hung w/a double row of spear-point prisms, 14" h., pr. 495.00

Pigeon blood, deep flaring bowl w/gently scalloped rim, raised on a pedestal base w/a large bulbous knop above the stepped, domed foot, the bowl decorated w/bands of fine dots dividing it into four panels each decorated w/clusters of blossomheads, gilt trim, hung w/clear facet-cut prisms, 19th c., 14" h., pr. 253.00

Pink, short & wide cylindrical shouldered bowl w/a flaring, slightly scalloped rim, raised on a waisted pedestal base w/flaring cushion foot, enameled decoration, hung w/facet-cut clear prisms, 19th c., 12¼" h., pr. 319.00

Pink, cylindrical bowl w/scalloped & flaring rim, raised on a footed cylindrical standard, enameled w/blue, white & gold floral decoration, hung w/a double row of spear-point prisms, 15¼" h., pr. . . . 910.00

Ruby-flashed cut to clear, the bowl raised on a baluster-form stan-

dard w/a circular foot, cut w/oval
& scroll designs, hung w/facet-
cut prisms, Bohemia, 19th c.,
12½" h., pr. 247.50
White opaque, flaring vase-form
w/scalloped rim, decorated overall w/small gold flowers, hung
w/5" l. spear-point prisms, overall
10" h., pr. 225.00
White opaque cut to emerald green,
lobed bowl w/scalloped rim above
a slender stem & flaring foot,
decorated w/enameled florals &
gilt trim, hung w/facet-cut spear-
point prisms, Bohemia, the tallest
13" h., set of 3 (ILLUS.) 1,540.00

MARY GREGORY

Glass enameled in white with silhouette-type figures, primarily children, is now termed "Mary Gregory" and was attributed to the Boston and Sandwich Glass Company. However, recent research has proven conclusively that this ware was not decorated by Mary Gregory nor was it made at the Sandwich factory. Miss Gregory was employed by the Boston and Sandwich Glass Company as a decorator, however, records show her assignment was the painting of naturalistic landscape scenes on larger items such as lamps and shades but never the charming children for which her name has become synonymous. Further, in the inspection of fragments from the factory site, no paintings of children were found.

It is now known that all wares now called "Mary Gregory" originated in Bohemia beginning in the late 19th century and were extensively exported to England and the U.S. well into this century.

For further information see The Glass Industry in Sandwich, Volume 4, by Raymond E. Barlow and Joan E. Kaiser, and the new book, Mary Gregory Glassware, 1880-1990, by R. & D. Truitt.

Box w/hinged lid, lime green, white
enameled young boy w/sprig
of flowers on lid, 3 1/8" d.,
2 1/8" h. $145.00
Box w/hinged lid, lime green, white
enameled young boy w/hat &
fishing pole sitting on tree limb
on lid, 5" d., 3" h. 245.00
Box w/hinged lid, golden amber,
white enameled young girl on lid,
ornate ormolu footed base, 4" d.,
4½" h. 365.00
Box w/hinged lid, footed, amber,
white enameled young child
w/hat sitting on a fence on lid,
brass feet & side ring handles,
4¼" d., 4½" h. 395.00

Butter dish, cov., clear, white
enameled boy kneeling by the
water's edge on cover 50.00
Carafe, water, cranberry, white
enameled boy, 11" h. 275.00
Creamer, cylindrical w/applied
clear handle, cranberry, white
enameled young girl, 2 1/8" d.,
3 5/8" h. 225.00
Cruet w/original stopper, clear,
white enameled young boy fish-
ing, 5½" h. 275.00
Cruet w/original clear bubble stop-
per, cranberry, Inverted Thumbprint patt., white enameled young
girl w/balloon by fence, 3 3/8" d.,
7½" h. 350.00
Cruet w/original amber bubble stop-
per, amber, w/applied amber
handle, white enameled young
boy, 3" d., 9¼" h. 250.00
Cup, cranberry, white enameled
young girl, 3½" h. 90.00
Dresser bottle w/original facet-cut
stopper, footed ovoid body tapering to a tall cylindrical ringed
neck, golden amber, white enam-
eled young boy, 2¾" d., 9" h. 185.00
Dresser tray, oval, ribbed edge,
lime green, white enameled
young girl & boy, 7 7/8" w.,
10½" l. 245.00
Ewer, cobalt blue, w/applied clear
handle & wafer foot, white enameled little girl in garden holding
roses, 6" h. 195.00
Lamp, table, kerosene-type, black
footed baluster-form base
w/white enameled girl carrying a
basket of flowers, clear shade
w/acid-cut decoration, original
chimney & brass fittings, 6½" d.,
20¼" h. 850.00
Liqueur set: 8½" h., 3 3/8" d., bul-
bous amber bottle-shaped decanter w/applied amber handle &
original teardrop-shaped amber
stopper, four 1 3/8" d., 1 7/8" h.
amber liqueur mugs w/applied
amber handles & a 9 1/8" d. amber tray; white enameled young
girl decorates the decanter & one
mug & white enameled young boy
decorates three mugs, 6 pcs. 525.00
Lustres, cylindrical bowl w/ruffled
rim, cranberry, white enameled
facing pair of girls, one holding a
flower & the other holding up her
apron, colorful flowers surround
both girls, white florals decorate
the rim, six 4½" l. prisms, overall
10¼" h., pr. 2,025.00
Mug, barrel-shaped w/applied am-
ber handle, golden amber, white

enameled young boy holding flowers, 3" d., 4¼" h. 85.00
Pitcher, 8¾" h., applied clear handle, clear, white enameled girl standing in a garden 125.00
Plate, 8½" d., cobalt blue, white enameled girl w/umbrella surrounded by delicate foliage & a gold rim 165.00
Syrup pitcher w/original lid, hourglass shape w/applied clear handle, clear, white enameled girl in flowing dress standing in foliage 225.00
Tumbler, juice, tapering cylindrical shape, champagne iridescent, white enameled young girl w/small basket, 2 3/8" d., 3¾" h. 50.00
Tumbler, barrel-shaped, sapphire blue, white enameled young girl standing under a canopy, 2½" d., 4¼" h. 55.00
Tumbler, cylindrical, Optic patt., amber, white enameled girl carrying a basket, 2½" d., 5" h. 55.00
Tumbler, footed, slightly flaring cylindrical shape, amber, white enameled young girl, 2¾" d., 5" h. 55.00
Tumbler, footed, cranberry w/gold trim, white enameled young boy & a butterfly, 5 5/8" h. 135.00
Vase, 3½" h., miniature, cranberry, white enameled little girl w/unusual headdress 125.00
Vase, 4" h., 2½" d., spherical base tapering to a cylindrical neck w/flared rim, sapphire blue, white enameled young boy holding a cane 95.00
Vase, 4½" h., 4" d., bulbous body, cranberry, white enameled young boy playing a horn 200.00
Vases, 5 7/8" h., 3¼" d., ovoid body w/cupped flaring rim, sapphire blue, white enameled boy on one & girl on the other, facing pr. 325.00
Vase, 6 7/8" h., 2¾" d., slightly flaring cylindrical body w/deep shoulder, short slender cylindrical neck w/cupped rim, cranberry, white enameled young boy, molded optic design 165.00
Vase, 7¼" h., 3½" d., amber ovoid footed body narrowing at the shoulder & flaring to a scalloped, ringed rim, shoulder applied w/snail-shaped golden amber handles, white enameled young boy, fine detailing 150.00
Vase, 7¾" h., 3¼" d., ovoid body w/a wide flat mouth, dark amethyst, white enameled young girl in a garden, raised in an ornate silver plate stand formed by two slender stylized storks holding the vase on their backs, vase 4½" h. 750.00
Vase, 11¼" h., footed ring-molded cylindrical body below a wide short neck w/flattened crimped rim, green opaque, white enameled young boy holding a bowl of flowers 245.00
Vases, 9" h., 3½" d., ovoid body tapering to a slender neck w/slightly flaring rim, cranberry, white enameled boy on one & a girl on the other, facing pr. 375.00

McKEE

The McKee name has been associated with glass production since 1834, first producing window glass and later bottles. In the 1850's a new factory was established in Pittsburgh, Pennsylvania, for production of flint and pressed glass. The plant was relocated in Jeannette, Pennsylvania in 1888 and operated there as an independent company almost continuously until 1951 when it sold out to Thatcher Glass Manufacturing Company. Many types of collectible glass were produced by McKee through the years including Depression, Pattern, Milk White and a variety of utility kitchenwares.

KITCHENWARES
Canister w/original glass cover, round, French Ivory, 10 oz. $16.00
Canister w/original glass cover, round, "Cereal," Seville Yellow, 40 oz. 48.00
Canister w/original glass cover, round, Poudre Blue, 48 oz. 195.00
Mixing bowl, Skokie Green, 11½" d. 22.00
Percolator, Range-Tec, clear w/multicolored concentric rings 65.00
Reamer, embossed "Sunkist," Chalaine Blue 195.00
Reamer, embossed "Sunkist," milk white, 6" d. 30.00
Reamer, embossed "Sunkist," Skokie Green 150.00
Refrigerator dish, cov., rectangular, Skokie Green, 4 x 5" 15.00
Salt & pepper shakers w/original metal tops, Roman Arch patt., Poudre Blue, 4½" h., pr. 90.00
Shaker w/original metal top, range-type, square, "Sugar," Skokie Green 25.00

Shakers w/original metal tops,
Roman Arch patt., "Salt" & "Pepper," black, 4¼" h., pr. 32.00

PRES-CUT LINES

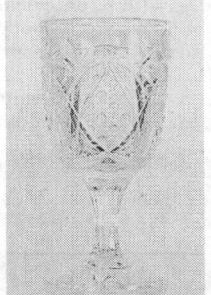

Sunbeam Pattern Wine

Bowl, 5" d., Rock Crystal patt.,
clear 11.50
Butter dish, cov., Sextec patt.,
amethyst 67.00
Candy jar, cov., Rock Crystal patt.,
ruby, 7" h. 40.00
Creamer, Rock Crystal patt., clear ..   40.00
Egg cup (or sherbet), footed, Rock
Crystal patt., amber, 3½ oz. 13.00
Egg cup (or sherbet), footed, Rock
Crystal patt., clear, 3½ oz. 12.00
Finger bowl, Rock Crystal patt.,
ruby, 5" d. 60.00
Goblet, Rock Crystal patt., ruby,
5" h. 42.00
Goblet, water, Rock Crystal patt.,
clear, 5¾" h. 12.00
Mayonnaise bowl & underplate,
Rock Crystal patt., ruby, 2 pcs. ...   50.00
Pitcher, tankard, 9" h., Rock Crystal
patt., clear 200.00
Plate, 7½" d., Rock Crystal patt.,
ruby 15.00
Plate, 11½" d., Rock Crystal patt.,
scalloped rim, clear 12.00
Relish, six-part, Rock Crystal patt.,
clear, 14" 25.00
Spooner, Toltec patt., clear 30.00
Toothpick holder, Aztec patt.,
clear 24.00
Toothpick holder, Toltec patt.,
clear 39.00
Tumbler, Plutec patt., clear 15.00
Tumbler, Rock Crystal patt., amber,
12 oz. 17.00
Tumbler, whiskey, Rock Crystal
patt., ruby.....................   45.00
Vase, 11" h., scalloped rim, Rock
Crystal patt., amber 80.00
Wine, Plutec patt., clear 16.00
Wine, Sunbeam patt., clear, 4½" h.
(ILLUS.).......................   32.00

MISCELLANEOUS PATTERNS & PIECES

Serenade Pattern Plate

Bowl, soup, Laurel patt., French
Ivory 20.00
Candleholders, Laurel patt., Jade
Green, 4" h., pr. 36.00
Cheese dish, cov., Laurel patt., Jade
Green..........................   65.00
Cup & saucer, Laurel patt., Skokie
Green..........................   15.00
Dresser tray, heart-shaped, Poudre
Blue 25.00
Lamp, table model, "Danse de Lu-
miere," a nude dancing lady
w/draperies hanging from her
outstretched arms, on an oval
deep flaring hollow base fitted
w/luminor lighting, frosted pink,
9½" w., 11" h................   330.00
Plate, 6" d., Serenade (Troubador)
patt., milk white (ILLUS.)........   150.00
Plate, dinner, Laurel patt., Skokie
Green..........................   9.00
Plate, grill, Laurel patt., Skokie
Green..........................   10.00
Platter, 10¾" oval, Laurel patt.,
French Ivory 23.00
Tom & Jerry bowl, French Ivory.....   25.00
Tumbler, whiskey, "Bottoms Up,"
frosted clear 57.00
Wren's Honeymoon Hut, hanging
birdhouse, clear................   75.00

MILK WHITE

*This is opaque white glass that resembles
the color of and was used as a substitute for
white porcelain. Opacity was obtained by adding oxide of tin to a batch of clear glass. It
has been made in numerous forms and shapes
in this country and abroad from about the
first quarter of last century. It is still being
produced and there are many reproductions
of earlier pieces. Also see HISTORICAL and
PATTERN GLASS.*

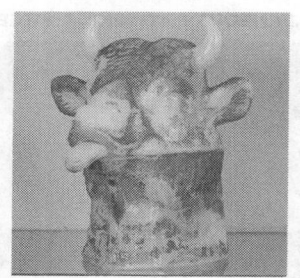

Bull's Head Mustard Jar

Animal covered dish, Bull's Head mustard jar, w/separate "tongue" spoon, original paint (ILLUS.) $250.00

Animal covered dish, Cat on Drum, Porteaux, France 135.00

Animal covered dish, Cat on split-ribbed base, 5½" l. 48.00

Animal covered dish, Crawfish on two-handled oblong base, overall 7½" l. 230.00

Animal covered dish, Dog on square base, Vallerysthal 200.00

Animal covered dish, Dog w/blue head, oval wide rib base, 5½" l. 75.00

Animal covered dish, Dove on basketweave base, round, marked "McKee," 4½" l. 135.00

Animal covered dish, Duck w/amethyst head, Atterbury, 11" l., 5" h. 225.00

Animal covered dish, Pintail Duck, 5¼" l., 4¼" h. 50.00

Animal covered dish, Elephant walking, England, 9" l. 340.00

Animal covered dish, Fox on ribbed base, patent dated 160.00

Animal covered dish, Horse on split-ribbed base, McKee 175.00

Animal covered dish, Owl Head on split-ribbed base, Atterbury 250.00

Animal covered dish, Quail on scroll-embossed oval base w/scalloped top, 6½" l., 4½" h. 65.00

Animal covered dish, Jack Rabbit w/laid-back ears on ribbed base, Flaccus 390.00

Animal covered dish, Robin on Nest, Vallerysthal 105.00

Animal covered dish, Rooster on basketweave base, painted comb & head, Challinor Taylor, 7" h. . . . 80.00

Animal covered dish, Squirrel on split-ribbed base, McKee, 5½" l. 375.00

Animal covered dish, Open Neck Swan on split-ribbed base, McKee, 5½" l. 460.00

Animal covered dish, Swan w/closed neck on split-ribbed base 46.00

Animal covered dish, Turtle on two-handled oblong base, overall 7½" l. 230.00

Bone dish, crescent-shaped, open-work border, 3" w., 9" l. 70.00

Bowl, 8½" d., 4½" h., Daisy patt., openwork edge, h.p. decoration . . 250.00

Bowl, 9" d., 4½" h., Waffle patt. . . . 43.00

Butter dish, cov., Apple Blossom patt. 60.00

Butter dish, cov., Blackberry patt. . . 65.00

Butter dish, cov., Tree of Life patt. . . 105.00

Trumpet Vine Cake Stand

Cake stand, Trumpet Vine patt., 6½" d., 9" h. (ILLUS.) 75.00

Candlestick, cruciform, twelve-sided base, tulip top w/crosses in panels, Christ & "INRI" on front, Sandwich Glass Co., 13" h. 85.00

Compote, open, 7" h., pedestal foot, open latticework, h.p. apple blossoms w/green leaves decoration, Atterbury 72.00

Compote, open, 8¼" d., 7" h., openwork edge, narrow-ribbed stem 55.00

Compote, open, 8¼" d., 8¼" h., Atlas stem, scalloped rim, Atterbury 95.00

Compote, open, Jenny Lind patt. . . . . .75.00 to 100.00

Covered dish, Admiral Dewey on tile base, 6½" l., 4" h. 65.00

Covered dish, Automobile, signed "Portieux," France 175.00

Covered dish, Battleship "Maine," 7½" l. 50.00

Covered dish, Battleship "Olympia," 6 3/8" l. 85.00

Covered dish, Beehive shape w/pyramidal cover, bees on hive & lid .35.00 to 45.00

Covered dish, Couch, w/original blue paint 150.00

Covered dish, Football, modern 85.00

Covered dish, Moses in Bulrushes, 5½" l. . . . . .150.00 to 200.00

Covered dish, Royal Coach, modern, 5¼" l 95.00

Covered dish, Sadiron 235.00
Creamer, Blackberry patt. 40.00
Creamer, Coreopsis patt., green
  band 95.00
Creamer, Paneled Wheat
  patt. . . . . .25.00 to 35.00
Creamer, Swan patt., 5" h. 35.00
Dresser box, cov., rectangular, em-
  bossed w/five kittens, 3½ x 10" . . 130.00
Dresser tray, Actress patt. 45.00
Jar, cov., Owl, Atterbury, 7" h. 130.00
Jar, cov., Owl, metal cover w/milk
  white insert w/embossed eagle,
  possibly Challinor, Taylor & Co.,
  6¼" h. (cover missing) 100.00
Lamps, footed, kerosene-type,
  boudoir-style, Block patt., pr. 140.00
Match holder, hanging-type, Indian
  Head, 4¾" w., 5" h. 65.00
Model of a baseball, maker un-
  known, modern 55.00
Pitcher, 7½" h., Owl w/glass
  eyes 150.00
Plate, 4 3/8" d., Rising Sun 65.00
Plate, 6" l., heart-shaped, openwork
  heart border 17.00
Plate, 6¼" d., Chicks on Wooden
  Shoe, heart-shaped lacy border . . . 85.00
Plate, 6¼" d., Chrysanthe-
  mums . . . . .25.00 to 35.00
Plate, 6¼" d., Easter Ducks 32.00
Plate, 7" d., Anchor & Belaying
  Pin 35.00
Plate, 7" d., Contrary Mule, w/gilt
  paint. 40.00
Plate, 7" d., Eagles, Flags & Stars
  border 32.50
Plate, 7" d., Owl Lovers . . . . .45.00 to 55.00
Plate, 7" d., Peg Border 19.00

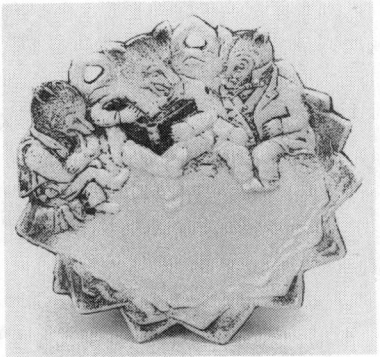

"Three Bears" Plate

Plate, 7" d., Three Bears, w/traces
  of original brown, green & gilt
  (ILLUS.). 37.50
Plate, 7" d., Three Kittens 35.00
Plate, 7¼" d., Chick & Eggs 35.00
Plate, 7¼" d., Little Red Hen, open-
  work lacy border. . . . . .50.00 to 75.00

Plate, 7¼" d., Marine Border,
  w/flags 50.00

"No Easter Without Us" Plate

Plate, 7¼" d., "No Easter Without
  Us," rooster & hens (ILLUS.) 55.00
Plate, 7¼" d., Paneled Peg 18.00
Plate, 7¼" d., Shell & Club border . . 18.00
Plate, 7¼" d., Spring Meets Winter,
  openwork border. 58.00
Plate, 7¼" d., Yacht & Anchor 32.50
Plate, 7½" d., "Easter Sermon,"
  preacher practicing sermon be-
  neath tree as rabbits listen 80.00
Plate, 7½" d., Hare & Cloverleaf
  center, scalloped & beaded bor-
  der 70.00
Plate, 7½" d., Indian Head center,
  Beaded Loop border 50.00
Plate, 8" d., Angel & Harp 35.00
Plate, 8" d., Single Forget-Me-Not,
  openwork border. 17.00
Plate, 8¼" d., Washington bust por-
  trait in relief, 13-star border 60.00
Plate, 9" d., California Bears 125.00
Plate, 9½" d., Columbus bust cen-
  ter, Club & Shell border. 42.50
Plate, 10½" d., Trumpet Vine,
  enameled flowers in center, Lat-
  tice Edge border 55.00
Relish dish, modeled as a bird,
  10¼" l., 5" w., 2" deep. 50.00
Relish dish, figural fish, inscribed
  "Pat. June 4, 1872," 4½ x 11" 40.00
Salt dip, figural Goose 30.00
Salt dip, footed, Strawberry patt. . . . 40.00
Smoke bell, w/applied ruby edge
  trim, 6" d., 2" h. 78.00
Spooner, Blackberry patt. 35.00
Spooner, Sunflower patt., Atter-
  bury 85.00
Sugar bowl, cov., Basketweave
  patt., dated 1874, 6" h. 100.00
Sugar bowl, cov., Blackberry patt. . . 60.00
Sugar bowl, cov., melon-ribbed body
  on three leaf-sprig feet, pressed
  Trumpet Vine patt., fired-on origi-

nal colors, impressed "S.V.,"
France 65.00
Sugar shaker w/original top, Chal-
linor's Forget-Me-Not patt. 110.00
Sugar shaker w/original top, Chal-
linor's Tree of Life patt.......... 85.00
Sugar shaker w/original top, Netted
Oak patt., Northwood 115.00

Alba Syrup Pitcher

Syrup pitcher w/original top, Alba
patt., decorated, Dithridge, 1894
(ILLUS.)........................ 75.00
Syrup pitcher w/original top, Chal-
linor's Banded Shells patt., h.p.
pink apple blossoms & green
shells 95.00
Syrup pitcher w/original top, Chal-
linor's Forget-Me-Not patt. 75.00
Syrup pitcher w/original top, Fishnet
& Poppies patt. 185.00
Syrup pitcher w/original top, Scroll
& Net patt. 95.00
Syrup pitcher w/original top, Wild
Iris patt., decorated w/red &
green 125.00
Tray, Lady & Fan patt., 5¼ x 7" 38.00
Whimsey, canoe, enameled flowers
& gold trim, 6" l................ 15.00
Whimsey, log cabin, w/original
"Prepared Mustard" paper label &
bank coin slot 95.00
Whimsey, model of Uncle Sam's hat,
color decoration, w/coin bank clo-
sure inside brim 40.00

MONT JOYE

*Cameo and enameled glass bearing this
mark was made in Pantin, France, by the
same works that produced pieces signed De
Vez.*

Cameo vase, 19" h., bulbous base
tapering to a tall, slender stick
neck, acid-textured brown ground
overlaid in green & cut w/large
horse chestnut leaf clusters &

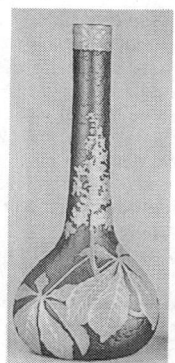

Mont Joye Cameo Vase

blossoms all trimmed w/gold,
signed in gilt (ILLUS.) $825.00
Vase, 4½" h., 4½" d., heavily
enameled flowers on a light ice
green ground 125.00
Vase, 6½" h., enameled gold trees
& green leaves on a deep amber
ground, signed................. 595.00
Vase, 10¾" h., cylindrical shape,
enameled green & gold floral
decoration on a raisin brown
ground, patterned gold band
rim 900.00
Vase, 11" h., enameled white orchid, green leaves & gold scrolls
on a red ground 285.00
Vase, 19 7/8" h., oviform w/everted
rim, etched & enameled w/poppy
blossoms against a heavily textured ground, the design & rim
trimmed w/gilt, gilt company
logo 935.00

MOSER

Moser Cordial Set
*Ludwig Moser opened his first glass shop
in 1857 in Karlsbad, Bohemia (now Karlovy*

Vary, Czechoslovakia). Here he engraved and decorated fine glasswares especially to appeal to rich visitors to the local health spa. Later other shops were opened in other cities and throughout the 19th and early 20th century lovely colorful glasswares, many beautifully enameled, were produced by Moser's shops and reached a wide market in Europe and America. Ludwig died in 1916 and the firm continued under his sons who were forced to merge with the Meyer's Nephews glass factory after World War I. The glassworks were sold out of the Moser family in 1933.

Bowl, 4½" d., heavily enameled oak leaves in blue, pink, green & yellow outlined in gold & gold branches & buds & six applied gold acorns.....................$175.00

Bowl, 8" d., 5" h., squatty bulbous body w/deep shoulder & a flat mouth, smoky amethyst ground decorated w/four banks of cut-back designs of fruit & foliage, signed "Moser"................ 795.00

Box w/hinged lid, lime green w/enameled yellow oak leaves & four applied glass acorns on the lid, 2½" d., 1¼" h. 595.00

Cordial set: 12½" h. decanter w/original hollow cylindrical stopper & six cordials; each piece in clear padded & engraved w/a cluster of three red cherries or three blue grapes, each cordial 6¾" h., 7 pcs. (ILLUS. of part) 715.00

Cup & saucer, demitasse, green shaded to clear ground w/gold trim........................... 80.00

Pickle castor, panel-cut insert, deep amethyst decorated w/a heavy gold band of embossed warriors, original gold-plated frame 350.00

Pitcher, tankard, 15¼" h., tall slender cylindrical body flaring at the base, applied clear gold-trimmed handle, the clear body ornately decorated w/gold, silver & copper-colored encrustations of blossoms, leaf swags & centering a royal bird.................... 880.00

Plate, wide green glass border w/ornate overall gilt scrolls, the white porcelain center h.p. w/the bust portrait of a brown-haired Victorian lady in a low-cut white gown (ILLUS. top next column) ... 300.00

Salt dip, cranberry decorated w/tiny gold florals, ferns & leaves, gold rim, 2 5/8" sq..................110.00

Sugar shaker w/original top, clear w/raised cranberry panels outlined w/heavy gold & traced flowers overall..................... 265.00

Moser Portrait-Decorated Plate

Tumbler, dark green w/multicolored enameled flowers & gold scrolling & borders, 5¼" h................ 295.00

Vase, 6¾" h., 3" d., ovoid emerald green panel-cut body w/a continuous gold band of Amazon warriors, signed "Moser" 245.00

Vase, 7 7/8" h., flat-bottomed bulbous body tapering to a tall slender neck w/widely flaring rim, blue & iridescent green cased glass, decorated w/gilt stylized vining flowers 440.00

Vase, 10" h., tall slightly tapering cylindrical form on a thick disc foot, topaz deeply cut-back w/a repeating design of sea horses among sea plants & snails, oval acid-stamped mark "Moser M (goblet) M" 715.00

Vase, 13 1/8" h., bulbous square body in clear shading to emerald green at the top, wheel-cut w/a pattern of tulip blossoms, buds & leafage on four sides & w/irregular top edge, inscribed "Moser - Karlsbad," ca. 1900 ....1,320.00

Moser Water Set
Water set: pitcher & four tumblers; each piece in green decorated

w/colored enamel flowers & bees,
the pitcher w/a funnel foot supporting the bulbous body tapering
to a flaring cylindrical neck &
w/an applied reeded green han-
dle, pitcher 8¾" h. (ILLUS.) 450.00

MT. WASHINGTON

*A wide diversity of glass was made by the
Mt. Washington Glass Company of New Bed-
ford, Massachusetts, between 1869 and 1900.
It was succeeded in 1900 by the Pairpoint
Corporation. Miscellaneous types are listed
below, but also see CROWN MILANO,
PEACH BLOW and SMITH BROTHERS.*

Boudoir bottles w/original blown
stoppers, creamy white ground
decorated overall w/enameled
florals, satin finish, 9¼" h., pr. ..$235.00
Cologne bottle w/original bulbous
stopper, bulbous mushroom-
shaped base tapering to a long
slender neck w/flared rim, white
satin ground, 10" h. 245.00
Rose bowl, "Verona," clear ground
w/heavy gold flowers & leaves,
6½" d. 295.00
Salt shaker w/original top, egg-
shaped, reclining-type w/a flat
base, decorated w/a spray of h.p.
pink & blue violets on a white satin ground 265.00
Salt shaker w/original top, egg-
shaped, reclining-type w/a flat
base, embossed "Merry Christmas" & trimmed in gold & gold
flowers on a white satin ground .. 195.00
Salt shaker w/original top, fig-
shaped, cranberry w/enameled
decoration 165.00
Salt shaker w/original top, Scroll &
Bulge patt., milk white w/enam-
eled florals & scroll trim 48.00
Salt & pepper shakers w/original
tops, green satin ground decorated w/enameled flowers, pr. 120.00
Salt & pepper shakers w/original
tops, tomato-shaped, h.p. daisies
decoration on a white satin
ground, 2½" d., 1¾" h., pr. 175.00
Salt & pepper shakers w/original
metal tops, tomato-shaped, h.p.
pansies decoration on a white satin ground, 2½" d., 1¾" h., pr. ... 175.00
Salt & pepper shakers w/original
tops, tapering six-lobed pear-
shaped body, h.p. yellow floral
decoration on a white satin
ground, 2 5/8" h., pr. 175.00

Sugar shaker w/original top, egg-
shaped, h.p. lavender spider
daisies w/yellow centers on shaded pink to white satin ground 195.00
Sugar shaker w/original metal top,
embossed Rib patt., pink blush
ground w/soft pink stripes, decorated overall w/enameled bouquets of blue & white forget-
me-nots 595.00
Toothpick holder, bulbous melon-
ribbed base tapering to a short
cylindrical neck, small blue flowers w/yellow centers on a white
shaded to yellow satin ground,
2¼" d., 2¼" h. 125.00
Toothpick holder, urn-shaped, small
pink daisies & green leaves on a
white shaded to yellow satin
ground 165.00
Tumbler, cylindrical, the glossy
white ground decorated w/a
Delft blue Dutch windmill scene,
3 5/8" h. 165.00
Vase, 11" h., jack-in-the-pulpit form,
"Verona," clear mold-blown rib
design decorated w/heavy enameled gold ribbons, scrolls, roses &
leaves 250.00

MULLER FRERES

Muller Freres Table Lamp

*The Muller Brothers made acid-etched cam-
eo and other fine glass at Luneville, France,
starting in 1910 and until the outbreak of
World War II in Europe.*

Cameo lamp, table-type, the bullet-
form shade & baluster base in
opalescent lemon yellow streaked
w/lemon yellow & sapphire blue,
overlaid in cherry red & maroon &
cut w/poppy blossoms, buds &
leafage, simple wrought-iron

mounts, acid-stamped "MULLER
FRES - LUNEVILLE," ca. 1920,
20¾" h. (ILLUS.) $15,400.00
Cameo vase, miniature, 1½" h.,
squat baluster-form, pink interior,
exterior overlaid in green &
white, etched w/Queen Anne's
lace, signed in cameo 264.00
Cameo vase, 10¾" h., pear-shaped,
light blue w/silver foil inclusions,
overlaid in deeper blue & etched
overall w/a confetti-like pattern
of dots, w/scalloped borders,
cameo signature 2,200.00
Cameo vase, 10 15/16" h., wide
squatty bulbous body w/a wide
shoulder to the short wide flat
mouth, rich creamy opalescent
streaked w/salmon, overlaid in
black & green & cut w/panels enclosing Japanese landscapes
w/figures, signed in cameo, ca.
1920 . . . . .4,950.00
Cameo vase, 17¾" h., wide ovoid
body w/a flaring base & a short
flaring neck, deep rich lemon yellow opalescent overlaid in salmon, olive green & forest green &
cut w/an Alsatian landscape
w/tall evergreens in the foreground by a brook & mountains in
the distance, signed in cameo
"Muller Fres - Luneville," ca.
1920 . . . . .4,950.00
Vase, 8" h., spherical body of cased
deep eggplant deeply etched
w/concentric arches, internally
decorated w/silver foil, engraved
mark "Muller Fres Luneville" 2,420.00
Vase, 11" h., cylindrical w/everted
rim, mottled orange & blue
ground, etched signature "MULLER
FRES LUNEVILLE FRANCE" 440.00

Bonbon, squatty bulbous form, pink
floral decoration on a shaded blue
ground, metal rim & high, arched
bail handle, 6" d., 6¾" h. to top
of handle $385.00
Box, cov., two angels w/harp on the
cover, white enamel dot decora-
tion overall, 3¾" d. 400.00
Box, cov., Bishop's Hat mold, pale
green ground w/pink & white
chrysanthemums trim & white
beading on cover, original lining,
5¾" w. 600.00
Box w/hinged cover, paneled oval
form, blue ground decorated
w/white scrolls & beading & pink
flowers, 6" l., 3" h. (ILLUS.) 225.00
Box w/hinged cover, shaded blue
ground w/Kate Greenaway scene
of three little girls having tea on
cover, florals & beading trim on
the cover & base, 6" d. 1,050.00
Box w/hinged cover, Octagonal
mold, h.p. floral & white beading
decoration on an olive green to
mauve ground, 6½" w., 3½" h. . . . 650.00
Cigarette holder, bulbous tapering
to a slightly flared rim, pink &
white daisies on a robin's egg
blue ground, white enameled dots
on the rim, beige interior 325.00
Cracker jar, cov., olive green
ground w/pink flowers, w/silver
plate cover, rim & bail handle,
6" d. 550.00
Hair receiver, Octagonal mold, pink
ground w/floral decoration 325.00
Vase, 13½" h., h.p. pink & white
lilies, signed 850.00

NAKARA

Paneled Oval Nakara Box

*Like Kelva (which see), Nakara was made
early in this century by the C.F. Monroe Company. For details see WAVE CREST.*

NEW MARTINSVILLE

Moondrops Decanter

*The New Martinsville Glass Mfg. Co.
opened in New Martinsville, West Virginia*

in 1901 and during its first period of production came out with a number of colored opaque pressed glass patterns and also developed an art glass line they named "Muranese" but which collectors today refer to as "New Martinsville Peach Blow." The factory burned in 1907 but reopened later that year and began focusing on production of various clear pressed glass patterns many of which were then decorated with gold or ruby staining or enameled decoration. After going through receivership in 1937 the factory again changed the focus of its production to more contemporary glass lines and figural animals. The firm was purchased in 1944 by The Viking Glass Company (now Dalzell-Viking) and some of the long-popular New Martinsville patterns are now produced by this still-active firm.

Basket, Janice patt. (No. 4500 Line),
  clear, 13" l., 10" h. $60.00
Book ends, figure of a hunter,
  No. 497, clear, 7 3/8" h., pr. 85.00
Book ends, Nautilus patt., shell-
  shaped, clear, pr. 120.00
Bowl, 9½ x 10", Janice-Swan patt.
  (S-J Line), swan-shaped, No. 4551-
  1SJ, clear.   60.00
Bowl, 10¾" d., Muranese line, ruf-
  fled rim, early 20th c. 60.00
Bowl, 11½" d., shallow, Prelude
  etching, clear 42.00
Butter dish, cov., Moondrops patt.
  (No. 37 Line), cobalt blue 475.00
Butter dish, cov., Moondrops patt.,
  pink 250.00
Cake plate, footed, Prelude etching,
  clear, 12" d. 48.00
Candlesticks, Prelude etching, clear,
  5½" h., pr. 48.00
Candlesticks, two-light, Flower Bas-
  ket etching, clear, pr. 38.00
Compote, open, 6" d., crimped rim,
  Radiance patt. (No. 4200 Line),
  light blue 45.00
Cordial, Moondrops patt., Prelude
  etching, ruby 15.00
Creamer & open sugar bowl w/tray,
  breakfast size, Janice patt., light
  blue, 3 pcs. 11.50
Creamer & open sugar bowl, Radi-
  ance patt., Florentine etching,
  clear, pr. 18.00
Cruet w/original stopper, Radiance
  patt., ruby 97.50
Decanter w/original clear stopper,
  Moondrops patt., ruby, 12¾" h.
  (ILLUS.) 225.00
Dresser set: two tall footed cologne
  bottles w/tall stoppers, a square
  w/rounded sides cov. powder jar,
  & tray; one cologne bottle jadite
  w/black stopper, one cologne bot-

tle all-black, powder jar w/jadite
  base & black cover & black tray,
  4 pcs. 165.00
Flower holder, figural Shawl Dancer,
  frosted clear 375.00
Mug, Moondrops patt., dark green,
  12 oz. 17.50
Mustard jar, cov., Janice patt.,
  blue 50.00
Relish dish, footed, three-part, Pre-
  lude etching, clear, 10" d. 45.00
Sandwich server w/center handle,
  Prelude etching, clear, 10½" d. . .   57.00
Sherbet, Janice patt., blue 22.00
Sherbet, Mt. Vernon patt. (No. 1600
  Line), amber, 4" h. 4.00
Tray, Janice patt., amber, 14" l. 24.00
Tray, oval, Radiance patt., ruby 35.00
Tumbler, juice, Moondrops patt.,
  blue, 5 oz.   15.00
Tumbler, whiskey, Moondrops patt.,
  amber 8.00
Vase, 10" h., crimped rim, Radiance
  patt., ruby 65.00
Vase, 10½" h., Prelude etching,
  clear 95.00
Water set: pitcher & five tumblers;
  Klear-Kut (No. 705) patt., clear,
  ca. 1910-20, 6 pcs. 350.00
Wine, footed, Mt. Vernon patt., am-
  ber, 5" h. 6.00

NORTHWOOD

Cherry & Cable Creamer

Harry Northwood (1860-1919) was born in England, the son of noted glass artist John Northwood. Brought up in the glass business, Harry immigrated to the United States in 1881 and shortly thereafter became manager of the La Belle Glass Company, Bridgeport, Ohio. Here he was responsible for many innovations in colored and blown glass. After leaving La Belle in 1887 he opened The Northwood Glass Company in Martins Ferry, Ohio in 1888. The company moved to Ellwood City, Pennsylvania in 1892 and Northwood moved again to take over a glass plant in Indiana, Pennsylvania in 1896. One of his major lines made at the Indiana, Pennsylvania plant was Custard glass (which he called "ivory"). It was made in several patterns and some pieces were marked on the base with "Northwood" in script.

Harry and his family moved back to England in 1899 but returned to the U.S. in 1902 at which time he opened another glass factory in Wheeling, West Virginia. Here he was able to put his full talents to work and under his guidance the firm manufactured many notable glass lines including opalescent wares, colored and clear pressed tablewares, various novelties and, probably best known of all, Carnival glass. Around 1906 Harry introduced his famous "N" in circle trade-mark which can be found on the base of many, but not all, pieces made at his factory. The factory closed in 1925.

In this listing we are including only the clear and colored tablewares produced at Northwood factories. Specialized lines such as Custard glass, Chrysanthemum Sprig, Blue, Carnival and Opalescent wares are listed under their own headings in our Glass category. Also see under Pattern Glass ROYAL IVY and ROYAL OAK.

Berry set: master bowl & four sauce
  dishes; Atlas patt., clear, 5 pcs. . . . $70.00
Berry set: master bowl & four sauce
  dishes; Cherry & Cable (Cherry
  Thumbprints) patt., clear w/ruby
  & gold trim, 5 pcs. 125.00
Berry set: master bowl & six sauce
  dishes; Gold Rose patt., clear
  w/rose & gold trim, 7 pcs. 125.00
Bowl, 7½" d., flattened shape, Chi-
  nese Coral. 45.00
Bowl, master berry, 7½" d., Leaf
  Umbrella patt., ruby 165.00
Bowl, 9" d., Plums & Cherries patt.,
  clear 50.00
Bowl, master berry, 10" d., Leaf
  Medallion (Regent) patt., clear
  w/gold trim 55.00
Bowl, Valentine (No. 14) patt.,
  clear 69.00
Butter dish, cov., Leaf Medallion
  (Regent) patt., green w/gold
  trim. 350.00
Butter dish, cov., Netted Oak patt.,
  milk white. 55.00
Butter dish, cov., Peach patt., green
  w/gold trim 145.00
Candy jar, cov., Chinese Coral,
  10½" h. 110.00
Celery vase, Leaf Umbrella patt.,
  vaseline w/cranberry spatter 235.00
Celery vase, Ribbed Pillar patt.,
  pink & white spatter. 85.00
Compote, open, 6" d., 4" h., Spool
  patt., Mosaic (purple slag) 48.00
Compote, open, shape No. 656, Chi-
  nese Coral. 45.00

Creamer, Atlas patt., clear w/gold
  trim. 30.00
Creamer, Cherry & Cable (Cherry
  Thumbprints) patt., clear w/ruby
  & gold trim (ILLUS.). 45.00
Creamer, Leaf Mold patt., vaseline
  w/cranberry spatter 160.00
Cruet w/original stopper, Leaf
  Medallion (Regent) patt., green . . 450.00
Cruet w/original stopper, Venetian
  (Utopia Optic) patt., green 225.00
Finger bowl, Leaf Umbrella patt.,
  Rose du Barry (cased mauve). 25.00
Nappy, Sunflower patt., green 40.00
Pickle jar, cov., Paneled Sprig patt.,
  ruby w/enameled decoration, sil-
  ver plate cover 165.00
Pitcher, water, Gold Rose patt.,
  clear w/ruby & gold trim. 125.00
Pitcher, water, Leaf Medallion (Re-
  gent) patt., green w/gold trim . . . 150.00
Pitcher, 8¾" h., Leaf Umbrella,
  cased blue, satin finish 450.00
Pitcher, tankard, 9" h., Oriental
  Poppy patt., blue w/gold trim 350.00
Pitcher, water, Paneled Holly patt.,
  green w/gold trim 195.00
Pitcher, water, Paneled Sprig patt.,
  Rubina 225.00
Pitcher, water, Plums & Cherries
  patt., clear w/ruby & gold trim . . . 150.00
Salt & pepper shakers w/original
  tops, Leaf Mold patt., vase-
  line w/cranberry spatter,
  pr. . . . . .175.00 to 200.00
Salt & pepper shakers w/original
  tops, Flat Flower patt., opaque
  green, pr. 125.00
Salt & pepper shakers w/original
  tops, Quilted Phlox patt., milk
  white w/h.p. pink flowers, pr. . . . 135.00
Sauce dish, Peach patt., green
  w/gold trim, 5" d. 35.00
Spooner, Cherry & Cable (Cherry
  Thumbprints) patt., clear w/ruby
  & gold trim 45.00
Spooner, Leaf Medallion (Regent)
  patt., purple w/gold trim 75.00
Spooner, Leaf Mold patt., vaseline
  w/cranberry spatter 100.00
Spooner, Leaf Umbrella patt., vase-
  line w/cranberry spatter, satin
  finish 145.00
Spooner, Memphis patt., green
  w/gold trim 65.00
Sugar bowl, cov., Belladonna patt.,
  blue w/gold trim & enameled
  flowers. 75.00
Sugar bowl, cov., Leaf Mold patt.,
  pink satin 225.00
Sugar shaker w/original top,
  Leaf Mold patt., ruby, satin
  finish . . . . .400.00 to 450.00
Sugar shaker w/original top, Leaf

Mold patt., vaseline w/cranberry
spatter 450.00
Sugar shaker w/original top, Leaf
Umbrella patt., Rose du Barry
(cased mauve), 5" h. . . . . 350.00 to 375.00
Sugar shaker w/original top, Netted
Oak patt., milk white 95.00
Sugar shaker w/original top, Parian
Swirl patt., blue opaque 165.00
Sugar shaker w/original top, Quilt-
ed Phlox patt., blue opaque 225.00
Table set: creamer, cov. sugar bowl
& cov. butter dish; Peach patt.,
clear w/gold & red trim, 3 pcs. . . . 225.00
Table set: creamer, cov. sugar bowl,
spooner & cov. butter dish; Bel-
ladonna patt., blue, 4 pcs. 285.00
Toothpick holder, Cherry & Cable
(Cherry Thumbprints) patt., clear
w/ruby & gold trim 30.00
Toothpick holder, Flute (No. 21)
patt., purple 85.00
Toothpick holder, Leaf Mold patt.,
ruby 235.00
Toothpick holder, Ribbed Pillar
patt., pink & white spatter, satin
finish 85.00
Tumbler, Apple Blossom patt.,
clear 56.00
Tumbler, Cherry & Cable (Cherry
Thumbprints) patt., clear w/ruby
& gold trim 28.00
Tumbler, Diadem (Sunburst on
Shield) patt., blue opalescent 125.00
Tumbler, Intaglio line, Strawberry
patt., red & gold trim 40.00
Tumbler, Oriental Poppy patt.,
green w/gold trim 50.00
Tumbler, Peach patt., clear 20.00
Tumbler, Peach patt., green w/gold
trim 32.50
Tumbler, Plums & Cherries patt.,
clear w/ruby & gold trim 25.00
Tumbler, Teardrop Flower patt.,
blue w/gold trim 45.00
Vase, Grapevine Cluster patt., blue
opalescent 35.00
Vase, Ocean Shell patt., Mosaic
(purple slag) 45.00
Water set: pitcher & three tumblers;
Royal Art line (white cased
w/swirled pink & yellow spatter),
4 pcs. 350.00
Water set: pitcher & five tumblers;
Peacock at Fountain patt., green
w/gold trim, 6 pcs. 850.00
Water set: pitcher & five tumblers;
Plums & Cherries patt., clear
w/gold trim, 6 pcs. 275.00
Water set: pitcher & six tumblers;
Barbella patt., blue, 7 pcs. 325.00
Water set: pitcher & six tumblers;
Leaf Medallion (Regent)

Leaf Medallion (Regent) Water Set

patt., cobalt blue, 7 pcs.
(ILLUS.) . . . . 600.00 to 650.00
Water set: pitcher & six tumblers;
Memphis patt., green w/gold
trim, 7 pcs. 295.00

OPALESCENT

Presently, this is one of the most popular areas of glass collecting. The opalescent effect was attained by adding bone ash chemicals to areas of an item while still hot and refiring the object at tremendous heat. Both pressed and mold-blown patterns are available to collectors and we distinguish the types in our listing below. Opalescent Glass from A to Z by the late William Heacock is the definitive reference book for collectors. Also see PATTERN GLASS.

MOLD-BLOWN OPALESCENT PATTERNS

BULLSEYE
Bride's bowl w/ruffled rim, cranber-
ry, 9½" d. $265.00
Celery vase, canary yellow 110.00
Butter dish, cov., blue 180.00

CHRYSANTHEMUM SWIRL

Chrysanthemum Swirl Toothpick Holder

Celery vases, white, pr. 110.00
Creamer, blue 98.00
Pickle castor, blue insert in silver
plate frame w/matching tongs . . . 275.00
Salt shaker w/original top, blue 45.00
Sauce dish, blue 20.00
Sauce dish, cranberry 47.50
Sugar bowl, cov., blue 115.00

Sugar bowl, cov., white. 110.00
Toothpick holder, blue (ILLUS.) 150.00
Toothpick holder, white. 100.00
Tumbler, cranberry 115.00

COIN SPOT

Coin Spot Tumbler

Celery vase, ring neck mold,
   cranberry. 95.00
Finger bowl, blue 36.00
Pitcher, 6¾" h., cranberry 90.00
Pitcher, water, Jefferson variant,
   blue 150.00
Pitcher, water, square top mold,
   cranberry. 150.00
Pitcher, water, 'three-tier' tankard
   form w/bulbous base & high,
   arched spout, applied clear han-
   dle, blue 225.00
Sauce dish, ribbed mold, blue,
   4" d. 65.00
Sugar shaker w/original top, nine-
   panel mold, cranberry 140.00
Sugar shaker w/original top, ring
   neck mold, cranberry 145.00
Syrup pitcher w/original top,
   bulbous-based mold, blue. 155.00
Syrup pitcher w/original top, ring
   neck mold, blue . . . . 150.00 to 185.00
Syrup pitcher w/original top, ring
   neck mold, cranberry 345.00
Tumbler, cranberry (ILLUS.) 45.00
Water set: pitcher & four tumblers;
   white, 5 pcs. 165.00

DAFFODILS

Pitcher, water, blue 175.00
Tumbler, green 65.00

DAISY & FERN

Cruet w/original stopper, blue 150.00
Cruet w/original stopper, white 95.00
Pitcher, water, blue 245.00
Pitcher, 6" h., ball-shaped,
   cranberry. 500.00
Pitcher, water, ball-shaped, cran-
   berry (ILLUS. top next col-
   umn). . . . . 250.00 to 275.00
Syrup pitcher w/original metal top,
   applied clear reeded handle,
   blue 210.00

Daisy & Fern Water Pitcher

Syrup pitcher w/original metal top,
   white 135.00
Tumbler, blue. 35.00
Tumbler, cranberry 65.00

FERN

Barber bottle, square shape, blue . . 275.00
Barber bottle w/original stop-
   per, square shape, cran-
   berry . . . . 250.00 to 275.00
Celery vase, blue 90.00
Pitcher w/cloverleaf top, blue 125.00
Spooner w/ruffled rim, blue. 55.00
Toothpick holder, white. 195.00
Water set: pitcher & four tumblers;
   white, 5 pcs. 200.00

HOBNAIL, HOBBS

Barber bottle w/original stopper,
   cranberry. 192.00
Bowl, 6" d., 4" h., ruffled rim,
   cranberry. 60.00
Bowl, 9" d., ruffled rim, blue 55.00
Bowl, 10" d., ruffled rim, blue. 62.00
Bowl, centerpiece, 11½" d., blue . . . 85.00
Bowl, master berry, ruffled rim,
   cranberry. 100.00
Pitcher, 8 3/8" h., cran-
   berry . . . . 250.00 to 300.00
Pitcher, water, vaseline. 215.00
Sugar bowl, cov., white. 65.00
Table set: creamer, cov. sugar bowl,
   spooner & cov. butter dish; vase-
   line, 4 pcs. 430.00
Tumbler, blue. 57.00
Tumbler, cranberry, 4" h. 100.00
Tumbler, vaseline 40.00

POINSETTIA

Bride's bowl w/silver plate stand,
   cranberry. 365.00
Pitcher, tankard, blue . . . . .300.00 to 350.00
Sugar shaker w/original top, blue . . 235.00
Tumbler, blue. 54.00

REVERSE SWIRL

Creamer, cranberry 140.00

Lamp, miniature, kerosene-type, ca-
nary yellow 195.00
Salt shaker w/original top, blue 57.00
Salt shaker w/original top,
cranberry 40.00
Salt & pepper shakers w/original
tops, white, pr. 135.00

Reverse Swirl Sugar Shaker

Sugar shaker w/original top, cran-
berry (ILLUS.) 450.00
Syrup pitcher w/original top, blue . . 235.00
Toothpick holder, canary yellow 45.00
Tumbler, blue 95.00
Water set: pitcher & one tumbler;
blue, 2 pcs. 395.00

RIBBED OPAL LATTICE

Ribbed Opal Lattice Salt Shaker

Bowl, crimped rim, blue 150.00
Bowl, master berry, cranberry 250.00
Salt shaker w/original top, cranber-
ry (ILLUS.) 95.00
Salt shaker w/original top, white . . .   34.00
Sugar shaker w/original top, blue . . 295.00
Sugar shaker w/original top, cran-
berry 305.00
Syrup pitcher w/original top, blue . . 195.00
Toothpick holder, white 75.00
Tumbler, cranberry 135.00

SPANISH LACE

Bowl, 6½" d., ruffled rim, white 47.50
Bowl w/upturned rim, canary yel-
low 95.00

Celery vase, blue 80.00
Pitcher, water, 9½" h., ruffled rim,
blue 300.00
Rose bowl, canary yellow 37.50
Rose bowl, white 45.00
Salt shaker w/original top, white . . .   75.00
Spooner, canary yellow 80.00
Sugar shaker w/original top, cran-
berry 225.00
Tumbler, canary yellow 48.00

STRIPE

Barber bottle, cranberry 275.00
Pitcher, water, blue 180.00
Tumbler, cranberry 95.00
Vase, 9" h., 6" w., green 85.00

SWIRL

Pitcher, 4½" h., applied clear reed-
ed handle, blue 79.00
Pitcher, water, w/square ruffled
rim, blue 175.00
Pitcher, water, w/square ruffled
rim, cranberry . . . . 250.00 to 300.00
Rose bowl, white 45.00
Salt & pepper shakers w/original
tops, cranberry, pr. 275.00
Sugar shaker w/original top,
cranberry 450.00
Tumbler, cranberry 60.00
Tumble-up (water carafe w/tumbler
lid), cranberry, 2 pcs. 425.00
Water set: pitcher & one tumbler;
cranberry, 2 pcs. 365.00
Water set: pitcher & one tumbler;
green, 2 pcs. 585.00
Whimsey, model of a hat w/ruffled
rim, one side turned-up, blue,
6¼" w., 4" h. 145.00

PRESSED OPALESCENT PATTERNS

ARGONAUT SHELL

Creamer, blue 100.00
Cruet w/original stopper, white 110.00
Pitcher, water, blue . . . . 400.00 to 450.00
Sauce dish, blue 45.00

BEATTY HONEYCOMB

Sugar shaker w/original top,
white 195.00
Toothpick holder, blue 42.00
Toothpick holder, white 35.00

BEATTY RIB

Berry set: master bowl & 8 sauce
dishes; white, 9 pcs. . . . . 125.00 to 150.00
Bowl, master berry, 9½" d., white
(ILLUS. top next column) 35.00
Creamer, individual, blue 26.00
Sauce dish, white 30.00

Beatty Rib Master Berry Bowl

Sugar shaker w/original top, blue .. 195.00
Toothpick holder, white............ 30.00

BEATTY SWIRL
Bowl, master berry, white 35.00
Spooner, white.................... 35.00
Water tray, round, blue........... 40.00

CIRCLED SCROLL
Butter dish, cov., green......65.00 to 85.00
Creamer, green............70.00 to 100.00
Pitcher, water, green............. 160.00
Sauce dish, footed, blue 45.00
Sauce dish, footed, white 25.00
Spooner, green ....40.00 to 65.00
Table set: creamer, cov. sugar bowl,
　cov. butter dish, spooner; green,
　4 pcs. 595.00
Tumbler, blue.................... 75.00

DIAMOND SPEARHEAD
Bowl, master berry, vaseline 35.00
Butter dish, cov., vaseline 195.00
Creamer, cobalt blue 175.00
Creamer, sapphire blue........... 98.00
Goblet, vaseline 115.00
Mug, green...................... 45.00
Mug, vaseline.................... 50.00
Pitcher, water, vaseline........... 275.00
Salt shaker w/original top, vase-
　line 65.00
Table set, green, 4 pcs........... 575.00
Toothpick holder, cobalt blue....... 195.00
Tray, vaseline, 3 5/8 x 7" 55.00
Water set: pitcher & seven goblets;
　vaseline, 8 pcs................1,000.00

DRAPERY
Butter dish, cov., blue 155.00
Pitcher, 9½" h., ruffled rim,
　green 150.00
Table set, blue w/gold trim,
　4 pcs. 450.00
Tumbler, blue.................... 55.00

EVERGLADES
Berry set: master bowl & six sauce
　dishes; white, 7 pcs. 295.00
Bowl, oblong master berry,
　blue ....100.00 to 125.00

Bowl, oblong master berry, canary
　yellow w/gold trim.............. 195.00
Compote, jelly, blue.............. 78.00
Compote, jelly, blue w/gold trim ... 85.00
Compote, jelly, canary yel-
　low ....125.00 to 150.00
Pitcher, water, canary yellow 450.00
Sauce dishes, blue, set of 3 .... 60.00
Sauce dish, canary yellow......... 35.00
Table set, blue, 4 pcs. 550.00
Table set, canary yellow,
　4 pcs.................500.00 to 550.00
Table set, white, 4 pcs. 395.00
Tumbler, canary yellow 85.00
Tumbler, white................... 45.00
Water set: pitcher & four tumblers;
　white, 5 pcs.................... 600.00
Water set: pitcher & six tumblers;
　canary yellow, 7 pcs............. 695.00

FAN

Fan Sugar Bowl

Candy dish, green................. 40.00
Creamer, blue 65.00
Gravy boat, green 45.00
Sauce dish, blue 20.00
Sugar bowl, cov., blue (ILLUS.) 275.00

FLORA
Bowl, master berry, blue 115.00
Butter dish, cov., blue 295.00
Butter dish, cov., canary yellow 185.00
Compote, jelly, blue.............. 82.50
Spooner, blue.................... 80.00
Sugar bowl, cov., canary yel-
　low ....150.00 to 200.00
Table set: cov. sugar bowl, creamer,
　spooner; white, 3 pcs............ 225.00
Table set, blue, 4 pcs. 795.00
Tumbler, canary yellow 85.00

FLUTED SCROLLS
Berry set: master bowl & six sauce
　dishes; vaseline, 7 pcs. ..200.00 to 250.00
Butter dish, cov., blue (ILLUS. top
　next page) ....150.00 to 175.00
Butter dish, cov., vaseline 165.00
Creamer, blue 58.00

Fluted Scrolls Butter Dish

Epergne, two-piece, green, small . . .	125.00
Pitcher, water, vaseline	195.00
Sauce dish, blue	30.00
Sugar bowl, cov., vaseline	110.00
Table set, blue, 4 pcs.	475.00
Table set, vaseline, 4 pcs.	475.00
Tumblers, blue, set of 4 . . .150.00 to	200.00

INTAGLIO

Compote, jelly, blue	44.00
Compote, jelly, white	33.00
Creamer, blue	75.00
Cruet w/original stopper, canary yellow	175.00
Pitcher, water, blue	80.00
Spooner, blue	60.00
Table set: cov. sugar bowl, creamer, cov. butter dish & spooner; white, 4 pcs.	250.00

INVERTED FAN & FEATHER

Bowl, master berry, 10" d., blue	245.00
Butter dish, cov., blue	550.00
Creamer, blue	190.00
Spooner, blue	190.00

IRIS WITH MEANDER

Iris & Meander Table Set

Bonbon, canary yellow	35.00
Bowl, 8" d., canary yellow	135.00
Bowl, 9" d., footed, blue	35.00
Bowl, 9" d., footed, green	32.00
Compote, jelly, blue	65.00
Compote, jelly, canary yellow	85.00
Creamer, blue	125.00

Spooner, blue	85.00
Sugar bowl, cov., white	85.00
Table set, blue, 4 pcs. (ILLUS.)	685.00
Table set, canary yellow, 4 pcs.	510.00
Toothpick holder, blue	110.00
Toothpick holder, green	50.00
Tumbler, white	50.00

JEWEL & FLOWER

Bowl, master berry, blue	97.00
Butter dish, cov., white	62.00
Cruet w/original stopper, white	750.00
Salt & pepper shakers w/original tops, canary yellow, pr.	250.00
Spooner, white	75.00
Table set, canary yellow, 4 pcs.	495.00
Tumbler, blue	100.00

JEWELLED HEART

Jewelled Heart Berry Set

Berry set: master bowl & eight sauce dishes; white, 9 pcs. (ILLUS. of part)	210.00
Pitcher, water, blue	265.00
Sauce dish, blue	50.00
Tumbler, blue	60.00

PALM BEACH

Bowl, master berry, blue	95.00
Creamer & sugar bowl, blue, pr. . . .	250.00
Sauce dish, blue	50.00
Sauce dish, canary yellow	35.00
Water set: pitcher & five tumblers; blue, 6 pcs.	675.00

REGAL

Compote, blue	85.00
Table set: cov. butter dish, cov. sugar bowl & spooner; white, 3 pcs.	175.00
Table set, blue, 4 pcs.	375.00
Table set, green, 4 pcs.	450.00

RIBBED SPIRAL

Berry set: master bowl & six sauce dishes; blue, 7 pcs.	350.00
Bowl, 7½" d., blue	37.00
Bowl, 7½" d., canary yellow	38.00

Sauce dish, canary yellow	27.00
Sauce dish, white	25.00
Toothpick holder, blue	90.00
Tumbler, canary yellow	80.00

SHELL

Compote, blue	125.00
Sauce dish, blue	30.00
Sauce dish, white	25.00
Spooner, blue	55.00
Tumbler, blue	85.00
Tumbler, green	75.00

SWAG WITH BRACKETS

Berry set: master bowl & five sauce dishes; green, 6 pcs.	115.00
Butter dish, cov., green	115.00
Compote, jelly, blue	45.00
Compote, jelly, green	55.00
Creamer, green	60.00
Creamer & cov. sugar bowl, blue, pr.	200.00
Pitcher, water, canary yellow	200.00
Spooner, blue	49.00
Sugar bowl, cov., canary yellow	75.00
Sugar bowl, cov., green	75.00
Table set, canary yellow, 4 pcs.	450.00
Tumbler, canary yellow	55.00
Toothpick holder, canary yellow, 2½" h.	165.00

TOKYO

Bowl, master berry, green	55.00
Creamer, blue	95.00
Cruet w/original stopper, green	190.00
Spooner, blue	85.00

WATER LILY & CATTAILS

Bowl, 5 x 7½", green	37.00
Bowl, 11" d., amethyst	40.00
Butter dish, cov., blue	300.00
Table set, amethyst, 4 pcs.	850.00
Tumbler, blue	47.00

WREATH & SHELL

Bowl, master berry, canary yellow	75.00
Celery vase, blue	155.00
Cracker jar, cov., vaseline	950.00
Creamer, blue	120.00
Salt dip, blue	125.00
Sauce dish, blue	30.00
Spooner, blue	85.00
Spooner, canary yellow	88.00
Table set, vaseline, 4 pcs.	540.00
Toothpick holder, blue	215.00
Toothpick holder, white	125.00
Tumbler, footed, vaseline	85.00
Tumbler, collared base, vaseline	60.00
Tumbler, footed, white	55.00
Tumbler, collared base, white	35.00
Water set: pitcher & six tumblers; blue, 7 pcs.	600.00

MISCELLANEOUS PRESSED NOVELTIES

Maple Leaf Chalice

Astro bowl, 8" d., canary yellow	38.00
Beaded Cable rose bowl, green	38.00
Beads & Bark vase, footed, blue	55.00
Beads & Bark vase, footed, green	35.00
Corn vase, blue	110.00
Corn vase, vaseline	110.00
Corn vase, white	75.00
Diamond & Oval Thumbprint vase, 12" h., blue	33.00
Fancy Fantails rose bowl, canary yellow	50.00
Finecut & Roses sauce dish, footed, blue	35.00
Grape & Cable syrup pitcher w/original top, white	115.00
Grape & Cherry bowl, blue	80.00
Leaf & Beads rose bowl, blue	75.00
Many Loops dish, green	25.00
Maple Leaf Chalice, vaseline (ILLUS.)	35.00
May Basket w/twisted handle, green	85.00
Old Man Winter basket, footed, applied handle, vaseline, 7¾" h.	145.00
Palisades bowl, blue	24.00
Palisades vase, green	30.00
Palm & Scroll bowl, three-footed, blue	68.00
Peacocks on a Fence bowl, 9" d., blue	245.00
Piasa Bird cuspidor, lady's, footed, blue	45.00
Piasa Bird vase, blue	55.00
Rose Show bowl, 9" d., blue	300.00

Scheherezade bowl, blue (ILLUS.) . . .	65.00
Spokes and Wheels dish, tri-cornered, green, 8" w.	27.50
Spokes & Wheels plate, blue	40.00
Three Fruits bowl, 9" d., blue	225.00
Wheel & Block bowl, white	25.00
Windflower bowl, 9" d., blue	285.00
Winter Cabbage bowl, white	30.00

(End of Opalescent Glass Section)

OPALINE

19th Century French Opaline Lamp

Also called opal glass (once a name applied to milk-white glass), opaline is a fairly opaque glass with a color resembling the opal; however, pieces in such colors as blue, pink, green and others, also are referred to now as opaline glass. Many of the objects were decorated.

Lamps, table model, baluster form w/squared gilt-bronze handles & leaf-cast mounts on both sides, decorated w/colorful floral sprays within gilt & white scroll borders reserved on a *bleu celeste* ground, raised on a gilt-bronze plinth, France, 19th c., 19" h., pr. (ILLUS. of one) $3,190.00

Perfume bottle w/original tall, teardrop-shaped stopper, tapering cylindrical shape w/flat flared base, blue w/ring of white opaline around the stopper & neck of bottle, gold trim, 3 1/8" d., 7¾" h. 110.00

Salt dip, boat-shaped, blue decorated w/white enamel garland & scrolling 78.50

Vase, 7½" h., pink w/enameled decoration 125.00

ORREFORS

This Swedish glasshouse, founded in 1898 for production of tablewares, has made

decorative wares as well since 1915. By 1925, Orrefors had achieved an international reputation for its Graal glass, an engraved art glass developed by master glass blower Knut Bergqvist and artist-designers Simon Gate and Edward Hald. Ariel glass, recognized by a design of controlled air traps, and the heavy Ravenna glass, usually tinted, were both developed in the 1930's. While all Orrefors glass is collectible, pieces signed by early designers and artists are now bringing high prices.*

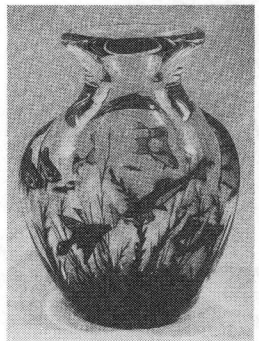

Orrefors "Graal" Vase

Centerbowl & underplate, flaring oval bowl engraved w/a nude couple on either side within a fanciful stylized border, the plate of conforming design, designed by Simon Gate, bowl inscribed "Orrefors S. Gate 147.26. A.D.," 1917-21, 15 1/8" l., the set $3,520.00

Model of a dove, pedestaled, clear, signed "Otte Riberius," 10" h. 300.00

Model of a fish, teardrop-shaped, marked "J GRAAL, ORREFORS," 6½" h. 650.00

Sculpture, abstract design in clear, a narrow swirled block molded w/concave circles at the front & back, inscribed "Orrefors Expo P787-72 Sven Palmquist," 2 1/8 x 8", 9¾" h. 302.50

Vase, 6¾" h., "Graal," baluster-shaped, clear w/an internal design of fish & sea plants, designed by Edward Hald, inscribed "Orrefors Graal No. 11632 Edward Hald" (ILLUS.) 825.00

Vase, 7 1/8" h., the cylindrical upper section in thick optically wavy clear glass engraved w/a nude male diver, raised on a black foot, designed by Vicke Lindstrand, ca. 1935, inscribed "Orrefors Lindstrand 1304. M. R." . . . 3,575.00

Vase, 9 5/8" h., "Ariel," tall ovoid thick-walled body, clear internally decorated w/trapped air bubbles.

blue & yellow striations, inscribed
"Orrefors Kraka N.411 Sven Palm-
quist" 357.50

OVERSHOT

Overshot Tankard Pitcher

*Popular since the mid-19th century, Over-
shot glass was produced by having a gather
of molten glass rolled in finely crushed glass
to produce a rough exterior finish. The piece
was then blown to the desired size and shape.
The finished piece has a frosted or iced finish and is sometimes referred to as "ice
glass." Early producers referred to this glass
as "Craquelle" and, although Overshot is
sometimes lumped together with the glass
collectors now call "Crackle," that type was
produced using a totally different technique.*

Banquet lamp, kerosene-type, ruffled Rubina shade, onion-form Rubina font w/lightly ribbed effect,
raised on a mottled brown marble
columnar stem w/ornate nickel-
plated metal embossed foot
& trim holding font, 7¼" d.,
19¾" h. $595.00
Basket, amethyst shaded to clear,
bulbous base flaring to a crimped
rim, applied clear twist handle,
5" d., 6¼" h. 118.00
Basket, Amberina Hobnail patt.
body w/ruffled rim, applied amber thorn handle, 7½ x 9½",
8½" h. 495.00
Cheese dish, domed cover w/ap-
plied clear faceted finial, cranberry body w/enameled crane & cat-
tails decoration, 8" d., 7" h. 425.00
Compote, open, 10" d., 10¼" h.,
cranberry, the wide rounded bowl
w/a scalloped 'crown' rim raised
on a compressed knop on the tall
cylindrical pedestal w/a widely
flaring base, gilt trim at the rim,
late 19th c. 302.50

Dish, ruffled & crimped rim, shaded
blue, in decorative ormolu stand
w/hanging side rings, 7½" d.,
overall 6½" h. 195.00
Epergne, single lily, clear w/applied
green snakes accented w/gold,
one snake coiled around the pedestal base & the other around the
lily-form, 9½" d., 17" h. 395.00
Pitcher, tankard, 7¼" h., 3¾" d.,
cranberry w/applied clear reeded
handle (ILLUS.) 138.00
Pitcher, 7½" h., blue w/applied am-
ber reeded handle, attributed to
Sandwich 135.00
Pitcher, cov., tankard, 9" h., 4" d.,
cranberry w/applied clear reeded
handle, hinged metal lid 175.00
Pitcher, 9 3/8" h., 5 1/8" d., bulbous
base tapering to a cylindrical neck
w/flaring pinched rim, cranberry
w/applied clear handle & wafer
foot 265.00
Pitcher, 12¾" h., clear, applied
clear twisted wrap-around
handle 225.00
Vase, 5½" h., pink w/applied ran-
dom amber threading 225.00
Wine set: 4½" d., 12½" h. footed
decanter w/original pewter
hinged lid & handle & four
2½" d., 4½" h. wines; cranberry
shaded to clear, 5 pcs. 525.00

PADEN CITY

*The Paden City Glass Manufacturing Com-
pany began operations in Paden City, West
Virginia in 1916, primarily as a supplier of
blanks to other companies. All wares were
hand-made, that is, either hand-pressed or
mold-blown. The early products were not particularly noteworthy but by the early 1930's
the quality had improved considerably and
the firm continued to turn out high quality
glassware in a variety of beautiful colors until financial difficulties necessitated its closing in 1951. Over the years the firm produced,
in addition to tablewares, items for hotel and
restaurant use, light shades, shaving mugs,
perfume bottles and lamps.*

Bowl, berry, 5½" sq., Crow's Foot
(No. 412) line, amber $7.00
Bowl, 9½" d., Party Line (No. 191)
line, amber 12.50
Bowl, cream soup, footed, Crow's
Foot (No. 412) line, amber 8.00
Bowl, cream soup, Crow's Foot
(No. 412) line, clear 10.00
Cake plate, open handled, etched
Gazebo patt., clear, 10" d. 35.00

Cake stand, low pedestal, etched
Ardith patt., topaz, 11¼" d....... 65.00
Cake stand, Crow's Foot (No. 412)
line, red, 12" d................. 77.00
Candlestick, etched Peacock & Rose
patt., cobalt blue, 5¾" h........ 70.00
Candlesticks, Crow's Foot (No. 412)
line, cobalt blue, 5¾" h., pr...... 75.00
Candlesticks, Maya (No. 221) line,
light blue, pr................... 70.00
Cheese & cracker server, cov.,
etched Gazebo patt., light blue... 90.00
Compote, open, 9¼" h., etched
Gothic Garden patt., yellow...... 30.00
Compote, open, 9½" d., 5¾" h.,
flared rim, etched Gazebo patt.,
clear.......................... 45.00
Console bowl, Crow's Foot (No. 412)
line, red...................... 28.00
Creamer & open sugar bowl, Crow's
Foot (No. 412) line, red, pr...... 50.00
Creamer & open sugar bowl, etched
Gothic Garden patt., yellow, pr... 75.00
Creamer & open sugar bowl, etched
Orchid II patt., clear, pr......... 165.00
Cup & saucer, Crow's Foot (No. 412)
line, clear, square.............. 11.00
Decanter w/stopper, Penny
(No. 991) line, red 55.00
Goblet, Penny (No. 991) line, blue,
5¼" h.......................... 22.00
Plate, 6" sq., Crow's Foot (No. 412)
line, clear 5.00
Plate, 6" d., Party Line (No. 191)
line, amber.................... 3.00
Plate, dinner, 9¼" d., Crow's Foot
(No. 412) line, clear 11.00
Plate, cheese & cracker, 10½" d.,
Archaic (No. 300) line, green..... 60.00
Sauce dish, Crow's Foot (No. 412)
line, clear, 4½" sq. 8.00
Tray, square, center handle, etched
Peacock and Rose patt., cobalt
blue 350.00
Tumbler, Georgian (No. 69) line,
red 15.00
Tumbler, footed, Party Line
(No. 191) line, amber, 3½" h. 9.50
Vase, 10" h., Regina (No. 210) line,
green 350.00
Vase, 10" h., paneled, etched Uto-
pia patt., black amethyst 160.00

PAIRPOINT

*Originally organized in New Bedford, Mas-
sachusetts, in 1880, as the Pairpoint Manufacturing Company, on land adjacent to the
famed Mount Washington Glass Company,
this company first manufactured silver and
plated wares. In 1894, the two famous factories merged as the Pairpoint Corporation and
enjoyed great success for more than forty
years. The company was sold in 1939 to a
group of local businessmen and eventually
bought out by one of the group who turned
the management over to Robert M. Gundersen. Subsequently, it operated as the Gundersen Glass Works until 1952 when, after
Gundersen's death, the name was changed to
Gundersen-Pairpoint. The factory closed in
1956. Subsequently, Robert Bryden took
charge of this glassworks, at first producing
glass for Pairpoint abroad and eventually, in
1970, beginning glass production in Saga-
more, Massachusetts. Today the Pairpoint
Crystal Glass Company is owned by Robert
and June Bancroft. They continue to
manufacture fine quality blown and pressed
glass.*

Box, cov., white opaque molded
quatreform oval w/a flat hinged
cover, the slightly flaring base
molded w/small scrolls around
the edge, decorated w/gold
enameled florals on the cover &
sides, signed on base "PMC 9524,"
7¼" l., 2¾" h..................$467.50
Candlesticks, tall slender baluster-
form stem below a tall cylindrical
candle socket w/flat rim, on an
applied disc foot, light green
engraved w/a Vintage patt.,
10½" h., pr. 375.00
Clock, table model, upright domed
clear case w/sawtooth edging,
round dial w/Arabic numerals
above engraved daisy blossom
w/leaf sprigs, one-day movement........................... 225.00
Compote, open, 8" d., 4½" h., amber w/cobalt blue "controlled bubble" ball connector 85.00
Compote, open, 8½" d., 7" h., cranberry cut to clear bowl & clear cut
stem 425.00
Cracker jar, cov., melon-ribbed
shape, light green body decorated
w/daisies, silver plate cover, rim
& handle, marked 395.00
Vase, 9½" h., trumpet-form ruby
red bowl, clear "controlled bubble" ball connector on a red
foot........................... 175.00
Vase, 10" h., footed, white ground
decorated w/tiny h.p. florals &
one large gold button on each
side, signed "Pairpoint".......... 375.00
Vase, 12" h., amethyst ground
w/engraved Vintage patt., clear
"controlled bubble" ball connector
& amethyst foot 125.00
Wine, Flambo Ware, tomato red
w/black stem 125.00

PATE DE VERRE

Pate de Verre Vase

Pate de Verre, or "paste of glass," was molded by very few artisans. In the pate de verre technique, powdered glass is mixed with a liquid to make a paste which is then placed in a mold and baked at a high temperature. These articles have a finely-pitted or matte finish and are easily distinguished from blown glass. Duplicate pieces are possible with this technique.

Bowl, 2 7/8" h., ovoid raised on a short cylindrical foot, thick clear walls streaked w/soft pink & rose, impressed "DECORCHE-MONT" within a horseshoe, underside inscribed "D47," ca. 1945 . . . . $1,980.00

Bowl, 3 7/8" h., stepped & flaring footed body w/a wide rim, mottled blue & white molded in high-relief w/overlapping deep indigo stars, signed in the mold "G. ARGY-ROUSSEAU" 6,050.00

Earrings, teardrop-form pendant molded as a tulip blossom in violet & rose, suspended by a rose-colored circle molded w/a spiral, 2¾" l., pr. 2,070.00

Figure of a bird, modeled in full-relief as a plump bird raised on a square base, grey streaked w/lime green, olive green & black, signed "A. WALTER NANCY," ca. 1925, 4¼" h. (rim ground) 880.00

Paperweight, "Papillon de Nuit," cast as a cube, grey internally streaked w/deep forest green & molded on one corner & top w/moths in full-relief, molded "G. ARGY- - ROUSSEAU," ca. 1923, 2 5/8" h. 2,200.00

Salver, circular, mottled amber & orange w/symmetrical handles, molded "A WALTER NANCY," 10" d. 352.00

Vase, 3 1/8" h., coupe-shaped, the deep rounded sides in grey molded in shallow relief w/three butterflies in shades of purple, red, black & green, molded "G.ARGY - ROUSSEAU," ca. 1915 . . . . 8,250.00

Vase, 4 5/8" h., ovoid body mottled w/cranberry, violet, green, orange, black & white & molded in low-relief w/two spiders seated in webs between leafy flowering branches, molded "G. ARGY-ROUSSEAU" & "FRANCE," ca. 1920 . . . . 13,800.00

Vase, 6" h., "Jeunesse," flattened oviform body w/flared rim, each side molded w/a seated nude female figure in white w/a circular frame, reserved against radiating dentils in mottled brown & orange, signed in the mold "G. ARGY-ROUSSEAU FRANCE" (ILLUS.) 15,400.00

Vase, 8¼" h., "Fougeres," ovoid footed body w/rounded tab handles flanking the flat mouth, mottled mauve & apricot body molded w/rows of dentils at the bottom & rim & w/coiled fern leaves at each side forming the handles, signed in the mold "G. ARGY-ROUSSEAU," France 4,620.00

Vase, 9½" h., ovoid, molded in low-relief w/striding black wolves above snowy drifts, in shades of pale green mottled w/purple, charcoal grey & frosty white, signed "G. ARGY-ROUSSEAU" & "FRANCE," ca. 1926 . . . . 27,600.00

Veilleuse (night light), "Papillons," the almost spherical shade in grey splashed w/lavender & Chinese red, molded in shallow relief w/three butterflies w/outspread wings reserved against a stylized foliate ground in shades of Chinese red, lavender, purple, black & chocolate brown, simple wrought-iron mount, signed "G. ARGY-ROUSSEAU," 1926, 5" h. . . . 8,800.00

Vide poche (figural dish), low rounded triangular form in mottled mauve, the apex w/a realistically molded bumble bee in green, yellow & black, signed in the mold "A. WALTER NANCY" & "h Berge' Sc.," 4 3/8" w. 1,650.00

Vide poche (figural dish), shallow oval form molded w/concentric waves & cast on one side w/acorns & oak leafage in shades of lemon yellow, emerald green & mustard, modeled by Henri Mercier, molded "AWALTER - NANCY" & "HM," ca. 1925, 6 7/8" l. 1,650.00

Special Focus: Pattern Glass

From Counterfeit to Collectible -

A Century of U.S. Coin Glass

by Tim Timmerman

The making of pressed glass is a peculiarly American art, one that came into its own in the 1820's. Shaping and patterning glass by "pressing" it was easier and cheaper than earlier methods of blowing the molten glass, then cutting the patterns by hand. Although manufacturers had been pressing glass for bases, feet and stoppers for blown glass pieces, the techniques necessary for creating fully pressed pieces developed over a period of decades.

Before 1864 most pressed pieces contained varying amounts of lead oxide. With the perfection of soda-lime glass, the production of pressed glass became cheaper and pieces were easier to mold, the thinness allowing for more intricate designs.

America's glass-making industry was revolutionized.

The history of the U.S. Coin pattern is rich in peculiarly American — and fanciful — tales, stories involving Wild West barrooms, hinting of treasure-filled cellars, and high-handed governmental edicts that may or may not have been obeyed.

It all started, or so the story goes, in early 1890, with a man named Albert Mader. A salesman for the Central Glass Company of Wheeling, West Virginia (later a part of the giant U.S. Glass Company), Mader was visiting a barroom in the West, reputedly the Silver Dollar Saloon of Spokane, Washington's Davenport Hotel. Intrigued by the saloon's use of actual money as floor decoration, Mader was inspired: Why not use coin impressions as a pattern for glass? Back home, the salesman's idea was greeted enthusiastically by Central Glass President Nathan B. Scott, who also happened to be West Virginia's U.S. Senator.

After months of experimentation, Central Glass went into production with what was soon to prove its most popular pattern: U.S.

Coin Glass. The pattern was designed by George Hipkins, 25, and the molds themselves produced by the Hipkins Novelty Mold Shop of Martins Ferry, Ohio.

Most of the coins used for U.S. Coin glass, or "Silver Age" as it was originally called, are dated 1892. Actually produced in 1891, was the glass planned to commemorate the great Columbian Exposition in Chicago, scheduled to open in 1892? Or was it made to celebrate the centenary of the U.S. Mint (the Fair, after all, didn't open until 1893)? One hundred years later, it's impossible to know. Record keeping was probably spotty and most glass companies were housed in wooden structures which were vulnerable to fire because of the high heat required for glassmaking.

Gathering the whole family around the dining table each evening, and welcoming the larger family for the ritual Sunday dinner, was a well-entrenched part of America's family life a century ago. Much more affordable than their blown and etched glass precursors, pressed glass serving pieces immediately found their place on middle class dining tables. With its charming coin-emblazoned pieces, it's no wonder that Central Glass' new line was an instant hit. In all, there were at least 88 different pieces to choose from.

The new line of pressed glass dishes was intended to grace the dining tables of ordinary American families. Pickle dishes, cruets, toothpick holders, goblets ... the festive glass pieces were inexpensive and sold in dime stores and general stores. According to a Central Glass catalog, *U.S. Coin* goblets wholesaled at 40 cents a dozen. A general store owner could order a dozen condiment dishes (epergne) for $3 a dozen from the manufacturer, and paid only $3.25 for a dozen of the plain 9" d. covered compotes.

Presuming that retail prices then, as now,

were double wholesale, 1892's thrifty housewife could buy a dozen goblets for about 80 cents, a condiment dish for 50 cents, and a 9" d. covered compote for around 55 cents. Orders flew in and were filled swiftly.

Average retail prices for 1892, when *U.S. Coin* glass made its brief appearance in those dime stores and general stores, seem astonishingly low today, a century later.

For the years 1888-91, the average annual income was $573.00 or about $11.00 a week for an average family of husband, wife and up to five children under 14. Their weekly food bill averaged $4.20 and they paid around $18.00 per month to rent a house. Five pounds of flour was 14 cents, a dozen eggs cost 22 cents, 10 pounds of potatoes were 14 cents, and the average milkman's delivery by the dawn's early light cost 13.6 cents for a half-gallon of milk.

Today, you can expect to pay $700.00 for that 50-cent condiment dish. A goblet retailing for 10 cents in 1892 sells for $150.00. The 50-cent goblet now fetches $350.00. If, and this is a big if, you could track down one of those 55-cent covered compotes, a $1,000.00 offer might be accepted.

While *U.S. Coin* glass was immediately popular with the public, its manufacture was destined to be brief. After only three or four (some say five) months, production was halted by the U.S. Treasury Department, which contended that the reproduction of U.S. coinage in any form constituted counterfeiting. The Central Glass Company was ordered to destroy not only all present inventory, but the very molds as well.

Or *was* that the order? Glass history gets a bit fuzzy here, namely about the exact nature of the pronouncement by the government inspector declaring the production of *U.S. Coin* glass illegal. Given that Central Glass President Nathan Scott was a U.S. Senator, it seems odd that he was unaware that it was illegal to reproduce replicas of U.S. coinage. Could it be that Senator Scott and the U.S. Glass Company thought their venture wouldn't bother the U.S. government? Some suspect political skullduggery behind the ban against the glass production.

The producers of *U.S. Coin* glass didn't give up without arguing that it would, after all, be impossible to pass coin glass for money. The coins were made of glass, not metal, and it was impossible to separate the designs from the object. Each coin was uniface, one having an obverse, the next a reverse. The government, however, won the argument.

One version has it that the federal agent ordered all finished pieces, both at the factory and in the hands of retailers throughout America, to be immediately destroyed. Another tale claims that the factories were allowed to complete all outstanding orders. The

molds were all destroyed, say some; they were simply retooled to accommodate the new version of coin glass, say others. Given that the molds cost around $20,000, a small fortune 100 years ago, it's easy to believe the manufacturer would recycle them for the new glass pattern, *Columbian Coin.*

Gaining credence through their endless retelling, intriguing rumors have survived the century since *U.S. Coin* was originally produced. Generous quantities of the original, swiftly-banned glassware, 'tis whispered, were safely whisked from factories under the cover of night, and straight into the cellars of enterprising, if dishonest, glassware workers. (Oddly enough, no such richly-laden cellars have emerged...)

At any rate, rather than cease production completely, demolishing expensive molds, the glass company, so the story goes, decided to replace the controversial coin design with others. Happily, the Columbian Exposition was celebrating the 400th anniversary of the discovery of America, providing a convenient alternative design idea. Obeying the governmental order to cease "counterfeiting," producing glassware with the American coin design, the glass company substituted Spanish coins with portraits of Christopher Columbus and Americus Vespucius, as well as with emblems of the coats of arms of both Spain and the United States. Thus was born the *Columbian Coin* pattern, also known as "Spanish Coin" and "Portrait."

Central Glass's *Columbian Coin* line is the same pattern as the earlier, short-lived *U.S. Coin*, with only a few variations, making it likely that the original molds indeed survived the federal interference. For example, the *Columbian Coin* spooner, as well as a few other pieces, has a flared top, while *U.S. Coin* versions of the same pieces do not. *Columbian Coin* pieces were manufactured in clear glass, with medallions in clear, frosted amber, gold and stained red; four, or possibly more, lamps were made in milk white glass.

In 1891, Central Glass Company had merged in a trust with 17 other glass companies to create the U.S. Glass Company of Tiffin, Ohio. Some *U.S. Coin* pieces were manufactured at the J.H. Hobbs, Brockunier Glass Company and the Nickel Plate Glass Company before the government's order to destroy the molds, but not before the production and distribution of vast quantities of the glass. How many pieces of the original *U.S. Coin* glass were produced? The exact number is unknown, but it is a fact that the popular pattern was shipped out by the railroad boxcar load.

Columbian Coin was probably produced through 1892. From 1893 through 1896, all production at both factories was stopped in a labor dispute. In 1896, a new company, the

Central Glass Works, was formed. Moved to Summitville, Indiana, it was not in full production until 1898.

It is not its age, but its scarcity, that makes *U.S. Coin* and *Columbian Coin* valuable. Not only was it made for a short time, but it was not then regarded as fine glassware. Thus, many of the pieces surviving the notorious federal agent did not survive America's late 19th century kitchen sinks. Eagerly collected in late 20th century America by both numismatists and lovers of antique glass, it has become nearly impossible to find through antiques dealers and shows. Much of what remains now rests safely in the hands of collectors.

Like many other collectors, I got hooked on coin glassware through an interest in coins. An avid collector of all kinds of coins since I was a boy, I came upon an 8" d. covered compote being sold by an antiques dealer. Perfect, I thought, to show off my gold coins at numismatic shows.

Now, 25 years later, my collection of *U.S. Coin* glass is almost complete except for a few pieces I *know* are out there. *Somewhere.* Over the years, my search for still more pieces to enhance my collection has me corresponding with dealers and collectors all over America.

As almost any collector can testify, the thrill of the chase never ends.

COIN DESIGN

The original design of Central Glass' unusual new glass included the application of medallions replicating, in different sizes, six denominations of U.S. coins: the "Liberty Head" dollar; the "Seated Liberty" with the "Eagle" reverse on the half-dollar, quarter-dollar and twenty-cent piece; the "Seated Liberty" with a "Wreath" reverse on the dime; and the "Wreath" reverse on the half-dime which is only on the champagne glasses.

Although nearly all pieces are dated "1892," except for the dollar in the tumbler, the design used on the glass was not that of coins minted in 1892. Some tumblers, probably produced at another plant, are dated "1878" and "1879." The champagne, claret and wine glasses show only the reverse of the coin. Since the glass was produced in 1891, the company may not have realized the "Liberty Seated" half-dollar, quarter-dollar and dime were set for an 1892 redesign with "Liberty Head" coinage.

The same front design is used on the glass half-dollar, quarter-dollar, twenty-cent and dime pieces, with little or no variation except for the size. On the reverse of the glass twenty-cent piece, the eagle is facing left, similar to all other reverses, but the minted twenty-cent piece has the eagle facing right. On the reverse of the minted dollar is the motto "In God We Trust," which is *not* on the glass design. On the reverse of the half-dollar, quarter-dollar and dime minted after 1866, a banner over the eagle's head, with the motto "In God We Trust," is *not* included in the coin glass design.

The reverse of the coin glass design is similar to pieces minted prior to 1866. Most of the minted half-dollars and some of the quarter-dollars, produced during different periods from 1853 to 1874 have arrows at the date. On the glass half-dollars and quarter-dollars, some have arrows and some don't. The front of the minted "Liberty Seated" coins has a ribbon across the shield; except for the half-dollar, the glass pieces do not. The "Liberty Seated" dime was minted from 1837 to 1891, and from 1838 to 1860 the outer edge of the coin face had stars. In 1860, and until 1891, the stars on the "Liberty Seated" dime were replaced with the motto "UNITED STATES OF AMERICA." While most of the glass design has the motto, the cruet and tumbler have the stars.

The variety of drinking vessels in the U.S. Coin pattern. Left to right: a mug, a straight-top goblet, a flared-top goblet, a goblet with the 10-cent piece, a flared-top claret and a wine glass.

Four types of U.S. Coin lamps. Left to right: a hand lamp with round bowl, a table lamp with flaring font, table lamp with round font and table lamp with square font.

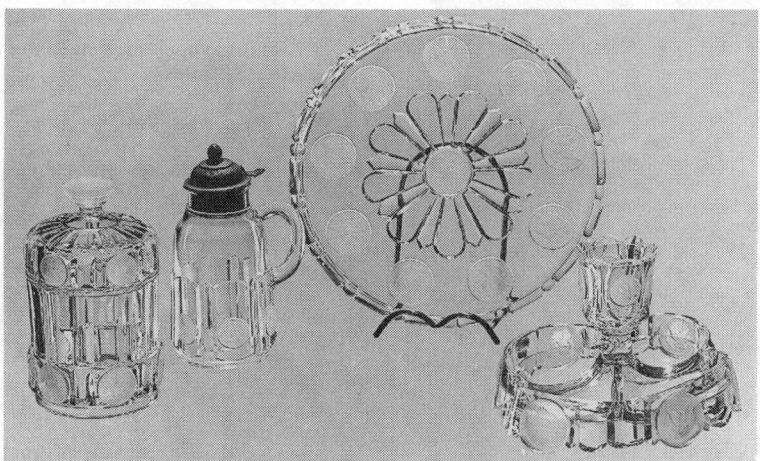

Some scarce pieces in the U.S. Coin pattern. Left to right: sugar bowl, syrup jug, water tray and epergne.

Although the "Indian Head" cent (1859-1909), the three-cent piece (1865-1889) and "Liberty Head" five-cent piece (1883-1913) were minted during the coin glass design period, they weren't used in coin glass. The five-cent, three-cent and one-cent are close enough in size to the ten-cent, leaving those pieces with only the "Liberty Seated" design. The coins they used — the half-dime and the ten-cent — gave the glass manufacturer the sizes required, with no design change necessary.

The size of the glass coins does vary, depending on the pieces used. It is puzzling why a twenty-cent piece (14/16" d.) was used on only four pieces, when a dime of the same size (14/16" d.) was used on the open compote.

The center of some of the "water trays" shows the reverse of the dollar with the eagle facing right instead of left; the "n's" in the words "one" and "United" are backwards. The backward "n's" also appear on the reverse of the glass coins on the corners of the butter dish — an easy error when designing the reverse side of a die.

FROSTED AND STAINED PIECES:

Coin glass was produced in clear glass, with either clear or frosted coins. I've been told that the clear pieces are less valuable than the frosted, but I haven't found a seller I could convince of this. The frosted pieces are both more available and more in demand. While the clear pieces, with fewer available, may not be quite as desirable to some collectors, their price seems to be the same. At any rate, there are not enough current sales records to establish a firm value difference between the two types.

The toothpick holder was made of clear glass with amber-stained coins, as well as in stained red with clear or frosted coins. The flat sauce dishes had amber and red coins. The 6" d. berry bowl had a red band around the rim, and other miscellaneous red staining has been found. According to Robert Bender of Zionsville, Indiana, whom I believe to be the foremost authority on coin glass, there's even one that is caramel-colored.

All lamps have been found with amber-stained coins. The 10" h. square font table lamp was produced with red coins, and supposedly only two were made. Coin glass lore has it that the pair was produced by a sly factory worker doing a little personal moonlighting, making a wedding gift for his own use. One is in the collection of James Simmons of Cambridge, Maryland. No one seems to know where the other one is.

An early reproduction of the U.S. Coin toothpick holder.

An original U.S. Coin toothpick holder.

REPRODUCTIONS:

Reproductions, except the early toothpick, were made in Japan and distributed by A.A. Importing of St. Louis, Missouri. The early toothpick was offered for sale in the mid-1960's and I don't know who the distributor was. The first item A.A. Importing introduced was the toothpick about 1967 of which about 2,000 to 3,000 were produced. The balance of the reproductions were produced through the mid-1970's and about 500 of each item were produced. The items were produced until the molds wore out and no additional molds were made. Prices quoted are from the wholesaler.

A late reproduction of the U.S. Coin toothpick holder.

Toothpick Holder:

Early reproductions have seven stars on the bottom of the reverse of the coin; this reproduction sold for $4.00. The later reproductions, also $4.00, show a very sharp definition of the coin, with both the date and picture well-defined. The original has two small stars on the reverse, one on each side under the "U" and "A," and the date is barely visible, if at all.

A close-up of the coin on the original U.S. Coin pattern compote.

A close-up of the coin on the reproduction U.S. Coin pattern compote.

Covered Compote - High-Standard:
The reproduction will have a ribbon over the eagle's head on the coin. The standard (behind the coins) is solid, while the originals are hollow. Reproductions cost $15.00 to $22.00. Diameter is six inches, height is nine inches.

Covered Compote - Flat:
Reproductions will have a ribbon over the eagle's head. Reproductions were $10.00 to $16.25. Diameter is six inches; height is five inches.

Creamer & Covered Sugar:
I have not seen these, and therefore cannot comment. Reproductions sold for $13.00 for the set of two.

Tumbler, Paneled Sides:
Reproduction is dated "1892" and frosted, whereas the original is dated "1878," and usually clear, although I have seen some frosted. Reproduction was sold for $2.50.

Bread Tray:
Reproduction is 8 x 10"; the original is 7 x 10". Both have dollars on the corners, with the original having the obverse and reverse on opposite corners, and the reproduction having the obverse on one end and the reverse on the other end. The dollars in the

bottom of the original lie vertically, while on the reproductions they lie horizontally. Reproductions were priced at $6.50.

Spooner:
Reproduction has four legs and eight points on the top. No original pieces were made in this design. Reproduction cost $6.50.

Candlesticks & Paperweights:
No original pieces were produced in these designs. Reproduced candlesticks were $9.75 per pair, paperweights were $7.50 per pair.

EDITOR'S NOTE: *Readers should remember that another pattern of "Coin" glass was produced by the Fostoria Glass Company from 1958 to 1982. This ware featured 'coins' not based on real money. Some are dated "1887," the year the Fostoria factory opened, and some are dated "1886." It was made in clear, and solid colors of ruby, emerald green, olive green, blue and amber.*

References:
Wheeling Glass by Josephine Jefferson (The Guide Publishing Company, 1947).
A Seventh Pitcher Book by Minnie Watson Kamm (Grosse Point, Michigan: Kamm Publications, 1953).
An Eighth Pitcher Book by Minnie Watson Kamm (Grosse Point, Michigan: Kamm Publications, 1954).

A special "thanks" to Mrs. Frances M. Burke.

For a more detailed book on U.S. Coin Glass, send $20.00 to: Tim Timmerman, 11655 S.W. Allen Blvd. #31, Beaverton, OR 97005-4850; (503) 646-8300.

PRICE LISTINGS:

Plain Top Berry Bowl

Berry bowl, plain top
6" d., quarters	$300.00
7" d., quarters	300.00
8" d., half-dollars (ILLUS.)	350.00
9" d., dollars	700.00

Berry bowl, scalloped top
  6" d., quarters 350.00

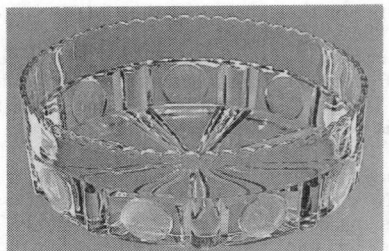

Scalloped Top Berry Bowl

7" d., quarters (ILLUS.) 350.00
8" d., half-dollars 400.00
9" d., dollars 800.00

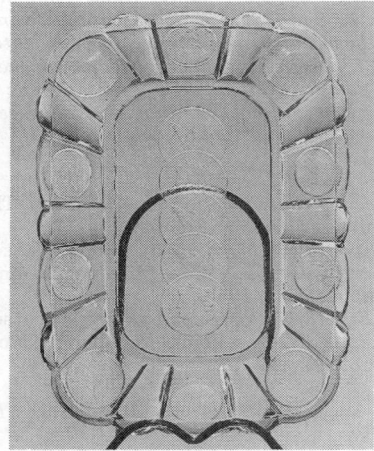

Bread Tray

Bread tray, dollars & half-dollars
  (ILLUS.) 325.00

Butter Dish

Butter dish, dollars & half-dollars
  (ILLUS.) 400.00
Cake plate, dollars & quarters
  (ILLUS. top next column) 400.00
Celery vase, quarters (ILLUS. next
  column) 300.00
Compote, covered
  High standard
    6" d., quarters & dimes 350.00
    7" d., quarters & dimes 400.00

Cake Plate

Celery Vase

  8" d., half-dollars & quarters
    (ILLUS.) 450.00
  9" d., dollars & quarters 1,000.00
Low standard
  6" d., twenty-cent pieces &
    quarters 350.00
Flat (nappy or covered dish)
  6" d., quarters 350.00
  7" d., quarters 400.00

8" d., half-dollars (ILLUS.) 450.00
9" d., dollars 800.00
Compote, open w/flared top
High standard w/plain rim
  7" d., quarters & dimes 300.00
  8¼" d., quarters & dimes 350.00
  9½" d., half-dollars & quar-
    ters 600.00
  10½" d., half-dollars & quar-
    ters 800.00
High standard w/scalloped rim
  7¼" d., quarters & dimes 500.00
Low standard w/scalloped rim
  7" d., twenty-cent pieces 450.00
Compote, open w/straight top
High standard w/plain rim
  7¼" d., quarters & dimes 300.00
  8½" d., quarters & dimes 350.00
  9¾" d., half-dollars & quar-
    ters 400.00

10½" d., half-dollars & quarters
  (ILLUS.) 500.00
Low standard w/scalloped rim
  6" d., twenty-cent pieces 450.00
Cruet w/original stopper, quarters
  (ILLUS. top next column) 650.00
Epergne, dollars & quarters
  (ILLUS. next column) 700.00
Goblet, ale, w/straight top, dimes,
  6½" h. (ILLUS. next column)...... 250.00
Goblet, ale, w/straight top, half-
  dollars, 7" h. (ILLUS. top next
  page left) 400.00
Goblet, ale, w/flared top, half-

dollars, 7" h. (ILLUS. top next
page right) 400.00

Cruet

Epergne

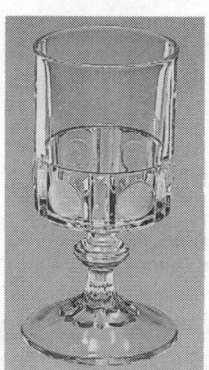

6½" h. Goblet

Lamps:
  Hand lamp, low footed, w/handle
  Round font
    4¾" h., twenty-cent pieces
      (ILLUS. bottom next page
      right) 400.00
    5½" h., quarters (ILLUS. bottom
      next page left) 400.00
  Paneled font
    4¾" h., twenty-cent pieces .. 400.00
    5¼" h., quarters 400.00
Table lamp, tall stem
  Flaring bowl

7" h. Goblets

8½" h., quarters (ILLUS.
  right) 450.00
9" h., quarters 450.00
9½" h., quarters (ILLUS.
  left) 450.00
10" h., quarters 450.00

Round bowl
  8" h., quarters 400.00
  8½" h., quarters 400.00
  9" h., quarters 400.00
  9½" h., quarters 400.00
  10" h., half-dollars 500.00
  10½" h., half-dollars 500.00
  11" h., half-dollars 600.00

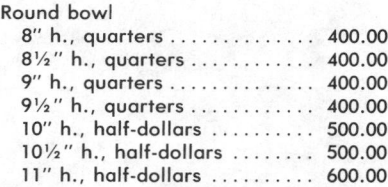

11½" h., half-dollars
  (ILLUS.) 600.00
Square bowl
  8" h., half-dollars & quar-
    ters 400.00
  8½" h., half-dollars & quar-
    ters 400.00
  9" h., dollars & quarters 400.00
  9½" h., dollars & quarters . . . 400.00
  10" h., dollars & half-
    dollars 500.00
  10½" h., dollars & half-
    dollars 500.00
  11" h., dollars & half-
    dollars 600.00
  11½" h., dollars & half-
    dollars (ILLUS. below) 600.00

U.S. Coin Pattern Hand Lamps

Mug, dollars (ILLUS.) 350.00

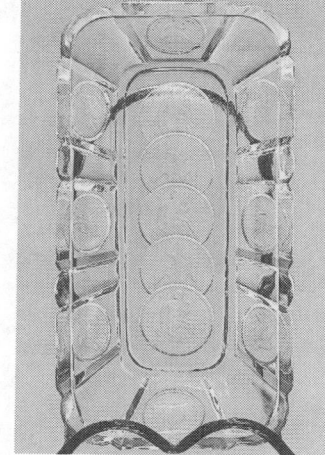

Pickle dish, half-dollars (ILLUS.) 200.00

Pitcher
    Water, dollars (ILLUS.) 500.00
    Milk, half-dollars 600.00
    Creamer, quarters 400.00
Preserve dish, half-dollars (ILLUS.
    top next column) 300.00
Salt & pepper shakers w/original
    pewter tops, quarters, each
    (ILLUS. of one next column) 150.00

Preserve Dish

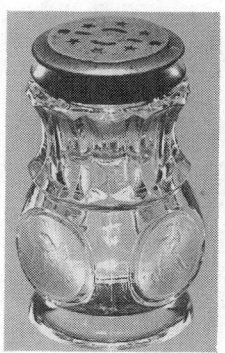

Shaker

Sauce dish, flat
    Plain top
        4" d., quarters 120.00

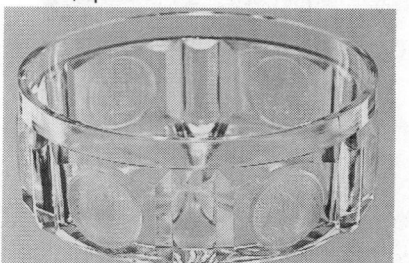

    4½" d., quarters (ILLUS.) 150.00

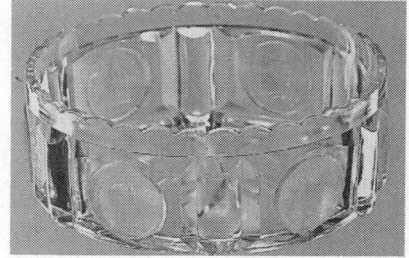

Scalloped top
    4" d., quarters 350.00

4½" d., quarters (ILLUS.) 400.00
Sauce dish, footed

4" to 4½" d., plain top, quarters
   (ILLUS.)...................... 150.00

4" to 4½" d., scalloped top,
   quarters (ILLUS.) 350.00

Spooner, quarters (ILLUS.)......... 250.00
Sugar bowl, cov., half-dollars &
   quarters (ILLUS. top next column)........................ 350.00
Syrup jug w/original dated metal
   top, quarters (ILLUS. next column)........................ 500.00
Toothpick holder, dollars (ILLUS.
   next column) 150.00
Tumbler, paneled sides, 1878 dollar
   in base (ILLUS. top next page).... 200.00

Covered Sugar Bowl

Syrup Jug

Toothpick Holder

Tumbler, clear sides, 1879 dollar in
   base, clear coin................. 200.00
Tumbler, clear sides, 1882 dollar in
   base, frosted coin 200.00

Tumbler with Paneled Sides

Tumbler, dimes on side (ILLUS.) 200.00
Waste (or finger) bowl
    4" d., 2½" h., straight top,
       quarters 350.00

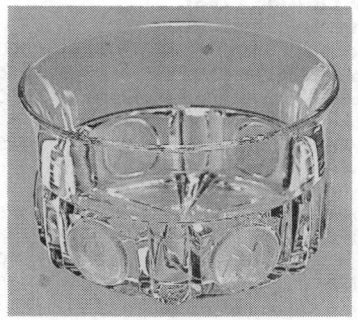

    4¼" d., 2½" h., flared top, quar-
       ters (ILLUS.) 350.00
Water tray, dollars, 10" d. (ILLUS.
    top next column) 450.00
Wine glasses
    Champagne, half-dimes, 5½" h. . . 450.00
    Claret, w/flared top, half-dimes,
       4¾" h. (ILLUS. left) 400.00
    Claret, w/straight top, half-dimes,
       4¾" h. 400.00
    Wine, half-dimes, 4¼" h. (ILLUS.
       right) 350.00

Water Tray

Claret & Wine Glasses

(End of Special Focus)

PATTERN GLASS

    Though it has never been ascertained whether glass was first pressed in the United States or abroad, the development of the glass pressing machine revolutionized the glass industry in the United States and this country receives the credit for improving the method to make this process feasible. The first wares pressed were probably small flat plates of the type now referred to as "lacy," the intricacy of the design concealing flaws.

    In 1827, both the New England Glass Co., Cambridge, Massachusetts and Bakewell &

Co., Pittsburgh, took out patents for pressing glass furniture knobs and soon other
pieces followed. This early pressed glass contained red lead which made it clear and reso-
nant when tapped (flint). Made primarily in
clear, it is rarer in blue, amethyst, olive green
and yellow.

By the 1840's, early simple patterns such
as Ashburton, Argus and Excelsior appeared.
Ribbed Bellflower seems to have been one of
the earliest patterns to have had complete
sets. By the 1860's, a wide range of patterns
was available.

In 1864, William Leighton of Hobbs, Brockunier & Co., Wheeling, West Virginia, developed a formula for "soda lime" glass which
did not require the expensive red lead for clar-
ity. Although "soda lime" glass did not have
the brilliance of the earlier flint glass, the formula came into widespread use because glass
could be produced cheaply.

An asterisk (*) indicates a piece which has
been reproduced.

ACTRESS

Actress Celery Vase

Bowl, cov.	$110.00
Bowl, 6" d., footed	50.00
Bowl, 7" d., footed	45.00
Bread tray, Miss Neilson, 12½" l.	90.00
Butter dish, cov., Fanny Davenport & Miss Neilson	75.00 to 110.00
Cake stand, Maude Granger & Annie Pixley, 10" d., 7" h.	125.00
Cake stand, frosted stem	165.00
Celery vase, Pinafore scene (ILLUS.)	175.00
Cheese dish, cov., "Lone Fisherman" on cover, "The Two Dromios" on underplate	225.00 to 235.00
Cologne bottle w/original stopper, 11" h.	47.00
Compote, cov., 6" d., 10" h.	100.00
Compote, cov., 7" d., 8½" h.	145.00
Compote, cov., 8" d., 12" h.	160.00
Compote, open, 6" d., 11" h.	130.00

Compote, open, 7" d., 7" h., Miss Neilson	150.00
Compote, open, 7" d., 7" h., Maggie Mitchell & Fanny Davenport	110.00
Compote, open, 8" d., 5" h.	75.00
Compote, open, 10" d., 6" h.	80.00
Compote, open, 10" d., 9" h.	100.00
Creamer, clear	65.00
Creamer, frosted	125.00
Goblet, Lotta Crabtree & Kate Claxton, clear	82.00
Goblet, frosted bowl	120.00
Marmalade jar, cov., Maude Granger & Annie Pixley	110.00
*Pickle dish, Kate Claxton, "Love's Request is Pickles," 5¼ x 9¼"	45.00
Platter, 7 x 11½", Pinafore scene	85.00
*Relish, Miss Neilson, 5 x 8"	35.00
Relish, Maude Granger, 5 x 9"	95.00
Sauce dish, Maggie Mitchell & Fanny Davenport, 4½" d., 2½" h.	24.00
Spooner, Mary Anderson & Maude Granger	74.00
Sugar bowl, cov., Lotta Crabtree & Kate Claxton	97.00

ADONIS (Pleat & Tuck or Washboard)

Celery	27.50
Creamer, blue	35.00
Creamer, clear	25.00
Plate, 10" d., clear	13.50
Plate, 10" d., green	35.00
Relish dish	9.50
Salt shaker w/original top	27.50
Sauce dish	7.00
Sugar bowl, cov.	28.00

ALASKA (Lion's Leg)

Banana boat, blue opalescent	175.00 to 200.00
Banana boat, emerald green	185.00
Banana boat, vaseline opalescent	200.00
Banana boat, vaseline opalescent w/enameling	325.00
Berry set: master bowl & 4 sauce dishes: emerald green, 5 pcs.	250.00 to 275.00
Bowl, 8" sq., blue opalescent	150.00 to 200.00
Bowl, 8" sq., emerald green	55.00
Bowl, 8" sq., emerald green w/enameled florals	122.00
Bowl, 8" sq., emerald green w/gold & enameling, w/silver plate stand	145.00
Bowl, 8" sq., vaseline opalescent	140.00
Bowl, 8" sq., vaseline opalescent w/enameled florals	225.00
Butter dish, cov., blue opalescent	375.00
Butter dish, cov., emerald green w/enameled florals	140.00 to 160.00
Butter dish, cov., vaseline opalescent	268.00

Butter dish, cov., white w/enameled
florals 85.00
Celery (or jewel) tray, blue
opalescent 132.00
Celery tray, blue opalescent
w/enameled florals 250.00
Celery tray, emerald green 75.00
Celery tray, emerald green
w/gold 85.00
Celery tray, vaseline opalescent
w/enameled florals 170.00
Creamer, blue opalescent 75.00
Creamer, clear opalescent 55.00
Creamer, emerald green 48.00
Creamer, vaseline opalescent 68.00
Cruet w/original stopper, blue
opalescent 260.00
Cruet w/original stopper, emerald
green 275.00
Cruet w/original stopper, vase-
line opalescent w/enameled
florals . . . . 200.00 to 250.00
Pitcher, water, blue opalescent 350.00
Pitcher, water, blue opalescent
w/enameled florals 550.00
Pitcher, water, clear opalescent
w/enameled florals & gold trim . . 125.00
Pitcher, water, emerald green
w/enameled florals 285.00
Pitcher, water, vaseline opales-
cent 350.00
Pitcher, water, vaseline opalescent
w/enameled florals . . . . . 425.00 to 500.00
Salt shaker w/original top, blue
opalescent 85.00
Salt shaker w/original top, emerald
green w/enameling 75.00
Salt shaker w/original top, vaseline
opalescent 75.00
Sauce dish, blue opalescent 38.00
Sauce dish, clear opalescent 25.00
Sauce dish, clear opalescent
w/enameled florals 35.00
Sauce dish, emerald green 20.00
Sauce dish, emerald green
w/enameled florals & leaves 38.00
Sauce dish, vaseline opalescent 38.00
Sauce dish, vaseline opalescent
w/enameled florals 48.50
Spooner, blue opalescent 62.00
Spooner, clear opalescent 42.00
Spooner, emerald green 34.00
Spooner, emerald green w/enam-
eled florals 70.00
Spooner, vaseline opalescent 60.00
Spooner, vaseline opalescent
w/enameled florals 75.00
Sugar bowl, cov., blue opalescent . . 150.00
Sugar bowl, cov., clear opalescent
w/enameled florals 65.00
Sugar bowl, cov., emerald green
w/enameled florals 73.00
Sugar bowl, cov., vaseline
opalescent 185.00

Sugar bowl, cov., vaseline opales-
cent w/enameled florals 245.00
Table set, blue opalescent,
4 pcs. . . . . 650.00 to 700.00
Table set, vaseline opalescent,
4 pcs. . . . . 550.00 to 600.00
Tumbler, blue opalescent 65.00
Tumbler, vaseline opalescent 67.50
Tumbler, vaseline opalescent
w/enameled florals 75.00
Water set: pitcher & 6 tumblers;
vaseline opalescent, 7 pcs. 850.00

ALEXIS - See Priscilla Pattern

AMAZON (Sawtooth Band)
Banana stand 67.00
Bowl, 6" d. 22.00
Bowl, 8" d., scalloped 24.00
Butter dish, cov. 90.00
Cake stand, 8" to 9½" d. 36.00
Celery vase 33.00
Champagne 30.00
Claret 37.50
Compote, open, jelly, 4½" d. 22.50
Compote, open, 6" d., high stand . . . 28.00
Compote, open, 9½" d., 8" h. 55.00
Cordial, ruby-stained 38.00
Creamer 45.00
Cruet w/bar in hand stopper 55.00
Goblet 32.00
Pitcher, water 53.00
Spooner 30.00
Sugar bowl, cov. 40.00
Tumbler, engraved 39.00
Tumbler, plain 22.00
Vase, double-bud 75.00
Wine 24.00

ANIMALS & BIRDS ON GOBLETS & PITCHERS

Goblets:
Bird & roses, acid-etched 30.00
Deer & Doe w/lily-of-the-valley,
pressed 100.00
Dog w/rabbit in mouth, acid-
etched 105.00
Flamingo Habitat, acid-etched 43.00
Frog & Spider, pressed 126.00
Giraffe, acid-etched 75.00
Ibex, acid-etched 86.00
Lion in the Jungle, acid-etched 90.00
Ostrich Looking at Moon, pressed . . 125.00
Owl-Possum, pressed 90.00
Pigs in Corn, pressed . . . . . 250.00 to 350.00
Squirrel, pressed, non-Greentown . . 300.00
Stork & Flowers, acid-etched 65.00

Pitchers:
Bringing Home Cows, pressed 750.00
Flamingo Habitat, acid-etched 125.00
Fox & Crow, pressed 150.00
Heron, pressed 143.00
Squirrel, pressed, non-Greentown . . 175.00

APOLLO

Bowl, 8" d.	22.50
Bread tray, square	27.50
Cake stand, engraved, 9" d.	47.50
Cake stand, plain, 9" to 10½" d.	50.00
Celery tray	16.00
Celery vase	37.50 to 45.00
Compote, cov., 4¾" d., 8¾" h.	45.00
Compote, cov., 6" d.	45.00
Compote, cov., 8" d.	65.00
Compote, open, 5" d.	25.00
Creamer, engraved	57.50
Creamer, plain	45.00
Goblet, engraved	35.00
Goblet, frosted	47.50
Goblet, plain	32.00
Lamp, kerosene-type, clear, 7" h.	60.00
Lamp, kerosene-type, blue, 9" h.	265.00
Lamp, kerosene-type, clear, 10" h.	72.00
Lamp, kerosene-type, canary yellow w/frosted font & stem w/enameling, 12" h.	260.00
Lamp, kerosene-type, blue base w/vaseline font	245.00
Sauce dish, flat or footed	15.00
Spooner	40.00
Sugar bowl, cov., etched	75.00
Sugar shaker w/original top	37.00
Syrup pitcher w/original top	110.00
Toothpick holder	28.00
Tray, water	40.00
Tumbler, clear	21.00
Tumbler, frosted	30.00

ART (Job's Tears)

Banana stand	100.00
Bowl, 7" d., flared rim, footed	26.50
Bowl, 8" sq., shallow	34.00
Bowl, 8½" d.	40.00
Bowl, 9¾" d.	38.00
Bowl, rectangular	20.00
Bowl, triangular	45.00
Butter dish, cov.	45.00
Cake stand, 9" to 10½" d.	58.00
Celery vase	37.00
Compote, cov., 6" d., 10" h.	54.00
Compote, cov., 7" d.	65.00
Compote, cov., 8" d., high stand	99.00
Compote, open, jelly, 5" d.	27.50
Compote, open, 9" d., 7¼" h.	48.00
Compote, open, 10" d., 9" h.	50.00
Cracker jar, cov., 7" d., 8" h. to top of finial	95.00
Creamer	42.00
Cruet w/original stopper	88.00
Goblet	50.00
Pitcher, water, bulbous	82.50
Relish, 4¼ x 7¾"	18.50
Sauce dish, flat or footed	15.00
Spooner	27.00
Sugar bowl, cov., engraved	48.00
Sugar bowl, cov., plain	42.50
Tumbler	30.00

ASHBURTON

Ale glass, flint, 6½" h.	85.00
Celery vase, plain rim, flint	64.00
Celery vase, scalloped rim, flint	135.00
Champagne, barrel-shaped, flint	85.00
Claret, flint, 5¼" h.	65.00
Cordial, flint, 4¼" h.	45.00
Creamer, applied handle, flint	250.00 to 275.00
Decanter, bar lip, canary yellow, flint	550.00
Decanter, bar lip w/patent pewter stopper, clear, flint	125.00
Decanter, bar lip w/patent pewter stopper, canary yellow, flint	1,600.00
Decanter, bar lip & facet-cut neck, flint, qt.	55.00
Decanter w/original stopper, clear, flint, qt.	97.50
Egg cup, clambroth, flint	155.00
Egg cup, clear, flint	32.00
Egg cup, non-flint	15.50
Egg cup, disconnected ovals	35.00
Flip glass, handled, flint, 7" h.	212.00
Goblet, short, flint	42.00
Goblet, barrel-shaped, flint	44.00
Goblet, flared, flint, clear	50.00
Goblet, flared, flint, clear w/gold, 6" h.	95.00
Goblet, non-flint	30.00
Goblet, disconnected ovals	35.00
Honey dish, 3½" d.	9.00
Mug, applied handle, 3" h.	60.00
Mug, applied handle, 4¾" h.	110.00
Pitcher, water, applied hollow handle, flint	400.00 to 450.00
Pomade jar, cov., white opaque, flint	195.00
Sugar bowl, cov., flint	175.00
Tumbler, bar, flint	58.00
Tumbler, water, flint	59.00
Tumbler, water, footed	85.00
Tumbler, whiskey, applied handle, flint	100.00 to 125.00
Vases, 9¼" h., shaped pedestal base, flint, pr.	160.00
Wine, clear, flint	42.00
Wine, clear, knob stem	85.00
Wine, peacock green, flint	650.00
Wine, non-flint	25.00

ATLANTA (Lion or Square Lion's Head)

Bowl, 5 x 8" oblong, flat	50.00
Butter dish, cov.	125.00
Celery vase	60.00
Compote, cov., 5" sq., 6" h.	95.00
Compote, cov., 8" sq., 9½" h.	130.00
Compote, open, 4¼" sq., 4" h.	45.00
Compote, open, 6" sq., 7½" h.	75.00
Compote, open, 8" sq., high stand	95.00
Creamer	48.00
Egg cup	95.00
*Goblet	62.00

Marmalade jar, cov., w/lion's head finial	100.00
Pitcher, water	110.00
Relish, boat-shaped	30.00
Salt dip, master size	135.00
Sauce dish	23.00
Spooner	47.00
Sugar bowl, cov., engraved	140.00
Sugar bowl, cov., plain	95.00
Toothpick holder	60.00
Tumbler	35.00

ATLAS (Crystal Ball or Cannon Ball)

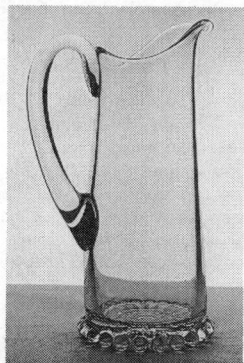

Atlas Pitcher

Butter dish, cov.	40.00
Cake stand, 8" to 10" d.	28.00
Celery vase	39.50
Champagne, 5½" h.	34.00
Cordial	42.00
Creamer, flat or pedestal base	22.00
Goblet, engraved	30.00
Goblet, plain	30.00
Pitcher, milk, tankard, applied handle	45.00
Pitcher, water, tankard, applied handle (ILLUS.)	50.00
Salt dip, individual size	15.00
Sauce dish, flat or footed	12.50
Spooner	30.00
Toothpick holder	25.00
Tray, water	65.00
Tumbler	28.00
Wine	25.00

BABY THUMBPRINT - See Dakota Pattern

BALDER - See Pennsylvania Pattern

BALTIMORE PEAR

Bowl, 4 x 8"	19.00
Bread plate, 12½" l.	48.00
*Butter dish, cov.	53.00
Cake plate, side handles, 10" octagon	38.00
*Cake stand, high pedestal	55.00

*Celery vase	50.00
Compote, cov., 7" d., high stand	75.00
*Creamer	32.00
*Goblet	35.00
*Pitcher, water	75.00 to 95.00
*Plate, 9" d.	28.00
Relish, 8¼" l.	22.50
*Sauce dish, flat or footed	18.00
Spooner	45.00
*Sugar bowl, cov.	53.00
Tray, water	28.00

BAMBOO - See Broken Column Pattern

BANDED PORTLAND

Berry set: master bowl & 8 sauce dishes; pink-stained w/gold trim, 9 pcs.	295.00
Bowl, berry, 9" d.	30.00
Butter dish, cov., pink-stained	150.00
Candlesticks, pr.	75.00
Celery tray, pink-stained, 10" oval	75.00
Celery tray, 5 x 12"	25.00
Celery vase	32.00
Cologne bottle w/original stopper	51.00
Compote, cov., 8" d., high stand	110.00
Creamer	35.00
Creamer, individual size	29.00
Cruet w/original stopper	60.00
Dresser jar, cov., 3½" d.	36.00
Goblet, clear	40.00
Goblet, pink-stained	68.00
Pitcher, water, 9½" h.	95.00
Pitcher, child's, pink-stained	32.50
Pomade jar, cov.	25.00
Punch cup, clear	12.50
Punch cup, clear w/gold trim	18.00
Relish, pink-stained, 4 x 6½"	28.00
Relish, clear, 4 x 8½" oval	14.00
Relish, pink-stained, 4 x 8½" oval	36.00
Salt & pepper shakers w/original tops, clear, pr.	55.00
Salt & pepper shakers w/original tops, pink-stained, pr.	100.00
Sauce dish, 4½" d.	15.00
Sauce dish, boat-shaped, pink-stained, 4¾" l.	25.00
Spooner, clear	35.00
Spooner, pink-stained	75.00
Sugar bowl, cov., pink-stained	112.00
Sugar bowl, individual size	22.50
Sugar shaker w/original top	50.00
Syrup jug w/original top, clear	75.00
Syrup jug w/original top, pink-stained	365.00
Toothpick holder, clear	41.00
Toothpick holder, pink-stained	50.00
Toothpick holder, purple-stained	28.00
Tumbler	35.00
Vase, 6" h., flared, clear	32.00
Vase, 6" h., flared, pink-stained	35.00
Vase, 9" h.	42.00
Wine, blue-stained	28.00

Wine, clear	30.00
Wine, gold-stained	35.00
Wine, pink-stained	75.00

BARBERRY

Barberry Pitcher

Bowl, 6" oval	18.00
Butter dish, cov., shell finial	50.00
Butter dish, cov., pattern on base rim	110.00
Cake stand, 9½" d.	48.00
Cake stand, 11" d.	125.00
Celery vase	38.00
Compote, cov., 8" d., high stand, shell finial	95.00
Compote, cov., 8" d., low stand, shell finial	77.50
Compote, open, 8½" d., 7" h.	42.00
Egg cup	20.00
Goblet	28.00
Pitcher, water, 9½" h., applied handle (ILLUS.)	84.00
Plate, 6" d., blue	50.00
Plate, 6" d., clear	20.00
Sauce dish, flat or footed	13.50
Spooner, footed	32.00
Sugar bowl, cov., shell finial	42.00
Tumbler, footed	28.00
Wine	35.00

BEADED DEWDROP - See Wisconsin Pattern

BEADED GRAPE (California)

Bowl, 5½" sq., green	19.50
Bowl, 6½" sq., green	30.00
Bowl, 8" sq., clear	28.00
Bowl, 8" sq., green	35.00
Bowl, 6¼ x 8½" rectangle, green	30.00
Bowl, 9" sq., four-footed	15.00
Butter dish, cov., square, clear	55.00
Butter dish, cov., square, green	82.00
Cake stand, clear, 9" sq., 6" h.	55.00
Cake stand, green, 9" sq., 6" h.	83.00
Celery tray, clear	33.00

Celery tray, green	40.00
Celery vase	32.00
Compote, cov., 4 7/8" sq., 6" h., green	55.00
Compote, cov., 6½" sq., high stand, clear	75.00
*Compote, cov., 8½" sq., high stand, clear	125.00
Compote, open, 8½" sq., high stand, clear	72.50
Compote, open, 8½" sq., high stand, green	85.00
Cordial	15.00
Creamer, clear	40.00
Creamer, green	45.00
Cruet w/original stopper, green	115.00
*Goblet	37.00
Pitcher, water, round, green	78.00
Pitcher, water, square, green	125.00
Pitcher, water, tankard, clear	78.00
*Plate, 8" sq., clear	27.50
*Plate, 8" sq., green	40.00
Relish, green w/gold, 4 x 7"	35.00
Salt shaker w/original top, clear	32.50
Salt shaker w/original top, green	47.50
*Sauce dish, clear	12.00
*Sauce dish, green	15.00
Sauce dish, handled, green	30.00
Spooner, clear	40.00
Spooner, green	48.00
Sugar bowl, cov., clear	54.00
Sugar bowl, cov., green	60.00
Toothpick holder, clear	23.00
Toothpick holder, green	55.00
*Tumbler, clear	27.50
*Tumbler, green	40.00
*Wine, clear	35.00
*Wine, green	60.00

BEADED LOOP (Oregon - U.S. Glass Co.)

Beaded Loop Goblet

Berry set, master bowl & 6 sauce dishes, 7 pcs.	65.00
Butter dish, cov.	46.50
Cake stand, 9" to 10½" d.	45.00
Celery vase, 7" h.	29.00

Compote, cov., 7" d.	95.00
Compote, open, jelly	38.00
Compote, open, 7" d.	25.00
Compote, open, 7½" d., low stand	38.00
Compote, open, 9" d., 7¼" h.	50.00
Creamer	38.00
Cruet w/faceted stopper	49.00
*Goblet (ILLUS.)	36.00
Goblet, w/gold trim	32.50
Mug, footed, clear	38.00
Mug, ruby-stained	25.00
Pickle dish, boat-shaped, 7¼" l.	12.00
Pitcher, milk, 8½" h.	35.00
Pitcher, water, tankard	50.00
Relish	18.00
Salt shaker w/original top	25.00
Sauce dish, flat or footed	10.00
Spooner, clear	26.00
Spooner, ruby-stained	65.00
*Sugar bowl, cov.	37.00
Toothpick holder	30.00
Tumbler	50.00
Vase, small	37.00
Wine	58.00

BEARDED HEAD - See Viking Pattern

BELLFLOWER

Bowl, 7½" d., 2" h.	110.00
Bowl, 8" d., 4½" h., scalloped rim	95.00
Butter dish, cov.	95.00
Castor bottle w/original stopper	38.00
Celery vase, fine rib, single vine	130.00
Compote, open, 6" d., low stand	59.00
Compote, open, 7" d., low stand, scalloped rim	90.00
Compote, open, 8" d., 5" h., scalloped rim, single vine	100.00
Compote, open, 8" d., 8" h., dome-footed, single vine	125.00
Compote, open, 8" d., high stand, flint	285.00
Compote, open, 9½" d., 8½" h., scalloped rim, single vine	162.00
Cordial, barrel-shaped, knob stem, rayed base	95.00
Cordial, fine rib, single vine, knob stem	150.00
Cordial, fine rib, single vine, plain stem	60.00
Creamer, fine rib, double vine, applied handle	150.00
Creamer, fine rib, single vine, applied handle	135.00
Decanter w/bar lip, patent stopper, double vine, qt.	385.00
Egg cup, fine rib, single vine	40.00
Goblet, barrel-shaped, fine rib, single vine, knob stem	52.00
*Goblet, barrel-shaped, fine rib, single vine, plain stem	48.00
Goblet, coarse rib	45.00
Goblet, double vine	62.50

Goblet, 5 7/8" h., fine rib, single vine, pale green	210.00
Honey dish, rayed center, 3¼" d.	22.50
Honey dish, ringed center, 3½" d.	22.50
Lamp, kerosene-type, 8½" h.	175.00
*Pitcher, milk, double vine	350.00
Pitcher, water, 8¾" h., coarse rib, double vine	300.00
Plate, 6" d., fine rib, single vine	100.00
Salt dip, open, master size, footed, scalloped rim, single vine	40.00
Sauce dish, double vine	20.00
Sauce dish, single vine	20.00
Spooner, low foot, double vine	50.00
Spooner, scalloped rim, single vine	40.00
Sugar bowl, cov., double vine	55.00
Syrup pitcher w/original top, applied handle, fine rib, single vine, clear	650.00 to 750.00
Syrup pitcher w/original top, applied handle, fine rib, single vine, fiery opalescent	1,100.00
Tumbler, bar, fine rib, single vine	90.00
Tumbler, coarse rib, double vine	105.00
Tumbler, fine rib, single vine, banded	150.00
Tumbler, whiskey	185.00
Wine, barrel-shaped, knob stem, fine rib, single vine, rayed base	125.00
Wine, barrel-shaped, fine rib, double vine, w/cut bellflowers	325.00
Wine, straight sides, plain stem, rayed base	55.00

BIRD & FERN - See Hummingbird Pattern

BIRD & STRAWBERRY (Bluebird)

Bird & Strawberry Tumbler

Berry set: master bowl & 5 sauce dishes; w/color, 6 pcs.	525.00
Berry set: master bowl & 6 sauce dishes; footed, 7 pcs.	150.00 to 200.00
Bowl, 5½" d., clear	27.00
Bowl, 5½" d., w/color	35.00
Bowl, 7½" d., footed	62.00
Bowl, 9" d., flat, w/color	75.00
Bowl, 9½" l., 6" w., oval, footed	65.00

Bowl, 10" d., flat, clear 62.00
Bowl, 10" d., flat, w/color & gold
    trim........................... 115.00
Butter dish, cov., clear 90.00
Butter dish, cov., w/color ..150.00 to 200.00
Cake stand, 9" to 9½" d. 55.00
*Compote, cov., 6½" d., 9½" h..... 125.00
Compote, cov., jelly 130.00
Creamer, clear.................... 48.00
Creamer, w/color 125.00
Dish, heart-shaped 48.00
Pitcher, water 275.00
Plate, 12" d. 75.00
Punch cup 20.00
Sauce dish, flat or footed, clear 26.50
Sauce dish, w/color 38.00
Spooner, clear 49.00
Spooner, w/color ....100.00 to 125.00
Sugar bowl, cov. 64.00
Sugar bowl, open 34.00
Table set, 4 pcs. 250.00
Tumbler, clear 50.00
Tumbler, w/color (ILLUS.) ...75.00 to 100.00
Wine............................ 52.00

BLOCK & FAN

Bowl, 9¾" d. 32.00
Butter dish, cov. 38.00
Cake stand, 9" to 10" d. 29.00
Celery tray 25.00
Celery vase..................... 35.00
Compote, open, 8" d., high stand ... 45.00
Cracker jar, cov. 75.00
Creamer 38.00
Cruet w/original stopper, small,
    6" h.......................... 25.00
Cruet w/original stopper, medium .. 45.00
Goblet, clear 52.00
Goblet, ruby-stained.............. 110.00
Ice bucket 45.00
Pitcher, water 48.00
Plate, 10" d. 25.00
Relish, 11½" l................... 45.00
Salt shaker w/original top 20.00
Sauce dish, flat or footed, clear 12.50
Sauce dish, flat or footed, ruby-
    stained....................... 30.00
Spooner 28.00
Sugar shaker w/original top 40.00
Syrup pitcher w/original top, 7" h... 140.00
Wine, clear..................... 50.00
Wine, ruby-stained 75.00

BLOCK & STAR - See Valencia Waffle Pattern

BLUEBIRD - See Bird & Strawberry Pattern

BROKEN COLUMN (Irish Column, Notched Rib or Bamboo)

Bowl, 7" d. 40.00
Cake stand, 9" to 10" d. 85.00
Celery vase, clear 55.00

Celery vase, w/red notches 155.00
Compote, cov., 5" d., high stand ... 80.00
Compote, open, jelly, w/red
    notches 195.00
Compote, open, 5" d., 6" h. 32.00
Compote, open, 5" d., low stand,
    flared rim 50.00
Compote, open, 6" d., high stand... 35.00
Compote, open, 7" d., low stand ... 55.00
Cracker jar, cov. 100.00
*Creamer, clear................. 38.00
Creamer, w/red notches 245.00
Cruet w/original stopper.......... 85.00

Broken Column Goblet

*Goblet (ILLUS.)................. 54.00
Marmalade jar w/original cover 85.00
Pickle castor, cov., clear, original
    ornate frame 250.00
Pickle castor, w/red notches,
    w/frame & tongs........400.00 to 425.00
*Pitcher, water, clear............. 86.00
Pitcher, water, w/red notches 225.00
Plate, 5" d. 32.00
*Plate, 8" d. 40.00
Punch cup, blue 95.00
Punch cup, clear 25.00
Relish, w/red notches, 9" l., 5" w.. 78.00
Salt shaker w/original top 55.00
*Sauce dish, clear 15.00
Sauce dish, w/red notches 32.00
*Spooner, clear 36.00
Spooner, w/red notches 125.00
*Sugar bowl, cov., clear 72.00
Sugar bowl, cov., w/red notches ... 150.00
Syrup pitcher w/metal top 130.00
Tumbler, clear 45.00
Tumbler, w/red notches 75.00
Vase, 6½" h. 30.00
Water set: pitcher & 5 tumblers;
    w/red notches, 6 pcs. 650.00
*Wine........................... 85.00

BRYCE - See Ribbon Candy Pattern

BUCKLE

Bowl, 10" d., 3½" h., flint 85.00
Butter dish, cov. 81.00
Cake stand, 9¾" d., 5¼" h. 30.00

Champagne, flint	75.00
Compote, open, 8" d., low stand, flint	38.50
Compote, open, 8" d., low stand, non-flint	17.50
Creamer, applied handle, flint	90.00
Egg cup, flint	37.00
Egg cup, non-flint	25.00
Goblet, flint	50.00
Goblet, non-flint	26.00
Lamp, kerosene-type, brass & iron base	125.00 to 150.00
Pitcher, water, bulbous, applied handle, flint	467.50
Salt dip, master size, footed, flint	35.00
Salt dip, master size, flat, oval, flint	22.50
Spooner, flint	37.50
Spooner, non-flint	30.00
Sugar bowl, cov., w/acorn finial, flint	95.00
Sugar bowl, cov., w/acorn finial, non-flint	43.00
Tumbler, bar, flint	90.00
Tumbler, non-flint	29.00

BUCKLE WITH STAR

Buckle with Star Compote

Cake stand, 9" d.	35.00
Celery vase	32.00
Compote, cov., 7" d. (ILLUS.)	60.00
Compote, open, 8" d.	37.50
Creamer	35.00
Goblet	24.00
Sauce dish, flat or footed	9.50
Spooner	30.00
Sugar bowl, cov.	42.50
Sugar bowl, open	24.00
Syrup pitcher w/metal top	70.00
Tumbler, bar	65.00
Wine	25.00

BULL'S EYE

Ale glass	45.00
Celery vase, flint	75.00
Cordial, flint	85.00
Cruet w/original stopper	195.00

Egg cup, clear, flint, 3¾" h.	55.00
Egg cup, jade green	385.00
Goblet, flint	72.00
Salt dip, master size, footed, flint	32.50
Tumbler, flat, flint	70.00
Wine, knob stem, flint	58.00

BUTTON ARCHES

Button Arches Tumbler

Berry set: 8" d. master bowl & 6 sauce dishes; ruby-stained, 7 pcs.	158.00
Bowl, 8" d., ruby-stained, souvenir	45.00
Compote, open, jelly, 4½" h., ruby-stained	40.00
Creamer, clear	18.50
*Creamer, ruby-stained	40.00
Creamer, ruby-stained, souvenir, 3½" h.	30.00
Creamer, ruby-stained, souvenir, 4½" h.	45.00
*Creamer, individual size, ruby-stained	28.00
Cruet w/original stopper, ruby-stained	175.00
Goblet, clambroth	26.00
Goblet, clear	24.00
*Goblet, ruby-stained	37.50
Mug, clear	18.00
Mug, ruby-stained	30.00
Mug, ruby-stained, souvenir, 3½" h.	30.00
Pitcher, tankard, 8¾" h.	117.00
Pitcher, water, tankard, ruby-stained, souvenir of Pan American Exposition	150.00
Punch cup, ruby-stained, souvenir	28.50
Salt dip	18.50
Salt shaker w/original top, ruby-stained	25.00
Salt & pepper shakers, w/original tops, small, pr.	35.00
Sauce dish, clear	15.00
Sauce dish, ruby-stained	30.00
*Spooner, ruby-stained	42.50
Spooner, ruby-stained w/clear band	62.50
Spooner, ruby-stained & engraved	44.00
Sugar bowl, cov., clear	45.00

*Sugar bowl, cov., ruby-stained 85.00
Syrup pitcher w/original top 40.00
*Toothpick holder, ruby-stained 30.00
Toothpick holder, ruby-stained,
   souvenir...................... 35.00
Tumbler, clambroth, souvenir 23.00
Tumbler, clear 16.00
Tumbler, clear w/frosted band 22.00
Tumbler, ruby-stained 42.50
Tumbler, ruby-stained, souvenir
   (ILLUS.)...................... 39.50
Wine, clear 27.50
Wine, ruby-stained 37.50

CABBAGE ROSE

Bitters bottle, 6½" h.............. 125.00
Butter dish, cov. 95.00
Cake stand, 9½" to 12½" d. 58.00
Celery vase..................... 62.00
Compote, cov., 6" d., low stand ... 95.00
Compote, cov., 6" d., high stand ... 110.00
Compote, cov., 7½" d., high
   stand 115.00
Compote, cov., 8½" d., 7" h....... 125.00
Compote, open, 7" d., low stand ... 38.00
Compote, open, 7½" d., high
   stand 60.00
Compote, open, 9½" d., low
   stand 90.00
Cordial 50.00
Creamer, applied handle.......... 55.00
Egg cup 33.00
*Goblet 45.00
Goblet, buttermilk 43.00
Pickle or relish, 7½" to 8½" l. 22.00
Pitcher, milk, qt. 125.00
Pitcher, 3 pint 165.00
Salt dip, master size............. 30.00
Sauce dish 15.00
*Spooner 40.00
Sugar bowl, cov. 70.00
Tumbler, bar.................... 42.00
Tumbler 42.00
Wine........................... 45.00

CABLE

Cable Egg Cup

Bowl, 8" d. 45.00
Butter dish, cov. 90.00

Celery vase..................... 82.00
Champagne...................... 250.00
Compote, open, 8" d., 4¾" h...... 70.00
Decanter w/stopper, qt. ...300.00 to 325.00
Egg cup, clambroth, flint 385.00
Egg cup, clear (ILLUS.) 53.00
Goblet 80.00
Honey dish, 3½" d., 1" h......... 15.00
Lamp, whale oil, 11" h........... 122.50
Plate, 6" d..................... 90.00
Salt dip, individual size 30.00
Salt dip, master size............. 36.00
Sauce dish..................... 21.00
Spooner, chartreuse green 1,200.00
Spooner, clambroth.............. 230.00
Spooner, clear 45.00
Spooner, starch blue w/original gilt
   decoration of grape leaves 1,500.00
Tumbler, whiskey 230.00

CABLE WITH RING

Creamer, applied handle, flint...... 165.00
Lamp, kerosene-type, w/ring han-
   dle, flint..................... 195.00
Sauce dish, flint................. 14.00

CALIFORNIA - See Beaded Grape Pattern

CANADIAN

Bowl, berry, 7" d., 4½" h., footed .. 63.00
Bowl, 9½" d. 55.00
Bread plate, handled, 10" d. 48.00
Butter dish, cov. 80.00
Compote, cov., 6" d., 9" h........ 124.00
Compote, cov., 7" d., 11" h........ 125.00
Compote, cov., 8" d., low stand 92.00
Compote, cov., 8" d., 11" h........ 150.00
Compote, open, 8" d., 5" h....... 55.00
Creamer 55.00
Goblet 56.00
Pitcher, milk, 8" h.........100.00 to 125.00
Pitcher, water 110.00
Plate, 6" d., handled 32.00
Plate, 7" d., handled 45.00
Plate, 8" d., handled 45.00
Sauce dish, flat or footed 20.00
Spooner 45.00
Sugar bowl, cov. 80.00
Wine........................... 49.00

CANNON BALL - See Atlas Pattern

CAPE COD

Bread platter 48.00
Compote, cov., 8" d., 12" h........ 130.00
Compote, open, 8" d., 5½" h...... 45.00
Cruet w/original stopper........... 43.00
Goblet 38.00
Pitcher, water 95.00
Plate, 6" d..................... 35.00
Plate, 10" d., open handles 48.00
Sauce dish, flat or footed 16.00

CARDINAL BIRD

Cardinal Bird Sauce Dish

Creamer	38.00
*Goblet	32.00
Sauce dish, flat or footed (ILLUS.)	16.00
Spooner	35.00

CATHEDRAL

Bowl, 6" d., crimped rim, blue	25.00
Bowl, 6" d., clear	16.00
Bowl, 7" d.	20.00
Bowl, berry, 8" d., amber	48.00
Butter dish, cov.	44.00
Cake stand, amber	55.00
Cake stand, clear, 10" d., 4½" h.	38.00
Cake stand, vaseline	60.00
Compote, cov., 7¼" d., 10½" h.	85.00
Compote, cov., 8" d., high stand, blue	185.00
Compote, open, 7" d., fluted rim, amber	30.00
Compote, open, 9" d., 5½" h., amber	65.00
Compote, open, 9" d., 5½" h., blue	65.00
Compote, open, 9" d., 7" h.	55.00
Compote, open, 10" d., 6" h., amethyst	58.00
Compote, open, 10½" d., 8" h., shaped rim, clear	55.00
Compote, open, 10½" d., 8" h., ruby-stained	125.00
Creamer	35.00
Cruet w/original stopper, amber	58.00
Goblet, amber	37.00
Goblet, clear	38.00
Goblet, ruby-stained	65.00
Goblet, vaseline	60.00
Pitcher, water, ruby-stained	145.00
Relish, fish-shaped, amber	40.00
Relish, fish-shaped, blue	42.50
Salt dip, master size, amber	25.00
Sauce dish, flat or footed, blue	25.00
Sauce dish, flat or footed, clear	10.00
Sauce dish, flat or footed, ruby-stained	22.00
Sauce dish, flat or footed, vaseline	20.00
Spooner, amber	42.50
Spooner, clear	28.00
Spooner, vaseline	48.00
Sugar bowl, cov.	50.00

Tumbler, clear	25.00
Tumbler, ruby-stained	42.50
Wine, amber	60.00
Wine, blue	55.00
Wine, clear	25.00
Wine, vaseline	65.00

CHANDELIER (Crown Jewel)

Chandelier Celery Vase

Butter dish, cov.	100.00
Cake stand, 10" d.	75.00
Celery vase (ILLUS.)	40.00
Compote, open, 9¼" d., 7¾" h.	57.00
Creamer	55.00
Goblet	50.00
Goblet, engraved	60.00
Inkwell	55.00
Pitcher, water, tankard, ½ pt.	65.00
Pitcher, water, tankard, ½ gal.	125.00
Salt dip, footed	36.00
Sauce dish, flat	16.00
Spooner	45.00
Tumbler	40.00
Waste bowl	25.00

CLASSIC

Bowl, open, 8" hexagon, open log feet	100.00 to 125.00
Butter dish, cov., open log feet	225.00
Celery vase, collared base	125.00
Celery vase, open log feet	155.00
Compote, cov., 6½" d., collared base	200.00
Compote, cov., 7½" d., 8" h., open log feet	220.00
Compote, open, 7¾" d., open log feet	150.00
Creamer, collared base	125.00
Creamer, open log feet	150.00 to 175.00
Goblet	295.00
Pitcher, water, collared base	225.00 to 275.00
Pitcher, water, 9½" h., open log feet	425.00
Plate, 10" d., "Blaine" or "Hendricks," signed Jacobus, each	215.00
Plate, 10" d., "Cleveland"	200.00

Plate, 10" d., "Warrior"....150.00 to 175.00
Sauce dish, open log feet 40.00
Spooner, collared base 95.00
Spooner, open log feet 135.00
Sugar bowl, cov., open log feet 185.00

COLLINS - See Crystal Wedding Pattern

COLORADO (Lacy Medallion)

Colorado Sugar Bowl

Banana bowl, two turned-up sides,
   blue 35.00
Banana stand, green 45.00
Berry set: 8" d. master bowl & five
   4" d. sauce dishes; green w/gold,
   6 pcs. 160.00
Berry set: master bowl & 6 sauce
   dishes; clear w/gold, 7 pcs. 125.00
Bowl, 4" d., blue 38.00
Bowl, 5" d., ruffled rim, blue 40.00
Bowl, 7" d., footed 25.00
Bowl, 7½" d., footed, turned-up
   sides, blue w/gold 50.00
Bowl, 7½" d., footed, turned-up
   sides, green 29.00
Bowl, 9" d., footed, three turned-up
   sides 32.00
Bowl, 9" d., green w/gold 45.00
Bowl, 9" d., footed, crimped edge,
   green 40.00
Bowl, 10" d., footed, flared & scal-
   loped rim...................... 45.00
Bowl, 10" d., footed, fluted, green .. 48.00
Butter dish, cov., blue w/gold 260.00
Butter dish, cov., clear 85.00
Butter dish, cov., green 125.00
Cake stand 65.00
Candy dish 15.00
Celery vase, green w/gold 70.00
Compote, open, 6" d., 4" h.,
   crimped rim 22.00
Creamer, blue 85.00
Creamer, blue, souvenir 60.00
Creamer, clear.................. 34.00
Creamer, ruby-stained 54.00
Creamer, individual size, green
   w/gold 42.00
Cup, punch, green 28.00

Cup, punch, green, souvenir 25.00
Cup & saucer, green............. 45.00
Custard cup, green, large 28.00
Mug, green, souvenir, miniature.... 25.00
Mug, green..................... 30.00
Mug, green, souvenir 32.00
Mug, ruby-stained 55.00
Nappy, tricornered, blue w/gold.... 40.00
Nappy, tricornered, clear 20.00
Nappy, tricornered, green w/gold .. 29.00
Pitcher, water, green w/gold....... 176.00
Rose bowl, blue................. 60.00
Salt dip, master size, footed 30.00
Salt shaker w/original top, ruby-
   stained, souvenir............... 75.00
Sauce dish, blue w/gold 30.00
Sauce dish, clambroth 20.00
Sauce dish, clear.............. 13.00
Sauce dish, green w/gold 24.00
Sherbet, blue w/gold 48.00
Spooner, blue w/gold 60.00
Spooner, clear.................. 40.00
Spooner, green w/gold 50.00
Sugar bowl, cov., clear, large 53.00
Sugar bowl, cov., green, large
   (ILLUS.)...................... 74.00
Sugar bowl, open, individual size,
   clear......................... 20.00
Sugar bowl, open, individual size,
   green 35.00
Sugar bowl, open, individual size,
   ruby-stained 50.00
Table set, green w/gold,
   4 pcs....................325.00 to 350.00
*Toothpick holder, blue w/gold..... 60.00
*Toothpick holder, clear w/gold 25.00
*Toothpick holder, green w/gold ... 35.00
Toothpick holder, green w/gold,
   souvenir...................... 24.00
Toothpick holder, ruby-stained,
   souvenir...................... 55.00
Tumbler, green w/gold 32.00
Tumbler, green w/gold, souvenir ... 30.00
Vase, 2½" h., green 45.00
Vase, 10½" h., blue 78.00
Water set: pitcher & 6 tumblers;
   green w/gold, 7 pcs. 450.00
Wine, clear.................... 28.00
Wine, green w/gold 40.00
Wine, green, souvenir 35.00
Wine, ruby-stained w/gold 40.00

COLUMBIAN COIN
Bowl, 8½" d., 3" h., frosted coins .. 75.00
Celery vase, frosted coins.......... 110.00
Compote, cov., 8" d., frosted
   coins 157.00
Compote, open, 8" d., clear coins .. 68.00
Creamer, gilded coins 125.00
Cruet w/original stopper, frosted
   coins......................... 195.00
*Goblet, gilded coins 80.00
Lamp, kerosene-type, milk white,
   8" h.......................... 400.00

Lamp, kerosene-type, 9½" h. 165.00
Lamp, kerosene-type, frosted coins,
    12" h. 180.00
Mug, frosted coins 120.00
Pitcher, milk, gilded coins 195.00
Relish, frosted coins, 5 x 8" 68.00
Sauce dish, flat or footed, frosted
    coins 42.00
Spooner, gilded coins 65.00
Syrup pitcher w/original top, frosted
    coins 180.00
*Toothpick holder, frosted coins 95.00
*Toothpick holder, gilded coins 135.00
Toothpick holder, red coins 195.00
*Tumbler, clear coins 30.00
*Tumbler, gilded coins 55.00
Wine, frosted coins 145.00

COMPACT - See Snail Pattern

CORD DRAPERY

Bowl, 6¼" d., footed, amber 175.00
Bowl, 10" d., 3½" h. 42.00
Butter dish, cov., clear 70.00
Butter dish, cov., green 175.00
Cake stand, amber 145.00
Cake stand, clear 40.00
Compote, cov., jelly 55.00
Compote, cov., 9" d. 70.00
Creamer, blue 125.00
Creamer, clear 40.00
Cruet w/original stopper, amber . . . 305.00
Cruet w/original stopper,
    clear . . . . 80.00 to 90.00
Goblet 85.00
Mug 40.00
Pickle dish, amber, 5¼ x 9¼"
    oval 85.00
Pickle dish, clear, 5¼ x 9¼" oval . . 40.00
Pitcher, water, amber 185.00
Pitcher, water, clear 68.00
Pitcher, water, cobalt blue 225.00
Pitcher, water, green 235.00
Punch cup 15.00
Salt shaker w/original top 55.00
Sauce dish, flat or footed 16.00
Sugar bowl, cov., clear 60.00
Sugar bowl, cov., green 165.00
Toothpick holder 95.00
Tumbler, blue 125.00
Tumbler, clear 37.50
Wine 90.00

CORONA - See Sunk Honeycomb Pattern

COTTAGE (Dinner Bell or Finecut Band)

Bowl, master berry, 9¼" l., 6½" w.
    oval 25.00
Butter dish, cov. 36.00
Cake stand, amber 50.00
Cake stand, clear 35.00
Celery vase, amber 85.00
Celery vase, clear 35.00

Champagne 65.00
Compote, open, jelly, 4½" d., 4" h.,
    clear 24.00
Compote, open, jelly, 4½" d., 4" h.,
    green 45.00
Creamer, amber 60.00
Creamer, clear 27.00
*Goblet, amber 45.00
*Goblet, blue 48.00
*Goblet, clear 25.00
Pitcher, milk, amber 60.00
Pitcher, milk, clear 35.00
Pitcher, water, 2 qt. 50.00
Plate, 6" d. 12.00
Plate, 7" d. 22.50
Plate, 10" d. 42.50
Sauce dish 12.50
Tray, water 40.00

Cottage Tumbler

Tumbler (ILLUS.) 19.00
*Wine, amber 53.00
*Wine, blue 45.00
*Wine, clear 21.00

CROESUS

Croesus Water Pitcher

Berry set: master bowl & 6 sauce
    dishes; clear, 7 pcs. 300.00
Berry set: master bowl & 6 sauce
    dishes; green w/gold, 7 pcs. 395.00
Berry set: master bowl & 6 sauce
    dishes; purple, 7 pcs. . . . . 400.00 to 425.00
Bowl, 7" d., 4" h., footed, purple . . . 68.00

Bowl, 7" d., 4" h., footed, purple
w/gold 225.00
Bowl, 8" d., purple 175.00
Bowl, berry or fruit, 9" d., green . . . 108.00
Bowl, berry or fruit, 9" d., purple. . . 165.00
*Butter dish, cov., green 165.00
*Butter dish, cov., purple . . 200.00 to 225.00
Celery vase, green w/gold 170.00
Celery vase, purple 300.00
Compote, open, jelly,
green . . . . .225.00 to 275.00
Compote, open, jelly, purple 280.00
Condiment tray, clear 27.00
Condiment tray, green 60.00
Condiment tray, purple 90.00
*Creamer, green 100.00
*Creamer, purple 145.00
Creamer, individual size, purple,
3" h. 135.00
Cruet w/original stopper,
green . . . . .200.00 to 225.00
Pickle dish, green w/gold 35.00
Pickle dish, purple 78.00
Pitcher, milk, green 89.00
Pitcher, water, green (ILLUS.) 275.00
Pitcher, water, purple . . . . .400.00 to 500.00
Relish, boat-shaped, green 60.00
Salt shaker w/original top, green
w/gold 98.00
Sauce dish, clear 23.00
Sauce dish, green w/gold 37.00
Sauce dish, purple w/gold 43.00
*Spooner, green 73.00
*Spooner, green w/gold 92.00
*Spooner, purple 80.00
*Spooner, purple w/gold 100.00
*Sugar bowl, cov., clear 78.00
*Sugar bowl, cov., green 110.00
*Sugar bowl, cov., purple . . 150.00 to 175.00
*Sugar bowl, cov., purple w/gold . . . 180.00
Table set, purple, 4 pcs. 630.00
*Toothpick holder, green 65.00
*Toothpick holder, green w/gold . . . 95.00
*Toothpick holder, purple 125.00
*Tumbler, green 42.00
*Tumbler, green w/gold 54.00
*Tumbler, purple w/gold 70.00
Water set: pitcher & 5 tumblers;
green, 6 pcs. 500.00
Water set: pitcher & 6 tumblers;
purple, 7 pcs. 900.00

CROWN JEWEL - See Chandelier Pattern

CRYSTAL BALL - See Atlas Pattern

CRYSTAL WEDDING (Collins)
Banana stand, 10" h. 110.00
Banana stand, low pedestal 95.00
Bowl, cov., 5" sq. 68.00
Bowl, berry, 8" sq. 48.00
Butter dish, cov., ruby-stained 135.00
Cake stand, 9" sq., 8" h. 66.00

Cake stand, 10" sq. 75.00
Celery vase 45.00
Compote, cov., 4" sq., 6½" h. 37.50
Compote, cov., 5" sq. 58.00
Compote, cov., 7" sq., low stand . . . 85.00
Compote, cov., 7" sq., 13" h. 105.00
Compote, open, 5" sq. 45.00
Compote, open, 6" sq. 48.00
Compote, open, 6¼" sq., 8" h.,
scalloped rim 45.00
Creamer, clear 45.00
Creamer, ruby-stained 125.00
*Goblet, clear 40.00
Goblet w/fern engraving 85.00
*Goblet, ruby-stained 62.50
Honey dish, cov., 6" sq. 90.00
Lamp, kerosene-type, 7" h. 100.00
Lamp, kerosene-type, 9" h., frosted
& clear 145.00
Lamp base, kerosene-type, square
font, 10" h. 285.00
Pitcher, water, square, engraved . . . 195.00
Pitcher, water, square, plain 175.00
Plate, 9" sq. 45.00
Salt shaker w/original top 125.00
Sauce dish 12.00
Spooner, amber-stained 45.00
Spooner, clear 35.00
Spooner, ruby-stained 60.00
Sugar bowl, cov., clear 48.00
Sugar bowl, cov., ruby-stained 100.00
Table set: creamer, cov. sugar bowl
& spooner; clear, 3 pcs. 185.00
Table set: creamer, cov. sugar bowl,
cov. butter dish & spooner; ruby-
stained, 4 pcs. 400.00
Tumbler 45.00

CUPID & VENUS (Guardian Angel)
Bowl, open, 8" d., footed 30.00
Bowl, 9" oval 50.00
Bread plate, clear, 10½" d. 38.00
Bread plate, vaseline, 10½" d. 145.00
Butter dish, cov. 110.00
Cake plate, 11" d. 45.00
Celery vase 62.00
Champagne 110.00
Compote, cov., 7" d., high stand . . . 110.00
Compote, cov., 7" d., low stand 65.00
Compote, cov., 9" d., low stand 82.00
Compote, open, 7" d., low stand . . . 30.00
Compote, open, 8½" d., low stand,
scalloped rim 40.00
Cordial 85.00
Creamer 48.00
Goblet 80.00
Honey dish, 3½" d. 15.00
Marmalade jar, cov. 125.00
Mug, 2½" h. 25.00
Mug, 3½" h. 50.00
Pitcher, milk 65.00
Pitcher, water 90.00
Relish, oval, 4½ x 7" 30.00
Sauce dish, footed, 3½" to 4½" d. . . 14.00

Spooner 40.00
Sugar bowl, cov. 70.00
Wine 85.00

CURRIER & IVES

Bowl, master berry or fruit,
   10" oval, flat w/collared base 35.00
Compote, cov., 11½" d., amber 145.00
Cup & saucer, blue 85.00
Cup & saucer, clear 45.00
Goblet, amber 95.00
Goblet, clear 32.00
Pitcher, milk 60.00
Pitcher, water, amber 145.00
Pitcher, water, clear 85.00
Salt shaker w/original top, blue 75.00
Salt & pepper shakers w/original
   tops, pr....................... 65.00
Sauce dish, flat or footed 13.50
Spooner 35.00
Sugar bowl, cov. .... 35.00 to 45.00
Syrup jug w/original top, blue 162.00
Syrup jug w/original top, clear 82.50
Tray, water, Balky Mule on Railroad
   Tracks, 9½" d. 49.00
Tray, water, Balky Mule on Railroad
   Tracks, blue, 12¼" d. 150.00
Tray, water, Balky Mule on Railroad
   Tracks, clear, 12¼" d. 65.00
Tumbler, footed 38.00
Waste bowl 42.00
Wine, clear 25.00
Wine, ruby-stained 85.00

CUT LOG

Cut Log Relish

Bowl, 7" d. 33.00
Bowl, master berry or fruit, 8" d.,
   footed 40.00
Butter dish, cov. 64.00
Cake stand, 9¼" d., high stand 62.00
Cake stand, 10½" d., high stand ... 77.00
Celery tray 45.00
Celery vase 40.00
Compote, cov., jelly, 5½" d., high
   stand 65.00
Compote, cov., 7¼" d., high
   stand 95.00
Compote, open, jelly, 5" d. 30.00
Compote, open, 6" d., flared rim,
   high stand 35.00

Compote, open, 9¾" d., scalloped
   rim, high stand 57.00
Compote, open, 10¾" d., scalloped
   rim, high stand 75.00
Creamer 35.00
Creamer, individual size 12.00
Creamer & cov. sugar bowl, pr. 125.00
Cruet w/original stopper, small,
   3¾" h. 36.00
Cruet w/original stopper, large,
   5" h. 55.00
Goblet 50.00
Mug, small 20.00
Olive dish, handled, 5" d. 25.00
Pitcher, water, tankard, clear 96.00
Pitcher, water, tankard, ruby-
   stained 240.00
Relish, boat-shaped, 9¼" l.
   (ILLUS.) 24.50
Salt dip, master size 65.00
Salt shaker w/original tin top 60.00
Sauce dish, flat or footed 20.00
Spooner 40.00
Sugar bowl, cov. 60.00
Sugar bowl, cov., individual size.... 30.00
Tumbler, juice 35.00
Tumbler, water 40.00
Vase, 16" h. 60.00
Wine 23.00

DAHLIA

Bread platter, 8 x 12" 45.00
Butter dish, cov. 52.00
Cake stand, amber, 9½" d. 75.00
Cake stand, blue, 9½" d. 52.50
Cake stand, clear, 9½" d. 30.00
Cake stand, blue, 10" d. 95.00
Cordial 40.00
Creamer 28.00
Goblet 38.00
Mug, amber 45.00
Mug, blue 60.00
Mug, clear 32.00
Mug, child's 20.00
Pickle dish 15.00
Pitcher, milk, applied handle 55.00
Pitcher, water, blue 120.00
Pitcher, water, clear 55.00
Plate, 7" d. 18.00
Plate, 9" d., w/handles, apple
   green 42.50
Plate, 9" d., w/handles, clear 18.00
Plate, 9" d., w/handles, vaseline ... 45.00
Relish, 5 x 9½" 13.00
Sauce dish, flat, amber 22.00
Sauce dish, flat, clear 15.00
Sauce dish, footed 7.00
Spooner 35.00
Sugar bowl, cov., vaseline 60.00
Wine, amber 55.00
Wine, clear 35.00

DAISY & BUTTON

Banana boat, 14" l. 45.00
Basket, silver plate handle, 6" h. 125.00

Berry set: triangular master bowl &
4 sauce dishes; vaseline, 5 pcs. . . 150.00
Berry set: octagonal master bowl &
10 sauce dishes; amber, 11 pcs. . . 140.00
Berry set: octagonal master bowl &
12 octagonal sauce dishes; vase-
line, 13 pcs. 225.00
Bowl, 7 x 9½", sapphire blue 30.00
Bowl, 8" w., tricornered 45.00
Bowl, berry or fruit, 8½" d. 35.00
*Bowl, 10" oval, blue 65.00
Bowl, 10 x 11" oval, 7¾" h., flared,
vaseline 95.00
Bowl, 11" d., amber 38.00
Bowl, 12" l., 9" w., shell-shaped
oval, blue 75.00
Bowl, fruit, rectangular, ornate sil-
ver plate frame 250.00
*Bread tray, amber 25.00
*Butter chip, fan-shaped 9.50
*Butter chip, round, clear 6.00
*Butter chip, round, vaseline 9.00
Butter chip, square, amber 15.00
Butter chip, square, Amberina 75.00
Butter chip, square, blue 17.50
Butter chip, square, clear 7.50
Butter chip, square, purple 15.00
Butter chip, square, vaseline 25.00
Butter dish, cov., scalloped base 65.00
Butter dish, cov., square, clear 45.00
Butter dish, cov., square, green 60.00
Butter dish, cov., triangular,
amber 60.00
*Butter dish, cov., model of Victori-
an stove, green 215.00
Cake stand, blue 50.00
Cake stand, 9" sq., 6" h., clear 45.00
Canoe, vaseline, 4" l. 18.00
Canoe, amber, 8" l. 35.00
Canoe, blue, 8" l. 46.00
Canoe, vaseline, 8" l. 100.00
Canoe, amber, 11" l. 60.00
Canoe, blue, 11" l. 70.00
Canoe, vaseline, 14" l. 85.00
Celery tray, flat, boat-shaped,
4½ x 14" 90.00
Celery vase, square 65.00
Celery vase, triangular, amber 85.00
Celery vase, triangular, clear 45.00
Cheese dish, cov. 62.00
Compote, cov., 8" d., 12" h. 55.00
Compote, cov., 8½" d., 4½" h.,
amber 60.00
*Creamer, amber 32.50
*Creamer, blue 40.00
*Creamer, clear 29.00
*Cruet w/original stopper, amber . . 100.00
*Cruet w/original stopper, blue 95.00
*Cruet w/original stopper, clear 49.00
Cuspidor, blue 38.00
*Dish, fan-shaped, 10" w. 35.00
*Goblet, amber 30.00
*Goblet, blue 28.00
*Goblet, clear 22.50

*Hat shape, canary yellow,
1¾" h. 22.50
*Hat shape, blue, 2½" h. 35.00
*Hat shape, clear, 2½" h. 20.00
*Hat shape, vaseline, 2½" h. 35.00
*Hat shape, from tumbler mold,
4½" widest d. 55.00
*Hat shape, blue, from tumbler
mold, 4¾" widest d. 45.00
Hat shape, clear, 8 x 8", 6" h. 85.00
*Ice cream dish, cut corners,
6" sq. 9.00
Ice cream set: 2 x 7 x 9½" ice
cream tray & two square plates;
amber, 3 pcs. 85.00
Ice tub, 4½ x 6¾" oval, amber 60.00
Inkwell w/original insert, cat seated
on cover 245.00
Match holder, wall-hanging scuff,
amber, 4½" l. 30.00
Match holder, wall-hanging scuff,
blue 75.00
Match holder, wall-hanging scuff,
clear 65.00
*Pickle castor, amber insert, w/sil-
ver plate frame & tongs 120.00
*Pickle castor, sapphire blue insert,
w/silver plate frame & tongs 238.00
*Pickle castor, vaseline insert,
w/silver plate frame & tongs 185.00
Pitcher, 5 1/8" h., applied handle,
amber 55.00
Pitcher, water, tankard, 9" h.,
amber 125.00
Pitcher, water, bulbous, applied
handle, clear 95.00
Pitcher, water, bulbous, applied
handle, ruby-stained buttons 325.00
*Plate, 6" sq., Amberina 85.00
Plate, 7" sq., amber 18.00
Plate, 7" sq., blue 20.00
Plate, 7" sq., clear 15.00
Plate, 9" d., vaseline 40.00
*Plate, 10" d., scalloped rim,
amber 28.00
*Plate, 10" d., scalloped rim, blue . . 35.00
Platter, 9 x 13" oval, open handles,
amber 35.00
Platter, 9 x 13" oval, open handles,
blue 40.00
Platter, 9 x 13" oval, open handles,
yellow 40.00
Powder jar, cov., amber, 3¾" d.,
2" h. 30.00
Powder jar, cov., blue 38.00
Relish, "Sitz bathtub" 145.00
*Rose bowl, vaseline 38.00
*Salt dip, canoe-shaped, amber,
2 x 4" 19.50
*Salt dip, canoe-shaped, clear,
2 x 4" 14.50
*Salt dip, canoe-shaped, vaseline,
2 x 4" 12.00

Salt dip, master size, vaseline, 3½" d.	22.50
*Salt shaker w/original top, corset-shaped, blue	25.00
*Salt & pepper shakers w/original tops, vaseline, pr.	30.00
Salt & pepper shakers, blue & amber, pr., w/clear glass stand	55.00
*Sauce dish, amber, 4" to 5" sq.	15.00
Sauce dish, Amberina, 4" to 5" sq.	115.00
*Sauce dish, blue, 4" to 5" sq.	16.00
*Sauce dish, clear, 4" to 5" sq.	6.00 to 12.00
*Sauce dish, vaseline, 4" to 5" sq.	20.00
Sauce dish, tricornered, clear	12.50
Sauce dish, tricornered, vaseline	16.00
*Slipper, "1886 patent," amber	46.00
*Slipper, "1886 patent," blue	47.00
Slipper, ruby-stained buttons	80.00
*Spooner, amber	40.00
Spooner, Amberina, 5" h.	150.00
Spooner, amethyst	30.00
*Spooner, clear	35.00
Sugar bowl, cov., amber	35.00 to 45.00
Sugar bowl, cov., barrel-shaped, blue	50.00
Sugar bowl, cov., clear	30.00
Syrup pitcher w/original pewter top, blue	175.00
Table set: creamer, open sugar bowl & spooner; vaseline, 3 pcs.	65.00
Toothpick holder (or salt dip), "Bandmaster's cap," blue	35.00
Toothpick holder, square, blue	25.00
*Toothpick holder, three-footed, amber	30.00
*Toothpick holder, three-footed, electric blue	55.00
Toothpick holder, urn-shaped, clear	25.00
Toothpick holder, urn-shaped, vaseline	30.00
Tray, clover-shaped, amber	50.00
Tray, vaseline, 10 x 12"	89.00
Tray, ice cream, handled, blue, 9¼ x 16½"	30.00
Tray, water, triangular, vaseline	95.00
Tumbler, water, amber	22.50
Tumbler, water, blue	30.00
Tumbler, water, blue, pattern half way up	30.00
Tumbler, water, clear	20.00
Tumbler, water, vaseline	32.50
Waste bowl, blue	28.00
Waste bowl, vaseline	30.00
Whimsey, "canoe," wall hanging-type, ruby-stained buttons, 11" l.	110.00
Whimsey, "cradle," amber	45.00
*Whimsey, "sleigh," amber, 4½ x 7¾"	225.00
Whimsey, "wheel barrow," vaseline	125.00
*Whimsey, "whisk broom" dish, blue	75.00
*Wine	20.00

DAISY & BUTTON WITH CROSSBARS (Mikado)

Bowl, 5 x 8"	20.00
Bread tray, amber, 9 x 12"	25.00
Bread tray, apple green, 9 x 12"	32.50
Bread tray, canary yellow, 9 x 12"	52.00
Butter dish, cov., blue	58.00
Butter dish, cov., canary yellow	65.00
Butter dish, cov., clear	45.00
Celery vase, amber	38.00
Celery vase, canary yellow	43.00
Celery vase, clear	27.00
Compote, open, 7" d., low stand, amber	38.00
Compote, open, 7" d., high stand, blue	85.00
Compote, open, 8" d., high stand, amber	45.00
Compote, open, 8" d., high stand, canary yellow	70.00
Compote, open, 8" d., high stand, clear	32.50
Creamer, amber	37.00
Creamer, canary yellow	40.00
Creamer, clear	30.00
Creamer, individual size, amber	21.00
Creamer, individual size, blue	24.00
Creamer, individual size, canary yellow	22.00
Creamer, individual size, clear	14.00
Cruet w/original stopper	55.00
Goblet, amber	40.00
Goblet, blue	45.00
Goblet, canary yellow	35.00
Goblet, clear	28.00
Mug, amber, 3" h.	18.00
Mug, clear, 3" h.	12.00
Pitcher, milk, amber	55.00
Pitcher, milk, blue	60.00
Pitcher, milk, canary yellow	45.00
Pitcher, water, amber	75.00
Pitcher, water, canary yellow	85.00
Pitcher, water, clear	52.00
Relish, amber, 4½ x 8"	30.00
Salt shaker w/original top, canary yellow	35.00
Salt & pepper shakers, blue & amber, pr., w/clear glass stand	85.00
Spooner, amber	32.00
Spooner, canary yellow	30.00
Spooner, clear	23.50
Sugar bowl, cov., amber	42.00
Sugar bowl, cov., blue	65.00
Sugar bowl, cov., clear	25.00
Syrup pitcher w/original top	50.00
Tumbler, canary yellow	24.00
Water set: pitcher & 6 tumblers; canary yellow, 7 pcs.	250.00
Wine, canary yellow	28.00
Wine, clear	25.00

DAISY & BUTTON WITH NARCISSUS

*Bowl, 6 x 9½" oval, footed	48.00
Decanter w/original stopper	52.00
Goblet	20.00
Pitcher, water	60.00
Punch cup	10.00
Sauce dish, flat or three-footed	13.50
Sugar bowl, cov.	35.00
Tumbler	17.00
Water set: pitcher & 5 tumblers; cranberry-stained, 6 pcs.	150.00
*Wine	19.00

DAISY & BUTTON WITH THUMBPRINT PANELS

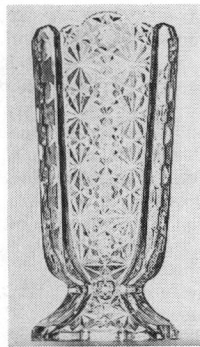

D. & B. w/Thumbprint Panels Celery

Bowl, 8" sq., amber	28.00
Bowl, 9" sq., amber	28.00
Cake stand, vaseline, 10½" d., 7¼" h.	75.00
Celery vase, amber panels (ILLUS.)	125.00
Celery vase, clear	28.00
Creamer, applied handle, amber panels	68.00
*Goblet, amber panels	55.00
Goblet, blue panels	60.00
Pitcher, water, vaseline	165.00
Salt shaker w/original top, amber panels	75.00
Spooner, amber panels	75.00
Tray, water, vaseline	95.00
Tumbler, amber panels	38.50
Tumbler, clear	20.00

DAISY IN PANEL - See Two Panel Pattern

DAKOTA (Baby Thumbprint)

Bowl, 7" w., heart-shaped, amber panels	42.50
Butter dish, cov., engraved	75.00
Butter dish, cov., plain	60.00
Cake stand, 8" d., engraved	50.00
Cake stand, 8" d., plain	45.00
Cake stand, 9½" d.	55.00
Cake stand, 10¼" d., engraved	67.00
Cake stand, 10¼" d., plain	58.00
Cake stand w/high domed cover . . .	295.00

Celery vase, flat base, engraved . . .	42.00
Celery vase, flat base, plain	35.00
Celery vase, pedestal base, engraved	50.00
Celery vase, pedestal base, plain . . .	42.00
Cologne bottle w/original stopper, 7" h.	135.00
Compote, cov., jelly, 5" d., 5" h. . . .	45.00
Compote, cov., 6" d., high stand, engraved	75.00
Compote, cov., 6" d., high stand, plain	58.00
Compote, cov., 8" d., high stand . . .	80.00
Compote, open, jelly, 5" d., 5½" h., engraved	35.00
Compote, open, jelly, 5" d., 5" h., plain	32.00
Compote, open, 6" d.	30.00
Compote, open, 7" d., engraved	40.00
Compote, open, 7" d., plain	38.00
Compote, open, 9" d., high stand, engraved	45.00

Dakota Engraved Creamer

Creamer, table, engraved (ILLUS.) . .	53.00
Creamer, table, plain	40.00
Creamer, hotel	110.00
Cruet w/original stopper, en- graved	145.00
Goblet, clear, engraved	35.00
Goblet, clear, plain	24.00
Goblet, ruby-stained, engraved	70.00
Goblet, ruby-stained, plain	65.00
Pitcher, milk, engraved	120.00
Pitcher, milk, plain	90.00
Pitcher, tankard, engraved	254.00
Pitcher, water, 10" to 12" h., clear . .	105.00
Pitcher, water, 10" to 12" h., ruby- stained	125.00
Pitcher, water, engraved, ½ gal.	95.00
Plate, 10" d.	63.00
Salt shaker w/original top	50.00
Sauce dish, flat or footed, clear, engraved	18.00
Sauce dish, flat or footed, clear, plain	12.00
Sauce dish, flat or footed, cobalt blue	55.00
Shaker bottle w/original top, 5" h.	68.00

Shaker bottle w/original top, hotel
   size, 6½" h. 65.00
Spooner, engraved 30.00
Sugar bowl, cov., engraved 62.50
Sugar bowl, cov., plain 48.00
Tray, water, piecrust rim, engraved,
   13" d. 125.00
Tray, water, piecrust-rim, plain,
   13" d. 95.00
Tray, wine, 10½" d. 100.00
Tumbler, clear, engraved 45.00
Tumbler, clear, plain 30.00
Tumbler, ruby-stained 45.00
Waste bowl, engraved 75.00
Waste bowl, plain 58.00
Wine, clear, engraved 40.00
Wine, clear, plain 30.00
Wine, ruby-stained 50.00

DEER & PINE TREE

Deer & Pine Tree Butter Dish

Bread tray, amber, 8 x 13" 82.00
Bread tray, apple green, 8 x 13" 125.00
Bread tray, blue, 8 x 13" 125.00
Bread tray, canary yellow, 8 x 13" . . 135.00
Bread tray, clear, 8 x 13" 50.00
Butter dish, cov. (ILLUS.) 105.00
Cake stand 100.00
Celery vase 80.00
Compote, cov., 8" sq., high stand. . . 185.00
Creamer 62.50
*Goblet 55.00
Marmalade jar, cov. 110.00
Mug, child's, apple green 45.00
Mug, child's, blue 45.00
Mug, large, blue 55.00
Pickle dish. 18.00
Pitcher, water 165.00
Sauce dish, flat or footed, clear 20.00
Spooner 45.00
Sugar bowl, cov. 62.50
Tray, water, handled, 9 x 15" 125.00
Vegetable dish, 5¾ x 9" 50.00

DELAWARE (Four Petal Flower)

Banana boat, green w/gold,
   11¾" l. 80.00
Banana boat, rose w/gold,
   11¾" l. 95.00
Berry set: boat-shaped master bowl

& 5 boat-shaped sauce dishes;
   rose w/gold, 6 pcs. . . . . . 250.00 to 300.00
Berry set: round master bowl &
   4 sauce dishes; rose w/gold,
   5 pcs. 250.00
Bowl, 8" d., clear 50.00
Bowl, 8" d., clear w/gold 55.00
Bowl, 8" d., green w/gold 55.00
Bowl, 8" d., rose w/gold. 57.50
Bowl, 9" d., scalloped rim, green
   w/gold 60.00
Bowl, 10" octagon, green w/gold . . . 95.00
Bride's basket, boat-shaped open
   bowl, green w/gold in silver plate
   frame, 11½" oval 160.00
Bride's basket, boat-shaped open
   bowl, rose w/gold, in silver plate
   frame, 11½" oval . . . . . . 200.00 to 225.00
Bride's basket, boat-shaped open
   bowl, green w/gold, miniature . . . 175.00
Butter dish, cov., clear 125.00
*Butter dish, cov., green w/gold. . . . 135.00
Butter dish, cov., rose w/gold 165.00
Celery vase, rose band w/gold 45.00
Celery vase, green w/gold 82.50
Celery vase, purple w/gold 59.00
Celery vase, rose w/gold 88.00
Claret jug, rose w/gold. . . . 150.00 to 175.00
Creamer, clear w/gold 45.00
*Creamer, green w/gold. 62.50
Creamer, rose w/gold 65.00
Creamer, individual size, clear
   w/gold 25.00
Creamer, individual size, green
   w/gold 55.00
Creamer, individual size, rose
   w/gold 60.00
Cruet w/original stopper, clear 100.00
Cruet w/original stopper, green
   w/gold 185.00
Cruet w/original stopper, rose
   w/gold 325.00
Marmalade dish w/silver plate
   holder, green w/gold. 45.00
Marmalade dish w/silver plate
   holder, rose w/gold 85.00
Pin tray, rose w/gold 90.00
Pitcher, tankard, green w/gold 150.00
Pitcher, water, bulbous, rose
   w/gold 100.00
Pomade jar w/jeweled cover, green
   w/gold. . . . . 185.00 to 200.00
Pomade jar w/jeweled cover, rose
   w/gold 335.00
Punch cup, clear 16.00
Punch cup, clear w/gold 30.00
Punch cup, green w/gold 40.00
Punch cup, rose w/gold 45.00
Salt shaker w/original top 85.00
Sauce dish, boat-shaped, clear 18.00
Sauce dish, boat-shaped, green
   w/gold 35.00
Sauce dish, boat-shaped, rose
   w/gold 40.00

Sauce dish, round, green w/gold ... 25.00
Sauce dish, round, rose w/gold 24.00
Shade, gas, rose w/gold 295.00
Spooner, clear w/gold 50.00
Spooner, green w/gold 55.00
Spooner, rose 60.00
Spooner, rose w/gold 75.00
Sugar bowl, cov., clear 62.50
Sugar bowl, cov., rose w/gold 90.00
Sugar bowl, individual size, rose
   w/gold 95.00
Table set, green w/gold, 4 pcs. 400.00
Table set, rose w/gold, 4 pcs. 450.00
Toothpick holder, clear 45.00
Toothpick holder, green w/gold 88.00
Toothpick holder, rose w/gold 125.00
Tumbler, custard glass w/stained
   florals 65.00
Tumbler, green w/gold 42.50
Tumbler, rose w/gold 43.00
Vase, 6" h., green w/gold 65.00
Vase, 8" h., green w/gold 105.00
Vase, 9½" h., amethyst 100.00
Vase, 9½" h., green w/gold 110.00
Vase, 9½" h., rose w/gold 115.00
Water set: pitcher & 3 tumblers;
   rose w/gold, 4 pcs. 295.00
Water set: pitcher & 4 tumblers;
   green w/gold, 5 pcs. 550.00
Water set: pitcher & 6 tumblers;
   clear w/gold, 7 pcs. .... 145.00 to 165.00

DEWDROP WITH STAR

Dewdrop with Star Sauce Dish

Butter dish, cov. 55.00
Cake stand, 11" d. 45.00
Celery vase 40.00
Cheese dish, cov. 130.00
Compote, cov., 7 1/8" d., 9½" h. ... 82.50
Compote, cov., 11" h. 77.00
Honey dish 13.50
*Plate, 7" d. 15.00
Relish, 9" l. 15.00
Sauce dish, flat .... 8.00 to 10.00
*Sauce dish, footed (ILLUS.) 7.00
Sugar bowl, cov. 50.00

DEWEY (Flower Flange)

Bowl, 8" d. 35.00
*Butter dish, cov., amber 85.00

Butter dish, cov., canary yellow 95.00
*Butter dish, cov., clear 55.00
*Butter dish, cov., green 80.00
Butter dish, cov., green, miniature .. 75.00
Creamer, amber 60.00
Creamer, clear 30.00
Creamer, cov., individual size 45.00
Cruet w/original stopper, amber ... 125.00
Cruet w/original stopper, canary
   yellow 170.00
Cruet w/original stopper,
   green .... 150.00 to 200.00
Mug, amber 60.00
Mug, clear 35.00
Mug, green 62.00
Parfait, amber 65.00
Parfait, clear 40.00
Pitcher, water, amber 110.00
Pitcher, water, canary yellow 145.00
Pitcher, water, clear 78.00
Plate, footed, canary yellow 85.00
Plate, footed, green 65.00
Salt shaker w/original top, amber .. 62.50
Sauce dish, canary yellow 35.00
Sauce dish, green 30.00
Sugar bowl, cov. 35.00
Tray, serpentine shape, amber,
   small 45.00
Tray, serpentine shape, clear,
   small 28.00
Tray, serpentine shape, green,
   small 38.50
Tray, serpentine shape, amber,
   large 55.00
Tumbler, amber 55.00
Tumbler, canary yellow 55.00
Tumbler, clear 45.00
Water set, pitcher & 6 tumblers,
   7 pcs. .... 300.00 to 350.00

DIAMOND POINT

Bar bottle, flint 125.00
Bowl, 8½" d., flint 95.00
Butter dish, cov., flint 82.50
Celery vase, pedestal base w/knob
   stem, flint 80.00
Celery vase, pedestal base w/knob
   stem, milk white 95.00
Champagne, flint .... 125.00 to 150.00
Claret, flint 100.00
Compote, open, 6" d., high stand,
   flint 75.00
Compote, open, 7" d., low stand,
   flint 67.50
Compote, open, 7" d., 7" h., milk
   white 175.00
Compote, open, 7½" d., 8½" h.,
   flint 150.00
Compote, open, 8" d., shallow bowl,
   high stand, non-flint 65.00
Compote, open, 10¼" d., 10" h.,
   milk white 350.00
Cordial, flint 195.00
Creamer, applied handle, flint 165.00

Cup plate, flint.................... 60.00
Decanter w/original stopper, pt..... 100.00
Decanter w/original stopper, qt..... 165.00
Egg cup, canary yellow,
    flint...................300.00 to 350.00
Egg cup, clambroth, flint........... 135.00
Egg cup, clear, flint 50.00
Goblet, clear, flint 58.00
Goblet, amber, non-flint 25.00
Goblet, blue, non-flint 32.00
Goblet, clear, non-flint 28.00
Honey dish, clear, flint 18.00
Honey dish, milk white, flint 60.00
Honey dish, coarse points, non-
    flint........................... 12.00
Lamp, whale oil, w/wafer connec-
    tor, flint, 10 1/8" h. 295.00
Pitcher, milk, applied handle, milk
    white, flint 550.00
Pitcher, water, bulbous, flint 350.00
Pitcher, water, non-flint 75.00
Plate, 8" d., milk white, flint 125.00
Salt dip, cov., master size, flint..... 195.00
Sauce dish, flint, 4¼" d. 20.00
Sauce dish, non-flint, 3½" to
    5½" d........................... 10.00
Spillholder, clear, flint 45.00
Spillholder, clear w/gold rim, flint .. 95.00
Spooner, non-flint 28.00
Sugar bowl, cov., flint 95.00
Sugar bowl, cov., non-flint 45.00
Toothpick holder, non-flint 35.00
Tumbler, flint 45.00
Tumbler, bar, flint................. 95.00
Tumbler, whiskey, handled, flint,
    3" h............................ 150.00
Wine, clear, flint 100.00
Wine, clear, non-flint 10.00
Wine, vaseline, non-flint 35.00

Champagne, clear 21.50
Champagne, turquoise blue
    (ILLUS.)........................ 37.50
Compote, open, 6" d., 6" h........ 22.50
Compote, open, 8" d., low stand,
    amethyst 45.00
Compote, open, 9" d., low stand,
    vaseline 38.00
*Goblet, amber 40.00
*Goblet, amethyst................. 38.00
*Goblet, blue 37.50
*Goblet, vaseline 35.00
Pitcher, water, amber 52.00
Pitcher, water, vaseline........... 75.00
Relish, amber, 4½ x 7½" 14.00
Relish, leaf-shaped, turquoise blue,
    5½ x 9"........................ 22.00
Relish, leaf-shaped, vaseline,
    5½ x 9"........................ 20.00
*Salt dip, vaseline, individual size .. 16.00
*Salt dip, amethyst, master size,
    rectangular 22.00
Sauce dish, flat or footed, amber ... 18.00
Sauce dish, flat or footed,
    amethyst ....12.00 to 18.00
Sauce dish, flat or footed, turquoise
    blue 13.00
Sauce dish, flat or footed, vase-
    line 12.50
Spooner, amber................... 28.00
Spooner, turquoise blue 38.00
Spooner, vaseline 40.00
Sugar bowl, cov., vaseline 60.00
Tray, water, cloverleaf-shaped,
    amethyst, 10 x 12" 45.00
*Tumbler, amber 30.00
*Tumbler, vaseline 26.00
Wine, amethyst 42.00
Wine, clear 18.00
Wine, vaseline 38.00

DIAMOND QUILTED

Diamond Quilted Champagne

Bowl, 6" d. 12.50
Bowl, 7" d., amber 25.00
Bowl, 7" d., vaseline 22.00
Butter dish, cov., vaseline ...:..... 75.00
Champagne, amethyst 37.50

DIAMOND THUMBPRINT

Diamond Thumbprint Spooner

Bowl, 7" d., footed, scalloped rim .. 95.00
*Butter dish, cov. ....150.00 to 200.00
Celery vase ....175.00 to 200.00
Compote, open, 8" d., high stand... 75.00
Compote, open, 8" d., low stand ... 65.00

Compote, open, 10½" d., high
   stand ....200.00 to 250.00
Compote, open, 11½" d., high
   stand ....300.00 to 350.00
Cordial, 4" h. 295.00
*Creamer, applied handle.......... 200.00
Decanter w/bar lip, qt., 10½" h. ... 195.00
Decanter w/original stopper, qt..... 225.00
*Goblet 450.00
Honey dish 25.00
Pitcher, water ....400.00 to 600.00
Sauce dish, flat 20.00
*Spooner (ILLUS.)................. 86.00
*Sugar bowl, cov. 150.00
*Tumbler ....50.00 to 90.00
Tumbler, bar, 3¾" h............. 150.00
Tumbler, whiskey 150.00
Tumbler, whiskey, handled........ 300.00
Wine............................ 235.00

DINNER BELL - See Cottage Pattern

DORIC - See Feather Pattern

DOUBLE LOOP - See Ribbon Candy Pattern

DRAPERY

Drapery Spooner

Creamer, applied handle........... 35.00
Goblet 28.00
Pitcher, water, applied handle 75.00
Plate, 6" d. 23.00
Spooner (ILLUS.).................. 28.00
Sugar bowl, cov. 40.00

EGG IN SAND

Bread tray, handled 36.00
Creamer 32.00
Dish, flat, swan center, 7" d....... 50.00
Goblet, blue 47.50
Goblet, clear 32.00
Pitcher, water (ILLUS. top next
   column) 38.00
Platter, 12½" oblong 42.00
Relish, 5½ x 9" 18.50

Egg in Sand Pitcher

Spooner, blue.................... 35.00
Spooner, clear 26.00
Sugar bowl, cov. 35.00
Tumbler 30.00

EGYPTIAN

Bread platter, Cleopatra center,
   9 x 12"....................... 57.00
*Bread platter, Salt Lake Temple
   center........................ 248.00
Butter dish, cov. 73.00
Celery vase...................... 105.00
Compote, cov., 7" d., high stand,
   sphinx base 195.00
Compote, cov., 8" d., high stand,
   sphinx base 185.00
Creamer 48.00
Goblet 45.00
Pickle dish..................... 20.00
Pitcher, water ....200.00 to 225.00
Plate, 10" d. 65.00
Plate, 12" d., handled 85.00
Relish, 5½ x 8½" 31.00
Sauce dish, flat 10.00
Sauce dish, footed 16.50
Spooner 40.00

EMERALD GREEN HERRINGBONE - See Paneled Herringbone

ENGLISH HOBNAIL CROSS - See Klondike Pattern

ESTHER

Berry set: master bowl & 5 sauce
   dishes; green, 6 pcs. 215.00
Bowl, 8" d., green w/gold 72.50
Butter dish, cov., clear 75.00
Butter dish, cov., green 145.00
Compote, cov., 8" d., high stand ... 100.00
Compote, open, jelly, 5" d., amber-
   stained w/enamel decoration 135.00
Creamer, green 90.00
Cruet w/original stopper, clear,
   miniature..................... 30.00
Cruet w/original stopper, green,
   miniature..................... 195.00

Cruet w/ball-shaped stopper,
clear 38.00
Cruet w/ball-shaped stopper,
green . . . . .200.00 to 225.00
Goblet, amber-stained w/enamel
decoration 150.00
Goblet, clear 60.00
Goblet, green 90.00
Pitcher, water, amber-
stained . . . . .200.00 to 250.00
Plate, 10¼" d. 30.00
Relish, clear, 4½ x 8½" 22.50
Relish, green, 4½ x 8½" 38.00
Relish, green, 5½ x 11" 40.00
Salt & pepper shakers w/original
tops, clear, pr. 95.00
Salt & pepper shakers w/original
tops, green, pr. 130.00
Sauce dish, green 25.00
Sauce dish, green w/gold 32.50
Spooner, clear 35.00
Spooner, green 68.00
Sugar bowl, cov., green 125.00
Toothpick holder, amber-stained 95.00
Tray, ice cream, clear 67.50
Tray, ice cream, green 145.00
Tumbler, clear 32.00
Tumbler, clear w/amber stain 45.00
Tumbler, green 50.00
Water set: pitcher & 6 tumblers;
green, 7 pcs. 545.00
Wine, clear 32.50
Wine, clear w/amber stain 75.00
Wine, ruby-stained, souvenir 75.00

EUREKA (McKee's)
Butter dish 80.00
Creamer 45.00
Egg cup 30.00
Goblet 35.00
Salt dip, master size 22.00
Spooner 50.00
Sugar bowl, cov. 55.00
Tumbler, footed 25.00
Wine 30.00

EYEWINKER

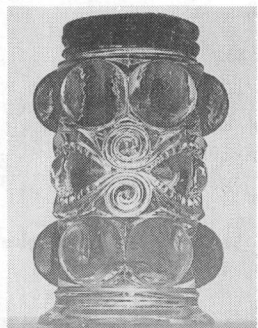

Eyewinker Salt Shaker

Banana boat, flat, 8½" 90.00

Banana stand 115.00
Bowl, 6½" d. 25.00
Bowl, master berry or fruit, 9" d.,
4½" h. 70.00
*Butter dish, cov. 68.00
Cake stand, 8" d. 58.00
Cake stand, 9½" d. 65.00
Celery vase, 6½" h. 55.00
*Compote, cov., 6" d., high stand . . 55.00
Compote, open, 5½" d., high
stand 60.00
Compote, open, 9½" d., high
stand 82.00
Compote, open, 10" d., high stand . . 75.00
Creamer 45.00
*Goblet 25.00
Pitcher, milk 70.00
*Pitcher, water 85.00
Plate, 7" sq., 1½" h., turned-up
sides 24.00
Salt shaker w/original top (ILLUS.) . . 35.00
*Sauce dish, round 34.00
Sauce dish, square 12.00
Spooner 45.00
*Sugar bowl, cov. 52.00
Syrup pitcher w/silver plate top 112.00
*Tumbler 28.00

FEATHER (Doric, Indiana Swirl or Finecut & Feather)

Feather Jelly Compote

Berry set, master bowl & 6 sauce
dishes, 7 pcs. 120.00
Bowl, 6½" d. 12.00
Bowl, 7 x 9" oval 20.00
Bowl, 7½" d. 35.00
Butter dish, cov., clear 60.00
Butter dish, cov., green 195.00
Cake stand, 8½" d. 38.00
Cake stand, clear, 9½" h. 47.00
Cake stand, green,
9½" h. . . . . .125.00 to 150.00
Cake stand, 11" d. 65.00
Celery vase 34.00
Compote, open, jelly, 5" d., 4¾" h.,
amber-stained 110.00
Compote, open, jelly, 5" d., 4¾" h.,
clear (ILLUS.) 20.00

Cordial 43.00
Creamer, clear 38.00
Creamer, green 75.00
Cruet w/original stopper, clear 45.00
Cruet w/original stopper, green 250.00
Doughnut stand, 8" w., 4½" h. 36.00
Goblet, amber-stained 140.00
Goblet, clear 60.00
Pickle dish. 15.00
Pitcher, milk 48.00
Pitcher, water, clear 70.00
Pitcher, water, green . . . . . . 175.00 to 200.00
Plate, 10" d. 45.00
Relish, 8¼" oval 18.00
Salt & pepper shakers w/original
    tops, green, pr. 225.00
Sauce dish, flat or footed, clear 14.50
Sauce dish, flat or footed, green . . . 45.00
Spooner 30.00
Sugar bowl, cov. 50.00
Syrup pitcher w/original top, clear . . 135.00
Syrup pitcher w/original top,
    green 315.00
Toothpick holder 85.00
Tumbler, clear 45.00
Tumbler, green 85.00
*Wine. 42.50

FINECUT & BLOCK

Finecut & Block Pitcher

Bowl, round, handled, pink blocks . . 50.00
Celery tray, clear w/amber blocks,
    11" l. 85.00
Champagne, amber 70.00
Compote, open, 8" d., 6½" h. 32.50
Cordial 70.00
*Creamer, clear 30.00
Creamer, clear w/amber blocks 50.00
Creamer, clear w/pink blocks 75.00
Egg cup, single 27.50
Egg cup, double. 29.00
*Goblet, amber 50.00
*Goblet, clear 40.00
Goblet, clear w/yellow blocks 52.00
Ice cream tray, clear w/amber
    blocks. 85.00
Ice cream tray, clear w/yellow
    blocks. 75.00

Pitcher, water, amber (ILLUS.) 85.00
Pitcher, water, clear w/blue
    blocks 125.00
Salt dip 12.00
Sauce dish, amber 15.00
Sauce dish, clear w/amber blocks . . 13.00
Sauce dish, clear w/blue blocks 22.50
Spooner, clear 40.00
Spooner, clear w/amber blocks. 45.00
*Sugar bowl, cov. 35.00
Tumbler, clear 17.50
Tumbler, clear w/blue blocks 40.00
*Wine, amber. 58.00
*Wine, blue 58.00
*Wine, clear 24.00
Wine, clear w/amber blocks 48.00
Wine, clear w/blue blocks 45.00
Wine, clear w/pink blocks 60.00
Wine, clear w/yellow blocks 35.00

FINECUT & FEATHER - See Feather Pattern

FINECUT BAND - See Cottage Pattern

FISHSCALE

Bowl, cov., 7" d. 55.00
Bowl, 8" d. 18.00
Bowl, 10" d. 22.50
Butter dish, cov. 42.00
Cake stand, 8" d. 33.00
Cake stand, 10" d. 35.00
Celery vase. 32.50
Compote, cov., 7½" d. 75.00
Compote, open, jelly 24.50
Compote, open, 6" d. 24.00
Compote, open, 7" d., high stand . . . 31.00
Compote, open, 9" d., high stand . . . 45.00
Condiment tray, rectangular. 32.00
Creamer 25.00
Goblet 32.50
Lamp, kerosene, hand-type w/finger
    grip 65.00
Mug 35.00
Pickle dish. 18.50
Pitcher, milk 35.00
Pitcher, water 55.00
Plate, 8" d. 35.00
Plate, 9" sq. 35.00
Relish, 5 x 8½" 22.50
Sauce dish, flat or footed 12.00
Spooner 21.00
Sugar bowl, cov. 38.00
Tray, water, round 35.00
Tumbler 95.00
Waste bowl. 50.00

FLORIDA - See Paneled Herringbone Pattern

FLOWER FLANGE - See Dewey Pattern

FLYING ROBIN - See Hummingbird Pattern

FROSTED LION (Rampant Lion)

Frosted Lion Oval Compote

Bowl, cov., 4 5/8 x 7 7/16" oblong,
  collared base 110.00
*Bread plate, rope edge, closed
  handles, 10½" d. 75.00
*Butter dish, cov., frosted lion's
  head finial..................... 90.00
Butter dish, cov., rampant lion
  finial......................... 140.00
*Celery vase..................... 73.00
Compote, cov., 5" d., 8½" h........ 175.00
*Compote, cov., 6¾" oval, 7" h.,
  collared base, rampant lion finial
  (ILLUS.) .... 150.00 to 175.00
Compote, cov., 7¾" oval, low col-
  lared base, rampant lion finial ... 128.00
Compote, cov., 8" d., 13" h., ram-
  pant lion finial 165.00
Compote, cov., 8¼" d., high stand,
  frosted lion head finial 145.00
Compote, open, 5" d., low stand ... 62.00
Compote, open, 7" d., 6¼" h. 80.00
Compote, open, 8" oblong, low
  stand 70.00
Creamer 75.00
*Egg cup 95.00
*Goblet 93.00
Marmalade jar, cov., rampant lion
  finial.......................... 125.00
*Pitcher, water .... 525.00 to 550.00
Platter, 9 x 10½" oval, lion han-
  dles............................ 95.00
Salt dip, cov., master size, collared
  base, rectangular 295.00
*Sauce dish, 4" to 5" d............. 25.00
*Spooner 53.00
Sugar bowl, cov., rampant lion
  finial.......................... 85.00
Table set, cov. sugar bowl, creamer
  & spooner, 3 pcs. 225.00

FROSTED WAFFLE - See Hidalgo Pattern

GALLOWAY (Mirror or misnamed Virginia)
Bowl, 6½" d. 17.50
Bowl, 9½" d., flat............... 30.00

Butter dish, cov. 55.00
Cake stand, 9¼" d., 6" h. 52.00
Compote, open, 4¼" d., 6" h. 33.00
Compote, open, 8½" d., 7" h. 60.00
Compote, open, 8¾" d., flared,
  rose-stained 85.00
Creamer, clear.................. 22.00
Creamer, rose-stained 75.00
Creamer, individual size 19.00
Cruet w/stopper 38.00
Goblet 90.00
Mug, 4½" d...................... 37.50
Pickle castor w/silver plate lid &
  frame 125.00
Pitcher, milk 68.00
Pitcher, water 50.00
Punch cup 8.00
Relish, 8¼" l.................... 14.50
Salt shaker w/original top 20.00
Salt & pepper shakers w/original
  tops, gold trim, 3" h., pr. 47.50
Sauce dish, flat or footed 12.00
Spooner, rose-stained 80.00
Sugar bowl, cov., clear 42.50
Sugar bowl, cov., rose-stained 85.00
Sugar shaker w/original top 35.00
Syrup pitcher w/metal spring top ... 75.00
Table set, cov. butter dish, cov.
  sugar bowl, creamer & spooner,
  4 pcs. .... 225.00 to 275.00
*Toothpick holder, clear 25.00
*Toothpick holder, green 50.00
Tumbler 30.00
Vase, 9½" h..................... 40.00
Water set: pitcher & 4 tumblers;
  rose-stained, 5 pcs. 495.00
Wine........................... 38.00

GARFIELD DRAPE
Bread plate, "We Mourn Our Na-
  tion's Loss," 11½" d. 55.00
Butter dish, cov. 75.00
Cake stand, 9½" d. 75.00
Celery vase, pedestal base......... 45.00
Compote, cov., 8" d.,
  12½" h................ 100.00 to 125.00
Creamer 40.00
Goblet 40.00
Pitcher, milk.................... 85.00
Pitcher, water 95.00
Sauce dish, flat or footed 9.00
Spooner 30.00

GEORGIA - See Peacock Feather Pattern

GOOD LUCK - See Horseshoe Pattern

GRASSHOPPER (Locust)
Bowl, cov., 7" d., footed 50.00
Butter dish, cov., no insect, clear ... 45.00
Butter dish, cov., w/insect, clear ... 70.00
Butter dish, cov., vaseline 95.00
Celery vase, w/insect 75.00
Compote, cov., 8¼" d. 65.00

Creamer, w/insect 57.50
Pitcher, water, w/insect 85.00
Plate, 8½" d., footed.............. 20.00
Plate, 10½" d., footed............. 28.00
Salt dip, master size.............. 38.00
Sauce dish, footed, no insect 14.00
Spooner, no insect 45.00
Spooner, w/insect................. 52.00
Sugar bowl, cov., no insect 40.00
Sugar bowl, cov., w/insect 70.00

GUARDIAN ANGEL - See Cupid & Venus Pattern

HALLEY'S COMET
Celery vase...................... 34.00
Goblet 32.00
Jar, cov., three-footed 49.00
Pitcher, water, tankard 92.00
Pitcher, water, tankard, engraved .. 105.00
Relish, 4½ x 7" 15.00
Spooner ....40.00 to 55.00
Tumbler 26.00
Wine............................ 22.00

HAND (Pennsylvania, Early)
Bowl, 9" d. 37.00
Bread plate, 8 x 10½" oval 38.00
Butter dish, cov.,................. 125.00
Cake stand, 12¼" d., engraved 175.00
Celery vase...................... 41.00
Claret 85.00
Compote, cov., 7" d., high stand ... 95.00
Compote, open, 7¾" d., 6¾" h. 45.00
Compote, open, 9" d., low stand ... 36.00
Cordial 85.00
Creamer 45.00
Goblet 55.00
Marmalade jar, cov............... 65.00
Mug 95.00
Pitcher, water 68.00
Relish 22.50
Sauce dish, 4½" d................ 12.50
Spooner 45.00
Sugar bowl, cov. 65.00
Tumbler, water ....100.00 to 125.00
Wine............................ 69.00

HEARTS OF LOCH LAVEN - See Shuttle Pattern

HEART WITH THUMBPRINT
Banana boat, 6½ x 7½" 115.00
Banana boat, 6½ x 11" 165.00
Barber bottle w/original pewter
  stopper 150.00
Bowl, 7" sq., 3½" h. 37.50
Bowl, 8" d., 2" h., flared rim 25.00
Bowl, 9" d. 38.00
Bowl, 10" d., scalloped rim........ 42.00
Cake stand, 9" d., 5" h. ...150.00 to 175.00
Card tray, clear 20.00
Card tray, green 55.00
Celery vase...................... 53.00

Compote, open, jelly, two handles,
  green 25.00
Compote, open, 7½" d., 7½" h.,
  scalloped rim 145.00
Cordial, 3" h. ....125.00 to 150.00
Creamer 39.00
Creamer, individual size 24.00
Cruet w/original stopper.......... 71.00
Goblet 55.00
Ice bucket 75.00
Lamp, kerosene-type, green,
  9" h. ....200.00 to 250.00
Mustard jar w/silver plate cover 95.00
Olive dish 19.50
Plate, 6" d. 22.50
Plate, 10" d. 34.00
Plate, 12" d. 58.00
Punch cup 22.50
Rose bowl, 3¾" d. 55.00
Sauce dish 15.00
Spooner 55.00
Sugar bowl, cov., large 95.00
Sugar bowl, open, individual size,
  green w/gold 45.00
Syrup jug w/original pewter top 108.00
Syrup jug w/original pewter top,
  miniature, 4" h. 85.00
Tray, 4¼ x 8¼" 30.00
Tumbler, water, clear w/gold 45.00
Vase, 6" h., trumpet-shaped, clear.. 32.00
Vase, 6" h., trumpet-shaped,
  green 65.00
Vase, 10" h., trumpet-shaped 65.00
Wine, clear 45.00
Wine, green w/gold 135.00

HICKMAN (Le Clede)
Bowl, 6" d., green 25.00
Bowl, 8" d. 16.00
Butter dish, cov. 35.00
Cake stand, 8½" to 9½" d. 38.00
Celery dish, boat-shaped, green 22.00
Celery tray 18.00
Compote, cov., 7" d., high stand ... 82.00
Compote, open, 7½" d., 5½" h. 19.50
Compote, open, 8½" d., 12" h. 65.00
Compote, open, 9½" d., 8" h. 45.00
Condiment set, miniature, salt &
  pepper shakers & cruet w/original
  stopper on cloverleaf-shaped tray,
  4 pcs.....................75.00 to 100.00
Creamer, clear w/gold 25.00
Creamer, green 27.00
Creamer & open sugar bowl, in-
  dividual size, oval, green, pr. 38.00
Cruet w/triple pouring spout &
  faceted stopper 31.00
Goblet, clear 35.00
Goblet, green w/gold 40.00
Ice tub, clear 48.00
Ice tub, green 60.00
Pitcher, water 60.00
Plate, 6" d..................... 11.00
Punch cup, clear 8.00

Punch cup, green 18.50
Relish, green 23.00
Sauce dish, clear 7.00
Sauce dish, green 12.50
Sauce dish, ruby-stained 18.50
Sugar bowl, cov. 37.50
Toothpick holder 32.00
Tumbler 25.00
Vase, 10" h., green 37.50
Water set: pitcher & 6 tumblers;
  clear w/gold, 7 pcs. 225.00
Wine, clear 27.00
Wine, green 45.00

HIDALGO (Frosted Waffle)

Hidalgo Compote

Bowl, 9" sq., clear & frosted 24.00
Butter dish, cov. 50.00
Celery dish, boat-shaped, 13" l. 45.00
Celery vase, amber-stained 47.50
Celery vase, clear 30.00
Compote, open, 7" sq., high stand
  (ILLUS.) 45.00
Creamer 35.00
Goblet, clear 20.00
Goblet, engraved 22.00
Goblet, frosted 45.00
Pitcher, water 43.00
Sauce dish, handled 15.00
Spooner 40.00
Sugar bowl, cov. 35.00
Sugar shaker w/original top 45.00
Tray, water 55.00
Tumbler, frosted 45.00
Waste bowl 25.00

HOBNAIL

*Butter dish, cov. 85.00
*Cologne bottle, amber, 6½" h. 37.50
*Cologne bottle, clear, 6½" h. 22.00
*Creamer, fluted top, applied han-
  dle, amber, 2 x 3" 25.00
Creamer, three-footed, blue 35.00
*Creamer, individual size, amber . . .   31.00
*Cruet w/original stopper, 4½" h. . . .   45.00
Egg cup, single 28.50
Egg cup, double 15.00
*Goblet 15.00

Hobnail Mug

Mug, amber (ILLUS.) 30.00
Mug, blue 21.00
Mug, clear 15.00
Pitcher, 8" h., square top, amber . . .   235.00
Pitcher, 8" h., square top, sapphire
  blue 265.00
Pitcher, water, blue 125.00
*Punch cup 22.50
*Rose bowl, 6" d., 5½" h. 85.00
Spooner, ruffled rim, amber 35.00
*Spooner, clear 30.00
Spooner, frosted 35.00
*Sugar bowl, cov. 20.00
Sugar shaker w/original top 42.50
*Toothpick holder, amber 39.00
*Toothpick holder, blue 22.50
Tray, water, amber, 11½" d. 55.00
Tray, water, blue, 11½" d. 55.00
Tumbler, seven-row, amber 20.00
*Tumbler, eight-row, amber 22.50
*Tumbler, ten-row, amber 60.00
*Tumbler, ten-row, blue 28.00
*Tumbler, clear 15.00
Tumbler, ten-row, ruby-stained 110.00
Tumbler, vaseline 38.00
*Vase, 5½" h., cone-shaped, ruffled
  rim, vaseline 45.00
*Wine, amber 25.00
*Wine, clear 20.00
Wine, green 22.50

HONEYCOMB

*Butter dish, cov., non-flint, clear . . .   45.00
Butter dish, cov., non-flint, clear
  w/gold 75.00
Cake stand, 9" d., 5¾" h., cable
  border 35.00
Celery vase, flint 75.00
Celery vase, non-flint 22.00
Celery vase, New York Honeycomb,
  non-flint 28.00
Champagne, flint 40.00
*Champagne, non-flint 30.00
Claret, flint 50.00
Compote, cov., 9¼" d., 11½" h.,
  flint 90.00
Compote, open, 7" d., 7" h., flint . . .   55.00
Compote, open, 9" d., 6" h., flint . . .   75.00
Compote, open, 11" d., 8" h.,
  flint . . . . 100.00 to 125.00
*Creamer, non-flint 45.00
Decanter w/bar lip, flint, 10½" h. . . .   110.00

Egg cup, flint 30.00
Goblet, flint 35.00
Goblet, flint, engraved 50.00
*Goblet, non-flint 12.00
Goblet, Laredo Honeycomb 45.00
Goblet, New York Honeycomb 22.00
Mug, flint 28.00
Mustard pot, w/original pewter lid,
   etched, flint 75.00
Pitcher, milk, flint 90.00
Pitcher, water, 8½" h., molded
   handle, polished pontil,
   flint....................150.00 to 175.00
*Salt & pepper shakers w/original
   tops, non-flint, pr............... 75.00
Spillholder, flint.................. 50.00
Spooner, non-flint 23.00
Sugar bowl, cov., flint 75.00
Tumbler, bar...................... 24.00
Wine, flint....................... 45.00
*Wine, non-flint 12.00

HORN OF PLENTY

Bar bottle w/original stopper, qt.... 165.00
Bowl, 7½" d. 70.00
Bowl, 8" oval 110.00
Butter dish, cov. 125.00
Butter pat 16.00
Celery vase...................... 175.00
Champagne....................... 155.00
Compote, cov., 6¼" d., 7½" h...... 250.00
Compote, open, 6" d............. 75.00
Compote, open, 7" d., 3" h....... 125.00
Compote, open, 7" d., 5½" h...... 225.00
Compote, open, 7" d., 7½" h., waf-
   fle base 110.00
Compote, open, 8" d., 6" h........ 110.00
Compote, open, 8" d., 8" h........ 115.00
Compote, open, 9" d.,
   8½" h..................150.00 to 200.00
Creamer, applied handle, 7" h...... 158.00
Creamer & cov. sugar bowl, pr. 325.00
Decanter, bar lip, pt. 110.00
Decanter w/original stopper, pt..... 150.00
Decanter w/original stopper, qt..... 175.00
Dish, 6¾ x 10", 2¼" h............. 140.00
Egg cup, 3¾" h. 48.00
*Goblet 70.00
*Hat whimsey..................... 350.00
Honey dish 20.00
*Lamp, w/whale oil burner, all-
   glass, 11" h..............200.00 to 225.00
Peppersauce bottle w/stopper 168.00
Plate, 6" d., canary yellow 247.50
Plate, 6" d., clear 95.00
Relish, 5 x 7" oval................ 95.00
Salt dip, master size, oval 85.00
Sauce dish, 3½" to 5" d........... 17.50
Spillholder, clambroth ....550.00 to 650.00
Spillholder, 4½" h., clear 75.00
Sugar bowl, cov. 135.00
*Tumbler, water, 3 5/8" h........ 78.00
Tumbler, whiskey, 3" h........... 130.00

Tumbler, whiskey, handled........ 220.00
Wine............................ 175.00

HORSESHOE (Good Luck or Prayer Rug)

Horseshoe Bread Tray

Bowl, open, 6" d. 12.50
Bowl, open, 7" d., footed 47.50
Bowl, open, 5 x 8" oval, footed..... 34.00
Bowl, open, 6 x 9" oval............ 27.50
*Bread tray, single horseshoe han-
   dles (ILLUS.) 50.00
Bread tray, double horseshoe han-
   dles.................65.00 to 85.00
Butter dish, cov. 90.00
Cake stand, 7" d. 35.00
Cake stand, 8" d., 6½" h. 58.00
Cake stand, 10" d. 90.00
Celery vase...................... 67.00
Cheese dish, cov., w/woman churn-
   ing butter in base 275.00
Compote, cov., 7" d., high stand ... 75.00
Compote, cov., 8" d., high stand ... 95.00
Creamer 38.00
Doughnut stand 95.00
Goblet, knob stem 40.00
Goblet, plain stem 25.00
Pitcher, milk 90.00
Pitcher, water 125.00
Plate, 7" d. 45.00
Plate, 10" d. 65.00
Relish, 5 x 8" 12.50
Salt dip, individual size 17.50
Sauce dish, flat or footed 14.00
Spooner 35.00
Wine........................... 165.00

HUMMINGBIRD (Flying Robin or Bird & Fern)

Butter dish, cov. 49.00
Celery vase, amber 68.00
Celery vase, clear................ 32.50
Creamer, amber ....75.00 to 100.00
Creamer, blue 85.00
Creamer, clear................... 50.00
Goblet, amber 62.00
Goblet, blue 65.00
Goblet, clear 50.00
Pitcher, water, amber 125.00
Pitcher, water, clear.............. 90.00
Spooner 30.00
Tray, water, amber............... 155.00

Tray, water, blue 125.00
Tray, water, clear 55.00
Tumbler, amber 60.00
Tumbler, clear 32.50
Wine.............................. 95.00

ILLINOIS
Basket, applied handle, 7 x 7" 95.00
Bowl, 6" sq. 26.00
*Butter dish, cov., 7" sq. 75.00
Celery tray 35.00
Celery vase 37.50
Cheese dish, cov., square 60.00
Creamer, small 25.00
Creamer, large 40.00
Cruet w/original stopper 110.00
Doughnut stand, 7½" sq., 4¼" h. .. 65.00
Pitcher, water, tankard 75.00
Pitcher, water, tankard, w/glass
  lid 125.00
Pitcher, water, squatty, silver plate
  rim, clear 95.00
Pitcher, water, squatty, silver plate
  rim, green 175.00
Plate, 7" sq. 25.00
Relish, 3 x 8½" 17.50
Sauce dish 15.00
Soda fountain (straw-holder) jar,
  cov., 12½" h. 250.00
Sugar shaker w/original pewter
  top 65.00
Toothpick holder 25.00
Vase, 6" h. 25.00
Vase, 9" h., 4" d. 40.00

INDIANA SWIRL - See Feather Pattern

IOWA (Paneled Zipper or Zippered Block)
Compote, jelly 24.00
Creamer, ruby-stained 65.00
Cruet w/original stopper 50.00
Lamp, kerosene-type 105.00
Olive dish, handled 16.00
Pitcher, water, gold trim 95.00
Punch cup 22.50
Salt shaker w/original top 25.00
Sauce dish, flat 7.50
Sugar bowl, cov., ruby-stained 75.00
Toothpick holder, clear 22.50
Toothpick holder, ruby-stained 74.00
Tumbler, clear 20.00
Tumbler, ruby-stained 37.50
Wine 32.50
Wine, w/gold trim 35.00

IRISH COLUMN - See Broken Column Pattern

IVY IN SNOW
Bowl, 7" d. 20.00
*Celery vase, 8" h. 35.00
Compote, open, jelly 25.00
*Creamer, clear 25.00
Creamer, ruby-stained ivy sprigs ... 85.00

*Goblet, clear 30.00
Goblet, green & red ivy sprigs &
  gold band at top & base 185.00
Honey dish, cov., amber-stained ivy
  sprigs 87.50
Plate, 10" d. 30.00
*Sauce dish, flat or footed 12.00
*Spooner 28.00
Sugar bowl, cov., ruby-stained 135.00
Syrup jug w/original top, clear 70.00
Syrup jug w/original top, ruby-
  stained ivy sprigs 295.00
Tumbler, clear 30.00
Tumbler, ruby-stained 40.00
Wine 38.00

JACOB'S LADDER (Maltese)
Bowl, 7½ x 10¾" oval 25.00
Bowl, 9" d., flat 40.00
Butter dish, cov., Maltese Cross
  finial 55.00
Cake stand, 8" to 12" d. 55.00
Celery vase 38.00
Compote, cov., 8¼" d., high
  stand 128.00
Compote, open, 7" d., high stand ... 35.00
Compote, open, 8" d., high stand ... 42.00
Compote, open, 10" d., high stand .. 55.00
Creamer 35.00
Cruet w/original stopper, footed ... 85.00
Dish, 8" oval 18.00
Goblet 65.00
Honey dish, open 9.00
Marmalade jar, cov. ....75.00 to 100.00
Pickle dish, Maltese Cross handle... 18.00
Pitcher, water, applied handle 145.00
Plate, 6" d., clear 24.00
Plate, 6" d., purple 110.00
Relish, Maltese Cross handles,
  5½ x 9½" oval 20.00
Salt dip, master size, footed 25.00
Sauce dish, flat or footed, blue 20.00
Sauce dish, flat or footed, clear 9.00
Spooner 25.00
Sugar bowl, cov. 65.00
Syrup jug w/metal top.....100.00 to 125.00
Tumbler, bar 75.00
Wine 35.00

JEWEL & DEWDROP - See Kansas Pattern

JOB'S TEARS - See Art Pattern

JUMBO and JUMBO & BARNUM
Butter dish & cover w/frosted ele-
  phant finial, oblong (ILLUS. top
  next page) 700.00
Butter dish & cover w/frosted ele-
  phant finial, round 450.00
Castor holder (no bottles) 100.00
Compote, cov., 12" h., frosted ele-
  phant finial............325.00 to 475.00
Creamer, w/Barnum head at han-
  dle 250.00
Goblet 700.00

Jumbo Butter Dish

Pitcher, water, w/elephant in
  base 695.00
Spooner 95.00
Spoon rack . . . . 500.00 to 750.00
Sugar bowl w/Barnum head handles
  & cover w/frosted elephant
  finial . . . . 350.00 to 450.00

KAMONI - See Pennsylvania Pattern

KANSAS (Jewel & Dewdrop)
Banana bowl. 55.00
Bowl, 8½" d. 35.00
Bread tray, "Our Daily Bread,"
  10½" oval 48.00
Butter dish, cov. 65.00
Cake stand, 8" d. 45.00
Cake tray, "Cake Plate,"
  10½" oval . . . . 60.00 to 75.00
Celery vase 45.00
Compote, cov., 7" d., high stand . . . 125.00
Compote, open, jelly, 5" d. 45.00
Compote, open, 8" d., high stand . . . 57.50
Creamer 47.00
Goblet 60.00
Mug, small, 3½" h. 32.00
Pitcher, milk 72.00
Pitcher, water 60.00
Relish, 8½" oval 32.50
Salt shaker w/original top 45.00
Sauce dish, 4" d. 15.00
Spooner 47.50
Sugar bowl, cov. 65.00
Toothpick holder 50.00
Tumbler, water, footed 55.00
Wine 52.00

KING'S CROWN (Also see Ruby Thumbprint)
Banana stand 130.00
Bowl, berry or fruit, 8¼" d., flared
  rim 27.00
Bowl, 9¼" oval, scalloped rim,
  round base 40.00
Butter dish, cov. 70.00
*Cake stand, 9" d. 76.00
Cake stand, 10" d. 85.00

Castor bottle, w/original top 16.50
Castor set, salt & pepper shakers,
  oil bottle w/stopper & cov. mus-
  tard jar in original frame, 4 pcs. . . . 325.00
Celery vase, engraved 60.00
Celery vase, plain 38.00
Compote, cov., 7" d., 7" h. 95.00
Compote, cov., 8" d., 12" h. 145.00
Compote, open, jelly 45.00
Compote, open, 7½" d., high
  stand 49.00
Compote, open, 8½" d., high
  stand 80.00
*Cordial 50.00
Creamer 35.00
*Creamer, individual size, clear 16.50
Creamer, individual size, clear
  w/gold 29.50
Creamer, individual size, w/green
  thumbprints 60.00
*Cup & saucer 55.00
*Goblet, clear 30.00
Goblet, clear w/engraved moose,
  doe & dog 95.00
Goblet, cobalt blue 165.00
Goblet, w/green thumbprints 25.00
Goblet, w/green thumbprints,
  souvenir 20.00
*Lamp, kerosene-type, stem lamp,
  10" h. 180.00
Mustard jar, cov. 62.00
Pickle, 5" h., souvenir 40.00
Pitcher, tankard, 8½" h. 65.00
Pitcher, tankard, 11" h. 110.00
Pitcher, tankard, 13" h., engraved . . 125.00
Pitcher, bulbous 125.00
Plate, 8" sq. 70.00
Punch bowl, footed . . . . 225.00 to 250.00

King's Crown Punch Cup

Punch cup (ILLUS.) 22.50
Relish, 7" oval 10.00
Salt dip, individual size 35.00
Salt & pepper shakers w/original
  tops, pr. 65.00
Sauce dish, blue 15.00
Sauce dish, boat-shaped 22.00
*Sauce dish, round 18.00
Spooner 35.00
Toothpick holder, clear 30.00
Toothpick holder, clear, souvenir . . . 50.00
Toothpick holder, rose stain,
  souvenir 30.00
Tray, square 29.00
Tumbler, amber 38.00

*Tumbler, clear 22.00
Water set, bulbous pitcher &
  6 goblets, 7 pcs. ....250.00 to 300.00
*Wine, clear 22.00
Wine, cobalt blue 200.00
Wine, cobalt blue, souvenir 165.00
Wine, w/green thumbprints 15.00

KLONDIKE (Amberette or English Hobnail Cross)

Klondike Boat-shaped Relish

Bowl, 6" sq., frosted w/amber
  cross 200.00
Bowl, 7¼" sq., scalloped top, clear
  w/amber cross 185.00
Bowl, master berry or fruit, 8" sq.,
  clear w/amber cross 85.00
Bowl, master berry or fruit, 8" sq.,
  frosted w/amber cross 250.00
Bread plate, clear w/amber cross,
  8½ x 11" oval 125.00
Butter dish, cov., clear 175.00
Butter dish, cov., clear w/amber
  cross ....250.00 to 300.00
Butter dish, cov., frosted w/amber
  cross 370.00
Butter pat, clear w/amber cross 35.00
Celery vase, clear w/amber cross .. 138.00
Condiment set: tray, cruet, salt &
  pepper shakers; frosted w/amber
  cross, 4 pcs. 1,350.00
Creamer, clear w/amber cross 90.00
Dish, oval, flat, shallow, clear
  w/amber cross 130.00
Goblet, clear w/amber cross 195.00
Jam dish, frosted w/amber cross,
  4¾" sq., 5½" sq., 5½" h., in sil-
  ver plate holder 118.00
Lamp, kerosene-type, clear w/am-
  ber cross, 10" h. 155.00
Pitcher, water, clear 50.00
Pitcher, water, clear w/amber
  cross ....250.00 to 275.00
Punch bowl, tulip-shaped, ped-
  estaled, slightly flared top 485.00
Punch cup, frosted w/amber cross .. 85.00
Relish, boat-shaped, clear w/amber
  cross, 4 x 9" (ILLUS.) 115.00

Relish, boat-shaped, frosted w/am-
  ber cross, 4 x 9" 129.00
Salt shaker w/original top, clear
  w/amber cross 68.00
Salt shaker w/original top, frosted
  w/amber cross 100.00
Salt & pepper shakers w/original
  tops, clear 145.00
Salt & pepper shakers w/original
  tops, frosted w/amber cross,
  pr....................200.00 to 250.00
Sauce dish, flat or footed, clear
  w/amber cross 22.50
Sauce dish, flat or footed, frosted
  w/amber cross 72.00
Spooner, clear w/amber cross 85.00
Sugar bowl, cov., clear w/amber
  cross, 6¾" h. 165.00
Sugar bowl, cov., frosted w/amber
  cross, 4" d., 6¾" h. 250.00
Sugar bowl, open, clear w/amber
  cross 75.00
Syrup pitcher w/original top, frosted
  w/amber cross 766.00
Table set: cov. butter dish, cov. sug-
  ar bowl, creamer & spooner;
  frosted w/amber cross, 4 pcs. 925.00
Toothpick holder, clear 125.00
Toothpick holder, clear w/amber
  cross 375.00
Toothpick holder, frosted w/amber
  cross 415.00
Tumbler, clear 25.00
Tumbler, clear w/amber cross 95.00
Tumbler, frosted w/amber cross 145.00
Vase, 8" h., trumpet-shaped, clear.. 50.00
Vase, 8" h., trumpet-shaped, clear
  w/amber cross 130.00

LACY MEDALLION - See Colorado Pattern

LE CLEDE - See Hickman Pattern

LIBERTY BELL
Bowl, berry or fruit, 8" d., footed ... 95.00
*Bread platter, "John Hancock,"
  shell handles, 7 1/8 x 11½" 150.00
Bread platter, "John Hancock," twig
  handles, 9½ x 13½", milk
  white 235.00
*Bread platter, "Signer's," twig
  handles 75.00
Bread platter, w/thirteen original
  states, twig handles, 8¼ x 13" ... 85.00
Butter dish, cov. 110.00
Butter dish, cov., miniature 150.00
Compote, open, 6" d............... 95.00
Compote, open, 8" d............... 65.00
Creamer, applied handle........... 115.00
Creamer, miniature 85.00
*Goblet 45.00
Mug, miniature, 2" h. 125.00
Pickle dish, closed handles, 1776-

1876, w/thirteen original states,
5½ x 9¼" oval 50.00
Pitcher, water ....550.00 to 850.00
Plate, 6" d., closed handles, scal-
loped rim, w/thirteen original
states 75.00
Plate, 6" d., no states, dated....... 62.50
Plate, 8" d., closed handles, scal-
loped rim, w/thirteen original
states 75.00
Plate, 10" d., closed handles, scal-
loped rim, w/thirteen original
states 95.00
Relish, shell handles, 7 x 11¼".... 70.00
Salt dip 28.00
Salt shaker w/original pewter top .. 110.00
Sauce dish.................... 25.00
Spooner 62.00
Sugar bowl, cov. 105.00
Table set, 4 pcs. ....400.00 to 450.00

LILY-OF-THE-VALLEY
Bowl, 5½ x 8" oval................ 32.50
Butter dish, cov. 115.00
Celery vase....................... 48.00
Champagne........................ 39.00
Compote, cov., 8" d., low stand 128.00
Compote, cov., 8½" d., high
stand 130.00
Compote, open, 7" d., low stand ... 47.50
Compote, open, 8½" d., 5" h. 42.50
Creamer, three-footed, molded
handle 65.00
Creamer, plain base, applied
handle 60.00
Cruet w/original stopper ..150.00 to 200.00
Egg cup 43.00
Goblet, plain 56.00
Pitcher, milk, applied handle....... 112.00
Pitcher, water, bulbous, applied
handle.................75.00 to 100.00
Relish, 4½ x 7" 25.00
Relish, 5½ x 8" 35.00
Salt dip, open, master size, three-
footed 60.00
Sauce dish....................... 17.50
Spooner, plain base 45.00
Spooner, three-footed 75.00
Sugar bowl, cov., three-footed 80.00
Wine............................. 155.00

LINCOLN DRAPE & LINCOLN DRAPE WITH TASSEL
Compote, open, 6¾" d., 5¼" h. 85.00
Compote, open, 7 1/8" d., 5" h. ... 110.00
Compote, open, 8" d., medium
stand 110.00
Compote, open, 8¼" d., 5 1/8" h.,
domed foot 87.50
Creamer 200.00
Egg cup 65.00
Goblet ....150.00 to 175.00
Goblet w/tassel................... 155.00
Salt dip, master size.............. 55.00

Salt dip, master size, w/tassel 125.00
Sauce dish, 4" d.................. 22.50
Spillholder....................... 54.00
Sugar bowl, cov. 165.00
Syrup pitcher w/original pewter top,
clear 150.00
Syrup pitcher w/original top,
opaque white 600.00

LION - See Atlanta Pattern

LION, FROSTED - See Frosted Lion Pattern

LION'S LEG - See Alaska Pattern

LOCUST - See Grasshopper Pattern

LOG CABIN

Log Cabin Sugar Bowl

Butter dish, cov. 295.00
Compote, cov. ....275.00 to 300.00
Compote, cov., "Lutteds Cough
Drops" 325.00
*Creamer, 4¼" h................. 132.00
Sauce dish, flat oblong 52.50
*Spooner, clear 115.00
*Spooner, sapphire blue 395.00
*Sugar bowl, cov., 8" h. (ILLUS.) 250.00

LOOP & DART
Bowl, 5 x 8" oval, round orna-
ments 37.50
Butter dish, cov., diamond orna-
ments, non-flint 38.00
Butter dish, cov., round ornaments,
flint........................... 80.00
Butter pat, round ornaments 35.00
Celery vase, diamond ornaments ... 28.00
Celery vase, round ornaments,
flint........................... 50.00
Celery vase, round ornaments, non-
flint........................... 44.00
Champagne, round ornaments,
flint........................... 85.00
Compote, cov., 6½" d., high stand,
round ornaments 90.00
Compote, cov., 7" d., 10" h., dia-
mond ornaments 65.00

Compote, cov., 8" d., 10" h., round
ornaments 90.00
Compote, cov., 8" d., low stand,
round ornaments 74.00
Creamer, applied handle, diamond
ornaments 32.50
Creamer, applied handle, round
ornaments 45.00
Egg cup, round ornaments 26.00
Goblet, diamond ornaments 40.00
Goblet, round ornaments 32.00
Pitcher, water, round ornaments ... 125.00
Plate, 6" d., round ornaments 30.00
Salt dip, master size, round
ornaments 45.00
Sauce dish, diamond ornaments 5.00
Sauce dish, round ornaments 6.50
Spooner, round ornaments 32.00
Sugar bowl, cov., diamond
ornaments 45.00
Sugar bowl, cov., round ornaments,
flint 75.00
Wine, diamond ornaments 32.50
Wine, round ornaments 45.00

LOOP & PILLAR - See Michigan Pattern

LOOP WITH STIPPLED PANELS - See Texas Pattern

LOOPS & DROPS - See New Jersey Pattern

MALTESE - See Jacob's Ladder Pattern

MANHATTAN

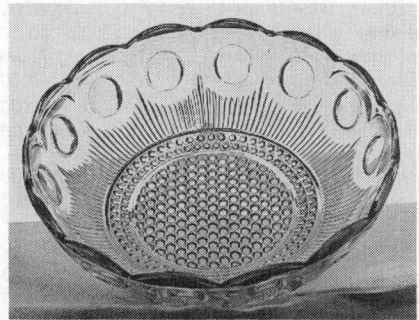

Manhattan Bowl

Basket, applied handle, 7 x 10",
11½" h. 145.00
Bowl, 8¼" d. 25.00
Bowl, 9" d. 22.00
Bowl, 10½" d. (ILLUS.) 15.00
Bread plate 20.00
Butter dish, cov. 48.00
Cake stand ....35.00 to 40.00
Carafe, water, pink-stained 65.00
Celery tray 26.00
Compote, open, large 47.50
Cracker jar, cov., pink-stained 85.00
Creamer 27.50
Creamer, individual size 25.00

Creamer & open sugar bowl, pr..... 55.00
Cruet w/original stopper 47.50
Goblet 25.00
Marmalade jar, cov. 37.50
Pickle castor in silver plate frame,
w/tongs 110.00
Pitcher, water, w/silver rim 95.00
Plate, 5" d., pink-stained 25.00
Plate, 8" d. 16.00
Plate, 10¾" d. 20.00
Punch bowl, 14" d., 8" h. 110.00
Punch cup 20.00
Salt shaker w/original top 24.50
Sauce dish, flat 12.50
Spooner 20.00
Sugar bowl, open 18.00
Toothpick holder, blue-stained...... 55.00
Toothpick holder, clear 25.00
Toothpick holder, purple-stained
eyes 30.00
Tumbler 12.50
Tumbler, footed 30.00
Vase, 6" h. 16.00
Violet bowl 20.00
Wine 25.00

MASCOTTE

Mascotte Cheese Dish

Bowl, cov., 7" d. 90.00
Butter dish, cov., engraved 85.00
Butter pat 12.50
Cake basket w/handle............. 55.00
Cake stand, 10" d. 48.00
Celery vase.................... 40.00
Cheese dish, cov. (ILLUS.) 65.00
Compote, cov., 5" d. 44.00
Compote, cov., 7" d. 45.00
Compote, cov., 8" d., 12" h. 65.00
Compote, open, jelly 20.00
Creamer 36.00
Goblet 32.00
Jar, cov., globe-type, embossed pat-
ent date, milk white............. 265.00
Pitcher, water 60.00
Salt shaker w/original top 14.00
Sauce dish, flat or footed, each 12.50
Spooner, clear 32.00
Spooner, vaseline 135.00
Sugar bowl, cov., engraved 48.00
Sugar bowl, cov., plain 39.00

Tray, water	58.50
Tray, water, engraved	75.00
Tumbler, clear	26.00
Tumbler, engraved	45.00
Wine, clear	26.00
Wine, engraved	45.00

MASSACHUSETTS

Banana boat, 6½ x 8½"	55.00
Bar bottle, bar lip, 11" h.	45.00
Bar bottle, green, 11" h.	60.00
Bar bottle w/original pewter top, 11" h.	80.00
Basket w/applied handle, 4½ x 4½", 4¾" h.	55.00
Bowl, 6" sq.	18.00
Bowl, master berry, 9" sq.	32.00
*Butter dish, cov., clear	55.00
Butter dish, cov., green	65.00
Champagne	45.00
Cologne bottle w/stopper	48.00
Cordial	45.00
Creamer	32.00
Cruet w/original stopper	42.00
Cruet w/original stopper, miniature, 3½" h.	55.00
Decanter w/stopper	88.00
Goblet	42.50
Mug, 3½" h., clear	20.00
Mug, 3½" h., clear w/gold trim	22.50
Plate, 8" sq.	35.00
Punch cup	15.00
Relish, 8½" l.	12.50
Rum jug, 5" h.	75.00
Sauce dish	15.00
Spooner	20.00
Sugar bowl, cov.	35.00
Tumbler, juice	22.00
Tumbler, water	25.00
Vase, 6½" h., trumpet-shaped, clear	25.00
Vase, 6½" h., trumpet-shaped, co-balt blue w/gold	40.00 to 60.00
Vase, 7" h., clear w/gold	24.00
Vase, 9" h., trumpet-shaped, clear	32.50
Vase, 9" h., trumpet-shaped, green	38.00
Vase, 10" h., trumpet-shaped, green	60.00
Whiskey shot glass	12.00
Wine, blue	110.00
Wine, clear	40.00

MICHIGAN (Paneled Jewel or Loop & Pillar)

Bowl, 8" d., clear	36.00
Bowl, 8" d., pink-stained w/gold trim	75.00
Bowl, 10" d.	32.00
Butter dish, cov., blue-stained	175.00
Butter dish, cov., clear	60.00
Butter dish, cov., pink-stained	375.00
Butter dish, cov., yellow-stained, enameled florals	150.00 to 175.00
Celery vase	50.00

Compote, open, jelly, 4½" d., blue-stained	125.00
Compote, open, 8½" d., high stand	65.00
Compote, open, 9¼" d.	85.00
Creamer, 4" h.	30.00
Creamer, individual size	35.00
Goblet, clear	35.00
Goblet, clear w/blue stain	40.00
Goblet, clear w/gold	42.00
Goblet, clear w/green stain, w/enamel	49.00
Mug, clear	20.00
Mug, yellow-stained, enameled florals	28.00
Pitcher, water, 8" h.	48.00
Pitcher, water, tankard, 12" h., clear	75.00
Pitcher, water, tankard, 12" h., pink-stained	245.00
Plate, tea, 6" d., yellow-stained w/pink florals	25.00
Punch bowl, 8" d., 4½" h.	50.00
Punch cup, clear	7.00
Punch cup, enameled decoration	12.00
Punch cup, pink-stained	30.00
Relish	20.00
Salt shaker w/original top, clear	27.50
Salt shaker w/original top, enameled decoration	32.00
Salt & pepper shakers w/original tops, individual size, pr.	75.00
Sauce dish, clear	13.00
Sauce dish, yellow-stained	19.50
Spooner, blue-stained	125.00
Spooner, clear	40.00
Spooner, pink-stained	71.00
Spooner, clear, child's	60.00
Sugar bowl, cov., blue-stained	150.00
Sugar bowl, cov., clear	75.00
Sugar bowl, cov., pink-stained, gold trim	100.00 to 125.00
Sugar bowl, cov., child's, 4¾" h.	40.00
Table set, pink-stained, 4 pcs.	350.00 to 375.00
Toddy mug, tall	45.00
Toothpick holder, blue-stained	75.00
Toothpick holder, blue-stained on top w/yellow enameled dots	100.00 to 150.00
*Toothpick holder, clear	37.50
Toothpick holder, clear, enameled florals	45.00
Toothpick holder, pink-stained, gold trim	265.00
Toothpick holder, yellow-stained	55.00
Toothpick holder, yellow-stained, enameled florals	60.00
Tumbler, clear	28.00
Tumbler, pink-stained, gold trim	70.00
Tumbler, yellow-stained, enameled florals	35.00
Vase, 6" h., clear	16.00

Vase, 6" h., pink-stained, enameled florals	40.00
Vase, 8" h., green-stained, white enameled dots	60.00
Waste bowl	68.00
Water set: pitcher & 3 tumblers; yellow-stained, enameled florals, 4 pcs.	225.00
Wine, blue-stained	55.00
Wine, clear	35.00
Wine, yellow-stained	50.00

MIKADO - See Daisy & Button with Cross-bars Pattern

MINNESOTA

Basket w/applied reeded handle	75.00
Bowl, 6 x 8¼"	45.00
Bowl, 8½" d., clear	50.00
Bowl, 8½" d., ruby-stained	100.00
Bowl, 7½ x 10½"	50.00
Butter dish, cov.	44.00
Carafe	36.00
Celery tray, 13" l.	40.00
Cheese dish, cov.	58.00
Compote, open, 7"	45.00
Compote, open, 9" sq.	50.00
Creamer, 3½" h.	40.00
Creamer, individual size	15.00
Cruet w/original stopper	50.00
Goblet	30.00
Mug	25.00
Nappy, 4½" d.	14.00
Pickle dish	12.00
Pitcher, water, tankard	50.00 to 75.00
Relish, 3 x 5"	10.00
Relish, 6½ x 8¾" oblong	25.00
Salt shaker w/original top, ruby-stained	50.00
Sauce dish	10.00
Spooner, clear	35.00
Spooner, clear w/gold	52.50
Sugar bowl, cov.	50.00
Toothpick holder, three-handled	35.00
Tumbler	22.50
Wine	25.00

MIRROR - See Galloway Pattern

MISSOURI (Palm & Scroll)

Bowl, 8¾" d., green	42.00
Butter dish, cov., clear	55.00
Butter dish, cov., green	85.00
Cake stand, 9" d., 4¾" h.	35.00
Cake stand, 10" d.	60.00
Celery vase	28.00
Compote, open, 9" d., 7½" h., green	120.00
Creamer, clear	25.00
Creamer, green	30.00
Doughnut stand, 6" d. (ILLUS. top next column)	38.00
Goblet	45.00
Mug	30.00
Pitcher, milk, clear	45.00

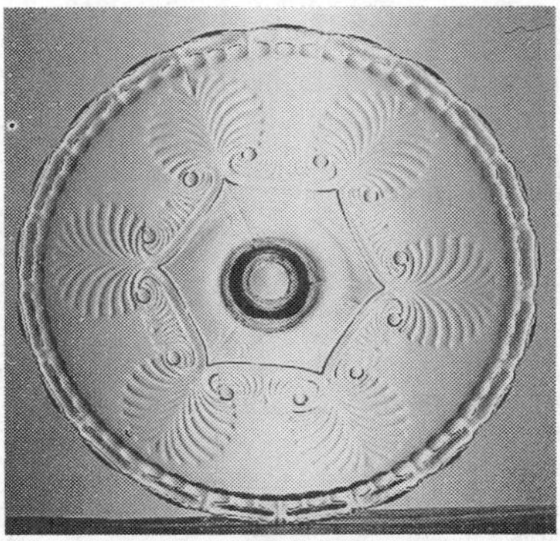

Missouri Doughnut Stand

Pitcher, milk, green	85.00
Pitcher, water	52.00
Pitcher, water, tankard, green	70.00
Salt & pepper shakers w/original tops, pr.	50.00
Spooner	24.00
Sugar bowl, cov.	47.00
Syrup pitcher	68.00
Table set, clear, 4 pcs.	195.00
Table set, green, 4 pcs.	250.00 to 300.00
Tumbler, green	35.00
Wine, clear	36.00
Wine, green	55.00

MOON & STAR

Bowl, cov., 6" d.	30.00
Bowl, cov., 7" d.	38.00
Bowl, master berry, 8¼" d., 4" h.	35.00
Bowl, fruit, 9" d., footed	35.00
Bread tray, scalloped rim, 6½ x 10¾"	50.00
*Butter dish, cov.	46.00
Cake stand, 9" d.	65.00
Cake stand, 10" d.	95.00
Celery vase	35.00
*Compote, cov., 6" d., high stand	55.00
Compote, cov., 7" d., 11" h.	70.00
Compote, cov., 10½" d., 16¼" h.	185.00
Compote, cov., 13½" h.	125.00
Compote, open, 7" d., 7½" h.	30.00
Compote, open, 8" d., 8" h.	58.00
*Creamer	52.00
Cruet w/original stopper, applied handle	55.00
Egg cup	28.00
*Goblet	45.00
Pickle dish, 8" l.	17.00
Pitcher, water, 9¼" h., applied rope handle	150.00
Relish, oblong	16.00
*Salt shaker w/original top	30.00
Sauce dish, flat or footed, each	12.00
*Spooner	38.00
*Sugar bowl, cov.	62.00
Syrup pitcher w/original top	125.00
*Toothpick holder	21.00
Wine	45.00

NEW JERSEY (Loops & Drops)

Berry set, master bowl & 3 sauce dishes, 4 pcs.	75.00
Bowl, 9" d.	25.00
Bread plate	28.00
Butter dish, cov., ruby-stained	150.00 to 200.00
Butter dish, cov., w/gold trim	75.00
Carafe, water	75.00
Celery tray, flat	25.00
Compote, open, jelly	20.00
Compote, open, 7" d., low stand	35.00
Compote, open, 7" d., high stand	60.00
Creamer	36.50
Cruet w/original stopper	50.00
Goblet, clear	32.50
Goblet, w/gold trim	36.00
Pitcher, water, bulbous	80.00
Plate, 10½" d.	32.00
Relish	12.50
Salt shaker w/original top	35.00
Sauce dish, flat	12.00
Spooner	27.50
Sugar bowl, cov.	45.00
Syrup pitcher w/original lid	115.00
Table set, 4 pcs.	215.00
Toothpick holder, clear	48.00
Toothpick holder, w/gold trim	65.00
Tumbler, clear	28.00
Tumbler, ruby-stained	50.00
Vase, 8" h., green	26.00
Vase, 10" h.	20.00
Water set, pitcher & 6 tumblers, 7 pcs.	200.00
Wine	41.00

OLD MAN OF THE MOUNTAIN - See Viking Pattern

OREGON No. 1 - See Beaded Loop Pattern

OWL IN FAN - See Parrot Pattern

PALM & SCROLL - See Missouri Pattern

PANELED FORGET-ME-NOT

Paneled Forget-Me-Not Goblet

Bread platter, 7 x 11" oval	35.00
Butter dish, cov.	40.00

Cake stand, 10" d.	50.00
Celery vase	35.00
Compote, cov., 7" d., 10" h.	67.50
Compote, cov., 8" d., high stand	78.00
Compote, open, 7" d., high stand	28.00
Compote, open, 8½" d., high stand	40.00
Creamer	34.00
Cruet w/original stopper	55.00
Goblet, amethyst	750.00
Goblet, clear (ILLUS.)	35.00
Marmalade jar, cov.	54.00
Mustard jar, cov.	40.00
Pitcher, milk	60.00
Pitcher, water, amethyst	175.00
Pitcher, water, clear	65.00
Relish, handled, 4½ x 7¾"	21.00
Relish, scoop-shaped, 9" l.	19.50
Salt & pepper shakers w/original tops, pr.	65.00
Sauce dish, flat or footed	12.00
Spooner	30.00
Sugar bowl, cov.	35.00

PANELED HERRINGBONE (Emerald Green Herringbone or Florida)

Paneled Herringbone Tumbler

Bowl, 6" d., ruby & amber-stained	55.00
Bowl, master berry, 9" sq., green	30.00
Butter dish, cov., clear	50.00
Butter dish, cov., green	73.00
Compote, open, jelly, 5½" sq., green	35.00
Cruet w/original stopper, green	100.00 to 125.00
Goblet, clear	19.00
Goblet, green	35.00
Pitcher, milk, green	75.00
Pitcher, water, clear	42.00
Pitcher, water, green	85.00
Plate, 9", green	35.00
Relish, 4½ x 8" oval, green	15.00
Sauce dish, green	12.50
Spooner, green	25.00
Sugar bowl, open, green	28.00
Syrup pitcher w/original top, green	150.00 to 200.00
Tumbler, green (ILLUS.)	21.00
Wine, clear	22.50
Wine, green	48.00

PANELED JEWEL - See Michigan Pattern

PANELED THISTLE

Bowl, 6" d., 2½" h., footed	12.50
Bowl, 7" oval, 1¾" h.	15.00
*Bowl, 8" d.	18.50
*Bowl, 8" d., w/bee	35.00
Bowl, 9" d., deep, w/bee	29.00
Bowl, 10" d., flattened rim	27.50
Bread plate	40.00
*Butter dish, cov., w/bee	50.00
Cake stand	38.00
Cake stand, w/bee	60.00
Candy dish, cov., footed, 5" sq., 6¼" h........................	30.00
Celery tray	13.50
Celery vase	45.00
*Champagne, flared, w/bee	37.50
Compote, open, 5" d., low stand ...	19.00
Compote, open, 5" d., high stand...	25.00
*Compote, open, 6" d., high stand..	45.00
Cordial	18.00
*Creamer	45.00
*Creamer, w/bee	60.00
Cruet w/stopper	50.00
*Goblet	34.00
*Honey dish, cov., square.........	60.00
Pitcher, milk	31.00
Plate, 7" sq., w/bee.............	23.00
*Relish, 4 x 8½"	16.50
*Relish, w/bee, 4 x 9½"	24.00
Rose bowl, 5" d., 2¾" h.	40.00
*Salt dip, master size.............	12.50
*Salt & pepper shakers w/original tops, pr.....................	65.00
*Sauce dish, flat or footed	16.00
*Spooner, handled	45.00
*Sugar bowl, cov.	45.00
*Tumbler, clear	30.00
Tumbler, ruby-stained	45.00
Vase, 9¼" h., fan-shaped.........	25.00
Vase, 13½" h., pulled top rim	35.00
*Wine	26.50
*Wine, w/bee	28.00

PANELED ZIPPER - See Iowa Pattern

PARROT (Owl in Fan)

Goblet	62.00
Pitcher, water	75.00
Spooner	25.00
Wine	75.00

PAVONIA (Pineapple Stem)

Butter dish, cov., clear, engraved...	90.00
Butter dish, cov., clear, plain.......	72.00
Cake stand, 10" d.	60.00
Celery vase, engraved...........	45.00
Celery vase, plain	38.00
Compote, cov., 6" d., high stand ...	60.00
Compote, cov., 7" d., engraved.....	100.00
Compote, cov., 8" d., engraved.....	125.00
Compote, open, 7" d.............	48.00
Creamer, engraved.............	42.00

Creamer, plain.................	38.00
Goblet, engraved	38.00
Goblet, plain	35.00
Pitcher, water, tall tankard, clear, engraved...................	75.00
Pitcher, water, tall tankard, clear, plain......................	60.00
Pitcher, water, tall tankard, ruby-stained.................125.00 to	150.00
Salt dip, master size............	16.50
Salt shaker w/original top	28.00
Sauce dish, flat or footed	15.00
Spooner, clear	35.00
Spooner, ruby-stained	45.00
Sugar bowl, cov., clear	55.00
Sugar bowl, cov., ruby-stained	85.00
Tray, water	68.00
Tumbler, clear, acid-etched	35.00
Tumbler, clear	32.00
Tumbler, ruby-stained	42.00
Tumbler, ruby-stained, engraved ...	47.50
Waste bowl...................	58.00
Water set: tankard pitcher & 6 tumblers; ruby-stained, 7 pcs...................325.00 to	350.00
Wine, clear, engraved	25.00
Wine, clear, plain	21.00
Wine, ruby-stained	40.00

PEACOCK FEATHER (Georgia)

Peacock Feather Compote

Bowl, 6 x 8" oval.................	27.50
Bowl, 8" d.	30.00
Butter dish, cov.	40.00
Cake stand, 8½" d., 5" h.	31.00
Compote, open, 6" d.............	18.00
Compote, open, 6¾" d., low stand	18.50
Compote, open, 8" d., high stand (ILLUS.)...................	42.50
Creamer	22.50
Cruet w/original stopper..........	40.00
Decanter, no stopper	30.00
Dish, tricornered	24.00
Goblet	25.00
Lamp, kerosene-type, low hand-type w/handle, 5½" h................	95.00
Lamp, kerosene-type, table model w/handle, 9" h., blue	220.00

Lamp, kerosene-type, table model
   w/handle, 9" h., clear 85.00
Lamp, kerosene-type, table model,
   10" h., amber.................. 275.00
Lamp, kerosene-type, table model,
   12" h., amber.................. 325.00
Mug 40.00
Pitcher, water 52.00
Relish, 8" oval 14.00
Salt & pepper shakers w/original
   tops, pr...................... 48.00
Sauce dish...................... 12.50
Spooner........................ 37.00
Sugar bowl, cov. 38.00
Tumbler 35.00
Water set, pitcher & 6 tumblers,
   7 pcs..................250.00 to 275.00

PENNSYLVANIA (Balder or Kamoni)
Bowl, berry or fruit, 8½" d., clear
   w/gold trim 30.00
Butter dish, cov. 58.00
Cake stand 45.00
Carafe 45.00
Celery tray, 4½ x 11" 28.00
Celery vase 22.50
Creamer, 3" h., clear w/gold trim,
   small 20.00
Creamer, 3" h., green w/gold trim,
   small 75.00
Cruet w/original stopper.......... 44.00
Decanter w/original stopper,
   10¾" h....................... 75.00
Goblet, clear 26.00
Goblet, clear w/gold 30.00
Pitcher, water 50.00
Punch cup, clear 12.00
Punch cup, clear w/gold 20.00
Relish.......................... 10.00
Salt shaker w/original top 30.00
Sauce dish, round or square...... 12.50
*Spooner....................... 22.00
Sugar bowl, cov., child's, green
   w/gold trim 135.00
Sugar bowl, cov. 45.00
Syrup pitcher w/original top 55.00
Table set, 4 pcs. 225.00
Toothpick holder, clear 35.00
Toothpick holder, green 100.00
Tumbler, juice 14.50
Tumbler, water, clear 23.00
Tumbler, water, clear w/gold trim .. 25.00
Tumbler, water, ruby-stained...... 49.00
Tumbler, whiskey............... 18.00
Vase, 5¾" h., clear w/gold trim.... 17.50
Vase, 5¾" h., green 60.00
Wine, clear..................... 18.00
Wine, green w/gold trim 58.00

PENNSYLVANIA, EARLY - See Hand Pattern

PILLOW ENCIRCLED
Bowl, 8" d., ruby-stained 51.00
Celery vase..................... 35.00

Condiment set: 5½ x 9½" tray, cru-
   et w/original stopper, salt & pep-
   per shakers w/original tops;
   ruby-stained, 4 pcs. 210.00
Cruet w/original stopper, clear
   w/enameled floral decoration 35.00
Mug 35.00
Pitcher, water, tankard, clear 42.00
Pitcher, water, tankard, ruby-
   stained....................... 102.00
Salt shaker w/original top 35.00
Sauce dish, footed 11.50
Spooner, ruby-stained 62.00
Sugar bowl, cov., clear 35.00
Sugar bowl, cov., ruby-stained 125.00
Tumbler, clear 35.00
Tumbler, ruby-stained 42.50

PINEAPPLE STEM - See Pavonia Pattern

PLEAT & PANEL (Darby)
Bowl, 7" d., 4½" h., footed 21.50
Bowl, cov., 8" rectangle, flat 90.00
Bowl, open, 8" rectangle, footed ... 35.00
Bread tray, closed handles,
   8½ x 13"..................... 48.00
Bread tray, pierced handles 35.00
Butter dish, cov., footed, tab han-
   dles ....75.00 to 100.00
Cake stand, 8" sq. 38.00
Cake stand, 9" to 10" sq. 65.00
Celery vase, footed 38.00
Compote, cov., 7" sq., high stand... 85.00
Compote, cov., 8" d., high stand ... 98.00
Compote, open, 7" d., high stand... 36.00
Creamer 28.00
*Goblet 27.00
Lamp, kerosene-type, stem base ... 125.00
Marmalade jar, cov............... 100.00
Pitcher, water 85.00
Plate, 5" sq. 22.00
Plate, 6" sq. 22.50
Plate, 7" sq., canary yellow 48.00
*Plate, 7" sq., clear 17.50
Plate, 8" sq. 32.00
Relish, cov., oblong, handled 65.00
Relish, open, handled, 5 x 8½".... 35.00
Salt shaker w/original top 35.00
Sauce dish, flat, handled.......... 18.00
Spooner 35.00
Sugar bowl, cov. 85.00
Sugar bowl, open 20.00
Tray, water, 9¼ x 14"........... 62.00

PLEAT & TUCK - See Adonis Pattern

PLUME
Berry set, 8½" sq. master bowl
   & five 4½" sq. sauce dishes,
   6 pcs........................ 95.00
Bowl, cov., 8" d.................. 42.50
Bowl, open, 6" d. 24.00
Bowl, open, 8½" sq. master berry .. 35.00
Bowl, open, 9" d. 30.00

Butter dish, cov.	43.00
Cake stand, 9" d., high stand	50.00
Celery vase	45.00
Compote, open, 6" d., collared base	36.00
Compote, open, 7" d., collared base	40.00
Compote, open, 8" d., high stand	50.00
Creamer, applied handle, clear	28.00
Creamer, ruby-stained	60.00
Cruet w/original stopper	38.00

Plume Goblet

*Goblet, clear (ILLUS.)	32.50
Goblet, ruby-stained & engraved	55.00
Pitcher, water, bulbous, clear, engraved	65.00
Pitcher, water, bulbous, clear, plain	65.00
Pitcher, water, bulbous, ruby-stained	200.00 to 250.00
Relish	26.00
Sauce dish, flat or footed	12.50
Spooner, clear	32.00
Spooner, ruby-stained	60.00
Tumbler, clear	35.00
Tumbler, ruby-stained, souvenir	40.00

POLAR BEAR

*Goblet, clear	120.00
Goblet, clear & frosted	150.00 to 175.00
Tray, water, clear, 16" l.	165.00
Tray, water, frosted, 16" l.	255.00
Waste bowl	90.00

PORTLAND

Portland Individual Creamer

Butter dish, cov.	48.00

Cake stand, 10½"	55.00
*Candlestick	50.00
*Celery tray	25.00
Celery vase	42.50
Compote, cov., 6½" d., high stand	125.00
Compote, cov., 8" d., high stand	40.00
Creamer	40.00
*Creamer, individual size (ILLUS.)	18.00
Cruet w/original stopper	40.00
Goblet, clear	35.00
Goblet, clear w/gold trim	38.00
Pitcher, water	52.50
Punch bowl, 15" d., 8½" h.	150.00 to 175.00
Punch cup	22.50
Salt shaker w/original top	16.00
Sauce dish, 4½" d.	12.00
Spooner	28.00
Sugar bowl, cov.	40.00
Sugar shaker w/original top	50.00
Table set: cov. butter dish, cov. sugar bowl, creamer & spooner; clear w/gold trim, 4 pcs.	350.00
Toothpick holder	28.00
Tumbler	24.00
Vase, 6" h., scalloped rim	22.00
Wine	27.50

PORTLAND MAIDEN BLUSH - See Banded Portland Pattern

PORTLAND WITH DIAMOND POINT BAND - See Banded Portland Pattern

PRAYER RUG - See Horseshoe Pattern

PRESSED LEAF

Pressed Leaf Spooner

Butter dish, cov.	60.00
Champagne	45.00
Compote, cov., acorn finial, low stand	47.50
Compote, cov., acorn finial, high stand	65.00
Egg cup	30.00
Goblet	45.00
Pitcher, water, applied handle	95.00
Salt dip, master size	30.00
Sauce dish	9.00

Spooner (ILLUS.)................... 28.00
Sugar bowl, cov. 45.00
Wine............................ 48.00

PRIMROSE

Primrose Sauce Dish

Bread plate...................... 30.00
Cake plate, two-handled, 9" d. 15.00
Creamer 30.00
Goblet 30.00
Pickle dish...................... 13.00
Pitcher, milk, blue 65.00
Pitcher, milk, clear 42.00
Pitcher, water, amber 55.00
Pitcher, water, clear............ 43.00
Plate, 4½" d., amber or blue 15.00
Plate, 4½" d., clear 13.00
Plate, 6" d., amber 16.50
Plate, 6" d., clear 13.00
Plate, 7" d., amber 22.50
Plate, 7" d., blue............... 16.00
Platter, 8 x 12", amber 22.50
Relish, amber, 5 x 9¼" 22.50
Relish, blue..................... 22.00
Relish, clear 12.50
Sauce dish, flat or footed (ILLUS.)... 10.00
Spooner 21.00
Sugar bowl, cov. 40.00
Tray, water, 11" d. 26.00
Wine, amber..................... 37.00
Wine, blue 45.00
Wine, clear 20.00

PRINCESS FEATHER (Rochelle)

Bowl, cov., 8" d. 85.00
Bowl, 5 x 7" oval............... 25.00
Bowl, 6 x 9" oval............... 30.00
Butter dish, cov. 50.00
Celery vase 40.00
Compote, cov., 8" d., low stand 100.00
Creamer 60.00
Egg cup 28.50
Goblet, flint (ILLUS. top next
    column) 35.00
Honey dish 12.50
Lamp, kerosene-type, 12" h. 75.00
Lamp, kerosene, hand-type w/finger
    grip handle.................... 120.00
Pitcher, water, bulbous, applied
    handle, flint 122.00

Princess Feather Goblet

Plate, 6" d., non-flint 29.00
Plate, 7" d., amber, flint 225.00
Plate, 7" d., clear, non-flint 22.00
Plate, 8" d., non-flint 24.00
Plate, 9" d., non-flint 32.50
Salt dip, master size.............. 29.00
Spooner, clear, non-flint 27.50
Spooner, milk white, flint 48.00
Sugar bowl, cov., clear, non-flint ... 60.00
Sugar bowl, cov., milk white, flint .. 135.00

PRISCILLA (Alexis - "Dalzell's")

Priscilla Sugar Bowl

Banana stand 95.00
Bowl, 8" d., 3½" h., straight sides,
    flat 38.00
Bowl, 8" d., 3½" h., w/pattern on
    base 45.00
*Bowl, 9" d., shallow 38.00
*Bowl, 10¼" to 10½" d. 38.00
Butter dish, cov. 95.00
Cake stand, 9" to 10" d., high
    stand 65.00
Compote, cov., jelly 55.00
*Compote, cov., 8" d. 100.00
Compote, cov., 12" d. 145.00
Compote, open, 4¾" d., 4 7/8" h.,
    flared sides.................. 35.00
*Compote, open, 8" d., 8" h........ 55.00
*Creamer 45.00
Creamer, individual size 28.00
Cruet w/original stopper 61.00

*Goblet	38.00
Pitcher, water, bulbous	120.00
Plate, 10½" d., turned-up rim	25.00
Relish	23.00
*Rose bowl, 3¾" h.	35.00
*Sauce dish, flat, 4½" to 5" d.	12.50
Spooner	28.00
Sugar bowl, cov. (ILLUS.)	45.00
Sugar bowl, cov., individual size	31.00
Syrup pitcher w/original pewter top, clear	135.00
Syrup pitcher w/original pewter top, green w/gold	450.00
Table set, 4 pcs. ....200.00 to	225.00
Toothpick holder	30.00
Tumbler	25.00
*Wine	35.00

PSYCHE & CUPID

Celery vase	36.00
Creamer	50.00
Goblet	45.00
Pitcher, water	85.00
Table set, spooner, cov. sugar bowl & creamer, 3 pcs.	185.00

PYGMY - See Torpedo Pattern

RED BLOCK

Bowl, berry or fruit, 8" d.	85.00
Butter dish, cov.	95.00
Celery vase, 6½" h.	135.00
Creamer, large	80.00
Creamer, small, applied handle	35.00
Cruet w/original stopper	150.00
Decanter, whiskey, w/original stopper, 12" h.	175.00
Dish, rectangular, 5 x 7½"	55.00
*Goblet	40.00
Mug, plain, 3" h.	27.00
Mug, souvenir, 3" h.	42.00
Pitcher, 8" h., bulbous	225.00
Pitcher, tankard, 8" h. .....175.00 to	200.00
Salt shaker w/original top	49.00
Sauce dish, 4½"	35.00
Spooner	35.00
Sugar bowl, cov.	70.00
Tumbler, souvenir	32.00
Tumbler	40.00
*Wine	40.00

REVERSE 44 (Paneled 44, U.S. Glass "Athenia")

Berry set: master bowl & 6 sauce dishes; clear w/gold or platinum stain, 7 pcs.	225.00
Butter dish, cov., clear w/gold or platinum stain	135.00
Champagne, clear w/platinum stain	75.00
Compote, jelly, clear w/gold or platinum stain	80.00
Creamer, berry, clear w/gold or platinum stain	95.00

Creamer, tankard, clear w/gold or platinum stain	30.00
Goblet, clear w/gold or platinum stain	60.00
Pitcher, tankard-type, footed, clear	105.00
Pitcher, tankard-type, footed, clear w/gold or platinum stain	155.00
Spoonholder, handled, clear w/gold or platinum stain	55.00
Table set: creamer, cov. sugar bowl & spooner; clear w/platinum stain, 3 pcs.	295.00
Toothpick holder, footed, handled, clear	35.00
Toothpick holder, footed, handled, clear w/gold or platinum stain	95.00

REVERSE TORPEDO (Diamond & Bull's Eye Band)

Reverse Torpedo Bowl

Banana stand	135.00
Basket, high stand	155.00
Bowl, 7½" d.	48.00
Bowl, 9" d., piecrust rim (ILLUS.)	75.00
Bowl, 10¼" d., piecrust rim	65.00
Butter dish, cov.	75.00
Cake stand	95.00
Celery vase	55.00
Compote, open, jelly	40.00
Compote, open, 5" d., flared rim, high stand	50.00
Compote, open, 7" d., smooth rim, high stand	55.00
Compote, open, 8" d., piecrust rim, high stand	62.50
Compote, open, 9" d., piecrust rim, high stand	82.00
Compote, open, 10" d., piecrust rim, high stand	125.00
Creamer	67.50
Goblet	85.00
Goblet, w/engraved flower	110.00
Honey dish, cov., square	145.00
Lamp, kerosene-type, 9" h.	145.00
Pitcher, water, tankard ....125.00 to	150.00
Salt shaker w/original top	40.00
Sauce dish	24.00
Spooner	52.00
Sugar bowl, cov.	72.50
Tumbler	50.00

RIBBED GRAPE

Goblet	62.50
Plate, 6" d.	28.00

Sauce dish, 4" d. 20.00
Spooner 45.00

RIBBED PALM

Ribbed Palm Goblet

Bowl, 8" d., footed 65.00
Butter dish, cov. 88.00
Celery vase...................... 75.00
Champagne....................... 125.00
Compote, open, 7¼" d., 4¼" h. 45.00
Creamer ....125.00 to 150.00
Egg cup 45.00
*Goblet (ILLUS.).................. 45.00
Pitcher, water, 9" h., applied han-
  dle ....250.00 to 300.00
Salt dip, master size............. 35.00
Salt dip, master size, footed 50.00
Sauce dish....................... 16.00
Spillholder...................... 57.00
Sugar bowl, cov. 68.00
Tumbler 110.00
*Wine 65.00

RIBBON (Early Ribbon)

Bread tray 35.00
Butter dish, cov. 72.50
Cake stand, 8½" d. 50.00
Celery vase...................... 40.00
Compote, cov., 8" d. 78.00
Compote, open, 8" d., low stand ... 40.00
Compote, open, 8" d., 8" h., frosted
  dolphin stem on dome base 295.00
*Compote, open, 5½ x 8" rectangu-
  lar bowl, 7" h., frosted dolphin
  stem on dome base 295.00
Compote, open, 8½" d., 4½" h..... 50.00
Compote, open, 10½" d., frosted
  dolphin stem on dome base 395.00
Creamer 34.00
Dresser bottle w/stopper 125.00
*Goblet 40.00
Pitcher, water 120.00
Plate, 7" d. 34.00
Platter, 9 x 13" 60.00
Sauce dish, flat or footed 12.50
Spooner 30.00
Sugar bowl, cov., 4¼" d., 7¾" h. .. 72.00

Table set, 4 pcs. ....200.00 to 225.00
Waste bowl...................... 45.00

RIBBON CANDY (Bryce or Double Loop)

Butter dish, cov., flat 48.00
Butter dish, cov., footed 55.00
Cake stand, 8" to 10½" d. 45.00
Celery vase..................... 50.00
Compote, cov., 7" d. 95.00
Compote, open, jelly 22.50
Creamer 32.00
Doughnut stand 32.00
Goblet 75.00
Pitcher, milk 50.00
Plate, 8½" d. 35.00
Relish, 8½" l.................... 14.00
Sauce dish, flat, 3½" d. 10.00
Sauce dish, footed, 4" d........... 12.00
Spooner 24.00
Sugar bowl, cov. 48.00
Syrup pitcher w/original top 85.00
Table set, 4 pcs. ....125.00 to 150.00
Wine........................... 95.00

ROCHELLE - See Princess Feather Pattern

ROMAN KEY (Roman Key with Flutes or Ribs)

(Frosted unless otherwise noted)

Celery vase..................... 70.00
Champagne...................... 94.00
Compote, open, 6½" d............ 78.00
Compote, open, 7¾" sq., 7¼" h. ... 65.00
Compote, open, 8" d., 6" h........ 60.00
Decanter w/stopper, qt. 252.00
Egg cup 35.00
Goblet 45.00
Salt dip, master size.............. 35.00
Sauce dish...................... 13.00
Spooner 32.00
*Sugar bowl, cov. 125.00
Tumbler, bar.................... 98.00
Tumbler, footed 63.00
Wine........................... 55.00

ROMAN ROSETTE (Late)

Bowl, 6" d. 16.00
Bowl, 8" d. 24.00
Bread platter, 9 x 11" 30.00
Butter dish, cov. 47.50
Cake stand, 9" to 10" d. 58.00
Celery vase, ruby-stained 95.00
Compote, cov., 5" d. 58.00
Compote, cov., 6" d., high stand ... 70.00
Compote, open, jelly, 5" d. 22.50
Cordial 47.50
Creamer 35.00
*Goblet 42.50
Mug, 3" h....................... 14.00
Pitcher, milk.................... 75.00
Pitcher, water 78.00
Plate, 7" d. 34.00
Relish, 3½ x 8½" 10.00

Sauce dish................................ 16.00
Spooner.................................. 21.00
Sugar bowl, cov. 40.00
Wine, clear............................. 48.00
Wine, ruby-stained 65.00

ROSE IN SNOW

Rose in Snow Compote

Bitters bottle w/original stopper 135.00
Bowl, 7" d., footed, canary........ 38.00
Bowl, 7" d., footed, clear 32.00
Bowl, 8½ x 11½" oval............. 47.00
Butter dish, cov., round............ 55.00
Butter dish, cov., square 50.00
Cake plate, handled, amber,
    10" d. 45.00
Cake plate, handled, blue, 10" d.... 35.00
Cake plate, handled, clear, 10" d. .. 25.00
Cake stand, 9" d. ....100.00 to 150.00
Cologne bottle w/original stopper .. 90.00
Compote, cov., 6" d., 8" h.......... 85.00
Compote, cov., 7" d., 8" h.......... 95.00
Compote, cov., 7" d., low stand 130.00
Compote, cov., 8" d., 10" h.,
    canary 155.00
Compote, open, 5" d., blue 110.00
Compote, open, 6" d., low stand
    (ILLUS.)................................. 50.00
Compote, open, 8" sq., low stand .. 110.00
Compote, open, 8" d., high stand ... 70.00
Creamer, round 35.00
Creamer, square 39.00
Dish, 8½ x 11" oval, 1½" h. 130.00
*Goblet, amber 41.00
*Goblet, blue 85.00
*Goblet, canary 65.00
*Goblet, clear 32.00
Mug, blue, large 110.00
Mug, clear, large 40.00
*Mug, applied handle, "In Fond
    Remembrance," canary 45.00
*Mug, applied handle, "In Fond
    Remembrance," clear............. 35.00
Pitcher, water, applied handle,
    amber 112.00
Pitcher, water, applied handle,
    blue 225.00
Pitcher, water, applied handle,
    clear.................................. 125.00

Plate, 6" d. 32.00
*Plate, 9" d., amber 40.00
*Plate, 9" d., clear 20.00
*Relish, 5½ x 8" oval, blue 65.00
*Relish, 5½ x 8" oval, clear....... 23.00
Relish, 6¼ x 9¼" 19.00
Sauce dish, flat or footed 11.00
Spooner, round 25.00
Spooner, square 28.00
Sugar bowl, cov., round 37.50
*Sugar bowl, cov., square 51.00
Tumbler 38.00

ROSE SPRIG

Rose Sprig Plate

Bowl, 6 x 9" oblong 27.50
Bread tray, two-handled, canary 40.00
Cake stand, canary, 9" octagon,
    6½" h. 85.00
Cake stand, 10" octagon 75.00
Celery vase.......................... 40.00
Compote, open, 8" oval............ 50.00
*Goblet, amber 50.00
*Goblet, blue 55.00
*Goblet, canary 60.00
*Goblet, clear 40.00
Pitcher, milk, blue 95.00
Pitcher, milk, canary 75.00
Pitcher, milk, clear 45.00
Pitcher, water, amber 60.00
Pitcher, water, clear............... 48.00
Plate, 6" sq., blue................. 45.00
Plate, 6" sq., clear (ILLUS.)........ 27.50
Relish, boat-shaped, amber, 8" l.... 35.00
Relish, boat-shaped, blue, 8" l.... 45.00
Relish, boat-shaped, canary, 8" l.... 40.00
Relish, boat-shaped, clear, 8" l. 32.50
Sauce dish, flat 13.00
Sauce dish, footed, amber 18.50
Sauce dish, footed, canary 20.00
Sauce dish, footed, clear........... 17.50
Tumbler 39.00
Tumbler w/applied handle 45.00
Whimsey, sitz bath-shaped bowl,
    canary, 7 x 10" 47.50
*Whimsey, sleigh (salt dip), amber,
    4 x 4 x 6" 47.00
Wine................................... 36.00

ROSETTE

Rosette Jelly Compote

Bowl, 7½" d.	16.00
Butter dish, cov.	40.00
Cake stand, 8½" to 11" d.	28.00
Celery vase	28.00
Compote, cov., 11½" h.	50.00
Compote, open, jelly, 4½" d., 5" h. (ILLUS.)	20.00
Compote, open, 7¼" d., 6" h.	30.00
Creamer	32.00
Goblet	32.50
Pitcher, milk	50.00
Pitcher, water, tankard	55.00
Plate, 7" d.	20.00
Plate, 9" d., two-handled	21.00
Relish, fish-shaped	12.00
Sauce dish	7.50
Spooner	31.00
Sugar bowl, cov.	32.00
Tumbler	16.00
Wine	25.00

ROYAL IVY (Northwood)

Berry set: master bowl & 6 sauce dishes; frosted rubina crystal, 7 pcs.	310.00
Bowl, 8" d., frosted rubina crystal	150.00 to 200.00
Bowl, fruit, 9" d., craquelle (cranberry & vaseline spatter)	235.00
Bowl, fruit, 9" d., frosted craquelle	150.00
Butter dish, cov., rubina crystal	150.00 to 175.00
Butter dish, cov., frosted rubina crystal	175.00
Creamer, clear & frosted	45.00
Creamer, rubina crystal	165.00
Creamer, frosted rubina crystal	185.00
Cruet w/original stopper, cased spatter (cranberry & vaseline w/white lining)	395.00
Cruet w/original stopper, clear & frosted	135.00
Cruet w/original stopper, craquelle (cranberry & vaseline spatter)	495.00
Cruet w/original stopper, rubina crystal	295.00
Cruet w/original stopper, frosted rubina crystal	375.00
Marmalade jar, w/original silver plate lid, clear & frosted	100.00
Pickle castor, frosted rubina crystal insert, complete w/silver plate frame	395.00
Pickle castor, cased spatter (cranberry & vaseline w/white lining) insert, complete w/silver plate frame & tongs	300.00 to 350.00
Pitcher, water, cased spatter (cranberry & vaseline w/white lining)	325.00
Pitcher, water, clear & frosted	90.00
Pitcher, water, rubina crystal	250.00
Pitcher, water, frosted rubina crystal	300.00
Rose bowl, clear & frosted	60.00
Rose bowl, rubina crystal	78.00
Rose bowl, frosted rubina crystal	95.00
Rose bowl, craquelle (cranberry & vaseline spatter)	180.00
Salt shaker w/original top, cased spatter (cranberry & vaseline w/white lining)	125.00
Salt shaker w/original top, rubina crystal	48.00
Salt shaker w/original top, frosted rubina crystal	80.00
Sauce dish, craquelle (cranberry & vaseline spatter)	45.00
Spooner, clear & frosted	50.00
Spooner, craquelle (cranberry & vaseline spatter)	150.00
Spooner, rubina crystal	65.00
Spooner, frosted rubina crystal	80.00
Sugar bowl, cov., rubina crystal	128.00
Sugar bowl, cov., frosted rubina crystal	200.00
Sugar shaker w/original top, cased spatter (cranberry & vaseline w/white lining)	300.00
Sugar shaker w/original top, rubina crystal	130.00
Sugar shaker w/original top, frosted rubina crystal	155.00
Syrup pitcher w/original top, cased spatter (cranberry & vaseline w/white lining)	490.00
Syrup pitcher w/original top, clear & frosted	100.00 to 150.00
Syrup pitcher w/original top, rubina crystal	250.00
Syrup pitcher w/original top, frosted rubina crystal	450.00
Toothpick holder, clear & frosted	47.50
Toothpick holder, craquelle (cranberry & vaseline spatter)	235.00
Toothpick holder, rubina crystal	80.00
Toothpick holder, frosted rubina crystal	125.00
Tumbler, clear & frosted	52.50

Tumbler, craquelle (cranberry &
vaseline spatter) 76.00
Tumbler, rubina crystal 64.00
Tumbler, frosted rubina crystal 69.00
Water set: pitcher & 5 tumblers;
rubina crystal, 6 pcs. 595.00
Water set: pitcher & 6 tumblers;
cased spatter (cranberry & vaseline w/white lining), 7 pcs....... 955.00

ROYAL OAK (Northwood)
Berry set: master bowl & 4 sauce
dishes; rubina crystal, 5 pcs. ... 290.00
Bowl, berry, 7½" d., frosted crys-
tal 65.00
Butter dish, cov., frosted crystal 55.00
Butter dish, cov., frosted rubina
crystal 250.00
Creamer, frosted crystal 75.00
Creamer, rubina crystal ...150.00 to 175.00
Creamer, frosted rubina crys-
tal.....................200.00 to 225.00
Pickle castor, frosted rubina crystal
insert, w/silver plate frame &
cover 225.00
Pitcher, 8½" h., frosted crystal 82.00
Pitcher, water, rubina crys-
tal....................200.00 to 250.00
Pitcher, water, frosted rubina crys-
tal....................275.00 to 300.00
Salt shaker w/original top, rubina
crystal 55.00
Salt shaker w/original top, frosted
rubina crystal 69.00
Sauce dish, frosted crystal 12.50
Sauce dish, rubina crystal 50.00
Spooner, frosted crystal........... 48.00
Spooner, frosted rubina crystal 95.00
Sugar bowl, cov., frosted rubina
crystal 180.00
Sugar shaker w/original top, frosted
crystal 95.00
Sugar shaker w/original top, rubina
crystal 138.00
Sugar shaker w/original top, frosted
rubina crystal ....145.00 to 165.00
Table set, frosted rubina crystal,
4 pcs............................ 595.00
Toothpick holder, frosted crystal.... 60.00
Toothpick holder, rubina crystal 150.00

RUBY THUMBPRINT
Berry set, round master bowl & 8
round sauce dishes, 9 pcs. 250.00
*Bowl, 8½" d. 90.00
Bowl, master berry or fruit, 10" l.,
boat-shaped ....100.00 to 125.00
Butter dish, cov., engraved 225.00
Butter dish, cov., plain 105.00
Celery vase (ILLUS. top next
column) ....100.00 to 125.00
Champagne, souvenir............. 45.00
*Claret........................ 65.00
Compote, open, jelly, 5¼" h. 49.00

Ruby Thumbprint Celery Vase

Compote, open, 7" d., engraved 150.00
Compote, open, 7" d., plain 145.00
Compote, open, 8½" d., 7½" h.,
scalloped rim ....200.00 to 225.00
Cordial, engraved 40.00
*Cordial, plain 28.00
Creamer, engraved................ 85.00
*Creamer, plain................... 60.00
Creamer, individual size 30.00
Creamer & sugar bowl, individual
size, pr......................... 80.00
Cup, engraved 35.00
*Cup, plain 25.00
Cup & saucer, engraved 65.00
*Cup & saucer, plain 62.00
*Goblet, plain 45.00
Goblet, souvenir 55.00
Pitcher, milk, tankard, 8 3/8" h. 125.00
*Pitcher, water, tankard, 11" h. 132.00
Pitcher, water, tankard, 11" h.,
w/engraved leaf band 190.00
*Plate, 5" d. 22.00
*Plate, 8¼" d. 22.00
Sauce dish, boat-shaped 32.00
*Sauce dish, round 20.00
*Sherbet 20.00
Spooner......................... 55.00
Toothpick holder, engraved 47.50
Toothpick holder, plain 45.00
*Tumbler, plain 36.00
Water set, bulbous pitcher & 6 tum-
blers, w/engraved family names &
dated 1897, 7 pcs............... 595.00
*Wine.......................... 35.00

SAWTOOTH
Butter dish, cov., clear, flint........ 78.00
*Butter dish, cov., clear, non-flint... 50.00
Butter dish, cov., sapphire blue,
non-flint....................... 230.00
Cake stand, non-flint, 7½" d.,
6" h. 30.00
*Cake stand, non-flint, 9½" d.,
4½" h......................... 75.00
Celery vase, knob stem, flint 55.00
Celery vase, knob stem, non-flint ... 40.00
Celery vase, stepped pedestal base,
notched rim, flint 125.00
Champagne, knob stem, flint....... 85.00

Champagne, non-flint.............. 35.00
Compote, open, 7½" d., 5½" h..... 38.00
Compote, open, 7½" d., 7½" h.,
    flint........................... 55.00
Compote, open, 9½" d., 10" h.,
    flint........................... 100.00
Creamer, applied handle, clear,
    flint........................... 75.00
Creamer, applied handle, cobalt
    blue, flint 230.00
Creamer, miniature, non-flint 29.00
Decanter w/original stopper, flint,
    14" h......................... 145.00
Egg cup, cov., canary yellow, flint .. 192.50
Egg cup, cov., clear, flint 100.00
Goblet, knob stem, flint 35.00
Goblet, knob stem, non-flint 25.00
Goblet, plain stem, non-flint 18.00
Lamp, whale oil, w/marble base ... 150.00
Pitcher, water, applied handle,
    flint........................... 215.00
Pomade jar, cov................... 60.00
Salt dip, cov., master size, footed,
    flint........................... 100.00
Salt dip, cov., master size, footed,
    non-flint...................... 35.00
Salt dip, master size, flint.......... 50.00
Salt dip, master size, non-flint..... 22.00
Spillholder, flint.................. 48.00
Spillholder, jagged sawtooth rim,
    sapphire blue, flint, 5½" h. 700.00
Spooner, clear, flint 24.00
Spooner, clear, non-flint 56.00
Spooner, cobalt blue, non-flint 85.00
Spooner, milk white, flint 75.00
Tumbler, bar, flint, 4½" h.......... 58.00
Tumbler, bar, non-flint............ 32.50
Wine, flint....................... 55.00
Wine, non-flint................... 18.00

SAWTOOTH BAND - See Amazon Pattern

SHELL & JEWEL (Victor)
Bowl, 8" d. 30.00
Bowl, 10" d. 25.00
Cake stand, 10" d., 5" h. 40.00
Compote, open, 7" d., 7½" h. 55.00
Creamer 25.00
Pitcher, milk, blue 75.00
Pitcher, milk, clear 32.00
Pitcher, water, blue 82.00
Pitcher, water, clear.............. 45.00
Pitcher, water, green 85.00
Sauce dish...................... 8.00
Spooner 30.00
Sugar bowl, cov. 42.50
Tumbler, amber 32.00
Tumbler, blue 32.00
Tumbler, clear 15.00
Tumbler, green 42.50
Water set, pitcher & 6 tumblers,
    7 pcs..................150.00 to 175.00

SHELL & TASSEL
Bowl, 7½" l., shell-shaped, three
    applied shell-shaped feet 55.00
Bowl, 9" oval, clear 50.00
Bowl, 9" oval, vaseline 175.00
Bowl, 10" oval, amber 90.00
Bowl, 10" oval, clear 50.00
Bowl, 6½ x 11½" oval, amber 90.00
Bowl, 6½ x 11½" oval, blue 125.00
Bowl, 6½ x 11½" oval, clear....... 45.00
Bread tray, 9 x 13" 55.00
Bride's basket, 8" oval bowl in silver
    plate frame.................... 150.00
Bride's basket, 5 x 10" oval am-
    ber bowl in silver plate
    frame.................250.00 to 275.00
Bride's basket, 5 x 10" oval clear
    bowl in silver plate frame 87.50
Butter dish, cov., round, dog
    finial...................150.00 to 175.00
Cake stand, shell corners, 8" sq. .. 42.50
Cake stand, shell corners, 9" sq. ... 62.00
Cake stand, shell corners, 10" sq. .. 85.00
Celery vase, round, handled 85.00
Compote, cov., 4¼" sq., 8" h....... 45.00
Compote, cov., 5¼" sq. 60.00
Compote, open, jelly 50.00
Compote, open, 6½" sq., 6½" h.... 45.00
Compote, open, 7½" sq., 7½" h.... 95.00
Compote, open, 8" sq., 7½" h..... 56.00
Compote, open, 9½" d., 9" h....... 82.00
Compote, open, 10" sq., 8" h. 75.00
Creamer, round 45.00
Creamer, square 50.00
Dish, 7 x 10" rectangle 35.00
Doughnut stand, 8" sq., signed 225.00
*Goblet, round, knob stem......... 60.00
Mug, miniature, blue ......100.00 to 125.00
Oyster plate, 9½" d. ......225.00 to 250.00
Pickle jar, cov. ....150.00 to 175.00
Pitcher, water, round 225.00
Pitcher, water, square 125.00
Plate, shell-shaped w/three shell-
    shaped feet, large 70.00
Platter, 8 x 11" oblong............ 52.00
Platter, 9 x 13" oval 60.00
Salt dip, shell-shaped 16.00
Salt & pepper shakers w/original
    tops, pr....................... 260.00
Sauce dish, flat or footed,
    4" to 5" d. 16.00
Sauce dish, footed, w/shell han-
    dle 15.00
Spooner, round 35.00
Spooner, square 50.00
Sugar bowl, cov., round, dog
    finial......................... 125.00
Table set, 4 pcs. 495.00
Tray, ice cream 60.00
Vase.....................175.00 to 200.00

SHOSHONE
Banana bowl, 8¼ x 10½".......... 45.00

Butter dish, cov., clear w/gold trim	70.00
Cake stand, clear	45.00
Cake stand, green	48.00
Carafe	38.00
Celery vase, ruby-stained	85.00
Compote, jelly	22.00
Compote, open, 7 x 9", scalloped rim	45.00
Creamer, amber-stained	47.50
Creamer, clear w/gold trim	35.00
Creamer, green	47.50
Cruet w/original stopper, clear	60.00
Cruet w/original stopper, green	135.00
Cruet w/original stopper, ruby-stained	195.00
Pitcher, tankard-type	50.00
Plate, 7½" d., green	35.00
Salt & pepper shakers w/original tops, ruby-stained, pr.	125.00
Salt dip, individual size	20.00
Sauce dish, clear w/gold trim, 5" sq.	12.50
Sauce dish, ruby-stained	23.00
Spooner, amber-stained	45.00
Spooner, clear	35.00
Sugar bowl, cov., clear w/gold trim	58.00
Table set, clear w/gold trim, 4 pcs.	200.00
Toothpick holder, clear w/gold trim	40.00
Toothpick holder, ruby-stained	95.00
Tumbler, ruby-stained	30.00
Wine, clear	45.00
Wine, ruby-stained	55.00

SHUTTLE (Hearts of Loch Laven)

Shuttle Creamer

Butter dish, cov.	110.00
Cake stand	125.00
Celery vase	46.00
Champagne	36.00
Cordial, small	32.00
Creamer, tall tankard (ILLUS.)	35.00
Goblet	60.00
Mug, amber	300.00
Mug, clear	28.00
Pitcher, water	140.00

Punch cup	12.00
Salt shaker w/original top	60.00
Spooner, scalloped rim	50.00
Tumbler	50.00
Wine	20.00

SNAIL (Compact)

Banana stand, 10" d., 7" h.	190.00
Bowl, 7" d., low	35.00
Bowl, 5¼ x 8" oval	35.00
Bowl, 9" d., 2" h.	50.00
Butter dish, cov.	78.00
Cake stand, 10" d.	120.00
Celery vase	50.00
Cheese dish, cov.	125.00
Compote, cov., 7" d., 8" h., engraved	185.00
Compote, open, 8" d., 6" h.	85.00
Compote, open, 10" d., 7" h.	145.00
Cracker jar, cov., 8" d., 9" h.	295.00
Creamer, clear	60.00
Creamer, ruby-stained	75.00
Cruet w/original stopper	125.00
Goblet	110.00
Pitcher, water, tankard	110.00
Pitcher, wine, tankard	125.00
Plate, 7" d.	46.00
Punch cup	32.50
Relish, 7" oval	22.50
Relish, 9" oval	31.50
Rose bowl, miniature, 3" h.	36.00
Rose bowl, 4½" h.	43.00
Rose bowl, double, miniature	35.00
Rose bowl, medium	55.00
Rose bowl, large	85.00
Salt dip, individual size	25.00
Salt dip, master size, 3" d.	40.00
Salt shaker w/original top, clear	40.00
Salt shaker w/original top, ruby-stained	65.00
Sauce dish	18.00
Spooner, clear	42.00
Spooner, ruby-stained	75.00
Sugar bowl, cov., individual size	75.00
Sugar bowl, cov., plain	60.00
Sugar bowl, cov., ruby-stained	95.00
Sugar shaker w/original top	115.00
Syrup jug w/original brass top	110.00
Tumbler	45.00
Vase, 12½" h., scalloped rim	75.00

SPIREA BAND

Berry set: master bowl & 6 footed sauce dishes; blue, 7 pcs.	150.00
Bowl, 8" oval, flat, amber	20.00
Bowl, 8" oval, flat, blue	39.00
Butter dish, cov.	45.00
Cake stand, blue, 10½" d.	80.00
Celery vase	25.00
Compote, cov., 7" d., low stand, amber	55.00
Compote, cov., 7" d., high stand, blue	65.00
Compote, open, 8" d.	25.00

Creamer, amber	36.50
Creamer, blue	35.00
Creamer, clear	28.00
Goblet, amber	31.00
Goblet, blue	33.00
Goblet, clear	20.00
Pickle dish	7.00
Pitcher, water	45.00
Platter, 8½ x 10½", amber	24.00
Platter, 8½ x 10½", blue	35.00
Platter, 8½ x 10½", clear	20.00
Relish, blue, 4½ x 7"	32.50
Salt shaker w/original top, blue	54.00
Sauce dish, flat or footed, blue	12.00
Spooner, amber	24.00
Spooner, vaseline	30.00
Sugar bowl, cov., blue	50.00
Sugar bowl, cov., clear	28.00
Wine, amber	23.00
Wine, blue	28.00
Wine, clear	15.50

SPRIG

Sprig Relish Dish

Bowl, 7" oval	25.00
Bowl, 8" oval, footed	35.00
Bread platter, 11" oval	35.00
Butter dish, cov.	65.00
Cake stand	44.00
Celery vase	42.50
Compote, cov., 6" d., low stand	50.00
Compote, cov., 6" d., high stand	85.00
Compote, cov., 8" d., low stand	76.00
Compote, cov., 8" d., high stand	95.00
Compote, open, 6" d.	32.50
Compote, open, 7" d., low stand	25.00
Compote, open, 8" d., high stand	39.00
Creamer	37.00
Goblet	35.00
Pickle castor, resilvered frame & tongs	85.00
Pitcher, water	55.00
Relish, 6¾" oval	14.00
Relish, 7¾" oval	18.00
Relish, 8¾" oval (ILLUS.)	22.00
Sauce dish, flat or footed	11.00
Spooner	25.00
Sugar bowl, cov.	55.00
Sugar bowl, open	20.00
Wine	52.00

SQUARE LION'S HEAD - See Atlanta Pattern

SQUIRREL - See "Animals & Birds on Goblets & Pitchers"

S-REPEAT

Berry set, apple green	85.00
Butter dish, cov., amethyst w/gold	125.00
Butter dish, cov., apple green	125.00
Carafe, water	550.00
Compote, jelly	40.00
Condiment set, apple green	200.00 to 250.00
Condiment set, clear	190.00
Condiment set, sapphire blue	200.00 to 250.00
Condiment tray, amethyst	37.50
Condiment tray, apple green	35.00
Decanter w/stopper, wine, amethyst	175.00
Decanter w/stopper, wine, apple green w/gold	125.00
Decanter w/stopper, wine, sapphire blue w/gold	195.00
Punch cup	16.00
Salt shaker w/original top, sapphire blue	40.00
Salt & pepper shakers, apple green, pr.	70.00
Salt & pepper shakers, clear, pr.	38.00
Sauce dish, amethyst w/gold	30.00
Sauce dish, apple green w/gold	27.50
Syrup pitcher w/original top	70.00
*Toothpick holder, amethyst	62.00
*Toothpick holder, sapphire blue	55.00
Tumbler, amethyst	40.00
Tumbler, sapphire blue	38.00
*Wine, apple green	50.00
*Wine, sapphire blue	50.00

STAR ROSETTED

Star Rosetted Goblet

Butter dish, cov.	55.00
Cake (or bread) plate, "A Good Mother Makes A Happy Home"	55.00
Compote, open, 6½" d.	16.00
Compote, open, 7½" d.	18.00
Creamer	30.00
Goblet (ILLUS.)	30.00
Plate, 7" d., amber	45.00

Plate, 7" d., apple green 35.00
Plate, 7" d., blue 12.00
Plate, 7" d., clear 10.00
Sauce dish, flat or footed 5.00
Sugar bowl, cov. 42.00
Sugar bowl, open 12.00

STATES (The)
Bowl, 7" d., three-handled 50.00
Bowl, 7½" d. 22.50
Bowl, 9" d. 45.00
Butter dish, cov. 56.00
Cocktail, flared 22.00
Compote, open, 5 x 5½" 36.00
Creamer 28.00
Creamer, individual size 30.00
Creamer & sugar bowl, pr. 65.00
Cruet w/stopper 55.00
Goblet 32.50
Pitcher, water 65.00
Punch bowl, 13" d., 5½" h. 95.00
Punch cup 11.00
Salt & pepper shakers w/original
   tops, pr. 60.00
Spooner 25.00
Sugar bowl, cov. 46.00
Syrup jug 95.00
Toothpick holder 32.00
Tumbler 26.00
Wine, clear 25.00
Wine, clear w/gold trim 30.00
Wine, green 60.00

STIPPLED FORGET-ME-NOT
Cake stand, 8" to 9" d. 90.00
Celery vase 31.00
Compote, open, 6" d., 6½" h. 32.50
Creamer 24.00
Cup & saucer 35.00
Goblet 45.00
Pitcher, milk 37.00
Pitcher, water 52.00
Plate, 7" d., w/baby in tub reaching
   for ball on floor center 65.00
Plate, 9" d., w/kitten center,
   handled 65.00
Plate, 11" d., w/stork center 85.00
Relish 13.00
Tray, water 125.00
Wine 42.50

STIPPLED IVY
Goblet 20.00
Salt dip, master size 28.00
Spooner 30.00
Sugar bowl, open 25.00
Tumbler, buttermilk 32.50
Tumbler, water 24.00

SUNK HONEYCOMB (Corona)
Cake stand, ruby-stained 125.00
Celery, ruby-stained 72.50
Cheese dish, cov., ruby-stained ... 170.00
Compote, cov., 7" d., 11" h. 165.00

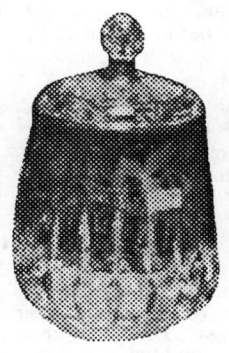

Sunk Honeycomb Cracker Jar

Cracker jar, cov., ruby-stained
   (ILLUS.) 485.00
Creamer, ruby-stained, 4½" h. 52.50
Cruet w/original stopper, clear 30.00
Cruet w/original stopper, ruby-
   stained, souvenir "Mother,
   World's Fair, 1893" 95.00
Cup & saucer, ruby-stained 35.00
Goblet, clear 39.00
Goblet, ruby-stained 45.00
Mug, ruby-stained, 3" h. 34.00
Pitcher, water, bulbous, ruby-
   stained 95.00
Punch cup 22.00
Salt dip, individual size 17.50
Salt shaker w/original top, ruby-
   stained 37.50
Sugar bowl, cov., hotel size, ruby-
   stained, engraved 195.00
Syrup pitcher w/original top, clear .. 135.00
Syrup pitcher w/original top, ruby-
   stained 175.00
Table set: cov. butter dish, cov. sug-
   ar bowl, creamer & spooner;
   ruby-stained, 4 pcs. 350.00
Toothpick holder, ruby-stained,
   souvenir 45.00
Tumbler, clear, engraved 24.00
Tumbler, ruby-stained 50.00
Water set, pitcher & 6 goblets,
   7 pcs. 350.00
Wine, clear 14.00
Wine, clear, engraved 22.00
Wine, ruby-stained 34.00
Wine, ruby-stained, engraved 40.00

SWAN
Celery vase, etched 40.00
Compote, cov., w/swan finial,
   8" d. 365.00
Compote, open, 8½" h. 44.00
Creamer, amber 55.00
Creamer, clear 45.00
*Creamer, milk white 35.00
Cup, handled 37.50
Goblet, canary yellow 70.00
Marmalade jar, cov. 110.00

Pitcher, water . . . . .200.00 to 250.00
Sauce dish, flat or footed 13.50
Spooner 42.00
Sugar bowl, cov. 185.00

TEARDROP & TASSEL

Berry set: master bowl & 6 sauce
   dishes; teal blue, 7 pcs. 395.00
Bowl, 7½" d., clear 38.00
Bowl, 7½" d., Nile green 35.00
Bowl, 8¼" d. 55.00
Butter dish, cov., clear 65.00
Butter dish, cov., cobalt blue 150.00
Butter dish, cov., emerald green. . . . 200.00
Compote, cov., 7" d., 11½" h. 95.00
Compote, cov., 9½" d. 95.00
Compote, open, 5" d. 25.00
Compote, open, 6" d. 35.00
Compote, open, 8½" d. 45.00
Creamer, amber 175.00
Creamer, clear. 45.00
Creamer, cobalt blue 125.00
Creamer, Nile green . . . . . .150.00 to 200.00
Creamer, white opaque 75.00
Creamer & cov. sugar bowl, emer-
   ald green, pr. 325.00
Creamer & cov. sugar bowl, white
   opaque, pr. 175.00
Goblet, clear 150.00
Goblet, emerald green 225.00
Pickle dish, amber 90.00
Pickle dish, clear. 29.00
Pitcher, water, clear. 70.00
Pitcher, water, cobalt blue 225.00
Pitcher, water, emerald green 295.00
Relish, clear 35.00
Relish, emerald green 100.00
Relish, Nile green 175.00
Relish, teal blue 175.00
Salt shaker w/original top 125.00
Salt & pepper shakers w/original
   tops, Nile green, pr. 350.00
Sauce dish, clear 13.50
Sauce dish, cobalt blue 35.00
Sauce dish, emerald green 75.00
Spooner, clear 50.00
Spooner, cobalt blue 90.00
Spooner, Nile green 175.00
Spooner, white opaque 65.00
Sugar bowl, cov., clear 60.00
Sugar bowl, cov., cobalt blue. 135.00
Sugar bowl, cov., Nile green 300.00
Tumbler, clear 38.00
Tumbler, cobalt blue 61.00
Tumbler, emerald green 165.00
Water set, pitcher & 6 tumblers,
   7 pcs. 285.00

TENNESSEE

Cake stand, 8½" d., high stand 32.00
Pitcher, milk, 1 qt. 110.00
Relish tray. 20.00
Toothpick holder 75.00
Wine. 125.00

TEXAS (Loop with Stippled Panels)

Texas Individual Creamer

Bowl, 8" oval 30.00
Cake stand, 9½" to 10¾" d. 62.50
Celery vase. 75.00
Compote, open, jelly 100.00
Creamer 26.00
*Creamer, individual size (ILLUS.) . . . 20.00
Goblet, clear 40.00
Goblet, ruby-stained. 110.00
Relish, handled, 8½" l. 20.00
Salt dip, master size, footed, 3" d.,
   2¾" h. 22.00
Sauce dish, flat or footed 25.00
Spooner 52.50
Toothpick holder, clear 35.00
Toothpick holder, clear w/gold 55.00
Vase, 7½" h., trumpet-shaped,
   pink-stained 95.00
Vase, bud, 8" h. 30.00
Vase, 9" h. 35.00
Vase, 10" h. 30.00
*Wine. 103.00
Wine, ruby-stained 125.00

THISTLE, PANELED - See Paneled Thistle Pattern

THOUSAND EYE

Thousand Eye Egg Cup

Bowl, 8" d., 4½" h., footed,
   amber 35.00
Bowl, 11" rectangle, shallow,
   amber 32.00

Bread tray, amber................. 32.00
Bread tray, apple green 52.00
Bread tray, blue 40.00
Bread tray, clear 28.00
Butter dish, cov., amber......... 115.00
Butter dish, cov., apple green 80.00
Butter dish, cov., blue 145.00
Butter dish, cov., clear 50.00
Cake stand, blue, 8½" to 10" d. 88.00
Cake stand, clear, 8½" to 10" d. ... 28.00
Cake stand, blue, 12½" d. 60.00
Celery vase, three-knob stem,
    amber 48.00
Celery vase, three-knob stem, apple
    green 55.00
Celery vase, three-knob stem,
    clear 40.00
Celery vase, plain stem, amber..... 45.00
Celery vase, plain stem, clear 35.00
Compote, cov., 12" h. 115.00
*Compote, open, 6" d., low stand,
    amber 22.00
*Compote, open, 6" d., low stand,
    apple green 31.00
*Compote, open, 6" d., low stand,
    blue 38.00
Compote, open, 6½" d., three-knob
    stem, blue 30.00
Compote, open, 7½" d., 5" h. 35.00
Compote, open, 8" d., 3¾" h., ap-
    ple green.................... 40.00
Compote, open, 8" d., 6" h., three-
    knob stem, amber 38.00
Compote, open, 8" d., 6" h., three-
    knob stem, apple green 65.00
Compote, open, 8" d., 6" h., three-
    knob stem, blue 65.00
Compote, open, 8" d., high stand,
    three-knob stem, vaseline 58.00
Compote, open, 9½" d., low stand,
    amber 27.00
Compote, open, 10" d., 6½" h.,
    three-knob stem, blue 85.00
Creamer, amber 42.00
*Creamer, clear 35.00
Creamer, clear opalescent 95.00
Creamer & cov. sugar bowl, amber,
    pr........................... 100.00
*Cruet w/original three-knob stop-
    per, amber 135.00
*Cruet w/original three-knob stop-
    per, apple green 135.00
*Cruet w/original three-knob stop-
    per, blue.............125.00 to 150.00
*Cruet w/original three-knob stop-
    per, clear 32.00
*Cruet w/original three-knob stop-
    per, vaseline ....100.00 to 125.00
Cruet stand w/pr. cruets w/original
    stoppers, knob stem, amber,
    set.......................... 210.00
Egg cup, blue 65.00
Egg cup, clear (ILLUS.) 25.00
*Goblet, blue 35.00

*Goblet, clear 28.00
*Goblet, vaseline 32.00
Honey dish, cov., apple green 125.00
Honey dish, cover w/knob finial,
    rectangular, vaseline 135.00
Lamp, kerosene-type, pedestal
    base, amber, 14" h. to collar 225.00
Lamp, kerosene-type, pedestal
    base, blue font, amber base,
    12" h........................ 195.00
Lamp, kerosene-type, pedestal
    base, blue, 12" h. 155.00
Lamp, kerosene-type, flat base, ring
    handle, amber 325.00
Lamp, kerosene-type, flat base, ring
    handle, clear 110.00
*Mug, amber, 3½" h. 29.00
*Mug, blue, 3½" h. 28.00
*Mug, clear, 3½" h............... 20.00
*Mug, vaseline, 3½" h........... 27.50
Mug, miniature, amber 30.00
Pitcher, water, three-knob stem, ap-
    ple green..................... 85.00
Pitcher, water, three-knob stem,
    blue 95.00
*Pitcher, water, clear............. 75.00
Pitcher, water, vaseline.......... 60.00
Plate, 6" d., amber.............. 22.50
Plate, 6" d., apple green.......... 17.00
Plate, 6" d., blue 22.00
*Plate, 6" d., clear 14.50
Plate, 8" d., amber.............. 22.50
Plate, 8" d., apple green.......... 25.00
*Plate, 8" d., clear 28.00
Plate, 8" d., vaseline 32.00
Plate, 10" sq., w/folded corners,
    amber 35.00
Plate, 10" sq., w/folded corners,
    clear........................ 28.00
Plate, 10" sq., w/folded corners,
    vaseline 35.00
Platter, 8 x 11" 30.00
Salt shaker w/original top, amber .. 21.00
Salt & pepper shakers w/original
    tops, blue, pr. 75.00
*Salt & pepper shakers w/original
    tops, clear, pr................ 65.00
Sauce dish, flat or footed, amber ... 12.50
Sauce dish, flat or footed, blue 16.00
*Sauce dish, flat or footed, clear ... 10.00
Spooner, three-knob stem, amber .. 52.00
Spooner, three-knob stem, clear.... 38.00
Spooner, three-knob stem, vase-
    line......................... 42.00
Sugar bowl, cov., three-knob stem,
    amber 55.00
Sugar bowl, cov. 37.50
*Sugar bowl, open, three-knob
    stem 25.00
Syrup pitcher w/original top,
    amber 100.00
Syrup pitcher w/original pewter top,
    footed, apple green 113.00
*Toothpick holder, amber 38.00

*Toothpick holder, blue 40.00
*Toothpick holder, clear 24.00
*Toothpick holder, vaseline 38.00
Tray, water, amber, 12½" d. 65.00
Tray, water, blue, 12½" d. 120.00
Tray, water, clear, 12½" d. 38.00
Tray, apple green, 14" oval 60.00
Tray, clear, 14" oval 50.00
*Tumbler, amber 24.00
*Tumbler, apple green. 39.00
*Tumbler, clear 18.00
*Wine, apple green 42.50
*Wine, blue 45.00
*Wine, clear 20.00
*Wine, vaseline 38.00

THREE FACE

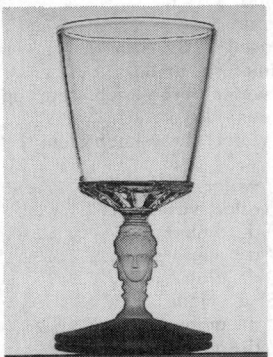

Three Face Claret

Butter dish, cov.,
   engraved . . . . .200.00 to 225.00
Butter dish, cov., plain 148.00
*Cake stand, 8" to 10½" d. 150.00
Celery vase . . . . 100.00 to 125.00
*Champagne 165.00
Claret (ILLUS.) 152.00
Compote, cov., 4½" d., 6½" h. 100.00
*Compote, cov., 6" d. 125.00
Compote, cov., 8" d., 13" h. 325.00
Compote, open, 6" d., high stand . . . 85.00
Compote, open, 7" d., high stand . . . 90.00
Compote, open, 8½" d., high
   stand 125.00
Compote, open, 9½" d., high
   stand 160.00
*Cracker jar, cov. 1,250.00
Creamer 90.00
*Creamer w/mask spout 150.00
Goblet, engraved 150.00
*Goblet, plain 72.00
*Lamp, kerosene-type, pedestal
   base, 8" h. 165.00
Marmalade jar, cov. 225.00
Pitcher, water 450.00
*Salt dip 44.00
*Salt & pepper shakers w/original
   tops, pr. 115.00
*Sauce dish. 30.00

*Spooner 60.00
Spooner, engraved 100.00
*Sugar bowl, cov. 140.00
*Sugar shaker w/original top 155.00

THREE PANEL

Berry set, master bowl & 5 sauce
   dishes, 6 pcs. 57.50
Bowl, 7" d., footed, blue 30.00
Bowl, 7" d., footed, vaseline 31.50
Bowl, 9" d., footed, amber 33.00
Bowl, 9" d., footed, blue 25.00
Bowl, 10" d., amber 49.00
Bowl, 10" d., blue 65.00
Bowl, 10" d., clear 20.00
Bowl, 10" d., vaseline 45.00
Butter dish, cov., amber 55.00
Butter dish, cov., clear 55.00
Celery vase, amber 47.50
Celery vase, clear 35.00
Celery vase, vaseline 55.00
Compote, open, 9" d., 4¼" h.,
   amber 40.00
Compote, open, 9" d., vaseline 45.00
Compote, open, 10" d., low stand,
   blue 65.00
Creamer, amber 35.00
Creamer, blue 45.00
Creamer, clear. 21.00
Creamer, vaseline 45.00
Cruet w/original stopper 155.00
*Goblet, amber 32.00
*Goblet, blue 48.00
*Goblet, clear 23.00
*Goblet, vaseline 40.00
Lamp, kerosene-type, amber 145.00
Mug, amber 35.00
Mug, clear. 30.00
Pitcher, milk, 7" h. 44.50
Pitcher, water, amber 85.00
Pitcher, water, vaseline 110.00
Sauce dish, footed, amber 17.00
Sauce dish, footed, blue 19.50
Sauce dish, footed, clear. 11.50
Sauce dish, footed, vaseline 15.00
Spooner, amber. 35.00
Spooner, blue. 38.00
Spooner, clear 15.00
Spooner, vaseline 35.00
Sugar bowl, cov., blue. 75.00
Sugar bowl, cov., clear 55.00
Sugar bowl, cov., vaseline 65.00
Sugar bowl, open 25.00
Table set, blue, 4 pcs. 245.00
Table set, clear, 4 pcs. 175.00
Tumbler, amber 35.00
Tumbler, blue. 40.00
Tumbler, clear 12.00

THUMBPRINT, EARLY (Bakewell, Pears & Co.'s "Argus")

Ale glass, footed, 5" h. 31.00
Bowl, 5" d., 5" h., footed 32.00

*Butter dish, cov. 115.00
*Cake stand, 8" to 9½" d. 275.00
*Celery vase, plain base 110.00
Celery vase, scalloped rim, pattern
    in base 155.00
*Compote, cov., 7½" d., high
    stand 85.00
*Compote, open, 6" d., low stand,
    scalloped rim 35.00
Compote, open, 7½" d., low
    stand 55.00
*Compote, open, 8" d., high stand .. 125.00
Compote, open, 8½" d., high stand,
    scalloped rim ....125.00 to 150.00
Compote, open, 14" d., 12" h. 600.00
*Creamer 60.00
Decanter, 11" h. 110.00
*Goblet, baluster stem 55.00
Goblet, plain stem 38.00
Inkwell 350.00
Pickle dish 40.00
Pitcher, milk 90.00

Early Thumbprint Water Pitcher

*Pitcher, water, 8¼" h.
    (ILLUS.) ....300.00 to 400.00
*Sauce dish, clear 8.00
Sauce dish, milk white 75.00
Spillholder 48.00
*Sugar bowl, cov. 60.00
Sweetmeat bowl, 6½" d., 7" h. 190.00
Tumbler, whiskey, handled,
    footed 150.00
*Wine, baluster stem 70.00

TORPEDO (Pygmy)

Bowl, cov., master berry 80.00
Bowl, 7" d., flat 15.00
Bowl, 8" d. 32.50
Bowl, 9" d. 32.00
Bowl, 9½" d. 42.50
Butter dish, cov. 75.00
Celery vase 40.00
Compote, cov., jelly 43.00
Compote, cov., 6" d. 78.00
Compote, cov., 7" d., 7¼" h. 65.00
Compote, cov., 8" d., 14" h. 135.00
Compote, open, jelly, 5" d., 5" h. ... 45.00
Compote, open, 7" d., high stand ... 52.00

Compote, open, 8 x 10½", 8" h.,
    ruffled rim 145.00
Creamer, collared base 55.00
Creamer, footed 37.50
Cruet w/original faceted stopper ... 75.00
Cup & saucer 65.00

Torpedo Goblet

Goblet, clear (ILLUS.) 50.00
Goblet, ruby-stained 80.00
Lamp, kerosene, hand-type w/finger
    grip, w/burner & chimney 115.00
Lamp, kerosene-type, 10" h. 185.00
Pickle castor, silver plate cover &
    tongs 135.00
Pitcher, milk, 8½" h. 95.00
Pitcher, water, 10" h. 84.00
Pitcher, water, tankard, 12" h. 75.00
Salt dip, individual size, 1½" d. 26.00
Salt dip, master size 45.00
Salt & pepper shakers w/original
    tops, pr. 95.00
Sauce dish 16.00
Spooner 40.00
Sugar bowl, cov. 95.00
Syrup jug w/original top, clear 135.00
Syrup jug w/original top, ruby-
    stained 250.00
Tray, 9¾" d. 70.00
Tumbler, clear 38.00
Tumbler, clear, engraved 45.00
Tumbler, ruby-stained 50.00
Waste bowl 60.00
Wine, clear 90.00
Wine, ruby-stained 125.00

TREE OF LIFE - PORTLAND

Butter dish, cov. 110.00
Celery vase 125.00
Celery vase, in silver plate holder .. 135.00
Champagne 75.00
Compote, open, 7" d., high stand,
    w/applied red serpent on stem ... 245.00
Compote, open, 7¾" d., 11" h.,
    Infant Samuel stand, signed
    "Davis" 125.00
Compote, open, 8½" d., 5" h.,
    signed "Davis" 60.00

Compote, open, 8¾" d., in two-handled Meriden silver plate holder, bowl signed "Davis" 185.00

Compote, open, 10" d., 6" h., signed "Davis" ....100.00 to 125.00

Creamer, signed "Davis" 55.00

Creamer, blue, in silver plate holder ....175.00 to 200.00

Creamer, clear, in silver plate holder 85.00

Creamer, cranberry in silver plate holder 190.00

Dish, leaf handle, blue 40.00

Epergne, single lily, red snake around stem, 18" h. 450.00

Goblet 60.00

Goblet, signed "Davis" 90.00

Ice cream set, tray & 6 leaf-shaped desserts, 7 pcs. 150.00

Mug, applied handle, 3½" h........ 45.00

Pitcher, water, applied handle 78.00

Plate, 7¼" d. 50.00

Powder jar, cov., red coiled snake finial on cover 350.00

Salt dip, individual size, footed, amber 65.00

Salt dip, footed, "Salt" embossed in bowl 135.00

Salt dip, footed, opaque green 95.00

Salt shaker w/original top 25.00

Sauce dish, leaf-shaped, blue 18.00

Sauce dish, leaf-shaped, clear 15.00

Spooner 30.00

Spooner, in handled silver plate holder w/two Griffin heads 110.00

Sugar bowl, cov., blue, in silver plate holder ....175.00 to 200.00

Sugar bowl, cov., clear, in silver plate holder 88.00

Sugar bowl, cov. 63.00

Table set, cov. sugar bowl, creamer & spooner, in ornate silver plate holders, the set 180.00

Toothpick holder, apple green 125.00

Toothpick holder, blue 75.00

Portland Tree of Life Tray

Tray, ice cream, 14" rectangle (ILLUS.)........................ 48.00

Waste bowl, amber 45.00

Waste bowl, blue 58.00

Waste bowl, blue, in ornate silver plate holder 175.00

Waste bowl, clear................ 28.00

TREE OF LIFE WITH HAND (Tree of Life-Wheeling)

Butter dish, cov. 125.00

Cake stand, frosted base, 11½" d... 75.00

Celery vase...................... 47.00

Compote, open, 5½" d., 5½" h., clear hand & ball stem.......... 48.00

Compote, open, 5½" d., 5½" h., frosted hand & ball stem......... 65.00

Compote, open, 9" d., frosted hand & ball stem 80.00

Compote, open, 10" d., 10" h., frosted hand & ball stem 95.00

Creamer, w/hand & ball handle 60.00

Mug, applied handle, 3" h.......... 125.00

Pitcher, water, 9" h............... 68.00

Sauce dish, flat or footed 19.00

Spooner 42.50

Waste bowl w/underplate.......... 60.00

TWO PANEL (Daisy in Panel)

Bowl, cov., 7" oval, vaseline 75.00

Bowl, 6 x 8" oval, blue 38.50

Bowl, 7½ x 9" oval, apple green ... 36.00

Bread tray, apple green 39.00

Butter dish, cov., blue 85.00

Butter dish, cov., vaseline 50.00

Celery vase, clear................ 30.00

Celery vase, vaseline 45.00

Compote, cov., 6½ x 8", 11" h., vaseline 85.00

Compote, cov., high stand, apple green 135.00

Compote, cov., high stand, blue 85.00

Compote, open, 9" oval, 4" h., apple green 60.00

Compote, open, 9" oval, 4" h., vaseline 45.00

Creamer, amber 45.00

Creamer, apple green 45.00

Creamer, blue 45.00

Creamer, clear.................. 22.50

Creamer, vaseline 35.00

*Goblet, amber 35.00

*Goblet, apple green 35.00

*Goblet, blue 48.00

*Goblet, clear 20.00

*Goblet, vaseline 32.00

Lamp, kerosene-type, pedestal base, blue, 7¾" h., No. 1 burner 145.00

Pitcher, water, blue 90.00

Pitcher, water, clear.............. 36.00

Pitcher, water, vaseline........... 65.00

Relish, blue..................... 30.00

Salt dip, master size, apple green .. 30.00

Salt dip, individual size, apple
green 14.00
Salt dip, individual size, blue 12.00
Sauce dish, flat or footed, amber ... 11.00
Sauce dish, flat or footed, apple
green 13.50
Sauce dish, flat or footed, clear 9.50
Spooner, amber 38.00
Spooner, blue 35.00
Spooner, vaseline 35.00
Sugar bowl, cov., amber 50.00
Sugar bowl, cov., apple green 55.00
Sugar bowl, cov., vaseline 54.00
Tray, water, blue 60.00
Tumbler, vaseline 40.00
Waste bowl, amber 36.00
*Wine, amber 35.00
*Wine, apple green 40.00
*Wine, blue 35.00
*Wine, clear 20.00
*Wine, vaseline 35.00

U.S. COIN - See Special Focus

VALENCIA WAFFLE (Block & Star)

Valencia Waffle Salt Dip

Bread platter 30.00
Butter dish, cov., apple green 55.00
Celery vase, blue 39.00
Celery vase, clear 30.00
Compote, cov., 7" sq., low stand,
amber 64.00
Compote, cov., 7" sq., low stand,
blue ....50.00 to 75.00
Compote, cov., 7" sq., low stand,
clear 50.00
Compote, cov., 8" d., clear 45.00
Compote, cov., 8" sq., low stand,
clear 125.00
Compote, cov., 8" sq., 9" h.,
amber 90.00
Compote, open, 6" d., low stand,
apple green 35.00
Compote, open, 7" sq., low stand,
amber 32.50
Compote, open, 7" sq., light blue ... 55.00
Compote, open, 8" d., 8" h.,
amber 60.00
Goblet, amber 35.00
Goblet, blue 35.00
Goblet, clear 30.00
Pitcher, water, 7½" h., amber 60.00
Pitcher, water, blue 72.00

Relish, amber, 5 3/8 x 9" 2
Salt dip, master size (ILLUS.) .... 15.
Salt shaker w/original top, apple
green 30.00
Sauce dish, footed, blue 14.00
Spooner, amber 38.00
Syrup jug w/original top, blue 75.00
Tray, water 25.00
Tumbler, ruby-stained 30.00

VICTOR - See Shell & Jewel Pattern

VIKING (Bearded Head or Old Man of the Mountain)

Viking Water Pitcher

Apothecary jar w/original stopper .. 75.00
Bowl, cov., 8" oval 100.00
Bread tray, cupid hunt scene
center 68.00
Butter dish, cov., clear 75.00
Butter dish, cov., frosted 85.00
Celery vase 60.00
Compote, cov., 7" d., low stand 82.00
Compote, cov., 9" d., low stand 110.00
Creamer 52.50
Egg cup 65.00
Goblet 95.00
Marmalade jar, cov., footed 75.00
Mug, applied handle 62.50
Pickle jar w/cover 95.00
Pitcher, water, 8¾" h. (ILLUS.) 110.00
Relish 25.00
Salt dip, master size 45.00
Sauce dish, footed 15.00
Shaving mug, milk white 62.50
Spooner 30.00
Sugar bowl, cov. 65.00

VIRGINIA - See Banded Portland Pattern and Galloway Pattern

WASHBOARD - See Adonis Pattern

WASHINGTON CENTENNIAL
Bread platter, Carpenter's Hall
center 100.00
Bread platter, George Washington
center 84.00

rge Washington
.... 130.00

endence Hall
.... 95.00

11½" d. 75.00

vase.................... 52.00
Champagne..................... 68.00
Compote, open, 7" d., low stand ... 45.00
Compote, open, 8" d., 6½" h. 37.50
Compote, open, 10½" d., high
  stand 70.00
Egg cup 39.00
Goblet 50.00
Pickle dish....................... 34.00
Pitcher, milk..................... 104.00
Pitcher, water 110.00
Relish, bear paw handles, dated
  1876 .... 35.00
Salt dip, master size............... 60.00
Sauce dish, flat or footed 11.00
Spooner 42.00
Sugar bowl, cov. 72.50
Sugar bowl, open 20.00
Syrup pitcher, w/dated pewter top
  w/tiny figural finial 165.00
Tumbler 58.00
Wine............................ 48.00

WESTWARD HO

Westward Ho Creamer

Bowl, 8"........................... 125.00
Bowl, 9" oval 95.00
Bread platter 115.00
*Butter dish, cov. ....125.00 to 150.00
*Celery vase...................... 135.00
*Compote, cov., 4" d., low stand ... 100.00
*Compote, cov., 5" d., high stand ... 95.00
*Compote, cov., 6" d., low stand ... 120.00
*Compote, cov., 6" d., high stand .. 325.00
*Compote, cov., 4 x 6¾" oval, low
  stand 145.00
Compote, cov., 5 x 7¾" oval, high
  stand 225.00
Compote, cov., 8" d., low stand 325.00
Compote, cov., 8" d., high
  stand ....275.00 to 325.00
Compote, cov., 5½ x 8" oval, high
  stand 440.00

Compote, cov., 8" d., 14" h........ 350.00
Compote, cov., 6½ x 10" oval, low
  stand ....225.00 to 250.00
Compote, open, 7" d., low stand ... 175.00
Compote, open, 9" oval, high
  stand 100.00
*Creamer (ILLUS.) ....125.00 to 150.00
*Goblet 70.00
Marmalade jar, cov. 295.00
Mug, child's, clear, 2½" h. 250.00
Mug, child's, milk white, 2½" h..... 175.00
Pickle dish, oval 65.00
Pitcher, milk, 8" h. 495.00
Pitcher, water 395.00
Platter, 9 x 13" 170.00
Relish, deer handles 100.00
Sauce dish, footed ....25.00 to 35.00
Spooner 75.00
*Sugar bowl, cov.........125.00 to 150.00
*Wine........................... 225.00

WILDFLOWER

Bowl, 5¾" sq. 15.00
Bowl, 7" sq. 17.50
Bowl, 8" sq., 5" h., footed, amber .. 22.50
Bowl, 8" sq., 5" h., footed, apple
  green 35.00
Bowl, 8" sq., 5" h., footed, vase-
  line 20.00
Butter dish, cov., flat, blue........ 50.00
Cake stand, apple green,
  9½" to 11" 66.00
Cake stand, clear, 9½" to 11" 48.00
Cake stand, vaseline, 9½" to 11" ... 82.00
Cake stand, blue, w/bail handle.... 225.00
Celery vase, amber 58.00
Celery vase, apple green 65.00
Celery vase, blue 75.00
Celery vase, clear................ 30.00
*Champagne, amber 50.00
*Champagne, blue 50.00
*Champagne, clear............... 30.00
Compote, cov., 6" d., amber 40.00
Compote, cov., 6" d., clear........ 49.00
Compote, cov., 7" d., amber 50.00
Compote, cov., 8" d., amber 90.00
Compote, cov., 8" d.,
  clear...................75.00 to 100.00
Compote, open, jelly 30.00
Compote, open, 9½" d., amber 45.00
Compote, open, 10½" d., 7½" h.,
  blue 125.00
Compote, open, 10½" d., 8¼" h.,
  amber 78.00
*Creamer, amber 38.00
*Creamer, apple green 40.00
*Creamer, blue 45.00
*Creamer, clear 35.00
*Creamer, vaseline............... 42.00
*Goblet, amber 32.00
*Goblet, apple green............. 42.50
*Goblet, blue 38.00
*Goblet, clear 30.00
*Goblet, vaseline 30.00

Pitcher, water, amber	50.00
Pitcher, water, apple green	95.00
Pitcher, water, blue	85.00
Pitcher, water, clear	48.00
Pitcher, water, vaseline	76.00
Plate, 10" sq., blue	45.00
Plate, 10" sq., clear	22.50
Platter, 8 x 11", blue	45.00
Platter, 8 x 11", clear	35.00
*Salt dip, turtle-shaped, amber	45.00
*Salt shaker w/original top, amber	35.00
Salt shaker w/original top, apple green	30.00
Salt shaker w/original top, blue	55.00
Salt shaker w/original top, vaseline	55.00
Salt & pepper shakers w/original tops, vaseline, pr.	110.00
*Sauce dish, flat or footed, amber	13.50
*Sauce dish, flat or footed, apple green	22.50
*Sauce dish, flat or footed, blue	17.00
*Sauce dish, flat or footed, blue	17.00
*Sauce dish, flat or footed, clear	12.50
*Sauce dish, flat or footed, vaseline	14.50
Spooner, amber	30.00
Spooner, blue	35.00
Spooner, clear	22.00
Spooner, vaseline	34.00
*Sugar bowl, cov., blue	54.00
*Sugar bowl, cov., vaseline	45.00
Sugar bowl, open, amber	20.00
Sugar bowl, open, blue	30.00
Sugar bowl, open, clear	19.00
Syrup pitcher w/original top, amber	140.00 to 160.00
Syrup pitcher w/original top, blue	350.00
Syrup pitcher w/original top, clear	115.00
Tray, dresser, blue, 4 x 9"	45.00
Tray, dresser, vaseline, 4 x 9"	28.50
Tray, water, amber, 11 x 13"	45.00
Tray, water, blue, 11 x 13"	75.00 to 100.00
Tray, water, clear, 11 x 13"	39.00
Tray, water, vaseline, 11 x 13"	50.00
Tumbler, amber	40.00
Tumbler, apple green	30.00
Tumbler, blue	35.00
Tumbler, clear	22.00
Tumbler, vaseline	30.00
Vase, 10½" h.	58.00
Waste bowl, amber	48.00
Waste bowl, clear	28.00
Water set: pitcher, tray & 5 tumblers; apple green, 7 pcs.	318.00
*Wine, amber	50.00

WISCONSIN (Beaded Dewdrop)

Banana stand, turned-up sides, 7½" w., 4" h.	72.00
Bonbon, handled, 4"	24.00

Bowl, 6½" d.	3
Bowl, 8" d.	42.
Bread tray	45.00
Butter dish, cov.	90.00
Cake stand, 8¼" d., 4¾" h.	42.50
Cake stand, 9¾" d.	45.00
Celery tray, flat, 5 x 10"	42.50
Celery vase	47.00
Compote, cov., 10½" d.	64.00
Compote, open, 6½" d., 6½" h.	26.00
Compote, open, 7" d., 4" h., tricornered, footed	25.00
Compote, open, 7½" d., 5½" h.	42.00
Cruet w/original stopper	40.00
Cup & saucer	55.00
Dish, cov., oval	26.50
Doughnut stand, 6" d.	40.00
Goblet	49.00
Marmalade jar, cov.	125.00
Mug, 3½" h.	34.00
Nappy, handled, 4" d.	20.00
Pitcher, milk	75.00

Wisconsin Water Pitcher

Pitcher, water, 8" h. (ILLUS.)	65.00
Plate, 5" sq.	24.00
Plate, 6½" sq.	26.00
Punch cup	16.50
Relish, 4 x 8½"	20.00
Salt shaker w/original top	55.00
Sauce dish	14.00
Spooner	38.00
Sugar bowl, cov., 5" h.	50.00
Sugar shaker w/original top	63.00
Syrup pitcher w/original top, 6½" h.	75.00
*Toothpick holder	41.00
Tumbler	45.00
Vase, 6" h.	58.00
Wine	60.00

X-RAY

Berry set: 8" d. master bowl & 6 sauce dishes; emerald green, 7 pcs.	155.00
Berry set: 8" d. master bowl & 8 sauce dishes; amethyst, 9 pcs.	295.00
Butter dish, cov., emerald green w/gold	92.00

erald green
· · · · · · · · · · · · · · · · · · 135.00
ld green · · · · · · · · 52.00
n stand, emerald
· · · · · · · · · · · · · · · · · · 65.00
..re, jelly, clear · · · · · · · · · · · · 42.00
Compote, jelly, emerald green · · · · · 47.00
Creamer, breakfast size, emerald
green w/gold · · · · · · · · · · · · · · · · 45.00
Cruet w/original stopper, emerald
green w/gold · · · · · · · · · · · · · · · · 100.00
Marmalade, cov., emerald green
w/gold · · · · · · · · · · · · · · · · · · 68.00
Pitcher, water, 9½" h., emerald
green, ½ gal. · · · · · · · · · · · · · · · 65.00
Rose bowl, emerald green w/gold · · 68.00
Salt shaker w/original top, ame-
thyst · 50.00
Salt shaker w/original top, clear · · · 18.50
Sauce dish, clear, 4½" d. · · · · · · · · 12.00
Sauce dish, emerald green,
4½" d. · 22.50
Spooner, emerald green w/gold · · · · 45.00
Sugar bowl, cov., emerald green
w/gold · 54.00
Sugar bowl, cov., breakfast size,
emerald green w/gold · · · · · · · · · · 65.00
Syrup pitcher, emerald green
w/gold · 110.00
Table set, emerald green, 4 pcs. · · · 300.00
Toothpick holder, emerald green · · · 60.00
Tray, condiment · · · · · · · · · · · · · · · 37.50
Tumbler, amethyst · · · · · · · · · · · · · 42.50
Tumbler, emerald green · · · · · · · · · · 25.00
Water set: pitcher & 4 tumblers;
emerald green w/gold, 5 pcs. · · · · 225.00

ZIPPER

Butter dish, cov. · · · · · · · · · · · · · · · 39.00
Celery vase · · · · · · · · · · · · · · · · · · 21.00
Cheese dish, cov. · · · · · · · · · · · · · · 45.00
Creamer · 18.00
Cruet w/original stopper · · · · · · · · · · 36.00
Goblet · 20.00
Relish, 6 x 9½" · · · · · · · · · · · · · · · 45.00
Sauce dish, flat or footed · · · · · · 6.00 to 8.00
Spooner · 20.00
Toothpick holder, green w/gold · · · · 45.00
Wine, clear · · · · · · · · · · · · · · · · · · 30.00
Wine, ruby-stained · · · · · · · · · · · · · 37.50

ZIPPERED BLOCK - See Iowa Pattern

(End of Pattern Glass Section)

PEACH BLOW

Several types of glass lumped together by collectors as Peach Blow were produced by half a dozen glasshouses. Hobbs, Brockunier & Co., Wheeling, West Virginia made Peach

Blow as a plated ware that shaded from red at the top to yellow at the bottom and is referred to as Wheeling Peach Blow. Mt. Washington Glass Works produced an homogeneous Peach Blow shading from a rose color at the top to pale blue in the lower portion. The New England Glass Works' Peach Blow, called Wild Rose, shaded from rose at the top to white. Gunderson-Pairpoint Co. also reproduced some of the Mt. Washington Peach Blow in the early 1950's and some glass of a somewhat similar type was made by Steuben Glass Works, the Boston & Sandwich Factory and by Thomas Webb & Sons and Stevens & Williams of England. Sandwich Peach Blow is one-layered glass and the English is two-layered.

Another single layered shaded art glass was produced early in this century by the New Martinsville Glass Mfg. Co. Originally called "Muranese," collectors today refer to it as "New Martinsville Peach Blow." We include it with other New Martinsville glass.

GUNDERSON - PAIRPOINT

Goblet, satin finish, 7¼" h. · · · · · · · · $245.00
Vase, 9¼" h., flaring tricornered
rim · 185.00

MT. WASHINGTON

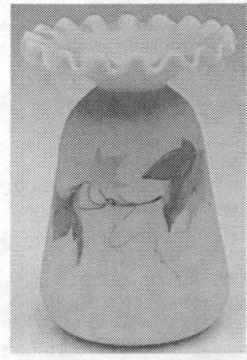

Mt. Washington Decorated Vase

Vase, 4¼" h., tapering ovoid body
w/pinched neck below a widely
flaring flattened & crimped rim,
decorated w/a band of green
leaves on brown stems w/trailing
tendrils, satin finish (ILLUS.) · · · · · 3,300.00

NEW ENGLAND

Celery vase · 975.00
Creamer, souvenir of Chicago
World's Fair marked "World's Fair
1893," 2½" h. · · · · · · · · · · · · · · · · 475.00
Creamer, a flat-bottomed domical
body below a wide cylindrical
neck w/pinched spout, applied
white handle, glossy finish,
3" h. · 385.00

New England Peach Blow Punch Cup

Punch cup, satin finish, 2 5/8" d.,
2 5/8" h. (ILLUS.) 425.00
Toothpick holder, square rim 350.00
Tumbler, glossy finish 445.00
Tumbler, satin finish 445.00
Vase, 4¾" h., squared-form w/gen-
tly rounded sides & flared ruffled
rim 635.00
Vase, 7½" h., jack-in-the-pulpit-
form, glossy finish 325.00

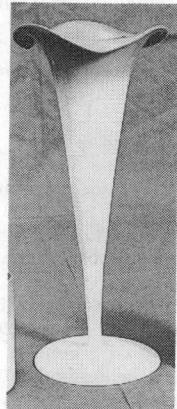

New England Peach Blow Vase

Vase, 10" h., trumpet-form w/un-
dulating trefoil rim, glossy finish
(ILLUS.) 550.00
Vase, 18" h., trumpet-form
w/tricorner rim, glossy finish 1,980.00

WEBB
Ewer w/gold-enameled metal cover,
decorated overall w/gold floral
decoration, 25" h. 895.00
Finger bowl, ruffled rim, decorated
w/heavy gold flowers, branches &
rim, creamy white lining, satin
finish, 2¼" h., 5" d. 425.00
Jar, cov., slightly swelled cylindrical
form, flattened dome cover, decorated w/gold pine needles, flowers & branches on jar & cover,
gold butterfly on the jar, 3" d.,
4 5/8" h. 675.00
Vase, 4¾" h., 2¾" d., footed ovoid
body w/crimped top, clear applied
Matsu-no-ke floral decoration &

applied clear thorny pedestal
base 365.00
Vase, 6" h., 5" d., decorated
w/raised gold bird sitting atop
gold branches & leaves, creamy
white lining 335.00
Vase, 7" h., 5¾" d., squatty bulbous
base tapering to a tall cylindrical
neck w/ringed & flared rim,
enameled gold floral & dragonfly
decoration 550.00
Vase, 12¼" h., 5" d., bulbous base
tapering to a slender cylindrical
neck, applied clear branches wind
around to form three feet, clear
applied leaves & flowers on the
branches, applied berry prunt on
base, creamy white lining 650.00

WHEELING
Creamer w/applied amber handle,
3½" h. 395.00
Pitcher, 5" h., bulbous body taper-
ing to a squared flaring neck, applied amber handle, satin finish . . 935.00
Salt & pepper shakers w/original
tops, pr. 675.00
Vase, 9¼" h., bulbous base taper-
ing to a long 'stick neck,' glossy
finish 985.00

PEKING

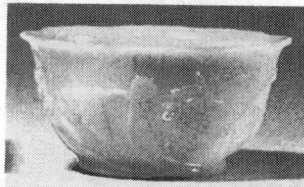

Peking Glass Bowl

*This is Chinese glass, some of which has
overlay in one to five colors, which has attracted collector interest. Peking Imperial
glass is the most valuable.*

Bowl, 4¼" h., deep squared form,
each side carved w/seasonal
flowering branches, including
chrysanthemum, lotus & prunus,
celadon green, 19th c. $1,320.00
Bowls, 4 3/8" d., deep rounded pink
sides w/a flaring rim, carved on
the exterior w/lotus leaves furled
& scalloped above thin stalks encircling the base & forming a
footring, the leafy stalks w/blos-
soms rising around the sides, pr.
(ILLUS. of one) 2,750.00
Jar, wide ovoid sea green body
tapering to a narrow short flared

neck, Qianlong mark & period,
5" h. 4,400.00
Jardiniere, flaring rectangular ruby
red sides finely carved w/season-
al blooms, borne on leafy stems,
comprising peony, prunus, chrysanthemum & narcissus, all supported on a recessed rectangular
base w/four "L"-shaped tab feet,
crizzled translucent, 18th c.,
5 1/8 x 7 3/8" 2,750.00
Vase, 5¼" h., three-color, bulbous
ovoid body on a thick applied
foot, tapering to a small, flat
mouth, the center w/a wide band
of opaque cream w/bands of
deep raspberry overlay above &
below carved w/a band of hooks
& volutes & *ruyi*-heads around the
top, a carved double row of overlapping lotus petals around the
base, w/an opaque blue thin neck
ring & an opaque blue flaring
base foot, incised on the bottom
w/a four-character mark, Qianlong mark & period (casting flaws
on base, neck reduced) 11,550.00
Vases, 6 3/8" h., baluster-form body
w/a widely flaring rim, carved
around the sides w/overlapping
upright lotus petals, all below the
flared neck w/pendent stiff
leaves, 19th c., pr. (one w/rim
chip) 3,025.00
Vases, 7¾" h., yellow baluster-form
body carved w/two birds amid
flowering peony & prunus
branches extending around the
sides & issuing from rockwork encircling the base, 19th c., pr. 1,650.00
Vases, 8½" h., cobalt blue, bottle-
form, bulbous footed base below
a tall cylindrical neck, 18th c.,
pr. 2,750.00

PHOENIX

*This ware was made by the Phoenix Glass
Co. of Beaver County, Pennsylvania, which
produced various types of glass from the
1880's. One special type that attracts collectors now is a molded ware with a vague
resemblance to cameo in its "sculptured"
decoration. Similar pieces with relief-molded
designs were produced by the Consolidated
Lamp & Glass Co. (which see) and care must
be taken to differentiate between the two
companies' wares. Some Consolidated molds
were moved to the Phoenix plant in the mid-
1930's but later returned and used again at
Consolidated. These pieces we will list under
"Consolidated."*

Ashtray, Phlox patt., deep burgundy
pearlized finish, 3" $35.00
Bowl, Tiger Lily patt., pink frosted
finish 203.00
Candy dish, cov., Phlox patt., frost-
ed clear blossoms on a blue
ground 135.00
Cigarette box, cov., Tiger Lily patt.,
overall aqua 195.00
Console bowl, Tiger Lily patt.,
pearlized flowers on a red
ground 183.00
Lamp base, urn-shaped, Dancing
Girl patt., pearlized white on a
nutmeg ground 400.00
Vase, 4¾" h., globular w/flaring
rim, Jewel patt., white design on
light green pearlized finish 95.00
Vase, 7½" h., Cosmos patt., white
blossoms & foliage on a brown
shadow ground 225.00
Vase, 7½" h., rounded rectangular
form, Cosmos patt., overall ivory
pearlized finish 75.00
Vase, 8¾" h., Primrose patt., milk
white flowers & leaves on a
brown ground 215.00
Vase, 9¼" h., 12" w., pillow-
shaped, Wild Geese patt.,
mother-of-pearl birds on a blue
ground 165.00
Vase, 10" h., Madonna patt., relief-
molded pearlized bust on a blue
ground 170.00
Vase, 11¼" h., baluster-form, Danc-
ing Girl patt., milk white figures
on a medium blue ground 485.00
Vase, 18" h., tall ovoid body, Thistle
patt., pearlized white figures on a
white ground 450.00

PILLAR-MOLDED

*This heavily ribbed glassware was
produced by blowing glass into full-sized
ribbed molds and then finishing it by hand.
The technique evolved from earlier "pattern
moulding" used on glass since ancient times
but in pillar-molded glass the ribs are very
heavy and prominent. Most examples found
in this country were produced in the Pittsburgh, Pennsylvania area from around 1850
to 1870, but similar English-made wares made
before and after this period are also available. Most American pieces were made from
clear flint glass and colored examples or
pieces with colored strands in the ribs are rare
and highly prized. Some collectors refer to
this as "steamboat" glass believing that it
was made to be used on American riverboats
but most likely it was used anywhere that a
sturdy, relatively inexpensive glassware was
needed, such as taverns and hotels.*

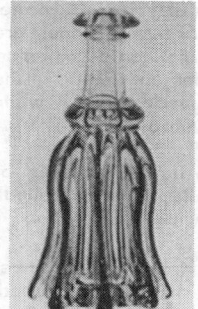

Pillar-Molded Decanter with Blue Ribs

Decanter w/bar lip, eight-rib w/co-
  balt blue ribs in a clear body, applied collar & lip, ground spot
  inside lip, 8¼" h. (ILLUS.) $957.00
Decanter w/bar lip, eight-rib, clear,
  tall conical form w/neck ring &
  panels cut around neck, polished
  pontil, 11¼" h. . . . . .75.00 to 100.00
Decanter w/bar lip, eight-rib, clear,
  tall conical form w/double applied
  neck ring & wide flat bottom,
  12¼" h. 135.00
Vase, 4¼" h., six-rib, clear bowl
  w/flared rim, on a pedestal
  foot 110.00
Vase, 9 5/8" h., eight-rib, clear, tall
  deeply waisted vase w/widely
  flaring ruffled rim, each pillar cut
  w/notches, on a short cylindrical
  standard & heavy disc foot, ca.
  1850-60 . . . . 115.50

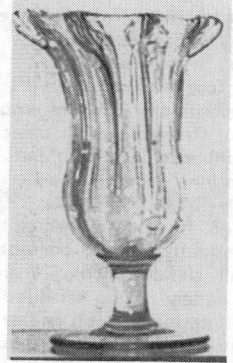

Pillar-Molded Vase

Vase, 10¼" h., eight-rib, clear, the
  tall body swelled at the bottom
  below a straight section ending
  w/a widely flared rim, on a plain
  applied stem & round foot, simple
  cut notches on the pillars, ca.
  1850 (ILLUS.) 192.50
Vase, 11 1/8" h., eight-rib, clear tall
  tulip-shaped bowl on an applied
  knop stem & round foot 150.00

POMONA

Decorated Pomona Punch Cup

*First produced by the New England Glass
Company under a patent received by Joseph
Locke in 1885, Pomona has a frosted ground
on clear glass decorated with mineral stains,
most frequently amber-yellow, sometimes
pale blue. Some pieces bore smooth etched floral decorations highlighted with staining.
Two types of Pomona were made. The first
Locke patent covered a technique whereby
the piece was first covered with an acid-
resistant coating which was then needle-
carved with thousands of minute criss-
crossing lines. The piece was then dipped into
acid which cut into the etched lines, giving
the finished piece a notable "brilliance." A
cheaper method, covered by a second Locke
patent on June 15, 1886, was accomplished
by rolling the glass piece in particles of acid-
resistant material which were picked up by
it. The glass was then etched by acid which
attacked areas not protected by the resistant
particles. A favorite design on Pomona was
the cornflower.*

Butter dish, cov., acanthus leaf
  decoration on cover, 1st patent,
  8" d., 4" h. $540.00
Carafe & matching tumbler, carafe
  w/tightly ruffled tricornered
  amber-stained neck w/applied
  clear band above the flared body,
  matching tumbler w/scalloped
  decoration, tumbler 3½" h., ca-
  rafe 6½" h., 2 pcs. 335.00
Celery vase w/ruffled rim & applied
  clear base, blue cornflower
  decoration, 1st patent,
  6¼" h. . . . . .400.00 to 450.00
Celery vase, Inverted Thumbprint
  patt., 2nd patent 125.00
Creamer, miniature, amber-stained
  rim, 1st patent 125.00
Creamer & open sugar bowl, squatty
  bulbous body tapering to a
  crimped & flared neck, decorated
  w/blueberries, red stems & gold
  leaves, 1st patent, 3" h., pr. 585.00
Cruet w/original stopper, blue cornflower decoration, 2nd patent 275.00
Goblet, amber-stained rim, 2nd
  patent 100.00

Pitcher, water, 7" h., Diamond
Quilted patt., 2nd patent 95.00
Pitcher, 11" h., blue cornflower
decoration, 2nd patent 495.00
Punch cup, blueberry decoration
w/red stems & gold leaves, 2nd
patent 125.00
Punch cup, blue cornflower decora-
tion, 1st patent, 2 5/8" d., 2¾" h.
(ILLUS.) . . . . .150.00 to 175.00
Punch set: 9½" h. tankard pitcher
& six punch cups; 1st patent,
7 pcs. 1,045.00
Tumbler, water, white cornflower
decoration, 1st patent 150.00
Vase, 6" h., ruffled rim, blueberry
decoration 195.00

QUEZAL

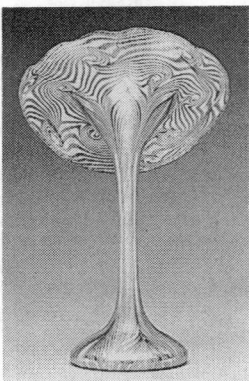

Quezal Jack-in-the-Pulpit Vase

*These wares resemble those of Tiffany and
other glasshouses which produced lustred
glass pieces in the late 19th and early 20th
centuries. They were made by the Quezal Art
Glass and Decorating Co. of Brooklyn, New
York, early in this century and until its closing in the mid-1920's.*

Compote, open, 6" h., the ovoid
bowl tapering to a short pedestal
on a cushion foot & flaring up to
a wide six-lobed fluted rim, the
exterior w/a series of green, amber & gold pulled-feather designs
running up from the base below
the white rim, stretched gold
iridescent interior, inscribed
"Quezal S 619" $880.00
Salt dip, individual, sixteen ribbed
panels, gold iridescent exterior,
interior highlighted w/deep
blue 245.00
Vase, 4" h., compressed bulbous
base w/a wide shoulder to the

narrow flaring neck, decorated
w/bands of silvery amber, green
& blue lappets on a rich emerald
green iridescent ground at the
base, the neck in pearly white,
signed "Quezal - 901" 1,320.00
Vase, 6½" h., baluster-form
w/slightly flared foot, blue, orange & gold iridescent pulled &
hooked swirling decoration,
signed 880.00
Vase, 7" h., trumpet-form amber
iridescent neck above a lobed
body, the lower section decorated
w/striated amber iridescent lappets edged in green & reserved
against an opalescent ground,
inscribed "Quezal - A982," ca.
1925 . . . . .1,380.00
Vase, 8¾" h., jack-in-the-pulpit
form, a squatty bulbous base
tapering up to a tall, slender neck
ending in a widely flaring & ruffled rim, the interior w/gold
iridescence, the exterior decorated w/mint green & gold striated
pulled-feather designs continuing
down to the base, signed "Quezal
P 663" (ILLUS.) 2,420.00
Vase, 9 5/8" h., ovoid body tapering
to a slender, waisted stick neck,
the lower section decorated
w/amber iridescent lappets &
silvery blue iridescent striated
feathering reserved against a caramel iridescent ground w/fine interior ribbing showing, the neck &
shoulder in creamy white, signed
"Quezal - A465," ca. 1920 . . . . . . .3,300.00
Vase, 10¾" h., pyriform body
w/squat foot, rich opalescent
sides decorated w/brilliant amber
iridescent striated feather devices
below amber iridescent lappets
edged in lime green, signed
"Quezal - 937," ca. 1920 . . . . .1,980.00
Vase, 11 7/8" h., jack-in-the-pulpit
form, a squatty bulbous base below a tall, slender stick neck ending in a widely flaring & ruffled
rim, the interior w/deep amber
iridescence, the exterior w/pearly
opalescence decorated w/winter-
green striated feathering edged in
amber iridescence continuing into
the neck & base, the base w/fur-
ther amber iridescent feathering,
the exterior rim w/an amber
iridescent chain decoration,
signed 3,300.00
Vase, 12½" h., wide ovoid body
w/a low, flared neck, the exterior
w/a creamy iridescent ground
decorated w/trailing gold vines

Flower-Decorated Quezal Vase

interspersed w/green flowers all above large pulled-feather designs around the bottom, signed (ILLUS.) 3,300.00

ROSE BOWLS

Spangled Glass Rose Bowl

Blue opalescent vertical stripes decoration, ovoid shape w/box-pleated top, attributed to Stevens & Williams, 4½" d., 4½" h. $145.00

Cased, brown decorated w/gold prunus blossoms & gold branches, creamy white interior, egg-shaped w/box-pleated top, attributed to Stevens & Williams, 3½" d., 5" h. 375.00

Cased satin, blue mother-of-pearl Ribbon patt., white interior, frosted clear applied wafer foot, three-crimp top, 2 5/8" d., 3¼" h. 125.00

Cased satin, rainbow Concentric Circles patt., white interior, squatty bulbous shape w/six-crimp top, 4 3/8''' d., 2 3/8" h. 850.00

Cased satin, rose mother-of-pearl Ribbon patt., white interior, nine-crimp top, 2½" d., 2¼" h. 265.00

Cased satin, shaded blue exterior enameled w/dainty white flowers & lacy gold foliage, white interior, applied frosted clear petal feet, eight-crimp top, 4¼" d., 5" h. 135.00

Cased satin, shad of-pearl exteri w/heavy gold creamy white form w/box-p ed to Stevens 4 7/8" h. ...

Cased satin, sh mother-of-pearl Herringbone patt., white interior, six-crimp top, 3½" d., 3½" h. 145.00

Cased satin, shaded pink mother-of-pearl w/embossed Basketweave patt., creamy white interior, tall ovoid form w/box-pleated top, attributed to Stevens & Williams, 4½" d., 6" h. 425.00

Cased satin, shaded yellow exterior decorated w/small blue & white flowers & foliage, white interior, applied frosted clear feet, eight-crimp top, 4¼" d., 5" h. 125.00

Cranberry decorated w/enameled white flowers w/yellow centers & gold leaves & trim, six-crimp top, 3" d., 4½" h. 350.00

Cranberry w/white "Arboresque" decoration overall, egg-shaped w/tightly ruffled top, applied feet, attributed to Stevens & Williams, 3 5/8" d., 5¾" h. 100.00

Spangled, rose w/silver mica flecks forming a coral-like pattern, egg-shaped, eight-crimp top, 3½" d., 3¾" h. (ILLUS.) 118.00

Verre moire (Nailsea) satin, blue & opaque white looping, egg-shaped, eight-crimp top, 5" d., 5" h. 195.00

ROYAL FLEMISH

Royal Flemish Ewer

This ware, made by Mt. Washington Glass Co., is characterized by very heavy enameled gold lines dividing the surface into separate

GLASS - ROYAL
areas or sec
ish, is va
Crack

...*ions. The body, with a matte fin-...iously decorated.*

...r jar, cov., ovoid body deco-...ted w/large Roman coins against a ground of stained panels divided by heavy gold lines, ornate silver plate cover, rim & bail handle, original paper label w/"Mt. W.G.Co. Royal Flemish," 8" h. $1,650.00

Decanter w/stopper, squatty bulbous body tapering sharply to a tall, slender stick neck w/small pointed stopper, pale grey acid-finished ground decorated on the obverse w/a peacock perched in a flowering branch, his crown applied w/opalescent glass beads, his plumage w/'eyes' of raised gilt roundels enameled in peacock blue, reserved against a paneled ground subtly enameled in palest charcoal & blue-grey & further gilt w/sprays of blossoms w/opalescent glass beaded centers, the neck w/gilt cartouches reserved against a deep puce ground further gilt w/pinwheels, enameled company monogram & "594," 16 1/8" h...................3,025.00

Ewer, wide flat-bottomed ovoid body tapering to a short narrow neck w/a cupped rim w/spout, gilt twisted rope handle around the neck & attached to the side, one side w/a large round reserve w/gilt decoration of cherubs slaying a dragon, the other side w/a similar reserve w/a fierce dragon-fish within a looped leafy scroll, the sides divided into angular panels by heavy gilt bands, each panel w/stained decoration & gilt scrolls, 8" d., 10" h. (ILLUS.) 3,600.00

Royal Flemish Pitcher with Fish
Pitcher, 8 5/8" h., bulbous spherical body w/a low cylindrical neck w/angled rim, applied rope twist handle, acid-finished & enameled w/two guppies swimming amid shells & undulating marine vegetation in rich shades of Chinese red, lavender, puce, chocolate brown, deep emerald green & lemon yellow trimmed w/gilding, reserved against a ground composed of irregularly shaped panels lightly enameled in pale yellow or lavender between raised gold borders conjoined by raised balls, the neck enameled w/scrolling coral edged in gilt & reserved against a strawberry ground, original paper label (ILLUS.) 5,775.00

Vase, 7½" h., 7½" d., squatty bulbous base w/a small squatty bulbous neck, decorated w/multicolored pansies all outlined w/gold over gold sunbursts & tracery 1,385.00

Vase, 13 7/16" h., a squatty bulbous footed base below a tall, slender & gently flaring neck w/a notched rim, acid-finished ground enameled w/Guba ducks in flight against a tooled gilt sun in shades of blue, black, charcoal, chocolate brown, white & Chinese red reserved against a ground composed of irregularly shaped panels enameled in pale yellow & grey between raised gilt borders conjoined by stellate devices or parallelograms, the neck decorated w/deep puce & gilt corkscrews, original paper label, ca. 1890.........................4,125.00

RUBINA CRYSTAL

This glass, sometimes spelled "Rubena," is a flashed ware, shading from ruby to clear. Some pieces are decorated, others are plain.

Cologne bottle w/original clear facet-cut stopper, cylindrical body w/deep shoulder, a short cylindrical neck w/a flat flaring rim, gold trim, 2½" d., 6½" h. $85.00

Condiment set: rectangular pepper pot & mustard jar w/silver plate tops, rectangular open salt dip, all in silver plate frame w/center handle; each piece w/overall cut diamond design, 3½" d., 4 3/8" h., the set 210.00

Jar, cov., clear facet-cut finial,

cylindrical body, gold trim, 3" d.,
5½" h. 75.00
Nappy, ruffled rim, applied clear
handle, 5" d. 80.00
Perfume bottle w/original facet-cut
stopper, tapering square shape
w/overall facet-cut decoration.... 110.00
Pitcher, water, 7¼" h., w/applied
clear handle, Inverted Thumbprint
patt. 145.00
Tumbler, Inverted Thumbprint patt.,
decorated w/enameled blue, gold
& white flowers & green & brown
leaves, 2 7/8" d., 4 1/8" h. 45.00
Water set: 9¼" h., 6" d. pitcher
w/applied clear reeded handle &
ten 3¾" h. tumblers; all decorated w/h.p. yellow roses, green &
yellow leaves & small blue, yellow & orange flowers, 11 pcs. 795.00

RUBINA VERDE

Rubina Verde Hobnail Tumbler

*This decorative glass, popular in the late
19th and early 20th centuries, shades from
ruby or deep cranberry to green or greenish-
yellow.*

Cheese dish, cov., Inverted Thumbprint patt. $250.00
Finger bowl...................... 145.00
Pitcher, 7¾" h., fluted & ruffled rim,
applied clear reeded handle,
molded Zipper patt. 450.00
Pitcher, 11" h., Inverted Thumbprint
patt. 400.00
Salt shaker w/original top, barrel-
shaped, Inverted Thumbprint
patt. 75.00
Toothpick holder, footed, egg-
shaped w/scalloped rim 285.00
Tumbler, Hobnail patt.
(ILLUS.) ....100.00 to 125.00

RUBY-STAINED

*This name derives from the color of the
glass — a deep red. The red staining was thinly painted on clear j...
refired at a low t...
were further engra...
were very popula...
1920's. This techn...
with "flashed" gl...
is actually dippe...
trasting color. A...*

Berry set: master bowl & six sauce
dishes; Carnation patt., gold trim,
7 pcs. $145.00
Bowl, 8½" d., 3¾" h., Box-In-Box
patt. 48.00
Butter dish, cov., Duncan's Empire
patt., 8" d., 6½" h. 110.00
Butter dish, cov., Loop & Block
patt. 65.00
Butter dish, cov., O'Hara Diamond
patt. 195.00
Butter dish, cov., Robinson's Puritan
patt., 7½" d., 6" h. 110.00
Celery vase, Box-In-Box patt., deco-
rated w/dainty enameled florals.. 95.00
Celery vase, Melrose patt., 3¾" d.,
6¼" h. 110.00
Creamer, Naomi patt. 65.00
Creamer, Triple Triangle patt. 45.00
Cruet w/original stopper, Big Button
patt. 75.00
Pitcher, tankard, Beaded Swag
patt. 125.00
Pitcher, water, Carnation patt.,
w/gold trim 265.00
Spooner, Beaded Swag patt. 50.00
Spooner, Naomi patt............... 35.00
Spooner, Saxon patt. 40.00
Spooner, Sheaf & Block patt. 40.00
Sugar bowl, cov., Crescent patt.... 140.00
Sugar bowl, cov., Loop & Block
patt. 80.00
Sugar bowl, cov., Scalloped Swirl
patt. 70.00
Syrup pitcher w/original top, Late
Block patt...................... 285.00
Syrup pitcher w/original top, Pi-
oneer's Victoria patt. 325.00
Syrup pitcher w/original top, Prize
patt. 295.00
Syrup pitcher w/original top, Trun-
cated Cube patt. 200.00
Table set: creamer, cov. sugar bowl,
cov. butter dish, spooner;
Bevelled Diamond & Star patt.,
4 pcs. 375.00
Table set, Framed Jewel patt.,
4 pcs. 375.00
Table set, Scalloped Six-Point patt.,
4 pcs. 400.00
Toothpick holder, Diamond Spear-
head patt., souvenir 55.00
Toothpick holder, Double Arch
patt. 175.00
Toothpick holder, Harvard patt. 62.50

holder, Pleating patt. 52.00

k holder, Prize patt. 130.00

pick holder, Zipper Slash patt.,

ouvenir....................... 38.00

umbler, Riverside's Victoria patt. .. 75.00

Water set: pitcher & five tumblers;
Klear-Kut patt., 6 pcs. 300.00

Water set: pitcher & six tumblers;
Art Novo patt., 7 pcs. 375.00

Water set: tankard pitcher & six
tumblers; Hexagon Block patt.,
7 pcs. 275.00

Water set: pitcher & six tumblers;
Loop & Block patt., 7 pcs. 450.00

Water set: tankard pitcher & six
tumblers; Pioneer's Victoria patt.,
7 pcs. 325.00

Wine, Co-Op's Royal patt. 55.00

Wine set: decanter w/original stopper & two wines; Model's Gem
patt., 3 pcs. 150.00

SANDWICH

Sandwich Tulip Vases

Numerous types of glass were produced at The Boston & Sandwich Glass Works in Sandwich, Massachusetts, on Cape Cod, from 1826 to 1888. Those listed here represent a sampling. Also see PATTERN GLASS and LACY in the "Glass" section, and PAPER-WEIGHTS.

All pieces are pressed glass unless otherwise noted. Numbers after salt dips refer to listings in Pressed Glass Salt Dishes of the Lacy Period, 1825-1850, *by Logan W. and Dorothy B. Neal.*

Bowl, 5½" d., footed w/flaring lattice openwork sides, rare ruby
(elongated chip on underside of
foot) $1,870.00

Bowl, 6" d., footed w/flaring lattice
openwork sides, clear 275.00

Candlestick, miniature, bell-shaped
socket on hexagonal base, blue

opalescent, 1 5/8" h. (underfill &
bubble in socket)............... 880.00

Candlesticks, Dolphin patt., petal
socket, square foot, sapphire
blue, 10 3/8" h., pr. (one w/re-
paired tail) 825.00

Candlesticks, Petal & Loop patt.,
electric blue, 6¾" h., pr. (one
w/tiny flake off one petal) 1,320.00

Cologne bottle w/original acorn
stopper, cut overlay, flaring base
tapering to tall slender body
w/neck ring & flat flared rim,
ruby cut to clear w/overall bull's
eye design & arches around the
base, ca. 1845-60, 3 3/8" d.,
6¼" h......................... 325.00

Compote, open, 6 5/8" d., 3 5/8" h.,
lacy, Oak Leaf patt., clear 247.50

Decanter w/original teardrop-
shaped stopper, green overlay cut
to clear in a grapevine design accented w/cut dots on the border &
stopper 400.00

Salt dip, lacy, boat-shaped, model
of a early sidewheel steamboat,
opalescent medium blue (similar
to BT-8) 880.00

Salt dip, lacy, scroll-ended sleigh
shape, Eagle patt., EE-3b (slight
roughage) 220.00

Salt shaker, "Christmas" salt w/dat-
ed metal top w/agitator, amethyst, 2½" h. 100.00

Salt shaker, "Christmas" salt w/dat-
ed metal top w/agitator, vaseline,
2½" h......................... 195.00

Sugar bowl, cov., lacy, octagonal
Gothic Arch patt., electric blue
(two minor upper rim flakes on
base, small flakes on cover on underside) 1,650.00

Tray, lacy, rectangular w/low flaring
sides, sailing ship & "U.S.F. Constitution" in the center, lacy heart
border, 7 1/8" l. (one small rim
chip & slight roughage) 5,775.00

Vase, 7" h., "Trevaise" art glass,
ovoid body tapering to a wide flat
rim, opal white cased to pale
green, the exterior w/gold &
green iridescent heart & leaf &
vertical vine designs, applied button pontil, early 20th c. 1,650.00

Vase, 9" h., Pineapple patt., white
opaque ovoid patterned body
raised on an applied blue pedestal base & w/a tall slender
trumpet-form blue neck w/a ruffled rim, ca. 1860 ....1,760.00

Vases, 9½" h., Three-Printie Block
patt., tall trumpet-form bowl
w/fluted rim, octagonal foot, elec-

tric blue, pr. (shallow chip on underside of one foot) 990.00
Vases, 10 1/8" h., tulip-form, octagonal body w/flared scalloped
rim, single wafer connecting bowl
to octagonal pedestal base, deep
amethyst, slight variation in
height, pr. (ILLUS.) 880.00
Vases, 10 1/8" h., tulip-form, octagonal body w/flared scalloped
rim, single wafer connecting bowl
to octagonal pedestal base, emerald green, pr. (slight variation in
height) 1,760.00
Whiskey taster, lacy, footed cylindrical form w/a geometric design,
deep amethyst 242.00

SATIN

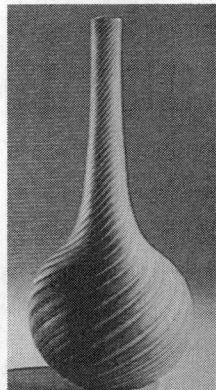

Tall Satin Glass Vase

*Satin glass was a popular decorative glass
developed in the late 19th century. Most
pieces were composed of two layers of glass
with the exterior layer usually in a shaded
pastel color. The name derives from the soft
matte finish, caused by exposure to acid
fumes, which gave the surface a "satiny" feel.
Mother-of-pearl satin glass was a specialized
variety wherein air trapped between the layers of glass provided subtle surface patterns
such as Herringbone and Diamond Quilted.
A majority of satin glass was produced in
England and America but collectors should
be aware that reproductions have been
produced for many years. Also see ROSE
BOWLS and WEBB under Glass.*

Basket, ruffled rim, shaded pink
mother-of-pearl Herringbone
patt., applied clear frosted handle
& feet, white interior, 3¾" d.,
6½" h. $265.00
Basket, crimped rim, applied frosted
clear thorn handle, shaded

heavenly blue mother-of-pearl
Herringbone patt., white interior,
8¼" d., 9¼" h. 595.00
Bowl, 5¼" d., 7¼" h., footed bulbous base w/a tricornered ruffled
rim, rainbow mother-of-pearl Diamond Quilted patt., applied vaseline feet, applied vaseline rigaree
edge trim & an applied frosted
berry prunt on the base 1,250.00
Bowl-vase, bulbous w/rolled rim,
brown mother-of-pearl Federzeichnung patt. w/gold enameled decoration, 7¼" d., 7" h. 1,995.00
Condiment set: open salt dip w/sil-
ver plate rim, cov. pepper pot &
cov. mustard jar w/silver plate
covers, spoon & frame w/center
loop handle, red mother-of-pearl
Ribbon patt., overall 6¼" h., the
set 840.00
Cracker jar, cov., shaded pink to
white & decorated w/yellow flowers & lavender foliage, silver
plate cover, rim & bail handle,
overall 9½" h. 525.00
Creamer, bulbous base tapering to
a slightly flaring cylindrical neck
w/pinched lip, applied clear frosted handle, shaded heavenly blue
& decorated w/dainty pink &
cream flowers & small green
leaves, white interior, 4¾" d.,
6" h. 235.00
Ewer, bulbous shouldered base w/a
tall cylindrical neck w/a bulbous
ring below the flaring ruffled rim,
applied frosted clear angled handle, shaded blue mother-of-pearl
Herringbone patt., white interior,
3½" d., 8" h. 195.00
Ewers, footed baluster-form body
tapering to a slender neck
w/pinched tricorner rim, applied
clear frosted handle, shaded
heavenly blue enameled w/pur-
ple, white & yellow flowers &
yellow scrolls, white interior,
3¼" d., 10" h., pr. 225.00
Flower frog, mushroom-shaped,
opaque white shaded to light
blue, decorated w/enameled blue
dot berries, white flowers &
brown leaves, 5" d., 3" h. 195.00
Lamp, kerosene table-type, shaded
maroon mother-of-pearl Swirl
patt. base, tapering cylindrical
form w/a wide shoulder & relief-
molded ribbing, raised on a
domed footed brass base & w/a
brass connnector & burner, w/a
rib-molded frosted spherical
shade, 6½" d., overall 20¾" h. .. $950.00
Perfume bottle, spherical body

w/original crown-shaped silver plate cap, white mother-of-pearl Peacock Eye patt., monogram "C" on the top of the cap, 3¾" h. 635.00

Pitcher, 7¼" h., bulbous ovoid body below a wide squared flaring mouth, applied reeded frosted clear handle, pink mother-of-pearl Zipper patt., bright yellow lining, attributed to Mt. Washington Glass Company 770.00

Plate, dessert, 6" d., ruffled rim, rainbow mother-of-pearl Diamond Quilted patt., creamy white underside 395.00

Plate, 7" d., shaded blue mother-of-pearl Drape patt. 195.00

Rose bowl, bulbous, eight-crimp rim, shaded brown w/gold prunus & butterfly decoration, white lining, 2½" d., 2½" h. 300.00

Rose bowl, squatty bulbous form, six-crimp top, rainbow mother-of-pearl Concentric Circles patt., white lining, 4 3/8" d., 2 3/8" h. 850.00

Salt dip, shaded pink to raspberry mother-of-pearl Diamond Quilted patt. 125.00

Sweetmeat jar, cov., pink mother-of-pearl Diamond Quilted patt., silver plate cover & rim w/stationary bail handle, 4¼" d., overall 7½" h. 500.00

Tumbler, shaded pink mother-of-pearl Coin Spot patt., white lining, 2¾" d., 3¾" h. 125.00

Tumbler, apricot mother-of-pearl Teardrops patt., white lining 95.00

Vase, 3½" h., 5½" d., squatty bulbous melon-lobed body w/low, ruffled neck, rose ground decorated w/alternating panels of pink & white leaves w/blue & yellow scrolls & blue flowers w/green foliage, white lining 195.00

Vase, 6" h., 3¼" d., bulbous base tapering to a cylindrical ringed neck w/a widely flaring ruffled rim, rainbow mother-of-pearl Diamond Quilted patt., white lining .. 895.00

Vase, 6 5/8" h., 4¾" d., bulbous body w/a stepped & flaring cylindrical neck, shaded chartreuse green mother-of-pearl Ribbon patt., white lining 325.00

Vase, 7¼" h., 4 5/8" d., footed wide ovoid melon-lobed body w/a short neck w/cupped rim flanked by applied white angled handles, blue & pink striped rainbow ground enameled w/pink & white roses, gold leaves & butterfly 295.00

Vase, 8½" h., 4" d., ovoid body tapering to a cylindrical neck w/flaring & crimped rim, creamy white mother-of-pearl Coin Spot patt., white lining 175.00

Vase, 9¼" h., Pompeian-style body, ovoid body tapering to a narrow neck w/a swelled base tapering to a flat rim, swirled mother-of-pearl satin glass design in Reverse Amberina coloring cased in white, attributed to Stevens & Williams, England 660.00

Vase, 10¾" h., footed slightly swelling cylindrical shouldered body w/a widely flaring crimped & ruffled rim, shaded pink mother-of-pearl Diamond Quilted patt. 310.00

Vase, 11½" h., tall ovoid body tapering to a short, wide cylindrical neck, brown mother-of-pearl Federzeichnung patt., overall gilt 'earthworm' design on brown ground, gilt painted mark "Patent 9159," ca. 1890 .... 2,200.00

Vase, 19¾" h., bulbous base continuing to a long slender cylindrical neck, spiral ribbed pale yellow & magenta, white interior (ILLUS.) 605.00

SCHNEIDER

Internally-Decorated Schneider Vase

This ware is made in France at Cristallerie Schneider, established in 1913 near Paris by Ernest and Charles Schneider. Some pieces of cameo were marked "Le Verre Francais" (which see) and others were signed "Charder."

Bowl, 5½" d., 3" h., Cluthra-type, bulbous tapering body w/wide incurved mouth, composed of irregular bubbles throughout in transparent amethyst, turquoise blue & clear, acid-stamped & underlined "Schneider" at the side & "France" on the base $467.50

Bowl, 11" d., 5½" h., Cluthra-type,
wide squatty bulbous body
w/closed rim, bubbled & striated
pink, white & clear, decorated
w/applied clear medial swagged
band, acid-stamped "Schneider"..1,045.00

Cameo vase, 7" h., spherical base
below a flaring trumpet-form
neck, mottled orange & yellow
overlaid in bluish brown & cut
w/a repeating design of stylized
leaves & blossoms, cameo-signed
"Charder" 412.50

Compote, open, 7½" h., circular
bowl in mottled orange & white,
supported by a mottled & striped
purple foot w/three applied rings,
etched signature "SCHNEIDER" ...1,760.00

Vase, 8 3/8" h., ovoid body
w/closed rim tapering toward the
base & set on a thick disc foot,
amethyst acid cut-back w/a
repeating Art Deco pattern of
arches & fanned ribbing, signed
"Schneider" 715.00

Vase, 8½" h., footed bulbous body
w/an etched surface, applied
w/purple spots of various sizes,
etched mark "Schneider" 2,990.00

Vase, 12" h., Cluthra-type, footed
slightly flaring cylindrical body
tapering to a short flared neck,
shaded & mottled pink, white &
clear swirling bubbles, etched
"Schneider" on foot & "France" on
the base 357.50

Vase, 15¼" h., the attenuated body
in clear internally decorated w/an
overall pattern of air bubbles, two
black handles applied at shoulder,
the terminals finely wheel-carved
w/a bouquet of flowers, a tendril
extending down to the mottled
purple circular foot, signed in intaglio "Schneider," ca. 1925 .....3,575.00

Vase, 16 3/8" h., large bulbous
ovoid body tapering to a thick
squared neck, thick clear walls
encasing brilliant pumpkin orange
mottled w/pale yellow & tangerine, the neck further mottled in
burgundy, signed "Schneider -
France" (ILLUS.) 2,420.00

Vase, 20 1/16" h., cylindrical body
on a circular foot, mottled clear &
pink w/an etched finish, applied
w/a wavy interlaced purple glass
band, etched signature.........1,610.00

SILVER DEPOSIT - SILVER OVERLAY

*Silver Deposit and Silver Overlay have
been made commercially since the last quar-*
ter of the 19th century. Silver is deposited on
the glass by various means, most commonly
by utilizing an electric current. The glass was
very popular during the first three decades
of this century, and some pieces are still being produced. During the late 1970's, silver
commanded exceptionally high prices and
this was reflected in a surge of interest in silver overlay glass, especially in pieces marked
"Sterling" or "925" on the heavy silver
overlay.*

Silver Overlay Bowl

Bowl, 8¼" d., compressed bulbous
form w/narrow flared rim, emerald green overlaid w/a scrolling
floral leaf design, raised on silver
bun feet (ILLUS.) $660.00

Bowl, 11½" d., fluted rim, clear
w/silver overlay leaves & berries
decoration..................... 110.00

Cordial set: 9¼" h. decanter
w/original stopper, six 2" h. cordials; cobalt blue w/silver overlay, 7 pcs...................... 365.00

Flask w/original silver plate screw
top, amber body w/silver overlay
depicting crossed fishing poles, a
long handled net & a shield lettered "Good Bait," 3¼ x 5¾" 195.00

Vase, miniature, 2¾" h., wide
shouldered ovoid body tapering to
a short, flaring neck, iridized
orangish amber overlaid w/over-
all Art Nouveau silver swirled
vines, leaves & blossoms, Austria,
early 20th c. 467.50

SLAG

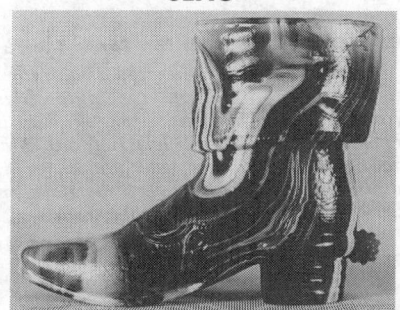

Boot-Shaped Toothpick Holder

Marble and Agate glass are other names applied to this variegated glassware made from the middle until the close of the last century and now being reproduced. It is characterized by variegated streaks of color. Pink slag was made only in the Inverted Fan & Feather pattern and is rare.

Cake stand, simple round top on a round pedestal above a domed round foot, purple, late 19th c. $55.00

Creamer, Sunflower patt., purple . . . 68.00

Punch cup, Inverted Fan & Feather patt., pink. . . . . .275.00 to 325.00

Salt dip, master size, oval wash-tub shape w/handles, marked "Sowerby," purple 70.00

Sauce dishes, footed, Inverted Fan & Feather patt., pink, set of 6 . . . . . . 995.00

Spooner, Fluted patt., purple 48.00

Spooner, Flying Swan patt., amber . . 90.00

Spooner, Inverted Fan & Feather patt., pink 375.00

Toothpick holder, rectangular, purple, 1¾ x 2", 3" h. 30.00

Toothpick holder, figural, model of a boot w/spur (British boot), purple, 4" l., 3¼" h. (ILLUS.) 50.00

Water set: pitcher & five tumblers; Inverted Fan & Feather patt., pink, 6 pcs. 2,200.00

SMITH BROTHERS

Plate Decorated with the Santa Maria

This company first operated as a decorating department of the Mt. Washington Glass Works in the 1870's and later on as an independent business in New Bedford, Massachusetts. The firm was noted for its outstanding decorating work on glass and also carried on a glass cutting trade.

Bowl, 3" d., melon-ribbed body, decorated w/blue scrolls & dainty yellow flowers, red rampant lion mark. $235.00

Box w/hinged lid, melon-ribbed body, pansy decoration, rampant lion mark. 175.00

Cracker jar, cov., barrel-shaped, creamy white w/shaded yellow daisies & green foliage, rampant lion mark, silver plate rim, cover & bail handle, cover marked "S.B.," 7" h. 375.00

Cracker jar, cov., square body, decorated w/enameled Shasta daisies & leaves on a tan & beige ground, silver plate rim, cover & bail handle, base signed 845.00

Plate, 6¼" d., scene of Christopher Columbus' ship "Santa Maria" (ILLUS.). 300.00

Rose bowl, creamy white ground w/shaded yellow daisies, green foliage & enameled white beaded rim, 4½" h. 195.00

Salt dip, melon-ribbed, decorated w/gold florals 75.00

Syrup pitcher w/original silver plate rim, cover & handle, bulbous melon-ribbed body decorated w/dainty flowers on a soft, creamy ground, 6" d., 6" h. 845.00

Vase, 5 7/8" h., 2¼" d., ring-type, cylindrical w/raised bands near top & base, h.p. colorful winter scene w/ornate house on a pale grey ground 75.00

Vase, 6" h., ring-type, tall conical body w/molded double rings near the top & base, tapering in at the bottom, the front decorated w/two large overlapping circles, one containing a scene of two red birds on a blossom-laden limb, the other w/a lake landscape, both framed by blossoming branches 385.00

Vase, 8½" h., 6½" d., wide ovoid shouldered body below a squatty bulbous neck w/a slightly raised rim, the creamy white body decorated w/three large shaded blue wisteria blossoms & green leaves trimmed in heavy gold, the neck molded w/a band of petals & scrolls below a band of short, wide ribs all brushed in pale green w/gold trim 845.00

SPANGLED

Spangled glass incorporated particles of mica or metallic flakes and variegated colored glass particles imbedded in the transparent glass. Usually made of two layers, it might have either an opaque or transparent casing.

The Vasa Murrhina Glass Company of Sandwich, Massachusetts, first patented the process for producing Spangled glass in 1884 and this factory is known to have produced great quantities of this ware. It was, however, also produced by numerous other American and English glasshouses. This type, along with Spatter, which see below, is often erroneously called "End of Day."

A related decorative glass, Aventurine, features a fine speckled pattern resembling gold dust on a solid color ground. Also see "Art Glass Baskets" under Glass.

Basket, lobed body w/applied clear handle, pink shading to white w/mica flecks, 9" w. $140.00

Bowl-vase, bulbous body w/ruffled rim, applied clear snail-shaped feet, clear-cased pink w/gold mica flecks, 5" d., 5" h. 235.00

Condiment set: cov. pepper pot, cov. mustard pot, cruet w/original stopper & original silver plate holder; cranberry & green spatter w/silver mica flecks, silver plate covers, 2 x 5½", 6" h., the set . . . 225.00

Creamer, bulbous ovoid base tapering to a short cylindrical neck w/pinched spout & applied amber angled handle, Inverted Thumbprint patt., orange & beige spatter w/mica flecks, 2" d., 3½" h. 65.00

Creamer, bulbous base w/molded swirled ribs below a cylindrical neck w/pinched spout, clear applied reeded handle, blue w/swirled mica flecks, 3¼" d., 4¾" h. 225.00

Ewers, pedestal cushion foot supporting a spherical body tapering to a ringed neck w/tricornered rolled & ruffled rim, applied clear thorn handle, heavenly blue w/silver mica flecks, white lining, 3½" d., 7½" h., pr. 165.00

Rose bowl, spherical, eight-crimp top, shaded blue exterior w/mica flecks, white lining, 3¾" d. 95.00

Rose bowl, spherical, eight-crimp top, oxblood, pink & cream spatter w/silver mica flecks in a swirling striped design, white lining, 4" d., 3¼" h. 110.00

Tumbler, chartreuse green & white spatter w/gold mica flecks, 2½" d., 3¾" h. 45.00

Tumbler, pink, gold & brown spatter w/mica flecks, white lining, 2¾" d., 3¾" h. 75.00

Vase, 8½" h., 4½" d., wide ovoid footed body narrowing at the shoulder to a square flared rim, applied arched clear handles,

deep rose w/overall coral design created by the mica flecks, white lining 135.00

Vase, 8 5/8" h., 2¾" d., small tapering baluster-form body raised on clear applied petal feet w/clear applied upright leaves around base above the feet, green w/deep green Aventurine swirl design, white lining 60.00

Vase, 9½" h., 6" d., squatty bulbous base tapering to a slender cylindrical body w/flaring rolled & crimped rim, pink w/silver mica flecks, cased in clear & w/clear applied trim around rim & fancy clear shell trim down each side, white lining 145.00

SPATTER

Spatter Glass Vase

This variegated-color ware is similar to Spangled glass but does not contain metallic flakes. The various colors are applied on a clear, opaque white or colored body. Much of it was made in Europe and England. It is sometimes called "End of Day."

Also see "Art Glass Baskets" under Glass.

Basket, bulbous w/ruffled rim, applied clear thorn handle, gold & pink spatter, white lining, 5 3/8" d., 5¾" h. $155.00

Basket, ovoid w/ruffled rim, applied clear rigaree edge trim & applied clear twisted thorn handle, maroon & white spatter, white lining, 6½" d., 7½" h. 175.00

Basket, bulbous mold-blown swirl design base w/crimped squared rim, applied clear twisted thorn handle, maroon, pink, yellow & green spatter, white lining, 5" d., 8" h. 165.00

Bowl, 8¼" d., 5¼" h., crimped rim, peach & white spatter, on an ornate footed ormolu base 225.00

Candlesticks, baluster-form, blue,
maroon & green spatter, 3¾" d.,
9" h., pr. 135.00

Creamer & sugar bowl, applied
clear handle & feet, red, orange &
yellow, white lining, pr. 120.00

Dish, cov., clear applied feet, cover
w/applied clear finial, applied
clear leaves on sides, pink &
green spatter, white lining,
4¼" d., 5¾" h. 75.00

Jar, cov., slightly domed cover
w/applied clear ball finial, cylindrical sides w/applied clear shell
trim beneath rim, maroon, yellow,
blue & white spatter, 3¼" d.,
5¾" h. 68.00

Pitcher, 5" h., 5" d., bulbous base
w/tri-lobed rim, applied clear
reeded handle, Swirl patt., maroon, yellow & white spatter,
creamy white lining 88.00

Tumbler, cylindrical, Inverted
Thumbprint patt., pink & cream
spatter, 2 5/8" d., 3¾" h. 45.00

Vase, 8" h., baluster-form w/ringed
neck & flared mouth, red, yellow
& green spatter, brown lining
(ILLUS.)......................... 85.00

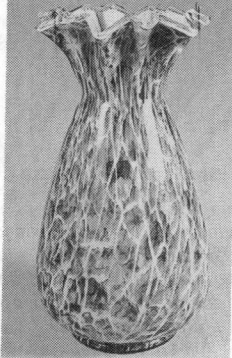

Large Spatter Glass Vase

Vase, 10½" h., elongated ovoid
base w/narrow neck & flaring
crimped rim w/applied clear edging, pink & brown spatter, white
lining (ILLUS.) 165.00

STEUBEN

*Most of the Steuben glass listed below was
made at the Steuben Glass Works, now a division of Corning Glass, between 1903 and
about 1933. The factory was organized by
T.G. Hawkes, noted glass designer, Frederick Carder, and others. Mr. Carder devised
many types of glass and revived many old
techniques.*

ACID CUT BACK

Vase, 7" h., 8" d., spherical body
w/closed rim, Jade green cut
back to Alabaster in a stylized Art
Deco style Oriental blossom
branch design....................$880.00

Vase, 9¾" h., cylindrical base below a widely flaring bell-form top,
frosted crystal decorated in stylized floral Mansard patt., signed
"Steuben" w/fleur-de-lis mark ...1,320.00

AURENE

Steuben Aurene Jar

Basket, flat-bottomed w/widely flaring sides folded-up on two sides
& joined by an applied handle
w/terminal prunts, gold w/overall
pink, orange & blue iridescent
highlights, marked "Steuben Aurene 153," 8¼" d., 8¾" h. 1,430.00

Bowl, cov., 7½" d., 6" h., squatty
bulbous base w/wide short rim inset w/low domed cover w/blos-
som & cone finial, overall blue
iridescence, signed "Steuben Aurene 6075" (small chips on rims
under cover) 660.00

Bowl, 11½" d., flattened globular
shape turning in to form a narrow
shoulder, overall gold iridescent
finish, signed, ca. 1900..........1,210.00

Candlestick, ovoid candle socket
w/a wide flat rim above a double
knop centered on a baluster-form
standard on a wide round foot,
silvery purplish blue iridescence,
signed "Aurene 2956," 9¾" h..... 467.50

Center bowl, a domed foot w/a
flattened flaring rim & molded
w/four pairs of ribs, the deep
flaring fan-shaped bowl also
w/pairs of ribs, overall blue
iridescence, foot engraved "Steuben" & w/partial silver paper
label, 6¼" h. 1,045.00

Compotes, open, 8" h., shallow
bowl on a tall stem, overall blue
iridescent finish, signed "AURENE
2642," pr. 1,540.00
Jar, cov., the shouldered ovoid body
raised on a ringed knob pedestal
w/a domed foot, the conical cover
w/a triple-loop finial, overall amber iridescence, signed "Aurene -
3114," minor chips on rim of cov-
er, 14" h. (ILLUS.) 2,090.00
Pitcher, 5¼" h., bulbous base taper-
ing to a wide cylindrical neck
w/small pinched spout, applied
handle, cobalt blue w/silvery blue
iridescence, marked "Aurene
3064" (slightly imperfect surface
coverage) 605.00
Salt dip, w/flared & scalloped rim,
gold iridescent finish, signed
"Aurene" 295.00
Tumbler, cylindrical w/flared rim,
gold iridescent finish, signed
"Steuben Aurene," 3¼" d.,
4 1/8" h. 225.00
Vase, 4¼" h., ovoid body taper-
ing to a flat rim, the shoulder
w/three small pulled loop handles alternating w/three dimples
around the body, blue iridescence, impressed "Aurene 2767,"
w/original Haviland paper label . . 825.00
Vase, 6½" h., tree trunk-form,
tripartite w/three tree trunks on a
circular base, blue iridescent finish, signed "Aurene 2744" 550.00
Vase, 8" h., wide ovoid body tapering slightly to short, flared rim,
overall blue iridescence, No. 7416,
signed 825.00

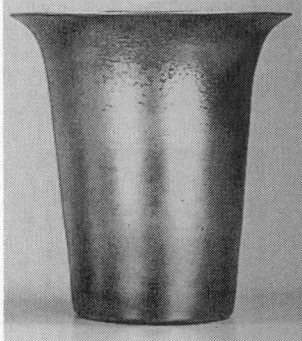

Cylindrical Aurene Vase
Vase, 10" h., flared cylindrical form,
iridescent blue w/pale green
highlights, signed "Steuben -
Aurene - 6127" (ILLUS.) 1,045.00
Vase, 12" h., wide-mouthed ovoid
body tapering to a knob pedestal
on a disc foot, iridescent blue

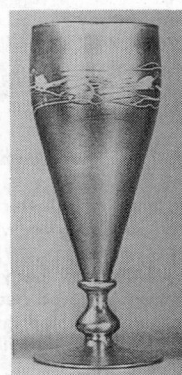

Aurene Vase with Trailed Decoration
decorated around the top w/ap-
plied threaded hearts & pulled &
trailed vines in Ivrene w/gold
iridescence, signed "Steuben -
Aurene - 8300" (ILLUS.) 2,860.00

BRISTOL YELLOW
Punch cup 195.00
Vase, 7¾" h., footed baluster-form
w/applied handles, shape
No. 6207 . . . . 125.00
Vase, 12" h., pedestal base w/con-
ical body, Optic patt., shape
No. 6034 . . . . 350.00

CALCITE
Bowl, 10½" d., Calcite exterior,
gold iridescent Aurene interior . . . 260.00
Compote, open, 8" d., 8" h., the
shallow wide bowl lined w/bright
gold iridescence, white exterior
continuing down the slender
swelled stem & applied disc
foot 357.50
Compote, open, 10" d., twelve
molded ribs, applied ring on
stem, Calcite exterior, gold irides-
cent Aurene interior 695.00
Finger bowl & underplate, the deep
bowl w/twelve molded ribs & a
widely flaring rim, set in a dished
underplate, each w/an iridescent
gold interior & white exterior,
each marked "Aurene" & numbered, bowl 4 7/8" d., underplate
6¼" d., 2 pcs. 275.00

CELESTE BLUE
Bowl, 10" d., 4" h., flaring body
w/domed foot 125.00
Candy dish, cov., footed, 8" h. 245.00
Compote, open, clear applied twist
stem, shape No. 5194 . . . . 250.00
Compote, open, footed, flared rim,
shape No. 112 . . . . 385.00

Salt dip, footed, deeply ribbed,
shape No. 2605, 2½" d., 1½" h... 150.00
Stemware set, eight goblets & eight
sherbets, 16 pcs. 635.00

CLUTHRA
Bowl, 7½" d., 2" h., mushroom-
shaped, pink................... 460.00
Vase, 7½" h., angular baluster-
shaped body, shaded from white
to black 1,200.00
Vase, 8¼" h., wide ovoid body
tapering to a short flared neck,
white w/irregular bubbled internal trapped-air decoration, fleur-
de-lis mark on base 935.00
Vase, 8½" h., baluster-form
w/slightly flared rim, light amethyst, shape No. 2683 ....1,200.00
Vase, 10 1/8" h., rose jar-form,
mottled lapis blue, signed 1,650.00
Vase, 10¼" h., wide ovoid body
tapering to a short widely flaring
neck, amethyst w/irregular bubbles & flowing mottling, acid-
etched script signature "Steuben" 1,320.00
Vase, 10½" h., tall slightly tapering
rounded triangular body, thick
walls in rose, pink & raspberry
mottling & irregular bubbles
throughout, clear rim & circular
foot, fleur-de-lis mark 770.00

GROTESQUE

Jade Blue Grotesque Vase

Bowl, 10" d., 6¼" h., four-lobed,
ruffled sides, blue shading to
clear, shape No. 7277 .... 475.00
Bowl, 13" l., 6½" h., clear oblong
eight-ribbed form w/symmetrically
ruffled edges, acid-marked
"Steuben" 330.00
Vase, 4½" h., folded handkerchief
design, amethyst, ca. 1920 ...... 440.00
Vase, 6¼" h., 11½" l., four-lobed
fanned & ruffled sides in Jade
Blue, marked w/the Steuben
fleur-de-lis mark on base
(ILLUS.) 3,850.00

Vase, 9 1/8" h., pedestal-based
ovoid quatreform body tapering to
a widely flaring ruffled rim, shaded green to clear, Steuben fleur-
de-lis mark on base 330.00

IVRENE

Fan-Shaped Ivrene Vase

Bowl, 12" d., 5½" h., deep flaring
four-lobed ruffled sides w/four
heavy ribs, shape No. 7449 ...... 395.00
Vase, 4" h., footed cylindrical base
w/flared ruffled rim, shape
No. 354, signed 225.00
Vase, 9½" h., 10½" w., deep flaring fan-shaped bowl w/ten lightly
molded ribs, raised on a short
stem & wide round foot, white
iridescence, partial paper label
on base (ILLUS.)................ 495.00
Vase, 10½" h., 10½" d., wide ovoid
body tapering to a short flared
neck, smooth creamy ivory
color......................... 770.00
Vase, 12" h., triple, trumpet-form
central vase flanked by two jack-
in-the-pulpit-form vases, all on
a circular base, etched Steuben
mark......................... 935.00

JADE

Green Jade Acid-Cutback Vase

Goblet, green Jade, 9" h. 500.00
Model of a duck, green Jade, shape
No. 6332 . . . . 550.00
Mug, iced tea, green Jade w/Ala-
baster handle 125.00
Vase, 7" h., footed ovoid body
w/flared rim, green Jade w/Ala-
baster base, engraved York patt.,
w/original label, shape No. 938 . . 875.00
Vase, 7" h., spherical, green Jade,
acid-cut fir cone decoration, shape
No. 6078 . . . . 950.00
Vase, 7" h., 7" d., spherical body
w/closed mouth, green Jade 330.00
Vase, 9 7/8" h., wide cylindrical
body w/rounded shoulder to a
wide cylindrical neck w/flared
rim, green Jade overlaid on
opalescent & acid-cut w/a design
of sparrows in blossoming prunus
branches against a stylized cloud-
ed sky between borders of
lappets, ca. 1925, unsigned
(ILLUS.) 1,320.00
Vase, 10" h., footed, green Jade
w/Alabaster base, Optic Fan
patt. 595.00
Vase, 10¾" h., classical urn-form
body in green Jade applied w/Al-
abaster double wishbone handles
at the shoulders, shape No. 2939,
signed in script 1,045.00
Vase, 11¼" h., tall baluster-form
w/a tall waisted neck, deep yellow iridescent ground, the sides
applied w/a dark blue iridescent
leafy vine winding up to the
shoulder, drilled & w/original
lamp fittings, ca. 1920 . . . . 1,920.00

MOSS AGATE

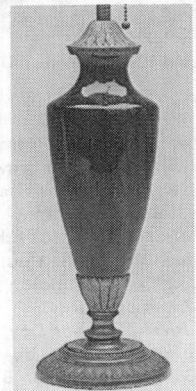

Moss Agate Lamp

Lamp, table model, the tapering
baluster-form body in unusual
silver speckled & cracked dark
amethyst w/swirls of blue, red,

amber, green & black, mounted
within beaded & foliate-molded
gilt-metal platform base & below
a conforming cap w/a two-socket
fitting, overall 25" h. (ILLUS.) 1,760.00
Vase, 11 7/8" h., tall ovoid body on
a domed foot & tapering to a
short neck w/a flattened flaring
rim, transparent amber cracque-
lure sides decorated internally
w/swirls in moss green, emerald
green, rust & amber, signed "F.
Carder - Steuben" 6,600.00

POMONA GREEN

Compotes, shallow circular bowl
raised on a columnar stem & pedestal base, shape No. 6044, pr. . . . 525.00
Dresser jar w/original self-threaded
stopper, swirl rib pattern, shape
No. 6887, 6" h. 165.00
Model of a cat, green & topaz,
shape No. 6044 . . . . 550.00
Pitcher, 9½" h., wide ovoid green
body w/a narrow shoulder below
the short cylindrical neck w/a
pinched spout, the interior molded
w/light ribbing, applied amber
handle, shape No. 6232 . . . . 275.00
Plates, 9" d., green rim on clear
bases, set of 10 . . . . 310.00

ROSALINE

Bowl, 3" d., 3" h., Rosaline bowl on
Alabaster pedestal foot, signed . . 245.00
Bowl, 8" d., 4½" h. 195.00
Bowl, 12" d., 4" h., widely flaring
pink bowl on a white Alabaster
foot 357.50
Finger bowls w/underplates,
conical-shaped Rosaline bowl on
Alabaster pedestal foot, shape
No. 3550, set of 12 . . . . 1,600.00
Powder jar, cov., bulbous ovoid
shouldered base w/a conforming
cover, 3¾" d., 3" h. 302.50
Vase, 4½" h., shaded Rosaline body
on Alabaster base 350.00

SILVERINA

Bowl, 10" d., Diamond Quilted
patt., blue, signed "Steuben - F.
Carder" 1,200.00
Vase, 10" h., conical body tapering
toward the foot, yellow molded
w/an air-trap diamond design &
flecked w/mica, acid-stamped
mark 330.00
Vase, 10" h., tall slightly tapering
cylindrical form w/a flared base,
yellow molded w/an air-trap diamond design & flecked w/mica,
signed (ILLUS. top next page) 660.00

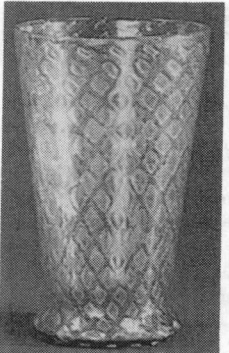

Silverina Vase

Wine, the slender bell-shaped citron
yellow bowl w/mica flecks in a
diamond air-trap design, raised
on a clear rib-molded stem on an
applied yellow foot, fleur-de-lis
mark on base, 6¾" h. 357.50

THREADED

Candlestick, clear w/a wide deep
flaring candle socket threaded in
green, the tall slender swelled
shaft in a swirled design applied
w/a band of four small green
prunts, on a domed base w/ap-
plied green rim thread, 12¼" h.
(some interior stain in shaft) 220.00
Compote, 6" d., 3" h., clear pedes-
tal, bowl w/pink threading. 150.00
Goblets, clear w/cranberry thread-
ing, pr. 180.00
Parfait & underplate, clear w/ruby
threading, signed, 2 pcs. 225.00
Vase, 6" h., clear body w/Flemish
Blue threading, unsigned 150.00
Vase, 6" h., waisted cylindrical clear
body w/green threading around
the top, shape No. 6817, signed . . 130.00

TOPAZ

Center bowl, domed foot w/deep
flaring fan-shaped bowl w/ribbed
design, shape No. 7463, 15" w. . . . 250.00
Goblet, footed w/wide stem, Topaz
w/applied Celeste Blue prunts &
rigaree on the stem 100.00

VERRE DE SOIE

Compote, cov., 6" h., squatty bulbous clear iridescent bowl w/a
short flared neck supporting a
low-domed cover button finial in
Celeste Blue, the bowl raised on
a slender tapering swirled Celeste Blue stem on a Celeste Blue
foot. 825.00
Flower bowl, optic panels, 6½" d.,
4¼" h., ... 110.00

Perfume bottle w/original teardrop-
shaped stopper, melon-ribbed
body, blue Jade stopper, shape
No. 1455, 5" h. 450.00
Perfume bottle w/original stopper,
clear iridescent slender slightly
tapering cylindrical body on a
round foot, a short cylindrical
neck w/flared rim fitted w/a hollow teardrop stopper, overall
8" h. 357.50
Perfume bottle & stopper, tall slen-
der teardrop-form body on a slender stem & disc foot, clear slightly
iridescent body, the pointed teardrop stopper in white Calcite
cased in deep red, overall
10" h. 1,760.00
Rose bowl, squatty melon-ribbed
body, shape No. 617 . . . . 110.00
Vase, bud-type, 10" h., footed, conical body tapering in at the neck &
flaring to a scalloped rim, engraved overall w/floral sprays,
shape No. 451 . . . . 275.00

MISCELLANEOUS WARES

Engraved Bicentennial Goblet

Bowl, 12½" d., clear crystal w/deep
slightly flaring sides above a high
domed base w/six wide buttress
ribs, the bowl centrally engraved
on the side w/a Christmas shepherd scene below "Christmas" &
w/small border designs for other
holidays which are spelled out
"Thanksgiving" - "Washington's
Birthday," "Memorial Day" -
"Fourth of July" & "Labor Day,"
exhibition piece No. 0061, designed by George Thompson &
Bruce Moore, 1954, w/original red
velvet box .6,600.00
Bust of an old woman, *cire perdue*
technique, her hair pulled back &
head slightly tilted up, clear frosted, executed by Frederick Carder,

ca. 1930, signed "F. Carder,"
5¼" h. . . . . .ɾ. 3,575.00
Candelabra, clear crystal, two-light,
a thick foot w/slightly flaring
sides supporting a tapering cylindrical stem w/a large interior air-
trap topped by a large teardrop
finial w/airtrap flanked by a pair
of thick, flat applied arms each
w/a flat-rimmed candle socket,
designed by George Thompson,
shape No. 8050, ca. 1952, 10" h.,
pr. 990.00
Center bowl, clear crystal, widely
flaring low sides tapering down to
six applied ball feet, designed
by John Dreves, marked, 15" d.,
5" h. 220.00
Champagnes, air-twist stems, clear
crystal, set of 8 . . . . 800.00
Goblet, clear crystal, Bicentennial
commemorative, the bell-form
bowl engraved w/an American
eagle emblem below a thirteen
star crest & dates "1776" & "1976,"
applied knopped stem w/airtrap
teardrop, applied disc foot, designed by Donald Pollard, 1975, in
original red velvet box, 8" h.
(ILLUS.) 1,650.00
Goblet, engraved Van Dyke patt.,
clear bowl w/amber stem, signed,
8" h. 350.00
Models of gazelles, clear crystal,
model No. 7399, pr. 460.00
Model of a partridge in a pear tree,
a crystal pear w/an applied 18kt
gold pear tree & partridge, w/red
leather case, 5¾" h. 2,200.00
Model of a songbird w/upright tail,
clear crystal, model No. 8112,
signed, 4½" l. 275.00
Plates, 10" d., clear crystal, "Au-
dubon" series, each engraved on
the reverse w/a different bird including a swallow-tailed kite,
ruffed grouse, osprey, white pelican, great blue heron, bald eagle,
flamingo, horned grebe, mountain
quail, Canada goose, barred owl
& wild turkey, each signed "S,"
ca. 1940, set of 12 . . . . .7,150.00

STEVENS & WILLIAMS

This long-established English glasshouse
has turned out a wide variety of artistic glass-
wares through the years. Fine satin glass
pieces and items with applied decoration
(sometimes referred to as "Matsu-No-Ke") are
especially sought after today. The following
represents a cross-section of its wares.

Stevens & Williams Rock Crystal Vase

Bowl, 7 3/8" d., 3¾" h., satin glass,
three-lobed clover leaf-form top
w/tightly crimped rim, shaded
gold to aqua mother-of-pearl satin
Swirl patt., robin's egg blue lin-
ing $895.00
Cameo vase, 4¼" h., heat reactive
dark red-maroon shaded to reddish orange overlaid in white &
cut w/jonquil bud & blossom
w/long spiked leaves, linear borders, circular mark "Stevens &
Williams Stourbridge Art Glass" . . 825.00
Cameo vase, 5¼" h., 2¾" d., squatty bulbous body w/clear wafer
foot, tall slender stick neck, white
overlaid w/pink & cameo cut w/a
fern decoration & white dots &
bands 275.00
Cameo vase, 12" h., tall double-
gourd shape w/slender neck,
bright turquoise blue layered in
white & extensively cameo-cut
w/nasturtium blossoms & embellished w/medial & rim borders of
repeating stylized floral designs,
stamped mark "Stevens & Wil-
liams Art Glass - Stourbridge" . . .3,575.00
Cracker jar, cov., barrel-shaped,
creamy white exterior w/applied
amber & green long ruffled
leaves, pink lining, silver plate
rim, cover & angled bail handle,
5½" d., 7¾" h. 275.00
Creamer, bulbous body w/ruffled
rim, opaque white exterior w/ap-
plied blue flower, green leaves
& amber handle, pink lining,
2¾" d., 2 7/8" h. 295.00
Cruet w/original clear facet-cut
stopper, footed amber ovoid body
w/overall white crackle design,
clear applied rigaree around rim
& base, applied cranberry handle,
3½" d., 9¼" h. 145.00
Jar, cov., cylindrical cranberry body
w/overall white crackle design,

domed cover w/clear facet-cut
knob finial, clear applied rigaree
band around base & rim, 3¾" d.,
5¾" h. 75.00

Rose bowl, 'Jewell' line, spherical
blue body w/molded Thumbprint
patt. & overall applied fine
threading, 2¼" h. 180.00

Rose bowl, six-crimp top, bulbous
shape, pink & white vertical
stripes in clear, 2¾" d., 2½" h. . . . 95.00

Rose bowl, satin glass, egg-shaped
w/box-pleated top, shaded brown
satin exterior decorated w/heavy
gold enameled branches & flowers, creamy white lining, 3½" d.,
4 7/8" h. 450.00

Tumbler, cut overlay, royal blue cut
to pink w/flowers & ovals design,
2½" d., 4¾" h. 60.00

Vase, 4½" h., 2" d., cylindrical,
grey background decorated w/a
white & grey bird perched on a
branch w/red berries & green &
blue leaves, gold trim 45.00

Vase, 5 1/8" h., 5" d., satin glass,
wide baluster-form body w/flaring
neck, green shaded to rose
mother-of-pearl satin Swirl patt. . . 895.00

Vase, 6" h., 5" d., bulbous spherical
creamy white body tapering to a
short cylindrical neck w/applied
transparent green edging &
flanked by applied green loop
stem handles, the body applied
w/a large ruffled amber & green
leaf w/a cranberry center wrapping around the sides, pink lin-
ing 165.00

Vase, 8¼" h., 5 7/8" d., 'Fibrilose'
line, bulbous body tapering to a
short neck w/flaring inverted rim,
clear w/heavy applied emerald
green random threading, marked
"#36653" 345.00

Vase, 9¼" h., 'Rock Crystal' line,
quintal-style w/a fan-shaped body
pinched into five openings at the
top, set on a stepped square platform base, intaglio cut in a scrolling floral design, engraved on
the base "S. & W. Patent N24048"
(ILLUS.). 495.00

Vase, 10¼" h., 4¼" d., tall ovoid
body tapering to a narrow neck
flaring to a ruffled rim, pink &
white swirled stripes in clear 195.00

Vase, 10¼" h., 5½" d., footed
baluster-form white cased body
w/applied angled amber thorn
handles, applied around the body
w/an amber branch w/three large
red cherries & blue leaves 895.00

Vase, 12" h., cut overlay, tall ovoid
double-gourd form body, intaglio
cut-back, crystal overlaid in bright
green & carved & engraved w/sin-
uous stylized flowers & leaves &
narrow geometric bands, a star-
cut base, late 19th c. 1,430.00

STRETCH

*Collectors have given this name to a
Carnival-type glass that is iridescent and
with a surface somewhat resembling the skin
of an onion. It was made in various glass factories and some is now being reproduced.*

Bowl, 8½" d., paneled, blue $50.00
Bowl, 8½" d., light blue 25.00
Bowl, 8½" d., white 25.00
Bowl, 9½" d., footed, ribbed interi-
or, blue 35.00
Bowl, 10" d., flared rim, green 20.00
Bowl, 10" d., rolled rim, green 25.00
Bowl, 10" d., flared rim, heavenly
blue 25.00
Compote, 6½" d., 5½" h., zipper
notched pedestal base, bright
green 48.00
Console bowl w/rolled rim, orange,
11½" d. 35.00
Console set: 10" d. bowl & pair of
candleholders; blue, 3 pcs. 35.00
Mayonnaise bowl w/underplate,
white 22.00
Sandwich server, center handled,
green, square. 25.00
Vase, 5" h., 8" w., fan-shaped,
white iridescent 110.00

TIFFANY

Tiffany Box with Enameled Cover

*This glassware, covering a wide diversity
of types, was produced in glasshouses operated by Louis Comfort Tiffany, America's
outstanding glass designer of the Art Nouveau period, from the last quarter of the 19th
century until the early 1930's. Tiffany revived
early techniques and devised many new ones.*

Bowl, 6" d., 3" h., flaring slightly undulating rim above deep sides w/ten molded swirled ribs, the interior wheel-cut w/a grapevine decoration, amber w/gold iridescent finish, signed "L.C. Tiffany Inc. Favrile - 5" $660.00

Box, cov., squatty circular footed body in gold iridescent glass, fitted w/a flattened circular copper cover enameled in ruby red, green, cobalt blue & salmon w/a swirled pattern, base engraved "5247D L.C. Tiffany - Favrile," cover stamped "A. DOUGLAS NASH CORP. 807," 5¼" d. (ILLUS.) 1,210.00

Cameo vase, 11 3/8" h., elongated ovoid footed body w/cylindrical neck in clear internally decorated w/olive green & lavender trailings, overlaid in deepest purple & grass green & intaglio carved w/pendent fruiting grapevines & leafage, designed for the Panama Pacific Exposition, inscribed "L.C. Tiffany Favrile 4327A" & "Panama Pacific Ex." 11,000.00

Candlesticks, paperweight-type, widely flaring rim decorated w/cobalt blue & green millifiore blossoms, emerald green trailing & leafage & radiating opalescent ribbing, continuing through the bulbous stem & base, each inscribed "L.C. Tiffany - Favrile," one numbered "3027P," ca. 1921, 4 1/8" h., pr. 5,228.00

Center bowl, ten-lobed body w/a very wide flat mouth above a deep swelled shoulder above gently tapering sides, transparent blue striped w/wide opaque opal-blue bands & further enhanced by swirled vertical ribbing, signed "L.C. Tiffany Inc. - Favrile - 5-7651 N," 8½" d., 4½" h. 2,750.00

Charger, circular, blue iridescent finish, carved w/vine leaves at the border, on three scrolled feet, engraved "L.C. Tiffany - Favrile," 10" d. 1,100.00

Compote, open, 5 1/8" d., 3" h., the shallow flaring opalescent bowl w/an internal leaf design & stretched iridescent bright green surface, raised on a short opal stem & disc foot, signed "L.C. Tiffany Favrile 5-1700" 770.00

Cordials, small bell-shaped bowl on a tall slender stem on a disc foot, overall gold iridescence, each marked "L.C.T. Favrile," 4½" to 4¾" h., set of 9 . . . . 1,100.00

Fingerbowls, round w/scalloped

rim, blue iridescent finish, each engraved "L.C.T.," 5" d., pr. 550.00

Goblet, Venetian-style, the delicate waisted cylindrical opalescent & ribbed bowl in transparent yellow raised on a double-bulbed hollow stem on a disc foot, marked "L.C. Tiffany - Favrile," 7¾" h. 440.00

Goblets, irregular rim in clear internally decorated w/mottled white radiating vertical streaks & edged in pale lavender, inscribed "L.C. Tiffany Favrile," ca. 1925, set of 8 . . . . 7,425.00

Inkwell, cased green body w/internal inclusions, vertical iridescent decorations, inscribed "L.C. Tiffany Favrile 112 A-Coll," 1 9/16" h. 495.00

Jar, cov., cylindrical, iridescent finish w/gold & green highlights, sterling silver rim, flat monogrammed mechanically-lifting cover & bail handle, glass marked "LCT," silver cover marked "Tiffany & Co.," 3¾" h. plus handle. . . . 550.00

Liqueur set: decanter w/original stopper & six stemmed cordials; the decanter w/a shouldered ovoid body w/a long cylindrical neck & knopped stopper, the cordials w/bell-form cup, rod standard & circular foot, rich amber iridescence, decanter inscribed "L.C. Tiffany Favrile," the cordials unsigned, 1892-1928, decanter 9 7/8" h., 7 pcs. 2,300.00

Ornament, leaded glass, constructed as a large moth w/body & wing centers of deep cobalt blue damascene decorated w/iridescent trailing, the outer wing sections in green & white mottled & striated opalescent, smoky grey section between wings, unsigned, 1899-1928, 11½" w. 3,575.00

Plaque, rectangular, mosaic landscape depicting a stream flowing through rolling hills, w/Lombardy poplars in the distance, all in iridescent glass w/Cypriote & damascene textures, the flowers in the foreground in shades of red, purple & rose, unsigned, 1899-1922, 7 5/8" w., 10 1/8" h. 10,350.00

Plate, 8" d., mold-blown w/18 light ribs in the white opal ground decorated w/a large central five-petal gold iridescent blossom framed by three gold iridescent rings, signed on the back "L.C.T. K2357" 715.00

Sherbets, Victoria patt., overall

amber iridescence, each signed
"L.C.T.," 3½" h., set of 5 . . . . 3,025.00

Sherry glasses, wide inverted bell-
form bowl on a slender faceted
stem, overall amber iridescence,
signed either "L.C.T. - Favrile," or
"L.C.T.," 3 7/8" h., set of 7 . . . . . . 1,870.00

Vase, 1 3/8" h., cabinet-type, the
squat waisted vessel in deep
iridescent red decorated about the
neck w/wavy trailing gold iridescent lines, inscribed "L.C.T.
Favrile 3918P" 1,860.00

Vase, 4" h., bottle-form w/bulbous
neck, amber iridescent decorated
w/iridescent loopings & pulled
trailings in olive green & silver
iridescence, inscribed "L.C.T.
B1638," w/original paper label,
ca. 1894 . . . . 2,588.00

Vase, 4 7/8" h., "Lava," irregular
ovoid body in amber distorted &
decorated w/thick amber iridescence randomly splashed over a
deep cobalt blue textured ground,
signed "L.C. Tiffany - Favrile
6025K," ca. 1916 . . . . 26,400.00

Vase, 7¾" h., paperweight-type,
shouldered ovoid body, pale yellowish green internally decorated
w/greenish ochre stems & leaves,
w/blossoms of giant molded
millefiori composed of thin
strands of purple, blue & green
encased in creamy white, the
whole cased in clear, the interior
in stretched iridescence, inscribed
"L.C. Tiffany-Favrile 8159D," ca.
1909 . . . . 8,800.00

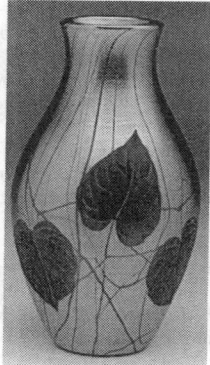

Tiffany Vase

Vase, 8 5/8" h., baluster-form body
in iridescent golden amber
w/green inclusions wheel-cut
w/broad naturalistic leaves &
vines, marked on base "L.C. Tiffa-
ny Favrile 3403L" (ILLUS.) 3,025.00

Vase, 13½" h., bell-form w/ruffled
rim, raised on a bulbous stem & a
gently waisted domical base,
opalescent body decorated
w/green feathering, the interior
in amber iridescence, opalescent
& green stem, the base further
decorated w/green feathering, inscribed "L.C.T. N4798," ca. 1900 . . 4,400.00

Vase, 19" h., jack-in-the-pulpit
flower-form, widely flaring flattened rim on a very slender stick
body over a squatty bulbous foot,
amber w/bright stretched iridescent finish, labeled & signed "L.C.
Tiffany Favrile 7783B" 3,300.00

Wall sconce, three-light, each bell-
form shade w/ruffled rim, pale
yellow opalescent decorated
w/feathering in golden yellow &
green, each fitting into a gilt-
bronze petal-form socket & curved
arm conjoined to a wall fitting,
shades inscribed "L.C.T.," 1899-
1928, 12½" w. 3,740.00

Water sprinkler, bulbous spherical
base w/a long slender curved
goose-neck w/jack-in-the-pulpit
rim, silvery blue iridescence over
turquoise blue, decorated in a
molded diamond quilted pattern,
inscribed "o1145," ca. 1894-1918,
14¾" h. 17,600.00

Wine, Rhine-type, blue opalescence,
signed "L.C.T. Favrile" 500.00

Wines, Royal patt., bell-form cup
raised on a spirally twisted stem
& circular foot, amber iridescent,
inscribed "L.C.T." & numbered, ca.
1900, set of 12 . . . . 5,500.00

TIFFIN

*A wide variety of fine glasswares were
produced by the Tiffin Glass Company of
Tiffin, Ohio. Beginning as a part of the large
U.S. Glass Company early in this century, the
Tiffin factory continued making a wide range
of wares until its final closing in 1984. One
popular line is now called "Black Satin" and
included various vases with raised floral designs. Many other acid-etched and hand-cut
patterns were also produced over the years
and are very collectible today. The three
"Tiffin Glassmasters" books by Fred Bick-
enheuser, are the standard references for
Tiffin collectors.*

Champagne, etched Adam patt.,
pink $30.00

Champagne, etched Cherokee Rose
patt., clear, 5½ oz. 20.00

Champagne, etched Flanders patt.,
yellow 22.50
Champagne, etched Persian Pheas-
ant patt., clear................. 25.00
Cocktail, etched June Night patt.,
clear 18.00
Compote, open, 7½" d., deep flaring bowl on a short twisted stem
& disc foot, Black Satin 40.00
Compote, open, 8½" d., 5½" h.,
Canterbury patt., clear 145.00
Console bowl, footed, etched Byzan-
tine patt., clear, 12" d. 40.00
Cordial, etched Cherokee Rose
patt., shape No. 17399, clear 45.00
Flower arranger, cut Twilight patt.,
No. 9115-112, clear 5" 55.00
Flower floater set: 14½" l. oblong
dish w/three candle sockets &
10" h. removable model of a
fawn; clear, late 1940s, 2 pcs..... 65.00
Goblet, water, etched Cherokee
Rose patt., clear, 9 oz. 25.00
Goblet, etched June Night patt.,
clear w/gold trim 25.00
Goblet, water, etched La Fleure
patt., topaz, 8" h. 32.00
Goblet, water, etched Persian
Pheasant patt., clear, 10 oz. 15.00
Goblet, cut Wisteria patt., Desert
Red, 1954-61 .... 25.00
Parfaits, etched Cherokee Rose
patt., clear, 4½ oz., set of 4 ..... 160.00
Plate, 6" d., etched Flanders patt.,
yellow 8.50
Plate, 8" d., etched Cherokee Rose
patt., clear 18.50
Plate, 8" d., etched June Night
patt., clear 10.00
Plate, 8" d., etched Persian Pheas-
ant patt., pink 23.00
Plate, torte, 14" d., etched Byzan-
tine patt., clear 45.00
Punch set: 10 qt. bowl, 20" d. un-
derplate & eleven cups; Williams-
burg patt., clear, 13 pcs.......... 180.00
Sherbet, Canterbury II patt.,
amber 8.00
Sherbet, etched June Night patt.,
clear 20.00
Sherbet, tall, etched Persian Pheas-
ant patt., clear................. 18.00
Sundae, etched Flanders patt.,
No. 24, clear 14.00
Tumbler, juice, etched Cherokee
Rose patt., clear, 5 oz. 25.00
Tumbler, juice, etched Coronada
patt., clear 45.00
Tumbler, iced tea, Diamond Optic
patt., Twilight (blue-lavender) 49.00
Tumbler, iced tea, etched Fuchsia
patt., clear 22.00
Tumbler, iced tea, etched Persian
Pheasant patt., clear, 12 oz. 20.00

Tumbler, iced tea, cut Wisteria
patt., Desert Red............... 25.00
Vase, bud, 8" h., etched Cherokee
Rose patt., clear 30.00
Vase, bud, 10" h., etched June
Night patt., clear............... 32.00
Vase, fan-shaped, pedestal base,
paneled flattened fan-shaped
body w/openwork scalloped rim,
Black Satin, No. 310 .... 60.00
Vase, tall trumpet-form body on a
disc foot, Black Satin ground
w/gold cattails decoration & gold
trim on the rim & foot 60.00
Water set: pitcher & six footed tum-
blers; etched Cadena patt., clear,
7 pcs. 185.00
Wine, etched Cherokee Rose patt.,
clear 30.00
Wine, etched Flanders patt., pink ... 60.00
Wine, etched June Night patt.,
clear 20.00

VALLERYSTHAL

Silver-Mounted Vallerysthal Vase

*Glass was made in Vallerysthal, France, for
several centuries until 1939 when the factory there was demolished during the war. Most
of its glass available to the collector today is
of fairly recent vintage.*

Animal covered dish, dog on rug,
amber, 5" $95.00
Animal covered dish, dog on rug,
blue opaque, 5"................. 95.00
Animal covered dish, fish, pink 75.00
Animal covered dish, hen, blue
opaque, 5" 85.00
Covered dish, model of a cabbage,
blue opaque 50.00
Plate, 8" d., Thistle patt., green 80.00
Sugar bowl, cov., embossed grape &
leaf design on top & base, green
opalescent..................... 50.00

Vase, 7 3/8" h., tapering cylinder, amber cased over white & clear, decorated w/an acid-etched design of wild grasses & blossoms, finely enameled in pale pink & blue & decorated at the top & base w/floral filigree silver mounts, signed in enamel "Vallerysthal," ca. 1900 (ILLUS.) 1,320.00

VAL ST. LAMBERT

This Belgian glassworks was founded in 1790. Items listed here represent a sampling of its numerous and varied lines.

Box, cov., ring-shaped finial, opaque blue w/fiery opalescent Basketweave patt., embossed "Val St. Lambert, Belgique," 4" d., 3¾" h. $85.00

Cameo vase, 6" h., 2½" d., barrel-shaped, intaglio-cut clear spear-shaped leaves connected by a center band on a ruby red ground, signed 225.00

Cameo vase, 10" h., an ovoid body w/a tall, slender cylindrical neck, frosted clear overlaid in lavender & cut w/sprays of wildflowers & leafage, signed in intaglio "Val - St. Lambert - Made in - Belgium," ca. 1900 . . . . .1,320.00

Cologne bottle w/original large spherical facet-cut stopper, cylindrical amber cut to clear overlay body w/Diamond & Arch patt., 6¼" h. 95.00

Cologne bottle w/original frosted sapphire blue ball stopper, cylindrical body w/deep shoulder to a short cylindrical neck w/a flat flaring rim, frosted sapphire blue w/embossed flower & leaf design, 2½" d., 5½" h. 85.00

Goblets, cut overlay, ruby cut to clear w/frosted panels decorated w/gold figures, set of 8 . . . . 960.00

VASELINE

This glass takes its name from its color, which is akin to that of petroleum jelly used for medicinal purposes. Pieces below are miscellaneous. Also see OPALESCENT GLASS and PATTERN GLASS.

Basket, bonnet-shaped, 8¾" h. $145.00
Cake stand, scalloped rim, opales-

cent William & Mary patt., England, 8 7/8" d., 4¼" h. 118.00
Celery vase, Beaumont's Columbia patt., Beaumont Glass Co. 70.00
Celery vase w/pedestal foot, opalescent Rib patt., England, 3 3/8" d., 6 7/8" h. 95.00
Cologne bottle w/original Maltese Cross-shaped stopper, octagonal body, 1¾" d., 4" h. 65.00
Creamer, block pattern bulbous base w/ribbed pattern flaring neck w/scalloped rim, applied vaseline handle, 2 1/8" d., 2¼" h. 44.00
Creamer & sugar bowl, opalescent Beaded Block patt., pr. 75.00
Paperweight, model of a book, intaglio cutting, 1¾ x 2¾ x 4¼" . . . 195.00
Plate, 8" d., Octagon patt. 12.00
Salt dip, master, w/clear applied rigaree edge trim, in silver plate footed frame, 3" d., 2¼" h. 110.00
Table set: creamer, cov. sugar bowl, spooner & cov. butter dish; Beaumont's Columbia patt., 4 pcs. 295.00
Water set: pitcher & six tumblers; Beaumont's Columbia patt., 7 pcs. . . . . .250.00 to 275.00

VENETIAN

Venetian Figure of Black Dancer

Venetian glass has been made for six centuries on the island of Murano, where it continues to be produced. The skilled glass artisans developed numerous techniques, subsequently imitated elsewhere.

Bowl, 7½" w., 6 1/8" h., applied rounded quatreform gold-flecked rim on a deep rounded conforming bowl of blue & clear internally decorated w/trapped air-bubble squares & circles & gold inclusions, ca. 1950's $357.50

Candelabrum, hyacinth blue ground decorated w/polychrome enamel figures of nude males in action poses holding weapons & animals, gold grisaille borders, 11" w., 14" h. 495.00

Compote, open, 6½" d., 8" h., eight-lobed bulbous bowl w/flanged rim & a swirled stem w/knob, gold "overshot" ground w/gold & aqua rim decoration 95.00

Console set: 9" l. rectangular bowl w/turned up sides & two 5¼" h. candlesticks w/applied leaf prunts; clear w/overall heavy gold swirled flecks, 3 pcs. 295.00

Decanter w/original stopper, head of a clown wearing a cone-shaped hat w/ball stopper at the top, decorated w/emerald & opaque white applied to apple green, overall 13" h. 275.00

Figure of a clown, standing, composed of multicolored blown glass w/a black hat & shoes, a horizontally striped suit, applied facial details & two applied dangling balls, w/original paper label, 7" h. 70.00

Figure of a lady, the black figure dancing, wearing a flaring dress & a broad-brimmed hat, ruffled sleeves & bodice trim, posed on a swirled clear foot w/gold flecks, 9½" h. (ILLUS.) 220.00

Goblet, red bowl, clear twisted stem highlighted w/gold flecks, 7" h. 155.00

Goblet, millefiori bowl w/gold dust flecks in stem, 7½" h. 210.00

Model of a bird, exotic creature w/tomato red back, aqua & grey breast w/silver dust accents & amber tail & crest, 15" 125.00

Model of an elephant, clear decorated w/red, amber, white & black accents, 8½" l. 110.00

Model of a fish, red & yellow w/controlled bubble decoration, 5" l. 100.00

Model of a pheasant, clear w/gold & deep brown flecks & controlled bubbles 100.00

Model of a rabbit, clear w/cobalt blue & gold ribbon design alternating w/white latticino bands, 8" l. 65.00

Sherbet, ruby bowl & clear stem w/gold knob, 4" d., 4½" h. 195.00

Vase, 8 3/8" h., wide ovoid body tapering to a short flared neck, Ercole Barovier design, brilliant cobalt blue applied w/white

Barovier-Designed Venetian Vase

wave-like bands up the sides divided by crude circles, engraved on the base "Barovier & Toso Murano" (ILLUS.) 1,210.00

Vase, 10 5/8" h., ovoid gourd-form tapering to a slender flaring slightly twisted neck, thick white textured walls cased within clear & enclosing scattered multicolored canes in yellow, orange, blue, black, pink & brown, designed by Ansolo Fuga, probably made by Arte Vetraria Muranese, ca. 1958 . . . . 1,100.00

VENINI

Founded by former lawyer Paolo Venini in 1925, this Venetian glasshouse soon developed a reputation for its fine quality decorative glass and tablewares. Several noted designers have worked for the firm over the years and their unique pieces in the modern spirit, made using traditional techniques, are increasingly popular with collectors today. The factory continues in operation.

Beverage set: tall slightly flaring cylindrical pitcher w/half the plain rim folded in to form a spout, & four slightly out-of-round cylindrical tumblers; each piece decorated w/narrow stripes alternating red, yellow, pink, blue & green, pitcher w/acid-stamped mark "Venini Murano Italia," 20th c., pitcher 6¾" h., 5 pcs. (spout lip of pitcher ground) $660.00

Bottle, Sommersi-type, flattened oval shouldered body w/a short flat neck, amber w/submerged opaque black decoration, acid-stamped mark w/"Venini Murano Italia," 20th c., 9" h. (some surface scratches) 1,210.00

Box, cov., circular, topaz bottom &
circular cover cased w/orange &
forming a pattern of irregular
spirals, engraved "venini italia,"
6¼" d. 660.00
Center bowl, "inciso," the deep
canoe-form vessel in thick grey
cased over orange, cut on the exterior w/fine concentric linear
striations, designed by Paolo
Venini, acid-stamped "venini -
ITALY - murano" within a circle,
ca. 1956, 11 3/8" l., 7¼" h. 4,400.00
Decanter w/original stopper, "bot-
tiglia con fascie," the waisted cylinder w/tapering neck & conical
stopper, decorated w/a vertical pattern in black & yellow,
designed by Fulvio Bianconi, ca.
1953, acid-stamped "venini
murano ITALIA," 17¾" h. 9,350.00

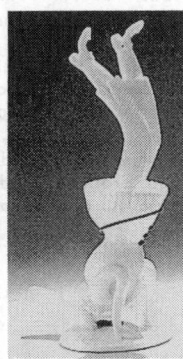

Venini "Commedia Dell'Arte" Figure

Figure, "Commedia dell'Arte" character in white, standing on its
head on a round base, black
detailing, designed by Fulvio Bian-
coni, 11½" h. (ILLUS.) 3,520.00
Model of a poodle, the black canine
w/white eyes, on a white base,
engraved mark "venini italia" &
original sticker, 5½" h. 440.00
Shade, hurricane-type, the double-
waisted cylindrical clear vessel
decorated w/red, blue & green
canes in a spiral pattern,
10½" h. .1,925.00
Vase, 4" h., "vaso a canne," flat
flaring sides in a compressed
cylindrical shape, composed of
translucent & transparent vertical
stripes of red, pale yellow, amethyst, blue, grey & green each
separated by clear narrow stripes,
1950's 330.00
Vase, 4¾" h., 9¾" d., "handker-
chief" style, a slumped bowl form
w/irregular flaring sides of brilliant orange & mauve-lavender

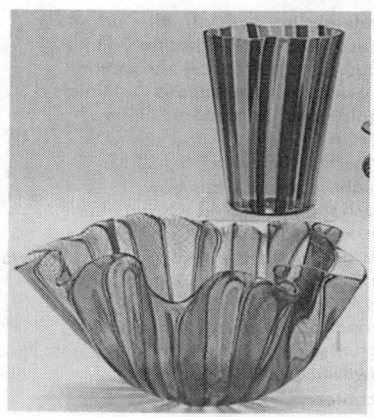

Venini Vases

latticino stripes, acid-stamped
mark "Venini Murano - Made in
Italy" (ILLUS. bottom) 495.00
Vase, 5¾" h., "vaso a canne," flar-
ing cylindrical body w/irregular
rim, striped design w/red, green,
grey, blue, amethyst & amber
stripes in recurring sequence, un-
signed (ILLUS. top) 660.00
Vase, 7½" h., "vetro pezzato arlec-
chino," free-form swollen cylinder, decorated w/a patchwork
pattern of irregular squares in
ruby red, sapphire blue, emerald
green & clear, designed by Fulvio
Bianconi, acid-stamped "Venini
Murano ITALIA" 10,450.00
Vase, 11¼" h., "fazzoletto,"
handkerchief-style w/a white &
light pink *zanfirico* design 1,650.00
Vase, 11 3/8" h., "vetro pezzato
arlecchino," swollen cylindrical
form, decorated w/a patchwork
pattern of irregular rectangles in
dark ruby red, emerald green,
sapphire blue & clear, designed
by Fulvio Bianconi, acid-stamped
"Venini Murano ITALIA" 8,800.00

VERLYS

*This glass is a relative newcomer for col-
lectors and is not old enough to be antique,
having been made since the 1930's in France
and the United States, but fine pieces are collected. Blown and molded pieces have been
produced.*

Ashtray, white opalescent
w/intaglio-cut butterflies & bevel-
cut rim, 3½ x 4½" $95.00
Bowl, 6" d., Cupid & Hearts patt.,
clear 40.00

Bowl, 8½" d., Thistle patt., clear ... 85.00

Bowl, 7 x 12", deep green, molded w/swimming fish, w/fin-shaped handles, raised signature "Verlys - France" 253.00

Console bowl, Birds & Bees patt., frosted clear, 11" d. 135.00

Console bowl, Tassels patt., clear, signed, 11" d..................... 100.00

Console bowl, Butterflies patt., clear, signed, 11½" d............ 115.00

Console bowl, Water Lily patt., amber, 14" d. 375.00

Console bowl, Water Lily patt., clear, 14" d. 110.00

Vase, 5" h., Butterflies patt., clear.. 225.00

Vase, 8½" h., clear ground decorated w/autumnal scene, signed 225.00

Vase, 9" h., Alpine Thistle patt., clear w/tan flowers & leaves 525.00

Vase, 9" h., Mandarin patt., clear...................275.00 to 295.00

Vase, 9" h., Thistle patt., beige ... 550.00

VICTORIAN COLORED GLASS

There are, of course, many types of colored glassware of the Victorian era and we cover a great variety of these in our various glass categories. However, there are some pieces of pressed, mold-blown and free-blown Victorian colored glass which don't fit well into other specific listings, so we have chosen to include a selection of them here.

Animal covered dish, Eagle on lacy base, blue opaque, Westmoreland Glass Co., marked "WG" on base, ca. 1970, 7½" l................. $70.00

Animal covered dish, Hen, black bird w/white head, basketweave base, Westmoreland Specialty Co., early 20th c., 5½" l. 250.00

Animal covered dish, Hen on basketweave base, blue opaque, Atterbury Glass Co., 7½" l. ....450.00 to 500.00

Animal covered dish, Hen on basketweave base, glass eyes, blue opaque, Challinor, Taylor & Co., 7½" l. 125.00

Animal covered dish, Owl Head on split-ribbed base, blue opaque, Atterbury...................... 150.00

Animal covered dish, Rabbit, iridescent caramel slag, Westmoreland Glass Co., marked "WG," ca. 1970, 5½" l. 45.00

Animal covered dish, Rooster on basketweave base, glass eyes, blue opaque, Challinor, Taylor & Co., 7½" l. 170.00

Animal covered dish, Swan w/raised wings on rectangular lacy base, blue opaque, Westmoreland Glass Co., marked "WG," ca. 1970 ..... 110.00

Bowl, 4¾" d., 5" h., spherical mold-blown sapphire blue optic pattern body w/flaring scalloped rim, body applied w/a clear flower & applied clear feet 165.00

Bowl, 5" d., 3" h., free-blown footed sapphire blue four-leaf clover shape w/fluted rim w/applied clear pointed edging, each corner decorated w/a h.p. gold bird perched on a branch 135.00

Box, cov., free-blown, sapphire blue decorated w/pink & yellow flowers & gold & yellow leaves & branches, 2½" d., 1¼" h.......... 145.00

Box w/hinged cover, free-blown, lime green decorated w/yellow buds, gold & silver flowers & leaves, 2¾" d., 1¼" h. 125.00

Box w/hinged cov., free-blown, lime green, cover decorated w/sanded gold panels containing dainty pink flowers, small daisies & gold & blue enameled trim & a small red jewel in the center, similar enamel decoration on sides, 3¾" d., 3¼" h. 110.00

Butter dish, cov., Georgia Gem patt., green opaque 165.00

Butter dish, cov., Scroll patt., blue opaque, Challinor, Taylor & Co. .. 175.00

Center bowl, mold-blown oblong pink opalescent diamond quilted body w/wide ribs, flaring crimped rim w/pulled-out end curls, on an applied leafy vaseline glass foot, 5½ x 10½", 6" h. 265.00

Cheese dish, cov., free-blown, emerald green, tall cylindrical cover w/deep shoulder & tall finial, matching underplate, each decorated w/white enameled fans, flowers & dots & gold scrolls & scallops, underplate 9½" d., overall 8¼" h. 195.00

Compote, open, Atlas patt., lace edge, blue opaque 180.00

Cracker jar, cov., free-blown, barrel-shaped, lime green enameled w/sprays of blue & pink flowers & green foliage overall, silver plate rim, cover w/finial & bail handle, 5" d., 6¾" h. 225.00

Cracker jar, cov., mold-blown Swirl patt., barrel-shaped, sapphire blue, ornate resilvered cover, rim & bail handle, 5" d., 7¾" h........ 245.00

Creamer & open sugar bowl, individual size, Georgia Gem patt., green opaque, pr................. 85.00

Cruet w/original stopper, Challinor's Tree of Life patt., blue opaque ... 95.00

Decanter w/original amber bulbous stopper, mold-blown, footed amber cut-paneled shouldered body tapering to a narrow cylindrical ringed neck w/flared rim, w/embossed scrolls & floral pewter overlay & pewter pedestal foot, 3¼" d., 8¾" h. 165.00

Decanter w/original sapphire blue steeple-shaped pointed stopper, mold-blown, footed ovoid golden amber body w/slender ringed neck w/flared rim, enameled w/white flowers & dots & gold trim, applied sapphire blue pedestal base, 3¾" d., 12½" h. 195.00

Goblet, free-blown, slightly flaring tall cylindrical cup raised on a pedestal foot, sapphire blue enameled w/large pink & white flower, sanded gold band & leaves & white enameled flowers w/orange centers decoration below, 2¾" d., 6 7/8" h. 75.00

Liqueur set: 8" h., 3" d. bulbous cruet w/three-petal top & original blue bulbous stopper & applied blue handle, six barrel-shaped mugs w/applied blue handles & 8½" d. tray; sapphire blue w/white lilies-of-the-valley & gold leaves decoration overall, 8 pcs... 325.00

Pitcher, water, 8½" h., 5" d., mold-blown optic design ovoid body w/a wide cylindrical neck, applied clear handle, sapphire blue decorated w/a band of large stylized blossoms 125.00

Pitcher, tankard, 12" h., 4½" d., mold-blown tall body w/bulbous wide rings around the bottom half, sapphire blue decorated w/panels of white flowers surrounding pink daisy-like blossoms, gold trim, applied blue handle ... 225.00

Pitcher, water, Georgia Gem patt., green opaque................... 95.00

Salt & pepper shakers w/original tops, Alba patt., blue opaque, 2½" h., pr. 45.00

Spooner, Waffle patt., green opaque....................... 35.00

Sugar shaker w/original top, Challinor's Forget-Me-Not patt., pink opaque......................... 165.00

Syrup pitcher w/original top, Grape & Leaf patt., blue opaque 295.00

Toothpick holder, Challinor's Tree of Life patt., apple green........... 45.00

Tumbler, Scroll patt., blue opaque .. 45.00

Tumbler, whiskey, free-blown, barrel-shaped, amber decorated

overall w/gold scrolls highlighted w/blue, yellow, lavender & orange dots, 2 1/8" d., 2¼" h. 40.00

Tumble-up (water carafe w/tumbler lid), free-blown, footed spherical body w/cylindrical neck fitted w/a tumbler, sapphire blue enameled w/large white flowers & gold leaves, 5" d., 8" h., 2 pcs. 210.00

Vase, 4½" h., 1¾" d., free-blown, footed slender cylindrical sapphire blue body cut w/panels & decorated w/gold bands & small enameled pink, blue & orange flowers w/green leaves 48.00

Vase, 8" h., model of a hand holding a scalloped rim cornucopia, blue opaque 45.00

Vase, 8 3/8" h., 3¼" d., free-blown, slender swelled cylindrical salmon pink body highlighted by mica flecks & applied w/a clear ruffled rigaree band down the sides, on applied clear swirl feet 55.00

Vases, 7" h., 3½" d., footed bulbous body tapering to a flaring neck w/scalloped rim, mold-blown Swirl patt., sapphire blue decorated overall w/dainty white enameled flowers & leaves & gold trim, pr............................ 245.00

Water set: 8½" h., 6" d. spherical pitcher w/cylindrical neck w/pinched spout & six 2½" d., 4 1/8" h. barrel-shaped mugs; all golden amber mold-blown Inverted Thumbprint patt., applied blue rope handles, 7 pcs.............. 225.00

WAVE CREST

Wave Crest Letter Holder

Now much sought after, Wave Crest was produced by the C.F. Monroe Co., Meriden, Connecticut, in the late 19th and early 20th centuries from opaque white glass blown into molds. It was then hand-decorated in enamels and metal trim was often added. Boudoir accessories such as jewel boxes, hair receivers, etc., were predominant.

Box w/hinged lid, Helmschmied Swirl mold, h.p. floral decoration on creamy white ground, 3" d. $150.00

Box w/hinged lid, Egg Crate mold, h.p. floral decoration on creamy white ground, 3" sq. 260.00

Box w/hinged lid, Embossed Rococo mold, cover decorated w/cupid & the side w/water scenes on a caramel ground, 3½" d. 325.00

Box w/hinged lid, Egg Crate mold, h.p. pink clover blossoms on a creamy white ground, 3½" sq., 3¼" h. 165.00

Box w/hinged lid, Embossed Rococo mold, h.p. pink flowers on a shaded aqua ground, 4½" d. 495.00

Box w/hinged lid, Embossed Rococo mold, h.p. floral decoration, red banner mark, 5½" oval 395.00

Box w/hinged lid, Egg Crate mold, the body decorated w/pink, white & amethyst vining florals, raised on an ornate gilt-metal scroll-footed base, 6" h. 605.00

Box w/hinged lid, Egg Crate mold, enameled floral decoration on the lid & gilt "Collars & Cuffs" on side, 6½" d. 950.00

Broom holder, embossed scrolling, h.p. floral decoration on a creamy white ground, w/ornate gilt metal frame 795.00

Cracker jar, cov., bulbous body, decorated w/clusters of blue flowers & green & brown foliage & scrolls on a soft blue ground, silver plate rim, cover & bail handle, 5½" d., 7¼" h. 295.00

Ewer, tall form w/an ovoid melon-lobed creamy white body decorated w/a transfer-printed scene of a young girl in a field, trimmed w/an attached gilt-metal high arched rim & spout & long S-scroll handle & raised on a scroll-molded footed gilt-metal base 115.00

Ewer, tall form w/an ovoid melon-lobed creamy white body decorated w/yellow flowers, trimmed w/an attached gilt-metal high arched rim & spout & long S-scroll handle & raised on a scroll-molded footed gilt-metal base 200.00

Ferner, Egg Crate mold, gilt-metal rim band & liner, h.p. dainty pink & blue flowers on a white ground, 7" w. 375.00

Ferner, round w/gilt metal rim band & liner, embossed scrolls & h.p. autumn leaves decoration 495.00

Jewel tray, Helmschmied Swirl mold, h.p. pink & white flowers & green leaves on a soft blue & white background, ornate ormolu handled rim, 5" d., 2" h. 275.00

Letter holder, plain rectangular form w/rounded corners, decorated w/a h.p. scene of a Victorian lady & girl w/butterfly net in a field, framed by a border of wavy leaves & blossomheads at the corners against a pale beige ground beaded overall w/white dots, gilt-metal arched backplate & rim band & footed base band (ILLUS.). 700.00

Napkin holder, Embossed Rococo mold, h.p. floral decoration, ormolu rim & lion head feet 395.00

Photo receiver, rectangular, Egg Crate mold, h.p. floral decoration on a creamy white ground, gilt-metal rim band 350.00

Salt & pepper shakers w/original tops, embossed tulip petal-shape, h.p. dainty floral decoration on a creamy white ground, pr. 50.00

Salt & pepper shakers w/original metal tops, tall cylindrical ring-neck mold, decorated w/cat sitting in foliage gazing at a spider web, pr. 195.00

Smoke set: cylindrical cigar holder & two match holders w/brass rims & bases, on the original round wooden tray; each creamy white w/delicate floral decoration, 4 pcs. 275.00

Sugar shaker w/original top, tapering cylindrical shape, enameled w/pastel fern decoration on a creamy white ground, 3" d., 4½" h. 195.00

Toothpick holder, cylindrical shouldered body w/beaded rim band, h.p. pink & yellow flowers on a creamy white ground, on a gilt-metal footed base 185.00

Tray, Helmschmied Swirl mold, decorated w/pink flowers on a light blue ground, ormolu trim & handles 375.00

Vase, bud, 3" h., scroll-molded elongated cylindrical neck on a squatty bulbous base, decorated w/pink flowers & green leaves on a creamy yellow ground, fitted w/a beaded embossed gilt-metal neck collar supporting two long, angled & scrolled handles, on an ornately molded, footed gilt-metal base 250.00

Vase, 3¾" x 4¼", squatty bulbous base tapering to a cylindrical neck

w/swelled inverted rim w/enam-
eled white beaded band, body
shaded green to white, lower
body decorated w/shiny green
lines forming random reserves,
each filled w/sea green floral
decorations, ormolu ringed base
w/paw feet.................... 525.00

Vase, 13¼" h., hexagonal body flaring at base, narrow shoulder &
short collared neck, pink shading
to blue ground decorated w/h.p.
florals & white enamel scrolling,
raised on ormolu footed platform
mount........................ 440.00

WEBB

Webb Cameo Vase

*This glass is made by Thomas Webb &
Sons of Stourbridge, one of England's most
prolific glasshouses. Numerous types of glass,
including cameo, have been produced by this
firm through the years. The company also
produced various types of novelty and "art"
glass during the late Victorian period. Also
see in "Glass" BURMESE, ROSE BOWLS,
and SATIN & MOTHER-OF-PEARL.*

Bowl, 7½" d., 5" h., crimped rim,
applied amber feet, the deep
sides decorated w/a wide band
of stylized draped multicolored
florals on a creamy white ground,
pink interior, signed............$450.00

Cameo bowl, 4¾" d., 2¾" h.,
squatty bulbous body w/a short
neck around the wide mouth,
raisin-mauve layered in white &
cameo-cut & completely carved
w/scrolling floral repetitive designs, stippled background in border execution, stamped "Thomas
Webb & Sons Gem Cameo" 7,150.00

Cameo scent bottle w/silver cap,
miniature, tiny ovoid body in yellow overlaid in white & cameo-cut
w/overall blossoms, decumbent
buds & leafy stems, hallmarked
sterling silver rim & cap, unsigned, 1¾" h.................. 550.00

Cameo vase, 6" h., footed bulbous
body w/a wide cylindrical neck,
frosted light blue ground overlaid
& cameo-cut in blue & white
w/morning glory vines & a flying
butterfly at the back, linear borders at top & base, semi-circular
early mark "Thomas Webb & Sons
Cameo" (ILLUS.) 1,650.00

Cameo vase, 6½" h., baluster-
shaped w/a wide flattened rim,
simulating carved ivory w/a scene
of three birds perched on a leaf &
berry-laden thorny branch against
an intricate lattice fence ground
below & stylized floral design
above, semi-circular impressed
mark "Thomas Webb & Sons" 6,600.00

Cameo vase, 8¼" h., bulbous conical body tapering to a flared rim
& raised on a wide flaring foot,
deep sapphire blue w/molded
neck ring, layered in sky blue &
white, hand-carved overall w/ap-
ple blossoms & buds on leafy
branches in high-relief w/excel-
lent detail, lappet borders above
& below, designed & carved by
George Woodall, signed "G.
Woodall" at lower side, base
marked "Thos. Webb & Sons
Gem Cameo" 23,100.00

Creamer, bulbous base tapering to
a tall cylindrical neck w/pinched
spout, w/applied clear frosted
handle, shaded heavenly blue
mother-of-pearl satin Diamond
Quilted patt., white interior,
3 1/8" d., 5" h. 325.00

Vase, 3¼" h., 2½" d., wide
baluster-form body w/slightly
flared rim, heavy gold decoration
overall w/gold butterfly on the
back, creamy ivory ground 195.00

Vase, 5½" h., 6½" d., squatty bulbous base tapering to a wide
cylindrical neck, shaded brown to
gold ground decorated w/heavy
gold prunus blossoms & feathery
flowers, gold trim, creamy white
interior....................... 595.00

Vase, 7½" h., 7 3/8" d., Rock Crystal, the wide flaring cylindrical
body engraved w/alternating
panels of bamboo latticework &
scenic reserves of Oriental landscapes including a fisherman,
pagoda, & storks, engraved by
William Fritsche & signed in script

Webb Rock Crystal Vase

"W. Fritsche" at the lower edge
(ILLUS.) 3,025.00
Vase, 9½" h., bulbous base taper-
ing to a long cylindrical neck,
decorated w/a gold, silver &
white bird on a yellow satin
ground, white interior, propeller
mark 415.00
Vase, 10¼" h., "Cluthra," slightly
tapering cylindrical body w/a
rounded shoulder to the cylindrical neck, mottled crystal incorporating shades of amethyst
w/yellow, red, blue & white striations & gold aventurine flecks,
signed "W & C England" 330.00

WESTMORELAND

*The Westmoreland Specialty Company was
founded in East Liverpool, Ohio in 1889 and
relocated in 1890 to Grapeville, Pennsylvania
where it remained until its closing in 1985.*

*During its early years Westmoreland
specialized in glass food containers and novelties but by the turn of the century they had
a large line of milk white items and clear
tableware patterns. In 1925 the company
name was shortened to The Westmoreland
Glass Company and it was during that decade that more colored glasswares entered
their line-up. When Victorian-style milk glass
again became popular in the 1940's and
1950's, Westmoreland produced extensive
amounts in several patterns which closely
resemble late 19th century wares. These and
their figural animal dishes in milk white and
colors are widely collected today but buyers
should not confuse them for the antique originals. Watch for Westmoreland's "WG" mark
on some pieces. A majority of our listings are
products from the 1940's through the 1970's.
Earlier pieces will be indicated.*

Animal covered dish, Cat on lacy
edge base, blue opaque w/glass
eyes, copied from the Atterbury
original . . . . $150.00 to 175.00
Animal covered dish, Fox on lacy
edge base, milk white, copied
from the Atterbury original 95.00
Animal covered dish, Fox on lacy
edge base, yellow slag, copied
from the Atterbury original 175.00
Animal covered dish, Hen on nest,
blue opaque, 5" l. 45.00
Animal covered dish, Hen on nest,
purple slag, 7½" l., 5¾" h. 55.00
Animal covered dish, Lamb on pick-
et base, blue opaque, copied from
antique original, 5½" l. 60.00
Animal covered dish, Lovebirds on
basketweave base, blue opaque . . 52.50
Animal covered dish, Rabbit on
picket base, purple slag, copied
from antique original, 5½" l. 50.00
Animal covered dish, Robin on Twig
Nest, Apricot Mist (frosted amber), copied from antique origi-
nal 65.00
Animal covered dish, Robin on Twig
Nest, light blue, copied from an-
tique original 55.00
Animal covered dish, Rooster,
standing, milk white, copied from
antique original 37.50
Ashtray, Paneled Grape patt., milk
white, 4" w. 10.00
Bowl, 3¾" d., Old Quilt (No. 500)
patt., milk white 12.00
Bowl, 6" d., Della Robbia (No. 1058)
patt., colored trim 25.00
Bowl, 8" d., Old Quilt patt., milk
white 32.50
Bowl, 10½" d., Paneled Grape
patt., milk white 70.00
Butter dish, cov., Paneled Grape
patt., clear, ¼ lb. 32.00
Butter dish, cov., Paneled Grape
patt., dark blue 45.00
Cake stand, Della Robbia patt.,
clear, 12" d. 35.00
Cake stand, Paneled Grape patt.,
milk white 85.00
Candleholders, English Hobnail
patt., clear, pr. 40.00
Candleholders, Lotus (No. 1921)
patt., pink opalescent, pr. 30.00
Candy dish, cov., Argonaut Shell
(No. 1048) patt., dolphin feet,
shell finial, milk white 38.00
Candy dish, cov., footed, Della Rob-
bia patt., clear, ½ lb. 40.00
Candy dish, cov., Della Robbia patt.,
milk white 10.00
Celery vase, Paneled Grape patt.,
milk white 28.00

Cologne bottle w/original stopper,
Lotus patt., black opaque 40.00

Compote, cov., 5 x 5", Beaded
Grape patt., clear 22.50

Console set: bowl & pair of candlesticks; Doric (No. 3) patt., Golden
Sunset (amber), 3 pcs. 50.00

Cookie jar, cov., handled, Cherry
(No. 109) patt., milk white 49.00

Creamer & open sugar bowl, Della
Robbia patt., colored trim, pr. 39.00

Creamer & cov. sugar bowl, Paneled
Grape patt., milk white, pr. 10.00

Cup & saucer, Beaded Edge (No. 22)
patt., milk white 10.00

Cup & saucer, Paneled Grape patt.,
clear 24.00

Goblet, water, Della Robbia patt.,
milk white, 6" h., 8 oz. 30.00

Goblet, Old Quilt patt., milk
white 20.00

Goblet, Paneled Grape patt., milk
white 15.00

Gravyboat & undertray, Paneled
Grape patt., clear, 2 pcs. 58.00

Mayonnaise bowl & underplate,
Paneled Grape patt., milk white,
2 pcs. 20.00

Pitcher, Old Quilt patt., milk white,
1 pt. 35.00

Pitcher, Paneled Grape patt., clear,
1 qt. 35.00

Planter, rectangular, footed, Paneled Grape patt., clear, 5 x 9" . . . 32.50

Plate, 10½" d., Beaded Edge patt.,
clear 18.00

Plate, torte, 15" d., Della Robbia
patt., clear 95.00

Punch set: punch bowl, undertray,
ten cups & ladle; Della Robbia
patt., colored trim, 13 pcs. 650.00

Sherbet, Della Robbia patt., colored
trim, 3½" h. 30.00

Table set: creamer, cov. sugar bowl,
cov. butter dish & spooner; Elite
(Pillow & Sunburst) patt., clear
w/gold trim, ca. 1890's, 4 pcs. 85.00

Tumbler, footed, Della Robbia patt.,
clear, 4¾" h. 12.00

Tumbler, footed, Della Robbia patt.,
colored trim, 6" h. 35.00

Tumbler, Paneled Grape patt., milk
white, 4¼" h. 15.00

Vase, 12" h., Paneled Grape patt.,
clear 12.00

Vase, 12" h., "swung"-type, Paneled
Grape patt., milk white 35.00

Wine set: decanter w/original stopper & five 2 oz. wines; Paneled
Grape patt., clear, 6 pcs. 110.00

(End of Glass Section)

GLOBE MAPS

English-made Terrestrial Globe

Celestial globe, floor model, the
globe turning in a mahogany
frame set upon a baluster-turned
pedestal raised on a tripod base
w/long curved spider legs ending
in spade feet, made by Cary's,
London, England, calculated to the
year 1800, late 18th c., globe
12" d., overall 34" h. (globe &
base restored) $3,575.00

Celestial globe, floor model, mounted within a brass meridian ring,
in a mahogany frame on turned
fluted legs joined by a compass
stretcher & brass feet on casters,
by G.F. Cruchley, London, England, first quarter 19th c., 28" d.,
4' h. 8,800.00

Celestial & terrestrial globes, floor
models, celestial globe marked
"Cary's New Celestial Globe, J.W.
Cary," the terrestrial globe signed
"Cary's New Terrestrial Globe,"
G. & J. Cary, England, each on a
similar mahogany tripod stand
w/horizon ring w/zodiacal calendar, first quarter 19th c., each
24½" h., pr. (losses, repairs) 8,800.00

Celestial & terrestrial globes, floor
models, terrestrial globe dated
1816, each mounted within a
brass meridian ring, on an urn-
form mahogany stand w/splayed
legs centered by a compass
stretcher, w/turned feet, by Cary,
Regency period, England, early
19th c., 16" d., 36" h., pr.
(repairs) 13,200.00

Celestial & terrestrial globes, table
models, mahogany, each globe
dated 1785 & mounted in a mahogany framework w/baluster-
turned legs joined by X-form
stretchers, by W. Bardin, George
III period, England, late 18th c.,
12" d., 13½" h., pr. (restora-
tions) 4,400.00

Terrestrial globe, floor model, globe
dated 1789, set within two brass
rings in a mahogany frame
w/square tapering legs joined by
arched stretchers centered by an
urn & compass, D. Adams, London, England, late 18th c., 24" d.,
43" h. 6,600.00
Terrestrial globe, table model, the
sphere pivoting within a circular
mahogany support ring on ring-
turned legs joined by turned
stretchers, globe dated 1833 &
marked w/"Terrestrial globe containing all the late discoveries
and geographical improve-
ments...," England, 17" d., 15" h.
(ILLUS.) 1,540.00

GOLLIWOGS

Chad Valley Golliwog Doll

*The Golliwogs, charming black characters
introduced in a book by Bertha Upton in 1889,
were as popular in England as were Raggedy Ann and Andy in the United States.
They were widely used as advertising premiums and also can be found in a series of books,
as banks, dolls and perfume bottles.*

Cup & saucer, child's, Staffordshire
china $75.00
Doll, black cloth sateen, applied
white oilcloth & blue felt eyes,
red felt applied mouth, black yarn
hair, body jointed at shoulders &
hips, dressed in original red
sateen pants, yellow felt vest &
blue felt jacket, 15" (light signs of
age) 125.00
Doll, stuffed cloth, black cloth head
w/blue & white felt eyes, red felt
nostrils, red velour oilcloth mouth,
synthetic black plush hair, clothing made as part of the body

w/red striped pants, yellow shirt,
blue jacket w/tails, white hands &
upper feet, marked "Chad Valley
- Chiltern Hygienic Toys - Made in
England," small spot of wear on
back, 24" h. (ILLUS.) 210.00
Perfume bottle, figural glass, clear
glass body & painted head stopper, made for Vigny, Paris, ca.
1922, 3½" h. . . . . .245.00 to 265.00
Postcard, Christmas, full-figure
w/black cloth face 28.00
Prints, from the series "Golliwog's
Polar Adventure," ca. 1900, matted, each 12½ x 15", group
of 11 . . . . 250.00
Valentine, full-figure Golliwog 45.00

GRANITEWARE

Graniteware Chamber Pot

*This is a name given to metal (customari-
ly iron) kitchenwares covered with an enamel coating. Featured at the 1876 Philadelphia
Centennial Exposition, it became quite popular for it was lightweight, attractive, and easy
to clean. Although it was made in huge quantities and is still produced, it has caught the
attention of a younger generation of collectors and prices have steadily risen over the
past five years. There continues to be a con-
sistent demand for the wide variety of these
utilitarian articles turned out earlier in this
century and rare forms now command high
prices.*

Bacon platter, blue & white swirl . . . $95.00
Baking pan, grey mottled, w/wire
handle, 11½" l. 19.00
Basin, miniature, heavy, white
w/royal blue rim 30.00
Basin, salesman's sample, blue &
white swirl, 3½" d. . . . . .150.00 to 200.00
Basin, blue & white swirl, 9½" d. 70.00
Basin, green & white swirl 65.00
Berry bucket, cov., black & white
medium speckled, tin lid, wire
bail handle 40.00
Berry bucket, cov., brown & white
swirl, tin lid, bail handle 95.00

Berry bucket, cov., grey mottled, tin lid, wire bail handle, 5" h. 55.00

Bread dough riser, cov., grey mottled 85.00

Bread pan, rectangular w/folded ends, top edge rolled over wire, grey mottled, early 23.00

Bread pan, robin's egg blue, 9" l. . . . 20.00

Cake pan, blue & white swirl, 8½" d., 3" h. 175.00

Cake pan, blue & white swirl, molded handles, 10 x 14" 140.00

Cake pan, grey & white swirl, large. 45.00

Candleholder, cobalt blue & white medium spatter 85.00

Candlestick, red w/black trim 35.00

Canteen, cobalt blue 58.00

Chamber pot, cov., brown & white swirl (ILLUS.). 185.00

Chamber pot, cov., robin's egg blue & white 125.00

Chamber pot, open, cobalt blue & white spatter 28.00

Chamberstick, light brown w/gold band 85.00

Clothes boiler, white w/brown lettering. 165.00

Coffee biggin, cov., red & white checked design, marked "Elite," 3 pcs. 275.00

Coffee boiler w/self-lid, blue & white speckled, large. 85.00

Coffee boiler, cov., Chrystolite 275.00

Coffee boiler, cov., grey mottled, wire bail handle w/wooden hand grip 50.00

Coffee flask, fine grey & white mottling, metal screw-on lid, 4½ x 5" (small dent on lid) 350.00

Coffeepot, cov., blue & white swirl, 9" h. 128.00

Coffeepot, cov., grey mottled, 11" h. 45.00

Coffeepot, cov., grey mottled, copper base 110.00

Coffeepot, cov., robin's egg blue, w/wooden handle 100.00

Coffeepot, cov., turquoise & white swirl, 11" h. 70.00

Coffeepot, cov., white decorated w/bluebirds & flowers, fancy tin cover, wooden handle & finial 145.00

Coffeepot, cov., white w/black rim, Pyrex cap in hinged cover 12.50

Colander, footed, blue & white mottled 65.00

Colander, footed, black & white mottled, large 60.00

Colander, blue & white speckled. . . . 25.00

Colander, blue & white swirl 87.00

Colander, white w/black trim 15.00

Creamer, end of day decoration 325.00

Cuspidor, blue & white swirl, large . . . . .250.00 to 325.00

Cuspidor, red & white swirl 150.00

Cuspidor, hotel-type, robin's egg blue 275.00

Dipper, blue & grey 27.00

Dipper, cobalt blue & white swirl . . . 25.00

Dipper, grey mottled 20.00

Double boiler, cov., blue & white swirl 165.00

Double boiler, cov., yellow & black 65.00

Dry measure w/lip, grey mottled, embossed "For Household Use Only," graduated to 1 qt. 95.00

Egg skillet, white, one-egg capacity 20.00

Frying pan, brown & white swirl 67.50

Funnel, grey mottled, 4" d. 40.00

Funnel, grey spatter 12.00

Griddle, oval, grey & medium blue mottled 55.00

Grater, cream & green, flat 95.00

Gravy boat, fine blue & white mottled 195.00

Jelly kettle, cov., brown & white swirl 75.00

Kettle, cov., Berlin-style, blue & white swirl 90.00

Kettle, cov., pale beige w/green trim, 8½" d. 25.00

Ladle, large blue & white swirl 69.00

Ladle, brown & white swirl 75.00

Ladle, white w/black trim, marked "Sweden" 20.00

Ladyfinger pan, grey mottled 200.00

Liquid measure, grey mottled, 1 gill 185.00

Liquid measure, grey mottled, 2 qt. 55.00

Loaf pan, lavender & white large mottled, folded corners 95.00

Lunch bucket, cov., light blue & white swirl 85.00

Lunch pail, cov., child's, grey mottled 125.00

Measure, grey mottled, 4 cup 98.00

Molasses pitcher, cov., white w/blue checkered pattern, marked "Elite" 175.00

Mold, grey on grey speckled, fluted, 8" d. 24.00

Muffin pan, 6 cup, grey mottled 28.00

Muffin pan, 8 cup, brown & white swirl 125.00

Muffin pan, 8 cup, dark blue & greyish white mottled inside & out 85.00

Mugs, cobalt blue & white swirl, small, pr. 98.00

Mugs, child's, grey mottled, set of 4 . . . . 69.00

Pail, blue & white mottled, white in-

terior, wire bail handle w/wood
grip, 12 qt. 48.00

Pie pan, cobalt blue 5.00

Pie pan, cobalt & white swirl, black
trim, white interior, large 55.00

Pie pan, Emerald Ware, green &
white swirl, Strong Mfg. Co.,
Sebring, Ohio 100.00

Pie pan, white w/rose decal in-
side 12.00

Pitcher, blue & white swirl, w/gra-
dation marks, 10" h. (some
wear) 80.00

Pitcher, milk, blue & white large
swirl, early shape 175.00

Pitcher, tankard, tapering funnel
shape w/long, angled rim spout,
pink, green & white speckled,
14" h. 675.00

Plate, blue & white swirl, 10" d. 15.00

Plates, Bluebelle Ware, shaded blue
w/black trim, Howell Shapleigh
Hardware Co., St. Louis, Missouri,
10" d., pr. 65.00

Plates, bluish grey speckled, 8" d.,
set of 4 . . . . 24.00

Plates, dinner, grey mottled, 10" d.,
set of 6 . . . . 150.00

Preserving kettle, cov., emerald
green & white swirl 135.00

Pudding pan, blue & white swirl 30.00

Roaster, cov., brown & white mottled, applied wire handles,
marked "Cream City Ware" 65.00

Roaster, cov., brown & white swirl . . 80.00

Graniteware Roaster

Roaster, cover & white insert, cobalt
blue & white swirl (ILLUS.) 375.00

Roaster, cover & white insert, light
blue & white speckled, Lisk Mfg.
Co., patent dated 1911, 18" l. 95.00

Salt box, cov., hanging-type, cream
& red 65.00

Soap dish, hanging-type, brown &
white swirl 155.00

Soup dish, turquoise blue 20.00

Stove, table top model, oil burning,
shaded brown, three burners, fancy metal castings w/matching
large coffeepot 450.00

Sugar bowl w/tin cover, grey mottled, marked "L&G Mfg. Co.,"

Lalance & Grosjean Mfg. Co.,
Woodhaven, New York 295.00

Tea kettle, cov., gooseneck spout,
orange w/black trim, marked
"20" 125.00

Tea kettle, cov., yellow & white
swirl 150.00

Teapot, cov., gooseneck spout, ap-
ple green 50.00

Teapot, cov., coil handle, blue &
white speckled (under base
wear) 35.00

Teapot, cov., gooseneck spout, blue
& white swirl, 3 cup 300.00

Teapot, cov., gooseneck spout,
brown & white swirl 145.00

Teapot, cov., gooseneck spout,
cream & green, 8½" h. 75.00

Teapot, cov., Pearl Ware, bulbous
body w/pewter trim, decorated
w/violets, General Steel Wares,
Ltd., Canada 295.00

Teapot, cov., red & white swirl 65.00

Tea steeper, cov., blue & white
speckled, marked "Corona
Ware" 79.00

Tea strainer, blue, star-form
perforations 55.00

Tea strainer, cream, fancy circle
perforations 39.00

Tea strainer, grey mottled, star-form
perforations 27.00

Tea strainer, white, fancy circle
perforations 28.00

Tumbler, blue & white swirl, 5" d.
top, large 65.00

Vegetable dish, open, aqua green &
white large swirl, deep sides,
oblong 85.00

Wash basin, blue & white swirl 45.00

Wash basin, green & white mot-
tled 50.00

Wash basin, handled, sky blue &
white swirl, Agate Ware, 19" d. . . . 175.00

Wash basin, grey mottled 15.00

Washboard, dark blue insert,
"Enamel King" 45.00

Washboard, grey mottled insert 50.00

Wash bowl & pitcher set, grey mot-
tled, the set 125.00

HATPINS & HATPIN HOLDERS

HATPIN HOLDERS

Bavarian china, floral decoration . . . $65.00

English china, corset-shape
w/hallmarked sterling rim, cobalt
blue band around the center, soft
blue to white background
w/hand-painted florals w/dotted
centers 185.00

English earthenware, cylindrical
body flaring at the rim & widely
flaring at the base, black satin
ground decorated w/scenes of
Oriental people, cork in base,
4" d., 4¾" h. 55.00

English earthenware, cylindrical
body flaring at the rim & widely
flaring at the base, black satin
ground decorated w/colorful pan-
sies, 3½" d., 5¼" h. 65.00

Nippon china, decorated around the
base w/a band of white storks
against the turquoise blue ground,
gold top, marked 85.00

Nippon china, h.p. pink roses, cobalt blue trim & gold bands,
marked 55.00

Royal Austria china, h.p. violets
decoration 75.00

Royal Bayreuth china, boy w/turkey
decoration 350.00

Royal Bayreuth china, figural grey
owl 495.00

Royal Bayreuth china, Goose Girl
decoration 325.00

R.S. Germany china, hexagonal
shape on tiny feet, roses decora-
tion, signed 85.00

HATPINS

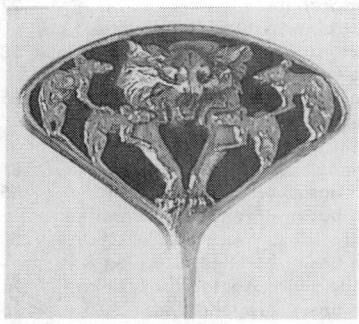

Lalique Gold & Enamel Hatpin

Brass, four kittens decoration,
9" l. 55.00

Brass filigree, Art Nouveau style
lacy design w/escutcheon head,
9" l. 65.00

Elk's tooth set in a gold head 125.00

Enameled metal, Art Nouveau style,
modeled in the form of an opening flower bud, enameled in
shades of green & orange & highlighted w/five small pearls, gold-
filled stem (minor enamel loss) . . .   550.00

Gold (10k), Art Nouveau style lady's
head decoration, all-original 185.00

Gold & enamel, the two-sided fan-
shaped head cast in low-relief
w/four muscular mice tormenting

a furry cat, the ground enameled in dark green, impressed
"LALIQUE," France, ca. 1900,
head 1¼" w., overall 9 3/8" l.
(ILLUS.) 5,500.00

Sterling silver, model of a bear
w/ruby eyes, hinged head, Eng-
lish hallmarks, head 1" l. 150.00

Sterling silver, model of a bulldog,
head 2¼" l.   85.00

Sterling silver, the head w/a
monogrammed top & tapering
sides w/engraving on all four
sides, head 2½" l., overall
11" l. 85.00

HEINTZ ART METAL WARES

Heintz Art Table Lamp

*Beginning in 1915 the Heintz Art Metal
Shop of Buffalo, New York began producing
an interesting line of jewelry and decorative
items, especially vases and desk accessories,
in brass, bronze, copper and silver. Their distinctive brass and bronze wares overlaid with
sterling silver Art Nouveau and Art Deco designs are much sought after today. Collectors
eagerly search for pieces bearing their
stamped mark consisting of a diamond surrounding the initials "HAMS." Around 1935
the firm became Heintz Brothers, Manufacturers.*

Book ends, sterling silver overlay
depicting pine cone & needles on
bronze, green patina $95.00

Cigar box, cov., rectangular, bronze
w/a sterling silver inlaid geometric chain band around the lid,
original wooden insert & screen,
signed, 6 x 10", 3¼" h. (slight
patina wear) 55.00

Console set: 9½" d. low bulbous
bowl w/incurved sides & a pair of
short 5½" h. columnar candlesticks w/flared bases; silver-inlaid

bronze, the silver design of bands
of long-leaved plants around the
sides of the bowl & base of the
candlesticks, holes in candlesticks
for electrification, all marked, the
set 467.50

Lamp, table model, mushroom-
shaped bronze shade w/a silver
overlay design around the rim
pivoting between an exaggerated
U-form support & continuing to a
cylindrical standard flaring at the
base w/conforming decoration
around the edge, 8¼" w., 9½" h.
(ILLUS.) 605.00

Loving cup, sterling silver decoration
on bronze, signed 85.00

Picture frame, sterling silver Greek
Key pattern decoration on bronze,
brown patina 195.00

Vase, sterling silver decoration on
bronze, 5" h. 150.00

Vase, cylindrical w/everted rim,
bronze decorated w/long-
stemmed silver primulas, impressed company mark & "Sterling
On Bronze 3807," 10¼" h. 132.00

Vase, bud-type, sterling silver decoration on bronze, 12" h. 150.00

HOLIDAY COLLECTIBLES

*For collectors Christmas offers the widest
selection of desirable collectibles, however,
other national and religious holidays also
were noted with the production of various
items which are now gaining in popularity.
Halloween-related pieces such as candy containers, lanterns, decorations and costumes
are the most sought after category after
Christmas and other holidays such as
Thanksgiving, Easter and the 4th of July
have relatively few collectibles available for
collectors. Also see CHRISTMAS TREE
LIGHTS and CHRISTMAS TREE ORNA-
MENTS, and VALENTINES.*

EASTER

Candy container, tin, egg-shaped,
depicts Victorian girl $20.00

Model of an egg, milk white blown
glass, pansy decoration, 5" l.
(worn) 32.00

Model of an egg, milk white blown
glass, horseshoe decoration,
6" l. 38.00

HALLOWEEN

Bell, chrome, w/scary cat perched
on top, 5" h. 95.00

Book, "Whitman Halloween Party,"

cut-out hang-up figures, uncut,
1953 .... 20.00

Candy container, "Brach's Trick Or
Treat Candy," model of a haunted
house, ca. 1940's 60.00

Candy container, celluloid, scarecrow w/pumpkin head 28.00

Candy container, papier-mache',
figural cone-shaped devil, West
Germany, ca. 1950's, 7" h. 28.00

Candy container, papier-mache',
figural pumpkin man, West Germany, ca. 1950's, 5½" h. 23.00

Candy container, papier-mache',
figural pumpkin man, Germany,
early 20th c. 425.00

Candy container, papier-mache',
figural witch, Germany, 4½" h. ... 265.00

Candy container, papier-mache',
figural cone-shaped witch, West
Germany, ca. 1950's, 7½" h. 26.00

Candy container, papier-mache',
Jack-o'-lantern w/wire bail handle, ca. 1930's 58.00

Candy container, papier-mache',
model of a black cat w/a spring
coil neck, West Germany, 5" h. ... 30.00

Candy container, papier-mache',
model of a black cat w/glass eyes
in the removable head, Germany,
1920's, 5½" h. ....150.00 to 175.00

Candy container, papier-mache',
model of a cone-shaped black
cat, West Germany, ca. 1950's,
7½" h. 26.00

Candy container, papier-mache',
model of a pumpkin, West Germany, ca. 1950's, 4" d. 18.00

Candy container, papier-mache',
model of a cone-shaped pumpkin,
West Germany, ca. 1950's, 6" h. ... 26.00

Candy container, papier-mache',
model of a pumpkin w/goblin on
top holding black cat 165.00

Coloring book, fuzzy black cat on
cover, Dell, 1955, mint uncolored
condition, 80 pp. 25.00

Costume, child's, Casper the Friendly Ghost, ca. 1950's 25.00

Costume, child's, Darth Vader, by
Ben Cooper 65.00

Costume, child's, Marie Osmond,
mint in box 35.00

Costume, child's, skeleton, w/mask,
in original box 25.00

Decoration, cardboard, model of a
black cat on orange honeycomb
tissue base, 12" h. 48.00

Die-cut decoration, cardboard, cat,
copyright by H.E. Lehrs, 22" l. 35.00

Die-cut decoration, cardboard, cat
on moon, copyright by H.E. Lehrs,
14" h. 35.00

Die-cut decoration, cardboard, owl,
copyright by H.E. Lehrs, 22" h. ...   35.00

Die-cut decoration, cardboard,
pumpkin, copyright by H.E. Lehrs,
13" h. 35.00

Die-cut decoration, cardboard,
skeleton, copyright by H.E. Lehrs,
5" h. 35.00

Die-cut decoration, cardboard,
witch, copyright by H.E. Lehrs,
20" h. 35.00

Figure of a witch, cardboard, black
& orange w/orange tissue pull-up
arms, 8" h. 39.00

Jack-o'-lantern, papier-mache',
w/a mean expression, ca. 1930's,
6" d. 65.00

Jack-o'-lantern, pressed cardboard,
laughing expression w/many
rounded teeth, round eyes
w/black glasses, trimmed w/col-
ored tinsel paper, wire bail handle, marked "Germany," 5½" h...   66.00

Lantern, black cardboard frame, orange tissue behind cut-outs of
witch, pumpkin, owl & cat,
w/wire hanger, 2½ x 3½",
6" h. 60.00

Lantern, model of a black cat's
head, Germany, 4" h. 165.00

Lantern, cardboard & tissue, model
of a skull.......................   55.00

Lantern, tin, ribbed model of a
pumpkin head w/large slanted
eyebrows & eyes & long mustache
over the serrated smiling mouth,
worn original goldenrod paint
trimmed w/black, friction-
fastened seam, 7" h. (broken
spot-soldering on seams) 440.00

Mask, cardboard w/honeycomb
crown, witch, orange & black 35.00

Model of a black cat holding a Jack-
o'-lantern, on a squeaker box,
Germany, 1920's, 6" h. 188.00

Model of an owl, papier-mache',
double-sided, w/glass eyes,
13" h. 125.00

Noisemaker, spaceman shooting
futuristic rifle in space, brightly illustrated, ca. 1950's 65.00

Noisemaker, tin, model of a witch
wearing devil hat, w/black cats,
etc., ca. 1940's 35.00

Parade lantern, tin & wood, a tin
Jack-o'-lantern top in orange &
black, mounted on a slender
wooden rod, overall 44" h........   770.00

Rattle, heavy molded paper, model
of an owl on a wooden stick handle, 1920's 65.00

Tambourine, metal, cat face,
w/original streamers 60.00

Tambourine, paper over wood

frame, decorated w/pumpkin
face, Germany 130.00

Trick or treat bag, paper w/handles,
decorated w/a witch & scared
moon in orange & black, large ...   6.00

HORSE & BUGGY COLLECTIBLES

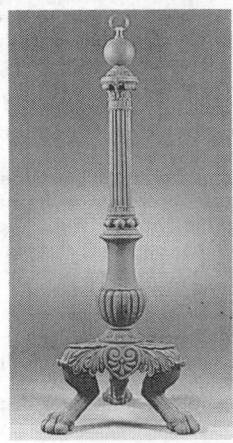

Tall Cast Iron Hitching Post

Bit, silver-mounted, lady's leg
shape, Crockett $250.00

Bit, steel, marked "U.S. Cavalry,"
w/leather bridle 38.50

Book, "Scientific Horseshoeing,"
by Cincy, 1899, first edition,
295 pp..........................   55.00

Bridle rosette, domed glass top,
horse head w/bridle & "N" in
black & gold, Plueger, early
1900's 55.00

Buggy step, cast iron w/cut-out
heart design 65.00

Chaps, leather, decorated w/a
snake, dice & swastikas, N. Porter, ca. 1920 ....4,950.00

Hearse, horse-drawn, the stepped
roof above glass sides w/a wide
arched center panel flanked by
narrower arched panels, large
rear wheels & smaller front
wheels, ca. 1880 (wheels re-
built) 6,500.00

Hitching post, cast iron, figure of a
black jockey standing w/one hand
on his hip & the other extended,
feet apart, wearing cap, long-
sleeved shirt, vest & long pants,
old polychrome repaint, 37" h.
(some rust) 500.00

Hitching post, cast iron, model of a
horse's head w/wavy mane &
molded features, retains traces of

yellow polychrome, marked "O.
Silberzahn Manfr., West Bend,
Wis," 19th c., 14" h. 880.00
Hitching posts, cast iron, urn-form
supporting a reeded pedestal
topped by a ball fitted w/a ring,
raised on a tri-form paw foot
base, 5' h., pr. (ILLUS. of one) . . .1,320.00
Lap robe, plush, floral border, wine
red w/beige flowers. 55.00
Lap robe, wool, muted red, green &
tan florals w/black veining on one
side, reverse side black w/a dog
w/glass eye (one missing) wearing a sleigh bell collar, marked
"Stroock, NY," 50 x 60" 275.00
Riding crop, leather w/sterling silver
handle, Victorian. 95.00
Saddle, "A" fork-type, marked "JTS
Co.Cal Oaktan," ca. 1890's 650.00
Salt lick holder, cast iron, marked
"Belmont Stable, Brooklyn". 50.00
Spurs, chiseled iron w/silver inlay,
w/leather fittings, marked "Chi-
huahua," rowel 2½" d., pr. 219.00
Spurs, nickel-plated steel, engraved
design, tooled leather fittings,
large rowel & chap guard, marked
"Crockett," pr. 229.00
Spurs, silver-inlaid steel, snake
design, August Buermann, ca.
1920, pr. 5,225.00
Spurs, silver-mounted steel, lady's
leg shape, Crockett, unused, pr. . .   295.00
Vest & chaps set, child's, leather,
ca. 1950's, the set 75.00
Wagon jack, wood & wrought iron,
ironwork w/tooled design &
"1814, P. Ordver," traces of old
red paint, 19½" h. plus adjustable
lift bar (wood very worn) 95.00

HOUSEHOLD APPLIANCES

Modern Style Teakettle

*Labor saving devices for the housewife as
well as appliances to improve the quality of*

*life of the American family began to prolifer-
ate in the 19th century. The introduction of
electricity helped expand the field even more
and today early appliances, especially electric
models, are increasingly collectible. Many
serious collectors search for early fans and
toasters in particular, but old coffee makers,
steam irons and vacuum cleaners also have
dedicated enthusiasts. All pieces listed are
electric unless otherwise noted. Also see
LAUNDRY ROOM ITEMS.*

Coffee mill, "Kitchen Aid," w/origi-
nal measuring glass $125.00
Fan, "Century," oscillating, brass
blades, patented in 1914, 10" h. . . .   85.00
Fan, "Westinghouse," vane-type,
12" h. 850.00
Hair dryer, "White Cross," Chicago
Stamping Co., in original case, ca.
1922 . . . .   15.00
Sewing machine, "Singer Feather-
weight Model 221," black,
w/case, attachments & instruction
book. . . . . .300.00 to 350.00
Teakettle, Modern style, chrome,
bulbous domical body on a molded foot, the sides tapering to a
small domed cover w/black Bakelite ball finial, fixed wicker overhead handle, short angled spout,
electric plug at back base, designed by Peter Behrens, marked
"A.E.G." & numbered "42112 -
47," made by A.E.G. Berlin, Germany, ca. 1909, electric element
missing, 8¼" h. (ILLUS.) 770.00
Television, "Emerson Model 1232,"
7" w. screen, in working condi-
tion 35.00
Toaster, "Bersted Mfg. Co. Model
68" 45.00
Toaster, "Pennsylvania Aircraft
Works Co.," unique 'pop-down'
type 45.00
Toaster, "Proctor Model 1445,"
chrome, w/bell 35.00
Toaster, "Sunbeam Model 4,"
patented January 30, 1923 . . . . . .   35.00
Toaster, "Sunbeam Model T9" 95.00
Toaster, "Sun-Chief Series 680,"
chrome, Art Deco style, two-door,
w/attached cord 45.00
Toaster, "Toastmaster Model 1A1,"
chrome, Art Deco style 70.00
Toaster, "Toast-O-Later," Crocker-
Wheeler Elect. Mfg. Co., Art Deco
styling, 1938 . . . .   195.00
Toaster, "Universal Model E7732"
(no cord) 175.00
Vacuum cleaner, hand-type, "Gilbert
#B112," ca. 1920 . . . .   45.00
Vaporizer, "KAZ," w/measuring la-

bel & full 2 oz. bottle of cold
inhalent in box 27.00
Waffle iron, "Sampson," round w/at-
tached tray, green handles....... 40.00

ICART PRINTS

Coursing II

The works of Louis Icart, the successful French artist whose working years spanned the Art Nouveau and Art Deco movements, first became popular in the United States shortly after World War I. His limited edition etchings were much in vogue during those years that the fashion trends were established in Paris. These prints were later relegated to closet shelves and basements but they have now re-entered the art market and are avidly sought by collectors. Listed by their American titles, those appearing below have been sold within the past eighteen months. All prints are framed unless otherwise noted.

Arrival, 1941,
11¾ x 16 7/8" ......$1,000.00 to 1,200.00
Attic Room, 1940, 14 7/8 x 17¼"
(laid down & glued)............3,080.00
Casanova, 1928, 14 x 21" 1,870.00
Coach (The), ca. 1948,
18 3/8 x 22 1/8" (darkening).....2,310.00
Coursing II, 1929, 15½ x 25"
(ILLUS.) 5,500.00
Dalila, 1929, 13½ x 20½" (foxing,
small margin tear) 1,650.00
Eve, 1928, 14 x 19¾" oval (two
margin tears) 1,760.00
Fair Dancer, 1939, laid down, glued,
19½ x 23" 3,300.00
Farewell, 1927, 14½ x 19".........1,320.00
Favorite (The), 1936, 15" d. (light
staining & foxing)...............2,420.00
Flower Seller, 1928, 14 x 19"
(margins trimmed) 1,980.00
Forsythia, 1926, 15½ x 19¼"
(foxing)........................1,650.00
Girl in Crinoline, 1937,
19½ x 23½" 2,640.00
Guardians, 1936, 15" d. (laid down,
pale light staining & foxing) 2,200.00

Gust of Wind, 1925,
17½ x 21"..........3,000.00 to 3,300.00
Joan of Arc, 1929,
15 x 21¾"..........2,200.00 to 2,500.00
Kittens, 1926, 9½ x 10" (minor surface abrasions, has been cleaned,
margins trimmed, loose sheet)...1,100.00
Little Butterflies, Butterfly Falls,
1926, 14 x 19" 1,925.00
Louise, 1927, 13 x 20" ..1,500.00 to 2,000.00
Melody Hour, 1934,
18½ x 23".........23,000.00 to 28,000.00

Orchids

Orchids, 1937, framed, 19 x 27¾"
(ILLUS.) 6,050.00
Recollections, 1928, framed,
12 x 17" (laid down on board,
glued to mat) 1,980.00
Salome, 1929, unframed, 14¾ x 20 7/8"
(foxing, small tears at edge).....1,925.00
Smoke, 1926, unframed, 15 x 20"
(foxing in margin & image) 1,650.00
Spanish Dance, 1929, framed,
13 x 20½" 1,210.00
Summer Birds, 1928, framed,
16¾ x 21" (mat burn, time-
darkening) 1,980.00
Tender Lesson, 1926, framed,
10¼ x 10 5/8" (laid down on
board, glued to mat) 1,430.00
Treasures, 1924, framed, 9 x 11"
oval (slight foxing in margin,
several creases) 1,210.00
Venetian Nights, 1926, framed,
13 x 21" cathedral 1,100.00
Venus in the Waves, 1931, unframed, 16 x 19" (slight mat burn,
margins slightly trimmed) 3,960.00
Winter Bouquet, 1924, framed,
11¾ x 16 5/8" 1,650.00
Zest, 1928, unframed, 15 x 20" (margin edges curled, very minor foxing, small corner scratch) 2,420.00

Special Focus:

Ice Skates &
Skating Memorabilia

by Ann J. Bates

Earliest references to skating are found in Scandinavian sagas and bone skates (cow, sheep, walrus teeth, red deer, elk, horse, etc.) measuring 11" to 12" l. have been discovered in Germany, Sweden, Norway, Denmark, Finland, Switzerland, the Danube Valley, and England. Archaeologists claim this method of transportation over snow, ice, and rough terrain has been used for 1700 years.

Snow skates were the forerunner of ice skates, and blocks of wood were carved out and shaped into a clog-form, into which the foot was slipped. The wooden clog was fitted with a metal strip and the foot was kept warm with animal hides.

Some of the probable origins of the word skate:

Low German: *Schake*, meaning "shank" or "leg bone"

Early Dutch: *Schenkel*, meaning "shank"

Danish and Norwegian: *Skoite*

Scots: *Sketcher*

French: *E'chasse*, meaning "stilt"

Modern Dutch: *Schaats*

Primitive peoples hunted with the use of skates and dogs. Gliding over ice on iron bladed skates was in vogue in Holland as early as the 14th century, and it is fairly certain that the use of iron as blades originated in the Netherlands. The high-curved prows helped skaters glide over rough ice. Some wrought-iron blades were attached to wooden soles, typically made from oak, walnut, rosewood, or beech. Leather thong harness fastenings passed through two or three holes drilled through the wooden sole (originally bone) to secure the foot to the skate. Small staffs or sticks were used for propulsion, steering, and braking.

Accounts of skating soldiers in 1572 at Amsterdam tell of their having successfully routed Spanish aggressors. Skating was also a means of transportation along canals and ditches. In early American colonial times, skates were used by Indians and white men, mostly for hunting down muskrats.

In the early days, 'great frosts' allowed skating in Europe and America. Speed skating, racing, and the "Dutch Roll" were developed in the 16th century in Holland, and both men and women competed for honors. In the 1600s, French and Flemish refugees in England introduced skating into the Fen (lakes) district of England. In 1662, in England, during a 'great frost,' people were seen "sliding with their skeets, which is a very pretty art." English skaters, influenced by the Dutch, skated at the "Great Frost Fair" on the Thames in 1683.

The first skates made in England prior to 1800 were modeled after Dutch patterns— long and low pitched—suitable for lengthy travel, sometimes 40 or 50 miles a day. Later, pond skating, requiring quick turns, led to producing the first English figure skate with iron blades that were short and circular in profile, with not more than 2" of their surface touching the ice at any one time.

In the 17th century, skating continued in Holland as an important recreation, and many artists painted happy and colorful skating scenes. Every class of society enjoyed this pastime, and nobility contributed to skating's beginning as a sport. The aristocrats influenced skating with elegance, grace, and good manners; they laid the foundation for artistic skating. Speed was an important aspect for peasants skating to market over frozen waterways to sell their wares.

The Edinburgh Skating Club in Scotland, formed during the second half of the 18th century, was the first such club in the world.

Tests had to be passed to gain admission to this club and its influence on skating contributed greatly to skating's role in modern times.

Of course, on those ancient skates, great skill was required to keep your balance. The tapes and leather thongs used to secure feet to skates became loose and frequent retightening was required. Screws were then developed to help hold the wooden base on the shoe or boot. This innovation was the forerunner of the modern figure skate, and was revolutionary in making possible new "exercises." The iron blade still extended over the front end of the boot and turned up, to create what is called the *prow*.

In 1772 Robert Jones wrote the first textbook on ice skating. Despite the fact that women skated during isolated periods in the past, figure skating in England was primarily a male sport. Mr. Jones suggested that pleasure skating be practiced by both sexes.

In the late eighteenth century figure skating took root in Germany and France. G.U.S. Vieth, an enthusiastic French skater, originated the skating of letters of the alphabet on ice. The English had created a science, and the French were to develop it into an art.

Competitions began in Vienna in 1871-2, and champions were born. English skaters living in St. Petersburg, Russia, in the early 1860s initiated the Neva Skating Association. Russian skaters became artistic and imaginative in the sport and by the early 1900s, St. Petersburg was the center of many international competitions.

Touring on skates along the long Dutch canals, over large stretches of frozen lakes (or fens in England), on the American Great Lakes, on the Hudson River, and lakes in Norway and Sweden, was another form of skating during the late 1800s and early 1900s.

Skating had become well established in North America by the beginning of the 19th century but most early American skates were imported from England, Germany, and Holland. This influence lasted for many years. E.V. Bushnell invented the first integral, all-metal footplate and blade skate. Straps were still used to secure feet to skates but soon after the clamp-on metal skate evolved. Between 1800 and 1850, good and bad models, 200 in all, came into the U.S. Patent Office.

An American, Jackson Haines, born in 1840, was the first of the world's great professionals. He gave exhibitions up and down the East Coast of America and Canada. He invented the 'Sit Spin' and created a new style of free skating which is still executed by contemporary skaters. Haines was the first to invent a new skate to help him improve his skill and technical abilities. In the 1860s, his blade was forged onto steel toe and heel plates which could be screwed directly and permanently onto the sole and heel of the boot. He also added teeth to the front of the blade to help in jumping. He gave skating shows in Europe, and became known as the founder of the international style of skating.

Following Haines' lead, various integral boot and blade skates were developed. In 1905 Gustav Stanzione opened a skating boot shop in New York City. Every part of the foot was measured for a custom fit. Blades were (and in good skates, still are) purchased and custom attached to the boots.

Norwegian Axel Paulsen, Norway's first skating champion, revolutionized speed skating techniques, as well as winning fame as a figure skater. The jump he developed is still a part of virtually every competitive figure skating program.

Another Norwegian skater, Sonja Henie, won her first World championship in figure skating at age 15. She went on to win 10 World championships (1927 to 1936), and six European championships (1931 to 1936), three Olympic gold medals (1928, 32, 36), and eight Norwegian championships. She continued her fairy-tale career as a professional in America starring in 10 Hollywood films and numerous ice shows. Sonja Henie was one of the greatest influences on the development and popularity of figure skating all over the world.

Several rather large collections of antique ice skates have surfaced in recent years, and there are several skate collectors interested in forming a national antique ice skate club. This brief summary may help such collectors establish guidelines in dating and evaluating their unusual skating treasures.

Because skates were developed in many places and for differing purposes, there are not any sharp cut-off dates between styles. Wood platform skates appeared in the same catalogs as all-metal, clamp-on skates, and clamp-ons coexisted with early shoe skates. Steel bladed, wood platform, strap-on skates reportedly were manufactured and used in Holland as recently as the 1950s.

Many skates, mostly of the steel (or iron) blade and wooden platform variety, were hand-crafted and are one-of-a-kind. Of these, the most pleasingly styled and artfully crafted, particularly in childrens' sizes, are the most desirable to collect, commanding prices of several hundred dollars. Others were more crude, but their uniqueness and the ingenuity of their workmanship can make them treasured by some collectors.

Because many skates have been destroyed or lost over the years, and because there were so many makers and styles, most specific, manufactured models have become rare. Any of the manufactured skates can increase sharply in value, perhaps by as much as 50%, if in mint condition and in their original boxes. Similarly, the presence of intact, original leather markedly increases value.

References and sources:

Ice Skating by Nigel Brown.

Nineteenth Century Games and Sporting Goods: The American Historical Catalog Collection.

The American Skating Mania, Smithsonian Institution.

Wonderful World of Skates by Arthur Goodfellow.

Skating in Art by Louise Wriedt & Robert Stheeman (based on the Gillis Grafstrom Collection).

Olympic Winter Sports in Norway.

The skate collections of the United States Figure Skating Association Hall of Fame in Colorado Springs, CO.

The author's own skate collection.

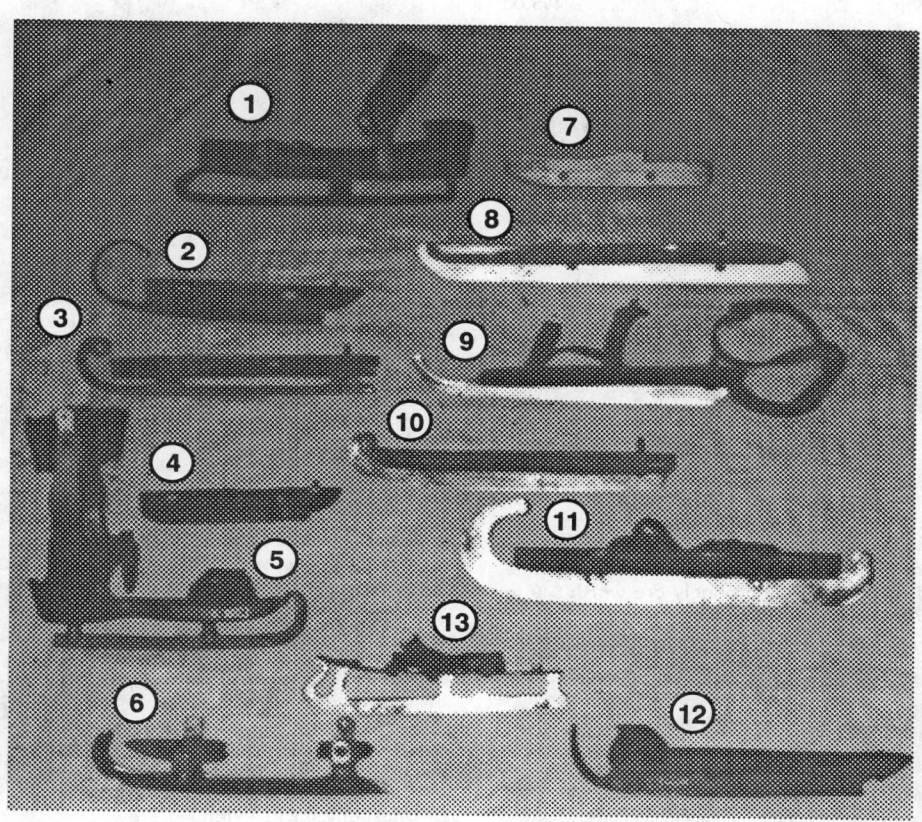

Price Listings:

Prices are for pairs, unless otherwise noted.

1. Hand-wrought blades with black-painted wooden footsole w/unique heel support $235.00

2. English gentleman's skate— Wirths & Bros., Germany, ca. 1833 (600 pairs were exported to Christian Hesser in Philadelphia on August 12, 1833 according to the Smithsonian Institution) 410.00

3. Dutch skate, ca. 1860—blue-painted wooden foot platform with thick blades and curled prow 375.00

4. Rare, tear-shaped cherry wood foot platform, child's skate, ca. 1870 . . . . 325.00

5. Blondin skate, Douglas Rogers & Co., Norwich, Ct., 1860 . . . . 600.00

6. German-made ("refined steel"), Jackson Haines era, with clamp attachment, ca. 1848 . . . . 250.00

7. Early primitive snow skate found in Denmark 350.00

8. Donoghue Racing Skate, Union Hardware, Torrington, Ct., red paint, ca. 1860s 195.00

9. England - Sheffield (Fred Harris) with decorated brass toe plate

and brass star on wood platform, early 1800s 425.00

10. Unusual swan-head on blade prow; all-metal skate; origin unknown 425.00

11. Rare, hand-wrought style of blade, found in Vermont, early 1800s 500.00

12. German skate showing Dutch design origins, 1826 .... 275.00

13. Beautifully shaped curved prow on a Philadelphia skate, late 19th c. 495.00

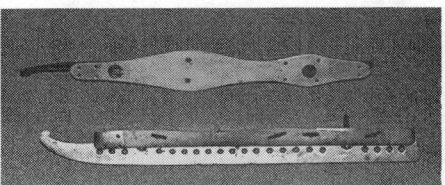

Whelpley, Boston, Ma., racing skate, mid-1800s 350.00

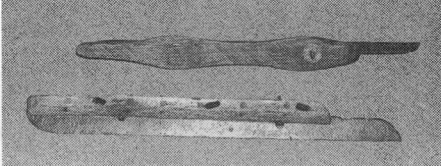

Unusually long-heeled touring skate, probably Dutch, early 1800s 185.00

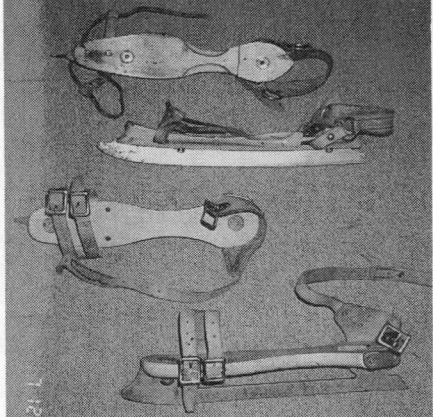

These skates are of recent, probably 1950s, manufacture and arrived in the U.S. from or via Holland. They are fully functional, and make very attractive wall hangings, but they are of little or no antique or collectible value at this time. They probably are worth $40 to $70 per pair as decorations.

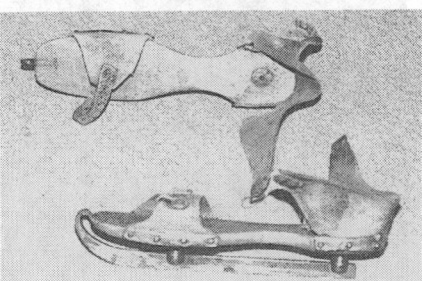

French polish, beech wood with broad toe straps with buckles, and brass heel bands ($2.00 per pair in 1886) 235.00

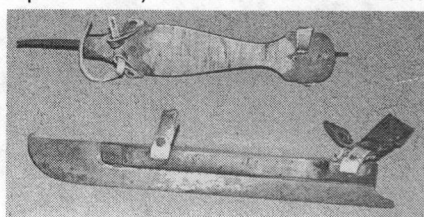

Unusually thick, extended prow w/curly maple footplate, brass trim on heel and toe; origin un- known, probably mid-1800s 250.00

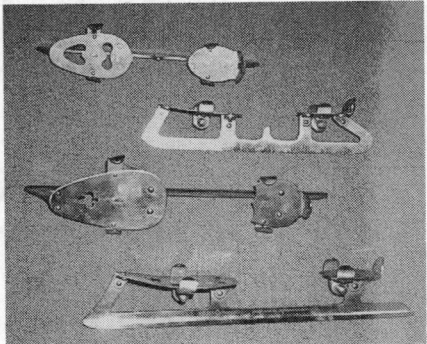

These are two pair of all-metal, clamp-on skates manufactured by Union Hardware of Torrington, Ct., about the turn of the century. The upper pair was relatively inexpensive, good, and popular and remain plentiful. They are probably worth $30.00 to $60.00 per pair. The lower pair is more elegant, much less of- ten encountered, and in fine condition, could sell for $125.00 or more.

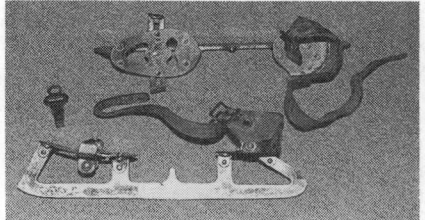

Hockey clamp-on skates, Union Hardware, Torrington, Ct., (fine quality), early 1900s 95.00

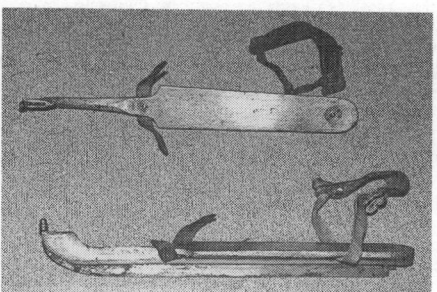

English skates of Dutch influence;
brass acorn on prow, early
1800s 235.00

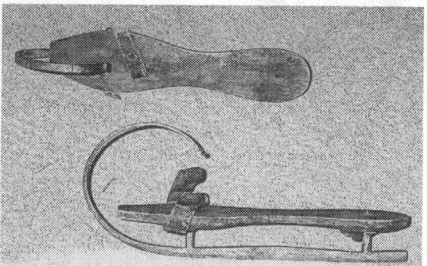

Rare, high stanchion model, refined
skates with notches in blades
(early toe picks ??), early 425.00

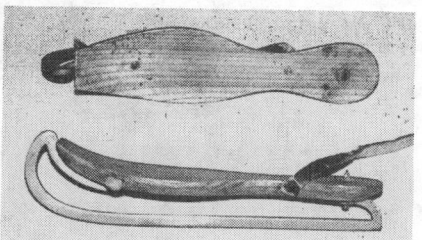

"Spring" (no center stanchions)
skate, early to mid-1800s 450.00

Early shoe skate, Wright & Ditson
(marked on blade: Synthite Steel
Tempered) "tuxedo model," early
1900s 60.00

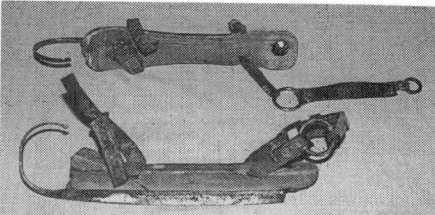

High prow-type with toe support in
front; modified soon after original
fabrication, late 1700s 475.00

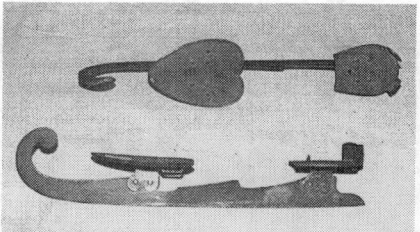

Jackson Haines era, all-metal skate
made in Sweden, marked on
blade "Staalsat," ca. 1855 .... 300.00

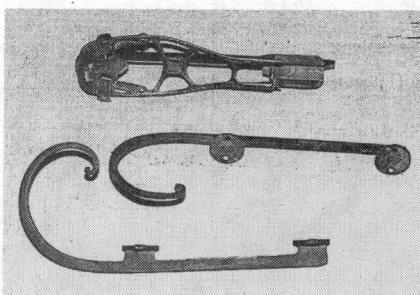

Upper: Very early, elaborately
fabricated all-metal, clamp skate,
Wm. Hawkins, Derby, Ct., ca. 1859-
1865, pr. 275.00
Lower: Hand-wrought iron blades
with high curved prow, radically
hollow ground (probably hand-filed,
and quite possibly well after initial
fabrication); apparently to be
screwed to wood platform; origin
and date unknown 400.00

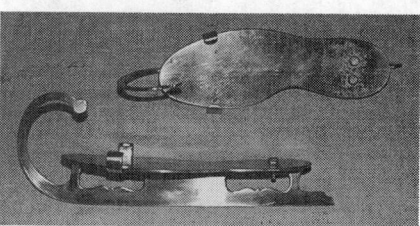

Custom-made of surgical steel for a
physician in Minnesota in the late
1930s, unique 375.00

Unusually thick, high-curved, hand-
wrought iron prow. New England,
late 1700s or early 1800s 395.00

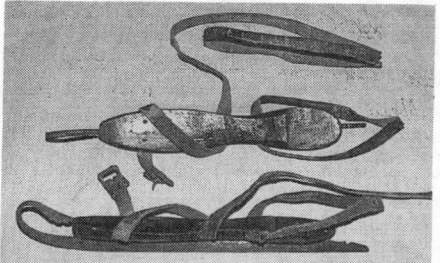

Unusual scalloped decorative pro-
files on front and rear of blades,
Pennsylvania, mid-1800s 325.00

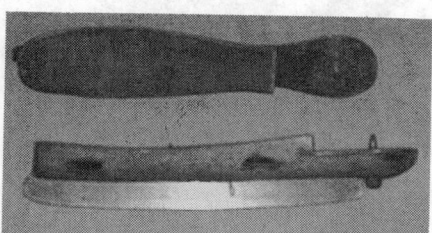

Early English figure skate (note
short blade and pronounced cur-
vature of blade bottom, brass
heel plate; blade stamped "Mars-
den Brothers & Silverwool, Skate
Manufacturers to His Royal High-
ness Prince Albert" 550.00

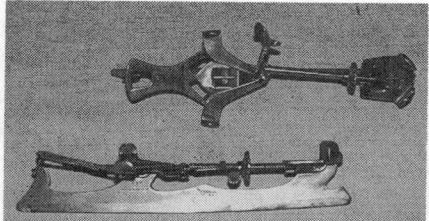

Unusual, fully lever-actuated, all-
metal clamp-on skate, "Whelpley's," Keene Mfg. Co., Keene,
N.H., 1884 . . . . 225.00

"Torpedo" racing skate (holes in

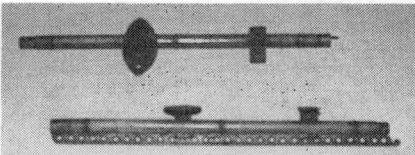

blade for weight reduction), unusual toe and heel plates, 1800s . . 210.00

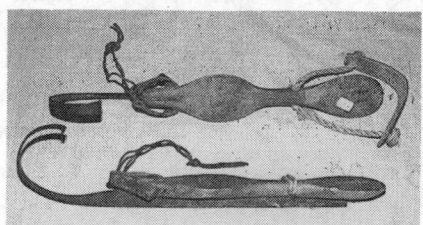

Rare, very early, extremely forward-
ly-extended, high-curved flat bladed prow, probably late 1700s 550.00

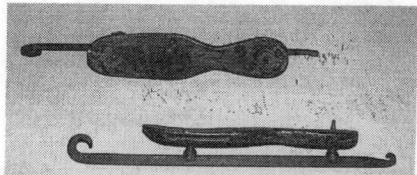

Rare, elongated, hand-wrought
blade, touring-type skate 450.00

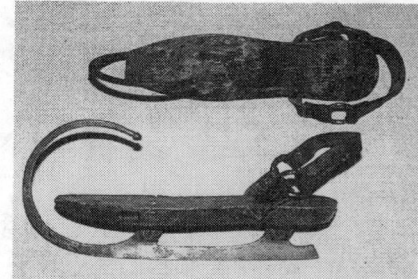

English cast-steel blade, high extended prow with small acorn tip,
dated "August 7, 1794" 575.00

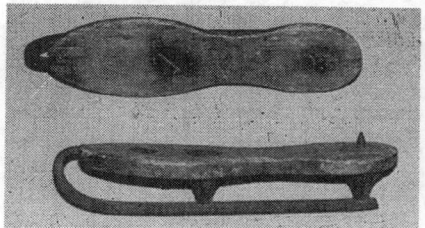

Child's skate with nice prow curva-
ture and elegant bell-shaped stanchions, Clarke's, Syracuse, N.Y.,
1860s 225.00

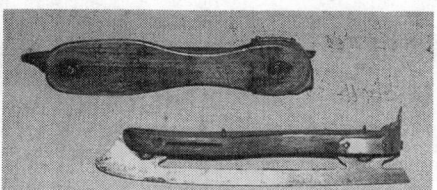

Skates made by Samuel Winslow in Worcester, Ma; sold for $1.50 per pair in 1886.................... 175.00

A more elaborate "torpedo" skate made by Raymond Skate Co., Boston, Ma., stamped "Warranted Tool Steel," 1800s 250.00

Sonja Henie Memorabilia:

Book, "Wings On My Feet," by Sonja Henie, 1940..................... 35.00
Coloring book featuring Sonja Henie, Merrill Publishing Co., 1941 .... 50.00

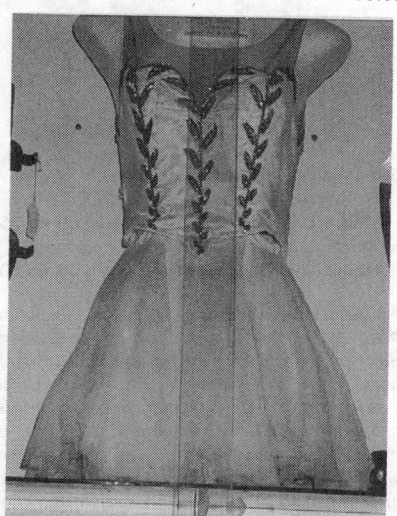

Costume, original beige skating costume worn by Sonja Henie (ILLUS.) ....2,000.00 to 3,000.00
Dolls, various Sonja Henie dolls by Madame Alexander, each.................275.00 to 500.00

Ice skates, Sonja Henie-endorsed pleasure skates, in box..100.00 to 125.00
Movie magazines with articles on Sonja Henie, each........15.00 to 25.00
Movie magazines with cover pictures of Sonja Henie, each 35.00
Paper doll set of Sonja Henie, Merrill Publishing Co., No. 3418, 1941, uncut 50.00

Program, "Hollywood Ice Productions 'Chicago' Presents - The Incomparable Sonja Henie," 1938 (ILLUS.)........................ 50.00

Program, "Fifth Transcontinental Tour - Sonja Henie - Presented by Hollywood Ice Productions, Chicago," 1941-42 (ILLUS.)............. 25.00
Program, "Sonja Henie - Sixth Triumphant Tour 1942-43," black velvet cover (ILLUS. top next page) 40.00
Program, "Sonja Henie - Seventh Triumphant Tour 1943-44," red velvet cover (ILLUS. next page) ... 50.00

Sonja Henie 1942-43 Program

Sonja Henie 1943-44 Program

Sheet music, "Later Tonight," from
the movie *Wintertime*, 1943
(ILLUS.)....................10.00 to 35.00

Sheet music, "Let's Bring New Glory
to Old Glory," from the movie
Iceland, 1942 (ILLUS.) .....10.00 to 35.00

Sheet music, "One in a Million,"
from the movie *One in a Million*,
1936 (ILLUS.) ....10.00 to 35.00
Souvenir pins, from various Sonja
Henie ice shows, each .....25.00 to 50.00

ABOUT THE AUTHOR: *Ann J. Bates is a long-time skating enthusiast and her collection of Sonja Henie memorabilia was begun by her parents in the 1930s and passed on to her.*

Although Ann passed up a career as a professional skater, she has maintained her interest in antique skates and skating memorabilia. Today she also has her own antiques business and promotes three antiques shows in Wisconsin during the summer and fall. She and her husband reside in Land O' Lakes, Wisconsin.

End of Special Focus

ICONS

Christ Pantocrator Icon

Icon is the Latin word meaning likeness or image and is applied to small pictures meant to be hung on the iconostasis, a screen dividing the sanctuary from the main body of Eastern Orthodox churches. Examples may be found all over Europe. The Greek, Russian and other Orthodox churches developed their own styles, but the Russian contribution to this form of art is considered outstanding.

Archangel Michael, depicted extracting the soul of an old man, Greece, ca. 1820, 18" w., 25" h. $2,200.00

The Assumption of the Virgin, painted wood, an ornate scene showing the reclining figure of the Virgin surrounded by numerous haloed figures & w/numerous angels overhead, Russia, ca. 1800, 13 x 16" 3,300.00

Christ Pantocrator, w/silver, partly gilded riza, Moscow, Russia, 1896, 8 7/8 x 10½" 1,760.00

Christ Pantocrator, gold border & halo, Russia, 19th c., 10 3/8 x 12¼" (ILLUS.) 1,045.00

Hodigitria Mother of God, w/carved wood frame, Greece, 19th c., 11¾ x 15¾" plus frame 1,760.00

The Holy Sabbath, painted wood w/ornate circle design framed by an inscribed border, Russia, 18th c., 11½ x 14" 7,700.00

The Holy Trinity, the three angels depicted seated at a table draped w/a blue cloth, Abram & Sarah are depicted offering food & wine, Russia, 19th c., 17¾ x 21" 5,720.00

The Resurrection, the central scene of the Resurrection and Descent into Hell surrounded by twelve Feasts, Russia, 19¼ x 25¼" 2,200.00

St. George Slaying the Dragon, painted wood, Greece, 19th c., 11¾ x 13¾" 1,870.00

St. Matthew, w/repousse' & chased silver-gilt oklad, by Alexander

Panfilov, Moscow, Russia, 1840, 9 x 10½" 1,980.00

St. Nicholas the Miracleworker, w/silver, partly gilded, oklad & w/enameled halo, Russia, ca. 1900, 8¾ x 10½" 1,870.00

Saints Zosima & Savati, painted wood, the standing saints facing each other w/a walled cityscape in the distance between them, Russia, 19th c., 10 3/8 x 12"...... 385.00

The Virgin & Child, w/fine silver-gilt oklad, repousse' & chased w/fruiting vine & flowers, the halos enameled w/scrolling flowering foliage in multicolors on a cream ground, A.F. Mishukov, Moscow, Russia, ca. 1910, 10¾ x 12¼" ..11,000.00

The Virgin Enthroned, the Virgin depicted seated on an elaborate carved wood throne w/angels holding a crown over the Mother of God's head, possibly Cyprus, 18th c., 13½ x 20½" 2,090.00

Vladimir Mother of God, w/silver-gilt oklad, the halo set w/emeralds, the Virgin's headdress sewn w/pearls, contained in a shadowbox, early 19th c., 4½ x 8¼"....5,500.00

INDIAN ARTIFACTS & JEWELRY

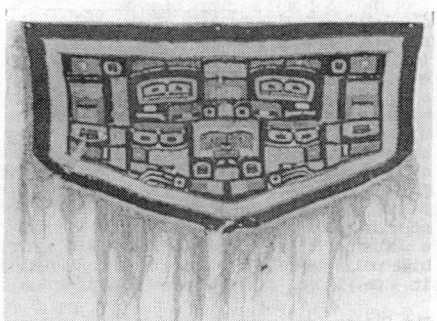

Rare Chilkat Blanket

Basket, Monache (Western Mono), gift-type, fine quality woven bracken fern & sedge, wide shallow rounded sides w/the top centered by a short, round neck, the upper side w/a border zigzag band, ca. 1900, 9" d., 4¾" h. ...$3,025.00

Basket, Papago, deep cylindrical sides, boldly woven pairs of floral & animal designs alternate w/tall triangularly-branched trees, flared rim w/rim handles, 18" d., 12½" h. (minor wear) 605.00

Basket, Pima, woven martynia &

willow, dark stepped diamond bands around the sides, 3½" d., 2 3/8" h. (small break in rim) 220.00

Belt, Plains, beaded leather, decorated w/dusty pink, various blues, white & white-heart red beads w/brass tack ornamented hanging end, purchased at Crow Agency, Montana, May 1888, 62" l. (several bead strips & brass tacks missing) 407.00

Blanket, Northwest Coast Chilkat, yarn on cedar bark warp, ca. 1890, very frail condition, damages, 58" l., 33" h. plus bottom fringe (ILLUS.) 2,970.00

Book, "Biography & History of the Indians of North America," by G. Drake, 1837 .... 125.00

Bowl, Apache, basketry, shallow sides woven w/a stepped geometric band in black martynia & willow, 13" d., 3½" h. 495.00

Bowl, Papago, basketry, woven martynia & yucca w/a stepped zigzag design, 7¾ x 10", 4½" h. 170.50

Bowl, Pima, basketry, geometric design in martynia, 11" d., 7¼" h. (1" area at rim & some spots in bottom missing stitches) 500.00

Bowl, Western Apache, basketry, woven in willow & martynia w/three circular bands of figures of men & horses, drips of green paint on rim & bottom, 11¾" d., 3¼" h. 1,485.00

Burden basket, Apache, twined weave w/worn dyed design, ca. 1900, 16¼" d., 15¼" h. (wear, missing stitches around rim & base, native leather repair) 220.00

Cradleboard cover, Sioux, Rosebud Indian Agency, beaded leather, typical geometric design in blues, green, faceted metallic & white-heart red beads on a white bead ground, attachment holes & parfleche hood stiffener, ca. 1900, 27¼" l. (damage to bead wrap at end of extension ornament) 6,600.00

Cribbage board, Eskimo, carved walrus tusk, carved w/seal heads & incised sleds, people, birds, an eagle & a shoreline map, 26" l. (prop peg broken off, chips at end) 880.00

Dance stick-rattle, Plains, probably Northern Plains Dog Society wand, wooden, one side stained green, the other striped diagonally w/red & black & w/an incised top, brass tack trim, brass bells & button dangles, dew claws &

buffalo hair braid w/abalone shell disc attachments, ca. 1900, 25¾" l. 2,640.00

Doll, Northern Plains, man w/buffalo hair braids, buckskin capote w/red & blue paint design, trade breech cloth, yellow ochre leggings fringed & beaded in black & white, grass-stuffed cloth body, early, 15" h. (wear, arms restitched) 950.00

Dress, Crow, black trade cloth w/red felt, ribbon binding & beadwork, cowrie shells sewn on heavy string across the bodice & shoulders, ca. 1925 (minor bead loss) 495.00

Food dish, Northwest Coast, carved wood, beaver w/abalone eyes & inset shell beads, 14 3/8" l., 1 15/16" h. (minor scratches) 450.00

Jar, Acoma, pottery, squatty bulbous shouldered body w/flat rim, painted paneled design of finely done birds in the style of Maria Poncho in orange & amber on a white slip ground, concave bottom, ca. 1930, 12½" d., 10 3/8" h. (minor firing clouds & glaze wear) 2,640.00

Jar, California, possibly Kern County, basketry, a wide slightly tapering cylindrical body w/a wide flat shoulder to a low wide mouth, woven w/a zigzag arrow design, 4 3/8" d., 2½" h. (stitch loss, stained, soiled) 412.50

Jar, Yokuts, basketry, canted sides, flat shoulders & short neck, woven designs include figures of men, women & animals within bands of geometric devices, redbud, dyed bracken fern root & sedge on grass foundation, woven in the King's River, California area, turn of the century, 18" d., 15" h. (one stitch missing at shoulder) 35,000.00

Jar, Zuni, pottery, polychrome designs, a high flaring body w/low shoulder curving into the high, tapered neck, painted red & black over chalky white slip w/three sets of two spiraling wings, the neck decorated in black & red w/six designs containing a flag w/hatched & crosshatched areas, wide vertical & hatched band extending to rim, 11½" d. 990.00

Knife sheath, woman's, Great Lakes, loom-beaded, alternating floral squares in red, gold, blue & white, square bottom, bordered w/fringe on three sides, together

w/old knife, 4" w., 10½" l.
w/straps (minor bead loss) 850.00
Knife sheath, Sioux, beaded leather,
bands of beading w/triangle designs in white-heart red, yellow,
green & blue beads, 8¾" l. 275.00
Loom basket, Eastern Woodlands,
hanging-type, stepped back
w/curlicue designs, rounded
sides, two high handles from front
to back, good color, 15" w.,
17" h. 38.50
Moccasins, Northern Plains, beaded
leather, floral bead design in
green, blues, yellow & white-
heart red, purchased at Crow
Agency, Montana in May, 1888,
10" l., pr. (soiled leather) 1,705.00
Moccasins, Sioux, beaded leather,
blues, white-heart red & yellow
beading on a white ground, yel-
low-ochre stained leather, 11" l.
(some bead loss on one) 600.00
Necklace, Zuni, squash blossom
type, sterling silver & turquoise,
sky blue stones in petit point set-
tings, signed "VMB" 330.00
Olla, San Ildefonso, pottery, red &
black design on greyish tan slip
ground, black rim & red under-
body band over a polished red
clay base, ca. 1910, 11¼" d.,
8½" h. (firing smudges & minor
rim damage) 900.00
Parfleche pouch, Northern Plains,
attributed to Nez Perce, leather
w/colorful geometric design,
20th c., 13½ x 26¾" 495.00

Photograph of Pete Mitchell (Dust Maker)

Photograph, "Pete Mitchell (Dust
Maker) - Tonca," platinum print,
by Frank A. Rinehart w/the photographer's 'Omaha' studio credit,
numbered in the negative, 1898,
matted, 7 x 9 1/8" (ILLUS.) 1,035.00
Photograph, "Zuni Governor," by Edward S. Curtis, platinum-silver

print on wove paper, numbered
"617-00" in negative, early 1900's,
9¾ x 13½" 6,325.00
Pipe, Sioux, Catlinite, black pipe
w/red Catlinite & lead inlay, stem
encased in leather decorated
w/stripes of green, greasy yellow, red, blue & white beading,
21½" l. 500.00
Pipe bag, Sioux, beaded leather,
decorated in yellow, dark blue,
Cheyenne blue, white, translucent
green & white-heart red, tab ornaments end in horsehair & tin
cones, green-stained fringe at
bottom, attributed to Brule Sioux
Chief Black Bear, 20½" l. plus
fringe 17,600.00
Pipe stem, Plains, possibly Sioux,
carved wood, spiral-carved &
painted in faded red & green,
marked "Bear Heart - Medicine
Priest - Cannonball Sun Dance -
July 3-4 1937 - He Topa," also
w/museum number "H321,"
23¾" l. 467.50
Pouch, Woodlands, beaded in an
ornate polychrome floral design
on black velvet w/edge beading & red binding, ca. 1890,
5 7/8 x 6½" (minor bead loss,
restitching, small split in cloth) . . . 247.50
Rattle, Iroquois, turtle shell w/ex-
tended head & neck wrapped for
the handle, False Face Society,
collected in Olean, New York,
signed "T.A. McKinron," 15½" l.
(two carapace breaks) 247.50
Rifle scabbard, Northwest Coast,
beaded leather, smoked & fringed
leather w/applied blue trade cloth
beaded in blue & red, tassels
w/larger blue & black beads
w/yarn ends, 19th c., 48" l. plus
fringe (minor cloth damage & a
few missing beads) 1,100.00
Rug, Navaho, Yei-type, decorated
w/a band of tall polychrome figures on a red ground, 35 x 42" . . . 412.50
Rug, Navaho, pictorial-type w/a
bold storm pattern adaptation
w/double-dye red, orange, dark
brown & natural hand-carded &
spun wool, ca. 1920, 35 x 61"
(very minor wear at corners) 1,320.00
Rug, Navaho, Third Phase Chief
blanket revival pattern featuring a
large "W" design at the top & bottom edge on a striped ground,
woven in hand-carded wool in
analine red, faded bluish green &
natural white, 47 x 65" (two small
holes, red slightly bled) 770.00

Rug, Navaho, room-sized, eye-dazzler serrate pattern in black, red, white, mustard yellow & grey, 90 x 216" 7,700.00

Sash, Eastern Woodlands, finger woven in red, blue & dark brown (faded black) wool w/white beads inserted in a diamond pattern & along edges of long strip tassels ending in yarn braid & fringe, 19th c. w/brass bells a later addition, band 5½ x 18", overall 94" l. 3,300.00

Totem pole, Northwest Coast (Haida), carved wood, bear over frog & raven, worn natural patina, ca. 1910, 10" h. 525.00

Vase, Hopi, pottery, cylindrical, decorated w/a bold stylized umber avian design w/red ochre on a shaded creamy orange slip, 9" h. (rim chips) 192.50

INRO

Four-Case Lacquer Inro

Originally used by the Japanese to carry a seal for signing documents, inro eventually were used to carry herbs or medicines in separate compartments. They are attached by cord to the sash and held in place by a netsuke. Finest examples are from the Edo and Meiji periods.

Inlaid silver, two-case, decorated in *katakiribori* & inlaid copper, gilt & *shibuichi* w/four Noh dancers (scratches & dents), w/matching silver *ojime* & silver bottle *netsuke* in the form of a double gourd incised w/*mon* & scrolling vine, signed "Masayoshi" w/kao, Meiji period, 2¾" h., the set ...$1,870.00

Inlaid wood, two-case, the burled veneer inlaid in tortoiseshell, mother-of-pearl, green stone & gilt w/a courtier's hat amid scattered cherry blossoms, the *himotoshi* consisting of silver flower- and leaf-form ringed mounts, unsigned, 19th c., 2 7/8" h. 6,600.00

Lacquer, three-case, decorated in gold *hiramake* & *kirikane*, each side carved w/a shaped panel containing a seated Chinese sage of inlaid tortoiseshell over foil on a ground of black lacquered cloth, the panels bordered by gold *karakusa*, w/silver cord runners, unsigned, 18th c., 2 5/8" h. (*kirikane* losses)....................3,740.00

Lacquer, four-case, carved as a cracked & chipped inkstick, one side showing a *shishi* perched on rockwork before a peony bush in relief, the reverse w/an inscription surrounded by a border of stylized instruments, w/reticulated gilt *ojime* of a *shishi* among peony, 19th c., signed "Mochuan" w/seal kan, 3½" h., the set 16,500.00

Lacquer, four-case, decorated overall w/horses in *hiramakie* & colored lacquers, w/*ojime* & *kagamibuta netsuke*, minor chips, 19th c. (ILLUS.) 770.00

Wood, three-case, each side carved in deep relief w/a dragon among scrolling clouds, the cord runners decorated in *chinkin-bori* w/*karakusa* on a *roiro* ground, red lacquer risers, w/*shakudo ojime* inlaid in silver & copper w/grasses, & wood *netsuke* carved w/a coiled dragon (one double-inlaid eye missing), 19th c., 3" h. (chips) 3,520.00

IVORY

Carved Whale Ivory Casket

Casket, carved whale ivory, rectangular coffered hinged lid above conforming sides w/flared, molded base, carved overall w/fanciful & erotic sea figures & mythological characters, American-made, 19th c., 6¾" l., 6½" h. (ILLUS.) $3,850.00

Chess set, carved figures of Chinese emperor & empress w/attendants, brown-stained & white, China, ca. 1930, in original fitted case, figures 2" to 4" h., the set 595.00

Figures of a girl & boy, each standing nude, she w/one hand raised to swat a colored bug on her arm, he holding a colored fish in one hand, each on an octagonal green onyx pedestal base, by F. Preiss, early 20th c., 7" h., pr...........3,080.00

Figure group, allegorical type w/a standing nude woman w/a cupid grabbing one of her legs, both raised on a carved cloud & drapery pedestal w/a wide scroll-trimmed socle base, Europe, late 19th c., 9½" h..................2,475.00

Jagging wheel, the long handle carved w/a bust portrait of a decollete' classical woman framed by leafy scrolls, notch-carved wheel w/pierced heart spokes, 19th c., 6½" l. 1,980.00

Mirror, the wide oval frame delicately carved overall w/pierced small leaves & figural putti, an armorial shield at the top flanked by female terms, small shields at each side & putti & an initialed plaque at the base, Dieppe, France, early 19th c., 33½" h. (losses) 3,300.00

Models of parrots, each carved w/wings folded back over the long tail, the feathers w/incised details, the undecorated head w/upcurled combs & curled beak, China, 9" l., pr. (cracks).........2,530.00

Plaque, rectangular, carved w/the figure of a seated Chinese lady playing a musical instrument in a garden landscape, seal signature, in a pierce-carved wooden frame, China, 19th c., 7 x 9" 825.00

Puzzle ball, sphere within a sphere, pierce-carved w/dragons & scrolling designs, on a carved stand w/a slender shaft & raised base, overall 8" h. (crack in base)...... 198.00

Triptych, ivory plaques mounted on wood panels, the arched center panel depicting The Adoration of the Magi, a figure of a Magi in

German Ivory Triptych

each half-round side wing, finely detailed & polychrome-painted on a wood ground inlaid w/ivory floral scrolls, monogrammed "T.S.," Germany, 19th c., some losses, 7¾ x 10¾" (ILLUS.) 990.00

Tusk, carved in relief w/scenes of Karako, on a pierced ivory & wood stand, signed "Gyokukan To," Japan, 19th c., 43" l. 4,400.00

JADE

Early Jade Vase

Bowl, low rounded sides w/closed rim, the exterior thinly carved w/the beribboned 'Eight Buddhist' symbols & cloud scrolls between *ruyi* & tasseled *vajra* borders, all reserved on a finely incised diaper ground infilled w/gilt, translucent pale green, China, 18th c., 5¾" d. (gilt rubbed) $6,600.00

Box, cov., round disc-form, the cover carved w/a raised circular medallion enclosing a butterfly above a leafy branch w/two peony blooms, supported on a circular ring foot, translucent pale greenish white, China, 2½" d. ... 990.00

Censer, cov., bulbous body carved w/wide horned monster-mask & loose-ring handles & raised on three scrolled legs w/pad feet, the domed cover surmounted by two lions, one w/paw resting on a ball, four-character Qianlong Yuzhi mark incised on the base & picked-out in red, white, China, 19th c., 4¾" h..................23,100.00

Figure group, horses, carved as a large recumbent horse w/head turned to one side, the incised mane trailing down the back, the tail swished to one side, & a recumbent foal to one side w/its front legs playfully over its mother, greenish white w/a spot of russet on the bottom, natural fissures, China, in the Ming style, 6" l............................4,510.00

Model of a water buffalo, well-carved recumbent animal w/legs tucked under, the head turned to one side, large curled horns & ears held back, centered by an incised flowerhead between the horns, incised jaw & neck folds, tail flicked to one side, greenish white tone w/a patch of brown on the reverse, China, 18th c., 5¼" l. (fissures) 7,700.00

Model of peaches & bats, oblong form carved as two peaches on a leafy stem w/two small bats clinging to the fruit, white, China, 18th c., 4" w. 3,850.00

Vase, archaic bronze form, carved around the sides w/flutes, below a wide band of archaistic decoration & two horned monster-head handles, the short waisted neck w/notches, polished grey-green w/russet & brown rivering, minute chips, China, Ming Dynasty, 17th c., 3 7/8" h. (ILLUS.)........3,080.00

Vase, cov., tall slender baluster-form, the cover w/a lion finial, the neck w/four monster-mask loose-ring handles, the body w/a wide low-relief band of archaistic bronze-style decoration above a lower border of lappets above the round, flaring foot, even pale greenish white, China, 19th c., 9¼" h. 4,675.00

JEWELRY

ANTIQUE (1800-1920)

Bar pin, amethysts, diamonds & platinum, seven collet-set round amethysts alternating w/twelve single-cut diamonds, in a platinum mounting, Edwardian $660.00

Bar pin, gold (14k) & demantoid garnet, demantoid model of a frog perched on a knife-edge bar pin offset w/two diamonds & a demantoid 715.00

Bracelet, bangle-type, garnets & gilt silver, hinged, set w/two rows of garnets, centered w/a stylized floral design set w/garnets, in gilt silver mounting, Victorian........ 275.00

Art Nouveau Bangle Bracelet

Bracelet, bangle-type, gold (14k), sapphire & diamond, Art Nouveau style, hinged, pierced openwork design highlighted w/three sapphires & one diamond, Whiteside and Blank (ILLUS.) 2,200.00

Bracelet, gold (14k) & diamond, each box link composed of chased scrollwork design enhanced w/five diamond center links, hallmarked, ca. 1900 .... 660.00

Bracelet, gold (14k), enamel & pearls, slide-type, gold mesh band, the ornate slide decorated w/half-pearls & black enamel tracery, small beaded tassel attached to slide & larger beaded tassel at end of mesh band, Victorian 1,485.00

Bracelet, sterling silver, Art & Crafts style, composed of alternating links of lightly hammered oblong organic curvilinear elements & small ball beads, impressed "Georg Jensen 9253 Denmark," 11" l. 275.00

Victorian Enamel Brooch

Brooch, enamel & 18k gold, round, depicting the profile of a Classical lady w/a blue ribbon accented by rose-cut diamonds, gold & black enamel mount, Victorian (ILLUS.)........................ 715.00

Brooch, glass, Art Nouveau style, circular embossed plaque of ivy

leaves w/blue foil backing, set
in a gilt metal mounting, signed
"Lalique" 605.00

Brooch, gold (14k), full-bodied model of a rose including petals on
stem, textured gold finish, Victo-
rian 275.00

Brooch, gold (14k) & gems,
butterfly-form silver-topped 14k
gold set w/oval & round sapphires
& rubies highlighted by round diamonds, in a silver-topped 14k
gold mounting, ca. 1900 . . . .   550.00

Brooch, gold (14k) & orange zircon,
Art Nouveau style, designed as
intertwined lotus blossoms highlighted by four round zircons 1,100.00

Brooch, sterling silver, enamel &
pearl, Art Nouveau style, centered by an oblong blister pearl
w/blue-green enamel surrounded
by a pierced sterling silver mount-
ing, hallmarked 522.50

Brooch, tortoiseshell, carved in the
form of a female head in high-
relief flanked by deer heads &
suspending three carved amphora, Victorian (tip of one am-
phora chipped) 1,320.00

Cameo brooch, gold (18k) & hardstone, depicting the full-length
figure of a woman in diaphanous
gown in a rectangular frame
w/wire twist borders set within
an oval mounting & accented by
pearls & rose-cut diamonds, Vic-
torian 990.00

Cameo brooch, sardonyx, pearls &
gold, depicting the bust profile of
a woman w/short curly hair &
wearing a necklace, set within a
frame highlighted by gold beadwork & half pearls, Victorian (oxi-
dation to surface) 715.00

Cameo earrings, gold (18k) & chal-
cedony, cameo framed w/seed
pearls, ornate scrolling & beaded
gold frame, ca. 1870, 2" l., pr. . . .   485.00

Cameo necklace, carved shell, centered by five oval cameos mounted in gold bead-edged frames
joined by florets, completed by a
14k yellow gold foxtail chain, in
original fitted box, Victorian,
16½" l. 880.00

Cameo pendant, hardstone, carved
w/a profile of a young woman
w/a band of ivy in her long curly
hair, mounted in an 18k gold
frame, cameo signed "Michelini,"
minute chip & repair to hair, Victorian (ILLUS. top next column) . .2,420.00

Chain, gold (14k yellow & pink),
composed of navette-shaped links

Victorian Cameo Pendant

joined by reeded links surmounted by a cross design, 20" l. (in-
cludes one additional link) 880.00

Chatelaine, sterling silver, large
heart-shaped pin w/ornate
pierced design suspending a similar smaller piece, the two suspending a pencil, card case,
corkscrew, rouge pot, vesta case,
compact & powder puff case,
maker's mark for Gorham Mfg.
Co. 1,430.00

Cloak pin, sterling silver, centered
by a 4½ x 5½ cm. oval amber
composition stone in a sterling silver frame set w/green stones,
marked "Georg Jensen," ca.
1905 . . . . .4,070.00

Cuff links, gold (18k) & diamond,
Art Nouveau style, designed as
stylized dragons highlighted by
round mine-cut diamonds, pr. 357.50

Cuff links, gold (18k) & enamel, concave yellow gold mountings joined
by a double bar fitting, enameled
w/a red, green, blue or white
scarab, ca. 1900, pr. (enamel
damage) 1,540.00

Earrings, gold (14k yellow), geometric design w/applied wire & beadwork, highlighted w/a 7 mm. ball,
Victorian, pr. 550.00

Earrings, gold (14k) & pearls, highlighted by granulation & twisted
wirework w/half-pearl accents,
kidney ear wires, Victorian, pr. . .   467.50

Earrings, gold (18k) & coral, teardrop shape w/beadwork & center
coral drop on a pierced conform-
ing disc, Victorian, pr. 770.00

Earrings, gold (18k) & porcelain,
drop-type, in a chased strapwork
frame, each plaque depicting a
woman in native Swiss Canton
dress, Victorian, pr. (ILLUS. top
next page) 1,320.00

Earrings, tortoiseshell, oval-shaped
links hanging from an abstract

Victorian Gold & Porcelain Earrings

open design, 10k gold screw-
backs, Victorian, pr. 357.50
Locket, gold (14k) & gems, oval,
hinged to reveal double compartment, decorated w/an applied
buckle accented by diamonds over
a horseshoe set w/pearls & ru-
bies, Victorian, in original case . . 1,870.00
Locket, gold (14k) & porcelain, portrait depicting a lady in 19th c.
dress, in a pierced frame w/seed
pearl border, on a gold-plated
chain, Victorian 605.00
Necklace, enamel, lapis, labradorite
& gold (18k), Egyptian Revival
style, centered by a polychrome
enamel plaque depicting a female
figure wearing an Egyptian headdress, the plaque suspended in
the center of the necklace by gold
chain drapery, highlighted by lapis beads & carved labradorite
scarabs, completed by a lapis
pompeII terminal, all in yellow
gold, signed "Soper 1872," Victo-
rian 2,750.00
Necklace, garnet & gold (14k), cen-
tered w/a row of round garnets,
suspending pear-shaped garnets &
clusters of round & pear-shaped
garnets, completed by a rope
chain, Victorian, 15" l. 385.00
Necklace, gold (14k) & pearls, highlighted by alternating pearl & gold
knife-edge batons, hallmarked,
Edwardian 1,100.00
Necklace, gold (14k) & turquoise,
Art Nouveau style, gold chain set
at intervals w/turquoise in stylized frames alternating w/pierced
gold spheres, 25½" l. 2,640.00
Necklace-pendant, gold, Etruscan
Revival style, a slender loop-in-
loop chain w/whiplash clasp suspending a double-hinged *bullah*,
the front decorated w/granulation
& wire twist in a radiating rose &

Etruscan Revival Necklace-Pendant

scroll design, the back w/gold
beads w/applied Greek letters Ep-
silon, Phi, Omega, Ze, highlighted
by interlocking leaves, in fitted
case marked "P. & P. Santamaria
Via Condotti 84 Rome," ca. 1850,
15½" l. (ILLUS.) 4,675.00
Pendant, gold (14k yellow), in the
form of a cross w/hinged glass
concealed compartment, suspended from a gold-plated beaded &
pierced chain, dated 1866, Vic-
torian 302.50
Pendant, gold (14k), pearl & ame-
thyst, Art Nouveau style, designed as a gold orchid, set
w/two pearls & suspending a
pear-shaped amethyst, suspended
from a link chain, Brassler
Company 330.00
Pendant, plique-a-jour enamel &
pink tourmaline, Art Nouveau
style, stylized foliate design set in
silver & highlighted by tiny pink
glass stones, suspended on a pa-
per clip chain 935.00
Pin, enamel & silver, Egyptian Reviv-
al style, rectangular plaque
depicting a sphinx & hieroglyphics
in brown, blue & green enamel,
Austrian hallmarks 357.50
Pin, gold (14k) & garnet, centered
by a cabochon garnet within a
twisted wire frame flanked by
two tulips, ca. 1900 . . . . 275.00
Pin, gold (14k), pearl & enamel, Art
Nouveau style, crescent-shaped
w/an enamel tulip highlighted by
a pearl 247.50
Pin, micro-mosaic & 14k gold, rec-
tangular black onyx panel inset
w/a design of birds & flowers, in
a multicolored enamel-trimmed
14k gold scrolling frame, 10k gold
finding, nick to onyx, minor sol-
der (ILLUS. top next column) 715.00
Pin, moonstone, heart-shaped

Micro-Mosaic Pin

moonstone within a beaded & wire-edged conforming frame surmounted by a cultured pearl crown, Edwardian 605.00

Pin, pearl, an 8 mm. white button pearl within a rose-cut diamond openwork mounting suspending a genuine natural 7.5 x 9.5 mm. black pearl, in a platinum top & 14k yellow gold mount, Edwardian 2,750.00

Ring, gold (14k yellow), memorial-type, navette-shaped mounting containing a painted miniature of a seated female figure & a dog, 19th c., in fitted case 522.50

Ring, gold (14k) & turquoise, Egyptian Revival style, bezel-set cabochon turquoise matrix within hieroglyphs flanked by Ptolemaic queens w/vulture headdresses, ca. 1900 ....1,320.00

Ring, gold (18k), modeled in the form of a snake w/rose-cut diamond eyes, English hallmarks, dated "1902" 522.50

Ring, gold (18k), man's signet-type, w/cypher monogram flanked by a lion & a tiger, ca. 1907 .... 330.00

Watch chain, gold (14k) & turquoise, gold link chain set w/seven oval cabochon-cut turquoise, Victorian, 50" l. 412.50

Watch chain & slide, gold (14k), rectangular slide accented by pearls & gold tassel pendant, Victorian .. 770.00

Watch chain & slide, gold (14k) rope chain & slide highlighted w/seed pearls, 48" l. 330.00

Watch chain & slide, gold (14k), w/double barrel slide highlighted by black enamel tracery & red stones, Victorian, 62" l. 880.00

SETS

Brooch & bracelet: gold & hardstone, Egyptian Revival style, the bracelet designed as alternating links w/lotus & cobra designs set w/blue hardstone scarabs, the winged brooch centered by a hardstone scarab, 19th c., the set (ILLUS.) 1,210.00

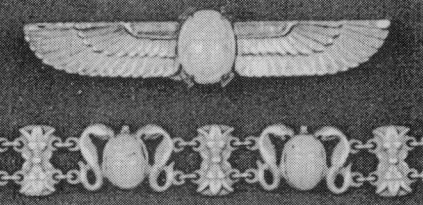

Egyptian Revival Brooch & Bracelet

Brooch & earrings: 18k gold, each designed as interlocking polished & reeded loops, each w/a central plaque highlighted by applied wirework, Victorian, the set 1,540.00

Necklace & earrings: gold (18k) & enamel, flat figure-eight segments alternating w/flat cartouche-form links, decorated & engraved w/birds in multicolor enamels, earrings of conforming design, the set.......................... 880.00

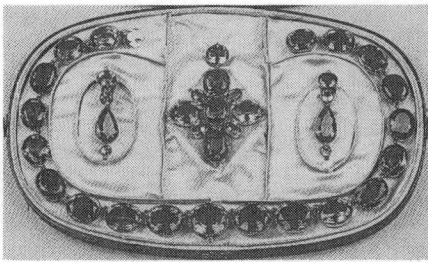

Amethyst Suite of Jewelry

Necklace, earrings & pendant: amethyst & 14k gold, the necklace composed of large, graduated oval stones, the earrings set w/large teardrop stones, the detachable pendant in the form of a cross set w/large oval stones, all set in 14k gold mountings, the earrings w/12k gold-filled findings, w/original leather case, 19th c., the set (ILLUS.)..........2,640.00

MODERN - 1920's - 1960's

The bright sparkling jewelry so popular from the 1920's through the 1960's has again come into its own. The baubles of rhinestones (faceted glass with a foil backing), colored glass stones and faux pearls were affordable to a large segment of the population with prices ranging from very low — less than a dollar for a rhinestone dress clip — to well over $100 for a well-designed article utilizing sterling silver mountings set with fine Austrian crystal. Some pieces were in excellent taste, resembling fine jewelry, while others were flamboyantly fake with a multitude of rhinestones interspersed with brilliantly colored glass stones. Also see BAKELITE.

Belt, rhinestone, w/799 claw-set
stones, marked "Christian Dior,"
23" l. 275.00
Bracelet, Austrian crystal, marked
"Eisenberg Ice," ½" w. 75.00
Bracelet, Bakelite, bangle-type,
carved acorns, cranberry,
1½" w. 175.00
Bracelet, Bakelite, bangle-type,
carved florals, translucent orange,
¾" w. 70.00
Bracelet, faux pearls w/rhinestone
clasp, two-strand, marked "Miriam Haskell" 125.00
Bracelet, gold (14k yellow) & citrine,
twelve square-cut citrines set
within a textured gold background
highlighted by small round diamonds in navette mountings, ca.
1950's 1,540.00
Bracelet, rhinestone, individually
set, three-row, flexible band, ca.
1940 .... 55.00
Bracelet, silver-tone metal, double
lion's head clasp, marked "Ken-
neth Jay Lane"................. 75.00
Brooch, baroque pearls & rhinestones, model of a flower w/leaf,
marked "Coro Craft" 75.00
Brooch, blue rhinestones, model of
a leaf, marked "Weiss" 38.00
Brooch, citrine & sterling silver,
model of a stag head............ 75.00
Brooch, gold (14k yellow), amethyst
& ruby, stylized swirl shape, Tiffany & Co., ca. 1950's 1,320.00
Brooch, red rhinestones & pearls,
model of a floral spray, marked
"Coro Craft" 100.00
Brooch, sterling silver, model of a
castle, marked "Trifari" 85.00
Brooch, sterling silver, model of a
floral bouquet, marked "Hobe" ... 275.00
Brooch, sterling silver & amethyst,
a two-leaf cluster surrounded by
thirteen individually set amethyst
quartz "berries" on slender stems,
by Frederick Davis, marked "FD -
FD Sterling Mexico," 3¼" l. 220.00
Brooch, sterling silver & colored
rhinestones, model of a bow,
marked "Eisenberg," 3½" l....... 200.00
Brooch, sterling silver w/gold wash,
model of a sailfish, marked
"Trifari" 125.00
Cuff links, celluloid, model of a bulldog, green, pr. 50.00
Dress clip, sterling silver, model of
a bird, marked "Trifari".......... 140.00
Earrings, Bakelite, clip-type, model
of a heart, red, pr.............. 38.00
Earrings, gold-tone metal w/pave'
set rhinestones, marked "Schra-
ger," pr. 20.00

Jade & Onyx Earrings

Earrings, jade & onyx, rectangular
cut-corner black onyx link joined
by diamond & platinum links &
suspending a jade drop, gold
wires, Art Deco style, pr.
(ILLUS.) 3,300.00
Earrings, pink, blue & clear rhinestones, dangle-type, marked
"Mosell," pr.................... 35.00
Earrings, sterling silver, model of
a tulip, marked "Georg Jensen,"
pr........................... 65.00
Locket, gold (14k) & diamonds,
hinged, heart-shaped w/diamonds
forming a small leaf shape, ca.
1920 .... 250.00
Necklace, abalone shell & silver,
choker-type, marked "Taxco,"
16½" l. 50.00
Necklace, Bakelite & celluloid,
models of carved acorns on a celluloid chain, amber.............. 125.00
Necklace, baroque pearls w/pearl-
ized castle-shaped pendant,
marked "Miriam Haskell," 20" l. ... 165.00
Necklace, colored beads & fresh-
water pearls, five-strand, marked
"Miriam Haskell" 58.00
Necklace, gold-tone metal, leaf
design, marked "Joseff of Hollywood" 302.50
Necklace, rhinestone, baguette-cut
& individually set, bow-shaped
fastener, marked "Christian Dior,"
18" l. 45.00
Necklace, rhinestone, choker-type,
individually set, six-strand,
marked "Kramer, NY.," 15" l. 65.00
Necklace, silver-tone metal & large
iridescent rhinestones, chunky design, marked "Schiaparelli" 345.00
Necklace, sterling silver chain,
beads & rhinestones, marked
"Alice Caviness" 50.00
Necklace, Venetian glass beads,
marked "Miriam Haskell," 30" l. ... 80.00
Pin, Bakelite, bar-type, carved,
red 38.00

Pin, Bakelite, model of a branch
w/four cherries, green & red 100.00
Pin, blue rhinestones, model of a
cat, marked "Alice Caviness" 25.00
Pin, Czechoslovakian crystal, model
of a leaf, marked "Miriam Haskell" 475.00
Pin, diamond, black onyx & platinum, Art Deco style, circular,
channel-set w/calibre-cut black
onyx, surmounted by two platinum scrolls highlighted by round
European- and single-cut diamonds, in a platinum mounting ..2,200.00
Pin, emerald green & clear rhinestones, model of a flower,
marked "Eisenberg" 90.00
Pin, enameled metal w/rhinestones,
model of a lobster, red, marked
"Hattie Carnegie," 4½" l. 95.00
Pin, gold (14k bi-color) & citrine, a
bi-color scrolled & fluted dome
enhanced w/a large oval citrine, signed "Seaman Schepps,"
1940's 990.00

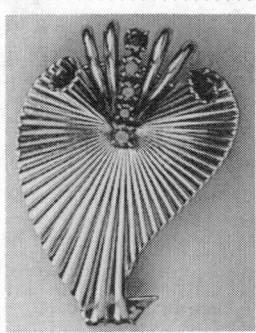

Gold & Ruby Pin

Pin, gold (14k yellow) & ruby, fluted
leaf form high-lighted by five
round rubies, engraved "Cartier
297," ca. 1940's (ILLUS.) 1,100.00
Pin, gold-tone metal & apple green
rhinestones, models of leaves,
marked "Corocraft". 50.00
Pin, gold-tone metal & rhinestones,
model of a leaf, marked "Pen-
nino" 90.00
Pin, gold-tone metal w/four topaz-
colored stones, model of a heart
& cherub, marked "Joseff" 125.00
Pin, multicolored stones & crystal,
model of a fish, marked "Coro,"
3" l. 125.00
Pin, red enamel, model of a flower
in a pot, marked "Coro Craft" 55.00
Pin, rhinestone, model of a bird on
a branch, marked "Trifari" 100.00
Pin, rhinestone, model of a snowflake, marked "Hattie Carnegie".. 35.00
Pin, rhodium, set w/large facet-cut

smoky-colored glass center & accented w/rhinestones, marked
"Sarah Coventry," ca. 1960 .... 29.00
Pin, rock crystal & gilt-metal, spherical rock crystal fruit suspended
from gilt-metal branches w/cabo-
chon rock crystal detailing, signed
"Mazer," ca. 1940, 2 x 4¼" 220.00
Pin, sterling silver, a circular
repousse' leaf wreath w/four
blossoms each formed by a cluster of five brilliant green cabo-
chons, impressed "Georg Jensen
Sterling - Denmark 4B," 1¾" d. .. 412.50
Pin, sterling silver, model of a donkey w/movable head, marked
"Martinez," Mexico 28.00
Pin, sterling silver, model of a flying
goose, marked "Coro," 4" l....... 125.00
Pin, sterling silver, model of an
orchid, marked "Maricella,"
Mexico 110.00
Pin, sterling silver & aqua glass center, model of a poodle, marked
"Trifari" 200.00
Ring, bi-colored tourmaline, enamel
& 14k yellow gold, central oval
cabochon set in a cut-corner rectangular gold mounting, accented
w/green & black enamel decoration 660.00

SETS

Pin & Earring Set

Bracelet & clip earrings: smoke,
emerald & rainbow-colored
stones; marked "Alice Caviness,"
bracelet 1¼" w., 3 pcs........... 75.00
Bracelet, pin & ring: silver w/disk-
form pearlized centers; marked
"Barclay," 3 pcs. 45.00
Brooch & earrings: clear & smoky-
colored rhinestones, wing-shaped
brooch & matching earrings;
marked "Weiss," 3 pcs. 40.00
Brooch & earrings: pave' set rhinestones, matching earrings, model of a leaf; marked "Trifari,"
3 pcs. 150.00
Brooch & earrings: sterling silver,
model of a floral bouquet, matching earrings; marked "Kalo,"
brooch 2 x 2", 3 pcs. 450.00

Brooch, bracelet & earrings: multicolored rhinestones, brooch &
earrings are models of a crown;
marked "Weiss," 4 pcs. 195.00

Necklace & earrings: amethyst glass
necklace w/three strands strung
on chain, matching earrings;
marked "Vogue," 3 pcs. 35.00

Necklace & earrings: Bakelite, red,
huge chunky style, matching earrings; 24" l. necklace, 3 pcs. 125.00

Necklace, bracelet & earrings:
chrome & marbleized Bakelite;
necklace composed of rectangular
chrome links alternating w/longer
rectangular Bakelite pieces
w/small link chain & closure,
w/matching 2" bracelet & ear-
rings, 4 pcs. 450.00

Pin & earrings: blue & green rhinestones, model of a circle; marked
"B. David," 3 pcs. 40.00

Pin & earrings: enameled metal,
model of a flower basket; marked
"Trifari," 3 pcs. 75.00

Pin & earrings: 14k yellow gold, fan-
shaped w/engine-turned striped
design; 1940's, 3 pcs. (ILLUS.)..... 495.00

JUKE BOXES

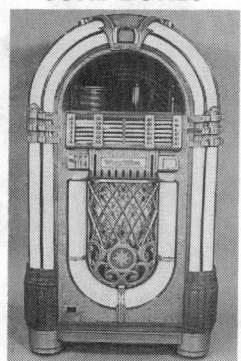

Wurlitzer Model 1015

Mills Model 801, 1927, original &
working condition $4,800.00

Ristaucrat, countertop model, 5c
play, 45 rpm, ca. 1950 .... 650.00

Rock-Ola Model 1426, 1947 (restored) 5,500.00

Rock-Ola Model 1496, "Empress,"
1962 (restored) 2,600.00

Seeburg Model KD 200, 1957 ...... 1,750.00

Seeburg "Selectophone," 1932,
green & gold paint, mint, original
condition 2,500.00

Wurlitzer Model 600, 1938, the

glazed front revealing twenty-four
selections flanked by columns of
illuminated plastics, within
veneered case ...... 2,500.00 to 3,000.00

Wurlitzer Model 700, 1940 (restored) 4,200.00

Wurlitzer Model 750, 1941 (restored) 7,900.00

Wurlitzer Model 850 (Peacock),
1941 .... 20,000.00 to 23,000.00

Wurlitzer Model 1015, 1946-47
(ILLUS.) .... 7,500.00 to 10,000.00

Wurlitzer Model 1100, 1948-49 (restored)............. 5,500.00 to 6,500.00

Wurlitzer Model 2304, 1959 .... 1,000.00

KEWPIE COLLECTIBLES

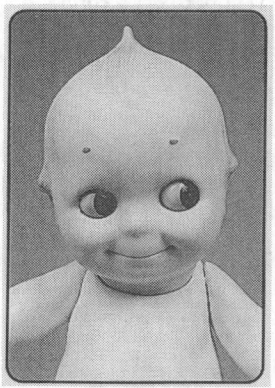

Large Kewpie Doll

*Rose O'Neill's Kewpies were so popular in
their heyday that numerous objects depicting them were produced and are now collectible. The following represents a sampling.*

Bowl w/domed cover, china, decorated w/three action Kewpies
on the cover, marked "J.C.
Bavaria"....................... $135.00

Creamer, china, depicts five Kewpies playing, Royal Rudolstadt 75.00

Doll, bisque w/jointed arms,
marked "Rose O'Neill" on the
right foot & "Japan" on the back,
7" h. 295.00

Doll, bisque socket head w/large
brown glass side-glancing eyes,
dot brows, closed watermelon
smiling mouth w/molded cheeks,
molded & painted tufts of hair,
jointed composition chubby toddler body w/starfish hands,
marked "Ges. gesch. O'Neill
J.D.K. 12," 13" h. (ILLUS.) 4,600.00

Figure, buttonhole-type, bisque, stiff

standing Kewpie w/arms raised, painted black side-glancing eyes, closed smiling mouth, molded & painted tufts of hair, painted blue wings, raised button extending from the back, 2" h. (tiny flaw on stomach) 105.00

Figure, bisque, standing w/jointed shoulders, molded & painted blue wings, painted black side-glancing eyes, dot brows, closed smiling mouth, molded & painted tufts of hair, marked w/paper label reading "Copyright Rose O'Neill" on back & "Kewpie Germany" on red heart label on stomach, 4" h. (very short firing line at neck).... 75.00

Postcard, Christmas, 1924 .... 31.00

KITCHENWARES

Also see METALS - IRON and WOODEN-WARES categories.

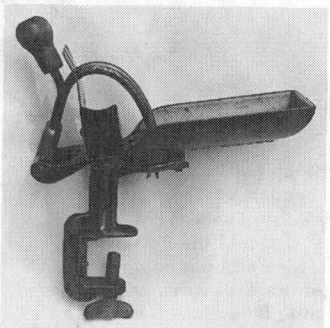

Cast-Iron Cherry Pitter

Aebleskiver pan, cast iron, "Griswold No. 32," round $55.00

Apple parer, cast iron, marked "Turntable 98," made by Goodell Co., Antrim, New Hampshire, 1898 patent date 55.00

Apple parer, White Mountain, Goodell Co., mint in original box w/instructions, 1940's 44.00

Batter bowl, spouted, green glass, Anchor Hocking Glass Corp., 7" d. 25.00

Bottle corker, cherry, turned cylinder w/plunger, mushroom knob handle, ca. 1870, 14½" l. 49.00

Bread box, white enameled metal w/cobalt blue Holland scene, Germany 80.00

Brownie pan, cast iron, "Griswold No. 9" 85.00

Butter churn, "Dazey No. 40," glass jar w/metal lid & mechanism &

wooden paddles, pat. Feb. 14, 1922 .... 85.00

Butter churn, "Dazey No. 80," glass jar w/metal lid & mechanism 88.00

Butter churn, "Fenner," wooden barrel-type on legs, Fredrickson Brothers, Cassadaga, New York .. 220.00

Butter churn, "Oakes Mfg. Co.," glass w/tin lid & cast-iron crank, 1 gal. 230.00

Butter churn, "Standard Churn Co.," wooden barrel-type w/oak staves & iron fittings 250.00

Canister set, china, colorful graduated square canisters in pearlized cream ground trimmed in red & yellow, Czechoslovakia, ca. 1920's, set of 12 (some inside cover chips) 275.00

Cheese grater, tin, slightly curved w/rolled edges, end hole for hanging, 5¼" w., 13¼" l......... 30.00

Cherry pitter, cast iron, "Goodell Co., Antrim, N.H. U.S.A.," clamp-on model, 1895 patent, 6¾" l. (ILLUS.)........................ 40.00

Cherry pitter, cast iron, "New Standard No. 50," clamp-on model.... 60.00

Cherry pitter, cast iron, "Rollman," clamp-on model 35.00

Cookie board, springerle-type, hand-carved wood, fish & birds designs in twelve blocks, 5½ x 8½"..................... 150.00

Cornstick pan, cast iron, "Griswold No. 22," pattern No. 954A, large letter mark 40.00

Cornstick pan, cast iron, "Griswold No. 282," Crispy Corn or wheat stick-type, seven compartments, 7 5/8 x 14" 65.00

Cream whip, cov., tin, cast iron & wood, crank mechanism on cover, four-footed, "Fries," ca. 1890, 6" l., 4½" w., 8" h. 92.50

Dutch oven, cov., cast iron, "Griswold No. 8" 72.50

Dutch oven, cov., cast iron, "Wagnerware No. 9" 45.00

Eggbeater, w/metal bowl, "A & J Full Vision Beater" 57.50

Eggbeater, "Ladd," spiral wire handle w/wooden knob, patented 1921 .... 14.00

Egg poacher, tin, arched long handle, holds four eggs in spring-loaded holder on round 7" disc w/drain holes for each, signed "Silvers," Brooklyn, New York 49.00

Food chopper, squared steel blade mounted w/a graceful baluster-turned wooden handle, blade marked "Brades Co., Cast Steel," 7½" l. 75.00

Food grinder, standing table-type, cast iron w/tinned finish, "Enterprise No. 12" 34.50

Food grinder, cast iron w/tinned finish, "Griswold No. 1" 25.00

Food grinder, cast iron, "Griswold No. 1111" 25.00

Food grinder, cast metal, "Keen Kutter No. 10" 20.00

Food grinder, cast iron, "Larkin," w/four blades 25.00

Food grinder, cast metal, "Winchester No. 12" 75.00

Griddle, cast iron, "Ballard & Ballard Company," Louisville, Kentucky, 10" d. 100.00

Horseradish grater, pine & pierced tin, w/arched ends & drawer front, ca. 1860, 5¼ x 6¾", 14" l. 295.00

Ice shaver, cast iron & steel, "Griswold No. 2" 125.00

Juice reamer, clear glass, "Radnt" .. 75.00

Juice reamer, transparent pink glass, "Radnt" 750.00

Juice reamer, transparent green glass, "Anchor Hocking" 15.00

Juice reamer, transparent green glass, "Federal" 7.00

Knife, pressed glass, plain handle, pink, w/box, 9" l. 15.00

Kraut cutter, rectangular pine board w/a rounded end w/a hanging hole, the edges w/reinforcing strips flanking the angled iron blade, red finish & scratch-carved date "1801," 19¼" l. 93.50

Ladle, clear glass, relief lettering on cup "Marbury patented 4/21/96," turned wood handle, handle 9" l. 100.00

Lemon squeezer, cast iron, "Ideal No. 12," w/glass insert 29.50

Mayonnaise jar & beater, clear glass, round, "Hutchinson" 150.00

Meat tenderizer, cylindrical stoneware head w/raised grids, marked "Pat'd Dec 25, 1877," w/turned wood handle, overall 9½" l. 71.50

Mixing bowl, amber glass, rolled rim, 9½" d. 12.00

Mixing bowls, nesting-type, Jadite Green glass, Swirl patt., Fire King line, Anchor Hocking Glass Co., 6", 8" & 9" d., 3 pcs. 16.00

Muffin pan, cast iron, "G.F. Filley No. 3," w/fourteen round cups, 7 5/8 x 11¾" 100.00

Nutmeg grater, tin & cast iron, wooden handle, marked "The Edgar - Edgar Mfg. Co.," w/patent dates, 7" l. 75.00

Pantry box, cov., round bentwood, stitched lappet construction w/two finger lappets on the base & one on the cover, painted grey, 19th c., 9½" d. 357.50

Pastry roller, wood, small wheel w/carved leaf & strawberry design in horseshoe-shaped holder w/short handle, 5 1/8" h. 75.00

Pepper shaker w/original metal lid, square, Delphite Blue glass, Jeannette Glass Co., 4½" h. 95.00

Pepper shaker w/original metal lid, Jadite Green glass, Jeannette Glass Co. 8.00

Pepper shaker w/original metal lid, milk white glass w/tulip decoration, Fire King line, Anchor Hocking Glass Co. 6.00

Pie baking tin, metal, "Ovenex No. 710" 18.00

Popover pan, cast iron, eleven-cup, "Griswold No. 10 949-b" 32.00

Old Chain Link Pot Scrubber

Pot scrubber, wire chain links, long iron loop handle (ILLUS.) 39.00

Raisin seeder, cast iron, marked "Ezy Raisin Seeder, Pat. May 21, 1895" & "Scald the Raisins," 6" l. (one wire prong missing) 104.50

Refrigerator dish, cov., rectangular, Delphite Blue glass, Jeannette Glass Co., 4 x 8" 55.00

Refrigerator dish, cov., transparent green glass, Crisscross patt., Hazel-Atlas Company, 8" sq. 30.00

Rolling pin, springerle-type, hand-carved wood, 20-block design 150.00

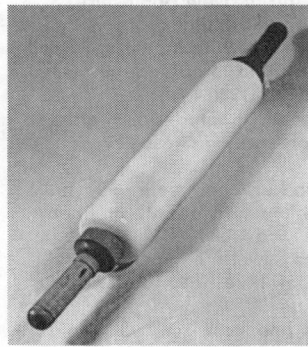

Milk White Glass Rolling Pin

Rolling pin, pressed milk white glass

cylinder w/turned wood handles, marked on end "Imperial Mfg. Co. - July 25, 1921," overall 22" l. (ILLUS.) 48.00

Rolling pin, stoneware w/blue bands decoration on the ends & wooden handles 175.00

Salt box w/wooden lid, hanging-type, ceramic, black lettering & decal decoration of long-tailed blue birds, Czechoslovakia 45.00

Salt & pepper shakers w/original metal lids, milk white glass w/swan decoration, one w/"Salt," the other w/"Pepper," Tipp City Glass Company, 3" h., pr. 25.00

Skillet, cast iron, "Griswold Erie No. 8" 28.00

Skillet, cov., cast iron, "Griswold No. 9," self-basting, patent dated 1920 . . . . 35.00

Skillet, cast iron, "Griswold No. 14" . . . . 125.00 to 150.00

Skillet, cast iron, "Griswold No. 666" 27.50

Skillet, cast iron, "Sperry No. 8," patent dated 1887 . . . . 65.00

Skillet, cast iron, "Wagner No. 2" . . . 85.00

Skimmer, wrought iron & brass, the round slightly dished brass bowl w/holes joined to a flattened iron handle w/a small inlaid heart & a heart loop at the end, 9 1/8" l. 467.50

KNIVES

Knives of all types are collectible today but especially popular are better quality pocket types from the late 19th and early 20th century. Even more modern knives by such makers as Case and Remington are sought after. Overall condition of the knife's blade(s) and handle are very important in pricing with mint, unsharpened knives bringing premium prices.

Advertising, "Kinney Shoes," pocket knife, unusual colorful marbleized case, blade embossed "Colonial-Providence, Rhode Island" $50.00

Case switchblade, No. 6161L, green bone handle, pre-1940, closed 4 3/8" l. 825.00

Case XX pocket knife, No. 62009, Barlow model, two-blade, bone handle, 1940-65, closed 3 5/16" l. 30.00

Case XX pocket knife, No. 62042, two-blade, bone handle, 1950-65, closed 3" l. 25.00

Case XX pocket knife, No. 5265SAB, two-blade, stag handle, 1940-65, closed 5¼" l. 85.00

Keen Kutter pocket knife, No. 882 . . 47.50

Moreley (W.H.) & Sons pocket knife, bone handle 22.00

Remington hunting knife, No. R1306, bullet emblem, stag handle, closed 5½" l. 125.00

Remington pocket knife, No. R603, shield emblem, small serpentine bone handle, closed 3 3/8" l. 50.00

Remington pocket knife, No. R6785, two-blade office knife 50.00

Robeson "Suredge" pocket knife, No. 922295, three-blade, brown "Shur Wood" handle, brass lining, closed 3 3/8" l. 30.00

Schmidt & Ziegler pocket knife, No. 4031, Germany 22.00

Winchester maize knife, No. 1614, single blade, cocobolo handle, closed 4 1/8" l. 55.00

Winchester pocket knife, No. 2303, "Small Senator" model, two-blade, pearl handle, closed 2 5/8" l. 40.00

LACQUER

Japanese Lacquer Saddle

Most desirable of the lacquer articles available for collectors are those of Japanese and Chinese origin, and the finest of these were produced during the Ming and Ching dynasties, although the Chinese knew the art of fashioning articles of lacquer centuries before. Cinnabar is carved red lacquer.

Basin, deep sides w/everted rim, supported on a tall slightly flared circular foot, decorated w/flower sprays in gold *hiramakie* on a deep red ground, Japan, 19th c., 14" d. (extensive wear) $137.00

Bowl, 10¾" d., 3" h., lotus-form, green w/a red blossom, Japan, 19th c. 605.00

Box, cov., cinnabar, round disc form, the cover carved w/a monkey seated on a gnarled trunk & holding a peach below a calligraphic inscription, all on a rolling wave ground, similarly repeated around the box w/three evenly spaced double flowerheads, lappets encircling the footring, China, 17th - 18th c., 2 7/8" d. (repairs) 1,760.00

Box, cov., gilt-decorated, rectangular, fitted on the interior w/four square silver-mounted clear glass bottles w/glass stoppers, Chinese Export, early to mid-19th c., 6" l., the set 275.00

Box, cov., cinnabar, ingot-shaped, the cover deeply carved, the panel of sages in a grove of bamboo trees, a further group to one side playing *go*, the foreground w/figures on a bridge, the sides w/continuous friezes of scholars & attendants & figures in boats on a lake within angular scroll bands, Qianlong Dynasty, China, 12¼" l. 4,400.00

Chair, black frame w/scrolled crestrail above a pierced fretwork back, the seat raised on square legs joined by stretchers, decorated w/mother-of-pearl inlay, Ming Dynasty, China, 16th c. (lacquer losses) 660.00

Food storage box, cov., rectangular, comprising four tiers of varying depths, a cover & shallow tray, all decorated in gold *togidashi*, *hiramake* & gold & silver *kirikane* w/scattered cherry blossoms & a meandering stream on a *roiro* ground, red lacquer interiors, Meiji period, Japan, 8" h. 2,750.00

Kimono stands, miniature, each decorated in gold *hiramakie* on a *roiro* ground, the first w/clusters of sea plants & shells, fitted w/gilt & *shakudo* mounts, the second w/scattered *aoi mon* amid *karakusa*, fitted w/chased brass mounts, Japan, 19th c., 23½" & 19½" h., 2 pcs. 2,860.00

Ring box, cov., rectangular w/rounded corners, the cover depicting a scene of a standing lady holding a flame aloft in one hand, a nobleman standing behind her, signed, Russia, 2 x 2 3/8" 385.00

Saddle, of gold & polychrome lacquers on *roiro* on metal, Meiji period, Japan, 24¼" l. (ILLUS.) ... 935.00

Tables, nesting-type, a rectangular top on an open trestle base w/pierced vasiform ends on flaring tapering legs, decorated

w/gilt foliate sprays on a black ground, China, 19th c., graduated nest of three, largest 12 x 21", 27¾" h., the set 770.00

Writing box, rectangular w/beveled edges & chamfered corners, decorated in gold & silver *takamakie*, *hiramakie* & *kirikane* on *nashiji* grounds, the exterior depicting a temple nestled among mountain peaks beside a stream, the interior w/a farmhouse amid rolling hills, fitted w/inkstone & silver waterdropper, 19th c., 8 1/8 x 9¼" (chips) 3,575.00

LAUNDRY ROOM ITEMS

The "good old days" weren't really all that good when Monday "wash day" and Tuesday "ironing day" came around. There was a lot of hard work involved in scrubbing clothes on the washboard and smoothing out the wrinkles with the hefty flatiron or "sadiron" (sad=heavy). Today collectors can look back with some nostalgia on those adjuncts of the laundry room, curious relics of the not too distant past.

IRONS

Electric iron, "Sunbeam Model A-9" $12.00

Fluting iron, "The Best," made by C.W. Whitefield, Syracuse, New York, cast iron, 5½" l., 4" h., 2 pcs. 85.00

Fluting iron, "Geneva Improved," w/brass inserts 195.00

Gas iron, "Royal," self-heating model, in original box 35.00

Sadiron, "Asbestos," w/detachable handle, patented May 22, 1900, 5" l. 39.50

Sadiron, child's, "Enterprise," 2¾" l. 165.00

Sadiron, child's, "Dover No. 602," w/matching trivet, 3¼" l., 2 pcs. 85.00

Sadiron, "Sensible No. 4," w/detachable handle, 5¼" l. 75.00

Sadiron, child's, swan-shaped, cast iron, 3" l. 95.00

SPRINKLING BOTTLES

Ceramic, figural Chinaman, California Cleminsons................. 28.50

Ceramic, model of a clothespin, yellow 79.00

Ceramic, model of an iron w/ivy vines on sides 36.00

Ceramic, Muggsy's "Myrtle," Pfaltzgraff Pottery 70.00

Hard plastic, figural girl w/hands on hips............................ 18.00

Soft plastic, model of an elephant, red 18.00

WASHBOARDS

Glass insert, child's, embossed "CRYSTAL," corrugated transparent green glass in wooden frame 95.00

Graniteware insert, cobalt blue 59.00

Roller-type, wooden frame w/turned wooden spools on rods laid in close rows, "Mother Hubbard's Patent Roller Washboard," late 19th c. 100.00

LEHN WARE

Wooden items made and decorated by Joseph Lehn, Lancaster County, Pennsylvania, command high prices. To supplement his income from farming, Lehn began making barrels for local gristmills in the mid-1850's and, a few years later, began to turn small wooden items as gifts for family and friends. The popularity of the small wooden items led him to begin to decorate these items for local stores in Lititz and New Euphrata, Pennsylvania. Today, these turned wooden bowls, buckets, boxes and covered, footed bowls, enhanced with hand-painted colorful stripes, stylized borders, floral or fruit designs, almost always on a salmon or dusty pink ground, will seldom be found for under $200 unless there is some damage to the piece.

Blanket chest, miniature, a rectangular top lifting above a case w/molded base, raised on short turned feet, decorated w/original red paint w/striping in green, white, yellow & black, a painted panel on the front decorated w/colorful floral transfer designs & an oval portrait of a lady, 9½" l. (escutcheon missing, lock loose)........................$850.00

Cup, wide rounded bowl on a short pedestal w/a round foot, original polychrome floral decoration on a light green ground, 2 7/8" h. (glued break in foot) 625.00

Cup, ovoid bowl w/flared rim on a short pedestal w/round foot, decorated w/original polychrome florals on a blue ground, 3 1/8" h. (minor wear, small flaked area) .. 925.00

Egg cup, footed, ovoid bowl w/original polychrome flowers on a salmon ground, 2¾" h. (wear) ... 225.00

Jar, cov., tall slightly flaring stave-constructed cylinder w/metal bands, flat turned cover w/porcelain knob, original red graining w/the black bands painted w/floral vines in yellow, green, white & red, alligatored surface, 8" h. (some wear) 2,000.00

Saffron jar, cov., deep rounded bowl on short pedestal & round foot, a slightly domed cover w/knop finial, decorated w/a polychrome design of flowers & strawberries on a salmon pink ground, 5 1/8" h. (minor wear, one foot chip & smaller nicks) 350.00

LIGHTING DEVICES

LAMPS

FAIRY LAMPS

These are candle burning night lights of the Victorian era. Best known are the Clarke Fairy Lamps made in England, but they were also made by other firms. They were produced in two sizes, each with a base and a shade. The Fairy Pyramid Lamps listed below usually have a clear glass base and are approximately 2 7/8" d. and 3¼" h. The Fairy Lamps are usually at least 4" d. and 5" h. when assembled and these may or may not have an additional saucer or bottom holder to match the shade in addition to the clear base.

Fairy Pyramid Lamps

Amber Diamond Point patt. glass shade on matching base, w/marked "Clarke" clear glass insert, 4" h. $250.00

Amber opalescent swirl glass shade, marked "Clarke" clear glass base, 2 7/8" d., 4" h. 95.00

Blue Diamond Quilted patt. mother-of-pearl satin glass shade w/white lining, marked "Clarke" clear glass base, 2 7/8" d., 3 5/8" h. 145.00

Cranberry Diamond Quilted patt. glass shade, marked "Clarke" clear glass base, 2 7/8" d., 3½" h......................... 95.00

Cranberry frosted glass shade w/opaque white spatter, marked "Clarke" clear glass base, 2 7/8" d., 3½" h. 125.00

Frosted sapphire blue Drape patt. glass shade, marked "Clarke" clear glass base, 4" d., 4 7/8" h. 145.00

Pink overlay w/rose swirl glass
shade w/embossed ribs, matching
self-base, white lining, 3" d.,
3½" h. 165.00
Spangled glass shade w/embossed
swirls, cranberry w/mica flecks
& irregular green threading,
marked "Clarke" clear glass base,
2 7/8" d., 3½" h. 165.00
Spatter glass shade in yellow &
white, marked "Clarke" clear
glass base, 2 7/8" d., 3½" h. 125.00
Yellow satin glass shade w/em-
bossed ribs, marked "Clarke"
clear glass base, 2 7/8" d.,
3½" h. 125.00

Fairy Lamps

Yellow Overshot Fairy Lamp

Baccarat clear embossed Sunburst
patt. glass shade on matching
saucer base, 5¾" d., 3 7/8" h. . . . 165.00
Blue Swirl patt. mother-of-pearl
satin glass shade, marked
"Clarke" clear glass base,
3 7/8" d., 5" h. 195.00
Burmese glass epergne, flared glass
base supports three metal rings
holding clear glass candle cups
w/Burmese shades, center
w/small turned-in bowl & ruffled
turned-down vase, marked "Thos.
Webb & Sons," 10¾" h. 2,130.00
Burmese glass shade w/matching
base & pleated skirt, base marked
"Thos. Webb & Sons Queen's Burmese Ware Patented," w/marked
"Clarke's Criklite Trade Mark"
clear glass candle cup w/fairy
logo, skirt 7½" d., 5½" h. 950.00
Frosted blue shaded to clear glass
shade w/embossed design & ruffled rim, shaded blue frosted
glass ruffled base, 6¼" d.,
7¼" h. 395.00
Green Diamond Quilted patt. glass
shade, clear glass base, 4" d.,
5" h. 145.00
Lacy brass openwork shade w/eight
large colored jewels on handled
brass saucer base w/place for

candle, 4 5/8" d., 4" h. 225.00
Lithophane shade w/three panels.
one of a young boy & his dog,
one w/two boys climbing a fence
& the third w/a young child looking out a window, marked
"Clarke" clear glass base, 4" d.,
4¾" h. 595.00
Overshot glass shade, frosted white
on yellow, in white porcelain base
marked "Clarke Patent," 3½" d.,
4½" h. (ILLUS.) 275.00

Peach Blow Shade on Ornate Base

Peach Blow glass shade decorated
w/enameled leafy vines, fitted
into clear glass candle cup raised
atop an ornate gilt metal figural
stand w/tall crossed palm trees
behind a prancing goat on a leaf-
molded foot, Thomas Webb &
Sons, late 19th c. (ILLUS.) 1,600.00
Ruby Bohemian glass shade
w/etched deer & castle scene, on
matching cup base, 4½" h. 275.00
Shaded blue satin glass epergne,
two shades w/white linings fitted
into marked "Clarke" clear glass
bases set into brass branch arms
supported by a tall, slender clear
cut glass columnar standard w/a
round foot, overall 14" w.,
16½" h. 550.00
Teal blue & white swirl overlay
glass w/embossed swirl pattern
shade w/white lining, marked
"Clarke" clear glass base, 4" d.,
4 7/8" h. 195.00
Verre Moire (Nailsea) glass shade,
frosted chartreuse green
w/opaque white loopings, marked
"Clarke" clear glass base,
3 7/8" d., 4½" h. 170.00
Verre Moire (Nailsea) glass shade,
frosted citron w/white loopings,
matching ruffled base, w/a

marked "Clarke's Criklite Trade
Mark" clear glass candle cup,
9½" d. base, 5¾" h. 845.00
Verre Moire (Nailsea) glass shade,
frosted cranberry w/opaque white
loopings, marked "Clarke" clear
glass base, 3 7/8" d., 4½" h. 175.00
Verre Moire (Nailsea) glass shade,
frosted cranberry shaded to clear
w/opaque white loopings, tightly
ruffled top, marked "Clarke" clear
glass base, 4" d., 5½" h. 195.00

HANDEL LAMPS

Handel Boudoir Lamp

Boudoir lamp, 7" d. domical
reverse-painted shade decorated
w/pond lilies & cattails, raised on
a bronzed metal baluster-form
base w/relief design of leafy
trees, on a low round footed
base, w/finial, shade signed
"Handel 6554," base signed "Han-
del," 13" h. (ILLUS.) 7,810.00
Candle lamp, a baluster-turned ma-
hogany candlestick w/brass-
rimmed bell-shaped socket fitted
w/a tall, slender bell-shaped hurricane shade of Teroma glass in
frosted clear w/chipped ice finish,
the exterior decorated w/a band
of stylized green & white birch
trees, a yellow ground inside,
shade 9" h., overall 19½" h. 550.00
Desk lamp, 8" d. conical caramel
slag glass shade formed of three
panels overlaid w/a brass-finished
hammered metal strap & floral
framing, grey patinated cast metal base, Handel shade tag, 16" h.
(ILLUS. top next column) 660.00
Table lamp, 14½" d. deep domical
reverse-painted shade w/a wide
border band of large yellow &
pink tea roses against a yellow
background enhanced by applied
highlighting on the exterior,
signed "Handel 6300" & artist-

Handel Slag Glass Desk Lamp

initialed "A," on a slender
bronzed metal baluster-form base
w/a round foot, overall 20" h. . . .2,310.00
Table lamp, 15" d. domical reverse-
painted shade decorated w/a continuous landscape of Dutch windmills in orange, brown, green,
red, yellow & blue, signed & numbered "Handel 6499," raised on a
slender metal base w/wide circu-
lar foot 1,980.00
Table lamp, 15" d. domical reverse-
painted shade decorated w/a continuous forest landscape at sunset
w/tall evergreens against a reddish orange sky, amethyst fields
in the distance, signed at the rim
"Handel 7045," mounted on a
slender bronzed metal base
w/molded slender lappets & a
flaring round foot impressed
"Handel," overall 21" h. 2,970.00
Table lamp, 17" d. domical leaded
glass paneled shade, six tapering
panels composed of amber slag
glass in a brickwork design above
a green & red swag & lappet repeating border, mounted on a
slender ring-segmented shaft on a
flaring disc foot w/a wave-design
edge band, both base & shade
marked, overall 23" h. 825.00
Table lamp, 18" d. domical reverse-
painted shade decorated w/four
birds-of-paradise amid multicolored leafy foliage in primarily
shades of blue, shade signed "ED
- Handel - 7120," raised on a slender tripartite gilt-metal Roman-
style base, overall 23" h. 13,200.00
Table lamp, 22" d. domical reverse-
painted shade decorated w/a
colorful Oriental dragon motif
w/exterior gold accents, raised on
original ring support & loving cup-
style base, 22" h. (ILLUS. top next
page) 880.00

Handel Table Lamp

Table lamp, 24" d. domical leaded glass shade composed of striated blue & white glass w/a border of pink flowers, reeded tapering standard w/flaring foot, shade & base signed, ca. 1900, 26" h. 2,640.00

MINIATURE LAMPS

Milk White Cosmos Miniature Lamp

Our listings are arranged numerically according to the numbers assigned to the various miniature lamps pictured in Frank R. & Ruth E. Smith's book, Miniature Lamps, *now referred to as Smith's Book I, and Ruth Smith's sequel,* Miniature Lamps II. *All references are to Smith's Book I unless otherwise noted.*

Blue opaque glass pedestal base, pressed clear glass font, Olmsted burner, milk white glass chimney-shade, No. 11 .... 350.00
"Little Twilight" embossed on clear glass ribbed pedestal base, Olmsted burner, white Bristol glass chimney-shade, 7" h., No. 19..... 120.00
"Improved Banner" & three stars embossed on milk white glass pedestal base, Olmsted burner, white Bristol glass shade, 3" h., No. 20 .... 145.00
Clear glass "Time & Light. Pride of

America. Grand Vals Perfect Time Indicating Lamp" & time marks from 8 to 6, unmarked burner, white embossed Shell patt. shade, 6¾" h., No. 23 ....155.00 to 170.00
Pewter base w/embossed rococo design, burner marked "Stellar. E.M. & Co." (Edward Miller & Co.), 3½" h. base, No. 68............. 75.00
Clear glass stem lamp w/square base, Acorn burner, clear glass chimney, advertised in Butler Brothers "Our Drummer" 1912 catalog, 4" h., No. 103 ....45.00 to 55.00
Green glass Beaded Heart patt. stem lamp, Acorn burner, clear glass chimney, 5½" h., No. 109 ....260.00 to 295.00
Cobalt blue glass Bull's Eye patt. variant stem lamp, Nutmeg burner, clear glass chimney, 5" h., No. 111 .... 115.00
Amber glass Bull's Eye patt. stem lamp, Nutmeg burner, clear glass chimney, advertised as "Daisy" in Butler Brothers "Our Drummer" 1912 catalog, 5" h., No. 112 ....100.00 to 120.00
Clear glass stem lamp w/embossed medallions, Acorn burner, clear glass chimney, 5½" h., No. 113 .. 75.00
Blue glass Waffle patt. font on embossed brass pedestal base, Acorn burner, clear glass chimney, 4½" h., No. 117 .... 95.00
Clear glass acorn-shaped lamp, Acorn burner, clear glass chimney, 4" h. base, No. 121 .... 125.00
Red-painted clear glass base & ball-shaped shade (resembling red satin glass), w/embossed flowers & designs, Acorn burner, clear glass chimney, 7¼" h., No. 135........ 150.00
Milk white glass w/ovoid footed base & matching ovoid chimney, each w/embossed flowers & scrolls painted in pink, brown & gold, Acorn burner, called "Jupiter" & pictured in Butler Brothers April 1912 catalog, 8" h., No. 156 .... 120.00
Milk white glass base & globe chimney w/embossed flowers & leaves trimmed in gold, Hornet burner, 8¼" h., No. 162 .... 175.00
Milk white glass mug-shaped base w/embossed Gothic Arch patt., w/matching milk white glass chimney, removable font, Acorn burner, 7¾" h., No. 163 .... 325.00
Pink glass Greek Key patt. stem lamp w/matching chimney-shade, Acorn burner, 8½" h., No. 166 ... 110.00
Milk white glass footed base &

matching globe-chimney w/embossed design highlighted in gilt, Acorn burner, 7¾" h., No. 173 ... 110.00

Milk white glass base and ball-shaped shade w/embossed & painted flowers & beading, sometimes called "Apple Blossom," Acorn burner, 7" h., No. 193 ..... 265.00

Blue glass base & globe chimney w/embossed Maltese Cross & other designs highlighted in gilt, Hornet burner, 9½" h., No. 214 ..... 150.00

Milk white glass base & ball-shaped shade w/embossed florals & wreaths highlighted w/pink, green & gold paint, Nutmeg burner, 7½" h., No. 224 .... 265.00

Milk white glass Acanthus Swirl patt. base & ball-shaped shade w/green-painted trim, Nutmeg burner, clear glass chimney, No. 230 .... 230.00

Green opaque glass w/embossed scroll leaf design, trimmed w/painted florals, Nutmeg burner, 8¾" h., No. 240 .... 410.00

Blue opalescent glass embossed overlapping leaves pattern, w/gold trim, Hornet burner, 9" h., No. 257 .... 265.00

Cobalt blue glass w/paneled & embossed design, trimmed in dark brown & gold, Hornet burner, 9" h., No. 262 .... 250.00

Milk white glass base & umbrella-type shade w/embossed design & painted blue bellflowers w/orange trim, Nutmeg burner, clear glass chimney, 9½" h., No. 266 .. 350.00

Milk white glass w/embossed overall fanned leaf design, fired-on red paint, Nutmeg burner, 7¾" h., No. 274 .... 395.00

Bluish green opaque glass w/embossed flowers, Nutmeg burner, 7¼" h., No. 282 .... 345.00

Milk white glass Cosmos patt. base & umbrella shade w/pink-stained band & colored florals, Nutmeg burner, 7½" h., No. 286 (ILLUS.) .. 305.00

Orange satin glass w/embossed design, P. & A. Victor burner, 11¾" h., No. 288 .... 425.00

Milk white glass w/embossed ribs, Nutmeg burner, 7¾" h., No. 297 .... 225.00

Cobalt blue cased glass Florette patt. ball-shaped base & shade, Nutmeg burner, clear glass chimney, 7" h., No. 388 .... 550.00

Blue satin glass melon-ribbed base & pansy-molded ball-shaped shade, Nutmeg burner, clear glass chimney, Consolidated Lamp &

Glass Co., Pittsburgh, 1894, 7" h., No. 389 .... 465.00

White satin glass w/embossed ribbing on base & shade, w/green fired-on paint decoration, Nutmeg burner, clear glass chimney, 7½" h., No. 393 .... 265.00

Cranberry glass w/compressed globular bottom beneath a spherical section, lightly paneled shade, Hornet burner, 9½" h., No. 442 .. 350.00

White cut velvet glass bulbous base w/applied blue feet, matching ruffled tulip shade, Nutmeg burner, No. 531 .... 2,100.00

Clear embossed glass shade, "Glow" thrift, brass hanging lamp, 3 1/8" to top of font, 6" to top of shade, Book II, No. 30 ... 125.00 to 150.00

White opaque glass, decorated overall w/multicolored nosegays, marked "Dresden" on bottom, Mt. Washington Glass Co., Acorn burner, 10½" h., Book II, No. 267 .... 845.00

White Bristol glass font & shade in black wrought iron pedestal holder, foreign burner, 8½" h., Book II, No. 452 .... 375.00

Amberina glass Quilted patt. shade & matching base w/applied shell feet, Nutmeg burner, 9½" h., Book II, No. 492 .... 950.00

PAIRPOINT LAMPS

Pairpoint Scenic Planter Lamp

Boudoir lamp, 9¼" d. domical "Puffy" shade w/irregular sides molded w/ribs & rose blossoms & butterflies, painted on the inside in red, green, yellow, blue, turquoise & brown against a white ground & trimmed w/gold on the exterior, raised on a four-armed support & a simple baluster standard above a circular base on four small cast scrolling feet, shade printed "The Pairpoint Corp.," base impressed "PAIR-POINT (monogram) 3047 1 - 2 - 8 1 - 2 - MADE IN U.S.A.," ca. 1920, 14¾" h. 3,850.00

Planter lamp, 16" d. mushroom-shaped 'Vienna' shade reverse-painted w/two landscape reserves of a New England village & sail-boat scene w/rose bouquets at each side & extensive gold trim on the exterior, signed "The Pairpoint Corp" on the rim, mounted on a gilt-metal four-columned base w/pierced scroll corner brackets & a wide, dished footed platform centered by a tapering round glass-lined planter, base impressed "Pairpoint C372," platform bent, metal plating worn, overall 14" h. (ILLUS.) 3,025.00

Table lamp, 12" d. domed mush-room-shaped cased glass shade in red over white, etched & gilt-enameled on the exterior w/a writhing dragon, fitted on a sup-port ring raised above a figural swirling poppy leaf & blossom metal base signed on the bottom w/the "Pairpoint Corp." diamond logo, overall 18" h.............. 770.00

Table lamp, 12" d. "Puffy" domical shade molded w/a profusion of red roses against a lush green foliate ground, the gilt-metal py-ramidal foot on the base decorat-ed w/scrolls, the openwork metal standard composed of a sinuous floral scroll design continuing to four upturned arms supporting a ring w/a cut-out design, shade stamped "The Pairpoint Corp," base stamped "PAIRPOINT MFG CO 3054," overall 22" h.........9,900.00

Pairpoint Lamp with "Puffy" Shade

Table lamp, 13" d. tapering cylindri-cal "Puffy" shade molded around the border w/a band of large blossoms & flying hummingbirds, reverse-painted in blue, yellow, green & purple on a blue & white striped background, on a footed trumpet-form silverplate signed Pairpoint base (ILLUS.) 5,500.00

Table lamp, 15½" d. "Puffy" domical 'Apple' reverse-painted shade, the fruiting branches, blossoms & but-terflies decorated in red, yellow, white & blue against lush green foliage, stamped "The Pairpoint Corp.," the brown patinated metal base w/four tall curved legs end-ing in leafy scrolls & resting on a squared & lobed disc foot im-pressed "PAIRPOINT MFG. CO. B3013," early 20th c., 20" h. 19,550.00

Table lamp, 16" d. flaring domical 'Tivoli' patt. shade, the acid-etched grey glass reverse-painted w/rose bouquets between scroll-ing cartouches in shades of yel-low, red, pink & green reserved against a combed creamy white ground, on a cylindrical standard & stepped shaped square base, shade signed "The Pairpoint Corp'n.," the base impressed "THE PAIRPOINT MFG. CO.," ca. 1920, overall 23½" h. 3,575.00

Table lamp, 18" d. domical reverse-painted 'Carlisle' shade in tex-tured grey painted on the reverse w/flower-filled urns & leafage al-ternating w/cartouche-shaped flower-filled reserves in shades of purple, blue, orange, yellow & mauve against an ochre ground, w/four exotic birds around the lower rim, raised on a tripartite patinated metal base composed of three scrolling legs cast w/leaf-age & set upon a three-part foot, w/finial, shade unsigned, base marked "PAIRPOINT - D3084," ca. 1915, overall 21½" h. 4,400.00

Table lamp, "Puffy" shade in the 'Stratford' shape molded on the lower rim w/rose blossoms & two hummingbirds & reverse-painted in white, pale green, brown, emerald green & crimson, raised on a cast metal baluster-shaped base, overall 24" h..............4,950.00

TIFFANY LAMPS

Candlestick lamps, conical shade w/rich caramel opalescent sides decorated on the lower section w/brilliant amber iridescent striat-ed lappets, fitting on a cylindrical

silvered metal & composition
support above an amber iridescent trumpet-form base molded
w/scrolling ribs, shades inscribed
"L.C.T.," bases inscribed "L.C.T.
Favrile 5," 1899-1920, overall
16 1/8" h., pr..................3,300.00
Desk lamp, the domical shade in
opalescent glass decorated w/ap-
plied pulled lily pads radiating
from the upper aperture, the
whole w/brilliant amber iridescence, pivoting within a harp support above an adjustable bronze
standard & base cast as an inverted lily blossom w/alternating petals extending to form eight feet,
shade inscribed "L.C.T.," base impressed "TIFFANY STUDIOS - NEW
YORK - 10991" & "470," 1899-1928,
shade 10" d., lowered 20" h. 6,600.00
Floor lamp, "Dogwood," 14" d. leaded glass ball shade composed of
an overall pattern of dogwood
blossoms in white striated opalescent glass tinged w/pink, tan,
pale amber & brown & w/water-
melon red streaks, the leaves in
white tinged w/pale green &
streaked w/various pastel hues,
fitting onto a tall bronze base
w/three slender rods conjoined at
the top & decorated w/applied
coiling & twisted wire, the rods
flaring toward the base & joined
by medial stretchers & ending
w/shell-like feet mounted on a
shaped tripartite base, w/finial,
unsigned, 6' 1½" h............53,900.00
Floor lamp, "Laburnum," 24" d.
domed leaded glass shade w/ir-
regular border decorated w/a
profusion of pendant laburnum
blossoms in shades of rich mottled yellow w/green leaves &
brown branches set against a
deep cobalt blue ground at top
shading to striated amethyst &
sapphire blue below, the bronze
base cast as a twisted stem on
flattened, circular foot, shade
stamped "TIFFANY STUDIOS NEW
YORK," the base stamped "TIFFA-
NY STUDIOS NEW YORK 645,"
w/'pigtail' finial, 6' h.........167,500.00
Hall lamp, hanging-type, the onion-
form shade in pale opalescent
glass decorated w/pulled feathering in pale green heightened in
gold iridescence, fitting into a
pierced circular bronze mount
w/beaded rim suspended from
three beaded chains above a central standard, w/ceiling mount,

unsigned, 1899-1928, 5" d., overall
18½" h. 2,475.00
Lily lamp, ten-light, consisting of ten
rainbow iridescent shades, supported by ten curving bronze
stems on a layered lily pad base
w/green-brown patina, shades inscribed "L.C.T. FAVRILE," one inscribed "L.C.T.," the base stamped
"TIFFANY STUDIOS NEW YORK,"
19¼" h. 23,000.00

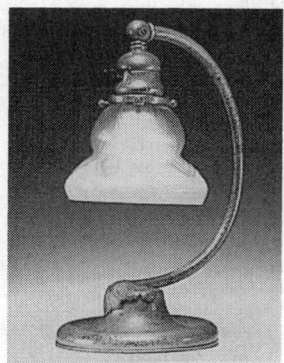

Tiffany Piano Lamp

Piano lamp, Favrile glass & gilt-
bronze, the lobed shade in rich
pearly opalescence decorated
w/amber & green striated
feathering, pivoting on an adjustable socket, the C-scroll arm
w/acanthus terminal raised on a
dished circular base, shade inscribed "L.C.T.," base impressed
"TIFFANY STUDIOS - NEW YORK -
687," 1899-1920, shade 5¾" d.,
overall 12¾" h. (ILLUS.) 2,200.00
Student lamp, a pair of 9¾" d. domical open-topped shades in green
& iridescent gold damascene
ribbed & wavy line designs lined
in white opal & fitted on metal
rings above short cylindrical burners extending from short arms
joined to & adjusting on tall slender uprights flanking a large suspended pine needle design bronze
cylindrical font, the support uprights fitted into a round disc
bronze base, shade signed
"L.C.T.," burners marked by the
Manhattan Brass Co., electrified,
overall 30" h. 11,000.00
Table lamp, "Azalea," 20" d. domical leaded glass shade composed
of red & green segments arranged
as blossoms on leafy branches,
signed & numbered "1918,"
mounted on a bronze base w/a
slender telescoping shaft & a
domed cushion base incised

w/stylized buds & raised on four small scroll feet, base signed & numbered "367," overall 34" h. 77,000.00

Table lamp, "Dragonfly," 17" d. conical shade composed of eight dragonflies w/overlapping outspread wings in emerald green striated opalescent glass overlaid w/bronze filigree, their bodies in mottled deeper green glass & w/red glass cabochon eyes, against a ground of striated green & reddish amber glass, raised on a three-arm support & gently waisted domical ribbed bronze base, further raised on five ball feet, shade impressed "TIFFANY STUDIOS NEW YORK 1462-12," base impressed "TIFFANY STUDIOS - NEW YORK - 29733" w/monogram, 1899-1928, overall 22¼" h. 18,700.00

Tiffany "Pansy" Table Lamp

Table lamp, "Pansy," the 16" d. leaded glass shade composed of segments arranged as four repeating clusters of pansy blossoms w/yellow & opal, pink slag & fiery amber petals & dark green & striated greenish amber leaves against a green & white slag background, rim tags marked "Tiffany Studios New York 1448-3," on three long arms extending from a slender reeded bronze shaft swelling to a wide bumpy cushion base on four small scroll feet, base impressed "Tiffany Studios New York 9939," overall 23" h. (ILLUS.) 11,000.00

MISCELLANEOUS LAMPS

Aladdin, Model B-62, short Lincoln Drape table lamp, ruby 425.00

Aladdin, Model B-75, tall Lincoln Drape table lamp, Alacite 185.00

Aladdin, Model B-85, Quilt table lamp, white Moonstone font & base 180.00

Aladdin, Model B-88, Vertique table lamp, yellow Moonstone 465.00

Aladdin, Model B-112, Cathedral table lamp, rose Moonstone 220.00

Alcohol lamp, Simplex Lamp Co., New York, warm vapor inhaler, fancy pierced tin holder w/burner, boiler, w/original tattered box, 1905, 7" h. 45.00

Anglo-Irish Cut Glass Lamp

Anglo-Irish cut glass lamps, gas-type, ovoid wide body tapering to a short neck supporting a domed cover tapering to a knob & pointed finial, body w/large star-cut blocks framed by criss-cross diamond bands, mounted on brass arm w/gas jet, one stamped "J.A. COX LONDON," 19th c., 26" h., pr. (ILLUS. of one) 4,180.00

Argand lamps, brass & glass, comprising one double-light & two single-light lamps, each surmounted by a flower & leaf finial flanked by two pair of serpents, the urn-shaped receptacle hung w/prisms, the light arms terminating in frosted & engraved clear glass shades, the fluted standard below on a square plinth base, each impressed "FRED. HANCOCK, PHILADELPHIA," mid-19th c., 15" w., 21¼" h., set of 3 (chips to prisms) 3,850.00

Arts & Crafts table lamp, a pair of pyramidal shades w/green slag glass panels mounted in paneled hammered brass frames suspended from shaped oak side arms

flanking a rectangular center oak
post w/a pointed finial & set
upon a rectangular oak base
w/small block feet, early 20th c.,
19½" h. 440.00

Banquet lamp, amber glass tulip-
shaped shade w/frosted panels
w/rose, lavender & blue alternating floral patterns, amber glass
font, figured nickel-plated metal
base w/variegated red marble
stem, original burner & chimney,
France, 6¼" d., 26½" h. 650.00

Banquet lamp, cranberry Peloton
glass wide cylindrical font w/blue,
pink, white & yellow "coconut"
decoration, raised on a slender
columnar brass standard & black
pottery foot, cranberry frosted
glass tulip-form w/flaring ruffled
rim, 6½" d., overall 21½" h. 550.00

Banquet lamp, deep cranberry glass
font w/cut panels above a
scrolled brass mount joining it to
a bulbous cranberry glass matching base tapering at the top,
fitted on a domed brass round
foot, 5" h., 15" h. (no shade) 495.00

Banquet lamp, lime green to clear
glass acid cut-back melon sectioned ruffled top shade w/overall
fine stippling, glass font w/em-
bossed nickel-plated foot &
mounts, tan variegated marble
stem, original burner & chimney,
France, 5¾" d., 23" h. 495.00

Banquet lamp, milk white glass
onion-form font decorated w/pas-
tel flowers in garlands w/bows
decoration & gold trim, raised on
an ornate brass stem w/embossed
design & a square, stepped &
footed brass base, w/a frosted
clear glass tulip-form shade
w/flaring ruffled rim decorated
w/gold enameled garlands &
scrolls & highlighted w/white
enamel, 7" d., overall 18½" h. 325.00

Banquet lamp, porcelain spherical
font decorated overall w/fine
beading & h.p. circular & diamond
reserves w/blossoms, a gilt-
bronze center band w/grotesque
face & ring handles & raised on a
short pedestal on a tripod claw
foot base, w/a frosted clear glass
ball shade decorated w/gilt blossom sprigs & grasses, France, ca.
1860 (ILLUS. top next column) 935.00

Betty lamp (early grease lamp)
w/wire hanger, wrought iron,
latch-type lid on font, 4½" h. plus
hanger 85.00

Betty lamp (early grease lamp)

Ornate French Banquet Lamp

w/hanger, wrought iron, chicken
finial on font cover, heart finial
on hanger arm, 7" h. plus twisted
hanger (pitted) 373.00

Bigelow, Kennard & Co. table lamp,
16" d. domical leaded glass shade
composed of whitish amber brickwork above a border band of
scrolled block devices in subtle
yellow variations, marked
"Bigelow, Kennard & Co., Boston,"
mounted on a slender four-lobed
bronze standard flaring to a four-
lobed foot, early 20th c., overall
20" h. 3,080.00

Bradley & Hubbard table lamp, Prairie School style, 16" d. conical
leaded glass shade w/four caramel slag panels bordered by narrow blue & red slag segments
under linear & geometric metal
gridwork, slender cylindrical metal standard on a round disc foot
w/similar geometric designs,
marked "B. & H. 222," overall
22½" h. 2,090.00

Bradley & Hubbard Table Lamp

Bradley & Hubbard table lamp, 20" d. reverse-painted domical shade composed of six bent glass panels decorated w/urns & floral arrangements & swags, mounted on a baluster-form bronzed metal ginkgo-decorated base, marked "Bradley & Hubbard Mfg. Co.," 24" h. (ILLUS.) 825.00

Duffner & Kimberly table lamp, 20¼" d. conical leaded glass shade w/uneven border, arranged in a design of a field of poppy flowers & leaves in white, yellow, pink, red, green & blue, on a bronze base molded w/poppies, overall 27" h. 18,700.00

Gilt-bronze table lamp, figural, cast as a young maiden in long flowing gown, waving a long scarf overhead & enclosing a small bulb, inscribed "E.Wante," France, ca. 1900, 12 5/8" h. (minor wear to gilt)........................6,050.00

Gone-with-the-Wind lamp, round relief-molded glass ball shade & base decorated w/a mythological scene of "The Muses," showing four muses w/musical instruments in various poses on the front & base, cherubs floating in clouds at the sides, in burgundy, pale aqua & white, burner dated "4/30/95," Consolidated Lamp & Glass Company, all original, 23½" h. 985.00

Gone-with-the-Wind lamp, clear satin glass ball shade & bulbous font relief-molded w/roses, brass flaring, ruffled collar & domed foot, electrified, 24" h. 645.00

Hall lamp, leaded glass, the closed inverted teardrop-form composed of a band of stylized floral rings in deep reddish amber framed by graduated light slag brickwork & diamonds, large domed metal cap at the top, attributed to Duffner & Kimberly, early 20th c., 12" h. 770.00

Jefferson table lamp, 16" d. domical reverse-painted glass shade decorated w/reddish orange poppy blossoms w/brown centers, leaves & border grasses against an orangish amber ground, numbered "2351," impressed "Jefferson" on metal rim, on a slender metal baluster standard & bell-form foot both divided by spaced ribs, overall 21" h. (ILLUS. top next column).......................1,210.00

Kerosene hand lamp w/finger grip, pressed glass, Beaded Swirl patt., green 350.00

Kerosene hand lamp w/finger grip,

Jefferson Table Lamp

pressed glass, Coolidge Drape patt., purple 175.00

Kerosene hand lamp w/finger grip, footed, pressed glass, Dart patt., clear......................... 125.00

Kerosene hand lamp w/finger grip, pressed glass, Queen Heart patt., w/old chimney, clear, Findlay 85.00

Victorian Hanging Kerosene Lamp

Kerosene hanging lamp, a domical pink Hobnail patt. shade fitted in a stamped brass shade ring suspending facet-cut prisms & supported by an ornate scrolling brass frame flanking the bulbous stamped floral & scroll brass font, w/brass crown, chains, upper ring & pink blown glass smoke bell, late 19th c. (ILLUS.) 1,700.00

Kerosene table lamp, blown glass, ruffled Rubina shade w/flower designs in frosted & clear, frosted Rubina font w/flower pattern, nickel-plated foot, original burner & chimney, 5¾" d., 14¾" h. 495.00

Kerosene table lamp, cut-overlay glass, the pear-shaped font w/cranberry cut to clear w/a

band of thumbprints near the top
& two bands around the base w/a
central band of worn gilt scrolls,
w/a brass connector to the tall
columnar hexagonal milk white
glass base w/a square foot, ca.
1860-70, 14" h. 550.00
Kerosene table lamp, mold-blown
glass, mother-of-pearl satin glass,
brownish mauve swirl design,
original ribbed clambroth ball
shade, w/brass mounts & feet,
complete w/chimney, 6½" d.,
20¾" h. 950.00
Kerosene table lamp, pressed glass,
Bows & Diamonds patt., apple
green, ca. 1880, 8¼" h. 165.00
Kerosene table lamp, pressed glass,
Daisy One-Piece patt., plain font,
patterned foot, clear, ca. 1880,
9¼" h. 33.00
Kerosene table lamp, pressed glass,
Feathered Arch patt., w/open-
work triple-loop stem, by Dalzell,
Gilmore & Leighton, clear, ca.
1890, 10 3/8" h. (slight base
roughage w/one small chip &
check) 71.50
Kerosene table lamp, pressed glass,
Peacock Feather patt., blue 250.00
Kerosene table lamp, pressed glass,
'Ripley marriage lamp,' a pair of
globular opaque blue fonts flanking a clambroth center section
w/covered match holder & raised
on a flaring brass pedestal base
w/square white marble foot, center section marked "D.C. Ripley &
Co. Patent Pending," ca. 1870s,
11" h. 1,210.00
Kerosene table lamp, pressed glass,
Sheldon Swirl patt., blue opalescent 150.00
Kerosene table lamp, pressed glass,
Swirled Rosettes patt., clear, ca.
1880-90, 8½" h. 55.00
Kerosene table lamp, pressed glass,
Teardrop w/Eyewinker w/Plume
font, clear w/frosted font 95.00
Kerosene table lamp, pressed glass,
Three Panel patt., canary yellow,
5" d., 8½" h. 350.00
Kerosene table lamp, pressed glass,
brass & marble, clear tapering
ovoid Bull's-Eye & Fleur-de-lis
patt. glass font on a spiral-pattern
cylindrical brass stem w/a domed
base mounted on a square white
marble foot, ca. 1870, 9½" h. 121.00
Kerosene table lamp, pressed glass
& iron, clear glass onion-form
font in the Feather Duster patt.,
mounted on a circular, flaring iron
base, ca. 1880, 8" h. 44.00

Leaded glass table lamp, 20" d.
broad conical shade composed of
radiating sections in deep green
opalescent glass between geometric borders in mottled lighter
green, the straight lower rim
w/irregular border composed of
stylized palmettes in the same
glass, raised on a fluted columnar
standard above a circular base,
w/finial, America, ca. 1925,
24½" h. 1,650.00
Leaded glass table lamp, 26" d.
broad parasol-domed leaded
shade composed of a yellow, red
& pink stylized tulip blossom border w/graduated brickwork at the
top, mounted on a slender bronze
standard w/a band of acanthus
leaf around the bottom above the
disc foot, attributed to Suess Ornamental Glass Company, Chica-
go, overall 25" h. 2,420.00
Moe Bridges table lamp, 15" d.
domical reverse-painted shade
decorated w/a riverside landscape w/autumn trees under a
yellow sky, signed on the rim
"Moe Bridges Co.," mounted on a
bronzed-metal base composed of
four slender straps curling up &
out at the base & fitted on a four-
lobed foot, blossom-form mounts
near the top & base of the standard, overall 21" h. 1,100.00

Moe Bridges Scenic Lamp

Moe Bridges table lamp, 18" d.
domical reverse-painted shade
decorated w/a mountainous winter landscape, mounted on a gilt-
metal tall urn-form base w/long
angled handles & a paw-footed
domed foot, base marked, overall
24" h. (ILLUS.) 1,980.00
Peg lamp, deep pink ribbed overlay
Bristol glass font with matching
ruffled-top mushroom-shaped
shade w/white lining, original

heavy brass candlestick, brass burner w/ring, original chimney, 5 5/8" d., 16½" h. 595.00

Peg lamps, shaded rich lemon yellow embossed Swirl patt. overlay satin glass font, matching ruffled-top mushroom-shaped shade, white lining, in brass candlestick, w/original brass fixtures & glass chimney, 5¾" d., 15½" h., pr...1,250.00

Perfume lamp, milk white glass, Art Deco design, tall slender cylindrical body flaring at the base, enameled all around in black & orange w/a stylized moonlit landscape, fitted on a gilt-metal rounded electrical socket base w/three small feet & a conforming perfume holder, the top fitted w/a domed, pierced gilt-metal cap, DeVilbiss, 8" h. (needs rewiring) 275.00

Phoenix table lamp, 18" d. domical reverse-painted shade decorated w/a continuous landscape of an Indian encampment by a lake in blue, green, orange, yellow & brown, raised on a cast-metal base w/a bulbous blossom-molded base tapering & swirling to a slender shaft, on a flaring round foot, early 20th c. 1,320.00

Polaroid No. 114 desk lamp, Bakelite & plastic, the black hooded shade supported by a slanted conical aluminum stem on a Bakelite raised round base, w/cooling vents in the hood & the stem, designed by Walter Dorwin Teague, ca. 1939, 13" h.........1,430.00

Quezal table lamp, bell-shaped shade w/gold iridescent finish on the inside, the exterior decorated w/pulled feather design in burgundy & gold against a white iridescent ground, signed "Quezal," on a trefoil-form metal base topped w/a dragonfly, early 20th c., overall 17½" h.........1,045.00

Unusual Conch Shell Lamp

Shell table lamp, cameo-carved conch shell w/three intricate classical vignettes w/sea nymphs & cherubs & a scroll-carved lower band, raised on a brass stand w/four dolphin feet, 13½" h. (ILLUS.) 1,210.00

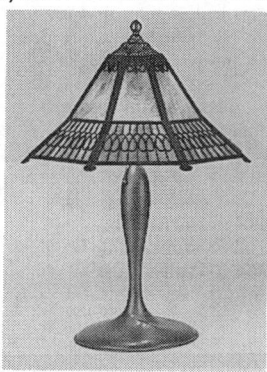

Slag Glass Table Lamp

Slag glass table lamp, 18" w. umbrella-form hexagonal paneled shade w/mottled green & white slag glass behind a pierced brass framework w/repeating spade & loop design, simple slender baluster-form metal standard w/wide disc foot, early 20th c., 25" h. (ILLUS.) 495.00

"Sparking" lamp, clear blown glass, a bulbous font on an applied ringed-stem & round foot, early 19th c., 3 5/8" h................. 330.00

"Sparking" lamp, pewter, ring handle, single spout burner w/chain, marked "M. Hyde" (Martin Hyde, New York City), 4¼" h.......... 280.50

Late Victorian Electric Fixture

Victorian electric lamp, three arched metal tubes w/metal leaves framing an electric socket around a central trumpet-form amber glass bud vase all above a hexagonal lantern w/cast-metal framing around reverse-painted floral glass panels enclosing an electric socket, raised on a square cast-metal pedestal base, attributed to Bradley & Hubbard, late 19th - early 20th c., overall 21" h. (ILLUS.)........................ 220.00

Whale oil lamp, clear pressed & blown glass, the four-lobed pressed foot w/stepped bands to a cylindrical top below two thick blown wafers supporting the free-blown spherical font w/a metal collar & ring w/a whale oil burner & supporting a frosted blown glass tulip-form shade, attributed to the New England Glass Co., ca. 1830-40, lamp base 8½" h., overall 13 3/8" h. (one minor flake & slight roughage on base) 412.50

Whale oil lamp, pressed flint glass, Bull's Eye & Fleur de Lis patt. font on brass standard w/square marble base, clear.................. 190.00

Whale oil lamp, pressed flint glass, Waffle patt. font in opaque blue, attached w/a wafer to a milky white pedestal base w/hexagonal foot, attributed to The Boston & Sandwich Glass Co., ca. 1850, 8½" h. 1,045.00

Whale oil lamp, tin, cast iron & pewter, a round ribbed flaring cast-iron foot below a slender tin shaft supporting the slightly tapering cylindrical tin font fitted w/a pewter burner, tin loop finger handle under font, burner marked "Perry's Patent," mid-19th c., 8½" h........................ 192.50

Whale oil lamps, pressed flint glass, Loop patt., canary yellow, fitted w/original wick support, attributed to The New England Glass Company, mid-19th c., 8¾" h., pr.........................2,090.00

Whale oil lamps, tole, conical font w/eared handle & hinged snuffer on saucer base, worn blue japanning, w/brass & tin burner, 3¾" h., pr..................... 242.00

Wilkinson table lamp, a 22" d. domical leaded glass shade composed of four repeating yellow, orange & green blossom clusters w/brown & white glass segments as a border & background, bent glass tuck-under edge, mounted on a simple ring- and rod-turned gilt-metal standard attributed to Wilkinson, assembled, overall 29" h. (ILLUS.) 2,530.00

Wilkinson Table Lamp

OTHER LIGHTING DEVICES

CHANDELIERS

Victorian Gilt-Bronze Chandelier

Arts & Crafts style, American Prairie School, leaded glass & bronze, the square fixture w/pyramidal lower section w/geometric leaded glass sections in mottled yellowish green opalescent, orange & ice-textured grey glass, the larger square mount enclosing a socket at each corner, the whole suspended from paired square chains & ceiling mount, ca. 1915, 19¼" sq., 21" h................2,200.00

Brass & glass, two-light, a central horizontal swelled brass two-arm disc w/a tall hanging ring at the top & a swag drop at the center bottom, each short, shaped arm suspending a bell-form socket fitted w/a slender bell-shaped white opalescent glass shade decorated w/gold pulled-feathers, shades signed "Quezal," w/a

chain, early 20th c., overall
14" h. 352.00
Daum Nancy signed, cameo glass &
painted metal, the onion-form
shade in grey glass mottled at the
rim w/soft mint green & tangerine
orange, the whole cut w/stylized
petals & leafage, supported in a
foliate mount suspended from
three chains below a foliate ceiling cap, shade signed in cameo
"DAUM - NANCY" w/the cross of
Lorraine, ca. 1910, shade 10" d.,
mount 25" h. 2,530.00
Gilt-bronze, eight-light, the eight
U-form scrolled arms issuing from
a wide central disc below a center
slender shaft mounted w/a band
of small embossed faces below
scrolls, pierced metal chains from
shaft to end of each arm, facet-
cut long prisms around base drop
at center, clear glass tulip-form
shades, mid-19th c. (ILLUS.) 3,575.00
Handel, bronze filigree & patinated
metal on slag glass, five-light, the
nine-sided central domed shade
w/slag glass panels in burgundy,
amber, cream & green overlaid
w/stylized palm trees on tropical
shores above a lower border
w/pierced whiplash designs over
striated green & white opalescent
slag glass panels, pendent from a
heavy chain & a four-armed support, each arm suspending a
smaller six-sided bell-form shade
of the same design, the upper rod
standard comprised of openwork
sections, w/molded ceiling cap,
large shade unsigned, small
shades impressed "HANDEL," ca.
1910, large shade 29" d., overall
38" h. 9,900.00

Louis XVI-Style Chandelier

Louis XVI-Style, gilt-bronze & glass,

six-light, a central standard supporting an annulus fitted w/can-
dle branches, overall hung
w/glass prisms & beads, 19th c.,
38" h., pr. (ILLUS. of one) 6,325.00

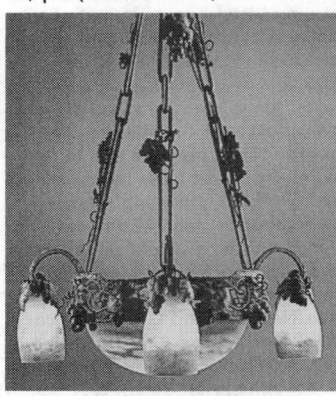

Muller Freres Chandelier

Muller Freres signed, glass &
wrought iron, the shallow domical
central shade in grey glass internally mottled w/lemon yellow, orange & purple, fitting into a
circular hammered iron framework wrought w/clusters of
grapes & leafage, w/three scrolling arms each supporting smaller
conforming shades, suspended
from elongated chain links similarly wrought w/grapes & leafage,
w/ceiling cap, shades acid-
stamped "MULLER FRES - LUNE-
VILLE," France, ca. 1900, 27" d.,
38" h. (ILLUS.) 3,025.00
Tiffany Favrile glass & bronze, four
shades, each composed of three
oval panels of yellowish green &
white striated opalescent glass
within a twisted wire framework
decorated w/coiling devices, each
fitting into a pierced socket above
a curved arm & conjoined to a
central sphere suspended from a
shaped cylindrical standard,
greenish brown patina, unsigned,
ca. 1899-1928, 17½" d., 24" h. . . . 6,600.00
Tin & wood, twelve-light, primitive
style w/a long central shaft boldly
ring- and knob-turned & issuing
twelve slender S-form wire arms
supporting tin candle sockets
w/crimped drip pans, wooden
center w/old worn patina &
dark paint, America, 19th c.,
29" h. plus wrought-iron hanging
chain 3,410.00
Toleware, six-light, Empire style,
the circular center band support
decorated w/trophies within

palmette-decorated diamonds in black on a yellow ground & fitted w/cylindrical upright sockets around the sides each w/a conical shade, the center band attached to a crown-form upper ring w/three heavy chains, France, early 19th c., electrified, 28" d., 20" h. 5,500.00

Toleware, eight-light, the faceted conical leaf-decorated standard centering a circular support w/serpentine projecting arms ending in dished drip plates each w/cylindrical candlecups, the ring mounted w/faceted upright stars, northern Michigan, first half 19th c., 38¼" d., 26½" h. (one star replaced) 8,800.00

Wrought iron, Art Deco style, eight-light, the wide flat pierced scrolling central section centered by opposing fleur-de-lis painted gold, supporting around the base eight curved candlearms w/wide bobeches, suspended at the top w/a circular chain below a foliate ceiling cap, painted verdigris finish, designed by Gilbert Poillerat, France, ca. 1930, 25 x 55", 5' 6" h. 7,150.00

LANTERNS

Punched-Tin 'Paul Revere' Lantern

Barn lantern, pine & glass, square wooden base & top w/slender corner posts notch-carved along the edge, glass sides w/one a hinged door, old natural finish, 9½" h. (old splits, tin repair on top).......................... 330.00

Barn lantern, wood & glass, the upright red-painted wooden framework w/chamfer-edged corner posts framing wavy glass sides, one side a door opening to a tin

socket, corner posts continue through base to form small knob feet, tin arched cap & wire bail handle, 19th c., 11" h. 522.50

Candle lantern, punched-tin, 'Paul Revere' type, cylindrical w/curved door & a conical top w/a short, angled cylindrical socket, overall punched designs, 12½" h. plus ring handle 181.50

Candle lantern, punched-tin, 'Paul Revere' type, cylindrical w/curved hinged door & conical top w/ring handle, the sides elaborately pierced w/hearts, diamonds, shields, arches & other Masonic devices, traces of old gilding, probably Pennsylvania, late 19th c., 16" h. (ILLUS.) 1,100.00

Candle lantern, tin, folding-type, "Minor's Patent/Jan. 24th/1865," w/attached match holder, original paint & stenciling, early 149.00

Candle lantern, tin, hand-type, conical body w/a hinged door glazed w/horn, the conical top pierced w/vent holes & w/a small curved cap, a strap handle opposite the door, 6" h. 236.50

Candle lantern, tin & glass, square form w/a red, a blue & a green glass side & a hinged tin door at the back, a pyramidal top pierced w/vent holes & a round ring handle, traces of paint, 19th c., 10" h. plus handle.................... 71.50

Candle lantern, tin & glass, pierced-tin pyramidal top w/large ring handle above a tin frame & glass sides, each w/two wire guards, old black paint, 11" h. plus ring handle 302.50

Candle lantern, tin & glass, round w/peaked top w/ruffled air vent & ring handle, a hinged door in one of the six glass sides, old black paint, 11¼" h. plus ring handle 220.00

Early Candle Lanterns

Candle lantern, tin & glass, a pyramidal pierced top above metal framework enclosing glass sides w/wire guards, a large ring handle at the top, minor damage, 11½" h. plus handle (ILLUS. right) 115.50

Candle lantern, tin & glass, an arched metal top w/open ends & small wire handle above a pierced metal framework enclosing glass sides, a hinged glass door & a metal back, old black paint, 13" h. (ILLUS. left) 137.50

Candle lantern, tin & glass, triangular, w/pierced circular chimney & circular ring handle, painted red, America, 19th c., 16" h. 550.00

Unusual Tin Candle Lantern

Candle lantern, tin & glass, hexagonal framework enclosed arched glass panels & a hinged door w/thin posts w/finials between each panel, a stepped geometrically-pierced top w/ring handle, probably American-made, late 18th - early 19th c., 18½" h. (ILLUS.) 2,640.00

Candle lantern, tin & glass, hexagonal, the metal frame holding six long tapering clear glass panels, a domed hexagonal top w/a conical vent cap, old black & gold repaint, raised on a long wooden pole, lantern 21½" h., overall 5' 3" h. (finial incomplete) 110.00

Hand lantern, kerosene-type, tin w/brass trim, a round slightly domed foot on the cylindrical font base supporting the clear glass globe w/a pierced cap & ruffled vent at the top, wire bail handle & wire globe guard, 12½" h. 126.50

Skater's lantern, tin & glass, tin font base & domed pierced vent cap w/wire bail handle, clear glass globe, 7" h. (light rust) 71.50

Skater's lantern, tin & glass, a domed tin font & burner below

the clear chimney & domed tin cap joined by wire supports to the base, 7¼" h. 82.50

Whale oil lantern, tin & glass, the circular font base w/a round domed foot below the clear blown glass ovoid globe topped by a cylindrical tin cap pierced w/a star & diamond design, a large ring handle at the top, tin w/original worn brown japanning, w/removable whale oil burner, probably New England Glass Co., mid-19th c., 13½" h. plus handle (minor base damage) 192.50

SHADES

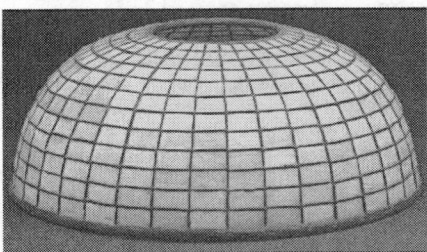

Bigelow-Kennard Leaded Shade

Amberina, bulbous-form in Diamond Quilted patt., 6" d. fitter, top 4¾" d., 5½" h. 175.00

Amberina, scalloped rim, 5" d. fitter, 7½" d., 5¾" h. 275.00

Bigelow-Kennard, 12¼" d. domical leaded glass shade composed of overall graduated bands of brickwork in pearl pink slag glass, rim tag-marked "Bigelow-Kennard & Co. - Boston," early 20th c., 5" h. (ILLUS.) 770.00

Leaded glass, 24" d. domical form w/uneven bottom rim & tapering to a central flaring crown cap, composed of a wide border of stylized pink rose blossoms, red cherries & green leaves below an upper section of graduated brickwork, late 19th c., 14" h. 440.00

Linden Glass Company Shade

Linden Glass Company, 27" d. conical leaded glass shade of mottled yellowish amber panels arranged in the Prairie School style w/triangular & rectangular segments of iridescent green, yellow & olive amber in narrow border bands at the top & near the rim, metal rim impressed "Linden Glass Co. Chicago, Ill.," design attributed to Frank Lloyd Wright for the Darwin D. Martin House, Buffalo, New York, early 20th c., some lead deterioration, no electrical fittings (ILLUS.) 3,575.00

Pairpoint, clear cut glass, mushroom-shaped, cut w/butterflies & flowers, 5" d. base, 4" h... 75.00

Quezal, ribbed trumpet-form, gold iridescent w/rich bronze satin lustre w/deeper bronze highlights, signed, 4 7/8" d., 5" h. 88.00

Quezal, lily-form w/ruffled rim, green & gold pulled-feather decoration on an opal ground, gold iridescent lining 350.00

Quezal, paneled bell-form, iridescent amber, signed, ca. 1920, 5 3/8" h., set of 6 .... 660.00

Steuben, bell-shaped w/relief-molded ribs, gold Aurene, fleur-de-lis mark, 5" d., 4½" h. 110.00

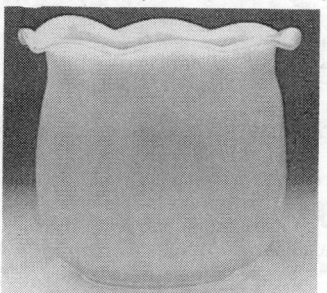

Tiffany Opalescent Shade

Tiffany, a wide, slightly tapering opalescent aquamarine body w/a wide, gently ruffled rim, slightly domed & tapered at the top, inscribed & labeled "TG & D Co. Tiffany Favrile Glass Registered - Mark," 5¾" d., 10" h. (ILLUS.) 412.50

Tiffany, 12" d. domical form, green & gold damascened decoration, unsigned....................1,760.00

Tiffany, domed & ruffled umbrella-shaped candlelamp-type, brilliant ruby red exterior cased in white, w/an overall stretched iridescence, one signed "L.C.T. Favrile" on the top rim, top opening 2 5/8" d., widest width 7¼" d., pr. 3,520.00

(End of Lighting Devices Section)

MAGAZINES

All magazines are in excellent, complete condition unless otherwise noted. Also see MOVIE MEMORABILIA, and PARRISH (Maxfield) ARTWORK.

Aldine, A Typographic Art Journal, 1872, Vols. V & VI, maroon covers, bound, 2 vols. $800.00

Amateur Photography Weekly, 1917, July 27 .... 5.00

American Girl, 1947, June 6.00

American Magazine, 1935, February 18.00

American Photography, 1930, August 6.50

American Printer, 1907, April, w/Ault Wiborg color ads 10.00

Arizona Highways, 1974, January, Indian jewelry 8.50

Atlantic Monthly, 1862, March 14.50

Boy's Life, 1960, March 3.50

Century, 1904-05, November through April, three color & one black & white Maxfield Parrish prints, article on Alphonse Mucha, ex-library 40.00

Collier's, 1899, October 14, Admiral Dewey front cover 12.50

Collier's, 1914, January 3 through March 14, bound 55.00

Collier's, 1916, January 8, Leyendecker cover, automotive ads, etc., 108 pp. 13.50

Collier's, 1952, March 8, Leo Durocher w/family 5.00

Cosmopolitan, 1912, December, Charles Dana Gibson cover & article...................... 25.00

Cosmopolitan, 1945, August 8.00

Cosmopolitan, 1953, May, Marilyn Monroe on cover 25.00

Country Gentleman, 1924, March 29 .... 7.00

Country Life, 1917, May 5.00

Delineator, 1910, January through April, bound 40.00

Esquire, 1934, September 12.00

Esquire, 1958, October, Silver Anniversary issue, w/original shipping box 25.00

Farm Journal, 1919, June 22.00

Federal Illustrator, 1928, Summer ... 3.00

Fortune, July, 1933, w/"Reign of Meiji," 13 color illustrations, 27 page history of Japan, etc. 15.00

Fortune, 1937, March, Paramount Movie Studios & Stars, four color posters by Cassandra 12.50

Frank Leslie's Popular Monthly, 1892, July through December, bound 45.00

Good Housekeeping, 1891, July through December, bound 40.00

Good Housekeeping, 1912, September, Coles Phillips cover (small crease at lower corner) 12.50

Good Housekeeping, 1920, May, Jessie Willcox Smith cover, two pages of dolls, S. Young & H. Cady pages 25.00

Graham's, 1847, January through June, bound 30.00

Harper's New Monthly Magazine, 1873-74, December through May, bound 75.00

Harper's New Monthly Magazine, 1886, May 11.00

Harper's Weekly, 1864, December 31, double-page Nast "Union Christmas Dinner" print 15.00

Harper's Weekly, 1865, May 6, Lincoln's funeral 75.00

Harper's Weekly, 1872, September 14, full-page Winslow Homer print entitled "Under the Falls, Catskill Mountains" 40.00

House & Garden, 1932, December .. 12.00

House & Garden, 1933, July 12.00

House & Garden, 1939, July, Gone With the Wind article 65.00

Illustrated London News, 1915, September 5.00

Inland Printer, 1900, September, color Will Bradley cover, Ault Wiborg ad 15.00

Jack & Jill, 1964, October, Halloween issue, w/removable Wrigley Gum Popup Zoo 18.00

Judge, 1926, May 15, Flapper in bathing suit & mermaid on cover 10.00

Ladies' Home Journal, 1892, July ... 15.00

Ladies' Home Journal, 1930, May, Art Deco ads 6.00

Liberty, 1941, August 5.00

Life, 1913, January 12 through May 22, bound 65.00

Life, 1930, April 11 .... 10.00

Life, 1937, September 6, Harpo Marx on cover 25.00

Life, 1938, August 22, Fred Astaire & Ginger Rogers on cover 20.00

Life, 1950, June 12, Hopalong Cassidy on cover.................... 25.00

Life, 1958, February 3, Shirley Temple on cover 8.00

Life, 1961, August 18, Mickey Mantle & Roger Maris on cover 20.00

Life, 1969, December 19, Charles Manson on cover................ 15.00

Look, 1949, April 26, Joe DiMaggio & Joe DiMaggio, Jr. 45.00

Look, 1960, July 5, Marilyn Monroe on cover & story inside 10.00

Look, 1971, May 4, Elvis Presley on cover 16.00

The Mentor, 1923, September 10.00

Midweek Pictorial, 1927, June 9, Charles Lindbergh on cover, Ovations in Paris, New York, etc., also Bobby Jones story 18.50

The Mother Magazine, 1915, June, fashions, Coca-Cola & other ads .. 19.00

National Geographic, 1935, July through December, bound 8.50

New Idea, 1907, June, complete w/full color fashion plate 12.50

Newsweek, 1939, December 25 ..... 30.00

Our Young Folks, 1870, January through December, bound 45.00

Outdoors, 1940, November 10.00

Physical Culture, 1904, August...... 15.00

Physical Culture, 1940, complete year bound 40.00

Pictorial Review, 1925, December, Christmas cover, two-page Dolly Dingle Christmas & Dolly Dingle cards, w/ads, fashions, gifts, etc. 55.00

Playboy, 1956, June 40.00

Playboy, 1960, June 17.00

Popular Science, 1936, June 12.00

Puck, 1894, February 7, color cover cartoon "Congress & Income Tax," 16 pp........................... 12.00

Punch, 1874, complete year bound .. 75.00

Radio Guide, 1939, February 25, Charlie McCarthy on cover 8.50

Recreation, 1896, June............. 6.50

Redbook, 1953, March, Marilyn Monroe on cover.................... 25.00

Red Cross, 1918, November, w/four full-page color illustrations by Norman Rockwell 10.00

Ring, 1935, June, special pictorial issue on Max Schmeling........... 18.00

St. Nicholas, 1915, May, T. Burgess story, Rockwell illustration, etc. .. 12.50

St. Nicholas, 1922, December, color Santa cover, stories, ads, etc. 8.50

Saturday Evening Post, 1912, January 6 through June 29, bound 150.00

Saturday Evening Post, 1923, May 12, w/double page Coca-Cola advertisement 18.50

Saturday Evening Post, 1956, November 17, complete, color Walt Disney & characters cover by Tenggren 10.00

Saturday Evening Post, 1977, August, Special 250th Anniversary Issue, w/Rockwell illustrations 8.50

Saturday Review, 1947, March 8, Albert Einstein on cover 15.00

Science & Mechanics, 1938, June.... 6.00

Scientific American, 1904, January through June, bound 40.00

Scribner's Monthly, 1880-81, November through April, bound 40.00

Sport, 1952, Jackie Robinson & Pee Wee Reese action cover 28.00

Sports Illustrated, 1965, Mickey
Mantle on cover 30.00
Stage, 1937, August 10.00
Success, 1903, November 12.00
Theatre Arts, 1940, September, Mar-
tha Graham front cover, Holm Li-
mon, Humphrey, St. Denis, etc.,
inside 15.00
Time, 1942, November 23, General
James Doolittle cover........... 15.00
Time, 1945, April, Armed Forces
edition, Truman cover, Franklin
Delano Roosevelt funeral cover-
age 33.00
Time, 1969, August 8, John Wayne
cover 10.00
Today's Housewife, 1924, March 5.00
True Experiences, 1934, July, Nitza
Vernille cover.................. 8.00
TV Guide, 1953, August 21, Super
Circus cover 35.00
TV Guide, 1957, June 8, Lassie
cover 30.00
TV Western Round-Up, Vol. 1, No. 1,
1957 .... 25.00
Vanity Fair, 1933, July 20.00
Woman's Day, 1963, August, w/12
page dictionary of Sandwich glass
in color 10.00
Woman's Day, 1965, October, w/dic-
tionary of French furniture 10.00
Woman's Home Companion, 1921,
February 8.00
Woman's Home Companion, 1936,
October 15.00

MARBLES

Guinea Marble

Glass, clambroth w/emerald green
swirled stripes, 13/16" d. $264.00
Glass, clear w/cobalt blue mica
flecks, 5/8" d. 25.00
Glass, comic strip type, "Sandy,"
white & blue w/dog's head &
name in black, 3/4" d............ 104.50
Glass, comic strip type, "Smitty,"
pale orange & red w/character in
black, 11/16" d................. 198.00
Glass, guinea-type, cobalt blue
ground w/orange, yellow & white
swirled spatter, 5/8" d. (ILLUS.) .. 210.00
Glass, latticino-type, yellowish
amber w/swirled white bands,
3/4" d. 66.00

Glass, latticino-type, deep turquoise
w/swirled white bands, 1" d...... 275.00
Glass, Lutz-type, swirled bands of
green, white & goldstone w/a
couple of pink bands, 5/8" d. 165.00
Glass, Lutz-type, thin swirled bands
of red, pink, white & goldstone,
5/8" d. 187.00
Glass, Lutz-type, opaque banded,
opaque jade green w/two goldstone bands trimmed in white
& four bright blue bands,
11/16" d. 330.00
Glass, Lutz-type, solid core, half
green & half yellow core w/wide
goldstone bands trimmed in
white, 7/8" d. 515.00

Lutz-Type Marble

Glass, Lutz-type, wide goldstone
center swirled band & narrower
yellow bands, 1½" d. (ILLUS.) 450.00
Glass, machine-made, multicolored splotches & swirls overall,
11/16" d. 286.00
Glass, mica-type, deep amber
w/overall fine mica flecks
throughout, 1¼" d.............. 258.50
Glass, "onionskin," red, white &
blue spatter, 2½" d. 135.00
Glass, open core-type, red, white &
dark blue core w/yellow middle
bands & red & green alternating
outer bands, 1 11/16" d. 187.00
Glass, open core-type, swirled
bands of yellow, red & white,
1 7/8" d. 198.00
Glass, peppermint swirl-type, white
bands w/thin swirled red stripes
& wide blue stripes w/mica flecks
mixed in, 3/4" d. 522.50
Glass, ribbon core-type, blue, white,
yellow & red bands, 13/16" d. 66.00

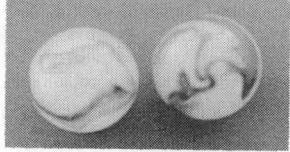

Slag Marbles

Glass, slag-type, carnelian & milky
white, 5/8" d. (ILLUS. right) 20.00

Glass, slag-type, oxblood & milky
white, 5/8" d. (ILLUS. left) 20.00
Glass, solid core-type, white core
w/red, green & blue bands & yellow outer bands, 1¼" d......... 60.50
Glass, spatter-type, swirled bands
of fine red, green & blue spatter
alternating w/white bands,
2 3/16" d. 440.00
Glass, spatter-type, swirled wide
bands of blue & white & yellow &
red spatter, 2½" d. 176.00
Glass, sulphide, w/boar, 1¾" d. ... 160.00
Glass, sulphide, w/cow, standing,
2¼" d. (sizable air bubble)....... 82.50
Glass, sulphide, w/dog, Huskie-
type, standing, light pink amethyst glass, 1 5/8" d. (air bubble
between legs) 110.00
Glass, sulphide, w/lion, standing,
2¼" d....................... 99.00
Glass, sulphide, w/owl, standing,
1 5/8" d., polished 180.00
Glass, sulphide, w/woman, sitting,
1 3/16" d. 198.00
Glass, sulphide, w/woman, standing, 1 7/16" d. 242.00

MATCH SAFES & CONTAINERS

Sterling Silver Safe with Golfer

Advertising safe, pocket-type, nickel
plate case w/celluloid over paper
wrapping, one side w/a colorful
portrait of a Victorian beauty, the
other w/"Buffum Tools - Louisiana, MO," 1½ x 2¾" ...$40.00 to 60.00
Advertising safe, pocket-type, silver
plate, "C.W.S. Crumpsall Biscuit
Co.," model of a pocket watch ... 195.00
Advertising safe, pocket-type, silver
plate, "Thorne's Whiskey is Match-
less" on front, model of a whiskey
flask, 1¼ x 2" 165.00
Brass safe, figural alligator, hinged
back & head, w/original paint,
8½" l. 95.00

Brass safe, figural fish, fine detail,
1¼ x 3¼"..................... 185.00
Brass safe, model of a camera case,
rectangular, 1¼ x 2½" 135.00
Cast iron container, table model,
double urn-form, 1867 patent..... 65.00
Cast iron safe, casket-shaped,
w/spaniel finial, Superior Foundry, Cleveland, Ohio 85.00
Copper safe, hinged cover, "Fifth
Massachusetts Regiment," proba-
bly issued at erection of monument at Gettysburg in 1880's, oval
on front w/soldier & "Hold Your
Ground"...................... 65.00
Porcelain container, saucer-type
w/striker sides, floral decoration,
Bavaria 45.00
Silver plate container, a pair of
figural cherubs hold the match
container at the center, Rogers,
Smith & Company (resilvered) 395.00
Silver plate safe, figural barrel,
1½ x 2¼"..................... 155.00
Silver plate safe, figural Rugby ball,
"Association" embossed front &
back, 1 5/8 x 2" 165.00
Silver plate safe, figural tusk w/a
small elephant figure on the end
lid, 1 x 3" 95.00
Sterling silver safe, Art Nouveau style lion holding shield,
2 1/8 x 2½" 90.00
Sterling silver safe, Art Nouveau
style w/woman on one side, deer
on the other, tobacco cutter on
bottom 65.00
Sterling silver safe, embossed dog's
head & florals, 2½ x 2 5/8" 110.00
Sterling silver safe, embossed scene
of Eros & Psyche ascending to
heaven, surrounded by dolphins,
griffins & shell 150.00
Sterling silver safe, embossed scene
of golfer swinging club framed by
bold leafy scrolls, early 20th c.
(ILLUS.)...................... 495.00
Sterling silver safe, embossed scene
of woman performing the dance
of seven veils amid rococo scrolling & florals 130.00
Wooden box, model of a low-
backed, low-heeled shoe, carved
w/a zigzag band along the bottom
of the uppers, painted w/contrast-
ing shades of yellow, black, red &
ochre, 19th c., 5¼" l., 2¼" h.
(paint loss) 605.00
Wooden container, table model,
turned container on short pedestal
base, smooth dark patina, ca.
1860, 3½" h. 28.00

MEDICAL COLLECTIBLES

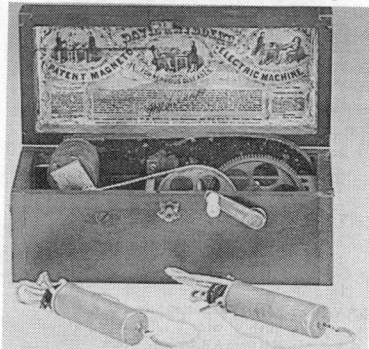

Early Quack Medical Device

Book, "Diseases of the Eye," by Nettleship, 1900 .... $10.00

Book, "Dr. Johnson's Method of Curing Piles," 1926 .... 10.00

Book, "The New Healing," by Streeter, about Osteopathy, England, ca. 1929 .... 32.00

Book, "New Truths in Ophthalmology," by Savage, 1893, signed by author, hard cover 25.00

Book, "Phrenology & Physiognomy," 1877, illustrated 25.00

Book, "Practice of Medicine," by William Osler, 1892, D. Appleton & Co., first edition (hinge cracking, spine getting loose, some corners chipped) 545.00

Books, "Atlas of Human Anatomy," by Tolt, Vols. I & II, 1942, illustrated, 956 pp. 25.00

Dose glass, embossed "Gavitt's Medical Topeka" 13.00

Examining table, chiropractic-type, two-piece collapsible model, folds into suitcase-sized case w/green velvet cover, ca. 1920's 95.00

Machine, "Davis & Kidder's Patent Magneto Electric Machine," quack medical device, brass mechanism, fitted in a mahogany case, exterior metal handle w/ivory knob, all-original except new wires to handle, ca. 1854, 4½ x 10", 4½" h. (ILLUS.) 385.00

Machine, "Renulife," violet ray machine, in fitted case, w/accessories & literature, dated "5-22-22" 320.00

Surgical knife, Civil War era, marked "Dove," w/wooden handle, 4½" l. 45.00

Syringe, infant's, "Goodrich," ca. 1940's, in original box 10.00

Vaporizer, milk white glass, ca. 1920's, in original box 25.00

METALS

ALUMINUM

Aluminum Service Plates

Coffeepot, cov., "Manning Bowman No. 3093," w/black wooden handle $30.00

Napkin holder, hammered, "Rodney Kent No. 405"................... 18.00

Pitcher, spun, cylindrical w/flaring rim & wooden ring handle, Russel Wright design, 10" h............. 145.00

Pitcher, water, hammered, Buenilum 15.00

Plates, service, circular, each embossed in the center w/either a fish, geese in flight, a deer, penguin, palm tree, swan, antelope or fox, pearlescent finish, designed by Oscar Bach, inscribed "Oscar Bach" & impressed "Sterling Bronze Co. - New York" & numbered, ca. 1930, 12" d., set of 8 (ILLUS. of part) 990.00

Punch set: spherical covered bowl, ladle & eight half-round cups; "Satellite" design, the bowl w/four round knob handles around the sides & a knob finial on the small cover, the cups w/round knob handles, w/a brushed finish, designed by Russel Wright & so-marked, bowl 10" d., cup 3¼" d., 2" h., the set........ 990.00

Tray, hammered, blackberry decoration, large double handles, "Farberware" 30.00

Warmer, cov., hammered, oak leaves & acorn pattern, w/Bakelite handles.................... 40.00

BRASS

Ashtray, round dished bowl flanked by a cigarette support at each side & raised on slender scrolling stylized rams' feet attached to a flat base ring, the bowl holding a green iridescent Steuben Aurene dish, by Oscar B. Bach, marked, 9" d., 5" h. 275.00

Candle snuffer & tray, w/scalloped

& scrolled edges, footed, early
19th c. 128.00
Flour scoop, patent dated "Dec. 8,
1868" 38.00
Kettle, spun, iron bail handle, la-
beled "Hayden's patent," 17" d.,
11" h. 75.00
Kettle, spun, iron bail handle, deep
cylindrical sides, marked "American Brass Kettle...," 26½" d.,
19" h. 125.00

Early Brass Ornament

Ornament, rectangular w/a rounded
lobe at the bottom, pierced w/let-
ters "I H" & engraved "EM - 1775"
& w/"Liberty" engraved on round
tab, three fastening loops on the
back, American-made, 2½ x 2¾"
(ILLUS.) 1,760.00
Spirits barrel, model of a keg w/a
domed lid at the top center,
bands around the body, a spigot
at one end & large ring handles
at the sides, raised on a short
pedestal w/a flaring, stepped
base on a rectangular plinth,
Regency period, England, early
19th c., 9" l. 1,045.00
Stencil, barrel-type, rectangular,
"Dick & Stout, 176, 186 Waslin St.,
N.Y.," 19th c., 4 x 8" 22.00
Tazza, low spreading foot, circular
top w/incised concentric decoration, probably Spain, early
18th c., 12¾" d. 880.00

BRONZE

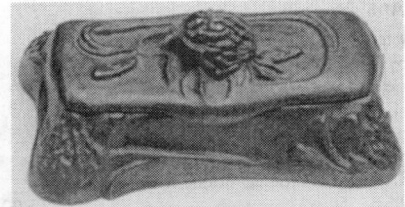

Decorated Bronze Box

Blotter ends, 'Abalone' patt., gilt
finish, impressed Tiffany Studios
mark & "1153," 12¼" l., pr. 330.00
Bowl, pedestal base, flaring rim,
decorated w/a dragon in relief,
pedestal further decorated w/a
dragon, signed "Toun Chu," Ja-
pan, mid-19th c., 9" h. 770.00
Box, cov., rectangular w/rounded
corners, the cover & corners of
the base cast w/large clover blossoms & vining stems, base incised
"J. Preston Chicago," 2 5/8 x 4¼"
(ILLUS.) 935.00
Bulb bowl, boat-form, decorated
w/turtle figures, signed "Seiryusai
chu," Japan, Meiji period, late
19th c., 16" l. 522.50
Ewer, Art Nouveau style, tall footed
ovoid body w/arched spout, the
whole cast w/maidens in waves
centered by a nude female in
high-relief, the handle in the form
of a second female grasping the
neck & spout cast w/lotus leaves,
stamped "Gorham Mfg. Co. - Spe-
cial 589," 23½" h. 6,600.00

Figural Bronze Jardiniere

Jardiniere, figural, wide footed
ovoid body tapering to a wide flat
mouth, the sides cast in relief
w/nude dancing ladies w/putti &
vines, mask handles at the sides,
after Gustave Joseph Cheret, inscribed "Joseph Cheret - E. Soleau
Editr Paris. - Copryght (sic) by
Soleau 1894 - 'To George Edwards
in recognition of his valued services as Art Director of Colliers
Weekly - May MCMI' " & stamped
"10," France, late 19th c., brown
patina, 12¼" h. (ILLUS.) 2,860.00
Loving cup, hand-hammered, three
strap handles, slightly ovoid body
w/round flaring base, unmarked
Stickley Brothers, numbered
"246," cleaned surface, 7½" d.,
9¾" h. 110.00
Paperweight w/calendar, Zodiac
patt., brown patina, Tiffany Stu-
dios, No. 929 . . . . 295.00

Plaques, one modeled in relief
depicting a sheik, the other a
harem girl, after Louis Hottot,
w/cold-painted detail, each in
a wooden frame w/metal Egyptian Revival mounts, late 19th c.,
15" w., 23½" h., pr. 3,190.00
Plate, the dished center cast w/a
stylized scroll pattern, the handles
formed by two facing venomous
snake heads w/their bodies
continuing as the rim of the
plate, Edgar Brandt, stamped
"E. BRANDT," early 20th c.,
13½" l. 2,200.00
Urn, a wide flat-sided bowl decorat-
ed on the outside w/a continuous
raised band of classical allegorical
figures, ornate scrolled handles,
on a short narrow ringed pedestal
on a circular socle on a marble
plinth w/incurved corners, gilt finish, inscribed "F. Barbedienne,"
France, late 19th c., 8¼" h. 4,675.00
Vase, cast as a stylized lotus bud,
highlighted w/gilt oval reserves
on a green patinated ground, inscribed "JEAN DUNAND," France,
ca. 1930's, 3 3/8" h. 880.00
Vase, footed ovoid body tapering to
a short flaring neck, the sides
cast w/a continuous woodland
landscape w/classical nude figures standing or seated playing
musical instruments, rich brown
patina, from a model by Henri
Cros, inscribed "H CROS" & "5" &
stamped w/the Hebrard Foundry
seal, early 20th c., 9" h. 2,750.00

CHROME

Chrome Cocktail Service

Candy box, cov., three-tier,
"Chase," catalog No. 90104 . . . . . . 30.00
Clock, table model, modeled as a
silhouetted stylized hand supporting a circular clock dial between

the thumb & forefinger, on a flat
rectangular base, impressed twice
"wHw FRANZ HAGENAUER WIEN -
MADE IN AUSTRIA," 12¼" h. 2,090.00
Cocktail service: tall cylindrical
cocktail shaker, eight stemmed
goblets & a rectangular tray; in
the "Skyscraper" design by Norman Bel Geddes, manufactured by
Revere Brass & Copper Co., tray
in the "Manhattan" pattern, w/Re-
vere marks, ca. 1930's, shaker
12¾" h., the set (ILLUS.) 3,520.00
Cocktail shaker, cylindrical w/in-
dented bands near the top & bottom, "Chase," 'Gaiety' model,
catalog No. 90034 . . . . 30.00
Coffee set: cov. coffeepot, creamer
& cov. sugar bowl; electric, red
Lucite handles, 3 pcs. 75.00
Coffee set: squatty cov. coffeepot,
cov. sugar bowl, creamer & large
oval tray; Universal Model
No. E9239, ca. 1924, 3 pcs. 75.00
Lamp, torchere-type floor model,
a slender reeded standard on a
disc foot on small knob feet, the
shade composed of three graduated widely flaring inverted cones
open to emit light between each,
by Walter Von Nessen, ca. 1928,
5' 7½" h. 7,150.00

COPPER

Copper Apple Butter Kettle

Apple butter kettle, deep cylindrical
sides, iron bail handle, set in a
forged iron three-legged stand,
ca. 1880, dents & stains, 19¾" d.,
13½" h. (ILLUS.) 82.50
Bowl, hand-hammered, shallow
footed petal-form w/eight wide
tapering lobes, hallmark of Karl
F. Leinonen, Boston, Massachusetts, ca. 1920, original dark patina, 8¼" d., 3" h. (some patina
wear) 412.50

Bowl, hand-hammered, wide shallow flaring sides raised on a brass footing, open box mark of Dirk Van Erp, natural repatination, early 20th c., 10¾" d. 440.00

Cauldron, deep sides w/rounded bottom & rolled rim, iron swing handle across the top, 28" d., 18" h. plus handle. 660.00

Centerpiece, Arts & Crafts style, hand-hammered, a flaring trumpet-form on tripod legs simulating bamboo, early 20th c., 9½" d. 154.00

Arts & Crafts Coal Bucket

Coal bucket, Arts & Crafts style, tapering cylindrical sides w/flaring foot & widely flaring spout, fixed iron handle near base & iron strap swing handle at the top, fine dark original patina, unmarked Stickley Brothers, numbered "116," 15½ x 17¼" (ILLUS.) 1,210.00

Measures, liquid-type, tall cylindrical body w/strap handle, half-gallon, quart & pint sizes, each w/excise marks & two bear maker's mark, C. Whitney & J.W. Cluett, Albany, New York, ca. 1869, 10½", 6" & 4¾" h., graduated set of 3 . . . . .1,100.00

Pitcher, footed ovoid body tapering to a wide rounded spout, thin strap handle, dovetailed construction, marked "China," 20th c., 7½" h. 25.00

Plate, hand-hammered, dished center w/a wide flanged rim decorated w/raised stylized dogwood blossoms & w/a rolled rim, dark original patina, by Karl Kipp, marked, 9¾" d. 412.50

Sauce pan, dovetailed bottom w/brass solder, iron handle attached w/copper rivets, stamped "B.D. & Co., Chicago & New York, IH Co.," 9½" d., 3½" h. 220.00

Teakettle, cov., dovetailed construction, straight sides, gooseneck spout, fixed overhead handle, 11" h. 150.00

Tray, elongated oval w/dished sides, shaped loop end handles, hand-hammered design, original patina, die-stamped mark of Gustav Stickley, early 20th c., 11 x 23" 660.00

Vase, hand-hammered, wide ovoid body tapering to a wide flat mouth, open box mark of Dirk Van Erp, original patina, early 20th c., 6½" d., 8¼" h. (cleaned) 907.50

Vase, hand-hammered, three sinuous high curved handles, flared base tapering to narrow neck surmounted by a ball-shaped mouth, original dark patina, unmarked Stickley Brothers, numbered "8," 5½" d., 10½" h. (small dents). . . . 302.50

Wall sconce, hand-hammered, a shaped wall plate w/a curved bar extending to support a knob-ended slender bar which supports a conical copper shade w/riveted bars separating the mica panels in the sides, unmarked Dirk Van Erp, original dark patina & mica, early 20th c., shade 9" d., overall 10½" h. 4,950.00

IRON

Cast Iron Cookie Board

Bill clip, cast, figural Indian Chief w/headdress & earrings, facing left, old brass color, w/hole for hanging, 2 x 2¾" 85.00

Birdhouse, cast, in the form of a two-story country cottage w/gabled roofs & covered porches, Miller Iron Company, Providence, Rhode Island, ca. 1868, 12" h. (loss of painted surface, oxidized) 3,850.00

Broom holder, cast, embossed "Gem Broom Holder," 2 pcs. 12.50

Card holder, cast, model of an elephant, Hubley. 150.00

Card holder, cast, model of a Pekingese dog, Hubley. 150.00

Cookie board, cast, rectangular, decorated w/a bird on a leafy branch surrounded by dots with-

in a sawtooth oval frame,
3¼ x 5¼" 150.00
Cookie board, cast, oval, decorated
w/the insignia of the Odd Fellows
& the initials "F.L.T.," 5 x 6¾"
(ILLUS.) 135.00
Dough scraper, hand-wrought, sim-
ple tooled snake head at join between handle & blade, 4¼" w. . . . 105.00
Hearth roaster, hand-wrought,
rotating-type, a narrow flat rotating bar decorated w/pairs of central upright scroll bars flanked by
double-arched & scrolled bars, on
a long slender three-footed bar
base w/a loop handle, early,
26" l. (pitted) 352.00
Kettle shelf, cast, reticulated top,
straight narrow legs, 11¼ x 17",
10" h. 65.00
Kettle tilter, hand-wrought, the long
slender gracefully upturned handle continuing to the arched
mechanism w/loop grip & braces,
23" l. (pitted, one end of hook
ended-out in copper) 225.50
Lighting stand, hand-wrought, tall
slender shaft, adjustable candlearms w/wide drip pans, on tripod
w/penny feet, 58" h. 900.00
Mailbox, cast, "Griswold No. 106" . . 75.00
Model of an eagle, cast, black
repaint, 33" h. 750.00
Model of a hatchet, cast, embossed
on handle "All Nations Welcome
But Carry," bust of Carry Nation
in blade, 12" l. 120.00
Paper clip, cast, wall-type, model of
a Collie dog 150.00
Pencil holder, cast, figural Indian
head, Hubley 175.00
Pipe tongs, hand-wrought, flattened
hinged handles w/curved tips &
simple round hooked finger rings,
6" l. 75.00
Popover pan, cast, "Griswold
No. 10" 32.00

Cast Iron Porringer

Porringer, cast, pointed tab handle
w/pierced design, wide shallow

round bowl, marked "Clark...
1 Pint," worn & flaked white
enamel interior, 5¼" d. (ILLUS.) . . 55.00
Roaster, cov., cast, Wagner Ware
"Drip-Drop Roaster," No. 8,
marked & patented "March
14 '22" 65.00
Rush light holder, hand-wrought, tall
pointed shaft, adjustable rush
holder has candle socket counter-
balance, on tripod w/penny feet,
47½" h. (pitted w/rust) 350.00
Shooting gallery figure, cast, mod-
el of a rooster, black finish,
4½" h. 29.50
Snow birds, cast, models of eagles,
5½" h., set of 6 . . . . 195.00
Spatula, hand-wrought, wide flat
fan-shaped blade tapering to
rounded base & continuing to a
long, narrow handle w/end loop,
11½" l. (pitted) 40.00
Stove pipe mitten shelf, cast, two-
part, half-round, "Woman's
Friend" in casting, each side
10½ x 20" 150.00
Tea kettle, cov., cast, squatty spher-
ical body w/short angled spout,
side-hinged slightly domed cover
w/embossed writing around edge
"A. Bradley & Co. - Pittsburgh,
Pa. 1866," w/wire bail handle,
9½" d., 8¼" h. (reblacked) 176.00
Umbrella stand, cast, in the form of
a cupid holding a snake, Victori-
an, late 19th c., 29" h. 880.00
Waffle iron, cast, "Wagner No. 0,"
patented February 22, 1910 . . . . . . 125.00

PEWTER

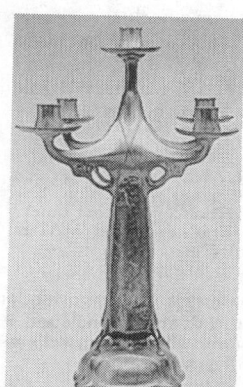

Kayserzinn Pewter Candelabrum

Basin, Thomas Danforth III, Philadelphia, Pennsylvania, ca. 1810,
12" d. (imperfections, polished) . . . 825.00
Beakers, flared cylindrical form,
w/wigglework portraits of King
William & Queen Mary within oval

reserves beneath a foliate border, on molded base, William & Mary period, England, ca. 1690, 5½" h., pr. 3,520.00

Candelabra, Art Nouveau style, five-light, shaped rectangular stem, the sides lightly molded w/differing undulating flowers, on molded raised circular base w/squared corners, the stem issuing four bold scroll branches, the underside w/open oval, the join w/ferns, rising to circular wax pan to the fluted urn-form socket, w/conforming central light, each impressed "KAYSERZINN" & numbered "4485" & "4486," early 20th c., 18¾" h., pr. (ILLUS. of one)........................5,500.00

Clock, table model, the tapering rectangular body w/raised tapering bands up the corners of the front supporting a slightly domed rectangular top, the circular clock dial inset near top of the front & decorated w/blue & green enamel & Roman numerals, Liberty & Company, England, stamped "MADE IN ENGLAND - ENGLISH PEWTER 0761," early 20th c., 8¾" h. 2,420.00

Coffeepot, cov., tall 'lighthouse' style, attributed to Israel Trask, Beverly, Massachusetts, w/bright-cut decoration, ca. 1825, 12¼" h. (polished) 605.00

Coffeepot, cov., tall octagonal pigeon-breasted form raised on a pedestal foot, domed cover w/button finial, C-scroll wooden handle, swan's-neck spout, applied on the side w/a medallion showing a cabin & an American flag, marked "Broadhead & Atkin, Sheffield," England, ca. 1840-50, 13¾" h........................ 250.00

Flagon, cov., tall tapering cylindrical form w/S-scroll handle & domed cover, Israel Trask, Beverly, Massachusetts, ca. 1813-56, 10½" h. (some battering) 300.00

Lamp, whale oil-type, cylindrical font raised on a tapering standard raised on a domed round foot, Rufus Dunham, Westbrook, Maine, 1837-60, 5 5/8" h. plus burner 330.00

Measures, bellied-form, England, ¼ gill to 1 qt., 2" to 6½" h., set of 6........................... 600.00

Mug, tapering cylindrical body w/a flared foot, slender scroll handle, Nathaniel Austin, Charlestown, Massachusetts, 1763-1807, 6" h. ...1,100.00

Pitcher, baluster-shaped w/angled

handle, Boardman & Hart, New York, 1828-77, 7¾" h. 990.00

Planter, rectangular, footed, a squirrel in relief at the four corners, marked "Kayserzinn," 7¾" l. 65.00

Plate, John Danforth, Norwich, Connecticut, ca. 1780, 8" d. 275.00

Plate, "Love" touch, Philadelphia, 18th c., 8½" d. 330.00

Plate, angel touch mark, Europe, 9" d. (scratches) 90.00

Plate, Roswell Gleason, Dorchester, Massachusetts, 1821-71, 9¼" d. (minor wear) 275.00

Plate, Thomas D. Boardman, Hartford, Connecticut, eagle in oval touch, after 1820, 9 3/8" d. 440.00

Porringer, flowered tab handle, Samuel Hamlin, Sr., Hartford & Middletown, Connecticut & Providence, Rhode Island, 1767-1801, 5½" d. (wear) 400.00

Tankard, cov., footed baluster-shaped body & rounded domed cover, bold S-scroll handle w/plume-shaped thumbpiece, "I & I" touch mark, England, 8" h. (somewhat battered) 375.00

Kayserzinn Tea & Coffee Service

Tea & coffee service: cov. teapot, cov. coffeepot, creamer, cov. sugar bowl & tray; all cast in low-relief w/bellflowers pendent from leafy branches, impressed "KAYSERZINN" & numbered "4263," ca. 1900, tray 15¾" l., teapot 7¼" h., 5 pcs. (ILLUS.)................... 660.00

Teapot, cov., pyramidal form w/angular wooden handle & pointed finial on the cover, hand-hammered finish, impressed mark "WM. HUTTON & SONS LTD. ENGLISH PEWTER 04787½," early 20th c., 6" h. 495.00

Teapot, cov., bulbous body tapering to a wide flaring foot & tapering up to a flaring neck w/inset domed cover, painted scroll handle & swan's neck spout, Samuel Simpson, Yalesville, Connecticut, 1835-52, 7¾" h. 319.00

Teapot, cov., footed cylindrical body below a swelled shoulder tapering to a widely flaring rim, inset conical cover, swan's neck spout, S-scroll handle, H.B. Ward & Co., Wallingford, Connecticut, ca. 1850, 8 3/8" h. (minor dents) 300.00

Teapot, cov., tall octagonal pigeon-breasted form raised on a domed foot, domed cover w/wooden button finial, wooden scroll handle, swan's neck spout, Roswell Gleason, Dorchester, Massachusetts, mid-19th c., 10" h. 330.00

Teapot, cov., elongated pear-shaped footed body w/low domed cover w/blossom finial, ribbed swan's neck spout, S-scroll handle, copper bottom, Homan & Co., Cincinnati, Ohio, ca. 1860, 10¼" h. 150.00

Vase, a pointed bullet-form body w/wide, flat mouth supported between three slender open buttress braces, the sides molded w/repeating Art Nouveau scrolling designs, impressed "Tudric 0223," Liberty & Company, England, ca. 1910, 7½" h. 165.00

SHEFFIELD PLATE

Sheffield Plate Coffeepots

Candlesticks, a flaring candle socket on a baluster-shaped shaft w/a gadrooned base on a flaring ribbed base w/plain disc foot, England, early 19th c., 7" h., pr. . .   165.00

Coffeepot, cov., urn-form, raised on a short pedestal w/ringed foot, hinged lid conforming to the rim spout, simple wooden handle, the lower body engraved w/floral swags, England, early 19th c., 13" h. (ILLUS. left) 385.00

Coffeepot, cov., urn-form, on a short pedestal w/domed round foot decorated w/a beaded band, domed cover w/urn-form finial, ornate scrolled wooden handle,

swan's neck spout, the tapering upper body chased w/narrow ribbing, the lower body engraved w/bold swags suspending lion head masks, engraved leaf band around the bottom edge of body, England, 19th c., 13" h. (ILLUS. right) 220.00

Dish cross, England, early 19th c., 12½" w. 302.50

Hot water urn, cov., wide stepped & domed cover w/ball finial, ring handles w/goat head terminals at the rim, the slender pedestal on a square base w/ball feet, England, 19th c., 13" h. 192.50

Soup tureen, cov., of bombe' oval form raised on four scroll supports decorated w/shells & leaves, reeded rod handles rising from lion masks, gadroon shell & foliate borders, matching ring finial, the body & cover engraved w/a crest & coronet within Garter motto, T. & J. Creswick & Co., England, ca. 1825, over handles 16" l. 3,850.00

SILVER, AMERICAN (Sterling & Coin)

Early American Caudle Cup

Asparagus tongs, Flemish patt., Tiffany & Company, New York, New York 412.50

Beaker, coin, tapering cylindrical form w/molded foot & rim, engraved w/initial "T," Samuel Kirk, Baltimore, Maryland, w/assay marks for 1824-27, 3½" h. 935.00

Bonbon scoop, decorated w/pierced neoclassical designs, Gorham Mfg. Co., Providence, Rhode Island, 9" l. 330.00

Bowl, "Martele'," a shallow shape w/a wide, flattened undulating rim decorated w/repousse' panels of flower clusters & leaves, Gorham Mfg. Co., Providence, Rhode Island, ca. 1905, 8 5/8" d. 2,640.00

Bride's basket, pierced & engraved boat shape, Whiting, 1916, 13½" h. 825.00

Butter dish, cov., a pierced cover on a footed bowl, both decorated w/chased florals, monogrammed, Jacobi & Jenkins, 1894-1908, 7¼" d. 412.50

Cake basket, coin, rectangular w/canted corners, raised on a similar spreading foot, w/stylized egg-and-dart die-rolled rims, w/elaborate acanthus scroll & rocaille side handles, the center engraved w/a monogram, William Gale & Son, New York, 1851, retailed by Gregg & Hayden & Co., Charleston, South Carolina, 15¾" l. 2,860.00

Caudle cup, coin, squatty bulbous body tapering to a wide, flat rim, slender scroll handles, engraved "NsM" at base, marked "I.D." in heart cartouche, Jeremiah Dummer, Boston, late 17th - early 18th c., repairs (ILLUS.) 2,090.00

Rare Silver Coffee Biggin

Coffee biggin, cov., coin, oval cylindrical stepped-form, a scrolled spout chased w/acanthus, plain sides, C-scroll wooden handle w/ornate chased terminals, the oval upper filter w/a pierced base & a domed cover w/wooden button finial, Garrett Eoff, New York, ca. 1820, 9½" h. (ILLUS.) 3,080.00

Coffeepot, cov., tall lighthouse form w/a wooden handle, monogrammed, Graff, Washbourne & Dunn, 20th c. 412.50

Compote, open, deep smooth rounded bowl w/a narrow stamped rim band & flanked by full-figural stag's head handles, raised on a short pedestal w/a wide domed foot, w/a monogram, Tiffany & Company, New York, New York, ca. 1875-91, 9" d., 7" h. 1,650.00

Creamer, coin, helmet-shaped, raised on a slender flaring pedestal w/a square foot, beaded rims, engraved under the spout w/a script monogram, John Baptiste

Dumoutet, Philadelphia, ca. 1800, 7 3/8" h. 1,760.00

Creamer & cov. sugar bowl, coin, lobed urn-form w/angular handles & reeded rims, raised on a short pedestal w/round foot, engraved w/collars of scrolling grapevine & w/contemporary initial "L," gilt interior, Charles Louis Boehme, Baltimore, Maryland, ca. 1805, sugar bowl 8 3/8" h., pr. 2,200.00

Cup, coin, presentation-type, octagonal body w/angled handle, engraved w/presentation dated "Jan. 8th 1845," marked on base "N.J. Bogert," Nicholas Bogert, New York, New York, 4" h. (minor dent) 1,045.00

Dish, heart-shaped, reticulated sides, Gorham Mfg. Co., Providence, Rhode Island, 5" l. 110.00

Fish slice, coin, the long wide blade w/curved edge pierced & engraved w/a fish framed by flowering leafy vines, the fiddle-and-thread handle engraved w/initials, James Conning, Mobile, Alabama, 1842-62, 11¾" l. 1,760.00

Tiffany Silver Flask

Flask, oblong, etched on one side w/a knight & on the other w/a squirrel above the initials "JH" on a shield enclosed by elaborate foliate scrolls & berries, w/hinged screw-on cap, Tiffany & Co., New York, 1891-1902, 7 5/8" h. (ILLUS.) 2,200.00

Goblet, coin, decorated w/chased flowers & C-scroll reserves, W. Gale & Son, New York, New York, ca. 1860, 6¼" h. 247.50

Ladle, coin, the deep rounded bowl w/a long slender down-turned rounded-end handle, Joseph Anthony, Philadelphia, 1785-1810, 10" l. 1,320.00

Ladle, coin, fiddle handle, deep round bowl, handle engraved

"T.V.," marked, ca. 1830, 12¾" l. (bowl battered) 220.00

Model of a bulldog, realistically modeled standing animal, wearing a collar, on a rectangular platform base, the base signed "E.E. Codman-Sc.," modeled by E.E. Codman, Gorham Mfg. Co., Providence, Rhode Island, retailed by Shreve, Crump & Low, ca. 1930, base 5¾" l. 4,125.00

Pitcher, cov., squared handle w/ivory heat stops, tapering sides, overall repousse' floral decoration, Gorham Mfg. Co., Providence, Rhode Island, 1884, 9" h. 1,210.00

Pitcher, coin, wide baluster-form body raised on a domed foot, a high arched wide spout & leafy S-scroll handle, elaborately chased around the body w/swirling sunflower-like blossoms & leafy vines, a similar band around the foot, a presentation inscription on the front under the spout, Krider & Co., Philadelphia, ca. 1851, 11" h. 990.00

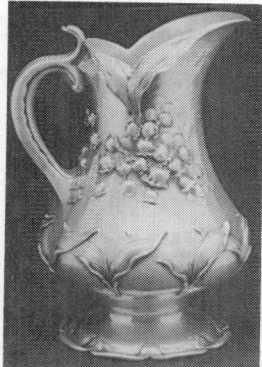

Tiffany Water Pitcher

Pitcher, water, footed tapering ovoid body w/a wide, arched spout & scroll-ended handle, boldly chased w/lily of the valley blossoms & leaves on a hand-hammered ground, w/Paris Exhibition mark, Tiffany & Company, New York, ca. 1891-1902, 12" h. (ILLUS.) 8,525.00

Platter, Chrysanthemum patt., Tiffany & Co., New York, 1891-1902, 16" l. 5,225.00

Porringer, coin, round bowl w/double arch handle pierced w/circles & crescents & engraved w/contemporary initials "A*N," the base w/a contemporary inscription, marked by Edward Webb, Boston, ca. 1700, 4¾" d. 11,550.00

Porringer, coin, w/keyhole handle, marked on underside, Bailey Chapman & Co., Boston, early 19th c., 5½" d. 770.00

Powder box, cov., squatty bulbous body decorated w/repousse' foliate & drapery swags below a laurel band, the similar domed cover decorated w/an enameled scene of a lady in a landscape, Gorham Mfg. Co., Providence, Rhode Island, 1895, 4½" d. 1,210.00

Punch bowl, the wide compressed ovoid body decorated around the rim w/large bold swirling daisy blossoms & stems w/a similar openwork design around the domed foot, Redlich & Co., New York, ca. 1900, 10½" d. 2,860.00

Salad serving fork & spoon, Repousse' patt., Kirk, Baltimore, Maryland, 2 pcs. 275.00

Sauceboat, coin, rounded body w/elongated lip, open handle, three legs w/hoof feet & shell terminals, attributed to Ebenezer Chittenden, Madison, Connecticut, marked three times w/"EC" in oval cartouche, early 19th c. 1,650.00

Smoking stand, a rounded rectangular tray-form on four ball feet, fitted w/three compartments w/silver-mounted glass hinged covers enclosing two removable silver-mounted glass ashtrays, a removable silver lighter in the center w/a ball-shaped lamp & two removable wicks, a flat fixed overhead strap handle, Gorham Mfg. Company, Providence, Rhode Island, 1912, 15" l. 3,520.00

Coin Silver Sugar Bowl

Sugar bowl, cov., coin, baluster-form, raised on four openwork scroll feet joined by an openwork foliate grapevine apron, the lower body repousse' & chased w/leaves beneath a band of foliate swags, acanthus scroll side handles, domed cover chased w/similar decoration & surmounted by a bud finial, Fletcher & Bennett, Louisville, Kentucky, ca. 1850, 7¾" h. (ILLUS.) 1,430.00

Sugar spoon, coin, Fiddle Tip patt., shell-shaped bowl, engraved "Lydia," David Kinsey, 6" l. 20.00

Sugar tongs, coin, shell-shaped ends, marked "J. Simpson," Philadelphia, Pennsylvania, engraved monogram, early 19th c., 6¼" l. 220.00

Sugar urn, cov., coin, body of inverted pear form w/presentation inscriptions, marked at the base "Lincoln & Reed - Pure Silver Coin - Boston," dated 1845, 8½" d. 247.50

Tablespoon, coin, bowl w/rounded drop & grooved rattail, engraved "M.P." at handle back, marked at stem w/crowned initials within a shield-shaped cartouche, John Edwards, Boston, early 18th c., 7 1/8" l........................ 660.00

Rare American Silver Tankard

Tankard, cov., coin, wide tapering cylindrical body w/a flat-domed cover, a corkscrew thumbpiece, an S-scroll handle engraved w/contemporary initials "IED," the "I" later converted to a "T," w/a scalloped terminal, on a molded base marked w/scratch weight "30 oz.," "IH" within heart touch on cover, sides & base, John Hastier, New York, ca. 1740, 7" h. (ILLUS.) 15,400.00

Tazza, classical design w/anthemion handles, Gorham Mfg. Co., Providence, Rhode Island, ca. 1870, 14" l. 605.00

Teapot, cov., coin, fluted oval body w/a shoulder curving up to a reeded rim band supporting the domed cover w/disc finial, the sides w/beaded bright-cut & roulette top & base border bands & centering a shield & ribbon emblem, straight spout & C-scroll

wooden handle, Isaac Hutton, Albany, New York, 1790-1810, 6¼" h. 4,950.00

Tea set: cov. teapot, creamer & open sugar bowl; each bulbous body lobed & hand spothammered overall, the teapot insulated, Dominick & Haff, New York, 1883, teapot 5¼" h., the set........................ 880.00

Tumbler, coin, short cylindrical form w/a rounded base, engraved w/a script monogram "JWK" within a circular bright-cut reserve, marked near the rim "A. BILLING" w/an eagle head, Andrew Billing, Preston, Connecticut or Poughkeepsie, New York area, 1775-1808 ....1,430.00

Vase, trumpet-shaped, scalloped spreading foot & rim, geometric & bead decoration, engraved w/monogram "AB," Gorham Mfg. Co., Providence, Rhode, Island, 1915, 8¾" h. 495.00

Vegetable dish, cov., shaped oval on rim foot, swirling fluted sides & foliate scroll rim, reeded foliate side handles, the domed cover w/similar decoration & a double-scroll ring finial, Tiffany & Co., New York, 1891-1902, overall 11¼" l. 3,300.00

SILVER, ENGLISH & OTHERS

Early English Cup

Bottle holder, formed as an upright dragon, w/claws holding the neck clamp, Arthur & Bond, Yokohama, Japan, early 20th c., 15" h. 5,500.00

Bread tray, oval, shallow boat-form, Blossom patt., No. 2, Georg Jensen Silversmithy, Copenhagen, Denmark, 1925-32, 11¾" l. 2,970.00

Butter pats, scallop shell-form, engraved w/a crest, raised on two hoof feet, George II period, Peter Archambo, London, England, 1747, 4 1/8" l., pr. 2,200.00

Castor, cylindrical form w/foliate chasing & piercing, Wilkinson & Co., Ltd., London, England, 1894, 6½" h. 357.50

Centerpiece bowl, bombe' sides decorated in high-relief w/irises on a hammered ground, plain tall rim foot, w/loose flower grid, Japan, early 20th c., 10½" d. 2,475.00

Chocolate pot, cov., pear-shaped body raised on three scroll supports, short spout rising from chased leaves & w/hinged flap, straight wooden handle projecting at right angle from body, the handle socket w/gadrooned border, flat-domed cover w/swiveling button finial & straight gadroon rim, engraved w/arms & initials below a coronet, Louis XV period, Nicholas-Hilaire Vilain, Paris, France, ca. 1730, 8 5/8" h. 8,800.00

Cocktail shaker, cov., the fluted lower body applied w/clusters of beads, tapered neck applied w/clusters of berries & scrolled wires to form handles, detachable cap w/bud finial, foliate pierced strainer, Georg Jensen Silversmithy, Copenhagen, Denmark, 1925-32, numbered 497, 9¼" h. .. 4,125.00

Coffeepot, cov., pear-form, lobed & fluted & w/a collar of foliage, flowers & shells, engraved w/contemporary arms, lion head spout, scroll handle rising from a dolphin head, Rehfuss & Co., Berne, Switzerland, ca. 1835, 8¾" h. 1,760.00

Coffeepot, cov., tapering cylindrical form, molded foot, acanthus-clad fluted scroll spout & wood scroll handle, hinged stepped domed cover w/urn finial, engraved w/a crest, George II period, Isaac Cookson, Newcastle, England, 1744, 9" h. 7,150.00

Creamer, helmet-shaped, engraved at front w/crest & motto surrounded by floral sprays, the rim of the gilt interior engraved w/running foliage spreading from the double scroll handle which is topped by a female bust turned to one side, pedestal foot, George III period, Thomas Heming, London, England, 1774, 5 5/8" h. 1,650.00

Cup, footed, handled, simple urnform w/raised center band, ornate scroll handles, maker's mark obscured, London, England, 1734-35, base dent, 7¼" h. (ILLUS.) 1,210.00

Cups & saucers, engraved floral de-

sign, maker "IS," Austria, ca. 1900, pr. 110.00

Dog collar, applied w/borders of shells, flowers & leaves, engraved w/inscription "BOWERS Coursing Meeting, 1819," adjustable for size & fitted w/a silver padlock, leather-lined, George III period, Charles Rawlings, London, England, 1819, 1" w. 1,980.00

Entree dishes, shaped rectangular form w/molded rim, the center engraved w/arms, Louis XVI period, Jean-Baptiste-Francois Cheret, Paris, France, 1781, 10" l., pr. ... 7,700.00

Ewer, helmet-shaped w/a long scroll handle & raised on a short pedestal w/a tiered lappet-stamped foot, the sides of the body decorated in bold relief w/a continuous overall leaf & berry vine, Italy, 20th c., 9¼" h. 1,045.00

Early Dutch Silver Goblet

Goblet, bulbous bowl on a wide stem & flared foot, the bowl & stem chased w/flowering scrolls, marked w/bird's leg, "D" & "K" in shield reserves, Dordrecht, Holland, 17th c., minor dents, 3¾" h. (ILLUS.) 440.00

Loving cup, Arts & Crafts style, spherical bowl w/trumpet base, applied w/three forked foliate scroll handles, hammered finish, engraved w/contemporary monogram, the base rim also engraved w/contemporary inscription, in fitted oak presentation box w/monogrammed brass plaque, lock w/key, Wakely & Wheeler, London, England, 1906, 8¾" h. ... 1,540.00

Monteith bowl, Queen Anne-Style, fluted & embossed w/a baroque cartouche, scalloped molded rim & applied w/lion-mask handles, Victorian, Edward Barnard & Sons, London, England, 1888, rim 12¼" d. 9,075.00

Salt dips, bombe' circular form, crested, raised on three short

scroll & pad feet, George II period, John Lingard, London, Eng-
land, 1730, 2¾" d., set of 4 .....1,760.00
Sugar box, cov., silver-gilt, in the
Charles II style, of shaped oval
form, raised on four scroll feet,
the sides w/lobed panels, the
hinged domed cover w/crenelated
rim below a band of lobed ovals,
w/oval acanthus calyx supporting
a snake loop handle, maker's
mark of John Bodman Carring-
ton, London, 1898, Victorian,
7 7/8" l. 1,100.00
Teapot, cov., lobed & fluted oval
vase form, C-form rosewood handle & lobed finial, designed by
Gustav Beran for Gerritsen & Van
Kempen, Zeist, Holland, 1947,
marked on base & struck w/Swed-
ish import marks, 7 3/8" h......1,320.00

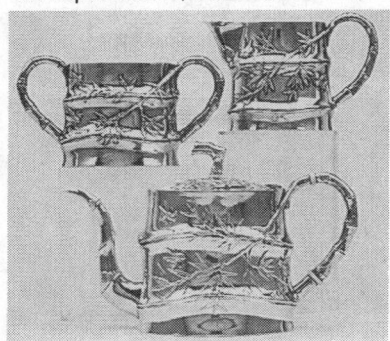

Chinese Export Tea Set

Tea set: cov. teapot, creamer &
open sugar bowl; each oval body
w/repousse' design of bamboo
stalks applied w/foliate bamboo
branches & dragonflies, bamboo-
form handles & teapot spout,
bamboo finial on teapot, maker's
mark "WHL," Chinese Export,
late 19th - early 20th c., teapot
5 7/8" h., 3 pcs. (ILLUS.) 1,870.00
Vase, tall ovoid body on a domed
foot & tapering to a short neck
w/a widely flaring rim, the body
elaborately chased w/a landscape
w/Chinese figures at battle w/dis-
tant buildings, a lappet leaf border around the shoulder, two
loose ring handles at the sides
suspended from grotesque animal
masks, marked "WH 90" w/chop
marks, Wang Hing & Co., Hong
Kong, China, late 19th - early
20th c., 15" h..................2,200.00

SILVER PLATE (Hollowware)

Bonbon basket, bail handle, grape
clusters & leaves on handle & pe-

rimeter of wire basket, 2 x 7½",
7½" h........................$275.00
Cake basket, embossed pedestal
base, swing handle, interior engraved w/four different birds,
leaves, Meriden Britannia Co.,
No. 1822, 10" d., 14" h. including
swing handle 175.00
Center bowl, shallow, supported by
a standing allegorical figure resting on a spreading circular foot,
Gorham Mfg. Co., Providence,
Rhode Island, ca. 1880, 13" h. 715.00

Art Deco Cocktail Goblets

Cocktail goblets, Art Deco style,
conical bowl raised on a triangular base & supported by a
tapering side bracket, Maison
Desny, France, unsigned, ca.
1925, 4 1/8" h., pr. (ILLUS.) 1,210.00
Coffee urn, cov., bulbous urn-form
body on tall decorated feet, a
crown-shaped rim w/rows of tiny
flowers, ornate curved handles &
a serving spout w/ivory handle,
the body chased overall w/florals,
w/burner in base, Hartford Silver
Plate Co., ca. 1880's, 17" h. 350.00
Coffee & tea service: cov. coffeepot,
cov. teapot, sugar bowl, creamer
& waste bowl; Remembrance
patt., Reed & Barton, 5 pcs. 500.00
Food warmer, ornately decorated
domed base & handle w/a hole
for a candle, three curved adjustable supports to hold various
sized vessels, Wilcox Silver Plate
Co., Meriden, Connecticut, late
19th c. 110.00
Jewelry box, cov., free-form ovoid
body w/heavily embossed overall
flowers, cover fitted w/pin-
cushion, original peacock blue
satin lining, Derby Silver Co., late
19th c., 3 x 5½" 175.00
Mirror plateau, inset mirrored top
surrounded by a frame of star-cut
medallions w/beaded outer bor-

der & petal-shaped prongs on inner border, raised on five feet, 12" d. 125.00

Mirror plateau, inset mirrored top surrounded by a frame of ornate scroll-cutting & raised on twelve cosmos blossom feet, tin back, 14" d. 115.00

Mirror plateau, elaborate scrolling & foliate decoration framing circular inset mirror, 20½" d. 440.00

Nut bowl, model of a nut w/a large seated squirrel on a branch forming the handle, Reed & Barton, late 19th c. (resilvered) 395.00

Spoonholder, round step-up base, figural stem of a Victorian lady in a fancy draped dress holding a large umbrella w/slots for twelve spoons, loop handle, 10" d. umbrella, 8" h. 285.00

Sugar bowl - spoonholder, the bowl decorated w/heavy repousse' designs, the rim w/prongs to hold twelve spoons, Meriden Silver Plate Co., ca. 1880 (resilvered) . . . 175.00

Tea set: cov. teapot, cov. sugar bowl & creamer; each of cylindrical oval form, the teapot & creamer w/stepped rectangular spouts, the covers w/spherical wooden finials, angular wooden handles w/a round opening, designed by Cornelius van der Hoef, made by Daalderop, stamped "Daalderop - Made in Holland," ca. 1930, teapot 5¼" h., the set 1,870.00

Tea table, tilt-top, the rectangular top w/hinged top w/locking screw & mahogany back-plate, shaped apron, all decorated in high- and low-relief w/sprays of different flowers & ferns on a matte ground, raised on a baluster-form standard molded w/fern leaves above the cruciform base w/scrolled leaves & flower clusters, on casters, Tiffany & Co., New York, ca. 1893, 23 x 28½", 29½" h. .29,900.00

Vase holder w/vase, modeled as a bushy-tailed squirrel seated on a mound base beside an opalescent pale green bud vase, Meriden (resilvered) 275.00

Vase holder w/vase, footed, ornate floral decoration & a ring handle, supports original robin's-egg blue vase enameled w/yellow flowers, Reed & Barton, late 19th c., vase 4" h., overall 9" h. 145.00

Vases, hexagonal slightly tapering form, decorated w/a band of incised Gothic-style design around

the rim, marked "GORHAM CO., SPECIAL, 1637," 6" w., 10" h., pr. 770.00

Ornate Victorian Water Set

Water set: a cylindrical covered pitcher w/finely ribbed upper & lower bands & a wide center band engraved w/cranes, tilting within an arched frame w/ornately scroll-molded feet set upon the rim of a flaring ribbed circular dish base w/inset drip tray & raised on paw feet, the rim of the base w/supports for two matching goblets & the front w/a full-figure flying horse projection, American-made, late 19th c., 21½" w., 25" h. (ILLUS.) 2,320.00

Wine coolers, pail-shaped, decorated w/a knotted rope design over raffia on matted ground, detachable liners w/fixed rims, Elkington & Co., Birmingham, England, ca. 1875, Victorian, 8" h., set of 4 . . .9,075.00

SILVER PLATE (Flatware)

ARBUTUS (Wm. Rogers Mfg. Co.)
Butter serving knife 9.50
Butter spreader 4.00
Tablespoon, pierced 19.00

BERKSHIRE (1847 Rogers Bros.)
Butter spreader 10.00
Cocktail fork 14.00
Server, trowel-shaped, concave, 8½" l. 40.00

CHARTER OAK (1847 Rogers Bros.)
Dinner fork, hollow handle 25.00
Meat fork 45.00
Salad fork 32.00
Teaspoon 11.00
Tablespoon, pierced 19.00

CHATEAU (Heirloom Plate)
Butter spreader 4.00
Jelly spreader 5.00
Sardine fork 6.00
Sugar spoon 4.00

ETERNALLY YOURS (1847 Rogers Bros.)
Butter spreader 12.50
Demitasse spoon 11.50
Dinner fork 12.00
Dinner knife 12.00
Salad fork 8.00
Tablespoon, pierced 19.00
Teaspoon 4.50

HERITAGE (1847 Rogers Bros.)
Butter spreader 12.50
Cocktail fork..................... 12.50
Dinner fork 12.00
Dinner knife 12.00
Dinner service, 53 pcs. (in box)..... 300.00
Salad fork 8.00
Teaspoon 4.50

MOSELLE (American Silver Co.)
Berry spoon 92.00
Butter serving knife 41.00
Cake fork 195.00
Cold meat fork 52.00
Dinner service, 6 each knives, forks
    & teaspoons, 18 pcs. 275.00
Gravy ladle...................... 93.00
Lemon fork 50.00
Pickle fork 45.00
Soup ladle, small................. 325.00
Tomato server 235.00

OLD COLONY (1847 Rogers Bros.)
Butter spreader 8.50
Gravy ladle...................... 30.00
Meat fork 30.00
Sauce ladle 20.00
Sugar spoon 11.00

REMEMBRANCE (1847 Rogers Bros.)
Butter spreader 12.50
Cocktail fork..................... 12.50
Dinner fork 12.00
Dinner knife 12.00
Salad fork 8.00
Teaspoon 4.50

VIOLET (Simeon L. & George H. Rogers Co.)
Serving fork, 5-tine, 10" l. 35.00
Soup spoon, round 8.00
Sugar spoon 8.00
Teaspoon 5.00

STERLING SILVER (Flatware)

ACORN (Georg Jensen)
Butter fork 50.00
Cocktail picks, set of 6 .... 240.00

Acorn Pattern

Demitasse spoon 31.00
Dinner service: 12 each dinner
    knives, luncheon knives, soup
    spoons, teaspoons, dinner forks,
    luncheon forks, butter spreaders,
    cocktail forks, salad forks, 18
    citrus fruit spoons, 2 serving
    spoons, 2 serving forks, pair of
    salad servers & 1 each cheese
    plane, cold meat fork, cake
    knife, butter knife, cream
    ladle & pierced serving spoon,
    138 pcs. 11,000.00
Pickle fork....................... 67.00
Sugar tongs...................... 125.00

CANTERBURY (Towle Mfg. Co.)
Beef fork 18.00
Bonbon scoop 75.00
Bouillon spoon 30.00
Gravy ladle...................... 50.00
Ice tongs 225.00
Pie server, silver blade 185.00
Punch ladle, gold-washed bowl 375.00

CHRYSANTHEMUM (Tiffany & Co.)

Chrysanthemum Pattern

Asparagus tongs 825.00
Cream soup spoon 85.00

Dinner service: 18 each dinner knives, fish knives, soup spoons, fruit knives, demitasse spoons, dinner forks, fish forks, dessert spoons, fruit forks & 12 tea-spoons, 1 cold meat fork & 1 sauce ladle, 176 pcs. 15,870.00
Fish fork 130.00
Gravy ladle 395.00
Tea infuser spoon 495.00
Waffle server 610.00

DRESDEN (Whiting Mfg. Co.)
Berry spoon 140.00
Bouillon spoons, gold-washed, set of 8 . . . . 250.00
Cream ladle 50.00
Gravy ladle 105.00
Jelly spoon 75.00
Luncheon fork 24.00

ETON (R. Wallace & Sons)
Butter fork 11.00
Dinner fork 40.00
Food pusher, child's 55.00
Salad fork 15.00
Sugar shell 30.00
Teaspoon 18.00

IMPERIAL or IMPERIAL QUEEN (Whiting Mfg. Co.)
Asparagus tongs, individual 70.00
Beef fork 55.00
Butter serving knife 55.00
Cheese scoop 125.00
Citrus spoon 14.00
Salt spoon, master size 45.00
Teaspoon 15.00

IRIAN (R. Wallace & Sons)
Berry spoon 225.00
Butter serving knife 60.00
Chocolate spoon 25.00
Lettuce fork 135.00
Pickle fork, gold-washed tines 85.00
Tablespoon 68.00
Teaspoon 25.00
Youth knife 60.00

MARIE ANTOINETTE (Dominick & Haff)
Asparagus fork 195.00
Gravy ladle 55.00
Salad fork 14.00
Salad serving fork 175.00
Sardine fork 55.00

NO. 10 (Dominick & Haff)
Bouillon spoon 18.00
Dinner fork 30.00
Gumbo spoon 29.00
Luncheon fork 21.00
Salad serving set 175.00
Seafood fork 18.00
Teaspoon 15.00

OLYMPIAN (Tiffany & Co.)
Berry spoon 795.00
Cheese knife 275.00
Gravy ladle 250.00
Ice cream server 795.00
Olive fork 125.00
Oyster ladle 950.00
Pie server 775.00
Sugar spoon 175.00

POPPY (Gorham Mfg. Co.)
Berry fork 44.00
Bouillon spoon 45.00
Butter spreader 15.00
Cold meat fork 85.00
Luncheon fork 15.00
Mustard ladle 65.00
Strawberry fork 30.00
Teaspoon 16.00

REPOUSSE (Samuel Kirk & Sons)
Butter spreader, flat handle 18.00
Cocktail fork 22.00
Food pusher, child's 26.00
Fruit knife, hollow handle 20.00
Gumbo spoon 55.00
Luncheon fork 28.00
Luncheon knife 28.00
Pea spoon 95.00
Punch ladle 295.00
Sandwich tongs, 9" l. 895.00

WATTEAU (Wm. B. Durgin Co.)
Butter spreader, flat handle 15.00
Coffee spoon 8.00
Fish knife 45.00
Gravy ladle 90.00
Ice cream spoon 35.00
Ice tongs 150.00
Mustard ladle 55.00
Sugar shell 40.00

TIN & TOLE

Tole Cake Basket

Box, cov., tole, ogee curved body w/hinged flat cover, cast feet, red & gold decoration on worn origi-nal black ground, 11¾" l. 55.00
Cake basket, tole, deep dished oval basket raised on a low pedestal

w/a rectangular foot, a swing strap handle across the middle, black ground decorated w/gilt peacocks & flowers within scrolling borders, England, mid-19th c., 13" l. (ILLUS.) 440.00

Candle box, tin, hanging-type, shaped crest above a cylindrical box w/curving lift lid, old worn dark brown japanning w/a polka dot design formed by removing spots of japanning, 14¼" l. (one crest brace & ring hanger missing, extra hole drilled for hanging) ... 160.00

Candle mold, tin, three-tube, on flat circular base, ring handle, 10¼" h....................... 75.00

Candle mold, tin, twenty-four tube, rectangular top & base framing the tubes, strap handle at top side, 10" h..................... 250.00

Candle sconces, tin, circular w/various arrangements of geometrically patterned tin cut-outs under glass, a short straight arm w/a candle socket projecting at the base of the sconce, 9½" d., pr. ...5,500.00

Canister, cov., tole, cylindrical w/small loop handles at sides near the top, brown ground decorated w/lobed floral design in yellow, white, red, green & black, 6" h........................... 300.00

Chandelier, miniature, tole, the circular candle support suspended by three wire uprights & six circular dished drip plates & candlecups, possibly Bergen County, New Jersey, early 19th c., 10¾" d., 26" h........................... 990.00

Coffeepot, cov., tole, tall slightly tapering cylindrical 'lighthouse' shape w/flared foot & low domed cover w/tiny looped finial, strap handle & curved spout, decorated w/bold stylized colored fruits on a black ground, early 19th c., 10½" h....................... 990.00

Creamer, cov., tole, slightly flaring cylinder, decorated w/stylized florals in red, green & yellow, on a worn brown japanned ground, 4 1/8" h....................... 450.00

Document box, cov., miniature, tole, rectangular w/a domed cover & small ring handle, original brown japanned ground w/a wide band around the upper sides decorated w/yellow striping & yellow, red & green leaf designs, 3" l. 330.00

Egg warmer, cov., tole, the tall oval cylindrical body w/a flat divided hinged top w/two finials opening to reveal a removable egg stand,

the body flanked by swan's head handles & raised on paw feet, the whole painted in red & trimmed w/bands of gilt baskets of fruit, exotic birds & foliate scrolls, Empire period, France, early 19th c., 10" h. 1,870.00

Match holder, tole, hanging-type, the wide flat back-plate w/a rounded top pierced w/a hanging hole over cut-out scrolled sides above the rectangular match bin w/an angled front, traces of original black paint & red & yellow decoration, 7 3/8" h. 60.50

Mug, tole, tall slightly tapering cylindrical form w/wide strap handle, original brown japanning w/an oval band filled w/stylized floral designs in red, yellow, green & white, 5 5/8" h. (minor wear) 625.00

Snuff box, cov., miniature, tole, rectangular w/rounded ends, floral decoration in red, black, green & white on a mustard yellow ground, 2" l. (some wear)....... 192.50

Tea caddy, cov., tole, miniature, cylindrical shouldered body w/a small domed cap, worn original black ground decorated w/a gold stenciled label reading "Tea," 2 7/8" h. 49.50

Tea caddy, cov., tole, oval cylindrical body w/a slightly round shoulder & short cylindrical neck fitted w/a domed cap, worn original black ground w/a large stylized blossom & leaf design in yellow & two shades of red, cap w/red ground w/black 'comma' design, 19th c., 4½" h. 165.00

Teapot, cov., tin, a wide oval cylindrical body w/a rounded shoulder to the short round neck & low domed cover w/small pewter finial, a C-form strap handle w/handgrip & a straight angled spout, 19th c., 8" h. 104.50

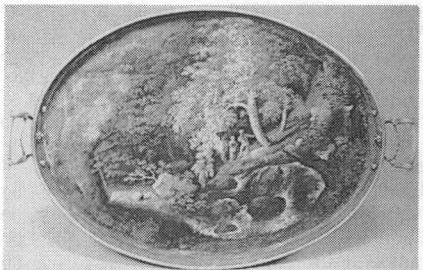

English Tole Tray

Tray, tole, oval w/dished sides & brass end handles, painted w/two figures in a wooded landscape, the end w/handles & applied lion's masks, now on a conforming mahogany stand, attributed to Pontypoole, England, early 19th c., restoration to paint, 28½" l. (ILLUS.) 3,025.00

(End of Metals Section)

MINIATURES (Paintings)

Profile Miniature of Col. John Cox

Bust portrait of child w/flute, on ivory, signed, rectangular ebonized frame w/brass liner, 3¾" w., 4 3/8" h. $165.00

Bust portrait of an elderly lady on ivory, oval, seated wearing a lace cap & shawl collar, in an upholstered chair, in a flat rectangular black wood frame, early 19th c., 3½" l. 137.50

Bust portrait of a gentleman in powdered wig on ivory, purported to be J. Bernard, shown three-quarters sinister, wearing a powdered white wig, bright blue jacket, white jabot & fichu, against a grey-beige background, in an oval gilt-metal frame w/subject's name in a banner across the bottom, engraved w/interlaced "B's" on the reverse, by Christian F. Zincke, ca. 1720, 1 7/8" h. 1,100.00

Bust portrait of a young lady on copper, shown three-quarters dexter, w/light reddish brown hair in ringlets to her shoulders, wearing pearl-drop earrings & necklace, white lawn fichu set

w/a brooch over a black dress, on a blue background, oval, in gilt-metal pendant frame, Dutch School, ca. 1645, 3½" h. 770.00

Bust portraits of George R. & Caroline Collyer Carter of Leominster & Boston, Massachusetts, on ivory, each dressed simply, she wearing a drop-shouldered gown w/puffy sleeves, her hair pulled up to form a knot, in gilt-metal locket frames, ca. 1840, unsigned, each 2¾ x 3¼", pr. (some paint loss) 770.00

Bust profile portrait of Colonel John Cox, facing left, grey hair & side-burns, wearing a dark blue jacket & white vest & cravat, against a shaded blue ground, oval brass liner in black leather frame, after James Sharples, late 18th - early 19th c., 2¾ x 3" (ILLUS.) 715.00

Bust profile portraits of man & woman, water-color & ink & graphite on paper, the gentleman facing right & wearing a dark coat & cravat, his short hair combed forward, the lady facing left wearing a closely-fitted lace cap w/trim, a lacy-trimmed collar & long-sleeved dress, each inscribed "Taken in Geneva Feb.22, 1845," in beveled wood frames, attributed to Justus Dalee, 2¾ x 3½", facing pair (pigment loss, soiled) 1,430.00

Full-length portrait of a little boy, water-color on ivory, the child wearing a blue gown & playing w/a dappled horse pull-toy, attributed to Joseph Whiting Stock, 1815-55, framed, 2½ x 3½" 7,700.00

Half-figure portrait of a blonde child, on ivory, the girl seated w/her chin resting on her raised hand, signed "E.E. Kaufer," in oval gold case, 3½" w., 4 1/8" h. 217.50

Half-length portrait of a gentleman facing right, pencil & ink on paper, wearing a high-collared coat & standing white collar, worn gilt-wood frame w/beaded inner & outer rim, 4½" w., 5 3/8" h. 247.50

Half-length portrait of a lady, three-quarters sinister, wearing a blue dress w/white chemise & matching mobcap, against a sky background w/clouds, the lady stated to be Mary Daves of North Carolina, in the manner of Edward G. Malborne, ca. 1805, in gold oval frame w/leatherette case, 3 1/8" h. 1,380.00

Half-length profile portraits of young

gentleman & lady, water-color on paper, one a profile of a young woman wearing a brown dress w/white lace collar seated in a green upholstered chair, the other a profile of a gentleman wearing a black coat seated in a green upholstered chair, signed & dated on verso "J.S. Ellsworth, Portrait Painter, July 5, 1851," framed facing in single frame w/center divider, 2½ x 3".................6,050.00

MINIATURES (Replicas)

William & Mary Dower Chest

Andirons, wrought iron, ring top w/simple tooling above baluster-form shaft, arched legs ending in penny feet, 8" h., pr............$500.00

Blanket chest, painted pine, rectangular thumb-molded & hinged lid fastened w/cotter pins opening to a deep well w/till, molded base, on bootjack feet, painted dark bluish green, Pennsylvania, 19th c., 7¾" l., 4¼" h...........440.00

Bookcase, Chippendale-Style, breakfront design w/tall narrow end cabinets w/capped tops above operational geometrically-glazed doors over lozenge-shaped paneled bases flanking the projecting center section w/a geometrically-glazed panel simulating two doors, w/a shelved interior, two lozenge-shaped panels in the center base, England, 19th c., 6¾ x 22", 22" h. (minor losses).................4,125.00

Box, cov., oval bentwood, single pointed lappet construction on top & case w/iron tacks, natural patina, 3½" l......................82.50

Carousel horses, carved pine, the spirited animals w/bridles & military saddles, mounted on a rod in

a black metal base, Muller-style, America, late 19th - early 20th c., 11" l., 13½" h., pr.............3,850.00

Chest of drawers, Classical (American Empire) style, carved mahogany, a serpentine step-back shelf fitted w/two short conforming drawers above a conforming top over three conforming long drawers flanked by free-standing tapering columns w/Ionic capitals, on carved paw feet, New York, ca. 1830-40, 13¾ x 23¾", 20¼" h.....................1,980.00

Chest of drawers, Federal style, mahogany, rectangular top over a conforming case fitted w/four long drawers, on turned feet, inscribed "Cooper" (Peter Cooper) on base board, New York, early 19th c., 9¼ x 17¼", 21¼" h. (minor damage)....................935.00

Cupboard, pine, dovetailed construction, rectangular top w/molded cornice above open section over two paneled cupboard doors, scalloped base, old dark finish, 7 x 21¾", 21¾" h..............270.00

Desk, pine w/mahogany lid, slant-front type w/pull-out lid supports & three dovetailed drawers, old dark finish, 7¼ x 10", 10½" h. (old repairs)...................200.00

Dower chest, painted wood, William & Mary style, rectangular lid w/molded edge lifting above a well faced by a pair of false drawers above a single true drawer at the base, molded base, on four heavy turned ball feet, New England, 1710-25, paint restored, 9¼ x 12¼", 13" h. (ILLUS.).......................4,620.00

Hat, man's fedora, olive green felt w/silk band & tassel, marked "Stetson," in original "Stetson" hatbox.........................121.00

Hat, man's top hat, black beaver, marked "Knox, New York," in worn original "Knox" hatbox.....137.50

Jar, cov., turned wood, small ring-turned bell-shaped bowl on domed foot, domed cover w/pointed button finial, attributed to Pease of Ohio, 19th c., 1½" h.............280.50

Kraut cutter, thin rectangular wood frame w/rounded corners, holds angled wrought-iron blade, old patina, 3½" l...................137.50

Ladle, pewter, round bowl & slender stem fitted w/a slender handle & shaped handle, 6" l. (some metal fatigue in handle)..............165.00

Mirror, wall-type, rectangular,

curly maple, wire hanging loop
at the top, early 19th c.,
3 7/8 x 4 7/8" 495.00
Mirror on stand, table model, paint-
ed wood, slender uprights on
shoe feet flanking a rectangular
ogee frame w/mirror, painted
red, backed w/wallpaper, 19th c.,
6" h. 715.00
Pressing iron, brass, simple en-
graved designs, w/turned wood
handle, compartment has small
iron ingot, 5¾" l. 170.00

Miniature Stagecoach

Stagecoach, painted & decorated
wood, metal & fabric, model of
the "Diamond Tally-Ho" coach,
typical of coaches made by Abbot
and Downing Coach Company of
Concord, New Hampshire in the
19th c., from plans published in
"Popular Science" magazine in the
1930's, in glass-sided case, 22" l.,
13" h. (ILLUS.) 1,100.00
Stool, wooden, thick round top
w/beveled edge & scratch-carved
date "1791," on three canted whittled legs, old dark patina, 5" d.,
3½" h. 258.50
Sugar bucket, cov., stave-
constructed w/two bentwood
bands, flat cover, bentwood
bail handle, America, 19th c.,
3½" h. 220.00
Tea kettle, cov., tin, wide cylindrical
short body w/molded bands & an
arched shoulder tapering to a
small fitted cover w/wooden knob
finial, fixed overhead strap han-
dle, straight spout, 4½" h. 85.00
Tea table, poplar, round top w/ta-
pered braces on underside tilts
above a baluster- and knob-
turned pedestal on a tripod base
w/spider legs, old red finish,
8" d., 8½" h. 875.00

MOLDS - CANDY, FOOD & MISC.

Cake, rabbit, cast iron, "Griswold
No. 862" . . . .$250.00 to 300.00
Chocolate, bulldog, tin, 5" h. 75.00

Chocolate, camel, tin, two-part,
6" h. 65.00
Chocolate, chick hatching, tin 80.00
Chocolate, chick w/hat, tin,
5½" h. 40.00
Chocolate, dog w/hat, tin, 6½" h. . . .   95.00
Chocolate, Easter egg, tin, molded
design at the center of the sides,
marked "Randle & Smith Birming-
ham," 6½" l. 70.00
Chocolate, hen on nest, tin, 5" h. 48.00
Chocolate, rabbit driving car, tin . . .   100.00
Chocolate, rabbit on large egg, tin,
8½" h. 68.00
Chocolate, rabbit sitting on stool
playing saxophone, tin 100.00
Chocolate, rabbit smoking pipe, tin,
7" h. 65.00
Chocolate, rabbit, standing w/bas-
ket on back, 16" h. 110.00
Chocolate, rabbits, tin-plate, a row
of four animals w/a hinged top,
9½" l. 45.00
Chocolate, rooster, tin, two-part,
American-made, 5½ x 6½" 75.00
Chocolate, Santa Claus, tin, standing
figure w/fur-trimmed robe, two-
part, 7½" h.   165.00
Chocolate, Santa Claus, tin, four
separate figures joined at top &
base w/a bar, top bar hinged to
open, marked "Made in Germa-
ny," 8" l. 55.00
Chocolate, Santa Claus & child, tin,
two-part, marked "Germany,"
7" h. 130.00
Chocolate, sheep, tin, 4½" h. 68.00
Chocolate, squirrel, tin, 4½" h. 42.00
Chocolate, three small girls, tin,
marked "U.S. Patent Pending,"
hinged, 9½" l. 45.00
Chocolate, zeppelin, tin 110.00
Food, crown & flutes, tin, cylindrical
w/fluted sides & a boldly stamped
crown in the top, 6½" h. 38.50
Food, ear of corn, copper, rectangu-
lar w/rounded corners, deep ruffled sides, design stamped in the
top, tin-washed, 4 x 6" (pinpoint
holes) 104.50
Food, ear of corn, yellowware, oval
domed shape w/the interior sides
paneled & the ear of corn molded
in the top, 3½ x 3¾", 2 1/8" h. . . .   82.50
Food, fruit & flutes, pewter, cylindrical body on a wide foot,
molded w/interior flutes & a
molded fruit design in the top,
England, 6½" h. 82.50
Food, pear, tin, oval w/deep ruffled
sides, design stamped in the top
& framed by a raised rim band,
3½ x 5¼" (light rust) 71.50
Food, pomegranate, tin, oval sides,

the inset top w/a boldly stamped
design of a large & small pomegranate & scrolling leaves,
7¼" l. 49.50
Food, sheaf of wheat, copper, rectangular w/rounded corners &
deep ruffled sides, stamped design in the top, tin-washed,
4½ x 6" 93.50
Food, swirl, copper, domed half-
round shape w/bold swirl design,
6 5/8" d. (pinpoint holes) 82.50
Food, Turk's turban, redware w/red-
dish glaze w/brown flecks &
daubs of white slip & dark brown
at the rim, 7½" d. (small chips) .. 60.50
Food, Turk's turban, redware, scalloped rim, amber glaze, 10¼" d.
(edge chips) 55.00
Ice cream, black man choking a turkey, pewter, E. & Co., No. 1089 .. 125.00
Ice cream, Cupid, pewter, No. 492 .. 55.00
Ice cream, doves, pewter, No. 177 .. 55.00
Ice cream, duck, pewter, hinged,
two-part, 4" l. 49.50
Ice cream, early steam engine, pewter, row of three engines, marked
"39," 1½" h. 38.50
Ice cream, engagement ring, pew-
ter, E. & Co. 45.00
Ice cream, golf ball, pewter, 2" d. .. 180.00
Ice cream, hen, pewter, two-part,
3¾" h. 82.50

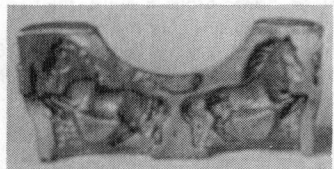

Rearing Horse Ice Cream Mold

Ice cream, horse rearing, pewter,
two horses shown, marked "118,"
soiling, 2½" h. (ILLUS.) 27.50
Ice cream, horse & rider, pewter,
three figures in a row, marked
"233," 2½" h. 22.00
Ice cream, opossum, pewter, two-
part, 5" l. 115.50
Ice cream, organ grinder w/mon-
key, pewter, row of three figures,
marked "159," 2" h. 27.50
Ice cream, race horse w/jockey,
pewter, No. 271 .... 125.00
Ice cream, rose, pewter, E. & Co.,
No. 295 .... 50.00
Ice cream, rose w/cupid's face,
pewter, No. 306 .... 60.00
Ice cream, sailboat, pewter, row
of three boats, marked "40,"
1¾" h. 88.00
Ice cream, Santa Claus, cast iron,
standing figure w/bag of gifts in

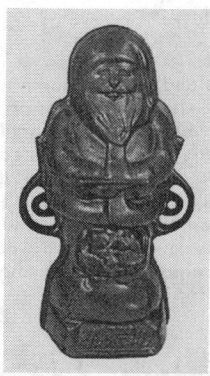

Griswold Santa Claus Mold

front & marked at base of front
"Hello Kiddies - 897 - Griswold
Mfg. Co. Erie, Pa.," open loop
side handles, 12" h. (ILLUS.) 275.00
Ice cream, slipper, pewter, three-
part, No. 899A 55.00
Ice cream, soldier in armor on
horseback, pewter, row of three
figures, 3" h. 22.00
Ice cream, Uncle Sam, pewter, three
figures in a row, marked "200,"
3" h. 110.00
Ice cream, woman churning butter,
pewter, row of four figures,
marked "30," 1" h. 33.00
Pastry, two-sided, cast iron, decorated w/a horse on one side &
two chickens on the other, late
19th - early 20th c., 6½ x 7" 275.00

MOVIE MEMORABILIA

*Also see AUTOGRAPHS, CHARACTER
COLLECTIBLES and DISNEY COL-
LECTIBLES.*

BOOKS

"Academy Award Winners," from
1928 to 1961, best actors & ac-
tresses, 9 x 11", w/original
jacket $35.00
"America," souvenir-type, making
of the D.W. Griffith silent film,
scenes, cast, etc., 1924 .... 85.00
"Betty Grable" coloring book,
1953 .... 35.00
"The Big Broadcast of 1938" press
book, in original envelope 90.00
"Carmen Miranda," coloring book,
1942 .... 45.00
"Deanna Durbin" coloring book,
1940 .... 25.00
"Don Juan," starring John Barry-

more, w/film scenes, soft cover,
1926 (several chipped pages) 30.00
"Knights of the Round Table" souvenir book, starring Ava Gardner,
1954 .... 24.00
"Mary Astor, My Story," w/dust
jacket, 1959 .... 15.00
"Noah's Ark," movie edition, Darryl
Zanuck production starring D.
Costello & G. O'Brien, w/dust
jacket, 1928 .... 20.00
"Romeo and Juliet," motion picture
edition, 1936, w/scenes.......... 33.00
"Theaters & Motion Picture Houses,"
A.S. Meloy, 1915, construction,
rules, designs, equipment, etc., 14
pages of ads, hardcover, 123 pp.,
7 x 10½" 60.00
"Wuthering Heights," Photoplay edi-
tion, photos of Merle Oberon,
Lawrence Olivier & David Niven .. 25.00

COSTUMES

John Barrymore, "Marie Antoi-
nette," MGM, 1938, bathrobe, red
satin w/blue satin lining & deep
orange velvet on lapels & around
the cuffs & pockets 660.00

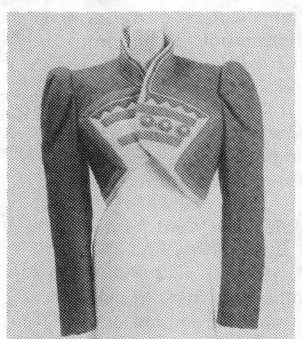

Wizard of Oz Costume

Emerald City inhabitant, "The Wizard of Oz," Metro-Goldwyn-
Mayer, 1939, bolero jacket, blue-
green felt w/elaborate tricolor geometric applique, 18" l. (ILLUS.) ..3,025.00
Judy Garland, "Meet Me in St.
Louis," Metro-Goldwyn-Mayer,
1944, rust silk long-sleeved dress
w/scoop neck, ornamented overall w/copper caviar beading, embroidery more concentrated at
bodice, faceted "moon stones" in
a foliate & squiggle design
throughout, w/Hattie Carnegie
Inc. label, together w/personal
presentation letter from Judy Garland, 2 pcs. 1,870.00
Charleton Heston, "Ben Hur," MGM,
1959, shirt, oatmeal colored cot-

ton blouse w/light blue embroidery down the neck, front & cuffs,
w/label sewn inside the neck
from "Western Costume Co.,
Hollywood," framed 770.00

Michael Jackson in Scarecrow Costume

Michael Jackson, "The Wiz," Universal, 1978, Scarecrow costume including a brown leotard, brown
leggings made w/hay & cloth
knots, two orange & white wool
sleeves, coated gauze body suit,
hat, tail, two mitts & two wrist
bands, 12 pcs. (ILLUS.) 1,650.00

Marilyn Monroe Costume

Marilyn Monroe, "Some Like It Hot,"
United Artists, 1959, sheer black
beaded & sequined cocktail dress,
chiffon w/dangling black beads &
sheer back (ILLUS.) 3,850.00
Munchkin fiddler, "The Wizard of
Oz," MGM, 1939, orange felt bolero jacket w/striped orange &
white tails, 40" l. 3,300.00
Paul Newman, "Butch Cassidy and
the Sundance Kid," Universal Studios, 1969, outfit including a cowboy hat, boots & cotton striped

shirt w/Western Costume Co. label inscribed "2471 - P. Newman," mounted in a display case, the group 8,250.00

Paul Newman Cowboy Boots

Paul Newman, cowboy boots, brown leather, w/a Paramount Studios tag, dirty, toes scuffed, pr. (ILLUS.). 220.00

Wedding Dress from "The Graduate"

Katherine Ross, "The Graduate," 1966, wedding dress, white lace w/scalloped neckline, high waistline, tightly fitting full-length sleeves, the cuffs & back w/tiny satin buttons, worn over an ivory underslip, handwritten w/"Katherine Ross, 1966 4-7" & the name "Vilolvi" on band near hem (ILLUS.). 880.00

Showgirl costume, "Guys and Dolls," Cinemascope, 1955, short dress w/fitted bodice, orange satin w/red & white plaid trim & red & white sequins, w/magenta velvet shoulder straps, framed 660.00

John Wayne, "Hatari," Paramount, 1962, jacket, together w/a lobby card from the film showing Wayne wearing the jacket, 2 pcs. 550.00

LOBBY CARDS

"A Night at The Opera" Lobby Card

"A Night at The Opera," starring the Marx Brothers, photo scene of the characters in a crowded dressing room, single card, MGM, 1935, 11 x 14" (ILLUS.) 3,080.00

"Broadway Scandals," starring Sally O'Neill, Jack Egan & Carmel Myers, Columbia, 1929, 11 x 14", set of 8 . . . . 495.00

"Cuban Pete," starring Desi Arnez, 1946 . . . . 65.00

"Dracula," starring Bela Lugosi, bust portrait of Lugosi at top & terrified heroine at the bottom, against a spiderweb-design background, insert card, Universal, 1931, 14 x 36" 33,000.00

"Go Around the World in a Daze," starring The Three Stooges, 1963, different colorful scenes, set of 8 . . . . 225.00

"Gone With The Wind," starring Clark Gable & Vivien Leigh, MGM, 1939, 11 x 14", set of 8 including title card, the set 3,300.00

"Hollywood," Paramount, 1923, 11 x 14", set of 8 . . . . .1,760.00

"It's A Wonderful Life," starring James Stewart & Donna Reed, Liberty Films, 1946, 11 x 14", set of 8 . . . . .4,400.00

"The Mummy," starring Boris Karloff, large bust portrait of the Mummy on the left side, title card, Universal, 1932, 11 x 14"..10,450.00

"Return of Captain Marvel," depicts Captain Marvel walking toward bad guys who are shooting at him, 1953 re-release 35.00

"Sinister Journey," starring Hopalong Cassidy, set of 8 . . . . 90.00

POSTERS

"The Adventures of Robin Hood," starring Errol Flynn & Olivia De Havilland, color portrait of Robin & Maid Marian on a large rearing white horse, three-sheet, Warner Bros., 1938, linen-backed, 41 x 81" 19,800.00

"All About Eve," starring Bette Davis, one-sheet, linen-backed, 1950, 27 x 41" 440.00

"An American in Paris," starring Gene Kelly & Leslie Caron, large full-length portrait of dancing couple, three-sheet, MGM, 1951, linen-backed, 41 x 81" 1,980.00

"The Birth of a Nation," by D.W. Griffith, colorful scene of Booth jumping to the stage after shooting Lincoln, one-sheet, Epoch Producing Corp., 1915, linen-backed, 27 x 41" 28,600.00

"Bus Stop" Poster

"Bus Stop," starring Marilyn Monroe, one-sheet, linen-backed, 1956, 27 x 41" (ILLUS.) 385.00

"Casablanca," starring Humphrey Bogart, Ingrid Bergman & Paul Henreid, black & white photo scenes w/captions, one-sheet, Warner Brothers, 1943, linen-backed, 27 x 41" 5,720.00

"Cat On A Hot Tin Roof," starring Elizabeth Taylor & Paul Newman, shows Taylor reclining in a sensuous pose, one-sheet, linen-backed, 1958, 27 x 41" 242.00

"Citizen Kane," starring Orson Welles, color bust portraits of the stars at top & bottom corners, one-sheet, RKO, 1941, linen-backed, 27 x 41" 22,000.00

"Creature From The Black Lagoon," starring Richard Carlson & Julia Adams, drawing of the Creature carrying the terrified heroine, one-sheet, Universal, 1954, linen-backed, 27 x 41" 4,620.00

"The Devil Is A Woman," starring Marlene Dietrich & Lionel Atwill, large portrait of the stars embrac-

ing as the background, one-sheet, Paramount, 1935, linen-backed, 27 x 41" 16,500.00

"A Dog's Life," starring Charlie Chaplin, half-length color portrait of Chaplin, the heroine & a dog, six-sheet, First National, 1918, linen-backed, 81" sq. 35,200.00

"The Fleet's In" Poster

"The Fleet's In," starring Clara Bow, Paramount, 1928, one-sheet, linen-backed, 27 x 41" (ILLUS.) . . . 2,200.00

"Gentlemen Prefer Blondes," starring Marilyn Monroe & Jane Russell, full-length portrait of Monroe & Russell in skimpy red & yellow dance costumes at the top, three-sheet, 20th Century Fox, 1953, linen-backed, 41 x 81" 1,430.00

"Godzilla," shows huge monster breathing fire & destroying Tokyo, one-sheet, Embassy, 1956, linen-backed, 27 x 41" 770.00

"The Grapes of Wrath," starring Henry Fonda, Jane Darwell & John Carradine, black & white photo portrait of the family across the center w/red & blue copy on a pale yellow background at top & bottom, one-sheet, 20th Century Fox, 1940, linen-backed, 27 x 41" 5,280.00

"Hard Days Night," starring The Beatles, one-sheet, 1964, 27 x 41" 66.00

"Hi-De-Ho," starring Cab Calloway, stylized full-length portrait of a dancing & singing black actress, photo of Calloway's head near the bottom, done in red, white & black, three-sheet, All-American, 1947, linen-backed, 41 x 81" 5,500.00

"High Noon," starring Gary Cooper, close-up portrait of Cooper, one-sheet, 1952, linen-backed, 27 x 41" 308.00

"Horse Feathers," starring the Marx

Brothers, caricature bust portraits of the four brothers at the top, one-sheet, Paramount, 1932, linen-backed, 27 x 41" 5,280.00

"How Could You, Jean?," starring Mary Pickford, color bust portrait of Pickford in the center, one-sheet, Artcraft, 1918, linen-backed, 27 x 41" 4,180.00

"Kick In," starring Betty Compson, Bert Lytell & May McAvoy, one-sheet, 1923, linen-backed, 27 x 41" 154.00

"King Cowboy," starring Tom Mix & Tony, large half-length color portrait of Mix forms the background, one-sheet, FBO, 1928, linen-backed, 27 x 41" 1,540.00

Rare "King Kong" Poster

"King Kong," starring Fay Wray & Robert Armstrong, dramatic color drawing of the huge ape holding the heroine at the top & fighting a dinosaur at the bottom, three-sheet, RKO, 1933, linen-backed, 41 x 81" (ILLUS.) 57,200.00

"Moon Over Miami," starring Betty Grable, Don Ameche & Robert Cummings, full-length sexy portrait of Grable in a tight black swimsuit against a black background, three-sheet, 20th Century Fox, 1941, linen-backed, 41 x 81" 13,200.00

"The Old Dark House," starring Boris Karloff, Universal, 1932, one-sheet, 27 x 41" (ILLUS. top next column) 48,400.00

"The Oregon Trail," starring John Wayne, large head portrait of Wayne at top above a racing covered wagon, one-sheet, Republic, 1936, linen-backed, 27 x 41" 10,450.00

"Patch Mah Britches," color anima-

"The Old Dark House" Poster

tion starring Barney Google, one-sheet, Columbia, 1935, linen-backed, 27 x 41" 1,650.00

"The Phantom of the Opera," starring Lon Chaney, Norman Kerry & Mary Philbin, a dramatic painted scene of the Phantom & the city of Paris, one-sheet, Universal, 1925, paper-backed, 27 x 41" ...38,500.00

"Queen Christina," starring Greta Garbo & John Gilbert, large dramatic bust portrait of Garbo above her name at the top, three-sheet, MGM, 1933, linen-backed, 41 x 81" 17,600.00

"Rebel Without A Cause," starring James Dean, three-quarter-length portrait of Dean w/hands in rear pockets on left side, six-sheet, Warner Brothers, 1955, linen-backed, 81" sq................4,400.00

"Son of Frankenstein," starring Boris Karloff, Basil Rathbone & Bela Lugosi, the standing monster as the background & the three main characters at the bottom, one-sheet, Universal, 1939, linen-backed, 27 x 41" 14,300.00

"Stormy Weather," starring Lena Horne, Bill Robinson & Cab Calloway, large portraits of Horne & Robinson above the title & credits w/other portraits scattered throughout, one-sheet, 20th Century Fox, 1943, linen-backed, 27 x 41" 3,520.00

"There's No Business Like Show Business," starring Ethel Merman & Marilyn Monroe, one-sheet, 1954, linen-backed, 27 x 41" 275.00

"Tire Trouble," an "Our Gang" comedy, bust portraits of the kids encircled by a large tire, three-sheet, Pathe, 1923, linen-backed, 41 x 81" 6,050.00

"Uncle Tom's Cabin," illustrated around the edges w/small color-tinted photo portraits of the various players, the title & credits in the center reserve, half-sheet, Universal, 1927, unfolded 22 x 28" 770.00

"The War of the Worlds," based on H.G. Wells' novel, color scene of large claw reaching down toward a tiny human couple, six-sheet, Paramount, 1953, linen-backed, 81" sq. 5,280.00

"The Wizard of Oz," starring Judy Garland, Frank Morgan, etc., colorful cartoon design w/the main characters on the yellow brick road at the bottom, three-sheet, MGM, 1939, linen-backed, 41 x 81" 25,300.00

"The Wolf Man," starring Lon Chaney, Claude Rains, Ralph Bellamy & Bela Lugosi, large head of the Wolf Man at the top, fainted heroine at the bottom, one-sheet, Universal, 1941, 27 x 41" 17,600.00

"Yellow Submarine," starring The Beatles, one-sheet, 1968, linen-backed, 27 x 41" 418.00

MISCELLANEOUS

Bela Lugosi Bust

Book ends, bronzed brass, figural Mary Pickford & Douglas Fairbanks, pr. 42.00

Booklet, "Pathex Motion Picture Films," complete list to 1927, listing hundreds of movies in all categories, 6 pp., 8 x 11" 25.00

Bust of Bela Lugosi in the role of Dracula, patinated resin prototype, shown wearing a bow tie & cape, inscribed "Langi, Hollywood 1940," 13" h. (ILLUS.) 1,320.00

"Change of Name" form for James Dean, paper, possibly for a club, states Dean's intention to change his name from "James Dean" to "James B. Dean," signed by Dean both ways, date "10/3/51" 2,640.00

Counter display box, cardboard w/colorful portrait of Barbara Stanwyck above the box w/original chocolate bars inside, 1940's, 6 x 7", 1" h. 65.00

Figure of Chico Marx, bisque, 7" h. 45.00

Handbill, "Texas Wildcats," starring Tim McCoy 22.00

Handkerchief, "Gone With the Wind," silk, four full figure depictions of Scarlett in different dress, original mint condition, 13 x 13" .. 125.00

Jigsaw puzzle, advertising "Man's Favorite Sport," starring Rock Hudson, unused 32.50

Magazine, "Modern Screen," 1940, July, Ann Sheridan cover 9.00

Magazine, "Movie Life," 1941, Gene Autry cover 23.00

Magazine, "Movie Radio Guide," 1941, October 24, Susan Hayward cover 10.00

Magazine, "Movies," 1948, April, Lana Turner cover 15.50

Magazine, "Movie Secrets," 1955, Vol. 1, No. 1, Marilyn Monroe issue 45.00

Magazine, "Photoplay," 1924, December 12.00

Magazine, "Photoplay," 1932, October, Ruby Keeler cover 15.00

Magazine, "Photoplay," 1941, Ginger Rogers cover, Karo "Dionne Quintuplets" ad 25.00

Magazine, "Photoplay," 1946, February, Van Johnson cover 5.00

Magazine, "Photoplay," 1953, Marilyn Monroe cover 25.00

Magazine, "Screen Book," 1939, April, article about Vivien Leigh as Scarlett O'Hara in "Gone With The Wind," also article about Shirley Temple in "Little Princess" 50.00

Magazine, "Screenland," 1936, December, Robert Taylor cover 27.50

Magazine, "Screen Parades," 1962, August, Natalie Wood cover 10.00

Magazine, "Screen Romances," 1940, January, color cartoon cover w/Disney's Pinocchio & 11 other pictures of movie, also pictures of the making of "Gone With the Wind" 60.00

Magazine, "Sheila Graham's Hollywood Romance," 1951, issue No. 1, Elizabeth Taylor cover 45.00

Magazine, "Time," 1938, Bette Davis "Jezebel" cover, "Flash Gordon Trip to Mars" movie review inside 31.00

Movie herald, "The Mark of Zorro," silent movie starring Douglas Fairbanks, 1921 .... 30.00

Movie herald, "Tugboat Annie Sails Again," starring Jane Wyman & Ronald Reagan 50.00

Movie prop, statue of the goddess Astarte, used in "The Prodigal" starring Lana Turner, resin & plaster, MGM Studios, 1955, together w/photo stills & title lobby card, 6" w., 31" h., the group 1,320.00

Movie theatre slide, glass, hand-colored, "Ken Maynard," ca. 1920's, 3¼ x 4" 45.00

Movie theatre slide, glass, hand-colored, advertising "Michelin Tires," ca. 1920's, 3¼ x 4" 45.00

Photograph of Cary Grant, black & white publicity photo from "Operation Petticoat" for a British film magazine, signed & inscribed "A Merry Christmas - To 'Picturegoer' and all of its readers! - Cary Grant," 1959, 8 x 10" 242.00

Marilyn Monroe Photograph

Photograph of Marilyn Monroe, black & white, showing the actress reclining on a silk pillow & wearing diamonds, signed & inscribed "To Bob Couture - Love and Kisses, Marilyn Monroe," small creases in lower corners, 7½ x 9½" (ILLUS.) 1,650.00

Photograph of Rudolph Valentino, black & white portrait of the actor as a young man, signed & inscribed "To My Dear Olga - Lovingly - Rodolph (sic) - X," 7 x 9½" 352.00

Postcard, Jeanette MacDonald, actual photo 18.00

Program, "The Big Parade," 1926 ... 25.00

Program, "The Covered Wagon," 1923 .... 35.00

Program, "Hunchback of Notre Dame," starring Lon Chaney 65.00

Sheet music, "Babes On Broadway," Mickey Rooney & Judy Garland on cover 25.00

Sheet music, "I Dood It," Red Skelton & Eleanor Powell on cover.... 25.00

Spoon, silver plate, Douglas Fairbanks 21.00

Writing tablet, Jeanette MacDonald on cover, unused................ 25.00

Writing tablet, Gregory Peck on cover 12.00

MUCHA (Alphonse) ARTWORK

Mucha Portrait Plaque

A leader in the Art Nouveau movement, Alphonse Maria Mucha was born in Moravia (now part of Czechoslovakia) in 1860. Displaying considerable artistic talent as a child, he began formal studies locally, later continuing his work in Munich and then Paris, where it became necessary for him to undertake commercial artwork. In 1894, the renowned actress Sarah Bernhardt commissioned Mucha to create a poster for her play "Gismonda" and this opportunity proved to be the turning point in his career. While continuing his association with Bernhardt, he began creating numerous advertising posters, packaging designs, book and magazine illustrations and "panneaux decoratifs" (decorative pictures).

Plaque, ceramic, pierced for hanging, round w/a colorful h.p. profile bust portrait of a young lady in the Art Nouveau style based on the 1899 lithograph "La Primevere Polyanthus," signed on the back "Peinture a La Main d'Apres Genre Pouruev 009," impressed underglaze "OB/M," minor paint loss, 16½" d. (ILLUS.) $1,210.00

Plaques, white metal, "Brunette and Blonde Tete Byzantine," after designs by Mucha, ca. 1900, framed, 9 x 16", pr. 2,875.00

Poster, "Champagne Ruinart," young woman w/long flowing hair standing & holding up a glass of champagne, printed in colors by F. Champenois, Paris, 1896, framed, 23" w., 68¼" h. (several repairs).........................4,400.00

Poster, "Flirt Bisquits - Lefevre-Utile," lithograph printed in colors w/a scene of a young lady & man standing among flowers, printed by F. Champenois, Paris, 1900, laid down, framed, 11¾ x 25¼"...................2,860.00

Poster, "Lorenzaccio...Theatre de la Renaissance," central scene of Sarah Bernhardt in her role from the play, printed in colors by F. Champenois, Paris, 1896, framed, 27¾ x 80¼" (several repaired tears along margins, creasing, minor abrasions)..............4,675.00

Poster, "Theatre de la Renaissance - La Samaritaine," 1897, lithographed in colors showing the standing figure of Sarah Bernhardt in the role of Photina, signed in the plate, 22½ x 68½".........7,475.00

Bernhardt - Hamlet Poster

Poster, "Tragique Histoire d'Hamlet - Prince de Danemark - Sarah Bernhardt - Theatre Sarah Bernhardt," standing portrait of Bernhardt in costume, printed in colors by F. Champenois, Paris, 1899, framed, some creasing & repaired tears, 29 3/8" x 6' 10" (ILLUS.)..........7,700.00

Print, "La Topaze (Topaz)," depicting a beautiful young woman seated in a large chair w/brilliant poinsettia-like blossoms in the foreground, printed in colors by F. Champenois, Paris, 1900, in origi-

nal period frame, 15¼ x 38¾" (staining, minor creases, small hole at top center, laid down on paper, margins trimmed)........3,575.00

Print, "Le Rubis (Ruby)," depicting a beautiful young woman seated on the floor w/legs drawn up to one side, stylized flowers in the foreground, printed in colors by F. Champenois, Paris, 1900, in original period frame, 15¼ x 38¾" (slight staining, minor losses to edges, laid down on paper, margins trimmed).................3,575.00

Print, "Redhead Among Flowers," printed on velveteen by the London firm of Hines, Stroud & Co., the image on a black ground, signed in the image, ca. 1900, framed, 24¼" sq. (trimmed).....3,080.00

Print, "Summer," scene of a beautiful young woman in a languid pose amid a summer garden setting, lithograph printed in colors by F. Champenois, Paris, France, 1898, framed, 22¾ x 43" (laid down, some staining, time darkened, margins trimmed).......4,025.00

Prints, "The Arts," each featuring a beautiful young woman depicting one of the arts, lithographed in color by F. Champenois, Paris, France, 1898, four scenes in a four-section frame, 20½ x 30"..13,800.00

MUSICAL INSTRUMENTS

Bass drum, cylindrical, bentwood w/hide heads, rope lacing & leather trim, the sides decorated w/the original red & black graining w/a gold stenciled eagle, stars & "E Pluribus Unum," interior label "G.D. Westlands, Rapids, O.," 19th c., 24" d., 19" h. (rope worn & repaired, one head torn).......................$1,250.00

Clarinet, "Paramount," in original case..........................100.00

Guitar, electric, "Fender Stratocaster"........................650.00

Guitar, "Gibson Model No. ES-295"...................1,250.00

Harmonica, Bugle Boy, w/illustrated box.............................30.00

Harmonica, miniature, Hohner, ca. 1930's, 1¼" l...................25.00

Harp, floor-model, ebonized & parcel gilt, "Sebastian Erards, patent harp No. 18, Great Marlboro St. London, No. 807," George III

period, 30¼" w., 67½" h.
(damages) 440.00
Mandolin, "Gibson, No. A-4" 1,450.00
Mandolin (Key of F), "Gibson,
No. A-28861," w/original case 750.00
Organ, pump-type, "Estey," elab-
orate walnut case 2,500.00
Organ, pump-type, "Ferrand &
Votey," ornate upright case
w/mirror, 36-note keyboard,
treble & bass coupler, knee
coupler, mirror 10 x 11", case
6' 7" h. 800.00
Piano, grand, "Bechstein," inlaid
walnut, overall bird's-eye veneering & painted band of putti & ribbon swags around the sides, on
rectangular tapering legs on
casters, late 19th - early 20th c.,
6' 8" l. 9,900.00
Piano, square, "Steinway & Sons,"
Style 3, rosewood case, w/double
round mouldings, Serial No. 27089,
ca. 1873 . . . . .2,750.00
Piano, upright, "W. Ritmuller &
Sohn," Art Nouveau style inlaid
walnut, mother-of-pearl & bronze-
mounted case, the upper section
inlaid w/sprays of spring flowers
in various woods & mother-of-
pearl, w/two three-light electric
fixtures cast w/foliate whiplash
designs, the ends of the keyboard
carved as stylized swans continuing down to webbed front feet,
the sides inlaid w/iris blossoms &
set w/bronze foliate handles, inlaid "W. RITMULLER & SOHN -
GOTTINGEN GEGR. 1795" & painted "Doppel Rosonaz System D.R.
Patent No. 108315," Germany, ca.
1900, 27½ x 60", 5' h. 8,800.00
Saxophone, soprano, "C.G. Conn
Co.," 1914 . . . . 750.00
Saxophone, baritone, "Martin" 275.00
Sousaphone, "C.G. Conn Co." 225.00
Trumpet, brass, "Bundy," w/original
case 120.00
Ukelele, "C.F. Martin & Co.," in
original case 275.00

MUSICAL INSTRUMENTS, MECHANICAL

Band organ, "Bursens Jazz Orchestra," console cabinet w/accor-
dion mounted on the front, eight
pipe ranks w/percussion, 98" w.,
9' 4" h. $29,500.00
Band organ, "Gasparini & Co.," con-
sole cabinet w/one moving figure,

52 keys & 138 pipes, 10' 6" w.,
7' 10" h. (restored) 29,500.00
Band organ, "Wurlitzer Style 150,"
w/organ, trombone, trumpet,
clarinet & piccolos, 27 x 98",
7' 2" h. (restored) 39,000.00
Barrel organ, "Diester," two barrel-
type, original condition 5,000.00
Caliola w/keyboard, "Wurlitzer,"
w/many rolls (restored) 16,000.00
Coin-operated piano, upright, "Capi-
tol Piano and Organ Co.," oak
case w/art glass, w/pipes 10,500.00

'Coinola' Player Piano

Coin-operated piano, upright, "Coinola," oak case inset w/three oval
stained glass panels, gold transfer
trade-mark over keyboard, w/pi-
ano, xylophone, drum & tambourine all visible above keyboard,
w/eleven rolls, early 20th c.,
63½" l. (ILLUS.) 4,125.00
Coin-operated piano, upright, "Cre-
mona Style 2 'A' Roll" 5,750.00
Coin-operated piano, upright, "See-
burg Style L," keyboardless, oak
case w/leaded glass panels (re-
stored) 12,500.00
Coin-operated piano, upright,
"Wurlitzer Style A," w/pipes,
quarter-sawn oak case (re-
stored) . . . . .20,000.00 to 24,000.00
Coin-operated piano, upright,
"Wurlitzer Style IX-B," w/bells attachment, direct drive mechanism
& roll changer 24,000.00
Orchestrion, "Link AX," w/xylo-
phone, tambourine, drum, wood
block, triangle, etc., art glass
case, w/many rolls 27,000.00
Orchestrion, "Link C," w/piano,
mandolin, flute pipes, etc., art
glass case, ca. 1920, 6' 4" h. 19,500.00
Orchestrion, "Seeburg Greyhound,"
player piano w/eight dog races, a
nickel starts the dogs racing
around the center post, race dis-
plays in the glass window, up-

right oak cabinet, 4' 3½" h.
(restored) .12,500.00

Orchestrion, "Seeburg Style K,"
w/piano, mandolin & flute, upright oak cabinet w/art glass win-
dows, 5' 2" h. 18,000.00

Orchestrion, "Seeburg Style KT,"
quartered oak rectangular cabinet
w/round columns down the sides,
an arched slag glass panel depicting a spread-winged eagle at the
top below two quarter-round
stained glass panels, quarter play,
w/three rolls, 5' ½" h. 25,000.00

Orchestrion, "Seeburg Style KT Special," w/piano, xylophone, mandolin, bass drum, snare drum,
tympani, cymbal, castanets, triangle, tambourine & Chinese block,
upright oak cabinet w/art glass
windows at top (restored) 26,000.00

Orchestrion, "Seeburg Style L,"
w/piano, mandolin & bells,
upright cabinet w/art glass
windows, 23½ x 36½",
4' 3½" h. . . . . .10,500.00 to 11,000.00

Orchestrion, "Western Electric Piano
Company," w/piano, snare drum,
tom-tom, reiterating xylophone,
cymbal, triangle & mandolin,
plays "G" rolls, upright oak case
w/art glass (restored) 24,000.00

Orchestrion, "Wurlitzer Bijou Orchestra," w/two ranks of violin &
flute pipes, xylophone, drum, automatic roll changer, rotating
"Wonder Light" at top, art glass
panel in quarter-sawn oak case,
8' 6" h. (restored) 45,000.00

Orchestrion, "Wurlitzer Style C," piano w/mandolin attachment, 38
violin pipes, 38 flute pipes, & bass
drum & snare drum, automatic
roll changer, Grecian-style case,
ca. 1921, 7' 4" h. 22,500.00

Orchestrion, "Wurlitzer Style CX,"
w/piano, mandolin, orchestra
bells, violin pipes, flute pipes,
bass drum, snare drum, cymbal &
others, automatic roll changer,
rotating "Wonder Light" at top,
ornate art glass front, in playing
condition (mostly restored) 25,000.00

Orchestrion, "Wurlitzer IX-B," one
rank of pipes, orchestra bells,
piano, etc., w/automatic roll
changer .24,000.00

Orchestrion, "Wurlitzer LX," piano
w/mandolin attachment, 38 violin
pipes, 38 flute pipes, orchestra
bells, bass drum & snare drum,
Turkish-style case, ca. 1921,
7' 9" h. .27,500.00

Organette, "Munroe Organ Reed Co.

- McTammany," two full sets of
reeds & sub-bass, wind motor
operated by bellows, plays sheet
music rolls, 12 x 14", 9" h. 495.00

Player concertina, "Tanzbar," power
provided by opening & closing the
instrument & the roll advances by
continually depressing & releasing
a lever, 1900-30 . . . . .1,100.00

Player organ, "M.P. Moller, Inc.,"
upright Art Deco style case,
w/two built-in roll cabinets & 145
boxed rolls, 7' 4½" h. 6,500.00

Player organ, "Welte Philharmonic
Organ," 32 pedals, 10 roll changer
& 3 manuals, w/300 original rolls
in metal boxes (restored) 68,000.00

Player piano, upright, "Capitol,"
w/27 violin pipes, oak case
w/stained glass insert, plays "A"
rolls 7,500.00

Player piano, child's, "Cheon Co. -
'Loden'," w/twelve rolls in original
boxes 700.00

Reproducing piano, grand, "Chicker-
ing Ampico A," w/rolls, 6' 5" (re-
stored) 16,000.00

Reproducing piano, grand, "Chicker-
ing Ampico B," walnut Sheraton
art case (unrestored) 9,000.00

Reproducing piano, grand, "Mason &
Hamlin Ampico Model B," walnut
case, 5' 8" (unrestored) 14,500.00

Reproducing piano, grand, "Steinway Duo-Art OR," mahogany
Louis XVI art case w/matching
bench, 1926, 6' 5", 2 pcs. 19,500.00

Reproducing piano, grand, "Steinway Duo-Art XR," Italian Renaissance walnut art case
w/matching bench, ca. 1928,
2 pcs. (restored) . . .20,000.00 to 22,000.00

Violano, "Mills Violano
Model No. S/N 232 (re-
stored) . . . . .50,000.00 to 75,000.00

MUSIC BOXES

American cylinder music box,
dovetailed fruitwood case
w/molded base & bracket feet,
the hinged lid opening to a printed paper-lined interior fitted
w/works, inscribed in script w/the
various dances, etc., the front of
the case fitted w/attached
wrought-iron & turned wood handle, Pennsylvania, 1780-1810,
9 x 15½", 9¼" h. $2,415.00

Polyphon (Polyphon Musikwerke,
Leipzig, Germany) table model
disc music box, mahogany case

Polyphon Disc Music Box

w/a wide, flaring cornice above a
glazed front w/an arched opening
w/carved corner brackets flanked
by turned columns above the
molded base w/drawer for discs,
on flattened bun feet (ILLUS.) 4,500.00
Regina (American subsidiary of Polyphon Musikwerke, Rahway, New
Jersey) Model 240 disc music box,
floor model, carved mahogany
case w/curved front & carved
lions' heads at the front corners,
20 x 22¼", 48½" h. 9,000.00
Regina (American subsidiary of Poly-
phon Musikwerke, Rahway, New
Jersey) disc music box, floor model, mahogany case w/a low gallery w/turned spindles around the
top above an arched, glazed front
w/carved corner brackets above
a paneled lower case, plays
23¾" d. discs 12,500.00
Swiss cylinder music box, twelve-
tune, inlaid rosewood case w/a
musical instrument inlaid on the
top of the lid, original tune card
inside the lid, patent dated 1896,
plays 9" l. cylinders, case 9 x 21",
6½" h. 1,050.00

Swiss Orchestral Music Box

Swiss orchestral interchangeable
cylinder music box, 30-tune, floor
model, burl walnut case w/fruit-
wood banding, lever-wound at
side, w/tune indicator, zither attachment, drum, six bells, castanets, stop/start & repeat/change
levers, the box within a case set
upon a table-form base w/taper-
ing knob- and block-turned legs
on casters, drawer in front of table for four of the five six-tune
15" l. cylinders, late 19th c.,
30 x 45", 39" h. (ILLUS.) 7,150.00
Symphonion (German) coin-operated
disc music box, mahogany case,
center-drive, double comb, crank-
wound at side, w/15" d. discs,
21 x 24", 11" h., the group 2,750.00
Symphonion (German) disc music
box, mahogany case, double
comb, crank-wound at side, plays
15¾" d. discs, w/12 discs, the
group 5,500.00

NAPKIN RINGS

*All napkin rings listed are silver plate un-
less otherwise noted.*

Children on Teeter-Totter Ring

Bear sitting on haunches w/paws on
ring $250.00
Bird on foliage engraved on ring,
coin silver 47.50
Bird perched on ring, small dog on
hind legs beside ring 200.00
Boy, Greenaway-type, standing in
front of a scrolled edged, six-
sided ring (resilvered) 275.00
Camel in front of ring on base,
Meriden 185.00
Cat, angry full figure animal w/or-
nately etched ring 210.00
Cherub carrying ring on back,
Victorian 250.00
Cherub sitting on stool reading book
next to ring, Victorian 225.00
Chicken foot holds ornate scalloped
ring, on heart-shaped base,

figural cupid tries to retrieve an arrow in front of foot............ 235.00

Children on teeter-totter w/ring between, on shaped base, Simpson, Hall, Miller & Co. (ILLUS.) 600.00

Dogs, one on either side of ring, four-footed base 275.00

Eagle on each side of ring, No. 148, Meriden 60.00

Griffins (2) w/ring between, Simpson, Hall, Miller & Co. 175.00

Horse, prancing & pulling wheeled sulky decorated w/flowers, Victorian, Rogers 275.00

Lily pad w/flower supporting ring, No. 168, Meriden 110.00

Long-tailed bird on leaf w/stem next to ring 125.00

Wolf baying at the moon, ornate freeform base on ball feet, floral etched ring 225.00

Wolverine pulling cart w/movable wheels carrying ring, Rogers & Bro......................... 300.00

NAUTICAL ITEMS

Cannon, ship's, for shooting line to shore, Coston Supply Co., 5" barrel, 41" l. $2,800.00

Deck watch, 21-jewel nickel lever movement, bi-metallic compensation balance, cam-wheel regulator, movement stamped "US NAVY BU Ships 1942," silvered matte dial w/Arabic numerals, subsidiary seconds & up-and-down indicator for 48 hours, mounted in gimballs, in two-tier mahogany box w/brass details, applied w/maker's plaque, Hamilton Watch Co., Lancaster, Pa., Model 22, ca. 1942, box 15 cm. w. ...2,420.00

Half-model of the schooner "Pilot" in a shadowbox frame, carved & painted wood on a seascape background w/stormy waves & distant ships, America, late 19th - early 20th c., overall 17½ x 23½" 1,072.50

Print, chromolithograph, "Palace Steamer Republic," identified in inscription beneath image, vessel identified on banner, bow, wheelhouse & sides, printed by Century Lithograph Company, Philadelphia, 19th - 20th c., framed, image 18¾ x 37½" 1,650.00

Sextant, ebony, labeled "Samuel Emery, maker, Water Street, Salem," w/ivory name plate inscribed "E. & Co W. Blunt," w/original case, 11½" h. 605.00

Ship model, bone, baleen & boxwood, model of a French man-of-war "L'Aurore," the finely fitted 52-gun ship w/planked deck, three boats in davits, a carved boxwood aft, the breakhead w/finely carved bone figurehead of a woman holding a wreath, w/copper-mounted hull, within a mahogany & glass case, the base inlaid & w/a plaque inscribed "L'Aurore," painted inventory number "L2561.47," France, early 19th c., ship 26½" l., case 30" l., 26" h. 12,100.00

Ship model, silver, model of a coastal freighter, the hull w/satin finish & oxidized polished band, this finish repeated on the funnel & upper deck details, accurately rendered w/windlasses, hatch covers, davits, lifeboats & fully rigged cargo booms, the front mast flying the flag of the line, the bow w/twin gilt anchors, the name of the ship inscribed in Japanese & English on the bow & stern "TOKIWASAN MARU," "MITSUI LINE" in English at mid-ship, on a stepped black lacquer base & within a matching vitrine, ca. 1930-35, Japan, ship 33½" l., stand 40¼" l., 3 pcs...........27,500.00

Ship's log, for the "Sarah Parker" of Portsmouth, Ichabod Goodwin, Master, entries from December 1820 to July 1831, voyages to New York, Mobile, Alabama & Liverpool, England, loose-leaf bound w/ribbon, 42 pp., 13 x 20" (some staining & paper loss) 247.50

NETSUKE

Ivory Netsuke of a Shishimai Dancer

These decorative toggles were used by the Japanese to secure an inro, tobacco pouch or other small personal article by means of a cord slipped through a kimono sash (obi). They are carved of ivory and other materials. There are many reproductions.

Figure of a boy standing holding a
	large daruma doll, ivory, 19th c. . . . $385.00
Figure of a cooper, inlaid wood,
	shown seated & working on the
	interior of a barrel, his head,
	hands & feet inlaid in ivory,
	signed "Yokosai," 19th c., 1" h. . . 1,540.00
Figure of Fukurokuju w/long head,
	w/turtle, signed 440.00
Figure of a monk w/a frog climbing
	on his back, ivory, 19th c. 385.00
Figure of a shishimai dancer, ivory,
	the dancer shown seated wearing
	a *shishi* mask, the mask w/inlaid
	eyes, deeply carved & stained
	details, unsigned, 18th c., age
	cracks, small chips, 2" h.
	(ILLUS.) 1,320.00
Figure group of Tenaga & Ashinaga,
	ivory, one standing long-legged
	figure holding the legs of the oth-
	er who bends down backward
	w/his long arms grasping the an-
	kles of the first, signed "Tomochi-
	ka," early 19th c., 2¾" h. 935.00
Figure group of two skeletons wres-
	tling, ivory, signed "Gyokosai,"
	19th c., 2¼" h. 880.00
Model of a chick coming out of an
	egg, ivory, inlaid eyes, signed
	"Shozan" 495.00
Model of a frog on a taro leaf,
	carved wood, Iwami School,
	signed "Seiyodo," 2¾" l. 11,000.00
Model of an octopus fighting a cat,
	ivory, signed "Masakazu," 19th c.,
	1" h. 1,540.00
Model of a recumbent boar, carved
	wood, inlaid eyes, signed "Ittan"
	w/*kakihan*, 19th c., 1¾" l. 7,150.00
Model of a seated puppy, carved
	wood, stained black, inlaid eyes,
	signed "Minko," 1 1/8" h. 660.00
Model of a snail & clam shell, bone,
	19th c., 1½" h. 165.00
Model of a squid, ivory, inlaid eyes,
	unsigned, 5" l. 3,575.00
Model of swan & her young, ivory,
	inlaid eyes, signed "Bisai"(?)
	w/*kakihan*, 20th c., 1½" h. 880.00
Model of a tapir, ivory, stylized ani-
	mal w/inlaid horn eyes, signed
	"Tadatoshi," crack, 2" l. 440.00
Model of water chestnuts & eels,
	ivory, signed "Gyokuhosai,"
	1¼" h. 137.50

NUTTING (Wallace) COLLECTIBLES

In 1898, Wallace Nutting published his first hand-tinted pictures and these were popular for more than 20 years. An "assembly line" subsequently colored and placed a signature and (sometimes) a title on the mat of these copyrighted photographs. Interior scenes featuring Early American furniture are considered the most desirable of these photographs.

Nutting's photographically illustrated travel books and early editions of his antiques reference books are also highly collectible.

BOOKS

"American Windsors," w/pages
	192a-d insert, 1917, first edition . . $104.50
"The Clock Book," second edition,
	1935 . . . . 55.00
"Furniture of the Pilgrim Century,"
	1924, 8½ x 11" 93.50
"Furniture Treasury," Vols. I, II & III,
	first edition, signed by Nutting . . . 176.00
"Ireland Beautiful," 1925, first
	edition 38.50
"Maine Beautiful," first edition 47.00
"New York Beautiful," 1927, first
	edition 30.00
"Pennsylvania Beautiful," first edi-
	tion, original dust jacket 50.00
"Virginia Beautiful," 1930, first edi-
	tion, signed by Nutting 93.50

PRINTS

(Framed unless otherwise noted)

Among Saffron Sails, 14 x 17", for-
	eign exterior scene, Italy 385.00
At the Fender, 13 x 16", interior
	scene 104.50
At the Well, Sorrento, 13 x 17", for-
	eign exterior scene w/children &
	adults, Italy. 577.50
Autumn Grotto, 16 x 20", exterior
	scene 77.00
Beech Borders, 9 x 11", foreign ex-
	terior, Ireland. 82.50
Best of the River (The), 11 x 14", ex-
	terior scene 132.00
Birch Bend, 16 x 20", exterior
	scene 110.00
Bit of Sewing (A), 14 x 17", interior
	scene 132.00
Blossoms by the Lake, 14 x 17", ex-
	terior scene 88.00
Boy's Joy (A), 8 x 10", exterior
	scene 44.00
Callers at the Squire's, 14 x 17", ex-
	terior scene 82.50
Call for More (A), 14 x 17", interior
	scene w/child. 577.50
Castle of St. Angelo, Rome (The),

10 x 12", foreign exterior scene, Italy 715.00

Cathedral Brook, 16 x 20", exterior scene 121.00

Coachford Bridge (A), 13 x 16", foreign exterior scene, Ireland 110.00

Comfort and a Cat, 12 x 15", interior scene w/cat.................. 286.00

Corner in China (A), 11 x 14", interior scene...................... 77.00

Dainty China, 14 x 17", interior scene 60.50

Dell Dale Road, 16 x 20", exterior scene 110.00

Dim Old Forest (The), 16 x 20", foreign exterior scene, Ireland 121.00

Distinction, 13 x 16", flowers in a vase 742.50

Dixville Shadows, 13 x 16", exterior scene 60.50

Elaborate Dinner (An), 14 x 17", interior scene 132.00

Eventful Journey (An), 14 x 17", exterior scene 577.50

Four O'Clock, 12 x 16", exterior scene w/cows 687.50

Gettysburg Crossing (A), 12 x 16", exterior scene 132.00

Golden Birches, 14 x 17", exterior scene 77.00

Grafton Windings, 15 x 22", exterior scene 176.00

Guardian Mother (The), interior scene, girl & mother in white flowing dresses (this picture is a reverse, girl is on left vs. right because the picture was developed w/the negative reversed), 9 x 14" 2,600.00

Guardian of the Road (The), 10 x 12", exterior scene in Oregon 176.00

Hall at Orvis Cottage, 13 x 16", black & white interior scene...... 220.00

Harpsicord (The), 11 x 17", interior scene 154.00

Isaac Walton Brook (The), 13 x 16", foreign exterior scene, England .. 143.00

Italian Spring (The), 10 x 14", foreign exterior scene, Italy 77.00

Jersey Blossoms, 11 x 14", exterior scene 71.50

Killarney Castle & Cove (A), 10 x 16", foreign exterior scene, Ireland 143.00

Knocking, 12 x 15", exterior scene, early pencil signature 418.00

Leanto Room, Goulding House, 12 x 16", black & white interior scene, signed by Nutting........ 286.00

Little River and Mt. Washington (A), 12 x 16", exterior scene 49.50

Long Island Shore, 7 x 11", exterior scene 187.00

Lorna Doone Brook, 10 x 12", foreign exterior scene, England 82.50

Manchester Battenkill (The), 16 x 20", exterior scene 82.50

Nest (The), 16 x 20", foreign exterior scene, England 286.00

Old Colony Home Room (An), 14 x 17", interior scene 187.00

Orchard Heights, 14 x 17", exterior scene 71.50

Pasture Dell (The), 13 x 15", exterior scene w/cows, early pencil signature 907.50

Rhode Island Coast (The), 9 x 18", exterior scene 522.50

Rhododendron Garden (A), 12 x 16", foreign exterior scene, Ireland ... 143.00

Rivals, 11 x 14", foreign exterior scene w/men, Italy 286.00

Rock Creek Banks, 9 x 12", exterior scene 87.50

Rock Creek Drive, 11 x 14", exterior scene 93.50

Sheltered Road (A), 11 x 17", exterior scene...................... 88.00

Sisters (The), 12 x 15", exterior scene w/girls on a porch, early pencil signature.................. 550.00

Spinnet Corner (The), 10 x 12", interior scene 132.00

Sunday Afternoon in the Old Home, 14 x 17", interior scene w/elderly lady & man 286.00

Unbroken Flow (The), 16 x 20", exterior scene 55.00

Vines & Thatch, 6 x 8", foreign exterior scene, Holland 187.00

Warm Spring Day (A), 10 x 16", exterior scene w/sheep 176.00

Wavering Footsteps, 13 x 16", exterior scene w/child 308.00

What a Beauty, 14 x 17", interior scene 143.00

Where Grandma Was Wed, 15 x 18", exterior scene 154.00

Whirling Candlestand (The), 13 x 15", interior scene.......... 121.00

Young River (A), 13 x 16", exterior scene 49.50

MISCELLANEOUS ITEMS

Envelope, for Nutting's publishing company, the "Old America Company," framed, 8 x 11" 15.00

Greeting card, interior scene at top of a girl looking into a mirror, a five-line verse below, 5 x 8" 231.00

Mirror, wall-type, w/an exterior blossom scene at the top, 8 x 28".......................... 220.00

Silhouette, "Girl on Iron Fence," 7 x 8".......................... 49.50

OCCUPIED JAPAN

American troops occupied the country of Japan from September 2, 1945, until April 28, 1952, following World War II. All wares made for export during this period were required to be marked "Made in Occupied Japan." Now these items, mostly small ceramic and metal trifles of varying quality, are sought out by a growing number of collectors.

Boxes, cov., bisque, one depicting a lady in a swing, the other a man in a garden, 7½" oval, pr. $120.00
Figure of a boy dressed as a cowboy w/gun drawn, china, matte finish, 6" h. 35.00
Figure of a clown, china, 6" h. 18.00
Figure, Cupid banjo player, bisque, 5½" h. 30.00
Figure, Hummel-style boy w/dog, porcelain, 5" h. 25.00
Figures, shepherd & shepherdess, bisque, 13" h., pr. 350.00
Lamp, table-model, figural bisque base w/Mary & her lamb, painted trim, 7" h. 95.00
Toy, windup tin, man playing xylophone 60.00
Trinket box, metal, model of a piano 20.00
Vases, figural, one with a standing Napoleonic gentleman beside a scrolly vase, the other w/a matching lady beside the vase, 8 x 10", pr. 200.00
Wall plaque, bisque, figural Colonial man in relief, 4½ x 6¾". 14.00

OFFICE EQUIPMENT

Early Merritt Typewriter

By the late 19th century business offices around the country were becoming increasingly mechanized as inventions such as the typewriter, adding machine, mimeograph and dictaphone became more widely available. Miracles of efficiency when introduced, in today's computerized offices these machines would be cumbersome and archaic. Although difficult to display and store, many of these relics are becoming increasingly collectible today.

Adding machine, "Dalton," w/beveled glass on all sides, 1912 patent $90.00
Calculator, "Monroe," electric semi-automatic, ca. 1930's 50.00
Check protector, metal w/walnut handle, "Chicago Check Protector," handle selects symbols, working condition 54.00
Handstamp holder, revolving-type, cast iron, fancy 65.00
Pencil sharpener, cast iron, "Webster," ca. 1892 . . . . 175.00
Safe, floor model, green ground w/decorative designs, decorated interior, marked "Hall Safe Co., Cincinnati, Ohio," patent dates of 1867, 1873 & 1878, 20 x 22", 35" h. 850.00
Typewriter, "Merritt," keyless model on rectangular wooden base (ILLUS.). 797.50
Typewriter, "L.C. Smith & Bros. No. 3," decals in good condition . . 45.00

Silver Smith Corona Typewriter

Typewriter, "Smith & Corona," encased in silver, the metal-rimmed keys including playing card suits, all centered by the Smith Corona emblem of a flying nude above the keys, engraved "L.C. Smith & Corona Typewriters Inc." below the keys, silver by Gorham Mfg. Co., Providence, Rhode Island, ca. 1930, overall 13½" l. (ILLUS.) 5,500.00

OPERA GLASSES, LORGNETTES & EYEGLASSES

Lorgnette, 14k gold, Art Nouveau style, oblong case w/ornate chased floral scrolls, monogrammed at the center, marked "Krementz" (ILLUS. top next column) $880.00
Lorgnette, 14k yellow gold, Art Nouveau style, scrolling design ac-

Art Nouveau Gold Lorgnette

cented by a faceted amethyst,
monogrammed 1,430.00
Lorgnette, platinum & diamond, Art
Deco style, rectangular frame
w/beveled corners, set w/rose-
cut diamond & diamond & black
enamel barrel slides completed
by a black cord, rose-cut diamond handle, signed "Cartier" on
bail 3,850.00

Edwardian Lorgnette

Lorgnette, platinum & diamond, Edwardian, diamond-set pierced
handle suspended from a collet-
set diamond & platinum chain,
England, early 20th c. (ILLUS.) ...1,980.00
Lorgnette, silver plate, floral engraved frame & a long spiral-
molded handle w/loop end,
19th c., 9½" l. closed............ 209.00
Lorgnette, sterling silver, folding-
type, openwork case w/marca-
sites, black velvet ribbon 85.00
Opera glasses, mother-of-pearl, gilt
& ebonized brass, the sides decorated w/panels of mother-of-
pearl, marked "Lemaire Fabt.
Paris," w/case 55.00
Opera glasses w/telescoping handle, gilt-metal w/inset abalone
shell, labels of maker & seller,

"Colmont, Paris" & "Leo Landro,
Indianapolis," w/drawstring
pouch 220.00

PAPER COLLECTIBLES

"Concord Grape" Broadside

*Also see CHARACTER COLLECTI-
BLES, FIRE FIGHTING COLLECTI-
BLES, FRATERNAL ORDER ITEMS,
MAGAZINES, MUCHA ARTWORK, PA-
PER DOLLS, POLITICAL ITEMS, RA-
DIOS, ROYCROFT ITEMS, SIGNS &
SIGNBOARDS, STEAMSHIP COLLECT-
IBLES and WORLD'S FAIR COL-
LECTIBLES.*

Admission ticket, U.S. Senate, to
the Impeachment of President Andrew Johnson, for the Gallery,
accompanied by a letter from
George H. French relating to it,
ticket dated April 14, 1868, letter
dated March 9, 1914, 2 pcs. $160.00
Bank note, National Bank of City of
New York, $1.00, 1918........... 28.00
Booklet, "Rose Parade," 1939,
Shirley Temple as Grand Marshall 30.00
Broadside, "The Concord Grape,"
promoting the growing of these
grapes, printed by B. Tolman,
Concord, Massachusetts, 1856,
staining, small tears & losses
along margins, glued down
corners, framed, 14½ x 20"
(ILLUS.)........................ 522.50
Broadside, concerning the Continental Congress, headlined "The following extracts from the votes
and proceedings of the American
Continental Congress we are in-
duced to publish early purely to
ease the impatience of our read-

ers. Association & C.," printed by
T.J. Fleet, Boston, 1774, framed,
9¾ x 15½" (discoloration, tears,
loss)...........................3,025.00

Broadside, stagecoach-related,
"North Danvers and Salem
Coach...," provides schedule of
the coach runs, printed by the
Salem Gazette Press (Massachusetts), dated July 20, 1849,
matted & framed, 8½ x 11"...... 275.00

Early Calligraphic Drawing

Calligraphic drawing, pen & ink on
paper, a large spread-winged eagle w/banner above the inscription "Designed and Executed by
H.G. Moore," New York, 19th c.,
framed, 26 x 39" (ILLUS.) 1,430.00

Cut-out picture, free-hand design of
rectangular outline w/pairs of
small birds & peafowl flanking a
central block surrounding pairs of
facing chickens & small birds in
leafy branches, on faded black
paper backing, 19th c., framed,
11½ x 13½"..................... 82.50

Estate appraisal, Enoch Womble estate, 98 entries, 26 slaves by
name, sex, color & value, Georgia, 1848, 7½ x 12½", 2 pp. 170.00

Exercise book, self-cover lettered
"Abigail Thayer's Cyphering Book,
began December 19th, 1820,"
neatly done in pen & ink but no
decoration, 30 pages w/no cover,
empty holes for thread stitching
at fold, 7¼ x 12" 35.00

Funeral poem, printed on rag paper,
titled "A Poem - Composed on the
sudden and surprising death of
Mr. Allen Merrells, who was
kill'd at the raising of a Meeting-
House in Farmington, July 1771,"
New England, late 18th c., unframed, discoloration, losses,
9½ x 11¼" 1,320.00

Land grant, Wind River Indian Reser-
vation, Wyoming, issued to
Sitting-in-the-Middle, w/a proxy

signature of President Theodore
Roosevelt, 1907 .... 80.00

Legal document, "Hire of Negroes,"
Dixon Plantation, Talbot County,
Georgia, 88 named slaves,
1857-58, 8 x 13"................ 210.00

Military commission, engraved Ohio
militia commission signed by
Thomas Worthington & dated
"1818," framed, 8½ x 12½" (dam-
age, paper tape repair, stains) ... 220.00

Military order of The Royal Legion of
the United States, to Brevet Major
George Henry French, as a Companion of the First Class, signed
by Beneroff Eherardis, Commander in Chief & John P. Nicholson,
Recorder in Chief, dated May 3,
1899, together w/related letters &
ephemera, unframed, the group .. 170.00

Mining prospectus, "Tres Amigos
Mining Company," complete
w/photographs & maps, 1904..... 60.00

Newspaper, "Boston Globe," August
14, 1945, "Japs Surrender"
headline 30.00

Newspaper, "Times Weekly Edition,"
London, January-June 1921, advertisements, Empire news, etc.,
six months bound, 512 pp. 43.00

Newspapers, "New Hampshire Sen-
tinel," April 16 & 23, 1863, Civil
War news, 2 pcs. 32.00

Paper money, South Carolina, frac-
tional currency, $.50, 1863 .... 7.00

Playbill, "Banjo Eyes," starring Eddie
Cantor, March 15, 1942 .... 20.00

Program, "Kentucky Derby," 1936,
winner Bold Venture 25.00

Slave document, acknowledgement
of receipt of one negro girl
named Kole, assigns forever the
rights & title to the said negro,
etc., Southhampton County, Virginia, brown ink on parchment
paper, 1784, 7 x 7¼"............ 180.00

Slave document, from estate of
Ephram Northern, 250 entries,
names five slaves w/values,
Georgia, 1829, 8 x 12", 6 pp...... 136.00

Stock certificate, "Lawrence & Topeka Coal Mining Company of Kansas," 1872 .... 186.00

Stock certificate, "Leavenworth &
White Oaks Gold Mining Co.,"
New Mexico Territory, 1882 ...... 127.00

Stock certificate, "Miner Boy Mining
Company," Colorado, 1881 .... 85.00

Theatre program, "Follow the Girls,"
w/Jackie Gleason & Gertrude
Niesen, 1944, 14 pp............. 15.00

Special Focus: Paper Collectibles

A Pack of Fun!
Collecting Playing Card Decks

by Ray Hartz

Imagine some early Caribbean natives strolling along the beach and finding some strange, tiny playing cards washed up with the surf. These would be the first imported playing cards to arrive in the Americas. Legend has it that crew members of Christopher Columbus' flotilla had encountered violent weather crossing the Atlantic in 1492, and the weather was blamed on an angry God who didn't like them playing with the tools of the devil (playing cards fashioned from leaves). To pacify God, they tossed the cards overboard.

Playing cards were considered works of the devil or a great boon to the common classes depending on your station in life. The very earliest cards were hand-painted little works of art made for the nobility, but with the advent of the printing press, playing cards became affordable to the common people.

The clergy felt that cards were the work of the devil because they often involved gambling or mysticism (tarot) which the church felt went against their teachings. Recorded history tells us that many a deck of cards was burned by religious zealots well before witches were burned.

The kings, princes and landlords felt cards were evil for commoners (but, of course, not their class) because they turned their peasants away from hard work to idleness. Peasants and common people thought they were a great form of relaxation after a day of toiling from sunrise to sunset. Early class struggle!

Probably the very early U.S. settlers didn't do much importing of playing cards because of religious admonitions against them, but our later colonists did bring or import cards, mostly from England. The American playing card manufacturing industry didn't get es-

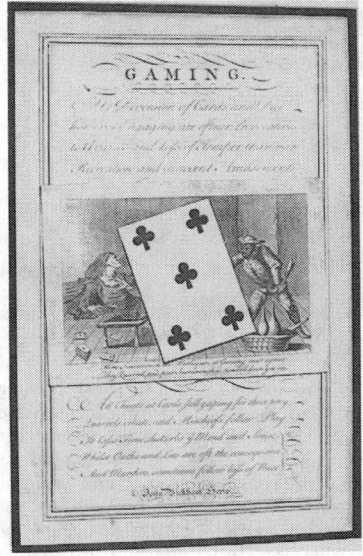

Framed warning against evils of gaming, ca. 1750.

tablished until the late 1700's, in Philadelphia and Massachusetts. Records show that Jazaniah Ford and Amos Whitney made playing cards in Massachusetts starting in the 1790's, and at about the same time playing cards were being produced in Philadelphia by others, followed shortly thereafter by New York City in the early 1800's.

But enough about the history of playing cards. As a collector, you should know that there have been American cards found which date back to the early 1800's but which are very rare and difficult to locate. You should also know that there were many ancillary uses for playing cards: advertising, souvenirs, games, artwork, fortune telling, history, political and celebrating war victories, to name some of the most popular areas of interest.

Collectors may find collectible playing card decks stuffed away in a "junk" drawer at home, in grandma's attic, at garage sales, flea markets, antiques shows and shops, auctions and collector clubs.

American decks will be found most often but don't limit your field of interest to only American decks. The foreign decks produced have been some of the most beautiful ever made. Their quality, artistry and imaginative work have seldom been excelled. You're into another more difficult ballgame when dealing with foreign cards, so beware of cards which are beautiful, which appear old, but which have been made in recent years. Check current catalogs or store offerings to see what's available new.

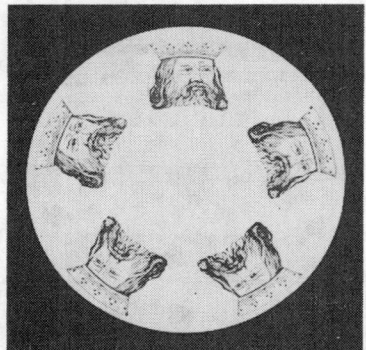

Round deck, I.N. Richardson, Boston, 1874.

Only a very experienced dealer or advanced collector can help with valuing foreign decks and sometimes they are stumped. It often comes down to a buyer and seller guessing at a fair market price. Sometimes you guess right, sometimes you don't. With my years of collecting experience, I still occasionally make mistakes, but I charge it up to educational expense. I learn quickly when it hits my pocketbook!

There *are* some methods to help identify, approximately date and, hardest of all, value your decks. Hopefully *The Antique Trader Price Guide* and this article will provide valuable practical assistance to you as a collector or dealer.

Playing card values have been soaring in recent years, but the hobby is really still in its infancy. It's a hobby where we hope most collectors will participate not because of the monetary return but because of the pleasure derived. However, it's nice to know that an outlay of funds for the purchase of cards is like putting money in the bank or a good investment vehicle with an excellent apprecia-

tion rate realized when you dispose of a duplicate or unwanted deck.

What should you look for when examining playing card decks? Study the following:

1. *Box or container.* As a general rule, the very earliest cards produced used wrappers rather than boxes, so many of the early decks are found with no box or container. The wrappers were fragile and did not often survive. Now, don't think that old-looking decks are antique and rare if you find the decks with no box. You'll often find decks, and rather common decks, missing their boxes. Many older, more valuable cards came in hard slipcases and these cases did a good job of preserving and protecting the cards.

Check the exterior of the box or container for valuable information about the deck name, manufacturer, place manufactured and date. Watch for mis-matched boxes as often cards get placed in a box which is not original to the deck. The condition of the box will affect the collector value and if it is missing may lower the value appreciably unless it was a very early deck which used wrappers.

2. *Tax stamps or seals.* Check the box or inner-wrapper for signs of a tax stamp. There may only be a portion of the stamp remaining but examine it closely for type of stamp, cancellation date, company initials, all of which will help in identifying the manufacturer and year of distribution. Check stamp collecting catalogs to further identify stamps, if interested. These revenue stamps are another area of specialization for some playing card collectors. The early makers used proprietary stamps which are very interesting. Foreign decks often used tax stamps on one of the playing cards. This is a field which requires special expertise and research but is very valuable in pinpointing age and value for some foreign decks.

Following is a listing of U.S. playing card revenue tax stamps from their inception in 1862 to 1965 when tax stamps were discontinued (Scott R2, R11, R12, R17, R21, R28 and Proprietary stamps RU1-RU16):

1862-1871　George Washington portrait with U.S. Inter. Rev. on top and Playing Cards at bottom, 1c, 2c, 3c, 4c, 5c.

1871-1883　Washington portrait in black with blue border, revenue stamp with no special mention of playing cards.

1883-1894　No tax.

1894-1918　Act of Aug. 1894, 2c stamp and this is a common stamp.

1918-1922　Vertical long blue stamps, "Class A" in center.

1922-1924　Small rectangular blue, "Class A" in center.

1924-1929   Small rectangular blue, "10 Cents" in center.

1929-1940   Long horizontal blue, "10 Cents" in center.

1940-1940   Small rectangular blue, "1 Pack" in center.

1940-1965   Long horizontal blue, "1 Pack" in center.

1965   Tax abolished. Some companies continued to make a stamp which acted as a seal for the deck.

The U.S. Playing Card Company uses a coding system at the bottom of their ace of spades. This letter code is only valid if followed by four numbers (ex: H4259). See the accompanying chart.

Letter Code System Used on the Ace of Spades

A	1920	1940	1960	1980	
B	1921	1976			
C	1922	1941	1961	1981	
D	1942	1962	1982		
E	1923	1943	1963	1983	
F	1924	1944	1964	1984	
G	1904	1925	1945	1965	1985
H	1905	1926	1946	1966	1986
J	1906	1927	1947	1967	1987
K	1907	1928	1948	1968	1988
L	1908	1929	1949	1969	1989
M	1909	1930	1950	1970	1990
N	1910				
P	1911	1931	1951	1971	1991
R	1912	1932	1952	1972	1992
S	1913	1933	1953	1973	
T	1914	1934	1954	1974	
U	1915	1935	1955	1975	
W	1916	1936	1956		
X	1917	1937	1957	1977	
Y	1918	1938	1958	1978	
Z	1919	1939	1959	1979	

To use this coding, you must have a rough idea of the age of the deck, but you can often tell a 1951 deck from a 1931 deck using tax stamps or other identifying means.

These methods of determining the age of a deck are only rough methods. Because the tax stamp did not have to be affixed until the deck was distributed, the year of manufacture as indicated by a letter code or by research may differ from the year of distribution. The affixed tax stamp may date years later than the deck. That's why you may find a deck with a 1940 tax stamp but codings or research tell you the deck was manufactured around 1900.

3. *Card design.* Square corners indicate probability of an older deck, pre-1880. In the 1880's manufacturers started to round off the corners of decks.

Faro casekeeper used for counting in game of Faro, with early Steamboat decks, late 1800's.

One-way or *one-headed* court cards were also mostly pre-1880 although some continued to be manufactured for Faro into the 1920's. Some *two-way* or *two-headed* court cards were made as early as the mid-1800's but as a general rule they didn't come into more accepted usage until the 1880's.

Non-indiced cards were also a pre-1880's feature. Indiced decks first appeared in 1875. These indices are numbers or letters showing the value of a card or the court card name in the corners of the card. This way they could be read easily without spreading your hand out to see the entire card. The smaller the number or letter, the earlier the deck.

Some manufacturers used miniature cards in the corner (Dougherty) which were called "Triplicates," and a rival company (NY Consolidated Card Co.), used numbers and called them "Squeezers," which became the industry standard.

4. *Paper stock.* The type of paper used in the manufacture of cards is an indicator of age. Early paper stock was more coarse and not polished. Polishing of the paper gave an appearance of a coated paper, followed by papers which actually were plastic-coated. Some cards were made of different materials: metal, aluminum and celluloid to name a few, but there were also cards individually handmade out of bone, leather, and other materials. Linen was used as a supplement in the manufacture of card paper from roughly 1910 to 1940, and the linen strands can be seen if the cards are examined closely. Some companies continued the use of linen even beyond 1940 but the costs were high.

5. *Printing techniques.* The type of printing and coloring is an indicator of age. Hand-

Jeu de Drapeaux (Game of Flags), French, late 1800's reprint of 1815 deck made in honor of Napoleon, hand-tinted.

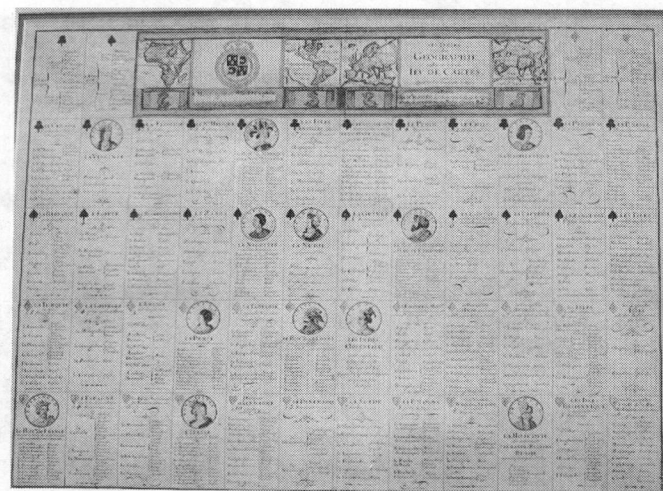

Framed sheet of geographical cards, hand-tinted, made ca. 1690.

Second Empire pack. French transformation deck, ca. 1860, hand-tinted, oversize card, Very rare.

painted cards came first but won't be found by collectors unless they frequent Sotheby's or Christie's auction houses. They were followed by wood-block printing and hand-coloring, copper and steel engraving, color by stenciling, and lithography.

6. *Ace of spades or other identifying card.* For American decks, always look for the ace of spades first when examining a deck. This is usually the key card which may show the name of the deck, the manufacturer and place of manufacture. Using this information and reference material on the design of the ace of spades will help to identify the deck.

Foreign cards placed identifying information on individual cards, varying by the manufacturer and country. Check all cards in the deck for information.

7. *Court cards.* The court cards (three or sometimes four cards in foreign decks depicting royalty) help to identify a deck when using various reference material. The courts are often beautiful and imaginative in design in some U.S. decks and many foreign decks, but card players are a conservative lot and don't especially like anyone to mess with their card designs because they feel it will change their luck. Many a new design has fallen by the wayside because of a lack of acceptance by customers.

8. *Jokers.* The 1870's produced many innovations in card design and the addition of a joker to decks was an important one. Some card collectors specialize in collecting jokers only, much to the chagrin of deck collectors who look for complete decks and often find the jokers missing. Jokers were more often not missing because they were removed by a joker collector but because they probably were tossed or removed and lost by a prior owner since their card games didn't require a joker.

A missing joker will lower the value of a deck, sometimes substantially if the joker is particularly interesting. An unusual railroad joker with black interest recently sold for $215 in an auction, Yes, folks, that's one card, the joker alone!

9. *Non-standard decks.* Most collectors look for playing card decks which have some type of obverse "face" interest and not just reverse or "back" interest. Other than truly early, antique decks, they seek cards with interesting court cards, nice aces of spades and, if an advertising deck, it should possibly have advertising on the ace of spades, joker, or other cards in the deck. Other interesting decks are pin-ups, tobacco insert

cards, tarot decks, souvenir and expo decks with photographs on each card, entertainment decks, and war cards.

10. *Suit signs.* We're all familiar with French suit signs, the standard *spades, hearts, clubs* and *diamonds* found in most U.S. decks. Foreign decks may use different signs, unique to their area or country. In Germanic countries the suit signs are *bell, acorn, leaf* and *heart*; in Spain and Italy the suit signs are *baton, cup, coin* and *sword*. Other decks have been made with innovative suit signs but they are usually short-lived and become collector items!

11. *Condition.* As in the real estate market which recommends three items to consider when purchasing a home: location, location, and location; with old and unusual collectible playing cards it's condition, condition, and condition.

Reference material recommended:

Encyclopedia of American Playing Cards, Hochman, 6 vols, soft-cover, 1976-1982. The Bible for American deck collectors.

Playing Cards of the Fournier Museum, Vol. 1, Fournier, Vitoria, Spain, 1982. Valuable for identifying foreign decks.

Cary Collection of Playing Cards, 4 vols, Keller, Yale University Library, New Haven, 1981. Excellent, expensive set for identifying worldwide cards.

Scott Specialized Catalog of U.S. Stamps, Scott Publ. Co, Sidney, OH. Reference for U.S. revenue playing card stamps.

Playing card collector clubs:

52 Plus Joker, The American Antique Deck Collector's Club, Ray Hartz, President, P.O. Box 1002, Westerville, OH 43081, Phone: (614) 891-6296. Write or call for information. Club was founded 1985 and has over 350 members worldwide. Furnish quarterly publication, member directory, several auctions yearly, conventions and free appraisals for members.

International Playing Card Society, 188 Sheen Lane, East Sheen, London SW14 8LF, England. Founded in 1972, international in scope, heavily into research and learned articles about playing cards.

ABOUT THE AUTHOR: Ray Hartz has been a playing card collector for over 10 years, a member of 52 Plus Joker since 1986, current president and past secretary/treasurer. He is also a member of the International Playing Card Society. Ray has addressed collector clubs in central Ohio on the subject of playing cards and is knowledgeable about U.S. and European playing cards. Above is a shot of the author in his "hunting outfit."

Price Listings:

The following prices are a composite of recent sales and auctions for the more "findable" playing card decks. Decks listed are complete with original boxes and no serious defects. Condition is excellent showing only light wear. For decks in better or worse condition substantial adjustments may be necessary. Mint decks may be 25-75% higher, rough decks 25-75% lower. Missing jokers or original boxes may reduce value 25% or more. The more rare the deck, the less important condition is to the value, and even a missing card or two for an important deck will not deter a collector. Collectors would like to find all their decks in "mint condition," but we have to be realistic when it comes to rare material. The mint condition mid-1880's rare deck may command a price in the thousands. On the other hand, age alone does not determine rarity or value to a collector. Decks from the turn of the century which are standard and not rare or highly collectible may be worth very little.

The following listings indicate the deck name, manufacturer, date, type of deck or design, and the number of cards and joker. "EC" means "extra card."

Bijou #1, USPC, ca. 1930, plaid back with coat of arms, includes extra cards, 11 & 12 for game of 500, 60+J (Not Illus.) 41.00

Blue Spade, Hanzel, 1925, non-revoke deck with blue spades, yellow diamonds and green clubs, unique courts, 52+J (Not Illus.) . . 111.00

Airplane Spotter, USPC, 1943,
plane silhouettes, 52+J+EC 25.00

American Airlines DH-4, USPC,
1972, standard, 52+JJ 7.00

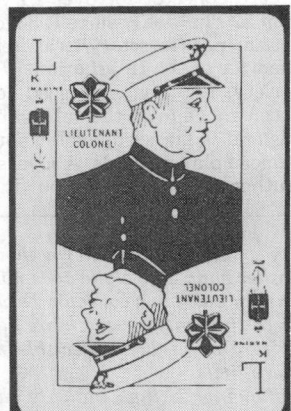

Anma, Anma Co., 1941, military
caricature courts, 52+Chief 50.00

Buster Brown, USPC, 1906, miniature, advertising, cartoons on
each card are based on comic
characters, 52+J (Not Illus.) 61.00

Harlequin by Tiffany & Co., Car-
ryl, 1879, transformation, 52+J
(Not Illus.).................... 935.00

Apollo, Nat'l Card Co., 1890,
52+J 50.00

Bicycle #808, USPC Co., 1895,
Wheel #1, 52+J................. 35.00

Cabinet, Russell & Morgan Ptg. Co.,
1890, 52+J 100.00

California, Rieder, 1911, souvenir
photos each card, 52+J 30.00

Coke, Brown & Bigelow, 1943,
advertising, girl & leaves,
52+J+EC 75.00

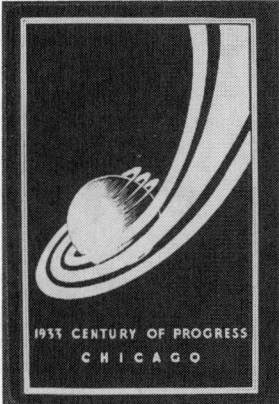

Century of Progress, WPCC, 1933,
photos, narrow, 52+J+EC 12.00

Columbian Exposition, Winters,
1893, drawn pictures, 52+J+EC .. 100.00

Cheer-up, Stancraft, 1960, hospital
cartoons, common, 52+JJ 5.00

Congress, USPC Co., 1947, narrow,
Minnehaha, 52+J 8.00

C & O, USPC, 1900, railroad, photos each card, 52+J 60.00

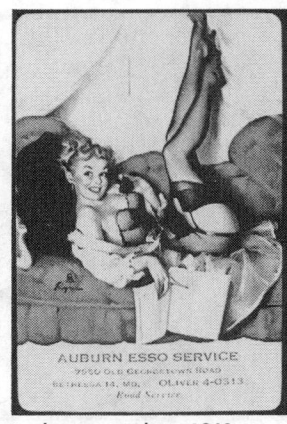

Elvgren, unknown maker, 1960, narrow, pin-up, girl on couch, 52+J 20.00

Cunard Line, Forman & Sons, 1900, steamship, 52+J 60.00

Excelsior, Dougherty Co., 1860, square corners, no indices, 52 . . . . 300.00

Double Action, Double Action Co., 1935, unusual, 52+J 35.00

Hunt & Sons, England, 1830, no indices, one-way courts, square cornered, 52 complete, no box (Not Illus.) 160.00

Flickers, Creative, 1974, photos movie stars, 52+JJ 12.00

Jack Daniel's, ca. 1970, advertising, unique design & courts (Not Illus.) 6.00

Florida E. Coast, Interstate, 1920, photos, common, 52+J 10.00

Fortune Telling, Whitman, 1931, 36+rules complete 6.00

Four Seasons, Piatnik, Austria, 1900, 32 complete 40.00

Franklin Cigars, unknown maker, 1900, advertising, gold edges, 52+J+EC 60.00

Grand Imperial Sec, USPC, 1900, wine advertising, 52+J+EC 60.00

Great Southwest, Harvey, 1901, photos, Indians, 52+J+EC 60.00

Mlle. Le Normand Fortune Telling, United Novelty, early 1900's, miniature, fortunes on each card along with miniature playing cards, 36+booklet complete (Not Illus.) 20.00

Hustling Joe, USPC Co., 1895,
semi-transformation, 52+J 600.00

Kem, Kem Co., 1950, narrow,
leaves on back, 52+JJ X2
double 6.00

Inca, Brown & Bigelow, 1948, original designs, 52+JJ 25.00

Kennedy Kards, Humor House,
1963, caricature courts, 52+JJ . . . 15.00

Jeu Louis XV, Grimaud, France,
1890, 52+EC 90.00
New York World's Fair, 1964-65,
color drawings of fair on each
card, 52+JJ (Not Illus.) 9.00

Nation's Capital, USPC, 1922, photos each card, 52+J+EC 40.00
Olea, Spanish, ca. 1900, Spanish
suits, square corners, 48 complete
(Not Illus.) 51.00

Ocean To Ocean, Goodall, Canada, photos each card, 52+JJ 35.00

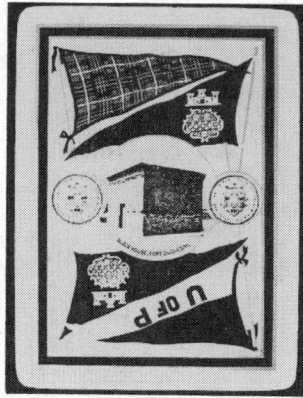

Pittsburgh, USPC, 1905, souvenir photos each card, 52+J 40.00

Panama, USPC, 1923, photos, fairly uncommon, 52+J+EC 50.00

Politicards, Politicard Co., 1971, caricature courts, 52+JJ 15.00

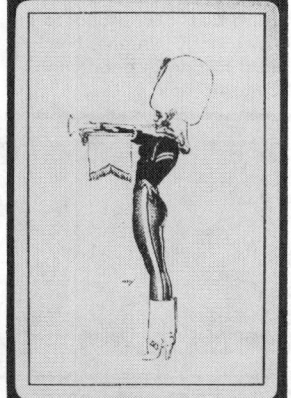

Petty, unknown maker, 1960, narrow, pin-up, girl with bugle, 52+J 20.00

Rhode Island, USPC, 1910, photos of the state on each card, 52+J+EC (Not Illus.) 77.00

Rockwell Int'l, 1980, original advertising and aerospace interest, 52+JJ 20.00

Van Camp's, ca. 1911, advertising deck with colorful back, unusual ace of spades and joker, 52+J (Not Illus.)...................... 73.00

Rubberset, unknown maker, 1920, advertising, 52 (missing joker)....   25.00

Tarot, DeLawrence, 1950, 78 cards complete, oversize 35.00

Stage #65X, USPC, 1908, photos stage stars, 52+J 90.00

Trumps Long Cut, 1886, tobacco insert, drawn early pin-ups, black back, hard to find in good condition, 52+J, no box 500.00

Swiss Costumes #174, Dondorf, Germany, 1906, 52+J 75.00

Vargas Girls, Stancraft, 1953, different pin-up color drawings each card, 52+J+info card (Not Illus.) 100.00

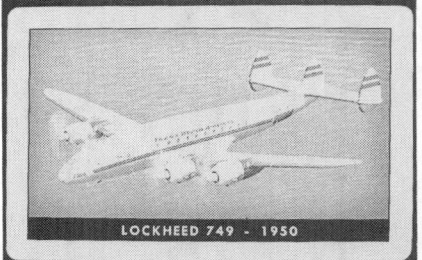

TWA Lockheed 749, USPC, 1970, standard, 52+JJ 4.00

Murphy Varnish, Dougherty, 1883, unique advertising/transformation deck, drawing each card, one of the most sought-after decks, 52+J (Not Illus.) 3,000.00

Victory, Arrco, 1945, unique patriotic courts, 52+JJ 60.00

Yellowstone, Haynes, 1925, photos, narrow, common, 52+J 15.00

(End of Special Focus)

PAPER DOLLS

(Also see CHARACTER COLLECTIBLES category.)

Advertising, "Clark's O.N.T. Thread," 'Minuet Series,' cut, nine dolls & a piano, ca. 1890's, the set $95.00

Advertising, "Mayer Shoes," Japanese girl w/separate kimono, 3" h. 15.00

"Air Hostess," uncut book, Saalfield, 1947 . . . .   29.50

Angela Cartwright, from "The Danny Thomas Show," boxed set, five dolls & 42 outfits, Transogram No. 4101, 1961 . . . .   85.00

"Baby Brother & Sister," uncut book, Whitman, 1958 . . . .   28.00

Bam Bam (Flintstones), uncut book, 1970, 12" h. 38.00

"Betty Bonnett's Brother Bob," uncut page, *Ladies' Home Journal*, 1917 . . . .   20.00

"Diane and Daphne, The Round About Dolls," uncut book, McLoughlin Bros., 1933 . . . .   45.00

Dionne Quintuplets, uncut book, Merrill Publishing No. 3488, 1935 . . . .   175.00

Doris Day, uncut book, Whitman No. 1179, 1954 . . . .   75.00

"Dresses Worn by the First Ladies," uncut, Saalfield, 1939 . . . .   85.00

Elsie Ferguson, uncut page, "Percy Reeves Movy-Dols," *Photoplay Magazine*, w/three outfits, 1919 . .   35.00

"Gulliver's Travels," uncut book, movie edition, Saalfield No. 1261, 1929 . . . . 150.00 to 200.00

Hedy Lamarr, uncut book, Saalfield No. 2600, 1951 . . . .   225.00

May Allison, uncut page, "Percy Reeves Movy-Dols," *Photoplay Magazine*, w/three outfits, 1919 . .   35.00

"My Twin Babies," uncut book, Whitman No. 970, 1940 . . . .   45.00

Norma Talmadge, uncut page, "Percy Reeves Movy-Dols," *Photoplay Magazine*, w/three outfits, 1919 . .   50.00

"Paper Dolls & Paper Toys of Raphael Tuck," uncut, Jendrick, 1970 . . . .   30.00

Partridge Family, uncut book, Artcraft No. 5137, 1971 . . . .   38.00

"Pert & Pretty," uncut, Merrill No. 1552, 1948 . . . .   95.00

"Pinocchio," uncut book, Walt Disney Productions, Whitman No. 6879, 1939 . . . .   275.00

Shirley Temple, uncut book, Saalfield No. 4420, 1959, 18" h. 40.00

"Sunny & Sue," uncut book, Abbot Publishing, ca. 1950's 28.00

"That Girl" (Marlo Thomas), uncut book, Saalfield No. 6066, 1967 . . . .   35.00

"The Twins," uncut book, Queen Holden, 1932 . . . .   40.00

"Wedding Party," uncut book, Saalfield, 1951 . . . .   30.00

"Welcome Back Kotter," uncut box, Toy Factory No. 106, 1976 . . . .   30.00

PAPERWEIGHTS

Advertising, lead, "Baltimore Polytechnic Institute," depicts drafting tools, embossed, dated 1889 . . . . . $20.00

Advertising, cast iron, "Wisconsin

Oxygen Hydrogen Co.," model of
an oxygen tank, early, 6" h. 45.00
Baccarat "Garlanded Double Clema-
tis" weight, clear glass set w/a
flower composed of two rows of
five red-ribbed & pointed petals
about a red & white stardust stamen, growing from a curved
green stem w/three leaves & a
red bud, w/four further leaves
about the flower, encompassed by
a garland of red, green & white
pastrymold canes alternating
w/coral & white canes, set on an
upset muslin ground, 3 1/8" d. . . .3,520.00

Baccarat Strawberry Weight

Baccarat "Strawberry" weight, clear
set w/a central green branch
w/seven leaves bearing three
strawberries in various stages
of growth, star-cut base, mid-
19th c., minor chips to base, 3" d.
(ILLUS.) 4,593.50
Baccarat "Yellow Wheatflower"
weight, the flower set w/two
rows of six black-spotted petals,
centered by two rows of white
stars & a red & white whorl,
growing from a green stalk &
surrounded by seven green
leaves, star-cut base, mid-19th c.,
2½" d. 2,488.00
Clichy "Faceted Garlanded Color-
ground Sulphide" weight, clear
glass set w/a sulphide depicting a
full-length portrait of Napoleon in
military dress encompassed by a
garland of pink & white cogwheel
canes divided by six pink & green
rose canes, set on an opaque cobalt blue ground, cut w/window &
five side printies, 3 3/8" d. 1,870.00
Clichy "Patterned Millefiori" weight,
the red ground set w/a central
pink, white & green cane surrounded by five looped garlands
of blue & white canes, each divided by white & green florets, mid-
19th c., 3" d. 1,053.00

Clichy miniature "Swirl" weight, alternating dark blue & white spiral
threads radiating from a central
pink, white & green floret, mid-
19th c., 2¼" d. 1,148.00
Kaziun (Charles) miniature "Millefi-
ori" pedestal weight, a cluster of
canes, one w/a gold "K," on a
pink torsade, clear pedestal base,
1½" h. 440.00

St. Louis Faceted Bouquet Weight

St. Louis "Faceted Upright Bouquet"
weight, clear glass set w/a central flower w/five red pointed
petals about a yellow stamen,
w/a blue & white flower to either
side & two similarly colored
millefiori canes, encompassed by
a white corkscrew cable & spiral
thread torsade at the periphery,
cut w/a decagonal window & geometric facets throughout, minor
chips, 2 11/16" d. (ILLUS.) 1,650.00
St. Louis "Fruit" weight, a white latticino basket enclosing a cluster
of fruit composed of two pears in
tones of green, a striped apple &
four cherries among green serrat-
ed leaves, mid-19th c., 3¼" d. 1,531.00
St. Louis "Honeycomb" weight, clear
glass set w/a carpet of numerous
hollow sienna canes about a central red, white & blue composite
cane, signed & dated "SL 1988,"
2 13/16" d. .1,100.00
Sandwich "Cherry" weight, clear
glass set w/two shaded red cherries pendent from a green branch
w/four serrated leaves, 19th c.,
2 15/16" d. 605.00
Sandwich "Poinsettia" weight, clear
glass set w/a flower composed of
two rows of six overlapping red
pointed petals about a red, green
& white "Clichy" rose cane stamen, growing from a curved
green stem w/four variegated
leaves & a leaf to the side,
19th c., 3 7/16" d. 605.00

Stankard (Paul) "Botanical" weight,
an upright rectangular clear casing enclosing a pine barren gentian root w/blue blossoms, seeds,
seed pods & root system, signed &
numbered "Bt.5, 1988," 5½" h. . .4,950.00

PAPIER-MACHE'

Papier-mache' Tea Caddy

*Various objects including decorative ad-
juncts were made of papier-mache', which is
a substance made of pulped paper mixed with
glue and other materials or layers of paper
glued and pressed and then molded.*

Candy container, model of a rabbit
w/basket on back, 7½" h. $65.00
Candy container, model of a rabbit,
removable clothes & head,
Germany 245.00
Center table, mother-of-pearl inlaid
& gilt-decorated black lacquer circular top, the top inlaid w/floral
sprays & geometric borders w/a
gilt-decorated frieze above a
baluster-form standard raised on
a three-sided concave plinth on
shaped & scroll feet, England,
third quarter 19th c., 55" d.,
30" h. (restorations to frieze) 4,950.00
Dresser set: rectangular cov. box,
oval cov. box, round cov. box &
rectangular tray; enameled pais-
ley design, Victorian, 4 pcs. 375.00
Model of a chicken, original polychrome paint, on a wire set into a
thin wooden base, 3 5/8" h. (mi-
nor wear, small chips) 75.00
Snuff box, cov., oval w/shaped front
rim, painted likeness of young
boy on cover, 3 3/8" l. (minor
wear) 145.00
Tea caddy, cov., cartouche-shaped
w/angled corners, decorated
overall w/gilt scrollwork & a
mother-of-pearl & h.p. circular
floral reserve on the cover, England, ca. 1820, 7¾" l., 4½" h.
(ILLUS.) 770.00

Tea table, tilt-top, octagonal top,
painted, parcel-gilt & mother-of-
pearl inlaid, the molded top decorated w/a capriccio above a
baluster-form standard on a
three-sided concave plinth on
scroll feet w/casters, England,
mid-19th c., 25" w., 28½" h. 1,870.00
Tray, rectangular w/rounded cor-
ners, chinoiserie-decorated dished
form w/reserves of peonies on a
cream ground w/gold speckled
borders, the center w/a border of
foliate scrolls, on a later rectangular stand w/bamboo-turned
legs, England, first quarter
19th c., 20½ x 25¾" 2,475.00

Victorian Papier-mache' Tray

Tray, cartouche-shaped w/scalloped
sides, a gilt-scrolled & mother-of-
pearl inlaid border, the center
painted w/a scene of a hunter
presenting his game to two figures, mounted on a later ebonized wood stand w/cabriole legs,
England, ca. 1840 (ILLUS.) 1,760.00
Tray on stand, rectangular tray
w/dished sides & rounded corners, painted overall w/gilt foliage & butterflies on a deep red
ground, impressed "Clay, King St.,
Cov. Gardens," raised on a red &
gold bamboo-turned stand, Regency period, England, early 19th c.,
tray 20½ x 28½" 11,550.00

PARRISH (Maxfield) ARTWORK

*During the 1920's and 1930's, Maxfield Par-
rish (1870-1966) was considered the most
popular artist-illustrator in the United States.
His illustrations graced the covers of the
most noted magazines of the day-Scribner's,
Century, Life, Harper's, Ladies' Home Journal and others. High quality art prints, copies of his original paintings usually in a range
of sizes, graced the walls of homes and offices*

across the country. Today all Maxfield Parrish artwork, including magazine covers, advertisements and calendar art, is considered collectible but it is the fine art prints that command the most attention.

Unusual Parrish Triptych

Advertisement for Hires, gnomes at
  a cauldron, ca. 1921, framed,
  7 x 9" $50.00
Book, "The Arabian Nights," illustrated by Maxfield Parrish, 1936 .. 70.00
Book, "The Golden Treasury of
  Songs & Lyrics," illustrated by
  Maxfield Parrish, 1911 ...150.00 to 200.00
Book, "Maxfield Parrish," by Coy
  Ludwig, color & black & white illustrations by Maxfield Parrish,
  1973, w/dust jacket 45.00
Calendar, 1923, for Edison-Mazda,
  entitled "Lamp Seller of Bagdad,"
  small, no pad 325.00
Calendar, 1927, for Edison-Mazda,
  entitled "Reveries," large,
  framed 595.00
Calendar, 1928, for Edison-Mazda,
  entitled "Contentment," large,
  framed 685.00
Calendar, 1930, for Edison-Mazda,
  entitled "Ecstasy," small,
  framed 500.00
Calendar, 1931, for Edison-Mazda,
  entitled "Waterfall," large 775.00
Calendar, 1940, for Brown & Bigelow
  Publishing Co., entitled "Evening
  Shadows," small 185.00
Calendar print, 1923, for Edison-
  Mazda, entitled "Lampseller of
  Bagdad," large 725.00
Calendar print, 1925, for Edison-
  Mazda, entitled "Dreamlight,"
  large 800.00
Calendar print, 1928, for Edison-
  Mazda, entitled "Contentment,"
  large 675.00
Calendar print, 1930, for Edison-
  Mazda, entitled "Ecstasy," large .. 625.00
Calendar print, 1959, for Brown &
  Bigelow Publishing Co., entitled
  "Under Summer Skies," 16 x 19".. 55.00
Magazine, Century, 1915, December,
  color frontispiece entitled "Pipe
  Night at the Players" 45.00
Magazine, Harper's Weekly, 1908,
  Dec. 12, cover by Maxfield
  Parrish 95.00

Magazine, Mentor, 1922, March,
  w/five Parrish illustrations 65.00
Magazine, Metropolitan, 1917, January, cover by Maxfield Parrish.... 325.00
Magazine cover, Collier's, 1905, September, Maxfield Parrish cover
  entitled "Harvest" 75.00
Magazine cover, Life, 1899, December 2, Christmas issue, framed ... 165.00
Magazine illustration, Ladies' Home
  Journal, 1915, December, "The
  Dream Garden," matted &
  framed 175.00
Playing cards, for Edison-Mazda,
  "Enchantment," 1926, full
  deck .... $175.00 to 200.00
Print, "Air Castles," for Ladies'
  Home Journal, 1904, 12 x 16",
  framed .... 175.00 to 200.00
Print, "Acussin Seeks for Nicolette,"
  Charles Scribner's Sons, 1905,
  11½ x 17" 575.00
Print, "The Broadmoor," Colorado
  Springs, 1921, framed, 7 x 8" 245.00
Print, "Cleopatra," House of Art -
  Reinthal Newman, 1917, large,
  framed, 24½ x 28" 1,400.00
Print, "Daybreak," House of Art -
  Reinthal Newman, 1923, large,
  18 x 30"............... 275.00 to 300.00
Print, "Evening," House of Art -
  Reinthal Newman, 1922, large,
  12 x 15" 260.00
Print, "Garden of Allah," House
  of Art - Reinthal Newman,
  1918, medium, original frame,
  9 x 18"............... 125.00 to 150.00
Print, "Hilltop," House of Art - Reinthal Newman, 1927, medium,
  framed, 12 x 20" 350.00
Print, "Spirit of Transportation,"
  1923, framed, 16½ x 20"........ 728.00
Print, "Wynken, Blynken & Nod,"
  from 'Poems of Childhood,'
  Charles Scribner's Sons, 1905,
  framed, 10¼ x 14½" 425.00
Print, triptych-style, a long arched
  central section flanked by smaller
  rounded arch side sections, the
  center section w/"Dreaming," the
  left section w/"Reveries," & the
  right section w/"The Lute Players," some wear on the molded
  frame, framed, 54½" w., 16¼" h.
  (ILLUS.)....................... 715.00

PERFUME, SCENT & COLOGNE
BOTTLES

Decorative accessories from milady's boudoir have always been highly collectible and in recent years there has been an especially strong surge of interest in perfume bottles. Our listings also include related containers such as pocket bottles and vials, tabletop containers & atomizers. Most readily available are examples from the 19th through the mid-20th century, but earlier examples do surface occasionally. The myriad varieties have now been documented in several recent reference books which should further popularize this collecting specialty.

ATOMIZERS

Blue opaque glass, long stemmed, "DeVilbiss" in gold on bottom, 6½" h. $195.00

Clear glass w/milk white feather design, DeVilbiss label, 4" h. 65.00

Cranberry cut to clear glass, facet-cut, attributed to Moser, 5¼" h. (needs new bulb) 95.00

DeVez cameo glass, dark green & orange cut w/scene of many sailboats & a rowboat on a lake, signed, 12" h. 875.00

Gold crackled glass, Art Deco style, 7½" h. 65.00

Opaque white shading to pink glass, twisted columnar form, w/Murano & DeVilbiss labels, 7½" h. 150.00

BOTTLES & FLASKS

Agate, flattened globular form, w/silver hinged rim & screw-on cap, marked "Black, Starr & Frost," 3" h. 247.50

Amethyst glass, twelve-sided tapered-form w/tooled lip, probably Boston & Sandwich Glass Works, Sandwich, Massachusetts, ca. 1860-80, 6 1/8" h............. 198.00

Bohemian glass, red cut to clear, globular base w/long slender neck, w/original matching stopper, 2½" d., 6" h. 95.00

Clear glass, "Bellodgia" by Caron, in original box 55.00

Clear cut glass, flask-shaped, Russian patt. w/1¼" sterling silver base, sterling silver screw-on top, marked "Tiffany & Co. Sterling," 3½" h. 395.00

Creamy opaque glass, decorated w/enameled pink flowers & brown leaves, w/matching stopper, 2½" d., 5¼" h. 85.00

English cameo glass, elongated tapering cylindrical lay-down type, yellowish amber overlaid in white & cut overall w/sweet pea blossoms, buds & leafy stems above a wide bottom border of vertical slats, hallmarked sterling silver screw rim & ball cap marked "SM," attributed to Thomas Webb, overall 11" l. 2,310.00

Frosted clear glass, "Three Flowers" by Richard Hudnut, ca. 1920's 50.00

Opalescent glass, lay-down type, multicolor stripe w/goldstone, 3¼" l. 34.50

Rubena frosted glass, squared form w/gold trim, w/original facet-cut crystal stopper, 2¼" w., 5¼" h. ... 80.00

Sterling silver, purse-size, oval, repousse' woman's bust.......... 70.00

Steuben glass, Jade Blue conical body tapering to a short cylindrical neck w/flared rim, a bulbous ovoid stopper in white opal, 4 5/8" h......................1,045.00

White overlay cut to clear glass, w/gold design, 5½" h. 235.00

PHONOGRAPHS

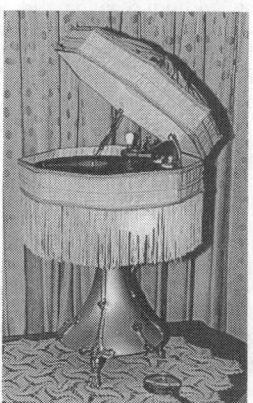

Burns-Pollock Electric Phono-Lamp

Burns-Pollock Phono-Lamp, electric, fabric-trimmed lift-top case w/tassel border above the light sockets & raised on a flaring gilt-metal pedestal base w/small claw-foot legs, w/exhibition reproducer (ILLUS.) $2,000.00

Columbia Type AG Cylinder Graphophone, w/original 4' "zinc" horn & stand, plays 5" cylinders, Serial No. 8,363, 1899 ....1,500.00

Columbia Type B Cylinder Graphophone, "Eagle," w/original aluminum horn, Serial No. 150,716..... 375.00

Columbia Type BF Cylinder Graphophone, "Peerless," w/original all-brass 25" horn, plays 6" cylinders, Serial No. 9,946, 1906 .... 425.00

Columbia Type BN Disc Graphophone, rear mount, w/oak horn........................1,300.00

Columbia Type BQ Cylinder Graphophone, "Rex," double spring,

w/original morning glory horn,
Serial No. 2,046, 1906 . . . .   975.00

Columbia Type CG Cylinder Graphophone, open works, wooden cov-
er, Serial No. 52,228, 1898 . . . . . .   425.00

Edison Amberola VI, gear drive,
w/Diamond B reproducer, mahog-
any finish, Serial No. 2,005. . . . . . .   450.00

Edison Amberola Model 30, table
model. 325.00

Edison Amberola Model 75 Floor
Model with Model C reproducer . .   475.00

Edison Concert Model C, Model B
reproducer, w/original 30" brass-
belled horn & floor stand, Serial
No. 9680, mint condition 2,400.00

Edison Gem Model B, black, key-
wind, w/Model B reproducer,
Serial No. 610625, 1903 . . . .   475.00

Edison Home Cylinder phonograph,
"Suitcase" model, w/shaver, 14"
brass-belled horn & automatic
reproducer, Serial No. 37,988,
1898 . . . .   425.00

Edison Home Cylinder phonograph,
w/30" flowered horn & 23" bell,
Model H reproducer, Serial
No. 321242, 1907 . . . .   775.00

Edison Standard "High Case,"
w/original 21" flowered horn,
1907 . . . .   550.00

Edison Standard Model A, w/origi-
nal red morning glory horn 625.00

Edison Standard square top, w/origi-
nal 14" brass horn & automatic
reproducer w/four clips. 400.00

Edison Triumph Model D2, w/origi-
nal Cygnet 10-panel horn & record
shaver 725.00

Edison Type C Concert model,
w/original 30" brass horn & floor
stand. 2,400.00

Heywood-Wakefield upright brown
wicker case w/Perfektone mecha-
nism, early 20th c.. . . . . .1,475.00

Thorens No. 15 Prizmaphone, brass
morning glory horn, two glass
sides, Serial No. 52251 . . . .   700.00

Victor II, w/original brass-belled
horn & exhibition reproducer,
Serial No. 1578A, 1902 . . . . .1,175.00

Victor III, w/black metal morning
glory horn & exhibition repro-
ducer, Serial No. 44566, 1906 . . . .1,200.00

Victor IV, solid red mahogany case
& horn, w/exhibition reproducer,
Serial No. 38419 . . . . .1,950.00

Victor V, oak case w/black morning
glory horn, 1906 . . . . .1,050.00

Victor M, w/black horn 1,450.00

PHOTOGRAPHIC ITEMS

19th Century Ambrotype

Ambrotype, depicting a dentist &
his instruments, in Union case
labeled A.P. Critchlow & Co.,
America, mid-19th c., 3¼ x 4¼"
(ILLUS.) $1,320.00

Ambrotype of Senator Stephen
Douglas, sixth-plate, in Union
case, ca. 1860 (some losses) 1,430.00

Beaker, glass, "Kodak," 4" h. 25.00

Book, "Complete Instructions in Photography," Sears Roebuck & Co.,
1907 . . . .   15.00

Camera, Ansco No. 1 Readyset Roy-
al, 1926 (minor wear outside) 65.00

Camera, Burke & James No. 3A
Ingento, folding-type, F4-F128,
1914 . . . .   50.00

Camera, Eastman Kodak Bantam
Special, the black-enameled body
divided by horizontal chromium-
plated metal bands, hinged lens
cover molded "KODAK BANTAM
SPECIAL MADE IN U.S.A. BY EAST-
MAN KODAK CO. ROCHESTER,
N.Y.," designed by Walter Dorwin
Teague, ca. 1935, 4½" l. 352.00

Camera, Eastman Kodak Brownie
No. 2A, in box, ca. 1907-24,
unused 80.00

Camera, Graflex Series II, 1942,
w/book, 2 1/8 x 2½". 325.00

Camera, Leica Model M-4, w/three
lenses, case, book & other acces-
sories 1,400.00

Camera, Premo No. 1 folding plate
camera, ca. 1913. . . . .   45.00

Camera, Rolleiflex 4 x 4, mint in
box 175.00

Camera, Speed Graphic 4 x 5, w/all
attachments including "HM" range
finder, "HR" flash, 4.7 graphic
lens, filters, ten cut film holders,
film pack holder, flash bulbs, etc.,
excellent condition, the group 350.00

Camera, Univex Model A, w/origi-
nal box & instructions 30.00

Camera, Zeiss Ikon Contessa 2.8,
  35mm 175.00
Carte de visite, Civil War drummer
  boy beating drum, R.H. Hender-
  shot, 2½ x 4¼" 85.00
Carte de visite, Tom Thumb w/wife
  & child, 2½ x 4¼" 60.00
Catalog, Kodak Supplies, 1930 ...... 25.00
Daguerreotype, baby sitting on
  nanny's lap (case has minor damage) 85.00
Daguerreotypes, elderly couple,
  duo-case 160.00
Magazine, Kodak News, 1949,
  September...................... 4.00
Movie camera, Kine-Exakta I, w/five
  lenses & case 250.00
Photograph, Natural Bridge of Vir-
  ginia by Burrows, hand-tinted,
  framed, 15 x 18½" 45.00
Scale, Eastman Kodak Co., boxed... 35.00
Tintype, portrait of a black woman
  wearing a long dress & gold
  jewelry, 7 x 9" 35.00

PINCUSHION DOLLS

*These china half figures were never intend-
ed for use as dolls, but rather to serve as ornamental tops to their functional pincushion
bases which were discreetly covered with silk
and lace skirts. They were produced in a wide
variety of forms and quality, all of which are
now deemed collectible, and were especially
popular during the first quarter of this
century.*

*Our listings are arranged numerically,
when possible, according to the code numbers
assigned in* The Collector's Encyclopedia of
Half-Dolls *by Frieda Marion and Norma
Werner.*

China half figure of a young girl
  w/shoulder-length loosely curled
  hair, arms away from body &
  slightly raised, Dressel & Kister
  (MW 147-302) $250.00
China half figure of Jenny Lind,
  ornate hair style w/bun at top
  of head & long sausage curls
  at her neck, arms away from
  body & hands raised, 4½" h.
  (MW 207-603) 150.00
China half figure of a court lady,
  her grey hair arranged in an ornate style w/rolled curls over the
  ears & sausage curls at the back
  of the neck, heavy eye make-
  up, hands raised & holding a
  flower in one, incised "16987"
  (MW 307-407) 195.00

China half figure of an elegant
  woman, so-called "Watteau
  bust," her hair arranged in an
  ornate coiffure, arms away from
  body & hands raised, 6½" h.
  (MW 507-601) 275.00
China half figure of a young woman wearing a bonnet, her
  arms akimbo, wearing a short
  sleeved top w/lacing at the front
  (MW 514-305) 40.00
China bust of Pierrette w/deeply
  ruffled collar, her hair peeking
  out from under skullcap at the
  forehead & above the ears
  (MW 770-331) 95.00

PIN-UP ART

Painting by Earle Bergey

*For most of the past century advertisers
have used sensuous depictions of young ladies to help sell their products. Modern "pin-
up" art really came of age about the 1920's
and soon artists such as Alberto Vargas,
George Petty, Rolf Armstrong and others
were churning out provocative portraits of
young beauties to grace calendars, magazine
covers and other advertising art. In more recent years male "beefcake" has also been
used to sell products, but it is the earlier female portraiture which is most sought-after
by collectors today.*

Calendar, 1945, George Petty, for
  "Esquire," w/envelope $62.50
Calendar, 1945, "Forever Yours,"
  Rolf Armstrong, full pad,
  16 x 33"....................... 150.00
Calendar, 1945, "The Toast of the
  Town," Rolf Armstrong, full pad,
  16 x 33"....................... 150.00
Calendar, 1951, "Esquire," in
  envelope 40.00
Calendar, 1954, T.N. Thompson stu-
  dio sketches w/Marilyn Monroe as
  Miss January 60.00

Calendar, 1955, Rolf Armstrong
girls, 15 x 33" 165.00
Calendar, 1955, desk-type, George
Petty girls 50.00
Calendar, 1955, "Sweet Dreams,"
Marilyn Monroe 125.00
Calendar, 1962, "Playboy Playmate
Calendar," w/Tina Louise,
w/jacket 55.00
Calendar, 1969, Curly Horse Ranch
cowgirl, Gillette Elvgren 46.00
Hot water bottle, figure of Marilyn
Monroe 125.00
Jigsaw puzzle, "Playboy Playmate
Puzzle," 297 die-cut cardboard
pieces, American Publishing Co.,
Waltham, Mass., 1967, in metal
canister 50.00
Magazine, "Flirt," 1947, December,
Vol. 1, No. 1, cover by Billy
DeVorss 32.00
Magazine, "Playboy," 1953, Decem-
ber, Vol. 1, No. 1, fair condition .. 400.00
Magazine, "Playboy," 1968, January,
Vargas girls special, 1930's to
present 35.00
Magazine, "Playboy," 1969, Febru-
ary, fold-out Vargas girls 12.50
Magazine, "Playboy," 1969, May,
Vargas girls prints 8.00
Matchbook cover, w/George Petty
illustration................... 1.50
Painting, oil on canvas, original de-
sign by Earle Bergey for book
cover for "Gentlemen Prefer
Blondes," Popular Library Cover
#221, artist-signed, 14¼ x 19¼"
(ILLUS.) 8,800.00
Playing cards, nude figures, Gillette
Elvgren, 2 decks 56.00
Print, "Dreamy Eyes," Rolf Arm-
strong, ca. 1920, 6 x 10" 45.00
Print, "Outside Chance," Gillette
Elvgren, 8 x 10"................. 20.00
Print, scene of girl talking on tele-
phone, George Petty, framed,
14 x 20" 69.00
Print, "Venus," Rolf Armstrong,
full-figure nude, ca. 1934,
10¾ x 13¾" 22.00
Windshield decal, Miss America,
1940, depicts bathing beauty 18.00

PIPES

Meerschaum, bowl carved w/a
bacchanalian scene of putti & a
reclining nude lady, amber stem,
w/a fitted case, 8 5/8" l. (ILLUS.
top next column) $660.00
Meerschaum, bowl carved as a

Meerschaum Pipe with Bacchanalian Scene

bearded, gruff looking man wearing a hat w/a sash hanging at the
back 50.00
Meerschaum, bowl carved as a
black man's head w/hat, amber
stem, 4¼" l.................... 300.00
Meerschaum, bowl carved w/deer,
a standing buck, doe & fawn beside the bellflower-form bowl,
amber & meerschaum stem, amber mouth piece, damages, w/fit-
ted case, 11 5/8" l. 467.50
Meerschaum, bowl carved as the
head of a gentleman in a plumed
beret, stained highlights, amber
stem, w/fitted case, 6 1/8" l. 330.00

POLITICAL, CAMPAIGN &
PRESIDENTIAL ITEMS

Early Andrew Jackson Lantern

CAMPAIGN ITEMS
Badge, 1900 campaign, Republican
National Convention............$150.00
Badge, 1928 campaign, Republican
National Convention alternate
delegate, Kansas City (ribbon
faded) 45.00
Ballot, 1880 campaign, Republican
presidential, Garfield (James)
& Arthur (Chester A.), paper,
w/electors plus state candidates,
Massachusetts (slight soiling,
glued to heavy paper) 30.00

Bank, 1972 campaign, Wallace (George), "Wallace for President," model of Liberty Bell 60.00

Book, "National Democratic Convention," 1948, hard cover, 574 pp. .. 35.00

Bubble gum cigars, 1968 campaign, Nixon (Richard M.), "Win with Dick," Nixon's photo on box, box of 24 .... 25.00

Compact, 1940 campaign, Willkie (Wendell), metal 40.00

Convention hat, 1964 campaign, Johnson (Lyndon B.), red, white & blue paper band w/black & white illustrations 30.00

Ferrotype, 1860 campaign, Douglas (Stephen A.) & Johnson (Herschel V.), two-sided 150.00

Lantern, candle-type, pierced tin, cylindrical w/conical top & hinged door, the pierced sides inscribed "ANDREW JACKSON FOREVER" flanked by stars, the door w/the initials "AJ" below the date "Jan 8th 1832," lacks ring finial, 13" h. (ILLUS.) 4,888.00

Lithograph, 1840 campaign, Harrison (William Henry), printed & hand-colored half-length portrait of "Genl. Wm. H. Harrison" in uniform, matted & framed, 14½ x 16½" (mat & print glued together, stains & minor paper damage) 104.50

Mechanical pencil, 1948 campaign, Republican Convention souvenir, Philadelphia 12.00

Medallion, 1840 campaign, Harrison (William Henry), metal, obverse w/bust of Harrison & inscription "Major General William Harrison - Born 1773," reverse w/a scene of a log cabin & cider barrel & "People's Choice in the Year 1840" 45.00

Necktie, 1956 campaign, Eisenhower (Dwight D.), "I Like Ike" 25.00

Newspaper, 1968 campaign, "The Nixon Nominator," published by the Nixon for President Committee, June 1968, 12 pp. 24.00

Pin, 1888 campaign, Harrison (Benjamin, cast eagle w/hanging pewter log cabin 75.00

Pin, 1940 campaign, Willkie (Wendell), metal, elephant head 15.00

Pin, 1960 campaign, Kennedy (John F.), figural PT 109, gold-colored metal 45.00

Pinback button, 1924 campaign, Coolidge (Calvin), "Hometown Coolidge Club - Plymouth, Vermont," w/picture.............. 200.00

Pinback button, 1936 campaign, Landon (Alfred) & Knox (Frank), model of a sunflower, "Landon - Knox" 12.50

Pinback button, 1940 campaign, Roosevelt (Franklin D.), "Our Gallant Leader" 14.00

Pinback button, 1940 campaign, Roosevelt (Franklin D.) & Wallace (Henry A.), jugate, 1" d. 35.00

Pinback button, 1940 campaign, Willkie (Wendell), "For President Willkie" & picture of Willkie 22.00

Pinback button, 1964 campaign, Goldwater (Barry), "Goldwater for President AUH2O," w/picture of Goldwater..................... 10.00

Pinback button, 1964 campaign, Goldwater (Barry), "Goldwater in '64," flasher picture-type 12.00

Pinback button, 1964 campaign, Goldwater (Barry), "Go Go Goldwater," gold & black 15.00

Pinback button, 1964 campaign, Johnson (Lyndon B.), "If I Were 21 I'd Vote for LBJ," depicts baby in highchair 9.00

Pinback button, 1968 campaign, Humphrey (Hubert) & Muskey (Edmund), jugate, 1¾" d. 8.00

Pinback button, 1972 campaign, McGovern (George S.) & Shriver (R. Sargent), jugate-type, w/"Come Home America," 3½" d. 25.00

Plate, 1908 campaign, Taft (William Howard), china, portrait of Taft & "Our Choice," 8½" d. 25.00

Plate, 1980 campaign, Reagan (Ronald W.) & Bush (George H.), chocolate glass, marked "Joe St. Clair" 25.00

Playing cards, 1964 campaign, Goldwater (Barry), "AuH2O"......... 45.00

Postcard, 1908 campaign, Bryan (William Jennings) & Kern (John), "For President Hon. William J. Bryan of Nebraska - For Vice President Hon. John W. Kern of Indiana," flags & shield decoration, pictures of both candidates .. 60.00

Poster, 1924 campaign, Coolidge (Calvin), "Calvin Coolidge for President," 14 x 22" (slight corner damage) 95.00

Poster, 1968 campaign, "McCarthy Year of the Dove," 20 x 26¼" 22.50

Poster, 1972 campaign, McGovern (George) & Shriver (Sargent), "Come Home America - Vote McGovern/Shriver," 11 x 17½" ... 7.50

Ribbon, 1880 campaign, Garfield (James), depicts Garfield, 5" l. .. 140.00

Sheet music, 1896 campaign, McKinley (William), "McKinley March" .. 20.00

Sheet music, 1924 campaign, Davis

(John), "John Davis March to the White House" 15.00

Stickpin, 1904 campaign, Roosevelt (Theodore), "Our Choice" 55.00

Textile block, 1840 campaign, Harrison (William Henry), white cotton square printed in blue w/a design of a log cabin & a barrel of cider in a landscape framed by scrolling floral vines & a partial bust of Harrison at the bottom edge, framed, 10¾ x 11" (stains) 137.50

Tie clip, 1956 campaign, Stevenson (Adlai), flasher-type, "Vote Adlai" 20.00

Toby mug, 1928 campaign, Smith (Alfred) & Robinson (Joseph), Syracuse China 85.00

Tumbler, 1952 campaign, Eisenhower (Dwight D.), glass 10.00

Walking stick, 1896 campaign, McKinley (William), a slender wooden shaft topped by a molded white metal knob-form handle decorated w/a bust portrait of William McKinley & marked "McKinley 1896," 33" l. 137.50

Watch fob, 1904 campaign, Roosevelt (Theodore), brass, "To the White House" 50.00

NON-CAMPAIGN

Commemorative Silk Handkerchief

Book, miniature, "The Inaugural Address of John Kennedy," by St. Onge, 1961 . . . . 35.00

Coloring book, "New Frontier Coloring Book," John F. Kennedy, by Arthur J. Weaver, 1962 . . . . 48.00

Fabric fragment, printed chintz, decorated in pink w/"Portraits of the First Seven Presidents of the United States," England, ca. 1830, 23½ x 24" (some discoloration) . . . 275.00

Handkerchief, commemorative, polychrome printed silk, the center w/a beardless portrait of Lincoln titled "Abraham Lincoln - Late President - The United States of America," framed by bust portraits of various Civil War Union officials & officers & oval reserves picturing various Northern cities, printed in blue, red, purple, green & yellow, some fiber wear, minor discoloration, ca. 1866, 30 x 32" (ILLUS.) 1,320.00

Inaugural ball program, 1897, for William McKinley, ornate engravings & gold leaf decorations, depicts the Capitol & White House, 5 pp. 150.00

Inaugural list, "General Order No. 1," Harry Truman, detailing complete inaugural parade order & participants, 1948 . . . . 125.00

Inaugural program, Roosevelt (Franklin) & Wallace (Henry A.) inauguration, dated January 20, 1941 . . . . 45.00

Map, tinted, depicts 1880 presidential vote, Old Honesty Plug Tobacco, copyright 1884 . . . . 45.00

Medal, dedication of McKinley Memorial, depicts McKinley & memorial, Canton, Ohio, 1907, 2" d. 65.00

Memorial picture for George Washington, printed silk, a scene of a classical figure mourning at a monument dedicated to Washington, backboard labeled "John Gibbs...Portsmouth," ca. 1800, 8 x 9 3/8" 1,100.00

Plate, china, Franklin Delano Roosevelt portrait, cobalt blue border, 12" d. 30.00

Plate, china, 1954 Republican Centennial commemorative, depicts Republican Presidents from Abraham Lincoln to Dwight Eisenhower, w/GOP elephant in center 50.00

Postcard, President Franklin D. Roosevelt speaking at dedication of Great Smoky Mountains National Park, 1930's 12.00

Punch-outs, "Sparton Cosmic Eye Television Party Animals Punch-Outs," "Demmie" the Donkey & "Goppie" the Elephant, mint & unpunched 25.00

Puzzle, depicts Spiro Agnew as Superman, in box, 1970 . . . . 35.00

Salt & pepper shakers, ceramic, model of President Kennedy in rocking chair, pr. 45.00

Scarf, silk, w/full color picture of John Kennedy w/flag border, ca. 1960's 10.00

Sheet music, "James Garfield Funeral March," 1881 . . . . 22.50

Song book, "Sing Along With Jack,"
John F. Kennedy, 1963 . . . . 35.00
Spoons, silver plate, representing
each of the Presidents from
George Washington through
Franklin Roosevelt, William
Rogers Manufacturing Co., set
of 32 . . . . 250.00
Stereoview card, President McKinley
& Major Generals Wheeler, Law-
ton, Shafter & Kieler 45.00

POSTCARDS

Advertising, "Hope Cotton Oil Co.,
Hope, Arkansas," 1911 . . . . $15.00
Advertising, "Hostetter's Bitters,"
depicts Panama Canal, unused . . . 28.00
Advertising, "Post Toasties Corn
Flakes," 1923 . . . . 15.00
Advertising, "Torpedo Roadster,"
real photo close-up of the 40 h.p.
Torpedo Roadster, Vincent, Ohio,
1913 . . . . 25.00
Animals Picnic (The), "Scorching,"
dressed bears riding bicycles,
printed by Ernest Nister, Germa-
ny, unused 18.00
Black women (2) on street in
Charleston, South Carolina,
1920 . . . . 15.00
Bonzo, comic dog w/"googlie" eyes,
ca. 1930's. 28.00
Boy in baseball uniform, dated
1909 . . . . 15.00
Christmas, depicts young boy & girl,
Clapsaddle artwork, 1914 . . . . 6.00
Christmas, Santa Claus in red suit,
w/four active small child angels . . 40.00
Christmas, Santa Claus on chimney,
1908 . . . . 10.00
Flood, great flood damage, etc.,
Troy, Ohio, two different real
photographs, 1913, pr. 20.00
Halloween, boy holding large pump-
kin face, Clapsaddle artwork 15.00
Halloween, embossed, lady & pump-
kin, two small men w/pumpkin
faces, colorful border, Clapsaddle
artwork, Germany 15.00
Halloween, depicts seductive wom-
an in red dress, Winsch back,
1911 . . . . 55.00
Hold-to-light, Brooklyn Bridge & Wil-
liamsburg Bridge depicted 25.00
Hotel ballroom, interior of ballroom
at the "Royal Poinciana," Palm
Beach, Florida, 1912 . . . . 25.00
Parade, Royal Parade, Wamba Car-
nival, Toledo, Ohio, 1913 . . . . 12.00
Puppies, scene of black & white
puppies, real photograph 5.00

RCA Recording Stars, color, ca.
1940's, set of 10 . . . . 30.00
Skiing at Mt. Washington, New
Hampshire, real photo, pre-1920,
mailed in 1948 . . . . 3.00
Ten Commandments, embossed,
Germany, set of 10 . . . . 175.00
Theatre, close-up of Illinois Theatre,
Chicago, Illinois, 1912 . . . . 8.00
Tours of the World by Woman's
Home Journal, early 1900's, pack-
et of 50 . . . . 30.00

POSTERS

*(Also see MOVIE MEMORABILIA and
DISNEY COLLECTIBLES.)*

Tiffany Glass Exhibit Poster

Cigarettes, "Chesterfield Cigarettes," w/Dean Martin & Jerry
Lewis pictured, 1951, 30 x 60" $135.00
Glass exhibit, "Tiffany Glass -
Chrysler Museum at Norfolk,"
water-color prototype for promotional signs showing colorful examples of Favrile glass, signed
"RB," 20th c., framed, 15 x 25"
(ILLUS.) 880.00
Magazine, "Harper's February," a
seated man reading w/a black cat
seated beside him, by Edward
Penfield, ca. 1900, framed (ILLUS.
top next page) 110.00
Masked ball, "Theatre de l'Opera
Bal Masque'," a design of
costumed partygoers by Jules
Cheret, lithographed in
color, Paris, 1898, framed,
33¾ x 48¼" 1,650.00
Railway, "Nord Express," depicting a
stylized black locomotive against
a blue sky w/a trail of white

Harper's Magazine Poster

smoke above, by A.M. Cassandre, printed in colors by Hachard et Cie, Paris, 1927, framed, 29½" w., 41¼" h. (minor creasing) 7,150.00

Steamship line, "Cie.Gie. Transatlantique - French Line," a large stylized ship sailing across a horizontal French flag background, designed by Paul Colin, ca. 1937, 15¾ x 23½" 1,093.00

Theatrical production, "The Great Emotional Drama - EAST LYNNE," the large title across the center flanked by colorful vignettes from the turn-of-the-century stage production, unframed, 28 x 41" (minor damage) 93.50

World War I, "Halt the Hun - Buy U.S. Government Bonds - Third Liberty Loan," scene of a standing U.S. soldier w/sword pulling a German soldier away from a crouching woman & child, by Henry Patrick Raleigh, 1918, 20 x 20½" 60.00

World War I, "I Want You for The Navy...," standing woman wearing a naval jacket & hat, signed "Howard Chandler Christy - 1917," cloth-backed edge tears & creases, touch-up on top center edge, 26½ x 41" (ILLUS.)......... 110.00

World War I, "Red Cross Christmas Roll Call," Red Cross nurse & Columbia w/arms raised & flanking a scroll, E.H. Blashford, 1918 .... 77.00

World War I, "Remember Belgium - Buy Bonds - Fourth Liberty Loan," silhouetted figure of a fat German soldier dragging a young screaming girl against a fiery background, by Ellsworth Young, 1918, 20 x 30"...................... 55.00

World War I, "Six Million Cheers - For Our Sailor Boys - The Best Ever," cartoon-style w/a marching sailor w/rifle & figures in colonial attire cheering in the background, in red, cream & blue, 27 x 40 7/8" (minor soiling & water marks) 66.00

World War I, "They Kept the Sea Lanes Open - Invest in The Victory Liberty Loan," submarine in the foreground w/other ships in the background, lower right corner damage, tears, framed, 29 x 39"....................... 35.00

World War II, "Because Somebody Talked," depicts dog in front of star, 1944, 14 x 20"............. 75.00

World War II, "Care Is Costly," scene of a wounded soldier, artwork by Adolphi Treider, 1945, 18½ x 26"..................... 50.00

World War II, "Under the Shadow of Their Wings," General Cable Corp., 1944 .... 145.00

POWDER HORNS & FLASKS

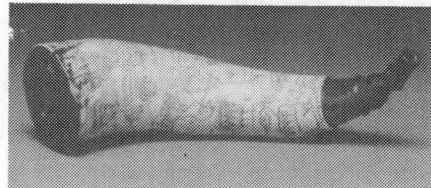

Early Powder Horn with Map

Brass flask, embossed w/a running rabbit $75.00

Copper flask, w/brass fittings, violin-shaped, embossed hanging stag, four different birds & florals (chain missing)................. 95.00

"I Want You" Poster

Copper & brass flask, embossed
shell design & engraved "W. A.
Pike 1887," 7" l. (minor solder repair) 60.00

Horn, engraved w/the crowned lion
of King George III & a map of
New York state military forts, dated 1780, England, 10½" l........ 880.00

Horn, engraved w/the depiction of
the British coat-of-arms above a
hunting scene w/a hunter, dog,
stag & boar beside the city & port
of Philadelphia, America, second
half 18th c., 11½" l. 2,420.00

Horn, engraved w/the British royal
arms above the inscription "New
Yorke" & a depiction of New York
City, a map w/towns & forts along
the rivers Mohawk, Mounitas &
Lorinse up the sides, inscribed &
dated "Joseph Clawton 1761,"
11¾" l. (ILLUS.) 5,280.00

Horn, engraved "R G Honesty and
Industry Peacham March 1847,"
further decorated w/American Indians, a spread-winged eagle,
various animals & figures,
w/brass spout & plug, America,
1847, 13" l. (surface abrasion) 330.00

Horn, engraved "Adam Hunt Cape
Freel's New Jersey Volunteers
1783," primitively decorated w/a
mermaid & church, America, 1783,
17" l. (split at plug end) 220.00

PURSES & BAGS

Ornate Victorian Purse

Alligator, envelope-style, brown,
leather-lined, inside zippered
compartment, adjustable strap,
ca. 1940's, 8½ x 13¼".......... $42.00

Beaded, Art Deco-style, colorful
scene w/peacocks, 7 x 9"........ 195.00

Beaded, black w/colorful Art Deco
design, clasp of gilt metal set
w/marcasite & a cameo, Paris,
France, 6½ x 8" 116.00

Beaded, black w/crystal beaded
loop design on front & flap,
3½ x 5"....................... 42.00

Beaded, blue & black checked design, w/fringe & drawstring 55.00

Beaded, Kelly green, w/drawstring
& five rows of beaded fringe 55.00

Beaded, pouch-type, blue, lavender,
pink, red & yellow flowers on
white ground w/multicolored tassel, crocheted closure w/lavender
drawstring, 5 x 8".............. 125.00

Beaded, silver & gold beading,
beaded tassels along bottom,
cloth-lined 60.00

Cotton homespun w/white silk facing, drawstring-type, wool & silk
floral embroidery in green, brown
& beige, 8½ x 8½" (fragile
w/stains & damage) 125.00

Enameled mesh, Art Deco style design in turquoise & green, tassels
at bottom 95.00

Enameled mesh, cream w/Art Deco
style goldtone & rhinestone clasp,
Whiting-Davis, 5 x 7" 40.00

Enameled silver, enameled w/color-
ful foliage on pale blue & deep
green ground, the borders enameled in cream, w/chain handle,
The Twentieth Artel, Moscow,
Russia, ca. 1910, 5" l. 2,090.00

German silver mesh, floral design
on frame, clasp w/two faux sapphires........................ 60.00

Gold mesh, Art Nouveau-style, the
18k gold frame set w/a round
ruby & highlighted by two diamonds & two rubies, the chain
mesh bag w/gold flowers, early
20th c. 825.00

Gold mesh, 14k, gold mesh strap,
monogrammed & jeweled frame,
mirror inside, hallmarked "P" 440.00

Gold mesh, the 14k yellow gold
purse frame set w/square facet-
cut sapphires & round single-cut
sapphires & round single-cut diamonds mounted in platinum, the
thumbpiece set w/round cabochon
sapphires, the change purse
frame set w/round diamonds,
in a fitted leather case marked
"Phelps & Perry Inc., 3 Maiden
Lane, New York" 1,650.00

Goldtone metal, basketweave box
purse, imitation tortoiseshell top,
fitted w/powder compact, Dorset
Fifth Ave., ca. 1950's 45.00

Petit point, multicolored flowers on

light brown background, marked
800 grade silver floral repousse'
frame, w/chain 130.00
Satin, black w/goldtone clasp set
w/clear rhinestones 50.00
Silver mesh w/enamel, black zig-zag
geometric design, large cabochon
on front & back, amethyst handle,
fancy fringe, Whiting & Davis,
4½ x 6" 250.00
Suede, black w/silver mounts
w/green stones & marcasites, Art
Deco-style 160.00
Tortoiseshell, the leather & suede
body covered w/tortoiseshell &
applied w/an ornate marine-style
metal monogram, the silver-gilt
mounts embossed w/flowerheads
on a hammered ground, woven
loop handle at top, by Tiffany &
Company, New York, numbered
"8306-6916," ca. 1885, 6½" l.
(ILLUS.) 1,100.00
Tortoiseshell, coin-type, the top
decorated w/a gold mono-
grammed crest "ENB," 19th c. 247.50
Velvet, black w/silver plated
repousse' frame, chain handle
w/medallion clip 125.00

RADIOS & ACCESSORIES

FADA Temple Model Radio

Catalog, "Motorola Radios," 1946,
floor & table models, record players, 32 pp. (cover worn) $23.00
Radio, Admiral Model 6C22N, Bakelite case, Art Deco style grill 50.00
Radio, Atwater Kent Model 76, console cabinet 350.00
Radio, Bendix Model 526C, marbleized green & black Catalin
case 750.00
Radio, Crosley "Musical Chef" Model
5TWE 30.00
Radio, DeWald Model B-512, clock-
radio, Catalin case, slide rule
dial, center clock, grill bars on
top of case, five knobs, 1948 ....1,500.00
Radio, Dumont "Tura" Model 103,
1947 .... 150.00
Radio, Emerson "Mickey Mouse"
Model 411, pressed wood case,

right round dial, center front
round grill w/Mickey cut-out.....1,200.00
Radio, Emerson Model 569, portable,
ivory Bakelite case, power supply
plug 115.00
Radio, FADA "Bullet" Model 115,
burgundy bullet-shaped Bakelite
case w/dial mounted on rounded
end, the dial frame & handle in
amber Bakelite, ca. 1941........ 935.00
Radio, FADA "Temple" Model 652,
maroon & butterscotch Catalin
case, 1946, 11" l., 6 5/8" h.
(ILLUS.) 440.00
Radio, FADA Model 740, plastic
case, right dial, left horizontal
wrap-around louvers, two knobs,
1947 .... 75.00
Radio, Garod "The Commander"
Model 6AU-1, red Catalin case
w/wrap-around grill, 1946.......1,700.00
Radio, General Electric Model 202,
brown plastic case, lower center
rectangular dial, upper metal
criss-cross grill, two knobs 35.00
Radio, Hallicrafters Model SX-28-A,
w/instruction booklet 500.00
Radio, Hibbard, yellow plastic
bullet-shaped case 125.00
Radio, Motorola Model 56L3, portable, pink 85.00
Radio, Philco Model 51-1731, console
radio-phonograph, mahogany
cabinet, 33 & 45 rpm record
changer 265.00
Radio, Philco Model 71, two-tone
wooden "cathedral" case, center
window dial, upper cloth grill
w/cutouts, four knobs, 1932 ...... 295.00
Radio, Pilot "Piloturner" Model
T-601, wooden case, center front
FM dial, two knobs, 1947 .... 50.00
Radio, RCA Model 8R75, brown marbleized Bakelite case, 1949....... 50.00
Radio, RCA Model 56X, plastic case,
upper dial w/red dot pointer, lower horizontal louvers, three
knobs, 1946................... 35.00

Unusual Radio by Sparton

Radio, Sparton, blue mirror, chromium-plated metal & wooden
case, the blue mirrored glass
rectangular body set onto a
black wooden 'sled,' five chrome

bands wrapping around the right side, designed by Walter Dorwin Teague, ca. 1936, 17½" l. (ILLUS.) 1,540.00

Radio, Stewart-Warner Model B61T2 .... 60.00

Radio, Western Auto Supply Model 557, table top model, pearly formica look, ca. 1950's 26.00

Radio, Zenith clock-radio Model L520R 35.00

RAILROADIANA

Pennsylvania Railroad Calendar

Award, "Missouri Pacific Lines," silver plated trophy-style, a small winged figure atop a slender reeded column set upon a pedestal base mounted w/a plaque engraved "Missouri Pacific Lines Safety Trophy - Award for Best Safety Record," w/pictures of railroad workers, signed by vice president & general manager, 26" h. (minor wear) $66.00

Badge, "Atlantic Coast Line," Police Patrolman No. 103, nickel silver, eagle shield w/custom logo seal, 1 3/8 x 2" 100.00

Badge, "Seaboard Air Line Railway," Police No. 377, nickel, plain die-cut w/embossed black enamel lettering, convex shape, 1¾ x 2¼" 75.00

Blotter, "Burlington Route - Ozark Zephyr," two-color 9.00

Book, "Returns of Railroad & Street Railway For Commonwealth of Massachusetts," September 1877, detailed description of mileage, debts, branches, accidents, etc., hard cover, 390 pp. 85.00

Book, "Santa Fe, The Railroad That Built An Empire," by James Marshall, autographed presentation copy, 1945 .... 43.00

Booklet, "Brotherhood of Locomotive Engineers Journal," March 1893, 80 pp. 9.00

Bouillon cup, "Pennsylvania Railroad," china, Broadway patt. 35.00

Bowl, "Baltimore & Ohio Railroad," china, Capitol - Black & Gold patt., 10" d. 95.00

Bowl, "SP" (Southern Pacific), china, Prairie-Mountain Wildflowers patt., 6" d. 35.00

Brochure, "The Oriental Limited - Great Northern Railway," 1924, pictures, 32 pp. 35.00

Butter pat, "Atlantic Coast Line," china, Flora of the South patt..... 89.00

Butter pat, "Chicago, Burlington & Quincy Railroad," china, Violets & Daisies patt. 35.00

Butter pat, "Atchison, Topeka & Santa Fe," china, Mimbreno patt. 45.00

Calendar, 1955, "Pennsylvania Railroad," large print w/group of trains at the top, calendar sheets for November & December 1955 & January 1956, two holes at top, creases, 28½ x 28½" (ILLUS.) 49.50

Calendar, 1964, Atchison, Topeka & Santa Fe, w/map & Kachina doll in color, Brown & Bigelow, 13 x 24" 15.00

Calendar-sign, "Mississippi Pacific Lines," metal, rectangular w/lithograph of a speeding locomotive at the top above a square pad of cardboard date & month cards, green ground w/red & cream lettering, 13" w., 19" h. (creases & tears on cards, very minor metal scratches) 93.50

Celery dish, "Southern Railroad," china, Peach Blossom patt., 12" l. 135.00

Coasters, "Mo Pac - Route of the Dome Liners" (Missouri Pacific), cardboard, set of 40 .... 25.00

Cocktail glasses, "Illinois Central," sides depict locomotive, logo & system map, set of 4 .... 30.00

Coffeepot, cov., "Southern Pacific Railroad," silver plate, Reed & Barton 75.00

Gravy boat w/attached undertray, "New York Central Railroad," silver plate, double-lipped 125.00

Lantern, "CCC&STL" (Cleveland, Cincinnati, Chicago & St. Louis), Dietz Vesta model, clear globe, 4½" h. globe 35.00

Lantern, "D&H RR Co." (Delaware

& Hudson), short clear globe,
Adlake 35.00

Lantern, "Lehigh Valley Railroad,"
w/embossed globe, Adlake 75.00

Lantern, "MOPAC" (Missouri Pacific), Corning glass orange-amber
globe, etched "M.P. Safety First,"
Handlan, 5 3/8" h. 225.00

Lantern, "Union Pacific RR," en-
gineer's presentation-type, clear
unmarked globe, Adams & West-
lake frame, lid engraved w/last
name & street address, dated
"1864" 525.00

Match holder, "Missouri, Kansas &
Texas Railroad," cast iron, table
model, lists company officials on
bottom, ca. 1905 .... 375.00

Match safe, "Frisco line RR," metal,
wall-type, telephone-shaped 350.00

Menu, "Missouri Pacific Railroad," a
steamer plate & state flowers pictured on the cover, ca. 1933 ..... 55.00

Monkey wrench, "CRI&P" (Chicago,
Rock Island & Pacific) 16.50

Padlock, "C.M.ST.P.&P.R.R." (Chicago, Milwaukee, St. Paul & Pacific
Railroad), brass, heart-shaped,
w/key 70.00

Padlock, "DL&WRR" (Delaware,
Lackawanna & Western Railroad),
brass, embossed "DL&WRR,"
w/original key 100.00

Padlock, "L&N" (Louisville & Nash-
ville Railroad), brass, w/key,
4" l. 75.00

Padlock, "NYCRR" (New York Central Railroad), moon-shaped,
w/original key 100.00

Photograph of locomotive & twelve
man crew (all identified), "#808
Southern Pacific, Los Angeles,"
1912 .... 30.00

Plate, dinner, "Atchison, Topeka &
Santa Fe," china, California Poppy
patt., 9¾" d. 35.00

Plate, "New York Central Railroad,"
china, DeWitt Clinton patt.,
9" d. 95.00

Plate, "Union Pacific Railroad," china, Harriman Blue patt., 7" d. 55.00

Platter, "Pere Marquette Railroad,"
china, Autoferry patt., 8" oval ... 95.00

Platter, "SP" (Southern Pacific), china, Prairie-Mountain Wildflowers
patt., 9½" d. 62.00

Playing cards, "Chesapeake & Ohio
Railroad," Chessie, the Cat
shown, sealed deck 35.00

Playing cards, "Norfolk & Western
Railroad," one deck showing 'The
Pocahontas,' the other 'The Pow-
hatan Arrow,' set of two decks ... 75.00

Playing cards, "Southern Pacific
Lines," pre-1909, views of Pittsburgh, ca. 1930s (box worn) 50.00

Postcard, "Burlington Railroad," dining car scene 8.50

Poster, "Illinois Central Railroad,"
colorful scene of Mardi Gras in
New Orleans & the World's Exposition of 1885, 10 x 30" 395.00

Print, yard-long type, "Missouri Pacific's Route of the Eagle Train,"
countryside scene 600.00

Ruler, marked w/table for determining train speeds, w/leather case,
6" l. 20.00

Sauce dish, "Atchison, Topeka
& Santa Fe," china, Mimbreno
patt., 5½" d. 70.00

Service plate, "C&O" (Chesapeake &
Ohio), china, George Washington
patt., portrait of Washington in
the center, a wide stamped gold
border band, Buffalo China 595.00

Sign, "Texas & Pacific Railway," porcelain, diamond-shaped, four
colors, early, 6 x 10", mint
condition 450.00

Soup bowl, "Baltimore & Ohio," china, Centenary patt., 9¼" d. 115.00

Soup spoon, "Union Pacific," silver
plate w/engraved winged streamliner logo, International Silver 25.00

Sundae dish, "Union Pacific Railroad," china, Streamliner patt.,
footed 25.00

Switch key, "At&SFRy" (Atchison,
Topeka & Santa Fe), brass, Adlake No. 14142 .... 20.00

Switch key, "D&H" (Delaware
& Hudson RR), brass, Adlake
No. 7076 .... 20.00

Switch lock, "Mobile & Ohio Railroad," heart-shaped, cast-iron,
shackle embossed "M&ORR,"
manufactured by Bohannon,
2½ x 3¾" overall w/chain 30.00

Tablecloth, "Chicago, Burlington &
Quincy," white cotton w/'California Zephyr' interwoven in center,
40 x 45" 25.00

Timetable, "Union Pacific Railroad,"
1947 .... 10.00

Timetable, "Union Pacific Railroad,"
1962 .... 5.00

Vegetable dish, "Chicago, Milwaukee, St. Paul & Pacific Railroad,"
china, Traveller patt. 35.00

Vegetable dish, "Union Pacific Railroad," china, Harriman Blue patt.,
6½" oval 75.00

Water glasses, "Santa Fe," clear
glass engraved w/stylized letters
on side, 4" h., set of 4 .... 35.00

ROYALTY COMMEMORATIVES

QUEEN VICTORIA (1837-1901)

1897 Diamond Jubilee Pitcher

Inkwell, white metal & brass, 1897 Diamond Jubilee commemorative, detailed bust of Queen Victoria in white metal, crown cover hinges back to reveal inkwell, square brass base, back w/"Victoria Regina 60 years 1897," w/registry mark & maker's marks, 6" d., 7¼" h. $350.00

Loving cup, pottery, 1897 Diamond Jubilee commemorative, Torquay, Allervale, 5½" h. 125.00

Pitcher, stoneware, 1897 Diamond Jubilee commemorative, the ovoid body embossed w/an oval reserve below the cylindrical neck w/embossed wording below the sterling silver rim band, dark brown glaze band around the neck & upper handle above a light tan body, the body w/Doulton - Lambeth marks, the silver w/London hallmarks for 1896, 5¼" h. (ILLUS.) .. 236.50

Plate, earthenware, octagonal, 1887 Golden Jubilee commemorative, black & white printed bust portraits of Queen Victoria & Prince Albert, also maps of the colonies, import & export totals & colored trim w/gold, 9¾" w. 165.00

Plates, porcelain, 1887 Golden Jubilee commemorative, blue & white design, Royal Worcester, 10½" d., set of 12 .... 165.00

Scarf, printed cotton, 1887 Golden Jubilee commemorative, w/Queen Victoria's portrait in the center framed by other smaller portraits, framed, 23 x 23½" (minor stains) 25.00

EDWARD VII (1901-1910)

Bowl, clear pressed glass, commemorative of the Silver Wedding anniversary of Prince Edward & the Princess of Wales, 1863-1888, 9" d. 185.00

Cup, child's, china, 1902 coronation commemorative, w/a lithophane in base.................... 100.00

Pinback button, celluloid, 1902 coronation commemorative, color portrait depiction of the King & Queen 38.00

King Edward Coronation Pitcher

Pitcher, stoneware, 1902 coronation commemorative, footed conical body w/a slightly flared rim & pinched spout, a dark tan neck band above the tan-glazed body, the front transfer-printed in bust portraits of King Edward VII & Queen Alexandra & "Coronation of King Edward VII - 1902," 8" h. (ILLUS.)........................ 247.50

GEORGE V (1910-1936)

Bowl, china, 1911 coronation commemorative, oval w/reticulated sides & rim, color decoration, 7 x 10½" 110.00

Cup, china, 1935 Silver Jubilee commemorative, portraits of King George & Queen Mary, Burleigh.. 22.00

Plate, china, 1911 coronation commemorative, depicts King George V & Queen Mary, ornate design, cobalt blue border 48.00

Tumbler, china, 1911 coronation commemorative, brown transfer-printed designs of King George & Queen Mary, the Crystal Palace & the inscription "June 30th, 1911," Royal Doulton.................. 65.00

EDWARD VIII (1936, abdicated)

Cup & saucer, china, 1937 coronation commemorative, Royal Chelsea 30.00

Mug, china, 1937 coronation commemorative, handled, Royal Doulton 125.00

Mug, earthenware, 1937 coronation commemorative, Lancaster & Sons, Ltd., England 55.00

Mug, earthenware, 1937 coronation commemorative, Myott, Son & Company 45.00

Phonograph record, abdication farewell address, 1938 .... 22.00

Pin tray, china, 1937 coronation commemorative, w/portrait of Edward VIII, scalloped edges, 5" sq. 30.00

Plate, china, commemorative of
Prince Edward's 1927 visit to
Canada, Paragon China 150.00

Plate, china, 1937 coronation commemorative, Cauldon China,
10½" d. 75.00

Tray, china, 1937 coronation commemorative, portrait of Edward
VIII, Grindley, 5" sq. 25.00

Tumbler, earthenware, 1937 coronation commemorative, Myott, Son &
Company 50.00

GEORGE VI (1936-1952)

George VI Glass Coronation Bowl

Ashtray, china, 1937 coronation
commemorative, Shelley 35.00

Basket, glass, 1937 coronation
commemorative 125.00

Booklet, "Coronation Arrange-
ments," map of routes, 1937 . . . . . 12.00

Bowl, glass, 1937 coronation
commemorative, shallow clear
sides w/scalloped rim, 9 5/8" d.
(ILLUS.) 49.00

Magazine, "Punch," 1952, February
13, memorial issue 12.00

Mug, china, 1937 coronation com-
memorative, portraits of King
George & Queen Elizabeth,
Myott 32.00

Pinback button, commemorative of
the 1939 royal visit to Canada &
the United States 25.00

Plate, china, commemorative of the
1939 royal visit to Canada & the
United States, depicts King
George & Queen Elizabeth
w/President Roosevelt in Washington, D.C., blue on white,
Mason's Ironstone, 10" d. 150.00

Program, 1937 coronation commemorative, w/photos of the roy-
al family & details, 9 x 11" 27.00

Stamp album, 1937 coronation commemorative, w/over 200 stamps . . 200.00

Tumbler, earthenware, 1937 coronation commemorative, relief-

molded bust portraits of King
George VI & Queen Elizabeth,
Crown Devon Mark 40.00

QUEEN ELIZABETH II (1952-   )

Book, "Elizabeth the Queen," by
Marion Crawford, 1952, first
American edition, many photographs of the young queen &
family, hard cover 10.00

Cup & saucer, china, 1953 coronation commemorative, Paragon
China 25.00

Dish, china, 1953 coronation
commemorative, Paragon China,
4½" l. 27.50

Mug, china, commemorating 1957
royal visit to Canada, Hammers-
ley, 3" h. 30.00

Pinback button, commemorative of
the 1959 royal visit to the United
States & Canada, portraits of
Queen Elizabeth & Prince Philip . . 8.50

Pitcher, earthenware, 1953 coronation commemorative, blue ground
w/a white embossed silhouette
portrait of the queen, Johnson
Bros. 40.00

Plate, china, 1953 coronation commemorative, brown transfer-
printed portrait of the queen w/a
fancy blue border, Crown Ducal,
10" d. 75.00

Plates, tin, one depicting Queen
Elizabeth, the other Prince Philip,
each 10" d., pr. 40.00

Tray, china, 1953 coronation
commemorative, Royal Winton,
3½ x 4½" 35.00

Tray, china, commemorating the
1959 royal visit to Canada & the
United States, Shelley, 4 x 4" 35.00

ROYCROFT ITEMS

*Elbert Hubbard, eccentric entrepreneur of
the late 19th century, founded Roycroft Shops
and established a craft community in East
Aurora, New York in 1895. Individuals were
trained in the trades of bookbinding, leather
tooling and printing. Craft-style furniture in
the manner of Gustav Stickley and known as
"Aurora Colonial" furniture was produced.
A copper workshop, begun in 1908, turned out
numerous items. All of these, along with the
Buffalo Pottery china which was produced exclusively for use at the Roycroft Inn and carries the Roycroft symbol, constitutes a special
category associated with the Arts and Crafts
movement.*

Ashtray, floor model, mahogany &
copper, a thick round foot sup-

porting a slender tapering turned pedestal supporting the rounded bowl top inset w/a copper ashtray centered by an upright matchbox holder, original patina, orb mark, 11" d., 29" h. $225.00

Book, "The Complete Writings of Elbert Hubbard - Author's Edition, Volume I," in half-levant binding designed by Dard Hunter, color-printed beginnings of chapters, autographed, number 852 of edition of 1,000, 8 x 11½" (minor wear to sides of spine) 99.00

Book, "Little Journeys to the Homes of Great Musicians," by Elbert Hubbard, 1901 .... 50.00

Book ends, hand-hammered copper, rectangular flat upright plate decorated w/a round, raised & tooled stylized flower blossom, simple raised line borders on sides & top, rivets along the base, No. 322, excellent new patina, early 20th c., 4" w., 5½" h., pr. ... 275.00

Bowl, copper w/hand-hammered finish, molded undulating rim band, original glossy dark patina, orb mark, 4½" d., 2½" h. 198.00

Box, cov., "goody"-type, mahogany, rectangular hinged top w/hammered iron & copper strap hinges, strap latch & end handles, metal-trimmed bottom corners, original finish, incised orb mark on top, 12 x 23", 9½" h. 550.00

Candlesticks, hand-hammered copper, 'Princess' model, slightly domed rectangular foot supporting two tall slender square stems holding a dished drip pan below the cylindrical candlecup w/flared rim, original dark patina, orb mark, 8" h., pr. 485.00

raised diamond cartouche on the front, fitted cover w/button finial engraved w/the monogram "GM," original dark patina, orb mark, 4¾" d., 7" h. (ILLUS.) 330.00

Lamp, table model, the 9½" d. domed shade composed of a brass-washed hammered metal frame set w/mica panels around the bottom rim, on a simple columnar hammered metal standard w/a wide round foot, original patina, orb mark, overall 14½" h. (minor wear) 1,870.00

Side chair, mahogany, a corseted flat splat between two slats flanked by tall flat stiles w/rounded tops, over-upholstered square seat, square tapering legs joined by rungs, old restored finish, No. 30, unmarked, 43½" h. 302.50

Tray, hand-hammered copper, long oval form, delicate incised & embossed stylized flower band near outer rim, glossy dark original patina, orb mark, 9¼ x 22½" 605.00

Vase, bud, hand-hammered copper & silver, a slender cylindrical body surrounded by four open buttress handles running from the rim to the base, the rim w/a band of applied silver squares, overall wood grain texture, heavy gauge, original dark patina, marked, 4¼" d., 8" h. 2,970.00

Vase holder, hand-hammered copper, a disc foot below a scalloped petal-form short pedestal supporting four tall slender, pointed leaf-shaped tabs flanking a green glass trumpet-form Steuben-marked vase, orb mark on the holder, early 20th c., 3½" d., 5¾" h. plus the vase 440.00

RUGS - HOOKED & OTHER

HOOKED

Roycroft Copper Humidor

Humidor, cov., hand-hammered copper, cylindrical body w/flared base decorated w/stylized trefoil blossoms in repousse' & w/a

Reindeer & Floral Urns Hooked Rug

Banded design, rectangular w/long
concentric rectangles composed of
thin bands of olive green, rose,
black & other colors, mounted on
a black cloth-covered stretcher,
23 x 38" (some wear)...........$110.00

Cat & kitten w/"Welcome" in a
semicircle, multicolored yarns on
an off-white ground, 24 x 39" 725.00

Conestoga wagon drawn by six
white horses, colorful scene
w/mill, trees & houses in background, mid-20th c., 25 x 48"
(minor edge damage)........... 265.00

Eagle & American shield, the center
w/a large spread-winged American eagle w/a shield on its
breast, in front of a banner reading "9th REGT US INFANTRY"
& a star-studded fan-shaped
background, a wide border
w/scattered stars, late 19th c.,
20 x 34" 1,100.00

Floral medallion, room-sized, rectangular, a large central floral
medallion in pale pinks, blues,
greens & browns on a cream
ground framed by a scrolling leaf
border, dark blue edging w/col-
ored leaf & flower spandrels at
each corner, late 19th - 20th c.,
106 x 146½" 6,050.00

Geese (two) flying above a marshy
scene of cattails, worked in greys,
green, brown, black & other accent colors, 26 x 41" (binding
worn) 150.00

Geometric 'Rose & Tile' patt., room-
sized, worked in brown, beige,
grey, black & red in an overall
pattern of squares framing stylized rose blossoms, early 20th c.,
108 x 140" (some repair & restoration).........................5,775.00

Goats, worked in tones of red, yellow, grey, blue & black w/two
large horned goats & three small
horned goats, the border w/large
scallops, ca. 1930, 35 x 39" (some
repairs) 880.00

Landscape & seascape, rectangular,
two rectangular sections, the upper one depicting a farm scene
w/a white house w/American
flag, a red barn, a woman & various animals in the yard, the lower
section w/a large white sailing
ship approaching a pier w/light-
house & rowboat, all within a
striped border, late 19th - early
20th c., 97 x 129"..............2,860.00

Lions, a large reclining lion in the
center foreground w/a smaller
walking lion in the left distance,
surrounded by palm trees & jungle plants, worked in shades of
brown, green, black, blue, red &
grey, dated "1922" in one corner,
from a pattern by Ebenezer Ross,
mounted on a burlap-covered
frame, 34½ x 63½" 700.00

Reindeer, floral wreath & floral urns
worked in shades of coral, green,
red, yellow, lavender & grey on a
black ground, bears fabric label
& string tag printed "Made in
Labrador - International Grenfell
Association," Labrador, Canada,
ca. 1925, 25¾ x 39½" (ILLUS.) ...3,410.00

Sleigh ride scene, worked in tones
of beige, orange, red, brown &
black, the silhouetted scene of
a man driving a sleigh pulled
by a single horse through a leaf-
less winter forest, mounted
on a stretcher, early 20th c.,
30 x 47" 1,430.00

Starburst filling the center w/a
small starburst at each corner,
room-sized, worked in dark
brown, white , beige, red, green
& blue against a dark brown &
green variegated ground, probably Pennsylvania, late 19th c.,
some repairs, restoration & discoloration, 70" sq. 1,650.00

Uncle Sam, flags & stars, worked in
red, white & blue, grey, yellow &
green, the small figure of Uncle
Sam standing above a rectangular platform w/the date "1900" &
wearing a blue swallowtail coat,
top hat & carrying a walking stick
& small American flag, flanked by
two large American flags on flag-
poles surrounded by floating red
& green five-point stars, a spread-
winged American eagle at the
center w/draped American flags,
the whole scene within a faith-
hope-and-charity chain border,
on a stretcher, 34 x 58" 16,500.00

OTHER

Art Deco rug, room-sized, a linear
check pattern in salmon, black,
green, light blue & brown,
8' 5" x 14' (minor wear)......... 275.00

Braided & shirred rug, the oval center section in shirred fabric
worked in blue, rose, beige, pink
& brown w/a footed bowl filled
w/sprays of stylized concentric-
ringed flowers & buds against a
dark brown ground, the whole
within red, white & blue braided
band borders, on a stretcher, mid-

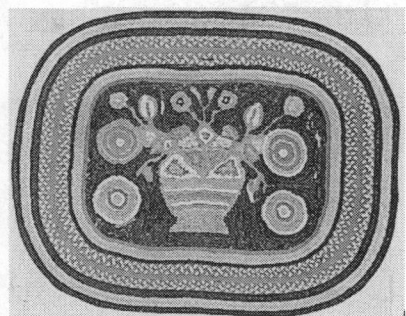

Braided & Shirred Rug

19th c., some repairs & fabric
loss, 27½ x 34" (ILLUS.) 2,750.00
Ingrain carpet, room-sized, woven
w/leafy scrolls & flowers & lyre
medallions in shades of green &
red wool, America, mid-19th c.,
14 x 15' (some fiber loss) 1,100.00
Needlepoint rug, room-sized, a serpentine lattice design w/a dark
blue ground w/light blue, celery
& olive green, enclosed by a tulip border in rust, light blue &
caramel, after a design of William Morris, early 20th c.,
4' 9" x 7' 10" 550.00
Shirred wool, red & pink stars on
a variegated green, cream &
brown field, America, 19th c.,
2' 2" x 5' 1" (some old repairs,
fading) 550.00
Wool felt, room-sized, rectangular,
printed w/a pattern of bowknots
& pine cones on a red ground,
America, 19th c., 7' 4" x 12' 3" . . . 770.00
Woven carpet, room-sized, Savon-
nerie, the grey-brown ground w/a
central pale blue roundel framed
by bold rose acanthus leaves
within a dentil border, France,
ca. 1900, 4' 6" x 6' 8" 5,500.00

SALESMAN'S SAMPLES

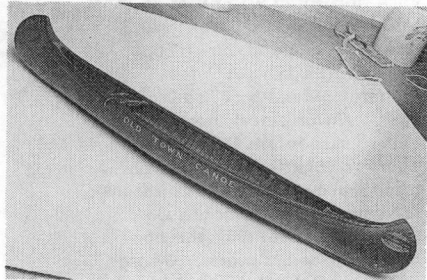

"Old Town Canoe" Sample

The traveling salesman or "drummer" has
all but disappeared from the American scene.
In the latter part of the 19th century and up
to the late 1930's, they traveled the country
calling on potential customers to show them
small replicas of their products. Today these
small versions of kitchenwares, farm equipment, and even bathtubs, are of interest to
collectors and are available in a wide price
range.

Blotters, "Wrenn's Blotters," sample
book, colorful, ca. 1920 . . . . $34.00
Canoe, "Old Town Canoe," wood,
printed marking along side & la-
bel on one end, 50" l. (ILLUS.) . . . 7,700.00
Clothes wringer, Lovell Manufacturing Co., Erie, Pennsylvania, adver-
tisement reads, "ANCHOR BRAND
- Best on Earth," patent dated
"June 20, 1899," 7½ x 8" 300.00
Coffin, wooden w/metal fittings,
removable top, all original,
3 x 22" 121.00
Furnace, "Anthanor Furnace," May &
Fiebeger, Akron, Ohio, cast alu-
minum, four-chamber, 17 separate
parts 550.00
Hat, man's, "Dobbs Fifth Ave., New
York," in original Dobbs hatbox . . 52.00
Plow, moldboard-type, w/decals 175.00
Roaster, graniteware, dark blue &
black speckled, 5" d. 115.00
Saddle, hand-sewn & tooled leather
conchos, white wool packing,
9" l. 300.00

"Eclipse" Kitchen Range

Stove, kitchen range-type, "Eclipse,"
cast iron w/silvered finish, ornate cast scrollwork, complete
w/stovepipe, late 19th c.
(ILLUS.) 910.00
Trash can, metal, embossed "Chief"
on lid, 4" h. 45.00

SCALES

Victorian Jockey's Scale

Baby scale, wicker top, painted white w/pictures of babies & toy animals $45.00

Balance scale, countertop, cast iron w/brass arm & weight, w/stenciling, Fairbanks 75.00

Balance scale, countertop, brass, tripod base w/openwork cross-arm suspending a shallow pan from each arm, marked "Doyles & Son London," 20" h. 220.00

Candy scale, countertop, brass, "Toledo No. 405A," weighs to 2 lbs. 165.00

Egg scale, galvanized zinc, "Oakes," oz. determines dozens, Tipton, Ohio 20.00

Jockey's scale, brass, oak & elm, a rectangular wooden bench w/a carved Jacobean-style flowerhead apron on heavy spiral-turned legs, one end of the top fitted w/a beige suede weighing seat, an etched brass scale w/tray & four weights at other end, marked "Young & Son, London," England, second half 19th c., 17½ x 34" (ILLUS.) 4,180.00

Postal scale, "Accurate," first class letter 3c 22.00

Postal scale, "IDL DeLuxe," ca. 1940 .... 20.00

Postal scale, tin & chrome, "W.M. Pelouze," patent dated 1897, small 22.00

Spring scale, hanging-type, polished brass face & hooks, "Chatillon," weighs to 30 lbs., 16½" l. 50.00

Spring scale, hanging-type, brass face, "Chatillon," weighs to 125 lbs., 14" l. 85.00

Spring scale, hanging-type, "Detecto No. 4100," weighs to 100 lbs., 11" l. 75.00

SCIENTIFIC INSTRUMENTS

Victorian Papier-Mache' Barometer

Barometer, pocket-type, brass pocket watch-shaped case, worn original cardboard case w/paper label marked "Henry J. Green, Brooklyn, N.Y. 1899," brass case marked "Made in England," 2¾" d. $203.50

Barometer, stick-type, gilt-bronze mounted mahogany, the round dial surmounted by two gilt-bronze putti & supported by winged busts jointed by drapery & continuing down the long rectangular drop framing the tube, Napoleon III period, France, mid-19th c., 3' 9" h. 3,025.00

Barometer, wheel-type, Directoire style, giltwood, the shaped rectangular frame w/palmette border enclosing a hexagonal barometer signed "Chevallier," surmounted by the top crest representing a science trophy incorporating a globe, books & palm fronds, France, late 18th c., 24¼" w., 39" h. (top crest associated) 8,525.00

Barometer, wheel-type, papier-mache' & black lacquer, a 10" silvered dial below an alcohol thermometer both within the shaped case decorated w/mother-of-pearl inlay & overall painted floral garlands, England, ca. 1860, 38½" h. (ILLUS.) 748.00

Barometer, wheel-type, satinwood case w/swan's-neck pediment over a serpentine case w/thermometer over etched steel barometer face w/'Rain-Fair' indicator, face signed "P. Barbon & Co., Edinburgh," Scotland, the back also inscribed "Barbon," George III period, late 18th c., 41" h. (later tube) 3,300.00

Compass, magnetic, brass-cased, made by W. & L.E. Gurley, New York, w/leaf sights, in fitted wooden case & w/fitted leather carrying case, 19th c. (crystal cracked) 450.00

Compass, surveyor's model, brass, face engraved "HM Poole, Easton, Mass.," 19th c., cased, 14½" l. 660.00

Microscope, brass, "Bausch & Lomb," straight neck, large single tube, ca. 1880, w/cherry box 550.00

Microscope, brass, "Spencer," professional-type, double tube, multi-lenses, ca. 1930's, w/cherry box 350.00

Octant, brass & ebony, made by W. & S. Jones, London, England, 19th c., w/fitted box, radius 14" (loose parts) 467.50

American Victorian Orrery

Orrery, a world globe rotating on an arm above a round base, marked "Joslin's Six-Inch Terrestrial Globe - Gilman-Joslin, Boston, 1860," 9" h. (ILLUS.) 1,980.00

Sextant, brass, signed by Dollard, London, England, 19th c., radius 8½" 330.00

Sundial & compass, pocket-size, silver, Butterfield-type, w/recessed compass, folding bird gnomon, the base engraved w/a list of cities & their latitudes, the compass housing brass (possibly replaced), in a later treen circular box, Macqart, Paris, France, early 18th c., 2½" l. 2,640.00

Telescope, brass, the barrel w/an adjustable eyepiece, raised on an ebonized tripod stand, Vickers, York, England, 19th c., barrel 44½" l., stand 52" h. 1,980.00

Telescope, brass & steel, refracting-type, triple-draw tube w/sighting scope inscribed "GALL & LEMBKE, N.Y.," the rim inscribed "JOHN BYRNE, NEW YORK 1895," on a

collapsible red-painted tripod stand, late 19th c., overall 5' 2" h. 2,640.00

Thermometer, ivory, the thermometer mounted on a column within a temple frame w/pierced tapering cupola, signed "Brinton, Brighton," England, 19th c., 8" h. (lacking finial)...................... 440.00

Transit level, brass, marked "J.T. Hobby, New York," ca. mid-1800's 750.00

SCOUTING ITEMS

Scout rules and regulations, handbooks and accouterments have changed with the times. Early items associated with the Scouting movements are now being collected. A sampling follows.

BOY SCOUT

Book, "Boy Scout Camera Club," by G. Harvey Ralphson, 1913 .... $6.00

Book, "Boy Scouts Life of Lincoln," by Tarbell, 1937, New York, w/dust jacket 10.00

Book, "Golden Anniversary, Book of Scouting," 1959, artwork by Norman Rockwell, w/dust jacket 35.00

Bugle, brass, Rex Craft, official model........................ 75.00

Calendar, 1936, illustrated by Norman Rockwell................... 185.00

Calendar, 1939, salesman's sample, illustrated by Norman Rockwell... 38.00

Calendar, 1944, illustrated by Norman Rockwell................... 42.00

Calendar, 1959, illustrated by Norman Rockwell, 16 x 33".......... 55.00

Charm, gold-filled, "National Scout Jamboree 1977"................. 20.00

Compass, aluminum on clear Lucite ruler base, Sylva Pathfinder 20.00

Explorer manual, 1955, by Ted S. Holstein 5.00

Game, "American Boy Game," Milton Bradley, ca. 1912, nice graphics 100.00

Handbook, 1919................... 30.00
Handbook, 1928................... 30.00
Handbook, 1935................... 10.00
Handbook, 1940, revised first edition in leather insignia jacket 25.00
Handbook, 1959, Norman Rockwell cover 5.00
Knife, fixed blade model, Remington, ca. 1920, w/sheath, 2 pcs. 125.00
Membership certificate, 1929 .... 7.00
Patch, 1953 National Jamboree 30.00

Phonograph record, cylinder-type, Sousa's "Boy Scouts of America March," w/the Boy Scout Chorus, Edison, ca. 1920 .... 48.00

Pin, enameled metal, Baden-Powell w/initials "B.P." & Scout knot, 1½" l. 30.00

Pocketknife, official Boy Scout model, unusual cream-colored handles, Imperial 25.00

Scarf, 1935 Jamboree 125.00

Scarf, 1953 Jamboree 35.00

Sheet music, "The Boy Scout March," by Macy, 1911 .... 25.00

Sheet music, "Scouting in the USA - Scout March," by Bartlett, 1917 ... 25.00

Signal set, Official Boy Scout, ca. 1950's 40.00

Tee shirt, 1957 Jamboree 29.00

BROWNIE SCOUT

Bank, model of a handbag, vinyl & hard plastic, 5 x 8" 60.00

Cookie cutters, ca. 1960's, the set .. 8.00

Doll, black girl in Brownie uniform, original clothes & wig, Effanbee, ca. 1965 .... 68.00

Handbook, 1951, hard cover 10.00

GIRL SCOUT

Calendar, 1946, w/original envelope 20.00

Camera, w/box, ca. 1950's 25.00

Handbook, 1917 .... 75.00

Handbook, 1932 .... 12.50

Handbook, 1947, hard cover, w/bookmark 15.00

Handbook, 1950 .... 5.00

Mess kit, Official Girl Scout, No. 15-3024, in original box 12.00

Pocketknife, "Utica Featherweight," ca. 1940's 26.00

Sash w/18 merit badges, 1964 ...... 30.00

Uniform, World War I era, w/hat & 15 badges 145.00

SCRIMSHAW

Scrimshaw is a folk art by-product of the 19th century American whaling industry. Intricately carved and engraved pieces of whalebone, whale's teeth and walrus tusks were produced by whalers during their spare time at sea. In recent years numerous fine grade hard plastic reproductions have appeared on the market so the novice collector must use caution to distinguish these from the rare originals.

Corset busk, engraved whalebone, decorated w/a fashionable lady & gentleman, inscribed "In God We Hope," 19th c., 12" l. (splits) $165.00

Corset busk, engraved whalebone, engraved w/a figure of Columbia, a bowl of flowers, a lighthouse & lady-slipper blossom, reverse initials "FS," late 19th c., 12½" l. ... 440.00

Corset busk, engraved whalebone, decorated w/a rising sun, a mourning scene & a bird & primrose, 19th c., 13¼" l............ 467.50

Whale's tooth, engraved on one side w/a bust portrait of Washington, the reverse w/a bust portrait of Lafayette, the borders w/laurel wreaths & scrolls, early 19th c., 5½" h. (some old chips & minor imperfections) 1,320.00

Whale's tooth, the side engraved w/a scene of a harbor & townscape which evolves in a spiral from the crown to the base, the top w/a series of frame buildings, houses & stores, a city hotel, a lighthouse & bath & w/various masted vessels in the harbor, 19th c., 7¼" h. 2,070.00

Scrimshaw Whale's Tooth
Whale's teeth, each decorated w/an engraved square-rigged sailing ship under full sail beneath a moon & stars, polychrome decoration, mounted on rosewood bases, American-made, 19th c., unobtrusive age cracks, 4¼" h., pr. (ILLUS. of one) 3,740.00

SEWING ADJUNCTS

Bodkin case, Tartanware, "Buchanan" $95.00

Book, "Lace Making & Needlework," by Barbours, color, 1896, 97 pp. .. 30.00

Crochet thread dispenser, Mauchlineware, round, colorful floral transfer, Coats label, 3½" d. 55.00

Darning egg, turned maple, 5" l. 25.00

Darning kit, leather folder, dog on cover 12.00

Pincushion, cast white metal, model of a recumbent lamb, a worn gold cloth pincushion forming the back, approximately 2" l. 49.50

Pincushion, cast white metal, model of a reclining cat, a worn pink cloth pincushion forming its back, marked "J.B. 681" & w/paper labels, 5¼" l. 71.50

Pincushion, embroidered silk, ball-shaped, embroidered w/chain-stitch in shades of green, yellow, peach & puce on a black silk ground, America, late 18th c., 2¼" d. (some wear, faded) 770.00

Sewing bag, ink-inscribed & decorated, decorated w/a verse, floral swag & birds on branches, inscribed "Martha Welsh Jackson to Miss Abigail Whitney Bancroft, 1818," Groton, Massachusetts, 7¾ x 9¾" 165.00

Sewing box, hardwood, top w/ball-turned column supporting a pincushion, holes for spool pins, one drawer, turned feet, dark finish, 7½" h. (pincushion worn) 40.00

Sewing box, cov., papier-mache' & mother-of-pearl, rectangular w/scalloped edges, the top inlaid w/mother-of-pearl roses on thorny gilt stems, opening to reveal a compartment interior, 19th c., 10 x 13" 220.00

Sewing box w/domed hinged lid, lacquer, opening to a tray w/open & lidded compartments & carved ivory sewing implements, the conforming case on carved dragon-head feet, decorated overall w/panels of chinoiserie figures on black ground, Chinese Export, early 19th c., 10½ x 15", 7" h. 2,420.00

Sewing kit, embossed leather, "Ladies' Companion," w/plaid lining, waxed writing card, floral engraved silver plate scissors, silver thimble, embroidery punch w/carved mother-of-pearl handle, red velvet pincushion & thimble holder, compartmented 275.00

Sewing kit, ivory, fitted w/14k gold thimble, gold-filled scissors, needle holder & bodkin, ca. 1850 .... 595.00

Silk winder, mother-of-pearl, petal shape 65.00

Tape measure, advertising, "Hoover Vacuum," 1950's 55.00

Tape measure, brass, model of a standing pig 85.00

Tape measure, celluloid, model of a kangaroo, pink 70.00

Thimble, sterling silver, wide band engraved w/holly & stork design............................ 25.00

Thimble case, vegetable ivory, mushroom-shaped, w/ivory thimble 85.00

SHAKER ITEMS

Shaker Butternut Stepladder

The Shakers, a religious sect founded by Ann Lee, first settled in this country at Watervliet, New York, near Albany, in 1774 and by 1880 there were nine settlements in America. Workmanship in Shaker crafts is an extension of their religious beliefs and features plain and simple designs reflecting a chaste elegance that is now much in demand though relatively few early items are available.

Box, cov., miniature, oval bent-wood, single lappet on base & cover, original yellow varnish finish, inside of cover w/pencil inscription "M. Catherine Allen, North Family 1882," four small wooden bobbins inside, 4 5/8" l. $4,070.00

Box, cov., painted oval bentwood, a single-lappet w/iron tacks on cover & double-lappets w/tacks on base, original green paint, 7 7/8" l. 412.50

Chest of drawers, painted pine & poplar, a low crestboard above the rectangular top over three long graduated drawers w/small wooden knobs, square tapering legs, decorated w/blue paint, possibly New York, 19th c. 2,090.00

Cream keeler, stave construction, two wide hickory buttonhole loops, fine patina, ca. 18th c., 16" d., 6½" h. 295.00

Cupboard, painted pine, rectangular
top above a pair of double-
paneled long doors w/a short
raised panel above a long raised
panel, a row of six small square
drawers w/small wooden knobs
across the bottom, bootjack feet,
old green paint, the interior
w/thirty pigeonholes & two
shelves, inside of one door branded "C.W. Durrell," used in the
dairy at Canterbury, New Hampshire, 19th c., 18½ x 38 3/8",
4' 9¼" h. (some damage to backboards, repairs to feet & edge
damage) 4,125.00
Desk, slant-top school-type, pine,
maple & ash, a low crestrail
above a pair of long rectangular
lift-lids above a wide apron over
a shaped support rail joining the
thick rectangular end legs on
arched shoe feet, early 19th c. ... 660.00
Medicine bottle, "Shaker Anodyne,"
aqua, Enfield, New Hampshire,
3½" h. 35.00
Pantry box, cov., miniature, oval
bentwood, lappet construction
w/two Harvard-style laps, New
England, late 19th - early 20th c.,
1¾ x 2½" 192.50
Rocking chair without arms, cylindrical back stiles w/turned acorn
finials above the woven tape back
above the woven tape seat,
turned legs joined by double
stretchers, painted brown, Mt.
Lebanon, New York, late 19th c.,
34" h. 880.00
Rocking chair w/arms, child's, the
tall back w/three arched slats below a slender blanket bar, slender arms w/mushroom handgrips
above baluster-turned arm supports, padded seat, size No. 0,
New Lebanon, New York, ca.
1900 ....3,080.00
Sewing carrier, open, oval bentwood, four-lappet construction,
w/bentwood swing handle, base
stamped "Sabbathday Lake Shakers Maine," early 20th c., 9" l.
(imperfections) 275.00
Side chair, ladder-back type, cherry
& tiger maple, three curved &
gently arched slats in the back
between plain turned stiles w/ob-
long turned finials, woven rush
seat, double rungs on the front &
sides, probably Harvard, Massachusetts, ca. 1840-60, old finish,
41½" h. 880.00
Stepladder, butternut, the shaped &
canted sides w/dovetailed side

braces centering three tapered
tiers, Alfred or Sabbathday Lake,
Maine, ca. 1840, 14" w., 23½" h.
(ILLUS.) 3,410.00

19th Century Shaker Stove

Stove, cast iron, long rectangular
body w/slightly canted sides, door
opening at one end above a semi-
circular shelf, raised on four slender slightly splayed legs, probably
New Lebanon, New York, 19th c.,
11 x 31", 18¾" h. (ILLUS.)....... 550.00
Work table, cherry & pine, rectangular top overhanging a deep apron
w/an end drawer, on turned &
slightly tapering legs, possibly
New York State, mid-19th c.,
25 x 36¼", 29¼" h. 3,850.00

SHEET MUSIC

"A Dream is a Wish Your Heart
Makes," 1949, from Disney's 'Cin-
derella' $10.00
"Ain't Dat A Shame," 1901, by John
Queen & Walter Wilson, black
comic cover................... 10.00
"Alexander Don't You Love Your
Baby No More?," 1904, by An-
drew Sterling & Harry Von Tilzer,
blackface cover 15.00
"All Aboard for Home Sweet
Home," 1918, by Burkhart, Statue
of Liberty, troop ship & Courtney
Sisters on cover 15.00
"Annie Get Your Gun," Ethel Mer-
man on the cover 15.00
"A Signal From Mars," 1901, cover
by E.T. Paull 15.00
"Back, Back, Back to Baltimore,"
1904, by Harry Williams & Egbert
Van Alstyne, black comic cover... 15.00
"Broadway Is My Home Sweet
Home," 1915, Charlie Chaplin on
cover (small tear) 10.00

"Chariot Race March," 1894, E.T. Paull cover 10.00

"Circus Parade March," cover by E.T. Paull 45.00

"Georgia Land," Sophie Tucker & blacks & cotton field photograph on cover 15.00

"Good-Bye Alexander," 1918, by Henry Creamer & Turner Layton, depicts World War I parade & black troops 15.00

"Heaven's Artillery," 1904, H. Lincoln 10.00

"The Home Coming March," 1908, cover by E.T. Paull 15.00

"I'd Leave My Happy Home For You," 1899, by William Heelan & Harry Von Tilzer, blackface cover 15.00

"Is It True What They Say About Dixie," Al Jolson on cover 25.00

"I Want My Mammy," 1921, colorful, blacks depicted on cover........ 13.00

"The Liberty Bell March," 1894, by John Philip Sousa 15.00

"The Little Ford Rambled Right Along," 1914, by Fay Foster & Byron Gay 22.50

"Little French Mother, Good Bye!," cover artwork by Norman Rockwell, World War I era 15.00

"Lovely to Look At," 1935, Ginger Rogers & Fred Astaire on cover... 15.00

"Meet Me in St. Louis," 1944, Judy Garland cover 25.00

"The Merry Widow," 1934, Jeanette MacDonald cover............... 10.00

"Motor King March," 1910, by Frantzen & Drislane, early auto cover .. 20.00

"Oh! Min," 1918, Andy Gump on cover 10.00

"Over Yonder Where the Lilies Grow," 1918, cover artwork by Norman Rockwell 12.00

"Pershing's Crusaders," 1918, cover by E.T. Paull 25.00

"The Race Course March," 1910, cover by E.T. Paull 35.00

"Roaring Volcano," 1912, cover by E.T. Paull..................... 30.00

"Salvation Lassie of Mine," 1919, by Jack Cuddigan & Chick Story 12.00

"Smokey Mokes," 1899, by A. Holzmann, blackface cover........... 10.00

"So Long, Mother," 1917, photo of Al Jolson & scene of a soldier saying goodbye 22.00

"Sympathy," 1937, from 'Firefly,' Jeanette MacDonald cover 10.00

"Tipperary Guards March," 1915, cover by E.T. Paull 25.00

"When That Midnight Choo Choo Leaves for Alabama," 1912, by Irving Berlin, depicts a train 15.00

"When the Car Goes By - The Motorman's Popular Song," 1897, by E.S. Ufford, open trolley on cover 35.00

"When You Wish Upon A Star," 1940, from Disney's 'Pinocchio' ... 18.00

"Where Did Robinson Crusoe Go With Friday on Saturday Night?," 1916, depicts Al Jolson in blackface 40.00

SIGNS & SIGNBOARDS

Columbia Beer Curved Sign

Animal medicine, "White's Golden Tonic for Horses, Out of Condition," lists cures w/picture of horse, framed, ca. 1900, 24 x 30".................. $75.00

Apothecary shop, molded zinc, large figural mortar & pestle, America, 19th c., 40" h. 467.50

Beer, "Carling's Ale," blue & creamy white enameled tin, scene of nine policemen sitting on a bench each holding a mug marked "Carling" & titled "Nine Pints of the Law," 12½ x 20"..................... 55.00

Beer, "Columbia Brg. Co. - Columbia Beer - Shenandoah, Pa.," vitrolite curved corner-type, a figure of Columbia standing behind a large shield, late 19th - early 20th c. (ILLUS.) 7,150.00

Beer, "Pabst - Milwaukee," leaded glass, at the center a large leaf & "B" framed by a ring w/lettering surrounded by scrolls & bands of "jewels," framed in wood, late 19th - early 20th c. 7,150.00

Blacksmith, painted sheet-iron, the silhouetted depiction of a large horseshoe centered by the figure of a prancing horse, painted black, late 19th - early 20th c.,

Sheet-Iron Blacksmith's Sign

some exfoliation & rust, 32" w.,
36" h. (ILLUS.) 2,310.00

Eyedrops, "Murine Eye Remedies,"
silvered glass, blue chipped lettering, resilvered & airbrushed in
original shimmering colors, ca.
1895-1910, ¼" thick, 6 x 38" 375.00

Grocery store, "Honor Brand is Better - Gowan-Peyton-Twohy Co.
Wholesale Grocers, Duluth," tin,
depicts a small blonde girl holding
red carnation-type flowers, 1907,
41½ x 17½" oval 525.00

Gun powder, "Dupont,"
lithographed canvas, wagon train
scene, signed & dated "1911,"
15 x 18" 285.00

Hair tonic, "Wildroot," cardboard,
w/nine color pictures of television's Robin Hood & Maid Marian,
w/facsimile autographs, ca.
1950's, 20 x 29" 50.00

Early Thomas Inks Sign

Inks, "Thomas Inks and Mucilage -
'Ask For Me,' " colorful embossed
tin, a grouping of bottles w/a
black cat spilling red ink, minor
corner damage, late 19th - early
20th c. (ILLUS.) 17,050.00

Marine lubricants, "Texaco Marine
Lubricants," tin, depicts five ships,
buoys, sea gulls, etc., 12 x 21" . . . 595.00

Motor oil, "McMillan Motor Oil,"
porcelain, authorized pump service, double-sided, depicts lepre-
chaun on each side 375.00

Olive oil, "Oliva Olive Oil," tin,
depicts can 95.00

Paint, "Lucas Paint," tin, colorful scene of giant-sized man
painting a miniature town, ca.
1904, 24 x 36" 750.00

Paint, "Martin Senour Paints & Varnish," cardboard, scene of the
ocean liner Queen Mary w/tug
boats & yachts, framed 3 x 4' 525.00

Physician, "Doctor C.O. Rogne,"
reverse-painted on glass within a
gilt reserve, 11 x 29" 175.00

Potato chips, "Wise Potato Chips,"
cardboard, depicts boy & girl in
store, 1940 . . . . 150.00

Service station, "Amoco," banner,
depicts man driving car, ca.
1940's, 36 x 36" 75.00

Service station, "Eveready Beam
Lamps," tin, "Installation & Aiming
Service" 30.00

Shoe repair shop, painted wood &
iron, double-sided model of a
large shoe, painted black & inscribed "shoes repaired while you
wait," late 19th - early 20th c.,
20½" h. 880.00

Poll-Parrot Neon Sign

Shoes, "Poll-Parrot," porcelain &
neon, red, orange, yellow, green
& blue parrot, dark red lettering
on white, parrot outlined in red
neon, very minor fading, 22" w.,
38" h. (ILLUS.) 1,265.00

Soft drink, "Dr. Pepper," double-
sided cardboard, depicts cheer-
leader on one side & square-
dancing couple on the other,
ca. 1950's 85.00

Soft drink, "Orange Crush," tin,
model of a bottle cap, 18" h. 165.00

Soft drink, "Pepsi-Cola," celluloid &
tin, illustration of a black couple

& "now it's Pepsi...perfect any-
time!," ca. 1960 .... 120.00
Soft drink, "RC Cola," cardboard,
Mona Freeman pictured, ca.
1940's, 26 x 39" 95.00
Soft drink, "7-Up," die-cut tin,
bottle-shaped, w/logo, 44" h. 150.00
Soft drink, "7-Up," neon, depicts
three-color fountain glass w/straw
& fizz bubbles 650.00
Soft drink, "Vitalized Ginger Ale,"
tin, depicts girl on surfboard,
6 x 9" 25.00
Table water, "White Rock," tin,
scene entitled "King of Hearts,"
signed August Hutaf, 8 x 13" 450.00
Tea, "Salada Tea," porcelain, in the
shape of a tea box 285.00
Tools, "Standard End Cutting Nipper," celluloid & tin over cardboard, depicts hand holding
nippers, 6 x 11" 225.00
Veterinary medicine, "Dr. Lesure
Veterinary Colic Cure," die-cut,
depicts two children giving medicine to one of three cats, ca.
19th c., framed, 15 x 18" 145.00
Whiskey, "Jack Daniels Old Tennessee Whiskey," tin, gold background w/corn stalks, black & red
letters, "Old No. 7 Brand," etc.... 125.00

SILHOUETTES

*These cut-out paper portraits in profile were
named after Etienne de Silhouette, Louis
XV's unpopular minister of finance and an
amateur profile cutter. As originally applied,
the term was synonymous with cheapness,
or anything reduced to its simplest state.
These substitutes for the more expensive oil
paintings or miniatures were popular from
about 1770 until 1850 when daguerreotype images replaced the vogue. Silhouettes may be
either hollow-cut, with the head cut away
leaving the white paper frame for mounting
against a dark background, or the profile itself may be cut from black paper and pasted
to a light background.*

Bust portrait of a man facing left,
hollow-cut, wearing a high white
collar, pencil detailing, in old
molded giltwood frame, early
19th c., 4¾ x 5 5/8" $150.00
Bust portrait of George Washington,
in a wide mahogany veneered
beveled frame, Philadelphia, portrait late 18th c., frame early
19th c., frame 8¼ x 9¾" (paper &
frame damaged) 154.00

Bust portraits of young ladies, one
hollow-cut, the other pen & ink,
each facing left, one w/her hair
pulled back w/curls, the other
w/short cut hair, one inscribed
"Miss Julia Wood," the other
"Miss Eliza Esther Wood," each
w/penwork details, in matching
beveled rosewood frames w/gilt
liners, ca. 1830, each 5 3/8" w.,
6" h., pr. 250.00
Full-length portrait of Alexander
McNair (1776-1826), the young
gentleman standing & wearing a
long frock coat & holding a top
hat & riding crop, mounted on a
black & white lithographed background, brief biography on back
of frame, mahogany veneer beveled frame, 12½" w., 16½" h.
(minor stains) 775.00
Full-length portrait of a boy playing
ball, details heightened in pencil,
applied to a lithographed scenic
ground, signed & dated "Aug
Edouart fait 1846 Boston," framed,
6 x 9" (imperfections) 302.50
Full-length portrait of a gentleman,
hollow-cut, standing facing left,
wearing a long-tailed jacket, giltwood frame, 5¾" w., 6 3/8" h.... 250.00
Full-length portrait of a lady standing & holding a book, cut black
paper heightened w/gum arabic &
laid on paper w/a grey-washed
foreground, unsigned, 19th c.,
framed, 6½ x 9" 275.00
Full-length portrait of a young lady,
standing facing left, wearing a
flounced dress & holding a closed
fan, oval mat opening in a narrow
rectangular frame, mid-19th c.,
framed, 15¼" h. 192.50
Full-length profile portrait of a
young man, standing facing left,
wearing a waistcoat w/long tails,
white painted detailing, in a narrow black wood frame, early
19th c., 9 x 13" 171.50
Full-length portraits of a lady & gentleman, cut black paper heightened w/white water-color & laid
on water-color trimmed paper,
signed "W.H. Brown 1846,"
stamped "Hartford, Connect.,"
framed, 7¾ x 9¾" 330.00

SODA FOUNTAIN COLLECTIBLES

*The neighborhood ice cream parlor and
drugstore soda fountain are pretty much a
thing of the past as fast-food chains have*

sprung up across the country. Memories of the slower-paced lifestyle represented by the rapidly disappearing local soda fountain have spurred the interest of many collectors today. Anything relating to the soda fountains of old and the delicious concoctions they dispensed are much sought-after.

APPLIANCES
Malted milk mixer, "Hamilton Beach," mint green enamel & chrome, w/three 7" h. stainless steel glasses, 18" h., the group ... $150.00
Malted milk mixer, "Hamilton Beach," triple-head, green enamel finish w/polished chrome nameplate band, each head w/three speed settings & operate independent of each other, mint condition 265.00
Malted milk mixer, "Hamilton Beach No. 18," porcelain finish 125.00

GLASSWARES
Root beer mug, "Dad's," barrel-shaped w/embossed staves, clear, 2" h. 40.00
Root beer mug, "Rochester," clear w/etched name & line borders ... 35.00

ICE CREAM SCOOPS & SERVERS
"Arnold No. 50," wooden handle, metal scoop marked "Patent Dated Feb. 1, 1927, Racine, Wis.," 10" l. 35.00
"Bohlig Mfg. Co.," round bowl, aluminum & white metal, patent dated "Oct. 6, 1908," 10" l. 1,950.00
Cone filler-type, unknown maker, chrome-plated white metal, tapering cylindrical head w/crossed spring handles, invented by Robert J. Price, patented in 1939, 7½" l. 350.00
"Fisher Motor Co., Ltd., Orilla, Ontario, Canada," 'Cold Dog' cylinder-type, German silver, wooden handle, 1920's, 9½" l. .... 600.00 to 675.00
"Gilchrist No. 31," size 8, nickel-plated brass, wooden handle, 11" l. 50.00
"Gilchrist No. 31," size 24, round, nickel-plated brass, wooden handle, patented in 1915, 11" l. 65.00
"Gilchrist No. 35," size 24, round, chrome-plated brass, wooden handle, patented in 1932, 10" l. ... 28.00
"Hamilton Beach Model 51," round, chromium-plated brass, Bakelite handle, 8½" l. 25.00
"Hamilton Beach Model 65," size 30, round, black Bakelite handle 20.00
"ICY-PI - Automatic Cone Co.," ice

cream sandwich scoop, German silver, plastic handle, ca. 1950 .... 125.00
"Kingery Mfg. Co., Cincinnati, Ohio," 'one-handed' conical-style, nickel-plated metal, patented September 1894, 8½" l. 180.00
"Lloyd Disher Co.," aluminum, 1940 .... 20.00
"Mayer Mfg. Co., Chicago, Illinois," 'Handy' ice cream disher, ice cream slicer for ice cream sandwiches, German silver, wooden handle, 1920's, 12" l. ....225.00 to 250.00
"McLaren's ICYPI," ice cream sandwich scoop, German silver, wooden handle, ca. 1929, 10" l. 198.00
"Mosteller Mfg. Co.," round bowl w/bowl-flip mechanism, aluminum & nickel-plated brass, wooden handle, patented in 1906, 10½" l. 195.00
"Zeroll Co., Toledo, Ohio," size 20, aluminum, 1930's, 7" l. 18.00

STORAGE CONTAINERS
Malted milk jar, "Horlick's," ½ gal. 25.00
Straw dispenser jar, cov., clear multi-paneled glass w/bulging base, metal cover w/brass ball finial to pull to dispense straws, patent dated 1912 .... 295.00
Syrup bottle, "Tango'la," label-under-glass 150.00

SYRUP & OTHER DISPENSERS

Hires "Punch Bowl" Dispenser

Carbonated Beverages, Sirups (sic) - Firm of John Matthews - 333 East 26th Street, New York, jug-shaped stoneware w/light brown glaze & bluish black lettering, 1 gal. 231.00
Hires Root Beer, pottery, punch bowl-form w/deep, rounded bowl raised on a tall, waisted pedestal base, domed cover w/pointed

knob finial, cover printed
w/"Drink Hires Rootbeer," bowl
printed w/"Drink Hires 5c" & portraits of the Hires boy, base printed w/"America's Health Drink -
Hires Rootbeer," w/long metal
spigot (ILLUS.) 28,050.00

Paper cone dispenser, "Vortex,"
wall-type, domed 11" glass tube
in metal holder, "...Soda Fountain
Drinks & Ice Cream Served in Vortex," gold label (wall bracket
missing) 40.00

Rochester Root Beer, pottery, barrel-
shaped on claw feet, complete
w/drip tray, small size 475.00

Rochester Root Beer, pottery, barrel-
shaped on stump base 325.00

SOUVENIR SPOONS

*All spoons are sterling silver and teaspoon
size unless otherwise noted.*

Ashtabula, Ohio, floral handle, pow-
er plant & boat in bowl $25.00

Battle scene on ornate handle,
"Vicksburg, Miss." in bowl 35.00

Belle Isle, Detroit on ornate handle,
island & boat in bowl 22.00

Ben Franklin, Liberty Bell & building
on handle, Independence Hall in
bowl 30.00

Brooklyn Bridge, floral handle,
bridge & boats in bowl 35.00

Buffalo cut-out figural handle,
McKinley Monument & buffalo in
bowl, 5½" l. 40.00

Bust of Longfellow w/book on handle, Longfellow's house in bowl . . 35.00

Donkey on handle, "Governor's Pal-
ace, Santa Fe" in bowl 20.00

Fish handle, "Oakland, California"
in bowl, 5" l. 30.00

Floral handle, "Williamsport, Pennsylvania, City Hall" in multicolor
bowl 35.00

Girl graduate figural handle, bowl
engraved "Hutchinson, KS" 55.00

"Illinois" in shield atop full-figure
semi-nude lady enameled handle,
bowl engraved "Chicago, 1908" . . . 75.00

Indian head figural & decorated
handle, engraved "Milwaukee City
Hall" in bowl 35.00

Indian totem pole figural handle,
Olympic Range from Seattle in
bowl, 5" l. 40.00

Lighthouse on handle, scene in bowl
w/"Longfellow's Home," Portland,
Maine 35.00

"Ohio" in shield atop full-figure

semi-nude lady enameled handle,
bowl engraved "Tyler Davidson
Fountain" 75.00

Portland, Maine - Henry W. Longfellow handle, "1892" in bowl,
demitasse 18.00

Prospector figural handle, Giroux
Mill, Ely, Nevada in bowl 18.00

Salmon figural handle, engraved
"Mt. Hood" in bowl 48.00

Salmon figural handle, engraved
"Mt. Rainier" in bowl 48.00

Space Needle figural handle, "Seat-
tle World's Fair" in bowl 20.00

Washington Monument entwined in
wreaths on handle, U.S. Capitol
Building in bowl 52.00

Whitman College, Walla Walla,
Washington pictured in gold-
washed bowl 25.00

SPINNING WHEELS

Flax wheel, turned hard & soft
woods, simple turned spindles in
wheel, simple turned distaff &
spindles on canted board raised
on three splayed legs joined by
foot pedal, old worn patina, overall 32" h. (distaff replaced, rod
from pedal to wheel replaced) . . . $325.00

Flax wheel, mixed hardwoods,
wooden wheel w/twelve baluster-
turned spokes, rectangular base
on three widely splayed baluster-
and ring-turned legs, chip-carved
detail, stamped mark "S.B.," old
brown finish, 35" h. (bobbin &
spinner missing, some edge dam-
age & repair) 150.00

Flax wheel, various hardwoods,
round wheel w/ten turned spokes
supported between turned uprights on a canted platform raised
on three canted baluster- and
ring-turned legs, good turned &
chip-carved detail, old brown pati-
na, 19th c., 38" h. 250.00

Flax wheel, turned hardwoods,
round wheel w/wide rim around
short, slender turned spindles,
baluster- and ring-turned uprights
& spindles on slanting body on
three baluster- and ring-turned
canted legs joined by the pedal,
turned end handle on body, old
dark patina, 39½" h. (distaff in-
complete) 200.00

Flax wheel, upright floor model,
various hardwoods, simple turned
spindles in wheel mounted in up-

right beside the distaff & above a crossbar w/spindles above the rectangular board base raised on four turned & canted legs joined by a pedal bar, old dark finish, overall 46" h. (one spinner missing) 245.00

STATUARY

Bronzes, and other statuary, are increasingly popular with today's collectors. Particularly appealing are works by "Les Animaliers," the 19th century French school of sculptors who turned to animals for their subject matter. These, together with figures in the Art Deco and Art Nouveau taste, are available in a wide price range.

BRONZES

Bronze Figure of "Chastity"

Aizelin, Eugene-Antoine, allegorical figure of "Chastity," a young woman seated on a tall stool holding her draped flowing gown over her bosom, brown patina, signed "E.Tne. Aizelin," 33" h. (ILLUS.) $3,850.00

Bochetti, B., figure of Marc Anthony, standing w/one arm raised, wearing body armor, w/a small cupid on a dolphin at his feet, golden patina, raised on a green marble pedestal, inscribed "B. Bochetti - Roma," overall 6' ½" h. 4,125.00

Carpeaux, Jean Baptiste, figure of a fishergirl, the young woman in peasant costume w/her dress tucked up into her waistband, walking & carrying a conical basket on one arm, brown patina, inscribed "Puys" & "Carpeaux,

Propriete' Carpeaux," France, 19th c., 28½" h. 2,970.00

Bronze Statue of Joan of Arc

Chapu, Henri Michel Antoine, figure of Joan of Arc, kneeling peasant girl w/her hands clasped in her lap, brown patina, signed "H. Chapu" & "F. Barbedienne, Fondeur, Paris 475" & stamped w/the collar reduction seal, 19th c., 22" h. (ILLUS.) 3,300.00

Chiparus, Demetre, "Fan Dancer," the kneeling figure clad in a beaded costume & holding two opened fans, her hands & face carved in ivory, silver, red & polished bronze patinas, mounted on a rectangular brown onyx base, inscribed "Chiparus," impressed "MADE IN FRANCE" & w/foundry stamp under base "L.N. - PARIS - J.L.," ca. 1925, 16½" l., 14¾" h. (minor wear to patina, chips to base) 24,200.00

Fremiet, Emmanuel, equestrian figure, a knight in full armor seated on a standing armored war horse & holding a lance in one hand, brown patina, inscribed "Fremiet," France, late 19th - early 20th c., 18½" h. (losses) 3,300.00

Harvey, Eli, model of a bull elk, standing on a rockwork base, inscribed "Eli Harvey Sc. 1904 - Copyright by Eli Harvey 1904," stamped "2 - GORHAM & CO. 435," underside inscribed "D.R.Y.," rich reddish brown patina, 16 5/8" h. 1,760.00

LeFaguays, Pierre, figure of an athlete, the muscular virtually nude figure straining against a lever, dark greenish brown patina, on an irregular oval base, inscribed "P LEFAGUAYS," impressed "BRONZE" & w/a circular foundry mark, ca. 1925, 18¾" l., 11 1/8" h. 1,925.00

Allegorical Bronze by Moncel

Moncel, A., Conte Alphonse Emmanuel de Marcel de Perrin, allegorical figure of a nude boy w/just a drape across his lap seated on a high-back stone seat w/one arm around a large jug, trailing vines on the seat & jug, green patina, signed "A. Moncel" & a foundry stamp, France, 19th c., 26" h. (ILLUS.) 7,150.00

Omerth, Georges, figure group depicting a young Turk carrying away a maiden on his fleet steed, their heads & hands carved in ivory, gilt & dark brown patinas, mounted on a red-veined marble base, signed "G. OMERTH," Germany, ca. 1900, 13½" h. 4,600.00

Parsons, Edith Barretto, models of Scottish terriers, one animal standing alert, the other twisting to look behind, on rectangular bases, one inscribed "E.B. PARSONS © - KUNST FOUNDRY N.Y.," the other "E.B. PARSONS © KUNST-FOUNDRY. N.Y.," reddish brown patina, 4 3/8" & 5½" h., pr. 1,045.00

Preiss, Johan P.F. (Fritz), "The Archer," the young Amazon wearing a short patterned tunic & headdress, a saber at her waist, poised to shoot an arrow through the air, her face, torso, arms & legs well-carved in ivory, painted in rust, orange & black w/gilt, raised on a rectangular onyx base on four compressed ball feet, inscribed "F. PREISS," Germany, ca. 1925, overall 9¾" h. 10,350.00

Roth, Frederick George Richard, model of a dog, reclining on a molded rectangular base, inscribed "FGR ROTH © 1916," reddish brown patina, 7 5/8" h. 3,080.00

Sicard, Francois Leon, figure group of Oedipus & the Sphinx, the nude youth leaning on a staff, one arm raised above his head while he kicks down on the fallen sphinx to one side, brown patina, inscribed "F. Sicard," France, late 19th - early 20th c., 27" h. 8,250.00

Vienna bronze, miniature model of a cat w/broom 190.00

MARBLE

Black Marble Bust of Antinous

Andraun, F., figure of Diana, the standing goddess nude except for a drapery partially wrapped around her body & held aloft in one hand, on a scrolling cloud base, inscribed "F. Andraun - Firenze," Italy, late 19th c., 40" h. (losses) 6,600.00

Bust of Antinous as an Egyptian, based on the antique, black marble three-quarter bust of a bare-chested young man, his head tilting forward w/downcast eyes, wearing an Egyptian *nemes* headdress, 19th c., 21¾" w., 27" h. (ILLUS.) 19,800.00

Marble Figures of Water Bearers

Figures of water bearers, depicting
a male & female, she in a knee-
length dress & he wearing knee-
length pants & a long coat, each
holding a handled pitcher on his
head, standing before a stump
w/a small child at one side, Continental, late 19th c., 4' 1" h., pr.
(ILLUS.) 7,700.00

Figures depicting the four seasons,
each classically draped female figure w/well-coiffed hair, holding
foliate attributes of the season,
Victorian, third quarter 19th c.,
approximately 45" h., set of 4
(damages) 14,300.00

Sandoz, Edouard-Marcel, figure of a
hare, depicting a plump crouching
hare w/its ears laid back, on a
rectangular base w/amber stain,
inscribed "Ed. M. SANDOZ" & "A
Mme. Hewitt 1929," dated 1929,
4 7/8" l., 4½" h. 3,575.00

Zoi, D., standing figure of a young
woman nude except for a draped
cloth at her waist, one hand holds
up a dove to her breast, raised on
a dark green marble rotating column, Florence, Italy, dated 1897,
column 30" h., figure 42" h. 6,160.00

OTHER MATERIALS

Terra Cotta Bust of a Lady

Alabaster, bust of a young peasant
woman, her head turned to the
right, wearing a headscarf & simple bodice, French customs seal
on the neck, w/a marble column
base, bust 18" h. (small edge
damage, wear) 605.00

Alabaster, figure of a woman in
classical garb by an urn-form lantern, seated w/a harp by her
side, inscribed "M. Traveli," late
19th c., 30½" h. (restorations) ...8,250.00

Brass, highly stylized figure of a
nude maiden astride a rearing

steed, rectangular base, impressed "KARL - HAGENAUER -
WIEN - MADE IN - AUSTRIA,"
numbered "1122" & w/impressed
monogram, ca. 1930, 9 7/8" h....1,320.00

Ivory, figure of a maiden, the nude
maiden, w/hair pulled into a top-
knot, standing w/one hand to her
face, the other hand resting on
her hip, inscribed "D. Chiparus,"
on an onyx base, ca. 1915, figure
5¼" h. 2,200.00

Terra cotta, bust of an 18th c. lady,
her slightly tilted head w/her hair
pulled back into long curls, wearing an off-the-shoulder drapery,
inscribed "Pajou Regis Sculptor -
1779," Louis XVI-Style, 19th c.,
raised on a mottled marble socle,
overall 25½" h. (ILLUS.) 3,575.00

STEAMSHIP MEMORABILIA

Liner "Normandie" Clock

*The dawning of the age of world-wide air-
line travel brought about the decline of the
luxury steamship liner for long-distance travel. Few large liners are still operating, but
mementoes and souvenirs from their glamorous heyday are much sought-after today.*

Activity schedules & menues,
"R.M.S. Mauretania Cruise News,"
for West Indies cruise February 18
thru March 8, 1954, loose leaf $40.00

Advertising folder, "U.S. Mail Line,"
rates, ship on cover, ca. 1900 .... 18.00

Ashtray, liner "RMS Queen Elizabeth," bone china, England,
4 x 5".......................... 38.00

Book, "Steamships," by Felix Riesen-
berg, 1933, w/tipped-in color Currier & Ives prints 30.00

Book, "Tragedy of the Lusitania,"
by Captain W. Ellis, illustrated
w/photographs & pen & pencil
drawings, 1915 . . . . 18.00
Broadside, depicts four-masted
steamship, "Red Star Line" carved
in frame, colorful lithograph, ca.
1870's, 2' 6" × 3' 6" 1,800.00
Clock, liner "Normandie," molded &
frosted glass, the circular chapter
ring molded w/"NORMANDIE" in
place of numerals, centered by
the prow of the ship coursing
through a wavy sea, pale blue
tint, molded "ATO" & "MADE IN
FRANCE," ca. 1935, 5 7/8" h.
(ILLUS.) 2,300.00
Directory, "Atlantic Coast Line, Trop-
ical Trips Directory," illustrated,
1930 . . . . 20.00
Doll, "Holland America Line," sailor
boy, 11" h. 65.00
Launch book, "Cunard Lines," liner
"Queen Elizabeth," elaborately il-
lustrated, 1938 . . . . 110.00
Medallion, "Cunard Lines," liner "Lu-
sitania," bronze, depicts sinking
ship & passengers buying tickets
from a skeleton, 2¼" d. 35.00
Mirror panel, liner "Normandie," reverse painted & gilt, from "The
Rape of Europa," the rectangular
panel painted & etched on the
reverse depicting a rising sun
over distant seas, w/sections of
masts in the foreground, one of
four panels designed by Jean
Dupas for the Grande Lounge,
the glass executed by Jacques
Charles Champigneulle, ca. 1935,
34¾" w., 4' 4½" h. 5,225.00
Passport cover, "Red Star Line," fab-
ric, depicts a ship, early 25.00
Playing cards, "Norwegian America
Line," double deck in holder
w/pad & pencil 25.00
Salt & pepper shakers, "M.S. Euro-
pa," china, one blue & one maroon, each lettered w/ship's
name, pr. 110.00
Souvenir book, liner "Queen Mary,"
pictorial, ca. 1930's 18.00
Tea set: cov. teapot, sugar bowl,
creamer, individual sugar bowl,
individual creamer, two 6½" d.
plates & one 8¼" d. plate;
"Cunard Lines," china, floral pattern, Tuscan, England, the set 135.00
Tie bar & cuff links, "Queen
Elizabeth," depicts ship on each,
ca. 1930's, the set 95.00
Tray, "Eastern Steam Ship Corp.,"
glass, advertisement for three

ships, route map in center,
6¾ × 8¾" 28.00
Vegetable dishes, silver plate,
slightly canted sides, narrow rim,
spherical side handles, made for
the Compagnie Generale Transatlantique for use on the liner
"Normandie," monogrammed
"CGT," impressed "CHRISTOFLE"
w/hallmarks, ca. 1935, across
handles 12¾" l., pr. 920.00

STEIFF TOYS & DOLLS

Steiff U.S. Navy Mascot Goat

From a felt pincushion in the shape of an elephant, a world-famous toy company emerged. Margarete Steiff (1847-1909), a polio victim as a child and confined to a wheelchair, planned a career as a seamstress and opened a shop in the family home. However, her plans were dramatically changed when she made her first stuffed elephant in 1880. By 1886 she was producing stuffed felt monkeys, donkeys, horses and other animal forms. In 1893 an agent sold her toys at the Leipzig Fair. This venture was so successful that a catalog was printed and a salesman hired. Margarete's nephews and nieces became involved in the business, assisting in its management and the design of new items. Through the years, the Steiff Company has produced a varied line including felt or plush animals, Teddy Bears, gnomes, elves, felt dolls with celluloid heads, Kewpie dolls and even radiator caps with animals or dolls attached as decoration. Descendants of the original family members continue to be active in the management of the company still adhering to Margarete's motto "For our children, the best is just good enough."

Cat: "Susi," grey & white mohair,
glass eyes, sewn nose & mouth,
4" $95.00

Cat: kitten "Tabby," grey & white striped plush mohair standing body, green glass eyes, pink floss nose & mouth, applied ears, original ribbon w/bell around neck, paper tag marked "Steiff - Original Marke - Tabby," 4" h. 95.00

Cat, black mohair plush, standing w/arched back & upright bushy tail, green glass eyes, red floss nose & mouth, velvet ears, unjointed, 8" h. 120.00

Dog: "Biggie," beagle, mohair plush head, brown glass eyes, black floss nose & mouth, jointed neck, in sitting position w/black, white & brown body, original red collar, button in ear & original paper tag w/"Steiff - Original - Marke - Biggie," 4½" h. 60.00

Dog, Collie, long & short mohair, glass eyes, sewn nose, felt mouth, ca. 1950-60s, 20½" l., 10" h. 225.00

Dog, Poodle, long & short black mohair, ca. 1940, 15". 125.00

Dog hand puppet, Cocker Spaniel. . . 35.00

Doll: "Der Captain," from the Katzenjammer Kids comic strip, cloth, wearing a navy jacket w/brass buttons & red & white gingham checked trousers, ca. 1905, 13" h. 825.00

Doll: "Mama Katzenjammer," from the Katzenjammer Kids comic strip, cloth, dressed in a red polka dot blouse w/a full white skirt, ca. 1905, 15½" h. 880.00

Doll: Santa Claus, felt w/rubber head, mohair beard, felt clothing, jointed, 1950's, 14" h. 295.00

Fish on wheels, w/ear button, on four rubber wheels 625.00

Giraffe, gold & brown mohair, w/original buttons, 1960's, 31" h. . . . . 450.00 to 500.00

Goat: "Snucki," white mohair body, black velvet legs, glass eyes, 5". . 75.00

Goat, U.S. Navy mascot, plush, cream & blue coat (ILLUS.) 235.00

Hedgehog dolls: 9" h. "Micki" & 4" h. "Mecki," "Macki" & "Mucki," felt jointed body w/rubber head, cotton & felt clothes & leather shoes, 1950-60s, set of 4 . . . . 340.00

Lamb, unjointed white mohair plush, green glass eyes, red floss nose & mouth, applied felt ears, airbrushed accent colors, blue ribbon w/bell around neck, silver button in ear & yellow tag reads "Steiff 6514.0 - Made in Germany," 6" h. 70.00

Monkey (chimpanzee): "Jocko,"

brown mohair, fully jointed, red chest tag "Made in U.S. Zone Germany," 7" h. 175.00

Monkey (chimpanzee) hand puppet: "Jocko," ca. 1950. . . . . 85.00

Panda bear, Dralon, fully jointed, glass eyes, 1950s, 8" 180.00

TEDDY BEARS

Teddy bear, white plush mohair body w/swivel neck, brown glass eyes, brown floss nose & mouth, applied ears, jointed shoulders & hips, gold Steiff button & yellow ear tag w/"Steiff - Knopf im Ohr - 0203/14," 5½" h. 85.00

Teddy bear, brown mohair plush, brown glass eyes, brown floss nose & mouth, applied ears, jointed neck, shoulders & hips, original felt pads, four brown floss claws, excelsior-stuffed, button in ear & yellow tag, "Steiff" printed in ink on bottom of right foot, 8" h. 150.00

Teddy bear, silver plush body, black shoebutton eyes, brown stitched nose & snout, slightly grumpy expression, swivel limbs, felt pads, no button, ca. 1910, 12½" h. 1,430.00

Teddy bear, white mohair w/black shoebutton eyes, gutta percha nose, brown floss mouth, applied ears, jointed at shoulders & hips, beige felt paw pads, kapok-stuffed body w/hump on back, working squeaker, black Steiff button in left ear, 14" h. (four small moth holes in a pad, mending on right ankle) 650.00

Teddy bear, golden brown plush mohair, excelsior-stuffed, swivel head, jointed shoulders & hips, black shoebutton eyes, applied ears, long nose w/black floss nose & mouth, vertical stitching on nose w/brown felt underneath, felt pads w/four black claws on each paw, large hump & elongated arms & feet, Steiff button in left ear, 21" h. (mohair worn & missing in spots, repaired areas & mended) 1,050.00

STEINS

Advertising, "Bartholomay's Rochester," w/winged wheel logo, Mettlach, pre-Prohibition (ILLUS. top next column) $145.00

Bartholomay's Advertising Stein

"Gentleman Dog" Stein

Character, "Gentleman Dog," porcelain, long-eared, sad-faced dog wearing spectacles, flaring hat forming the cover, tan, brown & green, C.G. Schierholz & Sohn, ca. 1900, ½ liter (ILLUS.) 2,640.00

Character, "Monk," pottery, rotund standing figure w/his hands across his ample stomach, cream w/brown trim, pewter thumbpiece, 4¼" d., 7" h., ½ liter 250.00

Character, "Mushroom Lady," porcelain, cylindrical dumpy body dressed in a green & pink floral shawl, lavender apron & grey skirt, tan slightly domed mushroom-shaped cover, impressed "124" & backward "E," 4 1/8" d., 6" h., ½ liter 1,800.00

Character, "Nun," porcelain, smiling figure of a standing nun in black habit w/white trim, lid w/pewter rim & thumblift, lithophane of a monk & lady in the base, 4" d., 7¼" h. 350.00

Character, "Rooster," porcelain, bird wearing glasses & a white coat w/a gold medal, marked "Musterschutz," 7¾" h., ½ liter..1,925.00

Delft pottery, a bulbous pewter-mounted base & cylindrical neck w/a pewter-hinged lid engraved "Johanne Margarette Elija" & mounted w/a coin, the body decorated w/a blue floral & leaf design on white, Holland, 18th c., 10½" h........................ 495.00

Mid-18th Century Faience Stein

Faience, slightly tapering cylindrical body painted w/a huntsman wearing a manganese hat, a yellow-collared green coat, yellow breeches & manganese boots, holding a spear & riding a manganese galloping horse beside a manganese hound in pursuit of a boar fleeing across yellow, ochre & green terrain sponged in the foreground in manganese beneath a blue-washed sky, the handle w/ochre foliate scrolls (seriously cracked), mounted w/a pewter footrim & hinged cover engraved "S B" flanking an anchor, mid-18th c., Crailsheim, 9 1/8" h. (ILLUS.) 6,050.00

Glass, amber encased in fancy figured pewter frame, 3" d., 8¼" h........................ 235.00

Glass, Bohemian-type, ruby red engraved w/a scene of a castle by a lake on front, applied ruby red handle, inset glass top, pewter mounts, 3½" d., 5½" h. 295.00

Fine Glass Stein

Glass, clear enameled w/a large oval reserve showing two small

children in 18th c. attire, framed
by scrolls, pewter lid (ILLUS.) 1,760.00
Glass: master stein & four small
steins; blue shaded to clear, master stein threaded, pewter figured
hinged lids, master stein 5¼" d.,
14½" h., small steins 3" d.,
7½" h., 5 pcs. 1,195.00
Ivory, wide cylindrical body carved
in high-relief w/a continuous
scene of the rape of the Sabine
women, the carved ivory handle
in the form of a full-figure warri-
or, set into a rounded banded
repousse' silver base decorated
w/fruits & leaves, domed
repousse' silver lid w/a fluted
edge & fitted w/a carved ivory
figural finial of a kneeling trumpeter, Europe, 18th - 19th c.,
11" h. 5,060.00
Mettlach, No. 817, relief-molded flo-
ral design & rams, inlaid lid,
½ liter 220.00
Mettlach, No. 1520, etched design
w/Prussian eagle on front & soldiers on sides, signed "Gorig,"
inlaid lid, ½ liter 385.00
Mettlach, No. 1695, four panels of
etched hunting scenes, inlaid lid,
½ liter 315.00
Mettlach, No. 1916, etched, footed,
bulbous flagon-shaped, design
of cavaliers drinking, signed
"Warth," inlaid lid, 2.15 liters 1,320.00
Mettlach, No. 1997, etched &
PUG, bust portrait of George
Ehret, brewer, inlaid lid, ½
liter . . . . .275.00 to 325.00
Mettlach, No. 1998, etched, "Trum-
peter of Sackingen," pottery inlaid
pewter lid, ½ liter . . . . . .450.00 to 500.00
Mettlach, No. 2001, modeled as a
shelf of books for Cornell Univer-
sity, inlaid lid, 1899, ½ liter 385.00

Mettlach "Chessboard" Stein

Mettlach, No. 2049, etched, a design
of a chessboard framed by scrolls
& chessmen, inlaid lid, ½ liter
(ILLUS.) 3,960.00

Mettlach 'Symphonia' & 'Germania' Steins

Mettlach, No. 2102, etched, Germania stein, coats of arms around
sides, signed "Schultz," pewter
lid, 5¾ liter (ILLUS. right) 6,600.00
Mettlach, No. 2126, etched, Sympho-
nia stein, composers around body,
signed "Schultz," pewter lid,
5½ liter (ILLUS. left) 6,875.00
Mettlach, No. 2249, relief tavern
scene, inlaid lid, .3 liter 275.00
Mettlach, No. 2359, relief four-panel
decoration w/figures in each, in-
laid lid, .3 liter 225.00
Mettlach, No. 2430, etched, scene
of Cavalier drinking, inlaid lid,
3 liter 495.00
Mettlach, No. 2582, etched, jester
performing on table in front of
tavern, signed "Quidenus," inlaid
lid, 1 liter . . . . .450.00 to 500.00
Mettlach, No. 2799, etched, overall
Art Nouveau design, inlaid lid,
2.1 liter 675.00
Mettlach, No. 2808, etched, girl
bowling, inlaid lid, ½ liter 475.00
Mettlach, No. 2921, etched, scene of
hunter drinking in front of camp-
fire, inlaid lid, 2.8 liter 900.00
Mettlach, No. 2936, etched, Elk's
Club stein, inlaid lid, ½ liter
(ILLUS. top next column) 495.00
Mettlach, No. 2966, tapestry, a
scene of a man seated on an upright barrel & holding a stein of
beer in one hand & a long cane
under his other arm, pewter lid,
½ liter 357.50
Mettlach, No. 3000, etched, three
panels w/women, pewter lid,
½ liter 300.00
Mettlach, No. 3251, etched, hunter
& young girl, inlaid lid, ½ liter . . . 345.00
Mettlach, No. 3254, etched, a scene

Mettlach Elk's Club Stein

of people eating & drinking, inlaid
lid, ½ liter 302.50
Porcelain, cylindrical w/a low flar-
ing foot, enameled scene of The
Kaiser Wilhelm monument in Berlin, lithophane in the base, molded domed pewter lid & thumbpiece, cover w/an engraved
German inscription dated 1898,
8¼" h. 165.00
Porcelain, scene of Rothenberg on
front, pink & purple flowers surrounding scene, cream background, brick trim, lithophane
scene of castle in base, marked
"M. Wossner, Rothenberg" on
base, Germany, 4" d., 9" h.,
½ liter 110.00
Pottery, incised decoration of violets
& green leaves against a grey
ground, pewter lid, marked
"1169C" under handle, Germany,
3 7/8" d., 8" h., ½ liter. 110.00
Pottery, cream background w/col-
ored figure of a man holding a
large goblet of beer on front, embossed pewter lid w/man riding
bicycle & "All Heil," 4" d.,
8 7/8" h., ½ liter 195.00

STEREOSCOPES & STEREO VIEWS

*Hand stereoscope viewers with an adjusta-
ble slide may be found at $30.00 to $50.00 each
in good condition. Elaborate table models are
priced much higher. Prices of view cards depend on the subject material and range from
less than $1.00 to $10.00, or more.*

STEREOSCOPES & VIEWERS
Stereoscope, Becker's Stereoscope,
wood & glass, tall upright case
w/view lens on side, brass plate
on side reads "Ales Becker's
Patents April 7, 1857 - Dec. 13,
1859," 10 x 11", 18" h. (patches
on lid hinges, one top board
replaced) $330.00
Stereoscope, Keystone Model 40,
w/three view cards, the group . . . 75.00
Stereoscope, Perfecscope, patented
1895 . . . . 65.00
Stereo viewer, Haneel Tri-Vision, in
box 45.00

STEREO VIEWS
Adirondack Mountains scenes, by
Stoddard, group of 19 . . . . 100.00
Albany, New York, new state capi-
tol, 1885, set of 8 . . . . 35.00
Battleship "Indiana," ca. 1898-99 . . . . 10.00
Black Cavalry soldiers on horseback,
Indian Wars period, late 19th c. . . 8.00
Black children (2) trying to ride pig,
1901 . . . . 6.00
Black woman washing dishes in riv-
er, 1907 . . . . 5.00
Cavalry troops on horseback, Ft.
Tampa, Spanish-American War
era, late 19th c. 6.00
Children (2) w/toys & costumes,
1898, pr. 8.00
City Hall Square, New York City,
1902 . . . . 4.00
Middle East views, complete num-
bered set of 30, w/original case . . 68.00
New England Glass Co. wareroom,
No. 235, ca. 1876, 3¼ x 6¾" 25.00
Niagara Falls, "Dixon Crossing Niag-
ara," 1895 . . . . 35.00
Parade view w/Admiral Dewey &
Fighting 10th on 5th Avenue, ca.
1899 . . . . 4.00
President Hayes & Mrs. Hayes, 1877
& 1878, pr. 30.00
President McKinley in his office, ca.
1900 . . . . 10.00
President Taft in his office, ca.
1910 . . . . 10.00
Russo-Japanese War battle scene,
Ricalton photograph, 1905 . . . . 6.00
St. Louis World's Fair scenes, 1904,
set of 3 . . . . 10.00
San Francisco, 1906 earthquake
views, five views 60.00
Watch maker & badge factory,
Reading, Pennsylvania, ca.
1880's 60.00
Yellowstone National Park views,
1904, 30 cards, boxed 125.00

STOVES

*The thought of a family gathered compan-
ionably around the parlor stove on a cold
winter's evening, or of an apple pie baking*

in the wood-burning cookstove, brings to some a longing for the "good old days." On a more practical note, many people turned to wood-burning stoves during the 1970's energy crisis when they discovered wood was plentiful and by far cheaper than commercial fuels. Aside from the primary function, a handsome old parlor stove adds a distinctive touch with its ornate design and an old cookstove can turn a kitchen into a real family room. Whatever the reason, there has been a renewed interest in old stoves of all types.

Cookstove, "Buck's Gem No. 122,"
cast iron, Buck's Stove & Range,
St. Louis, Missouri, 12" w., 29" l.,
22" h. $850.00
Cookstove, "Home Comfort," grey &
white enamel 985.00
Cookstove, "Quick Meal," light blue
granite w/nickel-plated trim, ca.
1910-1920...................... 850.00
Parlor stove, cast iron, "Stewart,"
hard coal burner, ornate nickel
trim w/gargoyles on each side,
96 mica windows, 6' h..........4,500.00

French Parlor Stove

Parlor stove, white porcelain, brass
doors & fittings, decorated
w/molded foliate designs, spiral
columns at the corners, grey-
veined white marble top, France,
19th c., 22 x 29", overall 4' 8" h.
(ILLUS.) 1,760.00

STRING HOLDERS

Before the widespread use of paper bags, grocers and merchants wrapped their goods in paper, securing it with string. A string holder, usually of cast iron was, therefore, a necessity in the store. Homemakers also found many uses for string and the ceramic

or chalkware wall-type holder became a common kitchen item.

Advertising, "O.L.O. Soap," tin $325.00
Advertising, "Red Goose Shoes,"
cast iron, model of a goose,
ceiling-type 950.00
Cast iron, model of a ball of twine
on a twin-molded domed foot,
painted black, 5" h. 49.50
Ceramic, bust of black bellboy
w/red cap, marked "Fredericks-
burg Art Pottery," ca. 1930....... 325.00
Chalkware, bust of a black mammy
wearing an orange bandana 269.00
Chalkware, bust of boy w/top hat &
pipe 35.00
Chalkware, bust of a chef.......... 35.00
Chalkware, bust of Spanish
woman........................ 59.00
China, model of a cat face, Holt
Howard, 1958 .... 25.00
Chalkware, model of a white kitten
& ball of yarn.................. 37.00
Chalkware, model of a large pear .. 25.00
Chalkware, model of a strawberry
face 20.00

TEDDY BEAR COLLECTIBLES

Rare Two-faced Teddy Bear

Theodore (Teddy) Roosevelt had become a national hero during the Spanish-American War by leading his "Rough Riders" to victory at San Juan Hill in 1898. He became the 26th President of the United States in 1901 when President McKinley was assassinated. The gregarious Roosevelt was fond of the outdoors and hunting. Legend has it that while on a hunting trip, soon after becoming President, he refused to shoot a bear cub because it was so small and helpless. The story was picked up by a political cartoonist who depicted President Roosevelt, attired in hunting garb, turning away and refusing to shoot a *small bear cub. Shortly thereafter, toy plush bears began appearing in department stores labeled "Teddy's Bears" and they became an immediate success. Books on the adventures of "The Roosevelt Bears" were written and illustrated by Paul Piper under the pseudonym of Seymour Eaton and this version of the Teddy bear became a popular decoration on children's dishes. Also see STEIFF.*

Book, "More About Teddy B and Teddy G, The Roosevelt Bears," by Seymour Eaton, illustrated by R.K. Culver, published by Stern, 1907 . . . .$170.00

Book, "The Roosevelt Bears, Their Travels & Adventures," by Seymour Eaton, illustrated by V. Floyd Campbell, 16 color plates, 1906 .90.00 to 125.00

Cookbook, "Prudential Cookbook," 1910, cover depicts little girl giving a tea party for her two Teddy bears 39.00

Cup & saucer, bone china, "Teddy's Playtime" & Teddy bear, puppy, kitten & toy decoration, turquoise trim, Great Royal Albert, ca. 1930's 65.00

Teddy bear, mohair, straw-stuffed body, fully jointed, shoe button eyes, back hump, America, ca. 1915-20, 14" 325.00

Teddy bear, brown mohair, w/cloth pads, glass eyes, growler, 18" 175.00

Teddy bear, cinnamon mohair, black feet, glass eyes, ca. 1940's, 18" . . 65.00

Teddy bear, pale golden plush, long muzzle, one glass eye (one missing), elongated limbs, back hump, felt pads w/stitched claws, early 20th c., 18" (patches of wear) 330.00

Teddy bear, yellow cotton, glass eyes, red felt mouth, 18" 155.00

Teddy bear, blue mohair, felt pads, growler, Germany, 19" 300.00

Teddy bear, yellow mohair, cloth pads, glass eyes, growler, Germany, 19" 200.00

Teddy bear, golden mohair plush, excelsior & kapok-stuffed, brown glass eyes, applied ears, elongated nose w/black floss vertically stitched, black floss mouth & five claws on each paw, original felt pads, large hump on back, swivel head & jointed shoulders & hips, elongated arms & feet, 21" (couple of small holes in pads, one claw on each paw worn off, left leg mended) 925.00

Teddy bear, golden mohair, jointed at neck, shoulders & hips, brown glass eyes, shaved snout, black

floss nose & smiling mouth, applied ears, shaved mohair pads on paws, unmarked Hermann, 26" (small spots of wear on chest) 275.00

Teddy bear, brown plush w/black shoe button eyes, black stitched nose, back hump, 30" (overall wear) 418.00

Teddy bear, two-faced, one side the face of a child w/large eyes, the reverse the face of a Teddy bear w/glass eyes & stitched nose & mouth (ILLUS.) 2,500.00

TEXTILES

BEDSPREADS

Chenille, pastel floral design $95.00

Chenille, large peacock decoration in center, 96 x 96" 95.00

Cotton, double-woven embossed, scalloped edges, 17" base tuck-in, white, 81 x 86" 95.00

Crewel-Embroidered Bedspread

Crewel-embroidered linen, composed of two 37-inch white linen panels embroidered w/an exuberant 'corkscrew' vine of blossoms & cone-shaped buds, in the center a large cross-hatched pot above sprouting buds above a pair of blue embroidered butterflies, berries, blossoms, surrounded by an inner embroidered border of berries, the whole within swag borders, tatted white cotton fringe, probably New England, late 18th - early 19th c., approximately 77 x 93" (ILLUS.) 3,575.00

Embroidered, red w/bird in center encircled w/flowers, featherstitch squares, grapes in corners, 62 x 86" 165.00

Embroidered silk, pheasants, other
birds & various flowers on a
champagne-colored ground, tasseled fringe, China, 75 x 92" 880.00
Hand-crocheted, crib-size, squares
w/flower designs & animals including rabbits, cats, squirrels,
deer, pigs & dogs, 40 x 66" 185.00
Hand-painted chenille, w/Mexican
woman design, never used....... 90.00
Linen, Prairie School design, woven
w/an overall square block design
w/crosses in various blocks,
in green & red on an ivory
ground, early 20th c., unmarked,
70 x 98" 412.50
Worsted wool, cut-corner style, mulberry ground decorated w/dia-
mond, flowerhead & feather quilting, America, early 19th c.,
74 x 104" (imperfections) 825.00

COVERLETS

Dated One-Piece Jacquard Coverlet

Jacquard, single weave, one-piece,
narrow bands of zigzags alternate
w/rows of sunbursts & running
vines, a wide border of overall
leafy florals, red & natural white,
71 x 77" (some wear)............ 125.00
Jacquard, single weave, one-piece,
bands of floral wreaths w/sun-
burst alternating w/bands of larger sunbursts across the center,
double birds & leaf sprig borders,
corners dated "1857," blue & natural white, some fringe damage &
minor wear, 66 x 90" (ILLUS. of
part) 577.50
Jacquard, single weave, two-piece,
bands of large rose clusters alternating w/small blossom & leaf
diamond-shaped clusters in the
center, undulating blossom & leaf
vine border, corner block signed
"Made by J. Wirick in St. Paris,
Champaign Co., Ohio 1855 for
Elizabeth Stuart," navy blue, olive

green, tomato red & natural
white, 68 x 76" (minor stains) 440.00
Jacquard, single weave, two-piece,
rows of four-rose clusters alternating w/rows of large flowerheads in feathery circles across
the middle, double-headed
spread-winged eagle border, corner blocks labeled "Gabriel
Rausher 1847," blue & natural
white, 66 x 86" (worn, stains,
some damage) 495.00
Jacquard, single weave, two-piece,
four central rose medallions, bird
borders w/corners labeled "J.C.
Adams 1859," red, navy blue &
natural white, 72 x 84" 495.00

Jacquard Coverlet Dated 1841

Jacquard, single weave, two-piece,
the center w/large four-rose leafy
clusters, double-headed eagle &
swag or potted flower & swag
borders, corner block signed "Peter Lorenz 1841," deep blue & natural white, overall wear, fringe
loss, stains, 78 x 88" (ILLUS. of
part) 467.50
Jacquard, double woven, one-piece,
overall central design of scattered
small stars, wide border of delicate looping vines w/perched
birds, corner block signed "Ohio
1843 by A. Allen," navy blue &
natural white, 78 x 88" (stains,
minor wear) 1,375.00
Jacquard, double woven, the center
composed of rows of large feather wreaths encircling a center
eight-point star & scattered
smaller eight-point stars, the
borders worked w/alternating
churches, houses & rose bushes,
the word "Ohio" across the top
along one border, two corner
blocks signed "C.L. Woodworth -
Wove by G.W. Lashels - Hunting-
ton - 1849," pink, green & navy
blue, 70 x 90" 485.00

Jacquard, double woven, center design of four-rose cluster rows alternating w/rows of large rounded diamonds & small octagonal panels w/stylized starbursts, eagles & urns along one border & stylized tables w/ewers or decanters on two other sides, signed & dated in corner block "William T. Williams, Dover Township, York County, PA 1849," red & white, 80" sq. 275.00

Jacquard, double woven, two-piece, bold geometric block design w/each block centering a leafy florette, wide flowering bush or daisy vine borders, a four-petal florette design in each corner w/the date "1848" divided between the petals, very dark blue, red & natural white, ends machine-sewn for stability, one end turned, 80 x 89" 522.50

Jacquard, double woven, two-piece, rows of floral medallions in the center, wide border & corner blocks w/birds, signed "J.B.M.Z. Fancy Coverlet Woven by G. Heilbronn, Lancaster, O. 1853," red, green & blue, 86 x 95" (overall & edge wear) 440.00

Jacquard, double woven, two-piece, a large central floral medallion surrounded by single flowers & pinwheels enclosed by a meandering grapevine & a further grapevine & chain, w/four corner blocks inscribed "Margaret Holderon 1838" on one & "Jane Holderon 1838" on the other, each w/a fringe border, dark & light blue, attributed to David Harring, Bergen County, New Jersey, pr. 2,200.00

Linsey-woolsey, blue w/Princess Feather patt., heart & flower quilting, America, early 19th c., 90¾ x 103" .4,950.00

Overshot, one-piece, optic design w/overall bands of star-like devices, red, navy blue, gold & natural white, 79 x 80" (minor fringe wear) 143.00

Overshot, optical pattern of rows of small diamonds alternating w/rows of eight-point stars, navy blue, tomato red, green & natural white, original sewn-on fringe, unused, 79 x 89" 375.00

Overshot, optic pattern w/varied block designs, medium blue, chocolate brown & natural white, no fringe, some edge wear, 68 x 82" (ILLUS. of part) 137.50

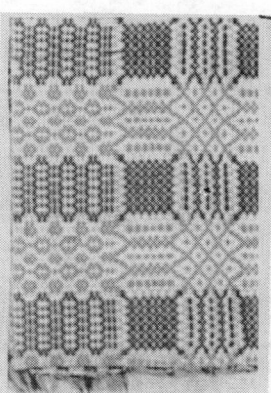

Two-Piece Overshot Coverlet

Overshot, summer-winter type, single weave, two-piece, optic crisscross designs, navy blue & natural white, good fringe, 80 x 96" (minor wear) 440.00

Overshot, two-piece, optic pattern w/bands of various block designs, gold, olive green & natural white, 80 x 96" (minor wear) 192.50

LACES
Battenburg

Doily, 6" solid center, 12" sq. 35.00
Doily, 20 x 20" 35.00
Table centerpiece, all-lace, diamond-shaped, 15" w., 25½" l. 98.00
Table centerpiece, all-lace, w/scalloped edge, 14" d. 45.00
Table centerpiece, 4" d. solid center, lace border, 12" d. 35.00
Tablecloth, 11" w. lace squares in corners, 28" sq. 168.00
Tablecloth, round, 60" d. 275.00
Tablecloth, 10" d. linen center, 68" d. 165.00
Table runner, flower design at each end, scalloped border, 13 x 38" . . 128.00
Table runner, three solid center medallions w/all-white embroidery, 18 x 52" 65.00
Tea cozy, all-lace w/flower center, double size, 10 x 13½" 52.00

Other

Filet lace table runner, cupids in center, cupids at each end, cupids & butterflies along sides, 18 x 42" 138.00
Pointe de Venise lace banquet cloth, w/12 matching napkins, 138" l., 13 pcs. 500.00
Quaker Lace tablecloth, designs of birds, swans, flower urns, etc., signed, 72 x 90" (needs soaking) 95.00

LINENS & NEEDLEWORK

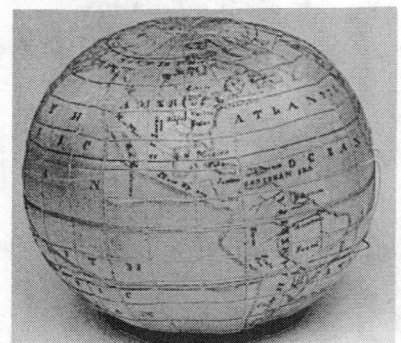

Rare Needlework Globe

Blanket, homespun linen, slate blue, mustard yellow, ecru & natural woven in a barred design, 44 x 91" (wear & small holes) 165.00

Blanket, homespun wool & cotton, grey & natural white stripes, hand-sewn center seam & machine-sewn hems, 68 x 75" 65.00

Blanket, wool & cotton, two-piece striped twill weave, in butternut, umber & natural fibers, America, 19th c., 78 x 95" 385.00

Bolster cover, homespun linen, dark navy blue & white tiny checked pattern, hand-sewn w/a tape closure, 23 x 56" (minor wear) 40.00

Clothing 'pocket,' quilted chintz, block-printed plum tree & pheasant pattern in madder, blue & drab, bound w/chintz tape & lined w/printed sepia feather & star patterned cotton, America, ca. 1825, two small slits at folds, 14" l. 880.00

Mattress cover, homespun linen, hand-sewn, blue & white small checked design w/white backing, tape closure, one off-center seam in blue, 19th c., 53 x 76" (small cut-out square in one corner)..... 125.00

Model of a terrestrial globe, embroidered & inked silk, the globe form w/a world map drawn in black, green & blue ink on a pale blue ground & embroidered w/pink, yellow & green silk threads, inscribed "Ann Baker 1818," Westtown School, Chester County, Pennsylvania, 5" d. (ILLUS.) 10,450.00

Napkin, homespun, blue & white checked pattern, hand-sewn hems, 18 x 19½" 55.00

Napkins, linen damask, w/narrow Greek Key & large fleur-de-lis pattern, set of 8 .... 35.00

Panel, silk & linen, embroidered w/a unicorn & lions w/a floral design, China, late 18th - early 19th c., 96" w., 24" h. 1,430.00

Pillow covers, homespun linen, navy blue & natural white small checked pattern, hand-sewn, 19 x 34", pr. (minor stains) 130.00

Pillow shams, turkey red embroidery on white w/a bird in the center & flowers all around, single thickness, 25½ x 27½", pr.... 98.00

Early Needlework Pocketbook

Pocketbook, embroidery on canvas, rectangular form folded down the center, worked w/crewel yarns in tent & cross-stitch in rich shades of blue, green, yellow, red, pink & lavender, lined w/blue silk, inscribed "Charles Williams 1757," New Castle County, Delaware, 7¾" w., opened 21" l. (ILLUS.)...9,350.00

Pot holder, crewelwork, shield-shaped linen ground embroidered in red, pink, yellow, gold & blue yarns, initialed & dated "H.W. 1767," 8" h. (losses) 770.00

Sheet, homespun, two-piece, hand-sewn hems & seam, red embroidered initials, 80 x 90" 65.00

Show towel, homespun linen, pink embroidery w/stars, pots of flowers, two chairs, inscribed "Lea Sartham 1834," single bottom fringe, 18½ x 51" 195.00

Show towel, homespun linen w/a cut-work panel w/embroidered stylized pots of flowers & birds, the top flap w/faded embroidery of a star, birds on stylized plants & "F.H.1818" in pale green & pink, faded stripes of pale blue & pink, Pennsylvania Dutch origins, 14½" w., 55" l. (minor stains & wear) 300.00

Tablecloth, hand-crocheted w/eagle, shield, flag, Statue of Liberty & serpent, scalloped edge, 40" sq. 50.00

Tablecloth, woven linen, decorated w/concentric squares in brown, ivory & mauve on a neutral ground, designed by Frank Lloyd Wright, marked "The Taliesin Line of Frank Lloyd Wright," 43" sq. ... 522.50

Tablecloth & napkins, ivory linen w/ecru lace inserts, further hand-embroidery around cloth & napkins, made in Spain, cloth 72 x 144", twelve 17" sq. napkins, 13 pcs. 225.00

Table cover, embroidered linen, round, Arts & Crafts design w/stylized foliate designs in red, yellow, blue & green, w/fringe, early 20th c., 44" d. 192.50

Towel, homespun linen, overall blue & white check pattern, hand-hemmed, w/hanging loops, 14½ x 44½" 60.50

Wall hanging, silk embroidery on a linen ground, a design of a large gold dragon on a field of peony blossoms & leaves, a variety of silk & gold thread stitches, Japan, 19th c., 53 x 81" (fiber loss) 3,630.00

NEEDLEWORK PICTURES

Silk-Embroidered 'Stumpwork' Picture

The art of embroidering scenes on backings of canvas, linen or silk dates back at least to the 17th century but became especially popular in England and America in the late 18th and early 19th centuries. Many young ladies were trained in this art at "schools" operated to train them in lady-like pursuits.

Needlework embroidery, scene depicting a maiden w/a basket of flowers by a river, a dog by her side, within a green velvet & giltwood frame, Queen Anne period, England, early 18th c., overall 8¼ x 10" 990.00

Needlework embroidery, 'stumpwork,' silk-embroidered scene depicting Abraham banishing Hagar & Ishmael, within borders of beasts, flowers, insects & a cottage, in an ebonized & parcel-gilt frame, Charles II period, England, third quarter 17th c., overall 19 x 22½" (ILLUS.) 3,080.00

Needlework embroidery on silk, "Shepherdess," a landscape scene with a young woman & small lamb in the foreground, a lake, building & trees in the distance, worked in silk threads in shades of yellow, green, blue & bittersweet, painted & velvet trim, within a black reverse-painted mat w/an oval opening & the title in gold, molded gilt frame, by Louisa Lathrop, probably from the school of Abby Wright, South Hadley, Massachusetts, early 19th c., 13¾ x 15¾" 4,950.00

Needlework embroidery on silk, depicting a basket of summer flowers, worked in silk threads on a black silk ground, in a painted & parcel-gilt frame, George III period, England, late 18th c., overall 20 x 23" 2,200.00

Needlework embroidery on silk, memorial picture, a landscape scene w/a large tree in each corner of the foreground beside a monument, each w/a lady standing beside it, a simple church in the center background, worked in water-color & silk & chenille threads, done by Eliza McMillan, Albany, New York, ca. 1820, original gilt plaster frame, 24 x 29" (some splits to fabric) ... 1,045.00

QUILTS

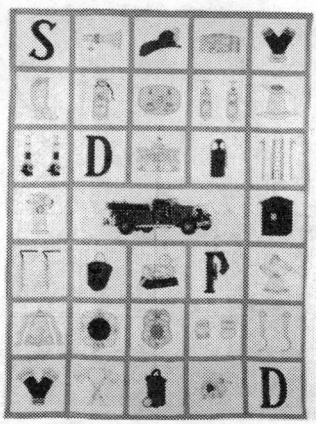

Appliqued Fire Fighting Quilt

Appliqued Album quilt, composed of red, green & yellow printed calico patches in a Snowflake & Oak Reel pattern, the central square w/large calico stars w/sprigs of buds within scallops, the broad outer borders w/snowflakes & oak reels, each center signed in India ink w/another name, the whole mounted on a white cotton ground heightened w/heart, flower & outline quilting, signed in the upper right "Rachel E. Coulter, Finished Her Work in 1850," probably Pennsylvania, 100 x 104" (some minor stains & discoloration)..........................4,180.00

Appliqued Cactus Rose patt. surrounding a central design of an eagle holding an olive leaf in its beak, encircled by the inscription "Virtue Liberty and Independence July Fourth 1776," the whole within a continuous tulip & swag border, worked in red & green calico on a white cotton ground, overall elaborate quilting, America, mid-19th c., 83 x 91"..............3,080.00

Appliqued fire fighting motifs, composed of 35 squares featuring various fire fighting designs including a bullhorn, hat, boots, hydrant, bucket, station house & a large truck in the center, large letters "S," "D," "F," & "D," blue banding on a creamy diamond-stitched ground, blue binding, made by Letha McLarney, San Diego, California, 1936, 63 x 86" (ILLUS.)....6,050.00

Appliqued Oak Leaf patt., red & green calico on a white ground arranged in four rows of five leaf clusters each, scalloped edges, early 20th c., 84 x 101"......... 440.00

Appliqued Quilt with Floral Sprays

Appliqued stylized floral sprays, composed of brightly colored yellow, red, pink, rose & green patches w/stylized floral blossoms, sprays & sprigs in the four quadrants, the whole mounted on a bright white cotton ground w/diamond, floral & scallop quilting, scalloped red-trimmed border, signed & dated in one corner "Olive McClure Cook - 1939," probably Pennsylvania, 84 x 88" (ILLUS.) 1,870.00

Victorian Crazy Quilt

Crazy quilt, composed of variously printed & woven brightly colored silk & velvet patches arranged in a random mosaic, the patches embroidered or painted w/horses, flowers, umbrellas, squirrels, bunches of berries & other decorative designs, at the center a black velvet square embroidered w/a bouquet of black-eyed Susans & other flowers entwined around a horseshoe, within black velvet borders w/rose blossoms & buds made from ruched pink silk w/green chenille leaves & stems, pink scalloped cotton eyelet border, probably Ohio, late 19th c., some minor discoloration & stain, 64 x 68" (ILLUS.)...............1,210.00

Crazy quilt, appliqued & embroidered silks & velvets, worked in forty-eight album squares w/a wide variety of designs including flowers, fans, butterflies, scenes of people dancing & portraits, all within a burgundy velvet & tasseled border, America, late 19th c., 59 x 90"...............3,300.00

Crib-size, pieced Sunburst patt., composed of red, yellow, pink, green, blue & white printed calico patches along w/a delicate blue & pink chintz border, the radiating starburst w/a rose & pink chintz rose blossom center, the field w/cube, outline & running cube quilting, tape binding, early 19th c., 48" sq. 4,400.00

Pieced Album Block patt., friendship-type, composed of blocks w/multicolored calico & white w/a pink calico grid, each center cross w/a printed name, 78 x 87" (binding replaced, some stains & fading) 220.00

Pieced Barn Raising patt., composed of brightly colored pink, blue, green, yellow & lavender patches, white cotton field w/diagonal line quilting, the whole within lavender borders, ca. 1935, 86 x 89" . .2,750.00

Pieced Checkerboard patt., composed of dark & light brown printed cotton patches in a large design, within broad borders of florally-printed brown & blue fabric, the reverse a blue & white printed toile fabric w/a repeating design of peasants in a landscape w/sheaves of wheat & berries, the field heightened w/cube & herringbone quilting, ca. 1820, 96" sq. (some minor stain & discoloration) 1,100.00

Pieced Concentric Square Quilt

Pieced Concentric Square patt. child's quilt, composed of red & white cotton patches, the field w/diamond quilting, on a stretcher, America, late 19th - early 20th c., 42" sq. (ILLUS.) 495.00

Pieced Nine Patch w/Stars of Le Moyne patt., composed of crisp red, white & blue patches, the *Star Nine Patches* alternating w/*Snowball* squares, the whole

within double flying goose border, backed w/brown linen, the field heightened w/cube & herringbone quilting, Ohio, ca. 1890, 71 x 80" 5,500.00

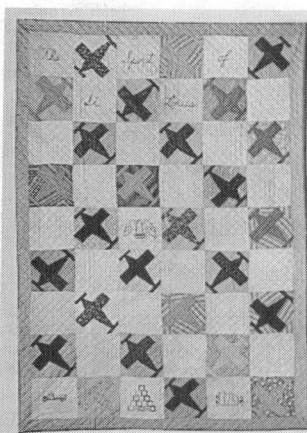

Spirit of St. Louis Quilt

Pieced Spirit of St. Louis patt., composed of brightly colored red, yellow, blue, orange & green-printed & solid cotton patches, each w/a silhouette of the airplane The Spirit of St. Louis, at the center an NRA spread-winged American eagle, along the bottom a barn w/silo & stalks of corn, a pick-up truck & building blocks inscribed "ADA," on a white cotton field made from re-used flour sack cloth & decorated w/large scale cube quilting, probably Midwestern, ca. 1930, 80 x 96" (ILLUS.) 2,310.00

Pieced Star of the East patt. child's quilt, composed of beige, black, terra cotta & lavender patches, the field w/cube, channel & diagonal line quilting, Amish, Pennsylvania or Ohio, late 19th c., 42½ x 69" (some fading, staining & fabric loss) 550.00

Pieced Wild Goose Chase patt., composed of purple, black, beige, emerald green, blue & white cotton patches, the black cotton field heightened w/concentric circle, cable & outline quilting, the back in pieced grey & plum cotton stripes, bright blue binding, Amish, Midwest, 68 x 80" (some wear) 2,750.00

White-on-white, embroidered overall w/boteh, feather wreath & flowerhead quilting, also embroidered "MAS 1833," worked by Mary Ann

Seeley, Orange County, New York, 88 x 90" (some discoloration) 715.00

SAMPLERS

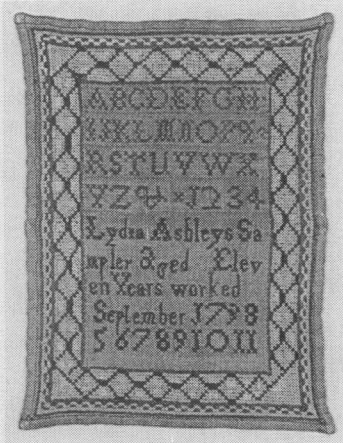

Late 18th Century Sampler

Alphabet & numerals above a bar of stylized roses above another alphabet sequence over a bar of strawberries above a pious verse over a bar of hearts & inscribed "Mary P. Anderson - Newbury port 1804," Newburyport, Massachusetts, worked in polychrome silk threads on linen, 11½ x 12½" 990.00

Alphabet & numerals centering "Lydia Ashleys Sampler aged Eleven years worked September 1798," all within a diamond border w/a narrow geometric outer border, stitched in silk threads in shades of pink, green, yellow & burnt umber, some color loss, 7 x 10" (ILLUS.) 1,045.00

Alphabets & numerals & a zigzag flower band above an inscription on the upper half above closely packed varied paired designs including birds, bowls of fruits, urns w/flower vines, fir trees & long-tailed birds all flanking a large center urn at the bottom issuing a tall scrolling floral vine, inscribed across the center "Hannah McCriller, her sampler, wrought in the 14th year of her age, A.D. 1795," worked in a variety of green, blue, pink, white & black silk stitches on a loosely woven linen ground, Canterbury, New Hampshire, framed, 17 x 17¾" (some stains & holes) 2,760.00

Cornucopias, clusters of grapes, blossoms & the figure of a small girl in a white dress standing next to an anchor, at center a large striped urn filled w/flowers above a yellow house flanked by weeping willow trees, the whole within a strawberry border trimmed w/ruched green silk & rosettes, executed in a variety of blue, green, yellow, pink & brown silk stitches on linen, signed at center "Harriet Weiser, 1830" & initialed "AW DW SW," probably Reading, Pennsylvania, ca. 1830, in original veneered frame, 17¾" w., 26¼" h. (some discoloration & minor fabric loss) 11,000.00

Family record, inscription & pious verse within a central square framed by a wide meandering flower & leaf vine border, worked in a variety of blue, green, yellow & pink silk stitches on a linen ground, the family record of the Jacob Bacon & Betsey Sawyer family, inscribed "Wrought by Rebeckah Bacon aged 11 years AD 1828," framed, 16½ x 17½" (some minor discoloration & fading) 3,450.00

Floral vining border on three sides w/floral sprigs centering a basket of flowers above a pious inscription framed by grapevines above an ornate landscape w/mansion across the bottom, scene titled "The Hermitage" & based on an erroneous view of Andrew Jackson's home, worked in silk threads in green, blue, yellow, cream & black & water-color-trimmed velvet on linen, inscribed "Rebecca Justice Aged 11 Years," ca. 1835, framed 9,625.00

Finely Detailed Sampler

Pious verses above two baskets

filled w/rose blossoms below a
farm scene w/blue house, trees,
a small pink house & a farmyard
w/sheep & cattle, the animals
w/bodies of painted & appliqued
paper, the lower border w/em-
broidered birds & flowers & a
paper cut-out swirl, the other
borders w/large rose blossoms &
buds, worked in a variety of pink,
blue, yellow, green, white & red
stitches on a loosely woven linen
ground, the whole w/the original
green silk ribbon trim, signed at
the center "Mary Clothilda Dare's
sampler, wrought in the year
1837," some minor fading & discoloration, Chester County, Pennsylvania, in the original frame &
glass, 23½ x 25 5/8" (ILLUS.) . . .22,000.00
Verse & "MaryAnn Jewell finished
this work, April 24th, 1817 at Mrs.
Venthams Boarding School, Winton, Aged _____ years," above cottage, barn, farm, people & wild
animals, worked in shades of
brown, gold, green, white, black
& light blue silk threads on homespun linen, framed, 12¾" w.,
17" h. (light stains & holes in
linen along bottom edge) 1,595.00

TAPESTRIES

Flemish Mythological Tapestry

Flemish mythological design, depicts
the reunion of Ulysses & Penelope
in front of a canopied bed, late
17th - early 18th c., 110" sq.
(ILLUS.) 4,400.00
Flemish "verdure" style, wide rec-
tangular fragment showing a
stand of tall, slender leafy trees,
large flowers in the foreground,
17th c., 58 x 78" (pieced, re-
pairs) 2,750.00

Flemish "verdure" style, rectangular, depicting various animals
within a wooded terrace w/village
& mountains in background, figural & fruit end panels, early
17th c., 89 x 158½" (repairs) . . .44,000.00
Franco-Flemish "verdure" style,
depicting a wooded scene
w/buildings in the distance, floral
border, early 18th c., 53" w.,
93" h. (minor areas of re-
weaving) 2,750.00

(End of Textiles Section)

THEOREMS

Basket of Fruit Theorem

*During the 19th century, a popular pastime
for some ladies was theorem painting, or stencil painting. Paint was allowed to penetrate
through hollow-cut patterns placed on paper
or cotton velvet. Still-life compositions, such
as bowls of fruit or vases of flowers, were the
favorite themes, but landscapes and religious
scenes found some favor among amateur artists who were limited in their ability and unable to do freehand painting. Today these
colorful pictures, with their charming arrangements, are highly regarded by collectors.*

Basket of fruit, water-color on paper, ornate low basket filled w/a
profusion of peaches, pears, berries, apples & a pineapple, America, ca. 1840, in probably original giltwood & gesso frame,
17½ x 23" (ILLUS.) $3,300.00
Bird w/long tail perched in tree
w/stylized flowers & leaves,
water-color on paper, Empire-
style frame w/half-round turned
pilasters & corner blocks &
old dark paint, mid-19th c.,
9½ x 12¾" 990.00
Family register on board, a water-
color & ink register of the Keith
Family, signed in pencil at the

lower margin "painted by... Allen... at Mrs. Ch... School Millbury
1836," unframed, 14 x 18" (areas
of staining & losses) 770.00

Fruit still life on velvet, inscribed on
reverse "Bridgewater Academy,
August 1824 Hannah Bassett,"
framed, 7½ x 9½" (darkened
ground) 412.50

Glass compote of fruit on paper, a
simple wide bowl on a low foot
filled to overflowing w/grapes,
pears, peaches & cherries, done
in water-color, signed "H.C.V.,"
19th c., framed, 9½ x 12" (discoloration) 467.50

Romantic landscape, water-color on
velvet, 19th c., framed, 17 x 21"
(discoloration) 330.00

Vase with flowers on paper, footed
white vase filled w/colorful garden blossoms, single blossom on
table beside vase, in original
grain-painted frame, 13 x 17¼"..1,100.00

TOBACCO JARS

Bisque, figural bust of a baby, Germany, 8 x 8" $125.00

China, figural bust of a black man,
very detailed hair, eyes & teeth,
glossy glaze, 9" h. 140.00

China, figural bust of a sea captain
w/pipe, matte finish, 7" h....... 225.00

China, model of a seated elephant,
6¼" h........................ 145.00

Glass, cylindrical w/hinged Art Nouveau-style brass lid, milk white
glass w/enameled floral decoration 90.00

Silver & glass, octagonal body, conforming silver lid w/ivory finial,
marked on lid & rim "950 standard," stamped "MADE IN
FRANCE FOR J.E. CALDWELL,"
Tetard Freres, Paris, France, ca.
1930, 8 1/8" h. 1,495.00

TOOLS

Alligator wrench, "Keen Kutter
No. 40" $125.00

Axe, safety-type, "Marbles No. 2,"
w/folding claw................ 280.00

Compass, carved & painted pine, a
large scale working-type w/iron
points, late 19th c., 29" l. 633.00

Hand saw, "Winchester No. 10,"
straight back, 7 points 72.50

Level, "Keen Kutter No. 3," cherry,
28" l. 70.00

Level, "Stanley No. 1194," brass-
bound, 28" l. 45.00

Pipe wrench, "Keen Kutter No. 14,"
Simmons Hardware............. 25.00

Plane, bench-type, "Auburn Tool
Co.," wooden, 28" l............ 45.00

Plane, box-type, whalebone, the
solid rectangular block stained
w/yellow pigment, 19th c., 2" w.,
8½" l. 660.00

Plane, jack-type, "Stanley 'Bailey'
No. 5¼," manual training-type ... 75.00

Plane, rabbet-type, "Ohio Tool Co.,"
wooden, 9½" l. 35.00

Plane, "Stanley No. 45," w/23 cutters, in original box 175.00

Plane, "Stanley No. 55," w/cutters &
instruction book................ 225.00

Plane, "Stanley No. 95," 6" l....... 80.00

Plane, "Stanley No. 604½C"....... 200.00

Plane, "Winchester No. 3026," corrugated bottom 60.00

Rule, caliper-type, "Stanley
No. 136," boxwood & brass,
4" l. 25.00

Rule, caliper-type, "Stanley
No. 136½," boxwood & brass,
5" l. 29.00

Rule, "Chapin-Stephens No. 036,"
rule & level, brass-bound 290.00

Rule, folding-type, "H. Chapin
No. 39," boxwood, 2' l. 25.00

Rule, folding-type, "Keen Kutter
No. 620," 2' l. 15.00

Rule, folding-type, "Lufkin
No. 1172," steel 12.00

Rule, folding-type, "Stanley No. 18",
boxwood & brass, two-fold....... 25.00

Rule, folding-type, "Stanley
No. 36½," brass & boxwood,
1' l. 28.00

Rule, folding-type, "Stanley No. 38,"
ivory, two-fold, German silver
trim, 6" l. 250.00

Rule, folding-type, "Stanley No. 39,"
ivory, four-fold, 1' l. 350.00

Rule, folding-type, "Stanley
No. 78½," boxwood, four-fold,
2' l......................... 87.50

Rule, folding-type, "Stanley No. 87,"
ivory, four-fold, 2' l. (some crazing) 150.00

Rule, folding-type, "Stanley No. 88,"
ivory, four-fold, 1' l............. 300.00

Rule, folding-type, "Stanley
No. 92½," ivory, four-fold, 1' l.... 275.00

Rule, folding-type, "Stanley No. 94,"
boxwood, four-fold, brass-
trimmed, 1' l. 100.00

Rule w/level & protractor, folding-
type, "Rabone No. 1190," four-
fold, 2' l. 70.00

Shingle measure, sliding-type, E.S.
Lane, Upton, Maine 75.00
Spoke shave, "Stanley No. 51," iron,
raised handles 15.00
Traveler (wheel gauge), wrought
iron, 12¾" l. 75.00
Wrench, "Keen Kutter No. 1837,"
curved, double open-end. 30.00

TOOTHPICK HOLDERS

Bees on a Basket Toothpick Holder

*Reference numbers listed after the holders
refer to the late William Heacock's books,* Encyclopedia of Victorian Colored Pattern
Glass, Book 1 *or* 1000 Toothpick Holders.

Amber cut glass, Art Deco-style,
squared shape, the square foot
w/cut diamonds, the tulip-shaped
diamond-cut sides below a scal-
lop-cut rim, 1 5/8" w., 2 5/8" h. . . $55.00
Amber glass, pressed Peek-A-Boo
patt. (1000, No. 327) 25.00
Apple green glass, pressed Bead-
ed Ovals in Sand patt. (1000,
No. 183) 175.00
Blue glass, pressed Hobnail patt. . . . 25.00
Blue opaque glass, Bristol-type,
blown hat shape w/rolled rim,
enameled floral decoration 48.00
Blue opaque glass, pressed Dutch
Kids patt. (1000, No. 258) 95.00
Clambroth glass, pressed Diamond
Point patt., signed "Baccarat," ca.
1900 . . . . 65.00
Clear glass, pressed Brilliant patt.
(Book 1, No. 135) 38.50
Clear glass, pressed Lean Queen
patt., w/gold trim (1000,
No. 782) 16.50
Clear glass, pressed Manhattan
patt., w/gold trim (1000,
No. 304) 20.00
Clear glass, pressed Scroll with
Cane Band patt. (Book 1,
No. 280) 30.00
Clear glass, pressed Toltec patt.
(1000, No. 268) 45.00

Clear glass, pressed Michigan patt.
(1000, No. 260) 42.50
Clear glass, pressed Wheeling Block
patt., w/pedestal base 110.00
Clear opalescent glass, pressed Idyll
patt. (Book 1, No. 149) 52.00
Cranberry-stained glass, pressed
Frazier patt., enamel-decorated
w/white & yellow flowers (Book 1,
No. 125) 28.00
Cranberry-stained glass, pressed
Swirl Two-Ply patt. (Book 1,
No. 302) 68.00
Custard glass, pressed Bees on a
Basket patt., 1000, No. 312
(ILLUS.) 60.00
Custard glass, pressed Washington
State patt. (Book 1, No. 319) 75.00
Emerald green glass, pressed Box-
In-Box patt. (Book 1, No. 31) 75.00
German porcelain, figural nude girl
in shell, marked "Glen Falls, NY,"
3½" h. 35.00
Green glass, pressed Fancy Loop
patt., w/gold trim (Book 1,
No. 108) 110.00
Green glass, pressed Pineapple &
Fan patt., w/gold trim (Book 1,
No. 235) 135.00
Green opalescent glass, pressed
Diamond Spearhead patt. (Book 1,
No. 75) 115.00
Green opaque glass, mold-blown
Palm Leaf patt. (Book 1,
No. 223) 38.00
Milk white glass, pressed Beggar's
Hand patt., w/green base (1000,
No. 370) 35.00
Milk white glass, pressed Tramp's
Shoe (1000, No. 390) 35.00
Pink opaque glass, pressed One-O-
One patt. (Book 1, No. 187) 70.00
Ruby-stained glass, pressed Sham-
rock patt., faint souvenir inscrip-
tion (Book 1, No. 284) 39.50
Ruby-stained glass, pressed Witch's
Kettle patt., souvenir inscription
(1000, No. 299) 15.00
Silver plate, figural, model of a bird
sitting next to a goblet engraved
"Take Your Pick" 80.00
Silver plate, figural, chick seated
next to half an eggshell resting
on a wishbone, shell engraved
"Best Wishes," Derby No. 2309
(1000, No. 768) 48.00
Silver plate, figural, a rat crouching
next to a pouch, Derby (Book 1,
No. 366) 59.00
Silver plate, figural, a pair of boots
on a base, Aurora 110.00

TOYS

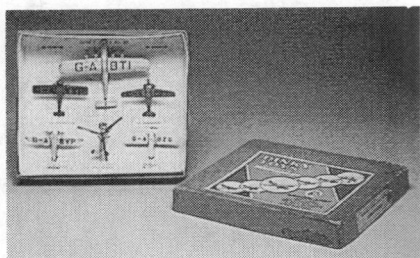

Dinky Toy Airplanes

African Safari animal, Hippopotamus, wooden, painted eyes, Schoenhut & Co. (Philadelphia, Pennsylvania), reduced size . . . .$350.00 to 400.00

African Safari animal, Zebra, wooden, glass eyes, Schoenhut, regular size 687.50

African Safari animal, Zebu, wooden, glass eyes, Schoenhut 2,200.00

African Safari figure of Arab chief, w/rifle, belt & cape, wooden, Schoenhut .1,430.00

African Safari native chief, wearing purple coat, wooden, Schoenhut . . 880.00

Airplane, metal, a monoplane w/a compressed air engine, silver body, wire framework wings, tail & wheel supports, fabric-covered wings & tail, designed to free-fly, Bing (Germany), ca. 1912, overall 51½" l. (some surface rust) 5,544.00

Airplane, "P-38," cast iron, Hubley Mfg. Co. (Lancaster, Pennsylvania), 9" l. 65.00

Airplanes, diecast metal, a set consisting of a four-engine Imperial Airways passenger plane in gold, a D.H. Leopard Moth in green, a Percival "Gull" in white, a Cieva "Autogiro" in gold, a "General" Monospar in silver & a low-wing monoplane in red, all still affixed in their original lithographed box, set No. 60, Dinky Toys (Meccano, England), box 8 x 9" (ILLUS.) 2,640.00

Armored bank truck, "Brinks," Dinky Toys, No. 275, w/original box 50.00

Automobile, Buick Club Coupe, cast iron, painted light blue & black, separate spare tire & four nickel-plated spoked wheels, w/driver, Arcade Mfg. Co. (Freeport, Illinois), ca. 1928, 8½" l. 3,850.00

Automobile, Ford Model T "Fordor" sedan, cast iron, painted black w/gold piping, plated wheels & driver, Arcade, ca. 1924, 6½" l. . . . . .350.00 to 400.00

Automobile, racer, cast iron, fantail model w/white rubber tires, Hubley Mfg. Co., 3½" l. 65.00

Battery-operated, airplane, "American Airlines," flagship "Carolyn," Line Mar (Japan), wingspan 19½" 385.00

Battery-Operated Automobile

Battery-operated, automobile, "Fregate" by Renault, tinplate, dark brown w/silver trim, ca. 1950, w/original box, near mint, 13" l., 4" h. (ILLUS.) 896.50

Battery-operated, automobile, "Opel Kapitan," tinplate, flashing dome light, Gama (Germany), mint in box, 10" l. 250.00

Battery-operated, "Balloon Blowing Teddy," plush & tin, feet kick forward, raises the balloon to his mouth & it inflates, eyes light up, w/box 150.00

Battery-operated, "Barney Drumming Bear," plush & tin, remote control, turns head, plays the drum & the eyes light up 75.00

Battery-operated, "Batmobile," Japan, 12" l. 150.00

Battery-operated, "Blushing Willy," eyes roll, pours from bottle & drinks, Y Company (Japan), 1960's, 10" h. 95.00

Battery-operated, "Bubble Blowing Monkey," plush & tin, w/light-up eyes, Alps (Japan), mint in box . . 145.00

Battery-operated, "Cycling Daddy," man pedals tricycle while waving & smoking a lighted pipe, mint in box 250.00

Battery-operated, "Dino Robot," grey tinplate & plastic, as Dino walks forward his head folds down to reveal a roaring dinosaur w/lighted mouth, Horikawa (Japan), w/original box, 11" h. 550.00

Battery-operated, "The Great Garloo," remote-controlled standing monster on wheels, ca. 1960, w/original box (ILLUS. top next column) 440.00

Battery-operated, "Hungry Baby Bear," mint in box 295.00

"The Great Garloo" Toy

Battery-operated, "McGregor,"
dressed in cloth Scotsman outfit &
smokes a cigar, Japan, 11" h. 175.00
Battery-operated, "Mighty Mike,"
plush bear w/lighted eyes, after
warming up, the bear lifts his bar-
bells over head & they light up,
stands on a tin base, Japan, ca.
1960 .... 475.00
Battery-operated, "Mr. Magoo Car,"
tin, plastic & cloth, auto wobbles
forward as Mr. Magoo bounces up
& down in seat, Hubley Mfg.
Co. ....325.00 to 375.00

Battery-Operated "Red Gulch Bar"

Battery-operated, "Red Gulch Bar,"
standing badman shoots bottles &
glasses off a bar as bartender
ducks, Sonsco (Japan), ca. 1950's,
mint in original box (ILLUS.) 495.00
Battery operated "Sleepy Baby
Bear," mint in box 325.00
Battery-operated, "Smoking Rabbit,"
plush head, pink coat & blue
pants, mint in box 195.00
Battery-operated, "Wild West Rodeo," tin & plush, tin cowboy
rides on a kicking bull w/bubbles
blowing from its nose, Line Mar,
mint in box 195.00

BB gun, Daisy Model 21, double-
barreled, Daisy Manufacturing
Co. ....350.00 to 400.00
BB gun, Daisy Model 105 .... 100.00
BB gun, King Model No. 2136 ...... 75.00
Blocks, building-type, "U-Build-Em,"
six different subjects, Playette
Corp. (New York), 1943, cardboard box torn on edges,
15" w. 40.00
Blocks, construction-type, "Richter's
Comet Blocks with Iron Construction," stone blocks in three colors,
in original wood box & w/original
illustrated idea booklet, dated
1900, box 6½ x 8½" 33.00
Blocks, puzzle-type, "Around the
World with Santa," by McLoughlin
Bros. (New York, New York), set
of 18 .... 425.00
Boat, battleship, lithographed paper
on wood, the deck details include
a smokestack, twin masts, venti-
lators, lifeboats on davits, rotating guns & sailors, early 1900's,
32" l. 1,100.00
Britains (soldiers), cast metal, Royal Marine Band, Set No. 1291,
w/original box, 12 pcs. 550.00
Bus, "Greyhound Lines," cast iron,
Arcade Mfg. Co., Model No. 438,
1937, 9" l. 875.00
Cap pistol, "American," cast iron,
Kilgore Mfg. Co. (Westerville,
Ohio), ca. 1940, 9 5/8" l. 625.00
Cap pistol, "Black Sambo," cast iron,
ca. 1890 .... 385.00
Cap pistol, "Daisy," cast iron, Ar-
cade Mfg. Co., 1925, 4" l. 35.00
Cap pistol, "Ric-O-Shay Jr.," cast
iron, Model No. 261 ......75.00 to 100.00
Cap pistol, "Spit Fire," cast iron
w/white plastic handles, ca. 1940,
5 5/8" l. 29.00
Cap pistols & twin holster set,
"Bull's Eye," silver plate w/orange
grips, Kenton Hardware (Kenton,
Ohio), 1940, 3 pcs., mint in box .. 295.00
Cap pistols & twin holster set,
"Westerns," Hubley Mfg. Co.,
1950's, 3 pcs. ....135.00 to 150.00
Carpet sweeper, "Busy Betty," litho-
graphed tin 32.00
Cash register, "Tom Thumb," metal
& plastic, light blue, ca. 1950's,
mint in box, 6 3/8 x 7½",
7½" h. 23.00
Circus animal, Buffalo, wooden,
carved mane, painted eyes,
Schoenhut, regular size (ILLUS.
top next page) ....350.00 to 400.00
Circus animal, Camel (Bactrian),
two-hump, wooden, painted eyes,
Schoenhut, regular size . .350.00 to 375.00

Schoenhut Buffalo

Circus animal, Camel (Dromedary), wooden, glass eyes, Schoenhut, regular size . . . . 375.00 to 400.00

Circus animal, Elephant, wooden, painted eyes, Schoenhut, regular size, 8¼" l. . . . . 125.00 to 150.00

Circus animal, Horse w/saddle (brown), wooden, painted eyes, Schoenhut, reduced size 150.00

Circus animal, Lion, wooden, painted eyes, Schoenhut, regular size 350.00

Circus animal, Rabbit, wooden, glass eyes, Schoenhut 1,760.00

Circus performer, Acrobat, lady, wooden w/bisque head, Schoenhut 412.50

Circus performer, Bareback Rider, lady, wooden w/bisque head, Schoenhut, 8½" h. . . . . . . 375.00 to 400.00

Circus performer, Lion Tamer, wooden, Schoenhut, regular size 330.00

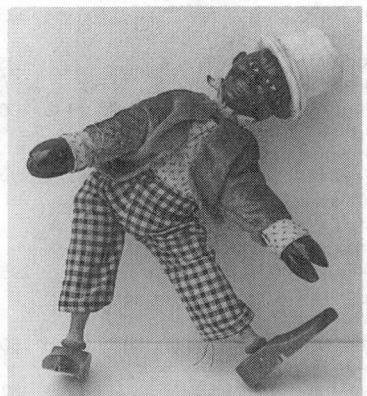

Schoenhut "Negro Dude" Performer

Circus performer, Negro Dude, wooden, Schoenhut, 8¾" h. (ILLUS.) . . . . 350.00 to 400.00

Circus prop, ball, wooden, Schoenhut 50.00

Circus set: two clowns in original costumes, a horse, an elephant, a poodle, assorted chairs, barrels & stands; painted wood, Schoenhut,

early 20th c., box size 12 x 20", the group 1,540.00

Circus tent, canvas, lithographed w/crowd in stands, complete w/frame & base, 1926, Schoenhut 1,450.00

Circus wagon, cast iron, "Overland Circus" animal wagon, pulled by a pair of white horses w/riders, w/driver, Kenton Hardware Co., 13¼" l. (bright paint worn) 400.00

Clicker, model of a jockey riding a horse, metal, ca. 1940 . . . . 10.00

Clockwork mechanism bus, double-decker, lithographed tin, open-top vehicle w/side seats on top, composition figures seated in them, winding rear staircase, dark green, yellow & grey, Bing, ca. 1912, 10" l. 2,860.00

Early Clockwork Limousine

Clockwork mechanism, limousine, tinplate, green & black lithographed body, red trim & yellow pinstriping, twin cowl lamps, twin large headlamps, original driver, brake, two opening doors, beveled glass in all windows & doors, original rubber tires on orange spoked wheels, Carette, ca. 1910, 15½" l. (ILLUS.) 6,820.00

Clockwork mechanism, ocean liner, tinplate, h.p. in beige, yellow & red, w/a single deck cabin, four lifeboats, aft cabin, ladder w/scrollwork at prow, two smokestacks, Bing, early 20th c., 25½" l. 13,200.00

Clockwork mechanism, "The Patriotic Boy," consisting of twin seven-inch diameter wheels which encase a keywind cloth-dressed painted doll w/tinplate arms & legs, holding a 13-star American flag, attributed to Altof, Bergmann & Co. (New York, New York), late 19th c., 9" h. (pants torn) 7,150.00

Clockwork mechanism, velocipede, a three-wheeled cast-iron cycle mounted by a figure w/composi-

Clockwork Velocipede

tion head wearing original jacket
& striped trousers, American-
made, late 19th c., 10" l.
(ILLUS.) 1,650.00
Coaster wagon, "Aeroflite," metal,
equipped w/electric headlights
(including bulbs), reflectors,
wiring switch & battery box,
8" disc wheels, pneumatic rubber
tires, Globe, 1937, 20" w.,
48" l. . . . . .400.00 to 450.00

Buddy L Concrete Mixer

Concrete mixer, pressed steel,
painted red, yellow & green, Buddy L (Moline Pressed Steel Co.,
East Moline, Illinois), ca. 1940's,
6½ x 9", 7½" h. (ILLUS.) 302.50
Delivery wagon, horse-drawn, paint-
ed wood, paneled wagon painted
white w/"Alderney Dairy Co. -
Grade A Milk" in color, w/horse
on wheeled platform, w/milk bottles & wooden crate, Schoenhut,
ca. 1910, the set 4,000.00
Erector set, "American Model
Builders Kit," steel, made by the
American Mechanical Toy Co.
(Dayton, Ohio), w/motor, instruction manual & original box, ca.
1915, the set 110.00
Farm equipment, wheelbarrow,
Schoenhut 396.00

Farm set: barn & animals; lithographed wood, Morton E. Con-
verse Co. (Winchendon, Massachusetts), ca. 1890-1910, the set . . 435.00
Fire aerial ladder truck, steelplate,
painted bright red, complete
w/ladder extension, decals
marked "CFD" & "Buddy L Aerial
Truck," Buddy L, ca. 1930's,
30" l. 605.00
Fire pumper wagon, hand-drawn
type, tinplate, on two large cast
wheels, painted red & gold w/a
polished brass top, Carette, ca.
1895, 8½" l. 825.00
Fire water tower ladder truck, steel-
plate, painted red, fitted w/full
extension ladder, decals marked
"CFD" & "Buddy L Water Tower,"
ca. 1930's, 32" l. 1,870.00
Friction-type, airplane, "Cessna Sky
Taxi," tinplate, Japan 145.00
Friction-type, automobile, Ford se-
dan, chromed surface, plastic
windshield, black rubber tires, ad-
justable front wheels, Marusan
(Japan), 1950's, 13" l. 3,366.00
Friction-type, automobile, Rolls-
Royce, tin, purple body w/silver
stripes, ca. 1940, 7½" l. 121.00
Friction-type, bus, "Greyhound
Scenicruiser," tin, Japan, w/box . . 125.00

Friction-type Motorcycle

Friction-type, motorcycle & rider,
tinplate, colorfully lithographed
w/"GMen" on sides, small rust
spots on left side, ca. 1950,
3¼" l. (ILLUS.) 44.00
Gas station, "Day & Nite Service
Station," lithographed tin, Louis
Marx & Co. (New York, New
York) 135.00
G.I. Jane figure, dressed in original
nurse's uniform, w/all accesso-
ries, Hasbro Mfg. Co. (Pawtucket,
Rhode Island) 1,200.00
G.I. Joe electric drawing kit, Hasbro
Mfg. Co., 1965 . . . . 40.00
G.I. Joe figure, action sailor, mint in
box w/original papers, Hasbro
Mfg. Co. 350.00

G.I. Joe figure, blond hair, dressed
in astronaut suit & helmet, Hasbro
Mfg. Co. 100.00
Horse-drawn cart, tin lithographed
cart & wooden horse, Gibbs Mfg.
Co. (Canton, Ohio), ca. 1910 ..... 195.00
Horse-drawn wagon, express-type,
tinplate, the long low-sided tinplate wagon in blue stenciled "Express Wagon" on the sides, on
four cast-metal wheels, driven by
a seated china head girl doll,
pulled by a pair of "Dexter" tinplate horses painted brown w/red
saddles, Altof, Bergmann & Co.
(New York, New York), ca. 1880,
overall 27½" l. 5,500.00
Ice wagon, cast iron, w/ice block &
tongs, rubber tires marked "Arcade Balloon," Arcade Manufacturing Co. (Freeport, Illinois),
7" l. 595.00

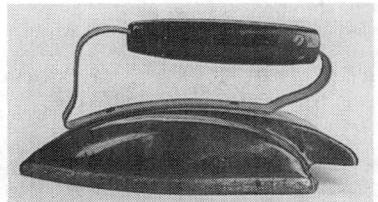

"Sunny Suzy" Toy Iron

Iron, electric-type, red-painted tin
w/black wood handle, "Sunny
Suzy," Wolverine Co. (Pittsburgh,
Pennsylvania), 1940's, 5½" l.
(ILLUS.)........................ 22.00
Ironing board w/picture of Bo Peep,
metal, Wolverine Co. 22.00
Jacks, w/original cloth bag, Arcade
Mfg. Co. 35.00
Juke box, "Junior Juke Box," by
Gong Bell Mfg. Co. (East Hamp-
ton, Connecticut), ca. 1950, mint
in box......................... 125.00
Kaleidoscope, "The Symmetro-
scope," tin, ca. 1899 .... 225.00
Marine toys set, painted tinplate, including a five-inch sailboat, two
smaller boats, an assortment of
fish, lobsters, ducks & swans, all
painted & embossed, Germany,
ca. 1900, w/box, box size 9 x 14"
(box cover torn)................. 165.00
Marionette, "Little Boy Blue," by
Hazelle's Marionettes, 1950's, mint
in box......................... 100.00
Marionette, composition, young
black boy dressed in bib overalls, checked shirt & straw hat,
14½" h. (some paint wear) 225.00
Motorcycle, cast iron, "Patrol Motor-

cycle" w/rider, Hubley Mfg. Co.
(Lancaster, Pennsylvania) 275.00
Moving van, "Allied Van," steel
plate, Tonka Toys, ca. 1950 ..... 225.00

"AMF Comet" Pedal Car

Pedal car, "AMF - Comet," royal
blue, 1948 (ILLUS.) 1,200.00

Two Early Pedal Cars

Pedal car, "Auburn Double Cowl
Phaeton," steel body painted dark
maroon & wine red, chromed details, disk wheels w/solid black
rubber tires, front bumper, trunk
at rear, two seats w/black leather
upholstery, windshield, cast steering wheel, single front pedal
treadle power, ca. 1932, fully restored & repainted, 62" l. (ILLUS.
left) 5,500.00
Pedal car, "Chrysler Airflow," Steel-
craft, 1937 ....3,800.00
Pedal car, "Duessenburg SSJ," dove
grey & red exterior w/chrome
trim including a windshield, headlights, radiator cap, spoked
wheels, rubber white-wall tires,
spare tire, brown leather interior,
steering wheel, front & back
bumpers, running boards, treadle
drive pedals, simulated gauges on
dashboard, mid-1930's, 58" l.
(largely rebuilt, repainted & restored) 14,300.00
Pedal car, "Durant," metal body
painted grey & black w/chromed
details, black leather seat, treadle
pedal motion, steel disk wheels
w/solid black rubber tires, windshield, luggage rack, side vents,
steering wheel, spare wheel, radiator cap, lettered "Durant" on

radiator, fully restored & repainted, late 1920's, 42½" l. (ILLUS.
right) 5,500.00
Pedal car, "Thunderbolt" series,
CT Convertible, BMC Toys (re-
stored) 1,500.00
Pedal fire truck, "Fire Patrol," red
w/white trim, electric headlights
& stoplight on cowl, nickel-plated
fire bell, V-8 radiator front, rear
platform, two extending ladders,
ball bearing drive rods, rubber
pedals & 9½" d. spoked wheels
w/rubber tires, American Juvenile
Vehicles, No. 5584, 1935, 51" l. . .3,500.00
Pedal tractor w/trailer, Internation-
al, No. 450, all-original 850.00
Pedal vehicle, Toledo bi-wing air-
plane, steel body painted bright
yellow w/red wings & tail, lined
in orange, chromed propeller, solid disc wheels w/black rubber
tires, w/steering wheel, adjustable smaller rear wheel, ca. 1920,
fully restored, wingspan 30",
41" l. 2,200.00
Penny toy, pool player standing in
front of pool table w/pool stick
pulled back aiming at a steel pool
ball on the table, Germany, ca.
1916, 4½" l. 150.00
Pistol, air-type, "Daisy Targeteer,"
Model 118, Daisy Manufacturing
Co., ca. 1940 . . . . 100.00
Pistol, automatic-type, "G-Man,"
Louis Marx & Co., ca. 1930, mint
in box. 85.00
Pistol, holster rig & shells, "Shootin'
Shell," Mattel Inc. (Hawthorne,
California), the set 55.00
Play set, "Fort Apache," Louis
Marx & Co., in original tin
box . . . . .150.00 to 200.00
Pop-Up Kritter, "Dizzy Donkey," light
blue w/black ears & red hooves &
tail, on dark blue guitar-shaped
base, Model 433, Fisher-Price, Inc.
(East Aurora, New York), 1939-42
(mint condition) 100.00
Pop-Up Kritter, "Tailspin Tabby,"
black cat w/yellow face & feet on
red guitar-shaped base, Model
400, Fisher-Price, Inc., 1931-39
(mint condition) 225.00
Pull toy, bear, gold mohair, glass
eyes, small metal wheels in feet,
w/worn brown collar, voice box
makes faint squeak when string is
pulled, Germany, 15" l. (one
wheel missing). 250.00
Pull toy, bee on wheels, "Buzzy
Bee," Model 325, Fisher-Price,
Inc., 1950-55 . . . . 35.00
Pull toy, dog, "Fido Zilo,"

lithographed puppy plays xylophone w/four nickel keys on a
pivoting platform, Model 707,
Fisher-Price, Inc., 1955-57 . . . . 75.00
Pull toy, dog, "Snoopy Sniffer,"
lithographed wood, Model 181,
Fisher-Price, Inc., 1961 . . . . 42.00
Pull toy, dog on wheels, mohair
excelsior-stuffed animal w/brown
glass eyes, brown floss nose &
mouth & applied ears, standing on
metal frame on wheels w/rods in
legs supporting animal, 19" l. (left
ear mended & reattached, some
patches of mohair missing, dam-
age around restitched). 250.00
Pull toy, duck, "Ducky Waddles,"
tin, Wyandotte Toys (Wyandotte,
Michigan) 150.00
Pull toy, fire patrol wagon
w/horses, cast iron, the open
wagon holds three seated firemen
& a driver, embossed on the side
"Fire Patrol," pulled by a black &
white horse raised on a single
wheel, original polychrome paint,
late 19th - early 20th c., 19½" l.
(paint wear) 900.00
Pull toy, giraffe on wheels, "Jingle
Giraffe," has loping gait, shiny
metal bell, spring tail, Model 472,
Fisher-Price, Inc., 1956, 8¼" h. 75.00

Early Horse Pull Toy

Pull toy, horse on wheeled platform,
carved & painted pine, dappled
grey animal w/real horsehair
mane & tail, leather ears & saddle, platform w/four cast-iron
wheels, late 19th c., 28½" l.,
31½" h. (ILLUS.) 1,760.00
Pull toy, horse on wheeled platform,
the tinplate animal h.p. brown &
naturalistically modeled w/paint-
ed mane, tail, eyes & bridle, a
separate tin collar, on a rectangular base w/small cast-
metal wheels, Lutz (Germany),
1870's - 80's, 7½" h. (slight paint
loss). 3,366.00

Pull toy, pelican on wheels, "Big Bill
Pelican," flipper-like feet, polyethylene bill that opens & closes
while emitting a call, Model 794,
Fisher-Price, Inc., 1961-69 . . . . 40.00

Pull toy, pig, "Peter Pig," wooden
beanie, vinyl ears & twirling polyethylene tail, w/"oink-oink"
sound, Model 479, Fisher-Price,
Inc., 1959-62 . . . . 48.00

Pull toy, rabbit, "Bunny Bell Drummer," hits a nickel bell in the cart
w/drumstick, Model 508, Fisher-Price, Inc., 1949-54 . . . . 50.00

Pull toy, rocket, "Space Blazer,"
spinning saucer w/plastic dome
that turns about a green-headed
man from Mars, w/warning bell,
springing radar antenna, rocket
engine lithograph & sound, wood
w/steel axles, Model 750, Fisher-Price, Inc., 1953-55, 14" l. 425.00

Pull toy, ship, sidewheel steamboat,
cast iron, embossed "Puritan" on
side of the wheel, w/animator
rocker bar, original polychrome
paint, late 19th c., 10½" l. (paint
wear) 600.00

Pull toy, train engine, "Looky Chug-
Pull toy, train engine, "Puffy Engine," lithographed engine
w/smiling face, acetate piston
arms, sound & wooden smokestack, Model 444, Fisher-Price,
Inc., 1951-55 . . . . 85.00

Puzzle, block-type, "Railway Picture
Block Puzzle," comprised of small
enameled tiles forming a scene of
a locomotive, in modern frame,
includes original decorative box
lid, C.B. Jr. (Germany), early
20th c., overall 21 x 32" 277.00

Puzzle, jigsaw-type, cardboard, pictures a train, Milton Bradley & Co.
(Springfield, Massachusetts), 20
pieces, 10 x 14", 1957 . . . . 25.00

Puzzle, jigsaw-type, "1897 Locomotive," McLoughlin Brothers (New
York, New York), complete
w/original box 325.00

Puzzle, jigsaw-type, "The Six-Day
War," box cover illustrates the
front page of the New York
Times, June 8, 1967, Parker
Brothers (Salem, Massachusetts),
unopened 16.00

Refrigerator, "Mary Lu Playthings,"
wooden w/metal trim, hinges &
latch, tin back, includes wooden
milk bottle & butter box, marked
by J.C. Penney, ca. 1930 . . . . 65.00

Rifle, cork shooting-type,
"Plymouth," red plastic handle,
Daisy Manufacturing Co., 14" l. 85.00

Robot, "Marvelous Mike," battery-operated, silver figure at the controls of a large yellow bulldozer,
mint in box 375.00

Robot, "Missile M Robot," battery-operated, tin & plastic, movement
activated by a radar antenna on
the robot's head, walks w/swinging arms, eyes light up & red
rockets shoot out of the chest &
go back in, Japan 95.00

Robot, "Space Robot," battery-operated, walks forward w/sparking action in chest, T-N Co. (Japan), 6" h. 275.00

"Tremendous Mike" Robot

Robot, "Tremendous Mike, The Robot," keywind, the orange metal
body w/red arms, w/a red transparent chest panel, by Aoshin (Japan), ca. 1960's, w/original box,
radar chest shield missing, 10" h.
(ILLUS.) 1,980.00

Rocking horse on rockers, the standing animal w/felt-covered body
w/hair mane & tail, fitted w/saddle & bridle, set upon a rectangular wooden platform base w/small
wooden wheels fitted atop a long
rocker base, late 19th c., 29" h. . . . 750.00

Painted & Carved Rocking Horse

Rocking horse on rockers, painted
& carved wooden body, fitted
w/glass eyes, hair mane & tail,
leather saddle & bridle, fitted

on long rockers w/striped trim, 19th c., imperfections, 59" l., 31" h. (ILLUS.) 935.00

Rocking toy, wood, silhouette rooster cut-outs flanking child's seat, on rockers, old red paint w/polychrome roosters, 39" l. (wear, some edge damage, hinges on backrest are loose) 700.00

Roller skates, ball-bearing type, w/original key, made in Torrington, Connecticut, 1930's, pr. 50.00

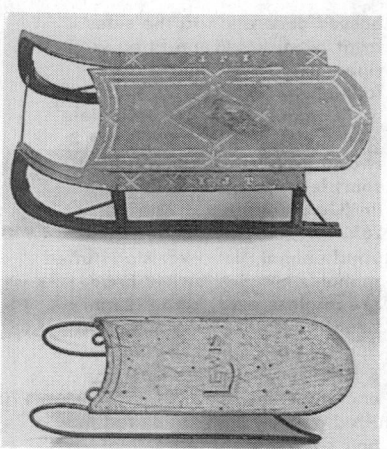

Early Sleds

Early Child's Scooter

Scooter, metal, red-painted w/wooden handles & ribbed metal footrest, on two wheels, J.G. Rideout, ca. 1930, 43" l., 32" h. (ILLUS.) 352.00

Sewing machine, "Princess," metal (mint in original box) 55.00

Sewing machine, "Sew Master," blue metal, wooden base, Kay-An-EE, Berlin, U.S. Zone, Germany, original box & instructions, 5½" h. 50.00

Roller skates, Winchester No. 10, mint in box, pr. 250.00

Roly poly clown, composition, h.p. in bright colors of red, yellow, green, blue & pink, painted face & wearing a peaked hat, ca. 1925, 12½" h. 308.00

Rug loom, wooden, Structo Mfg. Co. (Freeport, IL), ca. 1925 .... 185.00

Sand pail, lithographed tin, decorated w/scene of Humpty-Dumpty, Ohio Art Co. (Bryan, Ohio) 30.00

Sand pail, lithographed tin, pictures Jack & Jill, Ohio Art Co., excellent condition 15.00

Sled, child's size, painted & decorated, the red deck w/applied paint-enhanced print of a galloping horse & rider & inscribed "J.H.R. - 1831," decorated & inscribed on sides "Stampede," 13½ x 41" (surface imperfections) 412.50

Sled, child's size, painted pine, the platform painted yellow w/black pinstriping & "Lewis" in calligraphy, on simple wrought iron runners, America, late 19th c., 22" l., 8" h. (ILLUS. bottom) 605.00

Sled, child's size, painted & decorated pine, the wooden platform painted red w/a central yellow diamond, further decorated w/yellow pinstriping around the sides interrupted w/stellate devices, the gently curved wrought iron runners painted green w/stenciled initials "I J T" flanked by stellate devices, America, late 19th c., 37" l., 17¼" h. (ILLUS. top) 1,650.00

Sleigh, child's size, bentwood runners w/scrolled steel ends, original varnish & red paint w/striping, floral designs & landscape painting, 39" l. (some wear to decoration) 900.00

Sloop, painted wood & cloth, single mast fitted w/cloth sails & rigging, New England, early 20th c., 41" l., 5' h. 467.50

Steam shovel, painted metal, Buddy L (Moline Pressed Steel Co., E. Moline, Illinois), ca. 1925 (like new) 275.00

Stove, kitchen range, "Home," cast iron, w/seven cast iron cooking utensils (mint condition) 250.00

Stove, kitchen range, "Little Lady," electric-type, metal 37.00

Stove, kitchen range, tin, painted w/green & cream enamel, Kingston Products Corp. (Kokomo, Indiana), 12½" w., 10½" h. 105.00

Stove, kitchen range, the rectangular japanned-metal body w/em-

bossed decoration to the sides &
front, w/nickeled top fitted w/six
rings, rail, large central front-
falling oven door & five smaller
hinged doors, chimney, complete
w/a skillet, kettle, *bain-marie* &
two large pots w/lids, nickeled
short legs, spirit-fired, Mark-
lin (Germany), early 20th c.,
26¾" w. 4,950.00
Stuffed animal, cat, excelsior-stuffed
mohair animal w/swivel head,
green glass eyes, center seam on
head, pink floss nose & mouth,
applied ears, jointed at shoulders
& hips, four red floss claws on
each foot, overall 12" l. 270.00
Stuffed animal, cow, unjointed mo-
hair excelsior stuffed animal
w/glass eyes, red felt mouth,
beige felt horns, applied ears,
felt feet & udder, mohair tail,
19" l. (small moth holes on bottoms of feet, seam on left leg re-
stitched) 95.00
Stuffed animal, dog, golden mohair
animal in seated position, glass
oversized "googlie" eyes, floss
nose & mouth, red felt tongue,
darker mohair ears, jointed head,
unjointed front legs, 6" h. (mohair
a bit thin in places) 200.00
Target set, mechanical-type, "Rabbit
Hunt," w/double-barreled shotgun, Louis Marx & Co. (New York,
New York). . . . .:95.00
Telephone, wall-type, tin, Gong Bell
Mfg. Co. (East Hampton, Connecti-
cut) 35.00
Telescope, cardboard w/brass-
plated tin bindings at ends, three-
section, colorful label, Marks
Brothers Co. (Boston, Massachusetts), w/original (damaged)
box, 14¾" l. 65.00
Toaster w/flip side, electric, ca.
1920 . . . . 75.00
Tractor, "McCormick Deering," cast
iron, grey body w/red wheels, Ar-
cade Mfg. Co. (Freeport, Illinois),
4½ x 7" 225.00
Train accessory, "Electric Search
Light," No. 410, Louis Marx & Co.,
mint in box 20.00
Train car, Pullman, No. 710, Lionel
Mfg. Co. (New York, New York),
two-tone blue. 230.00
Train engine, Model No. 3242, Ives
Corp. (Bridgeport, Connecticut) . . . 225.00
Train station, tinplate, one-story
building w/low chimney, A.
Schoenhut Co. (Philadelphia,
Pennsylvania) 350.00

Tricycle, carved & painted wood, in
the form of a rearing horse, late
19th c., 35" h. 550.00

19th Century Tricycle Cart

Tricycle cart, carved & painted pine,
a shaped plank seat w/back w/a
bentwood crestrail on spindles,
the front tongue of the seat fitted
w/a small carved horse's head,
hand brakes flanking the seat,
the seat decorated w/a painted
yellow house on a red ground,
mounted on three red-painted
wooden wheels, late 19th c.,
37" l., 26" l. (ILLUS.) 5,750.00
Troll elephant, Dam Thing, Dam
Company, Denmark, ca. 1964 . . . . 80.00
Truck, "Bell Telephone," cast iron,
Hubley Mfg. Co. (Lancaster, Penn-
sylvania), 7" l. 450.00
Truck, dump, red cab & yellow box,
Buddy L (Moline Pressed Steel
Co., E. Moline, Illinois), ca.
1950's 125.00
Truck, dump, "Lumar," hydraulic
dump & scoop, Louis Marx &
Co. 175.00
Truck, gasoline tanker, "Texaco,"
Buddy L, sold only in gas stations,
ca. 1950, 25" l. 450.00
Truck, mail, six-wheel, "Buy U.S.
War Bonds," Buddy L 550.00
Truck, uranium hauler, all-steel, a
two-wheeled cab pulling a long,
deep trailer marked "Uranium
Hauler," army green w/yellow de-
cals, "USA 2700" on doors, yellow
rack on front of cab, Nylint #2700,
ca. 1960s, w/box, 23½" l., 6" h.
(minor wear, scratches & rust). . . . 33.00
Typewriter, "Tom Thumb," w/origi-
nal case 36.00
U.S. Mail cart, horse-drawn, tin &
lithograph on wood, Gibbs Mfg.
Co. (Canton, Ohio), No. 27,
11" l. 250.00
Wheelbarrow, wood, tin & iron,

wood frame w/iron front wheel & wrought-iron legs, the top w/a three-sided tin compartment decorated w/original worn brown paint & stenciled silver design of a running horse, 19th c., 31" l. 385.00

Windup celluloid "Dancing Sam," vaudeville-type figure dances on pedestal, AHI, Japan, mint in box 195.00

Windup celluloid "Hawaiian Dancer," pastel colors, Japan, in original box, 9" h. 145.00

Windup tin airplane, "Sky Hawk," Louis Marx & Co. 95.00

Windup tin automobile, "Rolls Royce," Wells Brimtoy (Hollyhead, Wales & Wells, London, England), ca. 1930, 14" l. 700.00

Windup tin automobile, "Varianto-Limo 3041," Schuco Toy Co. (Nuremberg, Germany) 75.00

Windup tin boy on tricycle, Unique Art Mfg. Co., Inc. (New York, New York), ca. 1930 . . . . 350.00

Windup tin bumper car, tinplate, red w/yellow trim & helmeted man & woman driver, key on top of hood, rotates in a circle, ca. 1930-50 (overall scratches) 77.00

Windup tin bus, "Express Bus," Wolverine Co. (Pittsburgh, Pennsylvania), ca. 1940 . . . . 210.00

Windup tin drummer, lithographed decoration w/a tall rounded hat & dress uniform, Louis Marx & Co., 9" h. (light wear on drum) 185.00

Windup tin "Farmer in the Dell," Mattell, Inc. (Hawthorne, California) 125.00

Windup tin ferris wheel, "The Giant Ride," Ohio Art Co. (Bryan, Ohio) 220.00

Windup Tin "Flapping Butterfly"

Windup tin "Flapping Butterfly," Yone (Japan), in original box, wings open 7" w. (ILLUS.) 50.00

Windup tin "George the Drummer Boy," w/moving eyes, Louis Marx & Co., ca. 1930, 9" h., mint in box 250.00

Windup tin "Jazzbo Jim on Roof," black figure dancing & playing a banjo on a rooftop, Unique Art, ca. 1921, 10" h. 440.00

Windup tin "Kiddy Cyclist," Unique Art, ca. 1930's 285.00

Windup tin "Merry-Go-Round," musical, w/four airplanes & five horses w/children riding, Wolverine Co. 510.00

Windup tin monkey, mohair w/glass eyes & jointed head & arms, jumping action, Gebruder Bing (Nuremberg, Germany), 1930's, 8" h. 395.00

Windup tin motorcycle, "Mac 700," driver mounts & dismounts, Arnold Co. (Nuremberg, Germany), 7½" l. 975.00

Windup tin "Native on Turtle," lithographed, ca. 1930 . . . . 225.00

Windup tin "Playland Merry-Go-Round," J. Chein & Co. (New York, New York), ca. 1930, 9½" h. 675.00

Windup Tin Race Car

Windup tin race car, red w/yellow trim & black wheels, "5" on hood, minor tire wear, Dubigo Mfg. Corp. (Long Island City, New York), w/original box (some tears), 10½" l. (ILLUS.) 71.50

Windup tin "Reading Elephant," Alps Shojo Ltd. (Tokyo, Japan) 75.00

Windup tin "Road Race," w/three cars, Ohio Art Co., mint in box . . . 125.00

Windup tin roller coaster, "Coney Island," w/two cars, Ohio Art Co., mint in box 250.00

Windup tin roller coaster, "Loop-A-Loop," includes small cars, Wolverine Co., ca. 1930, 19" l., mint in box 420.00

Windup tin "Rollover Cat," black cat holds ball, Louis Marx & Co., ca. 1930 . . . . 75.00

Windup tin "Sparkling Warship," Louis Marx & Co., w/box, 14" l. . . 300.00

Windup tin "Speed Boy Delivery," motorcycle w/attached delivery wagon, Louis Marx & Co., 1930's, 10" l. 395.00

Windup tin "Toe Joe Clown," acrobatic clown, Ohio Art Co. 95.00

Yo-yo, beginners model, Duncan

Yo-Yo Co., 1960's, unopened
package...................... 28.00
Zeppelin, tinplate, "Le Lepine,"
original rubber windup, rear oversized propeller, painted red &
gold, France, early 20th c.,
w/box, 10" l.................. 528.00

TRADE CARDS

Rare Clipper Ship Trade Card

*The Victorian trade card evolved from in-
formal calling cards and hand-decorated
notes. From the 1850's through the 1890's, the
American home was saturated with these
black-and-white and chromolithographed advertising cards given away with various
products.*

Axle grease, "Galena Axle Grease,"
colorful battleship picture &
"Remember the Maine," early
1900's $48.00
Carpet, "Crex Grass Carpet," hold-
to-light-type 14.00
Cigarettes, "Player's," 50 cards
depicting film stars, w/album, the
set........................... 45.00
Cigars, "Napoleon Cigars," meta-
morphic-type 18.00
Clipper ship, "Helen Angier," printed in gold, red & blue w/purple
lettering, a central oval medallion
w/a bust portrait of a pretty
young woman, the ship name
flanking it in large letters, by
Nesbitt & Co., ca. 1850's, slight
surface disturbance (ILLUS.)......1,200.00
Clipper ship, "Live Yankee," engraved scene of a striding Uncle
Sam figure holding a banner
above a scene of sailing ships,
printed by Nesbitt & Co. in red &
green, 1854 (corner flaws & a repair to one corner) 1,350.00
Clothier, "Marshall & Ball Clothiers,"
hand-colored Currier & Ives lithograph entitled "The Parson's Colt,"
3¼ x 5" (minor edge damage) ... 50.00

Glue, "Van Stan's Stratena," scene
of male black cook & little girl in
ship's galley, 1880's 32.00
Grocery store, "A & P," lithographed scene of firemen rescu-
ing Mary's little lamb from burning building.................... 20.00
Hotel, "The Windsor, Cape May,
N.J.," engraved scene of the
large hotel w/bustling carriages
& people in the oceanside foreground, 1884.................. 220.00
Ice cream maker, "Lightning," depicts black maid w/tray of ice
cream........................ 35.00
Insurance, "Prudential," depicts children playing w/blocks, signed by
Katherine Gassaway............. 7.50

Currier & Ives Trade Card

Lithographer, "Currier & Ives," a
lithographed river landscape w/a
heavily forested roadway shown,
titled "The River Road" under the
scene, early (ILLUS.)............. 400.00

"Speaking Dog" Bank Trade Card

Mechanical bank, "Speaking Dog,"
lithographed scene showing a
close-up of the toy bank sitting on
a table near a curtained window,
store advertising in the corner, by
Gast & Co. Lithographers, ca.
1880's, probably trimmed at left
(ILLUS.)...................... 880.00
Thread, "J. & P. Coats," color scene
of girl & rabbits 4.00
Tobacco, "Crescent Tobacco," depicts black men, mules & a poem,
4 x 4"........................ 5.00
Washing powder, "Gold Dust Washing Powder," die-cut, depicts
black twins in tub, ca. 1890's 55.00

Windmill, "Standard Vaneless Windmill," manufactured by the U.S. Wind Engine & Pump Co., Batavia, Illinois, set of 6 .... 90.00

TRADE CATALOGS

Sears, Roebuck & Co. "Modern Homes"

Abercrombie & Fitch, 1911, fishing supplies $100.00
Alden's, 1946, Christmas, nice doll cover, 1,970 pp. 45.00
American Cotillion Works, ca. 1900, carnival & holiday favors 45.00
Carson, Pirie, Scott & Co., 1915, "notions," sewing, spool cabinets, fancy buttons, etc., color, 172 pp. 65.00
Caulkins (H.J.), 1915, dental supplies, 982 pp. 69.00
Dennisons, 1901, holiday goods, window decorations, boxes, paper dolls, etc., color illustrations, 232 pp. 85.00
Frasse Co., 1900, bicycle supplies & fittings, illustrated, 96 pp. 80.00
Goldsmith Athletic Goods, color illustrations, 1922 .... 30.00
Hervey (W.) & Co., Boston, 1899, illustrated catalog of children's carriages, 56 pp. plus wrapper 75.00
Hibbard, Spencer & Bartlett Hardware, ca. 1907-12, 2,600 pp....... 200.00
Johnson Smith Novelties, ca. 1918, 292 pp. 28.00
Keating Bicycles, 1897, color-lithographed front & back covers, 32 pp. 125.00
Keuffel & Esser Co., 1909, drawing materials, instruments, surveying items, over 500 pp. 30.00
MacBeth Evans Shades & Globes, 1912, leaded, iridescent & decorated glass, etc., some color, 106 pp. 90.00
Mine Safety Appliance Co., 1919, 116 pp., 7¾ x 10½" 20.00
Montgomery Ward, 1933, Christmas, toys 45.00

Saalfield Publishing Company, 1950, paper dolls, coloring books, storybooks, character & celebrity items, 31 pp. 45.00
Sears, Roebuck and Co., 1915, "Baby Book," infant needs, dolls, carriages, etc., 68 pp. 48.00
Sears, Roebuck and Co., 1930, furniture, rugs, etc., color 50.00
Sears, Roebuck and Co., 1930-40, "Model Homes," house plans & prices, paper covers, minor edge tears & soiling (ILLUS.) 33.00
Sears, Roebuck and Co., 1945, Christmas 35.00
Simmons Hardware Co., "F," 1903, red leather covers, 1,400 pp. 350.00
Spiegel, 1947, Christmas, large doll & toy section 45.00
Stromberg-Carlson, 1948, "Album of Fine Radios," w/price listings, 60 pp. 21.00
Tammen Co., 1912, Indian & Mexican goods, agate, painted leather, beadwork, etc., color, 47 pp. plus supplement 120.00

Early Tobey Furniture Co. Catalog

Tobey Furniture Co., early 20th c., "The New Furniture - From the Shop of The Tobey Furniture Co. - Chicago," paper covers in green & fuchsia, 5¼ x 7¼" (ILLUS.) 935.00
Vogue Coiffures, 1924, wigs, hair pieces, excellent sepia illustrations, 46 pp. 60.00
Wallace Nutting Furniture, 1937, fully illustrated, 136 pp. 125.00
Western Electric, 1919, electrical supply yearbook, lighting, telephones, Lionel trains, Arresters, etc., 1,120 pp. 50.00
Wright & Co., 1910, Chicago, boys' merchandise, fabric samples, etc. 35.00

TRAMP ART

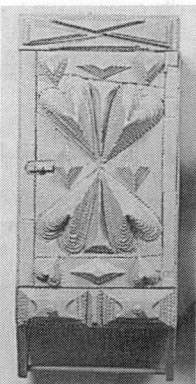

Tramp Art Hanging Cabinet

Tramp art flourished in the United States from about 1875 into the 1930's. These chip-carved woodenwares, mostly in the form of boxes or other useful items, were made mainly from old cigar boxes although fruit and vegetable crates were also used. The wood is predominantly edge-carved and subsequently layered to create a unique effect. Completed items were given an overall stained finish which was sometimes further enhanced with painted highlights. Though there seems to be no written record of the artists, many of whom were itinerants, there is a growing interest in collecting this ware.

Box, cov., rectangular, the sliding cover w/a pyramidal stack of narrow chip-carved blocks, similar tapering carved stacks around the four sides above a single drawer in the base w/chip-carved detailing, undulating base, 8" h. $137.50

Box, cov., rectangular w/boldly notched rim bands on base & lid, old brown alligatored finish, 8¼" l. 82.50

Box, cov., rectangular sides raised on a pyramidal pedestal base, each side w/graduated notched rectangles arranged to form pyramids, old finish, 9" h. 269.50

Cabinet, hanging-type, pine, rectangular w/hinged door decorated w/layered chip-carved hearts & diamonds above two small drawers & a slender roller, painted yellow, America, ca. 1930, 8 x 14", 34" h. (ILLUS.) 1,265.00

Chest of drawers, miniature, a triple-arched splashboard crest w/two small candle shelves above a rectangular top above three long drawers w/white porcelain pulls, double-arched apron &

bracket feet, all edges w/chip-carved designs, back labeled "I bought this July 2, 1955," old alligatored varnish finish, 13" h. (crest repaired) 137.50

Frame, rectangular w/a stepped chip-carved rectangular center opening & side panels w/chip-carved edges, each side w/a small chip-carved almond-shaped device in gold, old dark brown finish, 4½ x 6¼" 49.50

Frame, star-shaped, six-pointed w/notched stepped edges & a stepped oval center opening, old brown paint, 9 x 10¾" 330.00

Mirror, wall-type, a pointed crest w/a ball finial & flanked by short spires w/ball finials centering a diamond-shaped small mirror above an open compartment w/large rectangular mirror, the top tier supported by columns continuing to an open well & roller, all w/chip-carved layering forming designs of hearts, diamonds & balls, worn yellow paint, ca. 1930, 21" w., 34" h. 575.00

Shaving stand, wall-mounted, narrow rectangular border around a mirror plate over a stepped-out section w/two small center drawers w/applied diamonds flanked by small square mirrors, 9¼" w., 7" h. (some edge damage, mirrors discolored) 110.00

TRAYS, SERVING & CHANGE

Clysmic Table Water Tray

Both serving & change trays once used in taverns, cafes and the like and usually bearing advertising for a beverage maker are now being widely collected. All trays listed are heavy tin serving trays, unless otherwise noted.

Acme Beer, Los Angeles, California, aluminum w/red & blue enamel picture of a cowgirl bending over, 8½ x 15" $85.00

Allouez Mineral Water & Ginger Ale, portrait of an attractively dressed Victorian woman, ca. 1890 (change) 87.00

Anheuser-Busch, St. Louis, Missouri, colorful bust portrait of a beautiful young woman wearing a low-cut blouse, 12" d. 225.00

Clysmic, "King of Table Waters," scene of young woman in flowing drapery seated at the base of a waterfall beside an elk drinking from the water, American Art Works, Coshocton, Ohio, 1902, change (ILLUS.) 110.00

Deer Creek Ice Cream, depicts several elves eating & carrying ice cream, early 275.00

Dixie 45 Beer, Dixie Brewing, New Orleans, Louisiana, "The Beer That Speaks For Itself," 13" 40.00

Eagle Beer, Utica, New York, depicts eagle in center 95.00

Enterprise Brewing Co., San Francisco, California, color bust portrait of a girl w/flowers in her hair, ca. 1900, 12" d. 235.00

Goebel Beer, Detroit, Michigan, Dutch girls depicted 95.00

Grand Rapids Brewing, oval, depicts Victorian girl against a black ground 550.00

Hamm's Beer, scene w/two bears dancing & a half mug of beer against a lake background 25.00

Hershey's Ice Cream, depicts three ladies eating ice cream, dated "1915" 260.00

Hochgreve Beer, Green Bay, Wisconsin, "Drink Hochgreve Beer - Bavarian or Muenchner Style...," oval, scene of a brewery outlined in gold on a black ground, ca. 1900 .... 95.00

King's Pure Malt, lady w/beer tray depicted...................... 125.00

Lake Shore Ice Cream Co., "The Cream Supreme," lovely lady seated at table eating dish of ice cream...................... 350.00

Mellwood Distillery, Louisville, KY, bottle in center w/"Bottled in Bond" (change) 30.00

MoKa, round, depicts woman w/horse, large................. 325.00

Nu-Grape Soda, rectangular, hand holding a bottle of the product, "A Flavor You Can't Forget," 10½ x 13¼" 85.00

Pabst Beer, rectangular, vignette view of the brewery below "Pabst Perfected Brewing in America," a large round medallion in the upper left w/"Pabst - Milwaukee," pre-Prohibition, 12½ x 17½" 175.00

Pabst Blue Ribbon Beer, rectangular, elderly man pouring a glass of beer, 10½ x 13¼" 85.00

Pacific Beer, Tacoma, Washington, center w/round scene of "Mt. Tacoma" on wood-grained ground, "Best East or West," 1930's, 12" d..................70.00 to 100.00

Early Pepsi-Cola Tray

Pepsi-Cola, oval, center scene of a late Victorian lady standing & wearing a low-cut blue gown & a large feathered hat, holding a glass of Pepsi w/the bottle & another glass on a table beside her, a soda fountain scene behind her, ornate floral & scroll border band, ca. 1909 (ILLUS.) 1,550.00

Rainier Beer, Seattle Brewing & Malting Co., sexy Victorian girl resting on bearskin rug, 1900 .... 185.00

Reingold Beer, shows explorer & African native, artist-signed "O. Soglow"........................ 99.00

Rome Ale, Rome, New York, depicts gladiator holding glass 225.00

Ruhstaller's Lager, depicts waitress carrying six steins, some age (change) 120.00

Ruppert's Beer, Hans Flato pictured (change) 55.00

Slades Spices, shows game around the rim (change) 45.00

Smith Brothers Typewriters, depicts three horses & a typewriter (change) 250.00

Standard Brewing Co., Mankato, Minnesota, crowd scene & "The execution of 38 Sioux Indians at Mankato, Dec. 26th, 1862...," ca. 1905, 12" d. ....650.00 to 700.00

Success Manure Spreader, Kemp &
Burpee, Syracuse, New York,
team pulling wagon on red, yellow & white ground, oblong
(change) 150.00
Tamm & Wieting General Merchandise, Kaukauna, Wisconsin, colorful lithographed illustration
of a Victorian lady, ca. 1890
(change) 87.00
White Rock Beer, lady w/tiger
depicted...................... 125.00
White Rock Table Water, semi-nude
lady on rock (change) 155.00

VENDING & GAMBLING
MACHINES

Jenning's 'Little Duke'

Arcade, "Babe Ruth Baseball," a
baseball player moves into position to catch the falling ballbear-
ing, Stephens Novelty Co. $1,795.00
Arcade, "Blue Streak Digger," digger shovel-type, Exhibit Supply
Co. (restored) 2,000.00
Arcade, "Cail-O-Scope," Caille Bros.,
1904 ....1,500.00
Arcade, "Cent-O-Scope," floor model, oak cabinet on iron legs, Exhibit Supply Co. 1,200.00
Arcade, "Challenger Gun Shoot,"
floor model, 1-cent operation,
A.B.T. Mfg. Co. (restored) 250.00
Arcade, "Conquest," 5-cent play, Exhibit Supply Co., 1939, original
condition 450.00
Arcade, "Deliver the Punch," floor
model, Mills Novelty Co., 1904 ...2,600.00
Arcade, "Electricity Is Life," electric
treatment for headache, rheu-
matism. nervousness & neuralgia,
wooden pedestal base w/dia-
mond-shaped face w/knobs at

each side, Midland Mfg. Co., ca.
1900.........................8,500.00
Arcade, "Jewel Box Digger," digger
shovel-type, floor model, Buckley
Mfg.........................1,650.00
Arcade, "Jumbo Success," fortune
card-type machine, pedestal
based floor model, cast iron &
plated metal, Mills Novelty Co.,
1901-20.....................1,350.00
Arcade, "Mauser Gun Game," Exhibit Supply Co................ 150.00
Arcade, "Merchantman," digger
shovel-type, Art Deco style floor
model, Exhibit Supply Co., ca.
1942 (restored) 2,100.00
Arcade, Mutoscope, "Mills Viewer,"
15-views, 10-cent operation......1,900.00
Arcade, "Spirometer," lung capacity
tester, table model, oak cabinet
w/hose, National Spirometer Co.,
ca. 1899 ....4,500.00
Arcade, "Treasure Chest," digger
shovel-type, table model, Buckley
Mfg. (restored) 1,500.00
Arcade, "2c Strength Tester," tabletop metal case, Gottlieb Mfg. Co.
(restored) 250.00
Arcade, "Your True Horoscope," upright oak cabinet on iron legs,
upper vignette scene w/small
papier-mache' figures of a swami
& two female attendants, calendar
panels on front above paneled
base, ca. 1932, Exhibit Supply
Co...........................1,500.00
Candy vendor, "Stollwerck's Chocolate Confections," upright oak
cabinet, "Stollwerck's" on a blue
& white porcelain marquee sign,
two circular red glass plates
w/gold lettering, four columns
vending caramel, gum & chocolates, Volkmann, Stollwerck &
Co., patent dated "Sept. 27,
1892".......................1,400.00
Cigar vendor, "The Elm City," ornate
oak counter model w/scrolled
crest & finials above a large
diamond-shaped mirror over two
arched windows, patent dated
"Dec. 17, 1889," The New Haven
Car Register Co................2,500.00
Cup dispenser, "Dixie Cups," diecast metal mechanism mounts on
22" l. glass cylinder to hold cups,
1-cent operation 425.00
Gambling, Buckley's "Diamond
Fronts" countertop slot machine,
50-cent play, late 1940's 1,500.00
Gambling, Caille's "Aristocrat
Counter Roulette" machine,
1932-34 ....1,200.00
Gambling, Jennings' "Little Duke"

countertop slot machine,
1-cent play, ca. 1932, 22½" h.
(ILLUS.) . . . . .1,100.00 to 1,200.00

Gambling, Jennings' "Little Duke"
countertop slot machine, 25-cent
play, front case w/sunburst painted red, orange & yellow, ca. 1932,
22½" h. 1,525.00

Gambling, Jennings' "Operator Bell"
countertop slot machine, wood
front, 5-cent play, ca. 1920 . . . . . .1,800.00

Gambling, Jennings' "Victoria Silent
Vendor" ("Peacock Vendor") countertop slot machine w/front ven-
dor, 5-cent play, 1932-34 . . . . . . .5,500.00

Gambling, Mills' "Baseball" countertop slot machine, 5-cent play, ca.
1929. . . . . .3,500.00

Gambling, Mills' "Black Cherry"
countertop slot machine, 5-cent
play, 1945-48 . . . . .1,525.00

Gambling, Mills' "Blue Front" countertop slot machine, 10-cent
play 1,650.00

Gambling, Mills' "Brown Front"
countertop slot machine, 1-cent
play, ca. 1938, 26" h. 3,300.00

Gambling, Mills' "Dewey Twins,"
double upright slot machine,
5-cent & 25-cent play (re-
stored) . . . . .27,000.00 to 30,000.00

Gambling, Mills' "Golden Nugget
Conversion" countertop slot machine, made specifically for the
Golden Nugget Casino, 25-cent
play, 1947 . . . . .1,100.00

Gambling, Mills' "Jackpot Front"
countertop slot machine, 5-cent
play, 1930-33 . . . . . . .1,300.00 to 1,350.00

Gambling, Mills' "Jackpot" (Poinsettia front) countertop slot machine, 1-cent play, ca.
1929-31 . . . . .1,300.00 to 1,400.00

Mills' 'On-the-Square' Slot Machine

Gambling, Mills' "On-the-Square"

upright slot machine, 5-cent play,
restored (ILLUS.) 7,150.00

Gambling, Mills' "Q.T." countertop slot machine, 1-cent play,
1930s-50s 1,150.00

Gambling, Mills' "Q.T." countertop slot machine, 10-cent play,
1930s-50s 1,100.00

Gambling, Mills' "Silent Golden Bell"
(Roman Head front or Gold front)
countertop slot machine, 25-cent
play, ca. 1930s 2,200.00

Gambling, Mills' "Silent Gooseneck"
(Lion front) countertop slot ma-
chine, 25-cent play, ca. 1930s 1,100.00

Gambling, Pace's "Comet" countertop slot machine, 10-cent play,
1932-35 . . . . .1,100.00

Gambling, Rockola's "Four Aces"
countertop slot machine,
1932-34 . . . . .1,150.00

Gambling, Watling's "Baby Gold
Award" countertop slot machine,
5-cent play, 1932 (restored) 2,800.00

Gambling, Watling's "Rol-A-Top
Bell" countertop slot machine,
w/cornucopia of coins, etc., 5-cent
play, 1935-46 . . . . .3,100.00

Gambling, Watling's "Treasury"
countertop slot machine, 5-cent
play, 1936-41 . . . . .4,500.00

Gum "prize" vendor, "Prize King,"
vended prize ball gum, cast-iron
footed base & lid, tapering cylindrical clear glass dome, Automat-
ic Games Co., early 1940s 125.00

Gum vendor, "Columbus Model JM,"
1-cent operation, green porcelain
body & lid, No. 10 cylindrical clear
glass dome, Columbus Vending
Co., patented in 1934 . . . . .3,495.00

Gum vendor, "Cop & Robber (or
Hobo)," 1-cent operation, ca.
1930, Pulver Mfg. Co. 950.00

Gum vendor, "Master," Norris Mfg.
Co., 1-cent operation, ca. 1923,
16" h. 350.00

Gum vendor, "Northwestern Model
33 Gum," porcelain over cast iron
w/glass container, red & yellow,
1-cent operation, 1933, 14" h. 200.00

Gum vendor, "Yellow Kid," red case
w/"Yellow Kid" inside, Pulver
Mfg. Co., 1897 patent 525.00

Match vendor, "Knapsack Matches,"
glass, wood & metal, six-sided,
metal bars frame six glass
paneled sides printed in cream
outlined in red "Knapsack
Matches - Tin Box - One Cent," on
flaring metal & wood base w/dis-
penser chute, 10" w., 10½" h.
(soiling, minor scratches, overall
rust) 605.00

Peanut vendor, "Smilin' Sam - from Alabam," cast aluminum head, embossed "The Salted Peanut Man" on base, painted red, General Mds. Co., 1931 (restored) 750.00

Pinball, "Surf Queen," wooden rail, Bally Mfg. Co., 1946 . . . . 175.00

Popcorn vendor, "Popmatic 5c Popcorn Machine," cast-metal Art Deco floor model (restored) 2,500.00

Old Stamp Vendor

Stamp vendor, porcelain front & metal back, blue w/white letters & numbers, rust, chipping & one handle missing, overall rust on back, 7½" w., 16" h. (ILLUS.). 93.50

Trade stimulator, "American Eagle," Daval, 1940-52 . . . . 295.00

Trade stimulator, "Jumping Jack Dice" 275.00

Trade stimulator, "Kicker & Catcher," player kicks the ball & mechanical football player moves to catch it, Baker Novelty Co., ca. 1935 . . . . 400.00

Trade stimulator, National's "Monte Carlo" roulette wheel, nickel-plated cast-iron countertop model, allows five-way multiple play w/counter payouts of merchandise. 235.00

Trade stimulator, "Puritan," three-reel cast-iron countertop machine w/embossed scrolls & 'Puritan' across the top front, on feet, 5-cent play, Mills Novelty Co., 1905-33 (ILLUS. top next column) . . 700.00

Trade stimulator, "Puritan Baby Bell," three-reel w/standard slot machine symbols, front payout & last coin played window, 1-cent play, Midwest Novelty Co., dated 1929 . . . . 770.00

Trade stimulator, "Target Practice," 1-cent play, aluminum cast

Mills' 'Puritan' Trade Stimulator

w/scene of Olympic discus throwers, w/original decal & award card, Mills, ca. 1930, 18¼" h. 695.00

Trade stimulator, "Winner Dice," countertop, cast-iron base w/clear glass dome-shaped cover, Caille Brothers, ca. 1905 . . . . 475.00

VIENNA ART TIN PLATES

Louise B. Art Plate

These decorative tin plates were generally printed in the center with colorful bust portraits of lovely and exotic young ladies and were most often used as advertising promotional items in the early 20th century. The names used here are those given in Jane and Howard Hazelcorn's book Hazelcorn's Price Guide to Tin Vienna Art Plates *(H.J.H. Publications, 1987).*

"Apple Blossom," 'keyhole' style portrait of a standing young woman holding an urn filled w/flowers, H.D. Beach Co., ca. 1908, 10¼" d. $95.00

"Auf Capri, No. 101," portrait of a woman standing & holding an urn

filled w/flowers, Chas. Shonk Co.,
ca. 1907, 10¼" d. 95.00

"Claire," bust portrait of a young
woman w/her dark hair piled on
her head, wearing a low-cut
gown, H.D. Beach Co., ca. 1905,
10 1/8" d. 100.00

"Gypsy G.," bust portrait of a semi-
nude young woman w/a floral
band in her long dark hair & holding a rose in one hand, gold border band, H.D. Beach Co., ca.
1906, 10 1/8" d. 165.00

"Gypsy M.," bust portrait of a semi-
nude young woman w/a floral
band in her long dark hair & holding a rose in one hand, swirling
blossom border, H.D. Beach Co.,
ca. 1907, 10 1/8" d. 150.00

"Jill," bust portrait of a young woman w/a tiara in her hair & w/a
long neck scarf (based on the
Queen Louise portrait), H.D.
Beach Co., ca. 1906, 10 1/8" d. 135.00

"Louise B.," bust portrait of a pensive young woman w/a rose in
her long dark hair, wearing a
low-cut gown w/shoulder band
across her bosom, gilt leaf border, Meek Co., ca. 1907, 9 5/8" d.
(ILLUS.)........................ 125.00

"Marguerite," bust profile portrait of
a young woman wearing a cap on
her long, dark hair, in a low-cut
gown, gilt scroll border, "Western
Coca-Cola Bottling Co." advertising on the back, H.D. Beach Co.,
ca. 1906, 10 1/8" d. 300.00

"Marian," bust profile portrait of a
young woman w/long dark hair,
wearing an off-the-shoulder low-
cut gown, ornate patterned border, H.D. Beach Co., ca. 1908,
10 1/8" d. 95.00

"Poesie, No. 104," bust portrait of a
pensive young woman w/a laurel
wreath in her long dark hair,
wearing a low-cut gown, calendar
border, Chas. Shonk Co., ca.
1907, 10¼" d. 150.00

"Sara," bust portrait of a young
woman w/large blossoms in her
dark hair, wearing a low-cut
gown w/a shoulder strap, "Harvard Brewing Co." advertising at
the bottom front rim, calendar
border, H.D. Beach Co., ca. 1907,
10 1/8" d. 175.00

"Susanne M.," bust portrait of a
young woman w/a cap on her
long dark hair & wearing large
loop earrings, in a low-cut gown,
scalloped lobe & gilt swag border,

made for the Detroit Brewing Co.,
Detroit, Michigan, H.D. Beach Co.,
ca. 1907, 10 1/8" d. 165.00

WARTIME MEMORABILIA

*Since the early 19th century, every war that
America has fought has been commemorat-
ed with a variety of war-related memorabilia. Often in the form of propaganda items
produced during the conflict or as memorial
pieces made after the war ended, these materials are today quite collectible and increasingly important for the historic insights they
provide. Most commonly available are items
dating from World War I and II and since
the fall of 1989 marked the fiftieth anniversary of the beginning of World War II, there
should be added interest in this collecting
field.*

CIVIL WAR (1861-65)

Accounting sheet, for W. Henderson, I Co., 199th Reg., Pennsylvania Volunteers, 1864, w/a second
soldier's sheet on same page,
1864, 10 x 15" $32.00

Application for soldier's pension, for
the widow of B. Gray from Mississippi, 1862, Co. C, 1st Alabama
Battery P.R., 8½ x 14".......... 48.00

Book, "Civil War in Song & Story,"
by Moore, Colliers, 1889, illustrated, 560 pp. 28.00

Confederate bond, pink paper,
$1000 w/Jackson portrait, CSA
treasury seal, 1863 .... 65.00

SPANISH-AMERICAN WAR (1898)

Book, "Cuba In War Time," by
Frederick Remington, 1899 .... 25.00

Book, "History of the Spanish
American War," 1898, illustrated
w/many engravings, large 42.00

Book, "Uncle Sam's Navy," large
photos of battleships, officers,
etc. 20.00

Napkin holder, silver plate, decorated w/the U.S.S. Battleship Maine,
destroyed in Havana Harbor,
February 15, 1898 .... 22.00

Plate, china, "Remember the
Maine," illustrates the battleship
in the center, an American eagle
at the top & a banner at the bottom, 8½" d. 84.00

WORLD WAR I (1914-18)

Book, "History of the World War,"
by General Peyton March, 1919,
illustrated 30.00

Book, "Honor Roll of Ohio - Stark
County," 1917 edition, 1918 ...... 35.00
Book, "My Experiences in the World
War," by General Pershing, 1931,
first edition, 2 vols. 30.00
Book, "U.S. Fighting Men of Illinois,"
photographs & notations on all
servicemen from Illinois, hard
cover 48.00
Button, "Kick the Kaiser" 20.00

World War I Chess Set

Chess set, hand-carved & painted
wood, each of the pieces fashioned as various soldiers & per-
sonages of World War I, one side
being German soldiers & the Kaiser, the other side being British &
American soldiers, an American
general, British officers & a figure
of Columbia, American-made,
ca. 1920, each figure 5½" h.
(ILLUS.) 2,415.00
Handkerchief, silk, "Souvenir de
France," embroidered eagle
crest 15.00

WORLD WAR II (1939-45)

Book, "Pictorial History of the Second World War," Wise & Co., New
York, 4 vols.................... 37.50
Coin, bronze, commemorating "Allied Victory over the Axis,"
depicts MacArthur & Eisenhower,
1945, 1½" d. 15.00
Compact, wooden, "Until we meet
again," depicts sailor kissing a
girl goodbye, mint in box 110.00
Flag, "Welcome Navy," w/blue &
white battleship in center, Brooklyn Navy Yard origin, ca. 1940's,
3 x 4' 25.00
Map, illustrates the Pacific Theatre
of the war, Esso premium, 1945 .. 12.00
Matchbook w/matches, cover
marked "Remember Pearl Harbor
- Strike 'm Dead," each match a
Japanese soldier 40.00
Sign, tin, illustrated w/a flying eagle representing the so-called
'ruptured duck,' inscribed "Welcome back wearer of this badge
of honor. You have served your
country well, we thank you,"
6 x 16½".......................... 18.00

WATCHES

French Scottie Dog Watch-Pin

Hunting case, lady's, Patek Philippe
& Co., Geneva, Switzerland, nickel movement No. 60155, white
porcelain dial w/Roman numerals,
subsidiary dial for seconds, 18k
gold case, signed on dial, movement & front cover $825.00
Hunting case, man's, American
Waltham Watch Co., Waltham,
Massachusetts, 17-jewel movement, white porcelain dial w/Ara-
bic numerals, spade hands,
subsidiary dial for seconds, in a
14k yellow gold case w/engraved
decoration..................... 302.50
Lapel watch, lady's, Longines, engraved dial, within a guilloche'
bezel & case, highlighted by applied diamond initials, on a gold &
blue enamel dragonfly watch pin
set w/sapphires, Edwardian (minor enamel damage) 880.00
Open face, man's, Omega, Switzerland, serial no. 4493220, jeweled
nickel movement, chronograph,
15-minute recorder, white porcelain face w/Roman numerals,
two subsidiary dials, polished
18k yellow gold case engraved
"Omega Grand Prix Paris 1900" ..1,045.00
Open face, man's, Patek Philippe &
Co., serial no. 223714, white enamel dial w/Arabic numerals,
polished 18k gold case, signed on
case & movement................2,640.00
Open face, man's, Waltham,
17-jewel movement, white enamel
dial w/Arabic numerals, subsidiary dial, 14k yellow gold case 440.00
Watch-pin, sterling silver & marca-
site, modeled in the form of a
Scottie dog w/front paws on the
watch case, the watch w/round
dial marked "G.S. Paris," Arabic
numerals, onyx thumbpiece, the
whole set w/marcasites, French
hallmarks, ca. 1930 (ILLUS.) 550.00

WATCH FOBS

Gold & Sard Fob with a Compass

Advertising, "Avery Tractors," bull-
dog, metal w/celluloid insert $110.00
Advertising, "Bently & Olmstead
Company's Buffalo Calf Shoe,"
buffalo logo, w/leather strap 55.00
Advertising, "Heider Rock Island
Plow Co.," depicts a steam
tractor 85.00
Advertising, "Hupmobile," blue &
white enamel on gilt metal 60.00
Advertising, "Ingersoll-Rand,"
depicts man w/jackhammer 25.00
Advertising, "Poll Parrot," w/leather
strap 75.00
Bakelite, round w/bobcat head,
w/leather strap 90.00
Brass, relief decoration of an Indian
standing in & paddling a canoe,
tepees, lake & trees in background, 1½ x 1½" 20.00
Citrine & 14k gold, the oval intaglio-
cut citrine seal mounted in a
floral-chased gold mounting, suspended from black grosgrain ribbon, Victorian 330.00
Damascened gold, composed of
eight hinged plaques each w/a
damascened decoration of inlaid
vari-colored gold forming a long
Oriental landscape, 18k yel-
low gold mountings, w/chain..... 660.00
Fraternal, "Benevolent & Protective
Order of the Elk," sterling silver.. 79.00
Fraternal, "Loyal Order of the
Moose," w/tooth 40.00
Gold (14k), composed of scroll-
engraved hinged rectangular
panels completed by a pyramidal
fob 357.50
Gold (14k) & sard, the rectangular
stone in a gold mounting w/em-
bossed florals, a small compass
mounted on the handle, Victorian
(ILLUS.)........................ 220.00
Souvenir, "Civilian Conservation
Corps," bronze w/green enameled
center, 1935 .... 89.50

Souvenir, "1905 Lewis & Clark Exposition," aluminum-linked 45.00
Souvenir, "Newark, New Jersey
250th Anniversary, 1916," enameled metal.................... 35.00
Sterling silver, Art Nouveau-style,
composed of four plaques, two
w/female faces, suspending a circular medallion of a female figure, hallmarked................. 275.00

WEATHERVANES

Early Elephant Weathervane

Angel Gabriel, carved & painted
pine, the swell-bodied stylized figure of a flying angel blowing a
trumpet fashioned from sheet
metal painted white, continuing to
a sleeve encasing the forearm,
the angel w/incised ear, nose &
mouth detail, mounted on a
wrought-iron rod in a carved pine
ball, the whole on a black metal
base, probably New England, late
19th c., 22" l., weathervane 7" h.
(weathered paint) $4,400.00
Canada goose, carved & painted
pine, carved in the full round
w/outstretched wings, painted
black w/white markings, executed in the style of Ira Hudson,
mounted on a rod, possibly Maritime Provinces, early 20th c.,
40" l........................2,750.00
Codfish, molded & gilded copper,
the swell-bodied fish w/repousse'
scales & tail & applied sheet copper fins covered in much of the
original gilding & verdigris,
mounted on a rod continuing to a
white-painted turned pine urn,
attributed to J.W. Fiske & Co.,
New York, third quarter 19th c.,
23¾" l., weathervane 6" h.......3,300.00
Cow, molded copper & zinc, the full-
bodied standing animal w/cast
zinc head & molded copper body,

weathered to an overall verdigris,
mounted on a rod in a black metal stand, third quarter 19th c.,
29" l., 18½" h. 4,600.00
Dove, gilded copper, swell-bodied
flying bird, much original gilding,
mounted on a wrought-iron stan-
dard, 26" w., overall 6' 5" h. 1,955.00
Eagle, molded copper, molded in
the round, the figure w/open
beak & wings spread mounted on
a rod & horizontal perch above a
sphere supported on a wrought-
iron standard in a green-painted
wooden pedestal base, weathered
to an overall verdigris, probably
New England, third quarter
19th c., weathervane 20" h. (some
repaired bullet holes) 2,475.00
Elephant, gilded copper, swell-
bodied model of a walking elephant mounted on a rod on a
black metal base, attributed to
J.W. Fiske, New York, third quarter 19th c., restoration to gilding, 22¼" l., overall 17½" h.
(ILLUS.) 27,500.00
Goddess of Liberty, molded copper,
the swell-bodied standing figure
wearing a Phrygian cap & grasping a sheet copper American flag
standard in one hand while pointing into the distance w/the other,
mounted on a rod in a white-
painted pine pyramid-shaped
base, America, early 20th c.,
26" w., weathervane 51½" h.
(weathered w/verdigris) 7,975.00
Horse, trotting hackney-type, mold-
ed & sheet copper, the swell-
bodied animal w/sheet copper
ears, molded mane & cropped
tail, at full gallop, retains traces
of old brown paint & verdigris,
mounted on a rod in a cast-iron
base, together w/a harness packing box from Forest View Stud
Farms, J.W. Fiske & Co., New
York, ca. 1893, 51" l., 4' h.
(2 pcs.) 46,200.00
Pig, gilded sheet metal, silhouetted
animal w/curled tail, standing on
a rod continuing to an arrow finial
w/tulip bud arrowhead, retains
much of the original gilding,
late 19th - early 20th c., 28" l.,
9" h. 2,200.00
Polo player & pony, molded copper,
the swell-bodied figure of a helmeted polo player leaning forward on the neck of his pony,
w/mallet raised in his gloved
hand, the pony w/knotted mane,

flowing tail & perked ears, galloping, northern New York State, ca.
1920, 47" l., 37" h. 38,500.00
Rooster, cast iron, swell-bodied
form w/molded feather detail,
fitted w/a sheet iron tail, painted
yellow, mounted on a metal rod
above a sphere in a brown-
painted wooden pedestal base,
America, third quarter 19th c.,
35" w., weathervane 34¾" h. 9,350.00
Sailing ship, carved & painted pine
& sheet metal, the ship hull fashioned from a single wood plank
painted black supporting three
masts fitted w/white-painted
sheet copper sails, the whole
mounted on a horizontal arrow
w/black weight, early 20th c.,
31½" l., 17½" h. 7,188.00

Sedan Car Weathervane

Sedan car, sheet iron, silhouetted
seven-passenger sedan w/steer-
ing wheel visible, applied rings to
indicate tires, mounted on a rod
w/an arrow directional, ca. 1930,
31" l., 12" h. (ILLUS.) 990.00
Stag, leaping, molded copper, the
full-bodied animal in a leaping
pose, molded cast-zinc head &
antlers, retains much of the original gilding, mounted on a black
metal rod & base, third quarter
19th c., 34" l., overall 24½" h. . . .13,225.00
Weaver's shuttle, molded gilt-
copper, realistic model mounted
horizontally on a shaft w/a knob
finial, fine verdigris surface,
America, 19th c., 64" l. 2,750.00

WHISTLES

*There are many types of whistles—devices
used to produce whistling sounds by means
of breath, air or steam forced through them.
We distinguish between working steam whistles such as those used on boats, trains or in
early factories as a warning, summons or
command, and the small whistles used by individuals, some of which were meant to be a
whimsey or toy.*

Small Whistles
Brass, "Acme Thunder," England.... $16.50

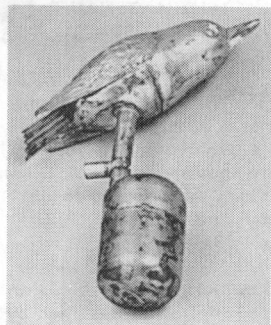

Figural Brass Whistle

Brass, figural, model of a bird
perched on a stem above a small
oblong tank, bird's beak & tail
feathers move as it chirps, original box marked "Victory Canary
Songster," made by the Victory
Sparkler & Specialty Co., Elkton,
Missouri, some tarnishing, ca.
1910, 4" h. (ILLUS.) 187.00
Brass, figural, model of dog's head
at end, 3½" l. 45.00
Pewter, figural, cast as a fat bird,
angled stem forms the tail,
2¾" l. 75.00
Pewter, figural, an angled stem to a
bulb cast as a dove perched on a
clump of foliage, 2 7/8" l. 70.00
Porcelain, figural, fat man, polychrome enamel decoration,
3½" h. (chips on base) 25.00
Pottery, model of stylized dog in
standing position on a small cylindrical base, mottled blue &
white glaze, 2¾" l. (wear, small
chips) 165.00
Redware, modeled as a large bird
w/brown slip eyes, the breast &
tail pierced w/whistle openings,
perched between two smaller
birds (one a plaster replacement)
& above two further small birds
on branches issuing from a central cone applied w/circular
growths, the whole covered in a
cream-colored slip glaze streaked
in manganese-brown, probably
Sussex, England, 19th c., 9 1/16" h.
(some abrasions & minor footrim
chips) 220.00

Silver Bosun's Whistle

Silver, bosun's model, of typical
form, the barrel terminating in
flowerheads, the panel tooled
w/trellis, Chinese Export, maker's
mark "CU" for Cutshing & pseudo-
hallmarks, Canton, China, ca.
1840, 4½" l. (ILLUS.)............. 770.00

Steam Whistles
Brass, locomotive, dome-type, sin-
gle-chime model, marked "Lunk-
enheimer," 11½" l. .....175.00 to 225.00
Brass, locomotive, dome-type,
three-chime model w/pigtail,
14" l. 275.00
Brass, locomotive, "Union Iron
Works, Erie, Pennsylvania,"
w/brass gauge, whistle 20" l.,
gauge 15" d.................... 450.00

WIENER WERKSTATTE

Wiener Werkstatte Carpet

*The Wiener Werkstatte (Vienna Work-
shops) were co-founded in 1903 in Vienna,
Austria by Josef Hoffmann and Koloman
Moser. An offshoot of the Vienna Secession
movement, closely related to the Art Nouveau
and Arts and Crafts movements elsewhere,
this studio was established to design and produce unique and high-quality pieces covering
all aspects of the fine arts. Hoffmann and
Moser were the first artistic directors and
oversaw the work of up to 100 workers, including thirty-seven masters who signed their
work. Bookbinding, leatherwork, gold, silver
and lacquer pieces as well as enamels and furniture all originated from these shops over a
period of nearly thirty years. The finest pieces
from the Wiener Werkstatte are now bringing tremendous prices.*

Basket, white-painted metal, tall
curved lozenge form w/a tall
loop handle, pierced overall w/a
square grill pattern, w/a glass liner, designed by Josef Hoffmann,
9 7/8" h. $880.00

Bowl, brass, lobed sides & scalloped
rim, a T-shaped handle at rim,
marked "Wiener Werkstatte - JH -
Made in Austria," designed by
Josef Hoffmann, early 20th c.,
4½" d., 1½" h. 495.00

Bowl-vase, brass, two-handled, the
ribbed half-melon form cup applied w/two looping & coiling
handles, raised on a ribbed inverted trumpet-form pedestal,
designed by Josef Hoffmann, ca.
1924-25, impressed "WIENER -
WERK - STATTE" w/"JH" monogram, & "MADE - IN - AUS-
TRIA," 11½" w. across handles,
7½" h. 12,100.00

Carpet, woven wool, linear border
design w/squares, ovals & rectangles in dark blues & tans framing
a large center circle all on a
grey ground, attributed to Otto
Prutscher, ca. 1905-07, 8' x 11' 5"
(ILLUS.) 15,400.00

Centerpiece, earthenware, designed
in the form of a kneeling farm
boy wearing a checkered shirt,
blue baggy pants & conical blue
hat, supporting two baskets on
his shoulder & head, another on
his knee & two at his feet, colorfully glazed in ochre, orange, blue
& yellow, designed by Gudrin
Baudisch, impressed "WW -
MADE IN - AUSTRIA - 367 - 2" &
w/artist's monogram, ca. 1915,
10¼" h. 2,875.00

Figure group of a horse & rider,
terra cotta w/a matte charcoal
glaze, impressed company monogram & "MADE IN AUSTRIA - 252,"
8¼" h. 385.00

Garniture set: flared square centerpiece & pair of flared vases; silver, decorated w/fan fluting &
hammered surface, designed by
Josef Hoffmann, marked on all
pieces, 900 standard, ca. 1910,
centerpiece 3½" h., vases
8½" h., the set...............12,100.00

Model of an elephant, painted
bronze, the silhouetted animal
w/his rear leg chained to a post,
impressed "HAGENAUER WIEN"
& w/ the Wiener Werkstatte -
Hagenauer mark & "MADE IN
AUSTRIA HANDMADE," 6¾" h. 352.00

Model of a fox, brass, the stylized

animal marked w/the impressed
Hagenauer - Wiener Werkstatte
mark & "FRANZ HAGENAUER
WIEN - MADE IN AUSTRIA,"
12¾" l........................1,100.00

Pendant, silver & mother-of-pearl,
the rectangular silver frame enclosing stylized heart-shaped
leaves & two oval mother-of-pearl
blossoms, has shaped bezel & thin
silver chain, designed by Josef
Hoffmann, unsigned, ca. 1912,
13/16 x 1 13/16" 2,185.00

Vase, bud, brass, the elongated
shaped cylindrical body raised on
a low pedestal base, designed by
Josef Hoffmann, impressed "WIE-
NER - WERK - STATTE," "JH"
monogram & "MADE IN AUSTRIA,"
ca. 1910, 12" h. 1,150.00

Vases, pottery, shaped square body
w/a wide angled shoulder to the
short round neck, glazed in pale
rose & decorated w/random abstract leaves, arrows, animals, a
city skyline, each side applied
w/a loop strap handle, by Hilda
Jesser, stamped w/the company
monogram & "874 - Austria," ca.
1925, 9" h., pr. 4,620.00

WITCH BALLS

*Several theories exist as to the origin of
these hollow balls of glass. Some believe they
were originally designed to hold the then precious commodity of salt in the chimney where
it would be kept dry. Eventually these blown
glass spheres became associated with ward-
ing off the "evil eye" and it is known they
were hung in the windows of homes of many
18th century English glassblowers. The tradition was carried to America where the balls
were made from the 19th century on. They are
scarce.*

Aqua ball w/wide bluish white loopings, sheared mouth, smooth
base, probably America, ca.
1850-80, 4½" d. (1/8" mouth
fissure).........................$341.00

Blue & white swirl ball, 5" d. 245.00

Clear ball, molded w/twelve vertical ribs, America, ca. 1830-80,
3½" d. 176.00

Clear ball w/pink & white loopings,
sheared mouth, probably Ameri-
ca, ca. 1850-80, 5" d. 715.00

Clear ball w/white loopings &
matching hollow sausage-turned
stand, 5¾" d. ball w/sheared

mouth & rim, overall 13¾" h.,
2 pcs. 1,045.00
Cobalt blue w/white loopings,
tooled mouth, smooth base,
probably America, ca. 1850-80,
3 1/8" d. 880.00
Cranberry ball, sheared mouth,
America, ca. 1850-80, 4¼" d. 357.50
Electric blue ball, molded w/sixteen
ribs swirled to the right, sheared
mouth, ca. 1850-80, 6¾" d. 396.00
Opaque green ball, sheared mouth,
America, ca. 1850-80, 5" d. 176.00
Opaque white ball w/opaque grass
green loopings, sheared mouth,
possibly America, ca. 1850-80,
4¾" d. (wooden stand included) . . 825.00
Opaque white ball w/opaque rose
loopings, sheared mouth, probably America, ca. 1850-80,
4½" d. 907.50
Opaque white ball w/pigeon blood
red loopings, sheared mouth,
probably America, ca. 1850-80,
4½" d. (black amethyst glass
stand included) 990.00
Opaque white ball w/salmon, green
& blue loopings, cased in clear
glass, probably America, ca.
1850-80, 2 7/8" d. 1,650.00
Opaque yellowish green ball, tooled
mouth, America, ca. 1850-80,
5" d. 110.00
Teal blue ball, tooled mouth, Ameri-
ca, ca. 1850-80, 3¾" d. 170.50
Teal green ball & matching hollow
sausage-turned stand, tooled
rims, 2 7/8" d. ball, overall
10 7/8" h., 2 pcs. 742.50

WOODENWARES

Early Cutlery Tray

*The patina and mellow coloring, along with
the lightness and smoothness that come only
with age and wear, attract collectors to old
woodenwares. The earliest forms were the
simplest and the shapes of items whittled out
in the late 19th century varied little in form
from those turned out in the American colo-*
nies two centuries earlier. Burl is a growth,
or wart, on some trees in which the grain of
the wood is twisted and turned in a manner
which strengthens the fibers and causes a
beautiful pattern to be formed. Treenware is
simply a term for utilitarian items made from
"treen," another word for wood. While maple was the primary wood used for these
items, they are also abundant in pine, ash,
oak, walnut, and other woods. "Lignum Vi-
tae" is a species of wood from the West Indies that can always be identified by the
contrasting colors of the dark heartwood and
light sapwood and by its heavy weight, which
causes it to sink in water.

*Also see KITCHENWARES and MOR-
TARS & PESTLES.*

Bowl, ash burl w/good figure, oval
w/canted sides, simple hollow
carved rim handles, 13½ x 17½",
5" h. $1,425.00
Bowl, ash burl w/good even figure,
curved sides, well shaped lip, soft
smooth finish, 18 x 19", 6¾" h. . .2,200.00
Bowl, burl, oval w/double long-
necked animal handles, simple relief & chip-carving, old worn finish
& dark stain in center of bowl,
carved initials "K.S.J." on bottom,
11¼ x 13¾", 9¼" h. 1,400.00
Bowl, hand-turned, deep rounded
flaring sides, old red on exterior,
interior w/scrubbed white patina,
19½" d., 6¼" h. 475.00
Box, cov., turned poplar w/original
reddish brown sponging, the
slightly tapering rounded sides
w/a turned band at the foot &
rim, the low domed cover w/but-
ton finial, 6" d., 4½" h. 357.50
Bucket, cov., stave construction,
iron band at top & bottom, wire
bail handle w/wooden handgrip,
old green paint w/black stenciled
label "1 gallon kerosene oil,"
7½" h. (some wear) 200.00
Butter churn, dasher-type, tapering
cylindrical shape, stave construction w/three steel bands, black
stenciled label "No. 0 - 4 gal. -
Mfd. by The American Wooden-
ware Mfg. Co., Toledo, O.," late
19th c., 18" h. plus dasher 240.00
Butter paddle, ash burl w/excellent
figure, well-shaped bowl, handle
w/curled end, old finish, 9" l. 475.00
Carpet beater, bentwood, "Good-
enough's Improved Carpet & Rug
Beater," made in Windsor, New
York, w/paper label, 41" l. 110.00
Compote, open, burl, deep flaring
bowl raised on a short ringed
pedestal on a wide stepped slight-

ly domed foot, worn original finish, 8¾" d., 5¾" h. 1,300.00

Cookie board, carved w/a running horse within a rectangular banded outline on one side, a star on the other, 6 3/8 x 9" 100.00

Cutlery tray, tiger stripe maple, rectangular w/deep slightly canted sides, divided down the center by an arched handle w/pierced handhold, New England, 1790-1810, 13½" l. (ILLUS.) 4,620.00

Cutting board, pine, pig-shaped, tail forms ring for hanging, 16" l. 55.00

Dipper, maple w/some curl, deep round body, flat & slightly curved handle, 9¼" l. 104.50

Dough box on stand, cov., Hepplewhite country-style, decorated poplar, rectangular one-board top lifting above a deep box w/canted sides on a stand w/a deep apron & slender square tapering legs, the sides of the box decorated w/large painted rectangles w/cut corners in old worn two-tone red paint w/yellow & white striping, the corners w/fan designs, similar decoration on the aprons & banding down the legs, decoration over early red, early 19th c., 17¾ x 38", 30¼" h. (age cracks, shrinkage) 575.00

Dough box on frame, cov., Queen Anne style, pine, rectangular top w/batten ends lifting above a deep trough, the sides continuing to trestle supports, 24 x 30¾", 28" h. 1,100.00

Drying rack, pine, four-section folding-type, three hanging rods in each section, old dark patina, 42" h. 65.00

Jar, cov., footed cylindrical body w/bulging base, worn original finish w/ebonized bands, canted cover w/flattened knob finial, 5½" h. 150.00

Jar, cov., bulbous ovoid body on a small footring, a small top opening w/a low domed cover w/knob finial, old varnish finish, wire bail handle w/wood hand grip, attributed to Pease of Ohio, 19th c., 6½" h. 295.00

Knife box, cov., painted poplar, rectangular w/a raised center handle w/pierced handgrip above slanted hinged lids opening to storage compartments, original brown graining on exterior, blue interior, 12½" l. (worn) 300.00

Kraut (or cabbage) cutter, walnut w/metal blade, cut-out "lollipop" handle w/hanging hole, old worn patina, 8 x 22½". 85.00

Mortar, burl, large heavy ovoid body tapering to a thick round foot, good figure, old soft finish, 7¾" h. 275.00

Noggin, hand-turned, the tall cylindrical body w/an integral carved loop handle along one side & a low rounded spout at the rim, refinished, 10¾" h. 71.50

Plate, good wear, early, 8 x 8 5/8" 300.00

Potato masher, shaped & turned handle, rounded pestle end, 11¼" l. 12.00

Rolling pin, beech & cherry, w/mortised handle mounted on wooden roller pins, America, ca. 18th c., 16" l. 340.00

Salt box, hanging-type, pine & poplar, long narrow crest, 35" h. (refinished) 130.00

Spoon, hand-carved, shallow round bowl, rounded handle stem flaring to a rounded flat end w/hanging hole, old varnish finish, 11" l. 82.50

Spoon, wide nearly round bowl continuing to a long flat handle w/pierced hanging hole, bowl w/some burl, carved date "1828," good old worn patina, 11" l. 220.00

Sugar bucket, cov., stave construction w/wooden banding secured w/copper tacks, wire bail handle w/wooden handgrip, old bluish grey paint, 6¾" h. 375.00

Sugar bucket, cov., stave construction w/wooden bands, bentwood swing handle, old green painted finish, 9½" h. (minor edge damage) 275.00

Early Cherry Tape Loom

Tape loom, cherry, the shaped plank w/slots drilled w/holes, the handle pierced w/a tulip blossom flanked by the initials "AK" on one side & "IK" on the other, fishtail handle, probably Pennsylvania, 1800-30, 24½" l. (ILLUS.) 275.00

Towel rack, mahogany, composed of slender rods, double end uprights on shoe-foot ends & joined by two short crossbars, three long crossbars from side to side, old finish, chamfered edges & mortised construction, 15 x 17½", 32¾" h. 127.50

Tub, cov., miniature, burl, tab handles, finely detailed w/turned rings, maple lid has "S"-shaped locking device, 6" d., 4" h. (putty filled hole in bottom) 525.00

Utensil rack, pine, scrolled edges, w/an arrangement of nine wrought-iron hanging hooks, old patina, 30" l. 200.00

Wall pocket, painted poplar, a wide backboard w/a cut sawtooth crest & scalloped sides flanking a canted board pocket w/scalloped rim above a deeper & wider pocket across the bottom, old blue repaint over green & gold, late wire nail construction, 7½ x 18", 24" h. 150.00

Wooden Watch Holder

Watch holder, hanging-type, painted, the rectangular crest centering a pierced heart above a rectangular case w/hinged door centering a glazed bull's-eye, 2 x 4¾", 10½" h. (ILLUS.) 660.00

WOOD SCULPTURES

American folk sculpture is an important part of the American art scene today. Skilled wood carvers turned out ship's figureheads, cigar store figures, plaques and carousel animals of stylized beauty and great appeal. The wooden shipbuilding industry, which had originally nourished this folk art, declined after the Civil War and the talented carvers then turned to producing figures for tobacconist's shops, carousel animals and show figures for circuses. These figures and other early ornamental carvings that have survived the elements and years are eagerly sought. Also see CAROUSEL FIGURES.

Carved & Painted Model of a Horse

Bust of Benjamin Franklin, carved & painted, 19th c., 8½" h. $935.00

Cigar store figure of an Indian chief, carved & painted, standing wearing a tall feathered headdress, long-sleeved robe & carrying a cluster of cigars, old painted surface, standing on a high flaring square base inscribed "Louis J. Lord Co. Cigars Tobacco," late 19th c., 5' 8" h. (replaced feathers in headdress, old repairs & bracing) 4,950.00

Cigar store figure of an Indian princess, carved & painted wood, the standing figure wearing a tall feathered headdress, a red & orange shawl over a green dress w/feather & jeweled ornaments & a checkered sash, the figure posed on a square base inscribed "Est. 1831 - Madden's Toys," on cast-iron rollers, attributed to Samuel Robb, ca. 1870, overall 6' 7" h. (some paint loss & chips) 17,600.00

Model of a bear, standing on its hind legs w/front legs stretched nearly straight out, chip-carved detailing for the fur & an articulated head w/tack eyes & features trimmed in polychrome, ca. 1910, 4' h. (some losses) 2,970.00

Model of a dog, carved & painted pine, stylized standing animal painted yellow w/black spots & scored fur & tail, standing on a green painted base, Wilhelm Schimmel, Cumberland Valley, Pennsylvania, ca. 1880, 6" l., 3½" h. (tail reglued) 6,600.00

Model of a horse, carved & painted, standing stylized animal on a rectangular base, attributed to George Avery, Massachusetts, ca. 1900, repaired break in foreleg, 7" l., 6" h. (ILLUS.) 275.00

Model of a parrot, carved & painted pine, the stylized figure of a standing bird w/head turned smartly to the right, painted yellow w/bright splashes of red & green, the wings & tail w/deep crosshatchings to indicate feathers, standing on a green painted circular mound, Wilhelm Schimmel, Cumberland Valley, Pennsylvania, ca. 1880, 5½" h. . .3,300.00

Model of a stag head, primitively carved w/the head looking down, mounted w/real deer antlers, on a shaped backplate, old pink & beige repaint, 17" h. (some flaking) 220.00

Whirligig, carved & painted pine, figure of a stylized man, carved in the round w/a flat white cap, facial features & ears carved in relief, articulated legs, two nail heads for front teeth, late 19th - early 20th c., 41½" h. (arms missing) 4,950.00

Whirligig of Men at Work

Whirligig, carved & painted pine, figures of men at work, two stylized figures in grey uniforms w/red caps w/their hands joined at a work wheel, the men 'pump' up & down as the front propeller turns; at the top (now separate) the small figure of a man w/a black-painted goatee & wearing a red-painted pointed sheet-iron cap, the arms form paddle blades & it stands on its own metal wire post, all on a rectangular planked base, America, 20th c., 38" l., overall 15¼" h. (ILLUS.) 825.00

WORLD'S FAIR COLLECTIBLES

There has been great interest in collecting items produced for the great fairs and expositions held through the years. During the

1970's, there was particular interest in items produced for the 1876 Centennial Exhibition and now interest is focusing on those items associated with the 1893 Columbian Exposition. Listed below is a random sampling of prices asked for items produced for the various fairs.

1876 PHILADELPHIA CENTENNIAL

Frank Leslie's 'Historical Register'

Book, "Burley's United States Centennial Gazetteer & Guide" $45.00

Book, "Frank Leslie's Illustrated Historical Register of the Centennial Exposition - 1876" (ILLUS.) . . . . .75.00 to 100.00

Book, "The Great Centennial Exposition Critically Described & Illustrated" 45.00

Book, "History of the Centennial Exposition" 45.00

Broadside, cloth, "Great Northern Railway," depicts Exposition buildings & railroad information, 27 x 34" (some taping) 200.00

Figure group, clear glass, boy & dog, Gillinder & Sons, base 3 x 5", 4½" h. 225.00

Match safe, silvered brass, depicts Administration Building 48.00

Lion Paperweight by Gillinder

Paperweight, frosted glass, model

of a reclining lion, Gillinder &
Sons (ILLUS.) 250.00
Puzzle blocks, "The Great American
Centennial Puzzle Blocks," paper
on wood, in original 11 x 22" box
depicting five fair scenes of the
Philadelphia Exhibition, the set . . . 185.00
Sheet music, "Centennial Music,"
w/black & white lithograph of
Memorial Hall 40.00
Shoe, lady's, clear glass, Gillinder &
Sons 55.00
Statuette, clear glass, Ruth the
Gleaner, Gillinder & Sons 50.00

1893 COLUMBIAN EXPOSITION
Admission ticket, "Chicago Day" 15.00
Badge w/bar hanger, brass, shield-
shaped & embossed w/a scene of
the landing of Columbus & "400th
Anniversary of Discovery of
America - Oct.1892," bar hanger
stamped "Souvenir" 65.00
Book, "Rand McNally's Guide to
Chicago and The World's Fair,"
complete w/colored map, personalized w/"Eugenia L. Williams"
in gold embossed letters, leather-
bound, 215 pp., 4¼ x 6½" 35.00
Book, "Shepp's World's Fair Pho-
tographed," over 500 pp. 75.00
Book, "The Vanished City," an elaborate collection of photo engravings of the fair, hard cover,
11 x 15" 100.00
Booklet, "Glimpses of the World's
Fair - A Selection of Gems of the
White city and Midway Plaisance,"
about 200 photographs including
several of the Ferris Wheel, given
by The Chicago Tribune, paper
covers 35.00

Silver Bookmark

Bookmark, sterling silver, shaped
rectangle, the center finely etched
w/a scene of the Fine Arts Building, scrolls at end & an ornate
scrolled handle, marked w/Co-
lumbian Exposition mark of Tiffany & Co., New York, 11½" l.
(ILLUS.) 1,760.00
Bookmark, woven silk Stevengraph,
a design of crossed American
flags at the top over "Souvenir
Woven in the Worlds Columbian
Exposition Chicago 1893" in color
above a black & white scene

Stevengraph Bookmark

of "Machinery Hall" & a black
& white train vignette at the
bottom, on original backing
(ILLUS.) 150.00
Cabinet photograph, depicts Ferris
Wheel, 4¼ x 6¼" 28.00
Coin purse, mother-of-pearl sides
w/souvenir inscription 45.00
Demitasse cup, china, tall cup decorated w/a scene of the Art Build-
ing 35.00

Silk Handkerchief with Scene

Handkerchief, silk, printed w/a
scene titled "Landing of Columbus" & at the top w/"Souvenir -
Worlds Fair - Chicago - 1492 -
1893" (ILLUS.) 50.00
Lamp, kerosene table-model, satin
glass, the shade decorated w/col-
ored transfers of the U.S. Government & Machinery Buildings,
another building shown on the
font, on gilt-brass feet, electrified,
18" h. 350.00
Mug, clear glass, embossed scene
of the Santa Maria on one side &
the Landing of Columbus on the

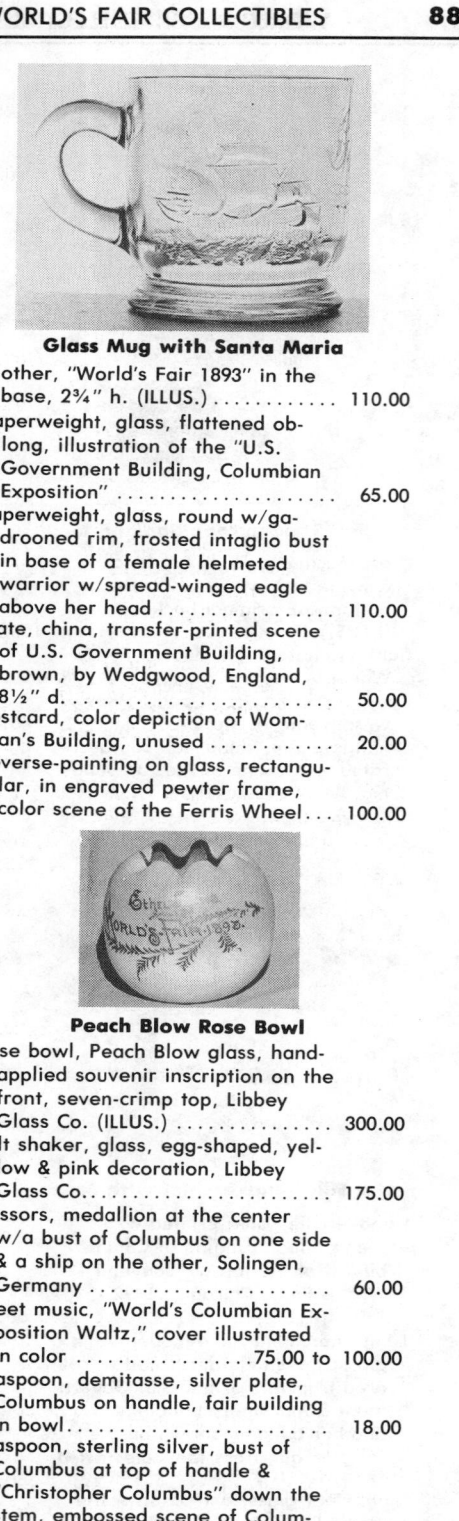

Glass Mug with Santa Maria

other, "World's Fair 1893" in the
base, 2¾" h. (ILLUS.) 110.00
Paperweight, glass, flattened oblong, illustration of the "U.S.
Government Building, Columbian
Exposition" 65.00
Paperweight, glass, round w/ga-
drooned rim, frosted intaglio bust
in base of a female helmeted
warrior w/spread-winged eagle
above her head 110.00
Plate, china, transfer-printed scene
of U.S. Government Building,
brown, by Wedgwood, England,
8½" d. 50.00
Postcard, color depiction of Woman's Building, unused 20.00
Reverse-painting on glass, rectangular, in engraved pewter frame,
color scene of the Ferris Wheel... 100.00

Peach Blow Rose Bowl

Rose bowl, Peach Blow glass, hand-
applied souvenir inscription on the
front, seven-crimp top, Libbey
Glass Co. (ILLUS.) 300.00
Salt shaker, glass, egg-shaped, yel-
low & pink decoration, Libbey
Glass Co. 175.00
Scissors, medallion at the center
w/a bust of Columbus on one side
& a ship on the other, Solingen,
Germany 60.00
Sheet music, "World's Columbian Ex-
position Waltz," cover illustrated
in color .... 75.00 to 100.00
Teaspoon, demitasse, silver plate,
Columbus on handle, fair building
in bowl 18.00
Teaspoon, sterling silver, bust of
Columbus at top of handle &
"Christopher Columbus" down the
stem, embossed scene of Colum-
bus & crew in the bowl, 6" l. 45.00

Watch fob & case opener, metal,
pocket watch-shaped, the front
w/a world globe surrounded by
"Compliments of Keystone Watch
Case Co.," the back w/the Keystone company logo 50.00

1901 PAN-AMERICAN EXPOSITION
Beer foam scraper, aluminum 48.00
Booklet, various photographic views
by Robert Allen Reid, 36 pp. 32.00
Pen tray, aluminum, depicts Elec-
tric Tower, Temple of Music &
Niagara Falls, w/scalloped rim,
3¼ x 9" 45.00
Plate, china, depicts the Temple of
Music, 6¼" d. 20.00
Teaspoon, sterling silver, Indian,
buffalo & Niagara Falls in relief .. 62.50

1904 ST. LOUIS WORLD'S FAIR
Book, "The Forest City - Official
Photographic Views of Universal
Exposition," oversized 60.00
Book, "History of the Louisiana Pur-
chase Expo," 4,000 engravings,
leatherbound, 1905, 800 pp. 300.00
Charm, composition, "Heinz," pickle-
shaped 17.00
Coin, elongated cent, Liberal Arts
Building depicted, 2½" l. 35.00
Guide, "Guide to St. Louis & World's
Fair," w/baseball season sched-
ule 10.00
Hatpin, metal, advertising "Ham-
mond Typewriters" 125.00
Jewelry box, clear glass, elegant
h.p. scene of Fair on top 125.00
Letter opener, metal, w/embossed
Fair buildings on handle 28.00
Mug, ruby-stained glass, souvenir-
type, Button Aches patt. 45.00
Plaque, ceramic, depicts Abraham
Lincoln, bisque finish, incised
"Weller," 4 5/8" 165.00
Postcard album, embossed front,
replica of official postcard in col-
or, 8½ x 11" 45.00
Stereo view cards, scenes of the
Fair, by T.W. Ingersoll, set
of 100 .... 200.00
Toothpick holder, wood, model of
an urn, stamped "1904 St. Louis
World's Fair" 18.00

1933-34 CHICAGO "CENTURY OF PROGRESS"
Bank, metal, model of Transporta-
tion Building, w/key, 3 x 5" 350.00
Book, "Our President, Franklin
Delano Roosevelt, A Biography,"
Century of Progress edition 25.00
Bookmark, goldtone metal, depicts
Hall of Science 20.00

Building ornament, cast iron, model
of a star & eagle, from a Fair
building, marked "I Will - 1933
Chicago World's Fair," 5" d. 200.00
Cane, wooden, w/"Century of Pro-
gress" decal, dated 10-12-33 . . . . . 20.00
Coaster, fiberboard, depicts a Fair
building 5.00
Coin, Chrysler exhibit 25.00
Compact, red faux leather covered,
Art Deco style floral top, "Century
of Progress World's Fair" plate on
bottom, 3 x 3½" 35.00
Incense burner, ceramic, modeled in
the form of Fort Dearborn 22.00
Mug, pottery, handle in the form of
a nude woman w/arched back,
embossed "World's Fair," 6" h. . . . 28.00
Panel, lace, depicts a Zeppelin over
Chicago 26.00
Pillow, leather, depicts Fair
scenes 75.00
Playing cards, colorful depiction of
Avenue of Flags, mint in box 35.00
Pocket watch, "Century of Pro-
gress," Ingersoll 295.00
Postcard, Sinclair exhibit, depicts
dinosaur 15.00
Postcards, souvenir pack of 18
different Fair views, 1934,
the set 16.00
Program, stage production of "The
Romance of Transportation" 25.00
Wagon, pressed steel, "Radio Flyer,"
red w/white rubber tires, w/all
decals, mint condition 225.00

1939-40 NEW YORK WORLD'S FAIR

Trylon & Perisphere Thermometer

Box, cov., chrome, depicts Trylon &
Perisphere, small 28.00
Flashlight, chrome, round, w/Trylon
& Perisphere, 4" 125.00
Hat, employee's, navy blue wool,
w/orange Trylon & Perisphere &
"1940" on front 40.00
Hot plate, silver plate, round, en-
graved Trylon & Perisphere, Reed
& Barton 42.00

Inkwell, metal, Art Deco style, model of the Trylon & Perisphere 110.00
Lapel pin, hand holding medallion
depicting the Trylon & Peri-
sphere 40.00
Nut dishes, tin, Planters advertising,
center w/Mr. Peanut standing in
front of Trylon & Perisphere, the
sides decorated w/peanuts, set
of 6 . . . . 50.00
Plates, commemorative, "Old New
York," dark blue transfer, Wedg-
wood, 10½" d., set of 12 . . . . 300.00
Puppet, hand-type, monkey w/patch
depicting Trylon & Perisphere 25.00
Razor, electric, "Remington Close-
Shaver," case w/Trylon & Peri-
sphere, razor w/Electrical
Products Building, 2 pcs. 165.00
Salt & pepper shaker, plastic, one-
piece, model of Trylon & Peri-
sphere, blue w/orange base 25.00
Thermometer, Bakelite, depicts
Trylon & Perisphere, 3¾" h.
(ILLUS.) 65.00
Uniform jacket, marked "Banking
Building," beige w/orange & navy
blue trim, orange buttons w/the
Trylon & Perisphere logo, excel-
lent condition 200.00

1962 SEATTLE WORLD'S FAIR

Cigarette lighter & ashtray, metal,
figural Space Needle 55.00
Model kit, plastic, Space Needle 35.00
Plate, china, made for Frederick &
Nelsons department store 15.00
Spoon, Space Needle figural handle,
World's Fair scene in bowl 20.00
Tumblers, glass, 22k gold-trimmed
w/Space Needle decoration, set
of 4 . . . . 20.00

1964-65 NEW YORK WORLD'S FAIR

Bank, plastic, model of an elephant
holding Unisphere, 10" h. 20.00
Bobbing-head figure, a couple
kissing 95.00
Booklet, "Progressland," by Walt
Disney 18.00
Candy dish, smoked glass 15.00
Fan, plastic, depicts buildings, opens
to 12" 15.00
Paper dolls, "Dress Up For New
York," uncut book 45.00
Plate, china, Masonic, depicts
Brotherhood World Peace Build-
ing 20.00
Postcard, Coca-Cola Pavilion, mint
condition 10.00
Salt & pepper shakers, ceramic,
model of "Unisphere," U.S. Steel
exhibit, pr. 16.00

On The Cutting Edge

Letter Openers

by Diane Levin

Collectors of antique and other old letter openers are lured by their wonderful designs, amazing variations and fascinating craftsmanship. They offer major contrast to today's common and sterile unadorned metal and plastic versions.

No wonder those of the past were desktop accessories while the modern adaptations are stashed in desk drawers, out-of-sight and out-of-mind.

The history of letter openers is sparse; there is little resource literature. Data relies upon conjecture, conversation, common sense and the little that is known.

Letter openers had their highest popularity between the development of envelopes (and initial use of skewers) in the late 1700's - early 1800's and the 1950's - 1960's when they gave way to modern communications.

Increasing reliance upon telephones and then the introduction and quick acceptance of facsimile machines offered faster alternatives to mail. Even electric/electronic envelope opening devices came along to displace the older form of letter opener.

The 150-year run started when envelopes, invented in England where cheap paper was first created, used a sealant that supplanted sealing wax and called for a new way to be opened.

At first, skewers were used. Even today, dealers, particularly English silver dealers, will suggest a skewer to letter opener seekers.

They were followed by the advent of dedicated letter openers in the early 1800's. Earliest versions were in silver and ivory, materials preferred by the wealthy. Tin also was among the very early materials applied to openers.

Toward the end of the 19th century brass letter openers featuring figural handles gained popularity. An early brass design was dagger-shaped, with crossbar and crusader figural handle; many are available today. Around the same time, letter openers became useful as an advertising and promotional medium.

An 1896 jewelry catalog from Marshall Field & Co., Chicago, featured sterling silver and sterling silver with mother-of-pearl letter openers. It also pictured dual purpose adaptations such as penknives, bookmarks and straight pens, to list a few, which were combined with letter openers.

The catalog also showed that the early intricate letter opener designs were the same as used for such other personal items as toothbrushes, shoehorns, nail files, crochet sets and more.

Sears, too, began early to market letter openers. Its 1902 catalog offered several, many as part of matching desk sets. Sterling silver, 14k gold and "pearl" paper cutters were shown.

Many widely-known "name" designers and manufacturers were involved with letter openers, among them notables such as Tiffany, Roycroft, Reed & Barton and Bradley & Hubbard.

Letter openers were given many names: office knife, envelope cutter, letter cutter, letter knife, envelope opener.

However, to call them "page cutter" or "page turner" is incorrect. The page cutter/page turner is distinguished by its rounded tip, as opposed to the pointed tip of letter openers. The rounded tip is designed to separate the uncut outer page edges; it also was used to turn the pages of important books to protect them from the damage that hands can inflict.

Through the years, many materials have

been used to make letter openers. Coupled with the design style, the materials are clues to the dating of letter openers.

Letter openers have been made of Bakelite, bone, brass, bronze, celluloid, copper, crystal, gold, ivory, lapis, Lucite, mother-of-pearl, pot metal, silver and silver plate, steel, tortoiseshell, wood ... and more.

Blades, too, exhibit differences, mainly in shapes and sizes. They are straight, tapered; dimensional, flat; scimitar-like, oval. Some carry out the handle's design motif.

Unfortunately, too many blades are being replaced by new ones before returning to the resale market. This is particularly evident among silver letter openers. Collectors be aware! It seems that non-collectors want the beauty of the old handles and the newness of blades, the best of both eras.

Letter openers have ranged from three or four inches to 12 and 14 inches long. It is written that "the ladies" used the smaller and more delicate versions.

There are certain letter openers that are easiest explained as novelties and feature unexpected combinations with objects made for other purposes. Thus, we find letter openers with bookmarks, tape measures and penknives.

Much sought after is the letter opener combined with both a straight pen and a Stanhope, or peephole, that reveals illustrations. Invented about 1820 by Lord Stanhope in England, the Stanhopes are a special interest of photographers-collectors, too. Lucky is the person who finds one of these intact, with an original pen point and the picture.

Also on the "endangered" list are the delicate celluloid letter openers with full form figural handles. Finely detailed, figurals include animals, people or inanimate objects. Happiness is multiplied by finding the celluloid figural that has a moving part.

With so many available choices among antique letter openers, many collectors elect to narrow their interests.

The advertising letter openers offer opportunities to doubly specialize. Some collections are eclectic, featuring a variety of products, services and firms. Others are built around a particular product or service. Another variety of collection is when the letter opener is germane to another collection, such as the collector of Titanic mementos who yearns for a letter opener from the ill-fated luxury liner.

Many people collect the plastic Fuller Brush letter openers that were issued in a plethora of colors and color mutations. It is the aim of this group of collectors to acquire the full range of colors. The most common Fuller Brush opener includes a handle featuring a salesman with attache case, depicted in outline design. A later version shows the salesman on one side and a saleswoman on the reverse, each carrying the signature attache case. These are created in relief on solid handles, one piece with the blades.

Patent attorneys turned to using letter openers to promote their services in the 1920's. Victor J. Evans and Clarence O'Brien, by virtue of their current easy availability, seem to have been heavy advertisers via this medium. Relatively rare and with a special character is the Clarence O'Brien and Hyman Berman version, apparently a short-lived association.

It is no surprise that banks and insurance companies were big users of letter openers. In keeping with their general imagery, the banks' letter openers were ornate and expensive looking, intended for their top customers.

Insurance companies were a factor in this arena. In the 1920's Prudential Life Insurance Co. inadvertently insured the demand for its letter openers in the 1990's by imprinting this message "Life Insurance Both Sexes."

A lot of the antique letter openers around still come from England, but other countries are represented.

There seems to be an abundance of openers that originated in China. There are two conjectures to explain this. One is that they were just one more product produced for that country's massive export business to the West. More "romantic" is the theory that Chinese aristocrats needed letter openers to protect their long ... very long ... fingernails.

Some collectors, including this author, try to trace the why and when a company issued a letter opener. This effort has been more fun than productive.

An inquiry to Phillips Milk of Magnesia about its small metal letter opener with magnifying glass brought a two-fold response. There no longer was anyone at the company who went back far enough to recall anything about it. However, the writer was "taking the liberty" of sending two product samples under separate cover!

A parting note about letter openers: Don't give them as gifts to Russians. Along with knives, letter openers signify the severance of a relationship.

Suggested Reading:

American Silverplate, by Dorothy T. and H. Ivan Rainwater, published by Schiffer Publishing Co., 1469 Morstein Rd., West Chester, PA 19380, 1988.

1896 Illustrated Catalog, Jewelry & Fashions, Marshall Field & Co., published in replica by The Gun Digest Publishing Company, 540 Frontage Rd., Northfield, IL 60093, 1970.

The Poor Man's Guide to Antique Collecting, by John Mebane, published by Doubleday & Company, Inc., Garden City, NY, 1969.

PRICE LISTINGS:

BAKELITE:

12" l., Art Deco style w/red & black handle w/a 1 oz. letter scale in the handle, mint in box (ILLUS.) . . $45.00

BONE:

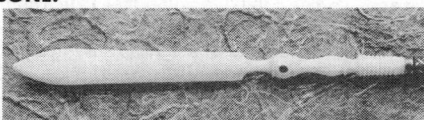

7¾" l., Stanhope-type, straight pen w/brass mounting, replaced pen point (ILLUS.) 43.00

8" l., bird design w/applied colored dots, w/brass 20.00

11¾" l., whalebone, oar-shaped, one-piece 10.00

BRASS:

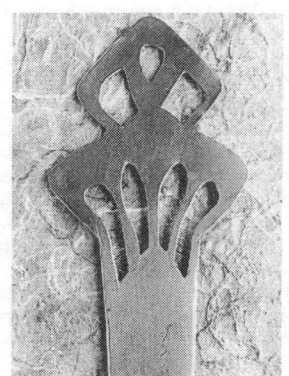

Arts & Crafts Style Opener

6" l., lacy design handle w/applied busts of Napoleon & Josephine, mother-of-pearl blade 65.00

6¾" l., Arts & Crafts style w/open-work handle, hand-made (ILLUS.) 5.00

6¾" l., full-form figural Napoleon handle 18.00

7" l., Art Nouveau-style flower, convex-shaped 10.00

7" l., figural owl handle, 1875 . . . . . . 130.00

7½" l., full-form horse on two legs 20.00

8" l., vertical dots & dashes impressed in handle, marked "Bradley & Hubbard" 20.00

8" l., Art Nouveau style w/cherub among flowers on handle, scimitar-shaped blade 45.00

8½" l., octagonal handle w/Hippocrates portrait & wreath design, for S.B. Penick & Company 20.00

8¾" l., Victorian design w/a bow knot & flowers, Belgium 85.00

9" l., two-dimensional flowers, stalk, bird's eye & feathers, fine detailing, ca. 1933 . . . . 120.00

9" l., dagger-shaped, inscribed "England" 18.00

9¼" l., circular cloisonne handle, China (ILLUS.) 25.00

9½" l., lion-form handle w/curlicues, arched blade 50.00

9½" l., advertising-type, "State Savings Bank Detroit, Mich.," dated "August 1897" (ILLUS.) 12.00

9¾" l., chameleon figural handle, Victorian, England 36.00

10" l., Art Nouveau stylized flower design handle 36.00

10" l., Dartmouth Pixie figural w/vertical handle design, England 13.00

10" l., woman's face, flowers & tendrils on handle, late 19th - early 20th c. (ILLUS.) 60.00

BRONZE:

6½" l., oval handle w/a robin inscribed "Robin," top inscribed "W.F.B." (ILLUS.) 10.50
6¾" l., Art Nouveau style w/flowers, leaves & curlicues, oval blade 12.00
8¼" l., Arts & Crafts style, Clark thread promotion 4.00
8½" l., Buddhist figure carved on ebony handle, Siam 10.00
8½" l., figural peacock, ca. 1920 ... 15.00
9" l., fish scale patterning on handle, scimitar-shaped blade, advertising The Metal Arts Co., Inc., Rochester, New York 14.00
9" l., magnifying glass inset in handle, advertising K-D Mfg. Co., Lancaster, Pennsylvania, ca. 1871 .... 4.50

9½" l., full-form figural sphinx han-

dle, scimitar-shaped carved blade, ca. 1937 (ILLUS.) 35.00

CELLULOID:

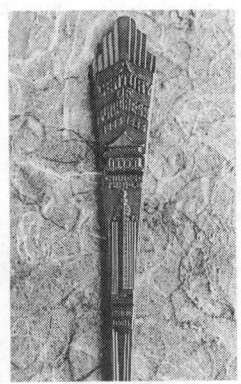

6 3/8" l., figural handle w/a Japanese home, terracing & a movable water wheel, Japan, ca. 1860 (ILLUS.)...................... 9.00
7½" l., figural Victorian lady's bust portrait 30.00
8½" l., figural kimono-clad Japanese lady playing a mandolin-like instrument...................... 35.00
9¼" l., figural dog stretched out on all four legs, advertising for "The Hub" 8.00

COPPER:

7" l., hand-made, over 120 years old, w/written provenance 4.00
7½" l., figural covered wagon handle, copper-plated (worn) 5.00
8" l., advertising for Clarence O'Brien, registered patent attorney, 1920's 22.00
8" l., advertising Griffith Laboratories, handle w/three-month 1934 calendar 7.50
8¾" l., Art Deco style, from the 1933 Century of Progress exhibition in Chicago (ILLUS.) 20.00

9" l., hand-hammered, Roycroft Copper Shop 48.00

GOLD:
8" l., full-form figural monkey w/golden topaz, 14k 3,800.00

IVORY:
5" l., ornately carved handle inset w/a garnet 35.00

6¾" l., carved two-dimensional camel on the top, six on the blade (ILLUS.) 6.50
8" l., hand-carved African woman's head 50.00
8¾" l., one-piece, tapered, blue & silver enamel band 25.00
9" l., elaborately carved handle, Dieppe, Normandy, France, ca. 1830 .... 695.00

METAL:

5" l., advertising Phillips Milk of Magnesia, magnifying glass in handle, England 3.00
7" l., green-painted aluminum, souvenir of Chicago Century of Progress, 1933 .... 13.00

7" l., horse's head on handle, Fort Knox, Kentucky 25.00
7¼" l., advertising Pfizer, medical caduceus on handle (ILLUS.) 35.00
7¼" l., marked "A Gift from Louis C. Tiffany - 1911," w/illustration of buildings, also w/"New York - Paris - London," fake 70.00

7½" l., advertising, tape measure handle, marked "Solvents & Thinners - 'Service Is My Specialty' - R.C. (Bob) Nash - 451-1174" (ILLUS.)........................ 9.00

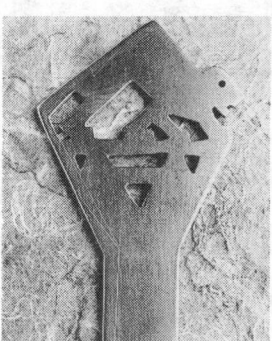

7 5/8" l., Art Deco design w/pierced stylized angular cat on handle (ILLUS.)........................ 20.00

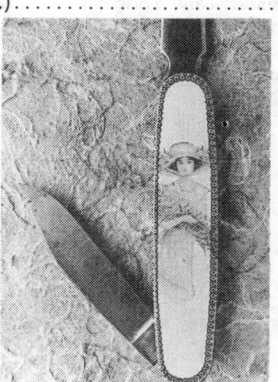

8½" l., penknife handle w/a picture

of a Victorian lady, advertising
George C. Bruen (ILLUS.) 24.00
9" l., Art Nouveau style w/metal
plates, S.D. Childs & Co., 1908 ... 15.00
9½" l., Art Nouveau design w/tulip
& sweeping tendrils 25.00
10" l., advertising, "The Prudential -
Life Insurance Both Sexes,"
1920's 15.00
10½" l., Trench Art, bullet casing
w/etched war scenes & names ... 40.00

PLASTIC:

7¼" l., advertising, figural Fuller
Brush man w/attache case han-
dle, brown (ILLUS.) 10.00

8¼" l., advertising, "Advance Aluminum Castings Corp. - 2742 West
38th Place - Chicago," grey rigid
handle w/shiny metal blade
(ILLUS.)....................... 22.00

8½" l., ivorene, raised design on
the handle showing an owl,
books, scrolls, an oil lamp & flowers (ILLUS.) 35.00
9½" l., ivorene, applied decoration
of a metal flower & leaf 20.00

SILVER:
5" w., boomerang-form w/kan-
garoo, souvenir of Australia 33.00

6½" l., figural Eiffel Tower handle,
w/metal blade, 1889 .... 30.00

6½" l., swirled scrolls on handle,
mother-of-pearl blade, hallmarks
on handle for Birmingham, England, 1901-02 (ILLUS.) 32.00
7½" l., Art Nouveau-style lady's
head on handle 48.00

7½" l., reserve on handle w/flying
bird holding an envelope framed
by scrolls & flower vines, Victorian (ILLUS.)..................... 32.00
8" l., fully detailed dog's head
w/collar on handle 50.00
8¾" l., enameled scenic design,
France, ca. 1895 .... 265.00
9½" l., advertising, marked "Armco
Steel," corded blade design 2.00
10" l., gold-colored metal quill
feather applied to handle, marked
"Ravin et Denfert," France 38.00

TIN:

4½" l., elaborate scrolled bright-cut
handle w/large initial "E," Victori-
an (ILLUS. previous page) 5.00

WOOD:

6½" l., black ebony handle w/ap-
plied metal scrolled initial plate,
scimitar-shaped blade, Victorian
(ILLUS.). 10.00

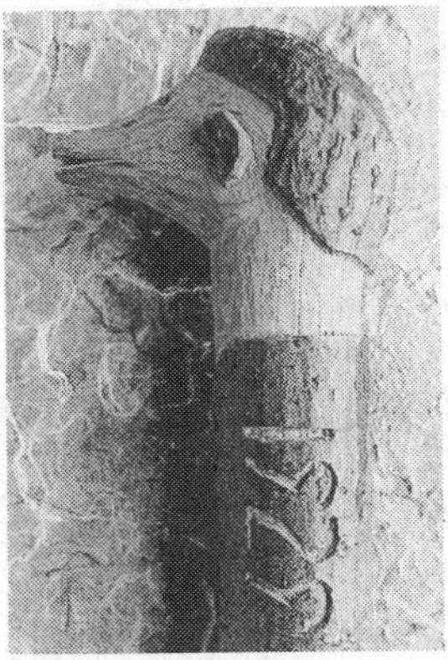

9" l., primitively carved bird's head
handle dated "1929," Africa
(ILLUS.). 20.00
10½" l., burnished two-dimensional
design of a man paddling a canoe, inscribed "Chicago 1933" &
"Wood Art Products - Chicago" . . .   12.00

OTHER MATERIALS:
6½" l., chrome, Art Deco design . . .   16.00

7½" l., greenish-black marble,
white-painted metal sailboat perpendicular to handle, worn paint
(ILLUS.). 10.00
7½" l., green onyx, carved handle,
scissor-like sterling silver blade,
Mexico 24.00

8" l., painted enamel handle
w/wooden blade, figural Breton
bust design, Quimper, markings
of French artist Paul Fouillet,
1930-40. . . . .   45.00
8¼" l., advertising, figural Uneeda
Biscuit boy handle, fine condi-
tion 80.00

8½" l., mother-of-pearl handle &
blade, carved fanned leaf designs
on handle (ILLUS.). 25.00
10½" l., emerald green Lucite,
twirled handle 15.00

ABOUT THE AUTHOR

*Diane Levin is a Chicago-based public re-
lations consultant and writer. She is an avid
collector of letter openers and has been identified as an authority on the subject.*

(End of Special Focus)

___

WRITING ACCESSORIES

*Early writing accessories are popular col-
lectibles and offer a wide variety to select
from. A collection may be formed around any
one segment—pens, letter openers, lap desks
or inkwells—or the collection may revolve
around choice specimens of all types. Material, design and age usually determine the value. Pen collectors like the large fountain pens
developed in the 1920's but also look for pens
and mechanical pencils that are solid gold or
gold-plated. Also see METALS and the "Special Focus," December - January 1993 issue.*

INKWELLS & STANDS
Blue cut glass well, diamond-
shaped, faceted hinged lid, cut
block pattern, small $225.00
Brass stand, an oblong dished tray
w/cast end handles supporting a
footed classical covered urn w/or-
nate cast details forming the ink-
well, late 19th c., 7¾" l. 150.00
Brass well, Art Deco style, ten
panels, brown satin finish w/wide
gold edge all around, scalloped

apron in front, hinged cover,
signed "Bradley & Hubbard,"
4¾ x 5" 110.00

Brass Ship Captain's Inkwell

Brass well, ship captain's-type,
spherical, hinged in the middle,
the exterior engraved w/scattered
small starbursts, the interior fitted w/a handblown glass ink bottle, marked "Geselzlich G.F.
Schutzt," Germany, ca. 1900, 2" h.
(ILLUS.)........................ 187.00

Bronze well, double, Chinese patt.,
gilt patina, w/liners, Tiffany Studios, No. 1763 .... 395.00

Bronze well, Venetian Zodiac patt.,
octagonal, lid decorated w/the
sign of Cancer, stamped "Tiffany
Studios New York 842," 4" d.,
2" h. (insert missing) 192.50

Bronze & glass well, Art Nouveau
style, lily pad-shaped base supporting a cranberry glass loop-
embossed bud-shaped well
w/hinged metal leaf-shaped
cover 275.00

Bronze & silver overlay well, Greek
Key patt., brown patina, Heintz
Art Metal...................... 195.00

Cut glass well, clear mushroom-
shaped, cut block pattern, hinged
brass lid, 2½" sq. 145.00

Cut glass well, clear Cane patt.,
Gorham sterling silver lid w/en-
graving, 3" sq. 170.00

Cut glass well, clear, square base
rising to pyramid shape, star-cut
base, teardrop insert well reflects
through entire well, ornate silver
plate hinged lid, 3" sq. base,
2¾" h. 265.00

Faience stand, rectangular body w/a
scallop-edged pen trough at the
front & an enclosed box at the
back pierced w/two circular apertures, the whole painted in manganese, green, ochre & blue
w/stylized floral sprays & sprigs
within manganese-edged rims,

now fitted w/a pair of faience
cylindrical inkwells mounted
w/hinged pewter covers, France,
probably Roanne, late 18th c.,
7 11/16" l. (minor abrasions, one
well w/chipped base)........... 330.00

Fruitwood stand, carved model of a
Boxer-like dog w/glass eyes, sitting by a tree stump-form well,
w/pen holder 450.00

Gilt-bronze well, figural Art Nouveau style, cast as a standing
nymph in a flowing gown supported by cyclamen, on a diamond-
shaped base enclosing a well w/a
leaf-form cover, after a model by
Charles Korschmann, signed in
the bronze "CH. KORSCHMANN,"
w/a Louchet foundry mark,
10¾" h. 1,320.00

Gilt-bronze well, cast as a maiden
emerging from a pond w/giant
water lily blossoms & leaves, a
single large blossom enclosing
an inkwell, worn gilt patina, inscribed "M. Bouval," impressed
"E. GOLIN & Cie - PARIS," ca.
1900, 9" l., 4¼" h. 935.00

Glass well, blown-three-mold, geometric, deep olive green, attributed to Keene, New Hampshire, ca.
1820, 2¼" d., 1¾" h. 104.50

Glass well, clear cylinder w/flat disc
base, marked "DAVIS' PATENT,
Feb. 14, 1893" 18.00

Glass well, lady's, dainty green
iridescent embossed Loetz-type
well in freeform shape, brass lid
w/figural chick atop, chick w/gold
cord w/red berry at end in mouth,
2¾ x 2¾"..................... 260.00

Glass well, pressed, figural, bust of
Admiral Dewey w/cap forming
lid, clear w/hat & jacket tinted
blue & face tinted flesh tone, ca.
1900, 3¼" h. 715.00

Ormolu well, urn-shaped body w/a
foliate cast lid centered by a
pomegranate finial, the body cast
w/foliate motifs & hung w/ribbon-
tied laurel swags, the twist-turned
socle cast w/beading & raised on
a square beaded base, Louis XVI
period, France, last quarter
18th c., 6¾" h................8,250.00

Porcelain well, light blue swirled
well on handkerchief-fold saucer
base, bluebird & flower decoration.......................... 145.00

Porcelain well, lobed form w/evert-
ed rim, decorated w/floral reserves against a royal blue
ground, Meissen, Germany, blue
crossed swords mark, 3" d. 275.00

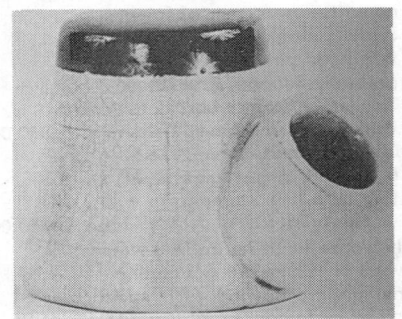

Pottery Inkwell

Pottery well, teakettle-form, cream-colored body w/dark brown slip at the top, faded gold lettering reads "Compliments of the Letort Hotel - Carlisle, Pa.," slight overall crazing, ca. 1890, 2½" h. (ILLUS.)...................... 82.50

Rockingham glazed pottery stand, arched molded & scrolling cartouche above a fitted compartment w/two ink chambers before a rectangular reserve, on yellowware, Chester County, Pennsylvania, 19th c., 5½" h. 165.00

Sheffield Plate & Mahogany Stand

Sheffield silver plate & mahogany stand, four silver plated bun feet support the rectangular mahogany base w/drawer supporting the Sheffield plate rectangular top w/a front well for pens & a central seal box topped by a taperstick flanked by a pair of cut glass bottles, all w/gadrooned borders, England, ca. 1810, 12¾" l. (ILLUS.) 3,410.00

Silver well, realistically modeled as a camel in a kneeling position, the back forming a hinged cover, engraved on interior "EHW, 1879, 1904," w/pitted white glass ink pot, maker's mark of Frederick H. Clark, Newark, New Jersey, retailer's mark of Theodore B. Starr, ca. 1904, 8" l. 1,980.00

Spatter glass stand, domed round base, raised serpent coiled as pen

holder, shades of white, red & blue, 3" d..................... 110.00

Sterling silver stand, a shaped rectangular base elaborately repousse' w/scrolls & *rocaille*, w/a pen well & openwork scroll pen supports in front of a pair of silver-mounted clear glass bottles w/fluted swirls, their silver hinged covers w/similar scroll & *rocaille* decoration, Shiebler & Co., New York, ca. 1900, 10" l. ...3,080.00

Sterling silver well, globular, chased w/floral scrolls, glass liner, Gorham Mfg. Company, Providence, Rhode Island, 1892, 4" h. (dent) 396.00

Wooden well, carved figural mountain goat w/glass eyes, 4¾" h.... 195.00

LAP DESKS & WRITING BOXES

Calamander wood & gilt-bronze, the rectangular calamander box mounted w/elaborately cast, pierced & scrolled mounts, each etched w/foliage, opening to an interior fitted w/a presentation plaque inscribed "Benjamin Disraeli First Earl of Beaconsfield (1804-1881)," opening further to a leather-lined writing surface hinged to reveal a satinwood veneered interior & small drawers, also fitted w/an inkwell & small lidded compartments, the underside of the lid leather-lined w/various document compartments & mounted w/a thermometer, J. Southcombe, Maker, 130 & 131 Jermyn St., London, England late 19th c., 14 x 24¾", 11½" h. 7,150.00

Inlaid satinwood, the rectangular hinged top centering an oval reserve inlaid w/a conch & beetle, opening to a blue baize-lined interior w/hinged writing flap, pencil, inkwell & sander wells, the sides fitted w/brass carrying handles, one side also w/a small drawer, ca. 1795, 10 1/8 x 20", 7¼" h. 2,750.00

Mahogany w/brass inlay, w/original inkwells & key, 6 x 8½ x 11½" .. 200.00

Papier-mache', the canted rectangular lid painted w/scene entitled "Deer Stalking" depicting hunters in Scottish costume w/hounds, the interior w/inkwells & velvet-covered writing surface, impressed "JENNENS & BETTRIDGE - BIRMN," together w/a letter indicating that the box was given as

a gift about 1846, England, second
quarter 19th c., 9½ x 11½" 1,980.00

French Porcelain Lap Desk

Porcelain & gilt-bronze, the central
porcelain panel decorated w/two
pairs of lovers in a pastoral landscape, the surrounding panels
decorated w/floral designs & gilt,
mounted w/gilt-bronze female
terms, France, 13" w. (ILLUS.)....2,860.00
Rosewood w/brass arabesque inlay
on the top, hinged top opening to
a fitted interior, Chinese Export,
19th c., 18" l. 770.00

PENS & PENCILS

Eclipse Pen & Pencil Set

Chilton "Wing-Flow" fountain pen,
black w/gold inlay body, excellent
working condition (slight plating
wear on some inlaid ribs) 475.00
Conklin fountain pen, 14-sided,
emerald marbleizing w/black
stripes, Nozac filler, 1935 .... 195.00
Conklin "Senior Endura" fountain
pen, sapphire blue body 450.00
Eclipse fountain pen & mechanical
pencil set, jade green body w/10k
gold scrolling overlay, light wear,
ca. 1923, pr. (ILLUS.) 192.50
Eversharp "Skyline" fountain pen,
1942 .... 40.00
Eversharp "Skyline" mechanical pencil, 14k gold body 175.00
Grieshaber "Umpire" fountain pen,
black body w/a ¼" fancy gold
band, 5¼" l..................... 95.00
John Holland lady's fountain pen,
green marbleized hard rubber
body w/gold-filled trim, lever-fill,
1915 .... 35.00
Mother-of-pearl & gold-filled
mechanical pencil, fancy engraving, in leather case w/chain loop

marked "Gold Filled & Pearl Patent 1871," contains original lead,
contracts & expands, 1¾ x 3¼" .. 130.00
Nardi "Tri-Kolor" mechanical pencil,
yellow marbleized body w/gold-
filled trim, in original box........ 75.00
Parker "Duofold Jr." fountain pen,
green marbleized body 110.00
Parker "Lucky Curve" lady's fountain
pen, green & white marbleized
body, 4½" l.................... 75.00
Parker "Duofold" mechanical pencil,
green mottled body w/gold top &
1¼" gold pencil point, incised
"Parker Duofold" on side of barrel, ca. 1920's, 4½" l. 75.00
Parker "51 Blue Diamond" fountain
pen, maroon................... 40.00
Parker "61" fountain pen, 12k gold-
filled body, never used 195.00
Pick "Exceptional" fountain pen,
green marbleized body, 5¼" l.
(some darkening) 50.00
Ronson "Penciliter," chrome body,
pencil & lighter combination...... 45.00
Sheaffer "Feather Touch No. 5"
fountain pen, gold vertical striping
on body 35.00
Sheaffer "Lifetime Triumph" fountain
pen, No. 1250, black body w/14k
gold tip 125.00
Sheaffer, "No. 46 Special" fountain
pen, jade green body, 1922 ...... 100.00
Wahl "No. 2" fountain pen, black
body, ca. 1925, 5¼" l.......... 50.00
Wahl "No. 2" fountain pen, gold-
filled body, ca. 1925 .... 105.00
Waterman "Ideal No. 94" fountain
pen, brown & green marbleized
body, ca. 1936 .... 55.00
Waterman "No. 554" fountain pen,
14k gold smooth body, ca. 1925 .. 500.00
Weidlich fountain pen, red hard rubber w/gold trim, lever-fill, 1924 .. 69.00

YARD LONG PRINTS

*These out of proportion colorful prints were
fashionable wall decorations in the waning
years of the 19th century and early in the 20th
century. They are all 36" wide and between
8" and 10" high. A wide variety of subjects,
ranging from florals and fruits to chicks and
puppies, is available to collectors. Prices for
these yard-long prints have shown a dramatic
increase within the past years. All included
in this list are framed unless otherwise noted.*

Advertising, "Pompeian Cosmetics,"
vertical, full-length portrait of
Mary Pickford................... $200.00

Birds w/butterflies, flowers &
violin 115.00

Glamorous 1920's Portrait with Calendar

Calendar, 1926, w/advertising below
a full-length color portrait of an
elegant 1920's lady (ILLUS.) 300.00

Chicks & Puppies Yard Longs

Chicks, numerous chicks emerging
from shells (ILLUS. top) 175.00
Girls (3) holding song sheets 100.00
Kittens 120.00
"Our American Poets," a row of
portraits, 1902 .... 55.00
Puppies, various colored puppies
playing (ILLUS. bottom) 175.00

YARN WINDERS

Floor model reel, painted hardwood,
a four-armed reel w/extended
end handle mounted horizontally
on plain uprights on a shoe-footed
trestle base, old worn blue paint,
22" l., 25½" h. (part of handle an
old replacement) $160.00

Floor model reel, turned hard- and
softwoods, six turned arms on
blocked upright above plank base
w/three turned canted legs, old
brown patina, w/geared counting mechanism, 30" d. wheel,
36½" h. (base may be old replacement) 75.00
Floor model reel, various hardwoods, six turned arms on upright, raised on a thick rectilin-
ear base w/four turned canted
short legs, old nut brown finish,
chip-carved detail, geared counter, 19th c., 43½" h. 65.00
Table model yarn "swift," clamp-on
type, all-wood, natural patina
(some damage) 110.00
Table model yarn "swift," turned
whalebone & ebony, 19th c.,
22½" h. (some replaced &
repaired ribs, age cracks) 935.00
Table model yarn "swift," whalebone, mounted atop a one-drawer
mahogany sewing box w/geomet-
ric mother-of-pearl, ivory &
baleen inlay, 19th c., 9 x 11",
overall 17½" h. (needs restoration).........................1,320.00

ZEPPELIN COLLECTIBLES

Airmail postal cover, from the 'Graf
Zeppelin,' w/the cancel of the
"Century of Progress Exposition,"
Chicago, 1933, w/a 50 cent green
zeppelin stamp.................. $65.00
Badge, German Zeppelin pilot's,
hallmarked 375.00
Book, "First Flight Around the
World," illustration of the "Graf
Zeppelin" on the cover 50.00
Bookmark, Duralumin, depicts air-
ship "Akron".................... 48.00
Button, tunic-type, brass, depicts
zeppelin, globe & swastika....... 35.00
Cap, leather; souvenir of airship
"Akron" 125.00
Key chain token, Duralumin, depicts
airship "Akron" 45.00
Needle book, "Air Fleet," Statue of
Liberty on cover................. 22.50
Pin, sterling silver, model of a
zeppelin, 3½" l. 85.00
Plate, china, souvenir of Lakehurst,
New Jersey, illustrated w/a zep-
pelin 75.00
Soda bottle, "Zep," depicts an
airship 85.00

INDEX

*Denotes "Special Focus" section

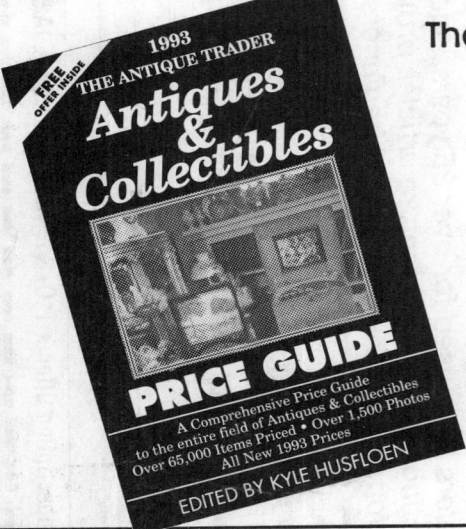